KEY TO EXERCISE ICONS

The exercises in this text are drawn from a variety of contexts—mostly business-related. One of these icons appears next to each end-of-chapter exercise to indicate its subject area:

- Accounting/Finance
- General Management
- Operations Management
- Marketing
- Economics/Policy
- Other Business
- Non-Business

STATISTICS FOR BUSINESS PROBLEM SOLVING

STATISTICS FOR BUSINESS PROBLEM SOLVING

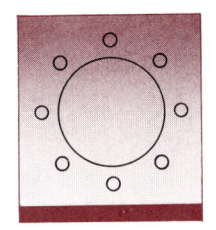

Harvey Brightman
Regents' Professor of Decision Sciences
Georgia State University

Howard Schneider
Associate Professor of Decision Sciences
Georgia State University

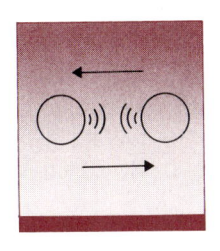

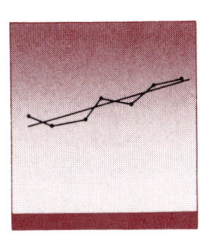

COLLEGE DIVISION South-Western Publishing Co.
CINCINNATI

Acquisitions Editor: James M. Keefe
Developmental Editor: Dennis Hanseman
Production Editor: Sharon L. Smith
Production Service: Susan L. Reiland
Marketing Manager: Tania Hindersman
Cover and Interior Designer: Ann Scheid

ME60AA
Copyright © 1992

by South-Western Publishing Co.
Cincinnati, Ohio

All Rights Reserved

The text of this publication, or any part thereof, may not be reproduced or transmitted in any form or by any means, electronic or mechanical, including photocopying, recording, storage in an information retrieval system, or otherwise, without the prior written permission of the publisher.

ISBN: 0-538-80286-3
2 3 4 5 6 7 MT 7 6 5 4 3 2
Printed in the United States of America

Library of Congress Cataloging-in-Publication Data

Brightman, Harvey J.
    Statistics for business problem solving/Harvey J. Brightman, Howard C. Schneider.
       p.   cm.
    Includes index.
    ISBN 0-538-80286-3
    1. Problem solving—Statistical methods.   2. Decision-making—Statistical methods.   I. Schneider, Howard C.,
II. Title.
HD30.29.B744   1992   91-2695
658.4'033—dc20   CIP

PREFACE

The study of statistics can be a rewarding experience. Over the years, statisticians have developed a powerful set of tools that have resulted in major contributions to human welfare. Statistical forecasting tools, for example, are in everyday use throughout the world. The quality control techniques pioneered by W. Edwards Deming are applied widely in Japan and are helping to revitalize the U.S. economy. Marketing research and opinion polling depend heavily on statistical sampling techniques. In fact, statistical methods have made major contributions to *all* areas of business.

But let's be frank. The first course in business statistics is often frustrating for both student and instructor. Students tend to view the course as an arbitrarily imposed hurdle that they must jump (or find a way around). They see no reason to study the subject, are often intimidated by it, and tend not to retain the material after the final exam. And teachers, who have felt the excitement of statistics, can be intimidated themselves by the prospect of conveying that excitement to students who would rather be elsewhere.

In this book, we propose to take a necessary and energetic step toward making the study of business statistics more rewarding for both students and their instructors. Above all, we aim to demonstrate that statistics is useful, not sterile; practical, not esoteric; and challenging, but rewarding.

We wrote this book for two reasons. In our own teaching, we have faced some of the problems just mentioned and believe we have overcome them. We hope we can translate some of our successes to a wider audience.

More recently, we have been heartened by the emergence of what might be called a statistics reform movement. A growing number of statistics instructors and business executives have been meeting in a series of conferences on Making Statistics More Effective in Schools of Business. The participants believe that statistics instruction can be made more vital and more relevant. Out of these meetings has emerged a new consensus. We have incorporated many elements of the consensus view in writing this book.

About This Book

This text is designed for a first course in statistics for students of business or public administration. It may be used for a one-quarter, one-semester, or two-quarter course aimed at students who will become business professionals. Its novel elements are:

1. A focus on using statistical methods to solve business problems
2. An early introduction to, and use of, time series data
3. An emphasis on graphics and descriptive statistics
4. Inclusion of nonparametric methods where appropriate (rather than in a separate chapter)

5. A chapter on data collection methods
6. Use of integrating frameworks to provide context and anchor the material
7. A stress on communicating statistical results to management
8. An extensive set of interesting, real-world problems
9. A readable and discovery-based presentation style

FOCUS ON PROBLEM SOLVING   Business professionals must be effective problem solvers and they must be able to find and exploit opportunities. The text demonstrates how probability and statistics can improve all phases of problem solving—sensing, diagnosis, and choice. Problem sensing, for example, involves detecting outliers that may signal an emerging problem or opportunity. The key statistical tools are histograms, box plots, line graphs, and residual plots. Diagnosis involves finding relationships among two or more variables. Here the relevant tools include cross-tabs, scatter plots, and correlation. Finally, the techniques of statistical inference are relevant in making choices.

To provide context, each chapter is problem-driven. It begins with a memo from a manager of a hypothetical firm, COMCEL. In it, the manager asks someone to identify an emerging problem, diagnose its root causes, take corrective action, or exploit an opportunity. The memo provides motivation for the chapter's material. The chapter concludes with a response memo outlining the findings and the statistical tools used.

TIME-ORDERED DATA   This text departs from the usual emphasis on cross-sectional data. The simple reason is that most data that cross a manager's desk are time-ordered (time series). It just makes sense to emphasize the situations and problems that managers most frequently face.

EMPHASIS ON GRAPHICS   We believe that graphical analysis is as important as more formal statistical methods. Throughout the book, we show how graphics and simple descriptive statistics can help summarize data quickly, identify emerging problems, or generate forecasts. Above all, we stress the need to examine the data *before* applying formal statistical methods.

TREATMENT OF NONPARAMETRICS   Where appropriate, we present both parametric and nonparametric methods in the same chapter. For example, in Chapter 7, we present confidence intervals on the mean followed by confidence intervals on the median. In Chapter 9, the usual one-way analysis of variance is followed by a discussion of the Kruskal–Wallis test and Dunn's multiple comparison method. This approach, we think, is far superior to the alternative of segregating nonparametrics in a single chapter that may not be covered.

DATA COLLECTION METHODS   Regardless of what textbooks may suggest, data do not just appear out of the void; they must be gathered. Consequently, we devote Chapter 6 to methods of data collection. We show how to plan a survey, write survey questions, and select the appropriate survey method and sampling design. We also discuss how to design planned change studies in order to minimize the most common validity-destroying errors.

COMMUNICATING RESULTS   Very little statistical analysis is useful unless the conclusions are communicated effectively to decision makers. As mentioned above, each chapter begins with a memo in which a manager describes a problem to be analyzed. The chapter ends with another memo, in which a subordinate reports the results of a statistical analysis. In that reply memo, the emphasis is on translating statistical results into managerial terms.

INTEGRATING FRAMEWORKS   To retain the material, readers must understand how the various subjects covered in the text are related. To help with retention, we have incorporated a variety of integrating frameworks. For example, hierarchical charts illustrate the organization of a particular subject and aid retention. Compare-and-contrast tables distinguish between two or more similar topics and aid comprehension.

INTERESTING PROBLEMS   Our book contains over 1,000 business-related problems and questions. Wherever possible, we have used real-world data. The end-of-section exercises stress the mechanics. The end-of-chapter problems require the student to (1) answer an important question, (2) investigate a statistical method, (3) draw inferences from samples to populations, or (4) verify a hunch or theory. Those problems were drawn from six broad subject areas: accounting and finance, marketing, general management, operations management, economics and public policy, and nonbusiness. To aid in comprehension, we define unfamiliar terms and describe how the data were collected.

PRESENTATION STYLE   Our style is business-oriented and not heavily mathematical. We have kept mathematical notation to a minimum because formulas can be a barrier to understanding. We often discuss a formula's underlying logic before presenting the mathematical notation. This book also avoids a lot of data-crunching that is best left to statistical software packages. The text's goals are to improve statistical reasoning and problem solving, skills that are essential to business success.

We have employed a writing style that reflects how business students learn best. Chapters are problem-driven, sections are highly structured with clear objectives, and the writing style is friendly and readable. We occasionally use discovery learning where we ask students to discover the key idea before we make the formal presentation. We have used this procedure in class with great success.

Each section includes a list of cognitive objectives that we believe are essential for mastery of statistics. Many of the objectives require that students translate statistical ideas among the three business languages—words, pictures, and mathematics.

Ancillaries

The text package contains a complete set of supplementary items. For the student, the Study Guide provides an additional set of explanations and problems. Each copy of the text comes with a copy of COM-STAT, a software package for IBM-compatible microcomputers. It can be used to solve many of the problems in the book.

The Instructor's Manual, prepared by the authors, contains suggested syllabi, chapter outlines, section summaries, additional problems, and a set of suggested readings. It also includes answers to all of the problems and exercises that appear in the text. A set of transparency masters is available to qualified adopters of the textbook. The Test Bank, prepared by Michael Broida, is also available in printed, MS-DOS, and Macintosh formats.

Finally, videotapes from the PBS series *Against All Odds: Inside Statistics* are available to qualified adopters of the textbook.

Acknowledgments

While this book is the sole responsibility of its authors, we wish to thank the following reviewers for their invaluable comments:

Frank Alt
University of Maryland

Michael Broida
Miami University

Margaret Capen
East Carolina University

William Carlson
St. Olaf College

Norm Chervany
University of Minnesota, Twin Cities

Terry Dielman
Texas Christian University

Rick Edgeman
Colorado State University

Noel Greis
University of North Carolina, Chapel Hill

Gudmund Iversen
Swarthmore College

Michael Jilling
University of South Carolina, Spartanburg

Lynn LaMotte
Louisiana State University

Martin Levy
University of Cincinnati

John McKenzie
Babson College

Michael Middleton
University of San Francisco

Thomas Moore
Grinnell College

Don Robinson
Illinois State University

Ralph Russo
University of Iowa

James Schlick
Kepner-Tregoe, Inc.

Lawrence Sherr
University of Kansas

Patrick Thompson
University of Florida

Mary Whiteside
University of Texas, Arlington

Wayne Winston
Indiana University, Bloomington

Vincent Yen
Wright State University

Dean Young
Baylor University

Douglas Zahn
Florida State University

We especially want to thank Mary Sue Younger of the University of Tennessee, Knoxville, and Dennis Hanseman of South-Western Publishing Co. for their exceptional help.

Lastly, we would like to dedicate this book to our wives, Arlene and Jane. They helped in so many ways, including reviewing and proofing. We are sorry for the many hours that we stole from our families in writing this book. We, however, believe it was worth it; we hope you will agree.

Harvey J. Brightman
Howard C. Schneider
Atlanta, Georgia

About the Authors

Harvey Brightman is Regents' Professor of Decision Sciences at Georgia State University. He is Past President and a Fellow of the Decision Sciences Institute. His work has appeared in *Decision Sciences, The American Statistician, Interfaces, Journal of the Academy of Management*, and many other journals. A renowned educator, Professor Brightman has won numerous teaching excellence awards at Miami University and at Georgia State. He has consulted with major corporations such as IBM, Armco Steel, ARCO Oil and Gas, and Georgia Power. His *Problem Solving: A Logical and Creative Approach* was a selection of the Executive Book of the Month Club and has been translated into Japanese.

Howard Schneider is Associate Professor of Decision Sciences at Georgia State University. Professor Schneider received his Ph.D. from the University of Virginia and is a specialist in multivariate statistics, forecasting, and survey design. He has served as a consultant to the U.S. Office of Personnel Management, Wachovia Bank, The Southern Company, Deloitte & Touche, General Electric, the U.S. Department of Transportation, and the Georgia Department of Offender Rehabilitation. He has developed and taught more than 100 seminars and short courses in statistical methods.

CONTENTS

1 Improving Business Problem Solving Through Statistics — 1

1.1 Introduction, 2
1.2 Problem Sensing in Business, 3
1.3 The Role of Statistics in Problem Sensing, 4
1.4 Problem Diagnosis and Alternative Generation in Business, 6
1.5 The Role of Statistics in Diagnosis and Alternative Generation, 7
1.6 Decision Making in Business, 12
1.7 The Role of Statistics in Decision Making, 13
1.8 Integrating Problem Solving and Statistics, 14
Appendix: Brief Description of the COMCEL Organization, 18

2 Descriptive Statistics I: Toward Managerial Problem Sensing — 20

2.1 Introduction, 22
2.2 Displaying Cross-Sectional Data Using Tables and Graphs, 24
2.3 Recognizing the Shape of a Histogram, 34
2.4 Displaying Time-Ordered Data: The Line Graph, 40
2.5 Summarizing Cross-Sectional Data: The Mean and Standard Deviation, 44
2.6 Interpreting the Mean and Standard Deviation: The Empirical and Chebyshev Rules, 51
2.7 Summarizing Cross-Sectional Data: The Median, Trimmed Mean, and Interquartile Range, 56
2.8 Interpreting the Median and Interquartile Range, 64
2.9 Summarizing Time-Ordered Data, 68
2.10 Key Ideas and Overview, 78

3 Descriptive Statistics II: Bivariate Data and Problem Diagnosis — 94

3.1 Introduction, 96
3.2 Types of Variables, 99
3.3 Analyzing Mixed Cross-Sectional Data, 100
3.4 Analyzing Categorical Cross-Sectional Data, 104
3.5 Analyzing Quantitative Cross-Sectional Data, 115
3.6 Analyzing Quantitative Time-Ordered Data, 127
3.7 Correlation and Cross-Correlation, 136
3.8 Key Ideas and Overview, 143

4 Basic Probability Concepts: The Study of Randomness — 160

4.1 Introduction, 162
4.2 Probability Concepts, 162
4.3 Picturing Probabilities: Introduction to the Probability Tree, 170
4.4 Joint and Union Probabilities, 177
4.5 Conditional Probabilities and Statistical Independence, 179
4.6 Computing Conditional Probabilities, 183
4.7 Using Probability Trees to Minimize Managerial Judgment Errors, 188
4.8 Nonstatistical Judgment Errors, 197
4.9 Key Ideas and Overview, 199

5 Probability Distributions — 212

5.1 Probability Distributions and Problem Solving, 214
5.2 Random Variables and Discrete Probability Distributions, 216
5.3 The Binomial Distribution, 223
5.4 Problem Solving and the Binomial Distribution, 231
5.5 The Poisson Distribution, 237
5.6 The Normal Distribution, 244
5.7 The Central Limit Theorem, 257
5.8 Integrating Framework and Key Ideas, 261

6 Data Collection Methods — 272

6.1 Data and Managerial Performance, 274
6.2 Sampling Principles and Statistical Inferences, 275
6.3 Basic Sampling Terminology, 279
6.4 Planning and Conducting a Survey: An Overview, 281
6.5 Simple Random Sampling Design, 284
6.6 Stratified Random Sampling Design, 287
6.7 Selecting a Survey Method, 292
6.8 General Principles in Writing Questions, 297
6.9 Basic Principles of Experimental Design, 303
6.10 Avoiding Problems in Experimental Design, 309
6.11 Key Ideas of Data Collection, 313

7 Making Inferences About One Population Parameter — 320

7.1 Problem Solving and Statistical Inferences, 322
7.2 The Sampling Distribution of the Sample Mean, 324

- 7.3 Confidence Intervals on an Unknown Population Mean, 329
- 7.4 One-Sided Confidence Intervals on an Unknown Population Mean, 338
- 7.5 The Hypothesis Testing Framework, 342
- 7.6 Stratified Random Sampling, 353
- 7.7 Confidence Intervals on an Unknown Population Proportion, 357
- 7.8 Determining the Sample Size, 360
- 7.9 A Nonparametric Confidence Interval for the Median, 364
- 7.10 Estimating the Population Variance and Standard Deviation, 369
- 7.11 Overview and Key Ideas, 373
- Appendix: Relationship Between Type I and Type II Errors, 384

8 Making Inferences About Two Populations — 388

- 8.1 Improving Departmental Performance, 390
- 8.2 Comparing Two Populations of Data, 390
- 8.3 Inferences on the Difference Between Two Population Means, 399
- 8.4 Inferences on the Difference Between Two Population Proportions, 409
- 8.5 A Nonparametric Confidence Interval for the Difference Between Two Population Medians, 412
- 8.6 Inferences on Two Population Variances for Normal Populations, 419
- 8.7 A Nonparametric Method for Comparing Two Population Variabilities, 425
- 8.8 Key Ideas and Overview, 431

9 Analysis of Variance — 444

- 9.1 The Role of Experimentation in Problem Solving, 446
- 9.2 Exploratory Data Analysis, 450
- 9.3 Analysis of Variance for a One-Factor, k-Level Study, 456
- 9.4 Testing for Significant Differences Between Pairs of Population Means, 467
- 9.5 The Kruskal–Wallis Nonparametric Analysis of Variance, 472
- 9.6 The Two-Factor, Completely Random Factorial Study, 479
- 9.7 Key Ideas and Overview, 489

10 Regression Analysis — 502

- 10.1 Looking for Relationships Among Variables and Problem Solving, 504
- 10.2 Collecting Data for a Regression Study, 509
- 10.3 Plotting Scatter Diagrams, 513
- 10.4 Curve Fitting, 520
- 10.5 Evaluating the Regression Model, 529
- 10.6 Evaluating the Regression Analysis Assumptions: Residual Analysis, 538
- 10.7 Using Regression Models for Prediction, 550
- 10.8 Indicator Variables, 555
- 10.9 Multicollinearity, 569
- 10.10 Regression Models and Problem Solving, 582
- 10.11 Determining Relationships Using the Chi-Square Test of Independence, 585
- 10.12 Integrating Framework, 591
- Appendix: Job Satisfaction Data, 607

11 Forecasting and Time Series Analysis — 610

- 11.1 Data Patterns and Forecasting, 612
- 11.2 Alternative Forecasting Approaches, 614
- 11.3 Forecasting Using Regression Analysis, 617
- 11.4 Forecasting Using the Classical Decomposition Method, 631
- 11.5 Qualitative Forecasting Methods, 655
- 11.6 Key Ideas and Overview, 659

12 Quality Control — 670

- 12.1 The Strategic Importance of Quality Control, 672
- 12.2 Types of Quality, 673
- 12.3 Control Charting for Variables, 676
- 12.4 Control Charts for Attributes, 692
- 12.5 Tools for Controlling and Improving Quality, 697
- 12.6 Vendor Certification and Acceptance Sampling, 708
- 12.7 General Principles, 713

Appendices — 727

- Appendix 1 The Binomial Table, A-1
- Appendix 2 Cumulative Poisson Distribution, A-16
- Appendix 3 The Normal Table, A-22

Appendix 4 Table of Random Numbers, A-23
Appendix 5 Student t Tables, A-25
Appendix 6 Percentiles of the χ^2 Distribution, A-26
Appendix 7 The F Distribution, A-27
Appendix 8 Table of Studentized Range Values, A-34

Answers to Odd-Numbered Exercises and Problems   B-1

Index   C-1

Improving Business Problem Solving Through Statistics

1.1 Introduction
1.2 Problem sensing in business
    Pounds's strategies
1.3 The role of statistics in problem sensing
    Data collection
    Data organizing and summarizing
    Data interpretation
1.4 Problem diagnosis and alternative generation in business
1.5 The role of statistics in diagnosis and alternative generation
    Data collection
    Data organizing and summarizing
    Data interpretation
1.6 Decision making in business
1.7 The role of statistics in decision making
    Data collection
    Data organizing and summarizing
    Data interpretation
1.8 Integrating problem solving and statistics
    Philosophy of data analysis
Chapter 1 Questions
Appendix: Brief description of the COMCEL organization

CHAPTER OUTLINE

1.1 Introduction

Statistics. We know what you're thinking—plugging numbers into unreadable formulas; sadistics; irrelevant. You are mistaken. Statistics can improve the problem solving performance of salaried and professional workers, supervisors, and managers in every business field.

Solving problems quickly is essential to business and personal success. Business professionals face two major types of problems. A *disturbance*, or *crisis*, problem is a gap between a previous or budgeted level of performance and the present performance. For example, when a retail department's sales show a sudden and dramatic decline from the previous quarter, we must diagnose the problem's causes and take corrective action to solve the problem permanently. A *managerial* problem, on the other hand, is a gap between the present level of performance and a desired higher level of performance. For example, a support staff takes 3 hours to type and mail a letter, a task that the supervisor believes should take only 1 hour. This is a managerial problem and we must seek ways to improve performance. In summary, solving a disturbance problem means asking, "How can we *restore* performance to previous levels?" Solving a managerial problem means asking, "How can we *improve* performance to the desired level?"

American managers and business professionals are often not effective problem solvers. One reason is that the mass of data that daily crosses their desks overwhelms them. But it need not! We can learn how to organize and analyze the data to develop *mental models* of the state of the department or firm. A mental model describes how an area is doing, where the opportunities lie, and what the emerging problems are. Mental models need not be complex or mathematical. Rather, they should be simple, verbal, or visual. In short, mental models describe how an area is operating, how it used to operate, and how it should operate. **Statistics** can play an essential role in building mental models.

Whether solving disturbance problems or managerial problems, we must follow a plan of attack. Consider the approach outlined in Figure 1.1. The three phases incorporated in this problem solving model are explained in this chapter.

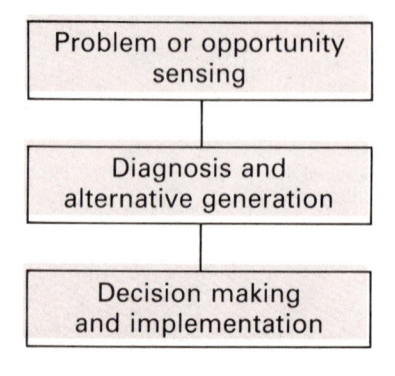

Statistics is a way of thinking that helps collect or create, organize, analyze, summarize, and interpret data to improve problem solving.

FIGURE 1.1 A Problem Solving Model

Problem or opportunity sensing
↓
Diagnosis and alternative generation
↓
Decision making and implementation

1.2 Problem Sensing in Business

Problem solving begins with problem finding. Problem sensing is crucial, because we cannot solve a problem until we know it exists. Effective business professionals detect emerging problems before they become crises. How do they do it? Management theorist William Pounds (1969) studied problem sensing and found that four strategies are used.

Pounds's Strategies

HISTORIC STRATEGY   Under the assumption that the best prediction of the future is the recent past, we expect continuity of performance: Whatever happened in the recent past should continue into the near future. If it does not, then a *performance gap* exists. For example, why is our safety record better this quarter than last quarter? Why is there a drop in the profits to earnings ratio? Why has the age of our accounts receivables increased? Much of the data necessary for problem solving can be found in a firm's management information system.

BUDGET VARIANCE STRATEGY   Plans and budgets provide detailed projections of performance for upcoming years. When actual performance falls short of budgeted levels, a *potential gap* may result. Unfortunately, budgeted performance levels are often set so low that departments easily exceed them. Thus, we detect few, if any, performance gaps. When planning is based on realistic goals, however, variances between actual and budgeted performance can help highlight hidden problems.

OTHER PEOPLE'S STRATEGY   Often, a problem comes to light from outside sources. A customer who purchases a product and is disappointed with it will notify the firm of his disappointment with the poor quality. Now the firm knows it has a problem! That is what happened to General Motors in the late 1970s and early 1980s. Potential customers told GM to make reliable, fuel-efficient, front-wheel-drive cars, or they would purchase them from firms that did. Another source of problem sensing is when a senior manager's brainstorm becomes an improvement project for her subordinates to investigate. The organization channels the problems identified by some (usually senior people) to others who are qualified to solve them (junior people).

EXTRA-ORGANIZATIONAL STRATEGY   Trade journals, competitors, other divisions within the organization, or professional conferences can sometimes identify performance gaps. Why is there a difference between our performance and our competitor's? Should we adopt a competitor's practices? Should we adopt a new procedure seen at a trade show? How do we compare with published performance levels for the industry? The extra-organizational strategy focuses on the external environment. Here the data in the management information system are less useful. Instead, a business person's informal network of contacts within the industry or country will provide much of the data needed for sensing problems or opportunities.

1.3 The Role of Statistics in Problem Sensing

Effective business professionals evaluate current performance using Pounds's four strategies. Next they identify important differences, select one for examination, and begin the problem solving process. Statistics can play an essential role in problem sensing, as we shall see next.

The following example illustrates how statistics helps in problem sensing. Note that problem sensing includes data collection, data organizing and summarizing, and data interpretation.

Data Collection

COMCEL's Norcross, Georgia, manufacturing plant employs 300 workers (see the Appendix at end of Chapter 1 for the organizational chart). Each month Sarah Teman, the manufacturing manager, receives two attendance reports from the management information system. The January 1992 monthly report just crossed her desk and showed that workers had only a 90% attendance rate. The second report, Table 1.1, shows the attendance percentages for the last 12 months. What, if anything, are the data trying to say?

Data Organizing and Summarizing

Statistics helps to organize and summarize the data. One simple and effective way to view a data set is to graph it. Using the data in Table 1.1, assign monthly

Table 1.1

1991 Monthly Attendance Data: Routine Management Information System Report

Period	Attendance
January	97.7%
February	99.0%
March	95.0%
April	98.3%
May	98.3%
June	97.0%
July	97.7%
August	95.0%
September	99.0%
October	96.3%
November	97.0%
December	95.1%

FIGURE 1.2

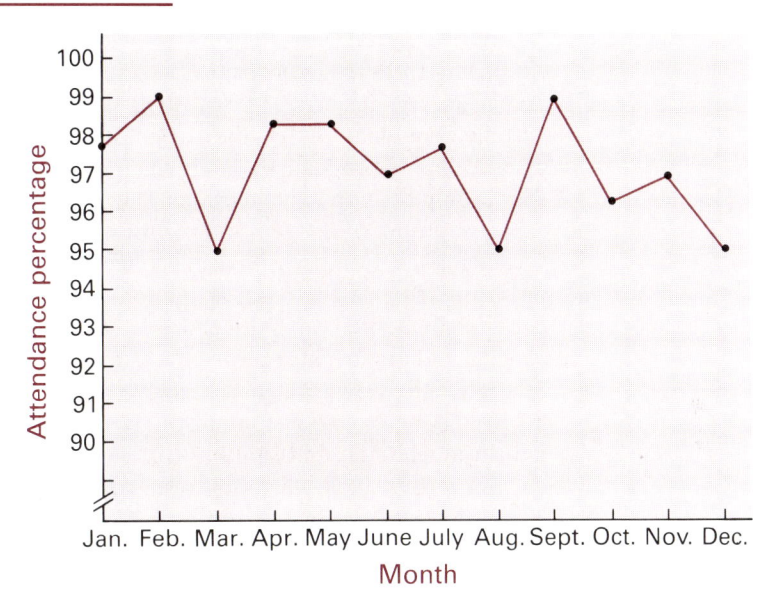

(Line chart: Attendance percentage by month, Jan–Dec, ranging roughly 95%–99%)

attendance percentages to the vertical axis, and months to the horizontal axis. Examining Figure 1.2, Teman develops the following mental model of how her plant has been operating:

> Using last year's data, I expect monthly attendance to be between 95% and 99%. The mean is slightly over 97%, and there is no upward, downward, or systematic pattern in the data. As long as monthly attendance is within the above limits, there is no disturbance problem. There is no need for problem solving.

Data Interpretation

January's attendance dropped to 90%. Is this an important, or major, deviation from the historic data? Does it signify a disturbance problem? That is, if Teman could afford to wait until next month without taking any action, would monthly attendance recover to historic levels?

There are two possible reasons why the January attendance fell to 90%. It may be due to **random variation** or to **assignable,** or **special cause variation**. Distinguishing between random and assignable cause variation is difficult, requires statistical training and insight, and is absolutely essential to problem sensing and effective performance. It may be the greatest contribution that statistics makes to business problem solving.

Margin notes:

★ Random variation is a minor departure from the average historic level of performance. Random variation results from the thousands of factors that make it impossible to predict exactly the level of a variable. Random variation does not require immediate problem solving action.

★ Special cause variation is a major departure from the average historic level of performance. The major departure is due to an assignable or special cause and must be corrected.

1.4 Problem Diagnosis and Alternative Generation in Business

According to Peter Drucker (1971), a leading management theorist, American managers are ineffective diagnosticians, being "solution-minded" instead of "problem-minded." Often they attempt (and fail) to solve a problem before considering its root causes. Even when they do manage to diagnose problems, they promptly jump to conclusions. Dewitt Dearborn and Herbert Simon (1958) asked a group of 23 senior executives to analyze the problems facing the Castengo Steel Company. Five of the six sales executives thought that the major problem was related to sales, but only five of the remaining 17 executives considered sales to be a major cause. When four of the five operations executives concluded that the major problem was related to production, only four of the 18 other executives agreed. Just three executives thought that the major problem involved human relations. Interestingly, their departments were public relations, industrial relations, and health.

As this example illustrates, our training dictates our view of a problem. However, just because we are accountants does not mean all problems are accounting problems! Decision scientists call this narrow view *selective perception*. Selective perception is hard to overcome because what is observed partly depends on who we are. We see with the mind as well as the eyes.

Another human failing that may hamper the search for causes of a disturbance problem is the tendency to blame others. If a worker's performance has dropped significantly, what may be the special (assignable) causes? The worker may initially blame such external factors as recent task changes: "I was doing fine until they changed my job. Now I don't know what they expect me to do." Supervisors whose bonuses depend on their workers' performances often blame their workers (Brown, 1984). The all-too-familiar scenario is to pass the buck: "I'm not to blame." The cause lies elsewhere, with other people, or in factors beyond our control.

Jumping to conclusions, like blaming others or dodging responsibility, is a common phenomenon. In fact, we may not be able to stop from jumping to conclusions—and sometimes true insights result. But it is not a formal method of analysis.

Once managers are able to perceive accurately the causes of a problem and thus understand it, they must seek or design potential solutions. In seeking a solution, we ask what has been done in the past to solve similar problems. In designing a solution, we ask what kinds of solutions could be designed if there were no constraints of time or money. Then we modify these creative options to reflect the actual constraints. Search is a logical process and design is a creative process.

Too often managers seek only one or two solutions to a problem. The second solution is typically no more than a clone of the first one: a variation on the same theme. Moreover, both are frequently recycled old solutions and often fail to solve the current problem.

Instead, managers should develop several different skeletal ideas, screen them, and select the best ones for further evaluation. A *skeletal idea* can be written on a single page. It includes a brief description of the idea, its rationale, and very rough estimates of the costs and benefits.

Alternative generation is related to problem diagnosis because the alternatives that are generated also depend on the perception of the root causes.

THE CASE OF THE MISSING INFORMATION   Many product managers within a firm were complaining that they did not have the necessary information to make good decisions when introducing new products. They had never complained before. Sensing that an important problem existed, the president contacted the information systems group. They, of course, chose to define the root causes as *technological* and proposed three alternative computerized systems. Each was very expensive and required extensive user training.

Despite some misgivings, the president installed one of the recommended systems. Although the product managers showed little enthusiasm during the 6-month installation, the president assumed that once the information system was in place it would be used. He was wrong. One year later, few product managers were using the computer system. Not even half had attended the training sessions. Moreover, the system had no impact on product decision making.

Perhaps the problem was not technological. The president had not considered that he might be facing a *human* problem. He sent a psychologist from corporate planning to interview the product managers. The psychologist concluded that the problem was not what they complained of, lack of information. Rather, the product managers were uneasy making risky decisions involving huge sums of money. Over the past several years the cost of introducing a new product had skyrocketed. The product managers realized that now any mistake could be costly to them and the firm. Viewing the problem as a human problem, the psychologist suggested two alternatives: either modify the reward system to emphasize overall departmental performance, or require managers to approve product introduction decisions jointly, in groups, rather than as individuals.

The president tried the shared risk approach, with astonishing results. Product managers grew enthusiastic and sought creative ways to promote their products. The supposed lack of information was never mentioned again.

The moral of the story: Almost any solution to the right problem beats the best solution to the wrong problem. A correct diagnosis is essential.

1.5 The Role of Statistics in Diagnosis and Alternative Generation

On reflection, Sarah Teman concludes that 90% attendance signifies a real problem. That is, it is due to a special or assignable cause. She must now determine this cause or causes.

Data Collection

Teman's hunch is that monthly attendance and workers' attitudes are related. When workers feel good about their jobs, they come to work; when dissatisfied with the job or management, they take paid sick leave. How can she test this belief? She needs a measure of workers' attitudes. Fortunately, COMCEL conducts a monthly worker attitude, or *climate*, sampling survey. Each month a sample of ten workers anonymously completes the survey shown in Table 1.2. The responses are stored in the management information system, which generates a routine monthly report on overall job attitudes. The Data Processing Department will also provide special reports on the responses to the eight questions, if requested. Teman obtains a summary of the overall attitudes averaged month by month over the past year, according to the 10-point rating system used in the survey. Table 1.3 displays the summary data.

Table 1.2

Climate Study Questionnaire

Instructions: For each of the following statements, please circle the number that best describes your situation.

          1 = Strongly disagree   4 = Agree
          2 = Disagree   5 = Strongly agree
          3 = Neutral

Workers in this plant:

1.	Help one another.	1	2	3	4	5
2.	Share information to help one another.	1	2	3	4	5
3.	Encourage creativity.	1	2	3	4	5
4.	Always try to improve.	1	2	3	4	5
5.	Join in social activities.	1	2	3	4	5
6.	Get to know one another.	1	2	3	4	5
7.	Comply with all rules.	1	2	3	4	5
8.	Live for their job.	1	2	3	4	5

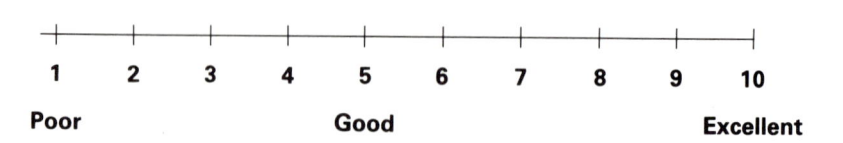

Overall Job Attitude:

```
   +----+----+----+----+----+----+----+----+----+
   1    2    3    4    5    6    7    8    9    10
  Poor                Good                    Excellent
```

Table 1.3

Mean Overall Job Attitude for Last 12 Months

Period	Mean Job Attitude
January	7
February	3
March	6
April	6
May	5
June	5
July	3
August	6
September	5
October	5
November	6
December	1

Data Organizing and Summarizing

Again we begin by graphing the data, assigning mean overall job attitude to the vertical axis and months to the horizontal axis. We have placed monthly attendance in the upper panel and overall job attitudes in the lower panel of Figure 1.3 on page 10.

The mean overall job attitude ranged from 1 to 7, with no obvious pattern. Overall, the workers had a good attitude, although in February, July, and December it deteriorated. The lower graph by itself is not very useful, but remember: Teman wants to determine if monthly attendance and overall job attitude are related. She will compare the two graphs in Figure 1.3.

Data Interpretation

Now a pattern emerges. In January the workers' mean job attitude was very good (a rating of 7). In February monthly attendance was also very high—99%. In February workers' attitudes dropped to a mean rating of 3, and one month later monthly attendance dropped to 95%. The pattern continued throughout the year. It appears that the mean attitude rating in one month predicts the monthly attendance in the following month. Thus the mean attitude rating *leads* monthly attendance by one month, or monthly attendance *lags* the mean attitude rating by one month. Given the lead–lag relationship, we should not be surprised that monthly attendance dropped to 90% in January 1992. After all, in December the plant had the worst attitude rating all year, predicting a major drop in the following month's attendance.

Now, what can Sarah Teman conclude about all this? The drop in monthly attendance was only a symptom of a more serious problem. Aided by statistical analysis and graphing, Teman has separated the symptom from its underlying cause. She must now refine her new diagnosis. If Teman is correct, she

FIGURE 1.3

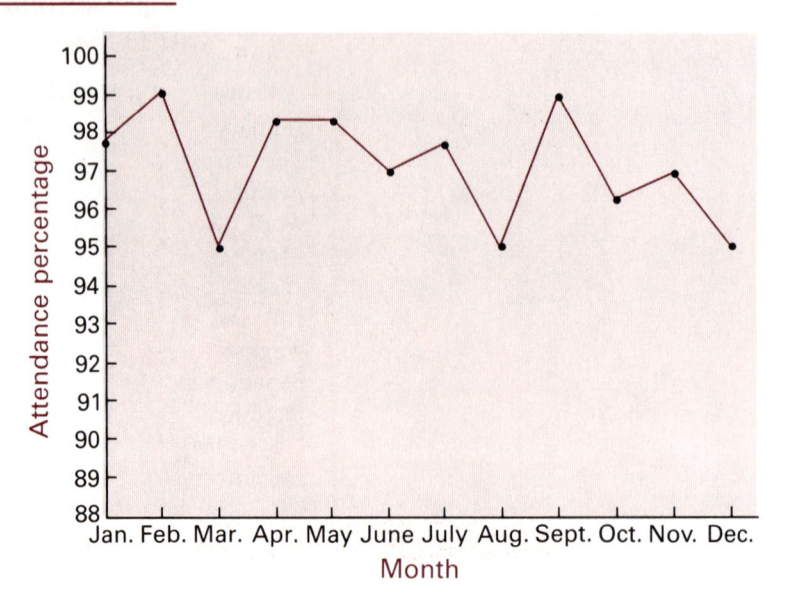

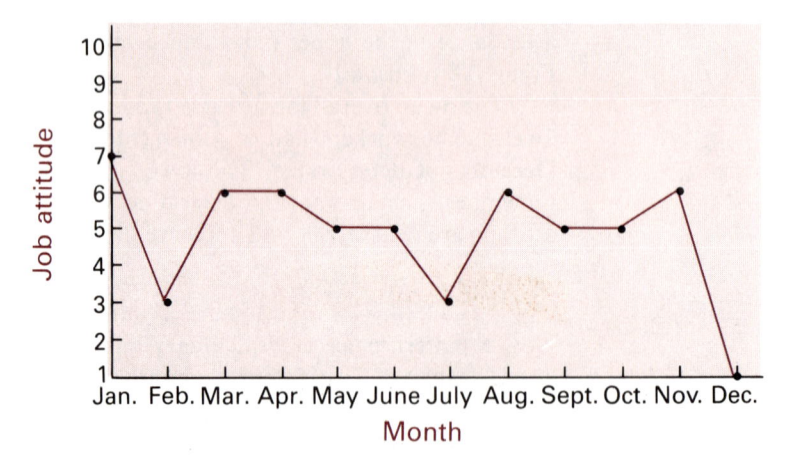

has to address the problem not of absenteeism but of improving workers' attitudes on the job. What causes their attitudes to vary monthly? Why were attitudes so positive in November and negative in December? The diagnosis is not yet complete. She must repeat the cycle of data collection, organization, and interpretation.

DATA COLLECTION Fortunately, the management information system preserved the workers' monthly responses to the eight climate questions shown in Table 1.2. Teman now requests a special report comparing the November and December data for all eight questions. The results are shown in Table 1.4.

Table 1.4

Raw Data on Responses to Eight Climate Questions: Special Report

Question	November Data (Sample size = 10)	December Data (Sample size = 10)
1	5, 5, 5, 4, 5, 4, 5, 4, 5, 5	2, 3, 2, 1, 2, 3, 3, 2, 1, 2
2	4, 4, 5, 4, 5, 4, 4, 5, 5, 5	1, 2, 2, 1, 2, 3, 2, 1, 1, 2
3	3, 3, 3, 4, 3, 2, 3, 4, 3, 3	3, 4, 3, 2, 3, 4, 3, 3, 4, 3
4	4, 4, 3, 4, 3, 3, 4, 3, 4, 4	4, 4, 4, 3, 3, 4, 3, 3, 4, 4
5	5, 4, 4, 5, 4, 5, 4, 4, 5, 4	4, 5, 5, 5, 5, 4, 4, 4, 5, 4
6	4, 4, 4, 5, 4, 4, 5, 4, 4, 5	4, 5, 4, 5, 4, 4, 4, 5, 4, 4
7	3, 3, 2, 3, 4, 3, 2, 3, 4, 3	3, 3, 4, 3, 2, 3, 3, 2, 3, 4
8	2, 3, 2, 3, 4, 3, 3, 3, 2, 3	3, 3, 2, 4, 3, 3, 2, 3, 3, 3

DATA ORGANIZING AND SUMMARIZING   The raw data in Table 1.4 are difficult to interpret. We need to organize and summarize them. One useful way is simply to compute means for the ten responses to each question. The means are given in Table 1.5.

DATA INTERPRETATION   The biggest change from November to December is the response to the first two attitude questions. Both concern *task support*, the degree to which workers cooperate with one another. Teman therefore suspects that a change in the level of worker cooperation caused the poor overall job attitudes. She reasons that some months the workers are cooperative and friendly to one another. Other months, it's like a war zone. After the bad times, the workers find reasons to stay home the following month.

Teman believes that when things are going well in the plant the workers get along fine. But when glitches occur—falling behind schedule or producing too many defective items—they often blame one another. She sees the work groups as too competitive, as if they were opposing teams rather than squads on the same side. Teman decides that the goal should be to develop a team spirit throughout the entire plant.

Table 1.5

Mean Responses to Climate Questions for November and December

Question	November	December
1	4.7	2.1
2	4.5	1.7
3	3.1	3.2
4	3.6	3.6
5	4.4	4.5
6	4.3	4.3
7	3.0	3.0
8	2.8	2.9

> A sample is a representative collection of some, but not all, elements of a population.
>
> A population is a collection of elements—people or objects—about which we wish to make generalizations.
>
> The margin of error is the possible difference we allow between the result obtained from a sample and what we would get if we could check the entire population.

Having completed the diagnosis, Teman asks the following question: How can we improve team spirit and cooperation within the plant? Let us pause here for two words of caution. First, Teman has *assumed* that worker competitiveness caused the levels of task support to vary within the plant. Perhaps she is right... or is she guilty of shifting the blame? Maybe poor management practices are to blame. Second, the data in Table 1.5 are based on a **sample** of only 20 workers. Yet Teman is making a generalization about a **population** of 300 workers in the plant. The generalization may be incorrect, for there are always differences between samples and populations. These differences are reflected in the **margin of error**.

Assuming that the sample results are indeed representative of the population, Teman seeks ways to improve cooperation within the plant. She asks the Human Resource Group (HRG) to develop two alternative solutions. Both its approaches involve training workshops on team building or on interpersonal communication. HRG is not sure which approach is better. How can it decide? We consider the process of decision making next.

1.6 Decision Making in Business

Decision makers should select those options that best accomplish their goals. Now that may seem obvious. Yet decisions are not always made that way.

Decision making is not usually a formal competition among competing ideas to accomplish a set of goals. Quite often managers do not set explicit goals in advance. Instead they create them once they have chosen a course of action. The goals then serve to justify the decision. For example, a chief executive officer (CEO) desires a sports franchise. To create a seeming need for action, he guides his Board of Directors to the discovery of a previously unknown crucial problem. Then he shows how the franchise would solve the problem. To the Board, the sports franchise will seem like a match made in heaven (Brightman, 1985).

That is not all. Sometimes the point in time when a decision is made cannot even be identified. It just happens. Marion Folsom (1962, p. 210), a top executive in business, has observed: It is often hard to pinpoint the exact stage at which a decision is reached. More often than not the decision comes about naturally during the discussions, when the consensus seems to be reached among those whose judgment and opinion the executive seeks.

By now, one wonders if decision making really can be treated as an orderly process. Yes, it can, despite all the problems in real-world practice, and statistics again plays an important role in sorting out the information. Statistics can provide objective and unbiased data that can influence the final decision. Properly used, statistics minimizes some of the problems in real-world decision making.

Even if a decision seems optimal—in accord with our goals as well as with our statistical data—we have another point to consider in decision making: **implementation**. Too frequently managers assume that they can easily install whatever option they select. But anyone who neglects implementation is living in a dream world. When the installation proves complex or the solution controversial, managers may face many problems, from coordination and scheduling conflicts to the political maneuverings of those opposed to the decision.

The decision maker should develop an *implementation plan* by:

1. listing every task required to install the option;
2. estimating the total installation time;
3. estimating the time to complete each task; and
4. comparing the time required to complete the tasks to the total time available.

Suppose there is insufficient time. Then various options exist. We may eliminate tasks, do several tasks simultaneously, obtain additional resources to reduce task time, or simply request more time to install the option.

The only sure thing in a complex installation is that something unexpected will occur. Be ready for it! Develop an implementation plan describing the steps to installing a solution. It should cover who, when, what, where, and how. Who will install the solution? What will motivate them to do their best? Who will oppose it? Why will they object? What are the crucial components in the installation? Why are they crucial? Where will the greatest coordination problems arise? Why will these coordination problems be so acute? When must each step of the installation be completed? Why can't the steps be rescheduled and thereby reduce potential problems? A decision that cannot be put into place solves no problems and meets no goals—except the unintended goal of exposing a poor decision maker.

1.7 The Role of Statistics in Decision Making

COMCEL's Human Resources Group has proposed two alternative workshops to improve worker cooperation. HRG is not sure which approach is better, so Teman authorizes a *pilot* (small-scale) study. Based on the results, she will make the final choice and then require all workers to attend the selected workshop.

Data Collection

HRG selects two work teams of five workers each. It assigns one team to the team building workshop and the other to the communication workshop. The workshop assignments are made by flipping a coin, to ensure that each work group has an equal chance of being in each workshop. HRG will evaluate both programs by comparing the mean job attitudes before and after the workshops.

Data Organizing and Summarizing

Table 1.6 on page 14 contains the results of the pilot study.

Data Interpretation

Table 1.6 indicates that members of team 1 appear to have improved their job attitudes, whereas members of team 2 show little overall improvement. Of course, these are inferences from a small sample and generalized to the entire

Table 1.6
Changes in Mean Job Attitudes of Teams by Workshop

	Before Means	Workshop	After Means
Team 1	4.50	Team Building	7.90
Team 2	4.57	Communication	4.65

plant. They may be wrong. Nevertheless, the data suggest that Teman should choose the team building workshop. She did, and the attendance problem was corrected.

1.8 Integrating Problem Solving and Statistics

Figure 1.4 integrates the problem solving model presented in this chapter with statistics. We begin with problem sensing. By organizing and summarizing routine reports, we can develop mental models that describe how a department operates under normal conditions. Chapters 2 and 11 are especially helpful for developing mental models. Any major disturbance signals a problem. Failing to sense a major disturbance (assignable cause variation) is as serious as sensing a

FIGURE 1.4 Integrating Statistics Within a Problem Solving Framework

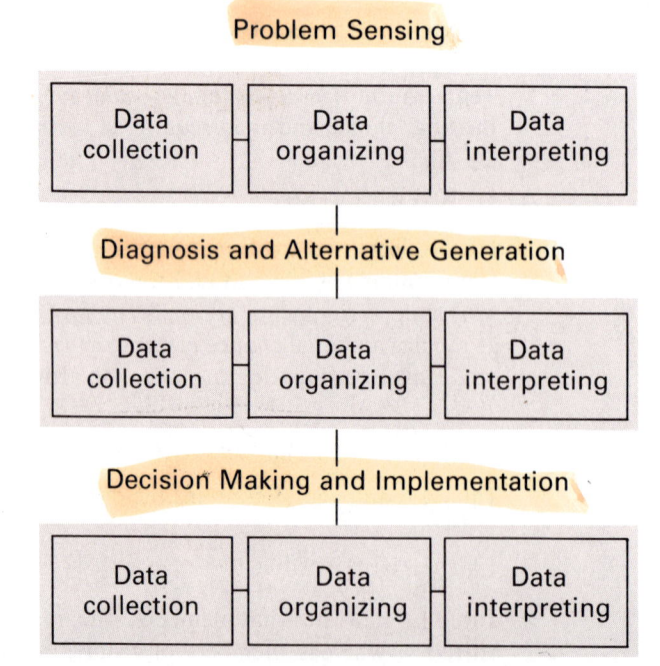

Problem Sensing

| Data collection | Data organizing | Data interpreting |

Diagnosis and Alternative Generation

| Data collection | Data organizing | Data interpreting |

Decision Making and Implementation

| Data collection | Data organizing | Data interpreting |

bogus problem (mere random variation). Chapters 2, 3, 11, and 12 will show how to distinguish between random and assignable cause variation, a critical skill in effective problem sensing.

Having detected a major disturbance, we must diagnose it. We ask: "What factor or factors caused the deviation from budgeted or historical levels of performance?" Seeking root causes is like finding a needle in a haystack—hard but not impossible, if we are methodical, persistent, and perceptive. Chapters 3, 10, and 12 focus on problem diagnosis.

After generating several possible solutions we must choose one and implement it. Chapters 4 and 5 provide basic probability concepts and the background to understand statistical analysis, a tool in making decisions. Chapter 6 shows how to collect data by conducting sampling surveys or pilot studies. Chapters 7–9 examine how we analyze and interpret the study results.

Philosophy of Data Analysis

The underlying theme of this book is that we must learn how to explore and analyze data to solve business problems. We suggest the following pattern of data analysis:

1. Plot or graph the data; then study it. What are the data trying to tell us? Do we have a problem or is the variation merely random?
2. If there is a problem, select an appropriate method of analysis.
3. Check the assumptions underlying the statistical method. If the assumptions are not valid, choose another method.
4. Collect or create the data, analyze them, interpret the findings, and take corrective action.

Data exploration and analysis can help in many ways: to separate opinions from facts; to develop mental models of departmental performance; to sense emerging problems long before they become crises; to prevent overreaction to random variation; to diagnose problems better by tracing causality, thus countering the tendency to jump from symptoms to false conclusions; and to make better decisions. In summary, statistics is a way of thinking about and improving business problem solving. It is too useful to be left only to statisticians.

CHAPTER 1 EXERCISES

1. For each statement indicate the source(s) of the implied standard. Use H, historical precedent; B, budgeted performance; O, other people; and E, external.
   a. "In our business, if labor costs exceed 10% of total cost, we can't make a profit." H
   b. "Japanese-managed plants making television sets in this country average only a 3% defective rate." E
   c. "I want the company I run to have a reputation for the highest quality product in the industry." O
   d. "Productivity has increased by only 1.5% this year, not by the 2% increase that was expected." B

e. "A major manufacturer monitors its service division by commissioning impartial quarterly telephone surveys of its customers." E
f. "We have received letters from our customers complaining that our warranty period is too short and coverage is too limited." D
g. "Our outside people should have some form of instant recognition just like the white shirts of IBM." D, E
h. "Our labor costs are expanding faster than those of anyone else in the industry. Profits would increase faster if we didn't insist on making the highest quality product in the industry." D

2. For each statement indicate whether the information received suggests an opportunity (O) or a problem resulting from a disturbance (D).
   a. "Weekly figures show we are 15% over standard cost." D
   b. "Weekly figures show we are 15% under standard cost." O
   c. "Customers have been telling our retail outlets that our two best-selling programs should be combined into one." O
   d. "If the mail-order catalog sent out last week was well received, our switchboard would be very busy by now." D
   e. "By this time of year, we should have $2 million in sales instead of $1.5 million." D

3. The accompanying table indicates your department's quarterly performance over the past three years. It shows the rate of return of items sold as a percentage of dollar value.

Quarter	Year 1	Year 2	Year 3
1	3.0%	3.5%	4.0%
2	4.5%	4.0%	4.5%
3	2.5%	2.5%	2.5%
4	6.5%	6.2%	7.0%

Write down the mental models you would use as standards for detecting problems or opportunities in these data.

4. The goal of statistics is to aid the manager in deciding which deviations from mental models are problems or opportunities and which are the result of random variation. A manufacturer produces an object that is supposed to be 100 cm wide. After hundreds of measurements, she has found that 68% of the items measured between 99.9 cm and 100.1 cm; 95% measured between 99.8 cm and 100.2 cm; and all of the measurements fell within the interval from 99.7 cm to 100.3 cm. Using this historical experience, should she conclude there is a problem if a selected item measures 100.7 cm? 99.5 cm? 100.25 cm? 100.05 cm?

CHAPTER 1
QUESTIONS

1. What is a mental model?
2. Describe how Pounds's four strategies help salaried staff, professionals, and managers sense problems and opportunities.
3. Distinguish between problem sensing and diagnosis.
4. Why is problem diagnosis essential to problem solving success?
5. How are disturbance and managerial problems similar? Different?
6. Name three sources of data that can be used to detect and solve problems.

7. We use historical data to form mental models of how things ought to be. For example, our mental model says that the defective rate should average 4%. But the actual rate will vary from day to day or week to week. If the primary use of mental models is to detect problems or opportunities, how can statistics be helpful?
8. Provide an example from your own experience that illustrates random variation and assignable cause variation.
9. How does statistics—data collection, data organizing and summarizing, and data interpretation—help identify and solve problems?
10. Looking for relationships between data sets is an essential diagnostic skill. For example, Sarah Teman had to determine what factor(s) affected monthly attendance. How can you generate these factors?

REFERENCES

BRIGHTMAN, HARVEY. "The Structure of the Unstructured Acquisition Decision." Presented at the Annual Meeting of the Decision Sciences Institute, Las Vegas, 1985.

BROWN, KAREN. "Explaining Group Poor Performance: An Attributional Analysis." *Academy of Management Review* 9, no. 1 (1984): 54–63.

DEARBORN, DEWITT, and HERBERT A. SIMON. "Selective Perception: A Note on the Departmental Identifications of Executives." *Sociometry* 21 (1958): 140–144.

DRUCKER, PETER. "What We Can Learn from Japanese Management." *Harvard Business Review* (March–April 1971): 110–122.

FOLSOM, MARION B. *Executive Decision Making.* New York: McGraw–Hill, 1962.

POUNDS, WILLIAM. "The Process of Problem Finding." *Industrial Management Review* (Fall 1969): 1–19.

APPENDIX Brief Description of the COMCEL Organization

COMCEL manufactures, sells, and services high-quality car phones and runs one of the major mobile phone communications networks in the United States. COMCEL's corporate headquarters are in Atlanta, Georgia, and it has about 1,000 employees. It has manufacturing plants in Norcross, Georgia, and Dallas, Texas. Both plants employ about 300 workers.

Ann Tabor is CEO of the firm and her senior team includes herself and five direct supports. Howard Bright, the plant manager in Norcross, and Arlene Taylor, the plant manager in Dallas, directly report to Nat Gordon, Vice President of Manufacturing. Pam Ascher, National Sales Manager, and Cherian Jain, Manager of Marketing Research, directly report to Bill O'Hara, Vice President of Marketing. Ms. Ascher manages four sales regions that include 30 markets. The Southern Region, which is the largest, includes 12 cities. The other three regions include six cities each. There are at least five to ten competitors in each sales region. However, COMCEL has been very successful. Sales have grown by 15–20% each year and recently exceeded $200 million.

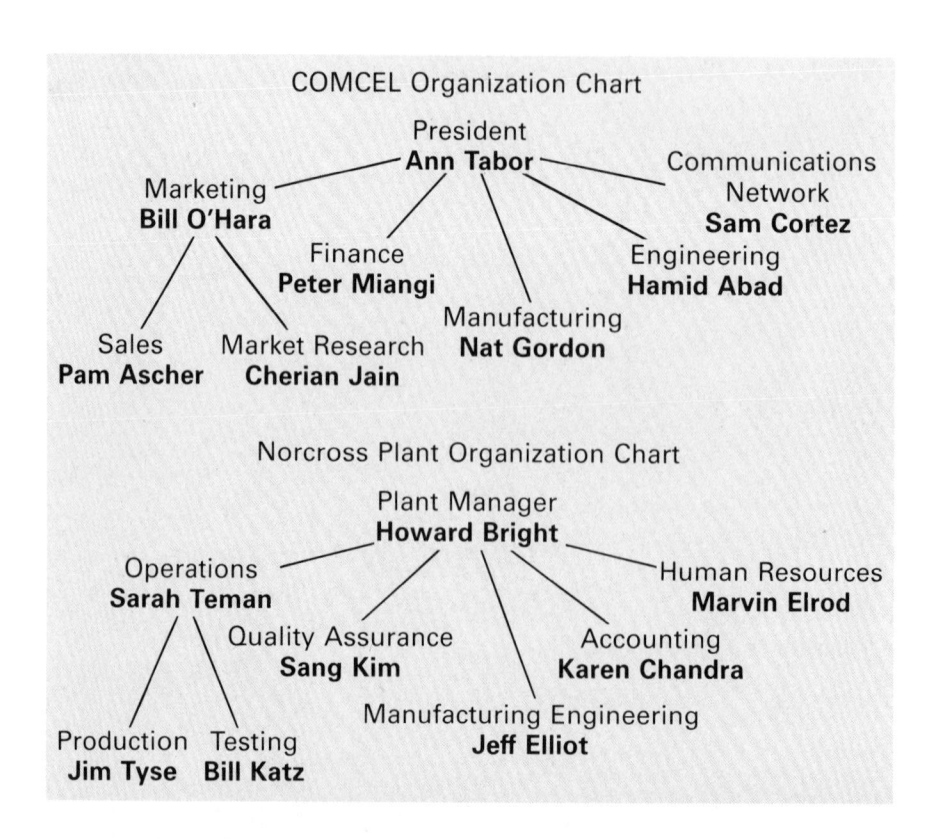

COMCEL Organization Chart

- President: **Ann Tabor**
  - Marketing: **Bill O'Hara**
    - Sales: **Pam Ascher**
    - Market Research: **Cherian Jain**
  - Finance: **Peter Miangi**
  - Manufacturing: **Nat Gordon**
  - Engineering: **Hamid Abad**
  - Communications Network: **Sam Cortez**

Norcross Plant Organization Chart

- Plant Manager: **Howard Bright**
  - Operations: **Sarah Teman**
    - Production: **Jim Tyse**
    - Testing: **Bill Katz**
  - Quality Assurance: **Sang Kim**
  - Manufacturing Engineering: **Jeff Elliot**
  - Accounting: **Karen Chandra**
  - Human Resources: **Marvin Elrod**

Descriptive Statistics I: Toward Managerial Problem Sensing

2.1 Introduction
   Cross-sectional data
   Time-ordered data
2.2 Displaying cross-sectional data using tables and graphs
   The stem-and-leaf display
   The frequency distribution and frequency histogram
   The relative frequency distribution and histogram
   The cumulative frequency distribution and ogive
2.3 Recognizing the shape of a histogram
   Symmetric histograms
   Bell-shaped histograms
   Impact of rescaling data
   Skewed or nonsymmetric histograms
   The outlier
2.4 Displaying time-ordered data: The line graph
   Stationary time-ordered data
   Nonstationary time-ordered data
2.5 Summarizing cross-sectional data: The mean and standard deviation
   Distinguishing the sample from the population
   The mean
   Approximating the mean of histogram data
   The range
   The variance and standard deviation
   Yes/No data
2.6 Interpreting the mean and standard deviation: The Empirical and Chebyshev rules
   Bell-shaped histograms: The Empirical rule
   The outlier
   Skewed histograms: Chebyshev's rule
   Weakness of the mean and the standard deviation
2.7 Summarizing cross-sectional data: The median, trimmed mean, and interquartile range
   The median
   Approximating the median of a frequency histogram
   Differences between the mean and median
   The trimmed mean
   The interquartile range
   Which set of summarizing measures?
2.8 Interpreting the median and interquartile range
   Identifying outliers using the median and interquartile range
   Drawing box plots
   Recognizing symmetry or skewness
2.9 Summarizing time-ordered data
   Are the mean and median informative for nonstationary data?
   Single moving averages
   Smoothing by moving averages
   Repeated smoothing by averages of three
   Residuals
   Impact of outliers on moving averages
2.10 Key ideas and overview
Chapter 2 Questions
Chapter 2 Application Problems

CHAPTER OUTLINE

COMCEL Interoffice Communication

Date: April 1, 1992
  To: Howard Bright, Manager, Norcross Plant
From: Ann Tabor, CEO
  Re: Analysis of Work Group Productivity

In looking over the most recent industrial engineering report for the work groups at the Norcross plant, I was disappointed to see that so many are performing below industry standards. I note on the positive side that one work group is performing at 123% of standard. If one group can perform this well, why can't they all?

Please look into this and report back as soon as possible.

2.1 Introduction

Aspiring managers must learn to identify opportunities as well as potential problems. Problem sensing is a crucial managerial activity, since we cannot solve a problem until we know it exists. Effective managers detect emerging problems long before they become crises; they also uncover opportunities before their competitors do.

How can managers become more effective in problem sensing? As noted in Chapter 1, they must learn to organize, summarize, and interpret large quantities of data. Simple descriptive statistics that organize and summarize data can help build mental models.

Where do managers get data to build their mental models? If they do not already have the data set, they create it or buy it. The firm's management information system provides much of the in-house data in the form of routine structured reports. Typically, these reports contain financial, accounting, marketing, and operations data. The data describe the state of the firm and are historical, aggregated, and internal to the firm. (An example is the monthly attendance report from Chapter 1.)

Managers can also purchase external data bases, undertake surveys, or conduct planned change studies. A *survey* is a sampling of facts or opinions that is used to estimate how an entire group would respond. Typical business examples are attitude surveys and marketing research studies. Surveys are especially important in uncovering emerging business opportunities. To seek ways of improving departmental performance, managers may run small-scale planned change experiments or pilot projects and study the results. If the planned change is an improvement, they may implement it permanently.

Once managers uncover problems, they must diagnose them quickly and accurately. Diagnosis is the ability to understand the problem and discover its root causes. Many managers are poor diagnosticians who jump to conclusions about problem causality, blame others, or totally ignore problem diagnosis in their rush to solve a problem.

Over the next two chapters, we will discuss the role of statistics—that is, of summarizing, organizing, and interpreting data—in problem sensing and diagnosis. The management information system, external data bases, surveys, and planned change studies are the sources of data. They provide two types of data—cross-sectional and time-ordered data. We shall examine each kind in turn.

Cross-Sectional Data

Cross-sectional data are measurements taken at *one time period* on different persons, places, or things, such as four plants, 50 workers, or several departments. Here are two examples.

EXAMPLE 1: Absenteeism data from four plants during January

EXAMPLE 2: Job attitude and productivity data for 50 workers during the second week of July

The cross-sectional data for the two examples differ. In Example 1 data are collected on only *one* variable—absenteeism. A *variable* is a characteristic that has different values, all measured in the same units, such as dollars, number of sales, productivity, sick hours lost, or consulting hours. In Example 2 data are collected on *multiple* variables—job attitude and productivity. Both examples contain cross-sectional data, however, since all the data describe a person, place, or thing at one point in time.

Time-Ordered Data

Time-ordered, or time series, data are data collected over time, in chronological sequence. Here are three examples.

EXAMPLE 1: Absenteeism data for plant 1 from March to December

EXAMPLE 2: Absenteeism data and productivity data for plant 1 from March to December

EXAMPLE 3: Absenteeism data and productivity data for plants 3 and 4 from March to December

The first example illustrates time-ordered data for one place (plant 1) on one variable (absenteeism). The second example shows time-ordered data for one plant on two variables (absenteeism and productivity). Example 3 involves *panel data*, which combine features of cross-sectional data and time-ordered data. The data are cross-sectional because measurements are taken in two plants in any one month. The data are time-ordered because the measurements are taken over time.

FIGURE 2.1 Differences Between Cross-Sectional and Time-Ordered Data

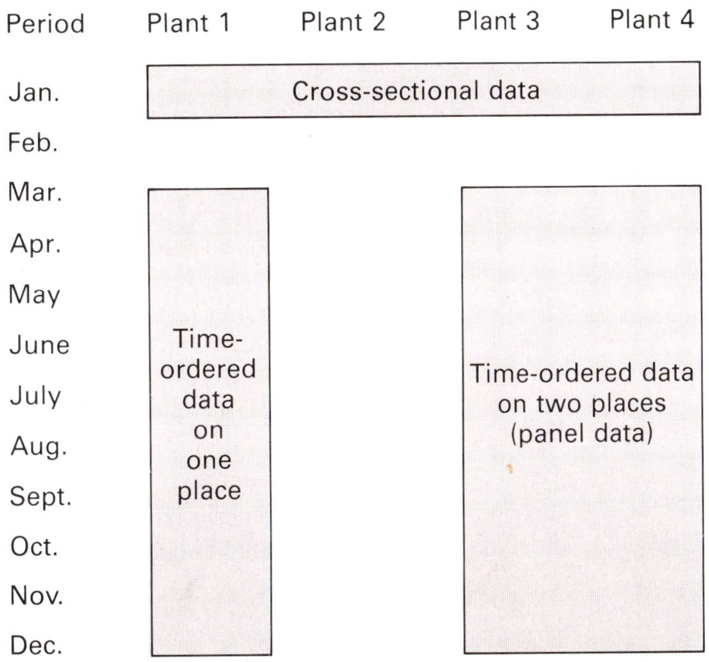

Period	Plant 1	Plant 2	Plant 3	Plant 4
Jan.	Cross-sectional data			
Feb.				
Mar.	Time-ordered data on one place		Time-ordered data on two places (panel data)	
Apr.				
May				
June				
July				
Aug.				
Sept.				
Oct.				
Nov.				
Dec.				

Cross-sectional and time-ordered data are both important to managers, but most routine data that management information systems deliver are time-ordered. Figure 2.1 visualizes the differences between time-ordered and cross-sectional data and how panel data are related to both.

It is the aim of these next two chapters to show how to decipher the information embodied by cross-sectional and time-ordered data. In plain English, what are the data trying to say, and what can be learned from them? The remainder of this chapter will demonstrate how to organize, summarize, and interpret cross-sectional and time-ordered data in order to *sense* problems. In Chapter 3 the emphasis will be on how to use the data to *diagnose* problems.

SECTION 2.1 EXERCISES

1. For each of the data sets listed indicate whether they are cross-sectional data (C) or time-ordered data (T).
    a. Daily Dow-Jones industrial averages
    b. The results of a Gallup poll on presidential preferences
    c. Mean salaries by department of a college for the academic year 1993–1994
    d. The Consumer Price Index by year since 1967
2. Explain the difference between problem sensing and problem diagnosis.
3. Explain why problem sensing can be done with one variable, while problem diagnosis usually requires the study of two or more variables.

2.2 Displaying Cross-Sectional Data Using Tables and Graphs

Displaying cross-sectional data helps managers see the structure underlying the data. They can then begin developing simple mental models of how their departments are operating—the first step of effective problem sensing. By the end of this section you should be able to:

1. draw a stem-and-leaf display for a small data set;
2. draw a frequency histogram for a large data set;
3. explain how the number of classes of a histogram affects the trade-off between seeing the data's structure and its detail;
4. convert a frequency histogram into a relative frequency histogram and interpret it; and
5. construct and interpret a cumulative frequency distribution, a cumulative percent distribution, and an ogive.

The Stem-and-Leaf Display

No matter how small the data set, always draw a diagram. A picture conveys more than words or numbers can. It can help you to see the structure or underlying pattern within the data, which is, after all, the purpose of organizing and displaying the data. For a small data set, consider the **stem-and-leaf display**.

A stem-and-leaf display shows the number of observations that share a common stem and the value of each observation.

Chapter 2 Descriptive Statistics I: Toward Managerial Problem Sensing

EXAMPLE: CLAIMS ADJUSTMENT DATA. As manager of an insurance claims department, you must set performance standards. You ask an experienced claims adjuster to record the number of claims she processes per day over a 30-day period. Her totals are listed in Table 2.1.

Table 2.1
Claims Processed per Day over a 30-Day Period

31	30	28	33	35	37
37	36	38	38	39	36
38	34	39	31	30	34
40	41	40	41	48	45
46	44	39	34	40	42

To create a stem-and-leaf display draw a vertical line, and separate each number into its first digit, the *stem*, and its second digit, the *leaf*. Put a stem on the left side of the vertical line and all of its attached leaves on the right. Do the same with the other stems and their leaves. The stem-and-leaf display should look like Figure 2.2.

In Figure 2.2, the stem-and-leaf display has only three stems, so much detail is lost. It is redrawn in Figure 2.3 with two improvements. First, the stem is repeated for the two large classes and the leaf digits are arranged in order from the smallest to the largest on each stem. Second, digits from 0 to 4 go in the first row of a repeating stem and digits 5 to 9 go in the second row. These changes make the display more understandable and will be useful later in calculating measures of the center and variability.

FIGURE 2.2 Stem-and-Leaf Display for Claims Data

		Number of Days
2	8	1
3	1035776889684910494	19
4	0101856402	10
		30

FIGURE 2.3 Ordered Stem-and-Leaf Display for Claims Data

		Number of Days
2	8	1
3	00113444	8
3	56677888999	11
4	0001124	7
4	568	3
		30

FIGURE 2.4 Ordered Stem-and-Leaf Display for Claims Data

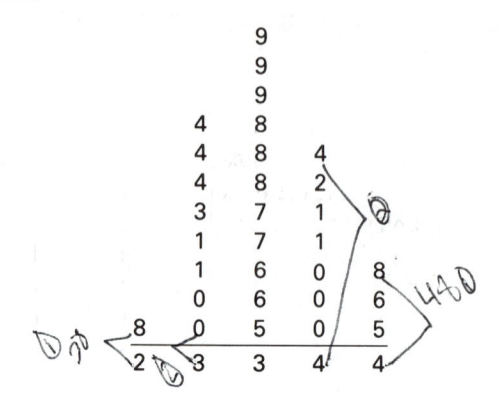

```
                9
                9
                9
        4       8
        4       8   4
        4       8   2
        3       7   1
        1       7   1
        1       6   0   8
        0       6   0   6
    8   0       5   0   5
    2   3       3   4   4
```

Now we can see the structure underlying the data. The number of claims processed varies from 28 to 48 claims per day. The lengths of the rows indicate the number and pattern of claims processed each day. On most days the adjuster processed between 30 and 44 claims, but on three of the 30 days she processed more than 44 claims.

Some managers grasp the data's structure more easily if the data are arranged in columns instead of rows. Figure 2.4 shows the ordered stem-and-leaf display rotated 90°.

The Frequency Distribution and Frequency Histogram

The stem-and-leaf display is very effective for small data sets—but imagine Figure 2.4 with 3,000 claims rather than 30! There would be so many stems and leaves that they would simply obscure the data's structure. In such cases, a more useful type of graphic display is a **frequency histogram**. This graph is similar to a stem-and-leaf display but does not provide information on the actual values. Instead it shows the number, or frequency, of observations in each class of values. We can readily construct a frequency histogram for the raw data on processed claims in Table 2.1.

Begin with a *frequency table*, or frequency distribution, showing how often the variable of interest assumes each value. The values for the variable of interest—number of completed claims processed—are grouped into ordered classes depending on how much data we have and how much detail we want to see. Construct the classes to meet these criteria:

1. They do not overlap.
2. They include all the observations.
3. They are easily interpreted.

If the classes overlap, then an observation may fall into two classes, and thus the total number of observations displayed in the histogram would exceed the number of observations in the original data set. If the classes exclude any ob-

A frequency histogram shows the number of observations that fall into each class. This frequency of occurrence is shown as the height of each block in the histogram. The area of each block is proportional to the number of observations within the class. The frequency histogram is simply a picture of a frequency distribution.

servations, then the histogram would show fewer items than given in the original data. Either way, the frequency table will not correctly represent the data.

For ease of interpretation choose integer class widths—such as 2, 4, 5, or 10. In general, unequal class widths are often misleading. Since the purpose of the display is to compare frequency counts between classes, the basis of comparison will not be the same when classes have unequal widths. Under certain circumstances unequal class widths are appropriate, however. For example, suppose that the claims data set also included several values between 100 and 300 and several values between 500 and 700. Since the bulk of the data is between 30 and 50 claims, consider a class width of 4 or 5 for this portion and above 50 use a class width of 350. This would cover all the data, yet be more readily interpreted than a series of empty classes, all equal in width.

DETERMINING THE CLASS WIDTH   Class width is an important consideration in constructing a frequency table or histogram because it affects our ability to see the data's structure and detail. To illustrate both issues, consider the following example. Assume that all members of a baseball team are batting under .400. We could divide the batting averages into two classes, the first ranging from .000 to .199 and the second from .200 to .399. However, all but a few averages will fall in the second class, which is not too informative. With class widths so wide, we cannot see the data's *structure*. We might want to know how many players have batting averages in the high 200s, but with only two classes, we cannot glean the answer. Now consider classes with widths of .02. It would take 20 classes to cover the range from .000 to .399 (.000–.019, .020–.039, .040–.059, ... , .380–.399). With so many classes, the *level of detail* can be overwhelming. Moreover, since the number of players on any team is usually under 40, many classes would be empty. It would be difficult to see the big picture. Our recommendation is 3 to 20 classes. This number of classes balances the number of data points against the level of detail we want to see.

In general, there are two approaches to determining the class width:

1. Decide on the number of classes; then determine the class width.
2. Decide on the class width; then determine the number of classes.

Both approaches can be illustrated with the claims data from Table 2.1.

Approach 1. Organize the claims data into six classes. Divide the data range—the highest data value minus the lowest data value—by the number of classes. The range for the claims data is 48 − 28 = 20, so the class width must be about 20/6 = 3.3. An easily interpreted class width would be 4, giving six classes: 26–29, 30–33, 34–37, 38–41, 42–45, and 46–49. We find the width of each class by subtracting the lower limits of adjacent classes: 30 − 26 = 4. These six classes do not overlap and will contain all the data values, because the claims processed are listed as integer values.

Approach 2. Organize the claims data into an interpretable class width of 5. This will give five classes: 25–29, 30–34, 35–39, 40–44, and 45–49. This approach, like the first one, creates a number of classes that is within our guidelines.

Table 2.2 presents the frequency distribution based on the first approach. The table shows the number of claims processed daily, grouped into six classes, and the number of days represented by each class. Note that the classes do not overlap, include all 30 data values, and have the same width of 4.

Figure 2.5 is a frequency histogram for the claims data set as grouped in the frequency table. The number of claims is on the horizontal axis. Place the lower limits of each class on the horizontal axis. The vertical axis shows the frequency count of each class (the number of days). In Figure 2.5, the height of the horizontal lines represents the number of observations in each class.

Table 2.2

Frequency Distribution for Number of Claims Processed over 30 Days

Claims Processed Classes	Number of Days
26 to 29	1
30 to 33	5
34 to 37	8
38 to 41	11
42 to 45	3
46 to 49	2
Total:	30

OPEN-ENDED CLASSES As noted earlier, sometimes it is impractical to use class intervals of equal width over the entire range of the frequency distribution. For example, how would we classify a sample of 1,000 household incomes ranging from $0 to $4,000,000 into ten classes? If we divide the range by 10, each class would have a width of $400,000. More than 99% of the data values would fall in the first class and less than 1% would be distributed over the other nine

FIGURE 2.5 Frequency Histogram for Number of Claims Processed over 30 Days

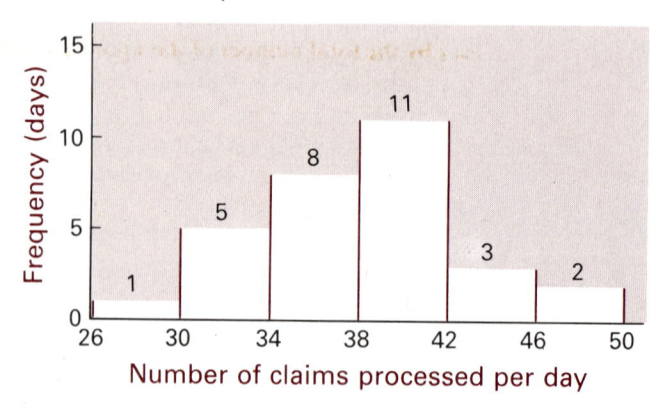

Table 2.3

Histogram for Income (in dollars) with an Open-Ended Class

Income Class ($)	Number of Families
$0 to 9,999.99	80
10,000 to 19,999.99	130
20,000 to 29,999.99	145
30,000 to 39,999.99	185
40,000 to 49,999.99	130
50,000 to 59,999.99	105
60,000 to 69,999.99	80
70,000 to 79,999.99	70
80,000 to 89,999.99	55
90,000 and above	20
Total:	1,000

classes—a very uninformative depiction of the data. How then should we set up the classes for a useful frequency distribution of household incomes? Table 2.3 shows one possibility. The last class is *open-ended*. This does not distort the frequency distribution, since the classes in the middle of the distribution all have the same width of $10,000, and 980 of the 1,000 data values fall into classes with equal widths. An open-ended class is a good solution for displaying some data sets.

The Relative Frequency Distribution and Histogram

A frequency table shows how many data points from the sample fall into each class. But the actual frequency counts would change as the sample size changed, thus obscuring the development of a simple mental model of the department's performance. One way around the problem of changing sample sizes is to construct a *relative* frequency table or *relative* frequency distribution.

Start with a frequency table as shown in Table 2.2. Divide each frequency count by the total number of data points and then multiply by 100. The resulting percentages are relative frequencies: the *proportional* occurrence of each class of observations.

Table 2.4 on page 30 shows the relative frequency or percentage distribution for the experienced claims adjuster. From it, the manager might formulate several mental models.

Model 1. Over one-third of the time (36.7%), an experienced claims adjuster can process from 38 to 41 claims per day.

Model 2. Over one-fourth of the time (26.7%), an experienced claims adjuster can process from 34 to 37 claims per day.

Table 2.4

Frequency and Relative Frequency Distribution

Claims Processed Classes	Number of Days	Percentage
26 to 29	1	1/30 = 3.3
30 to 33	5	5/30 = 16.7
34 to 37	8	8/30 = 26.7
38 to 41	11	11/30 = 36.7
42 to 45	3	3/30 = 10.0
46 to 49	2	2/30 = 6.6
Totals:	30	100.0

Model 3. An experienced claims adjuster rarely (3.3% of the time) completes fewer than 30 claims a day.

Model 4. An experienced claims adjuster seldom (6.6% of the time) completes 46 or more claims per day.

A relative frequency histogram is similar to a frequency histogram, as Figure 2.6 shows. The horizontal axis again represents the number of claims. The vertical axis shows the percentages (rather than the actual frequencies) of the data set falling into each class.

The Cumulative Frequency Distribution and Ogive

Problem sensing involves examining the numbers at the extremes, or *tails*, of a frequency distribution. By slightly modifying the relative frequency table we can

FIGURE 2.6 Relative Frequency Histogram for Number of Claims Processed over 30 Days

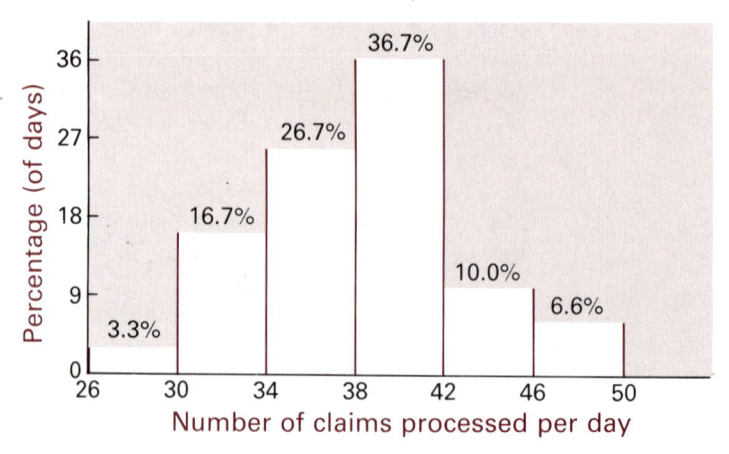

Chapter 2 Descriptive Statistics I: Toward Managerial Problem Sensing

Table 2.5

Constructing a Cumulative Frequency and Cumulative Percentage Distribution

Claims Processed Classes	Number of Days	Percentage	Cumulative Frequency	Cumulative Percentage
26 to 29	1	3.3	1	3.3
30 to 33	5	16.7	6	20.0
34 to 37	8	26.7	14	46.7
38 to 41	11	36.7	25	83.3
42 to 45	3	10.0	28	93.3
46 to 49	2	6.6	30	100.0

focus attention on the data at either tail of the distribution. The aim is to show how the data accumulate, their *cumulative distribution*.

In Table 2.5 two new columns have been added to Table 2.4. The first new column is labeled the *cumulative frequency*. Each row entry is the sum of the entries in the frequency column up to and including that row. For example, the entry in the third row of the cumulative frequency column is the sum of the entries in the first three rows of the frequency column, $1 + 5 + 8 = 14$. That is, in 14 days of the 30-day period the adjuster processed fewer than 38 claims. Similarly, the *cumulative percentage* column is the cumulative sum of the percentage column. Row 5 tells the manager that 93.3% of the time, the adjuster processed fewer than 46 claims a day.

An **ogive** is a graph of a cumulative percentage distribution. To plot the ogive for the processed claims, we must modify the first and fifth columns of Table 2.5 as shown.

> An ogive is a graph of the cumulative percentage distribution.

Claims Processed Class	Cumulative Percentage
Less than 26	0.0
Less than 30	3.3
Less than 34	20.0
Less than 38	46.7
Less than 42	83.3
Less than 46	93.3
Less than 50	100.0

The revised entries are then plotted in Figure 2.7 on page 32. To have the ogive start at 0, the first point is an additional one placed at the intersection of the horizontal axis value of 26 claims and the vertical axis value of 0%. The second point is at the intersection of the horizontal axis value of 30 claims and the vertical axis value of 3.3%. Recall that 30 is the smallest number of claims in the second class, so *less than* 30 matches up with the cumulative percentage in the first class, or 3.3%. The rest of the ogive is constructed in a similar fashion.

FIGURE 2.7   Ogive for Number of Claims Processed over 30 Days

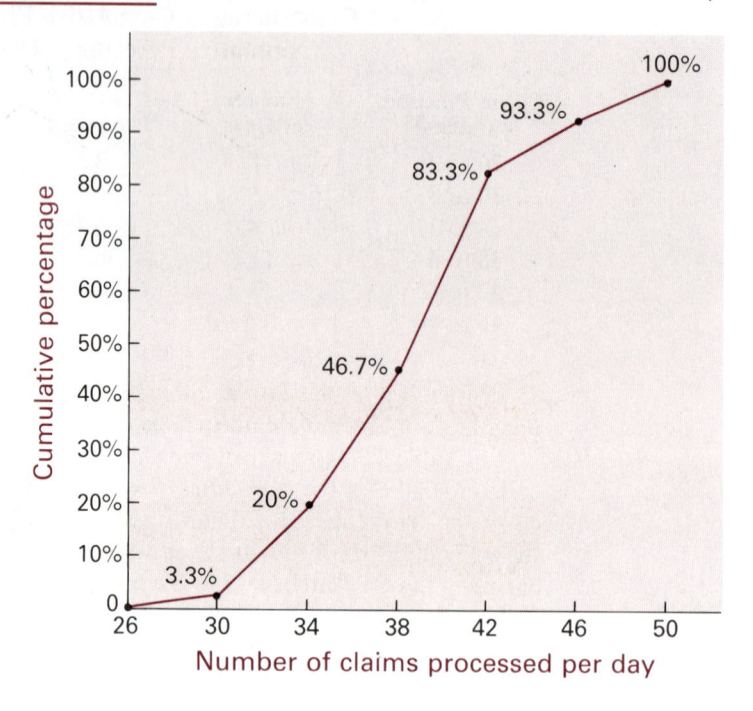

[Ogive chart showing cumulative percentage vs. number of claims processed per day. Data points: (26, 0%), (30, 3.3%), (34, 20%), (38, 46.7%), (42, 83.3%), (46, 93.3%), (50, 100%).]

Managers could use Figure 2.7 to sense problems and to make routine staffing decisions. Suppose that an experienced claims adjuster completed only 20 claims on Tuesday. Figure 2.7 shows that an experienced claims adjuster never completes fewer than 26 claims. The low value of 20 claims may signal a disturbance problem. Alternatively, if the adjuster completed 55 claims, this may signal an opportunity. Perhaps this worker does something differently that could improve the entire staff's productivity. Knowing that an adjuster processes under 38 claims per day about half the time (46.7%) will also help the manager determine staffing needs.

In summary, use stem-and-leaf displays, frequency histograms, or ogives to develop mental models. The mental models will then help to sense emerging disturbance problems, to recognize opportunities, or to make routine decisions.

SECTION 2.2 EXERCISES

1. In constructing a stem-and-leaf display or a frequency distribution you must decide how to group the numbers into classes. Each data point must belong to one and only one class. The classes should be of equal width unless there are open classes at the ends of the distribution. Suppose you are classifying sales receipts at a grocery store. Explain what is wrong with the class groupings shown.

Chapter 2 Descriptive Statistics I: Toward Managerial Problem Sensing   33

    a. $0 to $10   b. $0 to $19   c. $0 to $9.99
       $10 to $20 $20 to $59 $10 to $29.99
       $20 to $30 $60 to $79 $30 to $59.99
       $40 to $50 $80 to $99 $60 to $99.99
       Over $50 $100 and above $100.00 and over

2. Shown below are interest percentage rates charged on 30-year fixed-rate mortgage loans at 15 San Antonio banks. Construct a stem-and-leaf display to show the data.

10.75	10.25	9.75	11.1	13.0
10.5	9.85	12.25	10.25	10.5
10.1	10.75	12.0	12.75	10.75

3. A comparison shopper found the following prices per pound on the same cut of meat at 30 different grocery stores and specialty food shops.

5.23	5.65	6.30	6.72	7.00
5.26	5.95	6.50	6.72	7.00
5.30	5.95	6.65	6.74	7.15
5.45	6.13	6.69	6.90	7.15
5.49	6.20	6.70	7.00	7.20
5.55	6.30	6.70	7.00	7.20

    a. Make a stem-and-leaf display.
    b. Construct a frequency table with five classes.

4. The data shown below are price earnings ratios for 30 common stocks. Classify the data using the classes shown and determine the frequency and relative frequency distributions.

						Class	Frequency	Percentage
14.2	2.9	15.5	11.3	15.2	20.4	0 to 4.99	___	___
16.5	4.5	23.2	11.6	21.7	16.8	5 to 9.99	___	___
12.1	6.7	22.5	12.0	22.5	18.9	10 to 14.99	___	___
11.4	8.7	19.3	7.4	23.1	9.6	15 to 19.99	___	___
9.5	9.8	19.5	14.1	24.4	8.2	20 to 24.99	___	___

5. A plant manager recorded the number of accidents by month occurring in the plant over a 24-month period. The resulting frequency table is shown.

Accidents	Frequency	Accidents	Cumulative Frequency	Cumulative Percentage
1 to 2	6	Less than 1	___	___
3 to 4	10	Less than 3	___	___
5 to 6	5	Less than 5	___	___
7 to 8	2	Less than 7	___	___
9 to 10	1	Less than 9	___	___
	24	Less than 11	___	___

a. Complete the table and plot a graph of the cumulative percentages—the ogive.
b. What mental model could a manager develop based on these data?
c. Suppose next month 11 accidents happened. What might that suggest?

6. A company with two branch offices wished to compare sales commissions paid to employees during the 1990 calendar year. The data are shown.

Sales Commission	Office 1	Office 2
Up to $5,000	15	2
$5,000 to $9,999.99	100	23
$10,000 to $14,999.99	65	13
$15,000 or over	20	12
	200	50

a. Convert these frequency tables to percentage tables.
b. Convert these frequency tables to cumulative frequency tables.
c. Convert the percentage tables from part **a** to cumulative percentage tables.
d. Which of the tables provides the easiest means of comparison of sales commissions between the two offices? Explain.

2.3 Recognizing the Shape of a Histogram

The *shape* of a histogram is important in summarizing and understanding data. By the end of this section you should be able to:

1. recognize symmetric, bell-shaped, and skewed histograms;
2. explain how rescaling can affect the shape of a histogram; and
3. explain what outliers are and what they could mean.

Symmetric Histograms

In a symmetric histogram the classes left of center are mirror images of those right of center.

What characterizes a **symmetric histogram**? Consider the two frequency histograms shown in Figure 2.8. First find the centers, or balance points. Think of the number of observations in each class as weights and the horizontal axis of the histogram as a wooden board. In each class there is a stack of weights, one for each observation. Below the wooden board is a steel rod. Move the rod back and forth. The point where the board balances is the center of the frequency histogram and the mean of the data points, as depicted in Figure 2.9. It is evident that both histograms of Figure 2.8 balance at the value of 40. The classes to the right of the centers of both histograms are mirror images of the classes to the left. It is the mirror image characteristic of these histograms that makes them symmetric.

You should not expect real data sets to be perfectly symmetric. That happens only in statistics books. Yet many real-world histograms are close to symmetric.

Chapter 2 Descriptive Statistics I: Toward Managerial Problem Sensing

FIGURE 2.8 Two Frequency Histograms

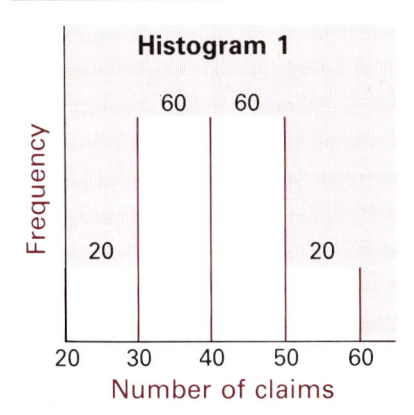

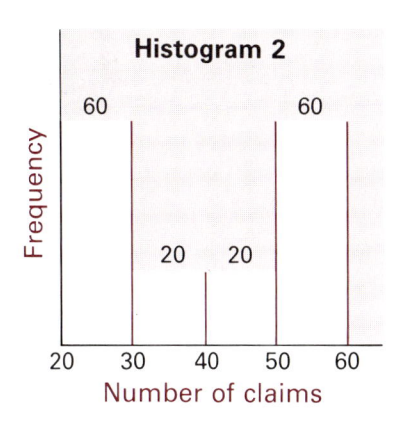

FIGURE 2.9 Balance Point for Histogram

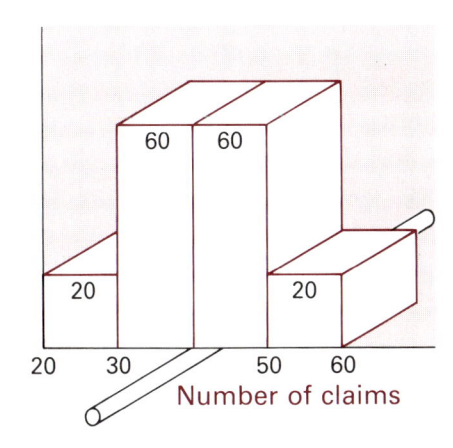

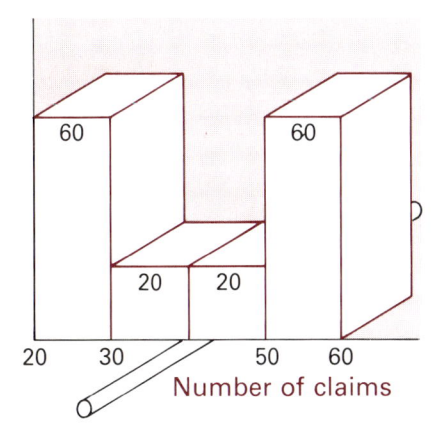

Bell-Shaped Histograms

Bell-shaped histograms are symmetric, have one peak, and are mound-shaped.

The **bell-shaped histogram** is one special type of symmetric histogram. One is presented in Figure 2.10 on page 36 for data on the values of loans at a bank. The center of the histogram is halfway between $500 and $550; that is, $525 is the mean loan. While the histogram is symmetric, it is also bell-shaped. Notice the following features:

1. Many of the dollar values of loans are at or near the center.
2. There are successively fewer values away from the center.
3. Moving in either direction from the center, the numbers of loans first drop off slowly, then more rapidly, and then more slowly again.

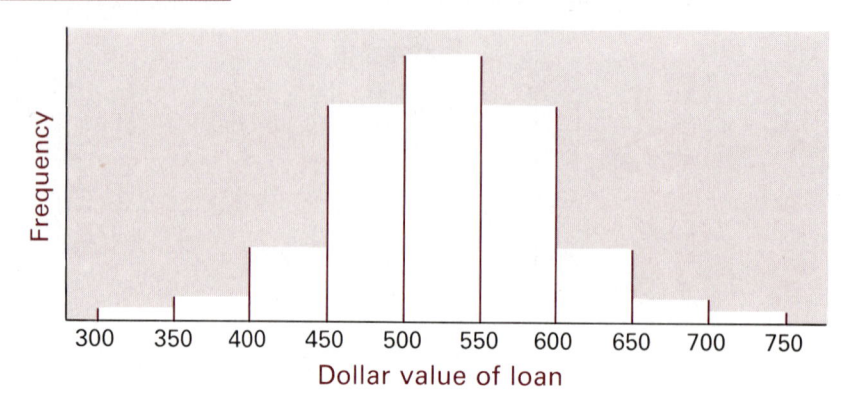

FIGURE 2.10 A Normal-Shaped Frequency Histogram

The bell-shaped histogram is very important in data analysis because it allows us to make precise statements regarding how far particular data values are from the histogram's center. This is a powerful way to summarize data, as will be shown in Section 2.6.

Impact of Rescaling Data

There are two reasons why a histogram may not look bell-shaped. One is that the scaling, or class widths, may hide the bell shape. The other, of course, is that data are *not* bell-shaped and no degree of rescaling them will make the histogram bell-shaped.

An example of the first situation can be demonstrated using the data in Table 2.6. The data represent the number of days needed to complete a project. By drawing two frequency histograms with different class widths, we can observe how the choice of class width can either mask or expose the underlying bell-shaped structure of the data. Begin by constructing two frequency distributions, one with a class width of 5 days and the other with a width of 4 days, as shown in Table 2.7. Note that the classes will contain all the data values because the days needed to complete the project are defined to the nearest .10 day. Figure 2.11 shows the two frequency distributions drawn as frequency histograms.

In the first histogram, the data are *not* bell-shaped. However, when the class width is reduced from 5 to 4 days, the distribution is symmetric and bell-shaped.

Table 2.6

Days Needed to Complete a Project

2.6	5.7	10.2	11.0	15.2
3.5	5.9	10.4	11.1	15.3
3.9	6.7	10.6	12.2	16.3
4.3	8.0	10.8	13.7	17.8
5.4	8.4	10.9	14.6	19.5

Table 2.7
Frequency Distributions of Class Width 4 and 5

Class	Days	Class	Days
0 to 4.9	4	0 to 3.9	3
5 to 9.9	6	4 to 7.9	5
10 to 14.9	10	8 to 11.9	9
15 to 19.9	5	12 to 15.9	5
	25	16 to 19.9	3
			25

FIGURE 2.11 Impact of Scaling on Shape of Frequency Histogram

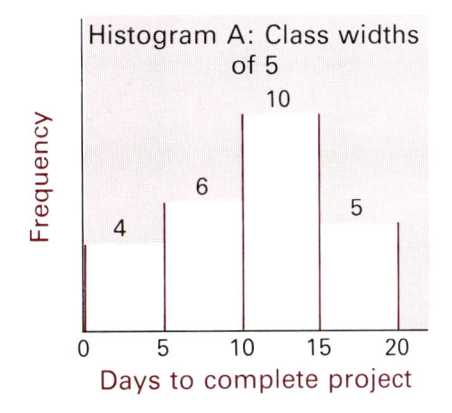

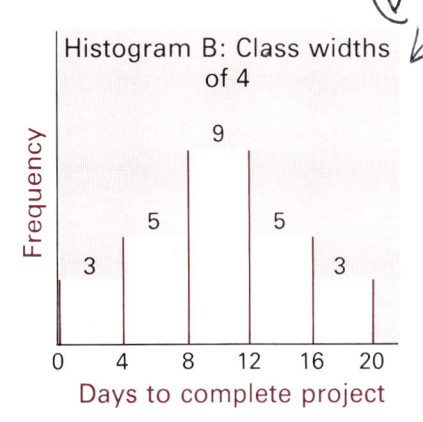

(Bell Shaped)

Histogram A: Class widths of 5

Histogram B: Class widths of 4

Days to complete project

The impact of scaling on the shape of a histogram is clearly significant. If rescaling does not result in a bell-shaped histogram, then the second situation—the underlying data are not bell-shaped—holds.

Skewed or Nonsymmetric Histograms

Skewed distributions fall off more slowly on one side of the class with the highest frequency than on the other side.

Skewed histograms are not symmetric. This can be seen readily by using the class with the highest frequency as a reference point. If more classes lie to the left of this class than to the right, then the distribution is *skewed to the left*. That is, the data values fall off more slowly toward the left than toward the right. If a histogram falls off more slowly toward larger values, it is *skewed to the right*.

Table 2.8 on page 38 shows COMCEL's productivity data for 36 work groups at its Norcross plant for the month of July. A frequency histogram for the cross-sectional data using a class width of 5 is shown in Figure 2.12. What does the histogram say about the various work groups?

Table 2.8

Work Group Productivity As a Percentage of Industrial Engineering Standards

Group	Productivity	Group	Productivity
1	106	19	110
2	95	20	123
3	103	21	104
4	95	22	100
5	95	23	101
6	97	24	95
7	95	25	97
8	105	26	94
9	102	27	102
10	89	28	102
11	105	29	106
12	99	30	110
13	95	31	97
14	100	32	101
15	106	33	95
16	101	34	98
17	97	35	97
18	104	36	94

FIGURE 2.12 Frequency Histogram for Productivity Data for 36 Work Groups

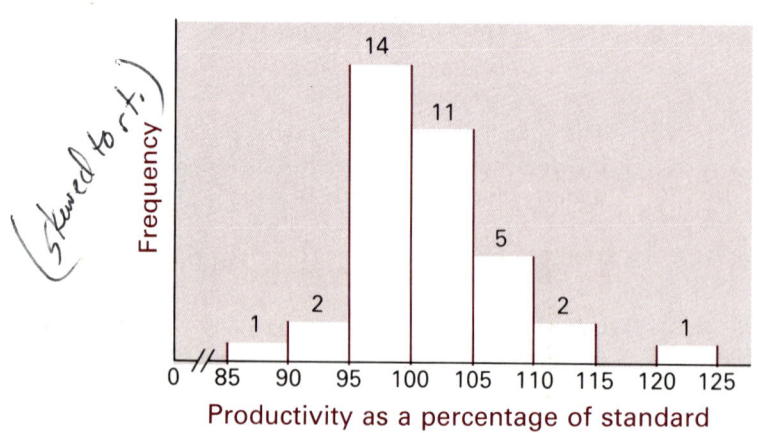

The histogram is skewed toward higher values, or skewed to the right. The frequencies for the higher productivity classes fall off more slowly than those for the lower classes. Most work groups produced from 95% to under 110%. The productivity of 123% for work group 20 stands out from the rest; perhaps it is an outlier.

The Outlier

A rudimentary definition of an outlier is any value that is much larger or smaller than most of the other values. Outliers *can* signify major deviations from standard or historic performance, and thus are essential to effective problem sensing. We say "can" for there are three possible explanations for an outlier.

1. The outlier is due to a coding error.
2. The outlier is due to chance, or random variation.
3. The outlier signifies the onset of a problem or an opportunity—assignable cause variation.

Outliers can be the result of coding errors in the form of inaccurate record keeping. A supervisor records work group 20's productivity as 123% when it is really 103%. If coding errors are eliminated as a cause, then the outlier may signify a chance happening. If a monkey sitting at a typewriter types the alphabet in the correct order, it is due to chance. We don't expect it to happen, but it could. Chance involves probabilities, which are presented in Chapters 4 and 5.

Assuming that chance can also be ruled out, then the outlier indicates either a disturbance problem or an opportunity. We must determine the cause(s) of the outlier. Suppose that the workers in group 20 had learned each other's jobs and thus could frequently switch jobs. Job switching might then account for their exceptional productivity. Alternatively, perhaps there is something distinctive about the group members—seniority, level of cooperation, or amount of schooling—that accounts for their high productivity. Later in this chapter we will demonstrate how to diagnose the causes of outliers using descriptive statistics.

In summary, knowing a histogram's shape is informative. For example, telling a colleague that COMCEL's work group productivities are skewed toward higher values provides him with a clear picture of the data. After identifying a distribution's shape, look for outliers, as they may signal an emerging problem or opportunity.

SECTION 2.3 EXERCISES

1. On a recent test in a statistics class of 20 students, 19 of the students scored between 70 and 95. One student scored 45 on the test and the teacher said that this student was an outlier. What questions would you ask to determine why the student did so poorly—that is, was an outlier?

2. A worker selects 30 items from the assembly line every hour and measures the width of the item to the nearest tenth of a centimeter. The width should be 15 ± 1 centimeters. The measurements for the first hour are shown below.

13.8	14.6	14.8	15.1	15.3	15.5
14.2	14.7	14.9	15.1	15.3	15.6
14.3	14.7	14.9	15.2	15.4	15.7
14.4	14.8	15.0	15.2	15.4	15.8
14.5	14.8	15.1	15.3	15.4	16.1

a. Construct a frequency table with four classes.
b. Sketch the histogram for the frequency table.
c. Construct a frequency table with six classes.
d. Sketch the histogram for the revised frequency table.
e. Do the data appear to be bell-shaped?

3. Must bell-shaped histograms be symmetric? Must symmetric histograms be bell-shaped?

4. Refer to Exercise 2. Suppose several hours later, you obtain the following frequency distribution on widths.

Class	Frequency
13 to 13.99	8
14 to 14.99	20
15 to 15.99	60
16 to 16.99	12

a. Given the acceptable width of 15 ± 1 centimeters, what can you conclude?
b. What action should you take now?

5. You are recording family incomes in a typical large city. Family incomes range from $7,200 to $750,000. Would you expect that the frequency histogram for family incomes would be skewed toward lower incomes, be symmetric, or be skewed toward higher incomes?

2.4 Displaying Time-Ordered Data: The Line Graph

For cross-sectional data, we draw histograms or ogives. For time-ordered data, we draw a line graph to display the data. Displaying time-ordered data helps managers see the structure underlying the data. Then they can develop simple models of how their departments are performing *over time*. By the end of this section you should be able to:

1. draw and interpret a line graph; and
2. explain the difference between stationary and nonstationary time-ordered data.

Stationary Time-Ordered Data

The following example illustrates how managers can use time-ordered data to develop simple mental models.

EXAMPLE: JOB ATTITUDE DATA. As part of its continual job climate assessment, COMCEL collects monthly data on the mean responses of ten workers to statement 4 from the climate study questionnaire shown in Table 1.2. The statement, "The workers in this plant always try to improve," is designed to assess the workers' attitudes toward improving productivity. COMCEL's monthly attitude data for the past three years are presented in Table 2.9.

Table 2.9
Mean of Ten Workers' Attitudes Toward Improving Productivity over the Past 36 Months

Year	Jan.	Feb.	Mar.	Apr.	May	June	July	Aug.	Sept.	Oct.	Nov.	Dec.
1990	4.81	2.60	3.12	3.66	2.80	3.60	2.94	1.87	2.30	1.80	4.60	2.56
1991	4.60	2.41	3.46	3.50	2.21	3.82	2.08	2.06	2.20	2.20	4.30	2.91
1992	4.60	2.73	3.38	3.46	2.43	3.60	2.39	1.99	2.17	2.01	4.40	2.36

A *line graph* to display the data's structure is shown in Figure 2.13. The horizontal axis measures time in months and the vertical axis is the level of the variable, attitude toward improving productivity. Attitude level varies from 1 (poor attitude) to 5 (very good attitude). Equal distances between grid marks on the horizontal and vertical axes should represent equal differences in amounts. Using unequal distances will distort the line graph.

FIGURE 2.13 COMCEL's Monthly Attitude Data, 1990–1992

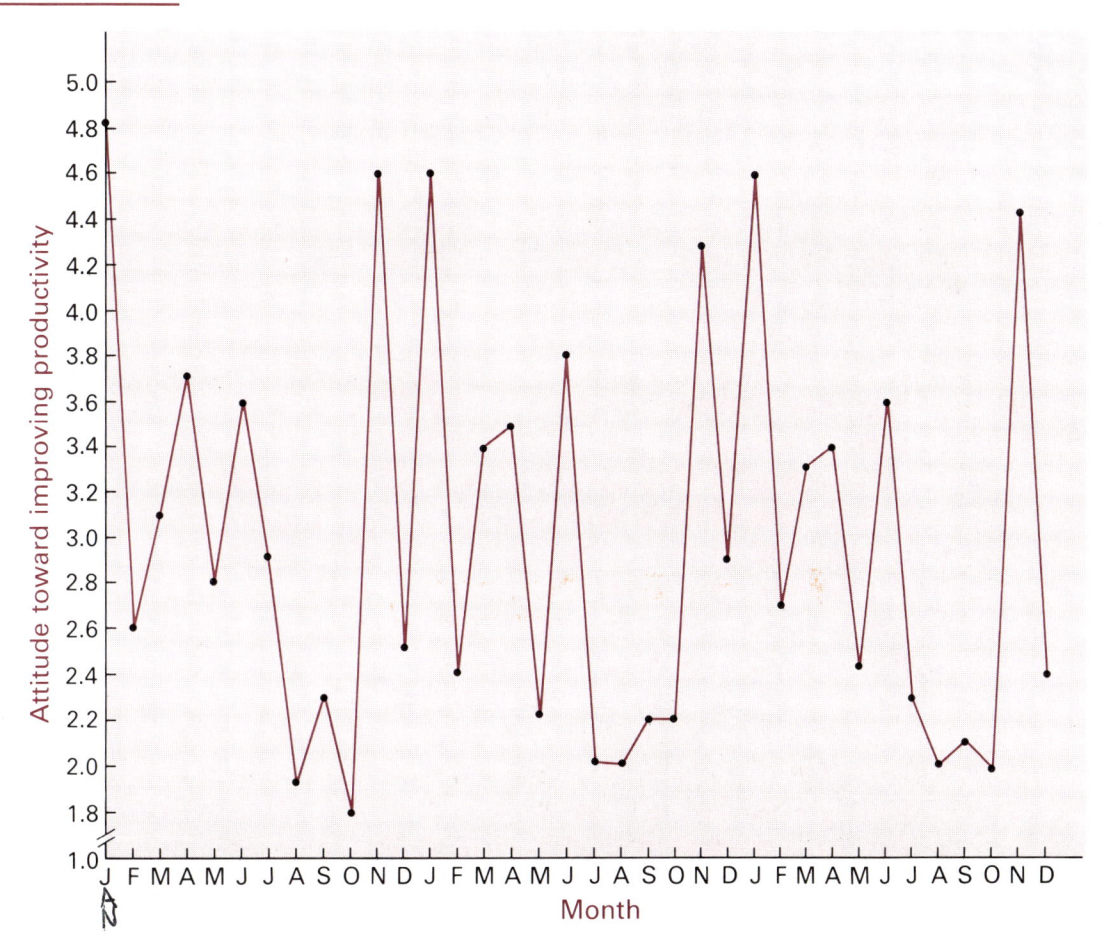

| A time-ordered series is stationary when the general level of the series remains nearly constant over the entire time period. The values of a stationary series fluctuate around a constant mean value.

What does the line graph reveal? Look for patterns! First, the data are **stationary**, because there is no upward or downward trend over time. While attitudes vary from month to month, the graph shows no systematic tendency for attitudes to improve or deteriorate over the 36 months. Specifically, the mean attitude score over the 3-year period is 3.00. The mean attitude scores for each of the 3 years, 1990, 1991, and 1992, are 3.06, 2.98 and 2.96, respectively. Thus the mean score over the 3-year period is virtually the same as that of any given year. The mean value of the series has remained constant over time.

The second thing to note is that attitudes are highest for the same two months—namely, January and November—each year. Monthly attitudes are also lowest from August to October each year. Effective managers should now ask why attitudes toward improving productivity are highest in January and November and lowest in August through October each year. Asking why is the beginning of problem diagnosis.

Nonstationary Time-Ordered Data

Next, consider the line graphs in Figure 2.14 and compare them with the line graph in Figure 2.13. Immediately, one notices that the line graphs in Figure 2.14

FIGURE 2.14 Examples of Nonstationary Time-Ordered Data

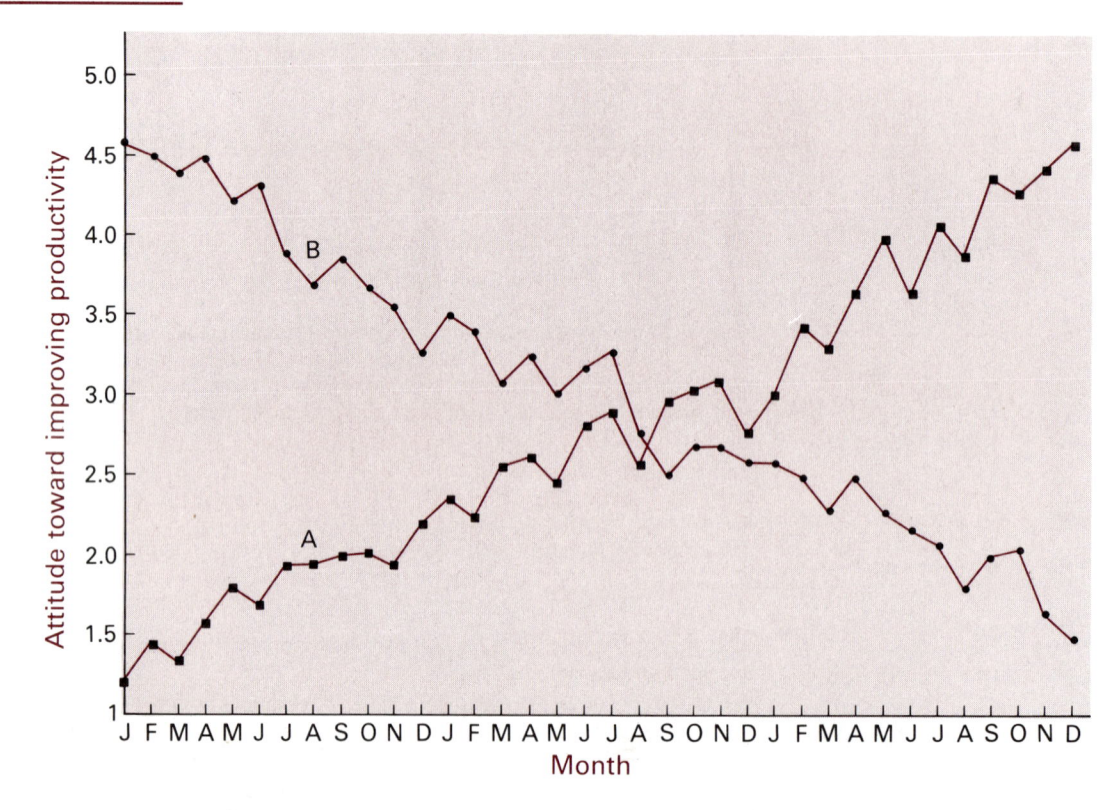

Chapter 2   Descriptive Statistics I: Toward Managerial Problem Sensing

display clear tendencies, in contrast to that in Figure 2.13. Line graph A shows an overall increase or upward trend in attitude scores over the three years. Although there are peaks and valleys throughout the three years, the attitudes tend to improve. In this case, the overall mean attitude for the 36-month period is *not* a good description of the level of the series from beginning to end. The mean attitude scores for each of the three years are increasing. The series is **nonstationary**.

Likewise, line graph B is also nonstationary, as it shows an overall decrease in attitude scores, or downward trend. The mean attitude scores for each of the three years are decreasing, rather than remaining stationary.

In summary, managers use stem-and-leaf displays or frequency histograms to display cross-sectional data and line graphs to display time-ordered data. Managers describe cross-sectional data as symmetric or skewed and time-ordered data as stationary or nonstationary. Both sets of descriptors are essential for obtaining a clear understanding of the data.

A time-ordered series is nonstationary when the general level of the series either systematically increases or decreases over time.

SECTION 2.4 EXERCISES

1. Explain what we mean by a stationary series.

2. Plot the following time-ordered data. Decide whether the series is stationary or nonstationary.

Quarter	1	2	3	4	1	2	3	4
Department 1	30	60	70	40	30	60	70	40

3. Plot the following time-ordered data. Decide whether the series is stationary or nonstationary.

Quarter	1	2	3	4	1	2	3	4
Department 2	12	24	25	30	28	48	45	50

4. Your summer job is to make sure a cola vending machine is working properly. For 50 cents, the machine should dispense 7 ounces of soda. Your job is to test the machine twice an hour and write down amounts of soda actually dispensed. The 16 measurements made over your 8-hour shift are shown here.

Time Period	1	2	3	4	5	6	7	8
Soda (ounces)	6.9	7.0	7.1	7.4	7.2	6.7	7.1	6.0

Time Period	9	10	11	12	13	14	15	16
Soda (ounces)	6.9	7.1	7.4	6.7	6.9	7.3	6.7	6.9

   a. Before plotting the data, would you expect this time series to be stationary or nonstationary? Explain.
   b. How is the concept of stationary related to your job as quality control inspector?
   c. Plot the data to check your expectations.

5. A sales manager was quoted as saying that sales of computer products have increased by 2% per month over the last 24 months. Would the sales data by month be stationary or nonstationary?

6. Two graphs are shown that record the percentage of pages with errors typed daily by the staff. Both graphs indicate that for the past week typists' errors are increasing. At week two, the firm took corrective action that solved the problem. Which graph reflects the successful problem solving?

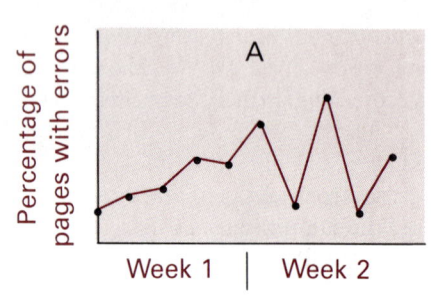

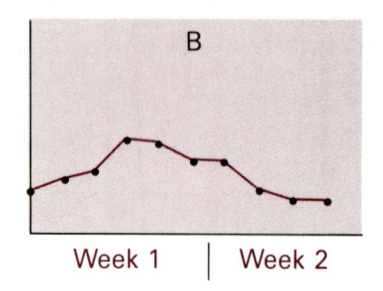

7. Shown are data of total production of electrical energy in trillion kilowatts-hours by utility companies for various years.

Year	1912	1920	1930	1940	1950	1960	1970	1980	1986
Energy	12	39	91	142	329	755	1,532	2,286	2,489

Sources: *Historical Statistics of the United States, Colonial Times to 1970*, p. 821; and *Statistical Abstract of the United States 1988*, p. 547.

   a. Plot the data in a scatter diagram. Is the line graph stationary?
   b. Describe the relationship.
   c. Estimate the time it has taken to double our energy production. For example, how long did it take to go from 100 trillion kw-hrs to 200 trillion? From 200 trillion to 400 trillion? From 400 trillion to 800 trillion? From 800 trillion to 1,600 trillion?
   d. Estimate the year when energy production should have reached 3,200 trillion kw-hrs. What are some reasons that it did not?

8. Shown are the percentages of people living in urban areas in the United States since colonial times.

Year	1800	1830	1860	1890	1920	1950	1980
Percentage	6	9	20	35	51	64	73.7

Source: *Statistical Abstract of the United States 1985*, p. 22.

   a. Plot the data. Are the data stationary?
   b. Describe the relationship.

2.5 Summarizing Cross-Sectional Data: The Mean and Standard Deviation

The main purpose of summarizing cross-sectional data is to help problem solvers answer the following questions more precisely:

How are we doing on the average? Most of the time? The majority of the time?

Is there much variation from one plant to the next, one work group to the next? If so, how much?

How far away from the rest of the data must a data value be before we label it as an outlier? What constitutes an extraordinary, or unusual, event?

We have shown how to organize cross-sectional data by drawing histograms and ogives. Now we will explain how to summarize the data to help the problem solver answer the questions. By the end of this section, you should be able to:

1. compute the sample mean;
2. approximate the sample mean of data that have already been displayed in a frequency histogram;
3. explain the need for a measure of spread;
4. explain why the range is not an effective measure of spread;
5. compute the sample standard deviation;
6. compute the mean and standard deviation for yes/no data;
7. use the standard deviation to explain how far particular data values are from the mean; and
8. explain why the mean can be misleading as a measure of the center.

Distinguishing the Sample from the Population

The sample mean is the sum of all the data values divided by the sample size.

Problem solvers generally deal with *sample data*. For example, COMCEL selects 10 workers and determines that their mean attitude toward improving productivity is 3.50 (on a 5-point scale). If COMCEL selected 10 other workers, the mean attitude might be 4.25. The two numbers are **sample means** and are affected by random events which include many factors that can cause the sample means to vary.

The *population mean* is the average attitude of *all* workers in the company. We rarely know the population mean for it is either too costly or too time-consuming to determine. We must use the sample mean to estimate the population mean. The distinction between samples and populations is very important in statistics, and will be discussed further in Chapters 6–12.

The Mean

Suppose we compute the sample mean for the 30 days of claims data displayed in Figure 2.4. To do so, we add up all the data values and divide by the number of observations. Use expression (2.1) to calculate the sample mean:

$$\text{Sample mean} = \bar{x} = \frac{\sum_{i=1}^{n} X_i}{n} \qquad (2.1)$$

The sample mean is called *x-bar*. The expression says: Sum the data values and divide by the total number of data values, *n*. The Greek letter sigma means "sum." The sample mean for the number of claims processed by the claims adjuster is

$$\bar{x} = \frac{28 + 30 + 30 + 31 + \cdots + 44 + 45 + 46 + 48}{30}$$

$$= \frac{1{,}124}{30} = 37.5 \text{ claims per day}$$

The adjuster processed, on the average, 37.5 claims per day over the 30-day period.

Approximating the Mean of Histogram Data

Suppose we are given only Figure 2.5, a histogram for the claims adjustment data, without the original data. We could *approximate* the histogram's mean by using the *balance point* idea, as shown in Figure 2.15.

Figure 2.15 shows a steel rod underneath a three-dimensional view of the histogram in Figure 2.5. Move the rod from left to right. At what claims processing rate would the frequency histogram balance? It wouldn't balance at 34 claims per day, for there would be too much weight (data values) to the right, and the histogram would tilt down to the right. It wouldn't balance at 42 claims per day, for there would be too much weight to the left, and the histogram would tilt down to the left. The balance point, or the approximate mean, is somewhere between 37 and 39 claims per day.

The sample mean is a very important measure in summarizing a data set. However, it does not measure the spread of values in a data set.

FIGURE 2.15 Frequency Histogram of Claims Adjustment Data

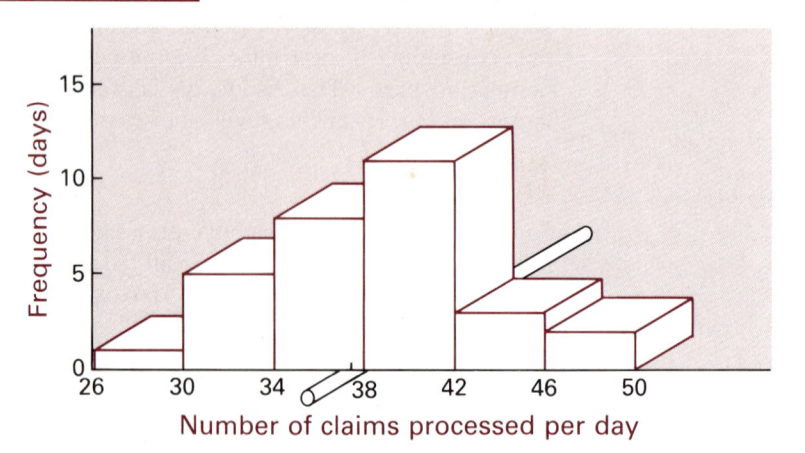

The Range

A new manager is placed in charge of two production lines. His goals are to increase the mean production rates to above 50 units per hour and to achieve a relatively constant hourly output. Table 2.10 presents data for the two departments.

Table 2.10
Two Production Data Sets

	Department A	Department B
	60	80
	59	40
	61	0
	60	120
	60	60
Mean	60 units per hour	60 units per hour

While both data sets have the same mean, the hourly production rate in department A is stable whereas that of department B is not. For department B, the sample mean simply does not typify the data. How can we measure the spread or variability in the two data sets?

The **sample range** is the simplest measure of spread. It equals the difference between the largest and smallest data values. The ranges for the two data sets are $61 - 59 = 2$ for department A and $120 - 0 = 120$ for department B. Thus, there is a very narrow spread in the production rate of department A and a very wide spread in that of department B.

Although the range is a useful measure of spread, it has three weaknesses. First, it uses only two data values, ignoring the remaining data. At best, it is a quick estimate of spread. Second, you can be easily misled by the range. Consider the two data sets in Table 2.11. While the range is 20 for both data sets, department D has a wider spread or variability, with all different values, while department C has only one value that differs from all the others. The third weakness is that the range ignores the mean in calculating the spread in a data set. A useful measure of spread should tell us how close the data values are to

The sample range is the difference between the largest and smallest data values.

Table 2.11
Two Additional Production Data Sets

	Department C	Department D
	60	40
	60	45
	60	50
	60	55
	40	60
Range	20 units per hour	20 units per hour

the mean. Why? In order to solve a problem, managers often need to know if groups differ in their mean performance or in their variability around that mean performance. We turn to such a measure next.

The Variance and Standard Deviation

The sample variance overcomes the three weaknesses of the range. The sample variance is the sum of the squared differences between each observation and the sample mean divided by the sample size minus 1:

$$\text{Sample variance} = s^2 = \frac{\sum_{i=1}^{n}(x_i - \bar{x})^2}{n - 1} \tag{2.2}$$

For example, compute the sample variance for the claims data in Table 2.1:

$$s^2 = \frac{(28 - 37.5)^2 + \cdots + (48 - 37.5)^2}{30 - 1} = 24$$

The variance has the following properties:

1. Unlike the range, all the data are used.
2. Unlike the range, the variance does not measure only spread or dispersion, but measures spread or dispersion around the *mean*.
3. The variance can never be negative because the *squared* differences around the mean are summed. When the variance equals zero, all the numbers are equal to the mean and there is no dispersion.

The sample variance has no direct physical meaning because it is measured in squared units such as claims^2 and dollars^2. A more informative measure of the spread is the **sample standard deviation**. The standard deviation is the square root of the variance. The standard deviation for the claims data is the square root of 24, or 4.9 claims.

What does this standard deviation tell us? Like the variance, the standard deviation measures the variability in the number of claims processed by the adjuster over the 30-day period. But the standard deviation is measured in the same units as the original data. It has a direct physical interpretation. It indicates how far away the numbers in the sample are from the sample mean. If the adjuster processed the same number of claims per day over the 30-day period, the standard deviation would be zero. The larger the standard deviation, the greater the spread in the 30 processing rates. As will be seen shortly, very few data values will fall beyond two or three standard deviations from the sample mean.

The sample standard deviation is the square root of the sum of the squared differences between the data values and the sample mean divided by the sample size minus 1.

Yes/No Data

Managers are often asked to respond to questions such as: Did your department have any discipline cases last year? Is your department planning to purchase additional computers? Do any of your employees use the firm's aerobic facilities? Unlike the previous examples, a response to any of these questions is either yes or no. Much of the data crossing a manager's desk are yes/no data. We must learn how to organize and summarize them.

EXAMPLE: COMCEL'S BENEFITS SURVEY RESULTS. COMCEL recently surveyed 500 employees to determine the number who are interested in a flexible benefits package. Presently, every employee has the same package. COMCEL is considering allowing employees to design their own benefits package. Thus, one worker could select the base life and health coverage insurance plans plus 3 weeks vacation, while another could select the extended insurance coverage and only 1 week vacation.

To quantify the yes/no data we assign a 1 to each person who said yes, favoring the proposed new benefits system, and a 0 to those who said no. The usual practice is to assign a 1 to the group of interest.

Figure 2.16 is a frequency histogram of the survey's results. Code the data as follows:

$$X = \text{the number of people who respond yes, assigned as the 1s}$$
$$Y = \text{the number of people who respond no, assigned as the 0s}$$
$$n = X + Y = \text{the total number of observations}$$

Use expression (2.3) to compute the sample mean, or the fraction of yes responses:

$$\bar{x} = \frac{\sum_{i=1}^{n} x_i}{n} \qquad (2.3)$$

The sum of x represents the number of people who responded yes to the survey. The sum of y represents the number of people who responded no. For the

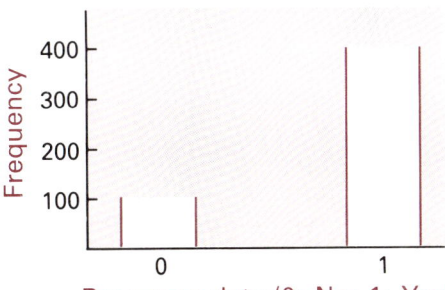

FIGURE 2.16 Histogram for Response to Proposed Flexible Benefits Package

benefits survey, the data and resulting sample mean are as follows:

$$x = 400 \text{ workers}$$
$$y = 100 \text{ workers}$$
$$n = 500 \text{ workers}$$
$$\bar{x} = \frac{400}{500} = .80$$

In other words, 80% of the workers want a flexible benefits package.

Use expression (2.4) to compute the sample variance:

$$s^2 = \frac{\sum_{i=1}^{n} x_i \cdot \sum_{i=1}^{n} y_i}{n \cdot (n-1)} \qquad (2.4)$$

For the benefits survey data we obtain the following:

$$s^2 = \frac{400 \cdot 100}{500 \cdot 499}$$
$$= .16$$
$$s = \sqrt{.16} = .40$$

What does the .40 mean? The standard deviation measures the variability in the attitudes of the 500 workers. If all favored (or did not favor) the new benefits package, the sample standard deviation would be zero (Please check this for yourself!). The smaller the sample standard deviation, the greater the workers' agreement about the new benefits package. But what does the .40 mean? We address that issue in the next section.

In brief, the three common measures used to summarize a data set are the sample mean, the sample range, and the sample standard deviation.

SECTION 2.5 EXERCISES

1. Three secretaries competing for a position are asked to type the same document. Their completion times are 1, 2, and 3 minutes, respectively. Find the mean, variance, and standard deviation.

2. Without doing any computation, what is the standard deviation of the following set of numbers: {1, 1, 1}?

3. The hourly wages of three employees are $4.00, $4.50, and $5.00. What would happen to the mean and standard deviation of these wages if the following occurred:
   a. each got a $.50 per hour raise?
   b. the hourly wage of each was doubled?
   c. What does adding a constant or multiplying by a constant do to the mean and standard deviation?

Chapter 2   Descriptive Statistics I: Toward Managerial Problem Sensing   51

4. Consider the following sample of data values: {4, 8, 6, 6, 5, 7, 3, 9, 2, 10}.
   a. Find the sample mean.
   b. Find the range.
   c. Find the sample variance and standard deviation.

5. Shown are two frequency histograms for the size of consumer loans at two banks. Without doing any computation, which has the greater mean and standard deviation?

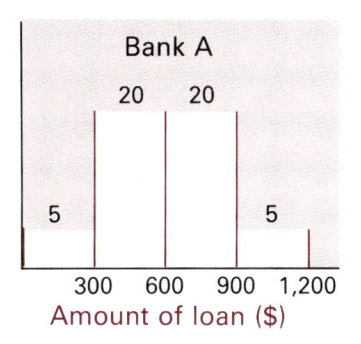

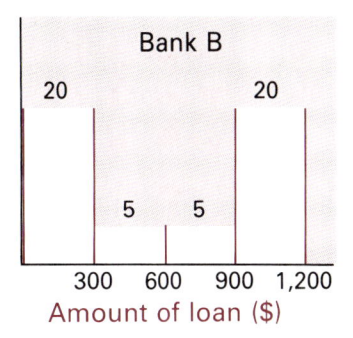

Bank A

Bank B

Amount of loan ($)

Amount of loan ($)

6. The following histogram shows the number of days to complete construction of houses in a development. One histogram block is missing. Given that the mean number of days to build a house is 75, how many houses took 60 to under 70 days to build?

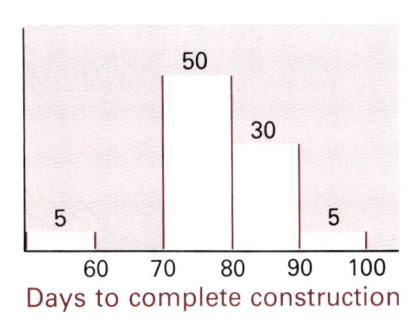

Days to complete construction

7. Workers in a nonunion company recently voted whether to join a national union. Of the 300 employees who voted, 90 voted in favor of union representation. Find the mean and standard deviation for the data set consisting of 210 values of 0 (those who did not favor union representation) and 90 values of 1 (those who favored union representation).

2.6 Interpreting the Mean and Standard Deviation: The Empirical and Chebyshev Rules

The sample mean and sample standard deviation quickly and accurately describe a data set. But what exactly does the standard deviation mean? How should we interpret it? It depends on whether the histogram for the data set is bell-shaped or not. By the end of this section you should be able to:

1. use the Empirical rule and the standard deviation to describe the variation of bell-shaped data around the sample mean;
2. use the Empirical rule and the standard deviation to detect outliers;
3. use Chebyshev's rule and the standard deviation to describe the variation of data that are not bell-shaped; and
4. use Chebyshev's rule and the standard deviation to detect outliers.

Bell-Shaped Histograms: The Empirical Rule

When a data set's histogram is approximately bell-shaped, we can use the mean and standard deviation to describe the distribution of values using the Empirical rule. The Empirical rule says that:

> About two-thirds of the data values will lie within a distance of one standard deviation on either side of the mean.

> About 95% of the data values will lie within a distance of two standard deviations on either side of the mean.

> Nearly all (99% or more) data values will lie within a distance of three standard deviations on either side of the mean.

Let's apply the Empirical rule to the project completion data in Table 2.6. Figure 2.11 (Histogram B) shows that the data set is reasonably bell-shaped. The mean and standard deviation for the data in Table 2.6 are given by:

$$\bar{x} = \frac{2.6 + 3.5 + 3.9 + 4.3 + \cdots + 15.3 + 16.3 + 17.8 + 19.5}{25}$$

$$= 10.2 \text{ days}$$

$$s = \sqrt{\frac{(2.6 - 10.2)^2 + \cdots + (19.5 - 10.2)^2}{25 - 1}}$$

$$= 4.7 \text{ days}$$

On the basis of the Empirical rule we can surmise that:

1. About two-thirds of the data will lie between 5.5 days and 14.9 days. This is a distance of one standard deviation on each side of the mean.
2. About 95% of the data will lie between .8 day and 19.6 days. This is a distance of two standard deviations on each side of the mean.

The Empirical rule is especially useful when we do not have the original data values. If we know only the mean and standard deviation of a bell-shaped data set, we could determine what percentage of the data lies within various distances from the mean.

The Outlier

If the histogram for a data set is approximately bell-shaped, a data value more than three standard deviations away from the mean should be considered an outlier.

Until now **outliers** have been defined as data values that lie far away from the mean. But how far is far? According to the Empirical rule, it would be rare for a data value to fall more than two standard deviations from the mean. We should expect this to happen only 5% of the time. Data values beyond three standard deviations from the mean are even rarer (occurring less than 1% of the time). This leads to the definition given in the margin.

But how do we handle data sets that are skewed? The next section will demonstrate the application of Chebyshev's rule for such data.

Skewed Histograms: Chebyshev's Rule

If a histogram is not bell-shaped, we can use Chebyshev's rule to determine what percentage of the data may lie at various distances from the mean. Chebyshev's rule states that:

At least $(100 - 100/h^2)$ % of the observations must lie within a distance of h standard deviations of the mean. This expression is true for all values of h greater than 1.

Table 2.12 illustrates how Chebyshev's rule summarizes data that are not bell-shaped.

Use Chebyshev's rule to summarize the work group productivity data in Table 2.8. The corresponding Figure 2.12 shows that the data are skewed toward

Table 2.12

Summarizing a Data Set with Chebyshev's Rule

Number of Standard Deviations	Computation	Interpretation
$h = 2$	$100 - \frac{100}{4} = 75\%$	At least 75% of the data values must lie within a distance of plus or minus *two* standard deviations of the mean.
$h = 3$	$100 - \frac{100}{9} = 88.9\%$	At least 88.9% of the data values must lie within a distance of plus or minus *three* standard deviations of the mean.
$h = 4$	$100 - \frac{100}{16} = 93.8\%$	At least 93.8% of the data values must lie within a distance of plus or minus *four* standard deviations of the mean.

higher values. Work group 20 was identified as a possible outlier. That is, based on the frequency histogram alone, work group 20's productivity was extraordinarily high. Now we can calculate the mean and standard deviation to check if it is an outlier:

$$\bar{x} = \frac{106 + 95 + \cdots + 97 + 94}{36}$$

$$= 100.42\% \text{ of industry standard}$$

$$s = \sqrt{\frac{(106 - 100.42)^2 + \cdots + (94 - 100.42)^2}{36 - 1}}$$

$$= 6.22\% \text{ of industry standard}$$

Now, using Table 2.12, we can determine if work group 20's productivity is an outlier.

For bell-shaped data, the rare data value or outlier is defined as happening 1% or less of the time. For non–bell-shaped data, rarely would a data value fall more than a distance of four standard deviations from the mean, or 100% − 93.8% = 6.2% of the time. If such an event happened, consider it an **outlier**.

When a data set is not bell-shaped, consider a value more than four standard deviations away from the mean as an outlier.

Let's determine the productivities that are four standard deviations on each side of the mean:

Four standard deviations below the mean: 100.42% − 4(6.22%) = 75.5%

Four standard deviations above the mean: 100.42% + 4(6.22%) = 125.3%

Work group 20's productivity of 123% is very close to four standard deviations above the mean and thus very close to being an outlier. Based on the frequency histogram, mean, standard deviation, and Chebyshev's rule, we can develop the following expanded mental model:

> The mean productivity for the 36 work groups is 100.42% of industry standard, and the standard deviation is 6.22% of industry standard.
>
> At least 75% of the work groups should have productivities between the mean minus two standard deviations and the mean plus two standard deviations—that is, between 87.9% (100.42% − 2(6.22%)) and 112.9% (100.42% + 2(6.22%)).
>
> Work group 20's productivity of 123% may be an outlier, since it is so close to a productivity of 125.3%, the value at four standard deviations above the mean.

Even without these statistical tools ($\bar{X}$, s, and Chebyshev's rule) a mental model of performance for the 36 work groups had been developed. However, the tools have refined and added precision to the initial mental model without an excessive amount of work.

In summary, we can apply Chebyshev's rule to any data set. When the data are bell-shaped, use the Empirical rule for a more precise description of the distribution. And what have we accomplished by using these rules? We have summarized a data set in terms of two numbers—the mean and standard deviation—without losing much information. Managers build their mental models about how their departments are doing from such summarizing statistics. Moreover, these rules help to define more precisely which data values are outliers.

Weakness of the Mean and the Standard Deviation

Sometimes the mean can be misleading. Suppose a company has 10 employees whose mean salary is $100,000 per year. Would you like to work for such a company? Your inclination is probably to say: "Where do I sign up?" But think again. Although the mean salary is $100,000, there is no guarantee that you will be getting the mean salary! One scenario for such a mean is that nine employees earn $10,000 per year and the boss earns $910,000 per year. The moral is that, unless you are the boss, the mean can be misleading.

A more informative measure of the average or typical salary for this company would be the mode. The mode is the data value that occurs most frequently. Since nine of the 10 salaries are $10,000, the mode of the data set would be $10,000.

The mode does have some drawbacks. If all data set values are different, there is no mode. Also, the mode has no corresponding measure of spread like the mean does. Thus, the mode provides no assistance in detecting outliers. We must look for another measure to overcome the shortcomings of the mean.

SECTION 2.6 EXERCISES

1. Given the following sample of {0, 3, 2, 6, 1, 2, 3, 4, 3, 5}.
   a. Find the mean.
   b. Find the variance and standard deviation.
   c. How many values fall within one standard deviation of the mean?
   d. How many values fall within two standard deviations of the mean?

2. The mean and standard deviation of a bell-shaped data set are 16 and 4, respectively. If an outlier is defined as any data point falling beyond three standard deviations from the mean, are any of these data points outliers: {3, 22, 28}?

3. Suppose you received a computer printout showing the mean and standard deviation for a variable as MEAN = 100 and S.D. = 10. Describe what the distribution for the variable looks like, first assuming that the histogram is skewed, and then assuming the histogram is bell-shaped.

4. The mean score on a college entrance examination is 500 and the standard deviation is 100. Assume that the test scores are bell-shaped.
   a. Approximately what percentage of the scores will fall below 400 or above 600?
   b. Approximately what percentage of the scores will fall beyond 700?

5. A set of measurements taken from an assembly line is bell-shaped with a mean of 65.0 inches and a standard deviation of .1 inch.

a. Approximately what percentage of the measurements will fall above 65.1 inches?
b. Between 64.6 and 65.2 inches?
c. Below 64.8 inches?

6. The mean amount paid out in worker's compensation claims is $750 and the standard deviation is $1,800. Is the distribution of claims bell-shaped? Explain.

7. A process control inspector reported that a sample of 50 fuses had a mean life of 96.5 hours and a standard deviation of .75 hour. He was later asked the fraction of the fuses that lasted more than 95 hours. The inspector did not have the data with him and could not answer the question. Can you place a lower and an upper bound on the desired proportion?

2.7 Summarizing Cross-Sectional Data: The Median, Trimmed Mean, and Interquartile Range

In the previous example, why did the mean fail to give an accurate picture of the average salary in the firm? It failed because the boss's salary was an outlier. Outliers strongly affect the mean and the standard deviation. One therefore needs alternative measures of the center and spread that are less affected by outliers. By the end of this section you will be able to:

1. determine the median;
2. approximate the median for data that have already been displayed in a frequency histogram;
3. compute the trimmed mean;
4. discuss when to use the mean, median, and trimmed mean;
5. compute the interquartile range; and
6. explain when to use the mean and standard deviation or the median and interquartile range.

The Median

An alternative measure to the mean is the median, the *middle data value* in an ordered stem-and-leaf display. Recall that we must rank order the data from the smallest to the largest value before drawing an ordered stem-and-leaf display.

Consider the data in Table 2.13. Is the median age of accounts receivable equal to 37 days? No, because there are four numbers below it—namely, 31, 33, 36, and 36—and five numbers above it—namely, 38, 39, 41, 44, and 47. The **median** is that number such that half the data values are larger and half are smaller than it. Thus the median must be between 37 days and 38 days. Arbitrarily we say that the median is halfway between the two values or 37.5 days.

How do we determine the middle value? Begin by distinguishing between the ranks of data values and the data values themselves. For example, in Table 2.13, data value 31 ranks first (the lowest) and data value 47 ranks 10th (the highest).

The median is the middle value in a rank-ordered data set. That means that half the data values are larger and half the data values are smaller than the median.

Table 2.13

Age of Accounts Receivable
Stem-and-Leaf Display

9	
8	
7	
6	
6	7
3	4
1	1
3	4

Formally, we can compute the rank using the following expression:

$$\text{Rank of median value} = \frac{1 + \text{Number of data values}}{2} \quad (2.5)$$

For the data in Table 2.13, the *rank* of the median value is $(1 + 10)/2 = 5.5$. Thus, a *rank* of 5.5 means that the median lies halfway between the fifth and sixth rank-ordered data values, or 37.5 days. Five data values are below 37.5 days and five data values are above 37.5 days.

Approximating the Median of a Frequency Histogram

How can we approximate the median of a histogram, such as the one shown for the work group productivity data in Figure 2.12? Use Figure 2.12 to develop the cumulative frequency table shown in Table 2.14. Note that the eight classes will contain all the data values because productivity data are integer values.

Table 2.14

Cumulative Frequency Table for
Work Group Productivity Data As Percentage of Standard

Productivity Classes	Number of Groups	Cumulative Frequency
85 to 89	1	1
90 to 94	2	3
95 to 99	14	17
100 to 104	11	28
105 to 109	5	33
110 to 114	2	35
115 to 119	0	35
120 to 124	1	36
Total:	36	

Cumulative frequencies are useful in approximating the median of frequency data. With 36 data values, expression (2.5) gives the rank of the median as $(1 + 36)/2 = 18.5$. The cumulative frequency column shows that the 17 smallest data values lie in the first three classes. The 18th and 19th data values are at the beginning of the 100% to 104% productivity class. In fact, they are the first two data values in that class. Therefore, we approximate the median to be just over 100% of industry standard.

We can check the approximation in this instance since the actual data are available from Table 2.8. In Table 2.15 the productivities of the 36 work groups are rank ordered. Notice that, since the rank is 18.5, the actual median is 100, which is very close to the approximation using the cumulative frequency table.

In summary, when only frequency data are available, develop a cumulative frequency table to approximate the median. The approximation will be almost as accurate as having the raw data.

Differences Between the Mean and Median

The mean and median were relatively close—38.2 days vs. 37.5 days—for the age of accounts receivable data set in Table 2.13. Please verify this. In the salary example the mean was $100,000, but the median was only $10,000. Why does the median not always lie close to the mean even though both are measures of the

Table 2.15
Determining the Actual Median for the 36 Work Group Productivities

Group	Data Value	Rank Order from Bottom	Group	Data Value	Rank Order from Bottom
10	89	1	22	100	19
26	94	2	16	101	20
36	94	3	23	101	21
33	95	4	32	101	22
24	95	5	9	102	23
4	95	6	27	102	24
7	95	7	28	102	25
5	95	8	3	103	26
2	95	9	21	104	27
13	95	10	18	104	28
6	97	11	8	105	29
17	97	12	11	105	30
35	97	13	29	106	31
31	97	14	1	106	32
25	97	15	15	106	33
34	98	16	30	110	34
12	99	17	19	110	35
14	100	18	20	123	36

center of a data set? Consider, what is the major difference between how we compute the mean and how we determine the median?

In determining the median, we are not concerned with the actual data values that lie above and below the median. We are concerned only that the *number* of observations that lie above the median be the same as the number that lie below it. In computing the mean, we sum the actual data *values* and divide by the sample size. If there are outliers or if the data are skewed, the median may differ widely from the mean.

The median is often used to summarize demographic data, such as the median family income level within a city. We use the median because a few, very rich families can distort the average. If a few wealthy families move into a small community, the mean income level will be shifted upward but the median will be relatively unaffected. Thus the median provides a more accurate picture of the typical income level. If there are no outliers, the mean and the median will be close to one another. In that case, we use the mean since it uses all the data values in its calculation.

In the presence of outliers the mean and median will be different. As has been shown in the varied examples, the mean is *sensitive* to outliers while the median is *robust*, or unaffected, by outliers.

The Trimmed Mean

Up to this point we have had two choices for determining the center of a data set. The mean is sensitive to outliers but sacrifices robustness. The median is robust against outliers but sacrifices sensitivity. A third choice, the **trimmed mean**, is a compromise. It is based on the actual data values, but ignores an equal number of the lowest and highest values. If there are no outliers, then the trimmed mean and the mean will be similar. If there are outliers, the two statistics will differ.

> To compute a trimmed mean: Rank order a data set from the smallest to largest data value. Delete an equal number of the smallest and largest data values. Calculate the mean for the remaining data.

The idea behind the trimmed mean is illustrated with the following two data sets. One has outliers and one does not. We will compute the mean, median, and the 10% trimmed mean. A 10% trimmed mean requires eliminating the lowest 10% and highest 10% of the data values. We ignore 20% of the data—the price of compromise.

Begin by putting the numbers in order from the smallest to the largest:

Data with Outlier

20, 40, 50, 80, 100, 130, 140, 190, 200, 300, 3,000

Data with No Outlier

20, 40, 50, 80, 100, 130, 140, 190, 200, 240, 300

There are 11 observations in each data set. To determine the 10% trimmed mean, trim, or eliminate, the one lowest and one highest data values. (Ten percent of 11 observations is 1.1, which is rounded to one observation.)

Statistics for the Data with Outlier

$$\bar{x} = \frac{20 + 40 + 50 + 80 + 100 + 130 + \cdots + 3{,}000}{11}$$

$$= 386.4$$

$$\text{Rank of median} = \frac{1 + 11}{2} \quad \text{or the sixth largest value}$$

$$\text{Median} = 130$$

$$\text{Trimmed mean} = \frac{40 + 50 + 80 + \cdots + 300}{9}$$

$$= 136.7$$

Statistics for the Data with No Outlier

$$\bar{x} = \frac{20 + 40 + 50 + 80 + \cdots + 300}{11}$$

$$= 134.5$$

$$\text{Median} = 130$$

$$\text{Trimmed mean} = \frac{40 + 50 + 80 + 100 + \cdots + 240}{9}$$

$$= 130$$

These statistics show that the mean and 10% trimmed mean are quite different when there is an outlier, but are very similar when there is none. In both data sets the median and 10% trimmed mean are similar or identical. This may not always be the case. It depends on the number of extreme values and the spread of the remaining 80% of the data values—those that were not trimmed.

One major advantage of the 10% trimmed mean over the median is that we use 80% of the actual data values to calculate it. When we ignore the values of the observations, some information is lost. It is as if the data are trying to speak but no one is listening. The trimmed mean has much to recommend it. It is less affected by outliers than the mean, but is more affected than the median. It is a compromise between the two traditional measures of the center.

Nevertheless, the median is still a commonly used and often appropriate alternative measure to the mean. We also need a measure of the spread around the median that, like the median itself, is unaffected by outliers.

The Interquartile Range

The interquartile range is a measure that is easy to determine and interpret, and unaffected by outliers. We begin by defining the *quartiles*. The quartiles are three numbers that divide a data set that has been rank ordered from the smallest to the largest value into four equal parts. The second quartile, Q_2, is the same as the median value. The first and third quartiles, Q_1 and Q_3, are the data values that are about a quarter of the way in from each end of the ordered data set. Just as the median is halfway in from each end, the quartiles are halfway between the end values and the median value.

The interquartile range measures the width of the middle half of the data between Q_1 and Q_3. Figure 2.17 shows a general diagram of the interquartile range.

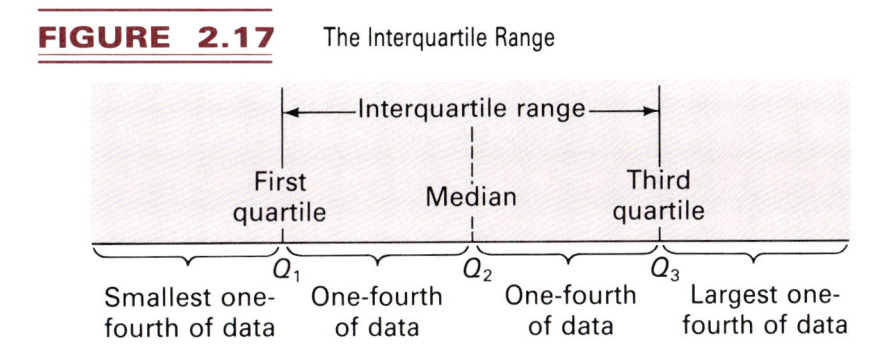

FIGURE 2.17 The Interquartile Range

In Table 2.16 the accounts receivable data from Table 2.13 have been ranked. The rank of the median is 5.5. Drop any fraction from the rank of the median value (drop the .5 and keep the 5), and use expression (2.6) to compute the rank of the quartile value:

$$\text{Rank of quartile value} = \frac{1 + \text{Median value rank}}{2} \quad (2.6)$$

Table 2.16

Ages of Accounts Receivable in Rank Order

Data Values	Rank of Data Values
31	1
33	2
36	3
36	4
37	5
38	6
39	7
41	8
44	9
47	10

The interquartile range measures the spread around the median in a data set and equals Q_3 minus Q_1.

Thus, the rank of the quartile value is $(1 + 5)/2 = 3$. Count up *three* data values from the lowest data value. The *first quartile* data value is 36. If the rank falls between two data values, take the mean as is done in finding the median. Now count down *three* values from the largest data value. The *third quartile* data value is 41. The **interquartile range** is the difference, or distance, between the first and third quartiles: $Q_3 - Q_1$, or $41 - 36 = 5$.

The interquartile range is less affected by outliers than the standard deviation is. Table 2.17 demonstrates this. Note that one data set has no outliers while the other has two outliers. For both data sets, the rank of the median value is $(1 + 6)/2$ or 3.5 for a median value of 350. The rank of first and third quartiles is $(1 + 3)/2 = 2$. For both data sets, the first quartile value is the second smallest data value or 200 and the third quartile value is the second largest data value or 500. For both data sets, the interquartile range is $500 - 200 = 300$. It is unaffected by the two outliers in data set 1. Thus, the interquartile range, unlike the standard deviation, is not affected by outliers.

Table 2.17

Impact of Outliers on Interquartile Range

Data Set 1 Two Outliers	Data Set 2 No Outliers
−20,000	100
200	200
300	300
400	400
500	500
60,000	600

In summary, the interquartile range has the following properties:

1. It must be greater than or equal to zero. Since the data are ordered from the smallest to largest value, the third quartile must always be greater than or equal to the first quartile. The interquartile range, like the standard deviation, can never be negative.
2. It is not affected by outliers.

Which Set of Summarizing Measures?

Suppose we want to summarize a data set. Should the mean and standard deviation or the median and interquartile range be used? It depends, of course, on whether there are outliers or the data are highly skewed. The mean and standard deviation are very sensitive to outliers or highly skewed data because the actual data *values* are included in the calculations. So if one or more values are very far from the rest of the data, both measures will be affected.

The median and interquartile range are insensitive to outliers because outliers are excluded in their calculation, which uses only the *ranks* of the data.

Chapter 2 Descriptive Statistics I: Toward Managerial Problem Sensing

In summary, use the following guidelines to treat a given data set:

1. If there are outliers or if the data are highly skewed, determine the median and interquartile range.
2. If there are no outliers or the data are nearly symmetric, calculate the mean and standard deviation.

SECTION 2.7 EXERCISES

1. The ages of 15 participants in a training seminar are shown. The data have already been rank ordered.

27	33	40
28	35	41
28	35	41
29	36	46
29	37	62

   a. Find the median age, the first and third quartiles, and the interquartile range.
   b. Find the mean age and the 10% trimmed mean age.
   c. How does the 10% trimmed mean compare to the mean and the median?

2. Given the following set of cross-sectional data values:

21	34	43
23	34	45
26	37	45
31	37	52
33	38	68

   a. Find the median.
   b. Find the interquartile range.

3. Complete the following table using the data: {6, 3, 2, 6, 1, 2, 3, 4, 3, 5, 7, 5}.

Class	Frequency	Percentage	Cumulative Frequency	Cumulative Percentage
0 to 1	___	___	___	___
2 to 3	___	___	___	___
4 to 5	___	___	___	___
6 to 7	___	___	___	___

   Use the table to *approximate* the median for the set of values. Now use the raw data to calculate the median.

4. The first quartile of a set of data values is 15, the median is 33, and the third quartile is 49.
   a. Find the interquartile range and explain its meaning.
   b. What fraction of the values are greater than 49?

5. Personnel managers usually want to know where a job applicant ranked in his or her graduating class. With a grade point average of 3.75, Mary Smith graduated above the 90th *percentile* of her graduating class. This means that 90% of the graduating class had GPAs of 3.75 or less. What percentile rank would a student be in if the student's GPA was:
    a. the median GPA?
    b. the first quartile?
    c. the third quartile?

2.8 Interpreting the Median and Interquartile Range

An important step in interpreting a data set is the ability to identify outliers. When the mean and standard deviation are used to summarize a data set, the Empirical rule helps to determine outliers. Recall that outliers in a bell-shaped distribution are data values that are more than three standard deviations away from the mean. This section shows how to determine outliers in a non–bell-shaped distribution using the median and interquartile range. By the end of this section you should be able to:

1. identify outliers using Tukey's rule;
2. draw a box plot to visualize the important features of a data set; and
3. distinguish symmetric and skewed data sets from a box plot.

Identifying Outliers Using the Median and Interquartile Range

Table 2.15 shows the productivities for 36 work groups at COMCEL's Norcross plant. Are any of the work group productivities outliers? Begin by computing the rank, quartiles, and interquartile range. In Table 2.15, the rank of the median value is 18.5, which leads to a median value of 100%. The rank of the first and third quartiles is $(1 + 18)/2 = 9.5$. Count up 9.5 values from the smallest value of 89% to the first quartile value of 95%. Count down 9.5 values from the largest value of 123% to the third quartile value of 104%. The interquartile range is $104 - 95 = 9\%$.

John Tukey, the creator of graphical analysis of data, has developed an approach to determine outliers. He uses the interquartile range and first and third quartiles to define outliers. In his definition of **outliers**, a *step* is the number that is 1.5 times the interquartile range.

> **Outliers** are data values that are more than one step lower than the first quartile value or more than one step higher than the third quartile value.

Now return to the productivity data. A step for the productivity data is given by

$$1.5 \cdot 9\% = 13.5\%$$

Thus, outliers are work groups whose productivities are

Lower than (First quartile value − One step) or $95 - 13.5 = 81.5\%$

Higher than (Third quartile value + One step) or $104 + 13.5 = 117.5\%$

By this definition, work group 20's productivity of 123% is an outlier. Next we will show how to draw a box plot that displays the quartile values, the median, and outliers, if any.

Drawing Box Plots

Refer to Figure 2.18 to see how the following directions for drawing a box plot are applied to the work group productivity data.

1. Draw a horizontal scale. Label its units and indicate the number of values in the data set.
2. Draw a rectangular box above the horizontal scale with sides at the first and third quartiles. The box height is unimportant.
3. Draw a vertical line through the box at the median value.
4. Draw horizontal lines from the box to the smallest and largest data values.
5. Draw a vertical line (called a fence) *one step* above the third quartile. Any data points to the right of this fence are outliers. Plot, circle, and label them.
6. Draw a vertical line (called a fence) *one step* below the first quartile. Any data points to the left of this fence are outliers. Plot, circle, and label them.

Box plots display important features of a data set. Figure 2.18 shows that:

1. The median work group productivity is 100% of standard and the productivity varies between 89% and 123% of standard.
2. The lowest one-quarter, or nine work groups, produces at between 89% and 95% of standard.
3. The middle half, or 18 work groups, produces at between 95% and 104% of standard.
4. The highest one-quarter, or nine work groups, produces at between 104% and 123% of standard.

FIGURE 2.18 Box Plot of Productivity Data for 36 Work Groups

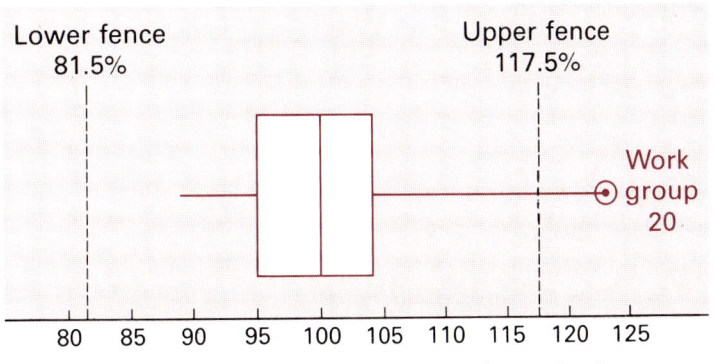

5. There are no outliers on the low side. None of the 36 work group productivities is below 81.5%.
6. Work group 20, which has the highest productivity at 123%, is an outlier. We should determine what factors account for this work group's high monthly productivity.

Given the above insights, the following mental models emerge:

> If a work group's productivity falls below 81.5%, we have a potential *disturbance problem* and we should take action. Unless someone has incorrectly coded a work group's monthly productivity, we should begin problem diagnosis. If we do not, we will fail to nip an emerging problem in the bud.

> If a work group's productivity exceeds 117.5%, we have a potential *opportunity*. If there is no coding error, begin problem diagnosis. If we do not, we may let an opportunity to improve the productivities of other groups slip through our fingers.

In summary, the box plot is a powerful visual way of summarizing data and of developing mental models. As we've said before, pictures are better than words.

Recognizing Symmetry or Skewness

Box plots show more than quartiles and outliers. They also indicate the distribution's shape—whether it is symmetric or skewed. Figure 2.19 shows two

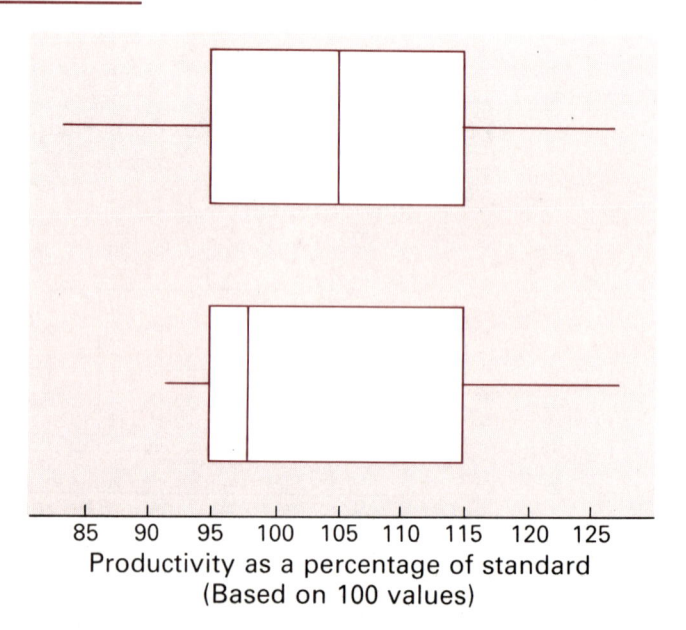

FIGURE 2.19 Two Box Plots

Productivity as a percentage of standard
(Based on 100 values)

box plots with the fences omitted. One box plot displays a nearly symmetric distribution and the other box plot displays a skewed distribution. Which is which? Think about it before reading on.

The top box plot shows symmetric data. Notice that the median is exactly in the middle of the box and the extreme values are at equal distances from the first and third quartiles. Using the median as the center, the left side of the plot is an exact mirror image of the right side of the plot. The data are symmetric.

The bottom box plot shows skewed data. Notice that the median is not in the middle of the box. Nor are the extreme values at equal distances from the first and third quartiles. The data are not symmetric. In fact, the data are skewed toward higher values, or to the right.

In summary, when using the median and quartiles to summarize data, *always* draw a box plot. We can determine if the data are symmetric or skewed and can easily spot outliers. Remember, outliers are data values that are above the upper fence or below the lower fence. A box plot provides much information about a data set in a single picture.

SECTION 2.8 EXERCISES

1. A manager received a report containing the following summary statistics on the number of complaints from customers from her 20 branch offices last month:

Minimum	0	First quartile	3
Maximum	22	Median	6
Mean	7.5	Third quartile	13

   a. Draw a box plot to display these data. Is the distribution symmetric or skewed? Why?
   b. Are either of the extreme values, 0 or 22, to be considered outliers?

2. A personnel manager is interested in the performance rankings assigned to middle-level managers. The performance scale ranges from 1 to 10, where a rating of 5 indicates average performance and 10 indicates exceptional performance. The summary statistics for 15 middle managers' ratings are shown.

Minimum	5	First quartile	8
Maximum	10	Median	9
Mean	8.7	Third quartile	10

   a. Draw a box plot to display these data. Is the distribution symmetric or skewed? Why?
   b. Should the minimum value be considered an outlier?
   c. Note that the median is 9 (on a 10-point scale). What are two possible explanations for this very high median value?

3. A marketing manager wishes to develop a box plot on the performance of his seven salespeople. The data are the number of sales in excess of $1,000 for the past week.

The data are shown here.

Salesperson	1	2	3	4	5	6	7
Number of Sales	3	6	2	4	5	15	1

    a. Why might the manager wish to develop a box plot?
    b. Determine the median, first quartile, third quartile, and interquartile range.
    c. Are there any outliers? If so, what action would you take?

4. You are recording times to build houses in a major development. You construct a box plot for the data and find one outlier, a point far below the first quartile. This means that one house took much less time to build than many of the other houses.
    a. Should you investigate the causes of this outlier?
    b. Do outliers always signify that something bad has happened?

5. Is it possible that the first quartile, median, and third quartile values are all the same? What does that tell you about the data?

2.9 Summarizing Time-Ordered Data

Summarizing time-ordered data enables problem solvers to answer the following questions more precisely:

How are we doing, on the average, over *time*?

Is our department's performance declining, staying the same, or improving over time?

Is there any pattern to our department's performance over time? When do we do well? When do we do poorly?

How can I identify an outlier? What constitutes an extraordinary, or unusual, event?

The first step in analyzing time-ordered data—drawing line graphs—was explained in Section 2.4. By the end of this section you should be able to:

1. explain why the mean and standard deviation, or the median and interquartile range, should not be used to summarize *nonstationary* time-ordered data;
2. compute a single, double, or triple moving average;
3. interpret a moving, or smoothed, average and use it to build a mental model;
4. explain the problems of computing double, triple, etc. moving averages;
5. compute residuals from the smoothed data;
6. interpret residuals to help sharpen mental models; and
7. explain how data outliers can distort the residuals.

Are the Mean and Median Informative for Nonstationary Data?

Two years of nonstationary monthly sales data are presented in Table 2.18 and graphed in Figure 2.20. We have computed the mean and median for each year and for the two-year period. Please verify the calculations.

Chapter 2 Descriptive Statistics I: Toward Managerial Problem Sensing

Table 2.18
Monthly Sales Data (in thousands of dollars) over Two Years

	Jan.	Feb.	Mar.	Apr.	May	June	July	Aug.	Sept.	Oct.	Nov.	Dec.
Year 1	100	90	80	80	60	70	50	60	50	45	50	45
Year 2	50	40	30	40	30	25	35	20	20	30	10	5

FIGURE 2.20 Nonstationary Data

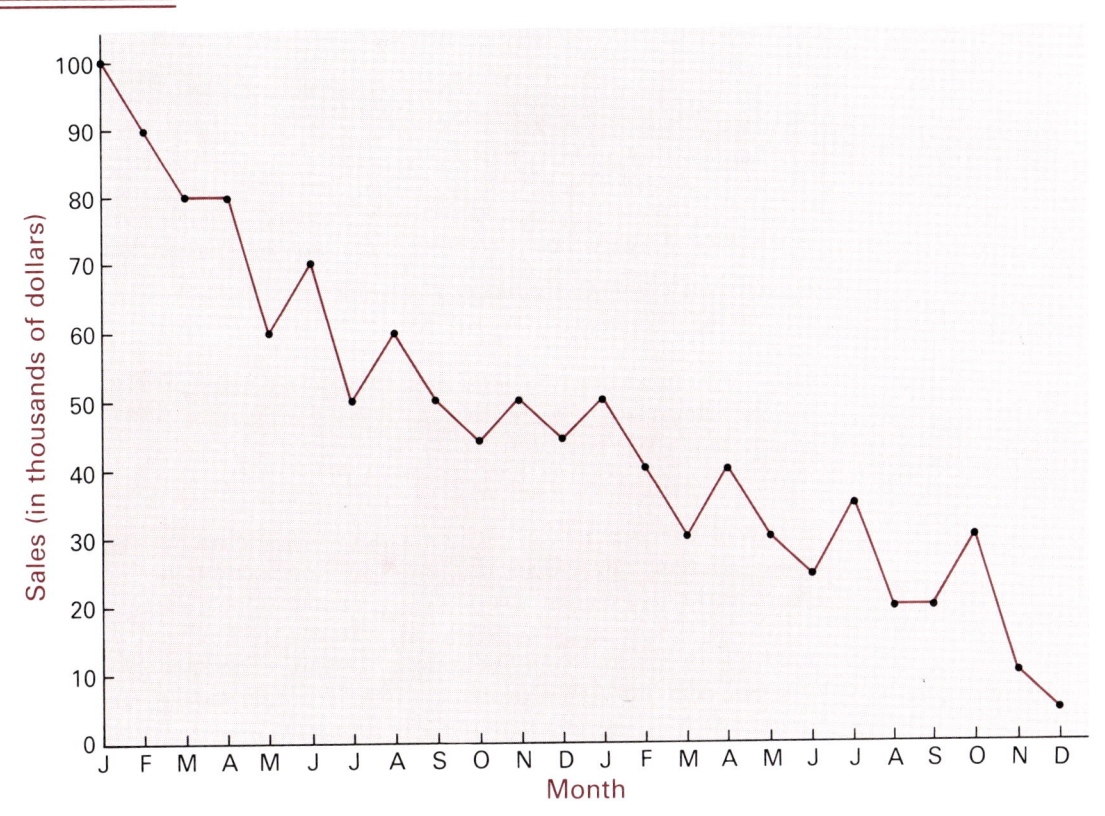

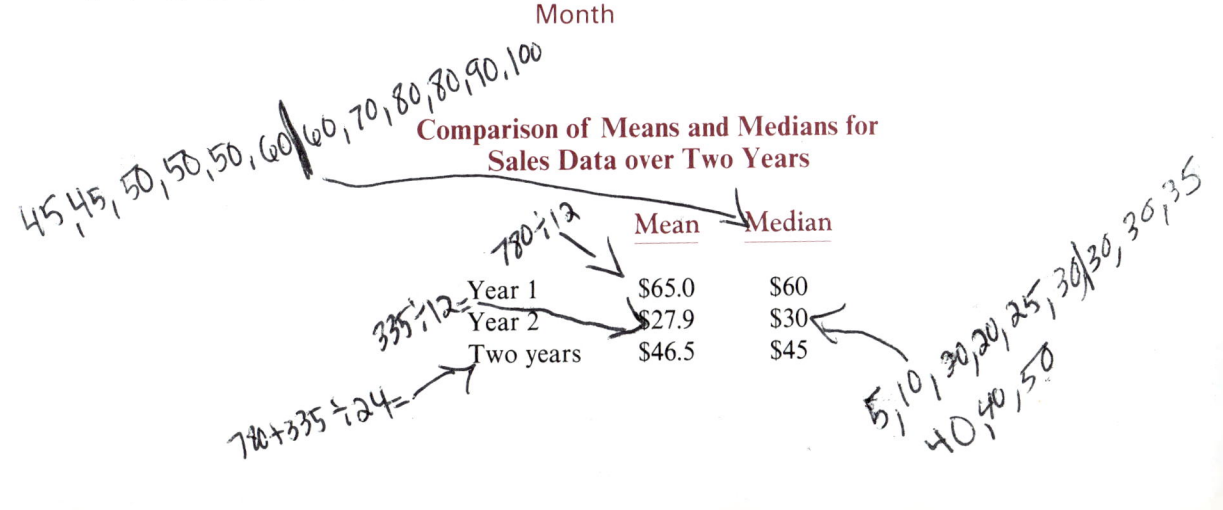

Comparison of Means and Medians for Sales Data over Two Years

	Mean	Median
Year 1	$65.0	$60
Year 2	$27.9	$30
Two years	$46.5	$45

Notice that the means and medians for each year differ dramatically from the mean and median for the entire 2-year period. The 2-year mean and median are *not* informative and useful for these data. Why? Please think about it before reading on.

An "average" should accurately summarize the data. It should provide a typical value that characterizes the series. The 2-year mean and median are too low for the first year and too high for the second year. In short, do not use the mean and median to summarize time-ordered data that are nonstationary. Nonstationary data do *not* have a constant mean or median over time.

If the data are stationary, then the overall mean or median will accurately reflect the average performance each and every year. Thus, we can use the mean and standard deviation or the median and interquartile range for stationary time-ordered data.

In conclusion:

Summarize stationary time-ordered data by computing either the mean and standard deviation or the median and interquartile range. Use the latter pair of statistics when there are outliers or highly skewed data. Treat stationary time-ordered data the same as cross-sectional data.

Do not compute the mean and standard deviation or median and interquartile range for nonstationary time-ordered data.

How then can we describe nonstationary time-ordered data? The solution is to use a moving average series.

Single Moving Averages

A moving average replaces each data value with a mean of what is happening around it. A moving average of three or five time periods (days, weeks, months, years, or the like) is often used to describe nonstationary data.

Table 2.19 contains nonstationary data for the number of personal hours taken for the past 48 months. Table 2.20, which contains only one of the four years of data, illustrates how to construct a **single moving average** of three months, MA(3). For now, ignore the double moving average column.

For a moving average of three periods, a period's moving average value is the mean of the values for that period, the period before, and the period after. Thus, February's moving average value is the mean of January, February, and

> A single moving average of length n, MA(n), contains a series of means based on n successive data points. The term "single" means that a moving average series is constructed from the original data.

Table 2.19

Personal Hours Taken

Year	J	F	M	A	M	J	J	A	S	O	N	D
1989	50	120	60	150	80	180	50	120	250	130	190	390
1990	120	200	270	150	280	290	200	350	300	310	400	350
1991	300	375	250	350	200	150	250	140	100	190	170	150
1992	250	200	150	170	270	170	200	300	150	250	250	200

Table 2.20

Moving Averages of Three Periods

Month	Time-Ordered Data Personal Hours	Single Moving Average of Three	Double Moving Average of Three
Jan.	50	Undeterminable	Undeterminable
Feb.	120	76.7	Undeterminable
Mar.	60	110.0	94.4
Apr.	150	96.7	114.4
May	80	136.7	112.2
June	180	103.3	118.9
July	50	116.7	120.0
Aug.	120	140.0	141.1
Sept.	250	166.7	165.6
Oct.	130	190.0	197.8
Nov.	190	236.7	220.0
Dec.	390	233.3	235.6

⋮

March's data values, and March's moving average value is the mean of March and its neighbors, February and April.

We cannot compute a moving average for the first data value (see Table 2.20, Undeterminable entry) and the last data value (not shown), since there are no values before the first data point or after the last data point. Two data values are lost when computing a single moving average of three.

In general, to compute a single moving average of 3, MA(3) series:

1. Set up a three-period moving average column.
2. Leave the first and last rows of the moving average column blank.
3. Any period's moving average is the sum of its data value, that of the period before it, and that of the period after it, divided by 3.
4. Place the mean of the three numbers opposite the middle of the three numbers averaged. This is called centering.

Smoothing by Moving Averages

Moving averages expose underlying trends, which tell whether the time-ordered data are increasing or decreasing over the long term. Sometimes the raw data contain many peaks and valleys, and it may be difficult to see the long-term upward or downward changes over time. Such is the case for the *rough* data from Table 2.19 graphed in Figure 2.21 on page 72. In contrast, Figure 2.22 shows the moving average of the original data.

What does the smoothed line graph in Figure 2.22 reveal? It shows that the mean number of personal hours increased from under 80 hours in February to about 350 hours in November of the second year, when it peaked. The mean

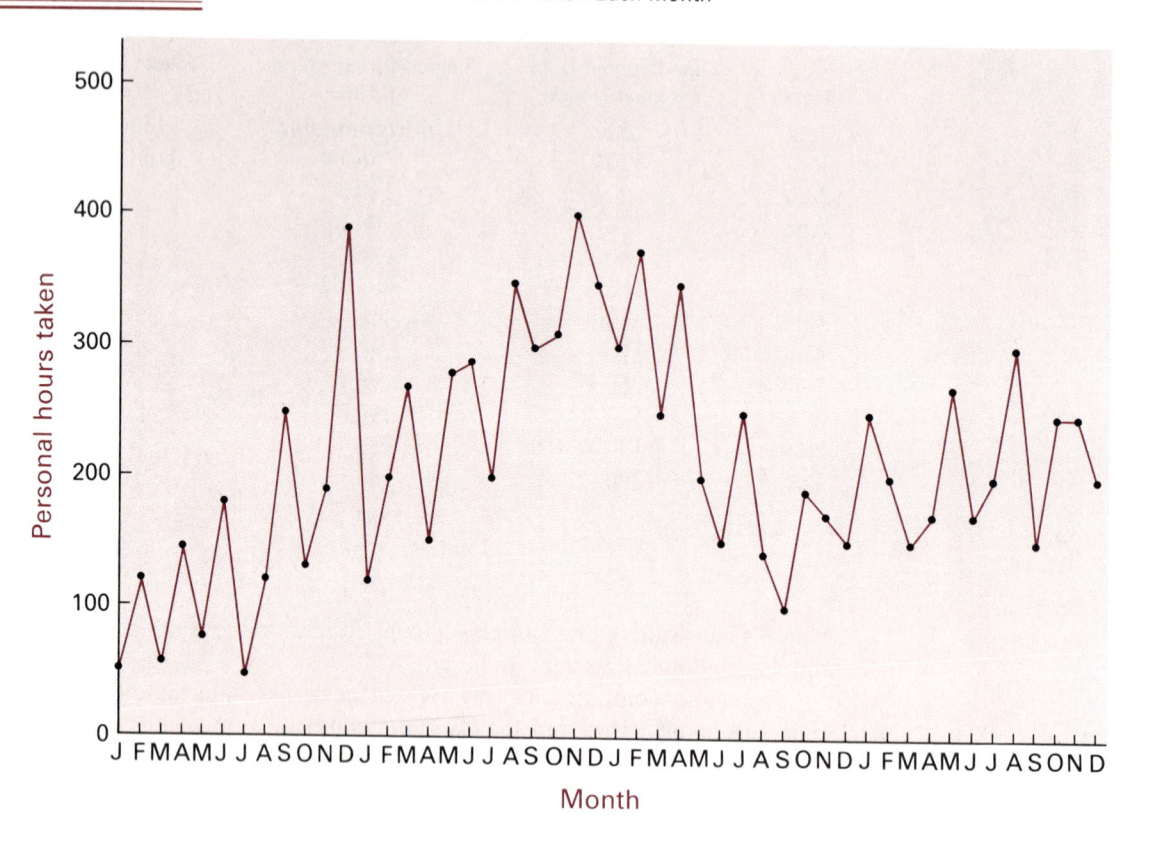

FIGURE 2.21 Raw Data—Personal Hours Taken Each Month

personal hours then dropped quickly and reached a low of about 150 hours in September of the third year. Since then, mean personal hours have increased to about 240 hours.

It's not that we couldn't see the pattern in Figure 2.21, but with all the roughness, it was somewhat hidden, and more difficult to detect. The underlying data pattern is more obvious in the smoothed line graph of the moving average.

Repeated Smoothing by Averages of Three

If smoothing the data once is useful, is smoothing more than once better? We can smooth the single moving average of three to reduce the remaining roughness. This is called a double moving average—a moving average of a moving average. For example, see the double moving average column in Table 2.20. The double moving average for March is simply $(76.7 + 110.0 + 96.7)/3 = 94.4$. The other double moving averages were computed in a similar fashion. The double moving average will be smoother than the MA(3). We can go a step further and also compute a triple moving average—a moving average of the double moving average.

Chapter 2 Descriptive Statistics I: Toward Managerial Problem Sensing

FIGURE 2.22 MA(3)—Personal Hours Taken Each Month

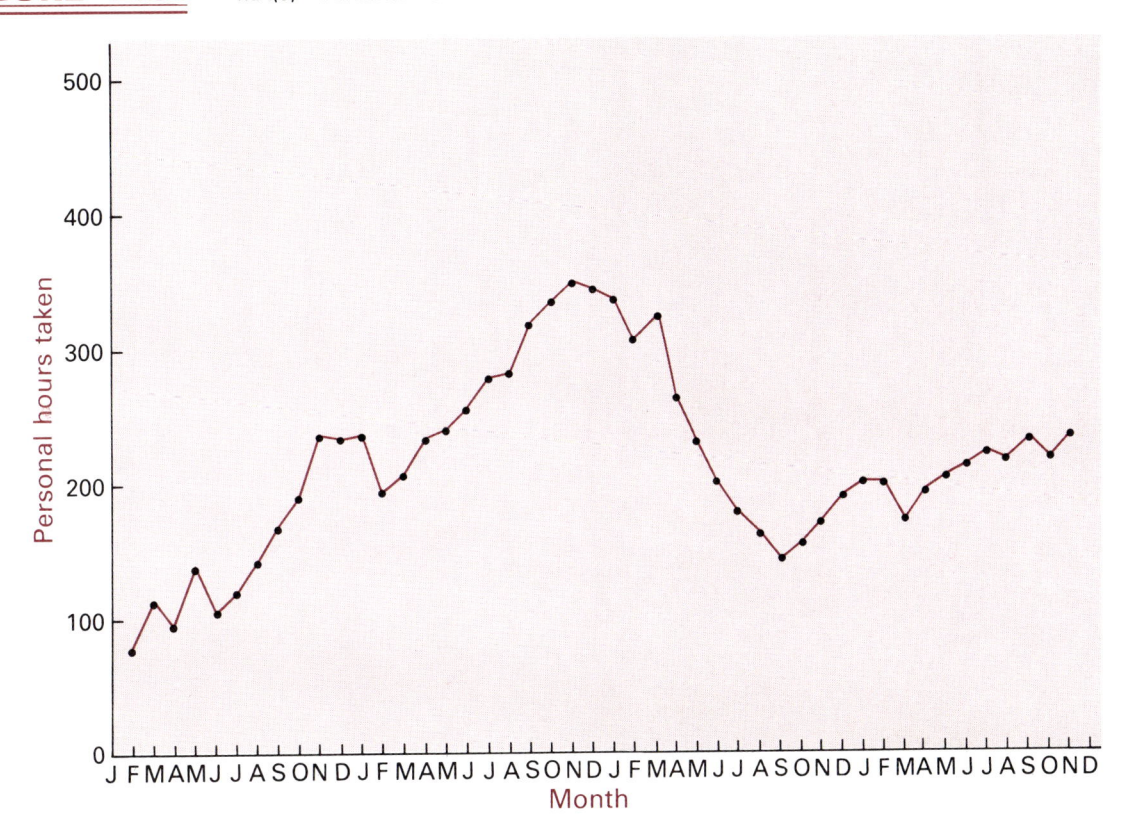

Figure 2.23 on page 74 shows a double moving average for personal hours data. Compare this line graph with the single moving average of Figure 2.22. The double moving average is indeed smoother. The big picture is very easy to detect.

Does this mean that we should always compute double or higher moving averages when looking for a pattern in the data? Are double or higher moving averages better than single moving averages? Not necessarily!

The unbroken line in Figure 2.24 shows a line graph of 48 numbers taken from the random numbers table in Appendix 4. Random numbers exhibit no pattern nor upward or downward trend. Then the data were smoothed five times using moving averages of three. The dashed line in Figure 2.24 illustrates this moving average. Note that the moving average smoothed five times suggests a pattern in the data. But there cannot be a pattern since the original data are random numbers. What is happening? The more moving averages we compute, the more likely we are to see bogus patterns.

The rougher—more peaks and valleys—the original data, the higher the moving average we must compute to smooth the data to see the data's pattern. However, be forewarned! In computing higher moving averages, we obtain

FIGURE 2.23 Double MA(3)—Personal Hours Taken Each Month

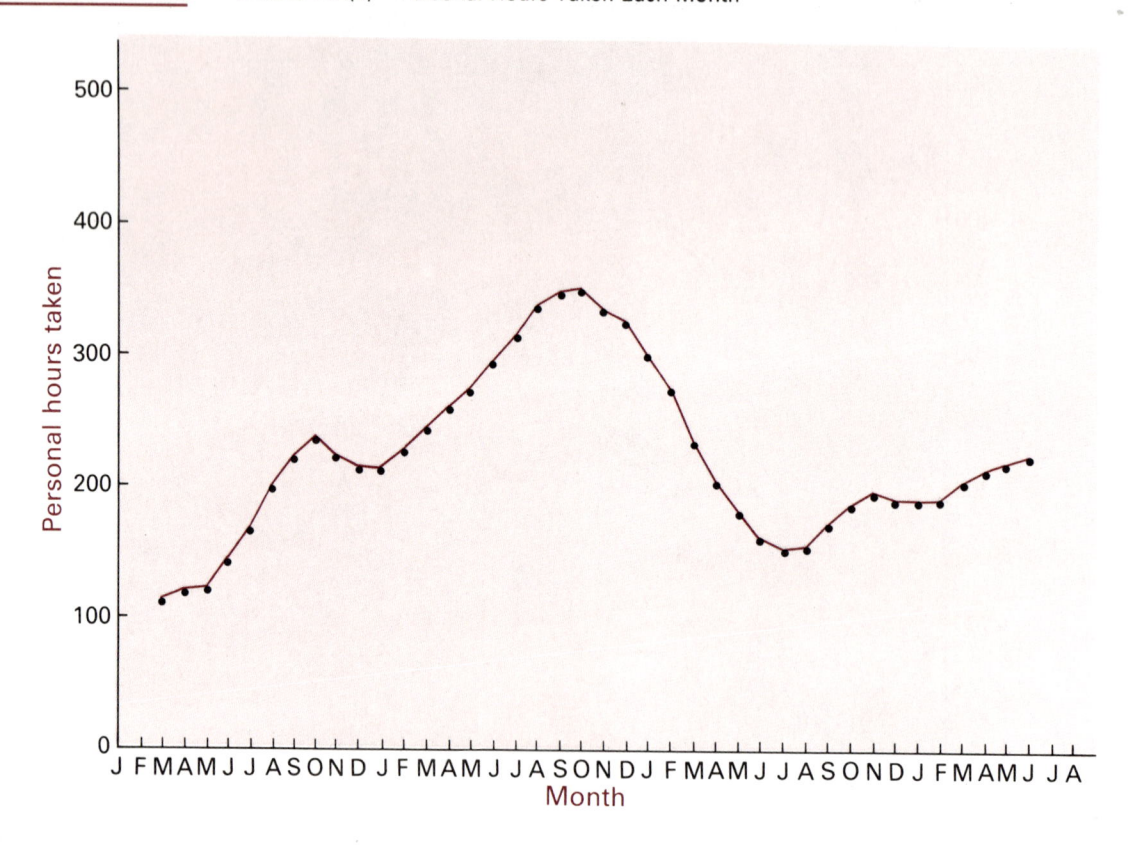

smoother line graphs that expose the underlying pattern—the good news; but we lose more data points at the beginning and end of the time-ordered data and begin to see nonexistent patterns—the bad news. Statistics alone cannot determine the right amount of smoothing. It is a judgment call, that comes with knowing the issues.

Residuals

The smoothed line graph is a crucial step in developing a mental model, but it is not the last step. We must also analyze the **residual**—the difference between the rough data and the smooth data.

The data for the 48 months of personal hours taken are used to illustrate residuals. Table 2.21 shows several calculated residuals. Figure 2.25 on page 76 is a residual plot for the 48 months of data. Time is on the horizontal axis, and the residuals are on the vertical axis.

Look for sudden jumps or drops in the residuals. They suggest something out of the ordinary happened. In Figure 2.25, two large residuals stand out from

A residual is the difference between an original data value and its corresponding smoothed value. A large negative or positive residual suggests that an extraordinary event has happened.

Chapter 2 Descriptive Statistics I: Toward Managerial Problem Sensing

FIGURE 2.24 Plot of Random Numbers and Moving Average of 3 Smoothed Five Times

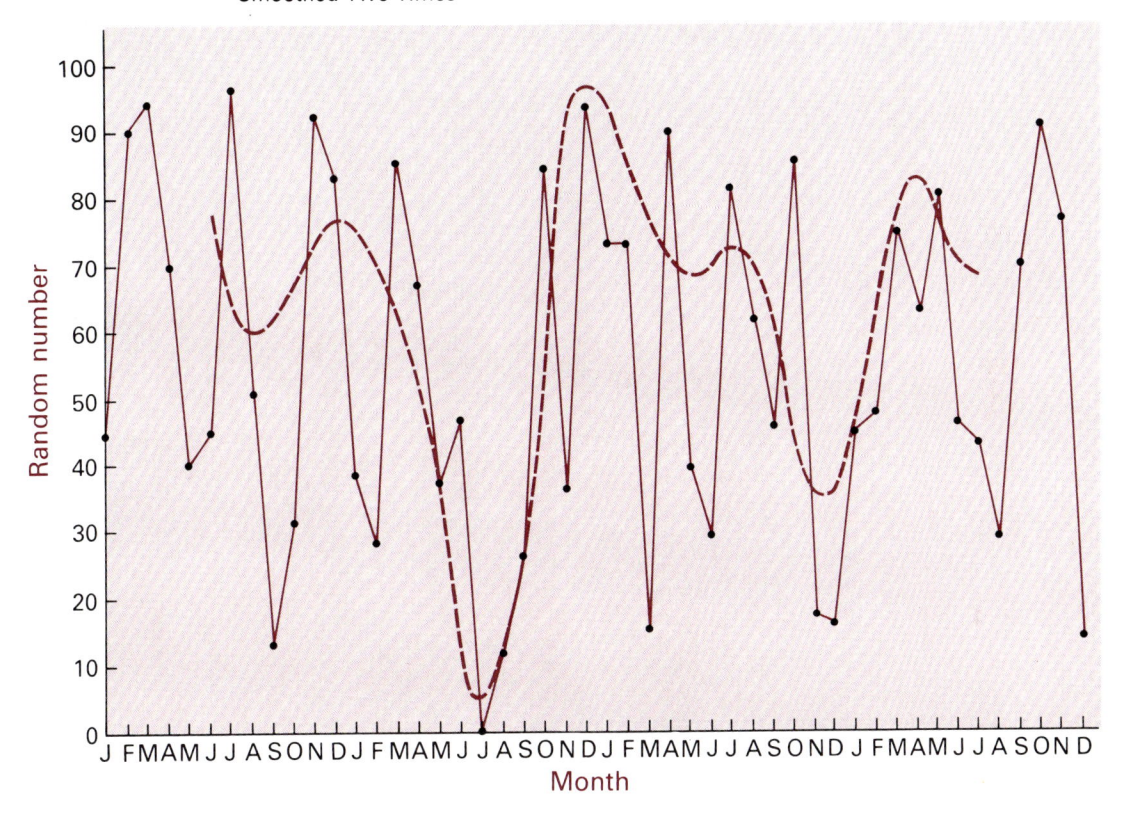

the rest. In December of the first year, the actual number of personal hours taken was much higher than the moving average. In the following month, the actual number of personal hours taken was much lower than the moving average. What has caused these extraordinary residuals? The moving average and residual line graphs suggest the two mental models described on page 76.

Table 2.21

Computing Residuals

Month	Original Data	Moving Average	Residual
Jan.	50	Undeterminable	
Feb.	120	76.7	+43.3
Mar.	60	110.0	−50.0
Apr.	150	96.7	+53.3
May	80	136.7	−56.7
June	180	103.3	+76.7
⋮			

FIGURE 2.25   Residual Plot: Personal Hours Taken

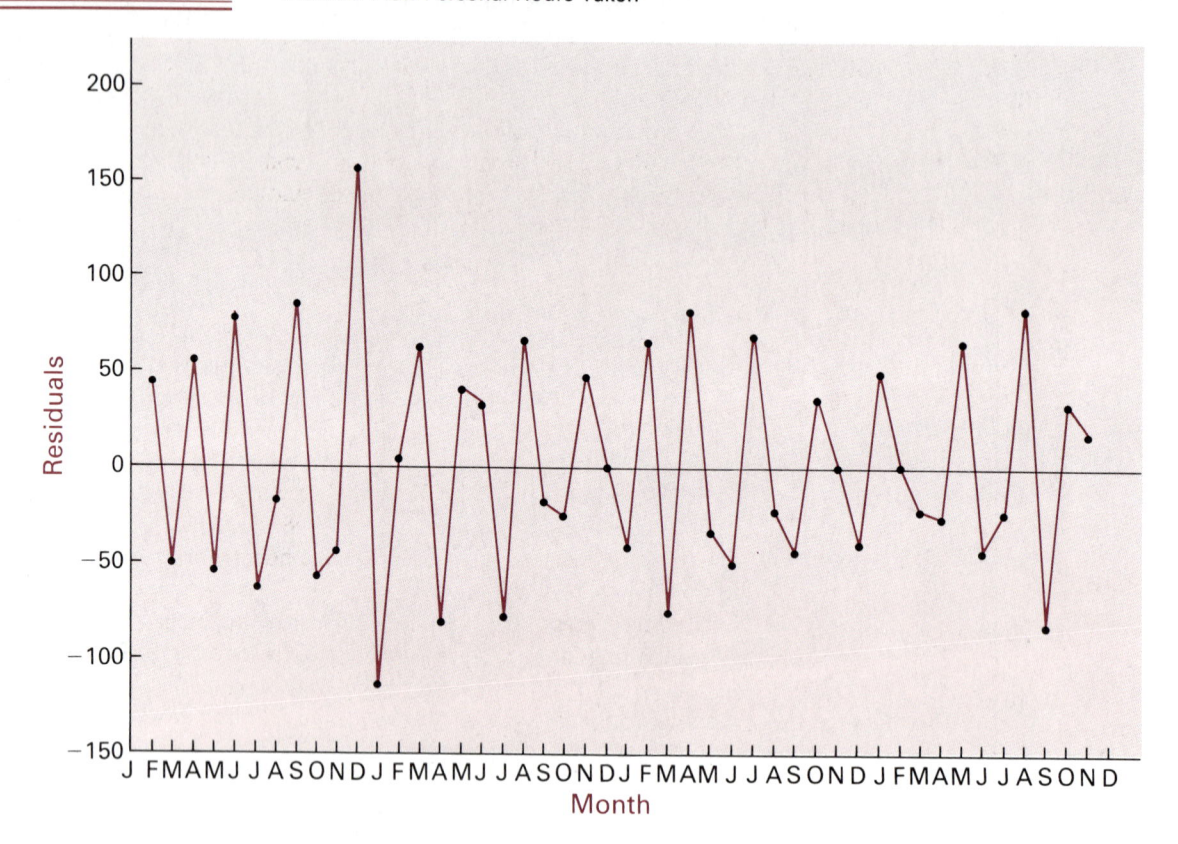

Insight from Smoothed Graph

Average personal hours increased steadily from under 80 hours in February to about 350 hours in November of the second year, when it peaked. Then they dropped quickly and reached a low of about 150 hours in September of the third year. Average personal hours have again increased steadily to about 240 hours.

What accounts for these changes over time?

Insight from Residual Plot

Workers took an unusually large number of personal hours in December of the first year. The next month they took an unusually small number of personal hours.

What could account for the large positive and negative residuals? Did this occur during the time when the firm considered and then rejected a wage cut? Did the Accounting Department mistakenly credit some of January's hours to December? Was there a flu epidemic?

The residual plot has sharpened the mental model first developed from the moving average line graph. Both moving averages and residual plots are essential tools in building mental models. The former reveals the big picture or pattern over time, and the latter identifies unusual events in the form of large positive or negative residuals.

The residual plot for the 48 months of personal hours data suggests that *both* in December of the first year and in January of the second year something out of the ordinary happened. However, as we will now demonstrate, only one month may have been an outlier.

Impact of Outliers on Moving Averages

In Table 2.22, the original data contain an outlier (see the data point for 1984). What impact does it have on the single moving average series and residuals?

The residual column indicates large negative and positive residuals for the three years from 1983 to 1985. Large positive and negative residuals suggest that something unusual happened over those three years. But we can see from the original data that in only one year was there an unusual happening, namely, 1984. But due to the smoothing by averages of three, the outlier's impact was spread over three years. Remember, *one* data value affects *three* moving average calculations.

Table 2.22 demonstrates that if we find large positive and negative residuals, one or more of them may not signify outliers. Here, the two large residuals for 1983 and 1985 are simply due to averaging. The large residual for 1984 signifies an outlier, and thus a potential real problem or opportunity.

In summary, smooth the data to detect the underlying data pattern. Develop a residual plot and identify large positive and negative residuals. Some of these

Table 2.22

Impact of an Outlier in Time-Ordered Data on the Residuals

Year	Original Data	Moving Average of Three	Residual
1980	10	Undeterminable	
1981	12	11.7	.3
1982	13	12.3	.7
1983	12	25.0	−13.0
1984	50	25.7	24.3
1985	15	27.0	−12.0
1986	16	15.0	1.0
1987	14	15.7	−1.7
1988	17	16.3	.7
1989	18	18.0	.0
1990	19	19.0	.0
1991	20	Undeterminable	

large residuals may not indicate outliers. But some do. Effective managers investigate all large residuals, determine which residuals suggest real problems, and then solve them.

SECTION 2.9 EXERCISES

1. Construct a 3-period moving average series for the sales data shown.

Time Period	Sales	Time Period	Sales
1	3	7	15
2	5	8	18
3	7	9	8
4	6	10	14
5	8	11	16
6	12	12	20

2. Using the same data given in Exercise 1, compute a 3-period double moving average series.

3. Compute the residuals for the data in Exercise 1. Do any residuals appear to be outliers?

4. Calculate a 3-month moving average series and the residuals for the given data. Describe the pattern in the data. Do any residuals appear to be outliers?

Month	J	F	M	A	M	J	J	A	S	O	N	D
Claims	4	8	7	15	6	9	5	3	8	7	6	5

5. Calculate a 3-quarter moving average series and calculate the residuals for the sales data shown. Describe the pattern in the data. Do any residuals appear to be outliers?

Year	Quarter	Sales	Year	Quarter	Sales
1989	1	240	1990	1	350
	2	260		2	330
	3	250		3	370
	4	290		4	390

6. Under what conditions will a moving average of three be a horizontal line?

2.10 Key Ideas and Overview

We conclude this chapter on problem sensing through descriptive statistics and graphics with the diagram in Figure 2.26. It will help integrate the material within Chapter 2.

Figure 2.26 recalls the following general ideas of this chapter:

1. As problem solvers, start with the following questions: How do we (myself, group, department, division, or firm) compare to others? Or, how are we

FIGURE 2.26 Integrating Framework for Chapter 2

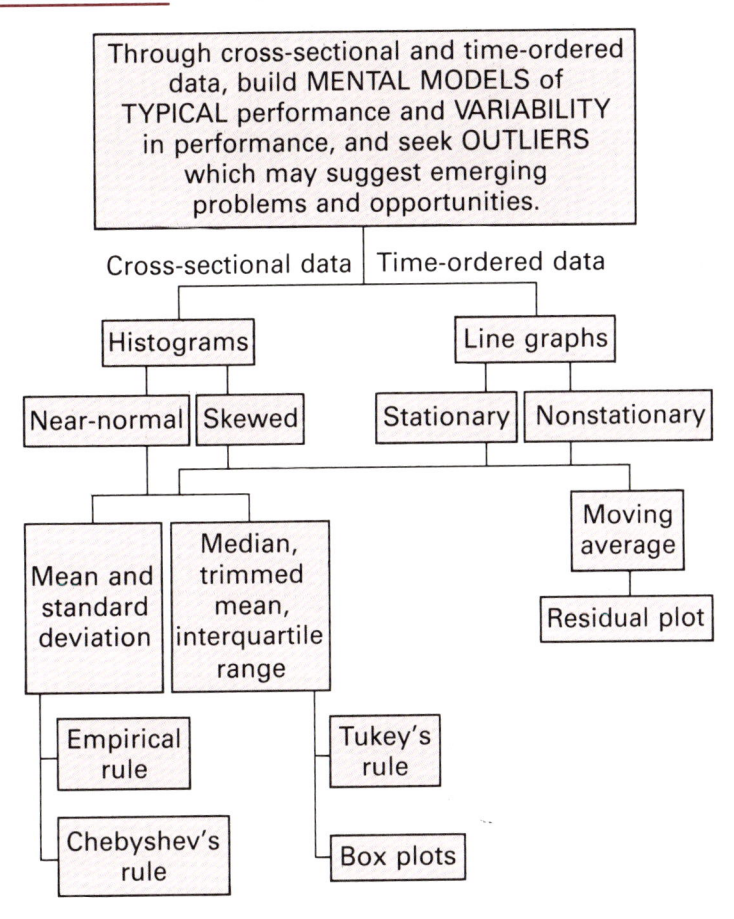

```
┌─────────────────────────────────────┐
│ Through cross-sectional and time-   │
│ ordered data, build MENTAL MODELS   │
│ of TYPICAL performance and          │
│ VARIABILITY in performance, and     │
│ seek OUTLIERS which may suggest     │
│ emerging problems and opportunities.│
└─────────────────────────────────────┘
        Cross-sectional data │ Time-ordered data
              │                      │
        ┌───────────┐          ┌───────────┐
        │Histograms │          │Line graphs│
        └───────────┘          └───────────┘
         │        │             │         │
   Near-normal  Skewed      Stationary  Nonstationary
         │        │                        │
  ┌──────────┐ ┌──────────┐          ┌──────────┐
  │Mean and  │ │Median,   │          │ Moving   │
  │standard  │ │trimmed   │          │ average  │
  │deviation │ │mean,     │          └──────────┘
  └──────────┘ │interquar-│                │
        │     │tile range│          ┌──────────┐
        │     └──────────┘          │ Residual │
        │         │                 │  plot    │
  ┌──────────┐ ┌──────────┐         └──────────┘
  │Empirical │ │Tukey's   │
  │  rule    │ │  rule    │
  └──────────┘ └──────────┘
  ┌──────────┐ ┌──────────┐
  │Chebyshev's│ │Box plots │
  │  rule    │ │          │
  └──────────┘ └──────────┘
```

doing over time? Have any extraordinary events happened? Are there outliers?

2. Organize cross-sectional data by drawing stem-and-leaf displays, frequency and relative frequency histograms, and ogives.
3. Summarize and interpret cross-sectional data by computing the mean and standard deviation or the median, trimmed mean, and interquartile range. Which statistics we use depends on the skewness of the data.
4. Use either the Empirical rule, Chebyshev's rule, or Tukey's rule to identify outliers in cross-sectional data.
5. Organize time-ordered data by drawing line graphs.
6. Treat stationary time-ordered data as cross-sectional data. Compute the mean and standard deviation or the median and interquartile range. Which set of descriptive statistics we use depends on the skewness of the data.
7. For nonstationary time-ordered data, use a single or higher moving average series to smooth the data and to detect its underlying pattern.
8. Use residual plots to seek outliers. Determine the root causes of the outliers.

9. Keep mental models simple. Use pictures (histograms or line graphs) when discussing a model with others. Many managers and business professionals prefer pictures or words to numbers alone.

COMCEL

```
Date:  April 15, 1992
  To:  Ann Tabor, CEO
From:  Howard Bright, Manager, Norcross Plant
  Re:  Analysis of Work Group Productivity Data
```

SUMMARY
Your April 1 memo asked why one group can perform at 123% of standard when so many work groups are producing below standard. Work group 20's performance is an outlier. They are an exceptionally high performing group.

I have found one difference between work group 20 and the other 35 groups. Group 20 members often switch jobs with one another. Apparently the group decided that job switching was something they wanted to do. Other groups have members that occasionally switch jobs, but not to the extent of work group 20. I am investigating this potential explanation. If job switching does explain their high performance, we should encourage and train other groups to do likewise.

SUPPORTING ANALYSIS
Since the productivity data pertain to a single month, I constructed a relative frequency table and histogram to understand the data. The distribution is skewed to the right and appeared to contain an outlier—the group that produced at 123% of industry standard.

Because of the potential outlier, I calculated the median and the interquartile range. The median is 100. The first quartile is 95 and the third quartile is 104. Thus the interquartile range is 9. Tukey's rule tells us that an outlier is any data point that is more than 1 step below the first quartile or more than 1 step above the third quartile. So an outlier is any number less than 81.5% (95 − 1.5 · 9) or above 117.5% (104 + 1.5 · 9). This analysis confirms that only work group 20's productivity is an outlier.

Chapter 2 Descriptive Statistics I: Toward Managerial Problem Sensing   81

CHAPTER 2 QUESTIONS

1. Why would you use histograms to display cross-sectional data?
2. How can a relative frequency histogram help you quickly and easily identify unusual or rare occurrences?
3. Why is it important to managers to identify unusual happenings?
4. A outlier might not signal the onset of a problem or opportunity. What are two other possible explanations for an outlier?
5. Why do we use line graphs for time-ordered data and histograms for cross-sectional data? That is, why can't we use line graphs for displaying cross-sectional data and frequency histograms for displaying nonstationary time-ordered data?
6. Distinguish between yes/no data and numerical data.
7. Why is the standard deviation more useful than the range as a measure of spread or variability?
8. Without resorting to math, how could you quickly approximate the mean of a frequency histogram?
9. What would a frequency histogram with a near-zero variance look like?
10. As the variance increases, what happens to the shape of the frequency distribution?
11. Explain the logic of defining an outlier as an observation that is more than three standard deviations away from the mean.
12. Under what conditions can the mean and standard deviation be misleading summary statistics?
13. The mean is *sensitive* to outliers and the median is *robust* to outliers. What do these terms mean?
14. Explain why the interquartile range is not affected by outliers.
15. When should you use the mean and standard deviation and when the median and interquartile range to summarize cross-sectional data?
16. Explain why Tukey's definition of an outlier as a data point that is either one step above the third quartile or one step below the first quartile makes sense.
17. What problems will you have if you use the mean and standard deviation or the median and interquartile range to summarize nonstationary time-ordered data?
18. What are two problems in using triple or higher moving averages to smooth time-ordered data to see the underlying pattern in time-ordered data?
19. How does a residual analysis aid in problem sensing?
20. What can go wrong if you use a moving average to smooth a time series that has outliers?

CHAPTER 2 APPLICATION PROBLEMS

1. Best Dairy Inc. has segmented its market into eight groups. Among these separate markets are the Machos and the Status Seekers. Machos are young males, blue-collar workers, with high school degrees who live in the city. Status Seekers are young males, white-collar workers, with college degrees who live in the suburbs. Best Dairy Inc. takes a sample of 10 from both market segments and asks each person his annual income. The data at the top of page 82 show the results. Are there any differences in incomes between the Machos and Status Seekers?

Machos	Status Seekers
$22,500	$29,000
22,000	28,500
21,000	28,000
22,000	27,500
23,000	28,500
23,750	29,000
20,000	27,500
22,500	28,000
23,500	28,000
21,500	28,000

    a. Draw stem-and-leaf displays.
    b. Compute the appropriate measures of the center and spread.
    c. What are the differences between the two segments?

2. The following list presents the number of computer crimes each year for the period 1962–1978. [*Source: Computer Crimes—Criminal Justice Resource Manual*; Bureau of Justice Statistics, 1979.] What is the underlying trend and are there any years when the number of crimes was unusual or extraordinary?

1962	2	1971	59
1963	2	1972	73
1964	6	1973	75
1965	8	1974	84
1966	3	1975	59
1967	4	1976	87
1968	12	1977	42
1969	20	1978	20
1970	38		

    a. Plot the raw data.
    b. Smooth the data with an MA(3).
    c. Develop a residual plot.
    d. Develop a mental model on the increase in computer crimes in the United States during 1962–1978.
    e. As director of the Computer Crimes Division, should you be seeking additional personnel for your department based on your answer in part **d**?

3. The administrator of the emergency room in Safehaven Hospital in Chicago has recorded the amount of time a patient waits before receiving treatment. The length of time that a patient must wait for treatment is important in determining the size of the emergency room staff. He records the wait times for 200 patients in a typical week. The data follow.

Class	Frequency
Less than 10 minutes	5
10 to 15 minutes	25
15 to 20 minutes	70
20 to 25 minutes	70
25 to 30 minutes	25
More than 30 minutes	5

a. What percentage of patients receive treatment in less than 10 minutes?
b. What percentage of patients receive treatment after more than 30 minutes?
c. Experience indicates that if 30% of wait times are less than 10 minutes, the emergency room is overstaffed. If 20% of the wait times are more than 30 minutes, the emergency room is understaffed. What can you conclude about Safehaven's emergency staffing?
d. Construct a frequency data set that would suggest that the emergency room is both understaffed and overstaffed.

4. Historically, over 40% of the accounts receivable at Apex Inc. have been in excess of 35 days. Apex recently started a program of inducements to reduce the age of the accounts receivable. Two months later a sample of 15 accounts receivable is taken. Given the following data, has the age of the accounts receivable been reduced?

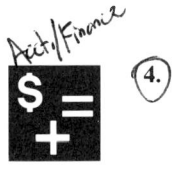

Number of Days

20	15	20	16	19
15	22	21	20	17
21	30	20	18	15

a. Plot a stem-and-leaf display.
b. Compute the appropriate measures of the center and spread.
c. Using either the Empirical or Chebyshev's rule, has the inducements program been successful? Explain.

5. Length-of-tenure discounts are the difference between the rents charged long-time tenants and newer tenants. Landlords give discounts because they want to keep good tenants and minimize turnover. The American Housing Group wants to know if the size of the discount is the same in Atlanta and Houston. It collects the following data, which are the percentage discounts at selected apartment complexes in the two cities. Do the discounts differ in the two cities?

Atlanta		Houston	
3.4	1.5	6.2	3.5
6.5	2.0	7.2	4.6
11.5	3.4	5.4	5.3
2.7	2.5	6.8	4.2
2.3	3.9	7.1	6.9
2.9	1.1	10.9	7.4
3.9	2.2	23.0	5.6
3.2		5.8	

a. Draw either a box plot or stem-and-leaf display, whichever is more appropriate.
b. Compute the appropriate measures of the center and spread.
c. Do the discounts differ between Atlanta and Houston? How?
d. What economic and demographic variables might account for the difference between Atlanta and Houston?

6. The financial manager at COMCEL wants to know how profit margins, net profit after taxes divided by sales, have done for the past 16 quarters. Data are given at the top of page 84. Are profit margins increasing or decreasing?

Quarter	Profit Margin	Quarter	Profit Margin
1	5.05	9	5.95
2	4.10	10	5.50
3	5.15	11	5.15
4	5.20	12	5.60
5	6.75	13	5.65
6	5.30	14	6.70
7	5.35	15	5.75
8	5.40	16	5.80

    a. Develop a line graph.
    b. Smooth the data using an MA(3).
    c. Develop a residual plot.
    d. Develop a mental model on profit margin performance.
    e. Based on your answer to part **d**, what do you expect should happen to profit margin for the next four quarters? If your expectations are not met, what might that mean?

7. American Breakfast sells 10-ounce boxes of its cereals. Each hour the Statistical Process Control Department takes a sample of four boxes from the production line and weighs the contents. They compute the hourly mean and the range in the four data values. This is to ensure that they do have 10 ounces in their boxes.

Hour	Weight of Four Boxes off the Line				Hourly Mean	Hourly Range
0800–0900	9.8	10	10.1	9.9	9.95	.30
0900–1000	9.9	10	10.2	10	10.03	.30
1000–1100	9.8	10	9.7	10.2	9.93	.50
1100–1200	10.1	10	9.9	9.8	9.95	.30
1200–1300	9.7	10	9.9	10	9.90	.30
1300–1400	10.4	10	9.8	9.8	10.00	.60
1400–1500	9.9	10.2	9.7	10.3	10.03	.60
1500–1600	9.8	10	10	10	9.95	.20
1600–1700	10	9.9	9.8	10.2	9.98	.40
1700–1800	9.9	10	10.1	10	10.00	.20

    a. Plot the hourly mean and range in two separate line graphs.
    b. Compute the mean and standard deviation of the hourly sample means and ranges.
Assuming that the means and ranges are bell-shaped, 95% of the hourly means (and hourly ranges) should lie within a distance of two standard deviations of their respective means.
    c. Suppose that the hourly mean weight of the four boxes for hour 1900–2000 is 9.5 ounces. What might that signify? Why?
    d. Suppose that the hourly mean range is 1.2 ounces for hour 2100–2200. What might that signify? Why?
    e. Given your answers to parts **c** and **d**, what action would you take if you were the plant manager?

8. Industry-wide figures show that for plants with 200–300 workers, the mean number of grievances filed per month is 75. Midwest Electric Company, which has 250 employees, has been tracking grievances. Data for the last 12 months are given. Do we have a possible disturbance problem?

Month	Grievances	Month	Grievances
1	75	7	97
2	70	8	94
3	73	9	99
4	78	10	93
5	65	11	100
6	73	12	93

    a. Use descriptive statistics and graphics to defend and support your position.
    b. How would you go about solving the disturbance problem?

9. Pan-Pacific Power Company wishes to know if its employees want the flexibility of designing their own benefits package. A flexible package allows employees to make choices among amount of vacation, type and amount of insurance, number of personal days, etc. Pan-Pacific conducts a survey of its managers and professionals, administrative support people, and hourly employees. The survey data are given here.

Group	Sample Size	Number in Favor
Managers and professionals	50	40
Administrative staff support	100	30
Hourly employees	1,000	250

    a. Compute the mean and the standard deviation for the three groups of data.
    b. Do the three groups appear to differ in the mean or the standard deviation?
    c. Based on your answers to parts a and b, how should Pan-Pacific deal with the flexible benefits issue?

10. For bell-shaped data, the mean and standard deviation together with the Empirical rule permit you to estimate specific values of the original data. I.Q. scores are bell-shaped with a mean of 100 and a standard deviation of 15.
    a. Describe the data using the Empirical rule.
    b. If 16% of the population has a higher I.Q. than Mr. Jones, what is Jones's I.Q.?

11. The sales of motor homes for Mobile Homes Inc. for a 20-month period are shown. The sales manager wants to develop a model of sales for the past 20 months. She may wish to use the model to make predictions for the next several months.

Month	Sales in Units	Month	Sales in Units
1	628 ✓	7	403 ✓
2	652 ✓	8	700 ✓
3	495 ✓	9	837 ✓
4	344 ✓	10	1,224 ✓
5	405 ✓	11	1,117 ✓
6	586 ✓	12	1,214 ✓

(*continued*)

Month	Sales in Units	Month	Sales in Units
13	762 ✓	17	1,396
14	846 ✓	18	1,174 ✓
15	1,228 ✓	19	628 ✓
16	937 ✓	20	1,753

    a. Plot the raw data.
    b. Compute the 10% trimmed mean, median, and interquartile range.
    c. Do any of the measures summarize the data accurately? Why?
    d. Compute an MA(3) series and plot it. Are the time-ordered data stationary? Describe the overall pattern of the moving average series.
    e. The moving average series graph suggests the moving average for period 20 will be about 1,200 units. Given this, what is the sales manager's prediction for sales in period 21, the upcoming month?

12. Centex Industries maintains data on the number of service calls its technicians make each day. Below is a frequency distribution of the data. The service manager wants to develop a simple mental model for the typical and the unusual number of calls per day (outliers).

Number of Calls	Frequency
0 to 4.99 calls	1
5 to 9.99 calls	3
10 to 14.99 calls	7
15 to 19.99 calls	17
20 to 24.99 calls	8
25 to 29.99 calls	2
30 to 34.99 calls	1

    a. Plot the frequency histogram.
    b. Develop a cumulative frequency distribution.
    c. Plot the cumulative frequency histogram.
    d. Develop a mental model on the typical and the rare or unusual number of calls per day.

13. The Arbitration Association collects data on the number of grievances filed by plants with between 200 and 300 workers. Shown are the data for the January survey. They want to identify firms with exceptionally low and high numbers of filed grievances. They plan to study these firms.

Firms	Grievances	Firms	Grievances
1	70	6	69
2	74	7	99
3	65	8	76
4	45	9	72
5	78	10	62

    a. Compute the median and interquartile range.
    b. Draw a box plot.

Chapter 2 Descriptive Statistics I: Toward Managerial Problem Sensing

    c. Identify outliers and label the box plot.
    d. Having identified two plants that are outliers (problem sensing), what would you do next?

14. The given data set is the number of children per household in a survey of 10 families taken in the 1950s.

$$0 \quad 1 \quad 1 \quad 1 \quad 2 \quad 2 \quad 2 \quad 2 \quad 3 \quad 3$$

    a. Compute the mean, 10% trimmed mean, and the median.
    b. The mean and median are relatively close. What does that imply about the data set?
    c. Compute the standard deviation and the interquartile range.
    d. The standard deviation and interquartile range are relatively close. What does that imply about the data set?

15. The data set below is the number of defective fuses in ten boxes of 100 fuses.

Box Number	Number of Defectives
1	0
2	1
3	1
4	1
5	2
6	2
7	2
8	2
9	5
10	25

    a. Compute the mean, 10% trimmed mean, and the median.
    b. The mean and median are relatively far apart. What does that imply about the data set?
    c. Compute the standard deviation and the interquartile range.
    d. The standard deviation and interquartile range are relatively far apart. What does that imply about the data set?

16. COMCEL wants to compare the sales-to-salary ratio for salespeople in two of its southern sales regions—Charlotte and New Orleans. Sales-to-salary ratio is an employee's sales divided by his or her base salary. Historically, New Orleans has had the highest sales-to-salary ratios. Recently, the Charlotte region has taken measures to increase the ratio. Summary data for all employees in both regions are presented.

	New Orleans	Charlotte	Charlotte (one year ago)
Sample size	5	5	5
Minimum	9	9	3
Maximum	25	22	15
First quartile	10	10	7
Median	12	11	7
Third quartile	15	15	11

a. Has Charlotte been successful? Defend your position.
b. How would you attempt to further improve both Charlotte's and New Orleans' sales-to-salary ratio?

17. Managers at Zentron Inc. maintain a data base of the number of personal hours taken in the plant at the end of each month. They want to determine the trend over the past two years. They also want to determine a normal number of hours taken so they can identify a month when the number of hours is out of line. If so, they will investigate.

Month	Number of Hours Taken	Month	Number of Hours Taken
Jan.	51	Jan.	65
Feb.	56	Feb.	66
Mar.	60	Mar.	65
Apr.	68	Apr.	68
May	69	May	67
June	69	June	63
July	57	July	66
Aug.	67	Aug.	63
Sept.	63	Sept.	59
Oct.	55	Oct.	60
Nov.	62	Nov.	65
Dec.	51	Dec.	59

a. Plot the data in a line graph.
b. Are the time-ordered data stationary? Why?
c. Compute the mean and standard deviation.
d. Assume that no changes occur within the plant. Use the Empirical rule to determine how many personal hours taken you should expect in 95% of the months.
e. If, in the following January, workers took over 100 hours, what might that mean? Why?

18. Each day the process control group takes ten cans of the company's best selling beverage and checks to see if the cans contain 300 ml. The mean results for a 10-day period on the filling volume are listed. This procedure is to ensure that proper filling volume is maintained.

Day	Filling Volume	Day	Filling Volume
1	301	6	295
2	300	7	290
3	297	8	291
4	299	9	287
5	295	10	285

a. Plot the daily means of the filling volumes in a line graph.
b. Compute an MA(3) and plot it.
c. Does it appear that the firm is having trouble with its filling volume operation? What action should the firm take? Explain your position.

19. The finance manager of XYZ Inc. wishes to compare her firm's current ratio to other firms in the industry. Current ratio is current assets divided by current liabilities. A frequency distribution for a sample of 32 firms' current ratios is presented.

Current Ratio	Frequency
Less than 1.0	1
1.00 to 1.49	2
1.50 to 1.99	7
2.00 to 2.49	14
2.50 to 2.99	7
Above 3.00	1

   a. Plot the frequency histogram.
   b. Develop a cumulative percentage distribution.
   c. Plot the cumulative percentage histogram.
   d. XYZ's current ratio is .95. How does XYZ compare with the other 32 firms? Is it typical or unusual? What action should XYZ take next if it concludes that its current ratio is out of line with the rest of the industry?

20. Financial analysts agree that for an industrial bond to be a safe investment, the firm's total income should be more than 3 or 4 times its interest payment. Shown are the interest coverage data, total income divided by bond interest, for the past ten years. Are the firm's bonds a safe investment?

Year	Interest Coverage	Year	Interest Coverage
1982	8.5*	1987	5.7
1983	7.9	1988	5.8
1984	8.2	1989	6.9
1985	6.5	1990	7.5
1986	6.6	1991	8.5

*In 1982 the firm's total income was 8.5 times as large as its interest on bonds.

   a. Plot the interest coverage for the past ten years.
   b. Compute an MA(3) and plot it.
   c. Describe the overall pattern of the interest coverage ratio for the past ten years. Using only the above time-ordered data, have the firm's industrial bonds been a safe investment for the past ten years?

21. The product life cycle tells us that the sales for a product are slow right after introduction, increase at an increasing rate, increase at a constant rate, begin to level off, and may even decline. Do the following sales data behave as the life cycle predicts?

Year	Sales (in thousands)	Year	Sales (in thousands)
1975	5	1979	31
1976	7	1980	47
1977	10	1981	49
1978	19	1982	52

(*continued*)

Year	Sales (in thousands)	Year	Sales (in thousands)
1983	50	1988	59
1984	54	1989	57
1985	57	1990	55
1986	61	1991	56
1987	60	1992	54

    a. Compute an MA(3) of the yearly sales and plot it.
    b. Use the moving average series to describe the growth of your product. Do sales follow the product life cycle model?
    c. Given the stage of the product, what actions should the firm consider?

22. Shown are two frequency distributions of cholesterol levels of 100 people who eat similar foods with only one exception. Group B people take 7 grams of fiber (oat bran) daily. Cholesterol levels over 200 indicate a potential problem. Levels over 240 are considered serious enough to warrant medication.

Group A Class	Frequency	Group B Class	Frequency
Under 160	5	Under 160	10
160 to 179	10	160 to 179	25
180 to 199	35	180 to 199	55
200 to 219	30	200 to 219	5
220 to 239	10	220 to 239	5
240 or over	10	240 or over	0

    a. Construct a frequency histogram for each group.
    b. Determine the approximate mean for both histograms.
    c. Does it appear that fiber affects a person's cholesterol level? Defend your position.

23. The accompanying scatter diagram contains a plot of the number of students in an elective Managerial Communications course in a College of Business Administration at an urban university. It also contains a plot of a moving average of length three. The instructor must make predictions on enrollment for the next year. If the class size tops 40, he will have to find a second instructor.

Term	Enrollment	Term	Enrollment
F88	12	SP90	12
W89	10	SU90	24
SP89	14	F90	30
SU89	20	W91	31
F89	17	SP91	34
W90	30	SU91	35

    a. Since the moving average series is much smoother than the original data, let's use it to make our predictions. What is the predicted enrollment for the Fall term of 91? Begin with an estimate of the moving average for SU91 and determine an estimate of enrollment for Fall 91.

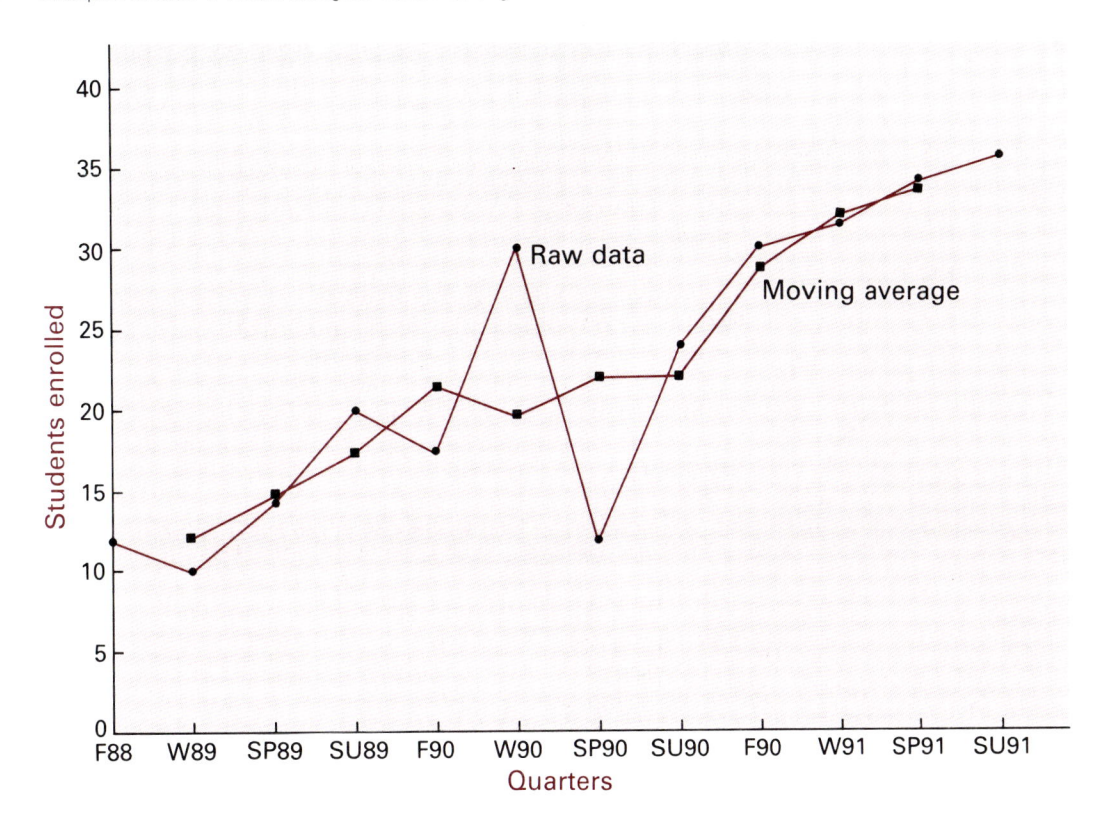

Chapter 2 Descriptive Statistics I: Toward Managerial Problem Sensing

[Graph: Students enrolled vs Quarters (F88 to SU91), showing Raw data and Moving average curves]

b. Now predict the enrollment for the Winter term of 92.
c. What have you discovered about the ability to use a moving average of length three to make predictions about the future?

24.

Date: June 5, 1992
To: Nat Gordon, Vice President of Manufacturing
From: Ann Tabor, CEO
Re: Monthly Attendance at Two Operating Plants

It has recently come to my attention that monthly attendance at our two operating plants may differ. Both may be below our desired goal of 98%. You will recall the emphasis that we placed on monthly attendance at our Annual Goal Setting Retreat. Please have one of your staff members look into the situation. I need the answers to the following questions:

1. Do both plants have similar monthly attendance figures?
2. Is monthly attendance of males and females or hourly and management employees the same?

Are there any other differences between the two plants? I need the report by June 12th.

Use Data Base I for your analysis. Your response to Ann Tabor should include a brief memo and your analysis.

25.

```
Date:  January 7, 1992
  To:  Pam Ascher, Manager—National Sales Manager
From:  Bill O'Hara, Vice President of Marketing
  Re:  Tracking Unit Sales in the Atlanta Sales Territory
```

Ann Tabor has asked me to provide her with an executive summary of our unit sales performance for Atlanta for the past 36 months. She wants to know how fast sales are increasing, what are our strong and weak quarters, and have there been any months when sales were unusually high or low. I'm sorry to add this to your other duties, but Ann needs the report on her desk by January 15th.

Use Data Base II for your analysis. Your response to Bill O'Hara should include a brief memo and your analysis.

3

Descriptive Statistics II: Bivariate Data and Problem Diagnosis

3.1 Introduction
    Univariate and bivariate data
    Problem sensing
    Problem diagnosis
3.2 Types of variables
3.3 Analyzing mixed cross-sectional data
    One-way table display
    Multiple box plots
3.4 Analyzing categorical cross-sectional data
    Cross-tabs tables
    Joint percentage tables
    Column percentage tables
    Row percentage tables
    Inductive inference
    Intervening variables
3.5 Analyzing quantitative cross-sectional data
    Scatter diagrams
    Linear relationships
    The circle vs. ellipse test
    Nonlinear relationships
    Clusters
3.6 Analyzing quantitative time-ordered data
    Multiple line graphs
    Lagged relationships
3.7 Correlation and cross-correlation
    The correlation coefficient
    Determining lagged relationships using cross-correlations
    Interpreting cross-correlations
3.8 Key ideas and overview
Chapter 3 Questions
Chapter 3 Application Problems

CHAPTER OUTLINE

COMCEL Interoffice Communication

Date: July 21, 1992
  To: Cherian Jain, VP Marketing Research
From: Ann Tabor, CEO
  Re: Market Share in the Southern Region

In checking the latest report on market share, I was pleased to see that we have captured 55% of the Dallas market and 50% of the Birmingham market. However, we have only 5% of the Washington market and 20% of the Atlanta market. What are we doing right in Birmingham and Dallas, and wrong in Washington, D.C., and Atlanta?

Please look into this for me and make some recommendations on how to improve our market share in the Southern Region.

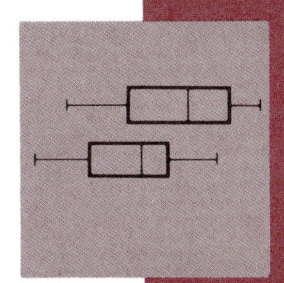

3.1 Introduction

There are two major differences between Chapters 2 and 3. From a *statistical* viewpoint, we focus here on *bivariate* data, whereas we focused on *univariate* data in Chapter 2. From a *problem solving* perspective, we focus now on both problem sensing and *diagnosis*, whereas we focused only on *problem sensing* in Chapter 2. By the end of this section you should be able to:

1. distinguish between bivariate and univariate data;
2. distinguish between problem sensing and diagnosis; and
3. distinguish between diagnosing disturbance problems and entrepreneurial opportunities.

Univariate and Bivariate Data

In Chapter 2 we presented productivity data for 36 work groups. Shown are data for four of these work groups.

Work Group	Productivity (% of standard)
1	106%
2	95%
3	103%
4	95%

These are univariate data. Each work group is described by *one variable*—group productivity. Thus, univariate data represent observations on *one* variable that are all measured in the same units, such as dollars, productivity, or personal hours taken.

Table 3.1 presents bivariate cross-sectional data for 12 sales regions of COMCEL. Each region is described by four variables—market share, advertising, mean years of experience of the sales force, and relative price of product as compared to the competition's price. Note that the units of the four variables need not be the same. Bivariate data represent observations on *two or more* variables that can be expressed in different units. However, each set of data values is measured on the *same* person, region, month, or thing. For example, the data set for the Atlanta region includes the following four values with different units: 20%, $13,000, 3 years, and 1.50.

Problem Sensing

Problem sensing is a critical managerial capability. Effective managers and business professionals must detect emerging disturbance problems and be *pathfinders*. They need to be able to create new opportunities and goals for their departments. Consider the market share data in Table 3.1. What are the data trying to say to the Charlotte regional sales manager?

The mean market share is 29.4% and the standard deviation is 15.2%. None of the data points is more than three standard deviations from the mean. Even

Table 3.1
Bivariate Data

Region	Market Share	Advertising	Mean Years Sales Experience	Relative Price
Atlanta	20%	$13,000	3	1.50
Birmingham	50%	$28,000	12	.60
Charlotte	30%	$17,000	15	1.00
Jacksonville	10%	$8,000	1	1.75
New Orleans	25%	$16,000	18	1.30
Orlando	30%	$18,000	7	.90
Miami	35%	$21,000	8	2.00
Washington	5%	$6,000	23	2.90
Baltimore	45%	$25,000	9	1.50
Dallas	55%	$32,000	11	1.10
Houston	20%	$11,000	20	2.50
Austin	28%	$16,000	17	2.25

$\bar{x} = 29.4\%$
$s = 15.2\%$

Washington's and Dallas's market shares are not outliers. Charlotte's market share is very close to the mean for the 12 regions. Should the Charlotte manager be satisfied to be in the middle of the pack? Perhaps, but he might also be curious to learn why the market shares vary so much among the 12 regions. If he can determine what causes market share to vary, he may be able to improve the Charlotte region's share. Looking for ways to improve performance is pathfinding.

Thus, a situation perceived as a problem can also be viewed as an opportunity. The Charlotte manager should ask himself: How can I improve my market share? Opportunity sensing begins with asking the question. Problem diagnosis involves answering the question.

Problem Diagnosis

Diagnosis begins once we have discovered a disturbance problem (an outlier) or have decided to attempt to improve performance (an entrepreneurial opportunity). For disturbance problems, diagnosis means determining the root causes of an outlier. To do so, ask the following two questions.

1. What is *unique* about the outlier group or the outlier time period?

   ### Examples

   What is unique or distinctive about work group 20 that might account for its very high productivity?

   What is unique or distinctive about December 1990 that might account for the unusually high number of personal hours taken that month?

2. What has *changed* that might account for the outliers?

Examples

Has work group 20 undergone any changes recently that might explain its very high productivity?

Were there any changes in the plant around December that might explain why so many personal hours were taken?

That is, when diagnosing disturbance problems, look for *differences* and *changes*.

Diagnosing entrepreneurial opportunities means determining what variables affect the goals we are trying to attain. Table 3.1 indicates that the Charlotte manager believes that market share is affected by level of advertising, mean years of sales force experience, and relative price. How do managers identify such potential variables? They draw upon their own judgment, creativity, and past experiences as well as advice from customers, vendors, and consultants. Diagnosis means identifying variables that might explain large variations from one region to the next in cross-sectional data or large variations from one time period to the next in time-ordered data. In short, diagnosis answers the question: "What affects what?"

In summary, you will learn how to diagnose disturbance problems and opportunities using bivariate cross-sectional and time-ordered data.

SECTION 3.1 EXERCISES

1. Why do we usually need to do a bivariate data analysis in order to perform problem diagnosis?
2. Suppose your univariate analysis has identified an outlier—a problem or an opportunity. What two questions will you ask in determining possible causes of the outlier?
3. A company has divided its market area into regions. For some time each region has contributed equally to the revenues of the firm. Last month one region's contribution to the company's revenue dropped. Assuming that this drop is more than a chance effect, how would you assist the company in diagnosing the causes of the problem?
4. Transform the following univariate data into bivariate data.

Salesperson	Ratio of Annual Sales to Total Salary
1	8.0
2	7.5
3	8.4
4	6.7
5	7.5

3.2 Types of Variables

Diagnosis means identifying variables that affect goals, such as improving market share or determining the reasons for one group's very high productivity. This section describes two types of variables—*quantitative* and *categorical*. By the end of this section you should be able to:

1. distinguish between quantitative and categorical variables;
2. explain why you might consider assigning numbers to categorical variables; and
3. explain why numbers you assign to categorical variables may not be meaningful.

A variable is a quantity that can take on more than one value. Consider the four variables—productivity, job switching, number of grievances, and leadership style—to describe three work groups. Productivity is measured as a percentage of the management standard. Job switching assesses whether work group members do or do not switch jobs. Grievances record the number of complaints filed against management. Leadership style assesses the managers' styles of supervision along two dimensions—importance in achieving production (high productivity) and concern for workers (high people).

Work Group	Productivity	Job Switching	Number of Grievances	Leadership Style
1	106%	Yes	4	High productivity/High people
2	95%	No	8	High people/Low productivity
3	103%	Yes	4	High productivity/Low people

Productivity and number of grievances are both quantitative variables. Group 2 filed twice as many grievances as groups 1 and 3. Work group 1's productivity is 11% higher than group 2's. Measurements for the productivity and grievances variables are meaningful because they are quantitative. That is, one can add, subtract, multiply, and divide two numbers, and the result makes sense.

The job switching and leadership variables are qualitative, or categorical, variables, because they cannot be meaningfully represented by numbers. Job switching within the group either has or has not happened. The group leadership style focuses on concern (or lack of it) for productivity and people. Differences in the leadership styles cannot be meaningfully expressed by numbers. Rather, we express the differences qualitatively, in words.

We can assign numbers to categorical variables, but the numbers are not quantitatively meaningful. For example, we can assign values from 1 to 4 to the leadership style categories:

Low on productivity and people	1
Low on productivity and high on people	2

Low on people and high on productivity 3
High on people and productivity 4

The four numbers are useful for *coding* the data in a management information system, as it takes less space to store the four numbers than it does to store the full leadership descriptions. However, the numbers are not meaningful as numerical measurements. We cannot say that a high on people and productivity leadership style has a value that is 3 more than a low on productivity and people style. The mathematical operations of addition, subtraction, multiplication, and division have no meaning for coded categorical variables.

SECTION 3.2 EXERCISES

1. Classify each of the following variables as either quantitative or categorical.
   a. age of employee
   b. monthly income
   c. gender
   d. leadership style
   e. race
   f. number of years of formal schooling
   g. month of the year
   h. occupation

2. Explain how educational level could be either a categorical variable or a quantitative variable.

3. For purposes of computer storage, the states are assigned numbers from 1 to 50 rather than typing the names of the states. On a computer output, the mean value of the state variable was $\bar{x} = 25.5$. What meaning can you place on this output?

4. Transform the quantitative variable, number of years with firm, into a categorical variable with three levels.

3.3 Analyzing Mixed Cross-Sectional Data

Why is it important to distinguish between categorical and quantitative variables? There are different ways to display and interpret categorical, quantitative, and mixed variables. We shall address these methods next. By the end of this section you should be able to:

1. explain what mixed data are;
2. explain what explanatory and dependent variables are; and
3. construct a one-way table and multiple box plot for mixed data.

In Chapter 2 a statistical analysis determined that work group 20's productivity of 123% of standard was an outlier. Assuming it was not due to a coding error or chance, what factor(s) might account for the very high productivity? Have there been any changes in the work group lately? Has it recently received specialized training? Have group members learned new techniques? Do group members switch jobs with one another to maintain their morale and skills? In short, what is *unique* or *different* about this group as compared with the other 35 groups?

Suppose further investigation of work group 20 revealed the following:

1. Its members continually switch jobs with one another. No other group does this as frequently. Job switching may be a cause of work group 20's very high productivity.
2. There are no other recent changes inside or outside the plant that might explain work group 20's high productivity.

We might surmise that job switching—a categorical variable—affects productivity—a quantitative variable. This pairing of different types of variables creates a *mixed data set*. One variable is categorical while the other is quantitative.

How can we determine if the two variables are related? The answer is to construct a *one-way table*.

One-Way Table Display

> A one-way table displays the impact of *one* categorical explanatory variable on a quantitative dependent variable. A one-way table contains the sample sizes and measures of the center and spread. Use a one-way table to determine whether an explanatory variable affects the dependent variable.
>
> An explanatory variable is a variable that affects the variation in another variable. It is also called the independent variable.
>
> A dependent variable is a variable whose variation depends upon another variable.

Before developing **one-way tables**, we must designate the **explanatory** and **dependent variables**. In the work group study, we should ask the following two questions. Could job switching explain why some groups are high producers and other groups are low producers? Could high or low production explain the absence or presence of job switching? The former makes more sense. Thus, job switching is the explanatory variable and productivity is the dependent variable. That is, productivity depends on job switching.

Table 3.2 contains the bivariate data on productivity and job switching.

Table 3.2

Bivariate Data for Productivity and Job Switching

Group	Productivity (%)	Job Switch	Group	Productivity (%)	Job Switch
1	106	Yes	19	110	Yes
2	95	No	20	123	Yes
3	103	Yes	21	104	Yes
4	95	No	22	100	Yes
5	95	Yes	23	101	Yes
6	97	No	24	95	No
7	95	No	25	97	No
8	105	Yes	26	94	No
9	102	Yes	27	102	No
10	89	No	28	102	Yes
11	105	Yes	29	106	Yes
12	99	Yes	30	110	Yes
13	95	No	31	97	No
14	100	Yes	32	101	Yes
15	106	Yes	33	95	No
16	101	Yes	34	98	Yes
17	97	No	35	97	Yes
18	104	Yes	36	94	No

Table 3.3

One-Way Two-Level Table for Work Group Productivity Data

	Categorical Variable	
	No Job Switching	Job Switching
Number of Groups	14	22
$\bar{x}$	95.5%	103.5%
s	2.8%	5.8%
Median	95.0%	102.5%
Interquartile Range	2.0%	6.0%

Table 3.3 is a one-way table for the same data which includes the sample sizes, the means, the medians, and measures of variability. Please verify the calculations for yourself.

One-way tables may contain more than two levels of a categorical variable. For example, to look for differences in sick leave hours taken by workers within a firm, we could divide the categorical variable—type of workers—into the three levels of management and professionals, administrative support, and production workers.

Multiple Box Plots

If we compute the median and interquartile range for a set of data, we can also draw a multiple box plot, with or without the fences. Figure 3.1 shows a multiple box plot for the bivariate data. The base line measures the quantitative variable—productivity. One box plot is drawn for each level of the categorical variable—job switching.

FIGURE 3.1 Multiple Box Plots Without Fences

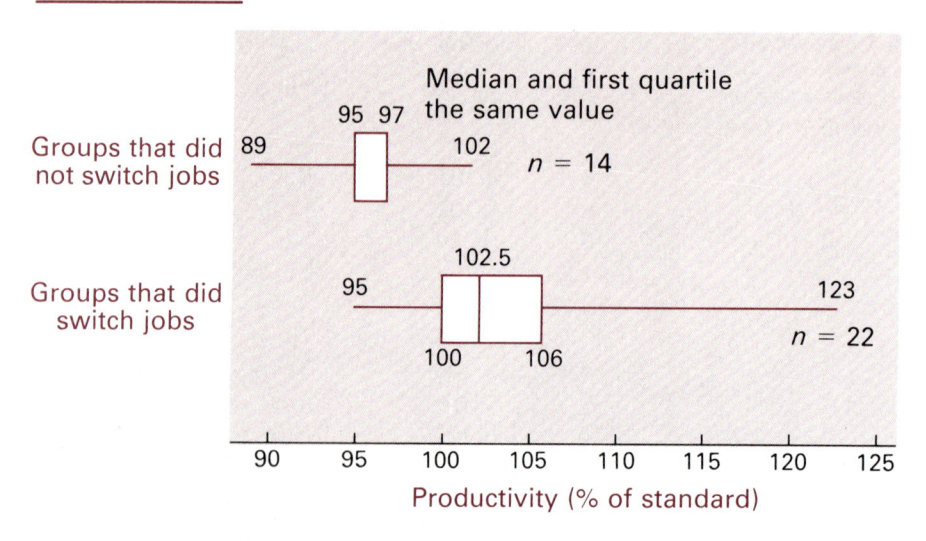

Both the one-way table and the multiple box plot suggest that the two measures of the center (mean and median) and the two measures of spread (standard deviation and interquartile range) *appear* to be different between the groups that did and did not switch jobs. Shortly, we will discuss why we must use the term *appears*. If job switching is a cause of high productivity, then management should encourage and train other groups to rotate jobs among their members.

SECTION 3.3 EXERCISES

1. A work group is composed of 11 men and 9 women. You want to know whether the number of sick days is related to gender. Listed are the number of sick days each person took during the past year.

Men	6	5	9	2	3	0	1	3	2	1	3
Women	0	2	1	3	4	8	2	11	2		

   a. Construct a one-way table by finding the mean number of sick days and standard deviation for each gender.
   b. Find the median number of sick days and interquartile range for each gender. Construct a multiple box plot.

2. The numbers of insurance claims processed by two branch offices for the past two weeks are listed. The general manager wants to know if the offices differ in their claims processing.

Office 1	25	30	32	38	37	31	33	29	32	34
Office 2	28	34	32	44	40	34	37	32	35	38

   a. Construct a one-way table of number of claims processed by each office using the mean and standard deviation for each group.
   b. Find the median number of claims processed and the interquartile range for each office. Construct a multiple box plot.
   c. Does it appear that one office processes more claims than the other?

3. An insurance association conference was held for agents specializing in life and property insurance. The ages of the attendees are shown.

Life		Property	
23	41	29	43
25	42	30	43
28	42	30	44
30	43	32	44
30	44	34	48
33	44	36	54
35	45	38	55
37	49	40	56
39	50	43	56
40	52	43	57

   a. Construct a multiple box plot for both groups.
   b. Does it appear that the distribution of ages differs between the two groups?

4. You find an unexpected large variation in salaries among 50 men, all working as loan officers in a major bank in Chicago. Suggest two potential explanatory variables that might account for the large variation.

5. Suppose you believe that previous performance rating—outstanding, good, mediocre, and poor—affects salary. You want to develop a one-way table. Which is the explanatory variable and which is the dependent variable? How many levels of the explanatory variable will there be?

6. Draw a multiple box plot that shows that outstanding performers have higher salaries and lower variability in salaries than poor performers.

3.4 Analyzing Categorical Cross-Sectional Data

Managers often collect categorical data on both the explanatory and dependent variables. Moreover, they sometimes convert quantitative variables into categorical variables. For example, we can convert the quantitative work group productivity variable into a categorical variable as follows:

Low-productivity teams   Teams whose productivity is *below* the median productivity of the 36 work groups

High-productivity teams   Teams whose productivity is *at* or *above* the median productivity of the 36 work groups

From Table 2.15 (page 58), the median productivity for the 36 work groups is 100%. Note that the above definitions ensure that all 36 work groups will fall into either the low- or high-productivity team subcategory.

When the explanatory and dependent variables are both categorical, managers use *cross-tabs* tables to determine whether two variables are related. By the end of this section you should be able to:

1. construct a cross-tabs table;
2. explain joint, row, and column percentages in a cross-tabs table;
3. determine whether two categorical variables *appear* to be related to one another by using the row or column percentages;
4. explain why you might need to qualify your conclusion about the relationship between two variables;
5. control for the impact of a potential intervening variable; and
6. assess the potential relationship between two variables after accounting for an intervening variable.

Cross-Tabs Tables

We want to determine whether productivity is in fact related to the absence or presence of job switching within work groups. The two categorical variables are job switching and level of productivity. The subcategories for both categorical variables should not overlap and should include all the observations. That is, the subcategories must be *mutually exclusive and exhaustive*. Job switching is assessed as yes or no, productivity as low or high.

Table 3.2 includes the data needed to count the number of work groups that fall into the following four subcategories. Remember, the median productivity for all 36 work groups is 100%. Please verify the counts.

Description of Work Groups Using Both Variables	Number of Groups
No job switching and low productivity	13
Job switching and low productivity	4
No job switching and high productivity	1
Job switching and high productivity	18

> A cross-tabs table shows the number of observations that have been cross-classified according to two categorical variables. Use a cross-tabs table to determine whether two categorical variables are related.

Table 3.4 is a two-by-two (2 × 2) **cross-tabs table**. Each categorical variable is broken down into two mutually exclusive and exhaustive subcategories.

What do the entries in the body of Table 3.4 represent? Entries within the table rules represent the number of work groups with two attributes—level of productivity *and* presence or absence of job switching. Thus, we see that there are 13 groups that had low productivity *and* did not switch jobs, while there are 4 groups that had low productivity *and* did switch jobs.

What do the entries in the margins represent? They are row and column totals found by summing across rows and down columns. Thus, there are 14 groups that did not switch jobs and 22 that did, while there are 17 groups that had low productivity and 19 that had high productivity. Margin entries represent the number of work groups with one attribute—level of productivity *or* presence or absence of job switching.

The 2 × 2 table is the simplest cross-tabs table. However, we can divide categorical variables into more than two subcategories. Table 3.5 on page 106 is a four-by-three cross-tabs table. We developed it to explore the impact of class standing on the desirability of an honor code. The undergraduate students were divided into four class standings and three opinions about having an honor code. An undergraduate student is either a freshman, sophomore, junior, or senior. A student either favors the code, does not favor the code, or has no opinion. Note that for both categorical variables, the subcategories are mutually exclusive and exhaustive.

Table 3.4

Cross-Tabs Table for Productivity and Job Switching Data

	No Job Switching	Job Switching	Total
Low Productivity	13	4	17
High Productivity	1	18	19
Total	14	22	36

Table 3.5
4 × 3 Cross-Tabs Table for Desirability of an Honor Code

	Favor	Do Not Favor	No Opinion	
Freshman	100	300	600	1,000
Sophomore	150	200	600	950
Junior	200	150	550	900
Senior	250	100	550	900
	700	750	2,300	3,750

Having developed the cross-tabs table, we can now determine whether the two categorical variables appear to be related. Does job switching seem to affect productivity? Or, does class standing affect one's position on an honor code?

To answer these questions, consider computing the following three important percentage tables:

1. Joint percentage table
2. Column percentage table
3. Row percentage table

Each table highlights a different aspect of the data. Use these three tables to answer the question: Does the absence or presence of job switching affect work group productivity?

Joint Percentage Tables

Table 3.6 shows joint percentages for the work group data. To create Table 3.6, Table 3.4, the initial cross-tabs table, was used. Each entry in Table 3.4 was divided by the total number of observations. For example, the top left entry in the joint percentage table is 13/36 = 36.1%. That is, 36.1% of the work groups had low productivity *and* did not switch jobs. The lower right entry indicates that

Table 3.6
Joint Percentages for Productivity and Job Switching Data

	No Job Switching	Job Switching	
Low Productivity	36.1%	11.1%	47.2%
High Productivity	2.8%	50%	52.8%
	38.9%	61.1%	100%

50% of the work groups had high productivity *and* did switch jobs. The marginal percentages found by summing across rows and down columns are also informative. They show that 47.2% of the work groups had low productivity and 38.9% of the work groups did not switch jobs.

While the joint percentages are informative, they do not tell whether productivity and job switching are related. We must explore further the cross-tabs data.

Column Percentage Tables

Table 3.7 shows the column percentages for the cross-tabs data. To obtain column percentages, divide each entry in Table 3.4 by its *column* total. For example, the top left entry in Table 3.7 is 13/14 = 92.9%. *One final note:* Notice that the marginal percentages on the right are not obtained by summing across the rows.

Table 3.7

Column Percentages for Productivity and Job Switching Data

	No Job Switching	Job Switching	
Low Productivity	92.9%	18.2%	47.2%
High Productivity	7.1%	81.8%	52.8%
	100%	100%	100%

This breakdown is very informative. We can analyze either *row* of the table. If we focus on the low-productivity teams in the upper row, we learn the following:

1. Overall, 47.2% of the work groups were low-productivity teams.
2. Of the groups that did not switch, 92.9% were low-productivity teams.
3. Of the groups that did switch, only 18.2% were low-productivity teams.

If job switching were not related to productivity, the above three column percentages would be similar.

Row Percentage Tables

Table 3.8 on page 108 shows the row percentages for the cross-tabs data. To obtain row percentages, divide each entry in Table 3.4 by its *row* total. For example, the top left entry in Table 3.8 is 13/17 = 76.5%. Again, note that the marginal percentages at the bottom are not obtained by summing down the columns.

This breakdown is also informative. We can analyze either *column* of the table. If we choose to focus on the job switching teams in the right column, we

Table 3.8

Row Percentages for Productivity and Job Switching Data

	No Job Switching	Job Switching	
Low Productivity	76.5%	23.5%	100%
High Productivity	5.3%	94.7%	100%
	38.9%	61.1%	100%

surmise the following:

1. Overall, 61.1% of the teams switched jobs.
2. Of the low-producing teams, only 23.5% switched jobs.
3. Of the high-producing teams, 94.7% switched jobs.

If productivity were not related to job switching, the above three row percentages would be about the same. Both row and column percentages suggest that job switching and productivity appear to be related.

Which percentages—row or column—are more informative? It is often a matter of individual taste. Which one is more helpful in understanding the potential relationship between the two categorical variables? A safe rule is to compute both.

Now consider how row and column percentage tables can be used to determine whether a firm has discriminated against women in its promotional practices.

EXAMPLE: GENDER DISCRIMINATION CASE   A large company is being sued for discrimination in its promotion practices. The suit alleges that women have been systematically denied promotion. The lawyers for the women have obtained access to the company's personnel records for the past 5 years. However, the court has allowed only limited access since the information is highly personal. It will allow the plaintiff to select a sample of 200 employees hired 5 years ago and follow their careers within the firm. The evidence from the sample will be used to determine whether the company is discriminating. Both sides have agreed to the procedure.

In this case, we are dealing with bivariate categorical data. We have two pieces of data for each employee: gender and whether the employee has been promoted. Note that the subcategories are mutually exclusive and exhaustive for each categorical variable.

Table 3.9 is a cross-tabs table for the gender discrimination suit data. Table 3.10 is the row percentage table for the data. It shows that 52.5% of the total sample were promoted. Of the males, 72.7% were promoted; of the females, only 27.8% were promoted. If there were no relationship between gender and

Table 3.9

Cross-Tabs Table for Gender Discrimination Suit Data

	Promoted	Not Promoted	
Male	80	30	110
Female	25	65	90
	105	95	200

Table 3.10

Row Percentages for Gender Discrimination Suit Data

	Promoted	Not Promoted	
Male	72.7%	27.3%	100%
Female	27.8%	72.2%	100%
	52.5%	47.5%	100%

promotion, we would expect the two row percentages to be relatively close to one another and to the overall percentage of 52.5%. In other words, whether an employee is a male or female, the chance of being promoted would be the same—52.5%. Thus it *appears* that the company is discriminating against women. Why is it again necessary to qualify the diagnosis with the word *appears*? The next two sections will shed some light on the types of arguments that could be used to call into question this *apparent* relationship.

Inductive Inference

The firm could make two arguments in its defense. One argument involves *inductive inference*, and the other involves the impact of *intervening variables*. Consider first the inductive inference argument. Table 3.9 is based upon only a *sample* of all the employees. Assume that the firm had not discriminated in its promotional practices. In that case, if Table 3.9 included data on *all* the employees, we would find that the row percentages were the same. Now take a *sample* of employees from the firm, assuming no discrimination. Will the row percentages for the sample equal the row percentages for all the employees? Not necessarily, because there could be differences depending upon which particular employees were selected for the sample. We would expect the two row percentages to be close but not necessarily equal. When we take a small sample and attempt to draw conclusions about the population from which the sample was taken, we must allow room for a *margin of error*. The margin of error is the difference between the sample result and what would be obtained if everyone in the population were sampled. Inductive inference involves making educated guesses about a population based upon a small sample.

Returning to the gender discrimination data, we must ask the following question: Is 72.7% so much larger than 27.8% that the difference is beyond the margin of error?

In Chapter 10 we will present the chi-square test for independence. It incorporates the margin of error into the analysis of row percentages. We can use the test for independence to answer the previous question. In summary, the judge would not use sample data alone to make a ruling. Rather, he or she would draw an inference from the sample data to apply to the target population.

Intervening Variables

The second argument that the firm could make follows this line of reasoning. It is true that, historically, a higher sample percentage of men have been promoted than women, but the difference in promotion percentages is not based on gender. Suppose that most promotions occurred in the firm's overseas divisions. Furthermore, suppose the promoted men had taken more course work in International Business (IB). The firm might argue that, therefore, the men were better qualified and thus more deserving of promotion. By so arguing, the firm would be suggesting reasons other than gender discrimination that could account for the differences in the promotion percentages of each gender. A judge would rule then on the validity of these alternative explanations.

The firm is suggesting that International Business course work is an **intervening variable**. That is, IB course work explains the difference in men and women promoted, not gender.

> Intervening variables are substitute explanatory variables. They are alternative variables that one can logically argue should have an impact on the dependent variable.

Can International Business course work explain why a higher sample percentage of men were promoted? Before developing cross-tabs tables, construct a *tree diagram*. Figure 3.2 displays a tree diagram, which is a breakdown of the total sample size according to the categorical variables of interest—IB course work, gender, and promotion status.

To construct a tree diagram, divide the entire sample of 200 into two groups by the intervening variable, IB course work. Then divide each of these groups into either male or female and then into promoted or not promoted or vice versa.

FIGURE 3.2 Tree Diagram for One Intervening Variable

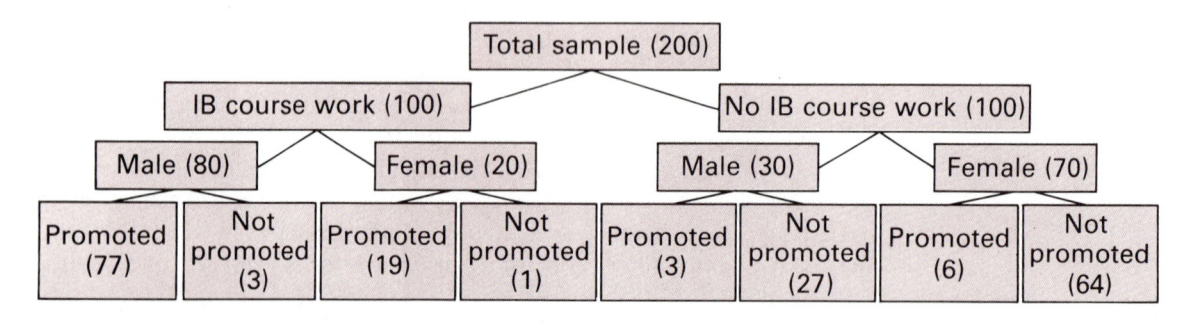

```
                         Total sample (200)
                    ┌────────────┴────────────┐
            IB course work (100)        No IB course work (100)
            ┌───────┴───────┐            ┌───────┴───────┐
        Male (80)       Female (20)   Male (30)       Female (70)
       ┌───┴───┐        ┌───┴───┐     ┌───┴───┐       ┌───┴───┐
   Promoted  Not    Promoted  Not  Promoted  Not   Promoted  Not
    (77)  promoted   (19)  promoted  (3)  promoted   (6)  promoted
            (3)              (1)           (27)              (64)
```

Use Figure 3.2 to construct Table 3.11, *two* cross-tabs row percentage tables. In this case, once we have accounted for the intervening variable—International Business course work taken—the row percentages within each cross-tabs table are very close. For example, of those who had IB course work, 96.2% of the males were promoted as were 95% of females. Of those who did not have IB course work, 10% of the males were promoted and 8.6% of the females. With inclusion of the intervening variable, there no longer appears to be a relationship between gender and promotion.

In summary, Table 3.10 suggests that gender and promotion are related. Males appeared to have a greater likelihood of being promoted than females. However, Table 3.11 indicates that after accounting for International Business courses, gender and promotion do not appear to be related.

How would the judge rule in the gender discrimination case? First, the judge would use the statistical test for independence to draw conclusions about company-wide discrimination. Second, if the test suggested discrimination, the judge would evaluate the *reasonableness* of the intervening variable. A variable such as International Business course work could be reasonably related to overseas promotions. However, height of the employee or color of hair would not be reasonable intervening variables. An intervening variable must pass the reasonableness test. Third, the judge would look for additional evidence of

Table 3.11

Cross-Tabs Tables and Row Percentages for Gender Discrimination Data with an IB Course Work Intervening Variable

IB Course Work

	Promoted	Not Promoted	
Male	77 96.2%	3 3.8%	80
Female	19 95%	1 5%	20
	96	4	100

No IB Course Work

	Promoted	Not Promoted	
Male	3 10%	27 90%	30
Female	6 8.6%	64 91.4%	70
	9	91	100

discrimination within the firm. This includes:

1. There are other gender-based harassment suits pending in the courts.
2. The company has an outdated maternity leave policy.
3. The firm was previously found guilty of racial discrimination in promotion practices.

Given that the intervening variable is reasonable and assuming that the company has no history of discrimination, the judge might rule in favor of the firm.

There can be more than one intervening variable. For example, we could classify people by course work and overseas experience. Here we are using two intervening variables as potential explanations for the differences in percentages of males and females that have been promoted. As more intervening variables are included, the number of cross-tabs tables increases while the sample size for each table decreases. The sample size for *each cell* of the cross-tabs table may become so small that we cannot reach valid conclusions about potential gender discrimination.

One final point remains. How do we determine potential intervening variables? They do not walk up and say: "Here I am!" Rather we must consider possible *logical* alternative variables that might account for the differences. Bear in mind that intervening variables must pass the reasonableness test.

SECTION 3.4 EXERCISES

1. A consulting firm administered the same questionnaire to 30 managers and 50 nonmanagers. On one of the yes–no questions, 15 managers answered yes and 15 nonmanagers answered yes. Construct a cross-tabs table to display these data.

2. A credit agency must distinguish good from bad credit risks. The credit manager believes that home ownership should be a good predictor of credit worthiness. The following table was constructed from the records of 300 previous clients.

		Credit Risk Group		
		Good	Bad	Total
Home	Owns home	225	30	255
Ownership	Rents	25	20	45
		250	50	300

   a. What percentage of the total sample are homeowners?
   b. What percentage of the good risks are homeowners?
   c. What percentage of the bad risks are homeowners?
   d. Based on parts **a**–**c**, does it appear that credit worthiness is related to home ownership?

3. A parole authority has constructed the next table showing success or failure in completing parole vs. the parolee's age at first conviction.

Chapter 3 Descriptive Statistics II: Bivariate Data and Problem Diagnosis

		Parole Outcome		
		Success	Failure	Total
Age at	Under 18	270	630	900
First	18–21	750	750	1,500
Conviction	Over 21	420	180	600
		1,440	1,560	3,000

    a. Of the parolees who were first convicted at age under 18, what percentage are successes?
    b. What percentage of the 18–21 age group are successes?
    c. What percentage of the over 21 age group are successes?
    d. What percentage of parolees are a success?
    e. Based on parts **a–d**, does it appear that age at first conviction is related to the success of parole outcomes?

4. The president of a university wants to know the extent to which undergraduates in the two largest colleges—Arts and Sciences, and Business—want a required course in interpersonal communications. A total of 100 students are surveyed. Complete the table by filling in the blanks.

Major		Position on Course Requirement		
		Yes	No	Total
Sciences	Count	10	___	___
	Row %	33.3	___	___
	Column %	25.0	___	___
	Cell %	10.0	___	___
Business	Count	___	___	___
	Row %	___	___	___
	Column %	___	___	___
	Cell %	___	___	___
		40	60	100

    a. What is the overall percentage that favor the communications requirement?
    b. What percentage of business students favor the communications requirement?
    c. What percentage of science students favor the communications requirement?
    d. From parts **a–c**, what can you conclude?

5. A small sample of consumers was selected for a pilot study to see if household income is related to whether the households owe money on revolving charge accounts. The data are shown here.

Household income (in $1,000s)	10	15	18	20	20	25	27	29
Owes money	N	Y	Y	Y	Y	Y	N	Y
Household income (in $1,000s)	32	35	35	35	37	39	35	40
Owes money	N	Y	Y	N	Y	Y	N	Y
Household income (in $1,000s)	42	43	50	55	60	62	70	80
Owes money	N	Y	N	N	Y	Y	N	N

a. Using the given data, complete the following table:

	Owes Money	Does Not Owe Money
Above Median		
Median and Below		

b. Does it appear that owing money is related to income level?
c. Why do we have to say *appear* in part **b**?

6. Three years ago 50 new people were hired at plant A and at plant B. A recent review showed that 15 of 50 are still working at plant A and 25 of 50 are still working at plant B.

Table 1

	Plant A	Plant B	Total
Still Employed	15	25	40
Left Employment	35	25	60
	50	50	100

Table 2

	Nonmanagers			Managers		
	Plant A	Plant B	Total	Plant A	Plant B	Total
Still Employed	7	9	16	8	16	24
Left Employment	33	21	54	2	4	6
	40	30	70	10	20	30

a. Based on the information in Table 1, does it appear that labor retention is related to place of employment? Explain using either row or column percentages.
b. Table 2 shows the same data broken down by whether the new employees were in managerial or nonmanagerial positions. Does it appear that employee retention is related to place of employment after controlling for type of position? Explain.

7. An aide to a state legislator is interested in determining attitude toward increasing starting salaries for teachers. One hundred people are interviewed on their position toward increasing starting salaries (for = 40, against = 40, no opinion = 20) and the party affiliation (Democrat = 30, Republican = 30, Independent = 40). Construct a 3 × 3 cross-tabs table that would indicate that the two variables are not related. Explain.

8. Using the same data as in Exercise 7, construct a 3 × 3 table that shows that Democrats prefer increasing starting salaries, but not Republicans and Independents. Defend.

9. Using the same data as in Exercise 7, construct a 3 × 3 table that shows that Republicans prefer increasing starting salaries, but not Democrats and Independents. Defend.

3.5 Analyzing Quantitative Cross-Sectional Data

One-way tables and cross-tabs tables are effective in showing relationships between two variables when one or more variables are categorical. However, when both variables are quantitative, we need an additional tool—the scatter diagram. By the end of this section you should be able to:

1. construct a scatter diagram;
2. interpret a scatter diagram;
3. apply the ellipse test to determine whether two quantitative variables appear to be related;
4. look for clusters in a scatter diagram; and
5. interpret clusters accurately.

We will use the data in Table 3.1 to introduce the scatter diagram. The table shows that last month the Charlotte sales region had a 30% market share and spent $17,000 on media advertising. Its sales force had, on the average, 15 years of experience. Charlotte's retail price for its product was $1,000 (not shown), and the mean competitors' retail price was also $1,000. Thus the relative price variable for Charlotte was 1.00. Atlanta, on the other hand, had a retail price of $1,000, but the mean price of its competitors was $667. So Atlanta's relative price was 1.5 (1,000/667).

Question: Do advertising expenditures, mean sales force experience, and relative price affect market share? *Answer:* Plot scatter diagrams.

Scatter Diagrams

A scatter diagram is a graph of two quantitative variables plotted against one another.

Since *all* the variables—advertising expenditures, years of experience, relative price, and market share—are quantitative, consider drawing **scatter diagrams** or XY plots.

Shown are the steps to construct a scatter diagram.

1. Place the dependent variable on the vertical axis and label it. The dependent variable is called Y and its values are denoted as y.

We believe that advertising expenditures affect market share, or market share *depends* on advertising expenditures. Therefore market share is the dependent variable, Y. Its 12 values are called $y_1, y_2, \ldots, y_{12}$.

2. Select one explanatory, or independent, variable. The explanatory variable is called X and its values are denoted as x. Place it on the horizontal axis and label it.

Advertising expenditure is an explanatory variable, X. Its 12 values are called $x_1, x_2, \ldots, x_{12}$. Average years of sales force experience and relative price are two other explanatory variables that could also be plotted against market share, Y.

3. Plot each observation by its x and y values. Each observation will be one point in the scatter diagram. Label each point.

Each observation is the advertising expenditure and market share for a city in the Southern Region. For example, the Charlotte observation is

$$x_1 = \text{Advertising} = \$17,000$$

$$y_1 = \text{Market share} = 30\%$$

Label the point ($17,000, 30\%) as CHAR.

Figure 3.3 is a scatter plot of market share and advertising expenditures for the 12 sales regions. What does a scatter diagram show? It may indicate that the

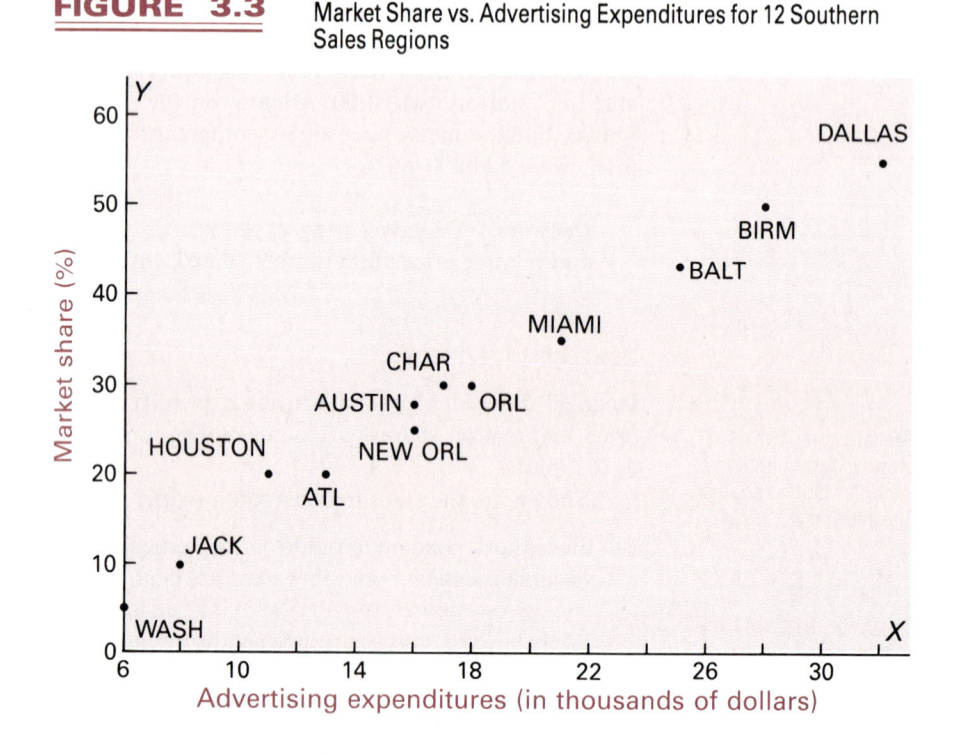

FIGURE 3.3 Market Share vs. Advertising Expenditures for 12 Southern Sales Regions

two variables are related to one another. However, as there are several types of relationships, look for:

1. a linear relationship between the two variables;
2. a nonlinear relationship between the two variables; and
3. clusters or groups of observations that are distinct from one another.

Linear Relationships

We can ascertain readily if there is a linear, or straight-line, relationship between two quantitative variables using a scatter diagram. In Figure 3.3, as advertising expenditures, X, increase, does market share, Y, increase by a *constant amount*? Yes. Moreover, there is a *positive* linear relationship. As advertising expenditures increase, so does market share. Advertising expenditures appear to be an important explanatory variable.

What could we conclude from the scatter diagram? Increasing advertising *may* improve market share. In other COMCEL markets, higher advertising expenditures result in higher market shares. However, do not jump to conclusions, since one or more intervening variables could account for this apparent relationship. Still, the relationship between these two variables makes marketing sense. As an initial action, we could present the scatter diagram to senior management and convince them to authorize the increased advertising expenditures on a *trial basis*. Then the impact of increased advertising could be determined. If the region's market share increases, more advertising dollars would be requested on a permanent basis.

Now consider the scatter diagram in Figure 3.4 on page 118, which plots market share against mean January temperature. It appears that there is no linear relationship between the two variables. As the mean January temperature increases, market share neither increases nor decreases. The diagram consists of a shapeless cloud of data points that slope neither up nor down in either direction. Mean January temperature does not explain market share variation. This is not a surprising finding.

One issue remains. Is there a more rigorous way to determine whether there is a linear relationship? Yes, we can use the quick and simple *circle vs. ellipse test*.

> If one can enclose all the data points in the scatter diagram with a tight ellipse, then the two variables are probably linearly related. If the ellipse is upward sloping to the right, then the two variables are positively related. If the ellipse is downward sloping to the right, the two variables are negatively related. If it takes a circle or an ellipse parallel to the horizontal axis to enclose all the data points, the two variables are probably not linearly related.

The Circle vs. Ellipse Test

This test is a graphical method for determining whether two variables are probably **linearly related**. It is not a substitute for the regression analysis to be discussed in Chapter 10.

To understand the logic of the ellipse test, look at Figure 3.4. In order to enclose the data, we need an ellipse that is parallel to the horizontal axis. There is no upward or downward pattern to the cloud of points; they are widely scattered. As the mean temperature increases, no systematic change occurs in the market share. Thus a horizontal straight line best represents the pattern, which means that as one variable changes, the other variable is unaffected. Subject to statistical verification using regression analysis, the two variables are not related.

FIGURE 3.4 Market Share vs. Mean Temperature

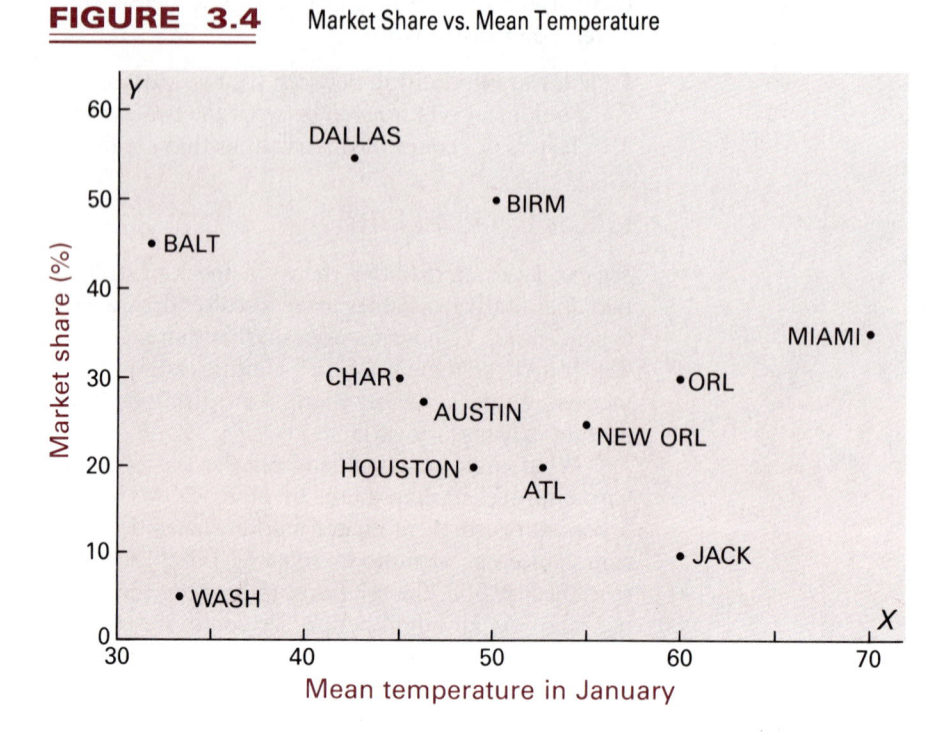

[Scatter plot showing Market share (%) on Y-axis (0 to 60) vs. Mean temperature in January on X-axis (30 to 70). Data points: DALLAS (~43, 54), BIRM (~50, 49), BALT (~33, 45), MIAMI (~70, 35), CHAR (~45, 30), ORL (~60, 29), AUSTIN (~47, 27), NEW ORL (~55, 24), HOUSTON (~46, 20), ATL (~52, 19), JACK (~60, 8), WASH (~34, 4).]

Figure 3.5 reproduces Figure 3.3, but with an ellipse drawn around the data. The data points lie on a path and are tightly clustered. An unbroken straight line running through the data would be upward sloping to the right. This indicates, subject to statistical verification, that the two variables are positively related. That is, as advertising increases, market share increases. When two variables are related, we can enclose their data points in a tight ellipse. The stronger the association between the two variables, the narrower the ellipse will be.

Although managers are not expected to actually draw ellipses or circles, this test is a visual way to help them learn to interpret scatter diagrams.

Given a set of data, always look first to see if the data exhibit a straight-line or **linear relationship**, since linear relationships are easiest to understand and explain. However, sometimes relationships are not linear, and we must learn how to identify and interpret those that are not.

A linear relationship means that as the explanatory variable increases, the dependent variable increases or decreases by a constant amount.

Nonlinear Relationships

Figure 3.6 is a scatter diagram of another quantitative variable, mean years of sales experience, vs. market share. Are the two variables related? Please think about it before reading on.

Using the circle vs. ellipse test, we would conclude that there is no straight-line relationship between market share and mean number of years experience.

FIGURE 3.5 Market Share vs. Advertising Expenditures

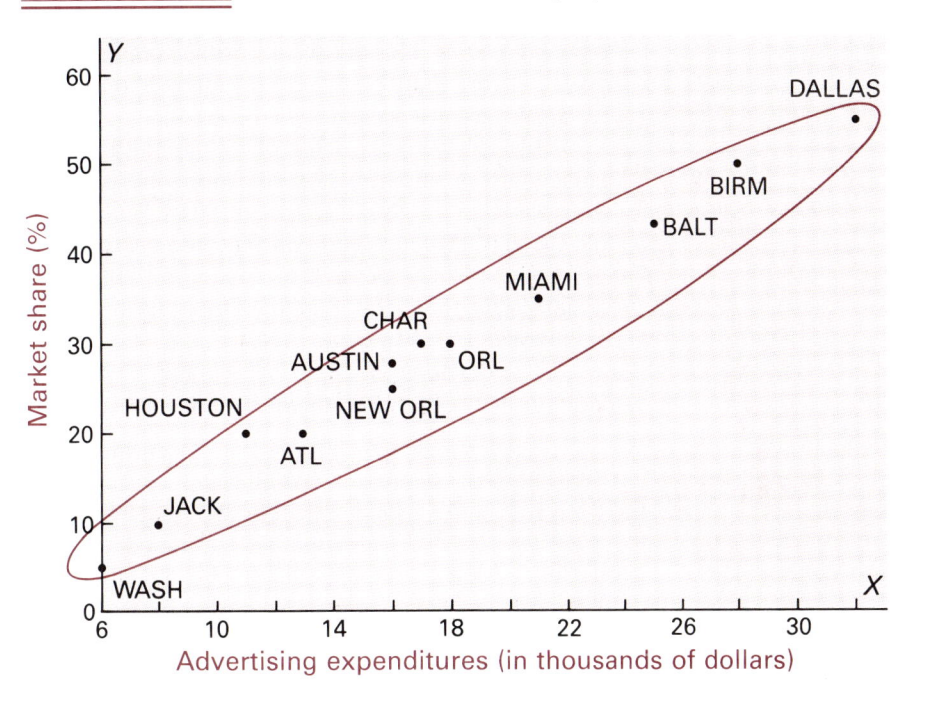

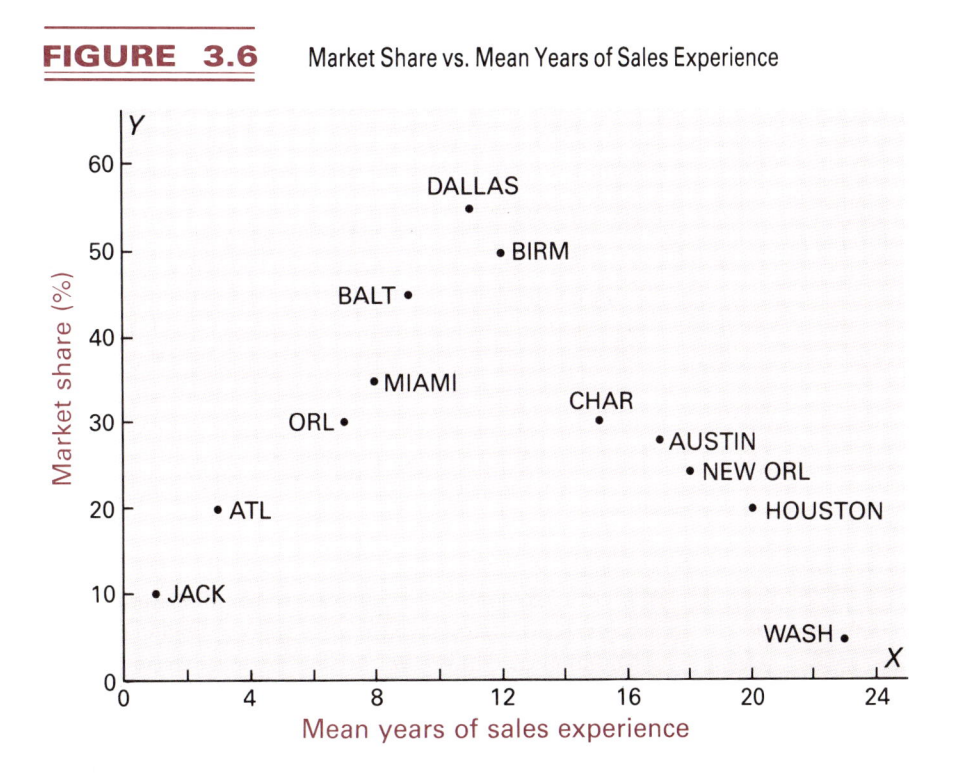

FIGURE 3.6 Market Share vs. Mean Years of Sales Experience

We would be right! But, there is a nonlinear relationship that can be represented by an inverted U. This means that as the number of years of experience increases, market share initially increases. Market share, however, peaks between 11 and 13 years of experience and then drops off.

How can we make sense of the nonlinear relationship? As the sales force gains more experience, it grabs more market share from the competition. However, after 13 years, sales people experience burnout; they lose enthusiasm, and the market share decreases. The nonlinear relationship does make sense.

For the Charlotte sales manager, how is the scatter diagram in Figure 3.6 useful? What managerial action should he take? Please think about the possibilities before reading on.

The sales force has, on the average, 15 years of experience. The scatter diagram shows that they are in the burnout stage. Here are several options.

1. Hire some new sales people who are enthusiastic.
2. Talk to the senior sales people and determine how they can regain enthusiasm. A different pay schedule, less travel within the region, earned days off, or vacation bonuses could be considered.
3. Pair junior and senior sales people in teams. Perhaps the enthusiasm of the junior people will spread to the senior staff. Of course, the opposite could also happen.
4. Review management practices. Perhaps the manager himself is an ineffective motivator or leader.

We are often inclined to blame poor performance on others, rarely looking at ourselves as a possible cause. Perhaps we should consider option 4 first! In summary, sales experience can either positively or negatively affect market share. Now we can generate alternative options to improve market share.

Here is another example of a nonlinear relationship. A market research firm wants to know how many times a television viewer would have to see an advertisement before that viewer could recall it. The firm selects 10 groups of 100 TV viewers. The firm assigns each group of 100 to one of the following 10 conditions—view ad once during test week, view ad twice, ..., view ad 10 times. One month later, all 1,000 people were asked to recall the ad. The market research firm recorded the percentages of each group who could correctly recall the ad. Figure 3.7 shows that only about 5% could remember an ad if it was viewed from one to three times a week. But above that level, the percentage increased as the commercial was aired more frequently. Above nine commercials per week, the graph appears to be leveling off at 35%.

These examples show nonlinear relationships and what they mean.

Clusters

Figure 3.8a is a scatter diagram of market share vs. relative price for the 12 sales regions. At first glance there appears to be no relationship between relative price and market share. We would need a circle to enclose all the data points. Moreover, there is not a nonlinear relationship. Can we conclude that the two variables are not related? Please think about it before reading on.

FIGURE 3.7 Percentage Recall vs. Number of Times Commercial Viewed per Week

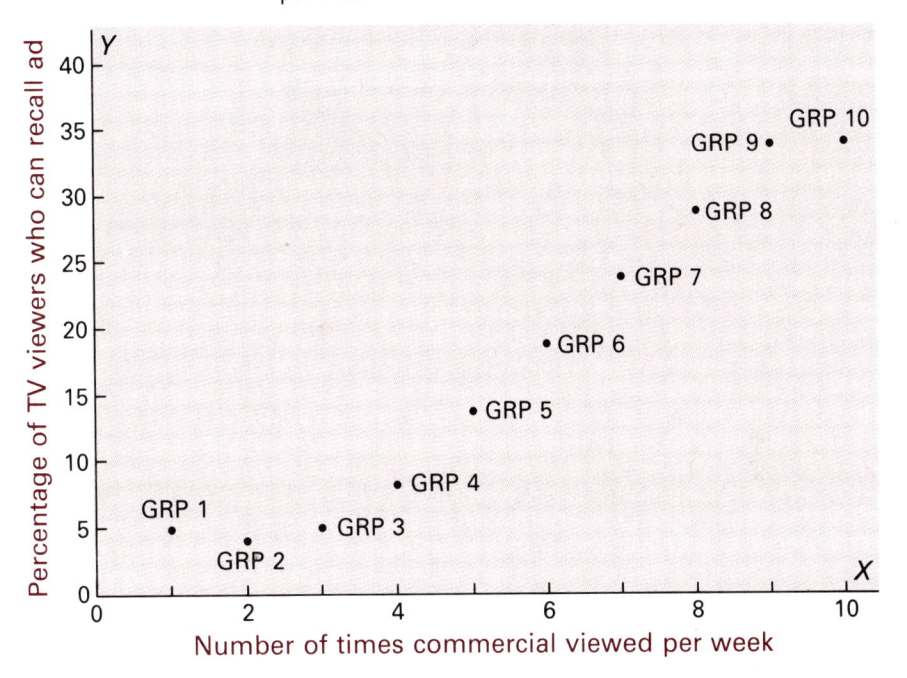

FIGURE 3.8a Market Share vs. Relative Price

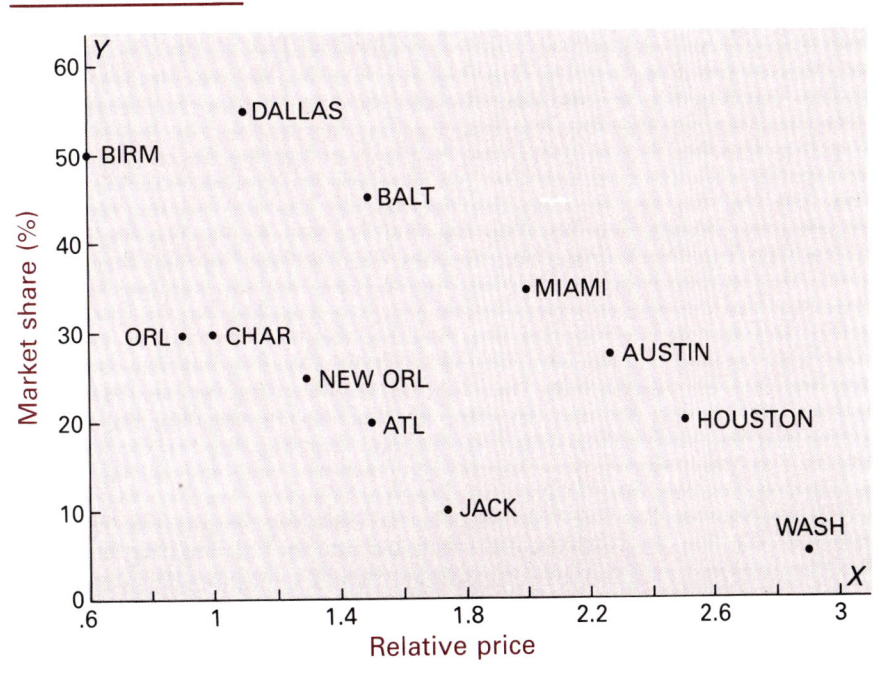

FIGURE 3.8b Market Share vs. Relative Price

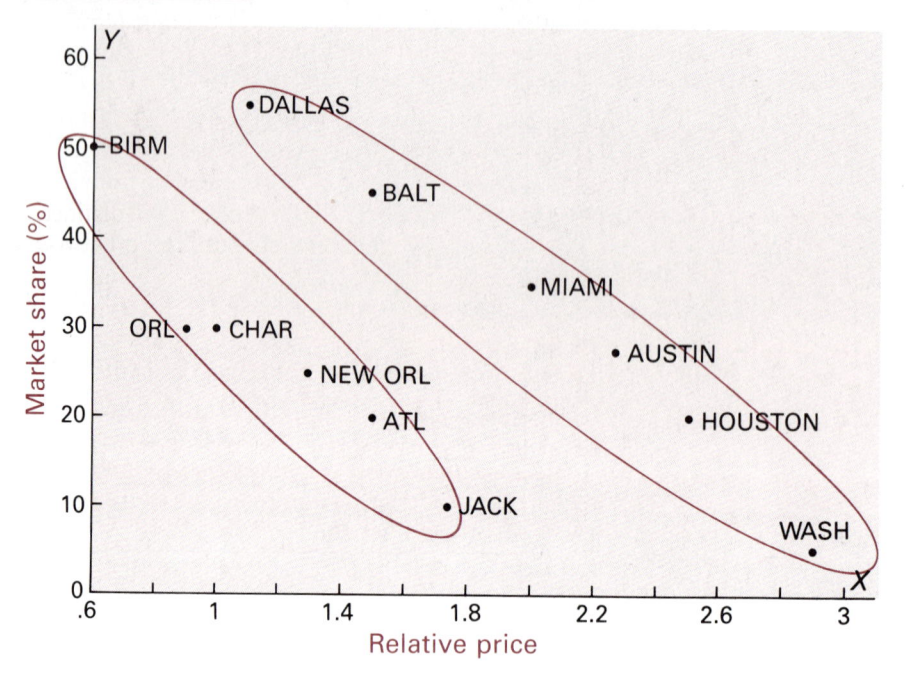

Look again carefully at Figure 3.8a. There are two distinct *clusters*, or groups, of data points, each consisting of six cities as shown in Figure 3.8b. The lower cluster includes the Atlanta, Birmingham, Charlotte, Jacksonville, New Orleans, and Orlando sales regions. The upper cluster includes the other six cities. What do the clusters mean?

Both clusters slope downward from left to right. Within each cluster, the higher COMCEL's price vs. the competitions' prices, the lower its market share. That makes economic sense. Now compare two cities—one in each cluster—that have the same relative price. In the lower cluster, Atlanta has a 1.5 relative price, as does Baltimore in the upper cluster. In both regions, COMCEL's price is 50% higher than the mean of its competitors. Then why does Baltimore have a 45% market share and Atlanta only a 20% share? There must be other variables that explain the different market shares for the same relative price.

Begin the diagnosis. First, what is similar about the six cities within each cluster? What is different between the two clusters? For example, perhaps sales offices in the upper-cluster cities provide better after-sales service, have a more effective reward structure, have more efficient sales organizations, or sell to different clientele. Second, have there been any changes in the six cities in the upper cluster that might account for their superior performance? For example, have they recently run sales promotion campaigns? Have they recently restructured their sales forces?

Sales managers in the lower-cluster cities should evaluate these potential differences and changes. If they find that the clustering is caused by factors over which they have control, they might be able to raise market share to the level of the higher cluster. They would have found a pathway to better sales performance.

Consider another example. Figure 3.9 shows productivity versus the number of training hours during the year for 12 work groups. Try to interpret Figure 3.9 before reading on.

Again, there appears to be no linear or nonlinear relationship between the two quantitative variables. But there are two distinct clusters. In the lower cluster of six work groups, there is no relationship between productivity and amount of training. Groups that had the most training, G7 and G9, had the same productivity as those with fewer hours of training, such as G2 and G11. However, the upper cluster does show a positive relationship between productivity and training. Groups that had the most training, G6 and G10, had higher productivities than those with fewer hours of training, G3 and G8.

The question to ask, of course, is: What is unique or distinctive about the six groups for which productivity varied with amount of training versus those that did not? Were both given the same type of training? Have there been any changes that might account for the two clusters?

In summary, diagnosing why a quantitative variable, such as market share,

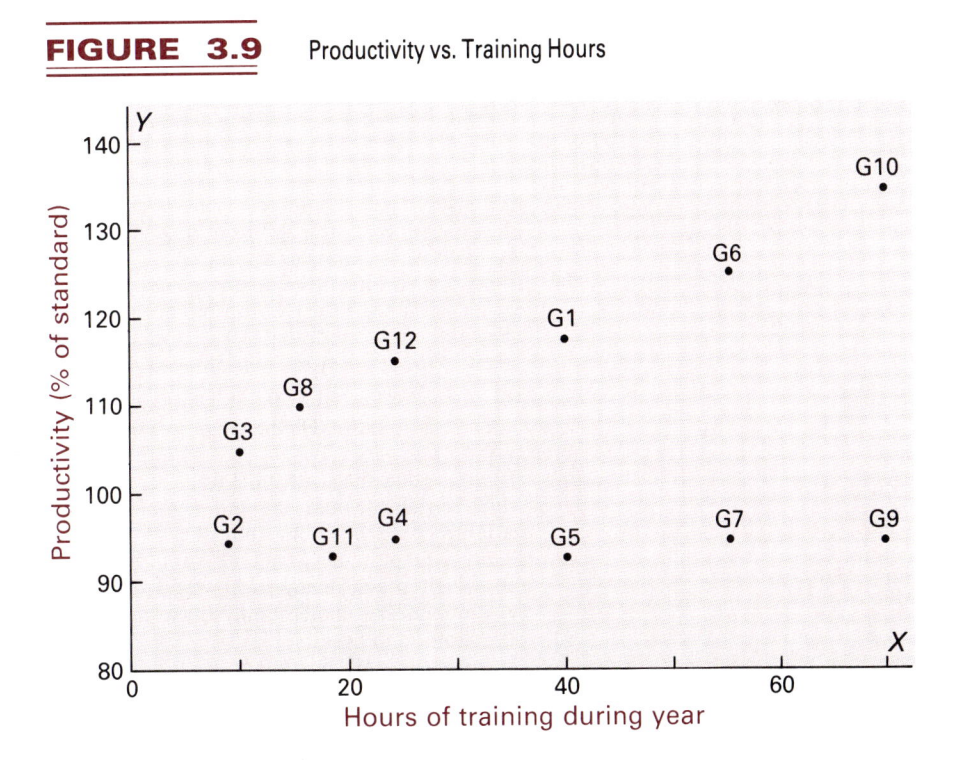

FIGURE 3.9 Productivity vs. Training Hours

varies involves (1) identifying potential explanatory variables, (2) looking for linear and nonlinear relationships and clusters, and (3) if clustering occurs, finding the reasons for it.

SECTION 3.5 EXERCISES

1. A survey was done to compare the base salaries (in hundreds of thousands of dollars) of chief executives in two industries. The results are shown.

Salary	Company Sales (millions of dollars)	Industry Type	Years with Company
4.6	60	1	8
14.3	400	2	3
5.4	90	1	12
5.6	150	1	12
4.1	180	2	18
4.8	75	1	6
5.6	130	1	10
21.5	500	2	9
3.3	130	2	12
8.1	300	2	15
5.7	105	1	16
5.6	100	1	14
5.6	230	2	8
5.7	115	1	15
9.7	330	2	20

    a. Plot salary against company sales for all the data. Does it appear that chief executive officers are paid according to the level of company sales? If so, is the relationship linear or nonlinear?
    b. Is experience with the company a factor in predicting the salary of the chief executive? If so, is the relationship linear or nonlinear?
    c. Does the type of industry (1 vs. 2) affect the relationship between sales and salary? Plot two scatter diagrams, one for each type of industry.

2. An instructor asked his students to record the number of hours spent studying statistics up to the first test. He then matched the grades made on the test with hours studied.
    a. If you plotted the scatter diagram of the scores against the hours studied, which variable would you put on the horizontal axis as the independent variable, grades or hours studied?
    b. Before you plot the graph of hours studied against grade, which of the following types of relationship would you expect to find?
        (1) nonlinear—increases rapidly at first and then levels off
        (2) linear and negative
        (3) no relationship
        (4) inverted U
    Explain.

3. An operations manager suspects a positive linear relationship between lot size and cost. Use the given data to plot a scatter diagram of lot size, X, and the cost to produce the lot, Y.

Lot Size (hundreds)	10	20	30	40	50	60	70	80
Cost (thousands)	34	47	53	68	75	88	98	110

Perform an ellipse test to determine if cost and lot size are linearly related. What do you conclude?

4. A publishing company measures the effectiveness of advertising on the sales of its magazine in 16 cities. It records the annual total spent in advertising in tens of thousands of dollars and the number of copies sold over the same period. The data are shown here.

City	A	B	C	D	E	F	G	H
Advertising ($10,000s)	4	5	10	15	16	12	20	6
Total Copies Sold (000s)	10	9	40	12	11	35	10	8

City	I	J	K	L	M	N	O	P
Advertising ($10,000s)	11	9	5	30	8	40	45	11
Total Copies Sold (000s)	38	38	8	7	41	6	7	47

a. Plot the data.
b. Describe the relationship between advertising and number of copies sold. If the data appear to cluster, explain how you would proceed from here.

5. Shown is a graph of students' SAT scores and their GPAs after the first year of college. Does SAT score appear to affect GPA? Based on the graph, is it the only variable that affects GPA?

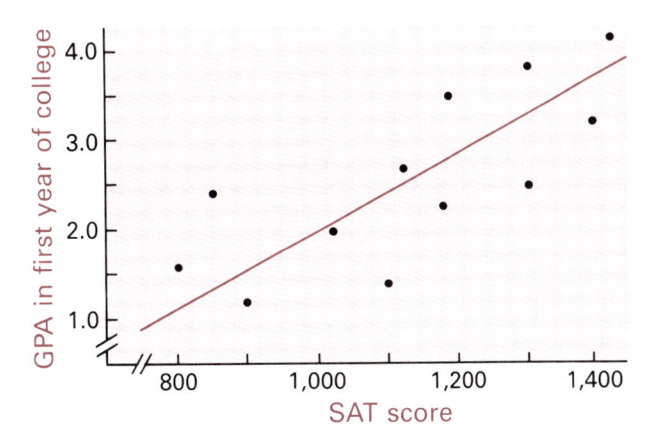

6. In 1982 American Telephone and Telegraph Company was required to break into 21 "Baby Bell" companies. Listed at the top of page 126 are data on revenue in billions and number of phones in millions in late 1982 for 10 of the 21 firms. [*Source: New York Times*, Jan. 9, 1982, p. 35.]

Firm	Telephones (in millions)	Revenues (billions $)
Bell—PA	8.0	1.97
Chesapeake	3.6	.96
Diamond State	.5	.14
Indiana Bell	2.7	.75
Mountain States	7.9	2.69
New Jersey	6.6	1.91
Northwestern	5.7	1.82
Pacific Northwest	3.9	1.39
South Central	10.6	3.56
Southwestern Bell	16.7	5.84

    a. Which variable should be the explanatory variable?
    b. Plot the data and describe the data set.

7. A market research firm wants to determine how much it must offer in dollars to get respondents to complete a survey and return it. The firm selects 11 groups of 100 people. One group receives no money, another group receives one dollar, and so on. The last group receives $10. The firm then distributes the survey and records the percentage of surveys returned in each group. The data are shown in the graph. What does the graph tell you?

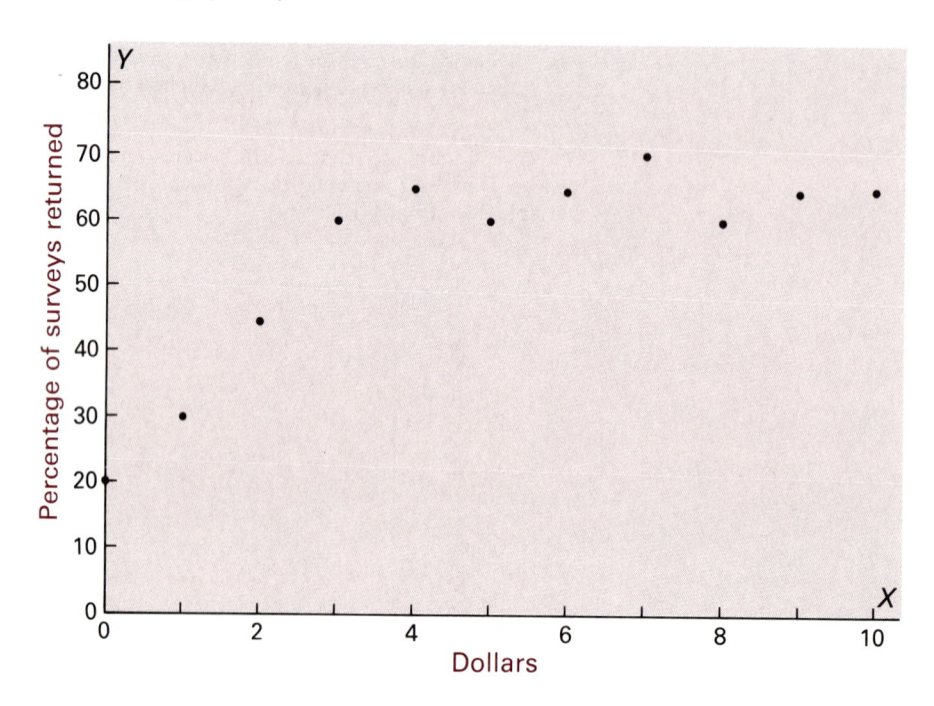

3.6 Analyzing Quantitative Time-Ordered Data

Cross-sectional data can be either categorical, as in the gender discrimination example, or quantitative, as in the market share example. Time-ordered data are generally quantitative. Thus, we can extend the cross-sectional quantitative techniques presented in the preceding section to time-ordered data also. These include drawing scatter diagrams and looking for linear or nonlinear relationships and clusters. But, because the data are time-ordered, we also recommend drawing *multiple line graphs*. By the end of this section you should be able to:

1. construct and interpret multiple line graphs for time-ordered data;
2. construct and interpret scatter diagrams for time-ordered data; and
3. explain a leading or lagging relationship between two variables.

An example involving time-ordered data analyzes COMCEL's Atlanta market share and advertising expenditures data for the past 16 months. The data are found in Table 3.12. The table shows that market share ranges from 15% to 25%. Suppose COMCEL believes that the dollars spent on advertising account for the large variation. How can COMCEL evaluate that potential relationship?

Table 3.12

Atlanta's Market Share for Past 16 Months

Period	Market Share (%)	Advertising Expenditures (thousands of dollars)
JA90	24	13
FE90	18	11
MA90	16	17
AP90	22	20
MY90	24	20
JU90	24	16
JL90	20	15
AU90	21	13
SE90	18	17
OC90	22	11
NO90	16	19
DE90	24	15
JA91	20	21
FE91	25	10
MA91	15	15
AP91	20	13
$\bar{x}$	20.56	15.38
s	3.24	3.44

FIGURE 3.10 Market Share vs. Advertising Expenditures from January 1990 to April 1991

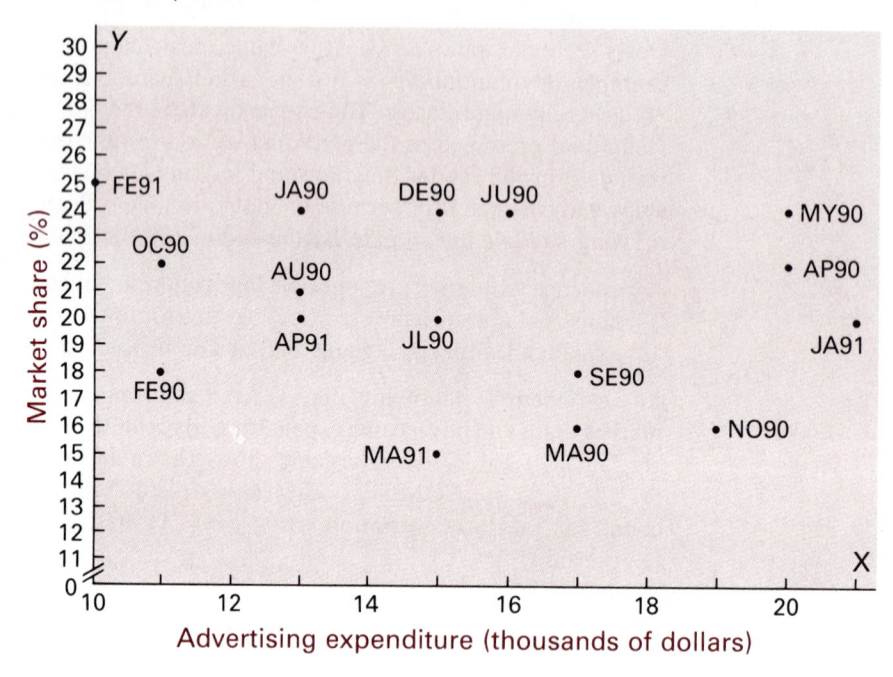

Begin by plotting a scatter diagram. As in cross-sectional scatter diagrams, each data point represents an X value, advertising expenditure, and Y value, market share. Remember to place advertising expenditures—the independent variable—on the horizontal axis, since COMCEL believes that it affects market share. After plotting the data, label each data point with its corresponding calendar date, as shown in Figure 3.10.

It is clear from the scatter diagram that there is no linear or nonlinear relationship, nor are there any clusters. The data are totally scattered. However, since the data are time-ordered, we should also draw a *multiple line graph* before reaching a final conclusion. A multiple line graph can help determine if the two variables have a leading or lagging relationship.

Multiple Line Graphs

We first presented line graphs in Chapter 2. In a line graph, the horizontal axis shows time measured in days, months, or years and the vertical axis shows the value of a quantitative variable. A line graph of the market share data would present months on the horizontal axis and the percentage market share on the vertical axis. Each data point would represent one month's experience. The line graph would show how market share changed *over time*.

Multiple line graphs contain more than one quantitative variable. Figure 3.11 is a multiple line graph of market share *and* advertising expenditures.

Chapter 3 Descriptive Statistics II: Bivariate Data and Problem Diagnosis   129

FIGURE 3.11 Multiple Line Graph—Market Share and Advertising Expenditure vs. Time

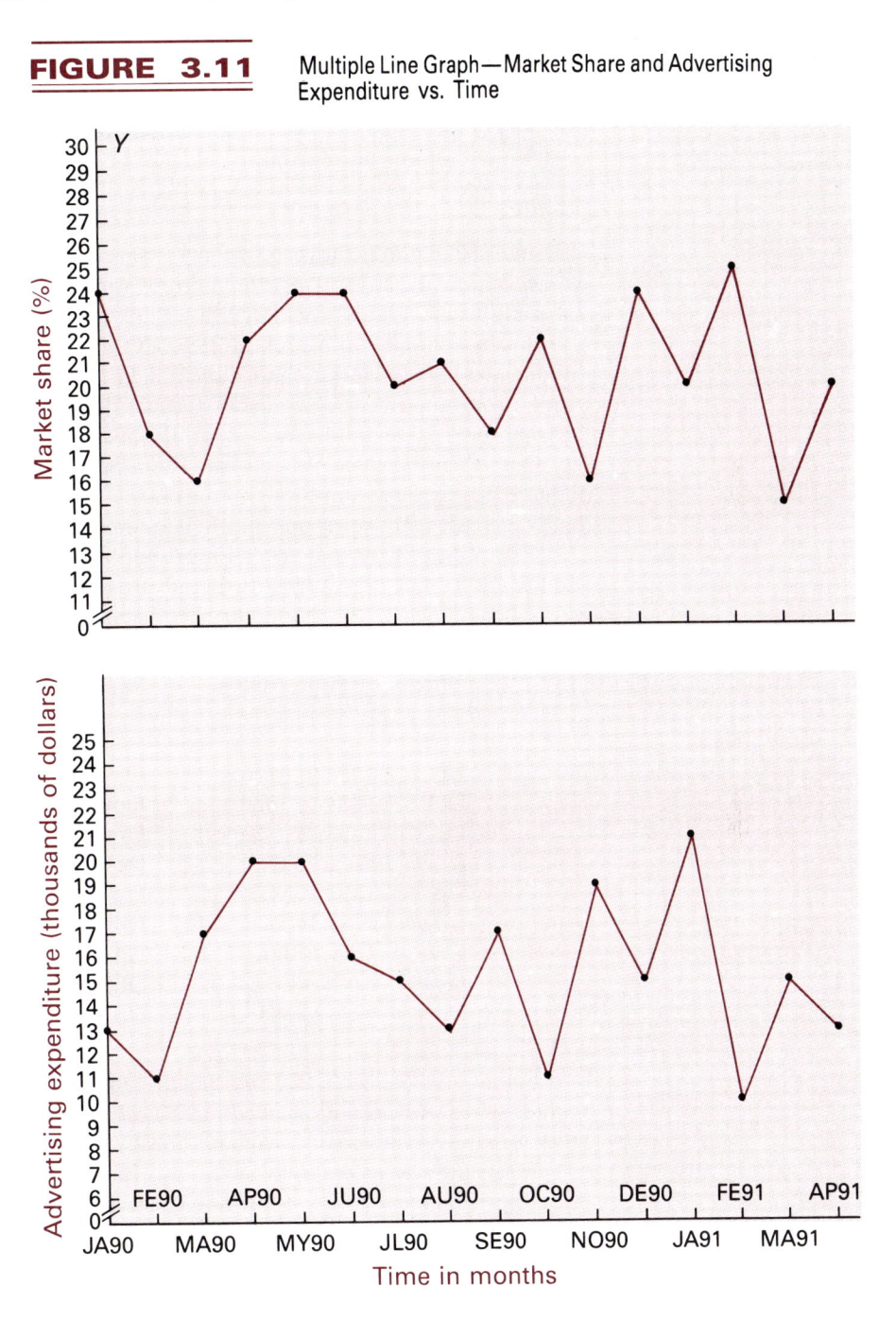

Time is still shown on the horizontal axis. The first variable—market share—is shown in the upper graph. The first data point is at the intersection of JA90 and 24%. The second variable—advertising expenditures—is shown in the lower graph. The first data point is at the intersection of JA90 and $13,000.

Lagged Relationships

The upper line graph shows how market share varied monthly. The lower line graph shows how advertising expenditures varied monthly. What insights does the multiple line graph provide? Please think about this before reading on.

From February to March of 1990 COMCEL increased advertising from $11,000 to $17,000. Market share did not increase in March, but it did increase in April. From August to September of 1990 COMCEL increased advertising from $13,000 to $17,000, but market share dropped in September. However, market share then increased in October. From September to October COMCEL reduced advertising from $17,000 to $11,000, yet market share in October actually increased. However one month later, market share dropped.

Figure 3.11 shows that advertising expenditures are related to market share. How? Upturns or downturns in the advertising line graph always occur *one month* before the corresponding turns in the market share line graph.

Turns in Advertising Line Graph	Turns in Market Share Line Graph
Up —Feb. to March	Up —March to April
Down—May to June	Down—June to July
Up —August to Sept.	Up —Sept. to Oct.
Down—Sept. to Oct.	Down—Oct. to Nov.
Up —Oct. to Nov.	Up —Nov. to Dec.
Down—Nov. to Dec.	Down—Dec. to Jan.
Up —Dec. to Jan.	Up —Jan. to Feb.
Down—Jan. to Feb.	Down—Feb. to March
Up —Feb. to March	Up —March to April

Figure 3.11 indicates that *one month's* advertising affects the *next month's* market share. Advertising expenditures *lead* market share by one month, or market share *lags* advertising expenditures by one month.

When the scatter diagram for a set of time-ordered data shows neither a linear nor nonlinear relationship nor clusters as in Figure 3.10, consider the possibility that one variable may lag the other. Draw a multiple line graph to verify.

Now that COMCEL knows that advertising expenditures lead market share by one month, it wants to predict market share using level of advertising expenditures. We recommend drawing a *lagged-variable* scatter diagram of advertising for each month vs. market share for the *following* month. Table 3.13 contains the data set for constructing such a lagged-variable scatter diagram.

Table 3.13

Advertising in a Month vs. Market Share in the Following Month

Month	Expenditures (thousands of dollars)	Market Share One Month Later (%)
JA90	13	18
FE90	11	16
MA90	17	22
AP90	20	24
MY90	20	24
JU90	16	20
JL90	15	21
AU90	13	18
SE90	17	22
OC90	11	16
NO90	19	24
DE90	15	20
JA91	21	25
FE91	10	15
MA91	15	20
AP91	13	Unknown

Note that the first month's advertising is paired with the second month's market share, the second month's advertising with the third month's market share, etc. See Table 3.12 for the original data.

The scatter diagram in Figure 3.12 on page 132 indicates that advertising expenditures for a month and market share one month later are linearly and positively related. We can envision the data encompassed by a tight ellipse that slopes upward to the right. We have drawn freehand a straight line through the data points in Figure 3.12. Note that it passes through many of them. The line seems to fit the data well, although some points are above or below the line.

COMCEL can now use Figure 3.12 to estimate its market share for different levels of advertising. For example, if it spends $16,000 for advertising this month, its market share next month should be between 20% and 21%. That is COMCEL's expectation based on the past 16 months of data. If it actually spends $16,000 and its market share is very much less or more than 20%–21%, there may be a disturbance problem. Recall that a disturbance problem is a deviation between expected and actual performance. Diagnosing a disturbance problem calls for determining why there was a deviation. For example, could competitors' price cuts explain the deviation between expected and actual market share?

Next, consider an example where two variables lag each other by two periods. We can detect this by drawing a multiple line graph. Table 3.14 contains the data for the two variables—monthly sales and research and development (R&D) expenditures for a firm. Figure 3.13 on page 133 shows the multiple line

FIGURE 3.12 Advertising Expenditure vs. Market Share One Month Later

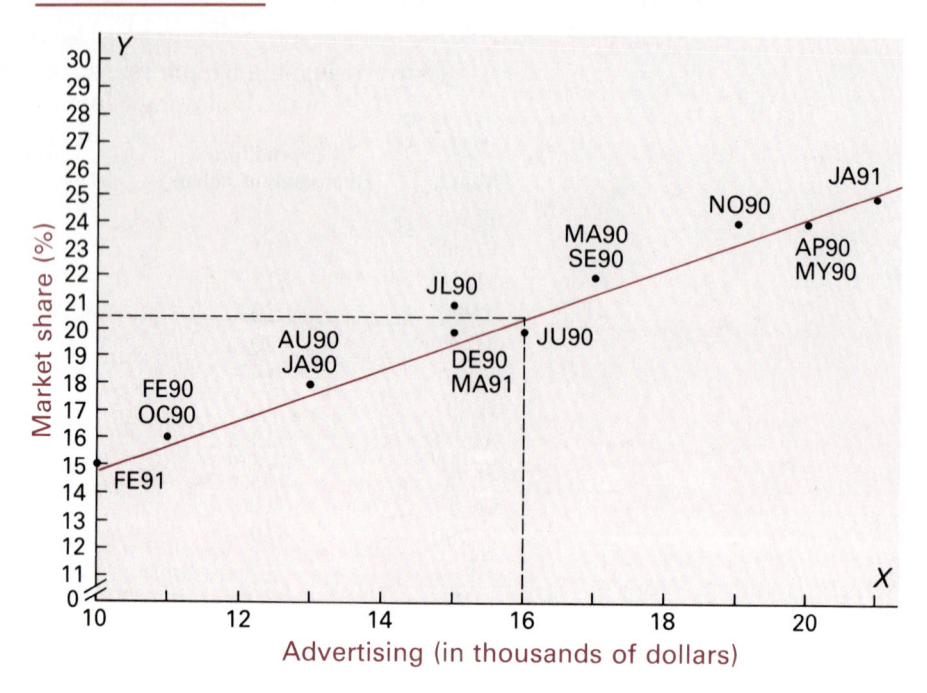

[Scatter plot with regression line: Market share (%) on Y-axis (0, 10-30) vs. Advertising (in thousands of dollars) on X-axis (10-20). Data points labeled: FE91 (10, 15), OC90 (11, 16), FE90 (11, 17), JA90 (13, 18), AU90 (13, 19), DE90 (15, 18), MA91 (15, 18), JL90 (15, 20), JU90 (16, 19), SE90 (17, 22), MA90 (17, 22), NO90 (19, 24), MY90 (20, 22), AP90 (20, 23), JA91 (21, 25). Dashed lines indicate advertising of 16 corresponds to market share of about 20.5.]

Table 3.14

Monthly Sales and R&D Expenditures

Month	Sales (thousands of units)	Research and Development (thousands of dollars)
JA91	26	5
FE91	24	3
MA91	23	4
AP91	14	8
MY91	18	8
JU91	36	9
JL91	36	5
AU91	41	4
SE91	23	6
OC91	18	10
NO91	27	11
DE91	45	12
JA92	50	5
FE92	54	6
MA92	23	5
AP92	27	11
MY92	23	12
JU92	50	11

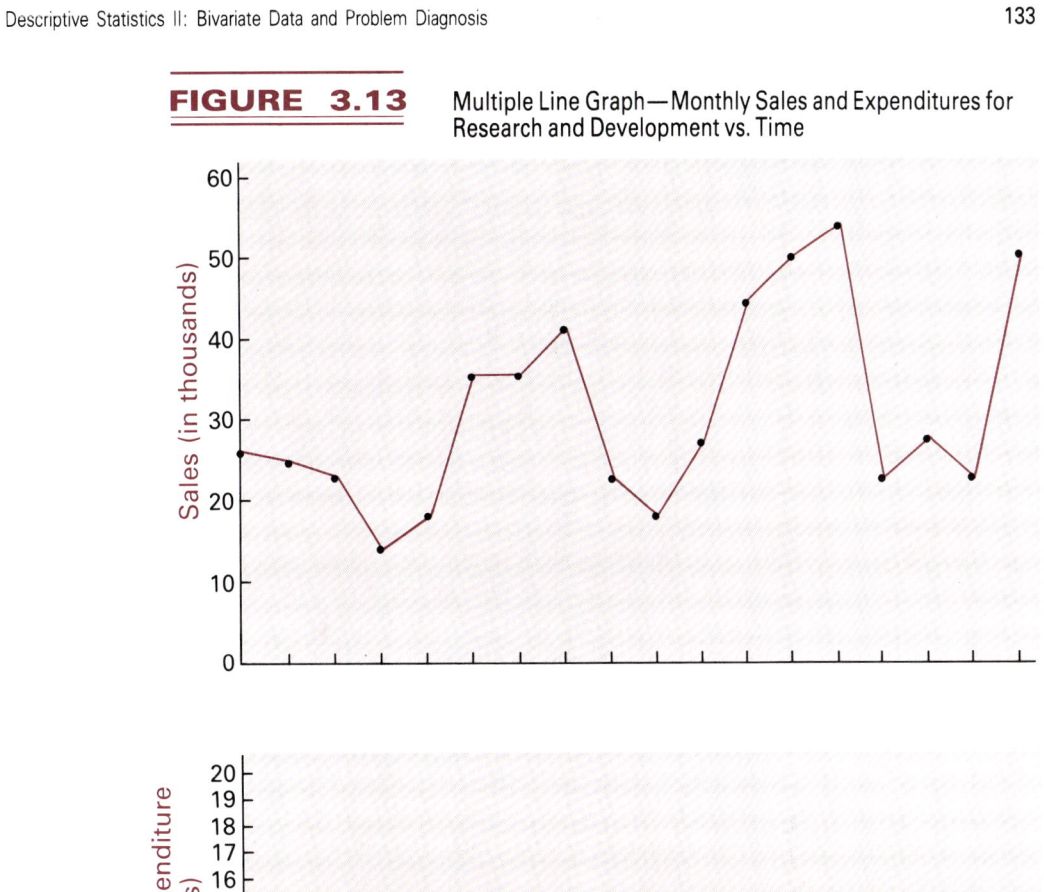

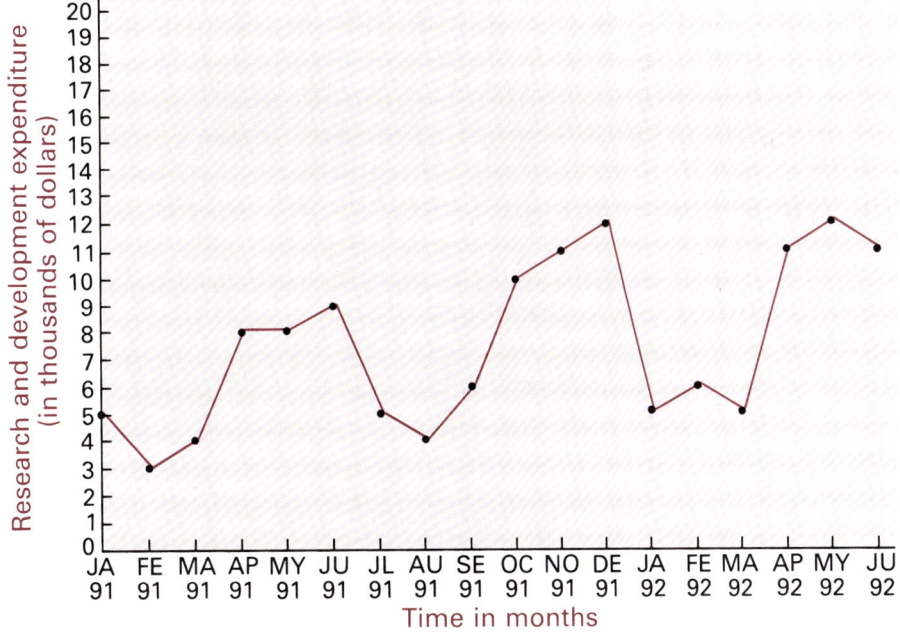

FIGURE 3.13 Multiple Line Graph—Monthly Sales and Expenditures for Research and Development vs. Time

graphs for these data. The upper line graph in Figure 3.13 shows how sales varied monthly. The lower line graph shows how research and development expenditures varied monthly. Are the two time series lagged and by how many periods?

The two time series are related. More specifically, R&D expenditures lead sales by 2 months. Note that R&D expenditures increased from February to June 1991. Sales increased from April to August—2 months later. R&D expenditures dropped from June to August 1991. Sales dropped from August to October 1991—2 months later. R&D again increased from August to December 1991. Sales again increased from October 1991 to February 1992—2 months later. In summary, one says that R&D expenditures lead sales by 2 months, or sales lag R&D expenditures by 2 months. On the basis of this analysis, we could develop a lagged-variable scatter diagram of R&D expenditures for each month vs. sales 2 months later from which future sales estimates could be made.

In summary, with time-ordered data, begin by plotting a scatter diagram to check for linear or nonlinear relationships or clusters. If no relationships or clusters are found, then plot a multiple line graph to determine if the two time series are lagged and by how many periods. If a leading relationship is found, then we can develop a lagged-variable scatter diagram. Draw a straight line through the data points in the lagged-variable scatter diagram. Use the line to estimate values of the dependent variable. *Warning:* Drawing a straight line through data by hand is easy to do, but different people will draw different straight lines. Different lines will yield different estimates. Chapter 10 presents a technique that produces the best fitting line for a set of data points.

SECTION 3.6 EXERCISES

1. An economist is studying the relationship between consumption, C, and disposable personal income, Y, over the past year.

Month	J	F	M	A	M	J	J	A	S	O	N	D
C	20	30	10	20	40	10	20	5	30	40	10	20
Y		15	16	21	9	16	23	11	14	7.5	28	26	10

   a. Plot a scatter diagram of Y against C using Y as the dependent variable. Perform an ellipse test to determine whether the variables are linearly related.
   b. Plot the C and Y series on a multiple line graph with time on the X axis. Does one series appear to lead or lag the other? If so, by how many months?
   c. If you notice a lead-lag relationship, reorder the data and pair the value of Y with the value of C that affects it. Plot the reordered pairs in a lagged-variable scatter diagram.
   d. What conclusions can you draw about the relationship between C and Y?

2. Consider the following time series data.

Month	Sales	Training Hours
Jan.	1.0	2
Feb.	.4	5
Mar.	2.5	10
Apr.	10.0	6
May	3.6	8
June	6.4	12
July	14.4	4
Aug.	1.6	9
Sept.	8.1	7
Oct.	4.9	15
Nov.	22.5	11
Dec.	12.1	13

   a. Plot sales vs. training hours as a scatter diagram with sales as the dependent variable. Can you draw any conclusions from the scatter diagram?
   b. Plot a multiple line graph of sales and training hours with time on the horizontal axis. Do you notice any lead-lag relationships?
   c. Reorder the data to match the value of sales with the value of hours the month before. Plot a lagged-variable scatter diagram for the reordered data.
   d. On the basis of your graphical analysis, how would you describe the relationship between sales and training hours?

3. What is the difference between a scatter diagram and a lagged-variable scatter diagram?

4. Why couldn't we develop multiple line graphs for the quantitative cross-sectional data?

5. Suppose that research and development expenditures lead sales by nine months—a positive relationship. Explain what that means to a sales manager.

6. Shown is a multiple line graph of two variables, sales of a firm and Gross National Product. Does it appear that the two series are related? Discuss.

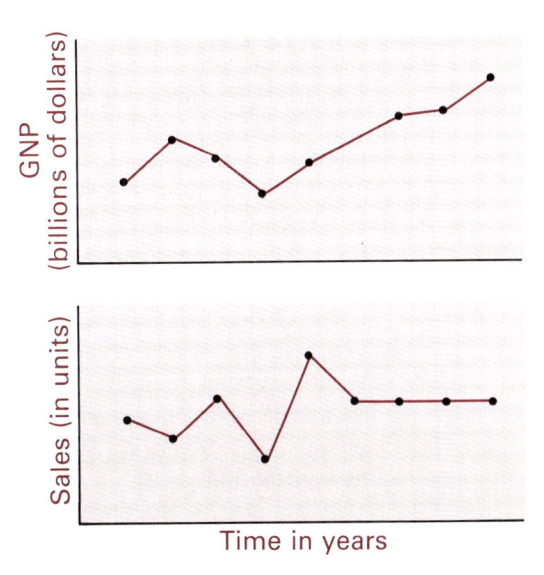

3.7 Correlation and Cross-Correlation

Graphs are useful in identifying lagged relationships between two time series. But an easier method can be used if a computer is available. We can calculate cross-correlation coefficients for the two series at different lags. Cross-correlation is an application of the general idea of correlation, a numerical index measuring the degree of linear association between two variables. By the end of this section you should be able to:

1. explain the relationship between the ellipse test and a correlation coefficient;
2. estimate the correlation coefficient for different data patterns;
3. define covariance and explain how it relates to the correlation coefficient;
4. explain when the cross-correlation coefficient should be used and how to interpret it; and
5. distinguish between correlation and cause and effect.

The Correlation Coefficient

The correlation coefficient, r, is a numerical measure of the strength of a linear relationship between two variables. Correlation coefficients can vary from -1 to $+1$. The graphs in Figure 3.14 show different degrees of *linear* associations and their r values.

In scatter diagram (a), $r = +1$. There is a *perfect positive* linear relationship between the two variables. It is perfect because r equals 1 and positive because of the plus sign. All the data points fall on a straight line. The relationship is perfect in the sense that if we knew the equation of the straight line and the value of the variable X, we could predict the Y value with perfect certainty. The relationship is positive because as variable X increases, variable Y also increases. Graph (e) shows a *perfect inverse* linear relationship, and r has a value of -1.

Scatter diagrams (b) and (d) show lines that fit the pattern of data points quite well, but not perfectly. A tight ellipse can enclose the data points. Correlation coefficients are close to $+1$ and -1. Scatter diagram (c) shows a pattern of points that can only be enclosed by a circle. The correlation coefficient is 0, indicating no linear relationship. That is, as variable X increases, variable Y neither increases nor decreases. A horizontal line is drawn to reflect the lack of a linear relationship between the two variables.

Correlations measure the linear association between two variables. **Cross-correlations** build upon the correlation concept.

Cross-correlations measure the linear association between two variables at different lags.

We will use Atlanta's sales data for the past 16 months found in Table 3.12 to compute cross-correlations between market share and advertising expenditures. Recall from Figures 3.10 and 3.11 that advertising expenditures do not affect market share in the same month, but rather in the following month. This example will demonstrate that cross-correlations of lag 0 and 1 provide the same information.

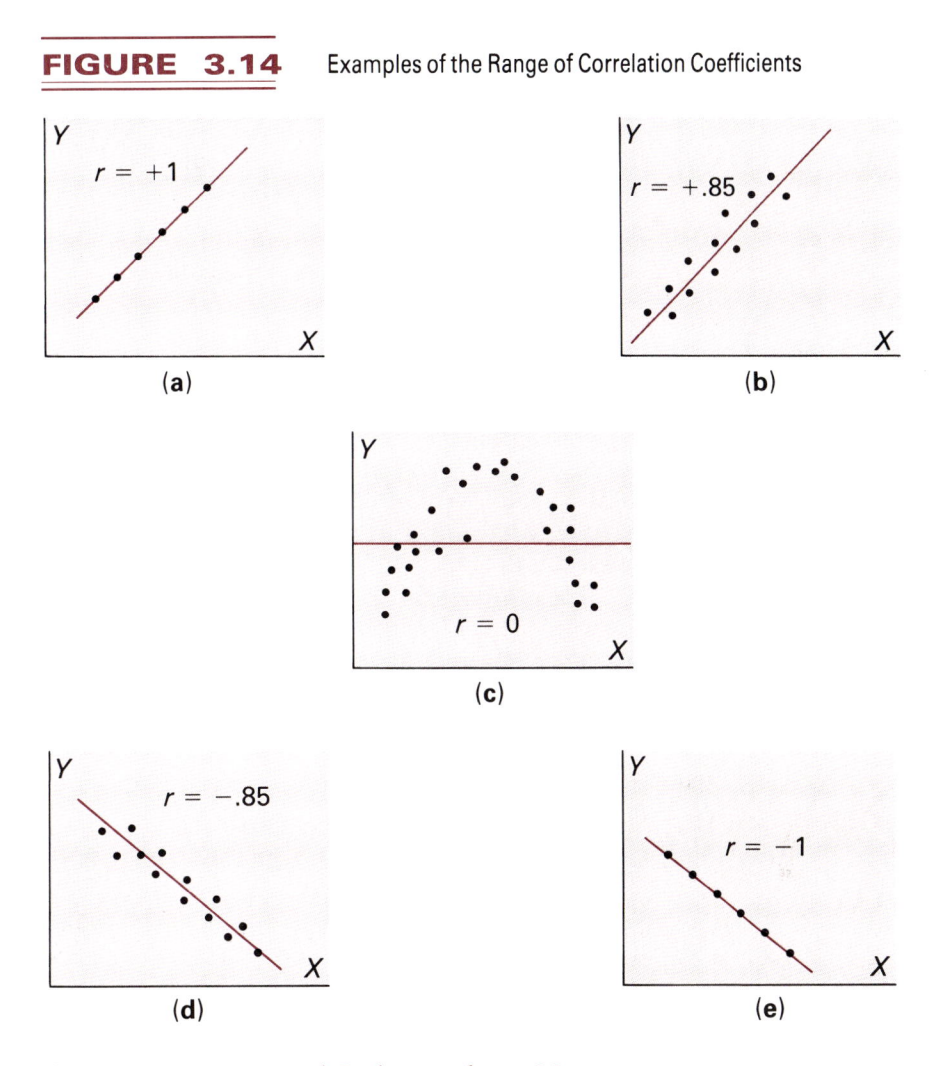

FIGURE 3.14 Examples of the Range of Correlation Coefficients

(a) $r = +1$

(b) $r = +.85$

(c) $r = 0$

(d) $r = -.85$

(e) $r = -1$

Determining Lagged Relationships Using Cross-Correlations

We will use expression (3.1) to compute the cross-correlation between market share and advertising expenditures for a lag of 0. Here we are determining if advertising expenditures in one month affect market share in the same month. Since Figure 3.11 indicates that the two variables are not linearly related, the correlation coefficient should be close to 0.

$$r = \frac{\text{Covariance}(X, Y)}{s_X s_Y} \tag{3.1}$$

The terms s_X and s_Y are the sample standard deviations for the advertising expenditures and market share data. The numerator, the *covariance*, is an extension of the variance. Covariance measures the extent to which the advertising and market share data move together, or covary. When the advertising and market share data points in a scatter diagram move upward to the right (as in Figure 3.14a or 3.14b), the covariance and the correlation will be positive. When the data points move downward to the right (as in Figure 3.14d or 3.14e), the covariance and the correlation will be negative. When the data points show no *linear* pattern (as in Figure 3.14c), the covariance and the correlation will be close to 0. Expression (3.2) shows how to compute the covariance.

$$\text{Covariance} = \frac{\sum [(x_i - \bar{x})(y_i - \bar{y})]}{n - 1} \qquad (3.2)$$

Visualizing the covariance graphically is important. Figure 3.15 reproduces Figure 3.10 with two additions. A horizontal line at the mean for market share, 20.56%, and a vertical line at the mean for advertising expenditures, $15,380, have been drawn. These two lines divide the scatter diagram into four quadrants labeled A, B, C, and D.

From expression (3.1), we see that the sign of the covariance determines the sign of the correlation coefficient, because the standard deviations in the denominator are always positive. In turn, the sign of the covariance depends on the cross-products term in the numerator of expression (3.2). To determine the sign of the cross-products, one can use the quadrants in Figure 3.15 to obtain the

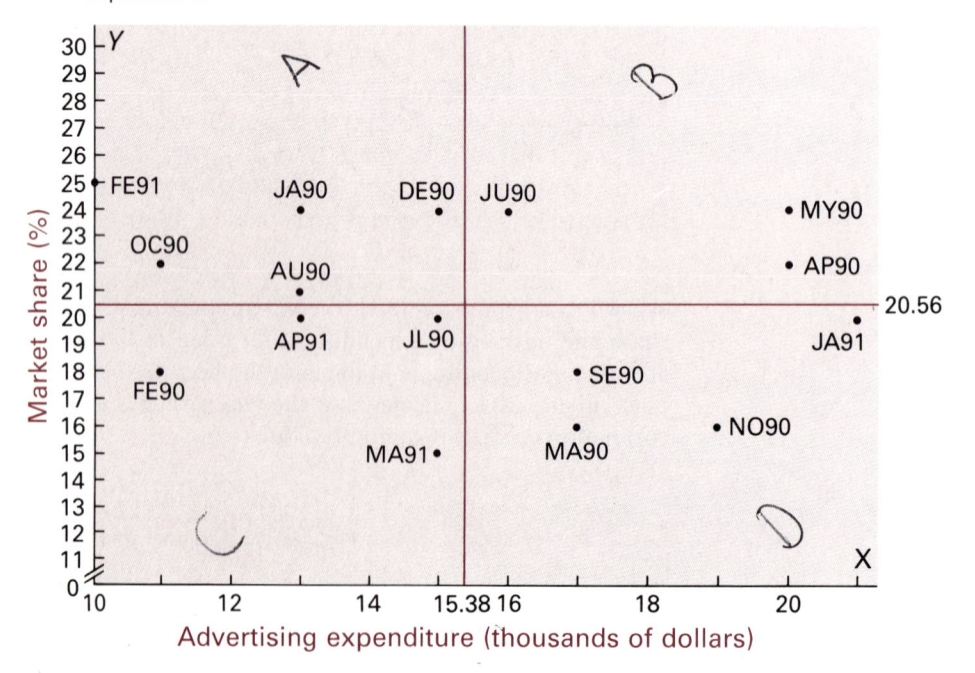

FIGURE 3.15 Four Quadrants of Market Share vs. Advertising Expenditures

following results:

Quadrant	$x - \bar{x}$	$y - \bar{y}$	Cross-Products $(x - \bar{x})(y - \bar{y})$
A	Negative	Positive	Negative
B	Positive	Positive	Positive
C	Negative	Negative	Positive
D	Positive	Negative	Negative

In quadrant B, both the advertising and market share values are larger than their respective means. From expression (3.2), the cross-products terms for these data points will be positive. In quadrant C, both the advertising and market share values are less than their respective means. The cross-products terms will also be positive. Cross-products terms for data points in quadrants A and D are negative.

When there is a positive linear relationship, most data points lie in quadrants B and C. The covariance term and thus the correlation will be positive. When there is a negative linear relationship, most data points lie in quadrants A and D. The covariance term and thus the correlation will be negative. When there is no linear relationship, it takes a circle or an ellipse parallel to the horizontal axis to encompass the data. That is, there are roughly equal numbers of data points in the four quadrants. The positive cross-products for data points in quadrants B and C will cancel out the negative cross-products from quadrants A and D. The covariance and thus the correlation coefficient will be approximately 0.

In Figure 3.15, we see that there are five data points in quadrant A, three data points in quadrant B, four data points in quadrant C, and four data points in quadrant D. Thus the correlation should be close to 0. Table 3.15 on page 140 shows the computations for the cross-correlation for the advertising and market share data for lag 0.

The cross-correlation at lag 0, $r(0)$, is only $-.19$, which suggests no linear relationship between market share and advertising expenditures, since r is close to 0. Advertising expenditures are not a *coincident indicator* of market share. A variable X is a coincident indicator when values of X in one period affect the values of Y in the *same* period.

Table 3.16 on page 141 contains the calculations for the cross-correlation for lag 1. Here we are determining if advertising in one month affects market share in the next month. As in Table 3.13, we match up January's advertising with February's market share, February's advertising with March's market share, etc. Note that we compute the cross-product terms about the means of the *original* two series even though one point has been eliminated due to lagging. We also divide the covariance by the product of the standard deviations of the *original* time series.

The cross-correlation at lag 1, $r(1)$, is $+.93$, which suggests a strong positive linear relationship between advertising in one month and market share one month later, since r is close to 1. Advertising expenditures are a *leading indicator* of market share. A variable X is a leading indicator when values of X in one period affect the values of Y in one or more *later* periods.

Table 3.15

Computing the Cross-Correlation at Lag 0 for the Variables X, Advertising Expenditures, and Y, Market Share

Period	x	y	$x - \bar{x}$	$y - \bar{y}$	Cross-Product Terms
JA90	13	24	−2.38	3.44	−8.19
FE90	11	18	−4.38	−2.56	11.21
MA90	17	16	1.62	−4.56	−7.39
AP90	20	22	4.62	1.44	6.65
MY90	20	24	4.62	3.44	15.89
JN90	16	24	.62	3.44	2.13
JL90	15	20	−.38	−.56	.21
AU90	13	21	−2.38	.44	−1.05
SE90	17	18	1.62	−2.56	−4.15
OC90	11	22	−4.38	1.44	−6.31
NO90	19	16	3.62	−4.56	−16.51
DE90	15	24	−.38	3.44	−1.31
JA91	21	20	5.62	−.56	−3.15
FE91	10	25	−5.38	4.44	−23.89
MA91	15	15	−.38	−5.56	2.11
AP91	13	20	−2.38	−.56	1.33
Sum					−32.42

$\bar{x} = 15.38$
$\bar{y} = 20.56$
Standard deviation in market share (see Table 3.12) = 3.24
Standard deviation in advertising expenditures (see Table 3.12) = 3.44
Covariance (see expression (3.2)) = −32.42/15
= −2.16
$r(0) = -2.16/[(3.24)(3.44)] = -.19$

These cross-correlations confirm that:

1. Advertising expenditures do not affect market share in the same month; $r(0) = -.19$.
2. Advertising expenditures in a month affect market share in the following month; $r(1) = +.93$.

Interpreting Cross-Correlations

Shown are cross-correlations at lags 0, 1, 2, ..., 6 for the advertising expenditures and market share data in Table 3.12.

Lag (months)	0	1	2	3	4	5	6
$r(k)$	−.19	+.93	−.20	+.11	−.48	+.10	−.20

Table 3.16

Computing the Cross-Correlation at Lag 1 for the Variables X, Advertising Expenditures, and Y, Market Share, One Month Later

Period	x	y	$x - \bar{x}$	$y - \bar{y}$	Cross-Product Terms
JA90	13	18	−2.38	−2.56	6.09
FE90	11	16	−4.38	−4.56	19.97
MA90	17	22	1.62	1.44	2.33
AP90	20	24	4.62	3.44	15.89
MY90	20	24	4.62	3.44	15.89
JN90	16	20	.62	−.56	−.35
JL90	15	21	−.38	.44	−.17
AU90	13	18	−2.38	−2.56	6.09
SE90	17	22	1.62	1.44	2.33
OC90	11	16	−4.38	−4.56	19.97
NO90	19	24	3.62	3.44	12.45
DE90	15	20	−.38	−.56	.21
JA91	21	25	5.62	4.44	24.95
FE91	10	15	−5.38	−5.56	29.91
MA91	15	20	−.38	−.56	.21
AP91	13	Unknown			
Sum					155.77

$\bar{x} = 15.38$
$\bar{y} = 20.56$
Covariance $= 155.77/15 = 10.38$
$r(1) = +10.38/[(3.24)(3.44)] = +.93$

Use the following rule to determine if a cross-correlation is large enough to indicate an important linear relationship between the two variables.

Based on n data points, two variables are linearly related at lag k if, ignoring the sign of the cross-correlation,

$$r(k)\sqrt{n - k} > 2$$

The largest of the above six cross-correlations are

$r(1) = +.93;\quad .93\sqrt{16 - 1} = 3.6 > 2$

$r(4) = -.48;\quad .48\sqrt{16 - 4} = 1.7 < 2$

The rule demonstrates that advertising expenditures affect market share at lag 1 but not lag 4. Advertising expenditures affect market share one month later. Moreover, the positive coefficient, +.93, means that increases in advertising expenditures are associated with increases in market share.

The cross-correlation for lag 4 does not indicate a relationship. However, suppose that $r(4)\sqrt{12}$ was greater than 2. How would you interpret a negative cross-correlation? Please think about it before reading on.

An important negative $r(4)$ cross-correlation would mean that an increase in advertising expenditures this month is associated with a *reduction* (negative coefficient) in market share *four* months later.

Warning: Correlation is different from cause and effect. A high correlation does not mean that one variable *causes* another to vary. The high cross-correlation for lag 1 of +.93 indicates only that variation in advertising is *associated* with variation in market share one month later. However, the term *cause* has been used because we can make a *logical* connection between the two variables. Marketing theory predicts that advertising expenditures should affect market share. However, if we computed cross-correlations for different lags between the Dow Jones Index and length of women's dresses, we might find one or more negative correlations. The shorter dresses are, the higher the stock prices. Yet no one would seriously argue that short dresses cause the Dow Jones Index to increase. Remember, high correlations only establish a linear association between variables. Judgment or theory establishes cause and effect.

In summary, when looking for relationships between two variables for which we have time-ordered data, compute cross-correlations for lags of 0, 1, 2, 3 or more periods. Use our rule to determine which cross-correlation coefficients indicate important linear associations between the two variables. Try to make sense of the cross-correlations. That is, why should variable X affect variable Y k periods later? Knowledge of cross-correlations helps managers understand their firm and its market place. For example, knowing that advertising expenditures lead market share by one month is essential to timing of advertising expenditures. Managers who understand their environment are better performers and can bring about better performance from others.

SECTION 3.7 EXERCISES

1. Explain the difference between variance and covariance. Which is likely to be more important in problem diagnosis?

2. A recent article in the newspaper noted: "There is a definite correlation between alcohol consumption and lung cancer." Does that mean that alcohol consumption causes lung cancer? Discuss.

3. Consider the following pairs of numbers:

x	1	3	5	7
y	5	9	13	17

    a. Find the mean and standard deviation for each variable.
    b. Find the covariance of the two variables.
    c. Find the correlation of x and y.
    d. Interpret the correlation and plot the data.

4. Consider the following data relating sales and advertising for six quarters.

Quarter	Advertising (millions $)	Sales (millions $)
1	2	8
2	3	9
3	4	11
4	5	12
5	6	13
6	7	14

Write the pairs of numbers you would use to calculate the covariance of the cross-correlation coefficient to determine whether:
   a. Advertising leads sales by one quarter.
   b. Advertising leads sales by two quarters.
   c. Sales lead advertising by one quarter.

5. Calculate cross-correlations at lags 0, 1, and 2 for the sales and training data in Exercise 2 of Section 3.6.

6. If $r = 0$ does that mean that two variables are not related? Discuss.

7. Draw a scatter diagram where the covariance is
   a. positive
   b. negative
   c. close to 0

   Defend your three diagrams.

3.8 Key Ideas and Overview

Table 3.17 on page 144 integrates problem sensing and diagnosis with the graphical techniques and descriptive statistics presented in the previous two chapters.

Managers and business professionals must learn to sense and diagnose problems quickly and accurately. Sensing begins with building mental models of the department's performance for a single time period (day, week, month) and over time. Sensing also involves looking for outliers in departmental, product, or people performance. The tools of Chapter 2 are essential. Diagnosis means finding potential explanatory variables that account for performance differences or outliers. Look for distinctions between groups or changes that might explain the performance differences or outliers. Collect data and use one-way or cross-tabs tables or scatter diagrams to display the findings. For time-ordered data plot multiple line graphs and compute cross-correlations.

We conclude this chapter with a set of key ideas:

> To answer the question of why two or more departments differ, first seek an explanatory categorical variable. Then compute descriptive statistics such as the mean and standard deviation or the median and interquartile range for different levels of the explanatory variable. Display the results in a one-way table.

Table 3.17

Integrating Framework for Chapters 2 and 3

Problem Solving Activity	**Typical Managerial Questions**	**Statistical and Graphical Tools**
Problem sensing	Sensing begins with understanding the performance of the department, product, people, etc. *Ask:* What is the	
	distribution of performances?	Stem-and-leaf, frequency, and cumulative histograms, ogives
	average performance?	Mean, median, or trimmed mean
	variability of performances?	Range, standard deviation, and interquartile range
	performance over time?	Line graphs
	Sensing continues with seeking outliers in departmental, product, or people performance. *Ask:* Are there	
	outliers?	Empirical and Chebyshev's rules, box plots
	outliers over time?	Moving average and residuals
Problem diagnosis	Diagnosis seeks variables that will explain differences between two or more departments or groups that have different performance distributions, averages, or variabilities. Diagnosis also seeks explanations for outliers. *Ask:*	
	Does an explanatory variable explain differences in average performance or variability in performance?	One-way tables
	Are two categorical variables related?	Cross-tabs tables, row or column percentages
	Are two quantitative variables related?	Scatter diagrams, ellipse vs. circle test, clusters, correlations
	Are two quantitative variables related over time?	Multiple line graphs, cross-correlations

Multiple box plots are an effective way of presenting one-way table data. Many managers prefer pictures to tables.

Cross-tabs tables help answer the question of whether two categorical variables are related to one another. Compute the row or column percentages.

Scatter diagrams help answer the question of whether two quantitative variables are related to one another. Look for linear or nonlinear relationships or clusters. The circle vs. ellipse test is effective for detecting possible linear relationships.

For time-ordered data, always draw a multiple line graph and scatter diagrams. Compute cross-correlations for zero, one, two, or more periods between the two variables.

High correlations do *not* mean that one variable causes another variable to vary. Correlation only establishes an association among variables. Judgment or theory establishes cause and effect.

COMCEL

```
Date:  August 10, 1992
  To:  Ann Tabor, CEO
From:  Cherian Jain, VP Marketing Research
  Re:  Analysis of the factors affecting market share
```

SUMMARY
Our recommendations are to:

1. increase advertising expenditures in selected cities on a trial basis; and
2. reduce burnout of our senior sales force and improve performance of more junior sales people.

We also found that the 12 cities form two distinct clusters when relative price and market share are plotted. We continue to seek an explanation. Finally, we discovered that advertising expenditures lead market share by one month. That is, a month's advertising affects market share in the following month.

SUPPORTING ANALYSIS
My staff brainstormed and generated three potential explanatory variables—advertising expenditures, mean years of sales force experience, and relative product price. We examined the relationship between market share and these variables from both a cross-sectional and time-ordered perspective.

CROSS-SECTIONAL ANALYSIS

Market share and advertising appear to be positively related, at least within the range of our data. Increasing advertising should produce market share increases.

Market share and mean years sales experience have an inverted U relationship. Regions whose sales force have 11 years' experience obtain the largest market share. More or less experience reduces market share. Intervening variable(s) may be responsible for this apparent relationship. But we should consider ways to season our younger sales forces and rejuvenate our more senior sales forces.

We found two distinct clusters when we plotted relative price vs. market share. We are looking for differences in the markets themselves and in our policies which would explain the two clusters.

TIME-SERIES ANALYSIS

Our data base included 16 months of market share and advertising data for Atlanta. Our initial scatter diagram found no relationship. Since this didn't make sense, we plotted both market share and advertising expenditures against time on a multiple line graph. Advertising expenditures appeared to lead market share by one month. That is, advertising in one month affects our market share the next month. The cross-correlation of lag 1, $r(1)$, of $+.93$ confirmed our analysis.

The analysis continues. We are working on a time-ordered analysis for relative price vs. market share for Washington for the past 16 months. Other reports to follow.

CHAPTER 3 QUESTIONS

1. What is the difference between univariate and bivariate data?
2. Why are bivariate data necessary in problem diagnosis?
3. In your own words, distinguish between quantitative and categorical data.
4. Explain how one-way tables or multiple box plots help in problem diagnosis.
5. Construct your own data to show how a column percentage table provides insight into the possible connections between two categorical variables such as homeowner and renter vs. for and against tax increase.
6. What are intervening variables?
7. What role do intervening variables play in a cross-tabs table analysis?
8. How can managers develop lists of variables that might help them explain variation among multiple groups?
9. Explain the logic of the ellipse test in determining if two variables are linearly related.
10. Does a finding of no linear relationship between two variables mean no relationship at all?
11. Explain how the presence of distinct clusters in a scatter diagram helps in problem diagnosis.
12. In simple terms, what are leading and lagging relationships?
13. How do multiple line graphs help in problem diagnosis?

14. Correct, if necessary, the following statement:

    Problem diagnosis determines if groups differ in their mean performance or how much variation there is among groups. Problem sensing determines why groups differ or explains the variation among groups.

15. Does a high correlation mean that one variable causes another variable to vary?

CHAPTER 3 APPLICATION PROBLEMS

1. Best Dairy Inc. knows that the Macho consumers have lower incomes than do the Status Seeker consumers. They wonder if Machos and Status Seekers also have different preferences for skim and whole milk. The marketing manager conducts a survey to determine if Machos and Status Seekers prefer skim and whole milk equally. He wants to verify that Best Dairy has meaningfully segmented its market. Best Dairy Inc. interviews 200 customers and cross-classifies them along the following two dimensions:

	Machos	Status Seekers	Total
Skim	30	80	110
Whole	70	20	90
	100	100	200

    a. Compute the row and the column percentages.
    b. Using either percentages, do Machos and Status Seekers prefer skim and whole milk equally?
    c. Why should you qualify your conclusion? That is, why could you be wrong?

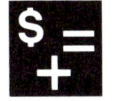

2. Length-of-tenure discounts are the difference between the rents charged long-time tenants and newer tenants. Landlords give discounts because they want to keep good tenants and minimize turnover. The length-of-tenure discounts in Chicago vary from 1.5% to 11.5%. Why is there so much variability? The American Housing Association believes that it is due to the size of the apartment complex. Larger complexes (more than 10 units) are owned by corporations and can afford to have vacant apartments. Thus they give smaller discounts. Small complexes owned by families cannot afford to have unrented apartments, and so give higher discounts for tenants to stay.

Discount (%)	Size of Complex	Discount (%)	Size of Complex
1.5	Small	6.5	Large
2.0	Small	11.5	Large
5.4	Large	2.7	Small
2.5	Small	10.7	Large
3.9	Large	2.9	Small
1.7	Small	6.7	Large
5.5	Large	3.2	Small
3.4	Small		

    a. Develop a one-way table using size of complex as the explanatory variable. Compute only the mean and standard deviation.
    b. Does complex size seem to explain why discounts vary widely in Chicago?
    c. Why couldn't you use a scatter diagram to organize and summarize the data?

3. Apex wants to reduce its age of accounts receivable from a mean of about 35 days. They try a program of inducements (discounts for prompt payment) in Hartford and no inducements in New Haven. They then select six accounts from both cities. Does the discount program appear to be successful?

Age of Accounts Receivable in Days	
With Inducement	No Inducement
20	30
15	28
20	31
16	35
19	25
24	30

    a. Set up a one-way table with presence or absence of inducements as an explanatory variable. Compute the mean and standard deviation for both groups.
    b. Has the inducement reduced the age of the accounts receivable? Explain in terms that an accounting manager could understand.
    c. Why couldn't you use a cross-tabs table to organize the above data?

4. The financial manager at COMCEL wants to know how profit margin, the net profit after taxes divided by sales, has done for the past 16 quarters in comparison to the industry average profit margin. Here are the data.

Quarter	COMCEL (%)	Industry (%)
1	5.34	5.40
2	5.19	5.45
3	5.17	5.60
4	5.41	5.55
5	5.25	5.56
6	5.49	5.65
7	5.46	5.80
8	5.34	5.75
9	5.40	5.80
10	5.47	5.85
11	5.20	6.00
12	5.12	5.90
13	5.28	6.00
14	5.21	6.10
15	5.31	6.30
16	5.16	6.20

    a. Draw a multiple line graph that shows the profit margin at COMCEL and the industry average for the past 16 quarters.

b. How do COMCEL's profit margins compare with the industry? Explain in terms that a financial manager could understand.
   c. Does the multiple line graph signal a problem for COMCEL?

5. Length-of-tenure discounts are the difference between the rents charged long-time tenants and newer tenants. Is the discount size related to length of residence? Shown are data taken from 15 San Francisco apartment dwellers.

Size of Discount (%)	Years in Residence	Size of Discount (%)	Years in Residence
1.5	2	6.5	7
2.0	3	11.5	10
3.4	3	2.7	3
2.5	2	7.6	8
3.9	4	2.9	1
10.0	9	3.9	5
2.2	3	4.7	6
3.4	4		

   a. Draw a scatter plot for the cross-sectional data. Which is the more likely explanatory variable?
   b. Do the variables appear to be related? Explain the relationship in terms that a real estate broker could understand.
   c. Why shouldn't you use a one-way table to organize the data?

6. An advertising manager wants to determine whether level of advertising is positively related to sales. If so, she may increase advertising. If the two variables are not related, she may reduce advertising. Shown are the most recent 20 months of sales and level of advertising data. Are the two variables related?

Month	Sales (hundreds)	Advertising (thousands $)
1	210	23.0
2	210	25.5
3	235	26.5
4	220	27.0
5	250	27.0
6	250	32.5
7	270	28.0
8	260	29.5
9	290	34.0
10	320	29.0
11	270	36.0
12	320	33.0
13	310	34.0
14	340	32.0
15	300	38.0
16	360	30.0
17	330	40.0
18	380	43.0
19	410	42.0
20	400	30.0

a. Draw a scatter diagram for sales and level of advertising.
b. Draw a scatter diagram for sales and the previous month's advertising.
c. Which scatter diagram is most suggestive of a relationship betweeen sales and level of advertising? Explain the relationship in terms that a marketing manager could understand.

7. A stock analyst specializing in the retail industry wants to know if chain stores, such as JC Penney, stress the same focus—service or price—as do independents. She surveys 30 independents and 20 chains and determines if they are price- or service-oriented. Here are the data.

	Service	Price	Total
Independents	25	5	30
Chains	4	16	20
	29	21	50

a. Compute either row or column percentages.
b. Do chains have a different orientation than independents? Explain in terms that a marketing manager could understand.
c. Why shouldn't you use a one-way table to organize the data?

8. Most experts believe that the number of grievances filed increases with increasing numbers of employees. You wish to determine if this is true. You suspect that the statement may be true for plants in the Midwest but not in the South. You collect data on the following ten plants, five in each region.

Plant	Region	Workers	Grievances
1	S	200	50
2	S	400	55
3	S	250	55
4	S	150	60
5	MW	160	60
6	S	300	65
7	MW	210	70
8	MW	240	85
9	MW	310	90
10	MW	390	100

a. Draw a scatter plot with number of workers as the explanatory variable and the number of grievances as the dependent variable. Be sure to label the ten data points as either a Midwestern or Southern plant.
b. Does there appear to be any relationship between number of grievances and number of workers? Describe how the two variables are related in terms that a personnel manager could understand.
c. What is a logical follow-up question given your answer in part b?

9. The Arbitration Association collects data on the number of grievances filed by plants with between 200 and 300 workers. It wonders why the number of grievances varies from 45 to 99 among the ten firms. Could the large variability be related to a

firm's use of participative management? It determines whether each firm uses participative management in the ten plants through a survey. Shown are the data.

Firms	Grievances	Participative Management
1	70	No
2	74	No
3	65	Yes
4	45	Yes
5	78	No
6	69	Yes
7	99	No
8	76	No
9	56	Yes
10	62	Yes

    a. Using the absence or presence of participative management as an explanatory variable, construct a one-way table for the mean and standard deviation in the number of grievances filed.

    b. Does it appear that participative management has an impact on the number of grievances? Explain in terms a manager could understand.

10. Is job attitude related to salary? Are people with higher salaries happier on the job than low-salaried people? Ten accounting managers are asked to indicate how satisfied they are on the job along a 5-point scale from 1 (very unsatisfied) to 5 (very satisfied). We also collect their salary data. Here are the cross-sectional data.

Manager	Salary	Job Attitude
1	38	1
2	38	4
3	40	3
4	36	2
5	46	2
6	43	5
7	50	2
8	52	2
9	54	4
10	56	2

    a. Plot a scatter diagram with job attitude as an explanatory variable.
    b. Does there appear to be a relationship between the two variables? Explain in simple terms.
    c. Why do we need to use the word *appear* in part **b**?
    d. Why can't you use a cross-tabs table to organize the data?

11. Do stress management programs minimize absenteeism? ABC Research conducts a study where it selects 200 firms. One hundred firms have stress reduction programs and 100 do not have programs. It subdivides each group into firms with high and low absenteeism using industry-wide average absenteeism figures.

	Absenteeism		
	Low	High	Total
Programs	40	60	100
No Programs	10	90	100
	50	150	200

a. Compute either the row or column percentages.
b. Do stress reduction programs appear to affect absenteeism? Explain your conclusion to a human resources manager.

12. Each day the U.S. Park Service recorded the number of cars entering a beach area. After day 10, the number of cars began to drop. Could that drop be related to the mean daily temperature?

Day	Cars (thousands)	Mean Temperature
1	20	75
2	21	77
3	19	74
4	21	75
5	20	78
6	18	82
7	22	78
8	21	75
9	20	77
10	21	72
11	19	68
12	17	63
13	16	64
14	15	65
15	14	60

a. Draw a multiple line graph for both variables—number of cars and mean temperature. Remember, time in days is the independent variable.
b. What does the multiple line graph tell you? Explain your conclusion to the park administrator.

13. Suppose a cross-tabs table suggests that market segment and milk preference appear to be related. Does including an intervening variable—weight of consumer—affect the relationship between the two market segments (Machos and Status Seekers) and their milk preferences (skim or whole milk)? Here are the data.

	Underweight Consumers		
	Machos	Status Seekers	Total
Skim	5	7	12
Whole	35	33	68
	40	40	80

Chapter 3 Descriptive Statistics II: Bivariate Data and Problem Diagnosis

	Overweight Consumers		
	Machos	Status Seekers	Total
Skim	50	48	98
Whole	10	12	22
	60	60	120

    a. Compute row or column percentages for both cross-tabs tables.
    b. With weight as an intervening variable, does it now appear that market segment and milk preference are related? Explain your conclusion to a marketing manager.

14. The production manager of a COMCEL division is looking for a better way to plan production and to reduce excess inventory. Sales of the division are generated by "cold calling" by the sales staff and from calls initiated by potential customers. The manager hopes she can predict sales based on the quotes made by the sales staff. She collected data on the total dollar value of quotes given to prospective clients and also recorded the dollar volume of sales in that month over the past year. The data are shown.

Month	Quotes (thousands $)	Sales (thousands $)
1	20	13
2	15	12
3	10	9
4	17	7
5	25	11
6	15	15
7	18	10
8	20	12
9	20	12
10	14	11
11	18	9
12	12	11

    a. Plot a scatter diagram for sales vs. quotes. Is quotes a coincident indicator of sales? Explain.
    b. Calculate the cross-correlation between sales and quotes at lag 1 and lag 2. Plot the scatter diagrams for lags 1 and 2.
    c. How would you describe the relationship, if any, between sales and quotes?

15. People with credit cards often mistakenly pay more than they owe and are given positive credit balances. Some people pay with bad checks, run up a credit balance, and then withdraw the credit balance in cash. An analyst with a small bank wonders whether there is a relationship between the number of credit balances over $1,000 in any week and the percentage of these accounts that are fraudulent. The only data at hand are the number of accounts showing credit balances above $1,000 and the number of fraud cases involving cash withdrawal for each week.

Week	Accounts with $1,000 or More in Credit	Fraud Cases Involving Cash Withdrawal
1	12	17
2	20	17
3	14	8
4	17	10
5	16	9
6	12	10
7	15	9
8	13	7
9	7	9
10	14	8
11	20	4
12	16	7

a. Plot scatter diagrams of the data at lags 0, 1, and 2. Treat cases as the dependent variable and accounts as the independent variable.
b. Calculate cross-correlations at these lags.
c. Does there appear to be a relationship between the number of accounts with credit balances over $1,000 and the number of fraud cases involving withdrawal of credit balances in cash?

16. A marketing manager runs a study in which he tries two advertising strategies to sell toothpaste. His goal is to increase market share. He selects 10 test markets and tries each marketing approach in five test markets. He records the change in market share from last quarter's market share.

Strategy	Test Market	Increase in Market Share (%)
Comparison to Other Brands	1	3
	2	4
	3	5
	4	6
	5	12
Use of Star Performers	6	0
	7	1
	8	1
	9	2
	10	5

a. Draw multiple box plots for both marketing strategies.
b. Which marketing strategy should the manager implement? Discuss.

Chapter 3   Descriptive Statistics II: Bivariate Data and Problem Diagnosis   155

17. A financial analyst believes that firms that produce higher-quality products have higher returns on investment than those firms that produce less reliable products. Product quality is rated from 50 for lower quality to 100 for high quality. Shown are data collected on 10 firms in two different industries.

Firm	Industry	Average Product Quality	Return on Investment (%)
1	Stereo	90	17.5
2	Stereo	50	8.7
3	Paper	50	8.8
4	Paper	70	7.8
5	Paper	90	8.0
6	Stereo	70	15.4
7	Stereo	100	22.5
8	Paper	100	7.8
9	Stereo	60	13.5
10	Paper	60	8.2

a. Plot the data.
b. Is product quality related to return on investment across both industries or in either industry?

18. Is the use of LIFO (Last In First Out) and FIFO (First In First Out) affected by the rate of inflation? That is, do firms tend to use LIFO in times of high inflation (above 6%) and FIFO in times of lower inflation ($\leq 6\%$)? Here are hypothetical results of a survey of firms.

	Low Inflation	High Inflation
LIFO	10	190
FIFO	100	100

a. Compute either row or column percentages.
b. Is use of LIFO or FIFO related to the level of inflation? Explain in terms that an accounting manager could understand.

19. Will small farms survive into the 21st century? The multiple line graph shown on page 156 illustrates the number of farms and the mean number of acres per farm since 1920. [*Source: Empty Breadbasket?*, The Cornucopia Project of the Rodale Press, 1981, p. 16.]
a. What does the multiple line graph show?
b. If both trends continue, describe the farming community in the 21st century.

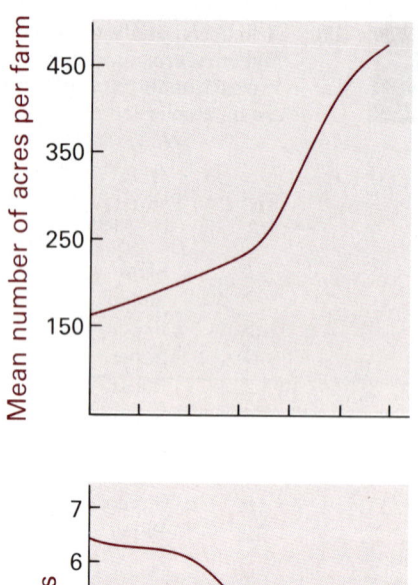

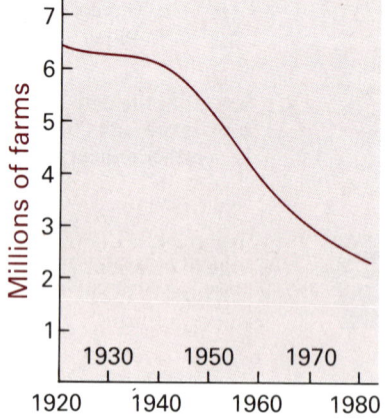

20. The Myers-Briggs Type Indicator (MBTI) measures four dimensions of human behavior. One dimension is how people make judgments. They are either thinkers (T) or feelers (F). Thinkers use logic and analysis; feelers stress feelings and impacts on people. Do thinkers and feelers choose different careers? One hundred preschool teachers and 86 computer systems analysts are interviewed. Each completes the MBTI. The cross-tabs data are shown here. [*Source: Manual: A Guide to the Development of the Myers-Briggs Type Indicator*, Myers and McCaulley, 1985, pp. 248–250.]

	Thinker	Feeler	Total
Preschool Teacher	21	79	100
Computer Analyst	66	20	86

- **a.** Is the thinker-feeler dimension related to job preference?
- **b.** Does it appear that thinkers and feelers choose different careers?
- **c.** Show that the above cross-tabs data make sense. That is, each group has chosen a job that is appropriate for them.

Chapter 3 Descriptive Statistics II: Bivariate Data and Problem Diagnosis

21. The Consumer Price Index (CPI) is the most commonly used measure of inflation. The index measures the average change in prices relative to a base year for a common bundle of goods and services bought by a consumer on a regular basis. Two important groups within the index are energy costs and medical care costs. Are both groups rising at the about the same rate over the past 27 years? Shown are data of the CPI for energy costs and medical care for 1960–1987. [*Source: U.S. Bureau of Labor Statistics, Monthly Labor Review, and Handbook of Labor.*]

Year	1960	1965	1970	1975	1980	1981	1982	1983	1984	1985	1986	1987
Energy	22.4	22.9	25.5	42.1	86.0	97.7	99.2	99.9	100.9	101.6	88.2	88.6
Medical	22.3	25.2	34.0	47.5	74.9	82.9	92.5	100.6	106.8	113.5	122.0	130.1

a. Construct a scatter diagram. Plot the energy price index on the horizontal axis.
b. Interpret the graph. What can you conclude?
c. What other format could you use to show how the two components of the CPI have varied over the past 27 years?

22. The multiple line graphs shown here and on page 158 contain the mean and standard deviation of weights of boxes of cereal taken each day off a production line. On day 5 the process mean was too low, meaning that the boxes were being underfilled. On day 10 the standard deviation increased, meaning the variability in weights was beyond what the firm desired. Again the firm took action. Did the actions correct the problem? Explain.

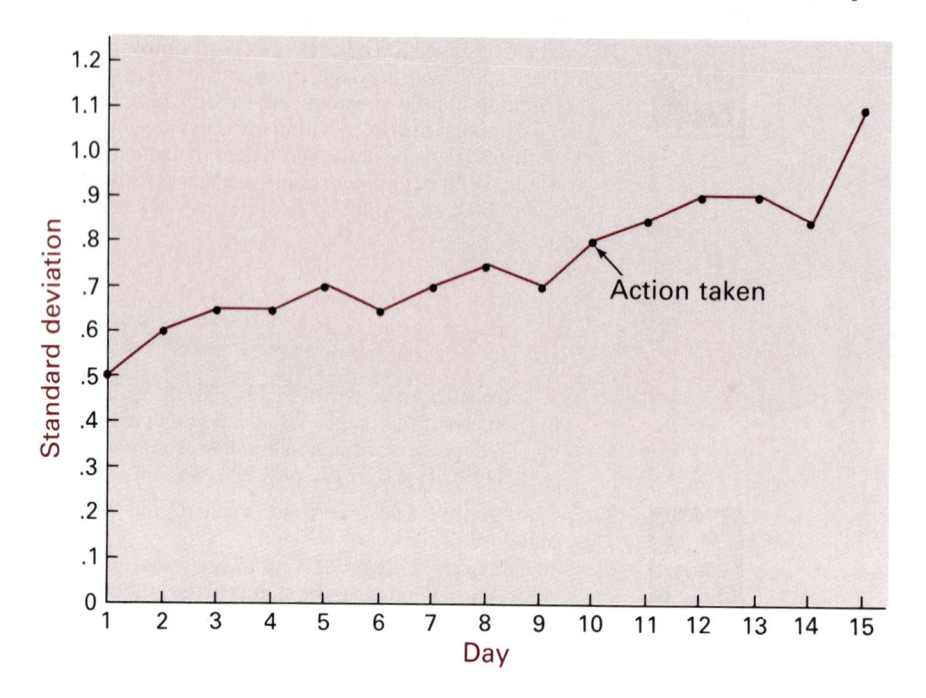

23. Franchised businesses represent about 40% of all U.S. retail sales. Is the franchise fee affected by the number of franchisers? Shown are data on the 10 largest franchisers in America. [*Source: The Franchise Handbook*, 1989.]

Name of Company	Franchise Fee (in dollars)	Number of Franchises
Century 21 Real Estate	18,000	7,005
Dairy Queen	30,000	5,122
Wendy's	25,000	2,597
TCBY Yogurt	20,000	1,240
Jiffy Lube	35,000	1,000
Computerland	25,000	800
West Coast Video	40,000	700
Thrift Rent-a-Car	7,500	655
Supercuts	17,500	508
Merry Maids	17,500	425

a. Is franchise fee related to the number of franchises? That is, do firms that have more franchises charge greater franchise fees?
b. If not, what might the cost of the franchise be related to?

24.

Date: June 23, 1992
To: Nat Gordon, Vice President of Manufacturing
From: Ann Tabor, CEO
Re: Monthly Attendance at Two Operating Plants

I received your report that noted that the Dallas plant monthly attendance figures exceed those of the Norcross plant. I noticed that management employees in both plants have higher monthly attendance figures. That, of course, does not surprise me. However, I am disturbed that there is so much variation in monthly attendance within each plant and between the two plants. We must determine the underlying root causes.

Please assign your best analysts to investigate the situation to determine possible reasons for the differences within and between plants. Once we know some causes, we can consider possible corrective actions. As always, I need your analysis quickly—no later than July 10th.

Use Data Base I for your analysis. Your response to Ann Tabor should include a brief memo and your analysis.

25.

Date: January 7, 1991
To: Pam Asher, Manager—South Marketing Region
From: Bill O'Hara, Vice President of Marketing
Re: Analysis of Atlanta Sales Growth

Both Ann and I appreciated your informative report. Also, congratulations on the excellent sales growth. We noted that sales have been steadily increasing and that the second and third quarters tend to be strong sales periods. What accounts for our increasing sales in Atlanta? What are you doing to obtain this growth? If we can determine what influences sales, we can help other regions experience the same growth as Atlanta.

I also noticed that you had unusually high and low sales in the fourth quarter of 1988 and the third quarter of 1990. Any ideas as to what caused these? Did anything unusual happen during those quarters? Did you or your competition make any changes? Don't spend too much on this as our first concern is to understand what factors influence your sales growth.

We will need a preliminary analysis by February 10th.

Use Data Base II for your analysis. Your response to Bill O'Hara should include a brief memo and your analysis.

4

Basic Probability Concepts: The Study of Randomness

4.1 Introduction
4.2 Probability concepts
   Event
   Frequency of an event
   Relative frequency of an event
   The law of large numbers
   Probability of an event
   Basic rules of probability
   What the law of large numbers does not say
   Personal probability
4.3 Picturing probabilities: Introduction to the probability tree
   Joint probability table
   Probability tree diagram
4.4 Joint and union probabilities
   Union probability: Combining two events using OR
4.5 Conditional probabilities and statistical independence
   Conditional probability
   Statistical independence and dependence
4.6 Computing conditional probabilities
   Distinguishing between conditional and joint probabilities
   Conditional probabilities and row or column percentage tables
4.7 Using probability trees to minimize managerial judgment errors
   The error of overlooking the base rate
   Noncoherency error
4.8 Nonstatistical judgment errors
   Availability error
   Concreteness error
4.9 Key ideas and overview
Chapter 4 Questions
Chapter 4 Application Problems

CHAPTER OUTLINE

COMCEL Interoffice Communication

Date: September 4, 1992
  To: Sarah Teman, Manager of Operations
From: Howard Bright, Plant Manager
  Re: Improving Work Group Productivity

An article in *Forbes* indicated that companies have been successful in improving productivity by encouraging members of work groups to learn each others' jobs. Switching jobs reduces the monotony and boredom of performing a single task, 8 hours a day, and leads to less reworking and improved productivity.

I know that some of our work groups have, on their own initiative, started switching jobs. Is there any evidence that these work groups have higher productivity levels than those groups that have not?

Please look into this for me, and give me your recommendation. The fact that job switching was successful in other companies does not mean it will work for us. However, if job switching is related to higher productivity, I will put it on the agenda for the next meeting of the Senior Team. We may want to make job switching a company policy.

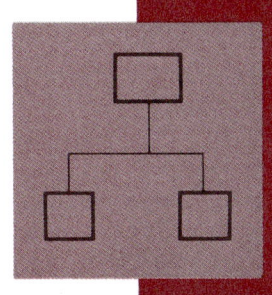

4.1 Introduction

Chapter 2 showed how to use the mean, range, standard deviation, trimmed mean, median, and interquartile range to sense possible emerging problems. Chapter 3 described how to organize and interpret data through one-way tables, multiple box plots, cross-tabs tables, scatter diagrams, and multiple line graphs. These tools help you sense and diagnose problems. Chapter 4 will help you use probability to make estimates, or judgments, under *uncertain* conditions.

Consider the following situation. The director of planning for a utility company must determine if additional power generating plants are needed for the year 2000. She believes that it depends on whether (1) consumers will increase their conservation efforts and (2) the federal government will change tax policy to permit taxpayers to deduct conservation costs, such as installing insulation, double-pane windows, and power-saving thermostats, from their tax bills.

The director is uncertain about future conservation efforts and federal tax policies. She personally believes there is a .50 chance of increased consumer conservation efforts and a .60 chance that the federal government will allow taxpayers to deduct conservation costs. If the federal tax policy does permit deductions for conservation costs, the chance of increased conservation will be higher than her .50 estimate, say .85.

The three chance estimates—.50, .60, and .85—cannot all be correct. They violate one of the rules of probability. You will know why by the end of the chapter.

Managers talk about chances everyday. What is the chance that consumers will increase conservation efforts? What is the chance that the federal tax policy will permit deducting conservation costs? The official name for chance is probability. Managers must understand probability. They may make poor decisions if they base future plans on questionable probabilities.

4.2 Probability Concepts

> A random experiment is an action that, when repeated over many trials, produces a set of definite outcomes or values. We cannot predict with certainty which value will occur on any trial. However, there is a predictable long-run pattern in the values.

To understand probability, we introduce the concept of a **random experiment**. Consider the following random experiment: Walk into a store that has 35 salespeople on its staff and count the number of salespeople on the floor. Now repeat this experiment many times. You will find that the number of salespeople on the floor can be one of 36 possible values—0, 1, 2, . . . , 35. However we cannot predict with certainty the number of salespeople we will find in any one visit. There is randomness or unpredictability. However, over many trials or visits, we would find a long-run pattern. Perhaps most of the time there are between 20 and 25 salespeople on the floor, and rarely are there fewer than 10 salespeople on the floor.

By the end of this section you should be able to:

1. explain in your own words the following terms: event, frequency of an event, relative frequency of an event, and probability of an event;

Chapter 4   Basic Probability Concepts: The Study of Randomness   163

2. distinguish between relative frequency and probability;
3. explain what the law of large numbers is and is not;
4. explain the two basic rules of probability; and
5. distinguish between relative frequency-based probability and personal probability.

Here are five random experiments that we have repeated many times and a list of their possible values.

Random Experiment	Possible Values	Example of Values
Walk in store with 35 salespeople once. Count the number of salespeople on the floor.	Any integer number between 0 and 35	0, 1, 6, 20
Select a work group. Record whether the group members switched jobs or not.	Two possibilities— Switch or Not switch	Switch
Flip a coin five times. Count the number of heads.	Any integer number between 0 and 5	0, 3, 5
Ask one family its annual income.	Any number between $0 and $100 million	$3,345, $152,000.06
Select one 12-ounce can of peaches and weigh the contents.	Any number between 11.90 ounces and 12.10 ounces	11.965 oz., 12.04 oz.

As was noted earlier, the number of salespeople on the floor can be any of 36 possible values—0, 1, 2, 3, 4, ..., 35. The status of job switching can be either of two possible values—yes or no. The number of heads in five flips can be any of six possible values—0, 1, 2, 3, 4, or 5 heads. There are millions of possible values for the fourth random experiment. Remember, one must include Bill Cosby's annual family income of over $70 million. The fifth experiment has an uncountable number of possible values. For example, the weight could be 12.00456745 ounces. If we round off weight to the nearest hundredth of an ounce, then only 21 values are possible—11.90, 11.91, 11.92, ..., 12.10.

Given the definition of a random experiment, we are now ready to define an **event**.

> An event is a collection of one or more values from a random experiment that has been repeated over many trials.

Event

There are several types of events. A *simple event* can take on only one value out of all possible values of the repeated random experiment. Finding exactly zero salespeople is a simple event. So is getting five heads in five coin flips or recording an income of $13,345.00.

A *compound event* includes two or more values from a repeated random experiment. Entering a store and finding between four and seven salespeople is a compound event. Selecting a family and recording an annual income between $10,000 and $15,000 is also a compound event. The first compound event contains four values—four, five, six, and seven salespeople. If we round off annual income to the nearest dollar and include the $10,000 and $15,000 figures, the second compound event contains 5,001 values.

For any simple or compound event there is a *complementary event* that consists of all other possible values of a repeated random experiment. Following is a list of two events and their complements. $13,454 is a simple event. Its complement is a compound event that includes all possible values of the repeated random experiment except $13,454. The event, more than 30 salespeople on the floor, is a compound event. Its complement is also a compound event—namely, 30 or fewer salespeople on the floor. Note that an event, simple or compound, and its complement together account for all possible values of a repeated random experiment.

Event	Complementary Event
Income of $13,454	All incomes other than $13,454
More than 30 salespeople on the floor	30 or fewer salespeople on the floor

Frequency of an Event

The frequency of an event is the number of times the event occurs over a number of trials, or repetitions, of a random experiment. Suppose we walk into a store 100 times and record the number of times we find at least 20 salespeople on the floor. Or suppose we interview 1,000 families and count the number of families whose income is greater than $50,000. We use the following notation to record the data.

$$\text{Frequency}_{100}(\text{at least 20 salespeople}) = 90$$

$$\text{Frequency}_{1,000}(\text{income greater than \$50,000}) = 50$$

In 90 out of the 100 trials, we counted at least 20 salespeople on the floor. In 50 out of the 1,000 trials, we found families with incomes greater than $50,000.

Relative Frequency of an Event

When we conduct a random experiment *n* times (over *n* trials), the relative frequency of an event *A* is equal to the number of times *A* happens divided by the number of trials.

The **relative frequency** of an event is the fraction of times that an event occurs in a given number of trials. The following notation is used to express relative frequency:

$$\text{Relative frequency}(A) = \frac{\text{Frequency}(A)}{n} \qquad (4.1)$$

The relative frequency of finding at least 20 salespeople is simply the number of times we found 20 or more salespeople divided by the total number of trials, or store visits. The relative frequency of finding families with incomes greater than

$50,000 is the number of times we found a family with an income greater than $50,000 divided by the total number of trials, or number of families interviewed. Thus,

$$\text{Relative frequency (at least 20 salespeople)} = \frac{90}{100} = .90$$

$$\text{Relative frequency (income greater than \$50,000)} = \frac{50}{1,000} = .05$$

Rare events, those that are not likely to occur, will have small relative frequencies. For example, in only 5% of the 1,000 trials or interviews did we find a family with an income greater than $50,000.

Common events, those which occur often, will have relative frequencies near 1. For example, the relative frequency of finding at least 20 salespeople on the floor is .90.

The Law of Large Numbers

According to the law of large numbers, every event has a fixed value called a probability, such that if a random experiment is repeated a very large number of times, then the relative frequency of the event will approach the fixed value. The more times the random experiment is repeated, the greater the stability of the relative frequency.

The relative frequency of an event is a useful indicator of the chance that an event will occur. But, relative frequency has one drawback. It will change as the number of trials of the repeated random experiment increases. Fortunately, the relative frequency is more stable if the random experiment is repeated many times. By stability is meant the following. If two people interview two sets of 10 families and count the number with incomes greater than $50,000, they may get very different relative frequencies. If they interview two sets of 100,000 families and count the number with incomes greater than $50,000, then the two relative frequencies will be nearly identical. This demonstrates the **law of large numbers**.

Figure 4.1 on page 166 illustrates the law of large numbers. Consider an event that has a probability of .8. The probability is represented by the horizontal line. The jagged line represents how the relative frequency tends to stabilize and in general becomes closer to the probability of the event. However, note that even after 150 trials, the relative frequency and probability of the event are not yet equal.

Probability of an Event

The probability, or chance, of an event represents the proportion of trials in which the event will happen in the long run. It is fixed, or nonchanging, number between 0 and 1 that represents the relative frequency of the event if the random experiment were repeated an infinite number of times.

Probabilities are precise descriptions of randomness. An event may be unpredictable and yet have a probability of .80. The event would occur in 80% of the trials if the random experiment were repeated forever and ever. A probability near 0 suggests a rare event, whereas a probability near 1 suggests a nearly certain event. A probability of .5 suggests an event that has the same chance of occurring as not occurring.

Basic Rules of Probability

In probability, there are two very basic and simple rules or principles to remember.

FIGURE 4.1

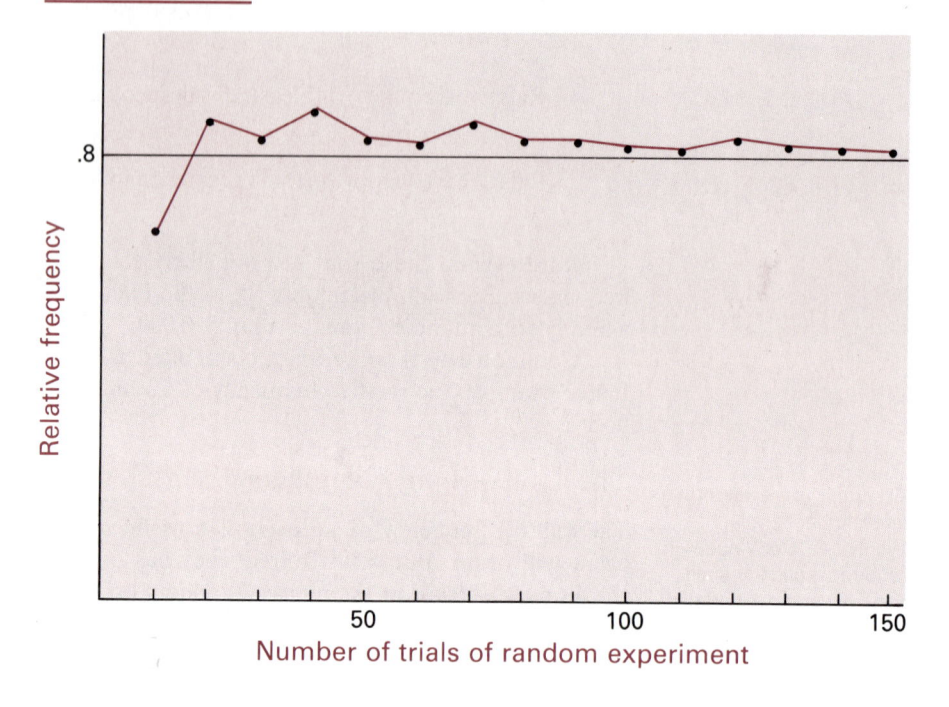

[Graph: Relative frequency vs. Number of trials of random experiment, showing values fluctuating around .8 for trials from about 10 to 150]

RULE 1: Probabilities are numbers whose values lie between 0 and 1.0 inclusive.

If there is absolutely no chance of an event occurring, it happens in 0% of the trials. If the event always occurs, it happens in 100% of the trials. Since an event cannot occur in less than 0% of the trials, it cannot have a negative probability, and since an event cannot occur more often than in all the trials, it cannot have a probability greater than 1.

RULE 2: The sum of the probabilities of all the possible events that can occur must be 1.0.

Recall the random experiment where 1,000 families were surveyed. Suppose we define two events—incomes of $50,000 or less and incomes greater than $50,000. Now we interview 100,000 families. Isn't it clear that the sum of the two relative frequencies must be 1.0? Similarly, the sum of the probabilities of the two events must also equal 1.0.

From Rule 2, we also know that the sum of the probabilities of an event, A, and its complement, $\bar{A}$, must be 1.0. Remember, an event and its complement include all the possible events. Thus, by Rule 2,

$$P(A) + P(\bar{A}) = 1.0 \qquad (4.2)$$

$$P(A) = 1.0 - P(\bar{A}) \qquad (4.3)$$

The notation $P(A)$ means the probability of event A happening.

What the Law of Large Numbers Does Not Say

What is wrong with the following reasoning? You toss a fair coin 10 times and get 10 consecutive heads. A friend argues that the "law of averages" says you are very likely to get a tail on the 11th flip. Is he correct?

Contrary to what would-be gamblers, muddleheaded managers, or confused friends say, the answer is no. The coin has no memory. It does not remember what happened on the first 10 trials. Statistically speaking, we say that the trials, or coin flips, are independent. The probability of getting a head with a fair coin always remains $\frac{1}{2}$. Now the chance of getting 10 heads in a row is very small. But if you did, the chance of getting a tail on the next trial does not increase.

Since the probability of getting a head for a fair coin is .5, shouldn't we expect some tails to balance out the 10 heads obtained? Yes, but that does not increase the probability of getting a tail in any individual trial. Suppose that we flip the coin an additional 9,990 times for a total of 10,000 flips. Imagine that half (4,995) of the next 9,990 flips are heads and the other half are tails. These events are tabulated here along with their relative frequencies of heads.

Number of Trials	Relative Frequency of Heads
10	10/10 = 1.0000
9,990	4,995/9,990 = .5000
10,000	(10 + 4,995)/10,000 = .5005

Now it is true that in the long run the relative frequency of getting a head must equal the probability of getting a head, which is .5. If you obtained an equal number of heads and tails over the next 9,990 flips, the relative frequency for the 10,000 trials would still be close to .5, specifically .5005, even though you began with 10 straight heads.

※ In short, there is no "law of averages" in probability.

Personal Probability

Until now, we have discussed relative frequency probabilities. The relative frequency viewpoint is useful when valid historical data are available. The relative frequency viewpoint is not useful when assessing the chance of a never-before-happened event. For example, what is the probability that a new boss will change the dress policy? What is the probability that a new microcomputer will outsell its major competitors in the next quarter? For a first-time event we need personal, or subjective, probabilities. Personal probabilities are also numbers whose values lie between 0 and 1, but they reflect one's personal beliefs and biases about the chance of an event happening.

Personal probabilities are still subject to the same two basic rules as are relative frequency probabilities. That is, personal probability is a number between 0 and 1, and the sum of the personal probabilities for all the possible events must be 1. We would assign a personal probability of 0 if we were *absolutely* sure that the event would not occur; we would assign a personal probability of 1 if we were *absolutely* sure that the event would occur. The more certain we are that the event will occur, the greater would be our personal probability of the event.

There's good news and bad news regarding personal probabilities. The good news is that they are very easy to assign. The bad news is that they are very easy to assign. Irrelevant factors (see Section 4.7) often influence a manager's personal probability estimates.

Let's illustrate how irrelevant factors may affect personal probability estimates. For example, is a person more likely to die from an accidental fall or from an accidental discharge of a firearm? What are your personal probability estimates for both events? Please think about it before reading on.

Many people believe that death due to an accidental discharge of a firearm is more likely. That is because such deaths make the evening news. According to psychologists Amos Tversky and Daniel Kahneman (1974, 1981), the probabilities of dramatic, sensational causes of death that get heavy media coverage are overestimated. Data from the U.S. Public Health Service show that the probability of accidental death from falling is many times greater than from a discharge of a firearm. People's probability beliefs may be biased by the amount of media exposure—an irrelevant factor.

Personal probabilities are subject to all the biases that humans have. A manager might overestimate future sales because he reads in *The Wall Street Journal* that a competing firm has recently had greater-than-expected sales, or a manager may underestimate sales because a friend's firm had a sudden drop in sales. The friend's firm is in an unrelated industry and so the manager has been influenced by what may be an irrelevant factor. Now it is true that there are no "correct" personal probabilities. Unlike relative frequency probabilities, we cannot determine them by running a random experiment over many trials. However, to be useful, personal probabilities must be free of irrelevant factors.

Managers often develop erroneous personal probability estimates. Previously a case was discussed where a director of planning generated three personal probability estimates—.50, .60, and .85. While these estimates reflect her thinking about the future, they are not valid for they violate the first rule of probability. This will be explained further in Section 4.7.

In summary, managers use relative frequencies to estimate probabilities of events. Managers also use personal probabilities when reliable historical data are unavailable. Both probabilities must obey the two rules of probability. However, personal probability has one singular drawback. Irrelevant factors may influence a manager's personal probability assessments. To avoid this problem to some degree, have several managers *independently* generate personal probabilities and then develop *consensus* probability estimates. This may minimize the impact of irrelevant factors on personal probabilities.

SECTION 4.2 EXERCISES

1. State which of the following could be classified as a random experiment and explain why.
    a. Buying five tickets at a movie theater and recording the amount charged
    b. Observing and recording the temperature at any time of the day
    c. Driving to work
    d. Watching the Kentucky Derby and recording whether a particular horse wins or loses
    e. Selecting an item from an assembly line and counting the number of defects
    f. Watching the World Series and recording whether the National League team wins or loses

2. Over the past year a firm has purchased 10,000 replacement parts from the Acme Company. Approximately 5% of these parts were defective and had to be replaced by Acme. A shipment of 20 parts has just arrived from Acme. Can you predict the *exact* number of defective parts in this shipment? Explain.

3. A group of five people contains three females and two males. Suppose we put the peoples' names in a hat and select three people. The following outcomes are possible.

    F_1 F_2 F_3 F_2 F_3 M_1
    F_1 F_2 M_1 F_2 F_3 M_2
    F_1 F_2 M_2 F_1 M_1 M_2
    F_1 F_3 M_1 F_2 M_1 M_2
    F_1 F_3 M_2 F_3 M_1 M_2

    a. Is selecting three people a random experiment? Why?
    b. Is selecting three people and counting the number of females a random experiment? Why?
    c. Suppose you decide to count the number of females in each outcome. List the possible range of outcomes.

4. Suppose you rolled a single fair die and recorded the number of times each side came up. A fair die is one in which the chances of getting a 1, 2, 3, 4, 5, and 6 are the same. After 60 rolls, the frequencies were as shown below:

Die Face	Frequency
1	5
2	8
3	12
4	6
5	10
6	19
Total:	60

a. Find the relative frequency of each outcome.
b. Is the relative frequency of the occurrence of 6 equal to the probability of rolling a 6? Why?
c. Make a relative frequency histogram of the data for 60 rolls.
d. Sketch what you think the relative frequency histogram might look like if you rolled the die 600 times. If it were rolled 6,000 times.

5. Suppose that 12% of U.S. households include four or more children. You select a random sample of 400 families and record the number of children in each household. The results are shown below.

Number of Children	Frequency
0	60
1	88
2	132
3	80
4 or more	40
Total:	400

a. What is the relative frequency of four or more children in the sample of households?
b. What is the probability of selecting a family with four or more children from the whole U.S. population?
c. Explain why the answers to parts **a** and **b** differ.

6. A newly formed consulting firm is preparing its first presentation to a prospective client. One member of the team says, "We have better than a 50% chance of making this sale." Why does this statement represent a personal probability, rather than a relative frequency probability?

7. An automobile salesperson claims to have a 20% chance of selling no cars today, a 50% chance of selling one car, and a 40% chance of selling two or more cars. Comment on the salesperson's knowledge of probability.

8. For Exercise 7, define a sample event and a compound event.

9. A random experiment involves selecting an item from an assembly line and counting the number of defects. Suppose that the number of defects can vary between 0 and 5.
   a. Is the event of one defect a simple event or a compound event?
   b. Define the complementary event to finding one defect.

10. We say that a probability is a fixed and nonchanging number between 0 and 1. Given that definition, why doesn't the relative frequency of an event generally equal the probability of the event?

4.3 Picturing Probabilities: Introduction to the Probability Tree

In Chapter 3 you learned how to develop cross-tabs tables to cross-classify groups using two attributes or variables. We now extend the cross-tabs table to the joint probability table and construct probability trees. Probability trees help to visualize probabilities. By the end of this section you should be able to:

Chapter 4 Basic Probability Concepts: The Study of Randomness

1. explain how the cross-tabs table and the joint probability table are similar and how they are different;
2. draw a probability tree from a joint probability table and vice versa; and
3. interpret the probabilities of a joint probability table or probability tree.

In Chapter 3, a 2 × 2 cross-tabs table for two categorical variables—productivity and job switching—was presented for 36 work groups. It is reproduced here.

Joint Probability Table

We can transform the cross-tabs frequency data in Table 4.1 into joint probabilities by simply dividing each entry by the total sample size, 36. The resulting numbers are between 0 and 1 and are shown in Table 4.2.

The four probabilities within the body of Table 4.2 are called **joint probabilities**. Let event A be a low-productivity group. Let event B be a group that does not switch jobs. Define a particular compound event as a group with low productivity and no job switching. From Table 4.2, that joint probability is .361. The joint probability is .50 that a work group will have high productivity and will switch jobs.

> A joint probability is the probability of the compound event, event A and event B. The joint probability of the compound event A and B is expressed as $P(A \text{ AND } B)$.

Table 4.1
Cross-Tabs Table for Productivity and Job Switching Data

	No Job Switching	Job Switching	
Low Productivity	13	4	17
High Productivity	1	18	19
	14	22	36

Table 4.2
Joint Probability Table for Productivity and Job Switching Data

	No Job Switching	Job Switching	
Low Productivity	.361	.111	.472
High Productivity	.028	.500	.528
	.389	.611	1.000

Table 4.1 is based on 36 work groups. Since there are only 36 work groups in COMCEL's Norcross plant, the sample equals the entire population. When cross-tabs tables are based on the entire population, frequency counts convert directly to joint probabilities. When cross-tabs tables are based on a portion of the population, dividing the frequency counts by 36 produces joint relative frequencies, which are only *estimates* of joint probabilities.

Probability Tree Diagram

We can use the joint probability table, Table 4.2, to build a probability tree as shown in Figure 4.2. In this case, it does not make any difference which categorical variable is placed near the top of the tree—productivity or job switching. In Figure 4.2, the productivity variable has been placed closer to the top of the tree. The two boxes are labelled low productivity and high productivity. For each level of productivity we draw two more boxes that represent no job switching and job switching. Thus there are four *end boxes* at the bottom of the tree.

Insert the following joint probabilities from Table 4.2 into the four end boxes of the probability tree.

Not switching jobs AND having low productivity	.361
Switching jobs AND having low productivity	.111
Not switching jobs AND having high productivity	.028
Switching jobs AND having high productivity	.500

FIGURE 4.2 Partially Completed Probability Tree for Productivity and Job Switching Data

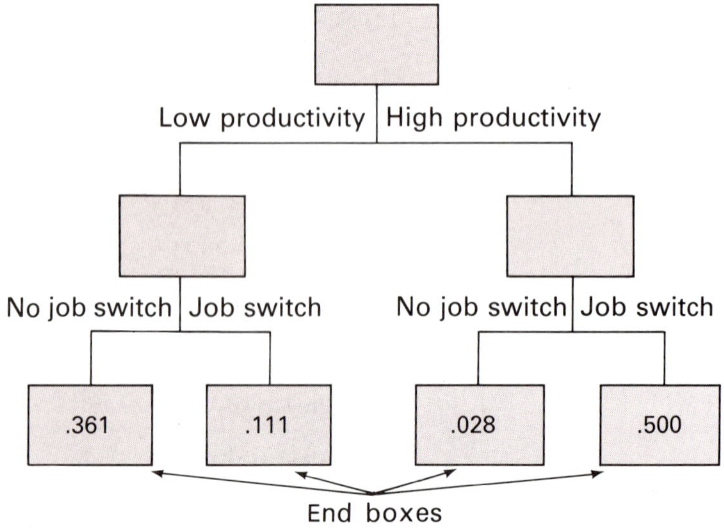

The four joint probabilities sum to 1.0, because these are the only four possible joint events. That is, two levels of productivity and two levels of job switching produce four possible events. Thus, by the second rule of probability, the four probabilities must sum to 1.0.

Now we can compute the probabilities for the remaining boxes as shown in Figure 4.3. The probability for the low-productivity box equals $.361 + .111 = .472$. The probability for the high-productivity box equals $.028 + .500 = .528$. The probability for the uppermost box equals $.472 + .528 = 1.0$, which is the sum of the probabilities of all boxes below it in the tree. Why? Please think about it before reading on.

There are two ways to be a low-productivity group:

1. Low productivity AND no job switch
2. Low productivity AND job switch

The sum of the two probabilities must be the probability of being a low-productivity group:

$$P(\text{low productivity}) = P(\text{low productivity AND no job switch}) + P(\text{low productivity AND job switch})$$

$$= .361 + .111 = .472$$

Similarly, the probability of being a high-productivity group must be the sum of the joint probabilities, $.028 + .500 = .528$.

Note that the probability of being a low-productivity or high-productivity group can also be found along the *row margins* of the joint probability table, Table 4.2.

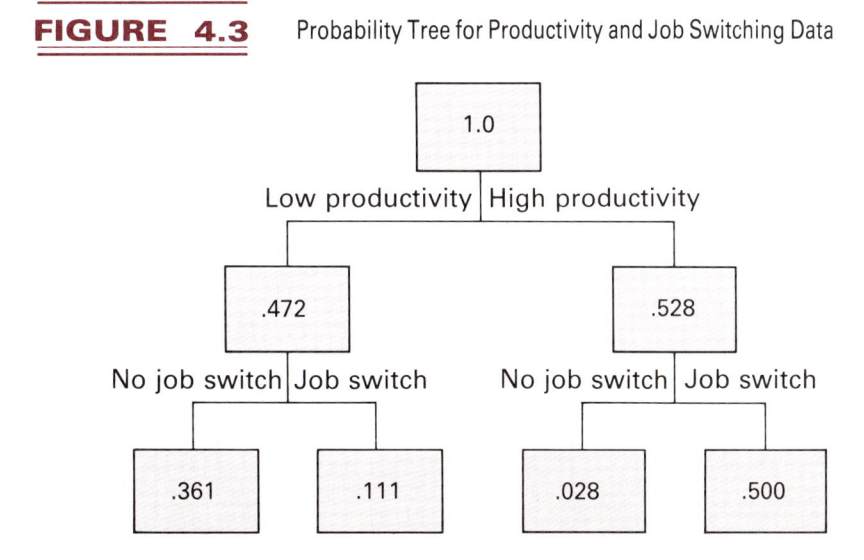

FIGURE 4.3 Probability Tree for Productivity and Job Switching Data

```
                        ┌─────┐
                        │ 1.0 │
                        └──┬──┘
           Low productivity│High productivity
              ┌────────────┴────────────┐
          ┌───┴───┐                 ┌───┴───┐
          │ .472  │                 │ .528  │
          └───┬───┘                 └───┬───┘
    No job switch│Job switch    No job switch│Job switch
         ┌──────┴──────┐           ┌─────────┴─────────┐
      ┌──┴──┐      ┌───┴──┐     ┌──┴──┐           ┌────┴──┐
      │.361 │      │ .111 │     │.028 │           │ .500  │
      └─────┘      └──────┘     └─────┘           └───────┘
```

But how can we determine the probability of job switch or the probability of no job switch from the probability tree?

There are two ways to be a no-job-switch group:

1. No job switch AND low productivity
2. No job switch AND high productivity

The sum of the two probabilities must be the probability of being a no-job-switch group:

$$P(\text{no job switch}) = P(\text{no job switch AND low productivity}) \\ + P(\text{no job switch AND high productivity})$$

$$= .361 + .028 = .389$$

Similarly, the probability of being a job-switch group must be the sum of the joint probabilities, .111 + .500 = .611. Figure 4.4 shows how the probabilities for the job-switch and no-job-switch groups are obtained from the probability tree. Please note that the probability of being a job-switch group or a no-job-switch group can also be found along the *column margins* of the joint probability table, Table 4.2.

In summary, this section has demonstrated how to convert cross-tabs tables into joint relative frequency or joint probability tables. Joint probabilities are probabilities of the compound event—event *A* AND event *B*. You can then

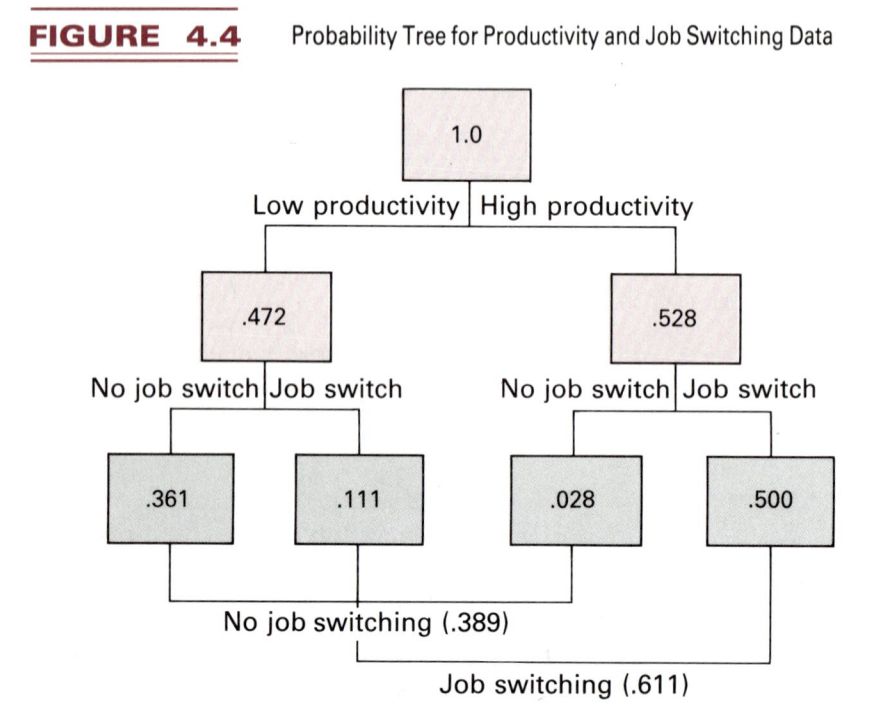

FIGURE 4.4 Probability Tree for Productivity and Job Switching Data

construct a probability tree from a joint probability table. Of course, you could convert a probability tree into a joint probability table. The probability tree helps to visualize probabilities.

SECTION 4.3 EXERCISES

1. Consider the following two categorical variables: gender and college major. Consider these four hypothetical joint probabilities:

    $$P(\text{male AND major in physical sciences}) = .35$$

    $$P(\text{male AND not major in physical sciences}) = .20$$

    $$P(\text{female AND major in physical sciences}) = .15$$

    $$P(\text{female AND not major in physical sciences}) = .30$$

    a. Construct a probability tree for the events shown. Place the gender variable higher in the tree.
    b. Find $P(\text{male})$ and $P(\text{female})$.

2. Using the joint probability information from Exercise 1, construct another tree by placing the college major variable higher in the tree. Find $P(\text{major in physical sciences})$ and $P(\text{not major in physical sciences})$.

3. Use the data from Exercise 1 to construct a joint probability table.

4. Suppose the data in Exercise 1 are based on a sample of 2,000 students. Use the data to develop a cross-tabs table.

5. A night student must decide whether to take a difficult course next term. If she gets promoted she will not be able to spend as much time studying and could get a grade of C or worse. She thinks that the probability of getting promoted and getting a grade of B or better is only .10. The probability of not getting promoted and getting a C or worse is only .05. She estimates that her overall probability of getting a B or better is .8.
    a. Construct a joint probability table from the data.
    b. What is the student's personal probability assessment that she will be promoted?

6. The day shift on a production line produced 400 units, of which 28 were defective. The night shift produced 350 items over the same time period, of which 35 were defective. The results are shown.

	Day	Night	Total
Acceptable	372	315	687
Defective	28	35	63
	400	350	750

    a. Of the 750 items produced, what percentage were defective?
    b. Of the 750 items produced, what percentage were defective and produced by the night shift?

c. What percentage of the 750 items were produced by the day shift and were acceptable? Is this percentage the same as the probability of selecting an item of output and finding that it was produced by the day shift and was acceptable? Explain.

7. A real estate company cross-classifies its 500 agents by experience and membership in the million dollar club. The results are shown.

Club Member	<2 Years	2 to 5 Years	Over 5 Years	Total
Yes	20	30	50	100
No	100	200	100	400
	120	230	150	500

a. Construct a joint probability table from the data.
b. If an agent is selected, what is the probability that the agent is a member of the million dollar club? The agent is not a member of the million dollar club and has more than 5 years' experience? The agent is a member of the million dollar club and has less than 2 years' experience?
c. Construct a probability tree from the joint probability table.

8. We wish to study two categorical variables: type of leadership (participative or autocratic) and level of employee morale (high or low). We have cross-classified 180 employees by type of leadership and level of morale and developed the following probability tree.

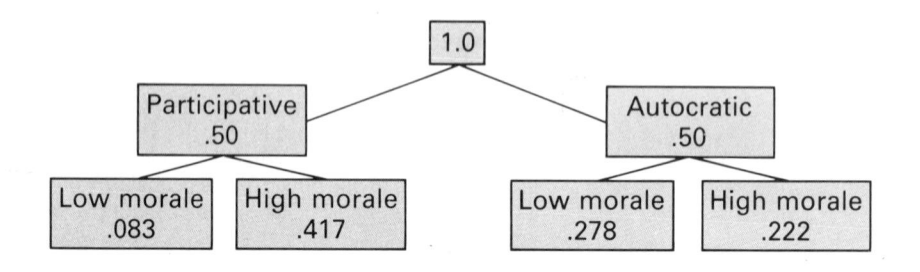

```
                            1.0
                    ┌────────┴────────┐
            Participative          Autocratic
                .50                   .50
            ┌────┴────┐           ┌────┴────┐
       Low morale  High morale  Low morale  High morale
          .083       .417         .278        .222
```

a. Develop a cross-tabs table from the probability tree.
b. Develop a joint probability table from the probability tree.

9. Using the data in Exercise 8, redraw the tree so that the morale variable is nearer the top of the tree.

10. We are preparing to develop a probability tree that represents methods of financing a car purchase and the cost of the car. What, if anything, is wrong with the following cross-classification?

Type of Financing	Cost of Car
Installment loan of 36 months or less	Less than $10,000
Installment loan of more than 36 months	$10,000 to under $25,000
	More than $25,000

4.4 Joint and Union Probabilities

Thus far in the discussion of compound events, we have focused solely on joint probabilities. They use the logical connector AND. Recall that joint probabilities are found at the end boxes of the probability tree. In this section we introduce another type of compound event, event *A* OR event *B*. By the end of this section you should be able to:

1. explain in your own words what a union probability is;
2. distinguish between joint and union probabilities;
3. determine union probabilities from a probability tree; and
4. explain the addition rule that relates joint and union probabilities.

Union Probability: Combining Two Events Using OR

The probability of event *A or* event *B* is called a union probability. Both union and joint probabilities are probabilities of compound events. So how are they different?

Begin by computing the union probability,

$$P(\text{low productivity OR no job switch})$$

In Table 4.3 are listed the joint events taken from the four end boxes of Figure 4.4. We then determine how many of the joint events are part of the union event—low productivity OR no job switch. The compound event—low productivity OR no job switch—is the sum of the probabilities for the first three joint events. The only joint event that is not part of the union event is where neither event happened—the fourth joint event.

From Figure 4.4, the union probability of low productivity OR no job switch is

$$P(\text{low productivity OR no job switch}) = P(\text{low productivity AND no job switch})$$
$$+ P(\text{low productivity AND job switch})$$
$$+ P(\text{high productivity AND no job switch})$$

$$= .361 + .111 + .028 = .500$$

Table 4.3

Joint and Union Events Table

Joint Events	Is Joint Event a Part of the Union Event, Low Productivity OR No Job Switch?
Low productivity AND no job switch	Yes, both events happened.
Low productivity AND job switch	Yes, first event happened.
High productivity AND no job switch	Yes, second event happened.
High productivity AND job switch	No, neither event happened.

Use Table 4.3 to compute P(high productivity OR job switch). This is the probability of selecting either a high-productivity group or a group whose members switch jobs. You should obtain .111 + .028 + .500 = .639.

In summary, a union event includes joint events where only event A happened, only event B happened, or both events happened.

Here's another way to compute the union probability. Expression (4.4) is called the *addition rule*.

$$P(A \text{ OR } B) = P(A) + P(B) - P(A \text{ AND } B) \qquad (4.4)$$

Verify it by recomputing P(low productivity OR no job switch). Use Figure 4.4 or Table 4.2 to obtain the three necessary probabilities.

$$P(\text{low productivity OR no job switch}) = P(\text{low productivity}) + P(\text{no job switch})$$
$$- P(\text{low productivity AND no job switch})$$
$$= .472 + .389 - .361$$
$$= .500$$

Note that we obtain the same answer as when Table 4.3 was used.

Why does the addition rule work? From Figure 4.4, note that P(low productivity) equals .361 + .111. Also note that P(no job switch) equals .361 + .028. Thus when these two probabilities were added, the joint probability—P(low productivity AND no job switching) = .361—appeared twice. Therefore we must subtract it once to correct for the double counting.

SECTION 4.4 EXERCISES

1. Consider the following probability tree that represents the two categorical variables: level of inflation and method for valuing inventories.

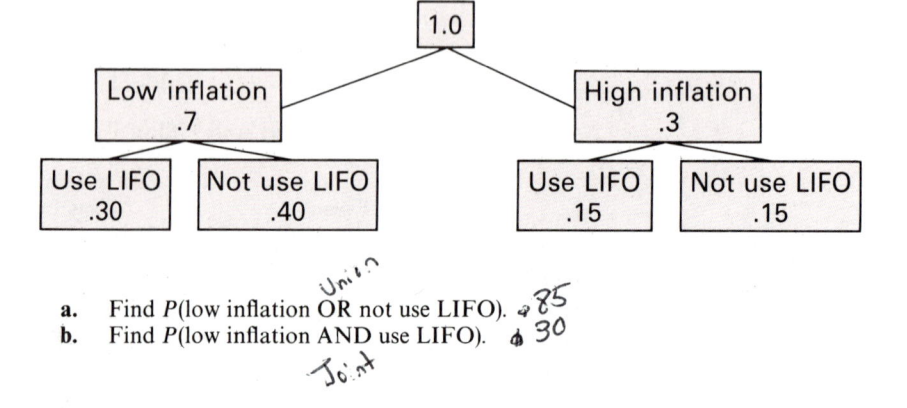

```
                    ┌─────┐
                    │ 1.0 │
                    └─────┘
           ┌───────────┴───────────┐
    ┌─────────────┐         ┌──────────────┐
    │Low inflation│         │High inflation│
    │     .7      │         │      .3      │
    └─────────────┘         └──────────────┘
      ┌─────┴─────┐             ┌─────┴─────┐
  ┌────────┐ ┌────────────┐ ┌────────┐ ┌────────────┐
  │Use LIFO│ │Not use LIFO│ │Use LIFO│ │Not use LIFO│
  │  .30   │ │    .40     │ │  .15   │ │    .15     │
  └────────┘ └────────────┘ └────────┘ └────────────┘
```

   a. Find P(low inflation OR not use LIFO).
   b. Find P(low inflation AND use LIFO).

2. A company has cross-tabulated its 350 employees by line/staff position and gender. The results are shown.

	Male	Female	Total
Line	40	10	50
Staff	230	70	300
	270	80	350

a. Construct a probability tree from the data. Place the gender variable nearer the top of the tree.
b. If one person is selected, what is the probability that the person is female and has a line position?
c. How many of the four joint events are members of the union event—male or a staff person?
d. Use the probability tree to determine the union probability in part c.
e. Use the addition rule to obtain the union probability in part d.

3. A restaurant has collected data on its customers' orders. They report that 30% had coffee only, 50% had dessert only, and 20% had both coffee and dessert.
a. Construct a probability tree.
b. What is the probability of a person ordering coffee?
c. What is the probability of a person ordering neither coffee nor dessert?
d. What is the probability of a person ordering coffee or dessert?

4. Suppose that a product manager estimates the following subjective probabilities for different levels of profit for a new product:

Event	Probability
Profit of $100,000 or more	.40
Profit of $50,000 or more but less than $100,000	.20
Profit of $0 or more but less than $50,000	.10
Loss of more than $0 but less than $50,000	.05
Loss of $50,000 or more but less than $100,000	.10
Loss of $100,000 or more	.15

a. What is the simple probability of making a profit of $100,000 or more?
b. What is the probability of losing $50,000 or more?
c. Explain how the probability in part b is a union probability.
d. What is the probability of making a profit of $100,000 or more and a loss of $100,000 or more on this product?
e. Explain how the probability in part d is a joint probability.

4.5 Conditional Probabilities and Statistical Independence

Thus far, in discussing simple events we have focused solely on simple probabilities, such as P(low productivity) or P(no job switch). In this section we introduce another probability for simple events, the conditional probability. By the end of this section you should be able to:

1. distinguish between conditional probability and unconditional, or simple, probability; and
2. explain, in your own words, what statistical independence is.

Conditional Probability

Here are three sets of statements describing probabilities regarding the job switching and productivity data example we have been using:

1. Select one team. Given no other additional information, what is the probability that it is a high-productivity group?
2. Select one team. Before assessing its probability of being a high-productivity group, we tell you that the members often switch jobs.
3. Select one team. Before assessing its probability of being a high-productivity group, we tell you that the group's mean shoe size is 7C.

All three statements describe probabilities of a simple, or single, event—a high-productivity group. What is different about the three statements? In the last two statements additional information about the group has been provided. The first statement provides no additional information. The first statement describes a **simple** or **unconditional probability**. The last two statements describe **conditional probabilities**. A conditional probability is the probability of a simple event, event A, given that event B is known. Event B in statement 2 is that team members switch jobs. Event B in statement 3 is that the mean shoe size is 7C. Following are the three statements translated into probability notation:

> The probability of event A is a simple probability and is denoted by $P(A)$.
>
> The conditional probability of event A given that event B is known is denoted by $P(A \mid B)$.

1. Simple probability P(high productivity)
2. Conditional probability P(high productivity | members switch jobs)
3. Conditional probability P(high productivity | mean shoe size is 7C)

From Figure 4.4 we can readily determine that the simple probability of being a high-productivity group is P(high productivity) = .528.

Section 4.6 will show how to use Figure 4.4 to determine conditional probabilities. But for now, use logic to approximate them. *Warning:* Logic is not a substitute for determining conditional probabilities from actual data. However, logic will help to intuitively understand the concept of statistical independence, which we will present shortly.

As mentioned before, the probability of being a high-productivity group is .528. Given in statement 2 that team members switch jobs, doesn't it seem logical that the conditional probability of being a high-productivity group should be higher than .528? That is,

P(high productivity | team members switch jobs) > .528

Exactly how much higher is not yet clear. But logically we expect it to be higher because groups whose members switch jobs may be more motivated, more knowledgeable about the group's jobs, and thus have higher productivities.

In statement 3, we are told that the team members of the high-productivity group have a mean shoe size of 7C. What would you logically say is the conditional probability of being a high-productivity group with this fact in mind? Think about it before reading on.

Presumably, you wouldn't change the probability figure of .528 upon knowing that the group's mean shoe size is 7C. After all, a team's mean shoe size should not affect its productivity. Thus, one might logically conclude that

$$P(\text{high productivity} \mid \text{mean shoe size is 7C}) = .528$$

So what has been learned? We have logically concluded that productivity and mean shoe size of 7C are *statistically independent* events. Knowing that event B happened did not cause us to revise the original simple probability of .528. We have also concluded that productivity and job switching are *statistically dependent* events. That is, the conditional probability is no longer .528.

Probability revision means that we believe that the two events, A and B, are statistically dependent. When event B is pertinent information, we should increase or decrease the simple probability. When the information is irrelevant, we do not revise the simple probability. The two events are statistically independent.

Statistical Independence and Dependence

> Events that are statistically independent are not related to one another and do not affect each other. Events that are statistically dependent are related to one another and the occurrence of one event affects the probability of the occurrence of the other event.

Two events can be **statistically independent** or **dependent**. The following table distinguishes independent and dependent events.

Independent Events	Dependent Events
$P(A \mid B) = P(A)$	$P(A \mid B) \neq P(A)$
The probability of the occurrence of A does not change if event B is known.	The probability of the occurrence of A changes if event B is known.
$P(B \mid A) = P(B)$	$P(B \mid A) \neq P(B)$
The probability of the occurrence of B does not change if event A is known.	The probability of the occurrence of B changes if event A is known.

When the conditional probability, $P(A \mid B)$, and simple probability, $P(A)$, are equal, event B is independent of event A. Knowing event B does not affect the probability that A occurs.

On the other hand, when the conditional and simple probabilities are *not* the same, then knowing event A or event B will cause us to revise the probability that the other will occur.

In summary, conditional and simple probabilities deal with a simple event. Conditional probabilities are denoted as $P(A \mid B)$, the probability of event A given that we know event B. If $P(A \mid B)$ does not equal the simple probability, $P(A)$, then events A and B are statistically dependent. In this section we have surmised statistical independence using logic and intuition. But in real-world situations logic and intuition are usually not enough. We must calculate conditional probabilities to establish statistical independence.

SECTION 4.5 EXERCISES

1. What does it mean to say that two events are statistically independent?
2. Given the following list of events, indicate whether you think the events A and B are likely to be independent or dependent.
   a. A = A two-spot face comes up on the first roll of a die.
      B = A two-spot face comes up on the second roll of a die.
   b. A = Accountant wears a red tie to work.
      B = Accountant passes CPA examination.
   c. A = Person enjoys work.
      B = Person does good work.
   d. A = Person owns place of residence.
      B = Person will pay credit card bills on time.
   e. A = Person has missed payments three times in the last six months.
      B = Person will pay credit card bill this month.
   f. A = Percentage of defects produced by the plant exceeds standard.
      B = Percentage of defects produced by less experienced workers exceeds standard.
3. A marketing organization varies its advertising among different zip codes to reflect differences in family income levels. Consider the following marketing research questions and state whether each suggests a simple, conditional, or joint probability.
   a. How many BMW 733s can we sell to families if their annual incomes are in excess of $100,000?
   b. How many potential car buyers are there who want a BMW 733 and have the $50,000 to pay for it?
   c. How many BMW 733s can we sell to the 50,000 families in this area?
4. Assume that the level of pollutants in the air depends on whether power is generated from coal-burning plants. Let:

   A_1 = Level of pollutants below Environmental Protection Agency standards

   A_2 = Level of pollutants above standards

   B_1 = Coal-burning plants used

   B_2 = Coal-burning plants not used

   a. Suppose $P(A_2) = .20$. Using only logic, would you estimate $P(A_2 | B_1)$ to be less than, equal to, or greater than .20? Explain.
   b. Explain why we cannot rely merely on logic to estimate the desired conditional probability.
5. Assume that the franchise fee is independent of the number of franchises that are currently operating. Let:

   A_1 = Franchise fee > $15,000

A_2 = Franchise fee ≤ $15,000

B_1 = Number of franchises > 2,000

B_2 = Number of franchises ≤ 2,000

Suppose $P(A_1 | B_1) = .45$. Using only logic, would you estimate that $P(A_1)$ is less than, equal to, or greater than .45?

4.6 Computing Conditional Probabilities

In the business world, we do not use logic or intuition to determine statistical dependence; we compute conditional probabilities. Why is it important to know whether two variables are statistically related? It is because managers are always looking for relationships between variables. For example, is job switching related to productivity? Does gender affect promotional status? Does advertising affect sales? Does serving internships during college help students obtain the jobs they want? By the end of this section you should be able to:

1. compute conditional probabilities using a probability tree and determine whether two events are statistically dependent;
2. distinguish between conditional and joint probabilities; and
3. explain in your own words how conditional probabilities are similar to and different from row or column percentage tables.

We continue to use the job switching and productivity data in this section. Recall from the previous section that logic was used to argue that the probability of high productivity, given that members switch jobs, should be greater than .528. Now use expression (4.5) to compute the desired conditional probability.

$$P(A | B) = \frac{P(A \text{ AND } B)}{P(B)} \quad (4.5)$$

Let event A = high productivity and event B = switch jobs. Then

$$P(\text{high productivity} | \text{switch jobs}) = \frac{P(\text{high productivity AND switch jobs})}{P(\text{switch jobs})}$$

The probability tree, Figure 4.4, provides the desired joint and simple probabilities. The simple probability of switching jobs is .611, which is the denominator for expression (4.5). The joint probability of high productivity and job switching is .500 (see the end box), which is the numerator of expression (4.5). Thus,

$$P(\text{high productivity} | \text{switch jobs}) = \frac{.500}{.611} = .818$$

There are two important observations. First, the calculated conditional probability is greater than .528. The data support our intuition. Second, the conditional probability of .818 is different from the unconditional probability of .528 of being a high-productivity group. Thus, high productivity and job switching are statistically dependent events.

Why does expression (4.5) work? What is the logic behind it? Although expression (4.5) deals with probabilities, we can understand its logic by studying the cross-tabs table, Table 4.1. The denominator of expression (4.5) focuses on event B—namely, groups whose members switch jobs. How many groups switch jobs? From Table 4.1, there are 22 such groups. Thus the denominator of expression (4.5) is 22/36. The numerator focuses on groups that switch jobs and have high productivity. How many of the 22 groups also had high productivity? Look at the job switching column of Table 4.1. Note that of the 22 groups, 18 also had high productivity. Thus the numerator of expression (4.5) is 18/36. Therefore, the conditional probability of having high productivity given that a group switches jobs is 18/36 divided by 22/36, or .818.

One additional example is presented to demonstrate how to calculate conditional probabilities from data.

EXAMPLE: INTERNSHIPS AND THE HIRING DECISION CASE   Does *serving internships* during college help graduates obtain their *desired jobs* upon graduation? That is, is the simple probability of obtaining a desired job the same as the conditional probability of obtaining a desired job given that the student had an internship? The placement officer has collected data on 500 students over the past 5 years. He recorded whether they had internships and whether they got their desired jobs upon graduation.

Table 4.4 is the joint probability table based on a sample size of 500 students. In the sample, 38% of the students had no internships *and* did not get their desired jobs; 28% had internships *and* did get their desired jobs.

Now we can build a probability tree. In this case, it makes no difference which categorical variable we place higher in the tree. In Figure 4.5, the internship variable is placed higher. We encourage you to build a different tree by placing the desired job event higher in the tree. Then it can be used to check the following calculations. The four joint probabilities have been inserted into the end boxes to complete the tree.

The simple probability of getting a desired job is

$$P(\text{desired job}) = .28 + .32 = .60$$

Table 4.4

Joint Probability Table

	No Internship	Internship	Total
No Desired Job	.38	.02	.40
Desired Job	.32	.28	.60
	.70	.30	1.00

FIGURE 4.5 Probability Tree for Internship and Desired Job Data

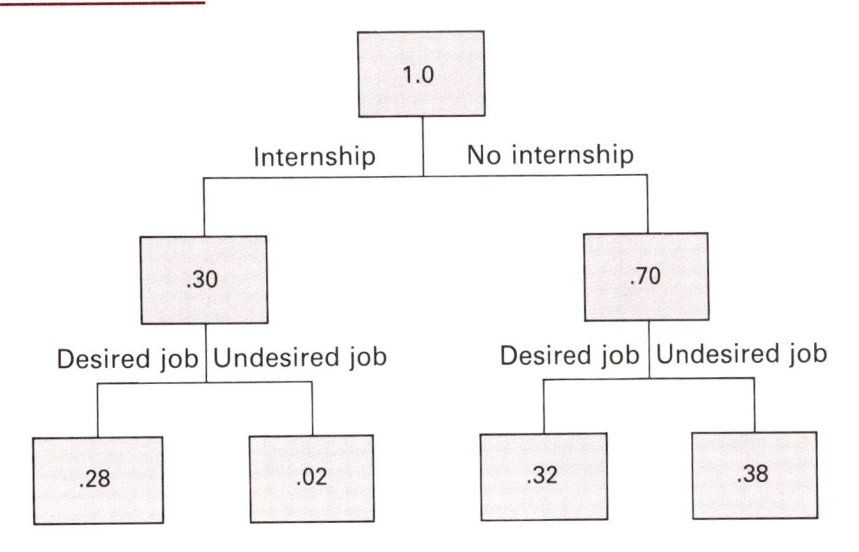

```
                    1.0
                   /   \
            Internship  No internship
                /           \
              .30           .70
            /    \         /    \
     Desired  Undesired  Desired  Undesired
       job      job       job       job
       .28      .02       .32       .38
```

Does an internship increase the probability of getting a desired job? If the conditional probability, $P(\text{desired job} \mid \text{internship})$, is still .60, then having an internship has no effect on getting a desired job. Now use expression (4.5) to compute the conditional probability:

$$P(A \mid B) = \frac{P(A \text{ AND } B)}{P(B)}$$

$$P(\text{desired job} \mid \text{internship}) = \frac{P(\text{desired job AND internship})}{P(\text{internship})} = \frac{.28}{.30} = .933$$

The denominator for expression (4.5) is $P(\text{internship})$, or .30. The numerator, the joint probability of getting the desired job and having an internship, is .28. The result yields a conditional probability of .933.

The conditional probability strongly suggests that internships do increase students' chances of getting desired jobs, because the conditional and unconditional probabilities of getting a desired job are very different. The chance of getting a desired job increases from .60 to .933 if students have had an internship. Thus, having an internship and getting a desired job are statistically related events.

Distinguishing Between Conditional and Joint Probabilities

It is easy to distinguish between a simple probability, $P(A)$, and a joint probability, $P(A \text{ AND } B)$. But differentiating between joint and conditional probabilities is more difficult. A joint probability is the probability of two or more events, A and B, happening. A conditional probability is the probability of a simple, or single, event A, given that we know event B happened.

Two statements are given here. One statement is a joint probability and the other is a conditional probability. Which is which and why?

1. The probability of selecting a person over 35 years old who favors increased spending on the environment
2. The probability of selecting a person who favors increased spending on the environment if he or she is over 35 years old

Statement 1 is the joint probability. It is a joint probability because two events describe the person—over 35 years old *and* in favor of increased spending. Statement 2 is a conditional probability because we are interested only in a simple event—a person who favors increased spending. However, we already know event B about the person—the person is over 35 years old.

In summary, joint probabilities deal with two or more events. Conditional probabilities deal with only one event, A, where we are given a second piece of information by way of another event, B.

Conditional Probabilities and Row or Column Percentage Tables

Conditional probabilities have been introduced before, although not in the same terms. We first presented them in the discussion of row and column percentage tables in Chapter 3. Row and column percentages are similar to conditional probabilities in the following respect.

Return to the job productivity and job switching data. First use Figure 4.4 to compute the following four conditional probabilities where event B is the level of job switching:

$$P(\text{low productivity} \mid \text{no job switch}) = \frac{.361}{.389} = .929$$

$$P(\text{high productivity} \mid \text{no job switch}) = \frac{.028}{.389} = .071$$

$$P(\text{low productivity} \mid \text{job switch}) = \frac{.111}{.611} = .182$$

$$P(\text{high productivity} \mid \text{job switch}) = \frac{.500}{.611} = .818$$

Now note that these four conditional probabilities are similar to the column percentages in Table 3.7 (page 107). One difference is that percentages are numbers between 0 and 100, and probabilities are numbers between 0 and 1. A second difference is that column percentages, which are based on a sample of the population, are only estimates of the true conditional probabilities.

Please verify that the four conditional probabilities where event B is the level of productivity are similar to the row percentages in Table 3.8.

Chapter 4 Basic Probability Concepts: The Study of Randomness

SECTION 4.6 EXERCISES

1. Decide whether each of the following is a conditional or a joint probability:
   a. The probability of selecting a promoted male   J
   b. The probability of selecting a male if the person has been promoted   C
   c. The probability of selecting an individual with high cholesterol if you already know that the person eats eggs six times a week   C
   d. The probability of selecting a six-times-a-week egg eater with high cholesterol   J

2. Consider the following probability tree:

   ```
                         1.0
              ┌───────────┴───────────┐
        Hospital bed occupied    Hospital bed not occupied
              .40                      .60
          ┌────┴────┐              ┌────┴────┐
        Urban    Rural           Urban    Rural
        .25      .15              .20      .40
   ```

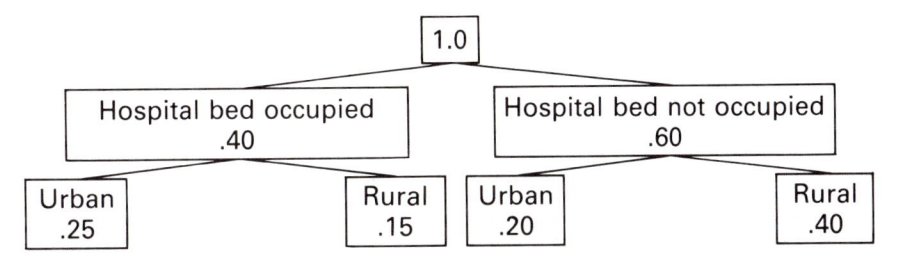

   a. Calculate P(bed occupied | urban county).
   b. Calculate P(bed not occupied | rural county).
   c. Are the events—hospital bed occupied and location of county—statistically independent?

3. Consider the following probability tree:

   ```
                         1.0
              ┌───────────┴───────────┐
       Inflation greater than 5%   Inflation less than or equal to 5%
              .2                         .8
          ┌────┴────┐              ┌────┴────┐
       ≤ 75 bank  > 75 bank      ≤ 75 bank  > 75 bank
       failures   failures       failures   failures
        .08        .12            .32        .48
   ```

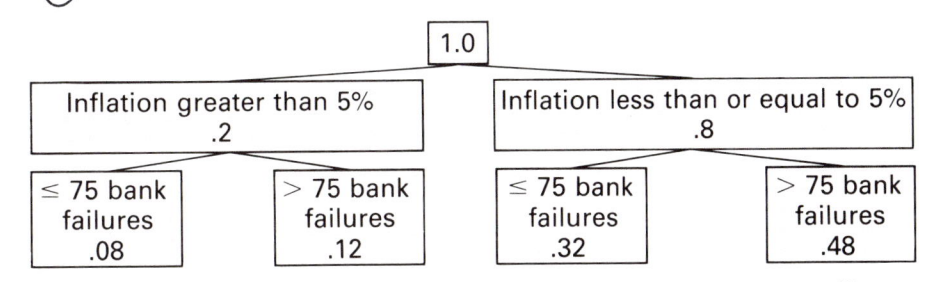

   a. Calculate P(inflation greater than 5% | ≤ 75 bank failures). .20 Pg 183
   b. Calculate P(> 75 bank failures | inflation rate less than or equal to 5%). .60
   c. Are the events—inflation rate > 5% and number of bank failures > 75—statistically independent? Independent
   d. Convert the probability tree into a joint probability table.

4. A major bank wishes to distinguish between good and bad credit risks. One variable the bank thinks might be related to credit worthiness is whether the applicant has worked for the same company for 5 years or more. The following joint probability (relative frequency) table was estimated based on the bank's experience with existing clients.

		Client Company Affiliation		
		<5 years	≥5 years	
Credit	Good	.25	.60	.85
	Bad	.10	.05	.15
		.35	.65	1.00

a. Determine the unconditional probability that an account will be a bad risk account.
b. Calculate the conditional probability that an account will be a bad risk if the applicant has worked for a company less than 5 years.
c. Are the events "Account will be bad" and "Applicant worked for the same company less than 5 years" statistically independent? Explain.

5. The following table shows the results of a sample of 200 students cross-classified on two variables: internship—yes or no—and grade point average—under 3.0 or 3.0 and above.

	Internship	No Internship	Total
Under 3.0	20	30	50
3.0 and Above	60	90	150
	80	120	200

a. Use these sample data to estimate the probability of an internship.
b. Estimate P(an internship | grade point average under 3.0).
c. Are the events in part **b** statistically independent?

6. Consider two variables: studied for exam—yes or no—and partied—yes or no. Based on historical data, we know the following three probabilities:

$$P(\text{studied}) = .40$$

$$P(\text{partied}) = .42$$

$$P(\text{partied} | \text{studied}) = .75$$

a. Construct a probability tree. Place the studied variable nearer the top of the tree.
b. Compute P(studied | partied).
c. Compute P(not studied | not partied).

4.7 Using Probability Trees to Minimize Managerial Judgment Errors

Managers have difficulties making judgments involving probability data. Their judgments are often plagued by inconsistency and systematic error. One source of error is that managers use rules of thumb. Probability trees can be used by managers to minimize such errors. By the end of this unit you should be able to:

1. explain in your own words the errors of *ignoring the base rate* and *noncoherency*;
2. construct a probability tree from unconditional and conditional probabilities; and
3. explain the logic of the two general principles of constructing probability trees.

A rule of thumb helps us to arrive at a judgment about some event or to make a decision. It serves to simplify making judgments. We all use rules of thumb. For example, in the child's game of tic-tac-toe, we learned that whoever goes first should place an X in the center square. This rule of thumb makes it difficult to lose the game. As another example, suppose you must develop a food expense budget for next year. You could develop 365 daily meal plans and then price them out. Or you could use the following rule of thumb: Take last year's food expenses and multiply by an inflation factor.

Rules of thumb are useful and they do simplify judgment making in some situations. However, they can also cause us to make mistakes in others. Fortunately, you can use the probability tree to help minimize some of the most common errors that managers make when using probability data.

The Error of Overlooking the Base Rate

Managers often use probability information poorly. They tend to develop rules of thumb based entirely on conditional probabilities and ignore unconditional probabilities or base rate information. The following example illustrates the error of overlooking the base rate data.

EXAMPLE: SEISMIC TESTING CASE   Before a well is drilled, oil companies often conduct seismic tests to determine if there is oil. They drill a hole in the ground, insert a dynamite charge, and detonate it. The sonic waves indicate whether oil is present or not. An *open structure* means that either oil, water, or air is present. A *closed structure* tends to rule out oil.

ABC Oil has drilled over 100 wells in a west Texas site. It has determined that the probability of finding oil at a given site is 20%. Furthermore, of those wells where oil was found, 70% had an open structure seismic test. Of those wells where oil was not found, 75% had a closed structure.

Estimate within 10% the chance of finding oil given that a site has an open structure.

Many managers would estimate the probability at between 70% and 80% because they are influenced solely by the 70% and 75% figures in the example. They formulate a rule of thumb that uses only the conditional probabilities and **ignore the base rate data**—the unconditional probability of finding oil, the 20% figure.

The rule of thumb given in the margin generates poor probability estimates. Instead we will use a probability tree to determine the probability of finding oil, given an open structure. The example deals with two categorical variables—presence of oil and seismic test results. Begin by dividing each variable into mutually exclusive and exhaustive levels:

The error of ignoring the base rate data occurs when managers use the following rule of thumb: When estimating probabilities, use only the conditional probabilities.

Categorical Variables	Levels
Oil found	Yes or no
Seismic test results	Open or closed

We have the following information:

1. The probability of finding oil at a site is 20%. This is an unconditional, or base rate, probability. It applies to all wells that ABC has drilled.

$$P(\text{oil found}) = .20$$

2. Of those wells where oil was found, 70% had an open structure. This is a conditional probability. We focus on *only* that *subset* of wells where oil was found.

$$P(\text{open structure} \mid \text{oil found}) = .70$$

3. Of those wells where oil was not found, 75% had a closed structure. This is also a conditional probability.

$$P(\text{closed structure} \mid \text{no oil found}) = .75$$

Until now, it made no difference which categorical variable we placed closer to the top of the probability tree. Is this still true? Before reading on, try constructing a probability tree in which the seismic test results—open or closed—are the first entries in the tree. You will find that you do not have enough information to fill in the probability boxes.

Now, draw the tree in which the results—oil or no oil—are the first data entered. You do have the unconditional probability data for these first entries—namely, the .20 and .80 base rate figures, as shown in Figure 4.6.

OIL ENTRIES   Next, consider the conditional probabilities. Of those wells where oil was found, 70% had an open structure. Simply multiply .20 · .70 to find the joint probability (.14) of having an open structure AND finding oil.

FIGURE 4.6   Probability Tree for Seismic Study: Base Rate Data Only

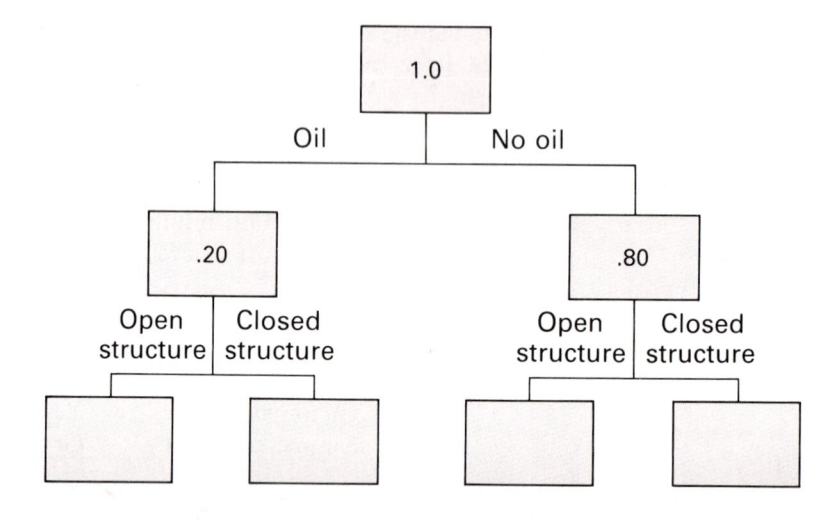

Insert the .14 figure into the end box that represents an open structure and oil found. The joint probability of finding oil AND having a closed seismic structure must then be .06.

Why do we multiply the .20 and .70 probabilities to get the joint probability? Please think about it before reading on!

The conditional probability expression (4.5) is used to calculate the joint probability by rewriting it in the form of expression (4.6). In this form it is called the *multiplication rule*:

$$P(A|B) = \frac{P(A \text{ AND } B)}{P(B)} \tag{4.5}$$

$$P(A \text{ AND } B) = P(A|B)P(B) \tag{4.6}$$

We can use the multiplication rule to determine the joint probability of an open structure and finding oil:

$$P(\text{open structure} | \text{oil found}) \cdot P(\text{oil found}) = .70 \cdot .20 = .14$$

That's why we multiplied the two probabilities.

NO OIL ENTRIES   Of those wells where oil was not found, 75% had a closed structure. In other words, 75% of the 80% that had no oil also had a closed structure. Therefore, the joint probability of having a closed structure AND finding no oil is .75 · .80 = .60. Insert the .60 figure into the end box. The joint probability of finding no oil AND an open structure must equal .20. This completes the probability tree for the seismic study, as shown in Figure 4.7.

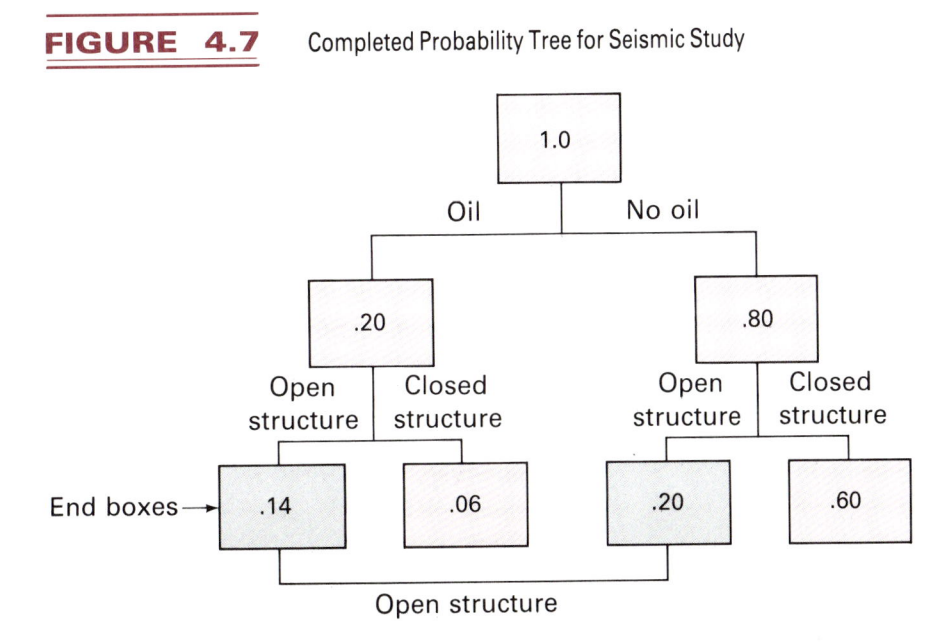

FIGURE 4.7   Completed Probability Tree for Seismic Study

Now compute the probability of finding oil given an open structure.

$$P(\text{oil found} \mid \text{open structure}) = \frac{.14}{.14 + .20} = .412$$

If you estimated that this probability would be between .70 and .75, you fell prey to the error of ignoring the base rate.

Consider a second case that illustrates the error of ignoring the base rate or unconditional probability data.

EXAMPLE: SCANNER PROBLEM CASE   A computer company uses a scanning device that places a mark on each defective chip it spots on the production line. The quality control department reports that 10% of all chips are defective. When a chip is good, the scanner correctly leaves it unmarked 90% of the time. When the chip is defective, the scanner marks it as defective 90% of the time.

Estimate within 10% the probability that a computer chip is really defective if the scanner marks it as defective.

The two categorical variables are chip quality and the result of the scanner test. Chip quality is good or defective—complementary events. The scanner results are marked defective or not marked—also complementary events.

Categorical Variables	Levels
Chip quality	Good or defective
Scanner result	Not marked or marked as defective

The categorical variable for which we have unconditional probability data, chip quality—good or defective chips—is placed closer to the top of the tree, which is shown in Figure 4.8. Ten percent of all chips are defective and 90% are good.

GOOD CHIP ENTRIES   Of the 90% good chips, 90% are not marked by the scanner. Thus the joint probability of a good chip AND not being marked is .90 · .90 = .81. Since the probability in any box must equal the sum of the probabilities below it, .09 is the joint probability of a good chip AND being marked defective.

DEFECTIVE CHIP ENTRIES   Of the 10% defective chips, 90% are marked defective by the scanner. Thus the joint probability of having a defective chip AND being marked as defective is .10 · .90 = .09. Then .01 is the joint probability of a defective chip AND not being marked. Therefore, the probability that a chip marked defective actually is defective is

$$P(\text{defective chip} \mid \text{marked defective}) = \frac{.09}{.09 + .09} = .50$$

FIGURE 4.8 Completed Probability Tree for Scanner Problem

```
                    1.0
           Good chips │ Defective chips
              .90            .10
        Not marked│Marked defective   Not marked│Marked defective
           .81        .09                .01           .09
                      └──────── Marked defective ────────┘
```

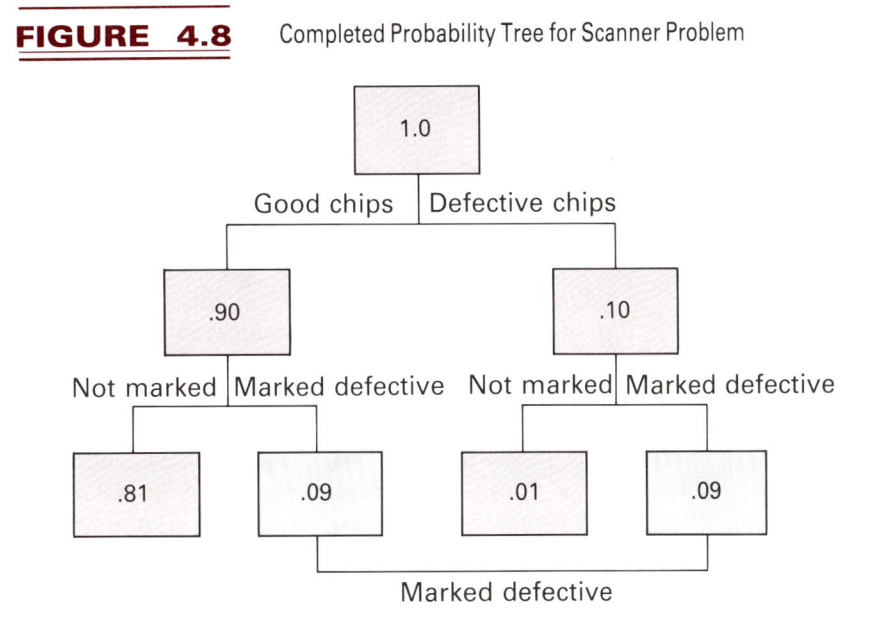

Again, if you estimated about 90%, you ignored the base rate data. By using a probability tree, you avoid the error of ignoring the base rate data.

Noncoherency Error

At the beginning of this chapter we discussed a director of planning who had made three subjective probability estimates about the future. All her estimates fell between 0 and 1. Nevertheless, all three probabilities cannot be correct. We will use a probability tree to show why.

Her three personal probability estimates are restated here:

Simple probability: $P(\text{increased conservation}) = .50$

Simple probability: $P(\text{deducting expenses}) = .60$

Conditional probability: $P(\text{increased conservation} \mid \text{deducting expenses}) = .85$

The three personal probabilities are numbers between 0 and 1. Taken together, do these three probabilities violate the two basic rules of probability? Might they imply that one or more joint probabilities are negative or greater than 1? If so, all three personal probabilities cannot be valid. Determining if joint probabilities are less than 0 or greater than 1 is very difficult by mere inspection. But we can use a probability tree.

As always, define the two categorical variables and divide them into mutually exclusive and exhaustive levels:

Categorical Variables	Levels
Increased conservation	Yes or no
Deducting expenses	Yes or no

Again, we place our base rate, or unconditional probability, data nearer the top of the tree. However, in this example there are two unconditional probabilities—*P*(increased conservation) and *P*(deducting expenses). Which categorical variable goes first? Please think about it before reading on.

We place the deducting expenses categorical variable nearer the top of the tree, as shown in Figure 4.9. Then we can use the conditional probability data (given deducting expenses) to determine the joint probabilities for the end boxes. If we place the increased conservation variable nearer the top of the tree, we cannot compute joint probabilities in this example. Try it and you'll see.

Now, we use the multiplication rule, expression (4.6). The joint probability of deducting expenses AND increased conservation is $.6 \cdot .85 = .51$. The second joint probability off the deducting branch, the probability of deducting expenses AND no increased conservation, is then $.60 - .51 = .09$. Remember, the director of planning estimated the simple probability of increased conservation as .50. Thus, the two shaded boxes must sum to .5. But that cannot be, because the third joint probability would need to equal $-.01$, which violates the first rule of probability. Therefore, the three personal probabilities are not valid. The director must change one or more personal probabilities.

FIGURE 4.9   Probability Tree for Conservation Problem

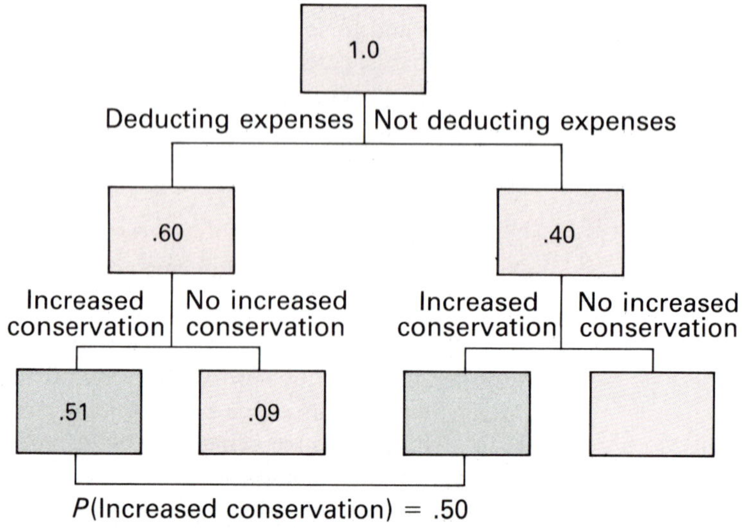

P(Increased conservation) = .50

Chapter 4 Basic Probability Concepts: The Study of Randomness

Let's consider a second case that illustrates the **noncoherency error**.

EXAMPLE: COMCEL AND THE KNOXVILLE MARKET CASE
COMCEL's senior management is discussing the possibility of entering the Knoxville, Tennessee, market. Management believes that its chance of successfully entering the market depends on whether COMCEL can develop a new communications technology that will significantly reduce its costs. The group has made the following personal probability assessments:

> Managers make the non-coherency error when they assign personal probabilities without determining whether these probabilities imply that one or more joint probabilities are less than 0 or greater than 1.

Unconditional probability: P(successful entry) = .70

Unconditional probability: P(technological breakthrough) = .20

Conditional probability: P(successful entry | technological breakthrough) = .95

Are these three probabilities valid? Do they imply that one or more of the joint probabilities are less than 0 or greater than 1? We begin by defining the categorical variables:

Categorical Variables	Levels
Successful entry into Knoxville	Yes or no
Technological breakthrough	Yes or no

Try to construct the tree before reading on. Then compare your tree to that in Figure 4.10.

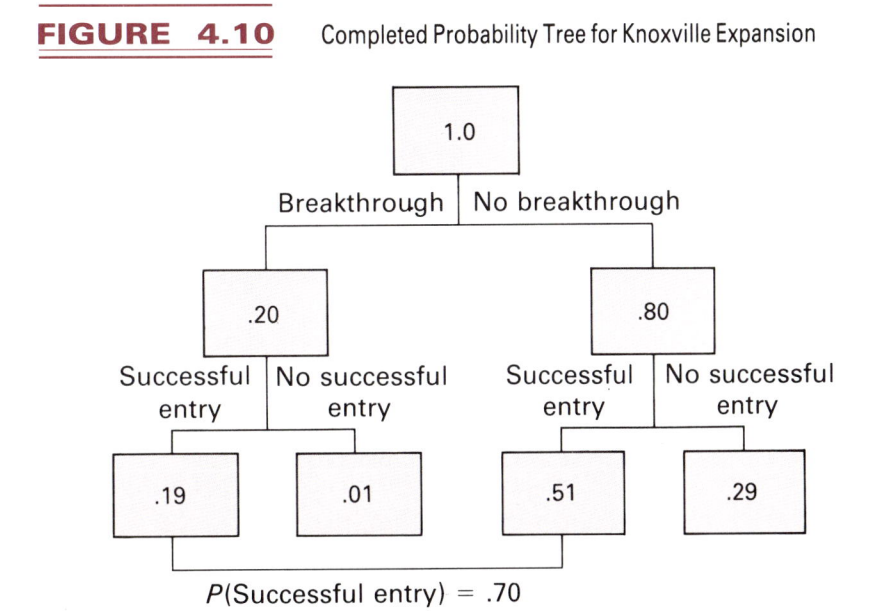

FIGURE 4.10   Completed Probability Tree for Knoxville Expansion

```
                        ┌───────┐
                        │  1.0  │
                        └───────┘
              Breakthrough │ No breakthrough
              ┌────────────┴────────────┐
           ┌─────┐                   ┌─────┐
           │ .20 │                   │ .80 │
           └─────┘                   └─────┘
      Successful│No successful  Successful│No successful
        entry   │   entry         entry   │   entry
        ┌─────┐   ┌─────┐        ┌─────┐   ┌─────┐
        │ .19 │   │ .01 │        │ .51 │   │ .29 │
        └─────┘   └─────┘        └─────┘   └─────┘
           └─────────────────────────┘
              P(Successful entry) = .70
```

Since none of the four joint probabilities is negative or greater than 1, there is no noncoherency error. Thus COMCEL can use the three probability estimates.

In summary, managers often fall prey to the errors of ignoring the base rate and noncoherency. They can use a probability tree to overcome these errors. In building a tree, place the categorical variable with known unconditional probabilities nearer the top of the tree. If the unconditional probabilities for both categorical variables are known, let event B from the estimated conditional probability dictate which categorical variable you place higher in the tree. For example, in the conservation problem, event B for the estimated conditional probability was deducting expenses. Thus we placed the deducting expenses categorical variable nearer the top of the tree. In the market entry problem, event B for the estimated conditional probability was technological breakthrough. We placed this categorical variable higher in the tree. Having constructed a probability tree, we can determine either (1) the desired conditional probability—avoiding the error of ignoring the base rate—or (2) the validity of all the personal probabilities—avoiding the noncoherency error.

SECTION 4.7 EXERCISES

1. A nationwide client survey showed that 5% of the clients were dissatisfied with the service received. Of those clients who were dissatisfied, 80% said they intended to change vendors. Of those who said they were satisfied, 90% said they did not intend to change vendors.
   a. Given the information above, what is the probability that a client from the survey list will be dissatisfied and want to change vendors?
   b. What is the probability that the person selected will be satisfied and not want to change?
   c. Construct a probability tree.
   d. Use the probability tree to find the probability that a person is dissatisfied, given that she tells you she intends to change vendors.

2. We survey firms to determine whether they use quality circles, small groups of employees who try to improve productivity, and their level of profitability. We obtain the following relative frequency-based probabilities.

$$P(\text{have quality circles}) = .10$$

$$P(\text{above average profit} \mid \text{have quality circles}) = .40$$

$$P(\text{average or below average profit} \mid \text{have no quality circles}) = .80$$

   a. Construct a probability tree.
   b. Construct a joint probability table.
   c. Calculate:

$$P(\text{have quality circles} \mid \text{above average profit})$$

$$P(\text{have quality circles} \mid \text{average or below average profit})$$

3. Three different managers were asked for their personal probabilities of events A, B, and the joint probability of A AND B. Their responses are shown. Event A is family branding and $\bar{A}$ is not family branding. Event B is 10% or less market share and $\bar{B}$ is more than 10% market share.

Manager	$P(A)$	$P(B)$	$P(A$ AND $B)$
1	.6	.4	.24
2	.8	.3	.70
3	.3	.5	0

   a. Construct a joint probability table for each set of probabilities.
   b. Are any of the sets of probabilities inconsistent or invalid?
   c. Do any of the managers think events A (family branding) and B (amount of market share) are unrelated? Explain.

4. An economist estimates that the probability that American exports will exceed imports in 1992 is .10. She also estimates that the probability that Japan will have a major recession in 1991 is .20. However, if Japan does have a major recession, she estimates that the probability that American exports will exceed imports in 1992 will increase to .50.
   a. Are the probability estimates coherent?
   b. Would the probability estimates be coherent if the economist estimated the probability that Japan will have a major recession in 1991 as .40? Assume all other probability estimates are unchanged. Explain.

5. Before the season begins, the manager of the Boston Red Sox estimates that the probability of winning the division is .65. He also estimates the probability of two new players on the team hitting 60 or more home runs is .70. Finally, he estimates that if the two new players do indeed hit 60 or more home runs, the chance of winning the division would then increase to .90.
   a. Are the probability estimates coherent?
   b. If the probability estimates are coherent, then compute the following probability:

   P(not winning the division | two new players hit less than 60 home runs)

4.8 Nonstatistical Judgment Errors

The probability tree is an effective tool for minimizing some managerial judgment errors. Managers can overcome other errors simply by knowing that they exist. We describe two common errors that managers make.

Availability Error

Please answer the following question:

Is the letter "k" more likely to be the first or third letter in an English word?

If you think that "k" is more likely to occur at the beginning of a word, you are not alone. That's how most people respond. When asked why, they usually say that they can recall more words that start with "k" than they can those that have "k" as their third letter. These people have made the **availability error**. The letter "k" is twice as likely to be the third letter as it is to be the first.

Ready recollections of an event happening do not mean that it has a high probability of happening. Likewise, vague or few recollections of an event happening do not mean that it has a low probability of happening. Memories are faulty and subjective. Instead, look for supporting data before making probability estimates.

> The availability error occurs when managers' judgments of an event's probability are based on or biased by the number of instances of that event that they recall and the ease with which these events come to mind.

Concreteness Error

Several years ago, a college professor decided to purchase a used automobile. He studied the surveys that *Consumer Reports* conducts to determine which cars have the fewest repair problems. He then decided to purchase one of their recommended vehicles. Several days before purchasing the car, he was discussing his choice with a colleague. The colleague happened to own that particular model car, and told the professor that it was the worst lemon in the world. In one instant the professor changed his mind. He made the **concreteness error**.

> The concreteness error occurs when a person places greater weight on highly personal data than on abstract or survey data. Decision making is erroneously based on the source of the data, rather than the sample size.

Review the professor's decision making process. The survey, based upon repair records from several thousand people, reported that the model needed very few repairs. On the other hand, a close friend told him that the car was a real lemon. The professor valued his colleague's information—a sample of one—much more heavily than the *Consumer Reports* data—a sample of several thousand. The professor did not know the survey people, but he knew his friend. His friend's personal and concrete experiences caused the professor to change his mind—the concreteness error in action. Unless survey data are questionable (see Chapter 6 for details), large size samples are more meaningful than a sample size of one.

The concreteness error occurs also in the business world. A pharmaceutical firm must reverse a precipitous drop in the market share of its major profit maker. Its patents had recently expired, and competitors who sold generic equivalents were eroding the firm's sales and profits. The company was considering maintaining its price in hopes of convincing doctors and pharmacists that it produced the high-quality product. It had recently conducted a scientific market research study showing that maintaining its current price would convince no one. During the deliberations, a senior manager strongly argued that he *personally* believed that the high-price strategy would work. Without much discussion, the group accepted his personal opinion and rejected the marketing research results. They had fallen prey to the concreteness error and as a result they suffered the consequences.

Do not value highly personal concrete data more than impersonal survey data. Rather, what is important is the validity of each, and the amount of evidence that supports each position. Generally, large size samples are more informative than small size samples. There is one exception to that rule. If the survey uses improper sampling designs or asks poorly worded questions, then of course do not trust the data.

Chapter 4 Basic Probability Concepts: The Study of Randomness

SECTION 4.8 EXERCISES

1. You tell a friend that 95% of all paroled felons complete parole without rearrest, thus saving millions of dollars of prison expenditures. The friend responds: "That's not true. There was a case reported in the paper where a parolee committed a heinous crime." Assuming you are correct, what's wrong with your friend's reasoning?

2. In a national survey, 93% of all customers surveyed reported being "satisfied" or "very satisfied" with the repair service of a major appliance firm, the best record of any major appliance company. A friend of yours tells you that he had a service call and the work was awful. Would you buy an appliance from this company if it had to service the appliance? Discuss your reasoning.

3. According to the National Safety Council's *Accident Facts* (1988 edition), the probability of death due to firearms is about one-eleventh of the probability of death due to falls. Explain why most people estimate the probability of dying due to firearms as higher than that of dying due to falls.

4. Tom Taylor has high intelligence. However, he lacks true creativity. He has a need for order and clarity, and for neat and tidy systems in which every detail finds its appropriate place. His writing is rather dull and mechanical, occasionally enlivened by flashes of imagination of the science fiction type. He has a strong drive for competence. He seems to have little feeling and sympathy for other people, and does not enjoy interacting with others. He has a deep moral sense of right and wrong. Tom is currently a graduate student. What is he majoring in?

    Suppose we asked you to rank the listed majors from 1 = most likely to 9 = least likely. You shouldn't rank the majors because you do not yet have enough information. You know much about Tom and his interests and this is important information. However, you are missing a second important piece of information—base rate data. What are the missing base rate data?

Business administration	———	Physical sciences	———
Engineering	———	Law	———
Computer sciences	———	Social work	———
Humanities	———	Library sciences	———
Education	———		

4.9 Key Ideas and Overview

Except in statistics books, managers are not given probabilities. So where do they come from? There are two methods for assigning probabilities:

1. the relative frequency approach, and
2. the personal, or subjective, probability approach.

Experience is the basis for the relative frequency approach. If we observe a random experiment many times, we can determine the relative frequency of an event. That, in turn, is an estimate of the probability. Relative frequency probabilities come from observation.

Intuition is the basis for personal probabilities. A manager "guesstimates" a probability based on knowledge and insight about an event. Managers' intuitive powers are often weak and so they make errors in assessing personal probabilities. Probability trees can improve their judgment making.

Any probability—relative frequency or subjective—must satisfy the following two rules of probability:

RULE 1: Probabilities are numbers between 0 and 1.0 inclusive.

RULE 2: The sum of the probabilities of all the possible events that can occur must be 1.0.

Table 4.5 captures some of the similarities between this chapter and the preceding descriptive statistics chapters.

Table 4.5

A Comparison of Descriptive Statistics and Basic Probability Concepts

	Descriptive Statistics	**Basic Probability**
Goals	To collect, organize, summarize, and interpret data. To detect possible relationships between variables. To describe a data set by a few numbers—mean, standard deviation, median, and interquartile range	To compute or assess probabilities. To detect possible relationships between variables. To describe the unpredictability of an event by its probability
Starting Point	A representative set of cross-sectional or time-ordered data. Compute measures of the central tendency and variability	A random experiment. Compute a relative frequency probability or estimate a personal probability.
Compound Events	Use a cross-tabs table to display descriptive data. Determine relationship by computing row or column percentages.	Use a probability tree to display probability data. Determine relationship by computing conditional probabilities.
Problem Solving	Helps managers build mental models, sense outliers, and diagnose root causes of disturbance problems.	Helps managers make decisions in a logical and systematic fashion. Probability trees help managers minimize information processing errors.

SECTION 4.9 EXERCISES

1. In each of the following scenarios, the word *probability* is mentioned. For each situation state whether the probability is a relative frequency or personal probability. Explain your answer.
   a. After producing 10,000 items over a period of 5 years, a manufacturer found that 5% of these items were defective. Therefore, the probability that any part is defective is 5%.
   b. A top executive states that there is an almost zero probability that her competitor will beat her firm to market with a competing product.
   c. The probability is greater than .5 that the Seattle Seahawks will win the Super Bowl by 1994.

2. The National Aeronautics and Space Administration (NASA) plans to purchase parts from several current vendors to construct its sixth space shuttle. Each vendor reports the probability that its part(s) will be defective. From these probabilities, NASA engineers calculate that the probability of a shuttle failure is .0001. Is this probability based on personal or relative frequency considerations?

COMCEL

```
Date:   September 10, 1992
  To:   Howard Bright, Plant Manager
From:   Sarah Teman, Manager of Operations
  Re:   Effects of Job Switching on Productivity
```

Summary. Although the work group productivity varies both by group and by month, work groups that switch jobs appear, on average, to outperform work groups that don't switch jobs. The Operations Analysis Group is now reviewing my analysis. Subject to their confirmation, I recommend you ask Marvin Elrod to determine the potential training costs as his Human Resources group will do the job training.

Supporting analysis. I obtained productivity data for all 36 work groups from the production information system. I assigned work groups to the "high" productivity category if they produced at the median level of productivity or higher. I assigned work groups to the "low" productivity category if they produced below the median productivity. I then determined how many groups in each category switched or had not switched jobs during the quarter.

Job switching appears to be related to high performance: 52.8% of my sample were high producers, but among the groups that switched jobs, 81.8% are high producers. So, the chance that a group is producing at or above the median level increases among the groups that switch jobs.

A note of caution. I have made two assumptions in my analysis. First, the above percentages are stable from month to month. Second, work groups worked on a normal mix of products.

Although the percentage of job switching groups that are high producers is dramatically higher than the percentage of high producers overall—81.8% vs. 52.8%—a definite conclusion must wait until we have more data. Since the total number of work groups is only 36, a shift of two or three groups from the high- to low-productivity categories could dramatically affect the percentages. All work groups have off-months, job switching or not. I have sent the data over to our statistical wizards to see what conclusions they can draw from the data. I will report as soon as I have their results.

CHAPTER 4 QUESTIONS

1. How do inaccurate probability estimates affect your problem solving ability?
2. Which of the following are random experiments and why?
    a. Determine the time it takes for products to reach the market place.
    b. Watch a ball game at a company picnic.
    c. Find out the promotional status of a worker.
    d. Assess the cholesterol levels of workers who exercise at least four times a week.
3. Illustrate a simple and a compound event for a random experiment where you interview random households and ask them how many cars they own.
4. Do relative frequencies of events always equal their respective probabilities? Explain.
5. How are relative frequency and personal probabilities similar and different?
6. The categorical variable, gender, has two levels: male or female. The two levels are mutually exclusive events. Are the events male and female also statistically independent?
7. Under what conditions can a joint probability be greater than 0?
8. Compare unconditional, joint, and conditional probabilities showing similarities and differences.
9. If $P(A|B)$ equals $P(A)$, what can you conclude about event B's impact on event A?
10. What is the multiplication rule? What is the multiplication rule when two events are statistically independent?
11. What is the addition rule? What is the addition rule when two events are statistically independent?
12. In your own words, what is the error of ignoring the base rate?
13. Explain the logic of placing the base rate, or unconditional probability, data as the first entry in a probability tree (nearer the top of the tree) when using it to overcome the error of ignoring the base rate.

Chapter 4 Basic Probability Concepts: The Study of Randomness

14. In your own words, what is the noncoherency error?
15. You must estimate the probability of an airplane crash. You read that morning of a major air disaster and you increased your original probability estimate. What error have you just made?

CHAPTER 4 APPLICATION PROBLEMS

1. Best Diary Inc. has collected the following frequency data on market segment and milk preference. Do different segments have different milk preferences?

	Machos	Status Seekers	Total
Skim	30	80	110
Whole	70	20	90
	100	100	200

   a. Develop a probability tree from the cross-tabs table.
   b. What is P(preferring skim milk OR being a Status Seeker)?
   c. What is the following unconditional probability: P(being a Macho)?
   d. What is the following conditional probability: P(being a Macho | preferring whole milk)?
   e. Are the probabilities in parts **b**–**d** true probabilities or only estimated probabilities—that is, relative frequencies?
   f. Based on your answers to parts **c** and **d**, does milk preference appear to be independent of market segment? Explain.
   g. Develop one marketing/advertising strategy the manager should consider given the answer in part **f**.

2. Based on 2,000 accounts, an accounting manager develops the following probability table on the size of accounts payable (rounded to the nearest dollar).

Less than $1,500	.05
$1,500 to $1,999	.15
$2,000 to $2,499	.30
$2,500 to $2,999	.30
$3,000 to $3,499	.15
$3,500 and above	.05

   a. What is the probability of an account payable being between $1,500 and $2,999?
   b. What is the probability of an account payable being less than $2,500?
   c. What is the probability of an account payable being more than $2,999?
   d. Why must the six probabilities in the table sum to 1? Explain.
   e. How would you develop the table?
   f. One year later, the manager finds that 40% of the accounts payable are $3,500 or more. Given the data in this problem, what might the accounting manager conclude?

3. A firm is considering using a nondiscriminatory test to predict which employees will be very successful on the job. Presently, 60% of the employees are very successful on the job. The firm asked each employee to take the test. The firm obtained the following conditional probability data:

$$P(\text{passing score} \mid \text{very successful}) = .80$$

$$P(\text{failing score} \mid \text{not very successful}) = .90$$

Is the test a good predictor? Can it be used to evaluate potential employees? That is, what is the probability of being very successful on the job given you get a passing score? What is the probability of not being very successful given you get a failing score?

   a. Construct a probability tree. *Hint:* Place the categorical variable—job success—nearer the top of the tree.
   b. Compute the following two conditional probabilities:

$$P(\text{very successful} \mid \text{passing score})$$

$$P(\text{not very successful} \mid \text{failing score})$$

   c. Is the test a good predictor of (1) very successful and (2) not very successful job performance? Explain in simple terms.

4. A civil rights group has collected the following hypothetical probability data on hiring practices in an industry:

$$P(\text{hiring an applicant}) = .10$$

$$P(\text{hiring an applicant} \mid \text{applicant is white male}) = .10$$

$$P(\text{hiring an applicant} \mid \text{applicant is black male}) = .10$$

The Civil Rights Act says that a person cannot be discriminated against in hiring based on sex, race, creed, or place of national origin. Given the above data, are hiring and the applicant's race statistically independent in the industry? Explain.

5. Restaurants must determine the number of waiters to hire. If there are too few, customers will have to wait more than 20 minutes for service. They may leave and never return. Too many waiters can increase the restaurant's operating costs. Consider the following wait times:
   less than 5 minutes
   5 minutes to 20 minutes
   more than 20 minutes
   a. What must the sum of the probabilities for the three events be?
   b. Assign personal probabilities that indicate that the restaurant has too few waiters. Discuss.
   c. Assign personal probabilities that indicate that the restaurant has too many waiters. Discuss.

6. A real estate manager provides personal, or subjective, probability estimates about the chances of selling several tracts of land to a major developer.

Tracts	Personal Probability
0	.05
1	.60
2	.15
3	.50
4	.35
5 or more	.45

   a. What, if anything, is incorrect about her six subjective probability estimates?
   b. How could you change the probability estimates to eliminate the problem you described in part **a**?

7. A product manager develops the following three personal probability estimates about the sales potential for high resolution TVs:

$$P(\text{meeting sales goals}) = .60$$

$$P(\text{positive market research finding}) = .70$$

$$P(\text{meeting sales goals} \mid \text{positive market research finding}) = 1.00$$

   a. Do the three probabilities imply that any of the joint probabilities is greater than 1 or less than 0? Use a probability tree to support your position.
   b. Suppose the product manager believes that the first and third probability estimates reflect his best thinking. Change the second probability estimate so that no joint probability is negative.
   c. Based on the third conditional probability, what is the product manager saying about the effectiveness or impact of the marketing research findings? Explain.

8. A stock analyst specializing in the retail industry wants to know if chain stores have the same focus—service or price—as do independents. In statistical terms, is focus statistically independent of type of store? The data are shown.

	Service	Price	Total
Independents	25	5	30
Chains	4	16	20
	29	21	50

   a. Develop a probability tree from the cross-tabs table.
   b. What is $P(\text{having a service focus OR being a chain})$?
   c. What is the following unconditional probability: $P(\text{having a price focus})$?
   d. What is the following conditional probability: $P(\text{having a price focus} \mid \text{being a chain})$?
   e. Based on your answers to parts **c** and **d**, is focus independent of type of store? Explain.
   f. Are the probabilities in parts **b**–**d** true probabilities or estimated probabilities—that is, relative frequencies? Explain.

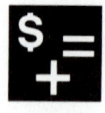

9. A firm is considering two methods for purchasing microcomputers. One method will permit divisions to centralize the purchases. That is, all division purchases will be made by one person. The second method will allow individual employees within a division to purchase any computer they wish. The MIS manager develops the following subjective joint probability estimates regarding the presence or absence of centralized purchasing and the purchasing of three different computer brands:

$$P(\text{centralized purchasing AND buy IBM micros}) = .30$$

$$P(\text{decentralized purchasing AND buy Macintosh micros}) = .20$$

$$P(\text{centralized purchasing AND buy Macintosh micros}) = .10$$

$$P(\text{decentralized purchasing AND buy other micros}) = .05$$

$$P(\text{centralized purchasing AND buy other micros}) = .05$$

$$P(\text{decentralized purchasing AND buy IBM micros}) = .20$$

   a. What, if anything, is improper about the six subjective joint probability estimates?
   b. The manager wants to maintain the relative sizes of the six probabilities. For example, she believes that the first probability is three times greater than the third probability and six times greater than the fourth and fifth probabilities. How can you do this without violating the basic rules of probability?

10. Does taking a workshop in problem solving improve on-the-job problem solving skills? Overall only 30% of all managers are rated as having high on-the-job problem solving skills. Of those who are highly rated, 90% took the problem solving course. Of those who are not highly rated, only 10% took the course. What is the conditional probability of being highly rated on the job if you have taken the problem solving course?
   a. Construct a probability tree.
   b. Compute the following conditional probability:

   $$P(\text{highly rated on the job} \mid \text{taken problem solving course})$$

   c. Would you recommend that the firm require the course of all managers? Assume that costs are negligible.
   d. Explain how you would collect the data in this problem.
   e. Use the probability tree to determine what $P(\text{taken problem solving course} \mid \text{not highly rated})$ must be if $P(\text{highly rated} \mid \text{taken course}) = .90$. Assume that all other probabilities remain the same.

11. Using data obtained from students at a college, you have computed the following three probabilities:

$$P(\text{GPA above 3.5}) = .15$$

$$P(\text{GPA above 3.5} \mid \text{SAT score above 1,200}) = .30$$

$$P(\text{GPA above 3.5} \mid \text{SAT score below 1,200}) = .03$$

   a. Does it appear that GPA and SAT scores are statistically dependent? Explain.
   b. How would you determine the above three probabilities for a college of 1,500 students?
   c. Are the probabilities true probabilities or relative frequencies? Explain.

Chapter 4   Basic Probability Concepts: The Study of Randomness   207

12. A project manager estimates the following three subjective probabilities for building a new warehouse:

$$P(\text{completing project on time}) = .90$$

$$P(\text{rainy weather}) = .50$$

$$P(\text{completing project on time} \mid \text{rainy weather}) = .80$$

   a. Do the three probabilities imply that any of the joint probabilities is greater than 1 or less than 0? Use a probability tree to support your position.
   b. Given your probability tree from part **a**, what is $P(\text{completing project on time} \mid \text{no rainy weather})$?

13. Do company-run stress management programs minimize absenteeism? ABC Research collects the following cross-tabs data. Low absenteeism is defined as less than 1% of total man-hours lost.

	Absenteeism Low	High	Total
Program	40	60	100
No Programs	10	90	100
	50	150	200

   a. Develop a probability tree from the cross-tabs table.
   b. What is $P(\text{having no stress management programs OR having high absenteeism})$?
   c. What is the unconditional probability: $P(\text{having low absenteeism})$?
   d. What is the conditional probability: $P(\text{having low absenteeism} \mid \text{having stress management programs})$?
   e. Based on your answers to parts **c** and **d**, is level of absenteeism independent of running stress management programs? Explain.

14. An airline's most popular flight is the shuttle from New York to Washington, D.C. Each plane can hold 150 passengers and each flight is always sold out in advance. However, the airline has noted that often there are one or more vacant seats. Apparently, some passengers catch an earlier flight or "double book" flights. The airline records the number of empty seats over a 1-week period.

Empty Seats	Probability
0	.10
1	.10
2	.20
3	.20
4	.20
5	.20

   a. Given the above data, is the airline losing revenues by selling only 150 seats per flight?
   b. Should the airline consider selling more than 150 tickets per flight? Discuss.
   c. Suppose it sells 155 tickets per flight. Given the above data, will it ever have any empty seats on a flight?
   d. What problem would the airline now experience if it sold 155 tickets per flight?

15. An economist makes the following subjective probability estimates. (High inflation is defined as an inflation rate over 5%.)

$$P(\text{high inflation next year}) = .20$$

$$P(\text{increased federal spending this year}) = .40$$

$$P(\text{high inflation} \mid \text{increased federal spending}) = .30$$

    a. Do the three probabilities imply that any of the joint probabilities must be greater than 1 or less than 0? Use a probability tree to support your position.
    b. Given the above data, what is $P(\text{high inflation} \mid \text{no increased spending})$?

16. The probability of having disease X in the general population is only .05. The Sagman Test is a newly discovered method for early detection. Of those who have disease X, the test indicates the disease for 90% of them. Of those who do not have the disease, the test indicates no disease for 90% of them. Is the test a good predictor of whether you actually have the disease or not? Should its use be widespread?
    a. Which of the following conditional probabilities is most appropriate to determine the test's effectiveness? Explain.

$$P(\text{have disease } X \mid \text{test says you have the disease})$$

$$P(\text{test says you have the disease} \mid \text{have the disease})$$

$$P(\text{test says you have the disease})$$

    b. Compare the unconditional probability of having the disease to the conditional probability of having the disease given the test says you have the disease.
    c. Compare the unconditional probability of not having the disease to the conditional probability of not having the disease given the test says you do not have the disease.
    d. Based on parts **b** and **c**, is the test a good predictor? Explain.
    e. Suppose that to use the test, $P(\text{have disease} \mid \text{test says you have disease})$ must be 90% or greater. What must the following conditional probability be: $P(\text{test says you do not have the disease} \mid \text{no disease})$?

17. An MIS manager had determined the following relative frequency probabilities for the age of microcomputers in the firm:

Age of Microcomputer	Probability
Less than 1 year	.05
1 year but less than 2 years	.10
2 years but less than 3 years	.10
3 years but less than 4 years	.15
4 or more years	.60

    a. Find the probability that a microcomputer is less than 2 years old.
    b. Find the probability that a microcomputer is at least 1 year old.
    c. Find the probability that a microcomputer is 3 years old or more.

d. Given that the mean useful life of a computer is 4 years due to technical obsolescence, what can you conclude about the need for capital investment in microcomputers from the probability data?

18. An organizational behavior consulting firm has collected the following data on leadership style for 200 firms in the United States and Canada. Do American and Canadian firms prefer the same leadership styles?

	Leadership Style	
	Participative	Autocratic
United States	30	70
Canada	50	50

a. What is the following unconditional probability: P(having participative leadership)?
b. What is the following conditional probability: P(having participative leadership | firm in United States)?
c. Based on your answers to parts **a** and **b**, is leadership style independent of the country where the firm is located? Explain in terms that a manager could understand.

19. You are told that men and women have the same chances of being promoted in a firm.
a. What must be true about the following three probabilities? Explain in simple terms.

$$P(\text{promoted})$$

$$P(\text{promoted} \mid \text{male})$$

$$P(\text{promoted} \mid \text{female})$$

b. Must the following two probabilities equal one another for gender and promotion to be statistically independent? Explain.

$$P(\text{promoted} \mid \text{female})$$

$$P(\text{female} \mid \text{promoted})$$

20. Fifty percent of all undergraduate students major in Business Administration. Given that you are a Business major, there is a .70 probability of being an extrovert—a person who likes to interact with others. If you are an Arts and Sciences major, there is an .80 chance that you are an introvert—a person who likes to concentrate on ideas. Suppose you select an extrovert; what is the chance that he or she is a Business major?
a. Write the unconditional probability in the first sentence in probability notation.
b. Write the two conditional probabilities in the next two sentences in probability notation.
c. Write the conditional probability in the last sentence in probability notation.
d. Develop a probability tree and determine the conditional probability.

21. Shown at the top of page 210 is a cross-tabs table of the age and race of the male inmate population in Georgia in 1988. [*Source: Georgia Criminal Justice Data–1988*.] Does it appear that race and age are statistically independent?

	Age				
	0–21	22–39	40–54	55–99	Total
White Male	639	4,335	1,224	270	6,468
Nonwhite Male	1,200	8,631	1,385	228	11,444
	1,839	12,966	2,609	498	17,912

a. What is the probability of a nonwhite male inmate?
b. What is the probability of a white male inmate?
c. What is the probability of an inmate being of age 0–21, given that he is a white male?
d. What is the probability of an inmate being of age 0–21, given that he is a nonwhite male?
e. Considering only your answers in parts **c** and **d**, does it appear that age and race are related? Discuss.

22. Cablebest is preparing to apply to the Federal Communications Commission (FCC) for a license. The FCC has three options: (1) grant a restricted license, (2) grant an unrestricted license, (3) do not grant a license. Cablebest believes that the FCC ruling will depend on its ability to recruit a knowledgeable general manager. Cablebest is presently seeking such a person. The firm is not sure whether it will have such a person when it submits the application. Following are the firm's subjective probability estimates.

$$P(\text{will recruit}) = .70$$

$$P(\text{won't recruit}) = .30$$

$$P(\text{unrestricted license}) = .50$$

$$P(\text{restricted license}) = .40$$

$$P(\text{no license}) = .10$$

a. Explain how a firm might estimate the probabilities.
b. The firm also estimates that $P(\text{unrestricted license} \mid \text{will recruit}) = .90$. Are all the probability estimates valid or coherent?

23. BHJ Inc. is one of Apex's largest customers. Here are historical probability data on the number of sales made to BHJ Inc. of more than 1,000 units over the 52 weeks of 1991:

$$P(\text{zero sales}) = .02$$

$$P(\text{one sale}) = .10$$

$$P(\text{two sales}) = .10$$

$$P(\text{three sales}) = .30$$

$$P(\text{four sales}) = .48$$

a. Suppose that in the first week of 1992, Apex has zero sales of more than 1,000 units to BHJ. Given the historical probability data, should Apex be concerned about lack of sales to BHJ Inc.? Discuss.
b. Suppose that for the first two weeks of 1992, Apex has zero sales of more than

1,000 units to BHJ. Should Apex now be concerned? Discuss. Assume that each week's sales are statistically independent events.

24. According to data from the National Center for Health Statistics, in 1986, the probability of an infant (one year old or less) dying in the United States was .0104. The probability of a white infant dying within the first year was .0089. The probability of a black infant dying within the first year was .0180.
    a. Which are unconditional probabilities and which are conditional probabilities?
    b. Given the above data, does it appear that infant mortality and race are related? Discuss.
    c. What might account for the fact that black babies are more than twice as likely to die within the first year as white babies?

25. A college tracks 200 students enrolled in a basic management course. Seventy percent of the students received a grade of B or better. Of those students who received a grade of B or better, 90% had prepared for exams by using study groups. Of those who received a grade of C or worse, only 30% had used study groups.
    a. What is the probability of receiving a grade of B or better if you use a study group?
    b. What is the probability of receiving a grade of C or worse if you do not use a study group?
    c. If you want to maximize your chance of receiving a grade of B or better, should you use a study group? Discuss.

REFERENCES

TVERSKY, AMOS, and DANIEL KAHNEMAN. "Judgment under Uncertainty." *Science* (September 25, 1974): 1124–1131.

TVERSKY, AMOS, and DANIEL KAHNEMAN. "The Framing of Decisions and the Psychology of Choice." *Science* (January 30, 1981): 453–458.

PROBABILITY DISTRIBUTIONS

5.1 Probability distributions and problem solving
5.2 Random variables and discrete probability distributions
   Random variables
   Relative frequency and personal probability distributions and histograms
   Mean and standard deviation
5.3 The binomial distribution
   Calculating probabilities
   The binomial expression
   The binomial table
   Mean and standard deviation of a binomial distribution
5.4 Problem solving and the binomial distribution
   Assessing consequences
   Problem sensing
   Assessing the Bernoulli process assumption
5.5 The Poisson distribution
   The Poisson expression
   The Poisson table
   Problem sensing and the Poisson distribution
   Assessing the Poisson process assumptions
   Mean and standard deviation of a Poisson distribution
5.6 The normal distribution
   Why is the normal distribution so useful?
   Characteristics of the normal distribution
   z-scores and finding probabilities
   The normal distribution and decision making
   Validity of the normal distribution assumptions
5.7 The central limit theorem
5.8 Integrating framework and key ideas
Chapter 5 Questions
Chapter 5 Application Problems

CHAPTER OUTLINE

COMCEL Interoffice Communication

Date: February 12, 1991
From: Howard Bright, Plant Manager
  To: Sang Kim, Quality Assurance
  Re: Quality of circuit breakers

I received a call from a good friend of mine who is also one of our best customers. She wanted to know if we are relaxing our quality control standards. In a box of 25 circuit breakers purchased from us last week, three turned out to be defective, a defective rate of 12%. She reminded me that our competitors guarantee a defect rate of no more than 5%.

Are our quality standards slipping? We should strive to ship no defective products, but we must certainly meet or exceed the quality levels of our competitors.

Please look into this and report back ASAP.

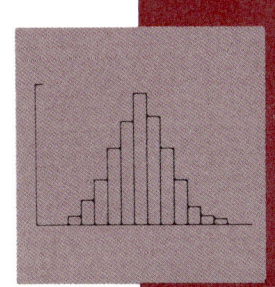

5.1 Probability Distributions and Problem Solving

Chapter 4 demonstrated two ways managers can obtain probabilities—namely, using intuition and judgment to generate personal probabilities, and survey data to provide relative frequency probabilities. Managers *generate* personal probabilities based on their knowledge and insight about an event. However, their intuitive powers are usually weak, and so they often make errors in determining personal probabilities. Survey data *provide* relative frequency probabilities. If we observe a random experiment many times, we can determine the relative frequency of an event, which is an approximation of the true probability.

In this chapter we will discuss a third probability source. Theoretical probability distributions are mathematical expressions that we use to *calculate* probabilities. These expressions are based on sets of underlying assumptions that must be satisfied if the calculated probabilities are to be valid. We will discuss three important theoretical probability distributions—the binomial, the Poisson, and the normal.

Thus, managers can use empirical, personal, or theoretical probabilities to become more effective problem solvers and decision makers. Figure 5.1 reproduces our problem solving model.

PROBLEM OR OPPORTUNITY SENSING   From Chapter 1, we know that effective managers use Pounds's four strategies to sense problems. The following example illustrates the historic model, in which managers look for deviations from past performance.

EXAMPLE 1:   From historical data, Georgia Stationery Supplies knows that 40% of orders received from ABC Inc. will be for more than 1,000 boxes of paper. Of ABC's last six orders, none has

FIGURE 5.1   Problem Solving Model

```
┌─────────────────────────┐
│ Problem or opportunity  │
│        sensing          │
└─────────────────────────┘
            │
┌─────────────────────────┐
│     Diagnosis and       │
│  alternative generation │
└─────────────────────────┘
            │
┌─────────────────────────┐
│     Decision making     │
│    and implementation   │
└─────────────────────────┘
```

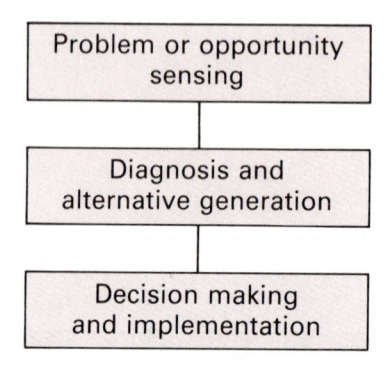

been for more than 1,000 boxes. Could Georgia Stationery Supplies be facing a problem with declining business from ABC Inc.?

DIAGNOSIS   Once a problem happens, managers suggest changes that might explain the deviation. After determining the root causes, they take corrective action and determine if the problem has been solved.

EXAMPLE 2: Recently the number of accidents per month on a highway has increased from one to ten per month. After a major investigation, the Highway Patrol thought they identified the cause—rapid road deterioration. They repaired the road and over the next month, there was only one accident. Was their diagnosis accurate?

DECISION MAKING—EVALUATING ALTERNATIVES   Managers must evaluate alternative actions before selecting the best one to implement. Evaluating alternatives sometimes means making predictions about the consequences of an alternative action. Theoretical probability models can provide objective and unbiased information.

EXAMPLE 3: COMCEL buys electronic components from ZT Audio for its cellular phones. COMCEL requires that each lot of 1,000 components contain 10% or fewer defectives. COMCEL inspects every shipment from ZT by selecting and testing a sample of 10 components. It is considering two acceptance rules: Accept the lot of 1,000 if (1) one or no components are defective or (2) two or fewer components are defective.

Evaluating alternatives sometimes means determining which action is more likely to accomplish the desired goals. Again we can use probability effectively.

EXAMPLE 4: Two overnight express services are in head-to-head competition. Federal Service advertises a mean delivery time of 30 hours, while United Express claims that its mean delivery time is 34 hours. However United Express's arrival times are more consistent because its standard deviation is only 2 hours, whereas Federal's is 5 hours. Which service should you use if your documents must always arrive within 36 hours?

Sensing problems, verifying diagnoses, evaluating alternative actions, and making choices are problem solving activities. Later, we will show how theoretical probability distributions can improve problem solving and decision making skills.

5.2 Random Variables and Discrete Probability Distributions

In Chapter 3 we introduced the random experiment. Now we build upon that idea and introduce two new terms—a random variable and its probability distribution. By the end of this section you should be able to:

1. explain what a random variable is;
2. explain the similarities and differences between discrete and continuous random variables;
3. describe the properties common to all discrete probability distributions;
4. draw a discrete probability histogram; and
5. compute the mean and standard deviation of a discrete probability distribution.

Random Variables

Table 5.1 lists four random experiments along with the variables for which we would like to compute probabilities.

How many values can the first variable take on? Since there are only 36 work groups in the plant, the variable can take on 37 different possible values: 0, 1, 2, 3, ..., 36.

In the second example the random variable is the number of correct answers obtained on a 15-question exam. If there is no partial credit, this variable can take on 16 possible values: 0, 1, 2, 3, ..., 15.

In the third example the random variable is the lifetime of a computer chip. Suppose that no chip has ever lasted less than 800 hours or more than 1,300 hours. What are all the possible lifetimes within this interval? Since fractions of hours are possible, the life of a computer chip can take on any value between 800 and 1,300 hours. There is an infinite, or uncountable, number of possible values.

In the last example the random variable is the box weight. Suppose that no box has ever weighed less than 15.9 ounces or more than 16.1 ounces. How many

Table 5.1

Variables Defined in Random Experiments

Random Experiment	Variable
From a total of 36 work groups, count the number of work groups that exceed 100% productivity.	The number of high-producing work groups
Count the number of correct answers on a 15-question exam.	The number of correct answers on an exam
Record the life of a computer chip.	The number of hours a computer chip lasts
Record the weight of a box of cereal that has a nominal weight of 16 oz.	The actual weight of the box

values are possible within this interval? There is an infinite, or uncountable, number of values.

In summary, the four random experiments in Table 5.1 have one thing in common. There may be a finite or an infinite number of outcomes, but the outcomes are numbers.

Now we are ready for a working definition of a **random variable**.

The number of high-producing work groups in a plant and the number of correct answers on an exam are examples of *discrete* random variables. Discrete random variables can take on a finite or countable number of values. Often the values are *counts*. For example, we can count the number of high-producing groups or the number of questions answered correctly on an exam. We write discrete random variables as follows:

> A random variable is defined in a random experiment that has numerical outcomes. Describing a random variable means (1) stating the variable for which we would like to determine or compute probabilities and (2) listing all its possible values.

The random variable X = the number of high-producing work groups
Listing of values   Possible values: $\{0, 1, 2, 3, \ldots, 35\}$

In the other two random experiments, the number of hours that a chip lasts and the weight of the cereal box are *continuous* random variables. They can take on an uncountable number of values. Other examples of continuous random variables are length, weight, and speed. Continuous random variables can be *measured*. In measuring weight, for example, the scale may permit a determination only to the nearest pound. Thus the resulting data will be discrete in units of 1 pound. Nevertheless we treat weight as continuous because it could take on an uncountable number of values. We write continuous random variables as follows:

The random variable X = the number of hours that a chip lasts
Listing of values   Possible values: $\{800 < x < 1{,}300\}$

The notation "<" indicates that there is an uncountable number of possible values between 800 and 1,300 hours.

Relative Frequency and Personal Probability Distributions and Histograms

Assume that no family in Omaha owns more than four cars. Consider the following discrete random variable:

X = the number of cars owned by families in Omaha

Possible values: $\{0, 1, 2, 3, 4\}$

> A discrete probability distribution consists of all the possible numerical values of a discrete random variable together with their associated probabilities.

We conduct a survey and obtain the relative frequency probabilities. Table 5.2 on page 218 presents the **discrete probability distribution** results. Note that the sum of the five probabilities equals 1. This is because of the families interviewed, all had either 0, 1, 2, 3, or 4 cars. These are all the possible events in the survey. As the second rule of probability says, the sum of the probabilities of all possible events that can occur must equal 1.

Table 5.2
Relative Frequency Distribution

Number of Cars	Relative Frequency Probability
0	.10
1	.40
2	.40
3	.08
4	.02

We can describe a discrete probability distribution by listing the allowable values and their probabilities or by drawing a picture called a *probability histogram.* We first talked about histograms in Chapter 2 to show how managers could use them to organize and summarize a mass of data into meaningful information. Figure 5.2 depicts a histogram for the number of cars owned by families in Omaha, using the same data given in Table 5.2.

Like frequency histograms, probability histograms consist of bars or rectangles. The base of each rectangle is centered on one of the values of the random variable—for example, 0, 1, 2, 3, and 4 cars in Figure 5.2. Each rectangle is 1 unit wide; its height is equal to the probability of getting that value. The total area under the probability histogram is 1 by the second rule of probability.

In Chapter 2, we analyzed groups of numbers using the mean and standard deviation. Now we extend these statistical tools to probability distributions for discrete random variables.

FIGURE 5.2 Probability Histogram: Survey of Number of Cars per Family in Omaha

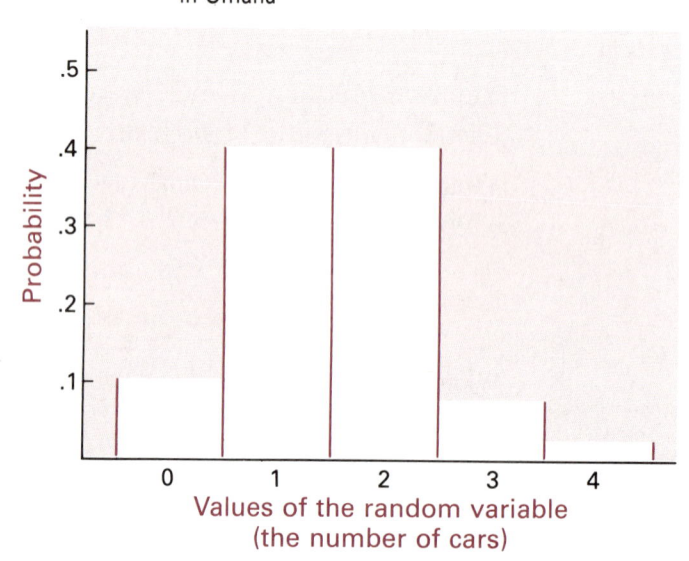

Mean and Standard Deviation

The mean is a measure of the central tendency of a probability distribution. As with frequency histograms, we can use the balance point idea from Chapter 2 to *approximate* the mean. Place a steel rod underneath the probability histogram in Figure 5.2 and move it from left to right. At what number of cars would the probability histogram balance? It would not balance at one car, for there would be too much weight (probability) to the right, and the histogram would tilt down to the right. It would not balance at three cars, for there would be too much weight to the left, and the histogram would tilt down to the left. The balance point is slightly more than 1.5 cars, and that is our approximation of the mean.

We can use expression (5.1) to compute the actual mean:

$$\text{Mean}^* = \mu = x_1 \cdot P(x_1) + x_2 \cdot P(x_2) + \cdots + x_n \cdot P(x_n) \qquad (5.1)$$

In expression (5.1), the term x_1 represents the first value that the discrete random variable X can take on. That is, we use capital letters to denote a random variable and lowercase letters to denote the individual values of the random variable. $P(x_1)$ represents the probability that the random variable takes on a value of x_1. We multiply each value, x_i, by its probability, $P(x_i)$, and then sum the products.

Now compute the mean for the discrete random variable—the number of cars owned by Omaha families. The results are shown in Table 5.3.

Does the mean indicate that each family owns exactly 1.52 cars? No, the mean value of 1.52 cars is the *long-run* average; it is the *average* number of cars per family over many thousands of families.

The mean, however, does not completely describe a probability distribution. It provides no insight about the amount of variability in the number of cars

Table 5.3

Computing the Mean

Value of x	Probability	Value · Probability
0	.10	.00
1	.40	.40
2	.40	.80
3	.08	.24
4	.02	.08
		Mean = 1.52 cars

---

*We use the Greek letter μ (mu) to denote a population mean or the mean of a probability distribution.

among families. That is, do *most* families own *close* to 1.52 cars? Figure 5.2 suggests that outcomes far away from the mean of 1.52 are not likely to occur. For example, owning four cars is not likely since the probability is only .02. Owning one or two cars is very likely since the probability is .40 + .40 = .80. The standard deviation, which is a measure of the concentration of the values about the mean, should be small. If numerical values far from the mean had large probabilities, then the standard deviation would be large.

For all types of data—whether raw data, histogram data, or probability data—the standard deviation is still the square root of the weighted sum of the squared deviations of the data around the mean. That is,

$$\text{Standard deviation*} = \sigma = \sqrt{\sum_i (x_i - \mu)^2 \cdot P(x_i)} \qquad (5.2)$$

where μ is the mean of the probability distribution. The results for computing the standard deviation for the number of cars owned per family in Omaha are given in Table 5.4.

In summary, the mean gives the long-run average, and the standard deviation describes the variability about that average. The Empirical rule aids in interpreting the standard deviation. It says that if the probability distribution for cars owned is normally distributed, 95% of the families will own between −.18 car (1.52 − 2(.85)) and 3.22 cars (1.52 + 2(.85)). Since a negative number of cars or parts of cars are not possible values for the random variable here, we would round off the values to between zero and three cars.

Our final example illustrates a subjective discrete probability distribution. Consider two possible stocks—U.S. Conversion and AeroTech. The rates of return on both stocks are uncertain since they depend on the state of the

Table 5.4

Computing the Standard Deviation

Value of x	Probability	Deviation $(x - \mu)$	Squared Deviation	Squared Deviation · Probability
0	.10	(0 − 1.52)	2.31	(2.31)(.10) = .231
1	.40	(1 − 1.52)	.27	(.27)(.40) = .108
2	.40	(2 − 1.52)	.23	(.23)(.40) = .092
3	.08	(3 − 1.52)	2.19	(2.19)(.08) = .175
4	.02	(4 − 1.52)	6.15	(6.15)(.02) = .123
				Variance = σ^2 = .729

$\sigma = \sqrt{.729} = .85$ car per family

---

*We use the Greek letter σ (sigma) to denote a population standard deviation or the standard deviation of a probability distribution. σ^2 is the population variance.

economy. There are three possible future economic scenarios—boom, neutral, and recession. A stock broker predicts the rates of return on both stocks as follows:

X = rate of return on U.S. Conversion stock
Possible values: $\{100\%, 15\%, -70\%\}$

Y = rate of return on AeroTech stock
Possible values: $\{20\%, 15\%, 10\%\}$

Table 5.5 shows the computations for the mean and standard deviation of rate of return for the U.S. Conversion stock. The subjective probability distribution shown in the second column is based on the stock broker's personal probabilities.

The mean rate of return for U.S. Conversion stock is 15% and its standard deviation is 65.8%. The mean rate of return for AeroTech stock is also 15% (calculations not shown) and its standard deviation is 3.9%. In the long run, both stocks have the same mean rate of return. But which stock is the riskier investment?

The U.S. Conversion stock is riskier because it has a much larger standard deviation. Its actual rate of return may be much higher or much lower than the mean rate of return of 15%. That is not true for the AeroTech stock. Its small standard deviation says that whether there is a boom, neutral, or recession economy, the actual return will be quite close to the mean return of 15%. Note that if both stocks had different mean rates of return, determining which is the riskier stock would be more difficult.

In summary, a discrete random variable can take on a finite number of numerical values. Its probability distribution includes the probability for each value of the random variable. Together with the mean and standard deviation, the probability distribution reveals nearly everything of interest about a random variable.

Table 5.5

Computation of Mean and Standard Deviation for Rates of Return on U.S. Conversion Stock

Value of x	$P(x)$	$xP(x)$	Deviation from Mean	Squared Deviation	Squared Deviation · $P(x)$
100%	.3	30%	(100 − 15)	7,225	7,225(.3) = 2,167.5
15%	.4	6%	(15 − 15)	0	0(.4) = 0
−70%	.3	−21%	(−70 − 15)	7,225	7,225(.3) = 2,167.5
		$\mu = 15\%$			Variance = σ^2 = 4,335

$\sigma = \sqrt{4{,}335} = 65.8\%$

SECTION 5.2 EXERCISES

1. Suppose a movie theater has 100 seats and movie tickets cost $6 each. Let X = number of tickets sold on a single Friday night. Let Y = total dollar sales resulting from selling the x tickets.
   a. Is X a random variable? If so, is it discrete or continuous? Describe the range of outcomes possible on any Friday night.
   b. Is Y a random variable? If so, is it discrete or continuous? Describe the range of outcomes on any Friday night.

2. Decide which of the following statements describe a random variable and whether the random variable is discrete or continuous.
   a. Number of accidents per month in a factory
   b. Time required to complete a typing test
   c. Selecting five items from an assembly line
   d. Dollar sales in a single week
   e. Return on investment for a company in a single year

3. What is the difference between a random variable and a probability distribution?

4. Sketch a probability histogram for the following probability distribution for X, the number of workshops offered during the quarter:

x	0	1	2	3
$P(x)$	.2	.3	.3	.2

5. Find the mean and standard deviation for the probability distribution in Exercise 4. Explain why the mean is *not* what you would expect as an outcome of any single quarter.

6. You are offered two investment opportunities:

I		II	
Outcome	Probability	Outcome	Probability
−$1,000	.6	−$500	.4
$0	.3	$0	.1
+$7,000	.1	+$600	.5
	1.0		1.0

   a. Find the mean and standard deviation of each investment opportunity.
   b. Which of the two investments would you prefer? Explain your choice.

7. Through careful record keeping over thousands of guests, a large hotel has determined the probability distribution for the random variable X, the length of stay (measured in days), as

x	$P(X = x)$	$P(X \leq x)$
1	.45	
2	.25	
3	.15	
4	.10	
5	.05	
	1.00	

a. In Chapter 2, you learned how to construct a cumulative percentage distribution. Construct a cumulative probability distribution by filling in the blanks.
b. What is the probability that a person about to check into this hotel will stay 3 days or less? .85
c. Find the probability that a new guest will stay more than 4 days.

8. Calculate the mean and standard deviation for the probability distribution in Exercise 7. Show that Chebyshev's rule applies to this probability distribution by showing that the probability that a length of stay will be outside 3 standard deviations from the mean is less than .11.

9. The number of defective parts produced per hour in a plant has the following empirical probabilities:

Defects per Hour	Probability
0	.50
1	.25
2	.15
3	.08
4	.02

a. Find the mean and standard deviation.
b. Why shouldn't you use the Empirical rule from Chapter 2 to interpret the standard deviation? That is, why can't you say that 95% of the number of defects per hour should be between the mean plus or minus 2 standard deviations?

10. Refer to Exercise 9. What is the probability that in a single hour more than one defective part will be produced? At least one defective part will be produced?

5.3 The Binomial Distribution

Probability distributions based on relative frequencies (Table 5.2) or intuition (Table 5.5) are useful. But there are other distributions—theoretical probability distributions—that play a critical role in business problem solving. We turn next to an important discrete theoretical distribution—the binomial distribution. By the end of this section you should be able to:

1. define a success and a failure;
2. calculate and interpret binomial probabilities;
3. use the binomial probability table in Appendix 1; and
4. compute and interpret the mean and standard deviation for a binomially distributed random variable.

Calculating Probabilities

To use the binomial probability distribution, a Bernoulli process must describe the repeated trials of a random experiment. A Bernoulli process has two characteristics:

1. The possible outcomes of a single trial must be classified into two mutually exclusive and exhaustive categories. For example: flip a coin—heads, tails; select a group—high productivity, low productivity; or inspect a product—good, defective.
2. The probability of any particular outcome (getting a head or finding a defective product) must remain constant from trial to trial.

The second condition requires that the probability of the outcome will not be affected by what happened on preceding trials. For example, suppose the probability of getting a head, p, on one flip of a fair coin is .5. The chance of getting a head on the first flip is .5. What is the chance of getting a head on the second coin flip *given* a head on the first coin flip? What is the chance of getting a head on the third flip *given* two heads on the first two flips? Since the coin has no memory, the probability of getting a head does not change over the three trials no matter what happens. It always remains .5. *Conclusion:* Flipping a fair coin is a Bernoulli process. Using terminology from Chapter 4, we say that a Bernoulli process requires that the outcomes on successive trials must be *statistically independent*. In actual business problems, we will settle for situations that are near-Bernoulli processes. We will discuss this important idea in Section 5.4.

Now we will derive the algebraic expression for computing binomial probabilities using the coin flip example. Flip a fair coin ($p = .5$) three times and compute the probability of getting exactly one head (and two tails). Since we are interested in computing the probability of getting *one* head in *three* coin flips, define the problem in terms of the following discrete random variable:

The random variable	X = the number of heads in three coin flips
Possible values	$\{0, 1, 2, 3\}$
Known quantities	$n = 3$, $p = .5$, $x = 1$
Unknown quantity	$P(X = 1)$

One way to get one head and two tails in three coin flips is H AND T AND T. We know from the multiplication rule (expression (4.6)) that

$$P(A \text{ AND } B) = P(A|B) \cdot P(B)$$

In a Bernoulli process, the conditional probability of event A given event B equals the unconditional probability of event A. Remember, event B has no impact on the probability of event A happening. Therefore, for statistically independent events, we can rewrite the multiplication rule as

$$P(A \text{ AND } B) = P(A)P(B) \tag{5.3}$$

Expression (5.3) says that the joint probability of two independent events is equal to the product of the unconditional probabilities for each event. Now extend the multiplication rule to more than two independent events:

$$P(H \text{ AND } T \text{ AND } T) = P(H)P(T)P(T)$$
$$= .5(1 - .5)(1 - .5) = .125 \tag{5.4}$$

The H AND T AND T sequence is only one of several ways of getting one head and two tails in three coin flips. In fact, there are three possible ways of getting exactly one head in three tosses of the coin, namely, HTT, THT, and HHT. Each sequence has the same probability, .125. Thus the probability of getting exactly one head in three coin flips, $P(X = 1)$ is $.125 + .125 + .125$, or .375. Alternatively, we can multiply expression (5.4) by 3:

$$P(X = 1) = 3(.125) = .375 \tag{5.5}$$

If we repeatedly flip a fair coin, for which $p = .5$, three times and count the number of heads, 37.5% of the time we will get exactly one head. We do not have to run a study or use intuition. We have used expression (5.5), which is the binomial probability expression, to determine the probability.

The Binomial Expression

Each flip of a fair coin is a single trial. On a single trial, two outcomes are possible. We define the outcome we are interested in as a "success" and the other outcome as a "failure." The terms are in quotes because a success could be selecting a defective item and a failure could be selecting a good item. The "success" outcome does not necessarily mean a desirable outcome. It is the one for which we want to calculate a probability.

Given that n is the number of trials, p is the probability of a success, and $(1 - p)$ is the probability of a failure, we can generalize expression (5.5) to get exactly x successes in n trials:

$$P(X = x) = {}_nC_x p^x (1 - p)^{n-x} \tag{5.6}$$

When the number of trials is small (for example, three coin flips), we can simply list the different sequences and count them. For a large number of trials, use the *combinations* expression (5.7) to determine the number of different ways to get x successes in n trials:

$$_nC_x = \frac{n!}{x!(n-x)!} \tag{5.7}$$

The term n is the number of trials and x is the number of successes. The symbol "!" stands for factorial, which means multiply the number before the factorial symbol by each positive integer lower than it. For example, 3! equals $3 \cdot 2 \cdot 1$

or 6. Zero factorial equals 1. In the coin flip example, we have

$$_3C_1 = \frac{3!}{1!(3-1)!} = \frac{3 \cdot 2 \cdot 1}{1 \cdot 2 \cdot 1} = 3$$

This is the number of different ways to get one head in three coin tosses.

Expression (5.6) generates binomial probabilities. We will now use the binomial expression for two mini-problems.

EXAMPLE: CREDIT CLASSIFICATION   A department store classifies its charge customers as either high-volume or low-volume purchasers. Ten percent are high-volume purchasers. If a sample of four charge customers is selected, what is the chance that none of them is a high-volume purchaser?

Define success as selecting a high-volume purchaser, and failure, the other outcome, as selecting a low-volume purchaser. For this example, the two assumptions underlying the binomial expression are the following:

ASSUMPTION 1:   There is a .10 chance of selecting a high-volume purchaser (success, $p = .10$) and a .90 chance of selecting a low-volume purchaser (failure, $1 - p = .90$).

ASSUMPTION 2:   Selecting high-volume purchasers from credit files can be represented as a Bernoulli process. The probability of selecting a high-volume purchaser does not change no matter how many high-volume purchasers have already been selected.

We can summarize the information we have as:

The random variable X = number of high-volume purchasers in a sample of four
Possible values $\{0, 1, 2, 3, 4\}$
Known quantities $n = 4$, $p = .1$, $x = 0$
Unknown quantity $P(X = 0)$

Substituting the known values into expression (5.6), we obtain

$$P(X = 0) = {_4C_0}(.10)^0(.90)^{4-0} = .6561$$

Thus, there is a .6561 probability that we would select no high-volume purchasers in a sample of four. The binomial probability is accurate if the two assumptions are valid.

EXAMPLE: MEETING CUSTOMER DEMAND   A bakery has five ovens. At least four ovens must be working in order to meet customer demand on a given day. The probability of a particular oven working is .90. What is the probability of meeting customer demand?

Define success as a working oven and failure as a nonworking oven. The two assumptions underlying the binomial expression for this example are given here:

ASSUMPTION 1: There is a .90 chance of an oven working (success, $p = .90$) and a .10 chance of an oven not working (failure, $1 - p = .10$).

ASSUMPTION 2: Working ovens can be represented as a Bernoulli process. The probability of an oven working does not change no matter how many ovens are already working.

The given information can be summarized as:

The random variable	X = the number of ovens working on a given day
Possible values	{0, 1, 2, 3, 4, 5}
Known quantities	$n = 5$, $p = .9$, $x = 4, 5$
Unknown quantity	$P(X = 4) + P(X = 5)$

Since *at least* four ovens must be working in order to meet customer demand, we must compute the probabilities of four or five ovens working and add them:

$$P(X = 4) = {}_5C_4(.90)^4(.10)^{5-4} = .3280$$
$$P(X = 5) = {}_5C_5(.90)^5(.10)^{5-5} = \underline{.5905}$$
$$.9185$$

Thus, there is almost a 92% chance of meeting customer demand. The binomial probability is accurate if the two assumptions are valid.

The Binomial Table

Recall that a probability distribution for a discrete random variable consists of all possible numerical values of the random variable and their associated probabilities. We now compute the probability distribution for the random variable—the number of high-volume purchasers of Example 1:

$$P(X = 0) = {}_4C_0(.10)^0(.90)^{4-0} = .6561$$
$$P(X = 1) = {}_4C_1(.10)^1(.90)^{4-1} = .2916$$
$$P(X = 2) = {}_4C_2(.10)^2(.90)^{4-2} = .0486$$
$$P(X = 3) = {}_4C_3(.10)^3(.90)^{4-3} = .0036$$
$$P(X = 4) = {}_4C_4(.10)^4(.90)^{4-4} = \underline{.0001}$$
$$1.0000$$

We could also have determined the five probabilities using the binomial table in Appendix 1. To use the appendix, perform the following steps:

1. Find the correct sample size, *n*. Sample sizes from 1 to 20 are the major column headings of the table.
2. Find the appropriate probability of success, *p*. The success probabilities are shown in increments of .01 from .01 to .50 and form the column subheadings.
3. Find the number of successes for which you wish to calculate probabilities. These are the row headings located along the extreme left-hand side of the table.
4. The desired probability is at the intersection of the appropriate value of *p* and the value of *x*.

We can use Appendix 1 to determine the probability of getting exactly zero high-volume purchasers in a sample of four when the probability of success is .10:

$$P(X = 0 \text{ for } n = 4, p = .10) = .6561$$

					$n = 4$					
$x \backslash p$	.01	.02	.03	.04	.05	.06	.07	.08	.09	.10
0	.9606	.9224	.8853	.8493	.8145	.7807	.7481	.7164	.6857	.6561
1	.0388	.0753	.1095	.1416	.1715	.1993	.2252	.2492	.2713	.2916
2	.0006	.0023	.0051	.0088	.0135	.0191	.0254	.0325	.0402	.0486
3	.0000	.0000	.0001	.0002	.0005	.0008	.0013	.0019	.0027	.0036
4	.0000	.0000	.0000	.0000	.0000	.0000	.0000	.0000	.0001	.0001

We can use Appendix 1 even when the probability of a success is greater than .5. Suppose the probability of selecting a high-volume customer was .7. We wish to compute the probability of selecting three high-volume customers—$P(Y = 3$ for $n = 4, p = .70)$. We cannot use Appendix 1 directly because it only goes up to a *p* value of .5. However, selecting three high-volume customers is the same as selecting one low-volume purchaser since there are only two types of credit customers. Thus,

$$P(Y = 3 \text{ for } n = 4, p = .7) = P(X = 1 \text{ for } n = 4, p = .3) = .4116$$

Mean and Standard Deviation of a Binomial Distribution

Consider again the problem of credit classification in Example 1. Figure 5.3 shows a probability histogram for the number of high-volume purchasers in a sample of size four.

We could approximate the mean in this figure visually by placing a steel rod under the probability histogram and moving it back and forth until we balance the histogram. It would balance near the value of .5 high-volume purchaser.

FIGURE 5.3 Binomial Probability Histogram: $n = 4$, $p = .10$

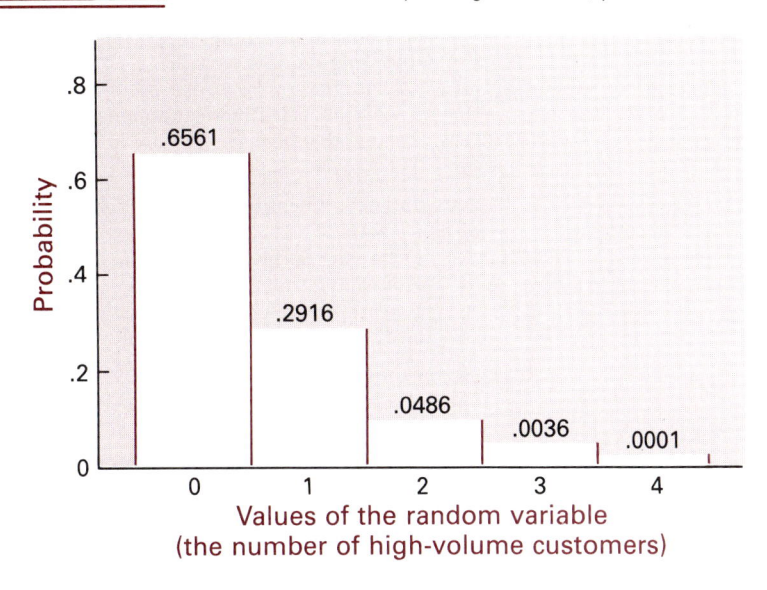

[Histogram showing probabilities: 0 → .6561, 1 → .2916, 2 → .0486, 3 → .0036, 4 → .0001]

Values of the random variable
(the number of high-volume customers)

We could also use expression (5.1) to compute the mean of the probability distribution shown in Figure 5.3. However, there is a simpler expression for binomial probabilities, given by

$$\text{Mean} = \mu = np \tag{5.8}$$

Remember, the term n is the number of trials and p is the probability of a success on a single trial. Thus, for the credit classification problem,

Mean number of high-volume purchasers $= 4(.1) = .4$

This agrees with our approximation. To compute the standard deviation we could use expression (5.2). But again, there is a simpler expression for binomial probabilities:

$$\begin{aligned}\sigma &= \sqrt{np(1-p)} \\ &= \sqrt{4(.1)(.9)} = .6 \text{ high-volume purchaser}\end{aligned} \tag{5.9}$$

The mean number of high-volume purchasers is .4 and the standard deviation is .6.

In summary, to use the binomial distribution, two assumptions must be true. First, only two outcomes can occur on a single trial. Second, the probability of any particular outcome must remain constant from trial to trial. If these assumptions are met, we can use the binomial expression or table to generate valid probabilities.

SECTION 5.3 EXERCISES

1. You are interested in computing probabilities. Define a success and failure for each of the following random variables.
   a. The number of workers present in a plant
   b. The number of American-made cars in the parking lot
   c. The number of loans that are in default at a bank
   d. The number of parcels of land that are valued above $100,000

2. A random experiment is counting the number of unoccupied beds in a university infirmary with 20 beds.
   a. Define the Bernoulli process involved.
   b. How many trials are involved?
   c. Explain the difference between a Bernoulli process and a binomial probability distribution.

3. Assume the probability of striking oil in a West Texas oil field is .10. Wildcatters Inc. plans to drill 10 wells in the oil field. They are interested in computing the probability distribution of striking oil in the 10 wells they will drill. Assume that striking oil is a Bernoulli process.
   a. Define the random variable of interest and its possible outcomes or values.
   b. What is the probability of not striking oil in any of the 10 wells?
   c. What is the probability of striking oil in two or three wells?
   d. How would Wildcatters Inc. establish that the probability of finding oil in the West Texas oil field is .10?

4. The probability of being involved in an auto accident each year is .1. Assume that involvement in an auto accident is a Bernoulli process.
   a. What is the probability of being involved in an auto accident in each of the next three years?
   b. What is the probability of not being involved in an auto accident in any of the next three years?
   c. What is the probability of being involved in an accident exactly once in the next three years?
   d. What assumptions did you make in answering parts a–c?
   e. What data would we need to estimate that the probability of being involved in an accident is .1?

5. Assume that the probability of obtaining a home equity loan is .40. Use the binomial table in Appendix 1 to determine the following probabilities if 10 people apply for a home equity loan.
   a. Exactly 4 will get a loan.
   b. Exactly 10 will get a loan.
   c. More than 7 will get a loan.
   d. Fewer than 6 will get a loan.
   e. Explain why the probability that 4 applicants obtain a loan should be higher than the probability that 10 applicants obtain a loan.

6. Accident claims are checked for completeness by a branch office before they are sent to the regional office for payment. Suppose the probability that a claim is complete is .7. Use the binomial table to determine the following probabilities.
   a. Of the next 5 claims processed, all 5 will be complete.
   b. Only 1 of the next 5 claims processed will be complete.
   c. One of the next 5 claims processed will be incomplete.

7. Refer to Exercise 6. What are the mean and standard deviation for the number of complete claims in a sample of 5 claims?

8. A good sales representative expects to make a sale on 25% of her calls. She plans to

make 10 calls over the next week. Assume that whether she makes a sale or not on each call is a Bernoulli process.
   a. Define a success and a failure.
   b. Define the random variable and its possible values.
   c. What are the mean and standard deviation of this random variable?
   d. What is the probability that over the next 10 calls, the sales representative will make more than 7 sales?
   e. What is the probability that the sales representative will make at least 2 sales, but not more than 6 sales?

9. A quality control worker for Xcel selects a sample of 10 items from a shipment from Supplyall and inspects for defects. Each item will be classified as either acceptable or defective. Supplyall claims that its defect probability is .10, but Xcel suspects that it might be .30. In the next shipment, the quality control worker finds 3 defective pieces in a sample of 10. Is Supplyall's claim or Xcel's claim more reasonable? Explain.

10. A market researcher plans to conduct a telephone survey of 100 customers to ask if they either favor or oppose a new customer policy. Suppose 70% of all customers favor the policy.
   a. Find the mean number of favorable responses in the sample of 100.
   b. Find the standard deviation.
   c. Explain the meaning of mean and standard deviation in the context of this problem.
   d. Suppose 45 of the 100 customers surveyed said they favor the new policy. According to Chebyshev's rule, what is the probability of observing 45 or fewer positive responses if 70% actually favor the new policy?

5.4 Problem Solving and the Binomial Distribution

In the previous section we presented the basics of the binomial distribution. Now we will demonstrate how the binomial distribution can improve problem solving and decision making. By the end of this section you should be able to:

1. use binomial probabilities to assess the consequences of decisions;
2. use binomial probabilities to sense emerging problems or opportunities; and
3. determine if real-world situations approximate a Bernoulli process.

Assessing Consequences

The following problem illustrates how binomially generated probabilities can help managers assess consequences of different strategies.

EXAMPLE: WHICH INSPECTION RULE TO CHOOSE?   COMCEL buys electronic components from ZT Audio for its cellular phones. COMCEL requires that each lot of 1,000 components contain 10% or fewer defectives. Inspecting every component is not practical. Thus COMCEL selects and tests a sample of 10 components. It is considering two acceptance rules: Accept the lot of 1,000 if (1) one or no components of the sample of 10 are defective or (2) two or fewer components of the sample of 10 are defective. If COMCEL rejects a lot, ZT must replace it.

Assume that ZT Audio can consistently produce acceptable lots—that is, lots with at most 10% defectives. Even so, a sample of 10 taken from a lot that contains 10% defectives could have two or more defective components. Given the first acceptance rule, what percentage of ZT's future shipments will be rejected even though they contain at most 10% defectives? COMCEL is interested in computing the probability of getting one or no defects in a sample of size 10. Thus a success is finding a defective component. Given here are the assumptions and the random variable of interest:

ASSUMPTION 1: There is a .10 chance that a component is defective (success, $p = .10$) and a .90 chance that a component is good (failure, $1 - p = .90$) in a sample of 10.

ASSUMPTION 2: Inspecting components is a Bernoulli process. The probability that a component is defective does not change no matter how many defectives COMCEL finds during inspection. We will examine this assumption shortly.

The random variable X = the number of defectives in a sample of size 10
Possible values $\{0, 1, 2, 3, \ldots, 9, 10\}$
Known quantities $n = 10, \quad p = .10, \quad x = 0, 1$
Unknown quantity $P(X = 0) + P(X = 1)$

Using Appendix 1, we find

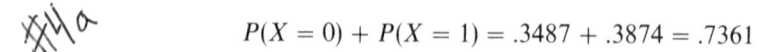

$$P(X = 0) + P(X = 1) = .3487 + .3874 = .7361$$

Assume all the lots of 1,000 contain 10% defectives. Remember, 10% defectives is acceptable, and so COMCEL should accept all of the lots. However, COMCEL's incoming component inspectors will find one or no defectives in a sample of 10 only about 74% of the time. Thus, COMCEL will actually accept only 74% of ZT's shipments even though 100% are good lots. Due to the sampling rule, $(1 - .7361)$, or approximately 26%, of acceptable lots will be rejected. This is called the *producer's risk*. The producer, ZT Audio, is at risk because although all the lots it has submitted are good lots, 26% of them will be rejected because of the sampling rule.

Now consider the second acceptance rule: Accept the lot if COMCEL finds *two or fewer* defectives. Now what is the producer's risk? Using Appendix 1, we determine that

$$P(X = 0) + P(X = 1) + P(X = 2) = .3487 + .3874 + .1937 = .9298$$

About 93% of the time, the COMCEL inspectors will find two or fewer defectives in a sample of 10. Thus, COMCEL will accept about 93% of the shipments from ZT. The producer's risk will drop to $1 - .93 = .07$. With only 7% of acceptable lots rejected by the second rule, ZT Audio would prefer rule (2), of course.

The second sampling rule reduces the producer's risk and is more agreeable for ZT, but what about COMCEL? It must be concerned about stopping lots that contain more than the acceptable 10% level of defectives. For example, suppose that ZT sends lots that all contain 20% defectives—twice the acceptable defective rate. These are all bad lots and should all be rejected. Analyze how successful the two acceptance rules are at stopping such lots from entering COMCEL. We have rewritten Assumption 1 to reflect the increased probability of a defective component, $p = .20$. Assumption 2 has not changed and so we have omitted it.

ASSUMPTION 1: There is a .20 chance that a component is defective (success, $p = .20$) and an .80 chance that a component is good (failure, $1 - p = .80$) in a sample of 10.

Known quantities $n = 10$, $p = .20$, $x = 0, 1$

On the basis of rule (1) and using Appendix 1, we find that

$$P(X = 0) + P(X = 1) = .1074 + .2684 = .3758$$

On the basis of rule (2) and using Appendix 1, we find that

$$P(X = 0) + P(X = 1) + P(X = 2) = .1074 + .2684 + .3020 = .6778$$

Under rule (1), COMCEL inspectors will find one or no defectives in a sample of 10 in lots that actually contain 20% defectives about 38% of the time. Thus 38% of the time, COMCEL will accept lots that contain 20% defectives.

Under rule (2), COMCEL inspectors will find two or fewer defectives in a sample of 10 in lots that actually contain 20% defectives about 68% of the time. Thus 68% of the time, COMCEL will accept lots that contain 20% defectives. Of the two sampling rules, COMCEL prefers rule (1).

The probability of accepting a bad lot is called the *consumer's risk*. The consumer or customer is at risk since it will accept bad lots. As we reduce the producer's risk, we increase the consumer's risk. COMCEL wants a sampling rule with a low consumer's risk whereas ZT Audio wants a low producer's risk. Expect serious negotiations between the two parties.

Problem Sensing

Problem sensing is a crucial managerial capability, since a manager cannot solve a problem until he or she knows it exists. We have already used descriptive statistics to sense problems; now we will use binomial probabilities.

EXAMPLE: DEVIATION FROM PAST PERFORMANCE?   ABC Inc. buys computer paper from Apex Stationery. From historical data, Apex knows that the probability that ABC will place an order in a given week is .40. There have been no orders from ABC in the last six weeks. Could Apex be facing a problem with a decline in orders from ABC Inc.?

Begin by stating the two assumptions and defining the random variable.

ASSUMPTION 1: In a particular week, there is a .40 chance that ABC Inc. will place an order (success, $p = .40$) and a .60 chance that ABC will not place an order (failure, $1 - p = .60$).

ASSUMPTION 2: Orders from ABC Inc. are a Bernoulli process. The probability of ABC placing an order in a week does not change no matter how many orders ABC Inc. has placed in previous weeks. We will discuss this assumption shortly.

The random variable	X = the number of orders in the last six weeks
Possible values	$\{0, 1, 2, 3, 4, 5, 6\}$
Known quantities	$n = 6, \quad p = .40, \quad x = 0$
Unknown quantity	$P(X = 0)$

Using Appendix 1, we find that

$$P(X = 0) = .0467$$

The chance of ABC placing no orders in the last six weeks is only .047. Yet, that is what actually happened. What could account for it? Please think about it before reading on! There are three possible explanations:

1. The probability of ABC placing an order is still .40, and there is *no problem*. The chance of getting no orders in the past six weeks is only .047. However, even though the probability is small, it is an event that could happen.
2. The probability of ABC placing an order has changed, and Apex does have *a problem* of declining sales. How does it know it has a problem? It is more likely to get no orders if the chance of getting an order dropped from the historic .40 to, say, .10. In that case, the chance of getting no orders in the last six weeks would have been .531 (a likely event) instead of .047. Please verify the .531 probability using Appendix 1.
3. Orders from ABC Inc. can no longer be modeled by a Bernoulli process. If this is true, then the .047 probability may not be meaningful. Apex *cannot tell* if it has a problem with declining orders.

If Apex believed that getting orders from ABC could still be modeled by a Bernoulli process, then it must choose one of the first two explanations. The chance of there being no problem is less than 1 in 20 (.047). The probability is so low that most managers would reject the "no problem" explanation. They would conclude that there is a declining order problem and would begin to diagnose its causes.

Assessing the Bernoulli Process Assumption

While we do not expect many real-world situations to be exactly a Bernoulli process, are they near-Bernoulli? Does the probability of a success remain *approximately* the same from trial to trial? If so, the binomial probabilities are meaningful and can be used in problem solving. We will examine whether the Bernoulli process assumption is justified for the Apex Stationery and COMCEL inspection examples.

APEX STATIONERY EXAMPLE   Does the probability of obtaining an order in a particular week from ABC Inc. remain the same no matter how many such orders ABC has recently placed?

To determine if this is a near-Bernoulli process, consider the two sets of time-ordered sales data shown in Table 5.6. Either ABC Inc. places an order in a week (O) or it does not place an order (NO). Both patterns show that in 40% of the weeks, ABC places an order. Yet one pattern is inconsistent with the requirements of a Bernoulli process. Can you tell which? Please think about it before reading on.

Pattern A is not representative of a Bernoulli process. Once ABC places an order, it does so for the next three weeks, and once ABC does not order in a week, it does not do so for the next five weeks. The trials are not independent.

Table 5.6
Possible Patterns of ABC Placing Orders over Time

Week	Pattern A	Pattern B
1	O	O
2	O	NO
3	O	NO
4	O	NO
5	NO	O
6	NO	NO
7	NO	NO
8	NO	O
9	NO	NO
10	NO	O
11	O	NO
12	O	NO
13	O	NO
14	O	O
15	NO	O
16	NO	NO
17	NO	NO
18	NO	O
19	NO	NO
20	NO	O

$$P(\text{order}) = \frac{8}{20} = .40 \qquad P(\text{order}) = \frac{8}{20} = .40$$

Pattern B is consistent with a Bernoulli process. Orders are interspersed among no orders. The .40 probability holds for the first five weeks, the second five weeks, the third five weeks, and the last five weeks.

COMCEL INSPECTION PROGRAM EXAMPLE   Is the probability that a component is defective the same no matter how many defectives COMCEL finds during inspection? That is, is the probability of a success, p, constant from trial to trial?

If lots of 1,000 are 10% defective, then COMCEL should expect about 100 defective components in each lot. Now ask the following questions:

1. What is the probability that the first component in a sample of 10 is defective?

$$p = \frac{100}{1,000} = .100$$

2. What is the probability that the second component is defective if the first component was defective?

$$p = \frac{99}{999} = .099$$

3. What is the probability that the tenth component is defective if the first nine components were defective?

$$p = \frac{91}{991} = .092$$

Since the three probabilities of success are very similar, we have a near-Bernoulli process. We may use the binomial expression or table to calculate meaningful probabilities. If the three probabilities of success varied greatly (a judgment call), we should not use the binomial expression to calculate probabilities.

SECTION 5.4 EXERCISES

1. COMCEL sells two phones—the standard and the deluxe. Historically, deluxe phones have accounted for 60% of sales. What is the probability that exactly 0 of the next 10 sales will be for deluxe phones? Suppose that in fact COMCEL does not sell any deluxe phones in its next 10 sales. What could that mean? Explain.

2. At every company-sponsored workshop, 15 workers sign up. However, most times, fewer than 10 workers actually attend. The manager of Human Resource Development is considering two strategies to improve actual attendance: (1) send constant reminders to registered workers and (2) have supervisors encourage their workers to attend programs. The manager estimates the following subjective probabilities of

workers actually attending a workshop for which they have registered:

$$P(\text{reminders}) = .50$$

$$P(\text{encourage}) = .70$$

What is the probability that the next workshop will have 10 or more workers attend if the manager uses the first strategy? The second strategy? Other things being equal, which strategy should the manager use?

3. Suppose that Joel Associates offers to buy each lot of 1,000 units from Gail Industries only if none of a sample of 5 units is defective. If Gail Industries expects 5% of the units to be defective, what percentage of the lots will Joel Associates reject over the long run?

4. A manufacturer claims that no more than 5% of its items are defective. You adopt the following decision rule: Reject a shipment of 500 items if more than 1 of the 10 sampled items is defective. Otherwise, you accept the shipment.
   a. What is the probability of rejecting the lot when in fact only 5% are defective? Is this a consumer risk or a producer risk?
   b. Suppose that 10% of the 500 items are actually defective. What is the probability of accepting the lot when it should be rejected? Is this a consumer risk or a producer risk?

5. A manufacturer claims that no more than 5% of its items are defective. You adopt the following decision rule: Reject a shipment of 500 items if more than 1 of the 20 sampled items is defective. Otherwise, you accept the shipment.
   a. What is the probability of rejecting the lot when in fact only 5% are defective? Is this a consumer risk or a producer risk?
   b. Suppose that 10% of the 500 items are actually defective. What is the probability of accepting the lot when it should be rejected? Is this a consumer risk or a producer risk?
   c. Compare the results of this exercise with those of Exercise 4. What is the effect of increasing the sample size on producer and consumer risk, everything else held constant?

6. A major appliance manufacturer conducts phone surveys each quarter to check customer satisfaction. One district has 100,000 customers. Suppose that 10% of its customers are dissatisfied. The company selects 50 customers from the district to check the number that are dissatisfied. Should the company use the binomial model to analyze the data for the district? Explain.

7. Assuming no other changes, would your answer change in Exercise 6 if the district has 100 customers? Explain.

5.5 The Poisson Distribution

Like the binomial distribution, the Poisson distribution provides probability values and is an alternative approach to obtaining probabilities through surveys or personal assessments. The Poisson distribution is a discrete probability distribution where the values of a random experiment may take on only positive whole numbers. By the end of this section you should be able to:

1. state the conditions for using the Poisson distribution;
2. calculate and interpret Poisson probabilities;

3. use the Poisson probability table in Appendix 2; and
4. compute and interpret the mean and standard deviation for a Poisson random variable.

Here are some examples of Poisson random variables:

Random Variable	Area of Opportunity
Number of accidents in a factory	per minute, hour, week, year
Number of defects	per foot, yard of cable
Number of errors	per line, page, 10 pages

A single trial is some fixed *area of opportunity* such as a fixed length of time (a day) or space (a page). The outcome on a single trial is a count of occurrences per area of opportunity, such as accidents per week. The possible values of each of these random variables are {0, 1, 2, 3, 4, ...} — any positive integer value.

For a variable to be Poisson distributed, three conditions must hold:

1. An event, such as an accident, has many opportunities to occur, but the probability that the event will occur at any opportunity is extremely small.

For example, there are many hours in a year, and most go by without accidents. There are many pages in a book, but very few have a typo.

2. The probability of an event is proportional to the size of the area of opportunity.

For example, the probability that an accident will happen in a COMCEL plant is greater over a period of one month than over a period of one week.

3. The events must be statistically independent.

The third condition requires that events do not occur in clusters. For example, if an accident occurs on Monday, this has no effect on the probability that other accidents will occur in the same week. If a spelling error is found on one page, it does not affect the probability of finding other errors on the same page.

The Poisson Expression

Use expression (5.10) for computing Poisson probabilities:

$$P(X = x) = \frac{e^{-\lambda}\lambda^x}{x!} \qquad (5.10)$$

λ (read as lambda) is the *average number* of occurrences over a given area of opportunity. The constant e equals 2.71828.

Consider the following problem, which involves a Poisson random variable.

EXAMPLE: DEFECTS PER STANDARD PHONE UNIT   Inspectors have kept careful records of the number of defects (scratches, paint flaws, etc.) over the last 500 standard car phones produced at COMCEL. The area of opportunity is a standard phone unit. One phone can have more than one defect. The inspectors recorded a total of 125 defects on the 500 sets, for an average of .25 defect per phone; $\lambda = .25$. What is the probability of finding no defects on the next phone inspected? What is the probability that the next phone will have exactly one defect?

$\frac{125}{500} = .25$

Begin by defining the random variable of interest.

The random variable	X = number of defects per standard phone
Possible values	$\{0, 1, 2, 3, 4, 5, \ldots\}$
Known quantities	$\lambda = .25$, $x = 0$, $x = 1$
Unknown quantities	$P(X = 0)$, $P(X = 1)$

From expression (5.10):

$$P(X = 0) = \frac{e^{-.25}(.25)^0}{0!} = .779$$

Note that $0! = 1$, since any number raised to the 0 power is 1, and that $e^{-.25} = \frac{1}{e^{.25}}$. There is a .779 probability that the next standard phone examined will have no defects.

$$P(X = 1) = \frac{e^{-.25}(.25)^1}{1!} = .195$$

There is a .195 probability that the next standard phone examined will have exactly one defect. Both probabilities are accurate if (1) the average number of defects per phone is .25 and (2) the defects are Poisson distributed; that is, the three conditions have been met.

The Poisson Table

We could also have determined the two probabilities using the cumulative Poisson table in Appendix 2. To use the table, find the average number of occurrences, λ. Values of λ are column headers. Values of x are the row headers. The intersection of a value of x and a value of λ is the cumulative probability, $P(X \leq x)$.

Use Appendix 2 to find the probability of finding no defects on a standard phone unit if the average number of defects per phone is .25.

$$P(X = 0 \text{ when } \lambda = .25) = .779$$

How do we find the probability of finding *exactly* one defect on a standard phone? The number at the intersection of λ equal to .25 and the row labelled 1 is

.974. The tabled number, .974, is a *cumulative* probability—the probability of observing one *or fewer* defects on a single standard phone. It is $P(X \le 1$ when $\lambda = .25)$. Note that

$$P(X \le 1) = P(X = 0) + P(X = 1)$$

Therefore,

$$P(X \le 1) - P(X = 0) = P(X = 1)$$
$$.974 - .779 = .195$$

λ x	.02	.04	.06	.08	.10	.15	.20	.25
0	.980	.961	.942	.923	.905	.861	.819	.779
1	1.000	.999	.998	.997	.995	.990	.982	.974
2		1.000	1.000	1.000	1.000	.999	.999	.998
3						1.000	1.000	1.000

That is, to find the probability of exactly one defect, we subtract the probability of finding exactly zero defects from the probability of finding either zero or one defect. In general, the way to find the probability of x defects is to subtract the cumulative probability of finding $x - 1$ defects from the cumulative probability of finding x defects.

Problem Sensing and the Poisson Distribution

In Section 5.4 we illustrated how the binomial distribution could be used to sense problems. We now demonstrate how the Poisson distribution can also be used to sense problems.

EXAMPLE: ACCIDENTS AT THE DALLAS PLANT The manager of COMCEL's Dallas plant notes that there have been 27 accidents within the plant over the past 36 months. Table 5.7 contains a breakdown of how many of the 36 months had 0, 1, 2, 3, 4, and 5 accidents. What is the probability that more than 3 accidents will occur next month?

Before using the Poisson probability table we must list the assumptions. If they are not reasonable, then calculated probabilities may not be meaningful.

ASSUMPTION 1: The average number of accidents per month is .75. There were no accidents in 18 of the months. There was 1 accident in 12 of the months. The total number

Table 5.7

Breakdown of the Past 36 Months According to Number of Accidents

Accidents per Month	Number of Months
0	18
1	12
2	4
3	1
4	1
5	0
	36

of accidents for the past 36 months is $0(18) + 1(12) + 2(4) + 3(1) + 4(1) + 5(0)$, or 27. Therefore, the average number of accidents per month, λ, is 27/36, or .75 accident per month.

ASSUMPTION 2: The probability of an accident occurring at any point in time is very small. The probability increases as the length of time increases. The area of opportunity is 1 month.

ASSUMPTION 3: The probability that another accident will occur is the same, no matter how many accidents have already occurred in that month.

Begin by defining the random variable of interest.

The random variable	X = the number of accidents in a month
Possible values	$\{0, 1, 2, 3, 4, 5, \ldots\}$
Known quantity	λ = .75 accident per month
Unknown quantity	$P(X > 3)$

From Appendix 2,

$$P(X > 3) = 1 - P(X \leq 3) = 1 - .993 = .007$$

The probability that the Dallas plant will experience more than 3 accidents next month is .007. This probability assessment will be accurate if the actual accident distribution is Poisson distributed with a mean of .75 accident per month.

Now suppose that next month there are more than 3 accidents at the Dallas plant. What could that mean? One possibility is that there is no increasing accident problem in Dallas. However, the computed probability of more than 3 accidents is only .007—a highly unlikely event. On the other hand, the high number of accidents could suggest that the Dallas plant has an accident problem. Most managers would choose the increasing accident rate explanation.

What should the manager do? He should investigate and seek possible root causes. He could ask: What changes occurred in Dallas this month? What is unique about this month in comparison to other months? For example, suppose that COMCEL installed new equipment. That might account for the higher-than-normal number of accidents. Perhaps new personnel have been assigned to the plant. That too might account for the problem. Effective managers, once they sense problems, investigate them.

Assessing the Poisson Process Assumptions

Suppose the number of accidents in a month in the Dallas plant is Poisson distributed. Then how many of the 36 months should have had exactly zero accidents? How many months should have had exactly one accident, two accidents, etc.?

Table 5.8 contains the plant accident data and the Poisson probabilities of having exactly 0, 1, 2, 3, 4, or 5 accidents. For example, from Appendix 2, the probability of having exactly one accident next month is .827 − .472 = .355. Please verify the other probabilities shown.

Table 5.8

Accidents at the Dallas Plant over 36 Consecutive Months

Accidents per Month	Actual Number of Months	Poisson Probability	Expected Number of Months
0	18	.472	36(.472) = 16.99
1	12	.355	36(.355) = 12.78
2	4	.132	36(.132) = 4.75
3	1	.034	36(.034) = 1.22
4	1	.006	36(.006) = .22
5	0	.001	36(.001) = .04
	36	1.000	36.00

The last column in the table contains the expected number of months that should have had 0, 1, 2, 3, 4, and 5 accidents if the number of accidents is Poisson distributed. For example, we would expect no accidents in 16.99 of the 36 months—that is, 36 months times the Poisson probability of .472. There were 18 months when there were no accidents. Note that all the actual and expected frequencies agree very well. It appears that the number of accidents at the Dallas plant is Poisson distributed.

Mean and Standard Deviation of a Poisson Distribution

The mean of a probability distribution is the long-run average value. The mean for any Poisson distribution is λ, the average number of occurrences per area of opportunity. To see that λ is the mean, use Table 5.8 to develop a probability histogram for the number of accidents. The histogram will balance at about .75 accident per month.

We could use expression (5.2) to compute the standard deviation, but there is a simpler one for a Poisson distribution:

$$\sigma = \sqrt{\lambda} \qquad (5.11)$$

The standard deviation for a Poisson random variable is simply the square root of its mean. For the Dallas plant's accidents study, the standard deviation is $\sqrt{.75} = .87$ accident per month.

In summary, we use the Poisson distribution when we must calculate probabilities for the number of events—an error, an accident—over a given area of opportunity—a page, a week, etc. A critical assumption is that the events must be statistically independent. The mean and standard deviation for a Poisson distributed random variable are λ and $\sqrt{\lambda}$, respectively.

SECTION 5.5 EXERCISES

1. Explain what an area of opportunity is.
2. A book editor expects to find one error per five pages of text. What is the probability that over the next five pages, the editor will find:
   a. At least one error?
   b. More than one error?
   c. Exactly one error?
   d. What is the mean number of errors over the next 15 pages?
   e. How could the editor estimate λ?
3. Suppose that the number of persons per car arriving at the entrance to One Flag over Guam amusement park is Poisson distributed with $\lambda = 3.2$. What is the probability that a car arriving at the entrance contains:
   a. One person?
   b. Fewer than four persons?
   c. What are the mean and standard deviation for the number of persons per car?
   d. How could the amusement park estimate λ?
4. A retailer sells office copiers. The problem facing the store manager is knowing how much inventory to stock. Large inventories tie up capital and increase insurance premiums. Alternatively, stockouts can result in lost sales. The store manager knows that it takes 5 business days from placing an order to delivery of a new supply of copiers. After an analysis of sales data she finds that she sold an average of five copiers per 5-day period.
   a. List the assumptions you must make before using the Poisson probability table. Be sure to define the Poisson random variable and describe its possible values.
   b. What is the area of opportunity?
   c. If she waits until five copiers remain in inventory before reordering, what is the probability that she will experience a stockout while she is waiting for new copiers to arrive?
   d. If she reorders when 12 remain in inventory, what is the probability that she will experience a stockout while she is waiting for new copiers to arrive?
   e. What should be her reorder point if she wants no than a 5% chance of stockout?

5. The factory has experienced an average of four accidents per month over the last three years. The manager decided to require each employee to attend an accident prevention workshop.
   a. Assuming that the workshop has no effect on the accident rate, what is the probability that next month there will be at least four accidents? At least two accidents?
   b. Suppose that next month there is only one accident. Would you conclude that the workshop was successful? Defend your answer.

6. Car phones are shipped in boxes of four. The average number of defects per phone is .5. Define the Poisson random variable, X, as the number of defects in a box of four phones.
   a. What are the mean and standard deviation of this random variable?
   b. Construct a probability histogram to display the distribution.
   c. According to Chebyshev's rule, at least 89% of the boxes will have fewer than how many defects over the long run?
   d. Suppose that the next box of four phones contained six defects. Could this suggest that something is wrong? Explain.

7. In an office the number of employees smoking in any 15-minute interval is Poisson distributed with a standard deviation of 3. What is the mean number of employees smoking in any 15-minute interval? What is the probability that during a 15-minute time period exactly three employees will be smoking?

5.6 The Normal Distribution

While the binomial and Poisson distributions are useful, many business problems involve continuous random variables. Continuous random variables can take on an infinite, or uncountable, number of values. For these cases, we will need a new probability distribution for problem solving—the normal distribution. By the end of this section, you should be able to:

1. explain the importance of the normal distribution;
2. describe the characteristics of the normal distribution;
3. explain what z-scores are;
4. compute normal probabilities;
5. use the normal distribution to help sense emerging problems and make decisions; and
6. explain why the mean and standard deviation of the normal distribution are not known *with certainty* except in statistics books.

Why Is the Normal Distribution So Useful?

There are many continuous probability distributions. Why single out the normal distribution? There are two reasons.

First, the normal distribution is an *approximation* to many probability distributions. For instance, we can use the normal distribution to approximate the binomial distribution when the number of binomial trials, n, is very large. The normal distribution involves much less computation.

To illustrate this idea, consider tossing a fair coin 100 times and counting the number of heads. The discrete random variable—the number of heads in 100

FIGURE 5.4 Probability Histogram for 100 Tosses of a Fair Coin

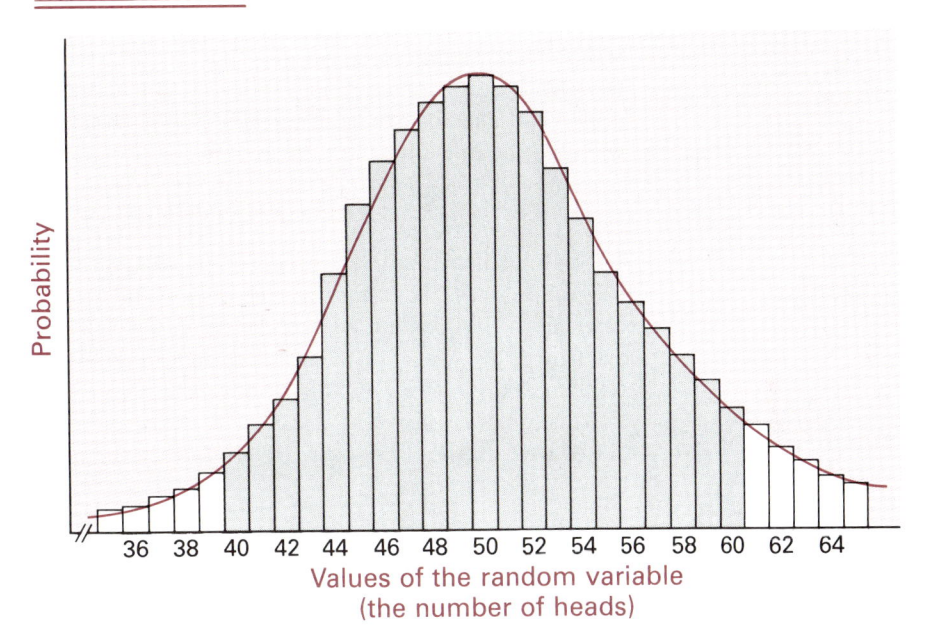

flips—can take on any of 101 values (0, 1, 2, 3, ... , 100). Figure 5.4 is a probability histogram of the 101 probabilities. We have drawn a smooth curve through the top of each rectangle. The probability histogram for 100 tosses is very close to the bell-shaped curve that we discussed in Chapter 2.

Now, we have two ways to compute the probability of getting between 40 and 60 heads:

1. Treat the random variable as discrete, use the binomial distribution, and determine the *exact* probability. This is the sum of the 21 shaded rectangles in Figure 5.4.
2. Treat the random variable as continuous, use the normal distribution, and *approximate* the probability. This is the area underneath the curve between 40 and 60 heads.

The binomial distribution requires that we compute factorials such as 100!. The normal distribution is a quick probability calculator for the binomial distribution.

The normal distribution is also used to *approximate* the distributions for variables such as IQ, height, grade point average, blood pressure, and the diameter of machined parts. All these variables share one thing in common: They are affected by a large number of independent factors. For example, blood pressure is influenced by genetic factors, diet, weight, lifestyle, aerobic conditioning, and other factors. A frequency histogram of the blood pressures of 1,000 people would be nearly bell-shaped. In summary, when many independent factors affect a continuous random variable, its behavior can often be described by the normal distribution.

Second, the *central limit theorem* states that the sampling distribution of the sample mean tends to be normal-shaped. This result is essential in marketing research, quality control, and political polling where it is important to be able to draw valid conclusions from samples about target populations of interest. We will describe this important theorem in the next section.

Characteristics of the Normal Distribution

The normal distribution is a *family* of bell-shaped curves. All have the same basic bell shape and differ only in their mean and standard deviation. The mean determines the location of the center of the bell, and the standard deviation determines the spread of the bell. Figure 5.5 presents three characteristic shapes. As the mean increases, the distribution shifts to the right. See Figures 5.5a and 5.5b for comparison. As the standard deviation increases, the distribution spreads out or flattens about the mean; see Figures 5.5b and 5.5c.

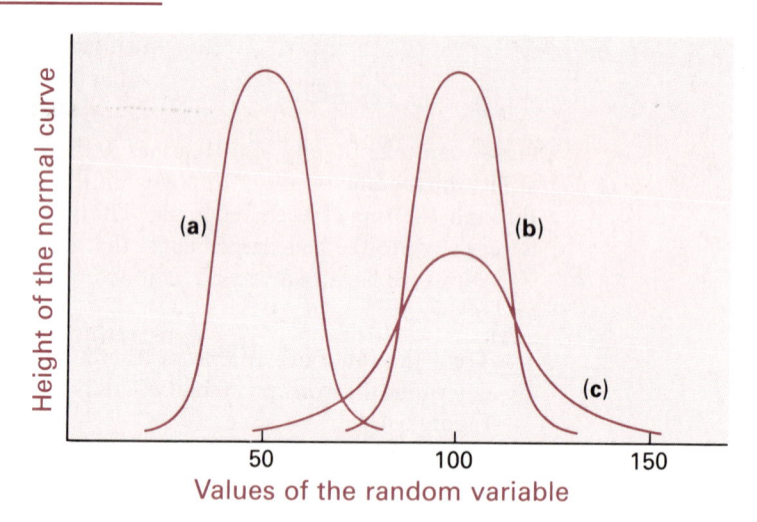

FIGURE 5.5 Three Normal Curves

All normal curves have the following characteristics:

1. They are symmetric.
2. The total area under the curve is 1. Probabilities are the areas under the normal curve. Recall that the second rule of probability states that the sum of the probabilities of all possible events is 1.0, and this idea extends to continuous probability distributions.
3. The values of x can range from $-\infty$ to $+\infty$. However, in practice, we rarely consider values of x lying at a distance beyond 3 standard deviations from the mean.

4. The normal curve is *asymptotic* to the horizontal axis. The curve gets closer to this axis as x gets very large or small, but never actually reaches the axis.
5. The probability that x will fall below (above) the mean is .5.
6. The probability that x lies within a distance of 1 standard deviation from the mean is .6826. The probability that x lies within a distance of 2 standard deviations from the mean is .9544. The probability that x lies within a distance of 3 standard deviations from the mean is .9974.

In Chapter 2 we used the Empirical rule to identify outliers. When a frequency histogram is *approximately* bell-shaped, about 68% of all data values fall within a distance of 1 standard deviation from the mean. Nearly all the observations fall within a distance of 3 standard deviations from the mean. When the histogram represents a perfect normal distribution, the exact percentages are 68.26% and 99.74%, respectively.

z-Scores and Finding Probabilities

Probabilities are the areas under normal curves, as shown in Figure 5.5. Because computing these areas requires calculus, statisticians have done the integration for us. However, instead of having one probability table for each normal curve (for each possible combination of a mean and standard deviation), we use only one table—the standard normal, or z, table. See Appendix 3.

The following example demonstrates how to use Appendix 3. Assume that a histogram for the weights of 1,000 female students is normally distributed. The mean and standard deviation are 120 pounds and 10 pounds. We wish to compute the probability that a female student weighs between 120 and 132 pounds, or $P(120 < \text{weight} < 132)$.

To determine the probability, we first convert the weights of 120 pounds and 132 pounds into z-scores using expression (5.12) and then use Appendix 3. A z-score for a value—say 132 pounds—is simply the number of standard deviations that the value is away from the mean:

$$z\text{-score} = \frac{\text{Value of normal variable} - \text{Mean}}{\text{Standard deviation}}$$

$$= \frac{x - \mu}{\sigma} \qquad (5.12)$$

Converting a 120-pound weight into a z-score: $\quad \dfrac{120 - 120}{10} = 0.0$

Converting a 132-pound weight into a z-score: $\quad \dfrac{132 - 120}{10} = +1.2$

To find $P(120 < \text{weight} < 132)$, we must find the area under the standard normal curve, $P(0 < z < +1.2)$, in Appendix 3.

In Appendix 3, the column labelled z contains values from 0.0 to 3.0 in increments of .10. The ten column headings indicate z-scores in increments

z	.00	.01	.02	.03	.04	.05	.06	.07	.08	.09
0.0	.0000	.0040	.0080	.0120	.0160	.0199	.0239	.0279	.0319	.0359
0.1	.0398	.0438	.0478	.0517	.0557	.0596	.0636	.0675	.0714	.0753
0.2	.0793	.0832	.0871	.0910	.0948	.0987	.1026	.1064	.1103	.1141
0.3	.1179	.1217	.1255	.1293	.1331	.1368	.1406	.1443	.1480	.1517
0.4	.1554	.1591	.1628	.1664	.1700	.1736	.1772	.1808	.1844	.1879
0.5	.1915	.1950	.1985	.2019	.2054	.2088	.2123	.2157	.2190	.2224

of .01. These permit finding probabilities for z-scores to two decimal places. The numbers in the table body are areas under the standard normal curve (probabilities) between z-scores of 0.00 and 3.09.

To determine $P(0 < z < +1.2)$, find the row z value of 1.2 and the column labelled .00. The value at the intersection is the area under the standard normal curve that lies between the mean of 0 and a z-score of $+1.2$, or .3849. The probability that a female student weighs between 120 and 132 pounds is thus .3849.

Compute the probability of selecting a female student who weighs between 92.4 pounds and 130 pounds, $P(92.4 < \text{weight} < 130)$. We again use expression (5.12) to convert weights into z-scores:

Converting a 92.4-pound weight into a z-score: $\dfrac{92.4 - 120}{10} = -2.76$

Converting a 130-pound weight into a z-score: $\dfrac{130 - 120}{10} = +1.00$

To find $P(92.4 < \text{weight} < 130)$, we must find the area under the standard normal curve, $P(-2.76 < z < +1.00)$ in Appendix 3. We find the area from 0 to -2.76 and the area from 0 to $+1.00$, and then add the two probabilities.

Since the normal curve is symmetric, areas under the curve are the same for positive and negative z-scores of the same magnitude. Find the row z value of 2.7 and the column labelled .06. The value at the intersection is the area under the normal curve that lies between the z-score of 0 and -2.76, or .4971. Find the z value of 1.0 and the column labelled .00. The tabled value at the intersection is .3413. Thus the desired probability is the sum of the two probabilities, .4971 + .3413, or .8384. The probability of selecting a female student who weighs between 92.4 and 130 pounds is .8384.

In summary, to find normal probabilities, we must find the areas under the standard normal curve. Thus, it makes no sense to talk about $P(\text{weight} = 125$ pounds). There is no area over a point. There is area only over an interval, say between 105 and 106 pounds.

The Normal Distribution and Decision Making

Normal probabilities are often used to help managers make decisions among alternative actions. Consider the courier service problem presented at the beginning of the chapter.

EXAMPLE: COURIER SERVICE PROBLEM   Federal Service advertises that its mean delivery time is 30 hours, while United Express claims that its mean delivery time is 34 hours. However, United Express's arrival times are more consistent because the standard deviation of its delivery times is only 2 hours, whereas the standard deviation of Federal's delivery times is 5 hours. Which service should we use if our document must arrive within 36 hours?

We recommend the following three-step process when using the normal distribution to solve business problems:

1. STATE THE ASSUMPTIONS AND DEFINE RANDOM VARIABLES

ASSUMPTION 1: If we drew a frequency histogram of document arrival times for both courier services for the past several months, the histograms would be nearly bell-shaped.

ASSUMPTION 2: The mean arrival times for the past several months are indicative of mean arrival times in the future. The mean arrival time for Federal Service is 30 hours and for United Express is 34 hours.

ASSUMPTION 3: The standard deviations in arrival times for the past several months are indicative of the standard deviations in the future. The standard deviation for Federal Service is 5 hours and for United Express is 2 hours.

The random variables	X = Arrival time for Federal Service
	Y = Arrival time for United Express
Possible values	X, Y: an uncountable number of values
Unknown quantities	$P(X < 36$ hours$), P(Y < 36$ hours$)$

2. SKETCH THE NORMAL CURVE(S)   This will help to visualize the probability we are trying to determine. The Federal Service curve is centered at the mean of 30 hours. The United Express curve is centered at the mean of 34 hours. The curves extend about 3 standard deviations on each side of their means. Figure 5.6 on page 250 depicts two such curves. We shade those areas that represent the desired probabilities. The figure indicates that Federal Service appears to have a higher probability of meeting the 36-hour maximum deadline.

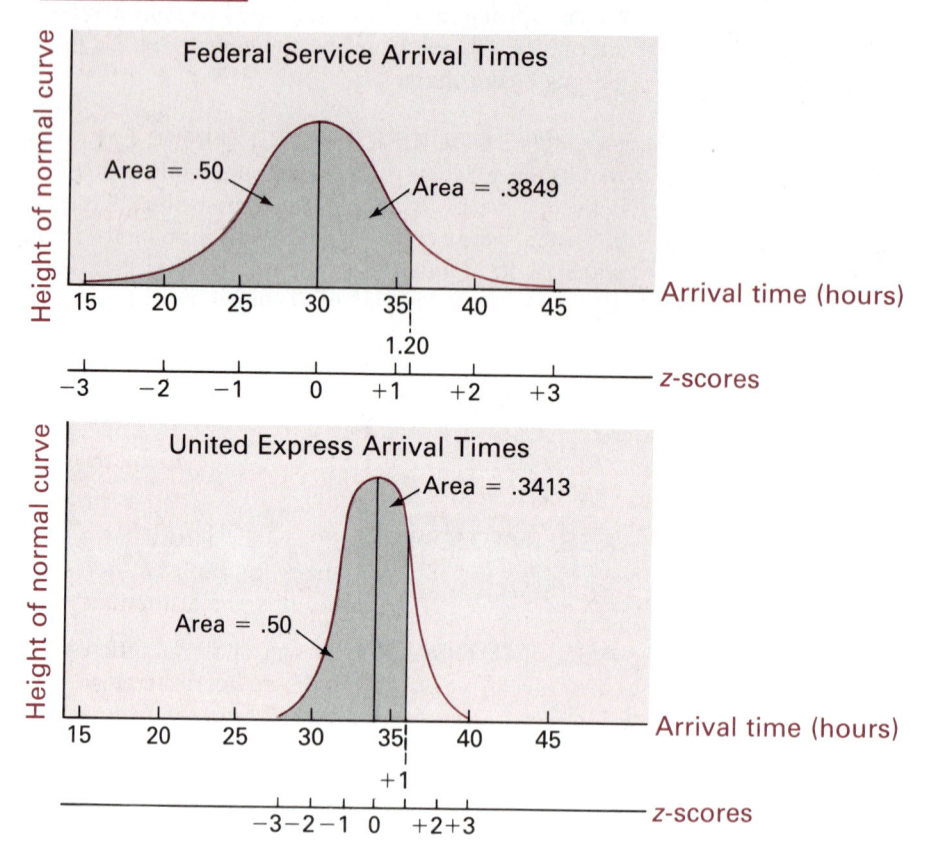

FIGURE 5.6 Distributions for Federal Service and United Express

Federal Service Arrival Times

Area = .50   Area = .3849

Arrival time (hours): 15, 20, 25, 30, 35, 40, 45
1.20
z-scores: −3, −2, −1, 0, +1, +2, +3

United Express Arrival Times

Area = .3413
Area = .50

Arrival time (hours): 15, 20, 25, 30, 35, 40, 45
+1
z-scores: −3, −2, −1, 0, +2, +3

3. CONVERT TO z-SCORES AND FIND PROBABILITIES *Computation for Federal Service* The probability that the arrival time is less than 36 hours is made up of two areas in the upper graph of Figure 5.6—the area below the mean and the area between the mean and 36 hours. The area below the mean is .50. The probability that the arrival time is between 30 and 36 hours is determined as

$P(30 < X < 36)$

$= $ Probability that the z-score is between $\dfrac{30 - 30}{5}$ and $\dfrac{36 - 30}{5}$

$= $ Probability that the z-score is between 0 and $+1.2$

$= .3849$ (from Appendix 3)

Thus, $P(X < 36) = .50 + .3849 = .8849$. The documents delivered by Federal Service will arrive in less than 36 hours 88.49% of the time.

Computation for United Express The probability that the arrival time is less than 36 hours is made up of two areas in the lower graph of Figure 5.6—the area below the mean and the area between the mean and 36 hours. The area below the mean is .50. The probability that the arrival time is between 34 and 36 hours is determined as

$$P(34 < Y < 36)$$
$$= \text{Probability that the } z\text{-score is between } \frac{34-34}{2} \text{ and } \frac{36-34}{2}$$
$$= \text{Probability that the } z\text{-score is between } 0 \text{ and } +1.0$$
$$= .3413 \quad \text{(from Appendix 3)}$$

Thus, $P(Y < 36) = .50 + .3413 = .8413$. The documents delivered by United Express will arrive in less than 36 hours 84.13% of the time.

Neither service is a certainty, but Federal Service is more likely to meet the 36-hour deadline. Therefore, we should select Federal Service as our courier.

Now we will illustrate how the normal distribution can help a marketing manager determine which of two marketing strategies to use in selling a product.

EXAMPLE: FAMILY VS. INDIVIDUAL BRANDING Family branding occurs when a firm applies one brand name to its entire product line, such as Levi's. Individual branding occurs when a firm uses individual brand names for its products—for example, Procter & Gamble's Pringles, Crisco, and Tide.

GSP, Inc. is trying family branding for a new toothpaste in 20 test cities. The mean and standard deviation in units sold per week are 2,250 and 250. GSP is also test marketing the toothpaste using individual branding in 20 similar cities. The mean and standard deviation in units sold per week are 2,250 and 500. GSP will select the strategy that maximizes its chance of selling at least 2,350 units per week. This will ensure that it meets its return on project investment goal. Which marketing approach—family or individual branding—should GSP select for mass marketing its product?

1. STATE THE ASSUMPTIONS AND DEFINE RANDOM VARIABLES

   ASSUMPTION 1: If we record toothpaste sales in units per week for both marketing strategies, the frequency histograms would be nearly bell-shaped.

   ASSUMPTION 2: The means from the marketing study are indicative of the mean sales when the product is mass marketed. The mean sales for both individual and family branding are 2,250 units per week.

ASSUMPTION 3: The standard deviations are indicative of the variability in sales when the product is mass marketed. The standard deviation for family branding is 250 units per week. The standard deviation for individual branding is 500 units per week.

The random variables	FB = Sales per week using family branding
	IB = Sales per week using individual branding
Possible values	FB, IB: several thousand values each
Unknown quantities	$P(FB > 2{,}350)$, $P(IB > 2{,}350)$

2. SKETCH THE NORMAL CURVE(S)   Figure 5.7 presents the normal probability distribution curves for the two marketing approaches.

3. CONVERT TO z-SCORES AND FIND PROBABILITIES   *Computation for family branding*   The probability that weekly sales exceed 2,350 units is the shaded area in the upper graph of Figure 5.7. The area between 2,250 and

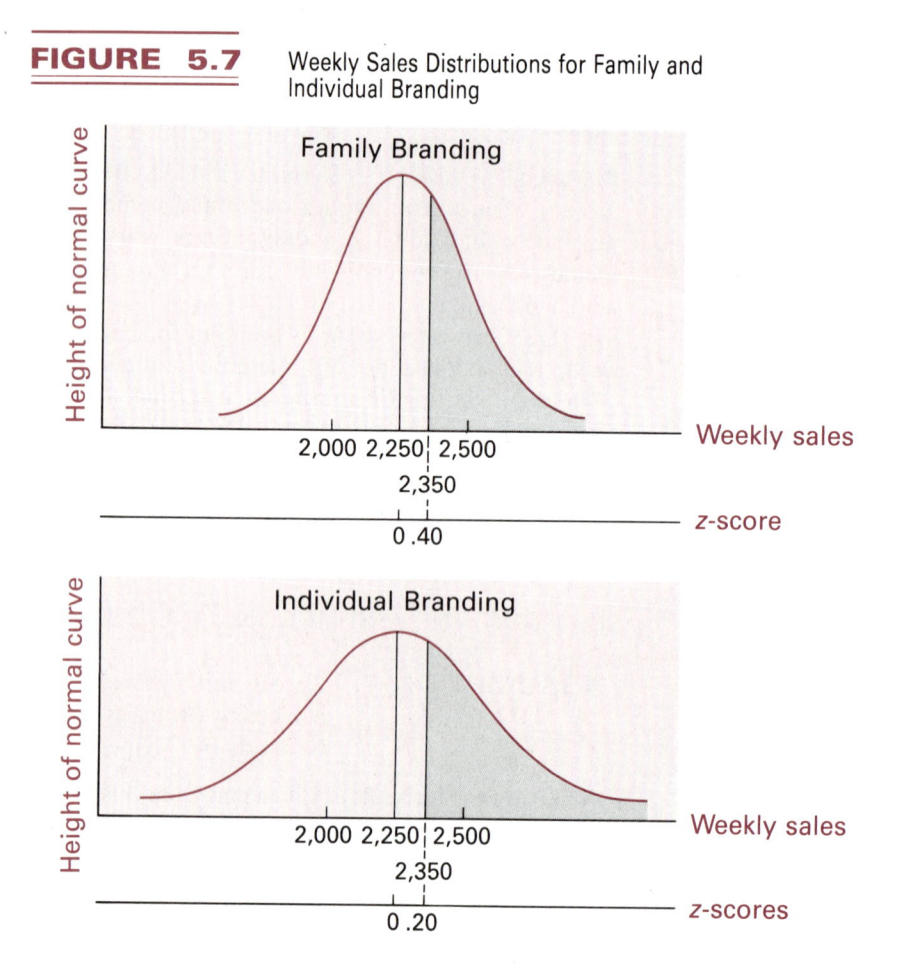

FIGURE 5.7   Weekly Sales Distributions for Family and Individual Branding

2,350 and the area above 2,350 total .5. Thus the desired area or probability is the area between 2,250 and 2,350 subtracted from .5.

The probability that weekly sales are between 2,250 and 2,350 is obtained as

$P(2{,}250 < FB < 2{,}350)$

$= $ Probability that the z-score is between $\dfrac{2{,}250 - 2{,}250}{250}$ and $\dfrac{2{,}350 - 2{,}250}{250}$

$= $ Probability that the z-score is between 0 and $+.4$

$= .1554$ (from Appendix 3)

Thus, $P(FB > 2{,}350) = .50 - .1554 = .3446$. There is a .3446 probability of selling more than 2,350 units per week using family branding.

Computation for individual branding The probability that weekly sales exceed 2,350 units is the shaded area in the lower graph of Figure 5.7. The desired area or probability is the area between 2,250 and 2,350 subtracted from .5.

The probability that weekly sales are between 2,250 and 2,350 is computed as

$P(2{,}250 < IB < 2{,}350)$

$= $ Probability that the z-score is between $\dfrac{2{,}250 - 2{,}250}{500}$ and $\dfrac{2{,}350 - 2{,}250}{500}$

$= $ Probability that the z-score is between 0 and $+.2$

$= .0793$ (from Appendix 3)

Thus, $P(IB > 2{,}350) = .50 - .0793 = .4207$. There is a .4207 probability of selling more than 2,350 units per week using individual branding.

With family branding, there is a .34 chance of meeting the minimum sales target, while with individual branding, there is a .42 chance of meeting the minimum sales target. Other things being equal, GSP should go with individual branding, unless it decides not to enter the market because neither probability is greater than .5.

Our final case illustrates how quality control personnel can use the normal distribution to determine if a firm can begin full-scale production.

EXAMPLE: PROCESS CAPABILITY STUDIES Before full-scale production begins, firms often run process capability studies to determine if the production process can produce products that meet engineering specifications. COMCEL's Engineering Design Group determines that the shatter strength for the cellular phone plastic handset must be between 4,600 and 4,900 pounds per square inch (ppsi). The *lower tolerance limit* (LTL) is 4,600 ppsi and the *upper tolerance limit* (UTL) is 4,900 ppsi.

The Quality Control Department conducts a process capability study by selecting five handsets from each of the first 15 production shifts. The mean and standard deviation of shatter strengths of the 75 handsets are 4,750 ppsi and 70 ppsi, respectively. What percentage of the handsets produced will have shatter strengths within the tolerance limits, between 4,600 and 4,900 ppsi? Should COMCEL begin full-scale production?

1. STATE THE ASSUMPTIONS AND DEFINE RANDOM VARIABLES

   ASSUMPTION 1: The histogram of 75 shatter strengths from the process capability study is nearly bell-shaped.

   ASSUMPTION 2: The mean shatter strength will be the same for the process capability study and full-scale production. The mean shatter strength is 4,750 ppsi.

   ASSUMPTION 3: The standard deviation of shatter strength will be the same for the process capability study and full-scale production. The standard deviation is 70 ppsi.

The random variable	SS = Shatter strength of handset
Possible values	An uncountable number of values
Unknown quantity	$P(4{,}600 < SS < 4{,}900)$

2. SKETCH THE NORMAL CURVE(S)   Figure 5.8 shows the normal probability distribution curve for the process capability study.

3. CONVERT TO z-SCORES AND FIND PROBABILITIES   The desired probability is the shaded area in Figure 5.8. It consists of two parts—the area between a z-score of -2.14 and the mean, and the area between the mean and a z-score of $+2.14$. These two parts have the same area. Thus we need to find only one area or probability and double it. The probability that shatter strength

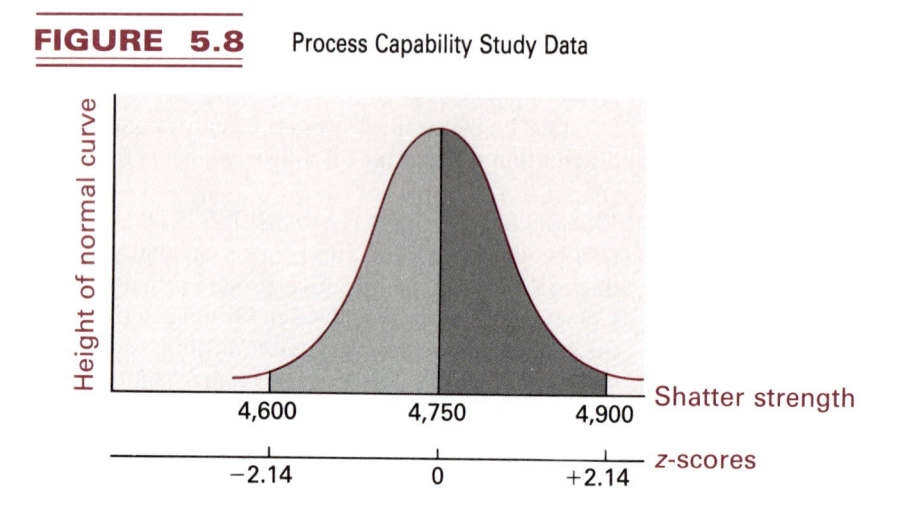

FIGURE 5.8   Process Capability Study Data

is between 4,750 and 4,900 ppsi is

$P(4{,}750 < SS < 4{,}900)$

$= $ Probability that the z-score is between $\dfrac{4{,}750 - 4{,}750}{70}$ and $\dfrac{4{,}900 - 4{,}750}{70}$

$= $ Probability that the z-score is between 0 and $+2.14$

$= .4838$ (from Appendix 3)

Thus, $P(4{,}600 < SS < 4{,}900) = .4838 + 4838 = .9676$. Therefore, 96.76% of the handsets will have shatter strengths within the tolerance limits. If COMCEL finds the 97% figure acceptable, it will start full-scale production. If this percentage is too low, COMCEL has two choices:

1. Widen the tolerance limits from 4,600–4,900 ppsi to 4,500–5,000 ppsi.
   Please verify that almost 100% of the handsets will then have acceptable shatter strengths. However, potential customers may not like the new tolerance limits. If customers do not care, then widening the limits makes sense.
2. Reduce the standard deviation of the process.
   Suppose that COMCEL reduces the standard deviation from 70 ppsi to 50 ppsi. Please verify that then almost 100% of its handsets will meet the 4,600 to 4,900 ppsi tolerance limits. This strategy can require extensive capital investment in new machinery or process improvements, but it is usually the better approach.

Validity of the Normal Distribution Assumptions

To use the z tables of Appendix 3 we must know the normal distribution's mean and standard deviation. How do we know these values? For example, how would we know the mean shatter strength of *all* plastic phone handsets—that is, the population of handsets?

The only way to know with certainty the population's mean and standard deviation is to test the entire population. With a few exceptions, this is not practical. Generally speaking then, we never know the population mean and standard deviation. However, there are two ways to *estimate* these values. First, we can assume that the sample and population have the same mean and standard deviation. That was our assumption in the process capability study. We took a sample of 75 handsets and assumed that its mean and standard deviation were equal to the corresponding population values. Second, we can estimate the population mean and standard deviation using methods of formal statistical reasoning. The latter approach is better. Formal statistical reasoning will be our topic for the remainder of the book.

In summary, using normal probabilities to make decisions assumes that the probabilities are meaningful. Computed normal probabilities will be meaningful only when the following three assumptions are true:

1. The random variable's frequency histogram is nearly bell-shaped.
2. The mean of the sample data is a good estimate of the mean of the population.
3. The standard deviation of the sample data is a good estimate of the standard deviation of the population.

SECTION 5.6 EXERCISES

1. Under what general conditions would you expect that a distribution will be normally distributed?

2. Refer to the standard normal table, Appendix 3. How much of the area under the curve lies:
   a. To the left of the mean of 0?
   b. Between 0 and 1 standard deviation above the mean?
   c. To the left of a point 1 standard deviation below the mean?
   d. To the right of a point 1 standard deviation below the mean?

3. Refer to the standard normal table. Find the following probabilities:
   a. $P(-1 < z < 1)$
   b. $P(-2.33 < z < 2.33)$
   c. $P(-2.58 < z < 2.58)$
   d. $P(-1.96 < z < 1.96)$
   e. $P(-3.00 < z < 3.00)$
   f. $P(z < -3.00)$
   g. $P(z > -3.00)$
   h. $P(1.2 < z < 2.3)$
   i. $P(.2 < z < 1.3)$
   j. $P(z = 1.3)$

4. Consider a normal distribution centered around a mean of 10.0 cm with a standard deviation of 1.0 cm. You are given the following set of observations: {7.5 cm, 8.2 cm, 10.0 cm, 12.0 cm}.
   a. Draw a picture of the normal distribution and place the observations on the graph.
   b. Place a standard normal, z-score, scale below the scale of the distribution in part **a** so the standard deviation units of the standardized normal scale correspond to the standard deviation distances of the original population.
   c. How far is each measurement from the mean of 10.0 cm as measured in standard deviation units?

5. The hours-to-burnout of fuses are normally distributed with a mean of 500 hours and a standard deviation of 25 hours. If a new fuse is installed, find the probability that it will last:
   a. At least 450 hours.
   b. More than 550 hours.
   c. Between 425 hours and 575 hours.
   d. Less than 425 hours.
   e. Between 425 and 450 hours.

   For each part above: (1) Draw and label the normal distribution. (2) Place the standard normal scale below the hours scale. (3) Shade the area corresponding to the desired probability.

6. Two companies are bidding to supply your company with computer chips. The first company claims the mean life of its chips is 1,000 hours and the standard deviation is

200 hours. The second company claims the mean life of its chips is 1,200 hours and the standard deviation is 300 hours. Which company would you buy from if a chip should last at least 800 hours? At least 400 hours?

7. Suppose the scores on a mechanical aptitude test are normally distributed with a mean of 50 and a variance of 25.
   a. What score would you have to make so that fewer than 1% of the scores are higher than yours?
   b. If a counselor told you that your z-score on the test was +1.4, what was your actual score?
   c. The counselor tells you that the company only hires applicants who score 60 or above. What percentage of the applicants will qualify for a job with the company?

8. The admissions office of a university had a policy of not considering an applicant who scores below 475 on the verbal portion of the SAT exam. Suppose verbal scores are normally distributed with a mean of 500 and a standard deviation of 100. Because of declining enrollment, in 1991 the administration lowered the cutoff score to 450. If the university has 10,000 applicants for the class of 1996, how many more will be accepted because of the revised policy?

9. A vending machine sells coffee in 6-ounce cups. If the machine is set to dispense 5 ounces of coffee, the amount of coffee dispensed per cup is normally distributed with a mean of 5 ounces and a standard deviation of .25 ounce. Assume that the standard deviation is .25 regardless of the mean amount dispensed.
   a. If the machine is set to dispense 5.75 ounces, what is the probability the dispensed coffee will overflow the 6-ounce cup?
   b. If the machine is set to dispense 5 ounces, what percentage of the customers will get only 4.5 ounces or less?
   c. Where would we set the mean amount dispensed so that only 2.5% of cups would overflow?
   d. Suppose you decide that overflows of hot coffee are worse for business than giving the customer a short cup. You set the machine to dispense 5.0 ounces and the next cup overflows. Would you conclude that the machine isn't working properly? Why?

10. Document arrival times are normally distributed with a mean of 30 hours and a standard deviation of 3 hours.
    a. What is the first quartile of document arrival times?
    b. What is the third quartile?
    c. Find the interquartile range.

5.7 The Central Limit Theorem

Many random variables are normally distributed. However, even when the population histogram is not bell-shaped, the *sampling distribution of the sample mean* may be approximately normal-shaped. Thus, we can use the standard normal tables to compute normal probabilities. By the end of this section you should be able to:

1. construct a sampling distribution for the sample mean and explain what it means; and
2. explain why the shape of the sampling distribution of the sample mean will be approximately normal, provided the sample size is sufficiently large.

FIGURE 5.9 Frequency Histogram of Days Absent for a Population of Six Workers

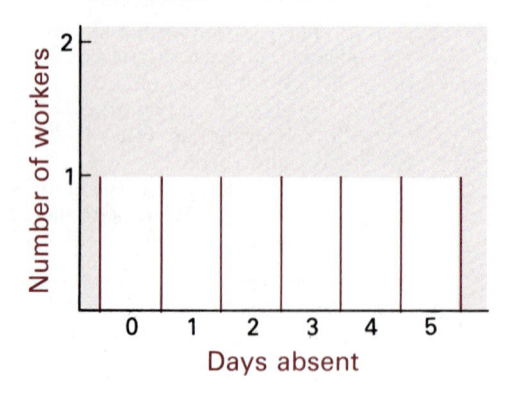

To illustrate a sampling distribution of the sample mean, start with a small population—the number of days each worker has been absent in the last quarter. The population histogram appears in Figure 5.9 and the data are presented here:

Worker	A	B	C	D	E	F
Days Absent	0	1	2	3	4	5

One thing is clear—Figure 5.9 is not a normal-shaped curve.

Now select a sample of three workers without replacement. For example, we might select workers A, B, and C. These three workers missed an average of one day each last quarter. If we select workers A, E, and F, they missed an average of 3 days each last quarter. Table 5.9 contains the 20 possible samples and their means; Figure 5.10 is a histogram for the 20 sample means.

Table 5.9

Sample Means for All Possible Samples of Size Three

Sample	Mean	Sample	Mean
A, B, C	1.00	B, C, D	2.00
A, B, D	1.33	B, C, E	2.33
A, B, E	1.67	B, C, F	2.67
A, B, F	2.00	B, D, E	2.67
A, C, D	1.67	B, D, F	3.00
A, C, E	2.00	B, E, F	3.33
A, C, F	2.33	C, D, E	3.00
A, D, E	2.33	C, D, F	3.33
A, D, F	2.67	C, E, F	3.67
A, E, F	3.00	D, E, F	4.00

FIGURE 5.10 Histogram of 20 Sample Means for n = 3

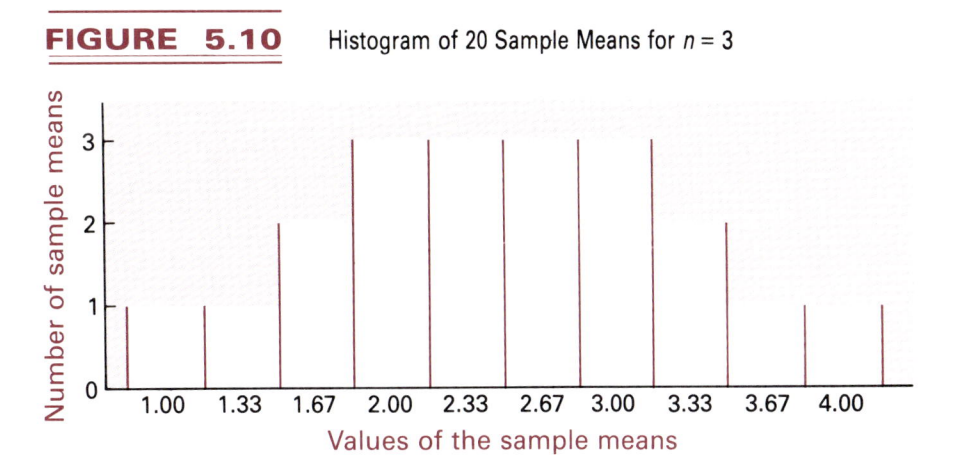

Figure 5.10 illustrates a sampling distribution of the sample mean. It is a sampling distribution because we took all possible samples of size three (without replacement) from the population and computed the sample means. It is a distribution because Figure 5.10 shows each sample mean value and the number of times it occurred.

Now take all possible samples of size four from the population without replacement. Again, we compute the sample means for the 15 samples. The results are given in Table 5.10; Figure 5.11 on page 260 shows the frequency histogram for the 15 sample means.

How do the shapes of the sampling distributions of the sample mean in Figures 5.10 and 5.11 compare to the shape of the population in Figure 5.9? The histogram of the population is definitely not a normal curve. Yet notice how the shape of the sampling distributions of the sample mean becomes more normal as the sample size increases from three to four. This is the idea behind the **central limit theorem**.

The central limit theorem states that even if the shape of the population distribution is not normal, the shape of the sampling distribution of the sample mean becomes more normal as we increase the sample size. For sample sizes larger than 30, the sampling distribution of the sample mean will be nearly normal-shaped.

Table 5.10

Sample Means for All Possible Samples of Size Four

Sample	Mean	Sample	Mean
A, B, C, D	1.50	A, C, E, F	2.75
A, B, C, E	1.75	A, D, E, F	3.00
A, B, C, F	2.00	B, C, D, E	2.50
A, B, D, E	2.00	B, C, D, F	2.75
A, B, D, F	2.25	B, C, E, F	3.00
A, B, E, F	2.50	B, D, E, F	3.25
A, C, D, E	2.25	C, D, E, F	3.50
A, C, D, F	2.50		

FIGURE 5.11 Histogram of 15 Sample Means for $n = 4$

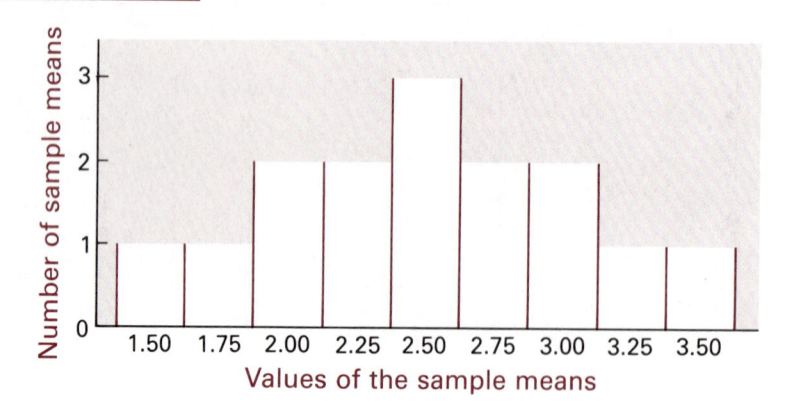

The central limit theorem is central because it deals with the mean, which is a measure of the center. It is a limit theorem because it describes what happens as the sample size increases.

Why does the central limit theorem work? As we take larger samples, more of the sample means are near or at the center of the sampling distribution—2.50 (see Figure 5.11). That is because a sample of size four that has a small value, such as 0 or 1, is likely to include a large value, such as 4 or 5. Thus the sample means will tend to cluster near the distribution's center. The further we move above or below the mean, the fewer the sample means. That is a description of a near-normal curve.

In summary, the central limit theorem states that, provided the sample size is greater than 30, the sampling distribution of the sample mean will be normal-shaped. We will make use of this theorem when we cover formal statistical inference in Chapter 7.

SECTION 5.7 EXERCISES

1. The numbers of years that Presidents Johnson, Nixon, Ford, Carter, and Reagan served are as follows:

    $$\{6, 5, 3, 4, 8\}$$

    a. Use the software included with the text to select all possible samples of size two without replacement.
    b. Use the software to develop a histogram showing the sampling distribution of the sample mean.
2. Repeat Exercise 1 for all samples of size $n = 3$.
3. Explain how the histogram of the population is related to the histogram of a sampling distribution of the sample mean. What happens to the spread of a sampling

distribution as the sample size used to calculate each mean is increased from two to three? What happens to the shape of the sampling distribution as the size of each sample increases?

4. In 1987, according to the *Bureau of Census Current Population Reports*, the median family income with two earners was $36,990 and the distribution was skewed toward higher incomes.
   a. Could you use the normal table to determine the probability of selecting a family with two earners that has an income between $30,000 and $40,000? Explain.
   b. Suppose we took a sample of 100 from the population of two-earner families and determined the mean of the 100 family incomes. Suppose we repeated taking a sample of 100 many times, each time recording the mean of the 100 family incomes. Could we then determine the probability of selecting 100 families with a mean family income between $30,000 and $40,000? Discuss.

5.8 Integrating Framework and Key Ideas

Managers build mental models of their firm's operations by collecting, organizing, and summarizing descriptive data, and by using probability distributions. Mental models help managers sense unusual occurrences, detect emerging problems, find relationships between variables, evaluate alternatives, and make decisions. Table 5.11 on page 262 summarizes some tools for improving problem solving.

We conclude with three key ideas which emerge from the two chapters on probability:

1. Managers must deal with uncertainty through probabilities. They should use empirical, subjective, or theoretical probability distributions to improve problem solving and decision making.

Often managers can collect data, calculate relative frequencies, and thereby estimate empirical probability distributions. They also rely on intuition and judgment and construct subjective probability distributions. Subjective probabilities are especially useful when no historical data are available. However, subjective probabilities can lead to flawed decisions if the rules of probability are violated. We have shown how decision trees can help guard against common managerial information processing errors (Section 4.7).

Finally, managers should use theoretical probability distributions to generate probabilities. We have presented three types of distributions—the binomial, the Poisson, and the normal.

2. Underlying the theoretical probability distributions are sets of assumptions. These assumptions must be reasonable if the calculated probabilities are to be meaningful. When properly used, theoretical probability distributions improve decision making.

In considering either the binomial or Poisson distribution, check for a near-Bernoulli or Poisson process. When considering the normal distribution, check that the data frequency histogram is almost bell-shaped.

Table 5.11
Using Chapters 2–5 to Improve Problem Solving

A. Sensing unusual occurrences—outliers

Cross-Sectional Data Use descriptive statistics, stem-and-leaf displays, and box plots. Outliers are data points that are more than 3 standard deviations from the mean or are outside the fences of a box plot.

Time-Ordered Data Use moving average and residual line graphs. Outliers are extremely large positive or negative residuals.

Probability Use subjective, empirical, or theoretical probability distributions. Outliers are events with low probabilities that actually happen.

B. Looking for relationships between variables

Cross-Sectional Data Use cross-tabs tables or scatter diagrams. Compute row or column percentages. Variables are related when all the row (or column) percentages are not the same.

Time-Ordered Data Use scatter diagrams, multiple line graphs, and cross-correlations. Two time series are related if $r(k)\sqrt{n-k} > 2$.

Probability Compute conditional probabilities. Events are related if the conditional and simple probabilities are not the same.

C. Evaluating alternatives and making decisions

Cross-Sectional Data Use one-way tables or multiple box plots to summarize impacts of alternatives. Select the alternative that has the highest mean or median or the lowest standard deviation or interquartile range.

Time-Ordered Data Use moving averages to assess impacts. Select the alternative that has the fastest increasing or decreasing moving average.

Probability Use probabilities to predict impacts. Select the alternative that has the highest probability of accomplishing the goals.

If managers are subject to using theoretical probability distributions improperly, why not rely on empirical or subjective distributions? Empirical distributions are based on sample data and are only estimates of relative frequencies of populations. In contrast, if a theoretical distribution accurately describes a population, then a manager can proceed to act with confidence that he knows the composition of the entire population and can predict the relative frequency of all possible outcomes. For example, the normal distribution will provide more meaningful probabilities than an empirical distribution.

Furthermore, collecting empirical probabilities on many events can be time-consuming. To use the normal probability distribution, all we need to know or estimate are the mean and standard deviation. We need to know only the probability of a success and the sample size to compute binomial probabilities, and the mean to compute Poisson probabilities.

3. The central limit theorem tells us that the sampling distributions of the sample mean will tend to be bell-shaped provided the sample size exceeds 30 observations.

Even though managers work with many data sets that are not normally distributed, the normal distribution is still very important. In Chapter 7 we will show how managers can use the central limit theorem to *estimate* unknown population means and percentages which are crucial in making decisions.

COMCEL

```
Date:   February 17, 1991
From:   Sang Kim, Quality Assurance
  To:   Howard Bright, Plant Manager
  Re:   Quality of circuit breakers
```

The Department of Quality Assurance does continuous monitoring of our circuit breakers. The defect rate has been approximately 5% for some time. Unfortunately, three or more defective items in a box of 25 must be expected at times. The fact that our customer found three defective circuit breakers does not suggest that the defect rate has increased.

We claim an *average* defect rate of 5% per sample of 25 circuit breakers. This means that, in the long run, our customers can expect an average of 1.25 defective circuit breakers in boxes containing 25 units. The average is 1.25 because most boxes will have no defective units or one defective unit. But some boxes will have two or more defective units due to chance.

If the underlying causes of the defects remain stable, and the defect rate remains constant at 5%, then approximately 13% of all boxes of 25 items will contain three or more defective units. On the other hand, only 3.4% of the boxes will contain four or more defective items in the long run. Since the cost of examining the whole manufacturing process is substantial, this department would examine the system only when the sampling process shows four or more defective items in a box of 25. We would reason that it is possible, but not very likely, to find four defective items in a box of 25 when the defect rate is 5%. In that case, something could be wrong, and we would examine the system. However, even if a box has four defective units, it isn't certain that the defect rate has increased.

We continue to look for ways—better materials, improved manufacturing methods—to reduce the average defective rate from 5%. Even if the rate could be reduced to 2% and the average number of defectives per box of 25 reduced to .5, some boxes (1.3%) would still contain three or more defective units over the long run.

CHAPTER 5 QUESTIONS

1. Can you change a continuous random variable into a discrete random variable? If so, provide an example.
2. Let X = the number of engines found in a standard passenger car. Is X a random variable? Why?
3. How are probability and relative frequency histograms similar and how are they different?
4. Correct, if necessary, the following statement:

    If two stock portfolios have the same *expected return*, but portfolio A has a larger standard deviation, then A is a *less* risky stock portfolio.

5. Explain what a Bernoulli process is.
6. When the standard deviation for a binomial distribution is very close to zero, what would the binomial distribution look like? Why?
7. Suppose that the binomial probability of an event happening is very low—.005. Yet the event does happen. From a problem sensing perspective, what can you conclude?
8. Referring to Question 7, what are two other possible explanations for an event that happens even though it had a low probability of happening?
9. Under what real-world conditions would you consider applying the Poisson distribution for problem solving?
10. The insurance industry knows that .005% of the population will die of a particular disease this year. Let X = number of people who die from the disease per 100,000 population. Is X a Poisson random variable? Why?
11. What happens to the shape of a Poisson histogram as the mean gets larger?

12. Compare the binomial and Poisson distributions. How are they alike and how are they different?
13. Explain what a *z*-score is.
14. Suggest a random variable from the business world not presented in the text that should be normally distributed. Explain your reason(s).
15. What is the probability that a normal random variable takes on a single specific value equal to 0?
16. If a process capability study indicates that the 3σ limits are inside the lower and upper tolerance limits, what can you conclude about the process? Explain.
17. Suppose the normal curve indicates that the chance of a project being completed in less than 40 days is .001. Yet your team actually completes its next project in less than 40 days. What should you conclude? Explain.
18. Explain in your own words why the central limit theorem works. That is, why will the sampling distribution of the sample mean be nearly normal-shaped, provided the sample size exceeds 30?

CHAPTER 5 APPLICATION PROBLEMS

1. A real estate salesperson can sell a home in Midtown about 25% of the time, a home in Buckhead about 50% of the time, and a home in West End about 10% of the time. In five attempted sales in a given section of the city, the salesperson sells exactly one home. Assuming a Bernoulli process, what is the probability of selling exactly one home in five attempts if:
   a. The home is in Midtown (all attempts are in Midtown)?
   b. The home is in Buckhead (all attempts are in Buckhead)?
   c. The home is in West End (all attempts are in West End)?
   d. What does it mean to say that selling a home can be modeled as a Bernoulli process?

2. Which of two approaches should we use to implement the installation of a new computer system? Approach A requires that *systems developers* manage the installation. Approach B requires that *system users* manage the installation. Based on previous installations, with systems developers the mean installation time is 20 weeks and the standard deviation is 2 weeks. With system users, the mean time is 16 weeks and the standard deviation is 4 weeks. Installation times are nearly bell-shaped for both approaches.
   a. What approach should we use to maximize the chance of completing the installation within 22 weeks? Explain.
   b. Explain how we could verify that the installation times for both approaches are nearly bell shaped.

3. Maky's department store has determined that demand for compact disk players is Poisson distributed with a mean of three per day.
   a. Construct the probability distribution for the daily demand for compact disk players.
   b. If the store stocks six players on a particular day, what is the probability that demand will be greater than supply?
   c. Explain what must be true if demand is Poisson distributed.

4. A franchise is planning to add as many as five additional outlets next year. The CEO has made the six personal probability estimates shown at the top of page 266.

Number of New Outlets	Subjective Probability
0	.02
1	.13
2	.40
3	.30
4	.10
5	.05

    a. Compute the mean number of new outlets.
    b. Compute the standard deviation in the number of new outlets.
    c. Suppose that the firm makes $150,000 net profit from each outlet. What is the mean net profit from the new outlets for next year?

5. An operations manager is considering two machines to fill 1-pound bags of coffee. She has received the following fill data from two vendors. Apex machine fills are close to normally distributed with a mean of 16.5 oz. and a standard deviation of 1 oz. Zenith machine fills are close to normally distributed with a mean of 15.5 oz. and a standard deviation of .25 oz.
    a. Which of the two machines has less variability in fills? Why?
    b. Suppose that a "1-pound bag" must have *at least* 16 ounces. Which machine has a greater probability of meeting that goal?
    c. Suppose that a "1-pound bag" must have at least 15 ounces. Which machine has a greater probability of meeting that goal?
    d. Explain why the best machine changes as we change the minimum number of ounces in the bag.

6. A new laptop microcomputer breaks down on the average once a month. During the past month the laptop has broken down three times. Assume breakdowns can be represented by a Poisson process.
    a. What is the probability of having three or more breakdowns in a month?
    b. This month the laptop did break down three times. From a problem sensing perspective, what might you conclude? Explain.

7. There are five stages in the consumer adoption decision—awareness, interest, evaluation, trial, and adoption. The chance of adopting a product increases, the more stages the consumer goes through. Here are relative frequency probability estimates:

$$P(\text{adopting} \mid \text{awareness stage only}) = .10$$

$$P(\text{adopting} \mid \text{awareness through trial stages}) = .80$$

We select five consumers. We are interested in computing probabilities that different numbers of consumers will adopt a product.
    a. Define the two random variables of interest and their possible values.
    b. Assume a Bernoulli process. What is the probability that *at least* four consumers will adopt the product if all five went only through the awareness stage? If all five went through the awareness through the trial stages?
    c. Given the two probabilities, what should you, the marketing manager, attempt to do? Explain.

8. Outel Corporation produces 80286 computer chips. Based on historical data, Outel knows that chip life (time to failure in hours) is near normally distributed with a mean of 2,000 hours and a standard deviation of 200 hours.
    a. What percentage of the chips will have times to failure below 1,550 hours?

b. Now suppose that in the past month, more than 20% of the chips have failed in under 1,550 hours in Outel's final inspection. From a problem solving perspective, what might that suggest? Explain.
c. How could Outel check whether time to failure is really normally distributed?

9. Cars arrive at a bank drive-in window at the rate of 10 per hour. Assume the arrivals are Poisson distributed.
a. Calculate the probability that one car arrives during a 6-minute period. .368
b. If more than three cars arrive during a 6-minute period, the customers will have to wait for service and may become annoyed. What is the probability that more than three cars arrive during a 6-minute period? .019

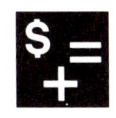

10. A stock analyst claims that he can accurately predict whether a company's return on investment (ROI) will increase from the previous year. He receives ten different company reports and is asked to determine which of the ten firms' ROIs will increase and which will decrease in the following year. Assume that none of the firms' ROIs stays the same. He predicts nine correctly.
a. If he were merely guessing, what is the probability that he would have made nine or more correct predictions?
b. Based on your answer, is the stock analyst an accurate predictor? Explain.

11. A vice-president of finance must decide which of two projects to implement. Shown are their net profits and subjective probabilities.

| Project A | | Project B | |
Net Profit	Probability	Net Profit	Probability
−$30K	.25	$ 0K	.4
$ 0K	.25	+$10K	.3
+$20K	.25	+$30K	.2
+$75K	.25	+$50K	.1

a. Find the expected net profit and standard deviation for the two projects.
b. Which project is riskier? Why?

12. Based on historical data, accidents on a certain highway occur at a rate of 5 per month. About three months ago the Highway Patrol began a driver awareness program to reduce accidents. Over the past month there was one accident. Has there been any reduction in accidents? Assume that accidents are Poisson distributed.
a. Compare the probability of having one or fewer accidents in a month if the average rate were still 5 per month.
b. What can you conclude about the effectiveness of the Highway Patrol program? Explain.

13. Savings and loan associations (S&Ls) were created to provide home mortgages for borrowers and long-term savings for individual investors. In the 1970s S&Ls were allowed to engage in riskier loans. By 1986 S&Ls started to collapse at an alarming rate. In 1988 the government dealt with 205 insolvent S&Ls. Suppose that an economist for the Federal Home Loan Bank System, which regulates federally chartered S&Ls, estimates that the mean number of remaining insolvent S&Ls is 350 and the standard deviation is 25. Assume that the number of insolvent S&Ls is normally distributed.
a. What is the probability that more than 300 S&Ls will fail in the upcoming years?

b. If the cost of bailing out each insolvent S&L is $500 million, what is the probability that the federal government will have to spend more than $175 billion in the upcoming years?

14. An owner of a small motel with 10 rooms is considering buying VCRs to rent to his customers. He estimates that half of his customers would be willing to rent a VCR. Therefore, he buys five sets. Define the random variable as the number of requests for a VCR in an evening. Assume 100% occupancy and only one request per room.
   a. What is the probability of meeting possible customer demand for VCRs?
   b. If the owner increases the number of VCRs to seven, what is the probability of meeting possible customer demand?
   c. If he increases the number of VCRs to nine, what is the probability of meeting possible customer demand?
   d. What other information would you need before you could decide whether to increase the number of VCRs from five to seven or nine?

15. A university economic forecasting unit indicates that next year's discount rate most likely will be 9%. The discount rate is the interest rate that the Federal Reserve banks charge their commercial bank customers to borrow money. Assume that the uncertainty about the discount rate can be represented by a normal distribution with a standard deviation of 1%. Assume that the forecast turns out to be accurate.
   a. Find the probability that the actual rate will be between 8% and 10%.
   b. Find the probability that the actual rate will be no higher than 10.5%.
   c. Suppose the forecasting unit changes its estimate of the standard deviation from 1% to some other figure. If the probability that the actual rate is less than 11% is .8413, what is the new estimate of the standard deviation?

16. A firm evaluates two different ways to manage a new product: (1) through a new product committee and (2) by a product manager. Shown are some comparative data on past attempts to use these approaches. Define the random variable of interest as sales performance.

Possible Outcomes		Committee	Product Manager
2% below target	−2	.05	.20
1% below target	−1	.10	.20
Meet target	0	.70	.20
1% above target	+1	.10	.20
2% above target	+2	.05	.20

   a. What are the mean sales performances for both strategies?
   b. What are the standard deviations of sales performance for both strategies?
   c. Which strategy is less risky? Why?

17. Telephone sales operators make on the average 1 call every 10 minutes. Assume that the number of calls made can be represented by a Poisson distribution. Recently, operators have become upset with their working conditions and you wonder if they are slowing down to retaliate. You observe one operator who has made no calls in the past 50 minutes. Assume that the average of 1 call every 10 minutes has not changed.
   a. What is the probability that no calls would have been made in the past 50 minutes?
   b. Given your answer in part a, what can you conclude?

18. Based on past records, National Telephone has bought at least 20 computers in 80% of its previous orders. However, in the past five orders, National has bought more than 20 computers only once. Does this mean that National is cutting back on the number of computers it purchases?

a. What are the chances of one or fewer orders for at least 20 computers in the past five sales to National?
b. Is National cutting back on the number of computers it purchases? Explain.

19. The number of hours before a battery must be replaced in Wellbuilt watches is normally distributed with a mean of 1,900 hours and a standard deviation of 145 hours.
   a. What proportion of watches will fail before 1,600 hours?
   b. Suppose that during the next six months, more than 50% fail before 1,600 hours. From a problem sensing perspective, what might you conclude? Explain.

20. How would you determine the root causes of the increased failures of Wellbuilt watches in Problem 19? What questions might you ask to help understand and solve the problem? Suggest several changes that might explain the onset of the problem.

21. According to the *New York Stock Exchange*, in 1985, the mean number of daily shares traded was about 110 million and the standard deviation was about 20 million. Assume that daily volume is near normally distributed. In 1988 we noted that the daily volumes were running at about 162 million shares.
   a. What is the probability that the daily volume will exceed 162 million shares if the mean and standard deviation are still 110 million and 20 million shares, respectively?
   b. How can you explain the 162 million shares a day in 1988?

22. Based on the 1987 *Bureau of the Census Current Population Reports*, an economist believes that the percentage of all races below the poverty level will most likely be 13% in 1992. She also believes that the probability that the percentage below the poverty level will exceed 14% is .20. Assume that the economist's subjective beliefs can be represented by a normal curve. Given this information, what is the economist's estimate of the standard deviation for the 1992 percentage below the poverty level?

23. The inventory manager at a retail farmer's market has just checked 100 50-pound bags from PacNorWest Potato Company.

Number of Rotten Potatoes in Bag	Number of Bags
0	45
1	37
2	13
3	4
4	1
	100

The manager believes that the number of rotten potatoes per bag is Poisson distributed with a mean of .8. Assume that the manager is correct.
   a. Calculate the probability of finding 0, 1, 2, 3, or 4 rotten potatoes per bag.
   b. How many bags would you expect to have 0, 1, 2, 3, or 4 rotten potatoes if the manager's assumption of a Poisson distribution is true? Compare the expected number to the actual number of rotten potatoes per bag. What can you conclude?
   c. Assume that the manager can live with a mean of .8 rotten potato per bag. How can the manager use the knowledge that the number of rotten potatoes is Poisson distributed to set a policy for inspecting and accepting 50-pound bags from PacNorWest? Assume that each bag will be inspected before the manager accepts it.

24. Consider the following three binomial probability distributions:

$$\text{Distribution 1:} \quad n = 5, \quad p = .5$$
$$\text{Distribution 2:} \quad n = 10, \quad p = .5$$
$$\text{Distribution 3:} \quad n = 20, \quad p = .5$$

Using Appendix 1, graph the three probability distributions. What can you conclude about the relationship between the binomial and normal distributions?

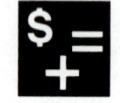

25. A CEO is considering several major strategic alternatives with respect to the product line. The firm can:

1. Choose to stay with its present products in its present markets.
2. Expand its line into either related or unrelated products.
3. Choose to expand its present line into new markets (international).

The CEO has developed the following subjective probabilities for each strategy and its impact on net profit after taxes over the next several years.

	Strategy 1	Strategy 2	Strategy 3
Increase net profit by $10 million	.20	.40	.50
No change in net profit	.60	.20	.40
Decrease net profit by $10 million	.20	.40	.10

a. Which strategy gives the highest mean increase in net profit for the firm?
b. One measure of a strategy's risk is the coefficient of variation, which is the standard deviation divided by the mean. The lower the coefficient of variation, the lower the risk. Compute the coefficient of variation for the three strategies. Which strategy is least risky?

6

Data Collection Methods

6.1 Data and managerial performance
6.2 Sampling principles and statistical inferences
    Sample size
    Level of confidence
    Variation of the target population
6.3 Basic sampling terminology
6.4 Planning and conducting a survey: An overview
    Margin of error
6.5 Simple random sampling design
    Selecting a simple random sample
    A note of caution
6.6 Stratified random sampling design
    When to consider stratified random sampling
    Selecting a stratified random sample
    A note of caution
    Other designs: Systematic and cluster designs
6.7 Selecting a survey method
    Obtaining a representative sample
    Questionnaire length and flexibility
    Obtaining accurate answers
    Administrative issues
6.8 General principles in writing questions
    Determining information needs: Diagnosing the problem
    Choosing the question format
    Avoiding wording errors
    A final thought
6.9 Basic principles of experimental design
    Basic terminology
    Experiments vs. non-experiments
    The importance of randomization
6.10 Avoiding problems in experimental design
    The history effect
    Diffusion of treatment
    Compensatory rivalry
    Trivial changes
    Random error
6.11 Key ideas of data collection
Chapter 6 Questions
Chapter 6 Application Problems

CHAPTER OUTLINE

COMCEL Interoffice Communication

Date: October 1, 1992
  To: Ann Tabor, President
From: Howard Bright, Norcross Plant Manager
  Re: Employee Morale

BACKGROUND
I have been monitoring the employee morale survey results to detect any sudden changes or downward trends. Because we give this test weekly to a random sample of employees, we can identify morale problems that inevitably affect productivity. I am happy to report that averages have remained stable for the past year.

I was discussing our morale scores with a friend of mine who works for a competitor that gives the same test. His firm's average scores are one point higher, which he attributes to the high level of employee participation in decision making.

AUTHORIZATION REQUEST
We should survey our employees to learn how many think there is not enough employee input into production decisions. We will develop a questionnaire and interview a random sample of our production employees in the Norcross plant. If low participation is the problem, we can hire a quality circle expert to help increase employee participation. Since employees would be interviewed on company time, I need your approval to proceed. Should we proceed if the project cost is under $50,000?

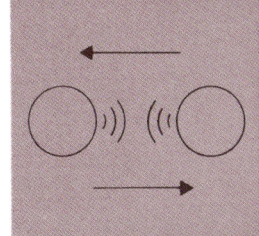

6.1 Data and Managerial Performance

Managers use data to understand their organization and its environment. Successful managers develop simple mental models of their departments. They ask themselves: "How is my department doing? How has it done in the past? At what levels could we perform?" Using these models, they sense when problem solving action is needed and when it is not.

As disturbance handlers, managers use data to determine what factors cause a significant deviation from historic or budgeted performance levels. For example, for the past two years the company's reject rate varied between 1% and 2%. This past quarter it jumped to 6%. Data help determine the root causes of such deviations.

As entrepreneurs, managers seek to improve departmental performance. They use data in evaluating planned improvements. For example, managers want to know: "Which of three material handling systems best reduces our level of inventory?" Without data, managers cannot evaluate the systems' costs and benefits, and will be unable to decide which to install.

How do managers obtain data? They have three sources. They already have it within their organization, create it themselves, or buy it from firms that specialize in selling data. Their firm's management information system (MIS) provides the first type of data in the form of routine structured reports. These reports contain financial, accounting, marketing, and operations data and describe the state of the firm. Managers should use these data to sense disturbance problems—gaps between actual and historical or budgeted performance.

Managers can create data by conducting *surveys* and *planned change studies*. A survey is a representative sampling of facts or opinions that is used to approximate what a complete collection and analysis might reveal. Typical business examples include attitude surveys and marketing research studies. Managers also seek ways to improve departmental performance by running small-scale planned change experiments or pilot projects and studying the results. If the planned change is an improvement, managers implement it permanently.

Finally, managers can buy data from outside sources. Often their own management information systems do not contain external data on industry-wide sales or local or national economic data. Thus firms purchase data from bureaus that sell specialized data bases. For example, Information Resources Inc. tracks every TV commercial played in the homes of its panelists and every purchase they make at the supermarket. Marketing managers find this information crucial in managing their products.

In this chapter we discuss survey sampling designs and methods, questionnaire design, and experimentation to obtain valid data. Statistics is a collection of powerful tools for data analysis, but these tools are not magic. If we collect invalid data, no analysis can make the results meaningful.

6.2 Sampling Principles and Statistical Inferences

Several weeks before the 1984 presidential election, most polling organizations were 95% confident that President Reagan would receive 59% ± 3% of the vote. He actually received about 60%. How can polling organizations be so accurate and confident when they interview fewer than 1,500 voters out of the target population of 90,000,000 voters? Sampling principles allow us to make *precise* and *highly confident* inferences from a sample to a target population. By the end of this section you should be able to:

1. explain what margin of error is;
2. explain how sample size affects the margin of error;
3. explain why increasing the level of confidence will increase the margin of error; and
4. explain why greater variation in the target population produces greater margins of error.

> The margin of error is the possible difference we allow between the sample result and the result we would obtain if we sampled the entire population.

Precise inferences have small **margins of error**. In the 1984 polling example, the margin of error was plus or minus 3%. That meant that the population percentage of voters supporting Reagan could vary by as much as ±3% from the sample result of 59%—from 56% to 62% of the votes. Pollsters were 95% confident in their prediction.

Meaningful inferences require small margins of error. What would be the value of knowing that a candidate will receive 59% ± 30% of the votes? The margin of error would be too wide to draw useful conclusions.

The level of confidence in an inference is also important. Higher levels of confidence are more meaningful. For example, it is not very informative to be only 20% confident that a candidate will receive 59% ± 3% of the votes. No one will listen to an organization that is not very confident in its inferences. Many organizations prefer to operate at a 95% level of confidence. They can accept a 5% chance that their inferences are wrong, but there is nothing sacred about a 95% level of confidence.

In summary, our goal is to show how to obtain highly confident inferences with small margins of error. Sample size, level of confidence, and variability of the target population affect the margin of error.

Sample Size

We will consider first the influence of sample size on the margin of error. We can reduce the margin of error by increasing the sample size. We illustrate this idea by considering a population with only five students:

Student	Age
A	18
B	19
C	20
D	21
E	22

The students' ages range from 18 to 22, with a mean age of 20. Suppose we write each student's age on a piece of paper, mix the papers well, and select three pieces of paper. We do not replace a slip of paper once it is drawn. This is *sampling without replacement*. Table 6.1 shows the ten possible sample means. These ten sample means are a *sampling distribution of the sample mean* (see Chapter 5).

The mean age of the three youngest students is 19.0 years; the mean age of the three oldest students is 21.0 years. Since the mean age of all five students is 20 years, the maximum margin of error is 1 year—the maximum difference between a sample result and the result that we would get if we sampled everyone in the population.

We could reduce the maximum margin of error by taking a sample of size four. There are five possible samples of size four—ABCD, ABCE, ABDE, ACDE, BCDE. The mean age of the four youngest students is 19.5 years, sample ABCD, and the mean age of the four oldest students is 20.5 years, sample BCDE. Thus, the maximum margin of error drops from 1 year to .5 year. Please verify our calculations before reading on.

LESSON 1: Increasing the sample size reduces the margin of error.

However, the disadvantage of larger sample sizes is that they increase the cost of the survey or planned change study.

Table 6.1

The Sampling Distribution of the Sample Mean for Samples of Size Three

Possible Sample	Sample Values			Mean
A, B, C	18	19	20	19.0
A, B, D	18	19	21	19.3
A, B, E	18	19	22	19.7
A, C, D	18	20	21	19.7
A, C, E	18	20	22	20.0
A, D, E	18	21	22	20.3
B, C, D	19	20	21	20.0
B, C, E	19	20	22	20.3
B, D, E	19	21	22	20.7
C, D, E	20	21	22	21.0

Level of Confidence

Suppose we draw a sample from the sampling distribution in Table 6.1, compute the mean, and insert it in the statement below.

> The mean age of the class is within the interval _____ years plus or minus a margin of error of .5 year.

The statement is true when the interval includes the population mean of 20. For example, if we obtain a sample mean of 19.7 (from sample ABE or ACD), then the statement is true since the interval includes 20 (19.7 − .5 = 19.2 years and 19.7 + .5 = 20.2 years).

What is the probability that the statement will be true? That is, from Table 6.1, what percentage of the sample means plus or minus .5 year contain the population mean of 20 years? Since 6 of the 10 intervals include 20 years, we are 60% confident that any interval would contain the population mean of 20 years.

Suppose we want to have 80% confidence that any interval would contain the population mean of 20 years. The interval will have to be wider than plus or minus .5 year. But how wide? An interval width of plus or minus .7 year will ensure that 8 of 10 intervals would contain the population mean of 20 years. Please verify this.

LESSON 2: If we increase the level of confidence in an inference, the price we pay is an increase in the margin of error.

We face a dilemma. We want a high level of confidence and a small margin of error. There is a solution: We could increase our sample size as we increase the desired level of confidence. However, that solution, as we have stated before, is costly.

Variation of the Target Population

The third factor that affects the margin of error is variation in the target population. Larger population variation produces greater margins of error. Consider another class of five students. Table 6.2 displays the age data for both classes.

Table 6.2

Two Populations with Different Variations

Class 1 Student	Age	Class 2 Student	Age
A	18	F	18
B	19	G	21
C	20	H	24
D	21	I	27
E	22	J	30

The ages in the second class range from 18 to 30, and the mean age is 24. There is greater variation in ages in the second class. How does this affect the maximum margin of error?

Again, we construct a sampling distribution of the sample mean. We take all possible samples of size three without replacement from the second population—samples FGH, FGI, FGJ, ..., HIJ—and compute the sample means. The smallest sample mean is 21 years (FGH). The largest sample mean is 27 years (HIJ). The maximum margin of error is 3 years, 27 − 24 or 24 − 21. This compares with 1 year for the first population, which has less variation in the five students' ages.

LESSON 3: As the variability of the target population increases, the margin of error increases.

In summary, managers need to have small margins of error. Realistically, they cannot reduce the variability of the target population. Reducing the level of confidence is not effective because it raises doubts about our assertions. The most effective way to reduce margin of error is to increase the sample size.

SECTION 6.2 EXERCISES

1. A telephone survey showed that 40% of a sample prefers brand X. The margin of error was ±5%. Explain what that means.

2. A political consultant proudly tells his client that a poll he conducted shows she will win the election with 53% of the vote. "What was the margin of error?" she asked. He said ±8%. She fired the consultant. Why?

3. An economist reports: "I am 95% confident that the sales revenue for the coming year will be $150 million ±$10 million." If the forecaster wanted a higher level of confidence, would the margin of error increase or decrease?

4. A population consists of the numbers {2, 4, 6}.
   a. Find the mean of these numbers.
   b. List all possible samples of size two without replacement.
   c. Find the sample mean for each of these samples.
   d. Find the mean of the sample means.
   e. If you selected one of the sample means as an estimate of the population mean, how far off could you be?
   f. State the relationship between the mean of the population and the mean of the sample means.

5. Consider the following population of numbers: {2, 4, 6, 8, 10}.
   a. List all possible samples of two and the mean of each sample.
   b. If your goal was to estimate the population mean and you selected one sample of size two, by how much could your sample mean differ from the population mean?
   c. List all possible samples of size four and the mean of each sample.
   d. If your goal was to estimate the population mean and you selected one sample of size four, by how much could your sample mean vary from the population mean?
   e. What happened to the maximum margin of error when you doubled the sample size?

6. Measurements from a production process are normally distributed with a mean of 20 cm. and a standard deviation of 2.0 cm. You select an item and make a measurement.

   The observation will fall between 20 cm. $\pm$ 2 cm.

   a. What level of confidence would you place on this statement?
   b. What is the level of confidence if the margin of error is ± 4 cm.?

7. Measurements from a production process are normally distributed with a mean of 20 cm. and standard deviation of 4.0 cm. You select one item and make a measurement.

   The observation will fall between 20 cm. $\pm$ 2 cm.

   a. What level of confidence would you place on this statement?
   b. What is the level of confidence if the margin of error is ± 4 cm.?
   c. Compare the results of this problem with Exercise 6 above. Why have the confidence levels declined when the margins of error have remained the same?

6.3 Basic Sampling Terminology

The field of sampling has its own set of terminology. Once you have mastered it, you can communicate intelligently with survey designers. By the end of this section, you should be able to:

1. explain sampling terminology; and
2. illustrate these terms with your own examples.

Consider three situations where sampling plays an important problem solving role. Each situation requires a different data source.

SAMPLING FROM THE MIS   An auditor wishes to determine if the monthly business expense reports in the management information system are accurate. The auditor will select a sample from last month's 1,500 business expense reports and compare the computer data to the actual expense reports. If the computer values are inaccurate, the auditor will conduct a more complete investigation.

OBTAINING DATA THROUGH SURVEYS   The Director of Automotive Safety at Alliance Motors is considering installing air bags in all the cars. There are no data on drivers' attitudes toward air bags. He will conduct a market research survey on a sample of drivers.

OBTAINING DATA THROUGH PLANNED CHANGE STUDIES   Compared to published industry figures, work teams at COMCEL's Norcross plant have not been as successful in reducing unit labor costs as have other firms. The manufacturing manager will test two possible methods of reducing labor costs:

1. Teaching work group members each other's jobs—job switching.
2. Teaching work group members creative methods.

280   Chapter 6   Data Collection Methods

She will select a sample of work groups for the study. If either workshop significantly reduces unit labor costs, she will require that all work groups attend the more effective workshop.

We will use these three examples to illustrate the following sampling terminology: element, target population, sampling unit, frame, and sampling design.

In the MIS study, an **element** is a single monthly business expense report. The measurement of interest is its dollar value. In the air bag study, an element is a registered driver. The measurement of interest is the driver's attitude toward air bags in cars. In the planned change study, an element is a work group. The measurement of interest is the reduction in unit labor costs.

> An element is an object on which we take a measurement. When the objects are people, we call them subjects.

In the MIS study, the **target population** consists of the monthly business expense reports for all 1,500 salespeople. In the air bag study, the target population is the group of all registered drivers in the country. (Note that we have ignored adults who do not drive a car, although they may be passengers.) In the planned change study, the target population is all the work groups in the Norcross plant.

> A target population is a collection of elements about which we wish to make an inference.

In the MIS study, **sampling units** would be individual monthly business expense reports filed by the 1,500-member sales force. Each expense statement is unique; they do not overlap. Each statement covers one salesperson's monthly expenses.

> Sampling units are non-overlapping collections of elements from the target population. A sampling unit can be an individual element.

Joe Smith, Sr., Mary Smith, and Joe Smith, Jr. are sampling units in the air bag study. They are different people. However, we could group the three Smiths into the Smith household. This would make sense if we plan to interview households. Often, grouping by household is more practical because it could be too costly to sample individual elements. Other possible groupings are all residents of a city block or of a political district.

When households are sampling units, we must define them so that no individual element can be sampled more than once. If Joe Smith, Jr. lives in a college dorm in town, is he a member of the dorm household or the Smith household? We must define household so that Joe Smith, Jr. cannot be selected more than once in the study. Double sampling would bias the findings.

The work groups within the Norcross plant are the sampling units in the planned change study. Work group membership must be unique. That is, the same worker cannot be in more than one group.

In the MIS study, the sampling **frame** is the list of 1,500 salespeople. If we specify the individual driver as a sampling unit, lists of registered drivers from the 50 states and the District of Columbia serve as a sampling frame. In the planned change study, the sampling frame is the list of work groups in the Norcross plant.

> A frame is a list of sampling units.

Sometimes we use *multiple* sampling frames. In sampling voters we could start with city blocks as sampling units and then sample voters within those blocks. Our first sampling frame is a list of city blocks, and the second frame is a list of voters within each block.

> The sampling design specifies the method of selecting the sample.

Later we will discuss the four most common **survey sampling designs**—simple random sampling, stratified random sampling, systematic sampling, and cluster sampling.

SECTION 6.3 EXERCISES

1. What is the difference between a target population and a sampling frame?
2. We want to estimate the proportion of registered voters who favor a proposed amendment to the state constitution. The frame for the study is the 36 books of registered voters from the 36 counties in the state. What is the sampling unit? Is the sampling unit the same as an element of the population?
3. The target population is all females in a city over the age of 40 years. The frame is a list of street addresses used by the Census Bureau. What is the sampling unit?
4. A company wishes to survey its employees concerning the choice of medical plans. A list of all employees is generated. What is the sampling unit? What is the element?
5. You work for a large bank that has 100 branch offices. You want to survey the opinions of employees about staying open longer on Saturdays. What would you use for a frame? What would be the sampling unit and element for the survey?

6.4 Planning and Conducting a Survey: An Overview

Conducting surveys involves more than selecting a survey sampling design. It requires planning. By the end of this section, you should be able to:

1. describe the nine-step procedure for planning a survey;
2. differentiate between selection, response, and nonresponse errors; and
3. differentiate between these errors and margin of error.

Scheaffer, Mendenhall, and Ott (1986) suggest the following nine-step procedure in planning a survey.

1. **STATE THE OBJECTIVES** In order to state the objectives, we often need to ask questions, such as: What is the survey's exact purpose? What specifically don't we know? What inferences do we need to draw? Begin by developing a specific list of information needs. Then write focused survey questions.

2. **IDENTIFY THE TARGET POPULATION** Whom are we interested in drawing conclusions about? All adults? Only adults aged 18–49?

3. **SELECT A SAMPLING FRAME** After identifying the target population, obtain a sampling frame. Three problems can occur at this stage.

   First, it may not be possible to find a perfect sampling frame. For example, in the air bag study lists of drivers from the 50 states and the District of Columbia could serve as a sampling frame. However, driver registration lists may not be complete because the states do not update them daily. Also some people on the lists have died. Even good sampling frames may have omissions. With this knowledge it may be possible to improve the sampling frame.

   A second problem is called selection error. For example, we are interested in determining filmgoers' attitudes toward horror films. Suppose that our sampling

Selection error occurs when the sampling frame is not a complete listing of the target population because some members of the target population are excluded from the sample.

Nonresponse error occurs when the respondents do not reflect the sampling frame.

frame is households that have purchased a VCR. We have just made a **selection error**. Many filmgoers do not own VCRs and thus our sampling frame is not a complete listing of the target population.

Increasing the sample size will not solve the problem. The problem is not the sample size, but who is included in the sampling frame.

A third problem is called the **nonresponse error**. This occurs when a large percentage of the sampling frame does not respond to the survey. Suppose that in the air bag study we ask respondents to call a 900 number to be interviewed. Because a 900 call costs $2 per minute, many drivers may not respond. Thus the final sample of respondents may not even represent the sampling frame.

Lower-income and upper-income families often do not answer mailed surveys. Thus, middle-income families are usually overrepresented in the final responses. Nonresponse error occurs even in face-to-face interviews. Those people who are not at home when the interviewer stops by may be systematically different from those who are at home. An example might be families with two wage earners vs. families with one wage earner. Families with two wage earners dine out more often and thus may be underrepresented in the final responses.

Selection and nonresponse errors are different. Selection error occurs when the sampling frame does not reflect the target population. Nonresponse error occurs when the respondents do not reflect the sampling frame.

In contrast to the selection error, increasing the sample size by resampling those who did not initially respond will reduce the nonresponse error. Furthermore, we should determine whether respondents and nonrespondents differ systematically in terms of age, race, or socioeconomic status. To do this, we compare the composition of respondents to census figures for the sampling frame. If they differ, we cannot draw inferences from the data.

4. SELECT A SAMPLE DESIGN   Decide how to select the respondents from the sampling frame and determine the sample size. In Sections 6.5 and 6.6 we will discuss four plans: simple random sampling, stratified random sampling, systematic sampling, and cluster sampling.

5. SELECT A SURVEY METHOD   Decide how to collect the data. In Section 6.7 we will discuss personal interviews, telephone interviews, and mailed questionnaires.

6. DEVELOP THE QUESTIONNAIRE   Write the questionnaire. Decide on the wording, the type of questions, and other issues discussed later in this chapter.

Response errors often occur in public opinion surveys. Roll and Cantril (1972) illustrate this error. They asked some citizens if they favored "adding to" the Constitution a one-term limit for the President. Others were asked if they favored "changing" the Constitution to include a one-term limit. Fifty percent were in favor when Roll and Cantril used the first wording and 65% were in favor when they used the second wording.

The order in which the candidates' names appear in a survey questionnaire can also affect a person's response. The name that is placed first can often pick up five percentage points more than if it were placed at the end of the list.

Response error occurs when respondents do not understand the question, are influenced by word variations, do not have enough information and guess, or do not want to give out information.

Race is another factor that can make a difference. A white interviewer of a black respondent may obtain a different response than a black interviewer would of a black respondent. This is especially true when the questions deal with black–white relations. Increasing the sample size will not eliminate response error. The problem lies not in the sample size, but with other factors such as questionnaire wording or the method of administering the questionnaire. Using valid survey sampling designs will not help either, for the problem is not how we selected the sample but how we worded or presented the questions.

7. **PRETEST THE QUESTIONNAIRE** Select a very small sample from the sampling frame. Conduct the survey and see what goes wrong. Correct any problems before carrying out the full-scale study.

8. **CONDUCT THE SURVEY** Monitor the interviewers to ensure consistent interviewing skills.

9. **ANALYZE THE DATA** Even before conducting the survey, determine how the data will be analyzed once collected. We will learn in future chapters how to use statistical analysis to draw valid inferences from the sample data to the target population.

Margin of Error

Selection, response, and nonresponse errors are mistakes made in conducting a survey. They are correctable. The margin of error is not a mistake. It is the possible difference we allow between the sample result and the result that would be obtained if we sampled the entire population. The sampling distribution in Table 6.1 included sample means that varied between 19 and 21. Most sample means were very close to the population mean of 20 years in this simple example. However, in a real-world study, a mean based on a small sample might vary considerably from the population mean. When drawing inferences about a large population, we must live with a margin of error. At this point, the most effective way to reduce the margin of error is to increase the sample size.

Choosing the appropriate sampling design can also reduce the margin of error. In the next two sections we cover simple random sampling, stratified random sampling, systematic sampling, and cluster sampling. Each sampling design differs in the method of selecting the sample, the ease of selecting the sample, and the accuracy of the inferences about the target population.

SECTION 6.4 EXERCISES

1. List the nine steps involved in planning a survey.
2. The first step in planning a survey is to get a group together and start hammering out a questionnaire. Do you agree?
3. When asked what his sampling method would be in an upcoming survey, the manager said, "We will use stratified sampling." Did the manager answer the question? Explain.

4. Suppose you want to test market a new safety razor by having prospective customers actually use the razor. What is the target population? What could you use as a frame?

5. What do we mean by response error? How is this type of error different from a nonresponse error?

6. For the following statements, state whether each involves a selection error (S), a response error (R), a nonresponse error (N), or some combination of these errors (C).
   a. Respondent misunderstands the question.
   b. Respondent wants to look good to the interviewer and lies about his income.
   c. Fearing for their safety, interviewers substitute high-income areas for low-income areas.
   d. Interviews are conducted at a supermarket only during the day on Saturday.
   e. Respondents hang up the phone when they realize it is another bothersome surveyor.
   f. The secretaries of company executives always complete mail questionnaires for their bosses.
   g. The telephone directory is used as a frame in a survey of all families in a county.
   h. The interviewer smiles whenever she gets a response she agrees with.
   i. The sampling frame bears only a slight resemblance to the target population.

7. A group of college students conducts interviews in an older part of a city where apartment buildings have no elevators. When instructed to go to the sixth floor of an apartment building, some students substitute apartments on the first floor rather than walk the stairs. The students argue that because the intended and substitute respondents live in the same building, this practice will not introduce error into the survey results. Do you agree? Discuss.

8. Television talk shows feature an author who claims that over half of all married women are dissatisfied with their marriages. This claim is based on the results of 3,500 responses obtained from 100,000 mailed questionnaires. What type of error might affect the conclusions from this survey?

9. A market research firm wants to survey the U.S. Hispanic population through a telephone survey. The firm uses the Miami telephone directory as its frame. List any errors of selection, response, or nonresponse that might be associated with the survey.

10. How is the margin of error different from selection, response, and nonresponse errors? Which error is easiest for managers to control?

6.5 Simple Random Sampling Design

The goal in obtaining data through survey sampling is to use a sample to make precise inferences about the target population. Moreover, we want to be highly confident of our inferences. We begin with the basic *probability* sampling design—**simple random sampling**. Other designs build upon it. By the end of this section, you should be able to:

Simple random sampling occurs when every possible sample of size n elements has the same chance of being selected from a target population of N elements. The sample is a simple random sample.

1. select a simple random sample using a table of random numbers;
2. explain why simple random sampling can sometimes produce poor estimates of the target population; and
3. explain the problems with using nonprobability samples.

Consider the following scenario. An auditor wishes to determine whether the monthly business expense reports for the 1,500-member sales force are accurate. If they are inaccurate, she will conduct a more complete investigation.

There are 1,500 monthly business expense reports in the target population. Examining every account would take too long and be too costly. The sampling frame is the list of 1,500 sales representatives. The auditor selects a **simple random sample** of size 10 from the sampling frame. Based on the 10 accounts, she can then estimate the total business expenses for the 1,500-member sales force.

Selecting a Simple Random Sample

To select a random sample, we need to know how to use a random numbers table. Think of the 1,500 business expense reports as being numbered 0001, 0002, 0003, ..., 1499, 1500. The number 0001 represents the first sales representative's report, the number 0002 represents the second report, and the number 1500 represents the 1,500th report. Now start at the upper left corner of the random numbers table (see Appendix 4) and select the first 30 five-digit numbers from the first column. See Table 6.3.

Table 6.3

Table of 30 Random Numbers

10480	22368	24130	42167	37570	77921
99562	96301	89579	85475	28918	63553
09429	10365	07119	51085	02368	01011
52162	07056	48663	54164	32639	29334
02448	81525	29676	00742	05366	91921

Since we are interested in numbers 0001 to 1500, eliminate the last digit in each group of five digits. If a random number occurs twice, ignore the second occurrence and select another random number. If the first four digits exceed 1500, go to the next number. Reading across the rows, we select accounts 1048, 942, 1036, 711, 236, 101, 705, 244, 74, and 536. These ten reports are a simple random sample.

What is the idea behind the random numbers table? Imagine we wrote the five-digit numbers 00000 to 99999 on 100,000 slips of paper, one number to a slip. We place them in a large barrel and rotate the barrel. Next we select one slip at a time, record its value, replace the slip in the barrel, and then select another slip until we record 100,000 numbers. We have just constructed a table of random numbers similar to Appendix 4—the hard way. Using a prepared table of random numbers is easier.

A Note of Caution

Probability sampling, such as simple random sampling, is more effective than nonprobability sampling designs. For example, in *convenience sampling* we select the first *n* customers who enter a store. Although such a sampling scheme would

Table 6.4

Years of Schooling Data Based on a Simple Random Sample of 10 Army People

	Enlisted Personnel	Officers
n	5	5
Grades Completed	10.0	16.0

be easy to carry out, we cannot legitimately calculate the probable margin of error. There is no guarantee that the first *n* customers represent the target population of all customers. The statistical expressions in the remainder of the book apply only to probability sampling.

A simple random sampling design can also produce very poor estimates. Suppose we want to estimate the mean grade level completed by army personnel. We select a simple random sample of 10 people and obtain the results given in Table 6.4.

Our sample includes 5 enlisted personnel and 5 officers. The enlistees, on the average, completed 10th grade. The officers, on the average, completed college—16th grade. The mean grade level for the 10 army people is 13th grade. Common sense tells us that this mean is too high for the army overall. Why might that figure be a poor estimate for the mean grade completed by people in the army? Please think about it before reading on.

Look at the target population. It has many more enlisted personnel than officers. Yet the sample has the same number of officers and enlisted personnel. As the sample does not mirror the target population, our estimate is not accurate. Nonrepresentative samples can occur in simple random sampling because each element has the same chance of selection. Even rare samples, such as those composed of all enlisted personnel or all officers can (but are not likely to) occur.

In summary, probability sampling is superior to nonprobability sampling. For some situations, simple random sampling is not the best type of probability sampling. We need additional survey sampling designs.

SECTION 6.5 EXERCISES

1. You want to draw a simple random sample of 10 people from a list of 520 people. You decide to use the last three digits of each group of five digits and read down each column. List the numbers of the 10 people selected.

10480	22368	24130	43167
37570	77921	99562	96301
89579	85475	28918	63553
09429	10365	07119	51085
02368	01011	52162	04056

2. What do you see as the major drawback of the simple random sampling design?
3. An appliance manufacturer has hired you to survey customers who have had a service call over the past two years. The frame is a list of names and addresses of service calls made. Some customers have had more than one call and are listed more than once. The list also includes calls made more than two years ago. What problems does this frame present to a sampler in selecting a simple random sample?

6.6 Stratified Random Sampling Design

The goal in obtaining data through survey sampling is to use a sample to make precise inferences about the target population. Properly done, *stratified random sampling* can produce more accurate inferences than simple random sampling. By the end of this section, you should be able to:

1. explain *when* to stratify a target population;
2. explain *how* to stratify a target population to obtain the most accurate inferences;
3. explain how to select a stratified random sample; and
4. explain when stratified random sampling can produce poor estimates of the target population.

When to Consider Stratified Random Sampling

We saw how a sample of 10 enlisted personnel and officers produced an inaccurate estimate of the mean years of schooling. The sample obviously did not reflect the true percentages of enlistees and officers in the army. How should we have selected the sample to ensure that it represented the target population? First, we should separate the target population into enlistees and officers. Then we should select a random sample from each group or *stratum*.

Why do we group the target population into the two strata? Not merely because enlistees and officers differ, but because they differ especially on what we wish to measure—years of schooling. Officers tend to have about 15–17 years of school. On the other hand, enlistees tend to have about 9–12 years of school.

Stratifying by military rank may not be useful if we are interested in determining attitudes toward increased pay. If the attitudes of officers and enlistees do not differ, then we can take a simple random sample.

Consider another problem. Howard Bright, manager at COMCEL's Norcross plant, plans to determine the employees' attitudes toward the firm. (See Table 1.2 for the nine questions in the climate survey.) He wants to know if the employee attitudes have worsened since last year's survey. If so, he will then determine the root causes and take corrective action. Although the total population is only 300 people, he decides to take a sample.

The plant consists of three groups—blue-collar, management or professional, and hourly support staff. Bright expects that job attitudes are similar within each group but different between groups. Thus, he divides the target population of 300 employees into three strata—blue-collar, management or professional, and hourly support staff. He will then select a simple random sample from each stratum.

A stratified random sample is one obtained by separating the target population into non-overlapping groups, or strata, and then selecting a simple random sample from each stratum.

Consider **stratified random sampling** when there are subgroups within a target population that are likely to have similarities—job attitudes or years of schooling—within a stratum but differences between strata.

Selecting a Stratified Random Sample

We begin the process of selecting a stratified random sample by determining the total sample size. Larger samples have smaller margins of error but are more costly. Thus, balancing precision and cost calls for managerial judgment.

After determining the total sample size, we must decide on the sample size per stratum. There are many ways to allocate the total sample among the strata or groups. Each allocation method may result in a different margin of error. Three factors affect the allocation:

1. the total number of elements in each stratum;
2. the variation in the measurements within each stratum; and
3. the cost of obtaining observations from each stratum.

Considering only the first factor, base the sample size on the number of elements in each stratum. Select larger size samples from strata with many elements. The logic is simple. A sample of size 50 from a target population of 500 is more representative than a sample of size 50 from a population of 50,000, so the margin of error will be smaller.

Considering only the second factor, select larger size samples from strata that have greater variability. Suppose that army enlistees have between 11 and 12 years (total range of one year) of schooling. To obtain an accurate estimate of enlistees' mean years of schooling, we need only a very small sample. If officers had between 16 and 20 years (total range of four years) of schooling, we must take a larger sample to get an accurate estimate. Remember Lesson 3: As the variability of the target population increases, the margin of error also increases. Taking larger samples will reduce the margin of error.

Considering only the third factor, select smaller size samples from strata when the cost of sampling is high. If one stratum is a large election district extending over 400 square miles, the travel costs for personal interviews will be high. Therefore, reduce the sample size in this stratum. Of course, if you use telephone interviewing, sampling costs for the large geographic stratum will be similar to the costs of sampling other strata.

In proportional allocation sampling, the percentage of each stratum in the sample mirrors its percentage in the population.

Use **proportional allocation sampling** when sampling costs are the same for all strata and when all strata exhibit the same variability. We will illustrate proportional allocation sampling for the job attitude study.

Howard Bright selects a total sample size of 10. There are 30 managers or professionals, 60 support staff, and 210 blue-collar workers. Since 10% of the plant population are managers or professionals, 10% of the sample will come from this group. Of the 10 people in the sample, one must be a manager or professional. Since 70% of the plant population are blue-collar workers, 70% of the sample will be blue-collar workers. Of the 10 people in the sample, 7 must be blue-collar workers. Similarly, 2 support staff will be randomly selected. Thus the sample should include 1 manager or professional, 7 blue-collar workers, and 2 support staff.

Now Bright can select a simple random sample from each stratum of employees using a random numbers table, Appendix 4. He assigns the numbers 001–030 to the 30 managers or professionals, the numbers 031–090 to the 60 support staff, and the numbers 091–300 to the 210 blue-collar workers. Then he selects a random starting point in Appendix 4—say, line 21, column 4—and reads across the row. The study participants are worker 143, worker 91, staffer 47, worker 221, worker 224, worker 253, worker 263, staffer 66, worker 215, and manager 002.

A Note of Caution

Properly used, stratified random sampling provides more precise estimates than simple random sampling. However, stratifying may produce worse results than simple random sampling if we stratify the target population incorrectly.

Consider the following problem. We want to estimate potential sales of a new product. We can test it in eight stores for one month. Since we sell to three retail chains, we choose to stratify the sample. The first chain has 20 stores and there are 10 stores in each of the other two chains. Using proportional allocation sampling, we randomly select four stores from the first chain and two each from the other two chains. Do not be surprised if the monthly sales estimate is inferior to that obtained by a simple random sample. Why? Please think about it before reading on.

Stratifying by chains may not be meaningful. Stratifying works best when the variability of the variable of interest is low within each stratum and high between different strata. Are sales of the 20 stores within the first chain very similar and are they different from sales of the other two chains? If not, then stratifying by chains is inappropriate.

Other Designs: Systematic and Cluster Designs

Two other commonly used survey sampling designs are *systematic* and *cluster sampling*. Systematic sampling occurs when we select one element at random from the first k elements in a sampling frame, and then select every kth element thereafter. This is a **1-in-k** systematic sample. Systematic sampling simplifies the selection process. This design is especially useful when we do not know the target population's size, and so simple random sampling is not possible.

Industrial quality control (QC) departments often use systematic sampling. These departments approve vendors, evaluate raw material component selection, do quality planning, analyze customer returns, and measure and report compliance with quality policies. In the compliance role, they select items from production lines or service centers and take measurements on variables such as product weight or the number of complaints. They compare the mean value of the measurements with the company standards to determine if quality is being maintained.

QC departments often use systematic sampling designs such as 1-in-100 items or one item per half-hour. These samples will include items from the beginning to the end of the shift. Thus if rejects increase over the shift as workers tire, the sample will reflect the target population. This target population is *ordered*. A simple random sample may not contain elements over the entire shift. The first hour of the shift may be overrepresented in the sample and the last hour may be underrepresented. Systematic sampling is useful for ordered populations.

Systematic sampling can sometimes produce poor estimates. For example, we must estimate a department store's weekly sales. Using a 1-in-7 systematic sampling design, we could select a day at random where $k = 1$ means Sunday and $k = 7$ means Saturday, and then sample the sales figures every seven days thereafter. If we randomly select Saturday, we will overestimate the weekly sales since Saturday and Sunday are by far the busiest shopping days. If we randomly select Wednesday, we will underestimate weekly sales. This target population is

Table 6.5

A Comparison of Four Survey Sampling Designs

Design	How to Select Sample	Strengths/Weaknesses
Simple random	Assign numbers to elements in sampling frame. Use random numbers table in Appendix 4 to select sample.	The basic building block. Simple, but often costly. Cannot use unless we can assign a number to each element in the target population.
Stratified	Divide population into groups that are similar within and different between on the variable of interest. Use Appendix 4 to select the sample from each stratum.	With proper strata, can produce very accurate estimates. Less costly than simple random sampling. Must stratify target population correctly.
Systematic	Select every kth element from a list after a random start.	Produces very accurate estimates when elements in a population exhibit *order*. Used when simple random or stratified sampling is impractical: e.g., the population size is not known. Simplifies the selection process. Do not use with periodic populations.
Cluster	Randomly choose clusters and sample all elements within each cluster.	With proper clusters, can produce very accurate estimates. Useful when sampling frame unavailable or travel costs high. Must cluster target population correctly.

periodic. The variable of interest varies in a predictable pattern. Therefore, do not use systematic sampling for periodic populations.

Cluster sampling occurs when we randomly select a set of m clusters from a target population and then examine or interview every element within each selected cluster. For example, we could divide a city into clusters of sampling units such as city blocks, groups of city blocks, or political districts. The sampling frame would then be lists of city blocks or political districts. Select a random sample of clusters and then interview *everyone* in the cluster.

The merit of cluster sampling is that it is cost-effective. By sampling all households within a cluster, we reduce travel costs. Consider cluster sampling when (1) a sampling frame listing population elements or sampling units is not available or is costly to obtain, or (2) travel costs are very high for other survey designs.

Clustering and stratifying are two different methods for grouping a target population. The elements within an ideal stratum should have similar measurements on the variable of interest, but there should be large differences on the variable of interest among strata. In contrast, the elements within an ideal cluster should have widely different measurements on the variable of interest, but there should be small differences in the variable of interest *among* clusters.

In summary, Table 6.5 compares the four survey sampling designs.

SECTION 6.6 EXERCISES

1. List the circumstances when you would prefer stratified random sampling over simple random sampling.

2. List the factors that determine the division of the total sample among strata.

3. What do we mean by proportional allocation of the total sample among the strata? Under what circumstances is this method the best one to use?

4. The federal government is planning to survey the 50 states and thinks that the measurement of interest will vary by the population of the state. They divide the states into three strata: five large states, 15 medium-sized states, and 30 small states. Budgetary restrictions limit the sample to a size of 10.
    a. How many states should be drawn from each stratum if the proportional allocation method is used?
    b. Why not use simple random sampling?

5. A company has divided a county into three strata of equal population size. The estimated income standard deviation for each stratum is $225. The standard deviation for the whole county is also $225. Should the firm use proportional allocation stratified sampling?

6. The IRS uses stratified sampling to audit tax returns. Suppose there are 120 million individual returns in any tax year and that the returns are stratified by adjusted gross income as follows.

$0–34,999	60 million
$35,000–49,999	40 million
$50,000–74,999	15 million
$75,000 and above	5 million

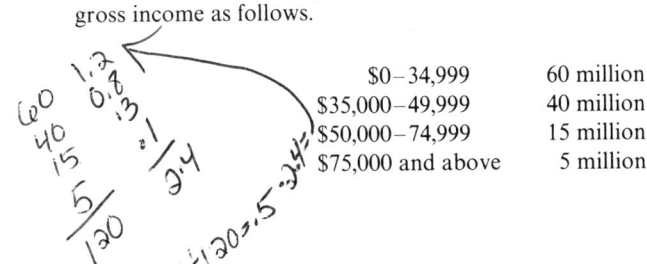

a. How many returns should be audited from each stratum if only 2% of the returns can be audited and the sample is allocated according to the size of the strata?
b. If you were making audit policy for the IRS, would you use proportional allocation to determine the composition of the total sample? Explain.

7. List the reasons for the popularity of systematic random sampling.

8. Distinguish between a random and a periodic population. Why might systematic sampling be a poor choice of a sampling plan when the population is periodic?

9. "My sampling frame is an alphabetized list of all my employees. Therefore, the frame isn't random." Comment.

10. Suppose the sampling frame consists of 10,000 residences listed by zip code. You are studying purchasing patterns of households and want to interview 250 families. Suppose you selected the 20th address, then the 70th, 120th, 170th, and so on over the entire list of 10,000 residences.
    a. What is the sampling constant, k, and what sample size would result?
    b. If you found you did not have the sample size you needed, should you begin again at the top of the list using the same sampling interval until you have the 250 residences? Why or why not?

11. Suppose your sampling frame is the white pages of the telephone directory. You are studying purchasing behavior of households. If the kth name in the directory is a business and is therefore ineligible, should you take the name listed right after the name of the business? Why?

12. List the conditions when you would consider using cluster sampling.

13. A company has 20 factories located in different parts of the country. It wants to survey its employees consisting of white-collar and blue-collar workers. Suggest a sampling plan **a.** if the measurement of interest is expected to vary more by factory than by type of worker and **b.** if the measurement of interest varies more by worker than by factory.

14. The target population consists of a list of 200 stores numbered from 001 to 200, from which 5 stores have been selected. Based on the numbers of the stores, indicate whether the sampling design was most likely to be a simple random sample, systematic sample, cluster sample, or a convenience (nonrandom) sample (one set of numbers represents each design).
    a. 110 111 112 113 114
    b. 098 099 156 157 158
    c. 037 063 110 139 181
    d. 025 065 105 145 185

6.7 Selecting a Survey Method

We have identified our sampling frame and selected a survey sampling design. Next we must decide which of three survey methods to use: personal interview, telephone interview, or mail questionnaire. There is no one best method for all situations. By the end of this section you should be able to:

1. compare and contrast the three methods; and
2. decide which method to use for a particular study.

Dillman (1978) points out how the three survey methods affect (1) obtaining a representative sample, (2) questionnaire length and flexibility, (3) obtaining accurate answers, and (4) administrative issues, such as how quickly we need the answers and how much we are willing to spend to get them. We will elaborate on these issues next.

Obtaining a Representative Sample

We must select samples based on chance and not personal bias. When we pick a specific individual or household from the sampling frame using a table of random numbers, that person or household should be interviewed. However, if that person is not available, we will need to select an appropriate substitute person or household. This is costly and time-consuming. Which of the three survey methods is best at avoiding substitutions?

Personal interviews. The advantage of personal interviews is that if the interviewee can be located, we are likely to get the interview. The interviewee will find it difficult to ask the interviewer to leave, whereas hanging up the telephone receiver or tearing up the mail questionnaire is easier to do. If we cannot locate the interviewee, then we can easily select a house three doors down the street. This should not present problems since people on the same street usually have similar social and economic characteristics. If the person is located but refuses to be interviewed, we should note the reason for refusal or the person's demographic characteristics.

The disadvantage of personal interviews is that locating a specific person may be difficult if the study covers a wide geographic area or the person is simply difficult to reach. Moreover, people who work during the day are difficult to locate. While they can be reached in the evening, many respondents are less willing to be personally interviewed after dark or after a hard day's work.

Telephone interviews. Telephone interviews are almost as useful as the personal interview in locating specific persons. They may even be better for locating persons who are geographically dispersed. Moreover, a telephone interview may require fewer substitutions than the personal interview because callbacks are much less expensive than return visits. Finally, people who work are more easily reached by telephone than by personal interview at night.

Unfortunately, not all people have telephones, and of those who do, some have unlisted numbers. Random-digit dialing reduces the latter problem as all possible numbers are randomly generated. For example, if the exchange number is 633-XXXX, we can program a computer to generate all possible sets of the last four numbers. Any unlisted number then has the same chance of selection as any other number with a 633 prefix.

Mail questionnaires. Even if busy schedules preclude a personal or telephone interview, people eventually pick up their mail. In surveys of homogeneous populations such as professional associations, the mailed questionnaire may do as well as other methods in getting a representative sample. However, a mailed questionnaire addressed to the "Director of Information Systems" or "Resident" may never reach the intended person. Even if it does, there is no guarantee that the recipient will complete the questionnaire. Often, unless we provide other incentives—money or a promise of sharing the survey results—the response rate may be significantly below that of personal or telephone interviews.

When the target population is the general public, the personal interview is the best method for getting a representative sample. Personal and telephone interviews are superior to the mail questionnaire in controlling selection of respondents, in response rates, and in avoiding unknown bias from refusals. With a homogeneous target population, such as a professional association, the mail questionnaire is almost as effective as the other two methods in obtaining a representative sample.

Questionnaire Length and Flexibility

The most difficult part of any survey is knowing *what* to ask and *how* to ask it. Later in this chapter, we will discuss the actual writing of the questions. Here we discuss how the survey methods affect the length and type of questions.

Personal interviews. Personal interviews permit more complex and open-ended (short essay) questions since we can prompt the respondent. The structuring of questions is less important than with the other two methods. *Screening questions*, which make some questions inapplicable to some respondents, are less likely to cause problems in the personal interview. For example, the following question can cause difficulty if it is part of a mail questionnaire, but should cause no difficulty for a trained interviewer:

Do you rent or own your place of residence?

1. RENT
2. OWN

IF RENT, GO TO QUESTION 12.

Telephone interviews. Telephone interviews should be shorter than the two other methods. As boredom or impatience sets in, respondents answer less carefully and may hang up. The telephone interview also requires the least complex questions. For example, a respondent asked to rank several items must retain the list in his head before ranking. In a personal interview, we can show the list to the respondent.

Mail questionnaires. The mail questionnaire requires the most careful construction. It must sell itself, be pleasing to the eye, and be constructed so responses can be given easily. Otherwise, the questionnaire will be discarded. Using open-ended questions is risky since respondents vary considerably in their writing skills. Many may answer in short and generally uninterpretable phrases when there is no interviewer present to probe for a fuller response. Use of screening questions, which requires bypassing some questions, can also lead to response errors. Finally, a higher nonresponse rate is more likely, since no interviewer is present to probe for answers or explain difficult questions.

The personal interview permits the longest and most detailed questionnaire, while the telephone method allows the shortest and least detailed questions. Personal and telephone interviews are both better than mail questionnaires at controlling the sequence of questions and are more successful in the use of screening questions. With respect to questionnaire flexibility and length, the personal interview is the best, the telephone interview a close second, and the mail questionnaire third.

Obtaining Accurate Answers

A successful study requires that we survey the right person, that the person have the information, and that he or she be willing to give it. How well do the three methods elicit a respondent's true attitudes, behaviors, and demographic characteristics?

Personal interviews. An interviewer who is helpful in *guiding* a respondent through complex and open-ended questions may also introduce serious bias. A disapproving facial expression or change in tone of voice can suggest the "correct" or socially desirable answer. In general, the socioeconomic status and race of the interviewer should not be too different from the respondent's or the respondent may distort answers to mislead the interviewer. Interviewers can be trained to minimize these problems, but it is expensive to do so.

Telephone interviews. Voice inflections from the interviewer can inadvertently bias responses. The problem is not as serious as in personal interviews since the interviewer's body language is not visible.

Mail questionnaires. Since no interviewer is involved, the respondent's willingness to provide true answers depends almost entirely on how the questions are presented. We say *almost* because the respondent may discuss the questionnaire with others before answering. This outside interference is most difficult to control in the mail survey, more easily controlled in the telephone interview, and most easily controlled in the personal interview.

Briefly, the mail questionnaire ranks highest in obtaining honest and unbiased answers, followed by the telephone interview, and then the personal interview. The opportunity for interviewer distortion is greatest in the personal interview.

Administrative Issues

The final issues to consider in selecting a survey method involve, of course, time and money. *When* do we need the information? *How much* is the budget? If we need the information in two weeks or a month, the best choice is a telephone interview. If potential respondents are spread over the world, the best choice is a mail questionnaire especially if the project budget is small. Here we discuss cost and other administrative issues related to the three survey methods.

Personal interviews. This is the most expensive method because of personnel costs, which include interviewers' salaries, travel, lodging, and meals. Finding and supervising qualified interviewers are difficult. They must be trained not to bias answers. We must verify that the interviews were completed as planned, and that the interviewer did not fill in the answers in the comfort of a hotel room.

Market research firms that have existing survey instruments will often allow their clients to add additional questions. "*Piggy-backing*" reduces client survey costs and allows several firms to survey the same target population with just one trip to a respondent. The interviewers should be professional, since the research firms offer steady employment and continual training.

Telephone interviews. This method is less expensive than personal interviews because fewer interviewers can call more people from one central location. In addition, the interviewers can be closely monitored, thus reducing the cost of recruiting, training, and supervision. WATS line technology reduces the cost per call even over great distances. Thus, larger samples can be taken in comparison with the personal interview.

Mail questionnaires. This is the least expensive method since it avoids the cost of training, supporting, and supervising interviewers. Mailing costs are uniform throughout the United States. Although the increasing use of facsimile machines may increase the cost of mail questionnaires, it will also reduce the time it takes to obtain the survey information.

In summary, the telephone is the fastest method and the personal interview is the slowest method. The least expensive method is the mail questionnaire and the most expensive is the personal interview. Considering speed and cost only, the personal interview should be avoided. Whether to telephone or mail the questionnaire depends on the trade-off between cost and time.

SECTION 6.7 EXERCISES

1. Which is the best survey method—personal interview, telephone interview, or mail questionnaire—for achieving each of the following objectives?
   a. Obtaining a representative sample
   b. Ease of questionnaire construction
   c. Obtaining accurate answers
   d. Minimum time and cost

2. Which is the worst survey method for achieving each of the four objectives in Exercise 1?

3. Your firm writes computer programs to help store and summarize residential sales data. You want to improve your current product to boost sales of the product and maintain customer loyalty. You want to survey current users and identify what they like and dislike about the current system. You have a list of names and phone numbers of all 1,500 licensed brokers in the target population. Considering all four of the general criteria for selecting a survey method, which method would you use?

4. Given each of the following characteristics of a proposed survey, which method would you think best to use?
   a. You need the information within a month.
   b. You are surveying the incidence of crime among new immigrants.
   c. Product usage survey
   d. Survey of attitudes of the members of the American Accounting Association
   e. Attitude survey with many complicated questions

f. Asks many personal or potentially embarrassing questions
g. Identifying the correct person to interview is not possible until after the sampling unit is selected.
h. Budget is very tight.

5. Explain the meaning of interviewer bias. How does it affect the results of surveys? How can you measure its effects?

6.8 General Principles in Writing Questions

Constructing the questionnaire is the most difficult part of any study since the wording of questions is more of an art than a science. We will cover how to determine the information needed, the type of questions to be written, and how to word the questions. After completing this section, you should be able to:

1. relate problem diagnosis to questionnaire construction;
2. determine what question format to use in a particular study; and
3. write questions that overcome the most common wording errors.

Determining Information Needs: Diagnosing the Problem

Companies do not conduct surveys merely to get data. They want to have important questions answered. They use surveys when diagnosing a problem. For example, suppose the firm must determine why sales of a recently introduced product are less than expected—a deviation from expected performance. Why aren't consumers buying the new product as rapidly as projected? What factors caused the deviation from expected sales?

Managers often focus too narrowly on the cause of a problem. They view a problem from the perspective of their own discipline. Marketers focus on consumer-oriented root causes. Engineers focus on poor product design root causes. To overcome a narrow view of a problem, we recommend using the "Alternative Worldview Method" to expose possible root causes (Ramakrishna and Brightman, 1986). This creative method requires that we brainstorm for multiple root causes in two distinct areas: internal to the firm and external to the firm. Internal root causes are those that originate inside the firm and over which we have control. External root causes are those that originate outside the firm and over which we have little or no control.

The root causes are explored at a brainstorming session, where no one criticizes any ideas. Participants just call out possible root causes in the two areas as fast as they can and list them on an easel pad. Afterwards, they can group similar causes together, identify the likely causes, and then address them in the survey. Shown here are the results of a brainstorming session for the sales deviation problem.

Internal factors: Poor product features, distribution channel failures, lack of product service support, poor product quality, or ineffective distribution.

External factors: Fierce competition, lack of consumer motivation to learn about the product, reduction in discretionary income, or fear of economic downturn.

Possible questions to ask include: Is the cause of lower-than-expected sales the consumers' lack of knowledge about the product? Does the product have the features they want? Is the service department at fault? Is the perceived quality lower than that of our competition? Before writing the first question, we must have a list of possible areas to investigate.

Surveys provide four types of information: (1) respondent behaviors, or what they say they do; (2) levels of knowledge, or what they know; (3) attitudes and opinions, or what they believe; and (4) socioeconomic characteristics, or who they are. These four types of information capture most of what we would need to know about an element in the target population.

Choosing the Question Format

Once the firm determines the information needed, what question format should it use? The choice depends on which survey method it selects—the personal interview, the telephone interview, or the mail questionnaire.

Most surveys consist of a combination of open-ended and closed-ended questions. Consider the questions in Table 6.6. From the table, we see examples of two basic formats for questions—open-ended and closed-ended.

Open-ended questions. Use open-ended questions when the list of all responses is very long or not obvious. For example, asking the question "What cigarette brand do you smoke?" would require too many alternatives for a complete list. Consider open-ended questions also for a pretest questionnaire

Table 6.6

Types of Question Formats in Surveys

Question	Format
Which country makes the best cars?	Open-ended
Which country makes the best cars? 1. USA 2. JAPAN 3. GERMANY	Closed-ended: Unordered alternatives
Which country makes the best cars? 1. USA 2. JAPAN 3. GERMANY 4. OTHER _____ (Please specify)	Partially closed-ended
If you own a Ford, how satisfied are you with its performance? 1. VERY SATISFIED 2. SATISFIED 3. UNSATISFIED	Closed-ended: Ordered alternatives
If you own a Ford, are you satisfied with it? YES _____ NO _____	Closed-ended: Binary alternatives

(Step 7 in planning a survey). In a pretest telephone interview, ask respondents to name all the radio stations they listen to. Use their responses in the major study as choices for a closed-ended question.

A disadvantage of open-ended questions is that answers depend on respondents' ability to write or speak as much as on their knowledge. Two respondents might have the same knowledge and opinions, but their answers may seem different because of their varying abilities. In interview surveys, the response accuracy also depends on the interviewer's ability to faithfully record everything the respondent says. Thus, considerable interviewer bias or error is possible. Finally, responses to open-ended questions are more difficult to interpret and analyze than are those to closed-ended questions.

Closed-ended questions. Use closed-ended questions when the full range of choices is known, when the list of questions is not too long, and when the questionnaires must be analyzed quickly.

However, there are several problems with closed-ended questions. First, we cannot determine the reasons behind a selection. A respondent could answer NO to the question "Do you intend to remodel your home this year?" for several reasons. He might not want to remodel his house or he is considering remodelling but he cannot afford it. Second, even when the DON'T KNOW option is offered, respondents will usually select from the other choices. They want to avoid the appearance of having no opinion. This is especially true when the wording of the question implies that they *should* know the answer.

Finally, the position of a choice affects the chances that it will be selected. This is called the *position bias.* For example, asked the amount of money spent each week for soft drinks, respondents will often pick the middle selection when they do not know the answer. Alternatively, where a long list of choices is *read* to respondents, they often select the last alternative. When the same choices are *visually* presented to the respondents, they will often select the first choice. Therefore, consider two approaches for minimizing the position bias. In mail questionnaires, print questionnaires with the choices in different sequences. In personal and telephone interviews, choose a different starting place every time you read the choices to a new respondent.

Avoiding Wording Errors

Suppose we know our information needs and have selected the question formats. Now we must write the actual questions. Remember that the respondent must (1) understand the question, (2) have the information, and (3) be willing to give it.

Table 6.7 on page 300 provides general guidelines for writing questions.

Understanding the question. Will the words have the same meaning to all potential respondents? Tailor the wording to the vocabulary of the potential respondents. If surveying a homogeneous population of doctors or lawyers, use technical language so that respondents will take the survey seriously. If the potential respondents are general public consumers, do not use specialized vocabulary.

Table 6.7

General Principles for Writing Questions

Understanding the Question

Match wording to the respondent's intelligence level or needs.
Avoid vague questions.
Avoid double questions.
Make the answers mutually exclusive.

Having the Information

Write questions that people can answer.
Write questions that people can answer without too much effort.

Willing to Give Information

Avoid questions that invade peoples' privacy.
Phrase questions so that social desirability does not play a role in selecting a response.
Never ask embarrassing questions.
Avoid questions that direct the respondent to select one answer over the others.

A question such as "Do you attend church regularly?" is vague. Respondents may define *regularly* differently. Rephrase the question this way.

How often did you attend church services in the past month?

1. NOT AT ALL
2. LESS THAN ONCE A WEEK
3. ONCE A WEEK
4. MORE THAN ONCE A WEEK

Ask only one question at a time. For example, "Do you own a second home or vacation home?" asks two questions.

Do not overlap answers in such a way that respondents could check two answers.

Where do you learn about sales in grocery stores?

1. FLYERS
2. NEWSPAPERS
3. RADIO
4. TELEVISION
5. FRIENDS AND NEIGHBORS

Since newspapers often contain insert flyers, choices 1 and 2 overlap.

Having the information. Have you assumed that respondents are more knowledgeable than they actually are or have greater access to information than they do? Respondents who do not possess the information requested, but who believe they should, will guess rather than admit they do not know. People often claim to subscribe to magazines that do not exist. Consider the following question.

Has your spouse read this issue of *Time*?

1. YES
2. NO

Trying to answer this question could pose one or several problems for some respondents. First of all, it assumes the respondent is married, which may not be the case. Second, it assumes that, if married, the person would know whether the spouse has read the magazine. Finally, it also assumes that the respondent knows what the term "spouse" means.

Even if respondents have the information, will it be "at their fingertips" and if not, will they be able and willing to find the information? For example, most people could not name the brand of tires on their car unless they went out and looked. But would they? Asking cigarette smokers to state the number of packs of cigarettes smoked last month will produce significant guessing since very few smokers are likely to know the exact number. Furthermore, they may not be willing to admit to themselves that they don't know the number!

Willing to give the information. Respondents will often lie when a truthful answer would adversely affect their prestige or invade their privacy. Personal questions may have higher rates of nonresponse and should be placed at the end of the questionnaire. Once the respondent has developed a rapport with the interviewer, he may provide truthful answers to prestige-laden or personal questions.

Unfortunately, it is not always obvious which questions are prestige laden. In one study, beer drinkers said they preferred light to regular beer but sales figures disagreed. Respondents lied because they perceived people who drank light beer as more discriminating and they wanted to be a part of that group.

People may also lie when the correct response would be embarrassing or make them appear to be members of an undesirable group, such as shoplifters, alcoholics, or drugs users. The following question might prompt the respondent to give answer 2 or 3 rather than admit to consuming the greatest quantity on the scale.

Approximately how many cans of beer do you consume each week, on the average?

1. NONE
2. 1 TO 3
3. 4 TO 6
4. MORE THAN 6

Consider extending the range of choices far beyond what is expected. Then the respondent can select an answer closer to the middle and feel more in the "normal" range.

Avoid biased questions. When a question or the list of responses seems to suggest a desired answer, respondents may give inaccurate information rather than disagree with the investigator's opinions. Suppose we handed out a questionnaire in a department store and one of the items was the following:

This store's merchandise is reasonably priced.

1. YES
2. NO

The item is heavily biased toward a YES response. It is clear how the researcher wants the shopper to respond. Revise the question as follows:

In comparison with other stores selling similar merchandise, would you say that our prices are higher, lower, or about the same?

1. HIGHER
2. LOWER
3. ABOUT THE SAME

A Final Thought

Managers are problem solvers. Surveys can help diagnose problem causes, identify current and future respondent needs, desires, and wants, and determine the effectiveness of managerial policies and actions.

Statisticians think of surveys in terms of survey sampling designs and sample size. Sampling designs and sample size affect the size of the margin of error and are crucial to the results obtained. In order to obtain true responses, managers must also consider question wording and format. Studies have shown that when the same people are reinterviewed, responses can change dramatically with a different interviewer or with a slightly different question wording. Therefore, it is very important to always pretest a questionnaire on a sample of respondents that have the same intellectual ability and knowledge of the topic area as the target population. We conduct the pretest as if it were the full study, and thereby we can discover question wording or format problems. There are two common ways of detecting wording problems. First, have respondents complete the questionnaire and then have them explain their answers. Second, ask respondents to think out loud as they answer each question. Finally, pretesting helps us find additional problems with questionnaire layout, question sequence, and branching instructions. Branching instructions direct respondents to answer certain questions depending on their responses to previous questions.

In addition, pretesting allows us to estimate response rates and the time needed to complete an interview. We can then compare this information with budgeted estimates to see if adjustments are needed.

Having followed our guidelines on (1) analyzing the problem before writing the questions, (2) selecting the proper survey sampling design, (3) selecting the best survey method, (4) choosing the proper question format, and (5) writing effective questions, we are now ready to obtain data through survey sampling.

For a more complete discussion of survey methods, question formats, and question wording, we recommend the work of Dillman (1978).

SECTION 6.8 EXERCISES

1. In order to give accurate responses, the respondent must (1) understand the question, (2) have the information, and (3) be willing to give it. With these criteria in mind, identify the flaws in the following questions.
    a. How many times did you visit a shopping mall in the past month?
    b. Do you use hairspray?
    c. Which is more important to you in purchasing foods, the caloric content or the levels of polyunsaturates?
    d. Have you been satisfied with the service provided by Rich's department store?
    e. Which car do you consider faster and more reliable, Porsche or BMW?
    f. Are you a frequent user of headache remedies?
    g. Listed below are stores generally considered to be upscale. Please check the ones you have shopped.

2. For each of the questions below, list the general source of error as not understanding the question (U), not having the information (I), or being unwilling to give the information (W).
    a. What is your income?
    b. Do you think that smoking ads should be banned or do you think that American businesses should have the right to advertise?
       1. YES 2. NO 3. NO OPINION
    c. How far would you drive to attend a cultural event?
    d. About how many alcoholic drinks do you consume on a week night?
    e. How many novels have you read in the last month?
    f. What percentage of your yearly income do you contribute to charitable causes?

3. Consider two forms of the same question shown here.
    (1) Which brands did you consider before you bought your last television? _____
    (2) Which of the following brands did you consider before you bought your last television?
       _____a. ADMIRAL _____b. RCA _____c. MAGNAVOX
       _____d. SONY _____e. OTHER
    The first version is referred to as *unaided recall* and the second is *aided recall*. What are the pros and cons of each form of this question?

6.9 Basic Principles of Experimental Design

Besides survey sampling, managers can obtain data by conducting *planned change studies*. Managers should continually seek ways to improve their workers' and their own performance, service, or product quality when needed. Unfortunately, they sometimes do not seek improvements. Some reasons are:

1. They have no time because they are always putting out brush fires—dealing with minor details and problems.
2. They assume that present performance, service, or quality cannot be improved. They are not innovators.

3. They are dissatisfied with present performance but do not have the courage to improve it. They fear that improving a system makes those who developed it appear incompetent—including themselves.
4. They are lazy or are looking for the easy way out.

To be innovative, managers need to continually ask questions, such as:

1. How can we improve production methods or service?
2. How can we train management and employees better?
3. How can we reduce marketing costs?
4. Will the customer use the product? How can we improve its present usage or make it more useful?

Once managers identify potential improvements, they should run planned change studies, preferably on a small scale, to determine if a potential improvement actually does improve performance or service. They should study the results. If the planned change is an improvement, they should implement it permanently. By the end of this section you should be able to:

1. define experimental design terms;
2. distinguish between an experiment and a non-experiment; and
3. explain how randomization helps rule out alternative explanations and why that is important.

Basic Terminology

What is an experiment, or planned change study? The "scientist image" represents experimentation in chemisty, physics, or psychology. However, managers also must run experiments to determine if planned changes do improve performance, service, or quality. So, what is an experiment? It's simply a *controlled study* in which a manager varies one or more factors and then measures the effects on the dependent variable.

Experimental factor. Factors, or treatments, are the planned changes that managers believe will improve performance, service, or quality. Factors could include different advertising approaches, production machine speeds, methods of cooking food, types of bonus systems, and so forth.

Level. Each variation of a planned change factor is a factor level. A marketing manager may try two different advertising approaches—two levels. A production manager may try three different speeds—three levels. We present some examples here.

Factor	Levels
Advertising approaches	Man-on-the-Street or Big Name Star
Polishing speeds	600 revolutions per min (rpm), 1,200 rpm, or 1,800 rpm
Cooking burgers	Broil or grill
Bonus systems	Individual or group bonus

Experimental unit. The entities that experience the planned change are the experimental units. They can be people, groups of people, or items on a production line. When the units are people, we call them subjects. Examples of possible experimental units for factors are the following:

Factor	Experimental Units
Advertising approaches	Customers
Polishing speeds	Eyeglass lenses
Cooking burgers	Burgers
Bonus systems	Workers

Dependent variable. Dependent variables are quantities that the manager measures to determine if the planned change has had any impact. We will limit our discussion to experiments that have only one dependent variable. Examples of possible dependent variables include:

Factor	Dependent Variable
Advertising approaches	Customer sales volume
Polishing speeds	Number of scratches on eyeglasses
Cooking burgers	Tastiness of burgers
Bonus systems	Number of units produced by workers

Experiments vs. Non-experiments

To run an experiment, the manager must meet two requirements:

1. assign experimental units to different factor levels, introduce a planned change, and measure the impact; and
2. control for extraneous factors.

We will illustrate both requirements in the following three scenarios.

SCENARIO 1   Max Drucker owns a rental car agency that provides four types of cars: Buick Regal, Oldsmobile Cutlass, Chevrolet Caprice, and Pontiac Grand Am. Max's major expense is unscheduled maintenance, which includes all repair work except routine oil changes, lubrication, etc.

Last year, Max asked himself if the cost of unscheduled maintenance was different for the four types of rental cars. He plans to drop those cars that have the highest costs. Max collected the unscheduled maintenance records for the past five years and then computed the total cost for each of the four types of cars. Since he owned an equal number of each type, Max compared the costs directly. Here are the results.

Buick Regal	Oldsmobile Cutlass	Chevrolet Caprice	Pontiac Grand Am
$3,950	$5,100	$5,300	$4,500

Question: Has Max run an experiment? Think about it before reading on.

He has not because he did not assign experimental units to factor levels, introduce a planned change, and measure the effects. First, there is no experimental factor since Max did not vary anything. Second, since there was no experimental factor, Max could not assign his cars (experimental units) to different factor levels. All he did was examine historical records. This is an *observational study* in which the manager collects data on an event that has already happened. Four types of cars have been used for five years and Max has merely collected the historical maintenance cost data.

Observational studies are not experiments and are difficult to interpret. The observational study suggests that the Buick Regal has the lowest unscheduled maintenance cost. If Max were naive, he would purchase only Buick Regals to reduce his maintenance costs. However, that may be an incorrect strategy! The Buick's low maintenance cost may be due to *extraneous factors*, factors beyond the car itself. Possible extraneous factors include:

1. Miles driven per year for each car type
2. Driver differences (abusive drivers, fast drivers, etc.)
3. Road surface differences (dirt, asphalt, concrete, etc.)
4. Operating environment differences (city, highway, etc.)
5. Type of gas and quality of oil differences
6. Customer neglect
7. Wrecks

On the basis of the cost data he has collected, Max cannot determine *why* the Buick Regal had the lowest cost. It may be that the Buick is indeed the least expensive car to maintain. On the other hand, its low cost may be due to at least seven other reasonable alternative explanations. For example, his Buick Regals may have been driven less than the other cars and thus lower mileage may explain the low maintenance costs. Max may *confuse* the effect of car manufacturer with mileage differences. Perhaps the Buicks may have been driven only on the highways and that accounts for their reduced maintenance cost. Again Max may confuse the car manufacturer and the operating conditions. In short, extraneous factors are possible alternative explanations to the factor under study—car type—that might account for the differences in the dependent variable—unscheduled maintenance cost.

If a manager does not introduce a planned change, there may be many alternative explanations to observed findings. Choose experiments over observational studies whenever possible as observational studies cannot control extraneous variation. However, simply introducing a planned change and measuring its effects do not control extraneous variation either.

SCENARIO 2   A university professor compares two teaching methods, lecture vs. case (the planned change), for an advanced business law course. Since he now teaches two sections, he uses the lecture method in the first section and the case method in the second section. After six weeks, he gives a different version of a chapter test to each section. The mean score in the lecture class is 83, as compared with a mean of 65 for the case method. *Question:* Has the professor run an experiment? Think about it before reading on!

The professor has introduced a planned change and measured the effects. He has taught sections using the case and lecture methods. He has measured the impact of different teaching methods by an examination. Therefore, he has met the first requirement of an experiment. However, his study is not an experiment. An experiment ensures that the measured effects result from the planned change and not extraneous factors, factors outside the experiment. The professor has not controlled for *any* potential extraneous factors. Therefore, he has not conducted an experiment.

Before reading on, generate a small list of potential extraneous factors that could explain why the lecture method produced better results, which may not be due to the method itself. This is difficult, so take your time.

Following is a list of potential extraneous factors that could have invalidated the experiment.

1. The professor may be a better lecturer than case teacher.
2. Students in the lecture class were smarter, more alert, or more motivated than students in the case method class.
3. The final exam in the lecture class was easier.
4. The lecture class met in the late morning and the case class met in the late evening. Students cannot think as clearly in the late evening.

Now compare this study with Scenario 3.

SCENARIO 3   Using *simple random sampling*, the professor selects two sections of business law from the five sections being taught at 10 A.M. The sections are scheduled in different buildings on campus. Students are not allowed to register for an individual class, merely the 10 A.M. class time. The professor selects a colleague who is equally effective in both teaching approaches. His colleague will teach both sections. The professor determines randomly which section his colleague will teach by the case method and which his colleague will teach by the lecture method. The professor then randomly assigns students to the two sections by using a random numbers table and the following assignment scheme:

First Two Digits of Random Numbers	Assignment
00–49	Lecture method
50–99	Case method

During the first class the instructor gives students in both sections the same pretest on business law fundamentals to determine their entry-level knowledge. After six weeks, the instructor gives the same post-test to both sections. Here are the results.

	Section 1—Case Method			Section 2—Lecture Method		
	Pretest	Post-test	Difference	Pretest	Post-test	Difference
Class Mean	48	76	+28	45	95	+50

This is an experiment. The instructor has controlled for the four previously mentioned possible extraneous factors. He used two different approaches: (1) eliminating potential extraneous factors and (2) randomization. Examples of the former approach are his use of the same pretest and post-test, using only one instructor, and selecting sections taught at the same time of day. The professor used randomization when he selected the two 10 A.M. sections, subdivided the students into two groups, and assigned them to the two sections.

Students in the lecture method class appear to do better. And it is unlikely that the lecture method class's superior performance is due to experimenter preferences, class section, test version, or time of day differences. Now there is no confusion as to why the lecture method students did better. All things being equal, lecturing is superior to the case method.

The Importance of Randomization

Randomization is essential to running a valid planned change study. Randomization minimizes the chance that two groups of students will systematically differ due to extraneous factors. In other words, randomization *tends* to equalize the groups on most potential extraneous factors. For example, randomization minimizes the chances that most of the better prepared, highly motivated, or smarter students are in the lecture method course. Thus, if we find a difference in the groups' performances, it is due to the planned change, not extraneous factors.

Randomize to the fullest extent possible in a planned change study. Use randomization to (1) select experimental units, (2) subdivide them into groups, and (3) assign the groups to the factor levels.

We conclude with several basic experimental design principles:

PRINCIPLE 1: Choose experiments over observational studies whenever possible. Observational studies collect past data and do not generate new data. They are after-the-fact studies and are not experiments.

PRINCIPLE 2: Conduct an experiment by assigning experimental units to different treatment levels, introducing a planned change, and measuring the impact. You must also control for extraneous factors.

PRINCIPLE 3: Control extraneous factors by using randomization and eliminating possible extraneous factors from the experiment. Both approaches ensure that the experimental factors caused the improvement in the product or service, and not some extraneous factor. We call this the *RO* **principle**— Ruling Out extraneous factors.

SECTION 6.9 EXERCISES

1. List the differences between an observational study and an experiment.
2. What is a factor? Is it a suspected cause or a symptom of the problem?

3. In order to solve a problem, a manager must first diagnose the causes. Explain how a properly conducted experiment helps to identify the real causes of a problem.
4. Explain how you would use a table of random numbers to assign 30 people to three equal-sized groups.
5. What is the purpose of randomization? Wouldn't it be better for a knowledgeable experimenter to place people in each group so the groups are equal except for the difference in treatment level? Explain.
6. In a recent telephone survey, a random sample of 400 respondents showed that men are more likely than women to vote for a Republican candidate. Is this an experiment? Explain.
7. A company wishes to study the relationship between job satisfaction and length of service with the company. The company decides to divide the length of service into two categories, under 5 years and 5 years and above. It randomly selects 20 employees from each of these two groups for testing and interviews.
   a. Is this an experiment or observational study? Explain.
   b. If the firm finds that people with longer tenure are more satisfied, can the company conclude that people who are new hires will automatically become more satisfied as time goes on? Why?
8. A consumer products testing laboratory wants to compare the wear on three brands of tires. The lab randomly assigns a different set of tires to each of three cars of the same make and randomly assigns one of three drivers to drive each car. After being driven around a test track for 10,000 miles, brand A has the smallest mean wear, and the lab concludes that brand A is the best tire. Do you think this conclusion is warranted? If not, what factors could have confounded the experiment, and how would you rule them out on the next experiment?

6.10 Avoiding Problems in Experimental Design

While the RO principle is essential for an experiment, it alone does not eliminate all planned change study problems. Next we consider several other serious problems and how to overcome them. By the end of this section you should be able to:

1. illustrate each potential experimental problem; and
2. correct each experimental problem.

EXAMPLE: COMCEL'S STUDY OF REDUCTION IN LABOR COSTS
According to published industry figures, work teams at COMCEL'S Norcross plant have not been as successful in reducing labor costs as have other firms. Recently, the plant manager asked Sarah Teman, Manager of Manufacturing, to design a plant-wide cost reduction program. First, Teman will conduct a small-scale study. Below are the two variations of her planned change:

1. Job switching within groups (JS workshop)
2. Teaching work groups creativity methods (CM workshop)

Teman identifies many teams in the plant that have a similar number of years of experience and prior success in implementing cost-saving ideas. From this pool, she randomly selects 10 work teams of five workers each. She

Table 6.8

One-Factor, Two-Level Planned Change Study

Factor: Type of Workshop

JS Workshop	CM Workshop
$1.30	$1.25
$1.35	$1.26
$1.10	$1.43
$1.15	$1.03
$1.02	$1.10

Dependent variable: Reduction in unit labor cost from January to June

---

randomly assigns the 10 teams to two groups of five teams each. She then randomly assigns one group of five teams to the JS workshop and the other group of five teams to the CM workshop. The dependent variable is the reduction in unit labor cost of producing a mobile telephone six months after the workshops. Table 6.8 presents the hypothetical data for the one-factor, two-level planned change study.

While Teman has ruled out some extraneous factors by eliminating them (similar years of experience and prior cost-savings idea success) and by using randomization, she can still improve her study. We will discuss some potential major problems that can spoil an experiment's findings.

The History Effect

ILLUSTRATING HISTORY   Both the JS and CM groups had similar reductions in unit labor costs. However, suppose that during the 6-month experiment the JS groups were given major bonuses for reasons that had nothing to do with the planned change study. Now we cannot be sure what their reductions in labor costs would have been had the JS groups received no bonuses during the experiment. The longer it takes to complete the study, the more likely it is that the **history effect** may occur.

> The history effect occurs when a change in the dependent variable is not due to the experimental factor, but an *unplanned* change that happened during the experimental period.

MINIMIZING HISTORY   The first way to minimize the history effect is to use randomization. Second, we should keep experiments as short as possible. Third, we should avoid running experiments during a period when there will be other major changes. For example, do not start a cost reduction study when the plant is switching to new production equipment. Finally, we should take frequent measurements on the dependent variable. Instead of just one measurement six months after the workshops, we should take measurements every week or month after introducing the planned change. Then if an unplanned major change does occur, we can determine whether the factor we varied appeared to be having any effect before the unplanned change happened. Showing that the JS groups' unit labor costs were already decreasing before they received their bonuses would probably rule out the bonus as the reason.

We can also determine whether there was a history effect by including *control groups* in the study. Control groups are work groups that receive no treatment—workshop, in this case. We would expect the control groups to experience no change in unit labor cost since they did not receive a planned change. However, if they showed a large reduction in unit labor cost, then history has affected the results. The experiment is flawed!

Diffusion of Treatment

ILLUSTRATING DIFFUSION OF TREATMENT   Suppose that members of the JS and CM groups tell each other what they have learned in their workshops. Now both groups have received the same factor level, or treatment. That may explain why the JS and CM groups had similar reductions in unit labor costs. **Diffusion of treatment** has ruined the experiment!

> Diffusion of treatment occurs when experimental groups that have received different treatments communicate with one another and thus the differences between factor levels become blurred.

MINIMIZING DIFFUSION OF TREATMENT   Ask members of the experimental groups not to talk with one another. Explain to them the need to maintain the purity of each factor level. If that does not work, physically separate the groups so they cannot talk to one another. It is critical that the differences between factor levels not be blurred.

Compensatory Rivalry

ILLUSTRATING COMPENSATORY RIVALRY   Suppose that the JS group members feel that they have been slighted. They wonder why *they* were not allowed to learn creative methods. In retaliation, they work extra hard to reduce labor costs. Now, the two groups differ in two ways: (1) different treatments and (2) different levels of motivation. We have a flawed experiment! Due to **compensatory rivalry**, the slighted groups may strive to do their best. This confounds the impact of the factor level with the level of the groups' motivation.

> Compensatory rivalry occurs when assignment of subjects to factor levels is made public, and subjects under one factor level believe they have received a second-class treatment.

MINIMIZING COMPENSATORY RIVALRY   First, do not make a public announcement about which groups are assigned to which factor levels. Second, assure all groups that all factor levels are equally worthwhile. Do not allow the groups to view one factor level as inferior. This may be difficult if one factor level really is inferior.

Trivial Changes

ILLUSTRATING TRIVIAL CHANGES   In the COMCEL study the two treatment levels differ significantly from one another. The premise of the JS workshop is that cost savings are achieved through job switching. The premise of the CM workshop is that creativity will help uncover new and innovative cost-saving ideas.

The following example illustrates a trivial change. We are varying car speed (factor) to determine its impact on gas mileage (dependent variable). We set the two factor levels at 20 mph and 21 mph—a **trivial change**. Since the difference is small, we cannot expect major changes in gas mileage. Consider running cars at 20 mph and at 50 mph.

> Trivial changes are differences in the factor levels that are so small that we cannot detect a difference in the dependent variable.

MINIMIZING TRIVIAL CHANGES   Be sure to make significant changes between factor levels to give the factor a reasonable chance to show its impact. "Pull apart" the levels of the experimental factor.

However, if we pull apart too far, we run into other problems. Suppose we randomly select people with IQs of 60 and 180 for a study on learning. We certainly have pulled apart the levels of the IQ factor. However, now we have two new problems: (1) finding people with such low and high IQ levels and (2) such people do not represent students in general, whose IQs vary between 110 and 140. Pull apart, but be mindful of the two problems.

Random Error

ILLUSTRATING RANDOM ERROR   From Table 6.8, the reduction in unit labor costs varies among the five teams within the JS treatment level (also among the five teams within the CM workshop). Random error or variation accounts for these differences since all five groups received the same JS treatment. The five values differ because of other factors not included in the study. These include level of worker motivation, skill level, and differences in workers' ages. There are many other differences among team members. Their net effect accounts for **random error**.

MINIMIZING RANDOM ERROR   Randomization tends to *equalize* the impact of extraneous factors over the factor levels. We will demonstrate in Chapter 9 that a multifactor design can reduce the impact of extraneous factors.

Multifactor designs have two or more experimental factors, each at two or more levels. Table 6.9 illustrates the design of a two-factor study with 12 work groups: (1) JS vs. CM workshop and (2) level of worker motivation—low and high. To run this study, Teman must first determine the level of motivation for *all* groups within the Norcross plant. She would then randomly select six groups with low motivation and six groups with high motivation. She would randomly subdivide each group of six into two sets of three work groups each and randomly assign each set of three low-motivation teams to either the JS or CM treatment. She would do likewise for the two groups of high-motivation teams. The dependent variable remains the reduction in unit labor cost from January to June.

> Random error causes the values of the dependent variable to differ within a factor level. Random error is due to the impact of all potential factors not included in the planned change study.

Table 6.9

A Two-Factor Design

Motivation Level	JS Workshop Group	CM Workshop Group
Low	1	3
	5	6
	9	12
High	4	2
	7	8
	11	10

SECTION 6.10 EXERCISES

1. Explain the *pull apart* principle.
2. Explain what the history effect is. Why is it a threat to the interpretability of an experiment? As a manager how can you control for history?
3. What is random error? Does randomization help to reduce random error?
4. A company is planning to purchase a single word processing package for the entire office. The office manager wants a package that is easy to learn and decides to compare two packages by means of an experiment. The manager selects 20 secretaries from the secretarial pool and randomly assigns ten to learn each package for a period of four hours. At the end of that time all are required to perform the same common word processing functions.
    a. List the factors, other than differences in the word processing packages, that might affect the outcome of this experiment.
    b. Would these factors ruin the validity of the experiment?
    c. Suggest ways to improve this experiment.
5. A State Patrol identifies 10 high-accident locations each month. The patrol wants to demonstrate that a program of selective enforcement is an effective way to reduce accidents. Under this program, a police car is placed at each location. Motorists see the patrol car and reduce speed. To show the effectiveness of selective enforcement, the total number of accidents from the 10 high-accident locations will be compared before and after the selective enforcement. Evaluate this experiment and suggest ways to improve it.

6.11 Key Ideas of Data Collection

We conclude this chapter with a set of important data collection ideas.

1. In drawing inferences, we must allow for a margin of error. However, we try to make it as small as practical. Margin of error decreases as sample size increases.
2. For the same level of confidence, different survey sampling designs may produce different margins of error.
3. There is no one best survey sampling *design*. Evaluate the four designs—simple random, stratified random, systematic, and cluster sampling. Select the one with the most advantages and the fewest disadvantages in a given situation.
4. There is no one best survey *method*. Evaluate the three methods—personal interview, telephone interview, and mailed questionnaire. Select the most advantageous method.
5. There is no one best *question format*. Select the one that will provide the needed responses.

6. Avoid the most common wording errors (see Section 6.8).
7. Observational studies collect past data and do not generate new data. They are after-the-fact studies and are not experiments.
8. Conducting an experiment means assigning experimental units to different treatment levels, introducing a planned change, and measuring the impact. We must also control for extraneous factors.
9. Control extraneous factors by using randomization and eliminating possible extraneous factors from the experiment. Both approaches ensure that the factor we varied caused the improvement in the product or service, and not some extraneous factor. We call this the *RO* principle—*R*uling *O*ut extraneous factors.
10. We should maximize the potential impact of a factor by pulling apart its levels.
11. We should minimize random error by using multifactor designs.
12. We should control for the history effect, diffusion of treatment, compensatory rivalry, and trivial changes.

COMCEL

```
Date:   October 6, 1992
  To:   Howard Bright, Norcross Plant Manager
From:   Ann Tabor, President
  Re:   Proposed Employee Morale Survey
```

I agree that raising the employees' morale is worth doing. But do we have a problem? Is there really a difference between this other company's average morale and ours? Our numbers are based on samples and therefore subject to a margin of error. Calculate the margin of error on past samples to see if our average plus the margin of error meets or exceeds their average morale score. There may be no problem.

SCOPE OF PROBLEM
You suggest interviewing a sample of production workers at the Norcross plant. What about our managerial staff and salaried workers? If we do have a morale problem, does it exist at all plants, among all shifts, and among all employees? Morale scores should be broken down by plant, shift, and employee type to see where we have a problem and where we don't.

PROBLEM CAUSES

If morale scores are lower than they should be, are you sure that the cause is too little participation in decision making? Maybe we give them too much decision-making responsibility, and not enough task support. Aren't there other explanations also, such as differences in training and experience, or physical working conditions?

SURVEY SAMPLING ISSUES

I discussed your memo with Cherian Jain, who is knowledgeable about different sampling designs. Since the morale gap might differ among departments and by type of worker, he recommends using stratified sampling instead of simple random sampling. Stratified sampling is effective when some subgroups are small and might be missed entirely, or when we want to draw a conclusion about a specific subgroup. Also, since we are trying to get honest feelings, perhaps we should use an outside consultant to ensure impartiality. You should also consider a questionnaire mailed to each employee's home by a consulting firm. People often answer sensitive questions more honestly when they are in the privacy of their own homes and no interviewer is present.

THE NEXT STEP

Prepare a final set of recommendations for my review by October 14th.

CHAPTER 6 QUESTIONS

1. What are three ways that managers obtain data?
2. Why do managers conduct surveys and run planned change studies? Why aren't all their information needs met by the management information system?
3. Explain margin of error and why it should be as small as possible.
4. Why does margin of error decrease as we increase sample size? Why does margin of error decrease as the variation in the target population decreases?
5. Suggest and defend a sampling frame for a job climate survey for COMCEL's Dallas manufacturing plant. The plant contains hourly, professional, and management personnel.
6. For a touchy subject such as attitude toward the job, what survey method should we use?
7. How are selection and nonresponse errors different?
8. Why doesn't increasing the sample size reduce the chances of selection error?
9. How does using a table of random digits ensure that we select a simple random sample?
10. What is wrong with convenience sampling?
11. In your own words, what is stratified random sampling?
12. Explain the logic behind the three rules for selecting the strata sample sizes.
13. When can stratified random sampling produce larger margins of error than simple random sampling?
14. How can a preliminary problem diagnosis help in designing your survey questionnaire?
15. How can the survey results help your final problem diagnosis?

16. What is the purpose of creating data through planned change studies?
17. How do experiments differ from observational studies?
18. Why can't managers always run experiments? That is, why must they resort to observational studies?
19. How can we accomplish the RO principle in planned change studies?
20. Why is the history effect more likely as the length of the planned change study increases?
21. What are the dangers in "pulling apart" an experimental factor—such as a personality or socioeconomic factor—too much?
22. Is compensatory rivalry likely when all treatment groups view their treatments as equally desirable?
23. Why is diffusion of treatment a serious problem in planned change studies?

CHAPTER 6 APPLICATION PROBLEMS

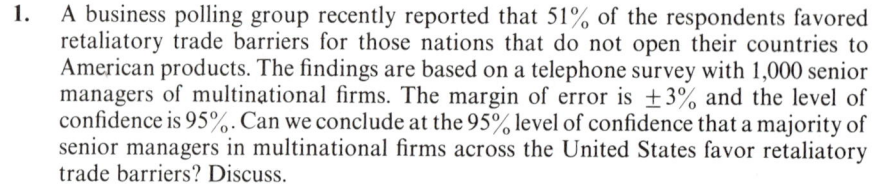

1. A business polling group recently reported that 51% of the respondents favored retaliatory trade barriers for those nations that do not open their countries to American products. The findings are based on a telephone survey with 1,000 senior managers of multinational firms. The margin of error is $\pm 3\%$ and the level of confidence is 95%. Can we conclude at the 95% level of confidence that a majority of senior managers in multinational firms across the United States favor retaliatory trade barriers? Discuss.

2. A marketing manager in charge of telemarketing—phone sales—wants to know the mean number of phone calls her operators make each month. While there is little variation within a month, there is much month-to-month variation. What sampling design would you recommend to estimate the overall mean number of calls made monthly? Explain.

3. Identify the sample and the population in the following situations:
   a. *Goal:* to study the problem of noise at major airports. You set up monitoring equipment at 10 randomly selected airports in the United States.
   b. *Goal:* to assess compliance with the revised tax code. You perform detailed tax audits on selected taxpayers' returns.
   c. *Goal:* to assess how a firm's hourly staff, support personnel, and professionals feel about a flexible benefits package. You send out a survey to selected workers.

4. Do soft-drink consumers prefer Pepsi or Coke? You are to design a one-factor planned change study. Describe the (1) experimental factor, (2) levels, (3) dependent variable, and (4) experimental units.

5. You want to select a simple random sample of eight states for a survey. Below are listed the abbreviations of 50 states in alphabetical order.

AL	AK	AR	AZ	CA	CO	CT	DE	FL	GA
HI	ID	IL	IN	IA	KS	KY	LA	ME	MD
MA	MI	MN	MS	MO	MT	NE	NV	NH	NJ
NM	NY	NC	ND	OH	OK	OR	PA	RI	SC
SD	TN	TX	UT	VT	VA	WA	WV	WI	WY

Let AL = 1, AK = 2, ..., WY = 50. Select eight states starting with the fifth entry in row 26 of the random numbers table and move across the rows—Appendix 4.

Use two-digit random numbers; eliminate the last three digits in each group of five digits. What states will be included in your survey?

6. About six months ago a firm installed a computerized inventory management system. The goal was to reduce inventory costs. The manager measured the reduction of inventory costs since the system was installed. Has the manager conducted a planned change study? Why or why not?

7. A multinational firm has divisions in the United States, Great Britain, Canada, Japan, and Egypt. The CEO wants to survey his workers on a proposed retirement plan. What would you suggest he use as a survey sampling design? What survey method would you recommend? Explain.

8. Shown are the before-treatment and after-treatment sample means of a study to improve consumer awareness of the attributes of a product such as mineral water. Different groups of consumers were given either the present advertising approach (control group) or the new advertising approach (treatment). The dependent variable is the number of product attributes that a consumer can correctly recall one week after the treatment. Do the study results indicate diffusion of treatment as a potential problem?

Group	Before Measure	After Measure
Control	2	2
Experimental	2	5

9. A marketing research firm wishes to estimate the number of New Yorkers who prefer the clarity of a new phone to that of a phone made by a major manufacturer. One hundred curious people enter a marketing research booth in a shopping mall and 65 prefer the new phone.
   a. What is the target population in this study?
   b. Did the marketing firm select a simple random sample?
   c. What problems are there in using this type of sampling?

10. You want to estimate the percentage of defects in a manufacturing plant that has four different production lines. You believe that the percentage varies greatly among the four lines. There is, however, little day-to-day variation within each of the four lines.
    a. What problem might you have if you use simple random sampling?
    b. What survey sampling design is appropriate for this study? Explain.

11. One hundred thousand families live in the two towns in a county. Town A has 70,000 families and town B has 30,000 families. The chairman of the county commission wants to determine the perceived need for additional fire and police services in the county. He plans to use stratified random sampling with each city as a stratum.
    a. Using stratified sampling means that he believes that each city has very different perceived needs for additional fire safety. Suggest several reasons why this might be so.
    b. The total sample size will be 1,000 families. What size sample should he take from each city? Assume that the variability of perceived need for additional fire and police services is similar in both towns. Explain.

12. You are running a planned change study on the impact of two leadership styles on worker productivity. Explain how you should use randomization in your study.

13. You take a simple random sample of 10 people from a population. Your goal is to estimate the mean weight of the population. The sample data are listed at the top of page 318.

	Men	Women
Sample Size	2	8
Weight (pounds)	170	120

The mean weight (weighted average) of the sample is 130 pounds. That seems too low for the target population. What might account for the simple random sample average weight being very different from the average weight of the population?

14. Shown are the before and after sample means from a study to improve consumer awareness of the attributes of a product such as mineral water. Different groups of consumers were given either the present advertising approach (control group) or the new advertising approach (treatment). The dependent variable is the number of product attributes that a consumer can correctly recall one week after the treatment. Do the study results indicate that the history effect is a potential problem?

Group	Before Measure	After Measure
Control	2	4.5
Experimental	2	5

15. You wish to estimate the number of coding errors made by a new data entry clerk. You suspect that at first he will make many mistakes, but over time, he will improve. The target population is 5,000 data entries. You cannot check them all, so you decide to take a sample.
   a. Why could simple random sampling generate a very poor estimate? Explain.
   b. What survey sampling design of the four presented is best at accurately estimating the number of data entry errors made by the clerk since he started?

16. An auditor selects a simple random sample from 500 accounts to check for compliance with audit control procedures and to verify the actual dollar amount in the accounts. Below are the data.

Account	Amount ($)	Compliance	Account	Amount ($)	Compliance
10	248	Yes	111	413	Yes
34	94	Yes	234	66	Yes
66	168	No	345	134	Yes
67	233	Yes	377	170	No
99	45	No	455	100	Yes

   a. Compute the sample mean dollar amount and the sample proportion of accounts in compliance.
   b. Why aren't the sample and population means the same, and why aren't the sample and population proportions the same?

17. In the legal case of *Amstar Corp. v. Domino's Pizza Inc.* (5th Circuit, 1980), Amstar Corp., producers of Domino sugar, attempted to show that the public might believe that Domino's Pizza was related to their product line. They wanted Domino's Pizza to change its name.

Amstar Corp. interviewed females who were responsible for making food purchases for their households. Each respondent was shown a Domino's Pizza box and asked if she believed the company that made the pizza made any other products.

If she answered yes, she was asked what other products were made by the company. Seventy-one percent of those answering the second question said sugar.

The 5th Circuit rejected Amstar's survey and said that it was seriously flawed. From a target population and sampling frame perspective, what is one major flaw in the study?

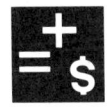

18. The five most common reasons why firms acquire other firms are:

Synergy	to increase the value of the combined enterprises
Tax considerations	to shelter the income of the acquiring firm
Assets	to obtain assets whose replacement value is higher than their market value
Diversification	to stabilize a firm's earning stream
Control	to gain control of the firm

You wish to determine which reasons have been the prime motivators for acquisitions that cost at least $100 million in the past five years. Discuss how you would select a simple random sample.

19. Does providing customer feedback on car service improve a car dealer's level of service? You are to design a one-factor planned change study. Describe the (1) experimental factor, (2) levels, (3) dependent variable, and (4) experimental units.

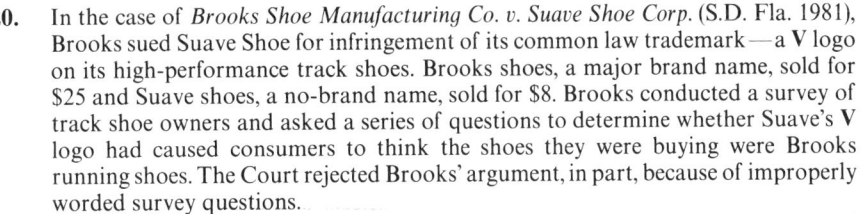

20. In the case of *Brooks Shoe Manufacturing Co. v. Suave Shoe Corp.* (S.D. Fla. 1981), Brooks sued Suave Shoe for infringement of its common law trademark—a **V** logo on its high-performance track shoes. Brooks shoes, a major brand name, sold for $25 and Suave shoes, a no-brand name, sold for $8. Brooks conducted a survey of track shoe owners and asked a series of questions to determine whether Suave's **V** logo had caused consumers to think the shoes they were buying were Brooks running shoes. The Court rejected Brooks' argument, in part, because of improperly worded survey questions.

Below are two forms of the same question. Version 2 is properly written and version 1 is improperly written. Why?

1. I am going to hand you a shoe. Please tell me what brand you think it is?
2. I am going to hand you a shoe. Do you know who makes or sells it?

Later in the survey, the following question was asked. What is improper about this question?

How long have you known about Brooks running shoes?

REFERENCES

DILLMAN, DON A. *Mail and Telephone Surveys: The Total Design Method.* New York: John Wiley & Sons, 1978.

RAMAKRISHNA, H., and H. BRIGHTMAN. "The Fact Net Model: A Diagnostic Approach." *Interfaces* 16, no. 6 (November–December 1986): 86–94.

ROLL, C., Jr., and A. CANTRIL. *Polls—Their Use and Misuses in Politics.* New York: Basic Books, 1972.

SCHEAFFER, RICHARD, WILLIAM MENDENHALL, and LYMAN OTT. *Elementary Survey Sampling.* Boston: Duxbury Press, 1986.

Making Inferences About One Population Parameter

7.1 Problem solving and statistical inferences
7.2 The sampling distribution of the sample mean
7.3 Confidence intervals on an unknown population mean
    t-Based confidence intervals
    Setting the level of confidence
    Confidence intervals and time-ordered data
7.4 One-sided confidence intervals on an unknown population mean
    The finite population correction factor
7.5 The hypothesis testing framework
    State hypotheses and managerial actions
    Determining the costs of the decision making errors
    Set a level of significance and determine a sample size
    Data collection
    Weigh the evidence and make a decision
    Prob-value
7.6 Stratified random sampling
    Impact of using simple random sampling
7.7 Confidence intervals on an unknown population proportion
    Estimated standard error of the proportion
7.8 Determining the sample size
    Two-sided interval on an unknown population mean
    Two-sided interval on an unknown population proportion
7.9 A nonparametric confidence interval for the median
    Constructing approximate 95% confidence intervals
    Assumptions for confidence intervals on the population mean and median
    Confidence intervals on the mean in the presence of outliers
7.10 Estimating the population variance and standard deviation
    The chi-square distribution
7.11 Overview and key ideas
Chapter 7 Questions
Chapter 7 Application Problems
Appendix: Relationship between Type I and Type II errors

CHAPTER OUTLINE

COMCEL Interoffice Communication

Date: July 21, 1992
To: Nat Gordon, V.P. Manufacturing
From: Ann Tabor, CEO
Re: Improving Quality and Reducing Breakdowns

The quality control department notified me that our mobile phones, on the average, experience a breakdown after 2,000 hours of service. According to published industry reports, the mean time-to-failure for phones from all manufacturers is 2,500 hours. I am not satisfied with our phones' performance.

I am authorizing you to set up a project team to improve phone performance. The project team will report directly to you. I want personnel from quality control, engineering, and manufacturing on the team. Improving time-to-failure has the highest priority, so assign your best people to the team. I won't be satisfied unless our time-to-failure exceeds 2,750 hours. If you need additional support personnel, let me know. I want the team's report by the end of March.

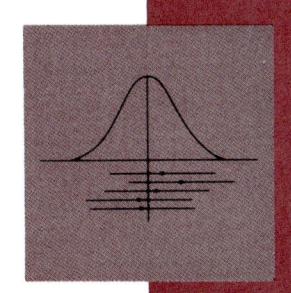

7.1 Problem Solving and Statistical Inferences

Managers use descriptive statistics to build mental models, sense and understand problems and opportunities, seek root causes, make decisions, and assess potential impacts. They do this by asking the right questions. For example:

What is our customers' mean income level?

What is the median number of days for parts to arrive from a vendor?

What proportion of the firm's employees favor a flex-time system?

What is the variability in the impact resistances of plastic TV cabinets made in the Springfield plant?

Managers realize it would be too costly to survey all customers, review all shipping records, interview all employees, or test all TV cabinets in order to answer their questions. As we learned from Chapter 6, cost is a key factor in survey considerations. We can, however, take a simple random sample from each target population and compute descriptive statistics. However, the sample mean, median, proportion, or standard deviation is *not* the target population's mean, median, proportion, or standard deviation. In this chapter we will use descriptive statistics and the method of confidence intervals to *estimate* target population parameters. In short, we will make *statistical inferences*. By the end of the section you should be able to:

1. distinguish between a target population and a sample;
2. distinguish between a population parameter and a sample statistic; and
3. explain what the population standard deviation really measures.

We begin with some very important definitions.

A *target population* is the entire group of elements about which we want information. An *element* is an object or subject on which we take a measurement. For example, all the employees in a firm and all the television cabinets produced in a plant are target populations. An element would be a *particular* employee (subject) or TV cabinet (object).

A *sample* is a part of the target population. We gain knowledge about the population from the sample. A sample is a number of elements taken from the population. For example, a sample might be 100 randomly selected employees or 50 randomly selected TV cabinets.

A *population parameter* is the information we want about the population. It could be the mean, median, proportion, or variance. Population parameters are fixed, or constant, values and are generally unknown. For example, population parameters would be the actual proportion of all employees who favor flex-time or the variance in impact resistances of all plastic TV cabinets.

A *sample statistic* is computed after obtaining the sample data. We use a sample statistic to *estimate* an unknown population parameter. While the population parameter is a constant value, the sample statistic will vary from sample to sample. For example, sample statistics are the sample proportion of the 100 employees who favor flex-time or the sample standard deviation of impact resistance of 50 TV cabinets.

It is important to remember the distinction that statistics describe samples and parameters describe populations. We estimate population parameters from sample statistics using statistical inference methods.

Statistical inferences permit us to assign a level of confidence that the inference is correct and to compute a margin of error. For example, we might be 95% confident that the mean income level of all our customers (target population) is $35,500 $\pm$ $5,000. The $5,000 figure is the margin of error (see Chapter 6). Margin of error measures the possible difference between the sample statistic and the population parameter.

Managers want small margins of error. Two effective methods are (1) to increase the sample size and (2) to select the proper sampling design. Recall from Chapter 6 that increasing a population standard deviation increases the margin of error. Unfortunately, there is little we can do to reduce a population standard deviation in the short run.

The population standard deviation measures the spread in the values within a population. The spread is not due to sampling mistakes made during data collection. Rather it is due to inherent variability. Suppose we tested the impact resistance of every plastic TV cabinet. Should we expect all cabinets to have the same impact resistance? Since there are many production factors that the firm cannot totally control, impact resistances will vary. For example, different assemblers worked on the cabinets at different times of the day. Some assemblers may have tired, and that affected the impact resistance. The raw material may have varied slightly among cabinets. If we could eliminate all sources of variability, the population standard deviation would be zero. In practice, this is impossible.

In summary, sample statistics describe a sample and population parameters describe a population. We use descriptive statistics and statistical inference methods to estimate unknown population parameters.

SECTION 7.1 EXERCISES

1. Explain the difference between a statistic and a parameter.
2. Consider a population of four data values, $\{1, 2, 3, 4\}$. The mean of these values is 2.5. The mean of a single sample of size two consisting of $\{2, 4\}$ is 3. Which of these two means is a parameter and which is a statistic?
3. A marketing research group is hired by a soft drink company to sample the preferences of consumers. The research company selects a random sample of 1,000 members of the general public and finds that 400 preferred brand A.

a. What is the target population?
b. What is the population parameter of interest?
c. What is the sample statistic?

4. A manufacturer wants to estimate the mean dollar loss from breakage resulting from shipping a product from New York to Detroit. As boxes are delivered, one in every 10 boxes is opened and the dollar value of broken contents is measured. In a sample of 50 boxes the mean dollar loss per box is $10.23.
a. What is the target population?
b. What is the population parameter of interest?
c. What is the sample statistic?

5. List the factors that affect the margin of error.

6. Explain why it is necessary to state a margin of error when estimating a population parameter.

7. An insurance company is about to do a planned change study. From a large group of experienced claims checkers, two groups of 15 are selected. One group will continue checking claims as usual. The other group will work in teams of three and specialize in some part of the claim form. After a period of three weeks, the claims manager intends to compare the mean number of claims checked per day between the two groups to see if specialization improves productivity.
a. What are the target populations?
b. What are the population parameters of interest?
c. What are the sample statistics?

8. You place four new and identical light bulbs into a light fixture. Why is it unlikely that all the bulbs burn out at the same time? What statistical measure would tell you how far apart the burnouts might be?

7.2 The Sampling Distribution of the Sample Mean

Suppose we took a sample of 50 TV cabinets and tested their impact resistance. Because this is one of many possible samples, the sample mean (a sample statistic) will probably not equal the population mean (a population parameter). The two means will differ because of variation within the population and because the composition of the samples varies. However, most sample means will be close to the population mean because of the sampling distribution of the sample mean.

From Chapter 5, the central limit theorem tells us that the sampling distribution of the sample mean will be normal provided we take a sample size greater than 30. Now you will learn some other properties of the sampling distribution. By the end of this section you should be able to:

1. distinguish between the mean and standard deviation of (1) a population, (2) a sample, and (3) the sampling distribution of the sample mean;
2. explain why the standard deviation of the sampling distribution, or standard error, must be smaller than the standard deviation of the population; and
3. explain how the parameters of the sampling distribution are useful in estimating an unknown population mean.

Table 7.1 contains data for a population of six workers and the number of days they have been absent in the last quarter.

Table 7.1

Absenteeism in One Quarter for a Worker Population

Worker	Days
A	0
B	1
C	2
D	3
E	4
F	5

Table 7.2

List of Sample Means for a Sample Size of Three

Sample	Mean	Sample	Mean
A, B, C	1.00	B, C, D	2.00
A, B, D	1.33	B, C, E	2.33
A, B, E	1.67	B, C, F	2.67
A, B, F	2.00	B, D, E	2.67
A, C, D	1.67	B, D, F	3.00
A, C, E	2.00	B, E, F	3.33
A, C, F	2.33	C, D, E	3.00
A, D, E	2.33	C, D, F	3.33
A, D, F	2.67	C, E, F	3.67
A, E, F	3.00	D, E, F	4.00

Table 7.2 contains the 20 sample means that comprise the sampling distribution of the sample mean for a sample size of three from the population described in Table 7.1.

Tables 7.1 and 7.2 will help distinguish the three types of distributions. First, there is the *population* distribution consisting here of six elements. Second, each *sample* is a distribution consisting of three values. Finally, there is the *sampling* distribution consisting of 20 sample means. From Chapter 2, we know that every distribution has a mean and a standard deviation. Table 7.3 contains the symbols and formulas for each mean and standard deviation.

The mean of the six observations of the population is μ and the standard deviation of the population is σ. Usually, the population mean and standard deviation are unknown and our goal is to estimate them. For the data in Table 7.1, we calculate

$$\mu = \frac{\sum_{i=1}^{N} x_i}{N} = \frac{0+1+2+3+4+5}{6} = 2.5 \text{ days}$$

$$\sigma = \sqrt{\frac{\sum_{i=1}^{N} (x_i - \mu)^2}{N}}$$

$$= \sqrt{\frac{(0-2.5)^2 + (1-2.5)^2 + \cdots + (5-2.5)^2}{6}} = 1.7 \text{ days}$$

Table 7.3

Terminology Table

	Mean	Standard Deviation
Population	μ	σ
Sample	$\bar{x}$	s
Sampling distribution of the sample mean	$\mu_{\bar{x}}$	$\sigma_{\bar{x}}$

Note that we use N, the population size, in the formulas for computing population parameters.

We can take one sample of size three (A, C, E) and compute a sample mean, $\bar{x}$, and a sample standard deviation, s:

$$\bar{x} = \frac{\sum_{i=1}^{n} x_i}{n} = \frac{0 + 2 + 4}{3} = 2 \text{ days}$$

$$s = \sqrt{\frac{\sum_{i=1}^{n}(x_i - \bar{x})^2}{n-1}}$$

$$= \sqrt{\frac{(0-2)^2 + (2-2)^2 + (4-2)^2}{2}} = 2 \text{ days}$$

Note that we use n, the sample size, in the formulas for computing sample statistics.

Instead of taking one sample of size three, suppose we took *all possible* samples of size three, without replacement, from the population and computed the sample means. That would give us a sampling distribution of the sample mean (Table 7.2). The *overall* mean of all the sample means is the mean of the sampling distribution, $\mu_{\bar{x}}$ (mu sub-$\bar{x}$).

We can now compute the mean of the sampling distribution in Table 7.2. Note that the denominator is the total number of possible samples—not the sample size—that we can take without replacement.

$$\mu_{\bar{x}} = \frac{1.00 + 1.33 + 1.67 + \cdots + 3.67 + 4.00}{20} = 2.5 \text{ days}$$

LESSON 1: The mean of any sampling distribution of the sample mean is the same as the mean of the population from which it was derived.

The standard deviation of the sampling distribution, $\sigma_{\bar{x}}$ (sigma sub-$\bar{x}$), measures the spread of the sample means around the mean of the sampling distribution. It is called the *standard error of the mean*. Will the standard error be larger, smaller, or the same as the population's standard deviation of 1.7 days? This is a difficult question so please think about it before reading on.

In the population, the number of days absent ranged from 0 to 5, and the mean was 2.5 days. In Table 7.2, the sample means for samples of size three ranged from 1.00 to 4.00 with a mean of 2.5 days. The 20 sample means cluster more closely around the overall mean of 2.5 days than do the population data. This brings us to the second lesson, which holds for all sampling distributions.

LESSON 2: The standard error of the mean is smaller than the standard deviation of the population.

Now compare the standard errors for the sampling distributions based on samples of size three and four observations. From Chapter 5, the sample means for sample sizes of four (Table 5.10) varied from 1.5 to 3.5 days. The sample means for samples of size three varied from 1.0 to 4.0 days. The standard error for a sample of size four is thus smaller than the standard error for a sample of size three. This brings us to the third lesson.

LESSON 3: The standard error of the mean decreases as the sample size increases.

When we select small samples from large populations, the standard error of the mean is

$$\sigma_{\bar{x}} = \frac{\sigma}{\sqrt{n}} \tag{7.1}$$

Our goal is to use the sample mean and standard deviation to estimate the population mean and standard deviation. How can knowing the properties of the sampling distribution of the sample mean help us estimate the unknown population mean?

To estimate an unknown population mean, should we take *one* sample of size three or *one* sample of size 30? Cost considerations aside, we would take the larger sample. How does this choice relate to the properties of the sampling distribution? These focused questions will help:

1. If we did take all possible samples of size three and all possible samples of size 30 from the population, what would the means of the two sampling distributions equal?

   From Lesson 1, they would both equal the unknown population mean.

2. Why is a sample mean based on 30 observations more likely to be closer to the unknown population mean? How can this be explained in terms of the standard error of the mean?

   The standard error decreases as we increase the sample size. Most means of samples of size 30 will be close to the unknown population mean. A sample mean based on only three observations could still be very far from the unknown mean.

In summary, we should take the largest sample size possible. We first learned that larger samples reduce the margin of error (see Section 6.2). Now we know the reason. As we increase the sample size, the standard error gets smaller.

SECTION 7.2 EXERCISES

1. Consider the population of data values, {2, 4, 6}. Suppose we select one item, write down the number, and replace it so it can be drawn again. The list of all possible samples of size $n = 2$ is shown here:

2, 2	4, 2	6, 2
2, 4	4, 4	6, 4
2, 6	4, 6	6, 6

   → sample

   a. Find the population mean, μ.
   b. Find the population standard deviation, σ.
   c. Find the means of the nine samples and the mean of the means, $\mu_{\bar{x}}$.
   d. Find the standard deviation of the sample means.
   e. What is the relationship between the population mean and the mean of the means?
   f. Show that the standard error of the sample mean is found by dividing the population standard deviation by the square root of the sample size.

2. Three distributions are involved in any inference. Refer to Exercise 1 and state the sizes of the population, the sampling distribution, and any sample distribution. → mean of each sample

3. All distributions have means and most distributions have standard deviations. Complete the table below by writing the symbol for each (please do not refer to the book).

	Mean	Standard Deviation
Population distribution	____	____
Sampling distribution	____	____
Sample distribution	____	____

4. As the sample size increases, the spread of the sampling distribution, as measured by the standard error, gets smaller. Suppose you selected a simple random sample of size 25 from a population and found that your standard error was too large to suit your needs. What size sample would you have to take the next time in order to cut the standard error in half?

5. The measurements taken on items from an assembly line are normally distributed with a mean of 50.0 cm. Consider the distribution of means based on all samples of size $n = 36$. If the population standard deviation is .5 cm, describe the sampling distribution of the sample mean in terms of shape, measure of central tendency, and measure of dispersion. Draw a picture and label all parts.

6. Refer to Exercise 5. According to the Empirical rule, 68% of all sample means will fall between what two numbers? Approximately 95% of the sample means will fall between what two numbers?

7. A sampling distribution of the sample mean is normally distributed with a mean of 20 pounds and a standard error of 4 pounds. Use your knowledge of the normal distribution to find:
   a. $P(\bar{x} > 24 \text{ pounds})$
   b. $P(\bar{x} < 19 \text{ pounds})$
   c. the probability that a sample mean selected at random will differ from the population mean by more than 6 pounds in either direction.

8. Using standard methods, a trained worker can complete a task in 12.0 minutes with a standard deviation of 2.1 minutes. An industrial engineer specializing in time and method studies suggests a new way of completing the task. A sample of 49 trained workers complete the task using the new system in an average of 11.4 minutes.
   a. If the new method is no better than the standard method, what is the probability of obtaining a sample mean of 11.4 minutes or less?
   b. As manager in charge, would you conclude that the new method is better than the existing method? Explain.

7.3 Confidence Intervals on an Unknown Population Mean

While we should always select the largest possible sample size, we cannot sample the entire target population because it would be too costly and too time-consuming. Rather we will use descriptive statistics and the method of confidence intervals to estimate an unknown population mean. By the end of this unit you should be able to:

1. explain what a confidence interval is and how it is derived from the sampling distribution of the sample mean;
2. explain the need for, and the impact of, using the t-table in constructing confidence intervals;
3. construct confidence intervals using the t-table;
4. make decisions based on interpreting confidence intervals;
5. distinguish between the degree of certainty and meaningfulness in constructing confidence intervals;
6. explain why it is impossible to construct a meaningful 100% confidence interval; and
7. explain why confidence intervals are inappropriate for nonstationary time-ordered data.

Consider the following situation of a tire manufacturer. The company will shortly announce a new Milemaster tire. The company must know the mean tire life so that it can set the limits for its treadwear warranty. If the warranty is set too low, the company may lose its competitive advantage. If it is too high, the company will have to replace too many tires.

Knowing the mean tire life with absolute certainty would require testing each and every Milemaster tire. Clearly this is not a practical approach. It takes too long, is too costly, and there would be no tires left to sell. A practical alternative is to take a simple random sample from the population of tires. We can then compute the sample statistics, $\bar{x}$ and s, and use them to estimate the population parameters, μ and σ.

The boss asks how we will arrive at an estimate. We tell him that we will take one simple random sample of size 900 from the population of tires in the warehouse. In a simple random sample, each possible collection of 900 tires has an equal chance of being selected. The boss nods his head in agreement.

We test the sample of 900 tires until the tread thickness is below federal standards. Here are the sample data:

$$\bar{x} = 47{,}500 \text{ miles}$$

$$s = 3{,}000 \text{ miles}$$

The unknown population mean is not 47,500 miles. That is, if we took another simple random sample of 900 tires, we would probably not get a sample mean of 47,500 miles again. The sample means will vary from one sample to another. The standard error reflects the sample-to-sample variation.

We tell the boss to imagine that instead of taking one sample of 900, we take all possible samples of 900 from the population and test the tires. When he complains that this is impractical, we respond that we aren't really going to do this; just imagine it.

We then tell him that from the central limit theorem, the sampling distribution of the sample mean based on 900 observations will be normally distributed and that the mean of the sampling distribution is the same as the unknown population mean. He is not impressed. He says that if he does not know the mean of the population, then he does not know the mean of the sampling distribution either.

Next we tell the boss that the standard error of the mean is much smaller than the population standard deviation. But since we do not know σ, we do not know the standard error either. However, we can use the *estimated standard error*, $s/\sqrt{n}$, to estimate the standard error, $\sigma_{\bar{x}}$. We will substitute the standard deviation for the one sample of 900 tires for the unknown population standard deviation. The estimated standard error is

$$\frac{s}{\sqrt{n}} = \frac{3{,}000}{\sqrt{900}} = 100 \text{ miles}$$

Figure 7.1 shows an approximate sampling distribution for the sample mean* tire life based on a sample of 900. The boss says that is a lovely picture, but

FIGURE 7.1 Sampling Distribution of the Sample Means for $n = 900$

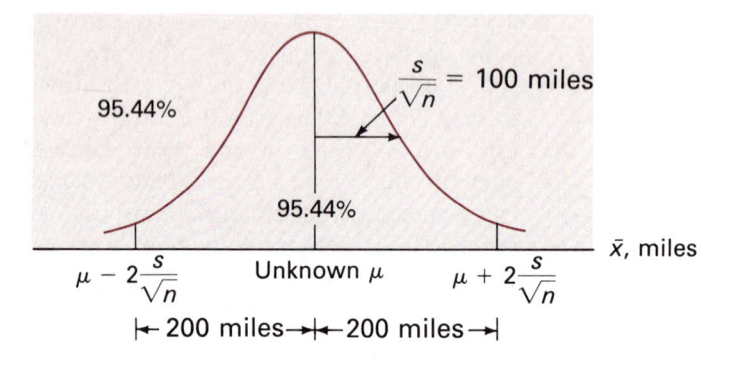

*The sampling distribution shown is not the true sampling distribution because σ is unknown.

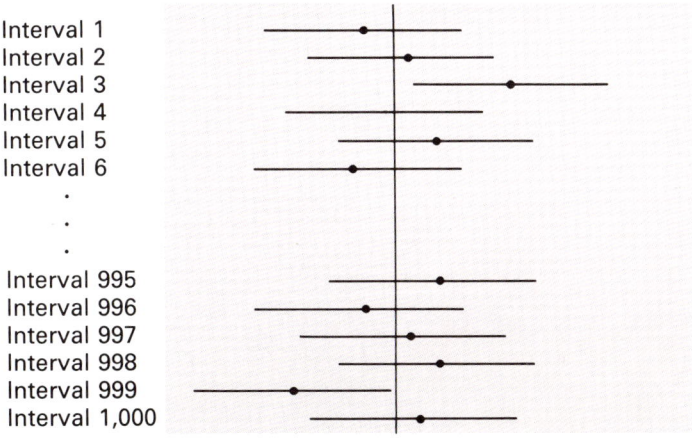

he still does not know the population mean, so what good is it? We present the following arguments, which are based on the normal distribution:

1. Theoretically, 95.44% of all sample means will be within two estimated standard errors (200 miles) of the unknown population mean.
2. The probability is .9544 that any sample mean will be within 200 miles of the unknown population mean.
3. The probability is .9544 that the actual sample mean we obtained will be within 200 miles of the unknown population mean.
4. We are 95.44% confident that our sample mean of 47,500 miles will be within 200 miles of the unknown population mean.
5. We are 95.44% confident that the interval 47,500 ± 200 miles contains the unknown population mean.

What does a 95.44% confidence level mean? If we constructed 1,000 confidence intervals based on 1,000 different samples we would expect that about 954 of these confidence intervals would contain the unknown population mean and 46 would not. We show this idea in Figure 7.2.

Assume that the population mean is 47,600 miles. Each of the 1,000 confidence intervals is centered at its sample mean, shown as an asterisk in Figure 7.2. 95.44% of the intervals would contain the value 47,600 miles. Thus, 954 intervals will contain the population mean. Notice that any sample mean that is beyond two estimated standard errors, or 200 miles in our example, from the population mean results in a confidence interval that does not contain the population mean. For example, see intervals 3 and 999 in Figure 7.2. From the normal curve we know that only 2.28% of the sample means will fall above 47,600 + 200 or 47,800 miles. Also only 2.28% of the sample means will fall below

FIGURE 7.2 1,000 Confidence Intervals

A confidence interval is a range within which we can say, with different levels of confidence, that the population parameter may fall.

47,600 − 200 or 47,400 miles. Thus, the **confidence interval** will *not* contain the population mean approximately 4.6% of the time, or 46 out of 1,000 times.

t-Based Confidence Intervals

We use the following expression to construct a two-sided ($\pm$) confidence interval for an unknown population mean:

$$\bar{x} \pm \text{Margin of error}$$

$$\bar{x} \pm (\text{Reliability factor})(\textit{Estimated} \text{ standard error}) \quad (7.2)$$

$$\bar{x} \pm t(\text{two-sided confidence \%}, n-1)\left(\frac{s}{\sqrt{n}}\right)$$

We already know how to compute the sample mean and the estimated standard error. That leaves only the reliability factor to discuss.

RELIABILITY FACTOR If we knew the population standard deviation and thus the standard error, we would use the normal table to determine the reliability factor. Since we know only the sample standard deviation and thus the estimated standard error, we use Appendix 5, the *t*-table, to determine the reliability factor. Table 7.4 is a portion of the *t*-table. *Warning:* We can use the *t*-table (or the normal table) only if the sampling distribution of the sample mean is near-normal shaped.

To use Table 7.4 we select a desired level of confidence and determine the degrees of freedom, which equal the sample size minus 1. The row labelled "infinity" contains the *z*, or normal, values. For example, the *t*-value for a sample size of 5 and a 90% confidence level is 2.132 (the intersection of the 90% column and 4 degrees of freedom). The *z*-value for a 90% confidence level is 1.645. For sample sizes of 50 or greater, the *t*- and *z*-values are essentially the same.

In general, *t*-table values are larger than normal table values. Thus from expression (7.2) the interval's margin of error is larger than it would have been if we could have used the normal tables. Wider margins of error are the price we

Table 7.4
A Short Table of *t*-Values

Degrees of Freedom	Desired Level of Confidence for Two-Sided Intervals			
	80%	90%	95%	99%
4	1.533	2.132	2.776	4.604
9	1.383	1.833	2.262	3.250
16	1.337	1.746	2.120	2.921
25	1.316	1.708	2.060	2.787
36	1.306	1.689	2.030	2.722
Infinity	1.282	1.645	1.960	2.576

must pay for not knowing the population standard deviation and thus the standard error. As we shall see shortly, wider margins of error provide less meaningful information.

EXAMPLE: ELIGIBILITY FOR FEDERAL AID   Is a census tract containing 5,000 families eligible for aid under Federal Program HR 247? Suppose that program eligibility requires that the mean income for a family of size four must be betweeen $7,500 and $8,500. There are other programs for poorer families. Only during a census year would the population mean income be known. In other years the program administrator must determine eligibility by estimating the population mean income using confidence intervals.

We begin by taking a simple random sample of 12 families of size four from the census tract. The sample data are cross-sectional. Recall that cross-sectional data are measurements from *one time period* taken on different persons, places, or things. Let's set up a 95% confidence interval on the population mean income. Table 7.5 contains the raw data.

First we compute the sample mean, $7,983, and sample standard deviation for the 12 observations, $441. The sample standard deviation is an estimate of the population standard deviation.

We must distinguish between the standard deviation of a single sample and the estimated standard error of the mean. We know the latter must be smaller. The sample standard deviation is $441 and the estimated standard error of the mean is $441/\sqrt{12}$ or $127.

The confidence interval will be valid only if the following assumptions hold:

ASSUMPTION 1:   The 12 families are a simple random sample taken from the census tract population.

ASSUMPTION 2:   The sampling distribution of the sample mean incomes is near-normal shaped.

Assumption 1 is valid since we did use simple random sampling to select the sample. Assumption 2 is necessary because we can use the *t*-table only when the sampling distribution is near-normal. The sample of 12 may be too small to rely on the central limit theorem to produce a normally distributed sampling distribution. Thus Assumption 2 will be valid only if the population of annual incomes is near-normal shaped. We check the normality assumption by constructing a stem-and-leaf display for the 12 sample data values, as shown in Figure 7.3 on page 334. Since Figure 7.3 shows that the sample data are near-normal shaped, the population may be also near-normal shaped.

Table 7.5

Incomes of 12 Randomly Selected Families

$7,300	$7,700	$8,100	$8,400
$7,400	$7,800	$8,300	$8,500
$7,600	$7,800	$8,300	$8,600

FIGURE 7.3 Stem-and-Leaf Display for Sample Income Data

	800	400	
	800	300	
400	700	300	600
300	600	100	500

| $7,000 | $7,000 | $8,000 | $8,000 |

Now we can substitute the descriptive statistics and the correct *t*-value into expression (7.2):

$$\bar{x} \pm t(\text{two-sided } 95\%, 11)(\text{Estimated standard error})$$

Lower limit: $7,983 − (2.201 · $127) = $7,703
Upper limit: $7,983 + (2.201 · $127) = $8,263

Interpretation: We are 95% confident that the unknown mean income is between $7,703 and $8,263. Alternatively, this confidence interval could be one of the 5 in every 100 that does not contain the unknown population mean.

Is the tract eligible for the program? It is, because we are 95% confident that the mean income for families of size four is between $7,703 and $8,263. Since every value within that range is between the program limits of $7,500 and $8,500, the tract is eligible.

Suppose we had obtained either of the following two intervals; what could we have concluded about the tract's eligibility? Please think it through before answering.

95% confidence interval ($6,810 to $7,390)
95% confidence interval ($7,310 to $7,890)

Since the upper limit of the first confidence interval is below $7,500, the tract is not eligible for this program. The second interval includes incomes less than and greater than $7,500. Thus, we *cannot* tell if the tract is eligible. If the population mean were below $7,500, the tract would not be eligible; otherwise it would.

If we obtained the second confidence interval, what should we do to determine if the tract is eligible? One possibility would be to increase the sample size. That would reduce the estimated standard error and therefore the margin of error. Eventually the margin of error will become so small that the upper and lower limits of the confidence interval would be either less than $7,500 (not eligible), between $7,500 and $8,500 (eligible), or greater than $8,500 (not eligible). Remember, we reduce the estimated standard error by increasing the sample size.

The next problem illustrates how we can use confidence intervals to detect changes from past performance levels—an important problem solving skill.

EXAMPLE: THE TENURE DISCOUNT PROBLEM   Length-of-tenure discounts are the differences between the rents charged long-time apartment renters and newer tenants. Discounts keep good tenants and minimize turnover. The American Housing Group wants to construct a 99% confidence interval on the population mean discount for renters who have lived in their present apartment for more than five years. The mean discount was 12% five years ago. Has it changed?

They select a simple random sample of 400 apartment dwellers from across the United States who have lived at their current addresses for more than five years. Given here are the sample mean and standard deviation for the cross-sectional discount data:

$$\bar{x} = 8\%$$
$$s = 2\%$$
$$\text{Estimated standard error of the mean} = \frac{2}{\sqrt{400}} = .1\%$$

The confidence interval will be valid only if the following assumptions hold:

ASSUMPTION 1: The 400 apartment dwellers are a simple random sample from the target population.

ASSUMPTION 2: The sampling distribution of the sample mean discounts is near-normal shaped.

Assumption 1 is valid since we used simple random sampling. Assumption 2 is also valid because with the sample of 400, the central limit theorem ensures that the sampling distribution will be near normal and thus we can use the *t*-table for determining the reliability factor.

Now we can substitute the descriptive statistics and the *t*-value into expression (7.2).

$$\bar{x} \pm t(\text{two-sided } 99\%, 399 \text{ or infinite df})(\text{Estimated standard error})$$

Lower limit: $8\% - (2.576)(.1\%) = 7.74\%$
Upper limit: $8\% + (2.576)(.1\%) = 8.26\%$

Interpretation: We are 99% confident that the unknown population mean discount is between 7.74% and 8.26%. There is a 1 in 100 chance that the interval does not contain the unknown population mean.

The tenure discount has dropped in the past five years. Five years ago it was 12%. Now we are 99% confident that it is between 7.74% and 8.26%. What might account for the drop? Is there greater demand for apartments? Is the perception that long-term renters should be rewarded with major discounts no longer valid? The American Housing Group must diagnose the possible causes for the discount drop.

Setting the Level of Confidence

Is it better to be 99% confident than 95% confident? Is it better to be 95% confident than 80% confident that an interval will contain the unknown population mean? Maybe not!

We have constructed 80%, 95%, and 99% confidence intervals for the following data:

$$\bar{x} = 100$$

$$n = 31 \quad \text{(degrees of freedom} = 30)$$

$$\frac{s}{\sqrt{n}} = 30$$

80% confidence interval:	100 ± 1.310(30)	(60.7 to 139.3)
95% confidence interval:	100 ± 2.042(30)	(38.7 to 161.3)
99% confidence interval:	100 ± 2.750(30)	(17.5 to 182.5)

The confidence interval gets wider as the level of confidence increases. Thus, the wider confidence intervals provide less meaningful information.

We have two choices in constructing a confidence interval. *Keeping the sample size constant*, we can construct either a narrower interval with a low level of confidence or a wider interval with a high level of confidence. Ninety or 95% confidence levels are often used by companies. However, there is no magic number to use. Each of us must decide upon the trade-offs between level of confidence and the width of the confidence interval.

Confidence Intervals and Time-Ordered Data

In Chapter 2 we learned that the mean and standard deviation summarize cross-sectional and stationary time-ordered data. A line graph for stationary time-ordered data will show no upward or downward pattern over time. Sample values fluctuate around a *constant* mean. Since the population mean is constant, we can construct confidence intervals to estimate it. Nonstationary data do not have a constant mean. The data increase or decrease over time. There is no constant population mean to estimate. Thus confidence intervals are valid only for cross-sectional and stationary time-ordered data.

SECTION 7.3 EXERCISES

1. What conditions must hold in order to construct valid confidence intervals?
2. You select a random sample of 10 observations from a normal population. The sample mean is 45, and the sample standard deviation is 15.
   a. Construct a 90% confidence interval for the population mean.
   b. Construct a 95% confidence interval for the population mean.
   c. Construct a 99% confidence interval for the population mean.

3. Repeat Exercise 2 but this time assume that the sample size is 50.
4. Explain why the confidence intervals in Exercise 2 are wider than the confidence intervals in Exercise 3.
5. A sample of $n = 9$ observations is selected from a normal population. The results are shown here:

$$\{2, 6, 7, 1, 4, 2, 5, 6, 3\}$$

a. Find the sample mean and the sample standard deviation.
b. What number will you use for an estimate of the population standard deviation?
c. Construct a 90% confidence interval for the mean of the population from which the sample was drawn.
d. State the assumptions you made in constructing the confidence interval in part c.

6. A manufacturing process is supposed to produce an item that measures 10 cm in diameter. A large amount of previous data suggests that the population standard deviation is .5 cm. The diameter measurements are normally distributed. In order to check that the process is working properly, a quality control expert selects 25 items from the assembly line and measures the diameters of these items. The sample mean is 10.3 cm.
a. Construct a 95% confidence interval for the population mean.
b. On the basis of this interval, do you conclude that the manufacturing process is working as it should? Explain.

7. A company purchases transistors from a large distributor. The distributor claims that the mean life of the transistors is 2,000 hours and the population standard deviation is 150 hours.
a. Consider the sampling distribution of all possible means of $n = 400$ transistors. If the distributor's claim is correct, what is the mean of the sampling distribution? What is its standard error?
b. You select a sample of 400 transistors and calculate the mean life of these units. If you then constructed a 95% confidence interval based on this sample mean, why would you expect the interval to contain the unknown population mean life?
c. Suppose the upper and lower bounds of a 95% confidence interval were 1,965 and 1,990, respectively. Does this confidence interval confirm the distributor's claim? Explain.

8. A random sample of 100 union plumbers in a large city showed that the mean weekly income was $525.75 with a standard deviation of $52.50. You want to estimate the mean weekly income of unionized plumbers.
a. What is the target population?
b. What is the parameter of interest?
c. What assumptions do you have to make in order to construct a confidence interval for this population mean?
d. Estimate the mean weekly income of all unionized plumbers in the city using a 95% reliability factor.

9. The Federal Trade Commission tests cigarettes to determine whether the level of nicotine agrees with the claims made by the manufacturer. A sample of 20 cigarettes of brand A showed that the mean level of nicotine was .5 mg per cigarette with a standard deviation of .01 mg. The FTC wants to estimate the mean level of nicotine per cigarette in brand A.
a. What is the target population?
b. What is the parameter of interest?

c. What assumptions do you have to make in order to construct a confidence interval for this population mean?
d. Construct a 99% confidence interval for the mean level of nicotine per cigarette for brand A.

10. In the past, the administrative office of a large military installation received a mean of 45 complaints a week. Four weeks ago the installation implemented Deming's quality management methods to reduce the number of complaints. The officer in charge plotted the total number of complaints per week. The graph is shown here.

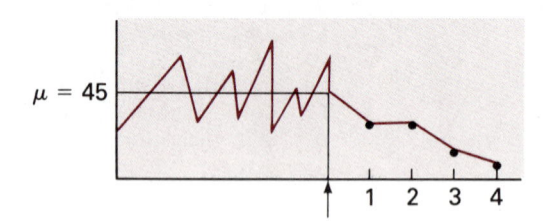

a. Would you characterize the time series before the quality program as stationary or nonstationary?
b. Would you use a confidence interval to estimate the mean number of complaints before implementation of the quality program? Why?
c. How would you characterize the series after implementation of the quality program?
d. Would you use a confidence interval to estimate the mean number of complaints after the implementation of the quality program? Why?

7.4 One-Sided Confidence Intervals on an Unknown Population Mean

Up to now, all confidence intervals have been two-sided; they extended an equal amount on each side of the sample mean (see expression (7.2)). Two-sided intervals have a lower and an upper limit. Sometimes we want to make statements such as: "I am 95% confident that the mean amount of personal time taken per week is *at most* 1.5 hours" or "I am 90% confident that the mean work group productivity is *at least* 30 units per hour." These are examples of one-sided confidence intervals; they do not extend an equal amount on each side of the sample mean. They do not have a lower and upper limit. By the end of this section you should be able to:

1. explain when to use a one-sided confidence interval; and
2. construct and interpret a one-sided interval.

We use the following expressions to construct a one-sided confidence interval for an unknown population mean. An "at least" interval has no upper limit; we use expression (7.3) to compute its lower limit. An "at most" interval has no lower limit; we use expression (7.4) to compute its upper limit.

$$\text{At least:} \quad \bar{x} - t(\text{one-sided confidence \%}, n-1)\left(\frac{s}{\sqrt{n}}\right) \quad (7.3)$$

At most: $\bar{x} + t(\text{one-sided confidence }\%, n-1)\left(\dfrac{s}{\sqrt{n}}\right)$ (7.4)

We use different *t*-table values to construct one-sided and two-sided intervals. Appendix 5 indicates which *t*-values to use for varying confidence levels for both types of intervals. Figure 7.4 shows that the *t*-value for a two-sided 90% confidence interval (Figure 7.4a) is the same as the *t*-value for a one-sided 95% confidence interval (Figure 7.4b). The *t*-value in expression (7.2) is based on the area between the mean and the lower limit and between the mean and the upper limit of the interval. Forty-five percent of the area is in each tail. Thus the limits of a two-tailed 90% confidence interval for 20 degrees of freedom are

Lower limit: $\bar{x} - 1.725(\text{Estimated standard error})$
Upper limit: $\bar{x} + 1.725(\text{Estimated standard error})$

A one-sided "at least" interval has no upper limit. The lack of an upper limit is

FIGURE 7.4   One- and Two-Sided Intervals

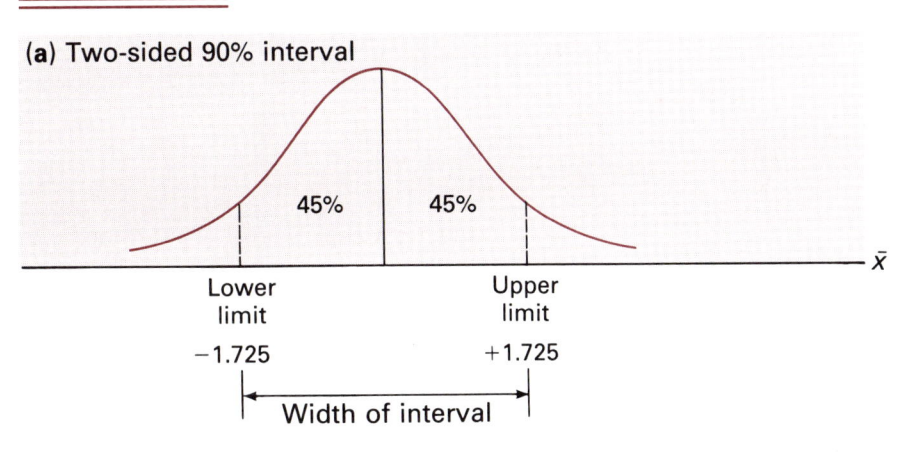

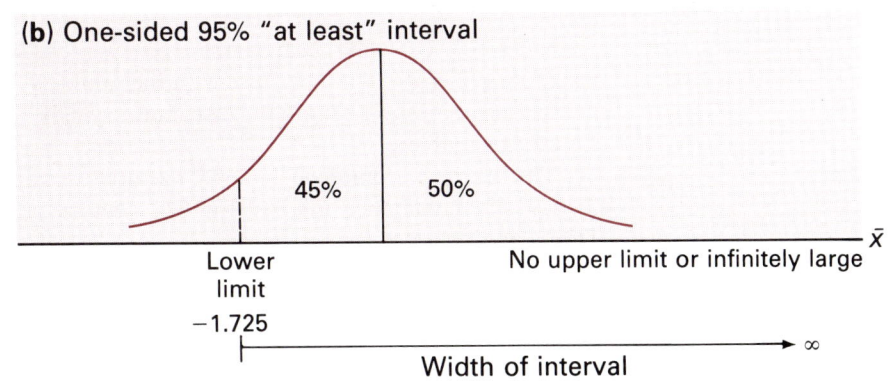

(a) Two-sided 90% interval

(b) One-sided 95% "at least" interval

represented by the 50% area in the upper tail of the distribution in Figure 7.4b. To obtain a one-sided 95% confidence interval, the lower tail of this distribution must contain 45% of the area. To find the lower limit for this interval, we must look up the *t*-value that represents 45% of the area shown. This is the same as the *t*-value for a two-sided 90% confidence interval. Thus, the lower limit of an (at least) one-sided 95% confidence interval is

Lower limit: $\bar{x} - 1.725$(Estimated standard error)

We have demonstrated that a one-sided 95% interval has the same *t*-value as a two-sided 90% interval. Thus, a one-sided $(100 - x)\%$ interval has the same *t*-value for its limit as a two-sided $(100 - 2x)\%$ interval.

Next we construct and interpret a one-sided interval to determine whether a firm's advertising is truthful.

EXAMPLE: TRUTH IN ADVERTISING   Howdy Burger is a local chain in St. Louis. Recently it introduced a new burger which it claims has no more than 120 calories. Is the firm's advertising truthful? A public policy watchdog agency conducts a study. Using a random numbers table, agency workers enter Howdy Burger's six stores at random times and purchase the new burger. They collect a sample of 225 burgers over several weeks and compute their caloric content. The agency will set up an "at most" one-sided 99.5% confidence interval. The descriptive statistics follow:

$$\bar{x} = 108 \text{ calories}$$

$$s = 60 \text{ calories}$$

$$\text{Estimated standard error of the mean} = \frac{60}{\sqrt{225}} = 4 \text{ calories}$$

ASSUMPTION 1:   The 225 burgers are a simple random sample taken from the new burger population.

ASSUMPTION 2:   The sampling distribution for the mean number of calories in 225 burgers is near-normal shaped.

Assumption 1 is valid because the agency used simple random sampling. Assumption 2 is also valid because with the sample size of 225, the central limit theorem ensures that the sampling distribution will be near normal. Therefore, we can use the *t*-table.

The "at most" confidence interval has no lower limit. The *t*-value for a one-sided 99.5% confidence interval for 224 degrees of freedom is 2.576. From expression (7.4):

Upper limit: $108 + 2.576(4) = 118.3$ calories

Interpretation: We are 99.5% confident—virtually certain—that the popula-

Chapter 7 Making Inferences About One Population Parameter

tion mean number of calories for the new burger is at most 118.3. Howdy Burger has been truthful in its advertising.

The Finite Population Correction Factor

Up to now, our sample sizes, n, have been very small in comparison to the population size, N. When the sample size is more than 5% of the population, we can use the *finite population correction factor* in calculating the estimated standard error of the mean. The estimated standard error is then given by

$$\frac{s}{\sqrt{n}}\sqrt{\frac{N-n}{N-1}} \quad \frac{750}{999} \tag{7.5}$$

The expression under the radical, $(N-n)/(N-1)$, is the finite population correction factor. Note that as the sample size n increases, the finite population correction factor gets smaller. This reduces the estimated standard error and ultimately the margin of error.

In summary, we use one-sided confidence intervals to make "at least" or "at most" statements. "At least" means the population mean is at least some number and "at most" means that the population mean is at most some number. When we are interested in making statements that the population mean is between two numbers, we construct two-sided confidence intervals.

SECTION 7.4 EXERCISES (one sided)

1. Ten items are selected from a normally distributed population. The mean of a sample is 15 and the standard deviation is 5.
   a. Construct a two-sided, 95% confidence interval for the population mean.
   b. Construct a 95% "at most" confidence interval to establish an upper bound for the population mean.
   c. Construct a 90% "at least" confidence interval to establish a lower bound for the population mean.

2. The finite population correction factor always reduces the size of the standard error of the mean. Explain in managerial terms why using the correction factor should reduce the standard error of the mean.

3. A sample of 250 bank loans was selected from 1,000 loans made during a given month. The mean loan made was $650 with a standard deviation of $450.
   a. Is the distribution of bank loans normally distributed? Why? [*Hint:* Can loan size take on negative values?]
   b. If the distribution of bank loans is not normal, then how can we estimate the mean loan size for the 1,000 loans?
   c. Estimate the standard error of the mean both with and without considering the finite population correction. How much is the standard error reduced by including the finite population correction factor?
   d. Construct a 95% confidence interval for the mean loan amount using the correction.
   e. Construct a 95% one-sided confidence interval to establish a lower bound on the mean loan amount.

f. Construct a 99% one-sided confidence interval to establish an upper bound on the mean amount of the 1,000 loans.

4. A soft drink machine is set to dispense a mean of 6.5 ounces of fill excluding ice. A sample of nine cups had a mean of 6.0 ounces with a standard deviation of .6 ounce. Construct a 99% one-sided confidence interval that will establish a lower bound on the mean amount actually dispensed.

5. A random sample of 100 bank depositors reveals a mean checking balance of $590 with a standard deviation of $720. Construct a 90% confidence interval that establishes an upper bound on the mean checking balance.

6. All employees of a company are required to take a battery of skills tests. The mean dexterity score is 70. An industrial psychologist believes that the mean score made by assembly line employees is higher than 70. A random sample of records of 25 assemblers showed a mean score of 77 with a standard deviation of 6.
    a. Construct a 90% confidence interval which will establish a lower bound on the mean dexterity score of assembly line workers.
    b. Based on your confidence interval, would you conclude that the psychologist is correct?

7.5 The Hypothesis Testing Framework

In Sections 7.3 and 7.4 we used confidence intervals to estimate an unknown population mean. The *hypothesis testing framework* is an alternative approach. By the end of this unit you should be able to:

1. distinguish between the confidence interval and hypothesis testing approaches;
2. formulate hypotheses and their associated alternative managerial actions;
3. explain what Type I and Type II errors are;
4. determine the costs associated with the two types of errors; and
5. test hypotheses and take managerial action.

We will illustrate the hypothesis testing approach using the Milemaster tire example from Section 7.3. Unless the mean tire life exceeds 47,000 miles, the project team will not market the tire. The engineering staff claims that the tire will exceed the 47,000 mile figure. Before the project team makes its final decision to market or not to market the tire, it can use the hypothesis testing approach. It involves the following five steps:

1. State hypotheses and alternative actions.
2. Determine the costs associated with the *two* types of decision making errors.
3. Choose the *significance level*, α, and the sample size.
4. Run the study, collect the data, and compute the sample mean and standard deviation.
5. Test the hypotheses and make a decision.

State Hypotheses and Managerial Actions

A hypothesis is a testable claim or statement about a population parameter. The null hypothesis is a statement of "no effect," "no change," "no improvement," or "I don't believe you." We also define a second hypothesis—alternative hypothesis—that we hope or suspect is true. We should also state what actions we will take if we reject the null hypothesis and what we will do if we fail to reject it.

The project team for Milemaster tire formulates the following two hypotheses and corresponding actions:

Null hypothesis:	The unknown population mean tire life is less than or equal to 47,000 miles—or, at most 47,000 miles.
Null action:	Failure to reject the null hypothesis means we won't market the Milemaster tire.
Alternative hypothesis:	The unknown population mean tire life is greater than 47,000 miles.
Alternative action:	If we reject the null hypothesis, we will market the tire.

Note several important features of the two hypotheses. First, the null hypothesis, H_0, assumes that the population mean will be at most 47,000 miles and therefore the tire should not be marketed. While the engineering department claims that the tire will last longer than 47,000 miles, the project team must be skeptical and assume that the tire cannot do what the engineering group claims. The null hypothesis reflects its skepticism. Without evidence to the contrary, the project team must assume that the tire does not do what the engineers claim. The project team hopes that based upon the study's sample evidence it will reject the null hypothesis and market the tire. In general, the null hypothesis is the "I-don't-believe-your-claims" hypothesis, whereas the alternative hypothesis is the "I-believe-your-claim" hypothesis. *Assume* the null hypothesis is true until evidence suggests otherwise.

Second, both hypotheses make claims about an unknown population mean. Unless we sample the entire target population, we are forced to draw statistical inferences. Hypothesis testing is an alternative to constructing confidence intervals.

Third, the two hypotheses are mutually exclusive and exhaustive. Either the unknown population mean tire life is less than or equal to 47,000 miles or it is more than 47,000 miles. Both hypotheses cannot be true, but one *must* be true.

Determine the Costs of the Decision Making Errors

We can be either right or wrong when we make statistical inferences about an unknown population mean. Table 7.6 on page 344 shows that there are *two* ways to be right and *two* ways to be wrong.

Correct decision:	Do not reject the null hypothesis when, in fact, it is true.
Correct decision:	Reject the null hypothesis when it is false.
Type I error:	Reject the null hypothesis when it is true.
Type II error:	Do not reject the null hypothesis when it is false.

Table 7.6

Types of Errors in Milemaster Example

Based on the Sample Data the Project Team	The Truth About the Unknown Population Mean	
	Null Hypothesis Is True (47,000 miles or less)	Null Hypothesis Is False (over 47,000 miles)
Doesn't reject the null (scraps the tire)	Correct decision	Type II error
Rejects the null (markets the tire)	Type I error	Correct decision

After running the study, the project team will either reject the null hypothesis or not reject it. Then only one error is possible. If it does not reject the null hypothesis, it will have either (1) made a correct decision or (2) made a Type II error. If it rejects the null hypothesis, it will have either (1) made a correct decision or (2) made a Type I error. Unfortunately, before collecting the data, the project team must be concerned about both errors and their associated costs.

Business errors are almost always costly. The project team would make a Type I error if it marketed the tire and the population mean tire life turned out to be 47,000 miles or less. The project team would make a Type II error if it did not market the tire and the population mean tire life turned out to be over 47,000 miles. What costs are associated with Type I and Type II errors?

COST OF TYPE I ERROR In advertising the tire, Milemaster will claim that, on the average, it will last longer than 47,000 miles. What if, in fact, the tire will last 47,000 miles or less? Milemaster will not discover this overnight but only after a large number of tires have been sold. Then problems will begin. Possible costs include reduced consumer confidence in the company, significant tire replacement costs under the tread warranty, and possible class action suits filed by irate consumers. A Type I error would be very costly for Milemaster.

COST OF TYPE II ERROR Here Milemaster does not market the tire when in fact the mean tire life would have been more than 47,000 miles. In failing to market a superior tire, Milemaster may have lost a real sales opportunity. The potential losses depend on how good the tire was. If the mean tire life was only 48,000 miles (only slightly better than currently available competitors' brands that have a 47,000-mile tread warranty), its losses might be small. But if the mean tire life was 75,000 miles, then failure to market this tire would be very costly.

Set a Level of Significance and Determine a Sample Size

The level of significance is the maximum risk we are willing to accept in making a Type I error. It is called the α (alpha) level.

No one likes making errors. However, when making statistical inferences, there is always the chance of making an incorrect decision. The **level of significance** focuses on the Type I error. We must rely on judgment to set the α level. How should we do it?

As shown in this chapter's Appendix, the chances of making Type I and Type II errors are related. As we reduce the chance of making a Type I error, the chance of making a Type II error increases. This inverse relationship leads to the following three guidelines:

PRINCIPLE 1: If a Type I error is costly and a Type II error is not costly, set a low level of significance—an α of 1% or less. Do not worry about making Type II errors.

PRINCIPLE 2: If a Type II error is costly and a Type I error is not, set α higher—at 10% or above. This reduces the chance of making a Type II error. Do not worry about a Type I error; it is not costly.

PRINCIPLE 3: When both errors are costly, set the level of significance, α, at 5% or 1%. Reduce the chance of a Type II error by increasing the sample size of the study.

Milemaster's project team concluded that a Type I error would be very costly. Therefore it set the level of significance very low, an α of 1%. Then if the team rejects the null hypothesis, the *maximum* chance of making a Type I error is 1 in 100. In other words, the project team can be 99% or more confident of having made a correct decision.

The project team must also determine the sample size for the study. How should this be done? We recommend the largest sample size that the project budget and time will allow. If this does not reduce sufficiently the chance of making a costly Type II error, then ask for a larger sample. In the tire study, the project team chose a sample size of 1,000 tires.

Data Collection

How do we obtain the data for testing hypotheses? We use data that already exist within the firm's information system, we run studies, or we purchase the data. Chapter 6 discussed how to conduct valid survey sampling or planned change studies.

The project team used simple random sampling to select 1,000 tires. It mounted the 1,000 tires on 250 randomly selected cars and recorded the mileage when each tire failed to meet federal standards for treadwear. Here are the study's sample statistics:

$$\bar{x} = 47{,}300 \text{ miles}$$

$$s = 3{,}162 \text{ miles}$$

$$\frac{s}{\sqrt{n}} = \frac{3{,}162}{\sqrt{1{,}000}} = 100 \text{ miles}$$

Weigh the Evidence and Make a Decision

If the *sample* mean had been 22,000 miles instead of 47,300 miles, should Milemaster reject the null hypothesis that the population mean is 47,000 miles or less? That is, is a sample mean of 22,000 miles more likely if the unknown population mean tire life was *at most* 47,000 miles or *greater than* 47,000 miles? Please think about it before reading on.

Milemaster should not reject the null hypothesis. A sample mean of 22,000 miles is more likely to occur when the unknown population mean is less than or equal to 47,000 miles than when it is greater than 47,000 miles.

However, a sample mean of 90,000 miles is more likely to occur when the unknown population mean is greater than 47,000 miles than when it is 47,000 miles or less. In the Milemaster study, as the sample mean increases, the evidence begins to favor the alternative hypothesis. How far above 47,000 miles must the sample mean be before the project team should reject the null hypothesis? That depends on the level of significance, α, that Milemaster chooses. Recall that it chose $\alpha = 1\%$.

Figure 7.5 shows the sampling distribution of the sample mean assuming that the null hypothesis is true—that is, the population mean is at most 47,000 miles. The area of rejection is the shaded area in Figure 7.5, which equals 1%, the α level. If the sample mean falls on the horizontal axis within the rejection region, the project team will reject the null hypothesis and market the tire. If the sample mean falls on the horizontal axis within the unshaded area, the project team will not reject the null hypothesis. It will scrap the Milemaster tire.

Here is the logic. There are two possible reasons why the sample mean could fall in the rejection region:

1. The null hypothesis is true. Obtaining a sample mean in the rejection region if the null hypothesis is true (population mean is at most 47,000 miles) will happen by chance no more than 1 in 100 times.
2. The null hypothesis is false. The reason that the sample mean was so large (so that it fell in the shaded area) is that the null hypothesis is incorrect. The alternative hypothesis that the population mean is greater than 47,000 miles is true.

Which explanation is more reasonable? The chance of getting a sample mean in the rejection region if the null hypothesis is true is 1% or less. It could

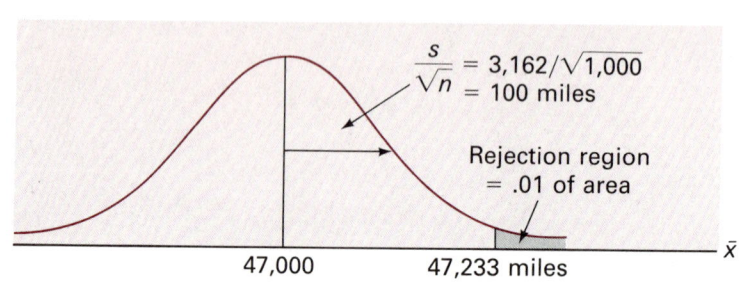

FIGURE 7.5 Sampling Distribution of the Sample Mean Assuming Null Hypothesis Is True

$\frac{s}{\sqrt{n}} = 3{,}162/\sqrt{1{,}000} = 100$ miles

Rejection region = .01 of area

47,000   47,233 miles $\bar{x}$

happen but it is very unlikely. Therefore, the second explanation is more reasonable.

We use expression (7.6) to determine the critical value for a one-sided, upper-tail hypothesis test. By replacing the plus sign with a minus sign, we have an expression for a one-sided, lower-tail hypothesis test.

$$\mu(H_0) + t(\text{one-sided}, (100 - \alpha)\%, n - 1)(\text{Estimated standard error}) \quad (7.6)$$

$\mu(H_0)$ is the population mean tire life under the null hypothesis. We look up a t-value for a one-sided, $(100 - \alpha)\%$ confidence interval for $n - 1$ degrees of freedom. In the Milemaster study, the t-value for a one-sided, 99%, $(100 - 1)\%$ confidence interval for an infinite number of degrees of freedom (999 df) is 2.326. The critical value for the Milemaster study is

$$47,000 + 2.326(100) = 47,233 \text{ miles}$$

Since the sample mean of 47,300 miles falls in the rejection region, the project team rejected the null hypothesis and marketed the tire.

Prob-Value

Milemaster has rejected the null hypothesis. At this point either it has made a correct decision or it has rejected the null when it should not have, a Type I error. It cannot have made a Type II error. What is the probability that Milemaster *actually* made a Type I error?

In the Milemaster study, the ***p*-value** is the probability of getting a sample mean of 47,300 miles *or larger* if the null hypothesis were true. Figure 7.6 illustrates the p-value for the Milemaster data. The p-value is the shaded area to the right of the actual sample mean of 47,300 miles. Even though we will not compute the p-value, graphically it is very much less than .01.

> The actual probability of making a Type I error is called the prob-value, or p-value. It can be determined only after the data have been collected.

FIGURE 7.6 Prob-Value for the Milemaster Study; Sampling Distribution of Sample Mean for Samples of Size 1,000

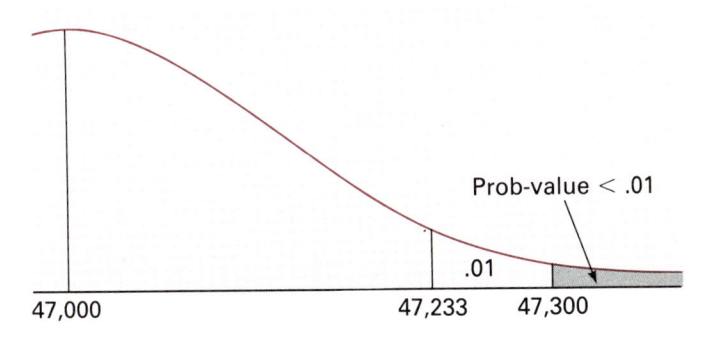

The *p*-value and the level of significance are different. We set the level of significance before running the study. It is the *maximum* probability of making a Type I error that we can tolerate given its costs. The *p*-value can be determined only after collecting the data. It is the *actual* probability of making a Type I error.

Some managers prefer computing *p*-values to setting a level of significance. That is, they do not set an α level before the study. Rather, after collecting the data, they determine the *p*-value. Then, based on the size of the *p*-value, they either reject or fail to reject the null hypothesis.

Whether we use *p*-values or level of significance, we must always determine the costs of Type I and Type II errors. These should dictate either the setting of the level of significance or the size of the *p*-value that will cause us to reject the null hypothesis.

In conclusion, based upon the sample evidence, the Milemaster project team rejected the null hypothesis and marketed the tire. Since its decision was based on a sample of 1,000 tires, it could be wrong. However, the actual chance that Milemaster has made a Type I error, the *p*-value, is much less than 1 in 100. Milemaster can be very confident that it made a correct decision.

We will use the following problem to illustrate a two-tailed hypothesis test.

EXAMPLE: THE VENDING MACHINE STUDY   Vendall leases soft drink vending machines to universities. The machines dispense exactly 10 ounces. Recently students have complained that the machines are dispensing either more or less than 10 ounces. When the machine dispenses more than 10 ounces, the soft drinks overflow the cup, and when the machine dispenses less than 10 ounces, students feel cheated. Vendall must decide whether to recall or not to recall the machines—that is the question.

As before, we will proceed using the five-step hypothesis testing approach.

STEP 1: STATE THE HYPOTHESES AND MANAGERIAL ACTIONS   The general rule is that a null hypothesis is the "I-don't-believe-what-you-are-telling-me" hypothesis. With this in mind, what are the null and alternative hypotheses and their associated actions? Please think about it before reading on.

	Hypotheses	Actions
H_0:	The machines are dispensing a mean of 10 ounces. $\mu = 10$ ounces	Do not recall the machines.
H_1:	Machines dispensing too little or machines dispensing too much. $\mu < 10$ ounces or $\mu > 10$ ounces	Recall the machines and adjust them to dispense 10 ounces.

Customers may claim that the machines are dispensing more or less than 10 ounces, but Vendall must *not* assume that their claim is true. Remember, be skeptical of others' claims.

Table 7.7

Examples of Costs of Making Type I and Type II Errors

Error	What Goes Wrong
Type I	Recall the machines to fix them. Then we find out that they are still dispensing a mean of 10 ounces.
Type II	Do not recall the machines when Vendall should have. The machines are dispensing more or less than a mean of 10 ounces, but Vendall does not correct the problem.

Type I Error Costs	Type II Error Costs
1. Cost of recall	1. If machines dispensing less than 10 ounces, many irate customers and potential lost sales
2. Cost of repairs to check machines that need no repairs	2. If machines dispensing more than 10 ounces, increased cost of goods sold, some unhappy customers, and some potential lost sales
3. Lost sales to competitors' vending machines during recall	

STEP 2: COSTS OF ERRORS   Table 7.7 lists some of the costs of making Type I and Type II errors.

STEP 3: α LEVEL AND SAMPLE SIZE   Balancing the costs of the two errors, Vendall sets α at 20%. This is the maximum risk Vendall is willing to tolerate of making a Type I error. Since the alternative hypothesis is two-tailed (greater than or less than), we divide the α level by 2. There will be two rejection regions—in the lower and in the upper tails. Each area will contain 10% of the area under the sampling distribution curve.

The study's budget allows for running 144 test dispensings from several randomly selected machines. The times of day when Vendall technicians dispense the drinks will also be determined using random numbers from Appendix 4.

STEP 4: DATA COLLECTION   Vendall technicians dispense 144 soft drinks from the test machines. The sample statistics are

$$\bar{x} = 9.98 \text{ ounces}$$

$$s = .35 \text{ ounce}$$

$$\text{Estimated standard error} = \frac{.35}{\sqrt{144}} = .029 \text{ ounce}$$

STEP 5: DECISION MAKING   Figure 7.7 on page 350 shows the sampling distribution of the sample mean for the drink dispensings assuming that the null hypothesis is true. Again, note that for a two-tailed hypothesis test, we divide α by 2. Ten percent of the area under the curve lies in each rejection region.

FIGURE 7.7 Sampling Distribution of Sample Mean—Vendall Study

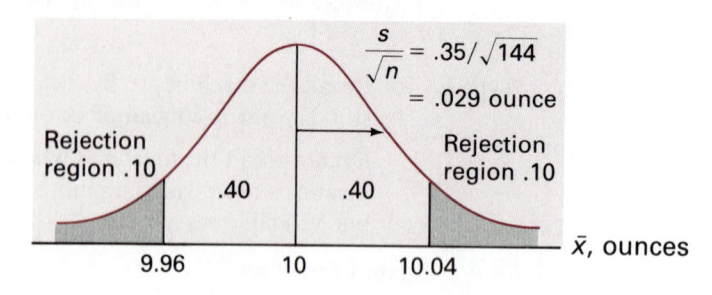

[Figure: Normal distribution curve centered at 10, with rejection regions of .10 at tails (below 9.96 and above 10.04), and areas of .40 between 9.96 and 10, and between 10 and 10.04. Standard error $\frac{s}{\sqrt{n}} = .35/\sqrt{144} = .029$ ounce. X-axis labeled $\bar{x}$, ounces.]

We use expression (7.7) to determine the lower and upper critical values for a two-tailed hypothesis test:

$$\mu(H_0) - t(\text{two-sided}, (100 - \alpha)\%, n - 1)(\text{Estimated standard error})$$
$$\mu(H_0) + t(\text{two-sided}, (100 - \alpha)\%, n - 1)(\text{Estimated standard error}) \quad (7.7)$$

For the Vendall study, we look up the *t*-value for an 80% two-tailed confidence interval and infinite (143) degrees of freedom. The value is 1.282. The critical values that separate the fail-to-reject region and the rejection regions in Figure 7.7 are given as

Lower critical value: $10 - 1.282(.029) = 9.96$ ounces

Upper critical value: $10 + 1.282(.029) = 10.04$ ounces

Since the sample mean, 9.98 ounces, does not fall in the rejection region, Vendall does not reject the null hypothesis. It should not recall the machines because the evidence suggests they may still be dispensing a mean of 10 ounces. Failing to reject the null hypothesis, Vendall has made either a correct decision or a Type II error.

Graphically, Figure 7.8 shows the *p*-value. It is twice the area to the left of 9.98 ounces. We say twice because we have a two-tailed test. Just as there are

FIGURE 7.8 Graphical Determination of the *p*-Value for Vendall Study

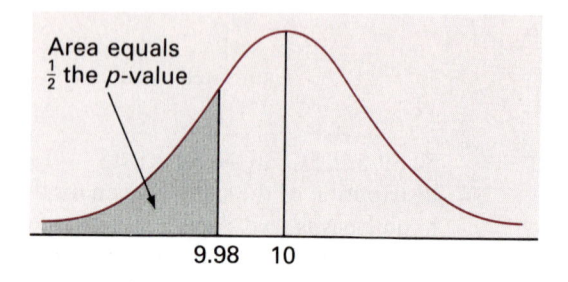

[Figure: Normal distribution curve centered at 10, with shaded area to the left of 9.98 labeled "Area equals $\frac{1}{2}$ the p-value".]

Table 7.8

Similarities Between Hypothesis Testing and Confidence Interval Methods

Confidence Intervals	Hypothesis Testing
Level of confidence	$(100 - \alpha)$ level
One-sided confidence interval	One-tailed test
Two-sided confidence interval	Two-tailed test

regions of rejection in the lower and upper tails of the sampling distribution curve, there must be two *p*-value areas as well. The area that represents 9.98 ounces *or less* is about 25% to 30%. Thus the *p*-value is between 50% and 60%. Given the sample data, had Vendall rejected the null hypothesis, the actual probability of making a Type I error would have been between 50% and 60%. Since Vendall had set the maximum risk of making a Type I error at 20% (the α level), Vendall did not reject the null hypothesis.

In summary, hypothesis testing highlights (1) that two different types of errors are possible, (2) that errors are costly and we should protect ourselves against making them, and (3) the idea of the *p*-value. These are important ideas. As Table 7.8 shows, the hypothesis testing and confidence interval approaches are similar. Researchers and scientists prefer the hypothesis testing approach. Managers and business professionals tend to favor the more intuitive confidence interval methods.

SECTION 7.5 EXERCISES

1. What, if anything, is wrong with the following pairs of null and alternative hypotheses?
   a. $\bar{x} \leq 2$
      $\bar{x} > 2$
   b. $\mu \geq 10$
      $\mu < 9$
   c. $\mu = 250$
      $\mu \neq 250$

2. Consumers who have seen the present advertising approach can recall two or fewer product attributes one month later. The marketing group has developed a new approach that it believes will increase the number of product attributes consumers can recall. Set up the null and alternative hypotheses and actions.

3. Over the past several years, car salesmen who worked on commission had a take-home pay that averaged $3,500 per month. This past year two things have happened that could change the mean take-home pay: (1) a slowdown in the economy and (2) car manufacturers bundling more expensive options in the base price. Has the mean take-home pay changed? The manager plans to take a simple random sample of car salesmen. Set up the null and alternative hypotheses.

4. Until this year the mean braking distance of a Nikton automobile moving at 60 miles per hour was 175 feet. Nikton engineers have developed what they consider a better braking system. They plan to test the new brake system on 100 cars and determine the braking distance at 60 mph. Set up the null and alternative actions.

5. Use the hypotheses in Exercise 2. The level of significance is .05. You take a sample of 100 consumers and obtain the following sample data:

$$\bar{x} = 2.8 \text{ attributes}$$

$$s = 5.0 \text{ attributes}$$

Based on your data should you reject or fail to reject the null hypothesis? What managerial action would you take?

6. Use the hypotheses in Exercise 3. The level of significance is .10. You take a sample of 36 car salesmen and obtain the following data:

$$\bar{x} = \$3,250$$

$$s = \$600$$

Based on your sample data, should you reject or fail to reject the null hypothesis?

7. Use the hypotheses in Exercise 4. The level of significance is .01. You test 81 sets of brakes and obtain the following data:

$$\bar{x} = 173 \text{ feet}$$

$$s = 27 \text{ feet}$$

Given these sample data, should you reject or fail to reject the null hypothesis?

8. Suppose you are a mountain climber. Your life depends on the strength of your rope. The mean strength of the rope must be at least 350 pounds per square inch. You plan to cut 10 pieces of rope from a long roll, test the breaking strength of each piece, and find the mean breaking strength for the sample.
   a. Set up the null and alternative hypotheses and actions.
   b. List the consequences of making either a Type I or a Type II error.
   c. With these consequences in mind, should your level of significance be small or large? Explain.

9. Every jury trial is a test of the null hypothesis that the defendant is innocent against the alternative that the defendant is guilty.
   a. What kind of error has the jury made if it convicts an innocent defendant? If they let Al Capone, the Chicago mobster, go free?
   b. Reducing the probability of making a Type I error increases the probability of making a Type II error. Thomas Jefferson, the third President of the United States, said, "It is better for 10 guilty men to go free than for one innocent man to be convicted." Would this statement translate to a small or large level of significance if jury trials could be translated to statistical tests?
   c. If the jury concludes with the verdict of "not guilty," has the trial proven the innocence of the defendant?

10. The level of significance chosen for a test is .10. The calculated p-value is .13. Should the null hypothesis be rejected? Explain.

11. The level of significance chosen for a test is .01. The calculated p-value is .0001. Should the null hypothesis be rejected? Explain.

12. A drug manufacturer claims that the mean potency of one of its heart stimulants is 90%. A random sample of 100 tablets is selected and tested. The sample mean

potency was 89.5% with a standard deviation of 2%. If the mean potency rate is less than 90%, the medicine is not as effective as it should be, and this could have serious consequences for heart patients.
   a. Set up the null and alternative hypotheses.
   b. Choose a level of significance of either .01 or .20 depending on the relative costs of making either a Type I error or Type II error.
   c. Test your hypotheses and state your conclusions. Do the data confirm the manufacturer's claim?
   d. Estimate the *p*-value for the test.

13. Refer again to Exercise 12. Suppose the mean potency rate was exactly 90% as the manufacturer claims. Is it possible to prove this using hypothesis testing methodology? Draw pictures to explain.

14. You are performing a one-tailed test of $H_0: \mu \leq 50$ versus $H_1: \mu > 50$. The level of significance is .05 and the estimated standard error of the mean is 3.2 based on a sample size of 100 observations.
   a. Draw a picture and label the critical value and the rejection region.
   b. Given a sample mean of 54.2, calculate the *p*-value for the test and state whether you would reject or fail to reject the null hypothesis. Draw a picture.
   c. Given a sample mean of 60.0, calculate the *p*-value for the test and state whether you would reject or fail to reject the null hypothesis. Draw a picture.

7.6 Stratified Random Sampling

Recall from Chapter 6 that we consider stratified random sampling when there are subgroups within a target population that are likely to have similarities on the variable of interest within a stratum but differences between strata. A stratified random sample is one obtained by separating the target population into nonoverlapping groups, or strata, and then selecting a simple random sample from each stratum. It can produce confidence intervals with smaller margins of error than simple random sampling. By the end of this section you should be able to:

1. construct confidence intervals on the population mean using stratified random sampling; and
2. explain the impact of using stratified random sampling on the width of the confidence interval.

When using stratified random sampling, we use expressions (7.8) and (7.9) to compute the sample statistics. Expression (7.9) assumes that the finite population correction factor is not needed.

$$\bar{x}_{ST} = \frac{N_1}{N}\bar{x}_1 + \frac{N_2}{N}\bar{x}_2 + \cdots + \frac{N_L}{N}\bar{x}_L \qquad (7.8)$$

$$\text{Est SE}_{ST} = \sqrt{\left(\frac{N_1}{N}\right)^2 \frac{s_1^2}{n_1} + \cdots + \left(\frac{N_L}{N}\right)^2 \frac{s_L^2}{n_L}} \qquad (7.9)$$

N_i is the number of sampling units in each stratum. N is the population size. n_i is the sample size in each stratum.

The estimate of the population mean is a weighted average of the sample means from the strata. While expression (7.9) is complex, it bears some similarity to the estimated standard error in simple random sampling. Note that the sample variances for each stratum are divided by their respective sample sizes.

We can substitute the above descriptive statistics into expression (7.10) to construct a two-sided confidence interval on an unknown population mean using stratified random sampling:

$$\bar{x}_{ST} \pm t(\text{two-sided confidence \%}, n-1) \cdot \text{Est SE}_{ST} \tag{7.10}$$

Consider the following example.

EXAMPLE: MEAN NUMBER OF SICK DAYS A recent report noted that firms within the mobile phone industry average 5.05 sick days per employee per year. COMCEL's Southern Region wants to estimate the mean number of sick days taken per employee last year. The region has 1,500 hourly workers, 200 managers, and 200 administrative support staffers. COMCEL believes that the three groups will differ greatly on the number of sick days taken. Hence, it uses stratified random sampling. COMCEL selects a 4% sample from each stratum of employees. The sample includes 60 workers, eight managers, and eight support staff—76 people. Within each stratum, a simple random sample is selected. COMCEL wants a two-sided 95% confidence interval on the mean number of sick days taken within the past year for all 1,900 employees.

Table 7.9 presents the descriptive statistics for the 76 participants in the study (raw data not shown). The closest t-value for a two-tailed 95% confidence interval and 75 degrees of freedom in Appendix 5 is the t-value for 60 degrees of freedom, 2.000. Alternatively, we could use the normal value of 1.96 since the sample size exceeds 50. We use the former to obtain

$$\bar{x}_{ST} \pm t(\text{two-sided 95\%}, 75)(\text{Estimated standard error})$$

Table 7.9

Descriptive Statistics for Number of Sick Days Taken

Statistic	Hourly Employees	Management	Support Staff
n	60	8	8
$\bar{x}$	4.85	8.88	6.63
s^2	.57	.41	.27
N	1,500	200	200

$$\bar{x}_{ST} = \frac{1{,}500}{1{,}900}(4.85) + \frac{200}{1{,}900}(8.88) + \frac{200}{1{,}900}(6.63) = 5.46$$

$$\text{Est SE}_{ST} = \sqrt{\left(\frac{1{,}500}{1{,}900}\right)^2\left(\frac{.57}{60}\right) + \left(\frac{200}{1{,}900}\right)^2\left(\frac{.41}{8}\right) + \left(\frac{200}{1{,}900}\right)^2\left(\frac{.27}{8}\right)} = .083$$

Lower limit: 5.46 − (2.000)(.083) = 5.29 days
Upper limit: 5.46 + (2.000)(.083) = 5.63 days

Interpretation: We are 95% confident that the mean number of sick days taken for all Southern Region personnel is between 5.29 and 5.63.

COMCEL's mean number of sick days is above the industry mean. How can COMCEL reduce it? Table 7.9 indicates that both managers and support staff are taking more sick days than hourly employees. If the overall mean is to be brought down, COMCEL must focus on the manager and support staff strata. It should ask the following diagnostic questions:

1. Have there been *any changes* lately that might account for the difference between the mean numbers of sick days taken by hourly employees and by management and the support people?
2. What (beyond the mean number of sick days) is *unique or distinctive* about hourly employees vs. management and the support people?

For example, suppose that for the past year, COMCEL's administrative offices have been undergoing extensive renovation. The noise levels, the erratic behavior of the heating and cooling equipment, and the constant departmental relocations have caused managers and support staff to take sick days. If the renovation was the cause, the number of sick days should now drop as the renovation has been completed.

Impact of Using Simple Random Sampling

Suppose that stratified sampling is called for in a study. What is the impact of using simple random sampling instead? Imagine that COMCEL had taken a simple random sample instead of a stratified random sample. Suppose that the same 76 people had been selected. Thus the 76 observations would be the same as those obtained by a stratified random sample. However, the sample standard deviation for the 76 employees would have been 1.51 days and the estimated standard error of the mean would have been .173 day (calculations not shown). This is more than twice as large as the estimated standard error using stratified random sampling. Using stratified sampling when it was appropriate reduced the estimated standard error by more than 50%. This cuts the margin of error for the confidence interval in half.

In summary, we use stratified random sampling when there are subgroups within a target population that are likely to have similarities on the variable of interest within a stratum but differences between strata. Stratified random sampling can produce narrower, and thus more meaningful, confidence intervals than simple random sampling.

SECTION 7.6 EXERCISES

1. You must decide between a simple random and a stratified random sampling plan. List the conditions under which you would prefer a stratified sampling plan.

2. Using stratified random sampling, a manager took a simple random sample from two plants and determined the mean number of minutes to assemble a VCR. The results are shown here:

	Plant 1	Plant 2
Population size (N)	3,000	7,000
Sample size (n)	30	70
Sample mean	120	135
Sample variance	25	144

    a. What is the sample mean for the stratified random sample?
    b. What weight should you give to the sample mean from plant 1? From plant 2?
    c. Estimate the variance of the sample mean for the stratified random sample in part **a**.
    d. Construct a 90% confidence interval for the population mean of the two plants.

3. A marketing research firm wishes to estimate the mean number of hours a week spent watching television. The firm believes that the mean will vary significantly by household income. Using census data, it divides a county into three income classes—low, medium, and high. A proportional sample from each stratum showed the following:

	Low	Medium	High
Sample mean (hours)	56	40.5	26.7
Sample variance	7.2	8.1	7.3
Proportion of the total population	.5	.3	.2
Sample size	300	180	120

Construct a 95% confidence interval to estimate the mean number of hours of television watched over the total population.

4. An auditor wants to estimate the mean age of the accounts receivable. He subdivides the population into three strata by size of account. He selects a simple random sample from each stratum. Here are the data:

	Small	Medium	Large
Sample mean (days)	33.9	25.1	19
Sample size	40	13	23
Sample variance	35.4	232	87.6
Population size	1,000	360	540

Construct a 99% confidence interval to estimate the mean age of accounts receivable.

Chapter 7 Making Inferences About One Population Parameter

7.7 Confidence Intervals on an Unknown Population Proportion

We have been dealing with quantitative data up to this point. In this section we focus on yes/no data—data often used to code responses to questionnaires. Typical yes/no questions include:

1. Do you use the firm's aerobic facilities?
2. Do you plan to vote for candidate A?
3. Is your department planning to purchase additional computers?

In Chapter 2, we organized and summarized yes/no data. Now we will estimate population proportions from sample yes/no data, or sample proportions. By the end of this section, you should be able to construct and interpret confidence intervals on population proportions using simple random sampling.

We begin by computing the sample mean and variance for yes/no data. The sample mean for yes/no data is called the sample proportion.

$$\text{Sample proportion} = \frac{x}{n} \qquad (7.11)$$

$$\text{Sample proportion variance} = \frac{xy}{n(n-1)} \qquad (7.12)$$

where x is the number of people who respond yes to the question
y is the number of people who respond no to the question
n is the sample size

x/n, or $\hat{p}$ (read as p-hat), is the sample proportion of people who said yes. y/n, or $\hat{q}$, is the sample proportion of people who said no. Sample proportions are similar to sample means. Both are measures of a data set's center. While sample means can take on all possible negative and positive values, sample proportions are numbers between 0 and 1. We can convert proportions to percentages by multiplying by 100.

Estimated Standard Error of the Proportion

The general expression for the estimated standard error is $\sqrt{s^2/n}$. Substituting expression (7.12) for s^2 yields the estimated standard error for the sample proportion.

$$\text{Estimated standard error of sample proportion} = \sqrt{\frac{\hat{p}\hat{q}}{n-1}} \qquad (7.13)$$

We can use expression (7.14) to construct two-sided confidence intervals on the population proportion:

$$\frac{x}{n} \pm \text{Margin of error}$$

$$\hat{p} \pm z(\text{Estimated standard error of sample proportion}) \qquad (7.14)$$

$$\hat{p} \pm z\sqrt{\frac{\hat{p}\hat{q}}{n-1}}$$

where z-values are from the standard normal table. These are the same as the tabled values in the bottom row (infinite degrees of freedom) of Appendix 5.

The following problem illustrates constructing a two-tailed confidence interval on an unknown population proportion.

EXAMPLE: JAPAN—THE LEADING ECONOMIC POWER? An international business council wants to estimate the population proportion of Californians who believe that Japan is the leading economic power. The council takes a simple random sample of 200 Californians. One hundred sixteen of those sampled said they believe Japan is the leading economic power. The council wants to construct a two-sided 90% confidence interval on the unknown population proportion.

Here are the assumptions:

ASSUMPTION 1: The sample of 200 Californians is a simple random sample from the population.

ASSUMPTION 2: The shape of the sampling distribution of the sample proportion of Californians who rank Japan as the leading economic power is normally distributed.

Assumption 1 is realistic because we used simple random sampling. According to Cochran (1977), our second assumption is also realistic. Cochran provides the following rules on the normality of the sampling distribution of the sample proportion, as given in Table 7.10. Since $\hat{p} = 116/200 = .58$, the necessary sample

Table 7.10

Cochran's Rules for Normality of the Sampling Distribution of the Sample Proportion

$\hat{p}$	Sample Size Needed to Ensure Normality
.5	30
.40 or .60	50
.30 or .70	80
.20 or .80	200
.10 or .90	600
.05 or .95	1,400

size is 50. The sampling distribution of the sample proportion will be normal and we can use Appendix 5 or the normal table to obtain the standard normal values, z.

Here are the descriptive statistics from the survey:

$$\hat{p} = \frac{116}{200} = .58$$

$$\text{Estimated standard error} = \sqrt{\frac{(.58)(.42)}{199}} = .035$$

From expression (7.14), the two-sided 90% confidence interval on the population proportion is

$$.58 \pm t(90\%, \text{infinite})(\text{Estimated standard error of sample proportion})$$

Lower limit: $.58 - (1.645)(.035) = .523$
Upper limit: $.58 + (1.645)(.035) = .637$

Interpretation: We are 90% confident that between 52.3% and 63.7% of Californians believe that Japan is the leading economic power.

In summary, just as we use the sample mean to estimate the population mean, we use the sample proportion to estimate the population proportion.

SECTION 7.7 EXERCISES

1. You believe that no more than 5% of a population prefer brand A, but want to confirm this belief by a telephone survey. If you are correct in your belief, would a sample of 40 respondents allow you to construct an at most confidence interval? Explain.

2. A marketing research study of 400 members of the general public indicated that only 86 respondents preferred brand A. Estimate the proportion of the population that prefers brand A. Use a two-sided 95% confidence interval.

3. A manufacturer claims that at least 90% of his electrical parts are defect-free. A sample of 600 parts showed that 78 were defective.
   a. Construct a one-sided 90% confidence interval that will establish a lower bound on the present number of defective items produced by the manufacturer.
   b. Based on your confidence interval, does it appear that the percentage of defective parts is greater than 10%? Explain.

4. An insurance agency that processed 25,000 claims last year wants to know the percentage of these claims that were processed incorrectly. A sample of 1500 claims showed that 93 had at least one error.
   a. The office manager wants to know how bad the error rate could be. Construct a 99% "at most" confidence interval for the percentage error rate for the population of 25,000 claims.
   b. What is the most likely error rate you would find if you did reexamine all 25,000 claims? Explain.

c. Construct a 95% "at least" confidence interval to establish a lower bound on the error rate.

5. Just-in-Time Inc. is a stock market timing service. It is interested in knowing the percentage of business economists who believe there will be a recession next year. Using the membership list of 4,500 members in the American Association of Business Economists as a sampling frame, the service calls 150 randomly selected members. Forty-three believe the country will experience a recession next year.
   a. Construct a 95% confidence interval to estimate the proportion of business economists who believe there will be a recession next year.
   b. Would this confidence interval apply to all economists? Explain.

6. According to a survey in *New Venture* magazine, 62% of 350 CEOs interviewed used company profitability as the most important factor in determining bonuses and perks. Assuming that the 350 CEOs constitute a simple random sample of the population of all CEOs, construct a 90% confidence interval for the proportion of CEOs who use profitability as the most important factor in determining bonuses and perks.

7.8 Determining the Sample Size

Early in a sample survey or planned change study, a project manager must *determine* the sample size. Up to now we have assumed that we knew the desired sample size. In this section we discuss how to determine the sample size so that we can be confident that the sample statistic will differ from the population parameter by no more than an amount that we specify. We want the margin of error to be as small as our budget and time allow. Observations cost time and money. Thus we try to keep the sample size small. On the other hand, if the sample size is too small, we will not get useful information and the entire survey or study will be for naught. We can reduce margin of error by increasing the sample size. But larger size samples increase the study's cost. There are no easy solutions. By the end of this section you should be able to:

1. determine the sample size for simple random sampling to limit the margin of error to some maximum value in estimating an unknown population mean;
2. determine the sample size for simple random sampling to limit the margin of error to some maximum value in estimating an unknown population proportion; and
3. explain without using formulas how to determine the sample size.

Two-Sided Interval on an Unknown Population Mean

To set up a confidence interval on an unknown population mean we have used the following expression:

$$\bar{x} \pm t(\text{Estimated standard error of the mean})$$

Since in most business applications the sample size exceeds 50, we can substitute the *z*-value for the *t*-value. The expression then becomes

$$\bar{x} \pm z\sqrt{\frac{s^2}{n}}$$

However, $z\sqrt{s^2/n}$ is simply the margin of error. To determine the necessary sample size, set $z\sqrt{s^2/n}$ equal to the desired margin of error and solve for *n*:

$$\text{Margin of error} = z\sqrt{\frac{s^2}{n}} \quad (7.15)$$

The term s^2 is the sample variance. We will not know what it is until we have taken our sample. At this point, we do not even know our sample size, so we must estimate s^2. Three common approaches are to

1. use the sample variance from a small *pilot* study;
2. use the sample variance from similar studies; or
3. estimate the range, which equals the estimated maximum value minus the estimated minimum value. Then divide the range by 6 and square that value to obtain the estimated sample variance.

We now illustrate how expression (7.15) can determine the sample size.

EXAMPLE: MILEMASTER TIRE STUDY   The population mean tire life of Milemaster tires must be estimated. Based on a small pilot study of 20 tires, the sample *standard deviation* is 800 miles. What must be the sample size to be 95% confident that the sample mean will be within 100 miles of the unknown population mean? In other words, what sample size provides 95% confidence that the margin of error will be ±100 miles?

Begin by substituting what we know into expression (7.15). Remember that the *z*-value for a 95% two-tailed confidence interval can be found in Appendix 5 and is 1.96. Now solve for *n*, the unknown sample size:

$$\text{Margin of error (ME)} = z\sqrt{\frac{s^2}{n}}$$

$$100 \text{ miles} = 1.96\sqrt{\frac{640{,}000}{n}}$$

In terms of a formula:

$$n = \frac{z^2 s^2}{\text{ME}^2} = \frac{(3.8416)(640{,}000)}{10{,}000} \quad (7.16)$$

$$= 245.86 \text{ or } 246 \text{ tires} \quad \text{(always round up when determining sample size)}$$

A simple random sample of 246 tires will allow us to be 95% confident that the sample mean will be within 100 miles of the unknown population mean tire life. The margin of error will be 100 miles. The pilot study sample size counts toward the 246 observations. Thus, we will need only an additional 226 tires to complete the study.

Now think about what the previous paragraph tells us. The population of Milemaster tires is very large. Yet if we take a simple random sample of 246 tires we are 95% confident that our sample mean will be within 100 miles of the unknown population mean. This demonstrates the power of the statistical inferences.

We can extend sample size determination to one-sided confidence intervals. Expressions (7.15) and (7.16) will not change, but we do need to adjust the z-value to reflect a one-sided confidence interval. For example, for a one-sided 95% confidence interval the z-value would be 1.645, not 1.96.

Two-Sided Interval on an Unknown Population Proportion

To set up a confidence interval on an unknown population proportion we have used the following expression:

$$\hat{p} \pm z \sqrt{\frac{\hat{p}\hat{q}}{n-1}}$$

However, $z\sqrt{\hat{p}\hat{q}/(n-1)}$ is simply the margin of error. To determine the necessary sample size, set $z\sqrt{\hat{p}\hat{q}/(n-1)}$ equal to the desired margin of error and solve for the sample size, n:

$$\text{Margin of error} = z \sqrt{\frac{\hat{p}\hat{q}}{n-1}} \tag{7.17}$$

In this situation, the problem is that we do not know what $\hat{p}$ is and we will not know it until we take our sample. So we must estimate $\hat{p}$. Four common approaches are to:

1. use the sample proportion from a small *pilot* study;
2. use the sample proportion from similar studies;
3. estimate the minimum and maximum possible values of $\hat{p}$ using managerial judgment or intuition. Use both estimates to determine sample sizes. To be on the safe side, select the larger sample size; or
4. use a $\hat{p}$ of .5, which will avoid underestimating the sample size. However, if $\hat{p}$ turns out to be very small (i.e., .01–.10) or very large (i.e., .90–.99) we will have significantly overestimated the sample size. This increases the study cost.

Now we can use expression (7.17) to determine the sample size.

Chapter 7 Making Inferences About One Population Parameter

EXAMPLE: AMBULANCE SERVICE STUDY We want to estimate the unknown population proportion of voters who favor improved ambulance service in the county. Based on a pilot study of size $n = 50$, we estimate $\hat{p}$ to be .40. What sample size is neeeded to be 99% confident that the sample proportion will be within .04 of the unknown population proportion? That is, we desire a margin of error of $\pm .04$.

Begin by substituting what we know into expression (7.17). Then solve for n, the unknown sample size:

$$\text{ME} = .04 = 2.576 \sqrt{\frac{(.4)(.6)}{n-1}}$$

In terms of a formula:

$$n = \frac{z^2 \hat{p} \hat{q}}{\text{ME}^2} + 1 = \frac{(6.636)(.4)(.6)}{.04^2} + 1 \qquad (7.18)$$

$$= 996.4 \text{ or } 997 \text{ people}$$

Thus, a simple random sample of 997 people provides 99% confidence that our sample proportion will be within .04 of the unknown proportion. In other words, the margin of error will be $\pm .04$. The pilot study of sample size 50 counts toward the overall sample of 997 people.

Again with a relatively small sample from a large population we can estimate the unknown population proportion quite accurately. That explains how the Gallup Organization can draw accurate inferences about all voters while interviewing only about 1,500 people.

We can also extend sample size determination to one-sided confidence intervals. Expressions (7.17) and (7.18) do not change, and we simply adjust the z-value to reflect a one-sided confidence interval.

In summary, once we set the maximum margin of error that we can tolerate—a manager's prerogative—and the desired level of confidence, we can determine the sample size to estimate the population mean or proportion.

SECTION 7.8 EXERCISES

1. List the factors that should be considered in calculating the required sample size.
2. A manager wants to estimate a population mean and asks your help. Here is the information at hand:

Population size (N)	50,000
Estimated population variance	2,500
Required margin of error	5
Required confidence level	95%

a. Calculate the necessary sample size.
b. Some people believe that a *good* sample size is about 10% of the population. Do you agree?

3. A marketing research firm wishes to estimate the percentage of homeowners who are dissatisfied with their present homeowner's insurance policy. The firm has no feel for what the percentage might be, but it wants to be within 2% of the true proportion with 95% confidence. Calculate the required sample size if the firm plans to use simple random sampling.

4. A major appliance dealer surveys its customers every quarter to determine whether its service department is doing a good job. The company wants to estimate the proportion of its customers who are dissatisfied with its service. The company wants to be 90% confident that the estimate will be within 1.5% of the true proportion. In previous studies the company found that approximately 10% of its customers were dissatisfied.

7.9 A Nonparametric Confidence Interval for the Median

In the examples we have covered, we assumed that either the population or sampling distribution of the sample mean was normal. This is a good assumption for most data. However, when there are outliers or the population is highly skewed, neither the population nor the sampling distribution may be normal. How then can we construct confidence intervals?

To do so, we will set up a *nonparametric* confidence interval on the *median*. *Nonparametric* refers to a set of statistical inference methods that do not require a normal population. By the end of this section you should be able to:

1. explain when to construct a confidence interval for the median;
2. construct a confidence interval for the median; and
3. explain the impact of constructing a confidence interval on the mean when an interval on the median should be constructed.

Constructing Approximate 95% Confidence Intervals

Constructing a confidence interval on a population median is relatively simple. The procedure uses ranks and guarantees that the level of confidence will be approximately 95%. This is the procedure:

1. Rank order the data from the smallest to the largest values.
2. Determine the sample median.
3. If there are data values that equal the sample median, delete them. Reduce the sample size by the number of deletions.
4. Look up the sample size in Table 7.11. Determine the *number of values* associated with the sample size.
5. Count up that many data values from the smallest value. This is the lower limit of the confidence interval for the population median.
6. Count down that many data values from the largest value. This is the upper limit of the confidence interval for the population median.

Table 7.11

Determining Limits of an Approximate 95% Two-Sided Confidence Interval on the Population Median

Sample Size	Number of Values	Sample Size	Number of Values
6–8	1	30–32	10
9–11	2	33–34	11
12–14	3	35–36	12
15–16	4	37–39	13
17–19	5	40–41	14
20–22	6	42–43	15
23–24	7	44–46	16
25–27	8	47–48	17
28–29	9	49–50	18

For larger samples—more than 50—determine the number of values as follows. Divide the sample size by 4, take the square root of that number, and multiply by 1.96. Then subtract the result from one-half of the sample size. Use the closest integer.

For example: For $n = 100$, $(100/2) - (1.96\sqrt{100/4}) = 40.2$ or 40. The lower limit of the confidence interval will be the 40th smallest data value and the upper limit will be the 40th largest value counting down from the top.

Next we illustrate the nonparametric method for constructing a two-sided 95% confidence interval on an unknown population median.

EXAMPLE: COMCEL WORKER ATTITUDE STUDY   COMCEL conducts a monthly worker attitude, or job climate, survey. Each month a simple random sample of 20 workers anonymously rate the job climate along the following 10-point scale. COMCEL wishes to construct a two-sided 95% confidence interval estimate on the unknown population median.

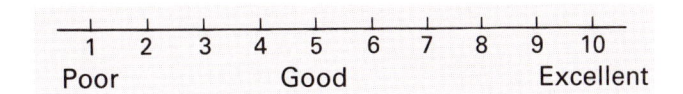

```
 1   2   3   4   5   6   7   8   9   10
Poor         Good              Excellent
```

Table 7.12 on page 366 contains the rank-ordered data for the latest month. Figure 7.9 shows that the attitudes of workers B, N, and Q are outliers; they have very poor attitudes in comparison to everyone else. The outliers suggest that the population from which the sample was taken may be long-tailed or non-normal. Given that there are outliers, we should construct a confidence interval on the population median.

From Chapter 2 we know that the rank of the sample median is $(1 +$ number of data values$)/2$. Given 20 data values, the median is halfway between the 10th and 11th ranked data values, or 8.5 (see Table 7.12). Since no sample value equals the sample median, the sample size remains 20. The tabled value (see Table 7.11) for a sample size of 20 is 6. Thus the lower limit of the confidence interval is observation 6 in the column labelled "Count from the Smallest Data Value,"

Table 7.12
Ranked Worker Attitude Data

Worker	Data	Count from the Smallest Data Value	Count from the Largest Data Value
B	1	1	20
N	1	2	19
Q	6	3	18
C	8	4	17
E	8	5	16
G	8	6	15
L	8	7	14
T	8	8	13
A	8	9	12
D	8	10	11
F	9	11	10
H	9	12	9
J	9	13	8
K	9	14	7
M	9	15	6
O	9	16	5
P	9	17	4
S	9	18	3
I	10	19	2
R	10	20	1

FIGURE 7.9 Stem-and-Leaf Display and Box Plot for Job Climate Data

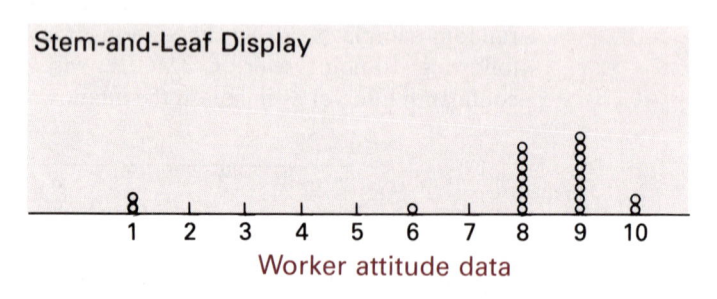

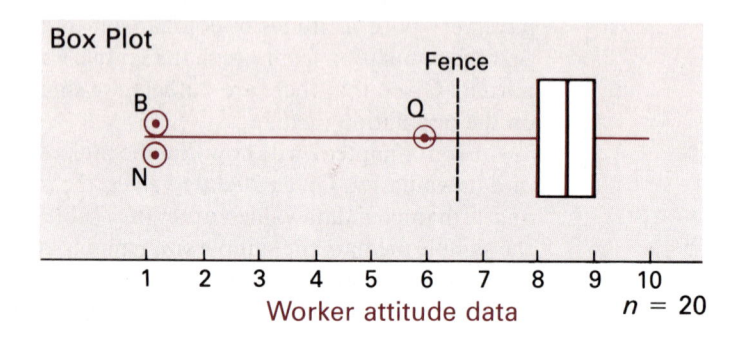

or 8. The upper limit is observation 6 in the column labelled "Count from the Largest Data Value," or 9.

Interpretation: We are about 95% confident that the unknown population median job climate attitude at COMCEL is between 8 and 9 on the 10-point scale. This is excellent!

We have the same interpretation for confidence intervals on the mean and median. If we collected 1,000 samples of 20 workers' attitudes, approximately 950 of the confidence intervals would contain the unknown population median. About 50 intervals would not. Therefore, we are about 95% confident that the interval we did construct does contain the unknown population median.

Assumptions for Confidence Intervals on the Population Mean and Median

We must make two assumptions in constructing confidence intervals on the population mean. First, the sample must be a simple random sample from the population. Second, the sampling distribution of the sample mean must be normally distributed. Only the former assumption is necessary for constructing confidence intervals on the population median. That is, every subgroup of size n from the target population must have an equal chance of being selected for the sample.

Confidence Intervals on the Mean in the Presence of Outliers

When the population has outliers, the size of the confidence intervals on the mean and median will differ. What effect will outliers have on the mean? What effect will they have on the standard error of the mean? Will a confidence interval for the mean be wider than for the median? Why? Please think about it before reading on.

Construct an approximate 95% two-sided confidence interval on the mean for the COMCEL worker attitude data.

$$\bar{x} = 7.80$$

$$s = 2.48$$

$$\frac{s}{\sqrt{n}} = \frac{2.48}{\sqrt{20}} = .55$$

$$\bar{x} \pm t(\text{two-sided } 95\%, 19)(\text{Estimated standard error})$$

Lower limit: $7.80 - (2.093)(.55) = 6.65$

Upper limit: $7.80 + (2.093)(.55) = 8.95$

Interpretation: We are 95% confident that the unknown population mean worker attitude rating is between 6.65 and 8.95 on the 10-point scale.

The results show that the mean—7.8—is smaller than the median—8.5. This is due to the effect of the three outliers—workers B, N, and Q. In determining the median, we are concerned only that the *number* of observations above and below the median be the same. In computing the mean, we sum the *actual* values of the observations and divide by the sample size. Thus if there are outliers, the median and mean may differ. Notice how the outliers—in this case, all very low values—*pulled* the mean toward them. Outliers will not affect the median. Remember, when we have outliers, the median is a better measure of the center for it is robust, or insensitive, to outliers.

Even more important to note is that the confidence interval for the mean is wider than that for the median. The outliers produce a relatively large estimated standard error. Even one or two outliers can significantly increase the sample standard deviation because we take the *squared* deviations around the mean. This yields a wider confidence interval for the mean, and wider confidence intervals are less meaningful.

In summary, when sample data contain outliers, construct confidence intervals for the population median using the nonparametric approach. However, when the population or the sampling distribution is near normal, confidence intervals for the mean will be narrower than when using the nonparametric method.

SECTION 7.9 EXERCISES

1. Explain when you should construct a confidence interval for the median rather than a confidence interval for the mean.

2. Consider the following sample of data points: {1, 2, 4, 6, 7, 20}.
   a. Find the sample median.
   b. Construct an approximate 95% confidence interval for the population median.

3. Participants in a training class are asked to rate a new instructor. The rating scale ranges from 0 = poor to 10 = outstanding. The following scores were obtained from 13 trainees:

$$\{1, 4, 5, 5, 6, 6, 6, 7, 7, 7, 7, 8, 9\}$$

   a. Find the sample median.
   b. What is the resulting sample size after adjustment for the repeating median?
   c. Construct an approximate 95% confidence interval for the population median.
   d. What practical meaning could the director of training assign to this confidence interval?

4. A shop steward wants to estimate the mean number of days of sick leave taken by the workers in a large plant. He selects a random sample of 50 employees and records the following numbers of days over the past month:

0	0	0	1	1	2	3	3	3	5
0	0	0	1	1	2	3	3	4	6
0	0	1	1	1	2	3	3	4	7
0	0	1	1	1	2	3	3	4	14
0	0	1	1	1	2	3	3	4	18

After seeing the sample data, the steward decides to estimate the population median rather than the population mean. Do you agree with his choice? Explain.

5. Below are profit margins on sales—net income after taxes divided by sales—for 10 firms. Construct an approximate 95% confidence interval on the population median.

5%   5.1%   5.5%   5.9%   6%   6.3%   6.6%   6.8%   7.7%   13.4%

7.10 Estimating the Population Variance and Standard Deviation

Up to this point, we have drawn inferences about the center of the population. For qualitative yes/no data we constructed confidence intervals on the population proportion. For quantitative data we constructed confidence intervals on either the population mean or median. However, sometimes we will be interested in making inferences about the population's standard deviation rather than its mean value. By the end of this section you should be able to:

1. explain the characteristics of the chi-square distribution; and
2. construct and interpret confidence intervals on the population standard deviation.

The following problem illustrates why constructing confidence intervals on an unknown population standard deviation is necessary.

EXAMPLE: JUST-IN-TIME MANUFACTURING SYSTEMS   COMCEL has recently installed a just-in-time (JIT) manufacturing system. COMCEL does not stockpile the materials needed to manufacture its mobile phones. Instead it relies on vendors to deliver the materials needed for daily production at noon every day. COMCEL's vendors have agreed to a delivery schedule with a maximum standard deviation in delivery times of 2 hours. Assuming a normal distribution, 95% of the time material should arrive within ± 4 hours of noon ($\pm$ two standard deviations). COMCEL collects the delivery times for the 10 most recent working days. Are its vendors able to meet the maximum 2-hour standard deviation around noon? COMCEL wants to construct a 90% confidence interval on the population standard deviation in delivery times.

How can COMCEL estimate the population standard deviation in delivery times? All inferences made in this chapter depend on prior knowledge of the sampling distribution of the sample statistic used to make the inference. We can construct confidence intervals for a population mean because we know that the sampling distribution of the sample mean is normally distributed. What would happen if we took repeated samples from a normal population and calculated the sample variance, s^2, for each sample? What is the sampling distribution of the sample variance?

Consider the following ratio: $(n-1)s^2/\sigma^2$. This ratio is a sample variance multiplied by the sample size minus 1, then divided by the population variance. Since the population variance is a fixed, but unknown, value, the ratio will vary as the sample variance varies. If we take repeated samples of size n and calculate the ratio, what would the resulting histogram look like? Would it be normal or skewed?

The answer is that it would be skewed toward higher values and here is why. The smallest value for the ratio is zero, which happens when all the sample observations are the same and therefore s^2 is zero. Since the variance cannot be negative, the ratio cannot be negative. The ratio can take on very large values when the sample data are very different from one another. Since the ratio's lower bound is zero and it has no theoretical upper bound, the histogram must be skewed toward higher values.

The Chi-Square Distribution

The histogram of this ratio is called a chi-square distribution. The chi-square distribution is a family of curves. While the curves vary in shape, all have a lower bound of 0 and are skewed toward higher values. If we took repeated samples of size 10 from a population with variance σ^2 and calculated the ratio, $(n-1)s^2/\sigma^2$, the distribution of ratios is chi-square distributed with $(n-1)$, or 9 degrees of freedom.

Please look at Appendix 6. Each row represents a different distribution within the chi-square family. Find the row labelled 9 degrees of freedom and the chi-square column labelled 2.5%. The tabled number is 2.70. If we took repeated samples from the population and computed the ratios, $9s^2/\sigma^2$, 2.5% of them will have values between 0 and 2.70. Moving over to the chi-square column labelled 97.5%, the tabled number is 19.02. Thus, 97.5% of the ratios will be less than 19.02. Since we have identified the 2.5 percentile and the 97.5 percentile, the *middle* 95% of all ratios will fall between 2.70 and 19.02. Figure 7.10 displays this chi-square distribution with 9 degrees of freedom. [*Note:* Chi-square is also written as χ^2.]

Thus, the lower and upper limits of a 95% confidence interval on a ratio are

$$2.70 < \frac{(n-1)s^2}{\sigma^2} < 19.02$$

FIGURE 7.10 χ^2 Distribution with 9 Degrees of Freedom

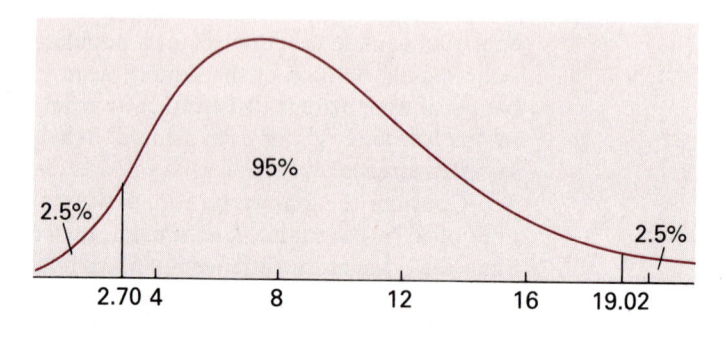

Generalizing, the lower and upper limits of a $(100 - \alpha)\%$ confidence interval on a ratio are

$$\chi^2_{\alpha/2} < \frac{(n-1)s^2}{\sigma^2} < \chi^2_{100-\alpha/2}$$

Rearranging terms, we obtain the following expression for constructing confidence intervals on the population variance:

$$\frac{(n-1)s^2}{\chi^2_{100-\alpha/2}} < \sigma^2 < \frac{(n-1)s^2}{\chi^2_{\alpha/2}} \qquad (7.19)$$

Expression (7.19) says we can construct a $(100 - \alpha)\%$ confidence interval for any population variance by multiplying the degrees of freedom by the sample variance and dividing by the appropriate percentile values from the chi-square table. To obtain a confidence interval on the population standard deviation, we simply take the square root of the lower and upper limits.

Now we can construct a 90% confidence interval on the unknown population standard deviation in delivery times. Before doing so, we state our assumptions:

ASSUMPTION 1: The 10 days for which we collected data are representative of vendors' typical delivery times.

ASSUMPTION 2: In the population, vendor arrival times are normally distributed.

To test the first assumption, COMCEL could compare these 10 arrivals with deliveries from other weeks. Assumption 1 would be met if there was no discernible difference. Assumption 2 is realistic since a stem-and-leaf display for the 10 delivery times is near-normal shaped. This suggests that the population may well be normal shaped. The raw data and corresponding statistics are presented here:

Day	1	2	3	4	5	6	7	8	9	10
Arrival time	Noon	Noon	1:00	11:00	Noon	11:00	1:00	2:00	Noon	Noon
Hours off target	0	0	1	−1	0	−1	+1	+2	0	0

$$\bar{x} = .2 \text{ hour off noon target}$$

$$s^2 = .84$$

$$s = .92 \text{ hour off noon target}$$

To construct a 90% interval, we need the chi-square values for 9 degrees of freedom at the 5th percentile and at the 95th percentile. Now substitute the sample variance and sample size into expression (7.19):

$$\frac{(10-1)(.84)}{16.92} < \sigma^2 < \frac{(10-1)(.84)}{3.33}$$

$$.45 < \sigma^2 < 2.27$$

To obtain a 90% confidence interval on the population standard deviation, σ, we take the square root of the lower and upper limits:

$$.67 \text{ hour} < \sigma < 1.51 \text{ hours}$$

Interpretation: We are 90% confident that the population standard deviation in vendor delivery about the noon target time is between .67 hour and 1.51 hours.

What can COMCEL conclude about the variability in delivery times? Since the confidence interval's upper limit is less than 2 hours, COMCEL's vendors are more than meeting the 2-hour standard deviation requirement.

Suppose that the lower and upper limits of the interval had been greater than 2 hours. What could COMCEL have concluded? Please think about it before reading on.

COMCEL could have concluded that it had sufficient reason to complain that its vendors are not meeting the agreed-upon reliability standards (standard deviation) in delivery schedules.

In summary, when we are interested in performance variability rather than mean performance, we construct confidence intervals on the population standard deviation. We use the chi-square distribution to construct the limits of the confidence interval.

SECTION 7.10 EXERCISES

1. For each of the following statements, indicate whether the z, t, or chi-square distribution applies. (One or more distributions may apply to each statement.)
    a. The area under the curve equals 1.
    b. The choice of the exact curve depends on the degrees of freedom.
    c. The distribution is symmetric about zero.
    d. The distribution is skewed to the right.
    e. The graph describes the sampling distribution of the sample mean.
    f. The distribution is used to estimate a population proportion.
    g. The distribution is used to estimate a population variance.

2. Complete the following table by finding the chi-square values for each of the sample sizes listed.

Sample Size	Degrees of Freedom	2.5 Percentile	97.5 Percentile
4	___	___	___
8	___	___	___
12	___	___	___

3. A quality control inspector wishes to estimate the population standard deviation of a set of measurements. A sample variance of 25 squared cm was calculated based on a sample of size 9. Construct a 95% confidence interval for the population standard deviation.

4. Consider the following set of data values selected from a normal population: {1, 4, 3, 2, 5}.
   a. Calculate the sample mean and sample variance.
   b. Estimate the population mean using a 90% confidence coefficient.
   c. Construct a 90% confidence interval for the population standard deviation.

5. A manufacturer makes a machine that injects a specified amount of heart stimulant into a patient's bloodstream. The manufacturer claims that the standard deviation of the amount injected is less than .05 milliliter. If the standard deviation is greater than .05, the patient may not get enough stimulant or get too much stimulant and die. The variance in a sample of 10 injections was .00587.
   a. Construct an 80% confidence interval to estimate the standard deviation of the amount injected.
   b. Construct a 99% confidence interval to estimate the standard deviation of the amount injected.
   c. Keeping in mind that people's lives depend on your decision, would you conclude that the machine is safe to use? Defend your position.

7.11 Overview and Key Ideas

We summarize Chapter 7 with the following four key ideas:

IDEA 1: We use sample statistics to estimate population parameters.

Population parameters are fixed but unknown values for which we obtain estimates by using:

1. the sample mean to construct a confidence interval on the population mean;
2. the sample proportion to construct a confidence interval on the population proportion;
3. the sample median to construct a confidence interval on the population median; and
4. the sample standard deviation to construct a confidence interval on the population standard deviation.

We use confidence intervals to estimate population parameters of cross-sectional and stationary time-ordered data.

IDEA 2: As the sample size increases the sample statistics tend to get closer to the unknown population parameters.

The estimated standard error of the mean and proportion is $s/\sqrt{n}$. As we increase the sample size, the estimated standard error gets smaller. Thus the sample mean (or proportion) tends to move closer to the unknown population mean (or proportion).

As the sample size increases, the sample variance also gets closer to the population variance. We can see this from expression (7.19). Set up two 95% confidence intervals for the population variance—one for 2 degrees of freedom and one for 120.

	2 Degrees of Freedom	120 Degrees of Freedom
Lower Limit	$\dfrac{2s^2}{\chi^2_{97.5\%}} = \dfrac{2s^2}{7.38}$ $= .27s^2$	$\dfrac{120s^2}{\chi^2_{97.5\%}} = \dfrac{120s^2}{152.21}$ $= .79s^2$
Upper Limit	$\dfrac{2s^2}{\chi^2_{2.5\%}} = \dfrac{2s^2}{.0506}$ $= 39.53s^2$	$\dfrac{120s^2}{\chi^2_{2.5\%}} = \dfrac{120s^2}{91.58}$ $= 1.31s^2$

For a sample size of 3 (2 degrees of freedom), the confidence interval is very wide. It ranges from .27 to 39.53 times the sample variance. For a sample size of

Table 7.13
Overview of Types of Confidence Intervals

Unknown Population Parameter	Survey Design	Assumptions	Sample Statistic	Two-Sided Confidence Interval (Correction Factor Omitted)
Population mean	Simple random	Sampling distribution of sample mean is near normal.	$\bar{x} = \dfrac{\sum_{i=1}^{n} x_i}{n}$	Lower limit: $\bar{x} - t\left(\dfrac{s}{\sqrt{n}}\right)$ Upper limit: $\bar{x} + t\left(\dfrac{s}{\sqrt{n}}\right)$
Population median	Simple random	Population shape is *highly* skewed or has outliers.	Sample median	Lower limit: see Table 7.11 Upper limit: see Table 7.11
Population mean	Stratified random	Sampling distribution is near normal.	Strata means $\bar{x}_1, \bar{x}_2, \ldots, \bar{x}_k$ overall sample mean $\bar{x}_{ST}$ see (7.8)	Lower limit: $\bar{x}_{ST} - t(\text{Est SE}_{ST})$ Upper limit: $\bar{x}_{ST} + t(\text{Est SE}_{ST})$
Population proportion	Simple random	Sampling distribution of sample proportion is near normal. Use Cochran's rules.	$\hat{p} = x/n$ $\hat{q} = y/n$ x = number of "yes" responses y = number of "no" responses n = sample size	Lower limit: $\hat{p} - z\sqrt{\dfrac{\hat{p}\hat{q}}{n-1}}$ Upper limit: $\hat{p} + z\sqrt{\dfrac{\hat{p}\hat{q}}{n-1}}$
Population standard deviation	Simple random	Population is normal.	Sample standard deviation	Lower limit: $\dfrac{(n-1)s^2}{\chi^2_{100-\alpha/2}}$ Upper limit: $\dfrac{(n-1)s^2}{\chi^2_{\alpha/2}}$

Chapter 7 Making Inferences About One Population Parameter

121, the confidence interval shrinks. It ranges from .79 to 1.31 times the sample variance. Idea 2 holds for all sample statistics.

IDEA 3: Confidence intervals provide a probable range within which the population parameter will fall.

Table 7.13 contains a summary of the types of confidence intervals covered in this chapter.

Regardless of whether we select a simple random sample or a stratified random sample, the general expression for any confidence interval involving means or proportions is simply

Sample statistic ± (Reliability factor)(Estimated standard error)

We cannot use the above expression for estimating the population median and standard deviation. When the population is highly skewed and the sample size is small, use the nonparametric confidence interval method. To estimate the population standard deviation, use expression (7.19) and the chi-square distribution.

IDEA 4: Confidence intervals measure only the effects of sampling error. They provide accurate and useful information only when the manager avoids the selection, response, and nonresponse errors discussed in Chapter 6.

COMCEL

Date: March 9, 1992
To: Ann Tabor, CEO
From: Nat Gordon, V.P. Manufacturing
Re: Project Team Report: Improving Time-to-Failure

SUMMARY
In November, the team installed new robotic manufacturing equipment to improve time-to-failure. We have just completed our final tests and the project team has achieved its goal. The mean time-to-failure is at least 2,813 hours.

SUPPORTING ANALYSIS
The team first reviewed all the causes of breakdowns for our phones. It appeared that improper welding was the major cause. Thus the team

chose to install additional robotics in the spot welding operation. By late January we were producing phones with the new equipment. Shortly thereafter we began running our time-to-failure tests. Two days ago we completed the final accelerated life testing. We selected a simple random sample of 61 phones from the over 300 phones produced on the new equipment. The sample mean and the standard deviation for the 61 phones were 2,855 hours and 200 hours, respectively. Given these data, we constructed a one-sided "at least" 95% confidence interval. The lower limit is 2,813 hours. Thus we are 95% confident that the population mean time-to-failure is at least 2,813 hours. There is a 5% chance that the population mean is not greater than 2,813 hours.

CHAPTER 7 QUESTIONS

1. You are interested in whether certified public accountants favor a recent change in the tax laws. What are the target population, the unknown population parameter, and the sample statistic for this study?
2. What does the population standard deviation measure?
3. Under what conditions must the sample statistic equal the corresponding population parameter?
4. Explain why the variance of a sampling distribution of the sample mean must be less than the variance of the population from which it was constructed.
5. You do not know either the mean of the population or the sampling distribution. Yet the sampling distribution of the sample mean is useful in drawing inferences about the unknown population mean. Why?
6. You select the first 20 people who exit a theater and ask them to rate the movie on a scale from 1 to 10. You wish to draw inferences from these 20 people to the theater-going population. Why will your confidence interval *not* be meaningful?
7. What information does a confidence interval provide that the sample mean does not?
8. The margin of error for estimating a population mean is $t \cdot s/\sqrt{n}$. Without changing the level of confidence, what is a practical way to reduce the margin of error?
9. Why would you want to reduce the margin of error?
10. Why is a *t*-based confidence interval larger than an equivalent *z*-based interval?
11. What would the limits be for a 100% confidence interval?
12. What is a one-sided confidence interval? When is it necessary?
13. What is wrong with the following hypotheses?

    Null: $\bar{x} \leq 4.7$ hours
    Alternative: $\bar{x} > 4.7$ hours

14. Why is it possible to make either a Type I or Type II error before a study, but only one error after the study?
15. If a Type II error is costly but a Type I error is not, why would you set the level of significance, α, at .10, .20, or even higher?
16. Correct, if necessary, the following statement: Hypotheses are *claims* about *sample statistics*.
17. What does the prob-value tell you?
18. Provide an example different from those in the book where you would recommend using a stratified random sample rather than a simple random sample. Discuss.

19. If a stratified sample is required but you select a simple random sample, what impact, if any, will this have on the confidence interval's margin of error?
20. Why does increasing the confidence level increase the margin of error?
21. Why do outliers or highly skewed populations require confidence intervals on the median rather than the mean?
22. Suppose you compute a mean-based confidence interval when there are outliers. What impact will this have on the sample mean, the estimated standard error, and the width of the confidence interval?
23. Provide an example different from those in the book where it would be important to estimate an unknown population standard deviation.
24. Even if the population is not normal shaped, you can use the z or t tables to construct confidence intervals. Why?
25. How are sample means and proportions similar and how are they different?

CHAPTER 7 APPLICATION PROBLEMS

1. An attempted hostile takeover occurs when the target firm's management resists acquisition. Maximizing share price is the most effective way to resist. Then the acquiring firm may have to pay too steep a price for the acquisition. Other less effective approaches are taking a *poison pill* or using *greenmail*.
   An investment banking house wants to estimate the proportion of firms that use the strategy to maximize share price. It takes a simple random sample of 1,000 firms. Eight hundred indicate that they use the strategy to maximize share price.
   a. Set up and interpret a 90% confidence interval on the population proportion that uses this strategy.
   b. What two assumptions must be true for the statistical inference to be meaningful?

2. The American Housing Association wants to estimate the mean length-of-tenure discount after five years across the United States. It selects a simple random sample of 900 tenants and finds that the mean discount after five years is 8% and the sample standard deviation is 5%. That is, tenants who have lived at an apartment for five years pay about 92% of the rent that new tenants pay at the same apartment complex. Set up and interpret a 95% confidence interval on the mean discount after five years.

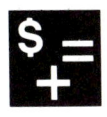

3. Historically, the mean age of accounts payable has been 22 days. For the past six months the firm has tried several ways to reduce the age of accounts payable.
   a. Set up the appropriate null and alternative hypotheses.
   b. In the problem context, what are the Type I and Type II errors?
   c. Identify one cost associated with each error.
   The accounting supervisor selects a simple random sample of 225 accounts payable. The sample mean age is 20.5 days and the sample standard deviation is 7.5 days. Given an α of .05, what can the accounting supervisor conclude?
   d. Show the region of rejection and indicate what action to take.
   e. Based on part **d**, is it now possible to make a Type II error? Explain.

4. A health care firm is considering introducing a home plaque removal system that is almost as effective as a dental cleaning. The systems will retail for $89. The firm will introduce the product only if the population proportion of potential customers who would buy the product is at least .22 (or 22%). The firm selects a simple random sample of 900 potential customers, and 234 indicate a willingness to buy the product.

a. Set up the appropriate 95% confidence interval.
b. Based on the confidence interval, should the firm introduce the product nationwide?

5. A firm is presently using family branding on a consumer product and selling about 1,750 cartons per week in the southeast United States. The marketing group has developed a new media campaign that it believes will increase sales substantially. It convinces management to try individual branding for six months.
   a. Set up the appropriate null and alternative hypotheses.
   b. In the problem context, what are the Type I and Type II errors?
   c. Identify one cost associated with each error.
   After the test period the firm selects a random sample of 400 and finds that these stores have sold a mean of 1,760 cartons per week; the sample standard deviation is 2,000 cartons per week. Given an α level of .10, what can the firm conclude from its test?
   d. Show the region of rejection and indicate what action to take.
   e. Why didn't you reject the null hypothesis? After all, the sample mean was greater than 1,750 cartons per week.
   f. Is it now possible to make a Type II error? Explain.

6. A quality control department takes a simple random sample of 2,000 TV cabinets each week (400 per day). They check for the presence of scratches or surface blemishes. If more than 5% of the production line's TVs have scratches or blemishes, the product does not conform to specifications, and the week's production is 100% inspected.
   Shown below are the daily defect figures for this week's production run:

Day	Number of Defects	Sample	Sample Proportion
Monday	13	400	.0325
Tuesday	11	400	.0275
Wednesday	14	400	.0350
Thursday	10	400	.0250
Friday	12	400	.0300
For week	60	2,000	.0300

   a. Plot the daily sample proportions. Place the days of the week on the horizontal axis and the daily sample proportions on the vertical axis. Do the daily sample proportions appear to be stable in the mean? [*Hint:* See Chapter 2 for line graphing.]
   b. What is the maximum proportion of nonconforming products for the week's production run? Set up and interpret an appropriate 90% confidence interval.
   c. Should the firm 100% inspect last week's production run? Discuss.

7. One hundred economic forecasters are interviewed and asked to make predictions as to whether the budget deficit will be reduced next year. The 95% confidence interval on the population proportion of forecasters who predict that the budget deficit will be reduced is .49 to .53.
   a. Can we say at a 95% level of confidence that a majority of the economic forecasters in the United States believe that the deficit will be reduced next year? Explain.
   b. Suppose the answer in part **a** does not allow you to say that a majority of forecasters believe that the deficit will be reduced next year. Would reducing the margin of error help, and, if so, how can it be reduced? Explain.

Chapter 7 Making Inferences About One Population Parameter

8. Industrial psychologists believe that stress is curvilinearly related to performance. That is, too little stress produces no drive to excel. Too much stress causes anxiety, which reduces performance. From 1989 to 1991, a firm worked to optimize the level of stress within a plant. At the beginning of the period, the level of stress was at 5 (on a scale of 1 to 10)—the optimal level. However, in the past nine months several things have happened that may have caused a change in the stress level.
   a. Set up the appropriate null and alternative hypotheses.
   b. In the problem context, what are the Type I and Type II errors?
   The firm's psychologist selects a simple random sample of 50 workers from the 1,000 employees and administers a stress test. The mean level of stress is 5.35 with a sample variance of .36. Given an α of .01, what can the psychologist conclude?
   c. Given the sample evidence, what action should the firm take?

9. The manager of a service center must estimate the mean time it takes for her telephone operators to handle a customer complaint over the phone. She has 50 operators in her department. She takes a simple random sample of 10 operators on a randomly selected day and obtains the following data on the time (in minutes) spent per call:

$$2 \quad 3 \quad 2 \quad 3 \quad 3 \quad 3 \quad 2 \quad 2 \quad 2 \quad 3$$

   a. Set up and interpret an appropriate 90% confidence interval.
   b. Last year the mean time was 3.2 minutes. Have the workers improved? Explain.

10. The manager of a repair center must estimate the mean travel time between customers for an 800-person repair force. From other repair firms' data, she estimates the standard deviation in travel times will be about 20 minutes. What size sample must she take so that she can be 90% confident that the sample mean will not vary from the population mean by more than 6 minutes?

11. A human resources manager wants to know the proportion of firms in the United States that have day-care facilities on their premises. His pilot study of 30 plants indicates that .20 have day-care facilities. What is the sample size needed to be 95% confident that the sample proportion will be within .05 of the unknown population proportion?

12. An arbitrator wishes to estimate the mean number of grievances per week in all plants with 1,000–5,000 hourly employees. He selects a simple random sample of 25 firms and obtains the following data:

$$\bar{x} = 9$$

$$s = 5$$

Set up and interpret an appropriate 80% confidence interval.

13. A vice-president of a large manufacturing firm wants to estimate the median productivity rate of his 2,000 work teams. He selects a simple random sample of 9 teams and obtains the following productivity data as percentage of standard:

$$92\% \quad 95\% \quad 89\% \quad 96\% \quad 104\% \quad 138\% \quad 99\% \quad 92\% \quad 101\%$$

   a. Set up and interpret an appropriate 95% confidence interval.

b. What must the vice-president have assumed about the 2,000 work groups' productivities that made him think that a confidence interval on the median, and not the mean, was appropriate?

c. Are the sample data consistent with his thinking?

14. Howard Bright, plant manager at COMCEL, wants to estimate how much variability there is in job climate among all blue-collar workers. He selects a simple random sample of 12 workers and obtains the following data on a 10-point job climate scale (higher numbers mean a more positive attitude toward the firm).

$$5 \ 6 \ 6 \ 7 \ 6 \ 5 \ 7 \ 6 \ 6 \ 5 \ 7 \ 6$$

a. Set up and interpret an appropriate 90% confidence interval on the standard deviation in job climate among all blue-collar workers.

b. Why must he set up a confidence interval? After all, he knows the sample standard deviation of the 12 blue-collar workers. Explain.

15. A firm wishes to estimate the mean weekly sales in cartons per week. The marketer selects a stratified sample of 25 firms from the low monthly sales stratum and 25 stores from the high monthly sales stratum. Each stratum has 1,000 stores. Shown below are the statistics for the weekly sales data (in cartons) for a randomly selected week.

	Stratum 1	Stratum 2
$\bar{x}$	45	100
s^2	60	150
n	25	25

Set up and interpret an appropriate 90% confidence interval on the mean weekly sales over all stores.

16. A quality control group checks the weight of automobile batteries. One major shipment contained the last two months' production. Since the group believes there is much month-to-month variation, the members select a stratified random sample using each month as a stratum. In January the firm produced 1,000 batteries and in February it produced 800 batteries. Here are the sample statistics:

	January	February
$\bar{x}$	15.0 lb	16.0 lb
s^2	.75	.90
n	30	24

a. Set up and interpret an appropriate 95% confidence interval on the mean weight of the shipment.

b. The engineering specification states that the mean weight of this battery is 15.6 pounds. Has the shipment met weight specification? Explain.

17. COMCEL's quality control department has set the mean impact resistance standard for plastic headphones at 4,660 pounds per square inch (ppsi). It has set the standard deviation in impact resistances at 22 pounds per square inch. During each shift the quality control department takes a sample of 10 phones (about one every

45 minutes) and tests their impact resistance. Shown below are the data for one shift:

Time	Impact Resistances (ppsi)
1	4,650
2	4,650
3	4,600
4	4,700
5	4,650
6	4,650
7	4,700
8	4,650
9	4,600
10	4,650

a. Plot the 10 time-ordered impact resistance data values. Place time into shift on the horizontal axis and impact resistance on the vertical axis. Is the production process stationary?
b. Set up and interpret an appropriate 95% confidence interval on the population mean.
c. Set up and interpret an appropriate 95% confidence interval on the standard deviation.
d. Are both manufacturing standards being met on this shift? Explain.
e. As a manager, what problem solving action should you take?

18. The U.S. Park Service takes a random sample of tourists entering a federal park to determine the mean length of stay (in days) of all tourists. It obtains the following responses:

$$2 \quad 3 \quad 4 \quad 2 \quad 40 \quad 3 \quad 4 \quad 5 \quad 4 \quad 3$$

a. Set up and interpret an appropriate 95% confidence interval on the population mean.
b. Set up and interpret an appropriate 95% confidence interval on the population median.
c. Given the raw data, which approach makes more sense? Explain.

19. The engineering manager has been testing a new brake pad. Because of its cost, the pad must last, on the average, at least 50,000 miles before replacement. The manager selects a simple random sample of 10 cars and fits them with 10 randomly selected new brake pads. The cars are tested in simulated city and highway driving until the pads need replacement. Here are the sample statistics:

$$n = 10$$

$$\bar{x} = 54{,}000 \text{ miles}$$

$$s = 3{,}162 \text{ miles}$$

a. Set up and interpret an appropriate 99% confidence interval.
b. What action should the manager take? Should he or she stay with the present brake pads or switch to the new pads? Explain.
c. Why did you need to construct a confidence interval? After all, the sample mean was much larger than 50,000 miles.

20. A food distributor claims that its frozen diet meals contain no more than a mean of 200 calories per serving. As head of a consumer watchdog group, you question this claim. You select a sample of 20 meals and determine the sample mean and standard deviation for the number of calories in a meal. Following are the sample statistics:

$$n = 20$$

$$\bar{x} = 195 \text{ calories}$$

$$s = 44.72 \text{ calories}$$

   a. Set up and interpret an appropriate 95% confidence interval.
   b. Is the food distributor's claim justified? Explain.

21. In *Swain v. Alabama*, the U.S. Supreme Court compared the fraction of grand jurors who are black (about 12%) with their fraction in the community (about 26%). The Court decided that the difference in percentages was insufficient to create a *prima facie* case. *Prima facie* means that the evidence appears to indicate that discrimination is occurring. If the plaintiffs demonstrate a *prima facie* case, then the burden of proof shifts to the defendant to explain or justify it.

   Assume that blacks formed 12% of the 2,000 jurors over the past 10 years.
   a. Assume for the moment that the population proportion of blacks in the community is unknown. Set up an "at most" 95% confidence interval on the unknown population proportion of blacks in the community based on the 12% figure.
   b. Relying on census data, the court knew that the population proportion of blacks in the community was 26%. Given your answer in part **a**, what could the court have concluded about the potential for racial discrimination in selecting juries?

22. The Securities and Exchange Commission (SEC) requires companies to file annual reports concerning their financial status. Firms cannot audit every account receivable, so the SEC permits firms to estimate the true mean. Suppose the SEC requires that a reported mean be within $5 of the true mean with 95% confidence.

   Given a small sample of 20, firm Y estimates the standard deviation to be $50. What must the total sample size be so that the firm can be 95% confident that the sample mean will be within $5 of the true mean?

23. In *Sears, Roebuck and Co v. City of Ingelwood*, Sears claimed that it had overpaid its sales tax because of an erroneous definition of what constituted an out-of-city sale. The law read that sales made to persons in the city limits were not subject to the tax. To support its claim, Sears selected a random sample of 900 sales slips and found that 330 of them were for sales to persons within the city and thus not subject to the sales tax. Set up a two-sided 95% confidence interval on the population proportion of sales to persons within the city.

24. In an antitrust case, *U.S. v. United Shoe Machinery Corp.*, the government estimated the market share United Shoe held on a variety of machines for the shoe industry. Using a simple random sample of 41 firms, United Shoe's sample proportion of fitting room machines was .41. Set up and interpret a 95% two-sided confidence interval on the population proportion (market dominance) of United Shoe's fitting room machines.

25.

Date: March 17, 1992
To: Cherian Jain, Manager of Marketing Research
From: Bill O'Hara, Vice-President of Marketing
Re: Partial Harrid Survey Data for Four Sales Regions

As you recall, COMCEL commissioned the Harrid Survey Group to conduct a survey in our four sales regions. Harrid took several different random samples from our four sales regions. Among other questions, the firm determined the importance that consumers place on the need to buy American-made phones and the need for FAX capability in mobile car phones. The Harrid Survey Group has sent me some preliminary data. I would like your people to review the data and answer the following questions:

1. How important is buying American-made phone sets to our customers nationally?
2. What proportion of all our customers desire FAX capability?
3. How much variation is there within the Southern Region customers in terms of their desire to *buy American*?

There is no rush since we will be receiving additional data from Harrid in several weeks. I would like to see your report within a month.

    Use Data Base III for your analysis. Your response to Bill O'Hara should include a brief memo and your analysis.

REFERENCES

COCHRAN, WILLIAM G. *Sampling Techniques,* 3rd edition. New York: Wiley, 1977.

MARASCUILO, LEONARD A., and MARYELLEN McSWEENEY. *Nonparametric and Distribution-Free Methods for the Social Sciences.* Pacific Grove, California: Brooks/Cole, 1977.

APPENDIX Relationship Between Type I and Type II Errors

Figure 7.11a (upper curve) shows the sampling distribution of the sample mean for the Milemaster study when the null hypothesis is true—that is, when the population mean is 47,000 miles or less. The α level is 1%. Figure 7.11b (lower curve) shows one of many possible sampling distributions when the alternative hypothesis is true and the population mean is greater than 47,000 miles. We have assumed the population mean is 47,300 miles, and thus we have shifted the lower curve to the right, centered at 47,300 miles.

Suppose the population mean is really 47,300 miles but the sample mean is less than 47,233 miles. According to the upper curve, we should fail to reject the null hypothesis. But the null hypothesis is false—the population mean is really 47,300 miles. The shaded area in the lower curve represents the chance of making a Type II error if the population mean is 47,300 miles.

Now suppose we increase the probability of making a Type I error. This will shift the critical value in the upper curve to the left. This will also reduce the shaded area in the lower curve. Thus the chance of making a Type II error becomes smaller. Figure 7.12 shows the chance of making a Type II error for an α level of 10%.

This is the logic. As we increase the rejection region in the upper curve (Figure 7.12a), we increase the chance of rejecting the null hypothesis. However, the only way to make a

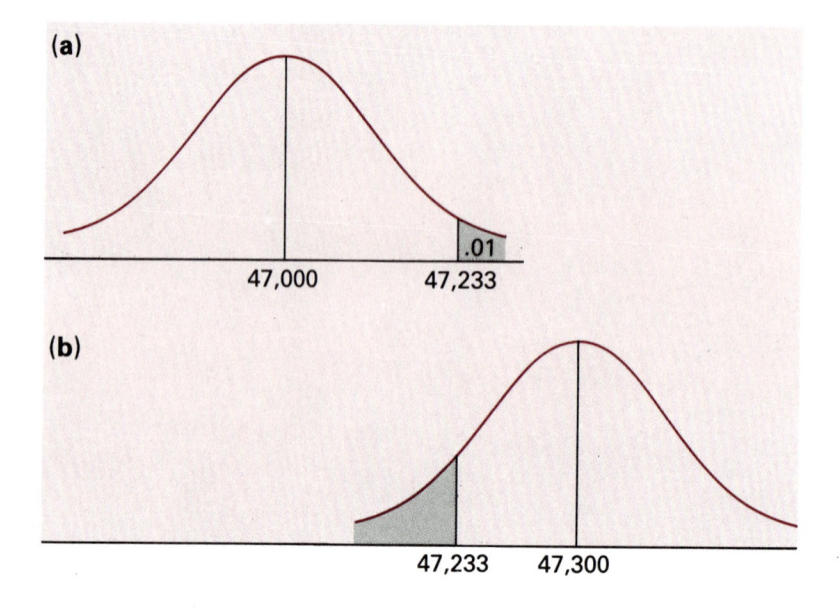

FIGURE 7.11   Type II Error for $\alpha = .01$

FIGURE 7.12 Type II Error for $\alpha = .10$

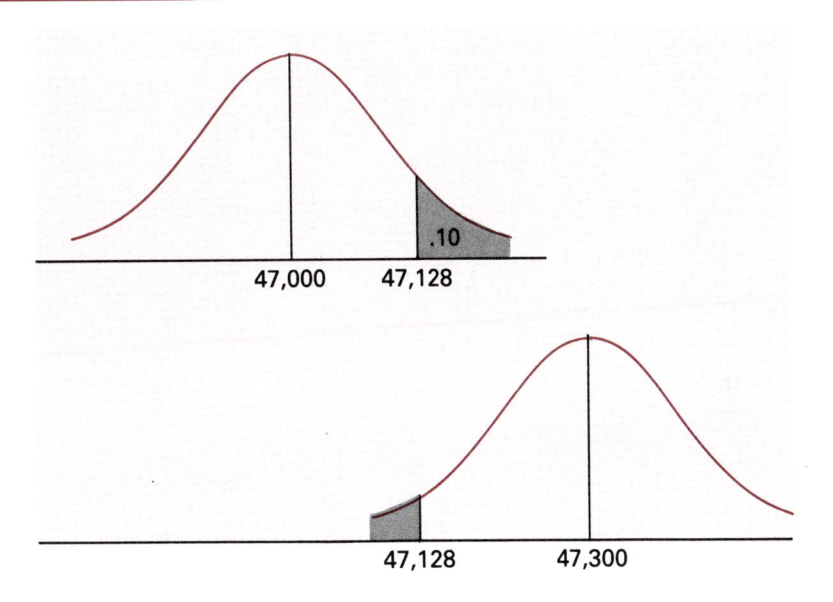

Type II error is *not* to reject the null hypothesis. Thus, by increasing the chance of rejecting the null hypothesis, we reduce the probability of making a Type II error.

Alternatively, as we increase the chance of making a Type I error, the critical value drops from 47,233 miles to 47,128 miles. The critical value shifts to the left. This reduces the fail-to-reject region in the lower curve (Figure 7.12b), thereby reducing the probability of making a Type II error.

We can also reduce the chance of making a Type II error by increasing the sample size. Figure 7.13 shows the sampling distribution for the Milemaster study when the null

FIGURE 7.13 Impact of Sample Size on the Type II Error

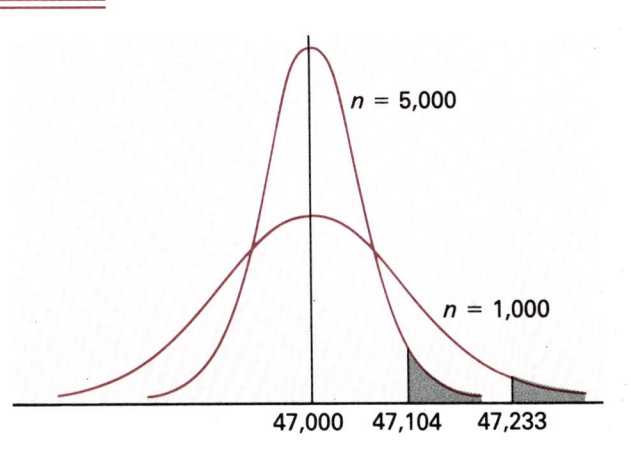

hypothesis is true for samples of size 1,000 and 5,000 tires. The region of rejection has an area of .01 for both sampling distributions. However, the sampling distribution for samples of 5,000 tires has the smaller estimated standard error. Thus its critical value will be less than for the sampling distribution for samples of 1,000.

Now assume that the population mean is still 47,300 miles. By shifting the critical value in the $n = 5,000$ curve to the left, we decrease the probability of making a Type II error.

In summary:

1. Increasing the probability of making a Type I error reduces the probability of making a Type II error.
2. For a constant α level, increasing the sample size reduces the probability of making a Type II error.

8

Making Inferences About Two Populations

8.1 Improving departmental performance
8.2 Comparing two populations of data
   Are both populations normal?
   Do both populations have the same mean?
   Transforming the data
   Do both populations have the same variance?
   Summary of data exploration principles
8.3 Inferences on the difference between two population means
   Sampling distribution of the difference between two sample means
   Estimated standard error of the difference between two sample means
   A two-sample t-based confidence interval
   Reducing the margin of error
   Beyond the normality and equal variance assumptions
8.4 Inferences on the difference between two population proportions
8.5 A nonparametric confidence interval for the difference between two population medians
   Confidence interval on the difference between two medians
   Interpretation of Mann-Whitney confidence intervals
   Logic behind the Mann-Whitney method
8.6 Inferences on two population variances for normal populations
   Sampling distribution of the variance ratio
   Constructing a confidence interval for the variance ratio
8.7 A nonparametric method for comparing two population variabilities
   Steps in the Mood test
8.8 Key ideas and overview
Chapter 8 Questions
Chapter 8 Application Problems

CHAPTER OUTLINE

COMCEL Interoffice Communication

Date: November 14, 1992
To: Sarah Teman, Manager of Operation
From: Howard Bright, Plant Manager
Re: Results of labor cost study at Norcross plant

In a conversation we had some months ago, you mentioned a study you were conducting to reduce unit labor costs. I believe you said that five work groups were assigned to a team-building workshop and five to a creative methods workshop. You said you would measure the success by comparing the cost of producing mobile phones six months after the workshops. I am anxious to know the results of your study. Please send an update on its progress.

I know you have training in statistics, but sample sizes of only five teams seem pretty small. Are you going to be able to make a judgment on the value of the two methods based on these small samples? And, if one method reduces labor costs more than another, how can you be sure that the difference is due to the difference between the workshops and not some other factor that has nothing to do with the study?

I look forward to receiving your update.

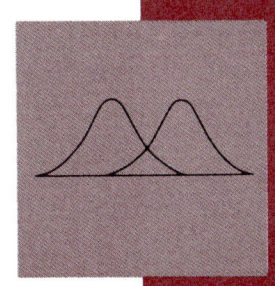

8.1 Improving Departmental Performance

Effective managers not only solve disturbance problems, but also initiate improvement projects. We showed how descriptive statistics (see Chapters 2 and 3) and probability models (see Chapter 5) are important in sensing and solving disturbance problems. A disturbance problem is a gap between a department's previous, expected, or budgeted performance levels and its present performance levels. Managers must eliminate the gap. For example, if a department experiences a sudden and dramatic decrease in productivity, a manager must diagnose the problem's causes and take corrective action to solve the problem permanently. Managers must put out brush fires whenever they occur.

However, a manager's ability to solve disturbance problems does not improve the firm's performance levels. It only restores service or productivity levels to previous levels. Consider this analogy. A hotel manager sees smoke, gets a fire extinguisher, and puts out the fire. Extinguishing the fire is important but it does not improve the hotel's service.

In order to be able to identify potential improvement projects, managers must be innovative and vigilant. One effective way is to use Pounds's *extra-organizational strategy* (see Chapter 1). Trade journals, competitors, other divisions within the firm, or professional conferences can sometimes suggest potential improvement projects. Questions regarding performance should be asked regularly. Is there a difference between our performance and that of our East Coast operations? Should we adopt competitor's practices? Should we adopt a new procedure seen at a trade show? How do we compare with published industry-wide performance levels?

When groups differ, the natural follow-up question is *why*. Asking that question is an essential step in identifying possible improvement projects. In this chapter we will compare the population means, medians, or variances of two groups. By comparing differences between groups statistically, we should be able to answer many of these questions.

8.2 Comparing Two Populations of Data

How should we compare two populations of data? How different are they? Are there differences between their shapes, means, or variances? In short, what is different?

Begin by exploring sample data. Draw stem-and-leaf displays or box plots. Graph the data before doing statistical analysis. Let the data speak. Look for outliers or different patterns in the two samples of data. Then apply confidence interval methods. By the end of this section you should be able to:

1. use stem-and-leaf displays or box plots to explore differences between the shapes, means, or variances of two samples of numbers;
2. transform the two samples of data to normalize the distributions and to equalize the variances; and

3. explain why the square root and logarithmic transformations may make a highly skewed population distribution more normal shaped.

Are Both Populations Normal?

To compare two populations of data, we start by drawing stem-and-leaf displays. Figure 8.1 shows a sample of quick ratios—current assets minus inventories divided by current liabilities—for manufacturing firms from two regions of the country. Are there any differences?

The data are not perfectly bell-shaped, nor should we expect them to be. Remember the data are only samples from two populations. Even if both populations were normal, we would not expect each sample to be *perfectly* bell-shaped. However, the samples should be near normal, as they are.

What can we conclude from Figure 8.1? Subject to statistical verification, there are no differences between the quick ratios of firms in the Northeast and firms in the Southeast.

Figure 8.2 on page 392 shows a sample of list prices for ball-point pens in two cities. Note that the two data sets have similar shapes, means, and variances. However, neither sample is normally distributed; both have outliers.

Why is it important that the population distributions be near normal? Recall that in constructing confidence intervals on the mean, we assume that either the population is normal or the sampling distribution of the sample mean is normal. For sample sizes greater than 30, the latter will be true unless the population is highly skewed. For highly skewed distributions, consider using *nonparametric* methods to compare population medians (Section 8.5) and population variabilities (Section 8.7). Remember first to construct stem-and-leaf displays of samples to check the population shapes before analyzing the data.

FIGURE 8.1 Stem-and-Leaf Displays of Quick Ratios from Firms in Two Regions

```
          Northeast
             9
             8
       9     7
       3     5     7
       1     2     4
      ---   ---   ---
       1.    2.    3.

          Southeast
             7
             5
             4     4
       6     3     3
       4     1     2
      ---   ---   ---
       1.    2.    3.
```

FIGURE 8.2   Two Similar Highly Skewed Groups

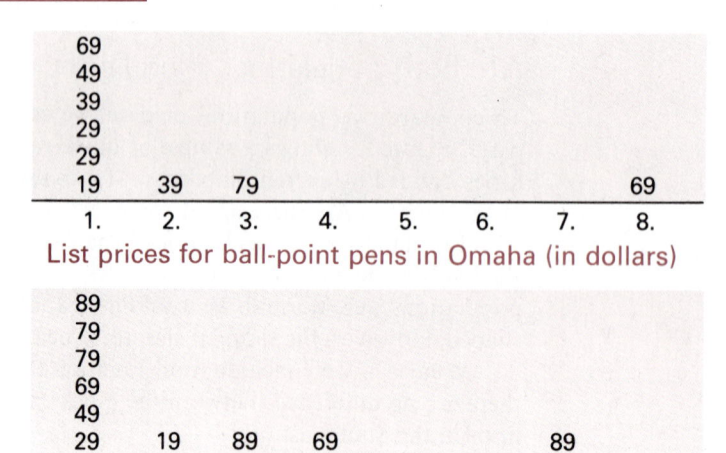

```
    69
    49
    39
    29
    29
    19    39    79                              69
─────────────────────────────────────────────────
    1.    2.    3.    4.    5.    6.    7.    8.
```
List prices for ball-point pens in Omaha (in dollars)

```
    89
    79
    79
    69
    49
    29    19    89    69                89
─────────────────────────────────────────────────
    1.    2.    3.    4.    5.    6.    7.    8.
```
List prices for ball-point pens in Columbus (in dollars)

Do Both Populations Have the Same Mean?

Potential improvement projects are often initiated by asking comparative questions, such as

1. Do the mean performances of the two groups differ?
2. If so, which group does better and why?

The confidence interval methods in this chapter that compare two population means assume that these populations have the same variances and are normally distributed. Figure 8.3 illustrates two sample data sets where these

FIGURE 8.3   Two Normally Distributed Groups with Different Means

```
                      8
                      7
                      7
                8     4
          1     2     2     1     6
─────────────────────────────────────────
          1.    2.    3.    4.    5.
```
Percentage reduction in unit labor cost for group 1

```
                            9
                            8
                            5
                            4     5
                5     2     2     1     9
─────────────────────────────────────────────
    1.    2.    3.    4.    5.    6.    7.
```
Percentage reduction in unit labor cost for group 2

FIGURE 8.4   Two Nonnormally Distributed Groups with Different Means and Variances

```
                    8
                    6
                    5
                    4
                    3   7
                    3   4
          3         2   2       8   1
          2         1   1       1   1   5
         ___       ___ ___     ___ ___ ___
          1.        2.  3.      4.  5.  6.
```
Percentage sales increase from previous year for group 1

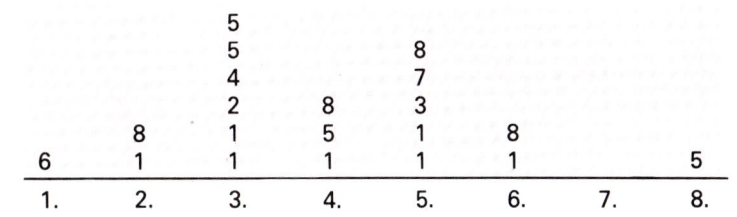

```
                    5
                    5           8
                    4           7
                    2       8   3
              8     1   5   1       8
      6       1     1   1   1   1           5
     ___     ___   ___ ___ ___ ___ ___     ___
      1.      2.    3.  4.  5.  6.  7.      8.
```
Percentage sales increase from previous year for group 2

assumptions are valid. Both data sets have the same near-normal shape and variance. Thus we can use the methods developed in Section 8.3 to determine whether the mean population performance levels differ.

What should we do when sample data suggest that the population shapes and variances differ? Consider the two data sets in Figure 8.4. The stem-and-leaf displays show that the samples differ markedly. We conclude that neither population distribution is normal. The means and variances are probably also different. The firms in the upper display have a lower sample mean sales increase, and the firms in the lower display have a greater variance.

As explained earlier, confidence intervals on the difference between two population means assume that both populations have normal (or near-normal) shapes and the same (or nearly the same) variances. Clearly, this is not true in Figure 8.4. What can we do? First, we can ignore the assumptions and apply the method described in Section 8.3. For highly skewed data this is risky since our inferences may not be valid. There are two other approaches to consider:

1. We could *transform* the data to make the population shapes more normal and the variances more equal. Then we could use the confidence interval method developed in Section 8.3.
2. If a transformation fails to make the population shapes near normal, we can use the *nonparametric* method developed in Section 8.5.

Transforming the Data

Transforming the data simply means changing the scale of measurement. Just as dividing each number by 12 in changing from feet to inches is a transformation, so is adding 10 to each data value a transformation. However, neither transformation will make a distribution more normal. Both transformations simply shift the distribution, but do not change its shape or its variance. This is seen readily in Figure 8.5.

In order to make the shapes more normal and help equalize their variances, we can use the square root and logarithm transformations. Consider these transformations when the data are highly skewed and consist only of positive numbers.*

In Table 8.1, we have used the square root transformation to rescale the two sets of sample data on percentage sales increase in Figure 8.4. Figure 8.6 presents the stem-and-leaf displays for the transformed data sets. Compare these with the displays in Figure 8.4. Note that both sample distributions are *more* normal. Also the variances are *more* alike. Now we will be able to use the confidence interval method in Section 8.3 on the *transformed* data to determine whether the means of the two transformed populations differ.

Why does the square root transformation work? The square roots of numbers between 0 and 1 are larger than the original raw values, and the square roots of numbers greater than 1 are smaller than the original raw values. In other words, data values in each tail are drawn toward the mean of the transformed data. We illustrate this feature in Table 8.2 on page 396. This transformation results in a more symmetrically shaped distribution.

The square root transformation works well when a distribution is skewed, but it is not a cure-all. The transformation may not normalize the data when there are outliers. Consider the size of contract award data in Table 8.3. Note that contracts 1 and 6 are outliers. Contract 1 is only about one-hundredth as large as the middle four contracts. Contract 6 is about 100 times larger than the middle four data values. Even after taking square roots, contracts 1 and 6 are still outliers. When one or more data values are outliers, consider using a *logarithmic base 10* transformation.

The logarithm base 10 (log base 10) of a number is the exponent or the power to which 10 must be raised to equal the given number. For example, 3 is

FIGURE 8.5   Transformation by Adding 10

9				9			
9				9			
7				7			
4	6			4	6		
2	3	2	1	2	3	2	1
1	2	3	4	11	12	13	14

Original data   Original data + 10

*The logarithm or the square root of a negative number is undefined.

Table 8.1

Square Root Transformation

Upper Stem-and-Leaf Display		Lower Stem-and-Leaf Display	
Original Data	Square Root Transformed	Original Data	Square Root Transformed
1.2	1.10	1.6	1.26
1.3	1.14	2.1	1.45
2.1	1.45	2.8	1.67
2.2	1.48	3.1	1.76
2.3	1.52	3.1	1.76
2.3	1.52	3.2	1.79
2.4	1.55	3.4	1.84
2.5	1.58	3.5	1.87
2.6	1.61	3.5	1.87
2.8	1.67	4.1	2.02
3.1	1.76	4.5	2.12
3.2	1.79	4.8	2.19
3.4	1.84	5.1	2.26
3.7	1.92	5.1	2.26
4.1	2.02	5.3	2.30
4.8	2.19	5.7	2.39
5.1	2.26	5.8	2.41
5.1	2.26	6.1	2.47
6.1	2.47	6.8	2.61
6.5	2.55	8.5	2.92

FIGURE 8.6 Stem-and-Leaf Displays After Square Root Transformation

		Group 1				Group 2		
		92						
		84					47	
		79					41	
		76				87	39	
		67				87	30	
		61	47			84	26	
48		58	26			79	26	
45		55	26			76	19	
14		52	19		45	76	12	92
10		52	02	55	26	67	02	61
1		1	2	2	1	1	2	2

Square root of the percentage sales increase from previous year

Table 8.2

Impact of Square Root Transformation on Data Distribution

Original Data	Square Root Transformed Data	
.25	.50	Shift upward
1.85	1.36	
2.50	1.58	
3.50	1.87	
8.00	2.83	Shift downward

Table 8.3

Size of Contracts Awarded to COMCEL

Contract	Size ($)	Square Root	Log Base 10
1	1,000	31.62	3.00
2	75,000	273.86	4.88
3	75,000	273.86	4.88
4	100,000	316.23	5.00
5	150,000	387.30	5.18
6	10,000,000	3,162.28	7.00

the logarithm of 1,000 to the base 10 because 10 raised to the power 3 equals 1,000.

Table 8.3 shows that a data set transformed by the log base 10 has no outliers. While the log base 10 transformation is generally effective, there may be times when other transformations should be considered. A readable source for other transformations is Siegel's *Statistics and Data Analysis* (1988).

Do Both Populations Have the Same Variance?

Managers are most often concerned about mean performance. However, when two groups or products have the same mean performance, managers want to know:

1. Do the two groups' variances differ?
2. If so, which group has the more consistent or less variable performance?
3. What accounts for a group's higher variance?

Table 8.4 contains the average collection period—receivables divided by mean sales per day—for a sample of firms from two industries. Both industries have about the same average collection period, 33.4 days. However, industry A firms exhibit more variance with the average collection period varying from 11 to 51 days. The average collection period for industry B firms varies from 22 to 41 days. Figure 8.7 highlights the differences between the variances for the two industries.

Table 8.4

Data Sets with the Same Mean but Different Variances

	Industry A	Industry B
	11	22
	22	31
	24	31
	32	32
	33	33
	34	33
	35	35
	36	35
	43	36
	47	38
	51	41
Mean	33.5 days	33.4 days

FIGURE 8.7 Two Normally Distributed Data Sets with Different Variances

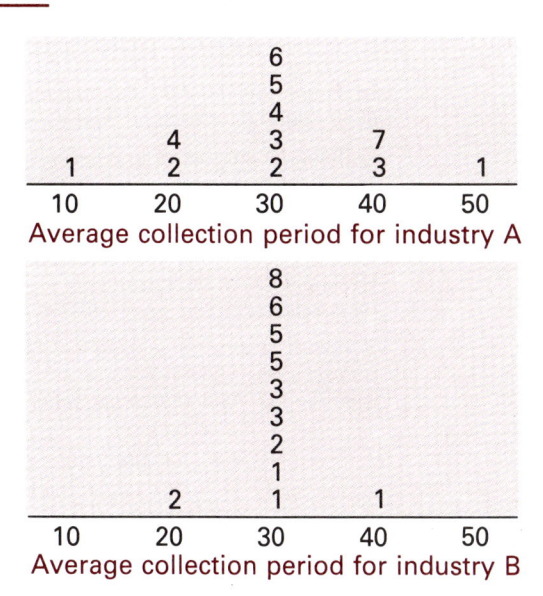

```
                        6
                        5
                        4
                4       3       7
        1       2       2       3       1
        ────────────────────────────────────
        10      20      30      40      50
        Average collection period for industry A

                        8
                        6
                        5
                        5
                        3
                        3
                        2
                        1
                2       1       1
        ────────────────────────────────────
        10      20      30      40      50
        Average collection period for industry B
```

If the sample data are near normal (as in Figure 8.7), we use the method of constructing confidence intervals in Section 8.6 to determine if the variances of the two populations are the same. When the sample data are highly skewed and a square root or log base 10 transformation does not work, we use the nonparametric method in Section 8.7.

Summary of Data Exploration Principles

We summarize the approach to comparing different populations with the following principles:

1. Use stem-and-leaf displays or box plots to compare the sample data visually. Are the samples normally distributed? If one or both distributions are highly skewed or contain outliers, apply a square root or log base 10 transformation. Transformations may make the data more symmetric.
2. Are the two population means the same? If the original or transformed sample data are near normal, use the method in Section 8.3 to construct confidence intervals and determine whether the two population means are the same. If the transformed sample data are still highly skewed, use the nonparametric method in Section 8.5.
3. Are the two population variances the same? If the original or transformed sample data are near normal, use the method in Section 8.6 to determine whether the two population variances are the same. If the transformed data are still highly skewed, use the nonparametric method in Section 8.7.

SECTION 8.2 EXERCISES

1. In comparing two data sets, managers compare their shapes, centers, and spreads. Give examples of each of these three distribution characteristics.
2. Explain the purpose of transforming data.
3. Suppose the following values were typical of a data set: {1.2, .5, 0, −.5, −1}.
   a. Would the log transform be useful for these data? Why?
   b. Would the square root transform be useful? Why?
4. Explain why it is important to explore the data with stem-and-leaf displays and box plots before selecting an estimation method.
5. You wish to construct a confidence interval on the population size of loans for used cars at the Jax Federal Savings and Loan. Here is a random sample of used-car loans from the Jax Federal loan portfolio.

$3,000	$4,200	$4,800	$6,000
$3,350	$4,500	$5,450	$6,500
$3,500	$4,500	$5,700	$8,000
$3,500	$4,800	$5,800	$13,500
$4,050	$4,800	$5,850	$15,500

   a. Why is it necessary to transform the data set before constructing a confidence interval?
   b. Use a square root transform and a log base 10 transform. Which transform appears to be better at normalizing the data?
6. Shown are loan portfolios of two savings and loans in Kansas City. Without

computing descriptive statistics, do there appear to be any differences between the distribution shapes, means, or variances of the two portfolios?

	950				
	900				
	875				
	650		810		960
	500		800		900
	350		400		400
450	150	900	275	800	175
250	100	250	100	200	150
3,000	4,000	5,000	3,000	4,000	5,000

8.3 Inferences on the Difference Between Two Population Means

When managers look at two groups or two products, they compare differences in performance, service level, or quality. For example, a manager asks: "Which group has a better mean performance—Los Angeles or Minneapolis?" or, "Does our product have, on the average, fewer breakdowns than that of our major competitor?" Remember, managers must compare the present level of performance, service, or quality to previous levels or to the levels of others. Major deviations signal the onset of a problem or an opportunity.

Sometimes we are interested only in whether two *sample* means differ. Here exploratory data analysis provides us with all the information. More often, we are interested in the populations from which the samples were taken. Drawing upon Chapter 7, we will set up a confidence interval on the difference between two population means. Even here, exploratory data analysis helps to assess the underlying assumptions of the confidence interval method. We assume that while the means of two population distributions may differ, the population distributions are near normal and the population variances are the same or nearly the same. By the end of this section you should be able to:

1. set up a confidence interval on the difference between two population means;
2. interpret the confidence interval and determine if two population means differ beyond mere sampling variability; and
3. explain how a confidence interval on the difference between two population means is an extension of a confidence interval on one population mean.

We introduce confidence intervals on the difference between two population means in the following example.

EXAMPLE: COMCEL STUDY OF REDUCING UNIT LABOR COSTS
According to published industry figures, work teams at COMCEL's Norcross plant have not been as successful in reducing unit labor costs as have other companies. Recently the manufacturing manager designed two cost reduction programs. Given here are her planned changes.

1. Improve team building to reduce labor costs—TB workshop.
2. Teach creativity methods that will help work groups to reduce labor costs—CM workshop.

Table 8.5 shows the results of the study.

Table 8.5

Results of Planned Change Study to Reduce Unit Labor Costs

	Factor: Type of Workshop	
	TB Workshop	CM Workshop
	$3.05	$4.12
	3.10	4.13
	3.13	4.21
	3.14	4.21
	3.18	4.22
	3.22	4.24
	3.22	4.26
	3.24	4.27
	3.29	4.27
	3.32	4.36
$\bar{x}$	$3.19	$4.23
s	$ .085	$ .070
s^2	.0072	.0049

Dependent variable: Reduction in unit labor cost from January to June

While the two groups have different sample means, do the population means differ? A formal statistical analysis begins by determining how different the two sample means are since we use the sample means to estimate the population means. The difference between the sample means is

$$\$4.23 - \$3.19 = \$1.04$$

Does a difference of $1.04 between the sample means suggest that the two population means differ? Or, is the $1.04 difference so small that it can be attributed to sampling variability?

Sampling Distribution of the Difference Between Two Sample Means

The difference between the sample means in the planned change study was $1.04. What would happen if we repeated the COMCEL study many times? The sample means for both treatments would change. Thus, the difference between the two sample means would vary with each study. Would the histogram of the difference between the two sample means be normal shaped? If we assume that

FIGURE 8.8 Sampling Distribution of the Difference Between Two Sample Means

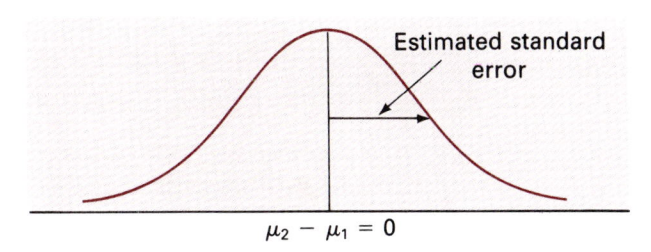

Estimated standard error

$\mu_2 - \mu_1 = 0$

the workshops are equally effective in reducing costs, what would the mean of the histogram equal? Please think about these questions before reading on.

The central limit theorem tells us that the histogram of differences would be normally distributed. Figure 8.8 depicts the histogram. Note that the mean of the distribution of differences in Figure 8.8 is 0.

When there is no difference between the two training methods for *all* the work teams, the mean of the sampling distribution is 0. Now the critical question is: How likely is an observed difference of $1.04—the sample difference—when the mean of the distribution is 0? To answer that question we must determine the estimated standard error of the difference between the two sample means—the standard deviation of the distribution in Figure 8.8.

Estimated Standard Error of the Difference Between Two Sample Means

From Chapter 7 the estimated standard error of the sample mean is $\sqrt{s^2/n}$. Now we extend the concept of the estimated standard error to the difference between two sample means *when the population variances are unknown but assumed to be equal*. Expression (8.1) is the estimated standard error of the difference between two sample means. Expression (8.2) is the pooled variance, s_p^2.

$$\sqrt{\frac{s_p^2}{n_1} + \frac{s_p^2}{n_2}} \tag{8.1}$$

$$s_p^2 = \frac{(n_1 - 1)s_1^2 + (n_2 - 1)s_2^2}{n_1 + n_2 - 2} \tag{8.2}$$

For equal sample sizes, expression (8.2) is simply the mean of the two sample variances.

For the COMCEL data, the pooled variance is

$$s_p^2 = \frac{(10 - 1)(.0072) + (10 - 1)(.0049)}{18} = .0061$$

From expression (8.1), the estimated standard error is

$$\sqrt{\frac{.0061}{10} + \frac{.0061}{10}} = \$.035$$

A Two-Sample t-Based Confidence Interval

We will build on what we already know from Chapter 7. We lay out, side by side, confidence intervals on one and two population means. We can use expression (8.3) to construct two-sided confidence intervals on the difference between two population means.

On One Population Mean	On Two Population Means
$\bar{x} \pm$ Margin of error	$\bar{x}_2 - \bar{x}_1 \pm$ Margin of error
$\bar{x} \pm ts\sqrt{\dfrac{1}{n}}$	$\bar{x}_2 - \bar{x}_1 \pm ts_p\sqrt{\dfrac{1}{n_1} + \dfrac{1}{n_2}}$

$$\bar{x}_2 - \bar{x}_1 \pm ts_p\sqrt{\frac{1}{n_1} + \frac{1}{n_2}} \tag{8.3}$$

Again, the margin of error is simply the *t*-value times the estimated standard error. In Chapter 7 the degrees of freedom for the *t*-value were $(n - 1)$. Since we pooled the sample variances, we also pool the degrees of freedom. The degrees of freedom are $(n_1 - 1) + (n_2 - 1) = n_1 + n_2 - 2$.

Next, we construct a two-sided 95% confidence interval for the difference between the two population means. Ninety-five percent of such intervals will contain the true difference between two population means.

Before constructing the interval, we must state our assumptions.

ASSUMPTION 1: The 20 work groups are a simple random sample taken from the Norcross target population.

ASSUMPTION 2: The sampling distribution of the difference between two sample means is normally distributed.

ASSUMPTION 3: We assume that the variances of the two populations are equal (or nearly so).

Assumption 1 is met because the project manager used randomization. Figure 8.9 verifies Assumption 2. The data are near-normal shaped. Thus the populations are probably near normally distributed. The sample variances (see Table 8.5), .0072 and .0049, verify Assumption 3.

For ease of interpretation, always subtract the smaller sample mean from the larger sample mean when computing the difference. Thus, the two-sided 95%

Chapter 8 Making Inferences About Two Populations

FIGURE 8.9 Stem-and-Leaf Displays for Sample Data for Team Building and Creative Methods Workshops

Team Building Workshop

```
              18   29
              14   24
              13   22
     05       10   22    32
     3.   3.  3.   3.
```
Reduction in unit labor cost

Creative Methods Workshop

```
                        27
                        27
                        26
                        24
                        22
                   13   21
                   12   21   36
              4.   4.  4.   4.
```
Reduction in unit labor cost

confidence interval is obtained:

($4.23 − $3.19) ± t(95%, 18 degrees of freedom)(Estimated standard error)

Lower limit: $1.04 − (2.101)($.035) = $.97
Upper limit: $1.04 + (2.101)($.035) = $1.11

There are two important things to notice about the confidence interval. First, since it does not include 0, there is a difference between the two *population* means, indicating that one training method is more effective in reducing unit labor costs. Second, it is the creative method workshop that is better. We are 95% confident that the creative training population mean minus the team building training population mean is between $.97 and $1.11. In other words, creativity training reduces unit labor cost by between $.97 and $1.11 more than team building training.

A second way to draw the same conclusion is to look at the estimated standard error of $.035. It measures the impact of all factors *except* training on the reduction in unit labor cost. Think of $.035 or 3.5 cents as the sampling error or variability. However, the difference between the means for the two training methods is $1.04, which is almost 30 times as large as the sampling variability. Thus we are 95% confident that there is a difference between the two population mean unit labor cost reductions.

There is yet a third way to draw the same conclusion. If the training methods were equally effective, then from Figure 8.8, the mean of the sampling distribution should be 0. That is, 95% of all differences between the two sample means should be within ±2 standard deviations of 0. Two standard deviations equal 2 · $.035 or $.07. But the difference between sample means is $1.04, which is well outside the two standard deviations range. In short, there is a difference between the two population means.

COMCEL is reasonably certain that creativity training is better than team building training. However, COMCEL should ask: "What other ways besides worker training would be even more effective in reducing unit labor cost?" Remember, managers must seek or design different ideas to evaluate. Avoid testing merely two or three similar approaches.

Consider another example.

EXAMPLE: GRILLING OR BROILING? Which method of preparing burgers is better? A market research firm randomly selects 30 people to taste burgers prepared by either grilling or broiling. The 30 people are randomly divided into two groups of 15. The research firm randomly assigns each group of 15 to the grill or broil test group. The people must rate the burger's tastiness on the following scale:

1	2	3	4	5
	Moderately	No	Moderately	
Terrible	terrible	taste	tasty	Tasty

Table 8.6 shows the data from the one-factor, two-level, completely random study. Set up a 90% confidence interval on the difference between the two population mean levels of tastiness.

Note that the two sample variances are nearly equal. The stem-and-leaf displays in Figure 8.10 suggest that the population distributions for tastiness for both cooking methods are near normal. The central limit theorem assures us that the sampling distribution of the difference between sample means will therefore be normal.

From expression (8.2), the pooled variance is

$$s_p^2 = \frac{(n_1 - 1)s_1^2 + (n_2 - 1)s_2^2}{n_1 + n_2 - 2}$$

$$= \frac{(15 - 1)(.96) + (15 - 1)(.69)}{15 + 15 - 2}$$

$$= .825$$

The estimated standard error is

$$\sqrt{\frac{s_p^2}{n_1} + \frac{s_p^2}{n_2}} = \sqrt{\frac{.825}{15} + \frac{.825}{15}}$$

$$= .332$$

Chapter 8 Making Inferences About Two Populations

Table 8.6
Taste Study Data

	Broil Method	Grill Method
	1	2
	2	2
	3	3
	3	3
	3	3
	3	3
	3	3
	3	3
	4	4
	4	4
	4	4
	4	4
	4	4
	4	4
	5	5
$\bar{x}$	3.33	3.40
s	.98	.83
s^2	.96	.69

FIGURE 8.10 Stem-and-Leaf Displays for Burger Study Data

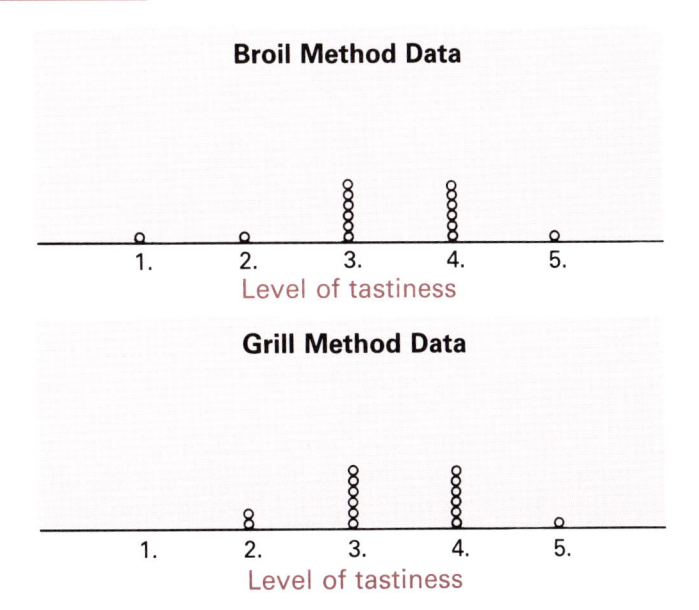

Broil Method Data

Grill Method Data

Level of tastiness

A two-sided 90% confidence interval on the difference between the two population means is obtained as

$$3.40 - 3.33 \pm t(90\%, 28 \text{ degrees of freedom})(\text{Estimated standard error})$$

Lower limit: $.07 - (1.701)(.332) = -.49$
Upper limit: $.07 + (1.701)(.332) = +.63$

Since the interval includes 0, we cannot conclude that the two population mean tastiness levels are different. In other words, there is *no statistically significant* difference in tastiness between grilling and broiling burgers.

Here is the logic. The difference between sample means of .07 is less than the estimated standard error of .332. There is not enough evidence to conclude with 90% confidence that the two population means really differ.

The study results are inconclusive. Since the confidence interval contains both positive and negative values, grilling could be preferred to broiling, broiling to grilling, or there could be no difference. The problem is that while one mean could be larger than the other, the margin of error is so large that we cannot detect it.

Reducing the Margin of Error

Increasing the sample size reduces the estimated standard error, as we can see from expression (8.1). Increasing the sample size also reduces the *t*-value due to the increasing degrees of freedom. The net effect is to reduce the margin of error. As the margin of error shrinks, the confidence interval shrinks, making it less likely that 0 will be in the interval. Thus we are more likely to detect any difference between population means. In summary, increasing the sample size makes it more likely to find statistically significant differences between two population means.

Beyond the Normality and Equal Variance Assumptions

Thus far we have assumed that the two population distributions are near normal with near equal variances. When the sample variances indicate that one population variance may be several times as large as the other or the stem-and-leaf displays indicate highly skewed populations, there are two options:

1. Transform the raw data by taking the square root or log base 10. If both distributions become more symmetric and the variances are nearly equal, use expression (8.3) on the transformed data to construct a confidence interval.
2. If the sample sizes are small and the transformations do not normalize the data and equalize the variances, use the nonparametric method in Section 8.5.

Chapter 8   Making Inferences About Two Populations

SECTION 8.3 EXERCISES

1. t-Based confidence intervals on the difference between two population means are based on the assumption that the populations are normally distributed. Explain how a box plot can be used to judge whether this assumption holds.

2. Assume that the following data sets were the result of an experiment.

Experimental Group	Control Group
17, 17, 18, 22, 23, 25, 26, 28, 30, 30, 31, 33, 41, 52, 65	12, 22, 22, 32, 33, 38, 42, 43, 43, 44, 53, 54, 55, 56, 68

   a. Prepare stem-and-leaf displays to determine the characteristics of the two data sets.
   b. Does it appear that both groups could have been drawn from normal populations? Explain.
   c. Apply a square root transformation to the data and construct new displays for the transformed data. Does the transformation make the data more normal shaped?

3. Under what circumstances should you pool the variances of two samples when estimating the difference between two population means?

4. Given: $s_1^2 = 5$ $s_2^2 = 8$
   $n_1 = 10$ $n_2 = 12$
   Compute a pooled estimate of the common population variance and an estimate of the standard error of the difference of means.

5. An experiment was performed using an experimental (e) group and a control (c) group. The results are shown below.

   $n_e = 12$ $n_c = 8$
   $\bar{x}_e = 14$ $\bar{x}_c = 10$
   $s_e^2 = 25$ $s_c^2 = 36$

   a. Pool the sample variances to estimate the common population variance.
   b. How many degrees of freedom are there for the pooled sample variance?
   c. Use the results of part **a** to compute the estimated standard error.
   d. Construct a 95% confidence interval on the difference between population means.
   e. Does it appear from your confidence interval that there is a difference between the population means of the experimental and the control groups? Explain.
   f. What assumptions did you make in constructing your confidence interval?

6. Consider the following two data sets:

Group 1	Group 2
1, 2, 2, 3, 3, 3, 4, 5	3, 4, 5, 5, 6, 6, 7, 9

a. Calculate the means and variances for the two samples.
b. Calculate a pooled variance estimate for the standard error.
c. Construct a 90% confidence interval for the difference between population means. Does it appear that the population means are different?

7. A company decides to compare the mean lives of two brands of transistors. The company selects 50 transistors of each brand and measures the life in hours. The results are shown below.

$$\bar{x}_1 = 26.5 \text{ hours} \qquad \bar{x}_2 = 32.5 \text{ hours}$$
$$s_1^2 = 136 \qquad s_2^2 = 144$$

a. Construct a 95% confidence interval on the difference between the two population means.
b. Based on the confidence interval, does it appear that one brand of transistors lasts longer than the other?

8. An overnight package express service wants to determine if there is any significant difference in the numbers of packages delivered per day between experienced and novice drivers. It randomly selects one experienced driver and one novice driver. For each operator, the firm selects a random sample of 10 days over the past quarter. Given are the descriptive data for the 10 days.

Experienced Operator	Novice Operator
$n_1 = 10$	$n_2 = 10$
$\bar{x}_1 = 35$ packages	$\bar{x}_2 = 31$ packages
$s_1^2 = 17$	$s_2^2 = 19$

At the 99% level of confidence can we find a statistically significant difference between experienced and novice operators in the number of packages delivered per day? Explain.

9. The Environmental Protection Agency (EPA) routinely checks to ensure that Anderson Metals is treating its toxic waste before discharging it into the Ohio River. The EPA collects six samples of water upstream from the plant and six samples of water downstream from the plant. It runs a bacteria count on the 12 samples. Here are the data.

Downstream Data	Upstream Data
30	30
28	29
30	29
30	30
32	30
30	31

a. Construct a 90% confidence interval on the difference in the population mean bacteria counts.
b. Does the confidence interval indicate that Anderson Metals is still treating its toxic waste?

10. Do firms with sales under 25 million dollars that do strategic planning have higher returns on total assets—net income after taxes divided by total assets—than firms that do not do strategic planning? We select a random sample of 10 firms and obtain the following descriptive data:

Strategic Planning	No Strategic Planning
$n_1 = 5$	$n_2 = 5$
$\bar{x}_1 = 10\%$	$\bar{x}_2 = 6\%$
$s_1^2 = 1.2$	$s_2^2 = 1.0$

a. Construct a 95% confidence interval on the difference between the two population means.
b. Do firms that do strategic planning have higher returns on assets than firms that do not do strategic planning? Explain.

8.4 Inferences on the Difference Between Two Population Proportions

In Section 7.7 we constructed confidence intervals on an unknown population proportion. We extend that idea to intervals on the difference between two population proportions. Such confidence intervals are useful in answering questions such as: "Is the proportion of highly motivated workers the same in two plants?" or "Has our program to equalize the proportions of highly motivated workers in the two plants been successful?" Such questions are essential in problem sensing, diagnosis, and decision making.

Recall that sample proportions are similar to sample means. Both are measures of the center of a data set. While sample means can take on all possible negative and positive values, sample proportions are numbers between 0 and 1. By the end of this section you should be able to construct and interpret confidence intervals on the difference between two population proportions.

We introduce confidence intervals on the difference between two population proportions in the following example.

EXAMPLE: DEMOGRAPHIC STUDY: ARE MULTIPLE ADS NECESSARY? An ad agency surveys the demographic differences between subscribers to two magazines. It randomly selects 1,000 subscribers of *American Business* and asks: "Is your family income over $60,000?" Five hundred fifty subscribers respond yes. The agency randomly selects 500 subscribers of *The Entrepreneur* and finds that only 200 have family incomes over $60,000.

Is there a difference between the proportions of the two magazines' subscribers who have incomes over $60,000? If there is no difference, the agency can use similar ads for both target audiences. If there is a difference, the agency must create different campaign strategies for each magazine; that is, it must segment the market.

The agency wants a 99% confidence interval on the difference between the two population proportions of subscribers with annual incomes over $60,000.

Expression (8.4) is the estimated standard error of the difference between the two sample proportions. We assign $\hat{p}$ to be the proportion of people who respond yes and $\hat{q}$ to be the proportion of people who respond no. The subscripts refer to the two data sets. We use expression (8.5) to construct a two-sided confidence interval on the difference between two population proportions.

$$\sqrt{\frac{\hat{p}_1\hat{q}_1}{n_1-1} + \frac{\hat{p}_2\hat{q}_2}{n_2-1}} \quad (8.4)$$

$$\hat{p}_1 - \hat{p}_2 \pm z\sqrt{\frac{\hat{p}_1\hat{q}_1}{n_1-1} + \frac{\hat{p}_2\hat{q}_2}{n_2-1}} \quad (8.5)$$

Table 8.7 shows the computation of the estimated standard error for the market segment study data. Before constructing a confidence interval, we state the assumptions:

ASSUMPTION 1: The two data sets are simple random samples taken from the *American Business* and *The Entrepreneur* subscriber populations.

ASSUMPTION 2: The sampling distribution of the difference between two sample proportions is normal.

The two assumptions are realistic. The ad agency took a simple random sample and Assumption 1 is met. Cochran's rules for normality (Table 7.10) assure us that the sample sizes are sufficiently large to ensure normality.

Again, for ease of interpretation, always subtract the smaller sample proportion from the larger sample proportion when computing the difference.

Table 8.7
Hypothetical Data for Demographic Study

	American Business	*The Entrepreneur*
n	1,000	500
$\hat{p}$	$\frac{550}{1,000} = .55$	$\frac{200}{500} = .40$
$\hat{q}$	$\frac{450}{1,000} = .45$	$\frac{300}{500} = .60$

$$\text{Estimated standard error} = \sqrt{\frac{(.55)(.45)}{999} + \frac{(.40)(.60)}{499}}$$

$$= .027$$

Shown here is a two-sided 99% confidence interval:

$$.55 - .40 \pm (2.58)(.027)$$

Lower limit: $.15 - .07 = .08$
Upper limit: $.15 + .07 = .22$

Since the interval does not include 0, the two population proportions differ. We are 99% confident that the difference between the two population proportions is between 8% and 22%. In other words, we are 99% confident that *American Business* magazine has between 8% and 22% more subscribers making over $60,000 per year.

The conclusion should not be surprising. While the estimated standard error is only .027, the difference between the two sample proportions of .15 is over five times as large as the estimated standard error. That indicates that there is a statistically significant difference between the two population proportions.

In summary, we construct confidence intervals on the difference between two population means or proportions in the same way. The center point of each interval is the difference between the two sample statistics (subtracting the smaller from the larger sample value). The margin of error is simply the *t*-value or *z*-value times the estimated standard error. We also interpret confidence intervals on the difference between two population means or proportions in the same way. If 0 is in the interval, we conclude that the two population parameters do not differ at the desired level of confidence. If 0 is not in the interval, we conclude that there is a statistically significant difference between the two population parameters at the desired level of confidence.

SECTION 8.4 EXERCISES

1. Suppose you conducted a study of 50 men and 100 women to estimate the difference between the sexes in percentages who prefer brand A to its competitors. The results are shown here.

	Men	Women
Sample size	50	100
Number who prefer A	20	50
Sample proportion	.4	.5

   Construct a 95% confidence interval for the difference between the two population proportions. Interpret your confidence interval.

2. In preparing a defense against a hostile takeover, a firm's management wants to know if there is a difference between owners of common and preferred stock in attitudes toward the current management. The poll taken shows that 200 of 400 common stockholders surveyed were in favor of a change in management, while 130 of 200 preferred shareholders favored the change.

a. Construct a 90% confidence interval for the difference between population proportions.
b. Does it appear that there is a difference between the population proportions of common and preferred shareholders who favor a change in management? Explain.

3. A new drug is being compared to an existing drug for its effectiveness in curing an illness. Of 100 patients treated with the new drug, 63 were cured. Of the 60 patients treated with the existing drug, 33 were cured.
   a. Explain in managerial terms what population proportions would mean here, i.e., what are the populations we are studying?
   b. Construct a 90% confidence interval for the difference between population proportions. Would you conclude that the new drug is more or less effective than the existing drug?

4. You want to compare the population proportion of Business majors and Arts and Sciences majors who are intuitive according to the Myers-Briggs Type Indicator (MBTI). You randomly select 10 students each from the two majors at a large university and administer the MBTI. Eight Arts and Sciences majors are intuitive and three Business majors are intuitive. Although you have used randomization, you cannot construct a confidence interval on the difference between the two population proportions. Why?

5. Are the proportions of whites and blacks unemployed the same? The U.S. Bureau of Labor selects a random sample of 5,000 people from each race. Below are the descriptive statistics.

	Black	White
Sample size	5,000	5,000
Number of people employed	4,350	4,735

   a. Use a 90% confidence interval to estimate the difference between the population proportions of the races that are employed.
   b. Interpret the confidence interval.

6. After buying a product, the consumer may have postpurchase doubt. A consumer asks, "Did I make the right buying decision?" This doubt is called cognitive dissonance. A national tire dealer wants to estimate the difference between the proportions of consumers who experience cognitive dissonance after purchasing tires in two large retail outlets, one in Albany, New York, and one in Reno, Nevada. It asks 50 customers in succession (at both stores) on a Saturday, "Are you satisfied with your tire purchase?" Why shouldn't you set up a confidence interval on the difference between population proportions?

8.5 A Nonparametric Confidence Interval for the Difference Between Two Population Medians

Thus far, we have assumed in the data analysis that either the population was normal, the sampling distribution was normal, or the transformed data were normal. These are reasonable assumptions for most data. However, when the sample sizes are small and there are outliers, square root or log base 10 transformations may not make the data near normal. Consider the Mann-Whitney *nonparametric* approach. Nonparametric methods do not assume normal populations or normal sampling distributions. Use them when the samples are long-tailed, include outliers, or have unequal variances.

We use the Mann-Whitney method to construct confidence intervals on the difference between two population *medians*. Recall that in the presence of outliers, we use the median, not the mean, as a measure of a data set's center. By the end of this section you should be able to:

1. explain when to construct a confidence interval on the difference between two population medians;
2. construct and interpret a nonparametric confidence interval; and
3. explain the logic behind the method.

To use a nonparametric interval we must make two assumptions:

ASSUMPTION 1: The data sets are two random and independent samples taken from two populations.

ASSUMPTION 2: The two population distributions have similar shapes—they need not be normal—and variances.

Using simple random sampling ensures that the first assumption will be met. Construct stem-and-leaf displays or box plots to confirm the second assumption.

We introduce confidence intervals on the difference between two population medians in the following example.

EXAMPLE: COMCEL'S WELLNESS STUDY   Last year, as part of a physical fitness program, all plant personnel had their cholesterol levels checked. About 30% of the workers had high levels, in excess of 275 mg/dl. A medical consulting team suggested two approaches to reduce cholesterol levels—a diet program and a diet/exercise regimen. The team conducted a one-factor, two-level completely random study. It randomly selected 20 workers who had high cholesterol levels and randomly assigned them to one of two test groups. After 90 days, test subjects had their cholesterol levels checked. The dependent variable is the drop in cholesterol level. Is one approach better in reducing cholesterol levels?

Table 8.8 on page 414 contains the raw data and Figure 8.11 contains the box plots.

Both data sets have few observations ($n = 10$), as well as outliers. However, the box plots suggest that the two samples have similar shapes and equal interquartile ranges. Thus, we will use the Mann-Whitney nonparametric method for constructing a confidence interval on the difference between two population medians.

Table 8.8

Drop in Cholesterol Level (mg/dl) Data

	Diet-Only Subjects	Diet/Exercise Subjects
	11	14
	12	16
	13	17
	15	18
	16	18
	17	19
	18	20
	20	24
	24	25
	70	54
$\bar{x}$	21.60	22.5
s	17.44	11.57
Sample median	16.50	18.50

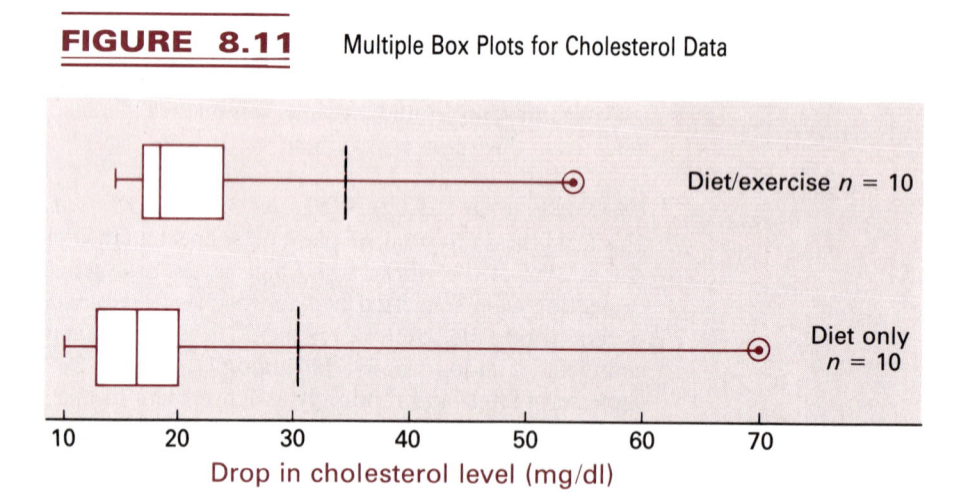

FIGURE 8.11 Multiple Box Plots for Cholesterol Data

Confidence Interval on the Difference Between Two Medians

1. Rank order each sample separately from the smallest to largest values.
2. Compute all possible differences between the data values in the two samples. For n observations per sample, there will be n^2 computed differences.
3. Look up the sample size in Table 8.9 and determine the *count* value. Call it K.

Chapter 8 Making Inferences About Two Populations

4. The Kth largest negative difference is the lower limit of the confidence interval for the difference between the two population medians.
5. The Kth largest positive difference is the upper limit of the confidence interval for the difference between the two population medians.

Table 8.10 contains the 100 computed differences for the wellness study data. To construct Table 8.10, we placed in ascending order the 10 data values for the diet-only sample in the leftmost column. We placed in ascending order the 10 data values for the diet/exercise sample in the top row. We then computed all 100 differences; that is, we subtracted the drop in cholesterol levels of those who only dieted from those who used diet and exercise.

Table 8.9

Constructing a 95% Two-Sided Confidence Interval on the Difference Between Two Population Medians

Sample Size per Group*	Number of Largest and Smallest Differences	Sample Size per Group	Number of Largest and Smallest Differences
5	3	13	46
6	6	14	56
7	9	15	65
8	14	16	76
9	18	17	88
10	24	18	100
11	31	19	124
12	38	20	128

*We assume equal sample sizes. For unequal sample sizes or sample sizes above 20, consult the tables in an applied nonparametric book.

Table 8.10

Table of Differences

Diet/Exercise

	14	16	17	18	18	19	20	24	25	54
11	3	5	6	7	7	8	9	13	14	43
12	2	4	5	6	6	7	8	12	13	42
13	1	3	4	5	5	6	7	11	12	41
15	−1	1	2	3	3	4	5	9	10	39
16	−2	0	1	2	2	3	4	8	9	38
17	−3	−1	0	1	1	2	3	7	8	37
18	−4	−2	−1	0	0	1	2	6	7	36
20	−6	−4	−3	−2	−2	−1	0	4	5	34
24	−10	−8	−7	−6	−6	−5	−4	0	1	30
70	−56	−54	−53	−52	−52	−51	−50	−46	−45	−16

(Diet Only)

With a sample size of 10 in each group, $K = 24$ from Table 8.9. First we find the 24 largest positive differences in Table 8.10 (see upper right-hand corner values). These are in descending order: 43, 42, 41, 39, 38, 37, 36, 34, 30, 14, 13, 13, 12, 12, 11, 10, 9, 9, 9, 8, 8, 8, 8, and 7. The value $+7$ is the 24th largest positive difference and so it is the upper limit of the confidence interval. Second, we find the 24 largest negative differences in Table 8.10 (see lower left-hand corner values). These are in ascending order: -56, -54, -53, -52, -52, -51, -50, -46, -45, -16, -10, -8, -7, -6, -6, -6, -5, -4, -4, -4, -3, -3, -2, and -2. The value -2 is the 24th largest negative difference and so it is the lower limit of the confidence interval.

In summary, the limits of the confidence interval on the difference between the two population medians is

Lower limit: -2 mg/dl

Upper limit: $+7$ mg/dl

Interpretation of Mann-Whitney Confidence Intervals

We interpret a nonparametric confidence interval just as we have other intervals. We are 95% confident that the difference between the two population medians is between -2 and $+7$ mg/dl. Since the interval includes 0, we conclude that there is *no statistically significant* difference between the population medians. Although the difference between sample medians was $18.5 - 16.5 = 2$, the population medians do not differ.

If both the upper and lower limits were positive, then we would be 95% confident that the median drop in cholesterol was larger for the diet and exercise plan than for the diet plan alone. Remember, we computed the drop in cholesterol for the diet/exercise group minus the diet-only group. If both the upper and lower limits were negative, we would be 95% confident that the median drop in cholesterol was smaller for diet/exercise than for diet only.

Logic Behind the Mann-Whitney Method

The Mann–Whitney method compares medians by determining the degree of overlap between *all the data values* of the two samples. Consider the two small data sets in Table 8.11. Clearly, the two samples in data set 1 have no overlap, while the two samples in data set 2 have complete overlap. Now we compute the two tables of differences and present the results in Table 8.12.

When there is no overlap, 100% of the differences will be positive. This suggests that the two population medians must be different. When there is considerable overlap, about 50% of the differences will be positive and 50% negative. This suggests that the two population medians will be the same. It is in this sense that the Mann–Whitney method uses the percentage of positive differences to determine whether the two population medians are different. Is the percentage closer to 50% (no difference) or 100% (a difference)?

Table 8.11

Illustrating the Overlap Idea for Two Small Data Sets

	Data Set 1		Data Set 2	
	Group 1	Group 2	Group 1	Group 2
	11	16	11	11
	12	18	12	12
	13	19	13	13
Median	12	18	12	12

Table 8.12

Tables of Differences for Two Small Data Sets

Data Set 1

	16	18	19
11	5	7	8
12	4	6	7
13	3	5	6

Data Set 2

	11	12	13
11	0	1	2
12	−1	0	1
13	−2	−1	0

Returning to the wellness study, we count 70 positive (70%) and 30 negative differences in Table 8.10. That was not quite enough for us to conclude, at the 95% confidence level, that the two population medians differ.

In summary, consider using the nonparametric confidence interval method when the sample size is small and the data contain outliers. If the confidence interval includes the value of 0, we conclude, at the 95% level of confidence, that we cannot detect any difference between the two population medians. In short, there is no statistically significant difference.

SECTION 8.5 EXERCISES

1. You are a manager looking for the best way to compare the centers of two populations based on two sample data sets. You have two choices—the t-test and a nonparametric alternative. Under what circumstances would you construct a confidence interval on the difference between population medians rather than on the difference between population means?

2. Consider the following sets of data points.

    Group 1:   1   3   5   10   3   4
    Group 2: 10 11 14   12 25 42

    a. Find the medians of the two groups and construct a table of differences between the two groups. Based on the percentage of the positive differences, would you say that the population medians of the two groups are different at the 95% level of confidence?

    b. Construct a 95% confidence interval on the difference between population medians using the Mann–Whitney method. Interpret this confidence interval.

3. Consider the results of an experiment that compared the time needed (in minutes) to produce an item under the current method with the time needed under a new method.

    Current: 68 70 72 73 77 85
    New: 60 63 64 65 70 79

    a. Find the medians of the two groups and construct a table of differences for the two groups. Based on the percentage of the positive differences, would you say that the population median time needed to produce an item is less under the new method at the 95% level of confidence?

    b. Construct a 95% confidence interval on the difference between population medians using the Mann–Whitney method. Does it appear that the new method reduces the median time to produce the item?

4. Consider the results of another experiment that compared the time (in minutes) needed to produce an item under the current method with the time needed under a new method.

    Current: 68 70 72 73 74 75 77 85
    New: 63 65 75 67 70 71 72 72

    a. Find the medians of the two groups and construct a table of differences for the two groups. Based on the percentage of the positive differences, would you say that the population median time needed to produce an item is less under the new method at the 95% level of confidence?

    b. Construct a 95% confidence interval on the difference between population medians using the Mann–Whitney method. Does it appear that the new method reduces the median time to produce the item?

5. You want to compare students' average grades for two different teaching methods — lecture vs. the case method. Assume that all students will obtain a grade between 70 and 100.

    a. Construct a data set that would suggest that you should set up a confidence interval on the difference between two population means.

    b. Construct a data set that would suggest that you should set up a confidence interval on the difference between two population medians.

6. Below are samples of student SAT scores from two public universities. At the 95% level of confidence, can we say that there is a difference between the population median SAT scores at the two universities?

University A	University B
800	850
900	875
950	910
975	950
1,150	1,050

8.6 Inferences on Two Population Variances for Normal Populations

Thus far, we have drawn inferences about differences in measures of the center—mean, median, and proportion. Now we ask whether two population variances are equal.

Why is it important to know whether population variances are equal? First, in constructing confidence intervals on two population means, we assume that the two population variances are equal or nearly so. It is time to verify statistically that assumption. Second, given that two groups have the same mean performance, managers want to know:

1. Do the two groups' variances differ?
2. If so, which group has the more consistent or less variable performance?
3. What accounts for a group's higher variance?

Consistent performance is an important managerial goal. Highly variable performance can cause great consternation for a manager. Some days performance is excellent, other days it is not. Consistent performance minimizes uncertainty and makes a manager's job easier. Also, highly variable performance signals a potential problem to a manager for which he needs to diagnose the causes and take corrective action.

Consistent product performance is also important from the consumer's perspective. If product workmanship varies greatly, consumers will look to other brands. Consumers want consistently good product workmanship and performance. By the end of this section you should be able to:

1. construct and interpret confidence intervals on the ratio of two population variances; and
2. explain what the *F*-distribution is and what it represents.

We introduce confidence intervals on the ratio of two population variances in the following example.

EXAMPLE: PRODUCTIVITY STUDY IN BALTIMORE AND DALLAS PLANTS   COMCEL's Dallas and Baltimore plants produce electronics for the mobile telephones. Are the means and variances in productivity similar for both plants? COMCEL randomly selects 21 workers from each plant and records their weekly productivity. Table 8.13 on page 420 contains the descriptive data.

Since the two sample means are similar, the two population means could be the same. However, the sample variance in the Dallas plant is 5 times as large as that in the Baltimore plant. Are the two sample variances so different that we should conclude that the two population variances differ? Before answering that question, we must introduce the sampling distribution of the ratio of two sample variances, or the *variance ratio*.

Table 8.13

Descriptive Data in Units per Hour (uph) for Two COMCEL Plants

	Dallas Plant	Baltimore Plant
Sample size (n)	21	21
Sample mean productivity ($\bar{x}$)	50.2 uph	50.3 uph
Sample productivity variance (s^2)	20	4
Sample standard deviation (s)	4.47 uph	2.00 uph

Sampling Distribution of the Variance Ratio

Assume that the workers' productivities in each plant are nearly normally distributed. Now run the productivity study and compute the following ratio of two sample variances:

$$\text{Variance ratio} = \text{VR} = \frac{s_1^2}{s_2^2}$$

Assume that the *population* variances are the same for the two plants. What should the value of the variance ratio be? Please think about it before reading on.

If the *population* variances are the same, most sample variance ratios should be close to 1. After all, if the two population variances are equal, the two sample variances should be similar and their ratio should be close to 1.

Now imagine taking another random sample from each plant and computing the ratio of the two sample variances. Continue to rerun the study and compute the sample variance ratios. We will obtain a sampling distribution of the variance ratios, which has a shape shown in Figure 8.12. The sampling distribution is called an *F*-distribution.

FIGURE 8.12 *F*-Distribution for 20 Degrees of Freedom in the Numerator and 20 in the Denominator. Assumption: Two Population Variances Are Equal

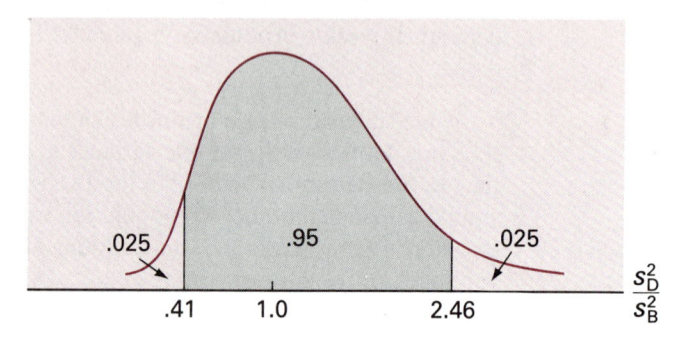

If the two population variances are equal, the mean of the sampling distribution is about 1 because most variance ratios should be close to 1. The sampling distribution shape is skewed toward higher values because when the numerator of the variance ratio is much smaller than the denominator, the ratio approaches 0. It cannot be negative since variances can never be negative! When the numerator is much larger than the denominator, the variance ratio becomes very large. That accounts for the skewed distribution.

The *F*-distribution is really a family of curves. The actual shape depends on the degrees of freedom for the sample variances in the numerator and the denominator. These are $(n_1 - 1)$ and $(n_2 - 1)$, respectively; n_1 is the sample size for one sample (for example, the Dallas plant) and n_2 is the sample size for the other sample (the Baltimore plant).

In the COMCEL study, the sample size from each plant was 21. Figure 8.12 represents an *F*-distribution that has 20 degrees of freedom for the numerator and 20 for the denominator. The total area underneath the curve is, of course, 100%. The curve shows that $2\frac{1}{2}\%$ of the variance ratios will have values below .41. How do we know this? Refer to Table 8.14. Find the intersection of 20 degrees of freedom for the numerator and 20 for the denominator in the .025 row. The value is .41. Likewise, the table indicates that 97.5% of the variance ratios will have values below 2.46. (See the intersection of 20 degrees of freedom for the numerator and 20 for the denominator in the .975 row.) Thus, 95% of the sample variance ratios will have values between .41 and 2.46 *if the two population variances are equal* (see shaded area of Figure 8.12). Also, since the total area is 100%, $2\frac{1}{2}\%$ of the variance ratios will have values above 2.46.

If the population productivity variances for both plants were the same, 95% of the time we would obtain a variance ratio between .41 and 2.46. However, the actual sample variance ratio in the COMCEL study was 5.* From Figure 8.12,

Table 8.14

An Abbreviated *F*-Table from Appendix 7

df for Denominator	Percentiles of the *F*-curve	df for Numerator 10	20	30
10	.025	.27	.36	.40
	.050	.34	.43	.46
	.950	2.98	2.77	2.70
	.975	3.72	3.42	3.31
20	.025	.29	.41	.45
	.050	.36	.47	.52
	.950	2.35	2.12	2.04
	.975	2.77	2.46	2.35

*The common practice is to place the larger sample variance in the numerator of the variance ratio.

that is a very rare happening—far out in the distribution's right tail. Yet that is what happened in the COMCEL study. What could account for such a large variance ratio? Think about it before reading on.

There are two possible explanations:

1. This is one of those very rare happenings. *Conclusion:* The two population variances are equal.
2. This is not one of those very rare happenings. *Conclusion:* The two population variances are not equal.

Although we could be wrong, we assume the latter is true. When the actual variance ratio falls above the upper *F*-value, we conclude that the two population variances are not the same.

Exactly how much greater is the productivity variance in the Dallas plant? The sample variance ratio is 5. However, if we took another sample we would probably not obtain the same sample variance ratio. Therefore we must construct a confidence interval on the sample variance ratio that incorporates the idea of the margin of error.

Before constructing the confidence interval, we state the assumptions:

ASSUMPTION 1: The two data sets are simple random samples taken from the Baltimore and Dallas plants.

ASSUMPTION 2: Worker productivities in both Baltimore and Dallas are normally distributed.

ASSUMPTION 3: Initially we assume that the two population variances are the same.

Assumption 1 will be met if we randomly select workers from the two plants. We can use two stem-and-leaf displays to check the second assumption. Finally, we will construct a confidence interval on the population variance ratio to test the third assumption.

Constructing a Confidence Interval for the Variance Ratio

The steps for constructing a confidence interval on the population variance ratio are presented here, along with their application to the COMCEL study.

General Procedure	For COMCEL Study
Set a desired confidence level.	We want a 90% confidence interval. Thus the *F*-curve should have 5% of the area in the lower tail, 90% of the area between the tails, and 5% of the area in the upper tail.

(continued)

General Procedure	For COMCEL Study
Compute the sample variance ratio.	Place the larger sample variance in the numerator.
$$VR = \frac{s_1^2}{s_2^2}$$	$$VR = \frac{20}{4} = 5$$
The lower limit of the confidence interval is	Both data sets have sample sizes of 21. Locate the *F*-value for 20 degrees of freedom for the numerator and 20 for the denominator in the .95 row (.05 + .90). The *F*-value is 2.12 (see Appendix 7).
$$\frac{VR}{F\text{-value from the upper tail}}$$	$$\text{Lower limit} = \frac{5}{2.12} = 2.36$$
Dividing the variance ratio by a number greater than 1 reduces its value and thus defines the confidence interval's lower limit.	
The upper limit of the confidence interval is	Locate the *F*-value for 20 degrees of freedom for the numerator and 20 for the denominator in the .05 row. The *F*-value is .47.
$$\frac{VR}{F\text{-value from the lower tail}}$$	$$\text{Upper limit} = \frac{5}{.47} = 10.64$$
Dividing the variance ratio by a number less than 1 increases its value and thus defines the confidence interval's upper limit.	

Thus, we are 90% confident that the ratio of the two population variances is between 2.36 and 10.64. Simply put, Dallas' variance is between 2.36 and 10.64 *times as large as* Baltimore's variance, or Dallas' standard deviation in units per hour is between 1.54 and 3.26 times that of Baltimore.

So what does that mean? What sample variance ratio value would we expect to see *within* the confidence interval if the two population variances were the same? When looking for differences between population means, we checked whether 0 was in the interval. If so, it meant that managers would act as if the population means were the same. What number should be in the interval if the two population variances could be the same? Please give it some thought before continuing.

A value of 1 indicates that the two population variances could be the same. Remember, we constructed a *ratio*, not a *difference*. Thus, if the confidence interval includes 1, we conclude that at the desired level of confidence, the two population variances could be the same. If the interval does not include 1, then the two population variances are different.

Based on the F-distribution, we are 90% confident that the Dallas workers' productivities exhibit more variance than their Baltimore counterparts. An effective manager now asks why and begins seeking possible reasons. Why are the Baltimore plant workers more consistent? What can we do to reduce the Dallas plant workers' variability?

In summary, we construct a confidence interval on the ratio of two population variances either to determine which of two performances, products, or services exhibits less variability or to verify an assumption underlying the confidence intervals on the difference between two population means.

SECTION 8.6 EXERCISES

1. Look up the following F-values.
   $F_{.95}$(10 degrees of freedom in numerator, 10 in denominator)
   $F_{.05}(5, 10)$
   $F_{.99}(20, 24)$

2. The purpose of an experiment is to compare two population variances. Six observations are drawn from population 1 and nine observations from population 2. The variance of the first sample is 82.5 and the variance of the second sample is 26.5. Assuming that the populations are normally distributed, construct both a 90% confidence interval for the ratio of the population variances and a 95% confidence interval.

3. Apex, Inc. is considering purchasing thermostats from two different companies, A and B. The quality of a thermostat is measured by the amount of variation between the actual temperature and the reading of the thermostat. Apex selects eight different thermostats from each vendor and puts them into a test chamber where the temperature is controlled at 70°. The recorded temperatures are shown.

   | Company A: | 68.5 | 69.0 | 70.0 | 70.1 | 70.4 | 70.6 | 70.9 | 71.5 |
   | Company B: | 68.9 | 69.5 | 69.9 | 70.1 | 70.1 | 70.1 | 70.2 | 70.8 |

   a. Assuming that the populations of measurements are normally distributed, construct a 90% confidence interval to estimate the variance ratio.
   b. Does one company produce thermostats that are less variable than the other? Explain.

4. What role do confidence intervals for variance ratios play in comparing the population means of two distributions?

5. Suppose that the monthly rates of return on stocks X and Y are normally distributed. From 60 months of data, random samples of six months of stock X and six months of stock Y showed the following percentage returns:

   | Stock X: | 1 | 7 | 6 | −5 | −1 | 10 |
   | Stock Y: | 4 | 3 | 2 | 3 | 8 | 10 |

a. Construct a 90% confidence interval to estimate the ratio of the population variances.
b. Does it appear that the variances in returns of the two stocks are different? Explain.

6. A pharmaceutical company purchases the same raw material from two different suppliers. The company is concerned that the level of impurities could vary considerably among shipments and could affect the quality of the end product. To compare the percentage levels of impurities between the two suppliers, the company selects 16 shipments from each supplier and measures the percentage impurities in each shipment. The results are shown here.

	Supplier 1	Supplier 2
$\bar{x}$	1.72	1.79
s^2	.156	.082
n	16	16

Construct a 90% confidence interval for the ratio of population variances. Does it appear that variation in impurities differs between the two suppliers? Explain.

7. Refer to Exercise 6. Suppose that the percentage impurities are as shown below. Should you construct a confidence interval on the population variance ratio? Explain.

| Supplier 1: | .30 .35 .37 .39 .40 .75 3.00 6.15 17.10 |
| Supplier 2: | .20 .25 .26 .27 .30 5.05 7.10 10.19 15.12 |

8.7 A Nonparametric Method for Comparing Two Population Variabilities

When constructing confidence intervals on the variance ratio using the F-tables, we must assume that the population distributions are near normal. When the data have outliers or when the distributions are highly skewed, we must use a nonparametric approach to compare population variability. Here, we choose the Mood (1964) test. Mood's test compares the dispersion (not variances) of two populations. By the end of this section you should be able to:

1. use Mood's test to determine if the dispersions in two populations are the same; and
2. explain why either very small or large test values indicate that two populations have different dispersions.

We illustrate the Mood test in the following example.

EXAMPLE: COMCEL SICK LEAVE IN BALTIMORE AND DALLAS PLANTS   Are the dispersions in sick leave (hours) taken in the two plants the same? COMCEL randomly selects the personnel records of 5 workers from each plant and obtains the descriptive data given in Table 8.15 on page 426.

Table 8.15

Hours of Sick Leave Taken Last Quarter

	Dallas Plant	Baltimore Plant
	.2	3.5
	1.2	3.6
	3.4	3.7
	14	6.9
	20	7.6
Sample size	5	5
Sample median	3.4 hours	3.7 hours

To use the Mood test, we must make two assumptions:

ASSUMPTION 1: The two data sets are independent random samples.

ASSUMPTION 2: The two populations have similar medians but may have different dispersions.

The first assumption is true because COMCEL used simple random sampling. Draw a multiple box plot to verify Assumption 2. The box plot in Figure 8.13 suggests that the two data sets have similar sample medians but different sample dispersions. Do the population dispersions differ?

Testing for equality of population dispersion begins by ranking the 10 data values. The ranked values are presented in Table 8.16, with B for Baltimore and D for Dallas. The Baltimore sample data have less dispersion than the Dallas data. The five values in the middle belong to the Baltimore workers, while the first three and last two data values belong to the Dallas workers.

Since we are dealing with ranked data, the second step is to find the *rank* of the median value. Given 10 data values, the *rank* of the median value is $(n + 1)/2$, or $(10 + 1)/2 = 5.5$.

FIGURE 8.13 Multiple Box Plot for COMCEL Sick Leave Data

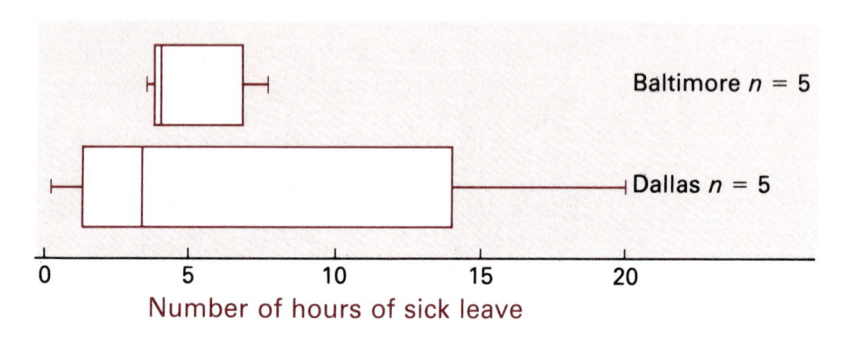

Chapter 8   Making Inferences About Two Populations

Table 8.16
Rank Ordering of Sample Sick Leave Data

Rank-Ordered Data		Rank
.2	D	1
1.2	D	2
3.4	D	3
3.5	B	4
3.6	B	5
3.7	B	6
6.9	B	7
7.6	B	8
14	D	9
20	D	10

The third step is to measure the dispersion of the ranked data. We cannot use the variance since we are using ranked data. However, we can make an analogy to the variance by computing the sum of the squared differences between the *rank* of each Baltimore data point (and each Dallas data point) and the *rank* of the median. Denote the sum of the squared differences as the computed M-value. Table 8.17 contains the computations for $M_{\text{Baltimore}}$ and M_{Dallas}.

Next we compare the computed M-value with the values in Table 8.18 on page 428. If the computed M-value is less than the lower limit, then the population from which the sample was taken has less dispersion than the other population at the 95% level of confidence. If the computed M-value is greater than the

Table 8.17
Computation of Sum of Squares for COMCEL Data Set

	Data Set Computation for Baltimore				Data Set Computation for Dallas		
	[R]ank	$R - 5.5$	$(R - 5.5)^2$		[R]ank	$R - 5.5$	$(R - 5.5)^2$
D	1			D	1	−4.5	20.25
D	2			D	2	−3.5	12.25
D	3			D	3	−2.5	6.25
B	4	−1.5	2.25	B	4		
B	5	−.5	.25	B	5		
B	6	.5	.25	B	6		
B	7	1.5	2.25	B	7		
B	8	2.5	6.25	B	8		
D	9			D	9	3.5	12.25
D	10			D	10	4.5	20.25
		$M_B = 11.25$				$M_D = 71.25$	

Table 8.18

Tabled *M*-Values for an Approximate 95% Level of Confidence*

Sample Size per Group	Lower Limit	Upper Limit
5	15.25	65.25
10	198.50	464.50
15	758.50	1,489.00
20	1,917.60	3,412.40
25	3,903.18	6,509.31
30	6,944.84	11,050.10
40	17,123.90	25,536.00
50	34,323.00	49,002.00

*For other sample sizes, see any book on applied nonparametric statistics.

upper limit, the population from which the sample was taken has more dispersion than the other population at the 95% level of confidence. If the computed *M*-value is between the lower and upper limits, the two populations could have the same dispersion at the 95% level of confidence.

The computed *M*-value for Baltimore is 11.25. Since it is less than the tabled *M*-value for a sample size of 5 (15.25), we are 95% confident that the population of workers in Baltimore has less dispersion in the number of sick days taken than their Dallas counterparts. Alternatively, we could reach the same conclusion by comparing the computed *M*-value for Dallas (71.25) to the tabled *M*-value in Table 8.18.

Table 8.19

Computation of Sum of Squares for Second Data Set

	Computation for Baltimore				Computation for Dallas		
	R	$R - 5.5$	$(R - 5.5)^2$		R	$R - 5.5$	$(R - 5.5)^2$
D	1			1	-4.5	20.25
B	2	-3.5	12.25	2		
D	3			3	-2.5	6.25
B	4	-1.5	2.25	4		
D	5			5	$-.5$	.25
B	6	.5	.25	6		
D	7			7	1.5	2.25
B	8	2.5	6.25	8		
D	9			9	3.5	12.25
B	10	4.5	20.25	10		
		$M_B = 41.25$				$M_D = 41.25$	

For a sample of size 5, computed M-values between 15.25 and 65.25 indicate that the two population dispersions could be the same. Suppose we illustrate this with the following ranked data set:

$$D, \ B, \ D, \ B, \ D, \ B, \ D, \ B, \ D, \ B$$

The Dallas and Baltimore data values alternate; the Dallas data values range from the first to the ninth observations while the Baltimore data range from the second to the tenth data values. That suggests that both populations have the same dispersion.

Now we will show that the computed M-values fall between 15.25 and 65.25. Table 8.19 shows the sum of squared differences between the ranks of the Baltimore data (or Dallas data) and the rank of the median. The median is still the 5.5th—$(10 + 1)/2$—largest data value. Both computed M-values are 41.25.

We summarize the Mood test procedure.

Steps in the Mood Test

1. Combine the two samples and rank order the data. Be able to identify which data values belong to which samples.
2. Determine the rank of the median value. This is $(n + 1)/2$.
3. Select one sample and compute the sum of squares (M) between the rank of its data values and the rank of the median value.
4. Compare the computed M-value to the upper and lower limits from Table 8.18.
5. If the computed M-value is less than the lower limit, then the population from which the sample was taken has less dispersion than the other population, at the 95% level of confidence.
6. If the computed M-value is greater than the upper limit, then the population from which the sample was taken has more dispersion than the other population, at the 95% level of confidence.
7. If the computed M-value is between the lower and upper limits, the two populations may have the same dispersion at the 95% level of confidence.

Note that in analyzing two population dispersions, it is not necessary to compute both M-values. If one M-value is below the lower limit, the other M-value will be above the upper limit.

In summary, when the data have outliers or are highly skewed, use the Mann-Whitney confidence interval method for comparing two population medians and the Mood test for comparing two population dispersions.

SECTION 8.7 EXERCISES

1. What are the assumptions behind the Mood method? When would you choose this method over the variance ratio method described in the previous section?

2. Consider the following data sets:

Group 1	Group 2
3	7
6	9
14	16
42	19
43	24

   a. Rank the observations from the two groups and find the sum of squared differences between the rank of each observation and the rank of the median for both groups.
   b. Compare the sums you found in part **a** to Table 8.18 in the text. What do you conclude from the table about the dispersions of the two populations from which the samples were drawn?

3. A cigarette manufacturer has produced two new brands of cigarettes—Clouds and Springs—with reduced tar and nicotine. Tests have shown that both brands have about the same average tar and nicotine content, so the manufacturer is interested in the variation in tar and nicotine of these two brands. They will market the one with the smaller variation. They select 10 cigarettes of each brand and determine the tar and nicotine content in milligrams. The results are shown here.

Clouds		Springs	
19.0	21.3	19.3	21.0
19.1	21.4	19.9	21.6
19.2	22.4	20.0	21.9
19.6	23.2	20.3	22.1
20.6	23.9	20.4	22.9

   a. Find the sample medians for the two brands.
   b. Suppose you were not willing to assume that samples were drawn from normal populations. Use the Mood procedure to determine if the variation in tar and nicotine differs between the two brands. State your conclusion.
   c. Suppose that you were willing to assume that the samples were drawn from normal populations. Construct a 95% confidence interval for the variance ratio. Does this confidence interval suggest that the population variances are different? Explain.

4. Is the assumption of normality of data sets in Exercise 3 reasonable? Construct two stem-and-leaf displays for Clouds and Springs to support your position.

5. An investor wishes to compare the risks associated with different stocks. Risk is measured by the variation in daily price changes. She selects a random sample of five daily price changes for two stocks. Below are the data.

Stock 1	Stock 2
.0	.625
.125	−.50
−.25	−.75
.50	.25
.75	1.50

Construct a 95% confidence interval on the difference between the two population dispersions. Can we say with 95% confidence that there is a difference between the two stocks in the risk associated with them?

8.8 Key Ideas and Overview

Managers must know when and how to improve departmental performance. They begin by conducting surveys to find potential improvement projects. Then they design potential improvements and run small-scale planned change studies to determine if they really improve performance or service. Finally, they analyze the data and study the results. They ask: What did we learn? If the planned change is effective, they implement it permanently.

Confidence intervals play an important role in improving departmental performance. Table 8.20 provides an overview of the confidence interval methods presented in the last two chapters. In Table 8.20 we have listed the chapter sections for constructing confidence intervals on the mean, median, proportion, variance, and dispersion for one or two data sets. It also shows the expressions for constructing confidence intervals on the various population parameters.

Table 8.20

Overview of Inference Methods

Center

	One Group	**Two Groups**
Normal Distribution	Mean Sections 7.3, 7.4, 7.6 t-based interval $\bar{x} \pm t(\%, \mathrm{df}) \cdot \dfrac{s}{\sqrt{n}}$ Proportion Section 7.7 z-based interval $\hat{p} \pm z \sqrt{\dfrac{\hat{p}\hat{q}}{n-1}}$	Means Section 8.3 t-based interval $\bar{x}_2 - \bar{x}_1 \pm t(\%, \mathrm{df}) s_p \sqrt{\dfrac{1}{n_1} + \dfrac{1}{n_2}}$ Proportions Section 8.4 z-based interval $\hat{p}_2 - \hat{p}_1 \pm z \sqrt{\dfrac{\hat{p}_1 \hat{q}_1}{n_1 - 1} + \dfrac{\hat{p}_2 \hat{q}_2}{n_2 - 1}}$
Nonparametric	Median Section 7.9 Rank-based interval Rank data. Determine the rank of the lower and upper limits from Table 7.11.	Medians Section 8.5 Mann–Whitney-based interval Compute table of differences. Determine the rank of the lower and upper limits from Table 8.9.

(continued)

Table 8.20 (Continued)

Dispersion

	One Group	**Two Groups**
Normal Distribution	Variance Section 7.10 Chi-square-based interval $$\frac{(n-1)s^2}{\chi^2_{100-\alpha/2}} \leq \sigma^2 \leq \frac{(n-1)s^2}{\chi^2_{\alpha/2}}$$	Variances Section 8.6 F-distribution-based interval $$\frac{s_1^2/s_2^2}{F_{100-\alpha/2}} \leq \frac{\sigma_1^2}{\sigma_2^2} \leq \frac{s_1^2/s_2^2}{F_{\alpha/2}}$$
Nonparametric		Dispersions Section 8.7 Mood test Rank data. Compute the sum of squares of the ranks about the rank of the median value. Compare the sum of squares to the tabled values from Table 8.18.

COMCEL
COMCEL

```
Date:   November 22, 1992
  To:   Howard Bright, Plant Manager
From:   Sarah Teman, Manager of Operations
  Re:   Report on labor cost reduction study in the Norcross plant
```

SUMMARY
Over the 6-month period, the five work groups that had team-building training reduced unit labor cost by an average pf $3.22. The groups that had creativity training reduced unit labor cost by an average of $4.26. The difference of $1.04 is too big to attribute to sampling variability, so the results are significant. I recommend that we provide creativity training for all work groups.

SUPPORTING ANALYSES
You asked how I could be sure that the results were due to the differences in the workshops and not some other factors. I can't be

absolutely sure, but I did everything feasible to protect against the common threats to the study's validity.

I selected 10 teams that had about the same experience working together and had about the same success in implementing cost-saving ideas. The teams were randomly assigned to the two workshops. This method of assignment prevented my biases from affecting the assignments. We chose only 10 groups because the workshops are expensive, in terms of both lost production and direct cost.

One problem I did have was convincing the participants not to discuss the training with members of the other treatment groups. Otherwise we would not get a clear picture of the impact of each training method. I told the 10 teams that when the study was completed, all groups would be given the workshop that resulted in the greater cost reductions. They agreed not to discuss the ideas they learned in the workshops for a period of 6 months.

I also made it clear that both workshops were effective in reducing costs and that neither method was inferior. I told them how they were selected for the study and how I assigned them to the two workshops by a flip of a coin. I made it clear that the study would be invalid if they assigned themselves to the workshops.

My biggest concern was that other cost-saving methods might be discovered by other work groups, vendors, or other divisions of the company and implemented during the study. This could make it difficult to determine the cost reductions due to the two training methods. Thus I took biweekly cost measurements rather than waiting until the end of the study.

In summary, I ran a valid study. The statistically significant differences in cost reduction between the two workshops is due to the type of training, and not other factors.

CHAPTER 8 QUESTIONS

1. In comparing two sets of data, what are we interested in? Why?
2. If two groups of data come from nonnormal populations with different variances, what can be done to make the data more normal and to make the variances more equal?
3. What assumptions are necessary in constructing confidence intervals on the difference between two population means?
4. If two sample means differ, must the two population means also differ?
5. What does the estimated standard error of the difference between sample means measure?
6. If the confidence interval on the difference between two population means does not include 0, what can we conclude?
7. Are you likely to conclude that two population means differ when the difference between their sample means is *much* larger than the estimated standard error?
8. Provide an example (different from those in the book) where we would need to draw inferences about two population proportions.

9. Correct, if necessary, the following statement:
   If the confidence interval on the difference in two *population* proportions includes the value of 0, we conclude that the two *sample* proportions are not different.
10. If the sample proportion is greater than 1, what can we conclude?
11. When should we use the Mann-Whitney confidence interval method?
12. Explain the logic of the Mann-Whitney method.
13. Why is consistent performance, product, or service desirable?
14. If the confidence interval on two population variances includes the value of 1, why would managers conclude that the two population variances are the same?
15. What are the differences between the assumptions underlying confidence intervals on the variance ratio and the Mood test?
16. When the computed M-value is either larger or smaller than the tabled values (Table 8.18), the population dispersions of the two groups differ. Explain the logic.
17. What role do stem-and-leaf displays and box plots play in constructing confidence intervals?
18. Why won't a square root or log base 10 transformation work on negative data values, such as dollar loss?
19. Why is it important to identify potential improvement projects?
20. What role can confidence intervals play in identifying potential improvement projects?

CHAPTER 8 APPLICATION PROBLEMS

1. Best Dairy Inc. has segmented its market into eight groups. Among these separate markets are the Machos and Status Seekers. Machos are young males, blue-collar workers with high-school degrees who live in the city. Status Seekers are young males, white-collar workers with college degrees who live in the suburbs. Best Dairy Inc. takes a sample of 10 from both market segments and asks each person his annual income. Below are the data. Is there a difference between the population mean incomes of the Machos and Status Seekers?

Machos		Status Seekers	
$22,500	$22,900	$29,000	$29,000
22,000	20,000	28,500	27,500
22,700	22,500	28,000	28,000
22,000	23,500	27,500	28,000
23,000	21,500	28,500	28,000

   a. Draw stem-and-leaf displays for both market segments. Do the shapes appear normal? Do the variances appear to be the same?
   b. Set up and interpret an 80% confidence interval on the difference between the two population means.

2. The Vice-President for Human Resource Development wishes to determine if the proportion of hourly employees who believe that senior management is open to their ideas is the same in two plants. He randomly selects 100 workers in each plant and asks them if senior management is open to their ideas. Shown are the sample proportions that respond yes.

	Plant	
	Hartford, CT	Austin, TX
n	100	100
$\hat{p}$	.56	.48

    a. Set up and interpret a 95% confidence interval on the difference between the two population proportions.

    b. Why can you assume that the sampling distribution for the difference between two sample proportions is near normal? Explain.

3. COMCEL buys the plastic for its mobile phone housings from two suppliers. It wonders if both suppliers' plastics have the same mean impact resistance. It takes a simple random sample of 10 phones made from each vendor's material and runs impact tests. Here are the data.

Impact Resistance in Pounds per Square Inch

Vendor A	Vendor B
4,600	4,700
4,650	4,750
4,700	4,600
4,650	4,650
4,750	4,650
4,850	4,675
4,600	4,800
4,900	4,625
4,650	4,675
4,600	4,690

    a. What is the appropriate confidence interval to construct for this problem? [*Hint:* Drawing a stem-and-leaf display or box plot may be helpful in answering the question.]

    b. Set up and interpret a 95% confidence interval.

4. A manager tests interacting and nominal group structures. The former is run by a directed leader who closely controls the meeting. Members speak when they have something to say; otherwise, they remain quiet. The nominal group provides time for all to think about the problem, the opportunity to share ideas with others, and to compare and contrast ideas and reach a consensus. The manager compares 10 groups with each group structure using the *Moon Survival* game. Groups must identify the top five items (from a list of 15) to help them travel from a crash site to the mother ship some 200 miles away. The groups' results are compared to those of NASA survival experts. Below are the number of correct items each group identified.

Interacting	2 3 2 5 2 3 4 4 3 4
Nominal	3 4 4 4 5 5 4 5 5 4

    a. Draw two stem-and-leaf displays for the number of correct items selected. Which group structure appears to produce more correct items and less variability in the number of correct items?

    b. Which group structure yields better mean results? Set up a 90% confidence interval on the difference between the two population means.

c. Which group has less variance in the number of correct items? Set up a 90% confidence interval on the ratio of the two population variances.

5. Shown are the number of months required for American firms to negotiate major contracts with firms in Europe and the Far East.

Europe	Far East
3	2
4	6
5	10
7	20
8	48

At the 95% level of confidence, are the dispersions in negotiating times the same for Europe and the Far East?

6. The American Housing Association (AHA) believes that the size of an apartment complex affects the length-of-tenure discount size. AHA takes a simple random sample of 10 small and 10 large apartment complexes and determines the mean discount within each complex for renters who have lived there five or more years. Here are the data:

Discount As Percentage of Normal Starting Rent

	Small Complex	Large Complex
$\bar{x}$	7.9%	2.5%
s^2	.8	.5
s	.89%	.71%
Sample size	10	10

a. Set up and interpret a 95% confidence interval on the difference between the two population mean discounts.
b. Set up and interpret a 95% confidence interval on the difference between the two population variances. Are discounts in large complexes more consistent than discounts in small complexes?

7. When team members learn to do each others' jobs, is the proportion of defects produced by the team reduced? An operations manager runs a planned change study in which she randomly selects 1,000 groups. Of these groups, 500 are given cross-job training and 500 are not. Several weeks after the training, she assesses the proportion of defects for both the study and control groups. Here are the data.

	Control Groups	Cross-Trained Groups
n	500	500
$\hat{p}$	.04	.01

a. Set up and interpret a 95% confidence interval on the difference between the two population proportions.
b. Has the cross training been successful in reducing the proportion of defects?

Chapter 8 Making Inferences About Two Populations

8. A nutritionist determines the impact of bran on reducing cholesterol levels. He randomly selects 10 people who have the same level of elevated cholesterol and randomly assigns them to one of two groups—the bran group and the control group. Each person in the bran group eats a bowl of bran every day for six weeks. The control group eats the same foods as the bran group except for the bran. After six weeks the researcher measures the drop in cholesterol levels of individuals in both groups.

| Bran group: | 10 | 15 | 20 | 10 | 80 |
| Control group: | 0 | 5 | 0 | 0 | 5 |

  a. Set up and interpret a 95% confidence interval on the difference between the two population medians (drop in cholesterol level).
  b. Does bran appear to reduce cholesterol levels? Explain.
  c. Why couldn't you set up a confidence interval on the difference between two population means? Explain.

9. FarWestern Power wants to even out commercial power usage during the day. Typically, power usage is very high during the day and very low in the evening hours. This forces FarWestern Power to use old and inefficient coal-burning plants to generate the necessary power to meet peak demand. FarWestern launches a new campaign to get commercial users to postpone some of their power needs until the evening hours. Have they been successful in reducing the variability in daily consumption? Below are day and evening power usages before and after the campaign for two randomly selected weeks.

Data in Thousands of Kilowatts for 12-Hour Periods

	Before Campaign	After Campaign
Monday A.M.	2,000	1,500
Monday P.M.	300	900
Tuesday A.M.	2,100	1,400
Tuesday P.M.	500	1,000
Wednesday A.M.	1,500	1,200
Wednesday P.M.	100	400
Thursday A.M.	2,500	1,700
Thursday P.M.	700	1,500
Friday A.M.	2,000	1,500
Friday P.M.	500	1,000

Set up and interpret a 90% confidence interval on the ratio of the population variances in power consumption. Has the campaign to even out daily power consumption been successful?

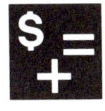

10. Apex must reduce its mean age of accounts receivable (A/R) from over 30 days. It tries a program of inducements—discounts for prompt payment—in Hartford and no inducements in New Haven. It then randomly selects 10 accounts from both cities. Does the program appear to be successful?

Age of A/R in Days	
With Inducement	No Inducement
20	30
21	28
20	31
16	35
19	30
24	30
21	29
22	34
25	32
21	32

    a. Draw stem-and-leaf displays for the two data sets. Do the data sets look normal and appear to have the same variance?
    b. Set up an appropriate 99% confidence interval.

11. An ad firm evaluates which of two approaches is more successful in helping potential consumers remember the advertising message. It tries a man-in-the-street approach using real customers talking about the product. The other approach uses movie stars and sports heroes talking about the product. The firm tries each approach in one city for one month. Two weeks later, it selects a simple random sample of 500 potential customers who have seen the ads and asks them what the ad's message was. Below are the proportions of consumers who correctly identified the ad's message.

	Man-in-the-Street	Stars and Sports Figures
n	500	500
$\hat{p}$	.40	.60

    a. Is there any difference between the two approaches at the 95% level of confidence?
    b. Why can we be reasonably sure that the sampling distribution of the difference in sample proportions is normal? Explain.

12. Are the average earnings per share for firms in the high-tech and heavy-industry market segments the same? Given are seven firms, selected at random from each segment, and their last year's earnings per share.

| High-Tech | .50 | 2.00 | 2.10 | 2.50 | 2.75 | 3.50 | 7.00 |
| Heavy Industry | 2.00 | 2.90 | 3.10 | 3.30 | 3.50 | 4.00 | 14.00 |

Set up and interpret a 95% confidence interval on the difference between the two population medians.

13. Which of two courier services has more consistent delivery times? Based on a sample of 21 days, Reliable Delivery's sample standard deviation is 1.0 hour and United Delivery's sample standard deviation is 1.20 hours. Set up and interpret a 95% confidence interval on the two population variances.

14. A poison pill is an action that a firm takes to make it unattractive to potential hostile takeovers. We wish to determine whether the proportion of firms that use a poison pill changed in the decade of the 1980s. Shown are hypothetical data for 1980 and 1990 surveys.

	1980	1990
	$n = 500$	$n = 500$
	$\hat{p} = .11$	$\hat{p} = .06$

At the 99% level of confidence, can we say that there has been a drop in the proportion of firms that have used the poison pill strategy from 1980 to 1990?

15. A firm tries two different leadership styles in two plants to determine their impact on productivity. Two plants are randomly selected. The project manager randomly selects 15 groups in plant A to be led by an autocratic leader and 15 groups in plant B to be led by a participative leader. Below are productivity data six months later.

Productivity As Percentage of Standard

	Participative Leadership	Autocratic Leadership
n	15	15
$\bar{x}$	105%	98%
s	1.5%	1%

a. Set up and interpret a 90% confidence interval. Which leadership style has the higher mean worker productivity? Explain.
b. The data are in percentages. Why did we set up confidence intervals on the population means and not the population proportions?

16. Given are daily outputs from two production lines. Which production line is more consistent?

Production in Units per Hour

Line A	Line B
50	47
53	55
60	57
61	62
65	66

Set up a 95% confidence interval on the difference between the two population dispersions.

17. Which fixed disk lasts longer? We have time-to-failure data in hours for two vendors' fixed disks. Which vendor has a higher average time-to-failure? Set up and interpret an 80% confidence interval on the difference between the two population means.

Time-to-Failure in Hours

	Vendor A	Vendor B
n	50	50
$\bar{x}$	1,000	800
s	50	40

18. Two universities wish to compare median Graduate Management Aptitude Test (GMAT) scores for their incoming graduate classes. Below are randomly selected samples from both universities.

    University A: 400 510 540 560 600 610 610 650 780
    University B: 410 500 550 560 600 600 610 630 680

    a. Draw box plots for the data sets.
    b. Set up and interpret a 95% confidence interval on the difference between two population medians.

19. In *Eison v. City of Knoxville*, a female candidate at the Knoxville Police Academy claimed that the physical qualification tests tended to reject female applicants. If Eison could show this, she would have established a *prima facie* case for discrimination. Then the city of Knoxville would have to demonstrate that the physical qualification test is crucial to on-the-job performance. Below are the data.

	Pass	Fail	Total
Female	32	9	41
Male	84	9	93

    a. Compute the sample proportions of both genders that passed the physical qualification tests.
    b. Set up a 95% confidence interval on the difference between the two population proportions. What can you conclude?

20. Two years ago, Alliance Motors launched the Luxor, a $50,000 two-door sedan to compete with the BMW 733. Alliance had targeted consumers who are 35–49 years old. Luxor car sales have been disappointing. Alliance suspects that the car is attracting older buyers, a market segment that is generally unwilling to spend $50,000 for a car. Alliance Motors randomly selects 100 Luxor owners and 100 BMW 733 owners. Shown are the descriptive data on owners' ages.

	Luxor	BMW 733
Sample size	100	100
$\bar{x}$	52.5 years	41.5 years
s	2.1 years	2.3 years

    a. Construct a 99% confidence interval on the difference between the two population mean ages.
    b. Is the Luxor attracting the same age buyers as the BMW 733? Explain.

21. In *Boykin v. Georgia Pacific Corporation*, two black plaintiffs complained that blacks were primarily assigned to low-level utility jobs. They presented the following data to support their position.

Race	Assigned to Non-Utility Job	Assigned to Utility Job	Total
Black	22	295	317
White	90	354	444

a. Compute the sample proportions of blacks and whites assigned to non-utility jobs.
b. Set up a 90% confidence interval on the difference between the two population proportions. What can you conclude?

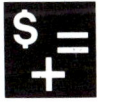

22. Do stocks in different industries have the same variance in their beta coefficients? The beta coefficient is a measure of the extent to which the returns on a given stock move with the stock market. A stock with a beta of 1 means that if the market rises (or falls) by 10%, the stock price will rise (or fall) by 10%. Below are hypothetical beta coefficients for stocks for two industries.

Computer	Public Utility
1.70	.55
1.20	.65
1.00	.60
2.10	.65
1.95	.62

Set up a 95% confidence interval on the ratio of the two population variances. What can you conclude?

23. Suppose we take two random samples of five male and five female full professors from state universities and we obtain the following nine-month salary information.

Males	Females
$47,000	$39,000
$53,000	$44,000
$59,000	$49,000
$65,000	$56,000
$79,000	$67,000

a. Set up a 95% confidence interval on the difference between the two population median incomes.
b. If your answer to part **a** indicates that there is a difference, does this mean that there is gender discrimination in salaries? Discuss.

24. Marketers who use price lining offer products in set price lines and target each line to a particular market segment. For example, a national retailer advertises car batteries as good or excellent. Below are hypothetical data on the number of seconds of cranking power for the good and the excellent brands.

Good Brand	Excellent Brand
65	140
78	146
85	148
85	148
88	148
94	149
100	155

a. Construct multiple box plots to compare the locations and dispersions of the two samples? What do you conclude?
b. Explain why it is unnecessary to construct a confidence interval for the difference between the population medians.
c. Explain why the Mood test for the difference of dispersions is inappropriate.

25. We randomly select 10 families in each of two cities and determine their family incomes. Are the dispersions in incomes the same in the two cities?

Eugene, OR	Akron, OH
$ 9,000	$11,000
$19,000	$14,000
$22,500	$19,500
$25,000	$24,500
$29,900	$27,500
$30,000	$35,000
$32,500	$37,000
$45,000	$47,500
$60,000	$55,500
$79,000	$82,000

Use Mood's method to set up a 95% confidence interval. Do the two population dispersions differ? Explain.

26.
```
Date:  September 7, 1992
  To:  Howard Bright, Norcross Plant Manager
From:  Sarah Teman, Manager of Operations
  Re:  Comparison of Dallas and Norcross Plants
```

I received a copy of Martin Young's analysis of the overall job attitude and the level of perceived task support within the Dallas plant. That got me to thinking that it would be informative to compare our performance with the Dallas plant's. In a couple of days I will be sending you my report. I'm looking forward to seeing how we compare to the Dallas operation. If you have any questions after receiving my analysis, please contact me.

Use Data Base I and develop a report that compares the Dallas and Norcross plants on overall job attitude and level of perceived task support. Write a memo summarizing the major findings to Howard Bright.

27.
```
Date:  April 15, 1992
  To:  Bill O'Hara, Vice-President of Marketing
From:  Cherian Jain, Manager of Marketing Research
  Re:  Additional Analysis of Harrid Survey Data
```

Having completed the initial analysis requested in your March 17 memo, I thought of some additional analyses we might do. It occurred to me that we should make comparisons among the various regions. I am especially interested in answering the following questions:

1. What is the buy—American attitude across the four regions? Is the pro buy—American attitude in the South found elsewhere?
2. Is the desire for FAX machines in the Northeast and West the same as in the South and Midwest regions?
3. Is the age of the accounts receivable the same in the South as in the other three regions?
4. Is the variation in the age of accounts receivable the same in the South as in the other three regions?

I'll have the additional report by the week of the 21st. Perhaps then we can discuss the marketing implications. Let's have several people from Peter Miangi's finance group sit in, for they may find the aging of the accounts receivable information informative.

Use Data Base III to analyze the data. Write a short memo to Bill O'Hara summarizing your response to the four questions. Include your statistical analyses to support your findings.

REFERENCES

MOOD, ALEXANDER. "On the Asymptotic Efficiency of Certain Nonparametric Two-Sample Tests." *Ann. Math. Statist.* 25 (1964): 514–522.

SIEGEL, ANDREW. *Statistics and Data Analysis.* New York: Wiley, 1988.

Analysis of Variance

9.1 The role of experimentation in problem solving
    Problem definition
    Problem diagnosis and solving
9.2 Exploratory data analysis
    Null and alternative hypotheses
    Spread charts
    Guidelines for interpreting spread charts
9.3 Analysis of variance for a one-factor, k-level study
    Total sum of squares and its components
    Degrees of freedom
    Hypothesis testing and the analysis of variance
    Summary of steps in the analysis of variance
9.4 Testing for significant differences between pairs of population means
    The problem of multiple comparisons
    Tukey HSD confidence intervals
9.5 The Kruskal–Wallis nonparametric analysis of variance
    Statistical hypotheses
    Logic behind the test
    Dunn's multiple comparisons
    Construction and interpretation of Dunn's multiple comparisons
9.6 The two-factor, completely random factorial study
    Designing a factorial study
    Exploratory data analysis: Graphing profiles
    Total sum of squares
    Sum of squares for main effects
    Sum of squares within
    Degrees of freedom
    Hypotheses
9.7 Key ideas and overview
Chapter 9 Questions
Chapter 9 Application Problems

CHAPTER OUTLINE

COMCEL Interoffice Communication

Date: November 15, 1992
  To: Bill Katz, Production Testing
From: Sarah Teman, Manager of Operations
  Re: Problem at Apex Plastics and Metals

Our Apex Plastics subsidiary is experiencing an excessive number of defects in its desk drawers. Over the last several years, Apex has been able to hold the percentage of defective cracked drawers to just 1%. Yesterday, the defect rate jumped to 6%, and they can't figure out why.

This has top priority as Apex has shut down its main production line. Please provide daily status reports.

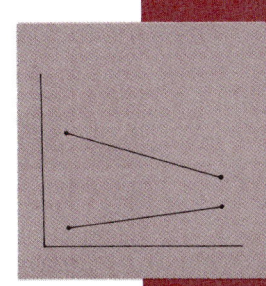

9.1 The Role of Experimentation in Problem Solving

Planned change studies or experiments are essential to determining root causes of disturbance problems. A disturbance problem is a sudden and significant deviation from historical or planned performance levels, such as a sudden increase in rejects or a major drop in service levels. Faced with a disturbance problem, the manager must be able to:

1. separate the symptoms from the facts—problem definition;
2. identify potential root causes—problem diagnosis; and
3. determine which are the true root causes—problem solving.

The first activity uncovers *what* happened. The last two activities seek to reveal *why* the problem happened.

The following example illustrates the role of experimentation in determining root causes.

EXAMPLE: THE CASE OF THE CRACKED TYPING TABLE DRAWERS
Apex Plastics and Metals, a COMCEL subsidiary, makes the housing for COMCEL's mobile phones. Apex also produces three sizes of drawers or compartments for typing tables sold by Contemporary Office Furniture, Inc. Model A is a 4-inch deep drawer, model B is a 7-inch deep drawer, and model C is a 10-inch deep drawer.

There are three steps in manufacturing drawers. At blanking, workers cut the raw material to the approximate drawer size. Next, workers use stamping presses that bend the blanked metal to form the drawer. Stamping press 3 makes the 4-inch drawer, presses 1 and 4 make the 7-inch drawer, and press 2 makes the 10-inch drawer. Finally, workers inspect for cracks and other damage. Defect-free drawers are then packaged for shipment to Contemporary. During stamping, cracking sometimes occurs at the lower corners of the drawer where the metal undergoes the maximum deformation and therefore stress. Over the past several years, the reject rate due to cracking has been about 1%.

At 8:00 A.M. on Tuesday, stamping press 2 started producing about 6% cracks. The line supervisor had Engineering check the press, but no problems were found. After the morning break (10:00 A.M.), stamping press 1 started producing about 4% rejects. Finally at 11:00 A.M., stamping press 4 started producing about 4% rejects. At noon, only stamping press 3 was still producing 1% rejects.

Apex has a severe disturbance problem. Why have there been fourfold and sixfold increases in reject rates on three of the four stamping presses? What is going on?

Before we can take corrective action we must understand the disturbance problem. The Kepner–Tregoe method is an effective tool for understanding disturbance problems.

Problem Definition

The Kepner and Tregoe method (1988) transforms ambiguous symptoms, facts, and assumptions into a clear statement of the disturbance problem. To define the problem, start by asking and answering the following questions:

What is the deviation (vs. what it isn't)?

When did the deviation occur (vs. when didn't it occur)?

Where did the deviation occur (vs. where didn't it occur)?

How much, how many, and to what extent did the deviation occur (vs. to what extent didn't it occur)?

Reject vague phrases. "Something is wrong" is an unacceptable answer to a "what is" question. Also avoid useless adjectives such as "We have *a lot of* defects." Be specific. Be precise. If the information is vague or imprecise, we need to do more detective work before entering the data into a problem definition worksheet, such as that in Table 9.1.

Problem Diagnosis and Solving

Diagnosing a problem begins with developing *problem solving hypotheses*. A problem solving hypothesis is a tentative statement of the cause of a problem that can be disproved. It is an informed guess that has a reasonable chance of being correct. It is an unproved assumption, a plan of attack. It is an alternative route to the solution.

Table 9.1

Problem Definition for the Cracked Typing Table Drawer Problem

	IS THE DEVIATION	IS NOT THE DEVIATION
WHAT	4%–6% cracks on 7" and 10" drawers	Excessive scratches Bent drawers 4%–6% for 4" drawers
WHEN	8:00 A.M. on press 2 10:00 A.M. on press 1 11:00 A.M. on press 4	No problems on press 3 On press 2 before 8:00 A.M. On press 1 before 10:00 A.M. On press 4 before 11:00 A.M.
WHERE	Presses 1, 2, 4 Lower four corners of drawers	Press 3 Cracks randomly distributed at blanking operation
EXTENT	Press 2: 6% Presses 1, 4: 4%	Press 3: normal 1%

We recommend the following problem diagnosis guidelines and demonstrate their application to the Apex drawer problem.

RULE 1: Generate many problem solving hypotheses.

Yesterday, 1% of Apex's typing table drawers had cracks. Today three presses are producing 4%–6% rejects. Something must have changed recently to cause the sudden increase in rejects.

The more hypotheses we generate, the more likely we are to solve the problem, because hypotheses point out directions in which to seek data to identify the real causes. Ultimately, we must select one or two hypotheses for serious analysis.

Think in terms of the following root cause areas: (1) *changes* in workers' or supervisors' motivations, likes/dislikes, etc., (2) *changes* in technology, processes, raw materials, or methods, and (3) *changes* in organizational structures or the external environment.

Apply this threefold strategy to Apex's problem. Table 9.2 presents a breakdown of the root cause areas, along with possible explanations.

RULE 2: Suspend judgment about the hypotheses until most of the facts are in. Keep an open mind.

Keeping an open mind is difficult. Many managers jump to conclusions about the root causes of a problem. A manager who had a recent problem with workers might jump to the conclusion that workers' stress or sabotage caused the cracked drawers. A manager who recently had a problem with raw material might jump to the conclusion that the raw material caused the cracked drawers. We must suspend judgment until we have collected Kepner–Tregoe problem definition data and have looked at all changes.

Table 9.2

Possible Root Causes

Root Cause Areas	Recent Change at Apex
People	Yesterday the company disciplined a worker who failed a random drug test. Perhaps a drug problem is the root cause.
Technology or methods	Today, Apex switched to a new raw material supplier. The new raw material is less costly. Perhaps the raw material is the root cause.
Organization or environment	Because of a drop in market share, Apex has recently laid off workers. Those still employed know that there will be more layoffs. Perhaps excessive worker stress is the root cause.

RULE 3: If possible, rigorously test hypotheses.

Testing runs the gamut from casual observation to formal studies or experiments. Casual observation is the weakest form of testing. Managers use casual observation when they say, "If event A and event B occur together frequently, then A is the cause of B." All of us use this form of "testing," but it is inconclusive. For example, alcoholics often have cirrhosis of the liver. Thus, we might conclude that excessive alcohol causes cirrhosis, but it does not. Rather, certain vitamin deficiencies cause cirrhosis. The problem is that alcoholics do not eat well-balanced meals. Casual observation is useful in *generating* problem solving hypotheses, not *testing* them.

Sometimes, all we can use is casual observation. How else could we test the sabotage or stress hypotheses? We could make observation more rigorous by generating other possible root causes. Then, *compare and contrast* the root causes and determine which one better explains the known facts.

Conducting formal planned change studies is the best way to test problem solving hypotheses. Suppose that based on the Kepner–Tregoe analysis, the plant manager believed that there were two root causes of excessive cracked drawers—(1) the new material and (2) the drawer depth. The drawer depth could be a cause since the excessive cracking did not occur on the 4-inch deep drawers, but did occur on the deeper 7- and 10-inch drawers. The manager could then run a two-factor planned change study. The factors would be material supplier and drawer depth. The raw material factor has two levels—old and new material supplier. The drawer depth factor has three levels—4″, 7″, and 10″ drawer depth. In Section 9.6 we will analyze the results of a two-factor study to determine the root causes of the excessive cracking of desk drawers.

Experimentation also plays an important role in evaluating potential management improvements in product, service, performance, or quality. For example, a manager believes that training in creativity or training in team building can reduce unit labor costs. The manager should run a planned change study and test three training variations—creativity training, team-building training, and no training (control groups). In Section 9.3 we will analyze the results of a one-factor, three-level unit labor cost study.

In summary, experimentation plays a crucial role in problem diagnosis, seeking root causes, and improving performance. In this chapter we will learn how to analyze experimental data. However, if we improperly design our studies, no analysis in the world can correct them. Please review the experimental design principles in Chapter 6.

SECTION 9.1 EXERCISES

1. What is a control group and what purpose did it serve in the reduction of unit labor cost study presented in the chapter?
2. According to Kepner and Tregoe, "A problem is a deviation from planned or expected performance" and "A problem is always caused by a change."

        a. What was the expected reject rate due to cracking at Apex Plastics and Metals?
        b. What was the problem?
        c. List some possible changes that may have occurred to produce the deviation.
3. Why is it as important to know where the problem does *not* exist as where it does exist?
4. Refer to the Apex Plastics example again. Suppose we learned that only press 4 started using raw material from a new vendor. Press 2, which makes 10-inch drawers, is still using the old material. How should we respond to someone who quickly concludes, "We made a mistake in changing vendors. The new vendor's material is defective."
5. What is the connection between managerial problem solving and design of experiments?
6. Why is it important to seek changes to explain a disturbance problem?
7. In the Kepner–Tregoe method we must not use vague phrases, such as "It is not working right," in defining a problem. Explain.

9.2 Exploratory Data Analysis

A central theme of this book is to use graphical tools to explore the data before analyzing them. In the last chapter we used stem-and-leaf displays and box plots. Here we introduce the *spread chart* as a graphical tool. By the end of this section you should be able to:

1. draw spread charts for a one-factor, *k*-level experimental data set;
2. visually determine if you are *likely* to reject (or fail to reject) the null hypothesis of no difference among the *k*-levels; and
3. explain when you are likely to reject (or fail to reject) the null hypothesis using the concept of spread both within and between factors.

Null and Alternative Hypotheses

From Section 7.5, we know that a statistical hypothesis is a testable claim or statement about one or more population parameters. The null hypothesis is a statement of "no effect," "no change," "no improvement," or "I don't believe you." We also define a second hypothesis—alternative hypothesis—that we hope or suspect is true. We should also state what actions we will take if we reject the null hypothesis and what we will do if we fail to reject it. Table 9.3 presents the null and alternative hypotheses for the unit labor cost reduction study mentioned in the previous section.

    Table 9.4 shows two possible data sets, as a result of the cost reduction study. When we complete our statistical analysis, we will reject the null hypothesis for one of the data sets. After drawing spread charts we will be able to make an educated guess as to which data set will cause rejection of the null hypothesis.

    The hypothetical data sets have some similarities and some differences. Both data sets have the same sample means. However, note that the spread in the values within each treatment level in data set 1 is much less than in data set 2.

Table 9.3

Null and Alternative Hypotheses for Cost Reduction Study

Null Hypothesis H_0: The effect of the three treatment levels is zero. Or, the population mean unit labor cost reductions are the same for the creativity training, team-building training, and the control groups.

Null Action A_0: All the workshops are equally effective in reducing labor costs. Since the control groups received no training but still obtained large cost reductions, we have a flawed study. The control groups should have had little or no reduction in unit labor costs.

Alternative Hypothesis H_1: The effect of the three treatment levels is not zero. Not all of the three population mean unit labor cost reductions are the same.

Alternative Action A_1: One (or more) workshop reduces unit labor cost more than the others. Determine which workshop is best and implement it throughout the plant.

Table 9.4

Two Sets of Hypothetical Data for Reduction in Unit Labor Costs

	Data Set 1 Workshop			Data Set 2 Workshop		
	Team-Building	Creativity	Control	Team-Building	Creativity	Control
	$3.05	$4.12	$.15	$−1.81	$8.23	$.10
	3.10	4.13	.07	10.19	−1.77	−3.90
	3.13	4.21	.30	9.19	7.23	10.10
	3.14	4.21	.05	.19	.23	−7.90
	3.18	4.22	.15	11.19	9.23	−1.90
	3.22	4.24	.02	−2.81	−2.77	.10
	3.22	4.26	.08	2.19	.23	7.10
	3.24	4.27	.03	.19	13.23	−7.90
	3.29	4.27	.05	3.19	.23	.10
	3.32	4.36	.10	.19	8.23	5.10
$\bar{x}$	$3.19	$4.23	$.10	$3.19	$4.23	$.10

Spread Charts

We begin a visual exploration of the data by translating each column of numbers into a spread chart. We do this in the following way:

1. Draw a horizontal line and scale it in the units of the dependent variable. In this case, the dependent variable is the dollar reduction in unit labor costs.

2. Place a "1" above the x-coordinate for each observation of the first treatment level—TB workshop. The actual height above the line is not important. Place a "2" above the x-coordinate for each observation of the second treatment level and a "3" above the x-coordinate for each observation of the third treatment level.
3. Place a labelled "$\bar{x}$" symbol at each of the three sample mean values, in this case, $\bar{x}_1$ at $3.19, $\bar{x}_2$ at $4.23, and $\bar{x}_3$ at $.10 for data set 1.

From Figure 9.1, we see that the data values for each workshop for data set 1 cluster together. There is very little spread in the data values within a treatment level. Also, the three sample means are quite different. What are the small spread of values *within* each treatment level and the large spread *between* sample means trying to tell us?

The large spread between sample means suggests that the dollar reductions in unit labor costs for the three types of training may be different. The small spread within each treatment level suggests that the data are *unchanging*. Even if we ran each treatment level 10 more times, the three sample means would not change very much from the present values. Thus the sample means in data set 1 will tend to maintain their rank order—lowest reduction for control groups, highest reduction for the creative methods workshop. Thus we will probably conclude that all population mean unit labor cost reductions are not the same at the three treatment levels. Remember that we are making inferences from this one study to the population. Statistically speaking, we will reject the null hypothesis for data set 1.

In contrast, the three sample means are quite different in data set 2. Note the large spread among the data values within each treatment level. Suppose we ran

FIGURE 9.1 Spread Charts for Unit Labor Cost Study

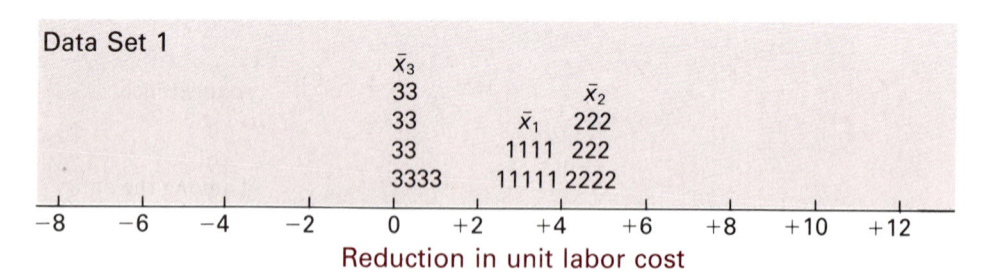

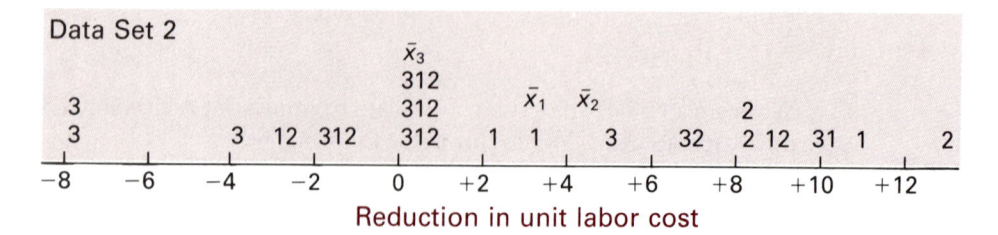

Table 9.5

Two Data Sets for Spread Charting

	Data Set 3 Workshop			Data Set 4 Display		
	1	2	3	1	2	3
	$.50	$.60	$.70	$180	$218	$210
	$.52	$.58	$.69	$200	$178	$215
	$.50	$.62	$.71	$200	$200	$170
	$.48	$.60	$.70	$220	$196	$213
$\bar{x}$	$.50	$.60	$.70	$200	$198	$202

each treatment level 10 more times and recomputed the three sample means. Would we expect them to be very close to the present values of $3.19, $4.23, and $.10? It is quite likely that the next 10 numbers within each level would be very different from the first 10 numbers. The three sample means could dramatically change. Thus, we cannot be sure whether the differences among the three sample means indicate real differences in the population mean unit labor cost reductions. We will probably conclude that the type of workshop has no impact on reducing unit labor costs. Statistically speaking, we cannot reject the null hypothesis for data set 2.

We use a spread chart and plot the data before beginning formal analysis to develop a feel for the data. Remember, however, that spread charting is not a substitute for a formal statistical analysis.

Table 9.5 contains two additional data sets. For which data set are we likely to reject a null hypothesis of no difference among population means? Again, we draw the spread charts.

The spread charts in Figure 9.2 on page 454 suggest that we would probably reject the null hypothesis for data set 3. Note that the spread in the unit labor cost data values *within* each treatment level is very small. The data are unchanging. Even if we collected more data, the sample means would probably remain quite constant. Moreover, there appear to be large differences among the three sample means. This suggests that not all three workshops have the same population mean unit labor cost reduction.

In data set 4 there is a large amount of spread among the data values *within* each treatment level. If we continued the study, the three sample means could change dramatically. Furthermore, there is little spread *among* the three sample means. The closer the sample means are to one another, the more difficult it is to reject the null hypothesis.

Guidelines for Interpreting Spread Charts

Table 9.6 on page 454 presents guidelines for interpreting spread charts. Based on the spread between and within treatment levels, we can make an educated guess as to whether the experimental factor has an impact on the dependent variable.

FIGURE 9.2 Additional Spread Charts

Data Set 3

```
                    x̄₁              x̄₂              x̄₃
                    1               2               3
                    111             222             333
         |----------|---------------|---------------|----------
        .40        .50             .60             .70
                    Reduction in unit labor cost
```

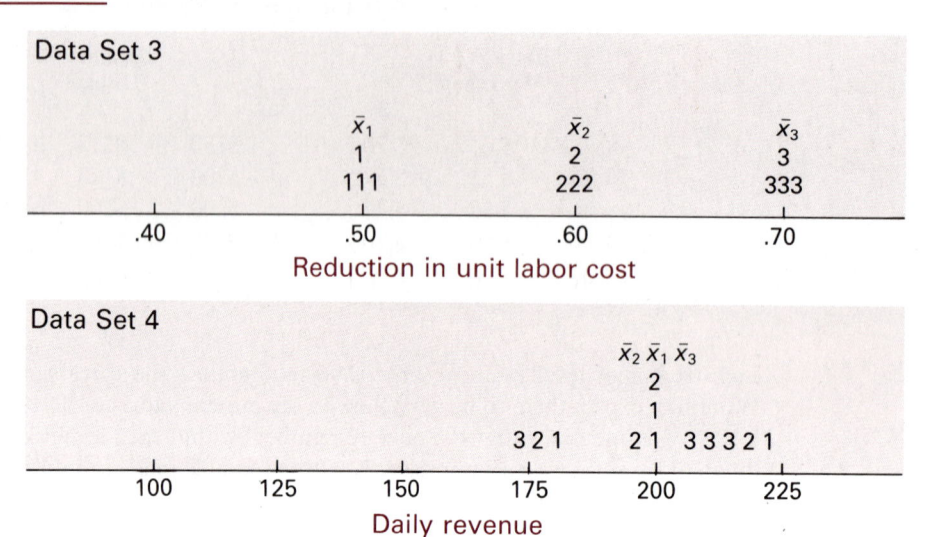

Data Set 4

```
                                            x̄₂ x̄₁ x̄₃
                                              2
                                              1
                                 3 2 1      2 1    3 3 3 2 1
         |----------|----------|----------|----------|----------
        100        125        150        175        200        225
                              Daily revenue
```

Table 9.6

Guidelines for Interpreting Spread Charts

When the spread between sample means is	and the spread within the levels is	then:
1. small	small	it is hard to tell if the factor has an impact.
2. small	large	the factor probably has no impact; do not reject the null hypothesis.
3. large	small	the factor probably has an impact; reject the null hypothesis.
4. large	large	it is hard to tell if the factor has an impact.

Data sets 1 and 3 illustrate the third guideline. There is little spread within each level and much spread among the three sample means. Data set 2 illustrates the fourth possibility. There is much spread both within and among the three treatment levels. Data set 4 typifies the second situation. There is much spread within each treatment level and little spread among the three sample means.

SECTION 9.2 EXERCISES

1. A grocery chain wants to test the appeal of three different sales promotions on soft drink sales. It selects three different stores in similar neighborhoods and randomly assigns one of the promotions to each store. Sales (in tens of bottles) are recorded over a period of five days.

	Type of Sales Promotion		
Day	Contest	Free Sample	Point of Purchase Display
1	8	12	16
2	8	15	18
3	9	11	18
4	10	13	19
5	10	12	20

    a. Plot a spread chart for this experiment.
    b. Does it appear that the three displays will produce the same mean sales over the long run? Explain your answer in terms of the relationship of the spread between to the spread within.
    c. If your graph suggests that one display is better than the others, which appears to be the best at producing sales?

2. COMCEL managers believe that all employees need to learn problem solving skills. It experiments with three different methods of teaching these skills. Five employees are randomly assigned to each method. After a specified period of instruction, each person is presented with the same set of problems. The employees' scores (coded) are shown below. Higher scores indicate greater problem solving ability.

	Teaching Method	
Lecture	Case	Role Playing
14	15	21
14	17	20
16	19	21
15	17	22
19	17	22

    a. Plot a spread chart for this experiment.
    b. Does it appear that any of the methods is more or less effective than the others in teaching problem solving? Explain your answer in terms of the relationship of the spread between to the spread within.
    c. Does the spread chart suggest which method would produce the highest mean problem solving score over the long run? Explain.

3. A telephone market research company has experienced a substantial rate of nonresponse on a question that is asked routinely. It experiments with three different forms of the question to try to improve response rates. The research firm records the nonresponse rates (in percent) for a five-day period. Below are the results.

<table>
<tr><td></td><td colspan="3">Question Format</td></tr>
<tr><td>Day</td><td>Open-Ended</td><td>Closed-Ended</td><td>Partially Closed-Ended</td></tr>
<tr><td>1</td><td>14</td><td>15</td><td>15</td></tr>
<tr><td>2</td><td>14</td><td>17</td><td>19</td></tr>
<tr><td>3</td><td>15</td><td>19</td><td>21</td></tr>
<tr><td>4</td><td>19</td><td>20</td><td>22</td></tr>
<tr><td>5</td><td>22</td><td>23</td><td>25</td></tr>
</table>

   a. Plot a spread chart for this experiment.
   b. Does it appear that any of the question formats is best at reducing nonresponse rates over the long run?

4. Explain why we had to use the word *appear* in Exercises 1–3.
5. Construct a data set for a one-factor, four-level study that would cause us to conclude that there is probably no difference among the four treatment levels. Defend.
6. Construct a data set for a one-factor, four-level study that would cause us to conclude that there is probably a difference among the four treatment levels. Defend.
7. Construct a data set for a one-factor, four-level study that would make it difficult to tell if there is a difference among the four treatment levels. Defend.

9.3 Analysis of Variance for a One-Factor, k-Level Study

The one-factor, k-level study is an important experimental design. The manager varies one factor or treatment and determines its impact on the dependent variable. The manager will implement the treatment permanently if it improves performance.

To determine if performance has improved, we conduct an analysis of variance (ANOVA). The analysis of variance compares two variances to determine whether k population means are the same. The ANOVA is an extension of material covered in Section 8.6. By the end of this section you should be able to:

1. explain why there are only two sources of variation that account for the total sum of squares in a one-factor, completely randomized study;
2. see the connection between the variance-within and variance-between terms and the spread charts;
3. explain the computation for the sums of squares;
4. explain why degrees of freedom equal the relevant sample size minus 1;
5. solve and interpret analysis of variance problems using our software; and
6. explain the use of the F-table in testing hypotheses.

Chapter 9 Analysis of Variance

To illustrate an ANOVA, we will analyze the cost reduction data for data set 1 in Table 9.4. The spread chart for these data in Figure 9.1 suggested that we would reject the null hypothesis of no differences among population mean unit labor cost reductions. Before beginning the analysis, we restate the null and alternative hypotheses. We also present the assumptions underlying the analysis.

H_0: The population mean unit labor cost reductions for the three workshops are the same. The experimental factor, type of workshop, has no effect on the population means.

H_1: The population means for the three workshops are not the same. At least one treatment level produces a different population mean unit labor cost reduction.

ASSUMPTION 1: The observations within each of the three treatment levels are independent random samples.

ASSUMPTION 2: The observations within each of the three treatment levels are near-normally distributed.

ASSUMPTION 3: The variances within each of the treatment levels are the same or nearly so.

The first assumption is true because we ran a one-factor, completely randomized study. We randomly selected the 30 teams from the population. We randomly divided the 30 teams into three groups of 10 teams each. We randomly assigned each group of 10 teams to a workshop (or no workshop in the case of control groups). The stem-and-leaf displays in Figure 9.3 on page 458 indicate that assumptions 2 and 3 are reasonable for the creativity and team-building workshops. However, the data for the control group may not be normal.

If either of the last two assumptions is seriously in question, consider transforming the raw data by a square root or log base 10 transformation. Alternatively, use the Kruskal–Wallis nonparametric test (Section 9.5). Serious doubts about these assumptions occur when:

1. outliers exist at one or more treatment levels; or
2. the largest range within a treatment level is more than 5 times the smallest range within a treatment level.

Applying Tukey's rule to the unit labor cost reduction data, there are no outliers in any group, including the control group. The data ranges for the three treatment levels are

Team-building training	$3.32 − $3.05 = $.27
Creativity training	$4.36 − $4.12 = $.24
Control groups	$.30 − $.02 = $.28

$$\frac{\text{Largest range}}{\text{Smallest range}} = \frac{.28}{.24} = 1.17$$

FIGURE 9.3 Stem-and-Leaf Displays

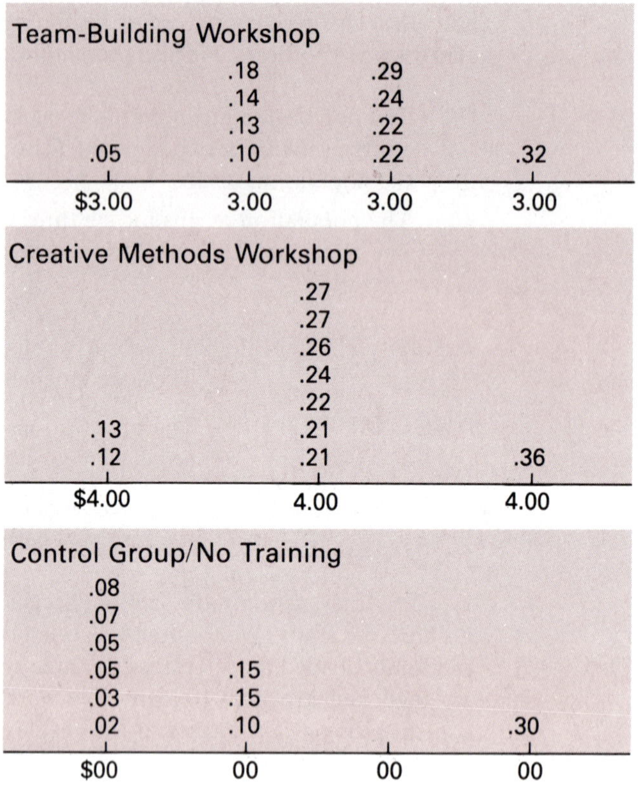

Team-Building Workshop

```
                    .18         .29
                    .14         .24
                    .13         .22
        .05         .10         .22              .32
        |_____|_____|_____|
       $3.00       3.00        3.00             3.00
```

Creative Methods Workshop

```
                                .27
                                .27
                                .26
                                .24
                                .22
        .13                     .21
        .12                     .21              .36
        |_____|_____|
       $4.00                   4.00             4.00
```

Control Group/No Training

```
        .08
        .07
        .05
        .05         .15
        .03         .15
        .02         .10                          .30
        |_____|_____|_____|
       $00         00          00               00
```

Therefore, we have no reason to doubt the validity of assumptions 2 and 3. We may continue the formal statistical analysis.

With spread charts, we compared the spread between the sample means to the spread within the treatment levels. If the former is much larger than the latter, we probably will reject the null hypothesis. In the formal analysis of variance we compute a ratio of two variances—the variance between the sample means divided by the variance within the treatment levels. The larger the ratio, the more likely we are to reject the null hypothesis.

Expression (9.1) is the equation for the variance. The numerator is called the sum of squares and the denominator is called the degrees of freedom. The sum

$$s^2 = \frac{\sum(x_i - \bar{x})^2}{n - 1} \tag{9.1}$$

of squares always equals the sum of squared differences between the *relevant* observations and their mean. The degrees of freedom equal the *relevant* sample size minus 1. We will soon explain the term *relevant*.

Total Sum of Squares and Its Components

The total sum of squares (SST) is the sum of the squared differences between each observation and the *overall* mean, the mean of all the observations.

Our goal is to compute the variance between and the variance within. We begin by computing the **total sum of squares**. The total sum of squares determines how much variability there is in the 30 data values of data set 1 in Table 9.4. Since we are interested in the sum of squares of all 30 numbers, the relevant mean is the mean of all 30 numbers or the overall mean, which equals 2.506. Thus,

$$SST = (3.05 - 2.506)^2 + (3.10 - 2.506)^2 + \cdots$$
$$+ (.05 - 2.506)^2 + (.10 - 2.506)^2$$
$$= 92.46 \text{ units of variability}$$

What accounts for the 92.46 units of variability? Why isn't SST equal to zero? In a one-factor completely randomized study there are two sources that account for the total sum of squares. Variability is due either to the factor we varied (the experimental factor) or to all other possible variables that we might have varied but chose not to. The sum of squares *between* the sample means (SSB) measures the impact of the experimental factor. The sum of squares *within* the treatment levels (SSW) measures the impact of all other variables. Expression (9.2) indicates that the total sum of squares can be divided into two components:

$$SST = SSB + SSW \qquad (9.2)$$

Next we determine SSB and SSW, divide each component by its corresponding degrees of freedom, and then compute a ratio of the two variances to test the null hypothesis.

The sum of squares within the treatment levels (SSW) is the sum of the squared differences between each observation within a treatment and the mean for that treatment, or column, summed over all the treatment levels.

First, consider the **sum of squares within treatment levels (SSW)**. How should we compute it? Why aren't the 10 data values for the team-building workshop (in Table 9.4, data set 1) the same? Since all 10 teams received the team-building training, any variation must be due to the impact of all other variables. Table 9.7 on page 460 shows the calculations for computing SSW. Note that the SSW term consists of three terms in this study, one for each level.

The sum of squares between sample means (SSB) is the sum of the squared differences between each sample mean and the *overall* mean, each weighted by the treatment sample size.

The sum of squares within (SSW) accounts for .17 of the 92.46 units of the total sum of squares. Since there are only two sources of variation for a one-factor study, the **sum of squares between sample means (SSB)** must equal 92.46 − .17 = 92.29. There is a more informative way to calculate SSB, which we will consider next.

The three sample means best represent the mean reductions in unit labor cost for the three treatment levels. These become the relevant observations in the sum of squares calculation. The mean of these three numbers is the overall mean of 2.506. (This is true only when the number of observations under each treatment level is the same.) The following expression for SSB is almost correct, but it disregards the sample size:

$$SSB \neq (3.19 - 2.506)^2 + (4.23 - 2.506)^2 + (.10 - 2.506)^2$$

Table 9.7

Computation of SSW for Unit Labor Cost Reduction Study

Team-Building Workshop	Creativity Workshop	Control Groups
$(3.05 - 3.19)^2$	$(4.12 - 4.23)^2$	$(.15 - .10)^2$
$(3.10 - 3.19)^2$	$(4.13 - 4.23)^2$	$(.07 - .10)^2$
⋮	⋮	⋮
$(3.32 - 3.19)^2$	$(4.36 - 4.23)^2$	$(.10 - .10)^2$
.065	.044	.063

SSW = .065 + .044 + .063 = .17 unit of variability

The three sample means in the study are based on only 10 observations each. Suppose we obtained the same sample means for 5,000 observations. Which case would provide more impressive evidence about whether the population means really differ?

A study based on 5,000 observations provides more impressive evidence, of course. Larger samples give us a better indication of the population than do small samples. Think about it. Which is more accurate—a Gallup Poll based on a sample of 10 or 5,000 people? Clearly, the latter. The point is that the above expression ignores the number of observations used to calculate the three sample means. Therefore, we must multiply each term of the previous expression by the number of data values used to compute each sample mean:

$$SSB = 10(3.19 - 2.506)^2 + 10(4.23 - 2.506)^2 + 10(.10 - 2.506)^2$$

$$= 10[(3.19 - 2.506)^2 + (4.23 - 2.506)^2 + (.10 - 2.506)^2]$$

$$= 92.29 \text{ units of variability}$$

Since there are 10 observations at each treatment level, the 10 in each term is called a *weighting constant*. If we had assigned 5,000 teams to each of the three types of training, the weighting constant would have been 5,000.

As the sum of squares computations are tedious, use our software package.

Degrees of Freedom

According to expression (9.1), to obtain the variance terms we must divide SSB and SSW by their corresponding degrees of freedom. The degrees of freedom for each sum of squares component equal $n - 1$, or the sample size minus 1. Why? Suppose we must compute the SSB for three sample means whose mean is 3. Could you correctly guess the three sample means if you had no hints? No, you could not. Even if we told you that one sample mean was 1, you still could not do it. However, if we told you that two of the sample means were 1 and 4, you would know that the third sample mean must be 4. This is because only 1 + 4 + 4 equals 9, and thus the mean is 3. Thus, when two (or $n - 1$) of the three numbers and the overall mean are known, the third sample mean is known. Once we know the first

Table 9.8

ANOVA Table for Reduction of Unit Labor Cost Study

Source of Variation	Sum of Squares	Degrees of Freedom	Variance	Variance Ratio
Between	92.29	2	46.145	7,325
Within	.17	27	.0063	
Total	92.46	29		

two sample means, the third number is automatically determined—thus, the loss of freedom.

The degrees of freedom are always the relevant sample size minus 1 $(n - 1)$. What are the degrees of freedom for SST? Since there are 30 numbers in the calculation, the relevant sample size is 30. The degrees of freedom are 29. In general, the total degrees of freedom are the total sample size minus 1.

What are the degrees of freedom for SSB? This term measures the differences in sample means between the treatment levels. Therefore the relevant sample size is the number of levels (3) minus 1. In our example there are then 2 degrees of freedom.

In determining the degrees of freedom for SSW, note that there are 10 observations for each treatment level. That produces 9 degrees of freedom for *each* level. Thus, there are 27 degrees of freedom for SSW. In general, the degrees of freedom for SSW equal the number of observations minus 1, times the number of treatment levels.

Table 9.8 is the analysis of variance (ANOVA) table for the reduction in unit labor cost study.

The variance between—impact of training workshops—is much greater than the variance within—impact of all other variables. The ANOVA table quantifies what we already knew from the spread chart in Figure 9.1 (the upper panel)—namely, the data exhibit a large spread between sample means and a small spread within treatment levels.

The variance ratio is the variance between divided by the variance within. In our example the variance ratio equals 46.145/.0063, or 7,325. The variance due to the training workshops is 7,325 times larger than the variance generated by all variables. The large value of the variance ratio suggests that the type of workshop affects the reduction in unit labor costs. In short, we should reject the null hypothesis.

Hypothesis Testing and the Analysis of Variance

Recall what the two variance terms measure. Variance within measures the impact of all other variables. Variance between measures the impact of all other variables *plus* the impact of the experimental factor, type of training. If the null hypothesis were true, then, except for sampling error, the numerator and denominator of the variance ratio should be the same. The ratio should be close to 1.

We could construct an *F-based* confidence interval on the ratio of the two variances (Section 8.6). If the confidence interval includes 1.0, the population variances could be the same and we fail to reject the null hypothesis. If the confidence interval does not include 1.0, the population variances are not the same, or the null hypothesis is false.

The more traditional approach is to determine whether the variance ratio falls in the region of acceptance or the region of rejection under the *F*-curve. When the variance ratio falls in the acceptance region, we fail to reject the null hypothesis. When the variance ratio falls in the rejection region, we reject the null hypothesis.

Here is how to determine the region of rejection. From Section 8.6, we know that if the null hypothesis is true, the sampling distribution of the variance ratio is *F*-distributed. For the unit labor cost reduction study, the variance ratio is *F*-distributed with 2 and 27 degrees of freedom. These are the degrees of freedom for the numerator and denominator of the variance ratio.

To determine the critical value that separates the region of acceptance and the region of rejection, we must set the level of significance. Recall from Section 7.5 that the level of significance is the *maximum* risk we are willing to accept in making a *Type I error*. It is called the alpha (α) level. A 5% α level is commonly used when the Type I error is costly. Thus, in the COMCEL study, the critical value is the *F*-value for 2 and 27 degrees of freedom and a level of confidence equal to $(100 - \alpha)\%$, or 95%. The critical *F*-value is 3.35 (interpolated from Appendix 7). The area to the right of 3.35 in Figure 9.4 contains .05 of the area and is the rejection region.

Since the variance ratio of 7,325 falls in the rejection region, we reject the null hypothesis. We conclude that the type of workshop does affect the unit labor cost reduction. The ANOVA has confirmed our spread chart analysis.

FIGURE 9.4 *F*-Distribution for 2 and 27 Degrees of Freedom

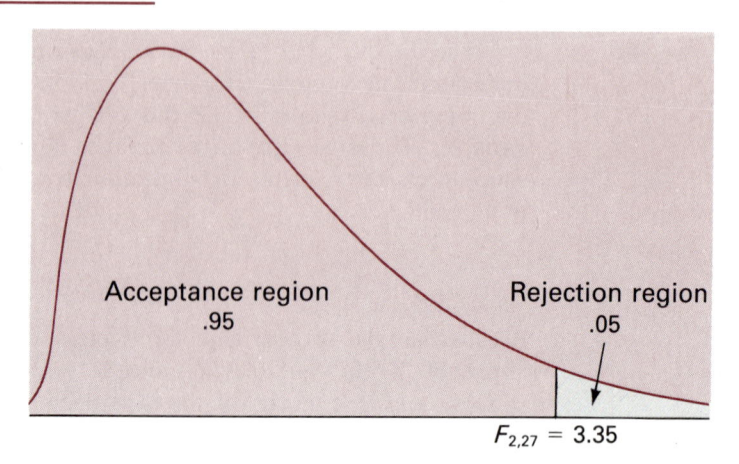

Acceptance region .95

Rejection region .05

$F_{2,27} = 3.35$

What is the logic behind rejecting the null hypothesis when the variance ratio falls in the rejection region? There are only two possible explanations for a variance ratio as large as 7,325:

1. The null hypothesis is *true*. The chance of getting a variance ratio of 7,325 or larger is the area under the curve in Figure 9.4 that lies to the right of 7,325. From Section 7.5, the area is called the *prob-value* and is almost zero.
2. The null hypothesis is *false*. A variance ratio of 7,325 or larger almost never happens if the null hypothesis is true. Therefore, the null hypothesis must not be true, and that is why we obtained such a large variance ratio.

The second explanation is the more reasonable one. After all, the prob-value is almost zero.

Next we will analyze the unit labor cost reduction data for data set 2 in Table 9.4, reproduced here in Table 9.9. The spread chart in Figure 9.1 (the lower panel) suggested that we would not reject the null hypothesis of no difference.

Table 9.10 on page 464 contains the ANOVA table for data set 2. The variance ratio is 46.15/31.11, or 1.48. From Appendix 7, for 2 and 27 degrees of freedom and a 95% level of confidence, the interpolated F-value is 3.35. The variance ratio falls in the acceptance region. Therefore we do not have sufficient evidence to reject the null hypothesis. We conclude that the type of workshop has

Table 9.9

Reduction in Unit Labor Costs—Data Set 2

	Team-Building Workshop	Creativity Workshop	Control Groups
	$-1.81	$8.23	$.10
	10.19	-1.77	-3.90
	9.19	7.23	10.10
	.19	.23	-7.90
	11.19	9.23	-1.90
	-2.81	-2.77	.10
	2.19	.23	7.10
	.19	13.23	-7.90
	3.19	.23	.10
	.19	8.23	5.10
$\bar{x}$	$3.19	$4.23	$.10

$\text{SST} = (-1.81 - 2.506)^2 + (10.19 - 2.506)^2 + \cdots + (5.10 - 2.506)^2$
$= 932.29$

$\text{SSB} = 10[(3.19 - 2.506)^2 + (4.23 - 2.506)^2 + (.10 - 2.506)^2]$
$= 92.29$

$\text{SSW} = (-1.81 - 3.19)^2 + \cdots + (.19 - 3.19)^2$ Team-building workshop
$\phantom{\text{SSW}} + (8.23 - 4.23)^2 + \cdots + (8.23 - 4.23)^2$ Creativity workshop
$\phantom{\text{SSW}} + (.10 - .10)^2 + \cdots + (5.10 - .10)^2$ Control groups
$= 840$

Table 9.10
ANOVA Table for Reduction of Unit Labor Cost Study—Data Set 2

Source of Variation	Sum of Squares	Degrees of Freedom	Variance	Variance Ratio
Between	92.29	2	46.15	1.48
Within	840.00	27	31.11	
Total	932.29	29		

no impact on unit labor cost reductions. The exploratory data analysis for data set 2 has been verified.

Summary of Steps in the Analysis of Variance

Here is a summary of how to conduct a valid planned change study and how to analyze the results.

1. Design a valid study. Use randomization whenever possible. Avoid problems such as history, diffusion of treatment, and compensatory rivalry. Refer to Sections 6.10–6.11 on designing valid planned change studies. If the study is not valid, the analysis of variance is not meaningful.
2. Set up null and alternative hypotheses and actions.
3. Decompose the total sum of squares into SSB(etween) and SSW(ithin).
4. Divide the sums of squares by their corresponding degrees of freedom to obtain variances.
5. Compute the variance ratio and determine if it falls in the 5% rejection region.

The logic behind the 5% α level is simple. It ensures that the maximum chance of rejecting a true null hypothesis is 5%. This protects against costly Type I errors. However, if the Type II errors are costly and the Type I error is not, we can set the α level at 10% and above. For a complete discussion of Type I and Type II errors and their costs, please review Section 7.5 and the Appendix of Chapter 7.

In summary, we use the analysis of variance to determine whether k population means are the same. If the population means differ, then we are interested in determining the best treatment level. That is our next topic.

SECTION 9.3 EXERCISES

1. Distinguish between sum of squares and variance.
2. What are the two sources of variation that explain the total sum of squares in a one-factor, k-level study? Explain.
3. Determine the total degrees of freedom, the within degrees of freedom, and the between degrees of freedom for the following one-factor, k-level studies.

a. Four-level study with five observations per treatment level
b. Three-level study with ten observations per treatment level
c. Two-level study with one observation per treatment level
d. Based on the answer to part c, what is the minimum sample size per treatment level? Explain.

4. Determine the critical value that separates the region of acceptance from the region of rejection for the study described in Exercise 3a for the given α values.
   a. 5%
   b. 1%
   c. 10%

   Draw the F-distribution for each α level and label the regions of acceptance and rejection.

5. A manager of a car service center wants to reduce the number of complaints about improperly made repairs. She tries two approaches: (1) a more detailed write-up of the car's problem and (2) a callback in which the repair person calls the customer two days after making the repairs to determine if the customer is satisfied. Given are the percentages of complaints over a three-week period. Assume an equal number of customers under each treatment. The manager sets an α level of 5%.

Week	Detailed Write-up	Callback	Control Group
1	1	6	8
2	5	2	10
3	3	4	12

a. Find the overall mean and the mean of each treatment level.
b. Find the total sum of squares for this data set.
c. Compute the sum of squares between and the sum of squares within.
d. How many degrees of freedom are there for the total sum of squares, the between sum of squares, and the within sum of squares?
e. Complete the following analysis of variance table.

Source	Sum of Squares	df	Variance	Variance Ratio
Between	_____	___	_____	_____
Within	_____	___	_____	
Total	_____	___		

f. Based on an α level of 5%, can we conclude that the population mean percentage of complaints under the three methods is the same? Explain.

6. Conduct an analysis of variance for the sales promotion study data in Exercise 1 of Section 9.2 Exercises. Use an α level of 1%. Do your results confirm the conclusions you made based on the spread chart alone?

7. Conduct an analysis of variance for the problem solving study data in Exercise 2 of Section 9.2 Exercises. Use an α level of 10%. Do your results confirm the conclusions you made based on the spread chart alone?

8. Conduct an analysis of variance for the telemarketing data in Exercise 3 of Section 9.2 Exercises. Use an α level of 5%. Do your results confirm the conclusions you made based on the spread chart alone?

9. A marketing report shows the prices of the same items charged by department stores and boutiques. Shown are the prices for the same bottle of perfume at four department stores and four boutiques. Assume that the prices are representative samples from their respective populations.

Department Stores	Boutiques
$13.50	$14.75
14.00	15.50
15.25	15.50
13.50	16.00

    a. Is the above study an experiment? Why?
    b. State the null and alternative hypotheses.
    c. State the assumptions we must make before using the ANOVA.
    d. At an α level of 5%, can we conclude that the population mean price for the bottle of perfume differs between department stores and boutiques?

10. COMCEL wants to reduce the unit labor cost of producing its mobile phones. It conducts a one-factor, three-level study. Below are the unit labor cost reductions for 12 work groups. Four groups attended either the team-building workshop, the creativity workshop, or both workshops.

	TB	CM	TB & CM
	$.50	$.60	$.70
	.52	.58	.69
	.50	.62	.71
	.48	.60	.70
Sample means	.50	.60	.70

    a. State the null and alternative hypotheses.
    b. Are the assumptions underlying the ANOVA realistic for the data in the study?
    c. Given an α level of 1%, should COMCEL fail to reject or reject the null hypothesis? Explain.
    d. If COMCEL rejects the null hypothesis, what action should it take?

11. A company is looking for a new chief executive. Each candidate must be evaluated by four committees of six members each. Each committee member independently rates the candidate's qualifications from 1 (unqualified) to 10 (highly qualified). Here are the evaluation scores on the first candidate.

Committee 1	Committee 2	Committee 3	Committee 4
5	4	6	8
2	6	4	9
3	8	5	5
4	5	5	7
4	7	7	7
4	6	8	8

a. Is this an experiment? Why?
b. State the null and alternative hypotheses.
c. Are the assumptions underlying the ANOVA realistic for the data in the study?
d. Perform an analysis of variance.
e. Given an α level of 5%, does it appear that the four committees are rating the candidate similarly?

9.4 Testing for Significant Differences Between Pairs of Population Means

The analysis of variance (ANOVA) does not always provide the answers that managers need. For example, someone asks: "Is the team-building workshop more effective than the creativity training workshop?" Remember, the alternative hypothesis says only that all k population means are not the same. If we reject the null hypothesis, it does not follow that all k means are different. A variance ratio that falls in the rejection region *signals* that we must conduct follow-up comparisons to determine which population means are different from each other. In managerial terms, we must know which treatment level is best, which is second best, etc. By the end of this section you should be able to:

1. explain the need for testing beyond the analysis of variance;
2. explain the need for an *experimentwise* protection level;
3. explain how the Studentized range statistic provides an experimentwise protection level; and
4. construct and interpret Tukey HSD confidence intervals.

We use COMCEL's one-factor, three-level, cost reduction study to illustrate how to construct Tukey confidence intervals, which are based on comparisons of pairs of population means. In that study, there are three possible comparisons we can make, namely,

1. Team-building workshop vs. control group
2. Creativity workshop vs. control group
3. Team-building vs. creativity workshop

The Problem of Multiple Comparisons

In comparing the team-building group vs. the control group, we can control the chance of making a Type I error by using a 5% α level. This is equivalent to a $(100 - 5)$%, or 95%, confidence level. The error for a single comparison is called the *per comparison error rate* and equals 5% when using an α level of .05. We could also use a 5% α level for comparing the team-building vs. creativity workshops. However, the chance of making a Type I error in one or both comparisons is not 5%; it is larger.

Keppel (1973) shows that for α levels of 5% or less, and for six or fewer comparisons, the *experimentwise error rate* is roughly

$$\text{Experimentwise error rate (EER)} = c \cdot (\alpha \text{ level})$$
$$\text{Experimentwise level of confidence} = 1 - \text{EER} \quad (9.3)$$

The α level is the per comparison error rate and c is the number of comparisons. The experimentwise error rate is the probability of making one or more Type I errors in a set of comparisons. Expression (9.3) says that the experimentwise error rate increases as we run more comparisons between treatment levels. As the experimentwise error rate increases, the experimentwise level of confidence decreases.

When comparing three sets of population means, each at a 5% α level, the chance of making one or more Type I errors increases from 5% to about 15% ($= 3 \cdot 5\%$). This is equivalent to a (100 − 15%), or 85%, confidence level for all three comparisons. The experimentwise error rate increases to roughly 30% ($= 6 \cdot 5\%$) when making six comparisons. This is equivalent to a 70% confidence level for all six comparisons. Most managers would consider 70% and 85% confidence levels too low.

Tukey HSD Confidence Intervals

John Tukey's (1953) honestly significant difference (HSD) method allows testing of all possible pairs of population means. It sets the experimentwise error rate (or confidence level) constant at whatever level we desire no matter how many comparisons we make.

Shown in expression (9.4) is the Tukey HSD confidence interval for an equal sample size per treatment level:

$$\bar{x}_1 - \bar{x}_2 \pm q(\text{Confidence level, within df}) \sqrt{\frac{\text{Variance within}}{n}} \quad (9.4)$$

The variance within comes from the analysis of variance table. The value of n is the common sample size of each treatment. We need the degrees of freedom associated with the sum of squares within term. Instead of the t-table, we use another table—the Studentized range distribution, symbolized by the letter q. An abbreviated portion is presented in Table 9.11. (See Appendix 8.)

For more than two treatment levels, the Studentized range-based margin of error is greater than the t-based margin of error. Moreover, the q-values (and thus the margins of error) increase as the number of treatment levels increases. There is both good and bad news in using q-values. The bad news is that larger q-values widen the confidence intervals, which are then more likely to include zero. This means that we must conclude that the pair of treatment means we are comparing are not statistically different. We are less likely to find a significant difference between treatment means using the q-statistic than the t-statistic. The good news is that if zero is not in the confidence interval, we can be 95%

Table 9.11

A Short Table for the Studentized Range Values

Within df	Experimentwise Level of Confidence	Number of Treatment Levels 2	3	4
10	95%	3.15	3.88	4.33
	99%	4.48	5.27	5.77
20	95%	2.95	3.58	3.96
	99%	4.02	4.64	5.02
27	95%	2.90	3.50	3.86
	99%	3.91	4.49	4.85

or 99% confident that there is a real difference, no matter how many pairwise comparisons of means we make. An experimentwise confidence level provides this assurance. For three *t*-based confidence intervals, our experimentwise confidence level would have been roughly 85% (100% − 3 · 5%) even though each comparison was made at a 95% level of confidence.

Table 9.12 on page 470 contains Tukey HSD 95% confidence intervals for the unit labor cost reduction study applied to data set 1. For ease of interpretation, we place the largest sample mean first in using expression (9.4).

The Tukey HSD intervals tell us that creativity training is better than team-building training in reducing unit labor costs and that both are better than no training. By using Tukey's HSD method, we have retained a 95% level of confidence for the family of three comparisons. Therefore, COMCEL should consider implementing creativity training throughout the plant.

The next example illustrates the application of the Tukey HSD method to a one-factor study with four treatment levels.

EXAMPLE: WHICH REGIMEN IS MOST EFFECTIVE IN REDUCING CHOLESTEROL? A health maintenance organization (HMO) tests three ways to reduce cholesterol levels: (1) diet, (2) diet and exercise, and (3) medication. They include a fourth treatment level—control group, consisting of people who receive no treatment. The project manager selects 20 people and randomly assigns them to the four treatment levels. The dependent variable is the drop in cholesterol level after three months. The HMO sets an α of 1%.

The resulting treatment level sample means are as follows:

Diet (D)	30-point drop
Diet and exercise (D/E)	31-point drop
Medication (M)	40-point drop
Control group (C)	5-point drop

Table 9.13 presents the analysis of variance for this study. The interpolated critical *F*-value for (3, 16) degrees of freedom and a $(100 - \alpha)\% = 99\%$ level of

Table 9.12

Summary Table of Three Tukey HSD Comparisons and Interpretations

Variance within (see Table 9.8)	.0063
Degrees of freedom for the variance within term	27
Desired *experimentwise* confidence level	95%
Number of treatment levels	3
Studentized range value (see Table 9.11)	3.50

Comparison	Tukey CI	Interpretation
TB vs. Control	$(3.19 - .10) \pm 3.50 \sqrt{\frac{.0063}{10}}$ $\$3.09 \pm \$.09$	Interval does not include zero. Team-building training is more effective than the control group in reducing unit labor cost.
CM vs. Control	$(4.23 - .10) \pm .09$ $\$4.13 \pm \$.09$	Interval does not include zero. Creativity training is more effective than the control group in reducing unit labor cost.
CM vs. TB	$(4.23 - 3.19) \pm .09$ $\$1.04 \pm \$.09$	Interval does not include zero. Creativity training is more effective than team building in reducing unit labor cost.

Table 9.13

ANOVA Table for Cholesterol Study

Source of Variation	Sum of Squares	Degrees of Freedom	Variance	Variance Ratio
Between	3,385	3	1,128	82.8
Within	218	16	13.63	
Total	3,603	19		

confidence is 5.29. Since the variance ratio, 82.8, is larger than the critical F-value, we reject the null hypothesis.

As there are four treatment levels, there are six possible comparisons. Table 9.14 contains the six 99% experimentwise confidence intervals. For ease of interpretation, we place the largest sample mean first in using expression (9.4).

These results show that medication is the most effective treatment. Diet and diet with exercise are equally effective, but both are less effective than medication. No treatment is the least effective way. Tukey's HSD method allows the family of six comparisons to be made at the 99% level of confidence.

Table 9.14

Summary Table of Six Tukey HSD Comparisons and Interpretations

Variance within (see Table 9.13)	13.63
Degrees of freedom for the variance within term	16
Desired *experimentwise* confidence level	99%
Number of treatment levels	4
Studentized range value (see Appendix 8)	5.19

Comparison	Tukey CI	Interpretation
D vs. D/E	$(31 - 30) \pm 5.19 \sqrt{\frac{13.63}{5}}$ 1 ± 8.57	Interval includes zero. No difference between diet and diet/exercise.
D vs. M	$(40 - 30) \pm 8.57$	Interval does not include zero. Medication is more effective than diet in reducing cholesterol.
D vs. C	$(30 - 5) \pm 8.57$	Interval does not include zero. Diet is more effective than control (no treatment) in reducing cholesterol.
D/E vs. M	$(40 - 31) \pm 8.57$	Interval does not include zero. Medication is more effective than diet/exercise in reducing cholesterol.
D/E vs. C	$(31 - 5) \pm 8.57$	Interval does not include zero. Diet/exercise is more effective than no treatment in reducing cholesterol.
M vs. C	$(40 - 5) \pm 8.57$	Interval does not include zero. Medication is more effective than no treatment in reducing cholesterol.

In summary, when we reject the null hypothesis, we should construct Tukey HSD confidence intervals on the difference between all pairs of population treatment means. When we reject the null hypothesis, we will find at least one significant difference between pairs of population means.

SECTION 9.4 EXERCISES

1. Explain why we cannot rely on the analysis of variance to tell us which population means are different for a one-factor, three-level study.
2. Explain why we can rely on the analysis of variance to tell us which population means are different for a one-factor, two-level study.

3. Whenever we make more than one inference from the same data set, the probability of making at least one Type I error increases. How does the Tukey confidence interval correct this problem?

4. Explain why it is unnecessary to use the Tukey procedure if we did not reject the null hypothesis based on the analysis of variance table.

5. Use the Tukey procedure to make all pairwise comparisons for Exercise 5 in Section 9.3 Exercises. Which population means are different? Set a 95% experimentwise level of confidence.

6. Use the Tukey procedure to make all pairwise comparisons for Exercise 6 in Section 9.3 Exercises. Which population means are different? Set a 99% experimentwise level of confidence.

7. Use the Tukey procedure to make all pairwise comparisons for Exercise 7 in Section 9.3 Exercises. Which population means are different? Set a 95% experimentwise level of confidence.

8. Use the Tukey procedure to make all pairwise comparisons for Exercise 10 in Section 9.3 Exercises. Which population means are different? Set a 99% experimentwise level of confidence.

9. The Tukey procedure controls the experimentwise Type I error rate by increasing the width of the confidence interval. How does increasing the confidence interval's width affect the probability of concluding that pairs of population means are different?

9.5 The Kruskal–Wallis Nonparametric Analysis of Variance

Now suppose that we have completed a one-factor, k-level, completely randomized experiment. Before analyzing the data, we test the following underlying assumptions:

ASSUMPTION 1: The observations within the k treatment levels are independent random samples.

ASSUMPTION 2: The observations within each of the k treatment levels are near-normally distributed.

ASSUMPTION 3: The variances within each treatment level are the same, or nearly so.

We construct k stem-and-leaf displays to assess assumptions 2 and 3. Suppose that the data are highly skewed with one or more outliers or that the range in the data at one treatment level is 5 times greater than the range at other treatment levels. What course do we follow?

We could try to transform the raw data using a square root or log base 10 transformation. If that makes the data more normal shaped and equalizes the variances, we can apply the F-based analysis of variance. Otherwise, we use the Kruskal–Wallis *nonparametric* analysis of variance. By the end of this section you should be able to:

1. explain when to use the Kruskal–Wallis test;
2. explain the logic of the Kruskal–Wallis test statistic;

3. apply the Kruskal–Wallis test; and
4. apply and interpret Dunn's follow-up test of differences between population medians.

We illustrate the Kruskal–Wallis test with the following planned change study.

EXAMPLE: DETERMINING THE BEST ADVERTISING APPROACH
Soky Inc. is considering three approaches for advertising its digital tape players: informative advertising, persuasive advertising, and retentive advertising. Soky randomly selects 28 people from its target population. It randomly assigns seven people to each of the three advertising methods. The remaining seven people will serve as a control group. Except for the control group subjects, each subject will be shown a tape player ad (developed using one of the three strategies) four times over a one-week period. Afterward, each person (including those in the control group) will indicate his or her intent to buy a digital tape player on a scale from 0 (definitely will not buy) to 100 (definitely will buy). Soky Inc. has set a 5% α level.

Table 9.15 contains the data for the advertising study.

The box plots in Figure 9.5 on page 474 indicate that each treatment level contains an outlier. The presence of outliers requires us to use the Kruskal–Wallis nonparametric analysis of variance method.

Statistical Hypotheses

We begin by stating the null and alternative hypotheses:

H_0: The four population *median* purchase intentions are the same.
H_1: Not all the population *median* purchase intentions are the same.

Note that the Kruskal–Wallis method tests population medians, not means. That is reasonable as we use the median as the measure of the center when the data have outliers.

Table 9.15

Data for One-Factor, Four-Level Marketing Study

Experimental Factor: Type of Advertising*

Informative	Persuasive	Retentive	Control Group
55	42	56	0
60	45	62	8
61	48	63	8
68	50	65	10
71	51	66	11
72	52	73	12
100	70	99	30

*Values represent intent to purchase on a 0–100 scale, where 100 indicates a definite intent to purchase.

FIGURE 9.5   Box Plots for Four-Level Planned Change Study

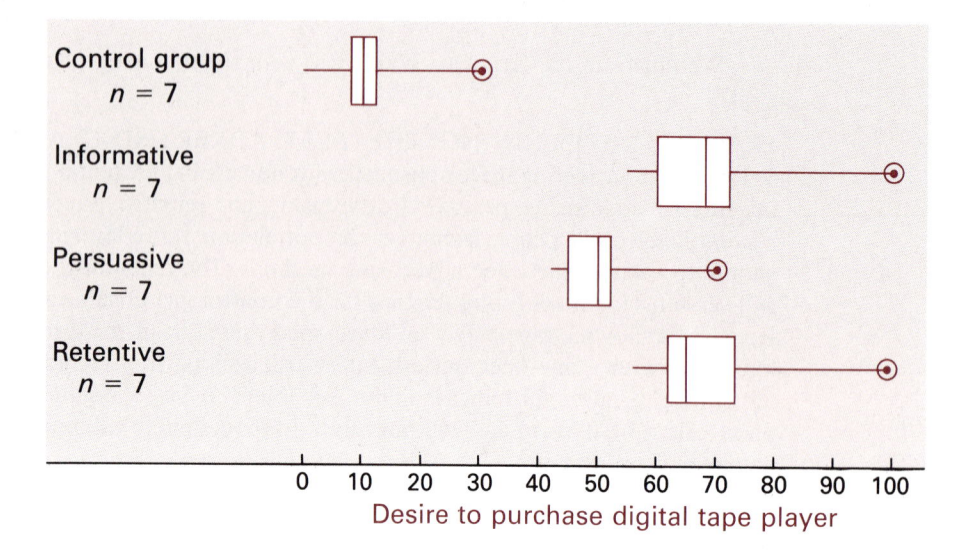

Next, we rank all the observations, as shown in Table 9.16, by assigning a 1 to the smallest of the 28 values, a 2 to the next higher value, and so forth. If two or more values are the same, assign each of them the mean of the two or more ranks. The numbers in parentheses in Table 9.16 are the data ranks.

Logic Behind the Test

Before proceeding with the logic behind the test, examine Table 9.16. If the four population medians are the same (the null hypothesis is true), the ranks should be randomly distributed among the four treatment levels. All the low ranks or high ranks would *not* be concentrated in one treatment level. However, notice that the control group contains all the low ranks while the informative and retentive

Table 9.16
Advertising Data Rank-Ordered

Informative	Persuasive	Retentive	Control Group
55 (14)	42 (8)	56 (15)	0 (1)
60 (16)	45 (9)	62 (18)	8 (2.5)
61 (17)	48 (10)	63 (19)	8 (2.5)
68 (22)	50 (11)	65 (20)	10 (4)
71 (24)	51 (12)	66 (21)	11 (5)
72 (25)	52 (13)	73 (26)	12 (6)
100 (28)	70 (23)	99 (27)	30 (7)

approaches contain most of the highest ranks. This indicates that we probably will reject the null hypothesis.

Instead of computing a variance ratio, we compute the following Kruskal–Wallis test statistic, H:

$$H = \frac{12}{N(N+1)} \sum_j \frac{R_j^2}{n_j} - 3(N+1) \qquad (9.5)$$

where N is the total sample size
R_j is the sum of the ranks for treatment level j
n_j is the sample size for treatment level j

Warning: This expression is valid only if less than one-fourth of the observations are ties.

Table 9.17 shows the calculations for the Kruskal–Wallis test statistic.

For sample sizes of 5 or more within each treatment level, if the null hypothesis is true, the H statistic is chi-square distributed with $k - 1$ (the number of treatment levels less 1) degrees of freedom. We first encountered the chi-square family of curves in Section 7.10.

As in the F-test, we must find the region of acceptance and the region of rejection. From Appendix 6, the chi-square value for 3 degrees of freedom and the $(100 - \alpha)\%$, or 95%, column is 7.81. We will reject the null hypothesis for H-values that are greater than 7.81. Since the value of the Kruskal–Wallis statistic is 20.27, we reject the null hypothesis. Not all of the four treatment levels produce the same population median intent to buy.

Having rejected the null hypothesis, the natural follow-up question is, "Which approach produces the largest intent to buy digital tape players?" We used Tukey's method to test for differences between pairs of population *means*. We use Dunn's method to test for differences between pairs of population *medians*. Both methods provide an *experimentwise* protection level.

Table 9.17
Computation of Kruskal–Wallis Test Statistic

Treatment	Rank Sums	Sample Size, n_j
Informative	$14 + 16 + 17 + 22 + 24 + 25 + 28 = 146$	7
Persuasive	$8 + 9 + 10 + 11 + 12 + 13 + 23 = 86$	7
Retentive	$15 + 18 + 19 + 20 + 21 + 26 + 27 = 146$	7
Control group	$1 + 2.5 + 2.5 + 4 + 5 + 6 + 7 = 28$	7

$$H = \frac{12}{28(29)} \left(\frac{146^2}{7} + \frac{86^2}{7} + \frac{146^2}{7} + \frac{28^2}{7} \right) - 3(28 + 1)$$

$$= 20.27$$

Dunn's Multiple Comparisons

Use expression (9.6) to construct either 90% or 95% experimentwise multiple pairwise comparisons of medians (Dunn, 1964):

$$\bar{R}_i - \bar{R}_j \pm D \sqrt{\frac{N(N+1)}{12}\left(\frac{1}{n_i} + \frac{1}{n_j}\right)} \qquad (9.6)$$

where N is the total sample size
$\bar{R}_i$ is the mean rank for treatment level i
n_i is the sample size for treatment level i
D is the appropriate value from the following table

Experimentwise Level of Confidence	Number of Treatment Levels		
	3	4	5
90%	2.13	2.39	2.58
95%	2.39	2.64	2.81

Note: Always place the higher mean rank first in expression (9.6). It makes interpreting the results simpler.

The term following the $\pm$ sign in expression (9.6) is the margin of error. As always, the margin of error is simply the reliability factor for the confidence level, D, times the estimated standard error, the remainder of the expression.

For the one-factor, four-level advertising study (Table 9.15), there are six possible pairwise comparisons:

1. Informative vs. control group
2. Persuasive vs. control group
3. Retentive vs. control group
4. Informative vs. persuasive
5. Informative vs. retensive
6. Persuasive vs. retentive

Given here are the mean ranks for the four treatment levels that we will need for expression (9.6).

Treatment Level	Mean Rank
Informative	$\frac{146}{7} = 20.86$
Persuasive	$\frac{86}{7} = 12.29$
Retentive	$\frac{146}{7} = 20.86$
Control group	$\frac{28}{7} = 4.00$

Construction and Interpretation of Dunn's Multiple Comparisons

Using expression (9.6)—Dunn's method—we can draw a comparison at the 90% confidence level on the difference between the informative strategy and the control group:

$$(20.86 - 4) \pm 2.39 \sqrt{\frac{(28)(29)}{12}\left(\frac{1}{7} + \frac{1}{7}\right)}$$

$$= 16.86 \pm 2.39(4.40)$$

$$= 16.86 \pm 10.5$$

Lower limit: $16.86 - 10.5 = 6.36$

Upper limit: $16.86 + 10.5 = 27.36$

Note that the comparison does *not* include the value of zero. Thus, we are 90% confident that the informative strategy produces a higher population median intent to buy digital tape players than no advertising—the control group.

Table 9.18 presents a summary of the six pairwise comparisons.

Table 9.18

Summary Table of Six Dunn Comparisons and Interpretations at a 90% Experimentwise Level of Confidence

Comparison	Dunn CI	Interpretation
Informative vs. control	$(20.86 - 4) \pm 10.5$ 16.86 ± 10.5	Interval does not include zero. The informative strategy produces higher intents to buy than the control group.
Persuasive vs. control	$(12.29 - 4) \pm 10.5$ 8.29 ± 10.5	Interval does include zero. Cannot detect any statistical differences.
Retentive vs. control	$(20.86 - 4) \pm 10.5$ 16.86 ± 10.5	Interval does not include zero. The retentive strategy is more effective than the control group.
Informative vs. persuasive	$(20.86 - 12.29) \pm 10.5$ 8.57 ± 10.5	Interval does include zero. Cannot detect any statistical differences.
Informative vs. retentive	$(20.86 - 20.86) \pm 10.5$ 0 ± 10.5	Interval does include zero. Cannot detect any statistical differences.
Persuasive vs. retentive	$(20.86 - 12.29) \pm 10.5$ 8.9 ± 10.5	Interval does include zero. Cannot detect any statistical differences.

The informative and retentive strategies are each more effective than the control group. There are no other significant differences at the 90% experimentwise confidence level.

In summary, when there are outliers at some or all of the treatment levels, we use the Kruskal–Wallis nonparametric method and Dunn's multiple comparisons to compare k population medians. If we reject the null hypothesis, we will find at least one significant difference between pairs of population medians in Dunn's follow-up method.

SECTION 9.5 EXERCISES

1. Explain when we should consider using the Kruskal–Wallis nonparametric procedure instead of the F-based analysis of variance.
2. Explain the logic of the Kruskal–Wallis test.
3. Here are data from a one-factor, three-level study.

Level		
1	2	3
26	12	22
28	14	42
30	18	42
31	20	46
46	40	47
27	15	44

   a. Why would we select the Kruskal–Wallis procedure over the F-based analysis of variance?
   b. State and test the null and alternative hypotheses.
   c. If we reject the null hypothesis at an α level of 10%, use Dunn's procedure to determine which population medians are different at an experimentwise 90% confidence level.

4. A coffee producer hires an expert taster to sample four new blends of coffee. The firm will market the best blend. Sixteen samples are placed before the taster, who is asked to rank the samples from 1 (best) to 16 (worst). The 16 samples actually contain the four different blends of coffee, four cups of each blend. The rankings are shown here.

Blend 1	Blend 2	Blend 3	Blend 4
1	4	6	12
2	7	8	14
3	9	11	15
5	10	13	16

   a. What is the null hypothesis being tested?
   b. For an α level of 5%, does there appear to be a difference in the blends of coffee? If so, rank the blends of coffee for the company. Use an experimentwise 95% level of confidence. Which coffee blend should the company introduce? Explain.

Chapter 9 Analysis of Variance

5. A manager wants to know whether there is a difference in the median number of days of sick leave taken by the employees in three different departments. It is well known that the distribution of sick leave days is skewed to the right. Based on the given data, does it appear that the median number of sick leave days varies by department? Set the α level at 5%.

Dept. A	0	1	3	6	9	14	16	19	25	38
Dept. B	0	.1	4	6	11	15	18	22	26	34
Dept. C	0	2	5	8	10	12	16	20	27	31

9.6 The Two-Factor, Completely Random Factorial Study

We have focused, up to this point, on one-factor, *k*-level studies. Sometimes managers run planned change studies that have two or more experimental factors. We now turn to these multifactor, or factorial, experiments. By the end of this section you should be able to:

1. draw a set of profiles for a factorial study and determine whether there is likely to be a significant interaction effect;
2. modify the basic analysis of variance to analyze a factorial experiment; and
3. explain what an interaction is and what are its decision making implications.

Return to the case of the cracked table drawers discussed in Section 9.1. Using the Kepner–Tregoe diagnostic method (Table 9.1), Apex suspected that the combination of new raw material and the 10-inch deep drawers had caused excessive cracking. This called for a two-factor study. Factor A, material vendor, has two levels and factor B, stamping depth, has three levels. Apex chose an α level of 1% for the 2 × 3 completely randomized factorial study, which is outlined here.

Factor A	Factor B
Material vendor	Stamping depth
Original vendor—old material	4 inches
New vendor—new material	7 inches
	10 inches

Apex tested all six (2 × 3) combinations of material and stamping depth. It ran each combination five times for one hour each. Apex randomly selected enough old raw material to make 15 one-hour runs and randomly assigned the old material to the three stamping depths. Next, the team randomly selected enough new raw material to make 15 one-hour runs and randomly assigned the new material to the three stamping depths. The team randomly determined the sequence of the six combinations of runs and recorded the percentage of cracks for each one-hour run. Table 9.19 on page 480 contains the results.

Table 9.19

Data for Two-Factor Cracked Drawer Study

	Stamping Depth (inches)			
	4	7	10	Means
Old Material	1	1	0	1
	0	0	0	
	0	1	2	
	2	2	1	
	2	1	2	
New Material	0	4	6	3.67
	2	5	5	
	0	3	7	
	2	4	6	
	1	4	6	
Means	1	2.5	3.5	2.33 overall mean

Dependent variable: Percentage of drawers cracked over a one-hour run. For example, using the old material to produce 4-inch deep drawers generated 1%, 0%, 0%, 2%, and 2% cracked drawers over five one-hour runs.

A factorial study has at least two experimental factors. Experimental factors are simply what managers vary in hopes of improving the product, service, performance, or quality. In a factorial study, every level of one factor is run in combination with every level of all other factors. Thus, each type of material will be tested at all three stamping depths. For example, the upper left-hand cell represents five one-hour runs using old material and stamping 4-inch deep drawers.

Designing a Factorial Study

In designing a factorial experiment, we must make decisions about the following:

1. the number of experimental factors
2. the number of levels of each factor
3. the sample size in each experimental cell
4. the design and execution of the study

With regard to the number of experimental factors, we need to include all factors that we believe affect the dependent variable. However, the study size increases very rapidly as we increase the number of experimental factors. For example, a study with five factors, each at two levels, has 32 cells, while adding one more factor with two levels doubles the number of cells. *A good rule of thumb*: Keep the number of factors to four or less.

Similarly, the study size increases as we increase the number of levels per factor. A five-factor study, each at four levels, has 1,024 cells. Unless there is a compelling need, we should consider only two levels for each factor. In the cracked drawer study, the compelling need is that three depths of drawers are produced. *A good rule of thumb*:   Limit to two, or at most three, the number of levels of each experimental factor.

A factorial study should have at least two observations in each of its experimental cells in order to get a measure of the sum of squares within variation. Without it, we cannot compute a variance ratio. While large sample sizes are desirable, they also increase the cost of the study.

To design and execute a valid study, we know, from Chapter 6, that we must control for history, diffusion of treatment, and compensatory rivalry, and use randomization whenever possible. The analysis of variance is meaningful only when the study is valid.

We consider a factorial study when we think that two or more factors affect the dependent variable of interest or when we suspect an interaction effect. We discuss interaction effects next.

Exploratory Data Analysis: Graphing Profiles

The factorial study introduces a new concept—the interaction effect. We will use Table 9.20 to illustrate the interaction effect for the cracked drawer factorial study. The tabled values are the mean percentages of cracked drawers over five one-hour runs. Profile graphs are an effective way of seeing (but not testing for) an interaction effect. Figure 9.6 on page 482 shows the *material vendor* profile graph for data set 1. It shows that the profiles are parallel. Irrespective of the stamping depth, the old material produces fewer defects than the new material. In short, the old material *appears* to be better. We say *appears* because we have only plotted profiles and not done the formal statistical analysis.

Figure 9.7 shows the material vendor profile graph for data set 2. In this case, the profiles are *not* parallel. That is, *it appears* that the better material *depends* on the stamping depth. The old material works best for the 10-inch drawers and the new material works best for the 4-inch drawers.

> Two factors exhibit an interaction effect when the effect of one factor changes at different levels of the other factor.

Figure 9.7 *suggests* an **interaction effect** while Figure 9.6 does not. When an interaction is present, the best level of one factor depends on the level of the other factor(s). We cannot make general statements such as "one material is best overall." The best material depends on the stamping depth.

It makes no difference which factor we graph. In Figures 9.6 and 9.7, we drew *material vendor* profiles. We would have drawn the same tentative conclusions had we drawn *stamping depth* profiles—that is, where we assign type of material to the horizontal axis and the profiles reflect the three different stamping depths.

Table 9.20

Data Sets to Illustrate the Absence and Presence of an Interaction Effect

	Data Set 1			Data Set 2		
	4 inches	7 inches	10 inches	4 inches	7 inches	10 inches
Old	1%	2%	1%	7%	5%	1%
New	4%	5%	4%	1%	6%	8%

FIGURE 9.6 Material Vendor Profile for Data Set 1

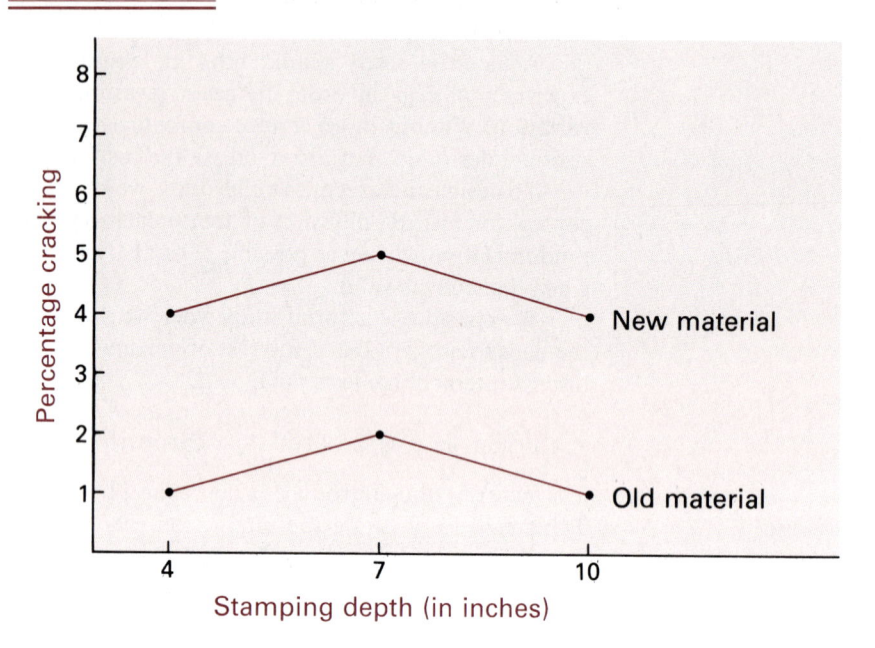

FIGURE 9.7 Material Vendor Profile for Data Set 2

Chapter 9　Analysis of Variance

FIGURE 9.8　Material Vendor Profile for Apex Study

[Figure: Profile plot with x-axis "Stamping depth (in inches)" ranging 4 to 10, and y-axis "Percentage cracking" ranging 0 to 8. "New material" line rises from 1 at depth 4, to 4 at depth 7, to 6 at depth 10. "Old material" line stays horizontal at about 1 across all depths.]

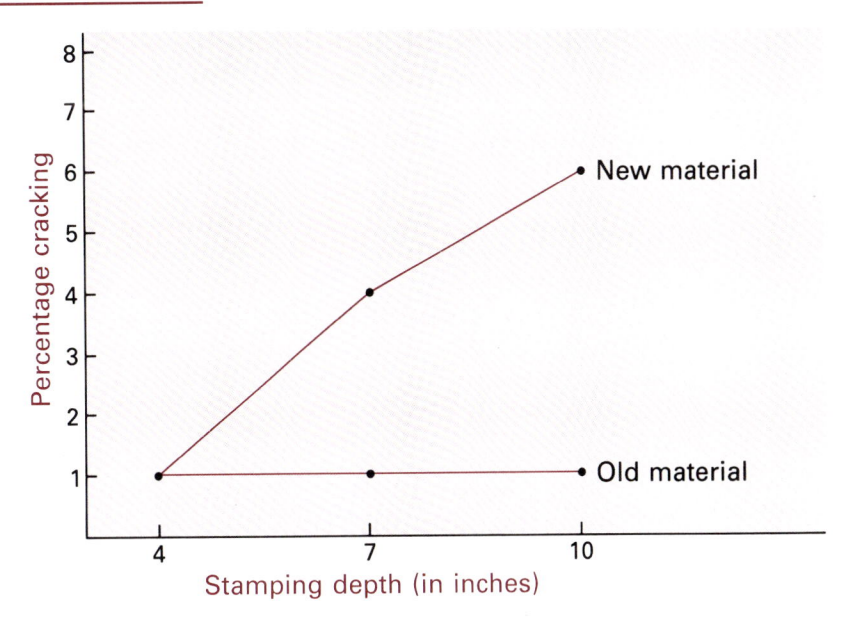

Now return to the actual study. Table 9.19 suggests that there is an interaction between the material vendor and the stamping depth. Figure 9.8 shows the profile plots. The old material vendor profile is horizontal while the new material vendor profile slopes upward to the right. Clearly, we have non-parallel profiles. Now we must do the analysis of variance to confirm the interaction effect.

Total Sum of Squares

As in the one-factor design, we begin by computing the total sum of squares. This represents the total variation in all 30 observations in Table 9.19 about the overall mean of 2.33%. It is given by

$$\text{SST} = (1 - 2.33)^2 + (0 - 2.33)^2 + \cdots + (6 - 2.33)^2 + (6 - 2.33)^2$$
$$= 134.67 \text{ units of variation}$$

What accounts for the 134.67 units of variation? It is due to four sources: the *main effects* of factor A (material vendor) and factor B (stamping depth), the *interaction effect* between material vendor and stamping depth, and all other possible variables that we might have varied but chose not to—the *within effect*. Let's compute the first two sources of variation. Although we are analyzing a new design, we can use our basic definitions for the sum of squares terms.

Sum of Squares for Main Effects

What two numbers best represent the main effect of the material vendor? The row sample means. The mean of these two row means is the overall mean of 2.33%. Remember that we will have to weight the squared differences by the number of observations used to calculate each of the two sample means, the *weighting constant*. Thus the sum of squares for the material vendor factor is

$$SSA = 15[(1 - 2.33)^2 + (3.67 - 2.33)^2]$$
$$= 53.46 \text{ units of variation}$$

We can likewise determine the sum of squares for the stamping depth factor:

$$SSB = 10[(1 - 2.33)^2 + (2.5 - 2.33)^2 + (3.5 - 2.33)^2]$$
$$= 31.67 \text{ units of variation}$$

Next we calculate the sum of squares within term. Look at the upper left-hand experimental cell in Table 9.19 where Apex ran old material and produced 4-inch deep drawers. The five data values are not all the same. The differences must be due to all the other variables we ignored in the study. These include stamping operators' levels of experience or skill, age of stamping equipment, closeness of supervision. The cumulative effect of all the ignored variables causes variation within an experimental cell. Given this, how should we calculate the within sum of squares? Please think about it before reading on.

Sum of Squares Within

We compute the sum of the squared differences between each cell value and its cell mean. The six cell means are 1%, 1%, 1%, 1%, 4%, and 6%. The calculation contains 30 terms since there are five observations in each of six experimental cells. This approach is identical to the way we calculated the within sum of squares for a one-factor, completely randomized design. The sums of the squared differences, along with their corresponding cell factors, are given by

$$
\begin{array}{ll}
(1-1)^2 + \cdots + (2-1)^2 & \text{old material and 4-inch drawers} \\
+ (1-1)^2 + \cdots + (1-1)^2 & \text{old material and 7-inch drawers} \\
+ (0-1)^2 + \cdots + (2-1)^2 & \text{old material and 10-inch drawers} \\
+ (0-1)^2 + \cdots + (1-1)^2 & \text{new material and 4-inch drawers} \\
+ (4-4)^2 + \cdots + (4-4)^2 & \text{new material and 7-inch drawers} \\
+ (6-6)^2 + \cdots + (6-6)^2 & \text{new material and 10-inch drawers}
\end{array}
$$

$$SSW = 18 \text{ units of variation}$$

SSA, SSB, and the within sum of squares have accounted for 103.13 of the 134.67 units of total variation. The remainder, or 31.54 units of variation, must be due to the possible interaction effect of factors A and B, the AB interaction. In general, the AB interaction effect equals

$$SSAB = SST - (SSA + SSB + SSW) \tag{9.7}$$

Degrees of Freedom

For the data in Table 9.19, the total number of degrees of freedom is the total sample size minus 1, or 29. The degrees of freedom for factor A is the number of levels minus 1, or 1. The degrees of freedom for factor B is $3 - 1 = 2$. The degrees of freedom for the within term is 24. Since there are five observations per cell, there must be $5 - 1 = 4$ degrees of freedom for each cell. There are six cells and therefore there are 24 degrees of freedom. The remaining 2 degrees of freedom belong to the interaction sum of squares term. Another way to compute the degrees of freedom for the AB interaction term is to multiply the degrees of freedom for factors A and B ($1 \cdot 2 = 2$).

Now it becomes clear why it is necessary to have at least two data values per experimental cell. With only one observation, there would be no degrees of freedom for the within term and we could not compute the variance-within term. Without the variance-within term, we could not compute a variance ratio.

Table 9.21 is the analysis of variance table for the cracked drawer study. The three variance ratios are simply the variances due to factors A, B, and AB, each divided by the variance-within term, .75. Now we can determine whether either the main effects or the interaction effect affects the dependent variable, the percentage of cracked drawers.

Table 9.21

ANOVA for the Cracked Drawer Study

Source of Variation	Sum of Squares	Degrees of Freedom	Variance	Variance Ratio
A: Material	53.46	1	53.46	71.28
B: Depth	31.67	2	15.84	21.12
AB interaction	31.54	2	15.77	21.03
Within	18.00	24	.75	
Total	134.67	29		

Hypotheses

For a two-factor factorial study, there are three sets of null and alternative hypotheses to test:

1. H_0: Material vendor and stamping depth do not interact to affect the population mean percentage of cracked drawers.
   H_1: There is an interaction effect.
2. H_0: Stamping depth (factor B) has no effect on the population mean percentage of cracked drawers.
   H_1: Stamping depth has an effect.

3. H_0:   Material vendor (factor A) has no effect on the population mean percentage of cracked drawers.
   H_1:   Material vendor has an effect.

As in the one-factor design, the denominator of the variance ratio is the within variance. We begin by testing for an interaction effect. If there is a significant interaction, then we know that the percentage of cracking depends on the combination of material and drawer depth. If there is no interaction, then we can determine if either factor has an impact on the dependent variable.

We will reject the null hypothesis for the interaction if its variance ratio falls in the rejection region. In the cracked drawer study, the critical value is the F-value for 2 and 24 degrees of freedom and a $(100 - \alpha)\% = 99\%$ level of confidence. The critical F-value is 5.61 (see Appendix 7). Since the variance ratio of 21.03 falls in the rejection region, there is a material vendor–stamping depth interaction effect.

The statistically significant interaction tells us that the percentage of cracks *depends* on the material vendor and the stamping depth. The material vendor profile graph presented earlier in Figure 9.8 helps us understand the managerial implications of the significant interaction.

The profiles in Figure 9.8 suggest that

1. with the old material, the percentage of cracks is 1% for all stamping depths; and
2. with the new material, the percentage of cracks increases with increasing stamping depth.

The two-factor study has verified that the root cause of the cracked drawers is the new material in combination with the 7-inch and 10-inch stamping depths. That is, the new material works well for the 4-inch drawers, but the metal cracks when used for the deeper drawers. Now Apex must take corrective action. They have two options:

1. Switch back to the original material vendor. Note that the percentage cracking is constant at 1% over all stamping depths with that vendor's material.
2. Ask the new vendor to adjust the composition of its material so that there will not be an increase in cracking at the 7-inch and 10-inch stamping depths.

Given a significant interaction effect, there is no need to test the remaining hypotheses—factor A or factor B. We already know the two factors interact to affect the dependent variable.

Suppose the variance ratio for the interaction effect had fallen in the acceptance region—that is, it was less than 5.61. Then we would have compared the variance ratio for each main effect against its corresponding critical value:

Factor	Variance Ratio	Critical Value
Material	71.28	F-value for 1 and 24 df at the 99% confidence level
Stamping depth	21.12	F-value for 2 and 24 df at the 99% confidence level

Chapter 9 Analysis of Variance

If we reject the stamping depth null hypothesis, at least one stamping depth produces fewer defects than the others, no matter which material is used. If we reject the material vendor null hypothesis, then one material produces fewer defects than the other at all stamping depths.

In summary, consider a factorial study when you think that two or more factors affect the dependent variable of interest or when you suspect an interaction effect. Always draw profile graphs before doing the analysis of variance. The profiles are necessary also to understand the managerial implications of a significant interaction.

SECTION 9.6 EXERCISES

1. How many independent variables are there in a 2 × 2 factorial experiment? How many levels of each independent variable are there? Can we have more than one dependent variable in a 2 × 2 experiment?

2. How many cells would a 2 × 3 factorial design have? How many experimental units would be needed if we wanted 10 observations per cell?

3. What are the main effects for a 2 × 2 factorial design?

4. What is an interaction? Why is it important to test for an interaction before testing the main effects?

5. Suppose that COMCEL tries two different promotions in two different market segments (income levels) to induce customers to increase car phone usage. The results of the analysis for the promotion–market segment factorial experiment are shown here.

Source of Variation	Sum of Squares	Degrees of Freedom	Variance	Variance Ratio
A: Promotion	2,530	1	2,530.00	_____
B: Income	1,050	1	1,050.00	_____
AB interaction	15	1	15.00	_____
Within	160	16	10.00	
Total	3,755	19		

   a. Complete the table by filling in the variance ratios.
   b. For an α level of 5%, is there an interaction between promotion and income?
   c. For an α level of 5%, is there a difference between the mean responses to the two different types of promotion?
   d. For an α level of 5%, is there a difference between the mean responses to the two different levels of income?

6. We have conducted a 2 × 2 factorial study on the effect of teaching method and students' SAT scores on test scores in a freshman history class. Here are the data.

		Factor A Lecture	Factor A Discovery	Means
Factor B	Less than 900	70	85	77.5
	More than 1100	80	95	87.5
	Means	75	90	

a. Plot a profile graph for this experiment. Does there appear to be an interaction? Explain.
b. It appears that mean performance under discovery teaching is greater than the mean performance under the lecture method. If this difference in means is statistically significant, can we conclude that discovery teaching is best overall? Explain.

7. We have conducted a 2 × 2 factorial study on the effect of teaching method and students' SAT scores on test scores in a freshman history class. Here are the data.

		Factor A		
		Lecture	Discovery	Means
Factor B	Less than 90	80	50	65
	More than 1100	70	100	85
	Means	75	75	75

a. Plot a profile graph for this experiment. Does there appear to be an interaction?
b. Does there appear to be one best teaching method? Explain.

8. We conduct a study to determine the number of trials needed to learn two different tasks by two methods of training. Four employees were randomly assigned to each task–method combination. The results are shown.

	Task 1	Task 2
Method 1	2, 3, 3, 2	4, 6, 6, 8
Method 2	5, 7, 6, 8	3, 2, 2, 3

a. Compute the cell means and plot the profiles for the two factors. What can we conclude from the profiles?
b. Perform an analysis of variance on these data.
c. Does it appear that one task takes fewer trials to learn than the other or that one method requires fewer trials to learn the two tasks? Explain.

9. Complete the following ANOVA table and answer the questions relating to it.

Source of Variation	Sum of Squares	Degrees of Freedom	Variance	Variance Ratio
Factor A	170	—		
Factor B	450	1		
AB interaction	14	2		
Within	—	24		
Total	950	29		

a. How many levels does factor A have?
b. How many observations per cell were there, assuming an equal number per cell?
c. Can the hypothesis of no interaction be rejected? Explain.
d. Is there a difference in the treatment means of factor A? Explain.
e. Is there a difference in the means of factor B? Explain.

10. We run a study to determine which type of clothes dryer, gas or electric, is better at drying clothes. At the same time, the purpose of the experiment was to determine which brand of dryer, A, B, or C, was most effective. The effectiveness of each dryer was measured by the percentage moisture that remained in the test clothing after 30 minutes. Here are the data.

		Brand		
		A	B	C
Type	Gas	17, 13, 21, 19, 15	7, 10, 6, 5, 7	12, 9, 13, 11, 15
	Electric	15, 11, 18, 12, 19	8, 12, 5, 8, 7	11, 8, 15, 10, 11

a. Plot a profile graph. Does it appear that there is an interaction between the type of dryer and brand? Explain what an interaction would mean in practical terms.
b. Use our software to perform an analysis of variance on these data.
c. Is there a significant interaction between type of dryer and brand?
d. Is one type of dryer better than the other?
e. Is there a difference among the three brands?

9.7 Key Ideas and Overview

In this chapter we have discussed the two most commonly used experimental designs, the one-factor and factorial designs. Both are alternatives to the survey-based random or stratified sampling data collection methods that were used in Chapters 6, 7, and 8. When designing *planned change* studies, use these two rules in deciding between the one-factor and factorial studies:

RULE 1: Design and run a one-factor study when there is reason to believe that only one factor will have a major impact on the dependent variable. You are assuming that all other variables do not have much impact on the dependent variable.

RULE 2: Design and run a factorial study when there is reason to believe that two or more factors will have a major impact on the dependent variable, when there is reason to suspect an interaction (nonparallel profiles) between two or more factors.

Good management has the capability to ask the right questions. In the last three chapters, we have learned the proper questions to ask when solving problems and making decisions. Tables 9.22 and 9.23 on page 490 summarize those questions and review the exploratory and analytical tools available to answer them. After all, good questions deserve good answers.

Table 9.22
Asking the Right Questions

Typical Managerial Questions	Statistical Questions
1. What is our customers' mean income?	What is the population mean, median, or proportion?
2. What is the median service time?	
3. What percentage of employees favor a flex-hours system?	
4. Which group has better mean performance—Chicago or Denver?	Are two population means, medians, or proportions the same?
5. Which plant has a higher median level of job satisfaction?	
6. Is the proportion of high-income car phone users the same in two regions?	
7. Which group's productivity shows less fluctuation?	Are two population variances or dispersions the same?
8. Does the Seattle plant have greater dispersion in sick leave taken than the Philadelphia plant?	
9. Which of three sales displays generates the highest income?	Are the main effects significant?
10. Do all employees respond best to one approach for improving morale? Or, does the best approach differ for hourly, professional, and management personnel?	Is there an interaction effect between two or more factors?

Table 9.23
Statistical Tools to Answer Managerial Questions

Statistical Questions	Exploratory Tools	Analytical Methods
What is the population mean, median, or proportion?	Stem-and-leaf displays Box plots	Confidence interval on one population parameter—Chapter 7
Are two population means, medians, or proportions the same? Are two population variances or dispersions the same?	Multiple stem-and-leaf displays Multiple box plots	Confidence interval on the difference between two population parameters—Chapter 8
Are the main effects significant? Is there an interaction effect?	Spread charts Interaction profiles	F-based or Kruskal–Wallis analyses of variance and Tukey or Dunn confidence intervals on differences between population means or medians—Chapter 9

COMCEL

Date: November 17, 1992
To: Sarah Teman, Manager of Operations
From: Bill Katz, Production Testing
Re: Resolution of Apex Material Cracking Problem

SUMMARY
Substandard material purchased from a new supplier caused the cracking problem. The new material cracked when drawers were stamped at a depth of greater than 4 inches. Apex has returned to its former supplier and the problem has not returned.

SUPPORTING ANALYSIS
A Kepner–Tregoe problem definition worksheet indicated that material from a new vendor had probably caused the increase in cracking. Since we suspected the new material, we ran a 2 × 3 factorial study to compare percentage cracking rates for the new and old materials for stamping 4-, 7-, and 10-inch drawers.

We conducted the study in the following manner. We used one operator and one machine. We randomly selected panels from stock and randomly assigned the panels to the six experimental cells. We then made six 1-hour production runs for each combination of material and drawer depth. We randomly determined the run sequence.

The statistical analysis indicated that the 7-inch and 10-inch deep drawers made with panels of the new material had cracking rates well beyond 1%. The 4-inch, 7-inch, and 10-inch deep drawers made with the old material had cracking rates of 1%. In short, the new material caused the excessive cracking.

CHAPTER 9 QUESTIONS

1. In the Apex Plastics and Metals case study, suggest several other possible causes for the increased cracking rate.
2. Why isn't it always possible to conduct planned change studies when testing problem solving hypotheses?
3. Explain why "no treatment effect" is the null hypothesis.
4. Why is it necessary to use the Kepner–Tregoe method in problem solving?
5. What source of variation does the spread within reflect?

6. What source of variation does the spread between reflect?
7. When the spread between is *much* larger than the spread within, we are likely to reject the null hypothesis of no treatment effect. Why?
8. Why must we do the analysis of variance? Can't spread chart exploratory data analysis replace the analysis of variance?
9. What do the sum of squares total, between, and within measure?
10. In a one-factor, *k*-level design, why are there only two sources of variation?
11. Why is a large variance ratio necessary to reject the "no treatment effect" null hypothesis?
12. What assumptions must we make about the data in order to use the analysis of variance?
13. If we reject the null hypothesis in an analysis of variance, why is it necessary to run Tukey's HSD comparisons?
14. Correct if necessary:

    If an HSD confidence interval contains the value of 1, we conclude that two sample means do not differ.

15. What is an experimentwise error rate?
16. If an exploratory data analysis indicates excessive outliers in a one-factor design study, what analysis should we do?
17. If we reject the null hypothesis of no difference in population medians, must we find differences in all the pairwise comparisons in Dunn's follow-up analysis?
18. Provide a business example where you would suspect an interaction between two factors.
19. What problems might we have if we ran a five-factor factorial study with each factor at three levels?
20. What does the expression, "there is no one best way," mean in a statistical sense?

CHAPTER 9 APPLICATION PROBLEMS

1. A firm wishes to compare three training methods to determine which is best in improving problem solving skills: lecture (L), role play (R), and case method (C). The spread chart shows the results on a common examination given to the 15 participants in the study.

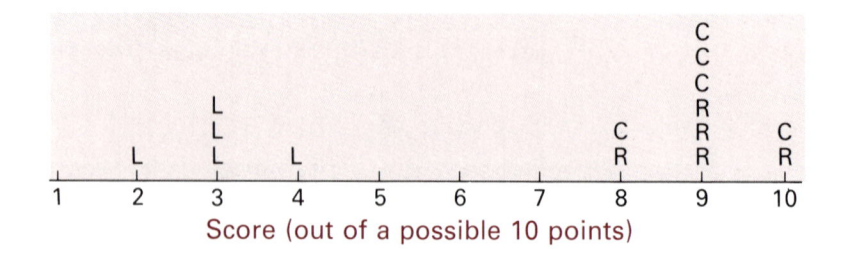

    a. Describe how the firm should have selected participants and assigned them to the three treatment levels.
    b. Does the spread chart suggest that the three teaching methods are equally effective?

2. Firms often use the Watson–Glaser Critical Thinking Appraisal to measure problem solving ability. The instrument measures the ability to make inferences, assess assumptions, draw conclusions, and evaluate arguments. Below are data from a study to determine whether the level of critical thinking affects the time to solve a complex disturbance problem.

Time in Minutes to Solve the Problem		
High Critical	Medium Critical	Low Critical
10	18	39
20	100	118
35	126	139
47	149	157
379	565	784

    a. Draw a multiple box plot for the three treatments.
    b. What analysis is appropriate? Why?
    c. Analyze the data using an α level of .05.

3. You believe that different types of managers learn problem solving best by different teaching methods. You will classify managers according to the Sensing–Intuition dimension of the Myers–Briggs Type Indicator. Sensing managers like presentations that are detailed and organized, while intuitive managers prefer to discover the important principles in a presentation. Thus you believe that sensing managers will prefer the lecture method, while intuitive managers will prefer the case method. You wish to test your beliefs.

    a. What type of experiment should you design?
    b. Construct a data table for the two-factor study that agrees with your beliefs. Show cell mean scores on the common final—from 0 to 100.
    c. Draw type of manager profile graphs for your data. That is, assign type of teaching method to the horizontal axis. Plot how sensing and intuitive managers perform when taught by the two methods.

4. You wish to reduce the time customers must wait to get their equipment repaired. You test three different strategies and include a control group—the present repair method. Shown is a multiple box plot of the results. What are you likely to conclude? Explain.

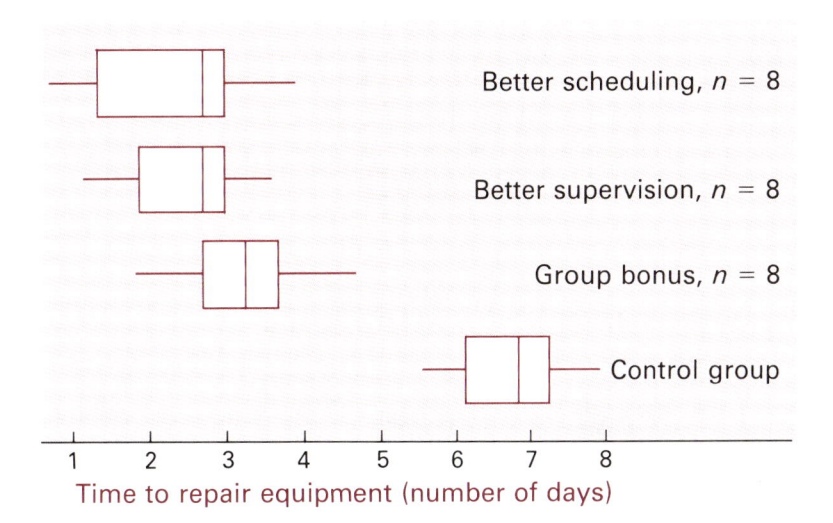

5. You believe that workers with both high and low need for independence work best under a participative style leader.
   a. How many factors should you have in your study to test your assertion? Why?
   b. How many levels of each factor should there be?
   c. If you believe that workers with low need for independence work best under an autocratic leader and workers with high need for independence work best under a participative leader, which experimental design is best? Why?
   d. Construct a data table for the two-factor study that agrees with your beliefs. Show cell mean scores (in productivity per hour).

6. Shown are two spread charts for a one-factor, three-level study conducted by a foundation on the effect of three types of TV ads on increasing awareness of sickle cell anemia. The three strategies are informative (I), persuasive (P), and emotional (E). Given the hypothetical data, for which study does it appear that we would reject the null hypothesis of no treatment effect? Defend your answer.

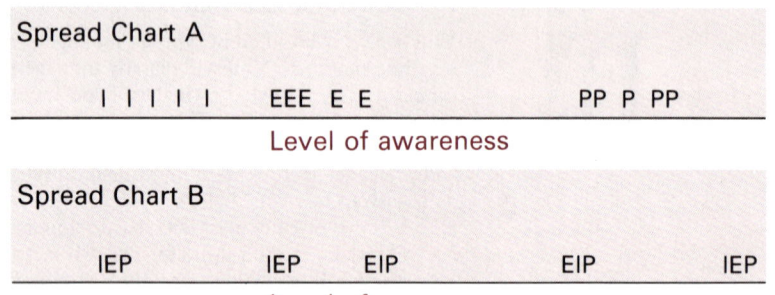

Spread Chart A

I I I I I   EEE E E   PP P PP

Level of awareness

Spread Chart B

IEP   IEP   EIP   EIP   IEP

Level of awareness

7. Which of three sales displays generates the largest revenue? Shown are the data from a one-factor, three-level planned change study.

	Daily Revenue	
Display A	Display B	Display C
$1,300	$150	$1,450
1,400	250	1,700
1,800	450	1,850
1,900	800	2,400
5,000	900	4,960

   a. Draw a multiple box plot.
   b. Are the three population median revenues the same for the displays? Use a 5% α level.
   c. Set up 95% Dunn multiple comparisons on the differences among all pairs of population medians.

8. Which computer has the longest time to failure? Shown are data on 15 randomly selected computers that have been tested until failure.

Chapter 9 Analysis of Variance

Time to Failure in Hours

Model A	Model B	Model C
105	35	143
4	2	66
65	110	15
197	145	99
56	76	80

    a. Draw a multiple box plot for the data.
    b. Is there any difference in time to failure among the three models? Use an α level of 5%.

9. You consider two possible improvements for razor blades that could increase the number of smooth shaves. The accompanying data are the results of a planned change study. The dependent variable is the number of shaves before the blade is no longer usable.

Plastic Coating on Blade	Lubricant on Blade	Standard Blade
15	15	7
13	17	9
11	15	8
13	11	8
13	12	8

    a. Are the three sample mean numbers of shaves different?
    b. Do you need an analysis of variance to answer part **a**?
    c. Are the three population mean numbers of shaves different? If we set α at 5%, can we reject the null hypothesis?
    d. Which type of improvement extends the life of blades the most? Use a 5% experimentwise error rate (95% experimentwise confidence level).

10. A capstone course for an undergraduate Decision Science major uses a business simulation game. Student teams make a set of decisions in a hypothetical, but competitive, environment. Final stock price is the measure of decision effectiveness.

Is there any difference in the performance among teams that do not use decision aids, those that use manual aids, and those that use computer-based decision aids? Here are the final stock prices of 15 teams under the three conditions.

No Aids	Manual Aids	Computer Aids
$ .12	$ .15	$1.00
1.59	3.16	4.10
3.50	3.60	6.20
3.52	4.70	6.30
13.55	16.25	22.40

    a. Draw a multiple box plot of the data.
    b. What analysis does the box plot suggest?
    c. Complete the suggested analysis. Set α at 5%.

11. Shown are data for a 2 × 2 factorial study on type of manager and teaching method first discussed in Exercise 3. The dependent variable is performance on the final exam.

	Score on Final Exam Out of a Possible 10 Points	
	Lecture	Case Method
Sensing	9	3
	9	5
	9	4
Intuitive	2	9
	5	10
	5	8

   a. Draw a type of manager profile graph.
   b. Having set an α level of 5%, is there a significant interaction effect?
   c. If you were in charge of training, what would the interaction effect mean for the way you run your training classes?

12. Groupthink is the tendency of groups to reach a quick consensus and generate poor decisions. Groupthink happens to groups under high stress that have poor leadership.

    Shown is a factorial study that tests for the necessity of both conditions—high stress and poor leadership. The dependent variable is the number of symptoms of groupthink that each group exhibits as it solves a complex business case.

	Number of Groupthink Symptoms	
	Poor Leadership	Good Leadership
Low Stress	2	1
	3	1
	3	1
	4	1
High Stress	7	1
	7	1
	7	2
	7	0

   a. Draw the type of leadership style profile graph.
   b. Draw the level of stress profile graph.
   c. Do an analysis of variance. Use a 5% α level.
   d. In simple terms, what does the interaction mean in terms of groupthink?

13. Which creativity method—brainstorming or analogy—is better? Fifteen managers are randomly selected and are randomly divided into three groups of five each. Each group is randomly assigned to one of two creative methods or the control group. After learning the assigned creative method (managers in the control group receive no creativity training), each manager is given a mini-case. At the end of 30 minutes we record the number of different ideas each manager has generated. Here are the data.

Control Group	Brainstorming	Analogy
1	7	9
2	11	9
3	12	11
5	12	12
7	13	14

a. Draw a spread chart.
b. Determine whether the three population mean numbers of alternative solutions are the same. Use a 1% α level.
c. Which method (or methods) is best at generating the largest number of different ideas? Set up 99% experimentwise confidence intervals.

14. Shown are the productivity cell means (units per hour) for a 2 × 5 factorial study.

|Length of Time Employed in the Firm (years)|				
	<1	1–3	4–6	7–9	10 or More
Individual Bonus	100	100	95	90	85
Group Bonus	85	90	95	100	110

a. Draw a length of time employed profile graph.
b. Draw a type of bonus profile graph.
c. Without doing a formal statistical analysis, does it appear that there is an interaction? Explain.

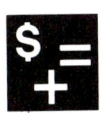

15. A firm is considering three different strategies to collect accounts receivable. All three strategies are effective in collecting overdue accounts. However, the firm wants to determine which strategy maintains the account holders' goodwill. Eighteen accounts which are 20 days past due are selected and subdivided randomly into three groups. Each group of accounts is randomly assigned to one strategy. The firm asks each account holder after it has received its treatment to indicate the level of goodwill on a 10-point scale (1 = poor goodwill to 10 = excellent goodwill). Here are the data.

Letter	Phone Call	Letter and Phone Call
7	5	2
8	5	2
7	6	3
9	7	4
9	6	3
8	6	3

a. Draw a spread chart.
b. Which strategy (or strategies) is best at maintaining goodwill? Use a 5% experimentwise error rate.
c. Explain why the letter and phone call strategy might have the lowest goodwill scores.

16. Three new drugs are tested for effectiveness at two different hospitals by two independent teams of doctors. Suppose both teams found the same variance ratio. Yet, one team rejected the null hypothesis and concluded that at least one drug's effectiveness is different from the other two. The other team, using the same level of significance, fails to reject the null hypothesis.
   a. Explain how this is possible.
   b. Construct a numerical example to support your explanation.

17. COMCEL is considering two promotion strategies to increase customer phone usage. The inverse rate promotion reduces the cost per minute with increasing phone usage. The free gifts promotion provides different gifts for different usage levels. COMCEL believes that the free gifts will work better with middle income users and the inverse rate promotion will work better with high income users.
   a. How many factors are there in the study?
   b. Assume COMCEL desires 50 subjects per cell. What is the total sample size for the study?
   c. Explain how COMCEL should select subjects for the factorial study and how they will be assigned to the experimental cells. Provide a detailed description.

18. Cola International wants to taste-test proposed reformulations of its major soft drink. It will try three types of sweeteners: sugar, saccharin, and aspartame. Twenty subjects rate each of the three formulations for tastiness on a scale from 0 = awful to 100 = very good.
   a. Shown are three 95% experimentwise confidence intervals for the difference between all pairs of treatment population means. What can you conclude?

Sugar vs. Saccharin	$(78 - 65) \pm 7$
Sugar vs. Aspartame	$(78 - 63) \pm 7$
Saccharin vs. Aspartame	$(65 - 63) \pm 7$

   b. Describe how Cola International should have conducted the study—that is, how it should have selected its sample, assigned the subjects to the three treatment levels, etc.

19. Refer to Exercise 18. Shown is a portion of the data in the cola reformulation study.

Sugar	Saccharin	Aspartame
80	65	65
75	66	70
81	61	62
78	65	65
75	60	63

   a. What variables might account for the fact that all the observations within each treatment level are *not* the same?
   b. Draw a spread chart. Which cola formulation do customers seem to prefer? Explain.

20. Does a stock's risk vary among industries? A stock analyst randomly selects five stocks from three industries—utilities, telecommunications, and computer technology—and records the historic beta coefficients. A beta coefficient measures a stock's volatility. Beta coefficients under 1.0 indicate stocks with very little risk; beta coefficients over 1.0 indicate risky stocks.

Given are the three 95% Tukey confidence intervals on the difference in population mean beta coefficients. What can you conclude?

Technology vs. Utilities	$(1.80 - .56) \pm .32$
Technology vs. Telecommunications	$(1.80 - 1.10) \pm .32$
Telecommunications vs. Utilities	$(1.10 - .56) \pm .32$

21. Is the infant mortality rate in the United States lower than in other Western countries? We collect data from five randomly selected cities in the United States (U), West Germany (W), and France (F). We record the number of infant deaths per 1,000 births. The data, which are based on a *UN Dept. of International Economic and Social Affairs* report, are shown in the accompanying spread graph. What conclusions can you draw from the spread chart? Discuss.

```
             F F           W             U
            F F F        W W W W        U U U U
    |----|----|----|----|----|----|----|----|----|
    6   6.5   7   7.5   8   8.5   9   9.5  10  10.5
                    Deaths per 1,000 births
```

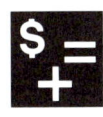

22. Does the mean indebtedness of delinquent card holders differ among the following three income classes?

Less than $20,000	$30,000–$50,000	Over $75,000
$146	$210	$585
124	156	708
178	112	606
156	165	647
145	110	578

a. Use our software to compute the variance ratio. Is the *p*-value less than .05? What can you conclude about the mean level of indebtedness and level of annual income?
b. Does the mean level of indebtedness differ among all income classes? Use an experimentwise error rate of 5%.

23. Suppose you believe that the mean level of indebtedness is affected not only by the credit card holder's annual income level (see Exercise 22) but also by his or her need for material goods—low or high need. Each factor affects the mean level of indebtedness. However, you suspect that high income card holders with high need for material possessions will have extraordinarily high mean levels of indebtedness.
a. What type of study should you consider running?
b. Develop hypothetical data that would support your position. Defend without doing the analysis of variance.

24. Do all states have the same mean cost per day for a hospital stay? A public policy watchdog group chooses three states—Alaska, South Dakota, and Georgia. It randomly selects six community hospitals and determines their mean cost per day.

The data taken from the 1987 report of *Health Statistics* are shown here.

Alaska	South Dakota	Georgia
$892	$318	$456
808	350	500
980	370	425
880	280	450
901	325	460
870	300	470

a. Using the spread within and spread between ideas, does it appear that the population mean costs per day at community hospitals in the three states are the same? Discuss.

b. If we are interested in drawing inferences only about the 18 hospitals in the study, do we need to conduct a formal analysis of variance?

25.

```
   Date: October 21, 1992
     To: Bill Katz, Supervisor of Testing
   From: Sarah Teman, Manager of Operations
Subject: Results of Planned Change Study
```

For the past 36 working days (since September 7th), we have been testing two new microchip circuits as well as the present circuit. Our goal is to increase the number of hours of operation for our telephone units to over 1,100 hours before failure. Bill O'Hara tells me that this is absolutely essential to maintain our share of market. It will also reestablish us as a leading technology firm in the industry.

Specifically I want the answers to the following questions:

1. Is either circuit better than our present one?
2. Which microchip circuit is better in terms of accomplishing our 1,100-hour goal?

I will need your analysis by the end of the week.

Use Data Base IV for your analysis. Your response to Sarah Teman should include a brief memo and your analysis.

REFERENCES

DUNN, O. J. "Multiple Comparisons Using Rank Sums." *Technometrics* 6(1964): 241–255.

KEPNER, BENJAMIN, and CHARLES TREGOE. *The New Rational Manager.* Princeton, New Jersey: Princeton Research Press, 1988.

KEPPEL, GEOFFREY. *Design and Analysis: A Researcher's Handbook.* Englewood Cliffs, New Jersey: Prentice-Hall Inc., 1973.

TUKEY, J. "The Problem of Multiple Comparisons." Unpublished manuscript. Princeton, New Jersey, 1953.

10

Regression Analysis

10.1 Looking for relationships among variables and problem solving
  Relationship detection tools
  Prediction, explanation, and control
10.2 Collecting data for a regression study
  Running experimental studies
  Running correlational studies
  Cross-sectional vs. time-ordered studies
10.3 Plotting scatter diagrams
10.4 Curve fitting
  Conditional means
  The method of least squares
10.5 Evaluating the regression model
  The need for statistical testing
  Decomposition of the total sum of squares
  Is the regression equation worth using at all?
  Are all predictor variables necessary?
10.6 Evaluating the regression analysis assumptions: Residual analysis
  Assumptions underlying regression analysis
  Examining residual plots
  Nonlinearity of regression curve
  Unequal variances
  Nonnormality
  Outliers
  Autocorrelation
10.7 Using regression models for prediction
  Prediction vs. extrapolation
  Differences between prediction and confidence intervals
  Reducing the width of confidence or prediction intervals
10.8 Indicator variables
  Representing categorical variables
  Significance testing
  Interaction
  Categorical variables with three or more classes
  Summary
10.9 Multicollinearity
  What is multicollinearity?
  Why is multicollinearity a problem?
  Detecting multicollinearity
  Minimizing multicollinearity
  Summary
10.10 Regression models and problem solving
  Steps in building valid regression models
  Using regression models to sense problems
  Using regression models in choice making
10.11 Determining relationships using the chi-square test of independence
  The need for statistical testing
  Chi-square test of independence
  Dangers of small expected frequencies
  Summary
10.12 Integrating framework
Chapter 10 Questions
Chapter 10 Application Problems
Appendix: Job satisfaction data

CHAPTER OUTLINE

COMCEL Interoffice Communication

Date: September 6, 1992
  To: Cherian Jain, V.P., Marketing Research
From: Ann Tabor, CEO
  Re: Increasing Retail Sales of Model 76 Car Phones

The sales and inventory reports over the last two months show that sales of the Model 76 car phone have been flat, and that inventory has been increasing. Perhaps we should lower the price or increase advertising or both to move this inventory. Is the unit price sensitive? Do sales increase with increases in advertising? We do not want to lower prices if sales are relatively insensitive to price changes, and we do not want to waste money on ineffective advertising.

Please look into this and report back as soon as possible.

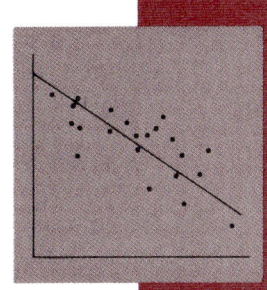

10.1 Looking for Relationships Among Variables and Problem Solving

Good managers know how to solve disturbance problems and initiate improvement projects. Looking for relationships among variables is essential to both of these tasks. For example, is there a relationship between the onset of more defective parts and the switch to a new raw material vendor? Can we increase sales by varying price and advertising? In short, we need to understand how variables affect each other.

Relationship Detection Tools

Managers can use at least three statistical tools to detect relationships among variables—namely, planned change studies, regression analysis, and the chi-square test of independence. Table 10.1 compares and contrasts these tools. We discussed planned change studies in Chapter 9. We will present regression analysis and the chi-square test for independence in this chapter.

Managers use planned change studies to answer the basic question: "Is there an effect?" Does type of training reduce unit labor costs? Does material from two different vendors affect the level of defects? Does leadership style affect job performance? Such questions are answerable by the use of planned change studies to determine if categorical independent variables affect a quantitative dependent variable.

Material vendors (firm A and firm B), type of training workshop (team-building, creativity, and skill training), and leadership styles (autocratic and participative) are examples of **categorical variables**. Productivity in units per hour, percentage defects, age in years, depth in inches, and price in dollars are examples of **quantitative variables**.

Planned change studies can also be used for quantitative independent variables. For example, in the study of the cracked desk drawers in Chapter 9, we determined whether the drawer depth—independent variable—affected the percentage defects—dependent variable.

A categorical, or qualitative, variable is one that is not measurable on a numerical scale.

A quantitative variable is one that is measurable on a numerical scale.

Table 10.1

Three Statistical Tools for Detecting Relationships Among Variables

Tool	Dependent Variable	Predictor, or Independent Variable
Planned change studies	Quantitative	Categorical or quantitative
Regression analysis	Quantitative	Quantitative or categorical
Chi-square test of independence	Categorical or quantitative	Categorical or quantitative

Managers use regression analysis when they want to know *how* variables affect one another, not merely whether they do or not. We develop an equation that *explains*, *predicts*, and *controls* the dependent variable. For example, a manager wishes to explain how price and advertising expenditures affect sales to set performance standards and to predict future sales levels. Price and advertising expenditures are the **predictor variables** and sales is the **dependent variable**. To explain, predict, and control, managers must determine (1) *if* two or more variables are related and (2) *how* they are related.

> Predictor variables are variables thought to affect the dependent variable.
>
> A dependent variable is a variable that we wish to explain, predict, or control.

Regression analysis is a mathematical technique for determining and measuring relationships among variables. It can be used whether the predictor variables are quantitative or categorical. Categorical variables may be converted to *dummy* or indicator variables so that they can be treated like quantitative variables.

Managers can also use the chi-square test of independence as a tool when the observations in a sample can be cross-classified according to two criteria. That is, managers can determine whether the two classification criteria are related. Suppose we study 1,000 customers to determine whether the level of product satisfaction is related to customers' income level. Product satisfaction is a categorical variable—a person is either satisfied or dissatisfied. Income level is a quantitative variable that can be transformed into distinct categories. The cross-tabs table, Table 10.2, presents the observations, which are *frequency counts*. Frequency counts are the *number* of people that fall into each cell of the cross-tabs table. For example, there are 390 people who earn less than $20,000 and are satisfied with the product, and there are 75 people who earn between $20,000 and $50,000 and are dissatisfied with the product. Table 10.2 suggests that product satisfaction is related to income level.

Despite their differences, planned change studies, regression analysis, and the chi-square test of independence are all useful in detecting relationships among variables. They are essential tools to managerial problem diagnosis and solving.

We illustrate the power of relationship detection in the following example.

EXAMPLE: INCREASING CAR PHONE SALES   COMCEL sells its entire line of car phones directly to the public through 60 retail outlets in shopping malls around the country. Recently, sales of the Model 76 have been flat, and inventory has been increasing. COMCEL is considering both price cuts and

Table 10.2

Cross-Tabs Table of Consumers by Level of Product Satisfaction and Level of Income

	Less than $20,000	$20,000–$50,000	$50,000 or More	Total
Satisfied	390	325	100	815
Dissatisfied	10	75	100	185
	400	400	200	1,000

radio ads to boost sales. However, it doesn't want to lower prices if sales are relatively insensitive to price changes. It also does not want to waste money on ineffective advertising.

COMCEL selects 24 outlets with comparable sales from different cities across the country. It will study the impact of four different prices and three different frequencies of ads on sales in the 24 outlets. It will test market each price and ad combination in two randomly selected stores for one week. The ads will be run during morning drive time on the most highly rated AM station in the test city. COMCEL will record the number of Model 76 phones sold during the test week. Based on the marketing study, COMCEL will apply the best price and advertising strategy to all 60 stores.

Table 10.3 contains the data for the marketing regression study.

Since the price and the frequency of ads will be used to predict units sold, and not the converse, the number of Model 76 units sold is the *dependent* variable. Price and number of ads per day are the predictor variables. Note that regression studies have only one dependent variable, but can have one or more predictor variables.

Table 10.3

COMCEL Marketing Study Data

Outlet	Price (dollars)	Number of Ads per Day	Model 76 Units Sold
1	100	1	9
2	100	1	11
3	100	3	19
4	100	3	15
5	100	5	26
6	100	5	24
7	90	1	14
8	90	1	19
9	90	3	24
10	90	3	28
11	90	5	31
12	90	5	32
13	85	1	17
14	85	1	19
15	85	3	29
16	85	3	25
17	85	5	30
18	85	5	30
19	80	1	26
20	80	1	23
21	80	3	26
22	80	3	24
23	80	5	37
24	80	5	34

Using regression analysis, the marketing research group obtained the following equation, which is based on a sample of 24 outlets for one week:

$$\text{UNITS SOLD-PRED} = 60.89 - .529\text{PRICE} + 3.312\text{ADS} \tag{10.1}$$

UNITS SOLD-PRED is the predicted or estimated number of units sold when PRICE and ADS are set at specific values. COMCEL will use equation (10.1) for predicting sales, explaining the effect of each predictor variable on units sold, and controlling the sales of their 60 retail outlets.

Prediction, Explanation, and Control

In general, we can use a regression equation to predict values of a dependent variable, to explain how each predictor variable and dependent variable are related, and to set standards to control performance. We will show how these three facets of regression analysis apply to the COMCEL study.

PREDICTION   The regression equation (10.1) predicts that, if we set the price at $85 and run two radio ads per day, stores like those in the study should sell a mean of 22.55 phones per week. We obtain this value of the dependent variable simply by plugging those particular values of the predictor variables into equation (10.1):

$$\text{UNITS SOLD-PRED} = 60.89 - .529(85) + 3.312(2)$$
$$= 60.89 - 44.96 + 6.624$$
$$= 22.55$$

EXPLANATION   To understand the numerical weights attached to the predictor variables, suppose management restricts the number of ads to one per day:

$$\text{UNITS SOLD-PRED} = 60.89 - .529\text{PRICE} + 3.312(1)$$
$$= 60.89 + 3.312 - .529\text{PRICE}$$
$$= 64.202 - .529\text{PRICE} \tag{10.2}$$

When *holding the level of advertising constant*, we estimate that each dollar increase in price reduces the mean number of units sold by .529 phone.

Figure 10.1 on page 508 is a graph of the regression equation (10.2). The straight line has a y-intercept of 64.202 and a slope of −.529. That is, when the price is $0, the straight line crosses the vertical axis—units sold—at 64.202 phones. Notice what happens when we increase the price by one dollar from $80 to $81:

At $80:   UNITS SOLD-PRED = 64.202 − .529(80) = 21.882

At $81:   UNITS SOLD-PRED = 64.202 − .529(81) = 21.353

Price change = +$1   Change in units sold = −.529 phone

FIGURE 10.1 Phones Sold vs. Price for One Ad Per Day

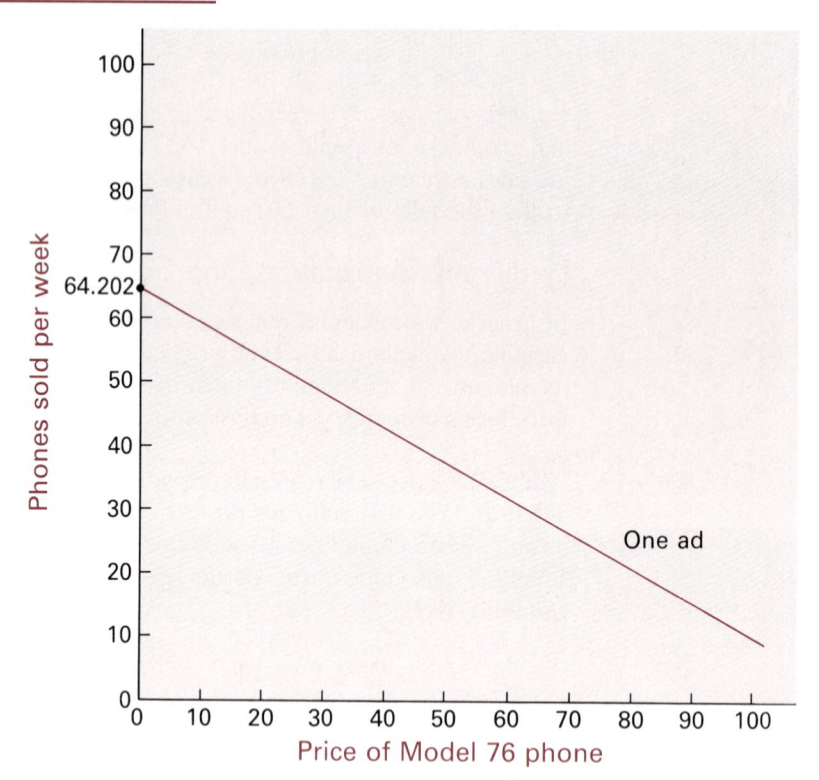

Price and units sold are *inversely* related. When price goes up, the number of units sold goes down. An inverse relationship is represented by the *negative sign* in equation (10.2) and by the negative slope in Figure 10.1.

Referring again to equation (10.1), suppose we charge $90 for the Model 76 car phone:

$$\text{UNITS SOLD-PRED} = 60.89 - .529(90) + 3.312\text{ADS}$$
$$= 60.89 - 47.61 + 3.312\text{ADS}$$
$$= 13.28 + 3.312\text{ADS} \qquad (10.3)$$

Holding the price constant, we estimate that each additional ad increases the mean number of phones sold by 3.312 units. The straight line in Figure 10.2 has an intercept of 13.28 and a slope of +3.312. When no ad is aired, the straight line crosses the vertical axis—phones sold—at 13.28 units. Sales increase from this point by 3.312 phones for each additional ad. There is a *positive* relationship between number of ads and number of units sold.

Thus, each regression coefficient (−.529 and 3.312) is a measure of the effect of a one-unit change in a predictor variable on the dependent variable when all the other variables in the equation are held constant.

FIGURE 10.2 Phones Sold vs. Number of Ads for a $90 Price

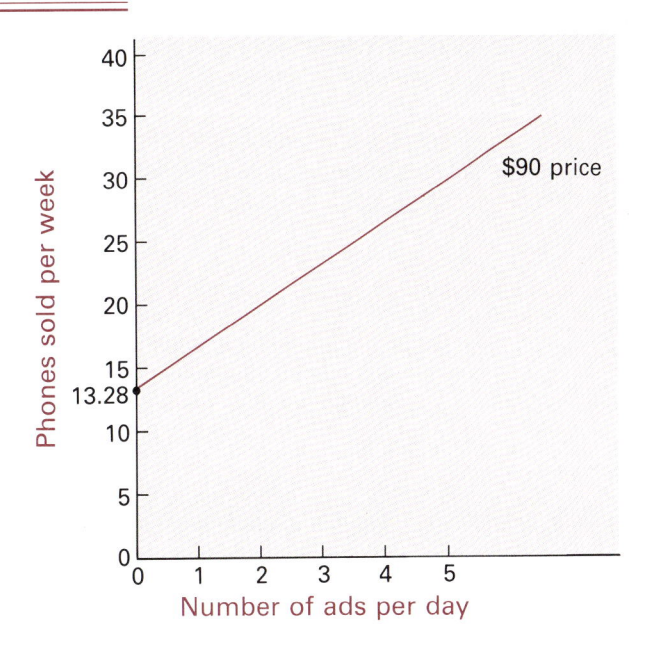

(Graph: Phones sold per week vs. Number of ads per day; line for $90 price starts at 13.28 when ads = 0 and rises to about 35 at 5 ads.)

CONTROL   COMCEL can use equation (10.1) to control sales. If a store charges $85 and airs two radio ads per day, it can predict that it will sell 22.55 phones per week. If the store does not come close, the store manager will want to know why. This is a deviation from expected performance and *may* signal the onset of a disturbance problem.

In summary, we can use a regression equation to predict values of a quantitative dependent variable based on the values of one or more quantitative or categorical predictor variables. We can determine the effects of each predictor variable on the dependent variable. That is, we interpret each regression coefficient as the effect on the dependent variable of a one-unit change in a predictor variable when all the other predictor variables in the equation are held constant. Finally, we can use a regression equation to set performance standards for the dependent variable. Failure to meet performance standards may signal the onset of a disturbance problem.

10.2 Collecting Data for a Regression Study

Managers must make a series of decisions in designing a regression study. First, they must decide on the type of study—either experimental or correlational. Then they must identify critical predictor and dependent variables, select a data source, determine the levels of the predictor variables (for an experimental study), and obtain the data. By the end of this section you should be able to:

1. explain what an observation is in a regression study;
2. explain the meaning of a unit of association;
3. distinguish between two types of regression studies—experimental and correlational;
4. select appropriate predictor variables and the proper number of levels for each variable in an experimental study; and
5. distinguish between a cross-sectional and a time series study.

Running Experimental Studies

In order to understand the decision making process behind running an experimental study, return to the COMCEL study. Recall that it was designed to measure the relationship of price and frequency of ads to the number of phones sold.

IDENTIFYING CRITICAL VARIABLES   COMCEL chose unit sales, a quantitative variable, as the dependent variable. It chose price and number of radio ads per day as the predictor variables because it believed that these variables affect unit sales. The choice of predictor variables is not always so obvious. We must always establish a logical connection between the dependent variable and each predictor variable.

SELECTING THE UNIT OF ASSOCIATION   COMCEL chose an individual store as the experimental unit or *unit of association*. The unit of association is the person, place, or thing on which we collect our data. At first, COMCEL had considered the region as the unit of association. All outlets in a region would charge the same price and run the same number of radio ads. The dependent variable would be the total number of units sold in the region. Thus, each region would become a single observation. However, COMCEL rejected this approach because there are only six regions, and a sample of six is too small.

Instead, COMCEL chose an individual store as the unit of association. It selected stores in 24 cities that had comparable sales to control for factors other than price and number of ads that might affect unit sales. It also chose cities that were far apart so that customers in one city could not hear the radio ads from other cities. COMCEL collected 24 observations, one for each of the 24 selected stores. Each observation included the value of the dependent variable and the values of the two predictor variables. For example, from Table 10.3, the observation values for store 1 were (9 units, $100, 1 ad).

DETERMINING THE LEVELS OF THE DEPENDENT VARIABLES   The present price of the Model 76 phone is $100. COMCEL needed to know how much it could charge and still make an acceptable profit. Eighty dollars was the lower limit according to the accountants. For the ADS variable, COMCEL determined that commuters generally hear five or fewer ads while driving to work. It then used the **pull apart strategy** and varied the predictor variables in the ranges of $80 to $100 and one to five ads.

The pull apart strategy says that the minimum and maximum values of the predictor variables should be spread apart as much as possible.

In selecting the actual prices and number of ads, COMCEL used the following two principles:

1. Use at least three equally spaced levels for each predictor variable.
2. Have the same number of observations for every combination of predictor variables.

COMCEL had originally considered three price levels—$100, $90, and $80. However, one manager was interested in studying the effects of a 15% discount, so COMCEL added a fourth price level—$85.

Note that in Table 10.3, each price was paired twice with each number of ads. Having an equal number of observations for every combination of predictor variables is called a *balanced design*. In Section 10.8, we will learn that a balanced design eliminates *multicollinearity*, a potentially serious problem in regression studies.

Running Correlational Studies

In experimental studies, the manager can pull apart the levels of the predictor variables and ensure a balanced design. In correlational studies, the manager cannot do either of these things. The manager merely records the data from historical records or sample surveys. We first discussed correlational studies in Chapter 6.

Many times it is either impractical or unethical to conduct experimental studies. Suppose we wanted to measure the effect of price and number of ads for all firms selling car phones. We could *record* the prices charged by our competitors and their number of daily radio ads, but we could not ask them to *vary* their prices or number of ads so that we could obtain a balanced design.

In correlational studies, managers must still select their critical variables and choose the unit of association. However, they cannot *pull apart* the levels of the predictor variables, nor can they obtain balanced designs. They simply collect the available data.

Due to the difficulties sometimes associated with carrying out experimental studies, correlational regression studies are more common. We discuss the unique problems of correlational studies in Section 10.8.

Cross-Sectional vs. Time-Ordered Studies

In Chapter 2 we first distinguished between cross-sectional and time-ordered data. Recall that cross-sectional data are taken from one time period whereas time-ordered data are collected over time.

The study conducted by COMCEL was a cross-sectional experimental study because it recorded sales for a single week. Alternatively, observations could have been collected in a time-ordered study over a period of several weeks or months. Consider the eight quarters of data shown in Table 10.4 on page 512. Working with time series data requires special care. We will cover this topic in Chapter 11. In this chapter we focus on cross-sectional regression studies.

Table 10.4

Industry-Wide Sales, Price, and Advertising Data

Year	Quarter	Predictor Variables Average Price	Advertising ($000s)	Dependent Variable Sales in Units (000s)
1991	1	97.5	2,568	40,000
	2	96.4	2,600	42,525
	3	96.0	2,612	41,980
	4	96.0	2,620	43,680
1992	1	95.0	2,625	44,000
	2	94.5	2,700	44,500
	3	94.5	2,703	46,000
	4	94.0	2,710	46,250

SECTION 10.2 EXERCISES

1. A human resources manager wants to determine whether age, salary level, and years on the job are related to job performance. He will randomly select 100 workers' records and determine whether the variables are related.
   a. What is the dependent variable?
   b. What are the predictor variables?
   c. What is the unit of association?
   d. What is an observation in the study?
   e. Is this an experimental or correlational study?
   f. Are the data cross-sectional or time-ordered?

2. The marketing manager wants to determine what affects share of market. She believes that relative price and relative level of advertising are critical variables. Relative price is the ratio of our price to the average of all our competitors' prices. The manager collects data on the three variables for the past 16 quarters.
   a. What is the dependent variable?
   b. What are the independent variables?
   c. What is the unit of association?
   d. What is an observation in the study?
   e. Is this an experimental or correlational study?
   f. Are the data cross-sectional or time-ordered?

3. An operations manager wants to determine whether the amount of plastic filler used to produce TV cabinets affects the percentage of cabinets rejected due to scratches or nicks. She plans to vary the amount of filler from 2% to 8% in 1% increments.
   a. What is the dependent variable?
   b. What is the predictor variable?
   c. What is the unit of association?
   d. What is an observation in the study?
   e. Is this an experimental or correlational study?
   f. Are the data cross-sectional or time-ordered?

4. Does advertising lead sales by one quarter? Does advertising in one quarter affect sales in the next quarter? The manager plans to collect data for 24 months to determine whether there is a relationship.
   a. What is the dependent variable?
   b. What is the predictor variable?

c. What is the unit of association?
d. What is an observation in the study?
e. Is this an experimental or correlational study?
f. Are the data cross-sectional or time-ordered?

5. You want to determine what quantitative factors affect grade point average (GPA) of students in accounting. Generate two variables that should explain GPA.
   a. What is the dependent variable?
   b. What are the predictor variables?
   c. Discuss why you believe there is a relationship between these variables and the dependent variable.

6. An operations manager wants to know if the production run size and age of equipment affect cost per unit of molded phone sets. He plans to vary production run size from 333 to 1,000 units and use equipment from 1 to 5 years of age.
   a. What is the dependent variable?
   b. What are the predictor variables?
   c. Suppose we decide on three levels of production run size and three levels of age of equipment. What values of each variable must we run to achieve a balanced design? Why?

7. Refer to Exercise 6. What questions should we ask to determine whether we have pulled apart (as much as possible) the levels of the two predictor variables? Explain.

10.3 Plotting Scatter Diagrams

The end result of a regression analysis is an expression relating the dependent variable to one or more predictor variables. Equation (10.1) for the COMCEL study, relating units sold to price and number of ads, is called a *multiple linear regression*. *Multiple* means that there is more than one predictor variable. By contrast, in a *simple* regression, there is only one predictor variable. *Linear* means *linear in the predictor variables*.* That is, if we plotted each predictor variable against the dependent variable, the scatter diagram would indicate a straight-line relationship. By the end of this section, you should be able to:

1. plot scatter diagrams and detect obvious departures from linearity in the predictor variables;
2. identify clusters in a scatter diagram; and
3. interpret clusters accurately.

Return to the COMCEL regression study. Figures 10.3 and 10.4 on page 514 are plots of each predictor variable against the dependent variable. In Figure 10.3, as price increases, units sold tend to drop. In Figure 10.4, as number of ads increases, units sold tend to increase. We can enclose the data points in both figures with a relatively tight ellipse. Recall that in Chapter 3 we first proposed the quick ellipse test, which we repeat here.

---

*Equation (10.1) is also *linear in the parameters*. We will discuss this idea in Section 10.4.

FIGURE 10.3 Price vs. Units Sold

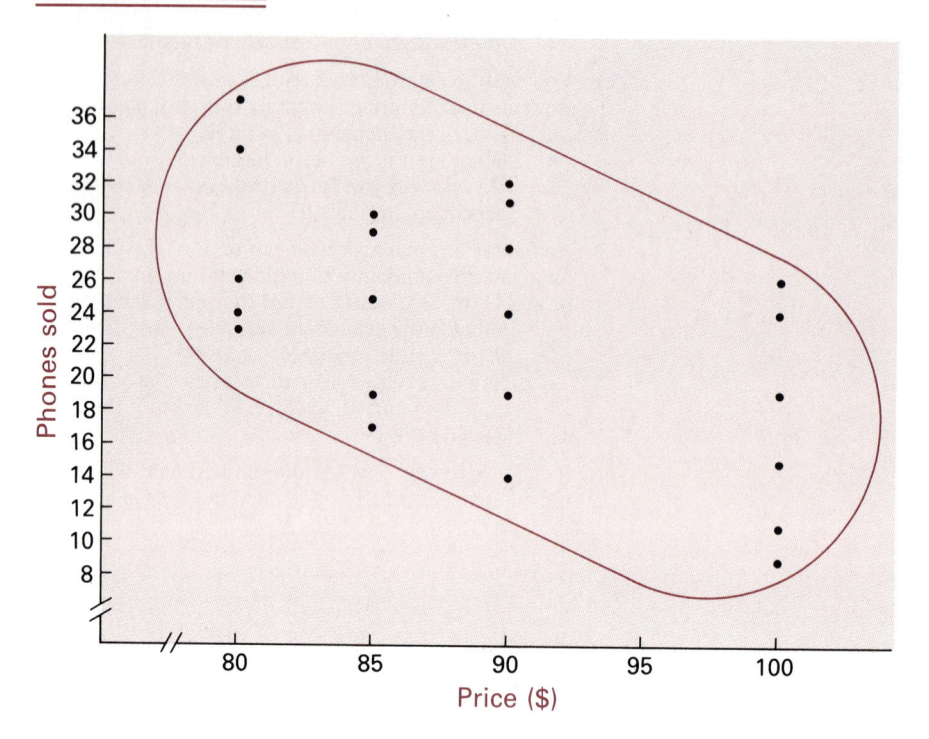

FIGURE 10.4 Phones Sold vs. Number of Ads Per Day

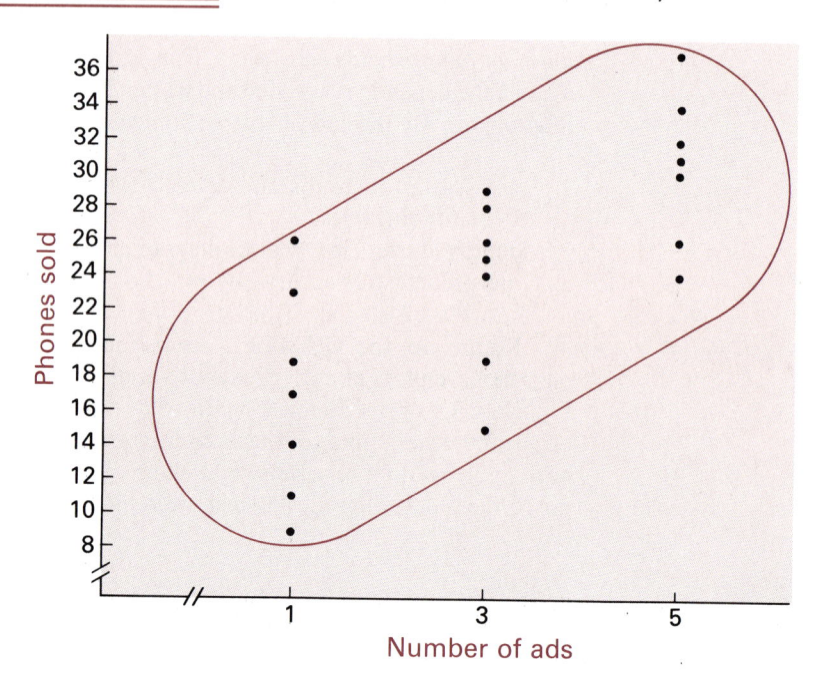

If we can enclose all the data in the scatter diagram with a tight ellipse, then the two variables are probably linearly related.

If the ellipse is upward sloping to the right, then the two variables are positively related.

If the ellipse is downward sloping to the right, then the two variables are negatively related.

If it takes a circle or an ellipse that is parallel to the horizontal axis to enclose all the data, then the two variables are probably not linearly related.

Figure 10.3 *suggests* a negative, or inverse, linear relationship between units sold and price. Figure 10.4 *suggests* a positive linear relationship between units sold and number of ads. We have used the word *suggests* because we cannot be certain until we have done the formal regression analysis.

What does "linear in the predictor variable" mean in management terms? Consider the following equation:

$$\text{UNITS SOLD-PRED} = 15.9 + 3.3\text{ADS}$$

It represents a *first-order* model because the predictor variable is raised only to the first power. This means that every time we run one more ad, we will *always sell an additional 3.3 units*. Even if we have run 100 ads, running the 101st ad will increase sales by 3.3 units. Of course, at some point, the regression equation will no longer be valid. That is, running one more ad will not increase sales by 3.3 units; it may even reduce sales. We discuss the limits to the validity of a regression equation in Section 10.7.

In some cases, first-order models are not appropriate. Consider the marketing data first presented in Chapter 3 and here in Table 10.5.

Table 10.5

Marketing Data for 12 COMCEL Regions

Region	Market Share (%)	Advertising ($000)	Predictor Variables Average Years of Experience	Relative Price
Atlanta	20	13	3	1.50
Birmingham	50	28	12	.60
Charlotte	30	17	15	1.00
Jacksonville	10	8	1	1.75
New Orleans	25	16	18	1.30
Orlando	30	18	7	.90
Miami	35	21	8	2.00
Washington	5	6	23	2.90
Baltimore	45	25	9	1.50
Dallas	55	32	11	1.10
Houston	20	11	20	2.50
Austin	28	16	17	2.25

FIGURE 10.5 Market Share vs. Years of Experience

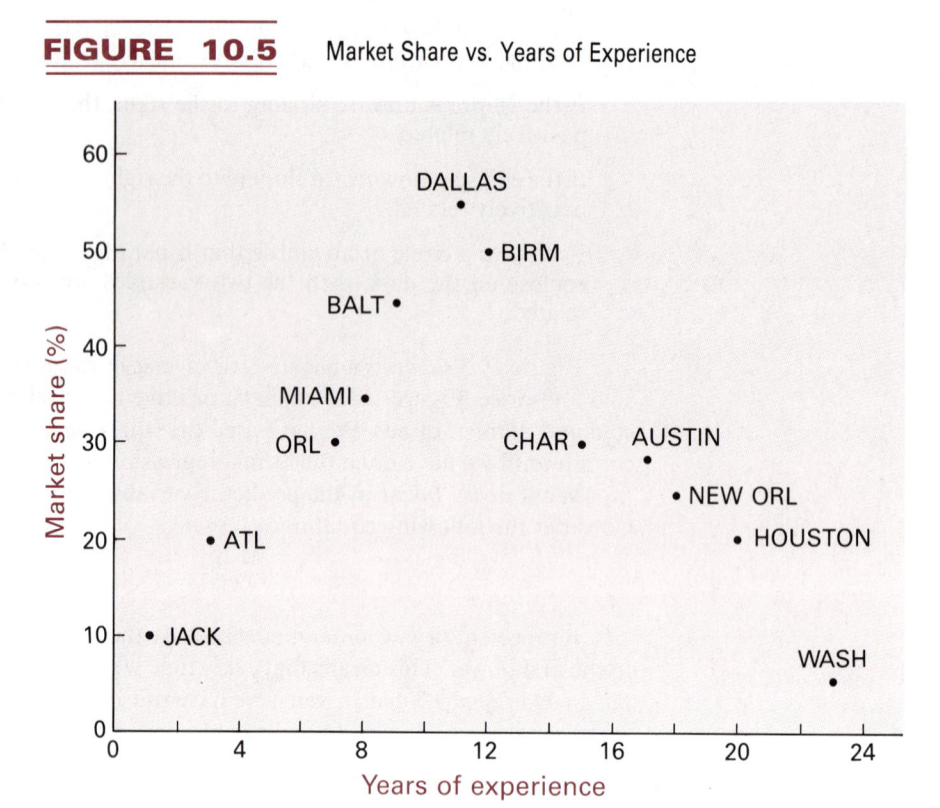

Figure 10.5 is a scatter diagram of market share versus years of sales experience. It shows a nonlinear relationship that can be represented by an inverted U. That is, as years of experience increases, market share increases initially. It peaks between 11 and 13 years of experience, and then drops off.

The nonlinear relationship makes sense. As the sales force gains more experience it grabs more market share from the competition. However, after 13 years, salespersons may begin to experience burnout—they lose enthusiasm, and market share decreases.

Using our software package, we obtained the following model:

$$\text{MRKTSHR-PRED} = 2.609 + 7.03\text{EXP} - .309\text{EXP}^2$$

Note that the predictor variable, experience, is raised to the second power. This is called a *second-order* model.

Figure 10.6, which relates market share and relative price, illustrates *clusters*. There is an overall inverse relationship between market share and relative price since we can enclose the data with an ellipse that slopes downward to the right. However, upon closer examination, there appear to be two distinct clusters of

Chapter 10 Regression Analysis

FIGURE 10.6 Market Share vs. Relative Price

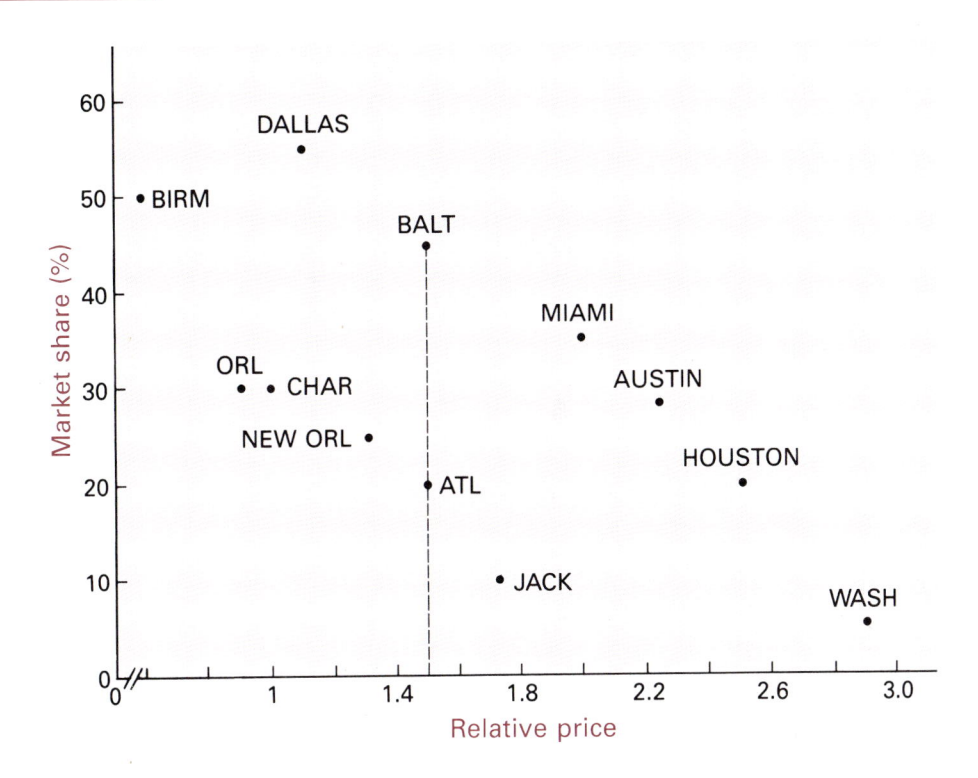

[Scatter plot showing Market share (%) on the y-axis (0 to 60) versus Relative price on the x-axis (0 to 3.0). Data points labeled: DALLAS (~1.1, 55), BIRM (~0.7, 50), BALT (1.5, 45), MIAMI (~2.0, 35), ORL (~0.9, 30), CHAR (~1.0, 30), AUSTIN (~2.2, 29), NEW ORL (~1.0, 25), HOUSTON (~2.5, 20), ATL (1.5, 20), JACK (~1.7, 9), WASH (~2.9, 6).]

data points, each consisting of six cities. The cluster closer to the origin (cluster 1) includes the Atlanta, Birmingham, Charlotte, Jacksonville, New Orleans, and Orlando regions. The other cluster lies further from the origin.

What do the clusters mean? Both slope downward to the right. Within each cluster, the higher the price is versus the competition's, the lower our market share. That makes economic sense. Now compare two cities—one in each cluster—that have the same relative price. In cluster 1, Atlanta has a 1.5 relative price. In cluster 2, Baltimore has the same 1.5 relative price. In both regions, COMCEL charges 50% more than the competitions' average price. Then why does Baltimore have a 45% market share and Atlanta only a 20% market share? There must be other variables that explain the significant difference in market shares for the same relative price. We have just sensed a potential problem or opportunity and should call a meeting to brainstorm for additional predictor variables.

In summary, regression analysis can handle both linear and nonlinear relationships. If the scatter diagram reveals clusters, we must seek additional predictor variables that explain the clusters. Always plot scatter diagrams for each pair of predictor and dependent variables before beginning the formal analysis.

SECTION 10.3 EXERCISES

1. Shown is a small data set on productivity in number of sales for over $100,000 made in a year and annual salary in thousands of dollars.

PROD	15	17	15	18	24	22	28	34	33	38
SALARY	20	22	26	30	32	35	35	40	45	47

   a. Develop a scatter diagram between PROD and SALARY.
   b. Does SALARY appear to be linearly related to PROD? Explain.
   c. Why must we qualify our analysis with the words *appear to be*?

2. Shown is a small data set on amount of study time (STUDYTIME in minutes) and test performance (TESTPERF).

STUDYTIME	30	60	75	90	100	135	160	200	240	300
TESTPERF	65	67	66	72	78	77	82	83	84	82

   a. Develop a scatter diagram between TESTPERF and STUDYTIME.
   b. Does STUDYTIME appear to be linearly related to TESTPERF? Explain.

3. Given is a time-ordered data set that includes quarterly sales, inventory, and net plant and equipment expenditures. The corporate economist believes that inventory and net plant and equipment expenditures can explain the level of sales.

Quarter	Sales	Inventory	NPEE
1	32,900	2,011	65
2	38,200	2,100	57
3	32,500	2,160	58
4	33,800	2,225	67
5	45,700	2,300	82
6	44,500	2,325	79
7	42,000	2,400	80
8	44,750	2,450	86
9	38,000	2,575	65
10	41,000	2,550	80
11	26,000	2,200	64
12	30,000	2,150	54

   SALES   Quarterly sales of capital equipment in millions of dollars
   INVENTORY   Mean level of inventory during quarter
   NPEE   Net plant and equipment expenditures in thousands of dollars

   a. Develop a scatter diagram between SALES and each predictor variable.
   b. Is either (or both) predictor variable linearly related to the dependent variable? Explain.

4. Given is a cross-sectional data set for 18 managers. It is a random sample of monthly salaries of managers at the same level within a major firm. The three independent variables are months on the job, level of interpersonal communication skill along a 1 (poor) to 10 (good) scale, and the manager's gender.

Manager	Monthly Salary	Months on the Job	Level of Communication Skill	Gender of Manager
1	2,000	14	3	Female
2	2,100	14	2	Female
3	2,150	12	3	Female
4	2,200	25	4	Female
5	2,300	27	6	Female
6	2,200	30	5	Female
7	2,400	32	7	Female
8	2,300	36	8	Female
9	2,500	40	9	Female
10	2,700	15	1	Male
11	2,800	16	3	Male
12	2,900	22	4	Male
13	3,200	27	5	Male
14	3,200	26	5	Male
15	3,100	30	6	Male
16	3,400	34	8	Male
17	3,600	32	7	Male
18	3,900	38	9	Male

a. Plot monthly salary vs. months on the job. Does there appear to be a relationship between the two variables?

b. Plot monthly salary vs. level of communication skill. Does there appear to be a relationship between the two variables?

c. Label each of the data points in the scatter diagram in part **b** as male or female (the gender variable). Are there distinct clusters when we include the gender variable?

d. What might clustering mean in the context of monthly salaries of men and women? Discuss.

5. Shown is a random sample of 12 physicians in the 45–50-year group. We have recorded their amount of life insurance, their annual income for the past year, and their marital status.

Physician	Amount of Life Insurance ($000)	Annual Income ($000)	Marital Status
1	250	60	Single
2	350	75	Single
3	450	85	Single
4	500	110	Single
5	650	130	Single
6	800	160	Single
7	790	60	Married
8	950	80	Married
9	1,200	90	Married
10	1,300	120	Married
11	1,400	140	Married
12	1,350	150	Married

a. Develop a scatter diagram between amount of life insurance and annual income. Does there appear to be a linear relationship between the two variables?
b. Label each point in the scatter diagram with the marital status of the physician—single or married. Are there distinct clusters? What can we conclude about the impact of marital status on the amount of life insurance purchased?

6. Here is a set of data showing the historic rates of return for stock Y (the dependent variable) and the New York Stock Exchange (NYSE)—the predictor variable.

Year	Stock Y	NYSE
1	3.0%	5.0%
2	8.2%	13.5%
3	−6.0%	−12.5%
4	−9.5%	−20.2%
5	13.5%	17.5%
6	7.5%	14.5%

a. Develop a scatter diagram between the rates of return for stock Y and the NYSE.
b. Does rate of return for stock Y appear to be linearly related to the rate of return for the entire NYSE? Interpret.

10.4 Curve Fitting

We have drawn scatter diagrams and plotted the variables to check for non-linearity or clusters. We are now ready to generate a regression equation with one or more predictor variables. In this section we will limit our discussion to regression equations in which the predictor variables are raised to the first power. By the end of this section you should be able to:

1. explain what conditional means are;
2. distinguish sample and population conditional means;
3. explain curve fitting to sample conditional means;
4. use the least squares equations for the two-variable case; and
5. explain what is meant by the term *least squares*.

Conditional Means

We have reproduced the COMCEL marketing study data in Table 10.6. Each column mean is the mean number of phones sold at a particular price. The six stores that charged $100 sold a mean of 17.33 phones in the study week. This mean of 17.33 phones is called a *sample conditional* (column) mean. The first row mean is the mean number of phones sold in the eight stores that ran one ad. That sample conditional row mean is 17.25 phones. The numbers in parentheses are the sample conditional means for a given combination of price and number of

Table 10.6
COMCEL Marketing Data in Table Format

Number of Ads Per Day	$100	$90	$85	$80	Row Means
1	9	14	17	26	17.25
	11	19	19	23	
	(10.0)	(16.5)	(18.0)	(24.5)	
3	19	24	29	26	23.75
	15	28	25	24	
	(17.0)	(26.0)	(27.0)	(25.0)	
5	26	31	30	37	30.50
	24	32	30	34	
	(25.0)	(31.5)	(30.0)	(35.5)	
Column Means	17.33	24.67	25.00	28.33	23.83

ads. For example, the two stores that charged $100 and ran one ad sold a mean of 10 phones during the test week.

In Figure 10.7 on page 522 we have plotted the sample conditional mean number of phones sold against the four price levels. Clearly, they do not all lie on a straight line. Since each sample mean is based on only six data points, it is subject to sampling error. The important question is, "Do the *population* conditional means all lie on a straight line?" Even if they do not, they may still fall close enough to use the straight line for prediction. In a linear regression model, we assume that the conditional population means of the dependent variable are linearly related to the predictor variables. Thus, in the COMCEL marketing study, we are assuming that if we tested all 60 stores—the population, the mean number of phones sold would be linearly related to price and number of ads.

The Method of Least Squares

The method of least squares is widely used for fitting linear or nonlinear equations to sample data. Since the method requires considerable calculation even when there is only one predictor variable, use our software package.

Consider the following set of five observations:

Data Set A

Predictor Variable x	Dependent Variable y
1	5
2	7
3	6
4	8
5	10

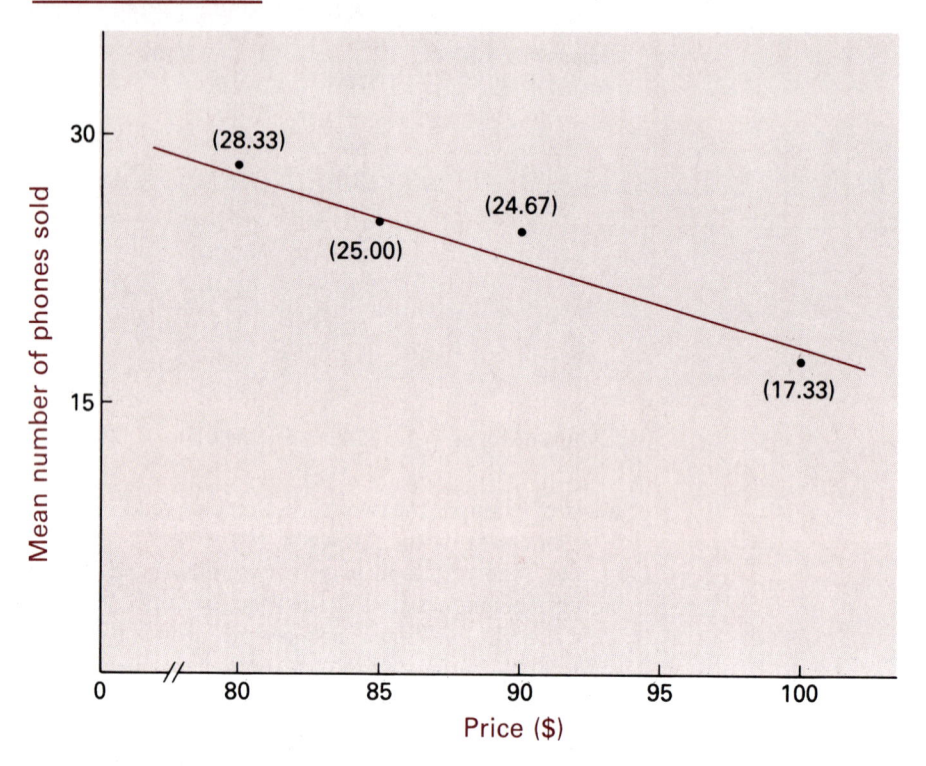

FIGURE 10.7 Fitting a Linear Equation to Sample Conditional Means

Suppose that for data set A, we believe that the population conditional means of y for the five values of x lie on a straight line. The equation for the straight line has the following form:

$$E(y) = \beta_0 + \beta_1 x \qquad (10.4)$$

The term $E(y)$ represents the population conditional mean of y (for example, mean units sold) for different values of x (for example, price). β_0 and β_1 are unknown population parameters, or constants. These would be known only if our sample were infinitely large.

Equation (10.4) is linear in the parameters and in the predictor variable x. It is linear in the predictor variable because the variable, x, is raised only to the first power. It is linear in the parameters because β_0 and β_1 do not appear as exponents.

We must estimate β_0 and β_1 based on information from only one sample. The sample linear regression equation has the following form:

$$y\text{-pred} = b_0 + b_1 x \qquad (10.5)$$

The term "y-pred" is an estimate of the population conditional mean of y for any value of x. The terms b_0 and b_1 are estimates of β_0 and β_1 and are called sample regression coefficients. The sample intercept is b_0 and the sample slope is b_1.

If we find values for b_0 and b_1 that best fit the sample data, these will also be our best estimates of β_0 and β_1.

A prediction error is the difference between the actual value of the dependent variable and the value predicted by equation (10.5):

$$\text{Prediction error} = y_i - y_i\text{-pred} \quad (10.6)$$

The method of least squares minimizes the sum of the *squared* prediction errors. It determines the values of b_0 and b_1 that minimize

$$\sum(y_i - y_i\text{-pred})^2 \quad (10.7)$$

The equation fitted to data set A is

$$y\text{-pred} = 3.9 + 1.1x \quad (10.8)$$

Table 10.7 contains the predictions and prediction errors—also called *deviations* or *residuals*.

Figure 10.8 on page 524 also shows the prediction errors. For example, when x is 3, the actual value of y was 6 and the predicted value of y based on the regression equation (10.8) was 7.2. Thus, the prediction error is $6 - 7.2$, or -1.2.

The sum of the squared prediction errors is 2.70, the smallest quantity possible for the sample data. If we changed the sample intercept and sample slope even slightly, the sum of the squared prediction errors would increase. We illustrate this in Table 10.8. For a sample slope of 1.1, when we vary the intercept around the least squares solution of 3.9, the sum of the squared prediction errors increases. For an intercept of 3.9, when we vary the slope around the least squares solution of 1.1, the sum of the squared deviations increases.

Table 10.7

Prediction and Prediction Errors for Data Set A

x	y	y-pred	Prediction Error	Squared Prediction Error
1	5	$3.9 + 1.1(1) = 5.0$	.0	.00
2	7	$3.9 + 1.1(2) = 6.1$	.9	.81
3	6	$3.9 + 1.1(3) = 7.2$	-1.2	1.44
4	8	$3.9 + 1.1(4) = 8.3$	$-.3$	.09
5	10	$3.9 + 1.1(5) = 9.4$	.6	.36
Sums			0.0	2.70

FIGURE 10.8 Illustrating Residuals or Prediction Errors

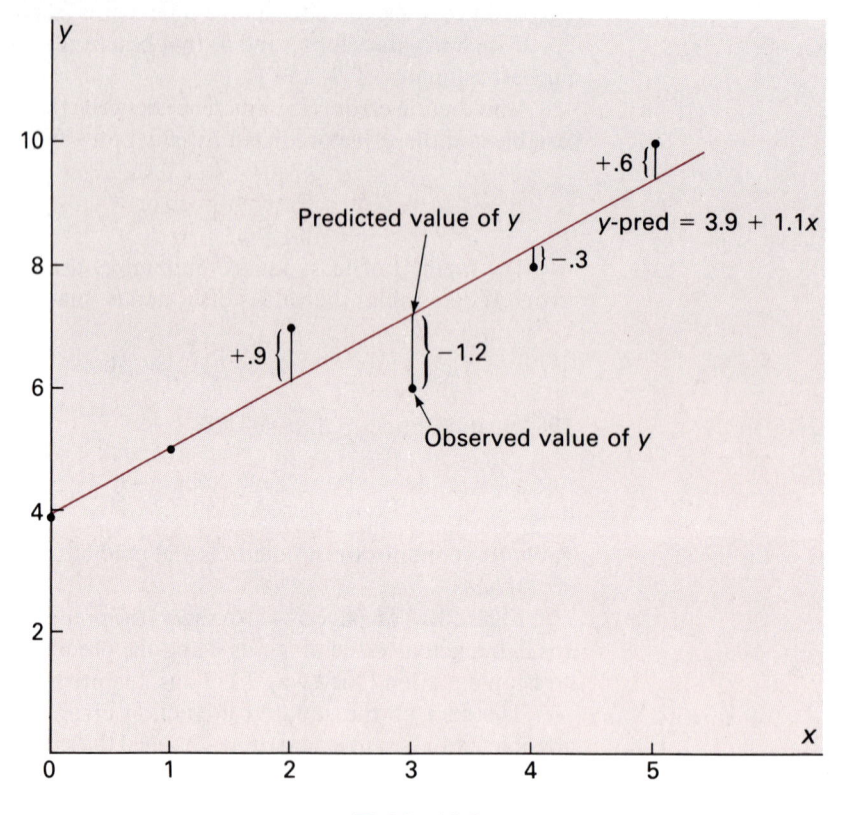

Table 10.8

Impact of Changing Least Squares Regression Coefficients

Intercept, b_0	Slope, b_1	Sum of Squared Prediction Errors
3.8	1.1	2.75
3.9	1.1	2.70 ←— Smallest
4.0	1.1	2.75
3.9	1.0	3.25
3.9	1.1	2.70 ←— Smallest
3.9	1.2	3.25

The method of least squares finds the sample regression coefficients that minimize the sum of the squared prediction errors. Here are the equations for the two-variable case:

$$b_1 = \frac{\sum x_i y_i - n\bar{x}\bar{y}}{\sum x^2 - n\bar{x}^2} \tag{10.9}$$

$$b_0 = \bar{y} - b_1 \bar{x} \tag{10.10}$$

Table 10.9

Calculations of Least Squares Sample Intercept and Sample Slope

Predictor Variable x	Dependent Variable y	Product of Variables xy	Square of x x^2
1	5	5	1
2	7	14	4
3	6	18	9
4	8	32	16
5	10	50	25
Sums 15	36	119	55

To calculate b_0 and b_1 we need to compute the product of each pair of x and y values and the square of each x value, as indicated in Table 10.9.

$$\bar{x} = \frac{15}{5} = 3, \quad \bar{y} = \frac{36}{5} = 7.2, \quad n = 5$$

$$b_1 = \frac{119 - 5(3)(7.2)}{55 - 5(3)^2} = 1.1$$

$$b_0 = 7.2 - 1.1(3) = 3.9$$

$$y\text{-pred} = 3.9 + 1.1x$$

Why is the best fitting linear line not the line that minimizes the *sum* of the prediction errors? That is, why must we use the least *squares* method? See Figure 10.9 on page 526. We have drawn two lines that each minimize the sum of the prediction errors. Neither line is a "best fitting line." The two lines are not even close to the actual data values. The problem with minimizing the sum of the residuals is clear. Positive deviations cancel out negative deviations and the sum is zero even though the two lines are not close to the actual data values. One way to solve the problem is to square the deviations and that is why we use the least squares method.

We could extend the least squares equations for multiple predictor variables. However, since multiple regression is too lengthy to do by hand, use our software.

We return to the COMCEL marketing study to illustrate the prediction errors in a multiple regression study. We used our software to find a least squares regression equation relating units sold to price and number of ads (see Table 10.3 for data). Recall that the regression equation for the data was given in expression (10.1) as

$$\text{UNITS SOLD-PRED} = 60.89 - .529\text{PRICE} + 3.312\text{ADS}$$

Table 10.10 presents the computer-generated results.

FIGURE 10.9   Graph Illustrating the Problem of Minimizing the Sum of the Prediction Errors

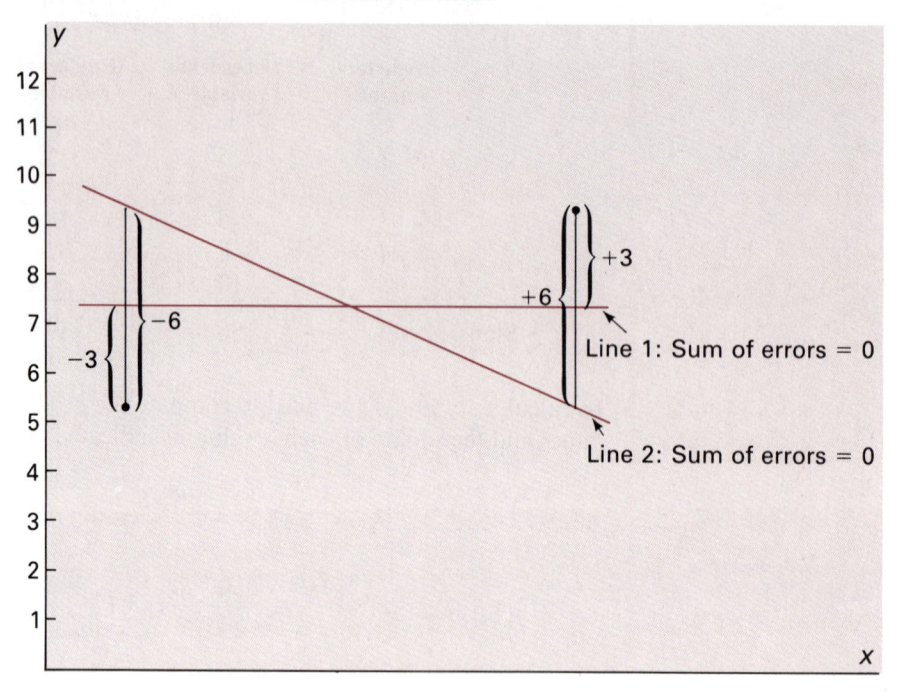

Table 10.10

Parameter Estimation for COMCEL Data

PARAMETER ESTIMATES

VARIABLE	PARAMETER ESTIMATE	STANDARD ERROR	t-VALUE	TWO TAIL p-VALUE
INTERCEPT	60.89107143	6.3527461	9.585	0.0001
ADS	3.31250000	.3193387	10.373	0.0001
PRICE	−0.52942381	.0705186	−7.509	0.0001

The sample regression coefficients came from the PARAMETER ESTIMATE section of the computer output. The INTERCEPT row shows a value of 60.89107143, which is rounded to 60.89; the ADS row shows 3.31250000, which is rounded to 3.312, and the PRICE row shows −.52942381, which is rounded to −.529.

The intercept value says that if we charged $0 and ran no ads we would sell (or give away) 60.89 car phones. In this example, the sample intercept has no meaning because $0 was far beyond the range of prices COMCEL varied ($80–$100). The sample intercept is simply a constant that is needed to make predictions. It would have a meaning only if the COMCEL data had contained observations that included $0.

The regression equation predicts the conditional cell means of phones sold for levels of price and number of ads (see Table 10.6). For example, when the price is $100 and the number of ads is one, it predicts a mean of 11.30 phones sold:

$$\text{UNITS SOLD-PRED} = 60.89 + 3.312\text{ADS} - .529\text{PRICE}$$
$$= 60.89 + 3.312(1) - .529(100)$$
$$= 11.30$$

Note that the actual conditional mean in Table 10.6 for the (1, $100) cell is 10 phones. The squared prediction error is $(10 - 11.30)^2$, or 1.69. There will be prediction errors for each conditional cell mean. However, equation (10.1) gives the best fit in the sense that no other straight plane could do a better job of minimizing the sum of the squared prediction errors.

In summary, we use the least squares software to determine the best fitting equation. It is the equation that minimizes the sum of the squared prediction errors or residuals. A residual is the difference between the actual sample value, y, and the value of y based on the regression equation, y-pred.

We can also use this software to obtain best fitting second-order (nonlinear) regression models. These are equations in which one or more predictor variables appear in the second degree, such as the market share (MRKTSHR) vs. experience (EXP) model.

SECTION 10.4 EXERCISES

Use the software for all the problems in this section.

1. Refer to the data set in Exercise 1 of Section 10.3 Exercises. Determine the linear regression equation between SALARY (dependent variable) and PROD. Interpret the sample intercept and sample slope. Draw the best fitting line in your scatter diagram of the data.

2. Refer to the data set in Exercise 2 of Section 10.3 Exercises. Determine the linear regression equation between TESTPERF (dependent variable) and STUDYTIME. Interpret the sample intercept and sample slope. Draw the best fitting line in your scatter diagram of the data.

3. Refer to the data set in Exercise 4 of Section 10.3 Exercises. Determine the linear regression equation between MONTHLY SALARY (dependent variable) and MONTHS ON THE JOB for men. Then determine the linear regression equation between MONTHLY SALARY (dependent variable) and MONTHS ON THE JOB for women. Draw both best fitting lines in your scatter diagram of the data. Given the two sample intercepts and sample slopes, does there appear to be equity in the salaries of men and women?

4. Refer to the data set in Exercise 5 of Section 10.3 Exercises. Determine the linear regression equation between AMOUNT OF INSURANCE (dependent variable) and INCOME for single physicians. Then determine the linear regression equation between AMOUNT OF INSURANCE and INCOME for married physicians. Draw both best fitting lines in your scatter diagram of the data. Given the two sample intercepts and sample slopes, does marital status appear to affect the amount of life insurance a doctor buys?

5. Refer to the data set in Exercise 6 of Section 10.3 Exercises. Determine the linear regression equation between the historic returns on stock Y (the dependent variable) and the returns on the NYSE, or market. Plot a scatter diagram.

In finance, the slope estimate is called the *beta coefficient*. It measures the extent to which returns of a given stock move with the stock market. Beta coefficients less than 1 indicate low-volatility stocks (such as utility companies); beta coefficients greater than 1 indicate risky or highly volatile stocks (high-technology companies). Interpret the beta coefficient for stock Y.

6. Shown are the results of an experimental regression study first discussed in Exercise 6 of Section 10.2 Exercises. The dependent variable is cost per unit. The two independent variables are the size of the production run and age of the equipment.

Cost Per Unit	Size of Production Run	Age of Equipment (years)
$1.50	1,000	1
$1.60	1,000	1
$1.75	1,000	3
$1.75	1,000	3
$2.10	1,000	5
$2.00	1,000	5
$1.70	670	1
$1.70	670	1
$1.85	670	3
$1.95	670	3
$2.30	670	5
$2.40	670	5
$2.00	333	1
$2.10	333	1
$2.25	333	3
$2.35	333	3
$2.50	333	5
$2.50	333	5

a. Develop a table of sample multivariate conditional means relating cost to production size and age of equipment. Determine the sample production-run-size conditional means. Determine the sample age-of-equipment conditional means. Determine the sample multivariate conditional means.

b. Determine the least squares linear regression equation. The dependent variable is COST PER UNIT and the two independent variables are SIZE OF PRODUCTION RUN and AGE OF EQUIPMENT. Interpret the sample intercept and sample slopes of the multiple linear regression equation.

c. Use the regression equation from part **b** to predict the COST PER UNIT for a run of 1,000 units using 5-year-old equipment. Compare the sample multivariate conditional mean to the prediction. Why aren't the two values the same?

7. Shown are the results of an experimental regression study. The dependent variable is JOB PERFORMANCE and the two independent variables are SKILL LEVEL and MOTIVATION LEVEL.

Job Performance (1 to 10)	Skill Level (0 to 100)	Motivation Level (0 to 100)
1	20	30
2	20	30
2	20	30
3	20	30
5	80	30
5	80	30
6	80	30
6	80	30
6	20	80
6	20	80
6	20	80
6	20	80
9	80	80
10	80	80
9	80	80
8	80	80

a. Develop a table of multivariate conditional means. Determine the sample skill level conditional means. Determine the sample motivation level conditional means. Determine the sample multivariate conditional means.

b. Determine the least squares linear regression equation. The dependent variable is JOB PERFORMANCE and the two independent variables are SKILL LEVEL and MOTIVATION LEVEL. Interpret the sample intercept and sample slopes of the multiple linear regression equation.

c. Use the regression equation from part **b** to predict the JOB PERFORMANCE for a worker with a SKILL LEVEL of 80 and a MOTIVATION LEVEL of 80. Compare the actual multivariate conditional mean to the prediction. Why aren't the two values the same?

10.5 Evaluating the Regression Model

In this section we discuss statistical tests and measures of fit that will answer questions such as: Is the regression model worth using at all? Do we need all of the predictor variables or can we predict just as well with a subset of these variables? By the end of this section you should be able to:

1. explain the decomposition, or partitioning, principle;
2. explain the role of analysis of variance in answering the question of whether a regression model is worth using at all;
3. and define the coefficient of determination and explain why it is a measure of fit; and
4. explain the role of *t*-tests in answering the question of whether all the predictor variables are needed.

The Need for Statistical Testing

One reason for building a regression model is to predict the dependent variable. Suppose that in the COMCEL study we wish to predict the unit sales for a store that will charge a price of $100 and run one ad. There are two ways to do this:

1. Use the mean number of units sold by the 24 stores in the sample. That is, in general, use the mean value of the dependent variable, $\bar{y}$, in the study.
2. Use the sample conditional means table (Table 10.6) or the regression equation (10.1) to predict units sold for PRICE = 100 and ADS = 1.

Which method provides better predictions? It depends on whether the dependent variable is *statistically* related to the predictor variables. If it is, then using the regression equation or the sample conditional means is better. We will illustrate this idea. We reproduce here the sample conditional means table as Table 10.11.

Strategy 1 uses $\bar{y}$ to make predictions. For the COMCEL study, the mean number of units sold was 23.83 phones. Using the data in Table 10.11, we computed the standard deviation of the 24 values of the dependent variable to be 7.25 phones:

$$s = \sqrt{\frac{(9 - 23.83)^2 + (11 - 23.83)^2 + \cdots + (34 - 23.83)^2}{23}}$$

$$= 7.25 \text{ phones}$$

The empirical rule (see Chapter 2) says that roughly 95% of the stores will sell between the mean number of phones plus or minus two standard deviations.

Table 10.11

COMCEL Marketing Data in Table Format: Multivariate Conditional Means

Number of Ads	$100	$90	$85	$80	Row Means
1	9	14	17	26	17.25
	11	19	19	23	
	(10.0)	(16.5)	(18.0)	(24.5)	
3	19	24	29	26	23.75
	15	28	25	24	
	(17.0)	(26.0)	(27.0)	(25.0)	
5	26	31	30	37	30.50
	24	32	30	34	
	(25.0)	(31.5)	(30.0)	(35.5)	
Column Means	17.33	24.67	25.00	28.33	23.83

Thus any store will sell 23.83 ± 2(7.25) phones, or between 9.33 and 38.33 phones. This is a wide—and not very informative—interval.

Strategy 2 uses either the sample conditional means or equation (10.1) to make predictions. We will use the former. The two stores that charged $100 and ran one ad sold 9 and 11 phones. The cell mean is 10 phones and the standard deviation is 1.41 phones:

$$s = \sqrt{\frac{(9-10)^2 + (11-10)^2}{1}} = 1.41 \text{ phones}$$

In this case, the empirical rule tells us that any store will sell 10 ± 2(1.41) phones, or between 7.18 and 12.82 phones. This is a narrow—and very informative—interval.

CONCLUSION We obtained a smaller interval by using the sample conditional means table (or the regression equation). This is true only when the predictor variables are *statistically* related to the dependent variable.

Analysis of variance is the formal way of determining whether the predictor variables and the dependent variable are statistically related. If *any* of the predictor variables is statistically related to the dependent variable, the regression model generates more accurate predictions than $\bar{y}$. If *none* of the predictor variables is statistically related to the dependent variable, we must use $\bar{y}$ (and accept a large standard deviation) or brainstorm for additional predictor variables.

Decomposition of the Total Sum of Squares

As in Chapter 9, the analysis of variance begins with a decomposition of the total sum of squares. Look at Table 10.11. Note that the dependent variable, units sold, varies among the 24 stores. How much variation is there? It is measured by the total sum of squares, SST:

$$\text{SST} = \sum (y_i - \bar{y})^2 \qquad (10.11)$$
$$= (9 - 23.83)^2 + (11 - 23.83)^2 + \cdots + (37 - 23.83)^2 + (34 - 23.83)^2$$
$$= 1{,}207.33 \text{ units of variation}$$

What accounts for the 1,207.33 units of variation? From Chapter 9, two sources that are represented by the right-side terms in expression (10.12) account for the total sum of squares:

$$\sum (y_i - \bar{y})^2 = \sum (y_i\text{-pred} - \bar{y})^2 + \sum (y_i - y_i\text{-pred})^2 \qquad (10.12)$$

The first right-side term is called the regression sum of squares (SSR). It measures the variation in *y* due to the two predictor variables, price and number of ads. In Chapter 9, the term SS(Between) was used. The second source is due to all other variables, called *extraneous variables*. That variation is called the error sum of squares (SSE). It measures the variation in *y* due to the many other variables we could have studied but did not. In the COMCEL marketing study, that is every variable except price and number of ads. In Chapter 9, the term SS(Within) was used. Thus,

$$\text{SST} = \text{SSR} + \text{SSE} \qquad (10.13)$$

In summary, we partition the total sum of squares into two components that reflect the impact of (1) the predictor variables and (2) all other variables not included in the study.

Having completed the decomposition, we must convert the sum of squares to mean squares, or variances (as in analysis of variance). We divide each sum of squares term by its appropriate degrees of freedom. The total degrees of freedom is always $n - 1$, or in the COMCEL study, $24 - 1 = 23$. The degrees of freedom for the regression is always equal to the number of predictor variables, *k*, or in the COMCEL study, $k = 2$. The remainder, $n - k - 1$, or 21, is the degrees of freedom for the error term. (See Section 9.3 for a discussion of the degrees of freedom concept and a complete discussion of the analysis of variance.)

Table 10.12 is the ANOVA table for the COMCEL marketing study. It shows that the variance or mean square due to the predictor variables is almost 82 times as large as the mean square due to all other variables. Is the regression model, equation (10.1), worth using to make predictions on units sold?

Is the Regression Equation Worth Using at All?

To determine whether the regression model is worth using, we begin by first stating the null and alternative hypotheses. (See Section 7.5 for a discussion of general principles.)

Table 10.12
ANOVA Table for COMCEL Marketing Data

Source of Variation	Sum of Squares	df	Mean Square	Variance Ratio
Regression or predictor variables	1,070.27	2	535.13	81.99
Error or all other variables	137.06	21	6.53	
Total	1,207.33	23		

Null hypothesis: *None* of the predictor variables in the regression equation affects the dependent variable.

Alternative hypothesis: *At least one* predictor variable affects the dependent variable.

As in Chapter 9, we use the variance ratio to either reject or fail to reject the null hypothesis. We ask the following question: "Does a variance ratio of 81.99 favor the null or alternative hypothesis?" The variance ratio is a ratio of the mean square-regression (MSR) to the mean square-error (MSE). MSE measures the impact of all potential predictor variables besides those in the study—extraneous variables. MSR measures the impact of extraneous variables *plus* the impact of the predictor variables, price and number of ads. If the null hypothesis is true, then, except for sampling error, the numerator and denominator of the variance ratio should be the same. The ratio should be close to 1, but it is not. MSR is almost 82 times as large as MSE. What is that telling us?

If the null hypothesis is true, the sampling distribution of the variance ratio is F-distributed. For the COMCEL marketing study (see Table 10.12), the variance ratio is F-distributed with 2 and 21 degrees of freedom. These are the degrees of freedom for the numerator and denominator of the variance ratio. The interpolated F-value for 2 and 21 degrees of freedom and a 99% level of confidence is 5.78 [$F(2, 21, 99\%) = 5.78$]. The area to the right of 5.78 in Figure 10.10 is 1% of the area beneath the entire curve. If price and number of ads had no impact on units sold (i.e., the null hypothesis is true), then only 1% of

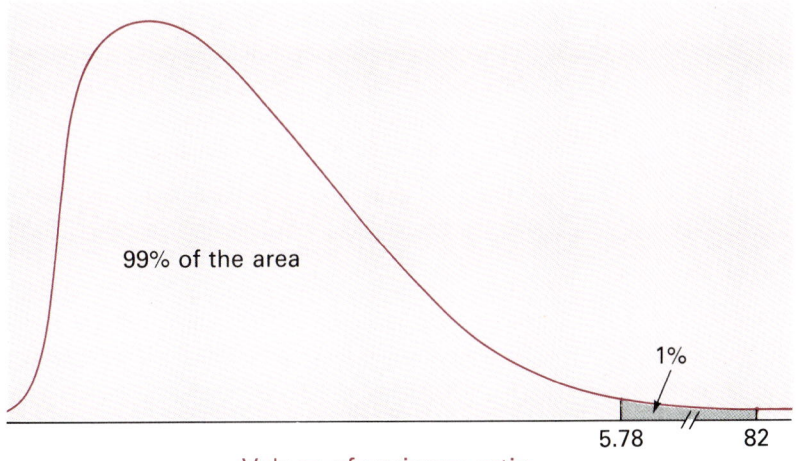

FIGURE 10.10 F-Distribution When Null Hypothesis Is True

Values of variance ratio

the time would we obtain a variance ratio of 5.78 or larger. If price and number of ads had no impact on units sold, the chance of getting a variance ratio of 82 or larger is even smaller than .01. It is the area under the F-distribution curve to the right of 82 in Figure 10.10. Recall from Section 7.5 that this area or probability is called the *p-value*. Managers often reject the null hypothesis when the *p*-value is .05 or less (the .05 rule).

The variance ratio tells us that at least one of the predictor variables is significantly related to the dependent variable. The variance ratio does not indicate how much of the dependent variable's total variation is accounted for by the two predictor variables. In short, how much of the variation in units sold do price and number of ads explain? For that we compute the **coefficient of multiple determination**.* It is given by

> The coefficient of multiple determination measures the percentage of the variation in the dependent variable accounted for by the predictor variables.

$$R^2 = \frac{\text{SS(Regression)}}{\text{SS(Total)}} \quad (10.14)$$

The possible range of values for the coefficient of multiple determination is between 0 and 1. The coefficient of multiple determination for the COMCEL data shown in the ANOVA table, Table 10.12, is

$$R^2 = \frac{1,070.27}{1,207.33} = .8865$$

The two predictor variables account for 88.65% of the variation in the 24 stores' sales figures. The remaining variation in units sold, 11.35%, is due to all other variables other than price and number of ads, and is still unaccounted for.

In conclusion, the *p*-value for the variance ratio of 82 is much less than .01. We are more than 99% confident that at least one of the predictor variables affects units sold. We can generalize our findings to all 60 stores in the COMCEL chain. The coefficient of multiple determination indicates that price and number of ads explain almost 89% of the variation in units sold.

If we fail to reject the null hypothesis, then the regression equation, or model, is not worth using. If we reject the null hypothesis, we will probably use equation (10.1) to explain what affects units sold and to predict and to control unit sales in COMCEL's 60 stores. We say "probably" for two reasons.

1. We must determine whether both predictor variables, ADS and PRICE, are necessary. Or, can we make accurate predictions of units sold using only one of the predictor variables?
2. Even if both variables are necessary, the prediction intervals generated by the regression equation (10.1) may still be too wide to provide meaningful information to managers. The decision to seek additional predictor variables

---

*When we have only one predictor variable, the symbol is r^2—the *simple* coefficient of determination. When there is more than one predictor variable, the symbol is R^2—the coefficient of multiple determination.

to increase R^2 depends on management's need for more accurate information and the cost of the search. (Prediction intervals are covered later in this chapter.)

Are All Predictor Variables Necessary?

To determine which predictor variables are necessary, we run *t*-tests. A *t*-test determines whether a particular predictor variable is necessary *after controlling for the impact of all other predictor variables*. It determines whether either of the population regression coefficients—β_1 or β_2—could be equal to zero. If a population regression coefficient for a predictor variable equals zero, then we remove the variable from the regression equation.

Table 10.13 shows the computer output for the parameter estimates and the *t*-statistics. The column labelled "Standard Error" measures the amount of uncertainty in the parameter estimates. For example, if COMCEL repeated the marketing study again, it would obtain different sales results. The parameter estimates would change and so would equation (10.1). Standard errors indicate by how much the parameter estimates are likely to change. Large standard errors (in comparison to the parameter estimates) mean that the parameter estimates would change greatly from study to study. Small standard errors mean that the parameter estimates would change little from study to study.

ADS VARIABLE The parameter estimate for the ADS variable is 3.312 with a standard error of .32, which is small relative to the parameter estimate. Thus, the parameter estimate is stable and would not change much if the study were repeated. We can be approximately 95% confident that the population regression coefficient would fall within the interval $3.312 \pm 2(.32)$. Since the interval does not contain zero, we can be 95% confident that the population regression coefficient for the ADS variable is not zero. We cannot remove the ADS variable from equation (10.1).

The *t*-value and *p*-value columns from Table 10.13 also indicate that the ADS variable cannot be removed from the regression equation. The *t*-value is the ratio of the parameter estimate to its standard error, $3.312/.32 = 10.37$. The regression coefficient of $+3.312$ is over 10 standard errors above a value of zero. The *p*-value is less than .0001. Using the .05 rule, we conclude that the ADS variable significantly affects units sold after controlling for the impact of price changes. Therefore, we must leave the ADS variable in the regression equation.

Table 10.13

Parameter Estimation Section of Computer Output (Rounded)

VARIABLE	PARAMETER ESTIMATE	STANDARD ERROR	*t*-VALUE	TWO TAIL* *p*-VALUE
INTERCEPT	60.891	6.35	9.59	.0001
ADS	3.312	.32	10.37	.0001
PRICE	−.529	.07	−7.51	.0001

*Assumes two-tail test of $H_0: \beta_i = 0$.

PRICE VARIABLE   The t-value for the price variable is -7.51. The regression coefficient of $-.529$ is over 7.5 standard deviations below zero. A coefficient of zero would mean that the price variable has no impact on units sold after controlling for the impact of number of ads. The p-value is .0001. Using the .05 rule, we conclude that price significantly affects units sold after controlling for the number of ads changes. Therefore, we must also leave the price variable in the regression equation.

We can ignore the t-value for the intercept term as it does not tell us whether price and number of ads are important predictor variables.

The t-tests indicate that we must use both predictor variables in the regression equation (10.1). If one t-test had a p-value that exceeded .05, we could eliminate that predictor variable and compute a new regression equation.

We can now answer the two questions that formed the basis for this section. Based on the ANOVA and the follow-up t-tests we conclude:

1. The regression model including both price and number of ads as predictor variables is worth using to predict units sold.
2. We need both predictor variables since both influence units sold.

SECTION 10.5 EXERCISES

Use the software for all the problems in this section.

1. We run a regression study with one dependent variable and four predictor variables. The total sample size is 45.
   a. What are the degrees of freedom for the numerator of the variance ratio? Explain.
   b. What are the degrees of freedom for the denominator of the variance ratio? Explain.
   c. What is the F-value for the appropriate degrees of freedom at the 95th percentile?

2. A variance ratio for (3, 30) degrees of freedom equals 4.52.
   a. Use Appendix 7 to determine the p-value for a variance ratio of 4.52. Is it less than .05? Is it less than .01?
   b. Interpret the p-value.
   c. Would you reject the null hypothesis and why?

3. The numerator of the variance ratio in Exercise 2 is 1,200 and the denominator is 265.50. Compute the multiple coefficient of determination. Given the size of the coefficient, would we expect that there are other predictor variables beyond the three presently in the regression model that are significantly related to the dependent variable? Explain.

4. Suppose that the variance ratio has a p-value of .10. Many managers use the .05 p-value rule and would not reject the null hypothesis. Make an argument about when a p-value of .10 could cause a manager to reject the null hypothesis.

5. A credit scoring model evaluates the credit worthiness of a loan applicant. We build a model of credit worthiness vs. salary, number of years living at present address, marital status, and number of years on present job. Set up the null and alternative hypotheses for this study.

6. Shown is a cross-sectional data set for 16 skilled laborers. Job satisfaction is the dependent variable and there are two independent variables. Closeness of supervision is the degree to which workers are constantly watched and supervised. A

score of 10 indicates very close supervision. Salary is the annual salary in thousands of dollars.

Job Satisfaction	Closeness of Supervision	Salary ($000)
1	10	22
2	9	20
3	7	38
3	9	36
5	7	27
4	7	25
6	5	30
6	6	31
7	4	28
7	5	32
8	4	34
9	3	25
8	4	36
9	2	24
10	2	38
10	1	39

    a. Determine the linear multiple regression equation.
    b. Develop an ANOVA table. Is the p-value for the variance ratio less than .05?
    c. Compute and interpret the multiple coefficient of determination.
    d. Determine whether both predictor variables are important. Explain.

7. In Exercise 4 of Section 10.3 Exercises, there is a cross-sectional data base for 18 managers. It contains a random sample of monthly salaries of managers at the same level within a major firm. Two of the independent variables are months on the job and the manager's gender. In Exercise 3 of Section 10.4 Exercises, you developed two regression models—one for males and one for females.
    a. Develop two ANOVA tables. Are the p-values for the variance ratios less than .01?
    b. Interpret the two simple coefficients of determination.

8. In Exercise 3 of Section 10.3 Exercises, there is a time-ordered data set for 12 quarters of data. SALES is the dependent variable and INVENTORY and NPEE are the independent variables.
    a. Determine the multiple linear regression equation.
    b. Develop an ANOVA table. Is the p-value for the variance ratio less than .01?
    c. Interpret the multiple coefficient of determination.
    d. Determine whether both predictor variables are important.

9. Shown is a time-ordered data set on company sales in millions of dollars (dependent variable) and disposable personal income in billions of dollars.

Year and Quarter	Sales	Disposable Personal Income
1990: 1	35.2	133.5
2	35.5	135.5
3	35.9	137.7
4	36.7	140.0

(continued)

Year and Quarter		Sales	Disposable Personal Income
1991:	1	37.7	143.9
	2	38.4	147.2
	3	39.2	148.9
	4	39.3	149.0
1992:	1	41.2	153.2
	2	41.4	155.6
	3	42.3	160.9
	4	43.1	163.5

    a. Determine the simple linear regression equation.
    b. Develop an ANOVA table. Is the *p*-value for the variance ratio less than .10?
    c. Why should the *p*-value for the variance ratio be the same as the *p*-value for the *t*-test when only one independent variable is in the regression equation?
    d. Interpret the simple coefficient of determination.

10. Refer to Exercise 6 in Section 10.3 and Exercise 5 in Section 10.4, in which we computed the beta coefficient for stock Y. Develop an ANOVA table. Is the *p*-value for the variance ratio less than .05?

10.6 Evaluating the Regression Analysis Assumptions: Residual Analysis

We have identified a regression model containing only significant predictor variables. Before using it to make predictions or to establish controls, we must verify the assumptions underlying the regression model. In this section, we discuss how an examination of sample prediction errors, or *residuals*, helps us test the assumptions. By the end of this section you should be able to:

1. explain the assumptions behind the linear regression model;
2. explain the symptoms of an inadequate model that are revealed by examining the residuals;
3. explain autocorrelation and why it suggests an inadequate model;
4. explain homoscedasticity; and
5. suggest remedies for problems identified by residual analysis.

Assumptions Underlying Regression Analysis

In Table 10.11, note that the eight stores that ran one ad sold between 9 and 26 units. The sample mean sales was 17.25 units. What would the population mean sales be if all 60 stores had run one ad? We cannot know its value unless we actually tested the population. The unknown population mean units sold for the 60 stores is denoted as $E(y_1)$ in Figure 10.11. Figure 10.11 illustrates the four assumptions—linearity, normality, equal variances, and independence—underlying the *simple linear* regression model.

FIGURE 10.11 The Simple Linear Regression Model

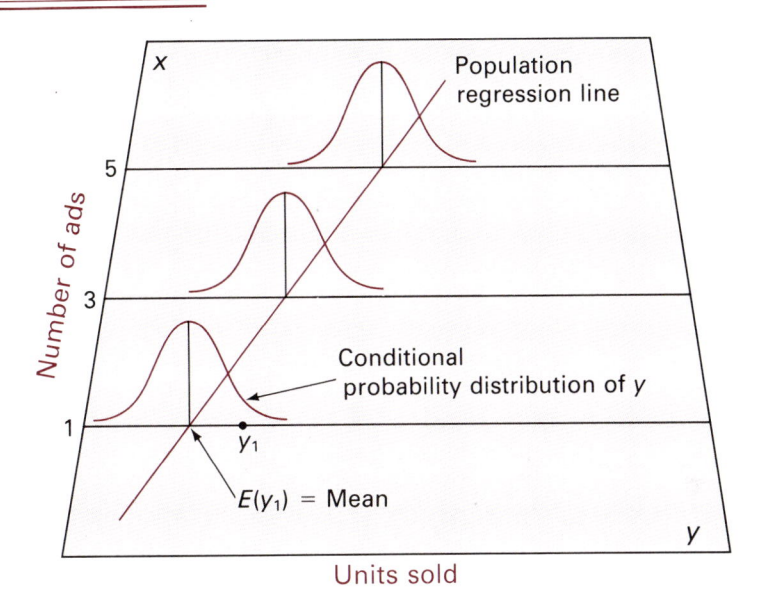

LINEARITY We assume that the population regression curve connecting the means of the conditional probability distributions is linear. Every point on the straight line is the population mean of the dependent variable, units sold, for a particular value of the predictor variable, number of ads. The multiple linear regression model assumes that the population multivariate conditional means lie on a plane.

NORMALITY We assume that each conditional distribution of units sold is normal. For example, units sold for all 60 stores that ran one ad would be normally distributed.

EQUAL VARIANCES We assume that the variances of the conditional distributions of units sold are equal. The variance in units sold for stores running one ad is the same as the variance for stores running three or five ads. The conditional means may be different, but the distribution variances are the same. This is the assumption of *homoscedasticity*.

INDEPENDENCE We assume that the y value from any conditional distribution must be unrelated to the y values from the same or other conditional distributions. For example, in Figure 10.11, if units sold for one ad (y_1) is above the mean of its distribution, the units sold for three ads or five ads may be above *or* below their respective means. Units sold by any store that runs one ad are unrelated to units sold by any other store. This assumption would not be true if two stores were located in the same small town and the town's major employer closed its doors. Sales of both stores would fall because of the town's drop in purchasing power.

Examining Residual Plots

A residual plot is a graph showing the residuals on the vertical axis and y-pred, a predictor variable, or time on the horizontal axis.

We use **residual plots** to determine whether a regression model meets the four assumptions. A prediction error or residual is the difference between the actual value of y and the value of y predicted by the regression equation. There is one residual for each observation in the sample:

$$\text{Residual} = y_i - y_i\text{-pred} \qquad (10.15)$$

We plot residuals against each predictor variable and against y-pred for cross-sectional data. We construct a residual plot against time when we have time-ordered data.

Figure 10.12 shows how a sample residual plot might look when all of the regression assumptions are met. The residuals oscillate within an equal-width horizontal band centered on zero and should display no systematic pattern of positive or negative residuals.

If each conditional distribution is normally distributed in Figure 10.11, then the residuals should be centered around zero. Why? Because y-pred is an estimate of the mean of each distribution, $E(y)$, in Figure 10.11. For a normal distribution, 50% of the values lie above and 50% lie below the mean. Thus, about half of the residuals should be positive and half should be negative.

If the assumption of equal variances is realistic, then the size of the errors above the mean equals the size of those below the mean. Thus the residuals should oscillate within a band of constant width around a horizontal line at a mean of zero.

We use residual plots to determine whether any of the following five problems exist for our fitted regression model:

1. The population regression curve is not linear.
2. The conditional distributions do not have equal variances.
3. The conditional distributions are not normal.
4. The conditional distributions contain outliers.
5. The model does not exhibit independence; the data exhibit autocorrelation.

FIGURE 10.12 Residual Plot When All Regression Assumptions Are Met

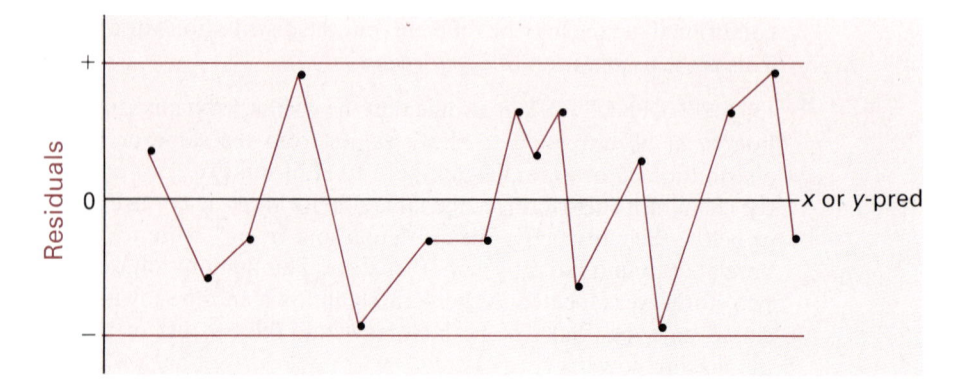

Nonlinearity of Regression Curve

Nonlinearity of the regression curve means that the relationship between the dependent variable and the predictor variables cannot be described by a linear curve. Table 10.14 contains a nonlinear data set for which we computed a linear regression line. Figure 10.13 shows a residual plot against the predictor variable, x. The residual plot shows a systematic pattern of positive and negative residuals. The residuals are first positive, then negative, and then positive again. The curvilinear pattern tells us that the form of the equation is wrong.

How can we correct the nonlinearity problem? A curvilinear pattern of residuals indicates the need to compute a curvilinear regression equation for the

Table 10.14

Residuals for a Linear Curve Fitted to Nonlinear Data

y	x	y-pred	Residual
1	1	$-12.71 + 8.25(1) = -4.46$	5.46
5	2	$-12.71 + 8.25(2) = 3.79$	1.21
8	3	$-12.71 + 8.25(3) = 12.04$	-4.04
14	4	$-12.71 + 8.25(4) = 20.29$	-6.29
26	5	$-12.71 + 8.25(5) = 28.54$	-2.54
38	6	$-12.71 + 8.25(6) = 36.79$	1.21
50	7	$-12.71 + 8.25(7) = 45.04$	4.96

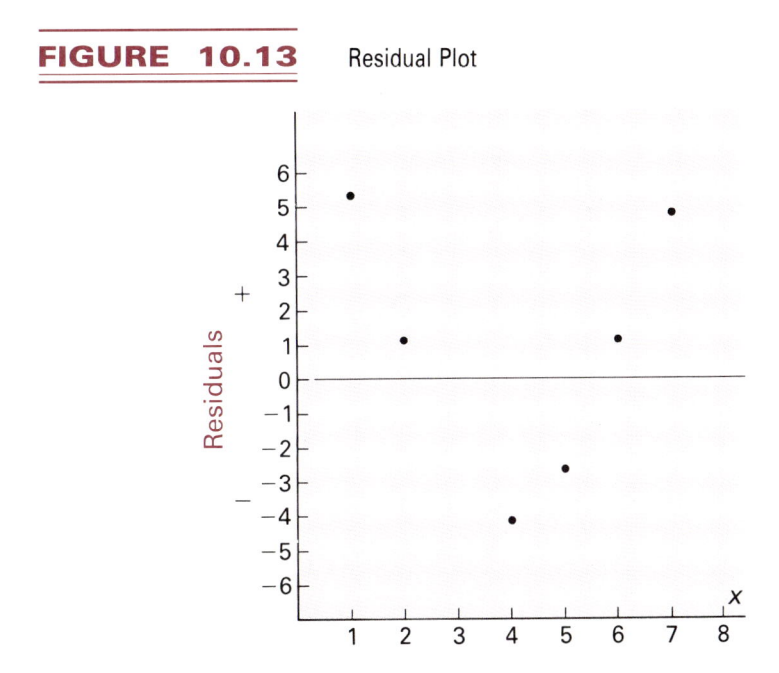

FIGURE 10.13 Residual Plot

Table 10.15

Residuals for a Nonlinear Curve Fitted to Nonlinear Data

y	x	x^2	y-pred	Residual
1	1	1	$1.14 - .98(1) + 1.15(1) = 1.31$	$-.31$
5	2	4	$1.14 - .98(2) + 1.15(4) = 3.78$	1.22
8	3	9	$1.14 - .98(3) + 1.15(9) = 8.55$	$-.55$
14	4	16	$1.14 - .98(4) + 1.15(16) = 15.62$	-1.62
26	5	25	$1.14 - .98(5) + 1.15(25) = 24.99$	1.01
38	6	36	$1.14 - .98(6) + 1.15(36) = 36.66$	1.34
50	7	49	$1.14 - .98(7) + 1.15(49) = 50.63$	$-.63$

data—for example,

$$y\text{-pred} = b_0 + b_1 x + b_2 x^2 \tag{10.16}$$

To obtain a curvilinear regression, we add another predictor variable that is the square of the x values. We then determine the best fitting multiple regression equation. Table 10.15 contains the residuals for the curvilinear regression equation. Now a residual plot would reveal an equal-width horizontal band centered on zero with no systematic pattern of positive or negative residuals.

Unequal Variances

When the variances of the normal distributions in Figure 10.11 are not the same, the residuals do not form an equal-width horizontal band. Rather, the residuals increase or decrease as the values of y-pred or the values of a predictor variable increase. Under these conditions, the statistical tests presented in the previous section and prediction intervals covered in the next section are invalid.

Table 10.16 contains a data set that violates the assumption of equal variances. We used our software to develop the least squares regression line, y-pred $= 2.28 + 2.67x$, for the seven data values. Figure 10.14 shows a plot of the residuals vs. x, the predictor variable.

Table 10.16

Data Set with Increasing Variances

y	x	y-pred	Residual
4	1	$2.28 + 2.67(1) = 4.95$	$-.95$
8	2	$2.28 + 2.67(2) = 7.62$	$.38$
9	3	$2.28 + 2.67(3) = 10.29$	-1.29
16	4	$2.28 + 2.67(4) = 12.96$	3.04
13	5	$2.28 + 2.67(5) = 15.63$	-2.63
24	6	$2.28 + 2.67(6) = 18.30$	5.70
17	7	$2.28 + 2.67(7) = 20.97$	-3.97

FIGURE 10.14　Residual Plot Illustrating Increasing Variances

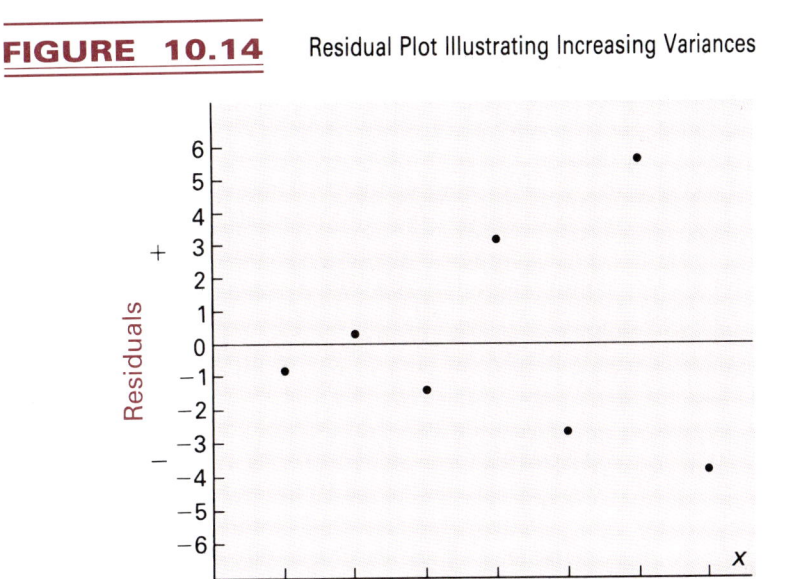

How can we fix the problem of unequal variances? One possibility, for data values that are positive, is to transform the dependent variable using the square root or log base 10 transformation. (See Section 8.2 for a review of transformations.) Use our software to take the square root of each value of the dependent variable. Calculate the least squares regression line with the transformed dependent variable. Check the residual pattern again.

We have taken the square root of the y values in Table 10.16 and recalculated the best fitting linear line. The transformed regression equation is now $\sqrt{y}$-pred $= 1.91 + .40x$. Note that the residuals in Table 10.17 now form an equal-width horizontal band.

Of course, we still want to estimate y, not its square root. To do this, substitute a value of x into the transformed regression equation and determine the square root of y. Then square this value to get an estimate of y. For example,

Table 10.17
Square Root Transformed Data Set

$\sqrt{y}$	x	$\sqrt{y}$-pred	Residual
2.00	1	$1.91 + .40(1) = 2.31$	$-.31$
2.83	2	$1.91 + .40(2) = 2.71$	$.12$
3.00	3	$1.91 + .40(3) = 3.11$	$-.11$
4.00	4	$1.91 + .40(4) = 3.51$	$.49$
3.61	5	$1.91 + .40(5) = 3.91$	$-.30$
4.90	6	$1.91 + .40(6) = 4.31$	$.59$
4.12	7	$1.91 + .40(7) = 4.71$	$-.59$

to estimate y when $x = 1.5$:

$$\sqrt{y}\text{-pred} = 1.91 + .40(1.5) = 2.51$$

$$y\text{-pred} = (2.51)^2 = 6.30$$

Nonnormality

Check for normality of the conditional probability distributions in Figure 10.11 by computing *standardized residuals*:

$$\text{Standardized residual} = \frac{\text{Residual}}{\sqrt{\text{MSE}}} \qquad (10.17)$$

The MSE term is found in the ANOVA table and is the variance due to all variables not in the model (see Table 10.12).

If the data are normal, about 68% of the standardized residuals should lie between -1 and $+1$. About 95% should lie between -1.96 and $+1.96$. If the data violate the normality assumption, try transforming the dependent variable using the square root or log base 10 transformation. These transformations, which often equalize the variances, also tend to normalize the data.

Outliers

Outliers will draw the computed regression equation away from the main body of points and distort the value of the regression coefficients. Use standardized residuals to check for outliers. An outlier is a value whose standardized residual lies outside the range of -4 to $+4$. If the standardized residuals indicate outliers, the ANOVA and t-tests discussed in the previous section will not be applicable.

How can we correct for the problem of outliers? First, check to make sure that they are not the result of a clerical error or an administrative decision, such as a one-time-only price clearance. If the observation is definitely in error or uncharacteristic of the population we want to describe with the regression model, then eliminate the data point and recompute the model. If we cannot discard the outlier, use a log base 10 transformation on the dependent variable, fit the new model, and check the residuals again. If that does not work, seek statistical help.

Autocorrelation

Nonindependence means that the residuals are related. They do *not* exhibit a random pattern when plotted against y-pred, a predictor variable, or time. Nonindependence often occurs in time-ordered data, but rarely in cross-sectional data. Thus, for time-ordered data, we should plot the residuals against time.

Consider the 16 quarters of firm and industry sales data in Table 10.18. We used our software to compute the residuals from the best fitting line, y-pred $= 1.502 + 1.766$IND. Figure 10.15 shows the residual plot vs. time.

Table 10.18
Data Set Illustrating Nonindependence

Year	Quarter	y Firm Sales (million $)	IND Industry Sales (million $)	y-pred	Residual
1992	1	20.96	127.3	20.98	−.02
	2	21.40	130.0	21.46	−.06
	3	21.96	132.7	21.93	.03
	4	21.52	129.4	21.35	.17
1993	1	22.39	135.0	22.34	.05
	2	22.76	137.1	22.71	.05
	3	23.48	141.2	23.44	.04
	4	23.66	142.8	23.72	−.06
1994	1	24.10	145.5	24.20	−.10
	2	24.01	145.3	24.16	−.15
	3	24.54	148.3	24.69	−.15
	4	24.30	146.4	24.35	−.05
1995	1	25.00	150.2	25.03	−.03
	2	25.64	153.1	25.54	.10
	3	26.36	157.3	26.28	.08
	4	26.98	160.7	26.88	.10

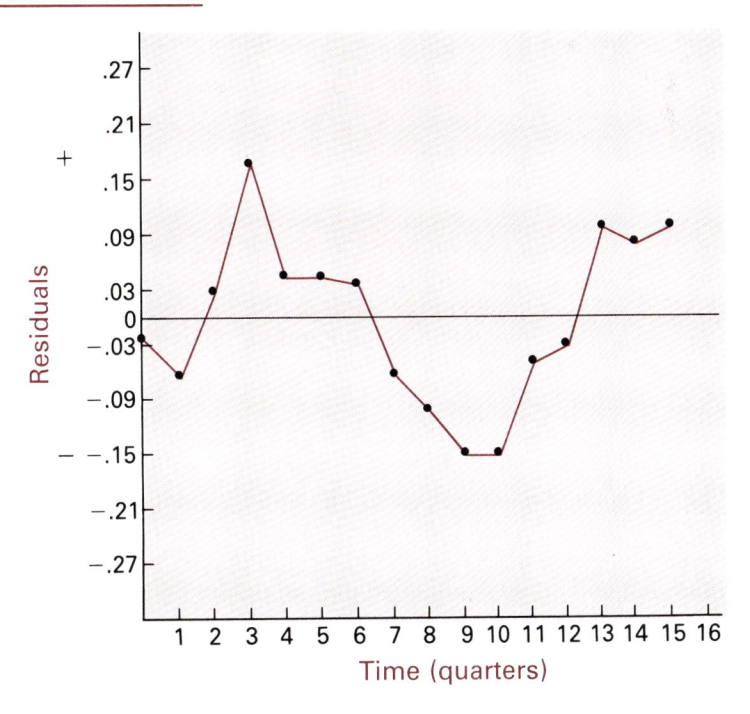

FIGURE 10.15 Residuals vs. Time

The plot of residuals vs. time shows long strings of positive and then negative residuals. The independence assumption is not satisfied. When there are long strings of positive and negative residuals, we have the problem of *positive autocorrelation*. If residuals bounce back and forth predictably between positive and negative values (sawtooth pattern), we have *negative autocorrelation*. In either case the regression model is invalid and should not be used.

How can we remedy this violation? We have three choices:

1. We can fit a curvilinear equation, equation (10.16), to the data. Then we reexamine the residual pattern.
2. We can brainstorm for additional predictor variables. We then include these predictor variables and reexamine the residual pattern.
3. We can develop an *autoregressive* model. Autoregressive models use previous values of the dependent variable as the predictor variable. Equation (10.18) is an autoregressive model which says that sales for a period depend on sales from one period earlier:

$$\text{SALES-PRED} = b_0 + b_1 \text{ SALES-1} \qquad (10.18)$$

We discuss autoregressive models in Section 11.3. After developing an autoregressive model, we reexamine the residual pattern.

In summary, never use a regression model without first checking the underlying assumptions. Begin by plotting the residuals against *y*-pred and against each of the predictor variables and, in the case of time-ordered data, against time. The residuals should be random, centered around zero, and should not contain outliers.

If there is an increasing (Figure 10.14) or a decreasing pattern to the residuals, use a square root or log base 10 transformation on the dependent variable's values. This will help also to normalize the data and minimize the impact of outliers. If there are long strings of positive or negative residuals, the data are autocorrelated. We have either the wrong form of the regression function—e.g., linear when it should be nonlinear; or we are missing one or more important predictor variables; or we should consider an autoregressive model. Statisticians use the Durbin–Watson test to assess autocorrelation. Neter, Wasserman, and Kutner's text (1985) presents a very readable discussion of this test.

RESIDUAL ANALYSIS OF COMCEL MARKETING STUDY DATA   Table 10.19 shows the original data values, the predicted values, and the residuals for each store in the COMCEL study. For example, the first store with a PRICE of $100 and one ad (ADS) sold 11 units. The predicted value derived from the regression equation (10.1), UNITS SOLD-PRED, is 11.2512. The residual is −.2512, which appears in the RESID column. We plotted the residuals against UNITS SOLD-PRED and each predictor variable in Figure 10.16 on page 548. We see that the residual plots contain no systematic patterns.

Table 10.19
Predictions and Residuals for COMCEL Data

OBS	PRICE	ADS	UNITS SOLD	UNITS SOLD–PRED	RESID	STD RESID
1	100	1	11	11.2512	−0.2512	−.098
2	100	1	9	11.2512	−2.2512	−.881
3	100	3	19	17.8762	1.1238	.440
4	100	3	15	17.8762	−2.8762	−1.126
5	100	5	26	24.5012	1.4988	.587
6	100	5	24	24.5012	−0.5012	−.196
7	90	1	14	16.5464	−2.5464	−.996
8	90	1	19	16.5464	2.4536	.960
9	90	3	24	23.1714	0.8286	.324
10	90	3	28	23.1714	4.8286	1.886
11	90	5	31	29.7964	1.2036	.471
12	90	5	32	29.7964	2.2036	.862
13	85	1	17	19.1940	−2.1940	−.856
14	85	1	19	19.1940	−0.1940	−.008
15	85	3	29	25.8190	3.1810	1.245
16	85	3	25	25.8190	−0.8190	−.320
17	85	5	30	32.4440	−2.4440	−.956
18	85	5	30	32.4440	−2.4440	−.956
19	80	1	26	21.8417	4.1583	1.627
20	80	1	23	21.8417	1.1583	.453
21	80	3	26	28.4667	−2.4667	−.965
22	80	3	24	28.4667	−4.4667	−1.748
23	80	5	37	35.0917	1.9083	.747
24	80	5	34	35.0917	−1.0917	−.427

There are also no outliers. From Table 10.12, the square root of the MSE term, 6.53, is 2.56. The standardized residuals are the actual residuals divided by 2.56. Table 10.19 shows that all the standardized residuals are between −2 and +2. Therefore, there are no outliers.

The normality assumption is probably met. We expect about 68% of the standardized residuals to lie between −1 and +1. Actually, there are 79% in that range. We expect 95% of the standardized residuals to lie between −1.96 and +1.96. We see that 100% fall in this range. Furthermore, the histogram of standardized residuals in Figure 10.17 on page 549 appears to be bell shaped. Therefore, we conclude that our model has met the normality assumption.

In summary, residual plots are like diagnostic indicators. They suggest whether our regression equation is in good shape or is in need of correction. The residual analyses presented above indicate that equation (10.1) is a valid model and can be used for prediction, explanation, and control.

FIGURE 10.16 Residual Plots

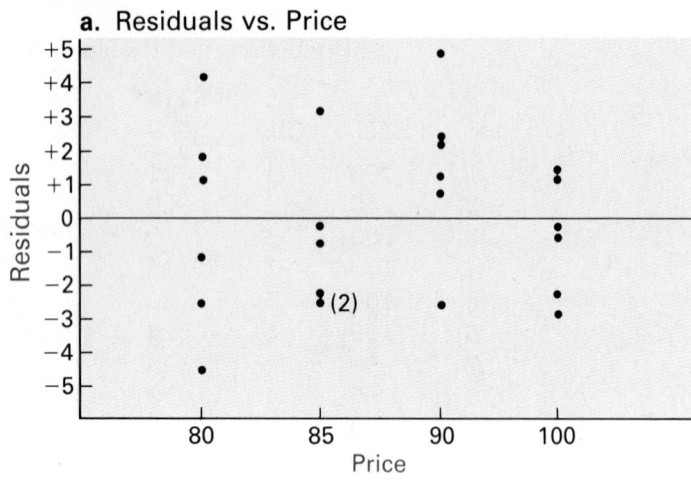

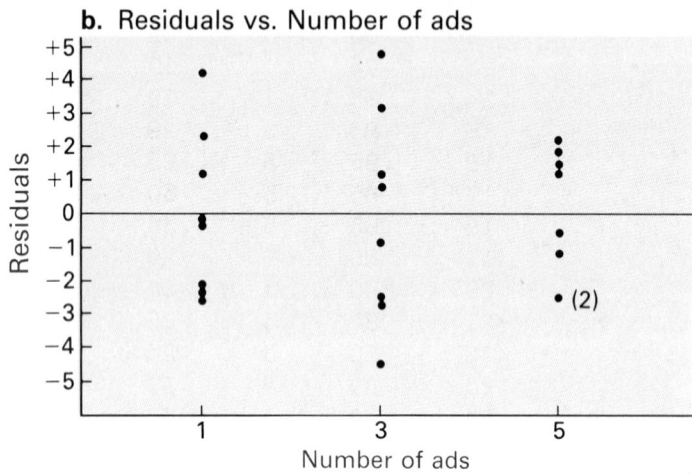

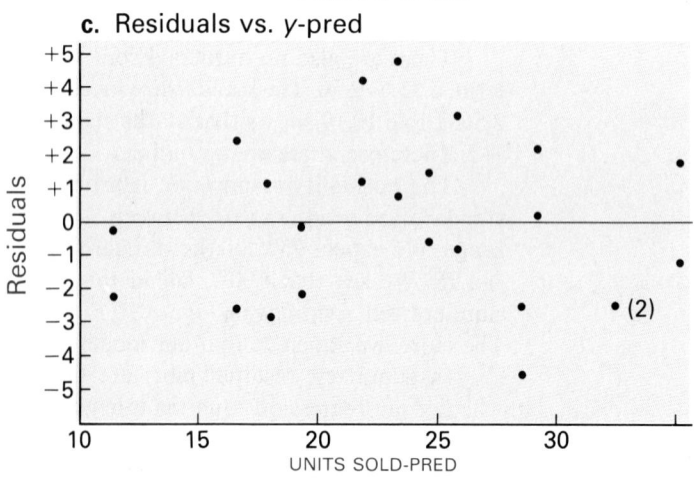

a. Residuals vs. Price

b. Residuals vs. Number of ads

c. Residuals vs. y-pred

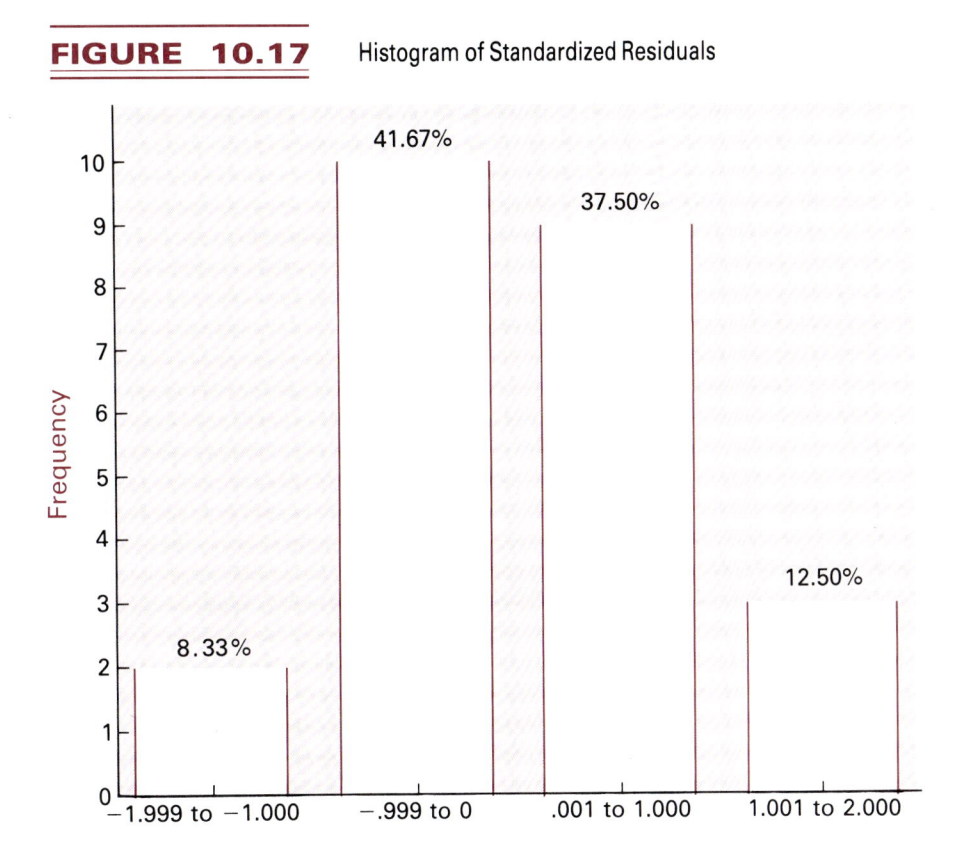

Chapter 10 Regression Analysis

FIGURE 10.17 Histogram of Standardized Residuals

Histogram showing frequencies across bins:
- −1.999 to −1.000: 8.33% (frequency 2)
- −.999 to 0: 41.67% (frequency 10)
- .001 to 1.000: 37.50% (frequency 9)
- 1.001 to 2.000: 12.50% (frequency 3)

SECTION 10.6 EXERCISES

Use the software for all the problems in this section.

1. If all the residuals from a best fitting line are zero, do any variables beyond those now in the regression model affect the dependent variable?

2. Shown is a small cross-sectional data set.

y	x
5	1
6	2
10	3
14	4
9	5
21	6
12	7
28	8

  a. Is the equal variance assumption reasonable? Plot residuals vs. the predictor variable.

  b. Use a log base 10 transform on the dependent variable, y. Recompute the best fitting line.
  c. Is the equal variance assumption reasonable for the transformed model? Plot residuals vs. the predictor variable.
  d. Use the transformed regression model to predict the value of y for $x = 5.5$.

3. Explain how to use standardized residuals to check for violations of the normality assumption.

4. Shown is a small cross-sectional data set.

y	x
3	1
10	2
20	3
31	4
51	5

  a. Is the linearity assumption reasonable? Plot residuals vs. the predictor variable. Draw a scatter diagram of y vs. x also.
  b. Draw a freehand nonlinear curve that is a good fitting line.
  c. Use our software to fit a second-order model. Do you still see a pattern in the residuals?

5. Fit a model to the job satisfaction, closeness of supervision, and salary cross-sectional data set in Exercise 6 of Section 10.5 Exercises.
  a. Are the linearity and equal variance assumptions reasonable? Plot residuals vs. both predictor variables.
  b. Is the normality assumption reasonable? Compute standardized residuals and construct a frequency distribution of the standardized residuals.
  c. Is autocorrelation likely to be a problem?

6. Fit a model to the time-ordered data set in Exercise 9 of Section 10.5 Exercises on company sales in millions of dollars and disposable personal income in billions of dollars.
  a. Are the linearity and equal variance assumptions reasonable? Plot residuals vs. the predictor variable.
  b. Is the normality assumption reasonable? Compute standardized residuals.
  c. Is the independence assumption reasonable?

10.7 Using Regression Models for Prediction

In regression analysis we use models that have met all the assumptions and are worth using (ANOVA and *t*-tests) to make predictions about the dependent variable. By the end of this section you should be able to:

1. distinguish between prediction and extrapolation;
2. explain the dangers of extrapolation;
3. explain the difference between a confidence interval and a prediction interval;
4. interpret prediction and confidence intervals; and
5. explain how to reduce the widths of prediction or confidence intervals.

Chapter 10 Regression Analysis

Prediction vs. Extrapolation

Regression models help us estimate values of the dependent variable. There are two types of estimation, which we will explain in the context of the COMCEL marketing study. **Prediction** means estimating units sold for prices between $80 and $100 and numbers of ads between 1 and 5—the predictor values are within the range of the original study. **Extrapolation** means estimating units sold for prices below $80 or above $100 and numbers of ads less than one or more than five—the predictor values are outside the range of the original study.

Figure 10.18 shows the danger of extrapolation. It illustrates a nonlinear relationship between two variables in the population. If we fit a linear model to data values between a and b, we see that the linear equation is a reasonably good fit within this range. However, the model would generate an inaccurate estimate of y for $x = c$. We have assumed that the linear relationship will continue, but it *may* not.

Extrapolation is risky. When extrapolating, be prepared to explain why the regression model can provide meaningful estimates outside the range of the original data. If good arguments cannot be made, do not use the model for extrapolation.

Prediction means estimating values of the dependent variable for values of the predictor variables *within* the range of the original study.

Extrapolation means estimating values of the dependent variable for values of the predictor variables *outside* the range of the original study.

FIGURE 10.18 Comparing Prediction and Extrapolation

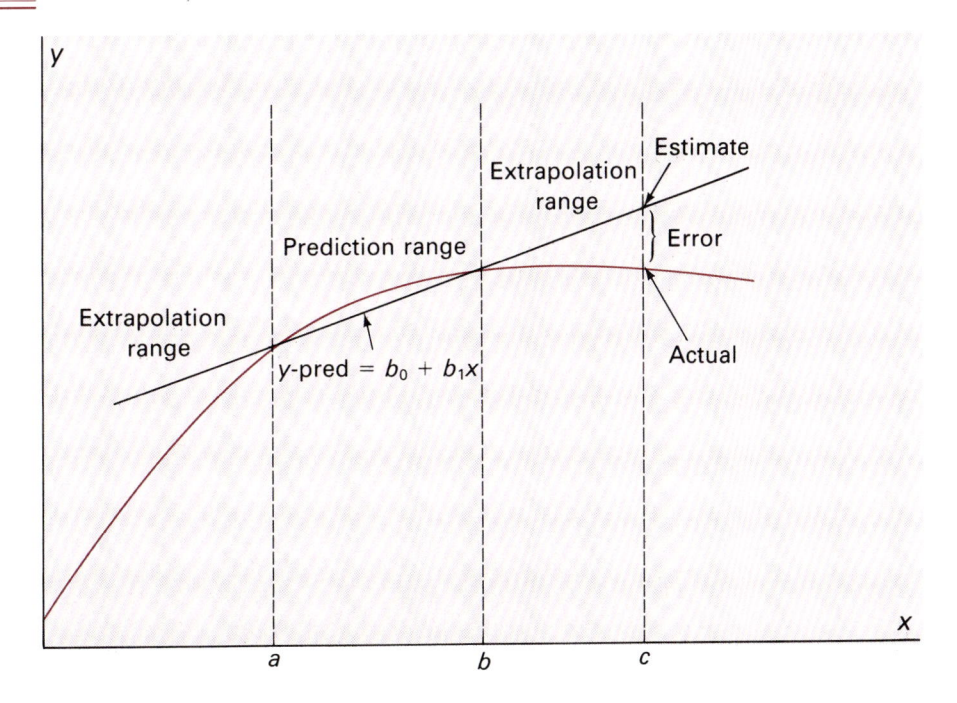

Differences Between Prediction and Confidence Intervals

Which would be easier to do: Predict the *mean* class grade or predict a *single* student's score? Predicting the class mean is easier for it usually ranges between 70 and 80. A student's score could range anywhere from 0 to 100. Thus estimation intervals for the class mean should be narrower than for a single student.

In regression analysis, we use a *confidence interval* to predict the mean value of y. The mean values of y are the conditional means of the probability distributions in Figure 10.11. We use a *prediction interval* to predict a single value of y. Using the test grade example for insight, we recognize that confidence intervals must be narrower than prediction intervals.

CONFIDENCE INTERVAL   We have set up a 95% confidence interval for the *mean* units sold for *all* stores that charge $100 and run one ad. Table 10.20 contains the output from our software. We are 95% confident that the mean units

Table 10.20

Confidence Intervals and Prediction Intervals for COMCEL Data

OBS	PRICE	ADS	UNITS SOLD	UNITS SOLD–PRED	L95MEAN	U95MEAN	L95	U95
1	100	1	11	11.2512	8.8717	13.6307	5.4298	17.0726
2	100	1	9	11.2512	8.8717	13.6307	5.4298	17.0726
3	100	3	19	17.8762	15.9019	19.8505	12.2083	23.5441
4	100	3	15	17.8762	15.9019	19.8505	12.2083	23.5441
5	100	5	26	24.5012	22.1217	26.8807	18.6798	30.3226
6	100	5	24	24.5012	22.1217	26.8807	18.6798	30.3226
7	90	1	14	16.5464	14.8219	18.2709	10.9607	22.1322
8	90	1	19	16.5464	14.8219	18.2709	10.9607	22.1322
9	90	3	24	23.1714	22.0716	24.2713	17.7459	28.5970
10	90	3	28	23.1714	22.0716	24.2713	17.7459	28.5970
11	90	5	31	29.7964	28.0719	31.5209	24.2107	35.3822
12	90	5	32	29.7964	28.0719	31.5209	24.2107	35.3822
13	85	1	17	19.1940	17.3933	20.9948	13.5843	24.8038
14	85	1	19	19.1940	17.3933	20.9948	13.5843	24.8038
15	85	3	29	25.8190	24.6031	27.0350	20.3688	31.2693
16	85	3	25	25.8190	24.6031	27.0350	20.3688	31.2693
17	85	5	30	32.4440	30.6433	34.2448	26.8343	38.0538
18	85	5	30	32.4440	30.6433	34.2448	26.8343	38.0538
19	80	1	26	21.8417	19.7000	23.9834	16.1133	27.5700
20	80	1	23	21.8417	19.7000	23.9834	16.1133	27.5700
21	80	3	26	28.4667	26.7866	30.1468	22.8944	34.0389
22	80	3	24	28.4667	26.7866	30.1468	22.8944	34.0389
23	80	5	37	35.0917	32.9500	37.2334	29.3633	40.8200
24	80	5	34	35.0917	32.9500	37.2334	29.3633	40.8200

sold for all stores that charge $100 and run one ad will be between 8.87 (L95MEAN) and 13.63 (U95MEAN) units per week. L95MEAN and U95MEAN are our symbols for the lower and upper limits for a 95% confidence interval on the conditional mean.

PREDICTION INTERVAL   Table 10.20 also shows 95% prediction intervals for units sold by a *single* store. For example, we are 95% confident that a single store that charges $100 and runs one ad will sell between 5.43 (L95) and 17.07 (U95) units per week. L95 and U95 are our symbols for the lower and upper limits for a 95% prediction interval for a single value of y.

Note that the prediction interval for sales of an individual store is wider than the confidence interval for the mean sales of all stores.

Prediction or confidence intervals—when does each (or both) make sense? That depends on the purpose of our study. Is our goal to explain, predict, or control the performance of a single store, person, production run, etc.? If so, construct prediction intervals. Or is our goal to explain, predict, or control the mean performance of all stores, persons, production runs, etc.? If so, construct confidence intervals.

Reducing the Width of Confidence or Prediction Intervals

We build regression models to predict values of the dependent variable. Since a wide confidence or prediction interval does not provide meaningful information, how do we reduce the width?

The expressions for confidence and prediction intervals for *simple* linear regressions are shown in equations (10.19) and (10.20), respectively. (Our software generates these intervals readily.) The expressions tell us how to reduce an interval's width. As we first learned in Chapter 7, narrow confidence (and prediction) intervals are more meaningful than wider intervals.

Confidence interval:

$$y\text{-pred} \pm t \sqrt{\text{MSE}\left[\frac{1}{n} + \frac{(x_p - \bar{x})^2}{\sum(x_i - \bar{x})^2}\right]} \quad (10.19)$$

Prediction interval:

$$y\text{-pred} \pm t \sqrt{\text{MSE}\left[1 + \frac{1}{n} + \frac{(x_p - \bar{x})^2}{\sum(x_i - \bar{x})^2}\right]} \quad (10.20)$$

The MSE is the mean square error term from the ANOVA table (Table 10.12). It is the denominator of the variance ratio. There is only one difference between the two expressions—an additional "1" term in expression (10.20). It is this additional term that increases the width of the prediction interval relative to the confidence interval.

There are three strategies to reduce a prediction or confidence interval's width:

1. Increase the sample size.

2. *Pull apart* (see Section 10.2) the values of the predictor variables.
3. Reduce the size of the MSE term.

The first strategy increases the size of the n term. As n increases, the interval widths shrink. The second strategy likewise increases the $\sum(x_i - \bar{x})^2$ term. Consider two different sets of predictor variables, x, as shown. Note that the values of x in the second column are further apart than those in the first column. The *pulled apart* values of x cause $\sum(x_i - \bar{x})^2$ to increase, which causes the interval to shrink.

	x	x
	1	1
	2	5
	3	9
$\sum(x_i - \bar{x})^2$	2	32

The third strategy rests on the following logic. MSE is the variance due to all extraneous variables—potential predictor variables *not* in the regression model. We can reduce the size of MSE by

1. *adding* significant predictor variables to the regression model, or
2. *eliminating* major sources of variation.

We will illustrate both approaches for the COMCEL marketing study. Suppose that COMCEL believes that the size of the shopping centers where its stores are located affects units sold. Larger centers generate more shopper traffic and therefore more phone sales. COMCEL could either (1) enter a SIZE of shopping center variable into the regression equation, or (2) select only stores from shopping centers of a similar size to conduct the study. The first approach seeks other predictor variables to explain the variation in units sold. The second approach reduces the variation in units sold by eliminating one source of variation—the impact of shopping center size.

In summary, we use prediction and confidence intervals to predict values of the dependent variable. Extrapolation is risky and should be done only when we can explain why the relationship between the variables should extend outside the range of the original study. Finally, we can increase sample size, pull apart the values of the predictor variables, or seek additional predictor variables to reduce the width of the interval. Remember, narrow intervals are more meaningful than wide intervals.

SECTION 10.7 EXERCISES

Use the software for all the problems in this section.

1. Refer to Exercise 6 in Section 10.5 Exercises.
    a. Set up a 95% prediction interval on job satisfaction for a closeness of supervision score of 6.5 and a salary of $30,000. Interpret the prediction interval.

Chapter 10　Regression Analysis

b. Set up a 95% confidence interval on the mean job satisfaction for a closeness of supervision score of 6.5 and a salary of $30,000. Interpret the confidence interval.
c. When would constructing each interval make sense? Discuss.

2. Refer to Exercise 9 in Section 10.5 Exercises. We expect the disposable personal income (DPI) in the first quarter of 1993 to be $165.2 billion. Set up a 95% prediction interval on sales for a DPI of 165.2. Interpret the prediction interval.

3. Refer to Exercise 3 in Section 10.4 Exercises. Develop a regression model for female employees in the sample.
   a. Set up a 95% prediction interval on monthly salary for a woman with 26 months of job experience. Interpret the prediction interval.
   b. Set up a 95% confidence interval on the mean monthly salary for all women with 26 months of job experience. Interpret the confidence interval.
   c. Is there any risk in using the regression model to construct a prediction interval on salary for 50 months on the job? Discuss.

4. Refer to Exercise 3. Develop a regression model for male employees in the sample.
   a. Set up a 95% prediction interval on monthly salary for a man with 26 months of job experience. Interpret the prediction interval.
   b. Set up a 95% confidence interval on the mean monthly salary for all men with 26 months of job experience. Interpret the confidence interval.
   c. Is there any risk in using the regression model to construct a confidence interval on salary for 5 months on the job? Discuss.

5. Refer to Exercise 3. Develop a regression model for female employees in the sample.
   a. Set up a 95% confidence interval on the mean monthly salary for all women with 14 months of job experience. Interpret the confidence interval.
   b. Set up a 95% confidence interval on the mean monthly salary for all women with 26 months of job experience. Interpret the confidence interval.
   c. Set up a 95% confidence interval on the mean monthly salary for all women with 40 months of job experience. Interpret the confidence interval.
   d. Look at the widths of the three prediction intervals. Are the widths different? When do you get the smallest width? When do you get the largest widths? What practical problems do you foresee in using the regression model to make predictions for either 14 or 40 months on the job? (*Hint:* How does confidence interval width affect the interval's meaningfulness?)

10.8 Indicator Variables

In the regression analysis studies up to now, all predictor variables have been quantitative. We now extend regression analysis to deal with one or more qualitative, or categorical, predictor variables, such as gender (male, female), department type (operations, accounting, marketing), or accounting method (LIFO, FIFO). To represent categorical variables, we create *indicator*, or *dummy*, variables. By the end of this section you should be able to:

1. represent categorical variables by creating one or more indicator variables;
2. interpret the regression coefficient of an indicator variable in a regression model;
3. explain the meaning of an interaction term; and
4. use indicator variables to compare regression equations for differences in intercepts and slopes.

In the first example, we explain how to code, or represent, a categorical variable with two classes and how to interpret a regression model with a coded indicator variable.

EXAMPLE: SMITH–JONES ACCOUNT EXECUTIVES DATA   We want to predict annual salary (dependent variable) using months of service and gender as predictor variables. We have included the gender variable because we want to learn how the salaries of the company's female account executives compare with those of their male counterparts. We select a stratified (by gender) random sample of 40 personnel records of account executives and record the annual SALARY (measured in thousands of dollars), the number of MONTHS with the company, and the GENDER of each employee.

Representing Categorical Variables

The GENDER variable is a categorical variable with two classes, males and females. We represent it as follows:

$$\text{GENDER} = \begin{cases} 1 & \text{if employee is female} \\ 0 & \text{if employee is male} \end{cases}$$

Table 10.21

Smith–Jones Salary Data for Account Executives

\multicolumn{3}{c}{Males}			\multicolumn{3}{c}{Females}
SALARY	MONTHS	GENDER		SALARY	MONTHS	GENDER
48.0	39	0		38.5	80	1
63.5	80	0		45.9	78	1
49.1	45	0		40.2	84	1
46.7	36	0		29.7	24	1
49.6	47	0		44.3	84	1
37.2	6	0		32.3	35	1
64.5	84	0		31.2	38	1
43.1	56	0		22.5	12	1
51.6	60	0		38.8	65	1
47.8	21	0		46.8	73	1
57.4	84	0		37.8	65	1
54.6	73	0		21.1	10	1
56.9	67	0		34.0	45	1
33.2	7	0		41.1	54	1
58.3	84	0		40.2	73	1
40.7	18	0		29.5	24	1
61.5	72	0		20.4	5	1
35.9	2	0		25.2	8	1
42.7	27	0				
35.0	12	0				
57.1	74	0				
43.8	36	0				

Chapter 10 Regression Analysis

In general:

> We represent a categorical variable with c classes by $c - 1$ indicator variables, each taking on the values of 0 and 1.

Table 10.21 contains the data for the Smith–Jones study. Once we code the gender of each employee as a 0 or 1, we treat the gender variable the same as months of service in the regression expression. We can measure the effect of the gender variable and evaluate its statistical significance.

Before computing a regression equation, we plot the salary vs. number of months for both males and females in Figure 10.19. The relationship between MONTHS and SALARY appears to be linear, but male (M) executives' salaries appear to be systematically higher than female (F) executives' salaries.

Using our software, we obtained the regression equation (10.21):

$$\text{SALARY-PRED} = 35.1 + .3\text{MONTHS} - 14.8\text{GENDER} \quad (10.21)$$

Significance Testing

We use the ANOVA table to determine whether MONTHS and GENDER are significantly related to SALARY. Then we use the t-test to determine whether each predictor variable should be retained in the model. See Table 10.22 on page 558.

FIGURE 10.19 Salary vs. Months of Service

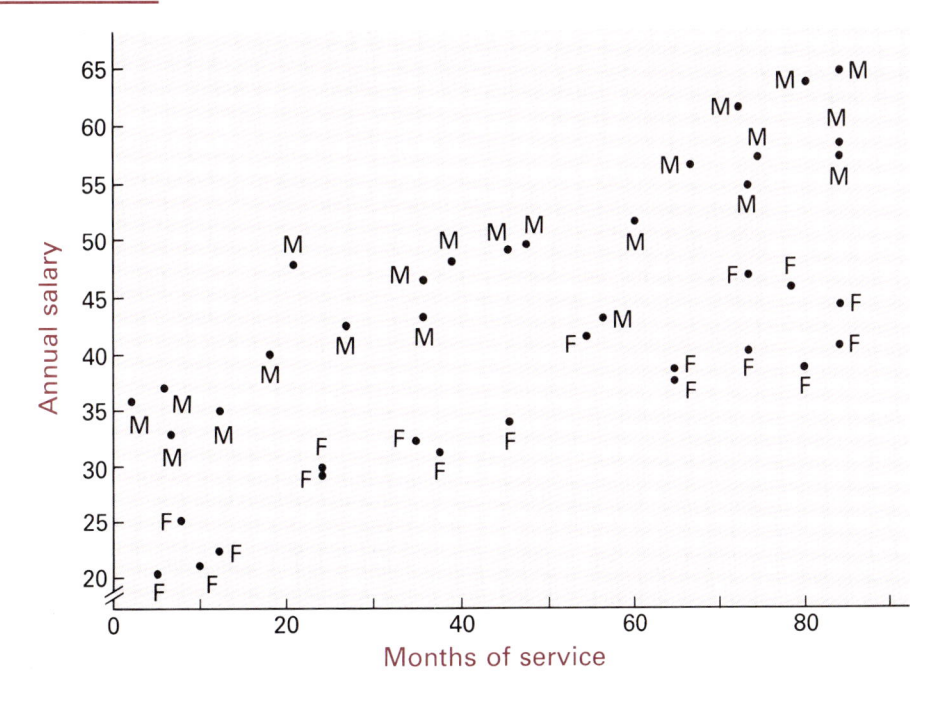

Table 10.22
ANOVA Table for Smith–Jones Account Executives Data

Source of Variation	Sum of Squares	df	Mean Square	Variance Ratio
Regression or predictor variables	4,793.88	2	2,396.94	231.47
Error or all other variables	383.14	37	10.36	
Total	5,177.02	39		

Parameter Estimates

Variable	Parameter Estimate	Standard Error	t-Value	Two Tail p-Value
INTERCEPT	35.149	1.103	31.87	.0001
MONTHS	.296	.018	16.44	.0001
GENDER	−14.832	1.023	−14.47	.0001

Equation (10.21) is a significantly better predictor of salary than $\bar{y}$, the mean salary for the sample. The F-value of 231.47 with 2 and 37 degrees of freedom has a p-value of .0001.

MONTHS is a significant predictor variable and should be retained in the model, equation (10.21). The parameter estimate of .296 (rounded to .3) is more than 16 times as large as its standard error. The p-value is .0001.

GENDER is also a significant predictor variable and should be retained in the model. The parameter estimate of −14.827 (rounded to −14.8) is almost 15 times as large as the standard error. The p-value is .0001.

Now we can use equation (10.21) to make predictions. To find the mean salary of males or females with a given length of service, we simply insert a 1 for female employees or a 0 for male employees for the GENDER variable and the appropriate number of months of service. For example, the mean salary of females with 36 months of service is

$$\text{SALARY-PRED}_{(F)} = 35.1 + .3(36) - 14.8(1)$$
$$= 20.3 + .3(36)$$
$$= 31.1 \quad \text{or } \$31,100$$

The mean salary for males with 36 months of service is

$$\text{SALARY-PRED}_{(M)} = 35.1 + .3(36) - 14.8(0)$$
$$= 35.1 + .3(36)$$
$$= 45.9 \quad \text{or } \$45,900$$

The interpretation of the GENDER variable regression coefficient is that after controlling for length of service, the mean salary of females is $14,800 lower than that of males. This difference in mean salaries does not depend on how we coded the GENDER variable. If we represented GENDER as male = 1 and female = 0, the regression equation would have been

$$\text{SALARY-PRED} = 20.3 + .3\text{MONTHS} + 14.8\text{GENDER}$$

The predicted mean salary for males with 36 months of service would be 20.3 + .3(36) + 14.8(1) = 45.9 or $45,900—the same result we obtained above. The predicted mean salary for females with 36 months of service would still be 20.3 + .3(36) + 14.8(0) = 31.1 or $31,100. In fact, we could use any two numbers to represent a qualitative variable with two classes, but 1 and 0 are the easiest to interpret.

Figure 10.20 shows the linear regression lines for males and females considered separately. The two lines are parallel, crossing the SALARY, or vertical, axis at different points. When MONTHS is zero, the graph for females (gender coded as 1) crosses the SALARY axis at $20,300. The graph for males (gender coded as 0) crosses the SALARY axis at $35,100. Smith–Jones pays female account executives lower starting salaries than males. However, since the lines are parallel, the $14,800 difference in salaries is maintained over the next several years. That is, the mean salary increase per month is the same. Salaries of males and females have increased at a mean rate of .3 thousand, or $300 per month.

FIGURE 10.20   Parallel Lines for Male and Female Executives

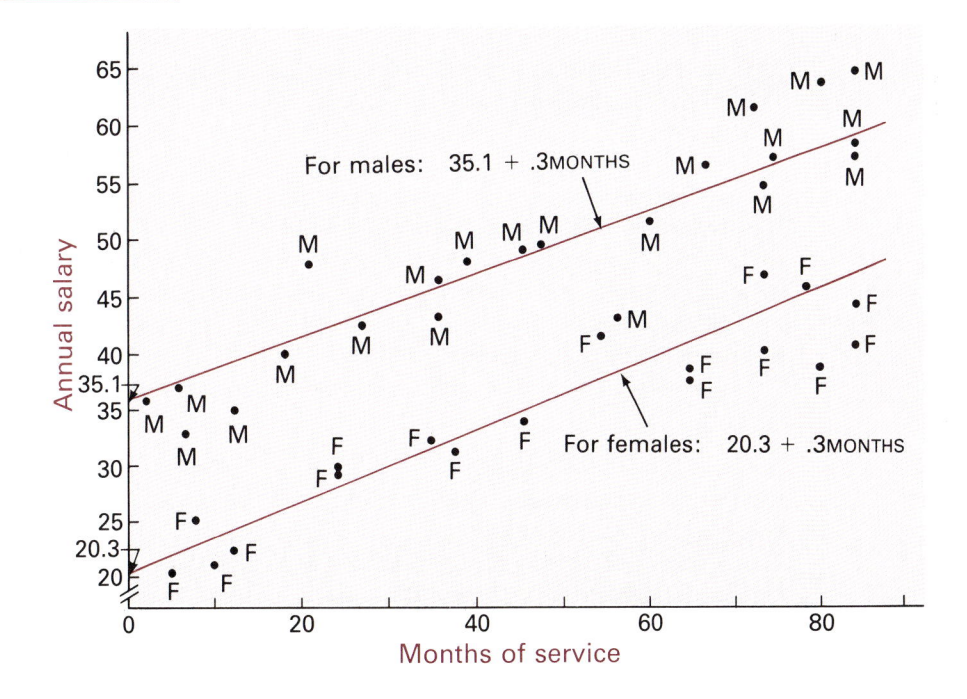

FIGURE 10.21 Nonparallel Lines for Male and Female Executives

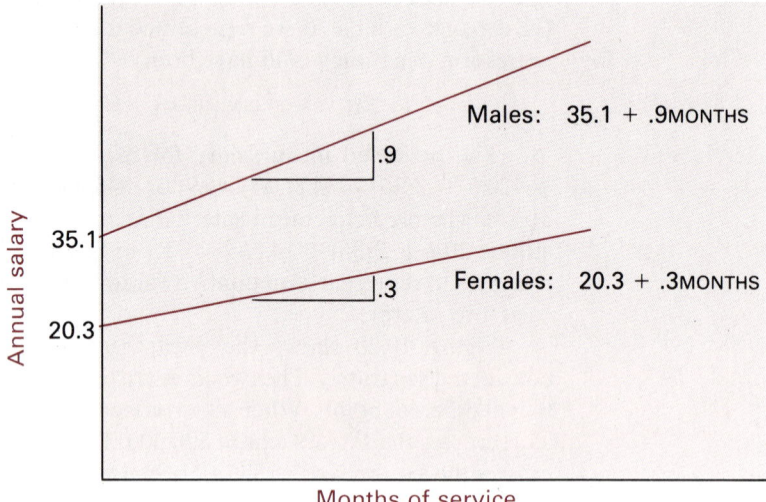

Annual salary vs. *Months of service*

Males: 35.1 + .9MONTHS (slope .9)
Females: 20.3 + .3MONTHS (slope .3)

Interaction

Suppose that male account executives at Smith–Jones not only had higher starting salaries (intercept), but also received salary increases at a higher mean rate than females. How would the parallel lines in Figure 10.20 change? Please think about it before reading on.

Figure 10.21 shows the plots in the case where the salaries of the males increase at the rate of $900 per month while those of the females increase at $300 per month. The two regression lines are no longer parallel. The slope of the equation for male account executives is steeper than that of females. The salaries of the males not only start off higher but also increase more rapidly.

We used a gender indicator variable to determine whether starting salaries (the intercepts) differed between males and females. We will use an interaction variable to determine whether the two slopes, the rates of salary increases, are the same. Alternatively, an **interaction** occurs when the regression lines for different levels of the indicator variable are not parallel. We first discussed the interaction concept in factorial experiments in Chapter 9.

We explain coding and interpreting interaction variables in the following example.

> An interaction occurs when the rate of change (the slope) of *y* vs. one predictor variable depends on the level of another predictor variable.

EXAMPLE: SMITH–JONES CREATIVE STAFF DATA   We select a stratified (by gender) random sample of creative staff personnel records. Figure 10.22 is the scatter plot. Note that females (F) appear to have higher starting salaries and their salaries increase faster than those of their male counterparts. Thus, we include an interaction variable in the regression equation.

FIGURE 10.22 Salary vs. Months of Service

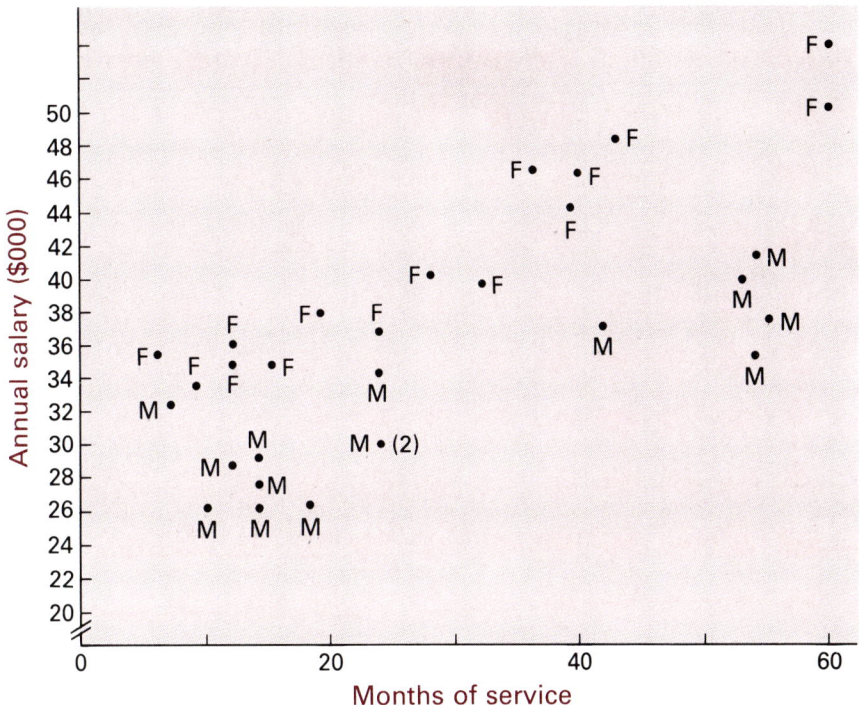

We create the interaction variable, GENDER × MONTHS, by *multiplying* the value of the MONTHS variable by the value of the GENDER variable for each observation in the sample. Table 10.23 on page 562 shows the values for the two original predictor variables and the created interaction variable. Equation (10.22) is the multiple regression model for the creative staff salary data:

$$\text{SALARY-PRED} = 25.3 + .2\text{MONTHS} + 5.4\text{GENDER} + .1\text{GENDER} \times \text{MONTHS} \quad (10.22)$$

Based on the ANOVA table and *t*-tests, the model is significant and all the predictor variables including the interaction variable are also significant.

Let's explore the significant GENDER variable and interaction term. Since females are coded GENDER = 1, the regression equation for annual salary vs. number of months of service for females is

$$\begin{aligned}
\text{SALARY-PRED}_{(F)} &= 25.3 + .2\text{MONTHS} + 5.4\text{GENDER} + .1\text{GENDER} \times \text{MONTHS} \\
&= 25.3 + .2\text{MONTHS} + 5.4(1) + .1(1) \times \text{MONTHS} \\
&= 30.7 + .3\text{MONTHS} \quad (10.23)
\end{aligned}$$

Table 10.23

Smith–Jones Salary Data for Creative Staff

	Males				Females		
SALARY	MONTHS	GENDER	GENDER × MONTHS	SALARY	MONTHS	GENDER	GENDER × MONTHS
26.4	10	0	0	35.0	15	1	15
26.4	18	0	0	39.8	32	1	32
32.2	7	0	0	35.7	6	1	6
35.5	54	0	0	40.2	28	1	28
37.2	42	0	0	32.7	9	1	9
29.3	14	0	0	37.0	24	1	24
34.3	24	0	0	38.0	19	1	19
27.8	14	0	0	36.0	12	1	12
30.0	24	0	0	50.4	60	1	60
37.5	55	0	0	54.0	60	1	60
30.0	24	0	0	46.4	40	1	40
26.2	14	0	0	46.5	36	1	36
28.9	12	0	0	44.1	39	1	39
40.0	53	0	0	35.0	12	1	12
41.5	54	0	0	48.3	43	1	43

The regression equation for annual salary vs. number of months of service for males is

$$\text{SALARY-PRED}_{(M)} = 25.3 + .2\text{MONTHS} + 5.4\text{GENDER} + .1\text{GENDER} \times \text{MONTHS}$$
$$= 25.3 + .2\text{MONTHS} + 5.4(0) + .1(0) \times \text{MONTHS}$$
$$= 25.3 + .2\text{MONTHS} \qquad (10.24)$$

The intercept for the regression line for the female creative staff is 30.7 ($30,700) as compared with 25.3 ($25,300) for the male staff. The difference in intercepts of 5.4 results from adding the value of the GENDER regression coefficient to the intercept for the female staff, but not for the male staff. The t-test indicated that the difference of $5,400 is statistically significant. The slope of the equation for females is .3 as compared with .2 for males. The difference in slopes of .1 results from adding the value of the GENDER × MONTHS regression coefficient to the slope for females, but not for males. The t-test indicated that the difference in slopes is statistically significant. Figure 10.23 shows the graphs of equations (10.23) and (10.24).

In summary, the statistical significance of the GENDER variable indicates that female creative staff do have higher mean starting salaries than male creative staff. The statistical significance of the GENDER × MONTHS interaction variable indicates that mean salaries of females have also increased at a faster rate than mean salaries of males.

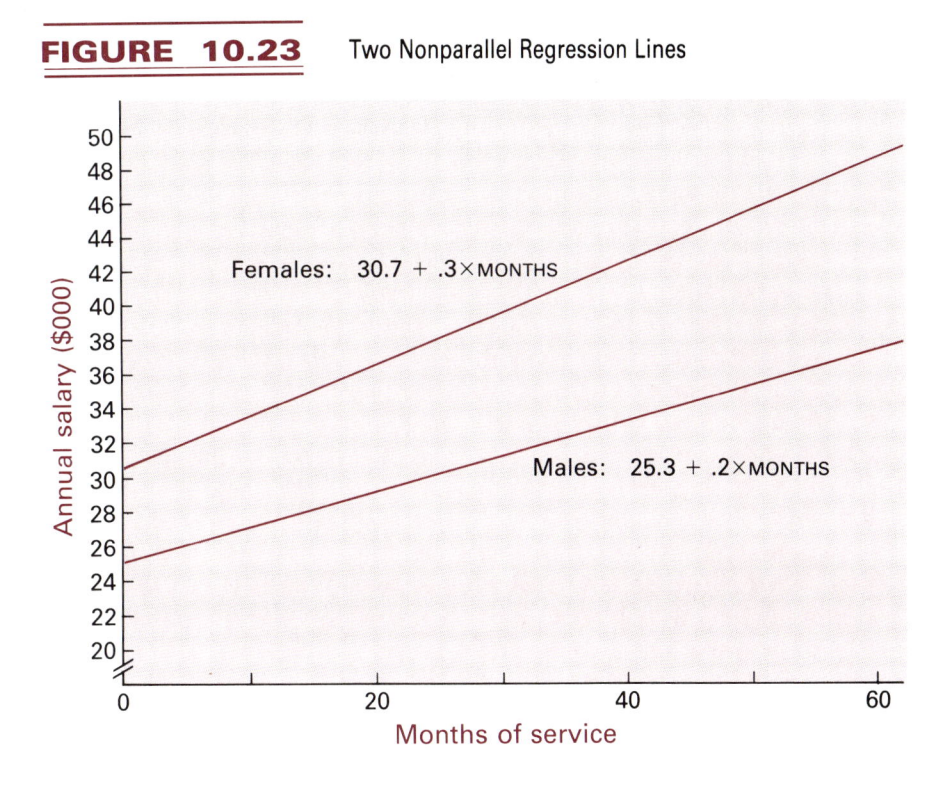

FIGURE 10.23 Two Nonparallel Regression Lines

[Graph showing two regression lines: Females: 30.7 + .3×MONTHS and Males: 25.3 + .2×MONTHS, with Annual salary ($000) on y-axis (20-50) and Months of service on x-axis (0-60).]

Categorical Variables with Three or More Classes

Up to now, we have considered only categorical variables with two classes, male and female. However, categorical variables often have three or more classes. This will require adding additional indicator variables to the regression model.

In our next example, we explain how to code a categorical variable with three classes and how to interpret a regression model with coded indicator variables. The example is taken from the health care industry, which accounts for approximately 10% of the U.S. gross national product, the dollar value of all goods and services produced each year.

EXAMPLE: PREDICTING THE NUMBER OF X-RAYS   Our goal is to predict the number of x-ray exposures taken per month (the dependent variable) from the mean daily patient load per month for three different classes of hospitals: private (for profit), public, and teaching. Mean daily patient load is the hospital's total number of inpatients and outpatients divided by the number of days in a month. Table 10.24 on page 564 contains hypothetical data for a stratified sample of five hospitals from each of the three categories.

Table 10.24
X-Ray and Patient Load Data by Type of Hospital

Hospital	Number of X-Rays Taken per Month	Mean Daily Patient Load	Hospital Type
1	2,105	15.5	Private
2	9,700	50.5	Private
3	17,800	100.5	Private
4	30,600	150	Private
5	61,600	300	Private
6	1,800	18.7	Public
7	7,000	45	Public
8	16,250	90.5	Public
9	48,950	250	Public
10	79,000	400	Public
11	26,000	50	Teaching
12	35,000	100.5	Teaching
13	56,500	200	Teaching
14	89,200	350.5	Teaching
15	118,100	500	Teaching

The hospital type variable is a categorical variable with three classes. Thus we must create two indicator variables. For example, we could represent the type of hospital categorical variable as follows:

$$\text{PRIVATE} = \begin{cases} 1 & \text{if hospital is private} \\ 0 & \text{otherwise} \end{cases}$$

$$\text{TEACHING} = \begin{cases} 1 & \text{if hospital is a teaching hospital} \\ 0 & \text{otherwise} \end{cases}$$

We have created two new indicator variables, PRIVATE and TEACHING, from the single categorical variable, hospital type, as shown in Table 10.25. *Note:* We have not created interaction variables because we do not believe that the relationship between mean daily patient load and number of x-ray exposures depends on the type of hospital.

We need only two indicator variables even though the categorical variable, type of hospital, has three classes. For example, we represent a private hospital as PRIVATE = 1 and TEACHING = 0, and a teaching hospital as PRIVATE = 0 and TEACHING = 1. A public hospital is neither a private hospital (PRIVATE = 0) nor a teaching hospital (TEACHING = 0). Thus public hospitals are represented by assigning the value 0 to each indicator variable. In other words, once we know a hospital is not a private or teaching hospital, we know that it must be a public hospital. Thus, we need only two indicator variables to represent a categorical variable with three classes.

Table 10.25

X-Ray and Patient Load Data by Type of Hospital

Hospital	Number of X-Rays Taken per Month	Mean Daily Patient Load	PRIVATE	TEACHING	Hospital Type
1	2,105	15.5	1	0	Private
2	9,700	50.5	1	0	Private
3	17,800	100.5	1	0	Private
4	30,600	150	1	0	Private
5	61,600	300	1	0	Private
6	1,800	18.7	0	0	Public
7	7,000	45	0	0	Public
8	16,250	90.5	0	0	Public
9	48,950	250	0	0	Public
10	79,000	400	0	0	Public
11	26,000	50	0	1	Teaching
12	35,000	100.5	0	1	Teaching
13	56,500	200	0	1	Teaching
14	89,200	350.5	0	1	Teaching
15	118,100	500	0	1	Teaching

Our software produced the following regression equation.

$$\text{XRAY-PRED} = -2{,}357 + 204.9\text{LOAD} + 2{,}488.9\text{PRIVATE} + 18{,}098.3\text{TEACHING} \quad (10.25)$$

The t-tests indicated that the LOAD, PRIVATE, and TEACHING variables should be retained in model (10.25). Shown are the three equations used to estimate the mean number of x-rays for each hospital type:

For public hospitals, PRIVATE = 0 and TEACHING = 0:

$$\begin{aligned}\text{XRAY-PRED}_{(PU)} &= -2{,}357 + 204.9\text{LOAD} + 2{,}488.9\text{PRIVATE} \\ &\quad + 18{,}098.3\text{TEACHING} \\ &= -2{,}357 + 204.9\text{LOAD} + 2{,}488.9(0) + 18{,}098.3(0) \\ &= -2{,}357 + 204.9\text{LOAD} \quad (10.26)\end{aligned}$$

For private hospitals, PRIVATE = 1 and TEACHING = 0:

$$\begin{aligned}\text{XRAY-PRED}_{(PR)} &= -2{,}357 + 204.9\text{LOAD} + 2{,}488.9\text{PRIVATE} \\ &\quad + 18{,}098.3\text{TEACHING} \\ &= -2{,}357 + 204.9\text{LOAD} + 2{,}488.9(1) + 18{,}098.3(0) \\ &= 131.9 + 204.9\text{LOAD} \quad (10.27)\end{aligned}$$

For teaching hospitals, PRIVATE = 0 and TEACHING = 1:

$$\text{XRAY-PRED}_{(T)} = -2{,}357 + 204.9\text{LOAD} + 2{,}488.9\text{PRIVATE}$$
$$+ 18{,}098.3\text{TEACHING}$$
$$= -2{,}357 + 204.9\text{LOAD} + 2{,}488.9(0) + 18{,}098.3(1)$$
$$= 15{,}741.3 + 204.9\text{LOAD} \tag{10.28}$$

Equations (10.26), (10.27), and (10.28) differ only in their intercepts. Private hospitals take, on the average, 2,488.9 more x-rays per month than public hospitals after controlling for daily patient load. The term 2,488.9 is the difference between the intercepts in equations (10.26) and (10.27): 131.9 − (−2,357). Teaching hospitals take, on the average, 18,098.3 more x-rays per month than public hospitals after controlling for daily patient load.

The differences in the mean numbers of x-rays taken would not change if we had used either of the following two possible codes to represent the categorical variable, type of hospital:

$$\text{PRIVATE} = \begin{cases} 1 & \text{if hospital is private} \\ 0 & \text{otherwise} \end{cases}$$

$$\text{PUBLIC} = \begin{cases} 1 & \text{if hospital is public} \\ 0 & \text{otherwise} \end{cases}$$

$$\text{PUBLIC} = \begin{cases} 1 & \text{if hospital is public} \\ 0 & \text{otherwise} \end{cases}$$

$$\text{TEACHING} = \begin{cases} 1 & \text{if hospital is a teaching hospital} \\ 0 & \text{otherwise} \end{cases}$$

We should conduct follow-up studies to determine why both private and teaching hospitals take more x-rays per month than public hospitals, after controlling for the mean number of patients treated. The greater numbers of x-rays may be due to the differing levels of care, the type and severity of diseases treated, or the profit orientations of each hospital type.

Summary

Recognizing when to include an interaction term in the regression model is important. Consider developing a regression equation to model the following beliefs:

1. Performance on a common final exam (dependent variable) depends on a student's level of critical thinking as measured by the Watson–Glaser Critical Thinking Appraisal (quantitative predictor variable) and the type of instruction, lecture vs. case method (categorical predictor variable). Students taught by the lecture method will outperform students taught by the case method by a constant amount irrespective of their level of critical thinking.

Since we do not believe there is an interaction between the two predictor variables, the following regression equation models these beliefs:

$$\text{PERF-PRED} = b_0 + b_1 \text{CRITICAL} + b_2 \text{LECTURE}$$

A significant indicator variable means that the two classes of the categorical variable affect the dependent variable. Graphically, the two regression lines are parallel. The intercepts of the two regression lines are different, but the slopes are the same.

Now consider developing a regression equation to model the following beliefs:

2. Performance on a common final exam depends on a student's level of critical thinking and type of instruction. Students with low critical thinking skills will do better when taught by the lecture method. Students with high critical thinking skills will do better when taught by the case method.

In the second situation the belief is that level of critical thinking and type of teaching interact. That is, the relationship between performance vs. critical thinking depends on the type of teaching. We should include an interaction variable, CRIT × LECTURE:

$$\text{PERF-PRED} = b_0 + b_1 \text{CRIT} + b_2 \text{LECTURE} + b_3 \text{CRIT} \times \text{LECTURE}$$

A significant interaction variable means that the two regression lines are *not* parallel. The two regression line slopes are different.

SECTION 10.8 EXERCISES

Use the software for all the problems in this section.

1. We believe that the number of product innovations for firms in the insurance industry depends on the firm's asset size and whether the firm is a mutual or stock company. Show two ways to code the qualitative variable, type of insurance company.

2. Shown are the data for a study of product innovations in the insurance industry. Code the type of insurance company as $x_2 = 1$ if stock company and 0 otherwise.

Firm	Number of Product Innovations Over a 3-Year Period	Asset Size	Type of Firm
1	10	500	Mutual
2	13	600	Mutual
3	14	575	Mutual
4	17	800	Mutual
5	20	1,100	Mutual
6	19	950	Mutual

(*continued*)

Firm	Number of Product Innovations Over a 3-Year Period	Asset Size	Type of Firm
7	4	400	Stock
8	7	500	Stock
9	8	700	Stock
10	10	650	Stock
11	13	950	Stock
12	14	1,000	Stock

    a. Plot asset size vs. number of product innovations. Use different symbols for stock and mutual firms. Does it appear that type of firm affects the number of innovations? Does it appear that asset size affects the number of innovations?

    b. Compute and interpret the multiple regression model for the above data (assuming no interaction term).

    c. Use the ANOVA table and the t-tests to determine which predictor variables are significantly related to the number of product innovations. Use a .05 p-value.

    d. Interpret the indicator variable regression coefficient. What does it mean? Explain it in terms that an insurance executive could understand.

3. Suppose we suspect an interaction between type of firm and asset size on the number of product innovations. Insert an interaction term into the model. That is, include an $x_1 x_2$ column in the input data for the multiple regression model. Test for the presence of an interaction term. Explain the lack of a significant interaction term in terms that an insurance executive could understand.

4. Change the data set in Exercise 2 to contain a significant interaction term. Plot the asset size vs. number of innovations data and show the nonparallel linear regression lines for stock and mutual firms.

5. Refer to Exercise 4. Verify the significant interaction term by the t-test output. Explain the significant interaction term in terms that an insurance executive could understand.

6. We believe that the qualitative variable, season of the year, affects air conditioner sales. Since there are four seasons, we will need three indicator variables. We use the following indicator variables:

$$x_1 = \begin{cases} 1 & \text{if season is winter} \\ 0 & \text{otherwise} \end{cases}$$

$$x_2 = \begin{cases} 1 & \text{if season is spring} \\ 0 & \text{otherwise} \end{cases}$$

$$x_3 = \begin{cases} 1 & \text{if season is fall} \\ 0 & \text{otherwise} \end{cases}$$

    a. How would we code the winter season, the spring season, the fall season, and the summer season?

    b. Suppose the population regression coefficient for the intercept is not zero but all three other population regression coefficients are zero. Are there any seasonal effects?

7. Auto firms use two different market segmentation approaches: (1) a concentration approach and (2) a multisegment approach. Rolls Royce is an example of the former strategy. It sells exclusively to the super-luxury market segment. Nissan uses the multisegment approach. It sells the Sentra to the economy-minded market, the Stanza to the mainstream family market, the 300ZX to the affluent sports car enthusiasts market, and the Infinity to the luxury market segment. Show two different ways to code the market segmentation approach. Interpret both coding schemes.

8. We believe that dollar sales volume in women's dress departments, SALES, depends on square footage, FEET, of the department. Larger departments tend to produce more dollar sales volume. Sales volume also depends on whether the salespeople are on commission. The presence of commission is thought to be positively related to dollar sales volume. Represent the categorical variable commission, COMM, as follows:

$$\text{COMM} = \begin{cases} 1 & \text{if salesperson is on commission} \\ 0 & \text{otherwise} \end{cases}$$

Does the following model represent our beliefs? If not, correct the model.

$$\text{SALES-PRED} = b_0 - b_1 \text{FEET} - b_2 \text{COMM}$$

9. Refer to Exercise 8. Suppose we believe that SALES depends not only on FEET and COMM but also on the interactive, or joint, effect of the two variables. Develop a proposed model that now reflects our beliefs. Describe the interaction term in words that a department manager could understand.

10.9 Multicollinearity

Regression analysis determines whether a set of predictor variables is related to a dependent variable. Often, in the fields of business and economics, predictor variables are related to one another. For example, the independent variables—store size and number of employees or salary and years of experience—may be highly related. Some problems arise when the predictor variables are correlated among themselves. By the end of this section you should be able to:

1. explain what multicollinearity is;
2. explain why multicollinearity is more likely to be a problem in correlational regression studies than in experimental regression studies;
3. explain the problems that multicollinearity causes;
4. detect multicollinearity; and
5. reduce the impact of multicollinearity.

What Is Multicollinearity?

The following equations show what happens for the COMCEL car phone sales data when we compute regression equations for: units sold and number of ads, units sold and price, and then units sold and both variables (see Table 10.3 for data).

$$\text{UNITS SOLD-PRED} = 13.9 + 3.312 \text{ADS} \qquad (10.29)$$

$$\text{UNITS SOLD-PRED} = 70.8 - .529 \text{PRICE} \qquad (10.30)$$

$$\text{UNITS SOLD-PRED} = 60.89 + 3.312 \text{ADS} - .529 \text{PRICE} \qquad (10.31)$$

Equations (10.29)–(10.31) exhibit a very important property—the regression coefficients remain the same as new independent variables are added to the regression model. UNITS SOLD drops by .529 for every one dollar increase in price regardless of whether we include the ADS variable in the regression equation. We get a clear measure of the effect of price (and number of ads) on the number of units sold.

From Table 10.3, note that COMCEL ran one, three, and five ads for every price level. This is a fully balanced study design. In experimental regression studies, the manager exerts experimental control and achieves a balanced design. The balanced design ensures that the regression coefficients will not change as we add or remove independent variables from the model.

Balanced designs are rare in business and economics. Instead, managers tend to run correlational studies. In correlational studies, the manager cannot exert control or achieve a balanced design. As a result, the regression coefficients change as predictor variables are added to the regression equation.

To see the effect of an unbalanced design, suppose that stores 5, 6, 19, and 20 close due to poor weather. Then observations (100, 5, 26), (100, 5, 24), (80, 1, 26), and (80, 1, 23) would be deleted from Table 10.3. The regression design is no longer balanced. Again we used our software and computed regression expressions for the remaining 20 observations for: units sold and number of ads, units sold and price, and then units sold and both variables:

$$\text{UNITS SOLD-PRED} = 10.52 \qquad + 4.38 \text{ADS} \qquad (10.32)$$

$$\text{UNITS SOLD-PRED} = 93.13 - .79 \text{PRICE} \qquad (10.33)$$

$$\text{UNITS SOLD-PRED} = 54.21 - .48 \text{PRICE} + 3.60 \text{ADS} \qquad (10.34)$$

The effect of removing four observations is dramatic. The PRICE coefficient changes from $-.79$ to $-.48$ when ADS is included in the equation. The ADS coefficient changes from 4.38 to 3.60 after PRICE is included. Adding or removing any predictor variable affects the size of the other regression coefficients in the equation. We do not obtain a clear measure now of the effect of price or number of ads on the number of units sold. For example, as we increase price by $1, how much does the number of units sold drop? Equation (10.33) says by .79, while equation (10.34) says by .48.

When the regression design is balanced, the predictor variables are *not* related to each other. Figure 10.24 is a scatter diagram of the *predictor variables*, price and number of ads, for all the data in Table 10.3. It shows a balanced design. Even without computing the regression coefficient, we can see that the best fitting line appears to be horizontal—a slope of zero. Graphically, the data can be enclosed only by a circle or a horizontal ellipse. Thus, the two predictor variables are not related to one another.

When the regression design is not balanced, the predictor variables are related to one another. Look at Figure 10.25, from which we have deleted the four data values previously mentioned. The best fitting line no longer appears to be horizontal, but a line with a negative slope. An ellipse that is slightly downward sloping to the right does a better job of enclosing the points than a circle does. When there is a linear relationship between the predictor variables,

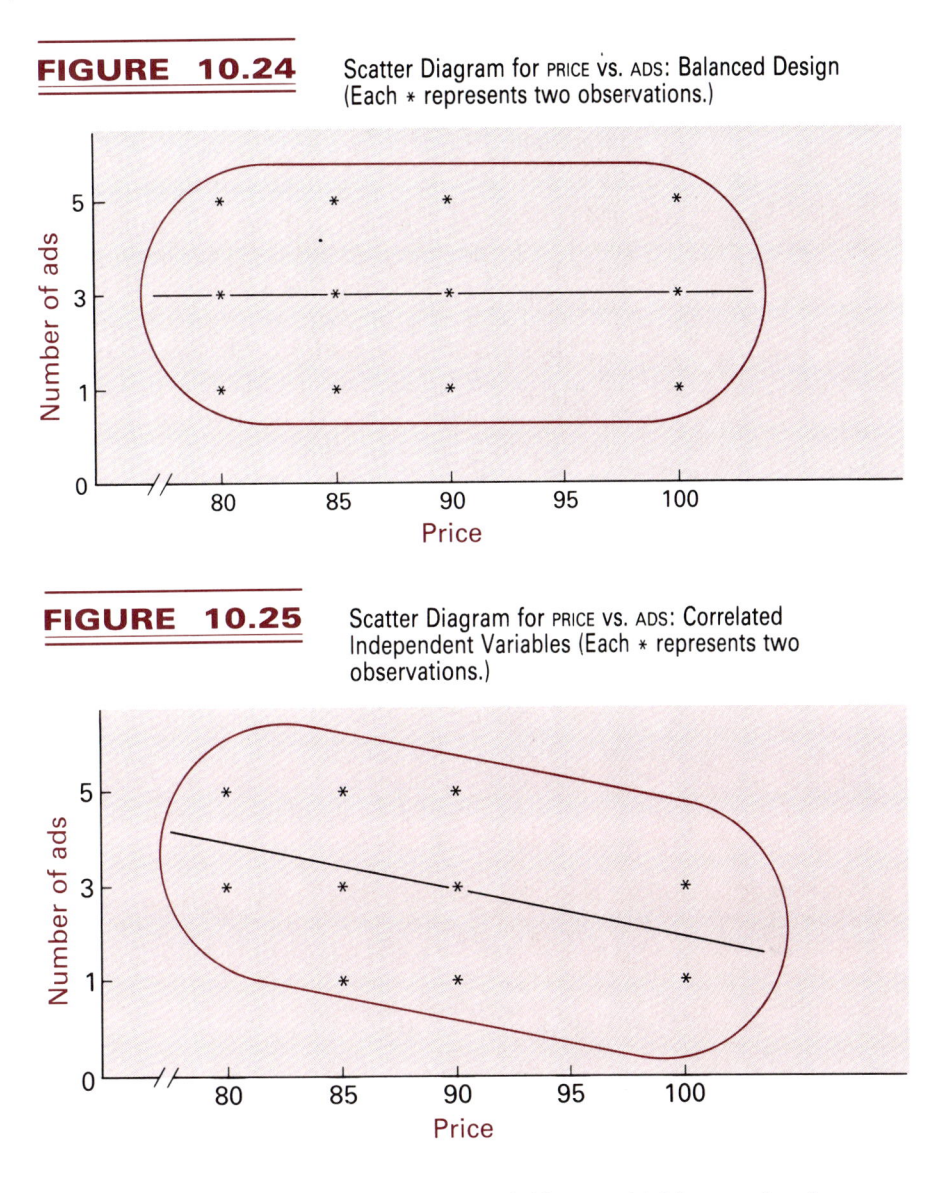

Chapter 10   Regression Analysis

FIGURE 10.24   Scatter Diagram for PRICE VS. ADS: Balanced Design (Each * represents two observations.)

FIGURE 10.25   Scatter Diagram for PRICE VS. ADS: Correlated Independent Variables (Each * represents two observations.)

they are *correlated*. When predictor variables are highly correlated, we can enclose the scatter plots of pairs of predictor variables by tight ellipses sloping upward or downward to the right or to the left. We have **multicollinearity**. This occurs frequently in correlational regression studies. Highly correlated predictor variables can cause problems in regression analysis.

Multicollinearity means that some or all of the predictor variables are highly correlated with one another.

Why Is Multicollinearity a Problem?

When the predictor variables are highly correlated, three problems can occur:

1. The signs (+ or −) of some regression coefficients may be the reverse of what logic suggests.

2. Important predictor variables may be erroneously removed from the regression equation in the follow-up *t*-tests.
3. The concept of measuring the effect of one variable while holding the other variables constant loses its meaning.

SIGN REVERSALS   Logically, UNITS SOLD in the COMCEL marketing study should be inversely related to the PRICE variable. The higher the price, the fewer phones sold. Be concerned if you run a regression analysis and obtain a positive price regression coefficient. The wrong sign could occur because price is highly correlated with other predictor variables in the equation.

The signs of the regression coefficients provide valuable information. They tell us whether the dependent variable is positively or negatively related to a predictor variable. Thus, sign reversals can cause problems in understanding relationships between variables.

UNUSUAL *t*-TEST FINDINGS   Consider the two data sets in Table 10.26. One set contains uncorrelated independent variables and the other contains highly correlated independent variables.

In the correlated data set, price and number of ads are positively related. As price increases, number of ads also tends to increase. In the uncorrelated data set, price and number of ads are not related.

We developed a regression model for units sold vs. price and number of ads for the correlated data set. The variance ratio of 33 (computer output not shown) has a *p*-value of less than .05. That is, at least one predictor variable is significantly related to units sold.

However, the follow-up *t*-tests in Table 10.27 show that neither predictor variable has a *p*-value of less than .05. Thus, for the correlated data set we reach a

Table 10.26

Correlated and Uncorrelated Data Sets

Correlated Data Set			Uncorrelated Data Set		
Units Sold	Price	Ads	Units Sold	Price	Ads
8	1	2	8	1	2
10	2	4	10	1	6
11	3	3	13	3	4
13	4	6	11	5	2
17	5	8	17	5	6

Table 10.27

Parameter Estimates and *t*-Tests

Variable	Parameter Estimate	*t*-Value	*p*-Value
INTERCEPT	5.256	5.967	—
PRICE	1.244	1.883	>.05
ADS	.611	1.408	>.05

strange conclusion: We have a good predictive model with no significant predictor variables.

Multicollinearity produced the strange results. Now we will illustrate how this occurred. We used our software to determine the sums of squares and regression models for both data sets in Table 10.26 for:

1. both predictor variables—price and number of ads—in a multiple regression model,
2. price only in a simple regression model, and
3. ads only in a simple regression model.

The results are given in Table 10.28.

UNCORRELATED DATA SET   The error sum of squares (SSE) for the PRICE-only model is 21.80. This amount is attributable to all variables not included in the model. One variable not in the model is the number of ads. When we included this variable, the error sum of squares dropped to 5.80. Thus, including the ADS variable reduced the error sum of squares by 21.80 − 5.80 = 16 units. Sixteen units is the impact of the ADS variable and is called the *extra sum of squares*-ADS (ESS-ADS). It is the marginal effect of introducing the ADS variable when the PRICE variable was already in the model.

The error sum of squares for the ADS-only model is 30.80. Again, this is attributable to all variables not included in the model. One variable not in the model is PRICE. When we included this variable, the error sum of squares dropped to 5.80. Adding the PRICE variable reduced the error sum of squares by 30.80 − 5.80 = 25 units. Thus, 25 units is the impact of the PRICE variable and is called the *extra sum of squares*-PRICE (ESS-PRICE). It is the marginal effect of introducing the PRICE variable when the ADS variable was already in the model.

The regression sum of squares (see Table 10.28) for the PRICE and ADS model is 41 units. Note that

$$\text{ESS-PRICE} + \text{ESS-ADS} = \text{SSR}(\text{PRICE, ADS}) \qquad (10.35)$$

$$25 \text{ units} + 16 \text{ units} = 41 \text{ units}$$

Table 10.28
Sums of Squares and Models for Data Sets in Table 10.26

Data Set	SSR	SSE	SST	Regression Model
Uncorrelated				
PRICE, ADS	41.00	5.80	46.80	4.05 + 1.25PRICE + 1.00ADS
PRICE only	25.00	21.80	46.80	8.05 + 1.25PRICE
ADS only	16.00	30.80	46.80	7.80 + 1.00ADS
Correlated				
PRICE, ADS	45.44	1.36	46.80	5.25 + 1.24PRICE + .61ADS
PRICE only	44.10	2.70	46.80	5.50 + 2.10PRICE
ADS only	43.04	3.76	46.80	5.53 + 1.36ADS

CORRELATED DATA SET   The error sum of squares for the PRICE-only model is 2.70. This quantity is attributable to all variables not included in the model. One variable not in the model is number of ads. When we included this variable, the error sum of squares dropped to 1.36. Adding the ADS variable reduced the error sum of squares by 2.70 − 1.36 = 1.34 units; the ESS-ADS is 1.34 units.

The error sum of squares for the ADS-only model is 3.76. When we included the PRICE variable, the error sum of squares dropped to 1.36. Adding the PRICE variable reduced the error sum of squares by 3.76 − 1.36 = 2.40 units; the ESS-PRICE is 2.40 units.

The regression sum of squares for the PRICE and ADS model is 45.44 units. Note that

$$\text{ESS-PRICE} + \text{ESS-ADS} \neq \text{SSR}(\text{PRICE}, \text{ADS}) \qquad (10.36)$$

$$2.40 + 1.34 \neq 45.44 \text{ units}$$

Why are both ESS-PRICE and ESS-ADS small for the correlated data set? Consider the model with the ADS variable only. When we include the PRICE variable, its impact is small (ESS-PRICE = 2.40 units) because the ADS variable was already in the model and the ADS and PRICE variables are highly correlated. Thus, much of the PRICE variable's impact is already in the model even before we include it. Now consider the model with the PRICE variable only. When we include the ADS variable, its impact is small (ESS-ADS = 1.34 units) because the PRICE variable was already in the model and the ADS and PRICE variables are highly correlated. Thus, much of the ADS variable's impact is already in the model even before we enter it.

So what are the implications? For uncorrelated data, equation (10.35) is true. If SSR(PRICE, ADS) is large, at least one of the extra sum of squares terms on the left-hand side must also be large. Since the t-tests use the extra sum of squares in their calculations, at least one of the predictor variables must be significant. For the uncorrelated data set, the extra sum of squares terms were 25 and 16. Both predictor variables will probably have p-values less than .05 in the follow-up t-tests. Thus, we cannot have a good predictive model with no significant predictor variables.

For correlated data, equation (10.35) is not true. Even if SSR(PRICE, ADS) is large, both extra sum of squares terms may be very small. That is why neither predictor variable was significant in the follow-up t-tests even though we obtained a significant variance ratio in the ANOVA. Thus we can have a good predictive model with no significant predictor variables.

In summary:

1. For uncorrelated predictor variables, a significant variance ratio means that there will be at least one significant predictor variable in the follow-up t-tests.
2. For highly correlated predictor variables, a significant variance ratio may *not* mean that there will be at least one significant predictor variable in the follow-up t-tests.

HOLDING ONE VARIABLE CONSTANT? When the data exhibit multicollinearity, the concept of measuring the effect of one predictor variable while holding the others constant is meaningless. We have interpreted each regression coefficient as the effect on the dependent variable of a one-unit change in a predictor variable while holding the other variables in the equation constant. However, if two predictor variables are highly correlated, then we cannot hold one variable at a fixed level and vary the others. In short, the regression coefficients lose their meaning.

In summary, multicollinearity may cause the signs of some regression coefficients to be the reverse of what logic suggests. It may lead to erroneous removal of important predictor variables from the regression equation in the follow-up *t*-tests. However, as Neter, Wasserman, and Kutner (1985) note, multicollinearity does not stop us from using the regression model for making predictions, provided we are not extrapolating.

Next we present a realistic correlational regression study that illustrates how to detect and minimize multicollinearity.

EXAMPLE: JOB SATISFACTION STUDY   COMCEL gives an annual job satisfaction questionnaire. By knowing which variables are related to job satisfaction, COMCEL can predict which employees are likely to become dissatisfied. It can then take preventive action.

COMCEL selects a random sample of 50 employees and matches the job satisfaction scores with biographical data in the employee's personnel file. Table 10.29 lists the potential predictor variables.

Unlike the marketing study presented in Section 10.1, COMCEL can neither vary nor pull apart the predictor variables. It cannot achieve a balanced design.

Table 10.29

Job Satisfaction Variables

Variable Name	How Measured
Predictor variables	
AGE	Years
SALARY	Yearly compensation (without overtime) in thousands of dollars
EXPER	Years of job-related experience employee had before working at COMCEL
EDUC	Years of formal education
GENDER	Indicator variable: 1 if male, 0 if female
MANAG	Indicator variable: 1 if employee has management responsibility, 0 if employee has no management responsibility
YEARS	Number of years at COMCEL
Dependent variable	
JOBSAT	Job satisfaction score

Table 10.30

First Regression Expression for Job Satisfaction Study

ANALYSIS OF VARIANCE

SOURCE OF VARIATION	SUM OF SQUARES	DF	MEAN SQUARE	VARIANCE RATIO
REGRESSION	151.24803	7	21.60686084	6.336
ERROR	143.23697	42	3.41040415	
TOTAL	294.48500	49		

PARAMETER ESTIMATES

VARIABLE	PARAMETER ESTIMATE	STANDARD ERROR	t-VALUE	TWO TAIL p-VALUE
INTERCEPT	13.71717028	3.87395583	3.541	0.0010
AGE	−0.03124251	0.05142448	−0.608	0.5468
GENDER	0.91858824	0.72037023	1.275	0.2093
SALARY	0.12835017	0.05117012	2.508	0.0161
YEARS	0.05920182	0.08559556	0.692	0.4930
EXPER	0.12844888	0.15979300	0.804	0.4260
EDUC	−0.63262474	0.32047721	−1.974	0.0550
MANAG	1.28045654	0.74564384	1.717	0.0933

Instead, it must simply use the available data, which may exhibit multicollinearity. See the chapter appendix for the data set.

JOBSAT(isfaction) scores range from 1 (highly dissatisfied) to 15 (highly satisfied). The predictor variables are all quantitative except MANAG and GENDER.

Table 10.30 shows the ANOVA table and the parameter estimate section of our computer output. The variance ratio of 6.336 has a p-value less than .001. (Compare to $F(7, 42, 99.9\%)$.) Thus at least one of the seven predictor variables is significantly related to JOBSAT(isfaction). The parameter estimates provide the regression coefficients for equation (10.37):

$$\text{JOBSAT-PRED} = 13.72 - .03\text{AGE} + .92\text{GENDER} + .13\text{SALARY}$$
$$+ .06\text{YEARS} - .63\text{EDUC} + .13\text{EXPER} + 1.28\text{MANAG} \quad (10.37)$$

The follow-up t-tests suggest that only SALARY and perhaps EDUC(ation) and and MANAG(ement) are important predictor variables. However, since the job satisfaction study is correlational, multicollinearity can cause misleading t-test findings. How can we detect multicollinearity?

Detecting Multicollinearity

We will discuss two methods for detecting multicollinearity—the correlation matrix method and the sign reversal method.

Table 10.31

Correlation Matrix for Job Satisfaction Study

	AGE	GENDER	SALARY	YEARS	EXPER	EDUC	MANAG	JOBSAT
AGE	1	.117	.619	.745	.659	.323	.134	.412
GENDER		1	.440	.361	.093	.437	.145	.401
SALARY			1	.559	.319	.815	.406	.574
YEARS				1	.235	.197	.144	.502
EXPER					1	.206	−.067	.216
EDUC						1	.246	.284
MANAG							1	.428
JOBSAT								1

THE CORRELATION MATRIX METHOD Our software developed a correlation matrix or table of correlation coefficients (Table 10.31). That is, each number at the intersection of a row and column represents the correlation coefficient of the row and column variables.

The correlation coefficient tells us the *direction* of the relationship between two variables. Recall from Chapter 3 that if all data points lie on a line with a positive slope, then the correlation coefficient is +1, a perfect positive relationship. If all data points lie on a line with a negative slope, then the correlation coefficient is −1, a perfect negative, or inverse, relationship. If the two variables are not related, the correlation coefficient is zero.

First, examine the correlations between the dependent and predictor variables. For example, the correlation between JOBSAT and AGE is about .41. Second, examine the correlations among all pairs of predictor variables. For example, the correlation between SALARY and EDUC is about .82. The correlation between SALARY and YEARS is about .56.

Here is a rule of thumb for assessing multicollinearity:

If the *absolute value* of any correlation coefficient between a pair of predictor variables is higher than the *absolute values* of the correlations between the predictor variables and the dependent variable, the pair of predictor variables is highly correlated. We have multicollinearity.

With the exceptions of EXPER and EDUC, the correlation coefficients between JOBSAT and the five other predictor variables range between .40 and .60. Four of the 21 correlation coefficients for pairs of predictor variables are above .60. These are the correlations between AGE and SALARY, AGE and YEARS, AGE and EXPER, and SALARY and EDUC. *Conclusion*: Four pairs of predictor variables are highly correlated.

THE SIGN REVERSAL METHOD If any regression coefficient signs differ from what we would expect from logic or from the correlation matrix, we may have multicollinearity. Here are two examples of regression coefficient signs that are contrary to logic:

1. *A positive relationship between price and number of units sold.* Microeconomic theory suggests a negative relationship when measuring a demand curve.
2. *A negative relationship between height and weight of children aged 5 to 20.* Logic and experience suggest a positive relationship.

Regression coefficient signs that are inconsistent with logic or theory do not always signal multicollinearity. Our logic or theory may be wrong; but, generally, a sign reversal is likely to be evidence of multicollinearity.

Regression coefficient signs that are inconsistent with the correlation matrix can also signal multicollinearity. The regression coefficient for the EDUC predictor variable is $-.63$ (see equation (10.37)). After controlling for the other variables (i.e., employees of the same gender, age, salary, years, experience, and level of management), job satisfaction *decreases* with increasing education. However, the correlation between JOBSAT and EDUC was about $+.28$ (see Table 10.31). The signs of the regression coefficient and the correlation coefficient are different. In summary, we may have multicollinearity when the sign of a regression coefficient for a predictor variable and the sign of the correlation coefficient for the predictor and dependent variables differ.

There are other methods for detecting multicollinearity, but for our purposes here we have limited our discussion to the correlation matrix and sign reversal methods. We next consider what can be done to reduce multicollinearity.

Minimizing Multicollinearity

Partial remedies for multicollinearity include: (1) obtaining additional data to *break the pattern* of the highly correlated predictor variables and (2) dropping one or more highly correlated predictor variables from the equation. The former strategy is more effective in reducing multicollinearity, but is also more difficult to implement.

BREAK THE PATTERN   The correlation matrix in Table 10.31 indicates that AGE is highly correlated with SALARY, with YEARS, and with EXPER. SALARY and EDUC are also highly correlated. Figure 10.26 shows a scatter diagram of the salary vs. education variables. Note that the two variables are highly correlated. The correlation coefficient is about $+.82$. The points can be encircled by a tight ellipse that slopes upward to the right.

We should seek additional observations (employees) for the study—specifically, employees with 12–14 years of education who have high salaries (cluster A) and employees with 17–19 years of education who have low salaries (cluster B). The extra observations would break the pattern between the education and salary predictor variables. By turning the ellipse into a circle, we can reduce the extent of correlation.

Breaking the pattern is not always feasible. There may not be any highly paid employees with 12–14 years of education in the firm, or there may not be any lowly paid employees with 17–19 years of education in the firm. In general, finding data to break the pattern may be difficult. Nevertheless, breaking the pattern is an effective strategy that we should always consider, if possible.

Chapter 10   Regression Analysis

FIGURE 10.26   Scatter Diagram of SALARY and EDUC for Job Satisfaction Study

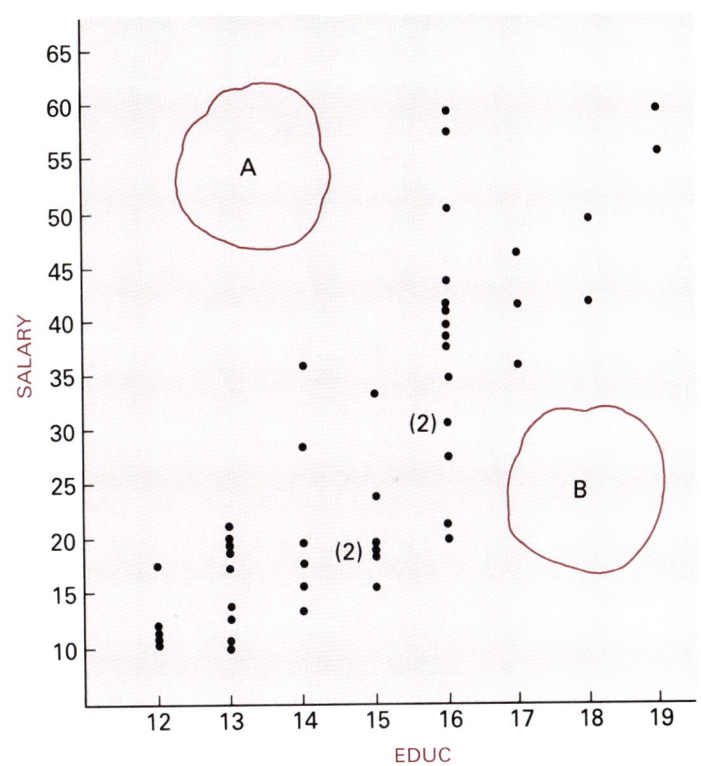

DISCARD HIGHLY CORRELATED PREDICTOR VARIABLES   We carry out the alternative strategy of discarding some highly correlated predictor variables by using the *backward elimination* approach:

1. Develop a regression equation between the dependent variable and *all* the predictor variables.
2. Drop the least significant predictor variable from the equation. This is the predictor variable with the highest *p*-value above .05 or whatever *p*-value you choose.
3. Recompute the regression model with the remaining predictor variables.
4. Again eliminate the predictor variable with the highest *p*-value above .05 and recompute the regression model.
5. Repeat until all the predictor variables have *p*-values less than .05 (or whatever *p*-value you choose).

From Table 10.30, the first variable we eliminate by this process is AGE with a *p*-value of .5468. We then recomputed the model with only six predictor variables. We continued eliminating variables until all the remaining predictor variables had *p*-values less than .05. The parameter estimates for these remaining variables are given in Table 10.32 on page 580. Equation (10.38) is our final model

Table 10.32

Parameter Estimates for Equation (10.38)

Variable	Parameter Estimate	t-Value	Two Tail p-Value
INTERCEPT	15.02477	5.005	.0001
GENDER	1.17926	2.022	.0491
SALARY	.16189	5.140	.0001
EDUC	−.79989	−3.236	.0022

and has a variance ratio of 13.96, which has a p-value of less than .01 (computation not shown).

$$\text{JOBSAT-PRED} = 15.02 + 1.18 \text{GENDER} + .16 \text{SALARY} - .80 \text{EDUC} \qquad (10.38)$$

Discarding highly correlated predictor variables is common practice, but it is not a solution. First, we derive no information about the impact of the discarded variables on the dependent variable. Second, the magnitudes of the regression coefficients for the predictor variables remaining in the model are affected by the correlated predictor variables removed from the model. Table 10.28 illustrates the second point. For the correlated independent variables, the PRICE regression coefficient is 1.24 when both independent variables are in the model. When we remove the ADS variable, the PRICE regression coefficient increases to 2.10. The same instability holds for the ADS regression coefficient. The magnitudes of the regression coefficients for the independent variables remaining in the model are affected by the correlated independent variables not in the model.

The backward elimination method reduces the number of independent variables in the model, thus reducing the model's complexity. It does little to eliminate multicollinearity.

Summary

Unless we run a balanced experimental regression study, the predictor variables will always be correlated to some degree. When the predictor variables are highly correlated (multicollinearity), regression coefficients are unstable and may be uninterpretable due to sign reversals. Some variables may be incorrectly deleted from the model during the follow-up t-tests.

Multicollinearity may be a problem if (1) the signs of regression coefficients are different from expected and (2) the correlations between pairs of predictor variables are greater than the correlations between the dependent and predictor variables.

Partial remedies for multicollinearity include (1) obtaining additional data to break the pattern and (2) dropping highly correlated predictor variables from the equation. For this latter approach, we illustrated the backward elimination method. See Neter, Wasserman, and Kutner's text (1985) for a discussion of the commonly used stepwise regression search method.

SECTION 10.9 EXERCISES

Use the software for all the problems in this section.

1. Suppose a plot of a pair of independent variables shows linearity. Describe what the scatter diagram would look like for the following correlation coefficients.
   a. $r = +1.0$
   b. $r = +.5$
   c. $r = 0$
   d. $r = -.5$
   e. $r = 1.0$

2. Shown is a small data set.

y	x_1	x_2
4	1	2
6	2	4
8	3	3
12	4	5
10	5	7

   a. Plot the predictor variables. Does the data set contain multicollinearity?
   b. Plot y vs. x_1. Plot y vs x_2.
   c. Compute the multiple regression equation for y on x_1, on x_2, and on x_1 and x_2.
   d. Why is the sign of the x_2 regression coefficient negative ($-.666$) in the regression model of y vs. x_1 and x_2 when the plot of y vs. x_2 shows a positive relationship?
   e. What conclusion can you draw about the meaningfulness of the regression coefficients when the data exhibit multicollinearity?
   f. Use the multiple regression model to predict y for $x_1 = 3$ and $x_2 = 3$.
   g. Is the predicted value of y close to the actual value of y? If so, what conclusion can you draw about the impact of multicollinearity on prediction?
   h. Use the correlation matrix output and show why the data exhibit multicollinearity.

3. Shown is a small data set.

y	x_1	x_2
4	1	1
6	6	2
7	4	4
8	2	7
12	7	7

   a. Plot the predictor variables. Do the data exhibit multicollinearity?
   b. Plot y vs. x_1. Plot y vs. x_2.
   c. Compute the multiple regression equation for y on x_1, on x_2, and on x_1 and x_2.
   d. Why do the signs of the regression coefficients not change? For example, the x_1 coefficient is $+.526$ with x_2 in the model. It is $+.769$ without x_2 in the model.
   e. Use the correlation matrix output and show why the data do not exhibit multicollinearity.

4. Refer to Exercise 2 in this set. What values of x_1 and x_2 should you seek to break the pattern?
5. If the dependent variable and one of the predictor variables have a correlation of +.95, can we conclude that the data exhibit multicollinearity? Discuss.
6. See Exercise 3 in Section 10.3 Exercises. Analyze the time-ordered data set for multicollinearity.
    a. Plot INVENTORY vs. NPEE. Does it appear that the two variables are highly related?
    b. Develop a correlation matrix for the data. Use it to determine whether multicollinearity is present.
7. Would it be possible to break the pattern for the data in Exercise 3 in Section 10.3 Exercises? Explain.
8. Refer to the data in Exercise 4 in Section 10.3 Exercises.
    a. Regress salary (dependent) on months on the job, level of communication skill, and gender. From a logical perspective, does the regression show any indication of multicollinearity?
    b. Use the correlation matrix to support your conclusion in part **a**.
    c. Suppose your purpose in fitting the regression model was to estimate the difference in monthly salary between males and females after controlling for months on the job and level of communication skill. Would multicollinearity prevent you from interpreting the regression coefficient of the gender variable in this instance? Explain.

10.10 Regression Models and Problem Solving

Before using a regression model in problem solving, we must ensure that the model is valid and meaningful. Otherwise, we use it at our own risk.

Steps in Building Valid Regression Models

Figure 10.27 illustrates the steps managers should follow in building valid regression models. Begin by constructing scatter diagrams. Do the predictor variables appear to be related to the dependent variable? Then develop a regression model and use the analysis of variance to determine if at least one of the predictor variables is related to the dependent variable at an acceptable level of confidence. If not, seek additional predictor variables. Then examine the data for multicollinearity, which is common in correlational regression studies. If the data contain multicollinearity, try to break the pattern. If that is not feasible, eliminate highly correlated predictor variables. Use the backward elimination method to develop a second-pass model. Then compute the residuals from the second-pass model. Check for linearity, normality, equal variances, and independence for time-ordered data. If the residual analysis indicates problems, correct them or seek statistical help. Now we can use the regression model for problem sensing and choice making—explanation, prediction, and control.

Regression analysis is very useful in sensing problems and making decisions. By the end of this section you should be able to make predictions with a regression model to (1) sense problems and (2) select effective alternative actions.

Chapter 10 Regression Analysis

FIGURE 10.27 Flowchart of Steps in Analyzing Regression Data

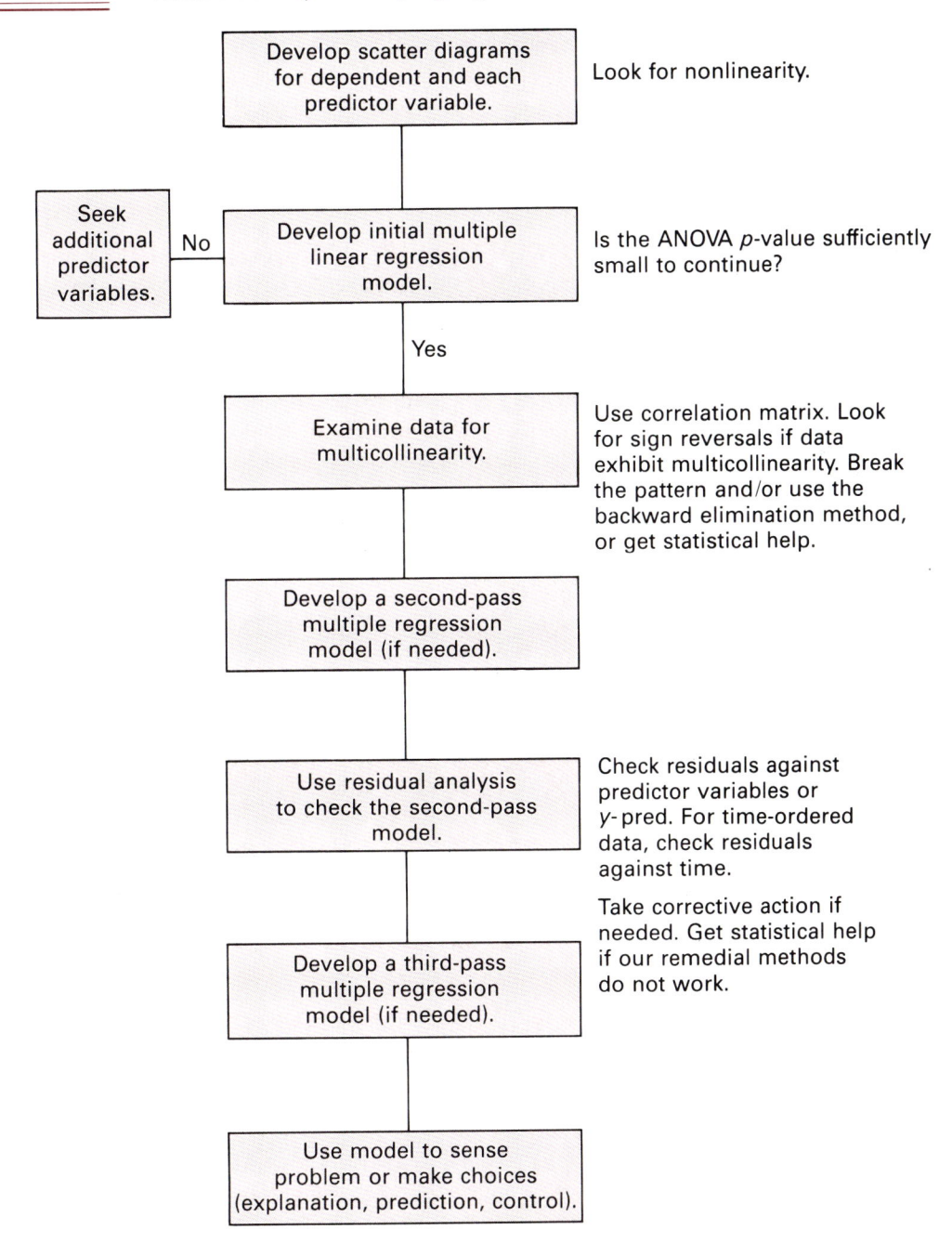

```
┌─────────────────────────┐
│ Develop scatter diagrams│    Look for nonlinearity.
│ for dependent and each  │
│   predictor variable.   │
└───────────┬─────────────┘
            │
┌──────────┐│┌─────────────────────────┐
│  Seek    │││                         │
│additional│ No  Develop initial       │    Is the ANOVA p-value sufficiently
│predictor │◄────multiple linear       │    small to continue?
│variables.│     regression model.     │
└──────────┘└───────────┬─────────────┘
                        │ Yes
            ┌───────────▼─────────────┐    Use correlation matrix. Look
            │   Examine data for      │    for sign reversals if data
            │   multicollinearity.    │    exhibit multicollinearity. Break
            └───────────┬─────────────┘    the pattern and/or use the
                        │                  backward elimination method,
                        │                  or get statistical help.
            ┌───────────▼─────────────┐
            │  Develop a second-pass  │
            │   multiple regression   │
            │    model (if needed).   │
            └───────────┬─────────────┘
                        │
            ┌───────────▼─────────────┐    Check residuals against
            │   Use residual analysis │    predictor variables or
            │  to check the second-pass│   y-pred. For time-ordered
            │         model.          │    data, check residuals
            └───────────┬─────────────┘    against time.
                        │                  Take corrective action if
            ┌───────────▼─────────────┐    needed. Get statistical help
            │  Develop a third-pass   │    if our remedial methods
            │   multiple regression   │    do not work.
            │    model (if needed).   │
            └───────────┬─────────────┘
                        │
            ┌───────────▼─────────────┐
            │   Use model to sense    │
            │ problem or make choices │
            │(explanation, prediction,│
            │        control).        │
            └─────────────────────────┘
```

Using Regression Models to Sense Problems

Consider equation (10.38), obtained by the backward elimination method for the job satisfaction study data:

$$\text{JOBSAT-PRED} = 15.02 + 1.18\text{GENDER} + .16\text{SALARY} - .80\text{EDUC} \quad (10.38)$$

This equation indicates that gender, salary level, and educational level affect job satisfaction. Examine each regression coefficient to determine what information a manager could obtain.

GENDER VARIABLE   After controlling for salary and education level, men (coded as 1) are more satisfied with their jobs than women (coded as 0) by a mean of 1.18 points on the 15-point job satisfaction scale.

While the impact of gender on job satisfaction is not great (only 1.18 points on a 15-point scale), women have less job satisfaction than their male counterparts. COMCEL should now diagnose the root causes. Perhaps a survey would be useful. Once COMCEL determines the root causes, it should design corrective actions to increase the job satisfaction level of women.

SALARY VARIABLE   After controlling for gender and education level, job satisfaction scores increase by a mean of .16 point for every additional $1(000) in salary. (Recall that salary was entered in units of $1,000.)

Should COMCEL consider paying higher salaries to its employees? Industry-wide statistics will be useful in determining whether COMCEL's salaries are out of line. If they are, it should consider higher salaries. This will increase job satisfaction and perhaps long-term retention of key personnel.

EDUC VARIABLE   After controlling for gender and salary, job satisfaction scores decrease by an average of .80 point for every additional year of education.

Why are more educated employees less satisfied at COMCEL? Are they underutilized? Are the jobs insufficiently challenging? Has COMCEL hired overqualified people? Before COMCEL can take corrective action, it must diagnose the root causes of the inverse relationship between job satisfaction and years of schooling.

Using Regression Models in Choice Making

We can also use regression models to help select effective actions. Here is the regression model for the COMCEL marketing study discussed in Section 10.1:

$$\text{UNITS SOLD-PRED} = 60.89 - .529\text{PRICE} + 3.312\text{ADS}$$

COMCEL's goal is to sell at least 40 phones per week per store. What price should the retail outlets charge and how many ads per week should they run? The negative price coefficient means that as COMCEL reduces its price, units sold increases. The positive ads regression coefficient means that as COMCEL increases the number of ads, units sold increases.

COMCEL developed this model for a price range of $80–$100 and for 1–5 ads per day. To increase sales, it should lower the price and increase the number of ads per day. The model predicts that COMCEL stores will sell 35.13 units at an $80 price and five ads per day:

UNITS SOLD-PRED $= 60.89 - .529(80) + 3.312(5) = 35.13$

The value of 35.13 units is below COMCEL's goal of 40 units. What should it do? It is considering charging less than $80 and/or running more than 5 ads per day. In statistical terms, COMCEL is now considering extrapolating the model. Recall that extrapolation is making predictions with a model outside the range of data used to construct it. Section 10.7 warned that a model may not yield valid predictions.

Extrapolating a regression model is a judgment call. However, because COMCEL's goal of 40 units has not been reached, it conducts a small-scale pilot study. It randomly selects several stores which try an $80 price and 7 ads per day. The model predicts that COMCEL will sell more than 40 units, but what are the actual mean sales in the test stores?

If the test stores' sales exceed 40 units per week, COMCEL will conclude that the same model yields valid predictions outside the range of the original study. It would then implement an $80 price and 7 ads per week in all retail stores or, if time permits, it could run additional pilot studies with more than 7 ads per day or charge a price of less than $80.

If test stores' sales fall significantly below 40 units per week, then COMCEL would conclude that it cannot use the same model to extrapolate. It will have to brainstorm for additional predictor variables apart from price and number of ads that may affect units sold. Then COMCEL can use the new regression model to determine how to achieve the goal of 40 units per week.

Problem sensing and choice making are essential managerial tasks. Regression models that detect and quantify relationships between variables are extremely helpful to problem sensing and choice making.

10.11 Determining Relationships Using the Chi-Square Test of Independence

ANOVA studies, regression analysis, and the chi-square test of independence are statistical tools used to detect relationships. The chi-square test of independence should be used when the observations in a sample can be cross-classified according to two criteria. The objective is to determine whether the two criteria of classification are related. We use a cross-tabs table to present the observations, which are data counts. By the end of this section you should be able to:

1. perform and interpret a chi-square test of independence; and
2. explain why mere differences among sample column percentages are not sufficient evidence of a relationship between two categorical variables.

In Chapter 3 we discussed a discrimination suit in which women claimed to have a smaller chance of being promoted than men. Table 10.33 on page 586 shows the results of a sample of 200 employees, cross-tabulated by gender and promotion status. Note that gender and promotion status are categorical vari-

Table 10.33

Cross-Tabs Data for Gender Discrimination Suit*

	Male	Female	
Promoted	80 (72.7%)	25 (27.8%)	105 (52.5%)
Not promoted	30 (27.3%)	65 (72.2%)	95 (47.5%)
	110 (100%)	90 (100%)	200 (100%)

*See Chapter 3 for information on how to construct cross-tabs tables.

ables with two levels each—male–female and promoted–not promoted—and that the data are counts. Is gender related to promotion status?

Table 10.33, a 2 × 2 cross-tabs table, shows the data counts for each combination of the two categorical variables. The numbers in parentheses are the *column percentages*. For example, 80 of the 110 males, or 72.7%, were promoted.

Suppose a person had just joined the firm and wanted to know the probability of being promoted. Would the answer vary depending on whether the person was male or female? Think about it before reading ahead.

Given Table 10.33, we would change our prediction based on the person's gender. The probability that any employee will be promoted is 52.5%. If the person is male, the probability increases to 72.7%. If the person is female, the probability decreases to 27.8%. Of the 90 females, only 25 were promoted.

The Need for Statistical Testing

If gender is not a predictor of promotion, then the *population* promotion rates for both males and females would be the same. Sample promotion rates of males and females will differ from the population percentages because of sampling error. For example, another sample of 200 employees would not yield exactly the same data as shown in Table 10.33. Remember, we are not interested in drawing conclusions about the sample of 200 employees. We wish to draw inferences about all employees in the target population.

In general, we ask the question: How different could the sample percentages be if the two categorical variables are really not related? In terms of Table 10.33, we ask the questions: Could the observed difference in promotion rates, 72.7% vs. 27.8%, be the result of sampling error? Is the population promotion rate the same for males and females?

Chi-Square Test of Independence

We studied statistical independence in Chapters 3–5. Two events are statistically independent when knowledge that one event has happened has no effect on the probability of the other event's happening. The null and alternative hypotheses for the discrimination data in Table 10.33 are given as:

Null hypothesis: Gender and promotion status are statistically independent (unrelated).

Alternative hypothesis: Gender and promotion status are statistically dependent (related).

The null and alternative hypotheses for ANOVA studies, regression analysis, and the test of independence are similar. All null hypotheses assume that the variables are not related.

If two events, A and B, are not related, then the joint probability of occurrence equals the product of the marginal probabilities:

$$P(A \text{ AND } B) = P(A) \cdot P(B) \qquad (10.39)$$

Assume that gender and promotion status are not related. That is, assume the null hypothesis is true.

1. What is the probability of selecting an employee who is male and promoted?
2. How many employees *should* have been males and promoted in a sample of 200?

We use expression (10.39) on the data in Table 10.33 to answer the first question:

$$P(\text{Male AND Promoted}) = P(\text{Male}) \cdot P(\text{Promoted})$$
$$= \left(\frac{110}{200}\right)\left(\frac{105}{200}\right)$$
$$= .55 \cdot .525$$
$$= .289$$

How many employees should have been males and promoted in a sample of 200 if $P(\text{Male AND Promoted}) = .289$? There should have been $.28875(200) = 57.75$ employees in the male and promoted cell of Table 10.33. This is the *expected frequency*, E. The *observed frequency*, O, was 80.

We compute the three remaining expected frequencies in a similar fashion:

$$E(\text{Male and Promoted}) = (.55)(.525)(200) = 57.75$$
$$E(\text{Male and Not promoted}) = (.55)(.475)(200) = 52.25$$
$$E(\text{Female and Promoted}) = (.45)(.525)(200) = 47.25$$
$$E(\text{Female and Not promoted}) = (.45)(.475)(200) = 42.75$$

Table 10.34 on page 588 shows the observed and expected frequencies for the discrimination data. The observed frequencies are in the upper left corner of each cell; the expected frequencies are in the lower right corner. If the observed and expected frequencies are similar, then we will fail to reject the null hypothesis of

Table 10.34

Observed and Expected Frequencies for Discrimination Study Data

	Male		Female		
Promoted	80	57.75	25	47.25	105
Not promoted	30	52.25	65	42.75	95
	110		90		200

statistical independence. If the observed and expected frequencies are very different, then we will reject the null hypothesis and conclude that gender and promotion status are related. But how different is very different?

The size of the following chi-square test statistic defines *very different*:

$$\chi^2 = \sum_i \sum_j \left[\frac{(O_{ij} - E_{ij})^2}{E_{ij}} \right] \quad (10.40)$$

Expression (10.40) says that for each cell: (1) subtract the expected from the observed frequency and square the result; (2) divide the squared result by the expected frequency; then (3) add the results from (2) for all cells.

Table 10.35 shows the calculation of the chi-square statistic for the discrimination data in Table 10.33.

Compare the value of the chi-square statistic against the chi-square tabled values found in Appendix 6. In general, the appropriate degrees of freedom for the test of independence are given by

Degrees of freedom = (Number of rows − 1) · (Number of columns − 1)

For the discrimination data, the degrees of freedom are (2 − 1)(2 − 1) = 1.

For the discrimination data in Table 10.35, we compare the test statistic value of 40.10 against the chi-square tabled values for one degree of freedom. The

Table 10.35

Calculations for Chi-Square Test Statistic for Discrimination Data

Cell	O(bserved)	E(xpected)	$(O - E)^2$	$(O - E)^2/E$
Male and Promoted	80	57.75	495.06	8.57
Male and Not promoted	30	52.25	495.06	9.47
Female and Promoted	25	47.25	495.06	10.48
Female and Not promoted	65	42.75	495.06	11.58
χ^2				40.10

test statistic is much larger than the 99.5th percentile value, which is 7.88. Thus the *p*-value is less than .005. Using the .05 rule, we reject the null hypothesis. We conclude that promotion status and gender are statistically related.

Is the firm guilty of discrimination? The fact that there is a significant relationship between gender and promotion status does not *necessarily* mean that gender is the cause of promotion status. There could be *intervening* variables. See Section 3.4 for a review of how to include intervening variables in the analysis.

We can use the chi-square test of independence when we have categorical variables with more than two levels. For example, is type of advertising (cooperative, comparative, or advocacy) related to level of product awareness (low, medium, or high)? Is level of social responsibility of a business (low, medium, or high) related to the type of business organization (proprietorship, partnership, or corporation)?

Dangers of Small Expected Frequencies

The test statistic, (10.40), is chi-square distributed *only* for large expected frequencies. We should use Appendix 6 to determine the *p*-value only when the expected frequencies are large. Just how large is large?

Do not use the chi-square test of independence under the following conditions:

1. For a 2 × 2 cross-tabs table when:
   a. the sample size, *n*, is less than 20.
   b. $20 < n < 40$ and any expected frequency is less than 5.
   c. $n > 40$ and any expected frequency is less than 1.
2. For larger than 2 × 2 cross-tabs tables when:
   a. more than 20% of the cells have expected frequencies less than 5.
   b. any cell has an expected frequency less than 1.

Summary

Use the chi-square test of independence to test for a relationship between two categorical variables. Calculate expected frequencies under the assumption (null hypothesis) that the two variables are statistically independent (unrelated). If the observed and expected frequencies are very different, the test statistic, (10.40), will be large and have a *p*-value less than an acceptable level of significance. Conclude that the assumption of independence is wrong. Reject the null hypothesis and conclude that the variables are dependent (related).

SECTION 10.11 EXERCISES

1. A chi-square statistic has a value of 5.78 for a 3 × 3 cross-tabs table.
   a. What are the degrees of freedom for a 3 × 3 table?
   b. Determine the *p*-value for the chi-square statistic.
   c. Would we reject the null hypothesis of statistical independence?

2. The larger the chi-square statistic, the more likely we are to reject the null hypothesis. Why?

3. We interview 1,000 investors. Six hundred have an annual income of over $50,000. Of these, 400 have invested in at least one real estate limited partnership. Of the 400 investors with incomes of $50,000 or less, 200 have invested in at least one limited partnership.
   a. Identify the categorical variables and their levels.
   b. Construct a 2 × 2 cross-tabs table.
   c. Compute the sample percentage of owning at least one limited partnership given that your income is less than or equal to $50,000.
   d. Compute the sample percentage of owning at least one limited partnership given that your income is more than $50,000.

4. Run the test of independence for the data in Exercise 3. Use a .01 p-value.

5. Shown is a 4 × 2 cross-tabs table on support for a balanced budget by region of the country. Two thousand registered voters are selected from the four regions.

	Strongly Support	Do Not Strongly Support	Total
Northeast	250	250	500
South	400	100	500
Midwest	300	200	500
West	250	250	500
	1,200	800	2,000

Perform a chi-square test of independence. Use a .10 p-value.

6. Employees of a multinational firm believe that an overseas assignment reduces the chances of promotion at the corporate headquarters. The Human Resources manager randomly selects a sample of 100 managers and develops the following 2 × 2 cross-tabs table.

	No Overseas Assignment	Overseas Assignment	Total
Promoted	16	24	40
Not promoted	22	38	60
	38	62	100

   a. Compute the sample percentage of being promoted given an overseas assignment.
   b. Compute the sample percentage of being promoted given no overseas assignment.
   c. Perform the chi-square test of independence on the two categorical variables. Use a .05 p-value.

7. Is level of information systems technology related to bottom-line performance of firms? The American Computing Group (ACG) conducts a survey of 100 firms in the banking industry. Fifty banks are performing above the industry median; 50 are not. The ACG asks each firm to indicate the highest level of information systems technology they have achieved. Shown are the cross-tabs data.

	Level of Information Technology		
	Transaction Processing	Decision Support	Executive Support
Below median	30	10	10
Above median	10	15	25

Perform the chi-square test of independence on the two categorical variables. Use a .10 p-value. What does the test tell you?

8. Is type of leadership related to level of worker job satisfaction? Shown are data for 50 workers.

	Autocratic Supervision	Participatory Supervision
Satisfied	11	26
Dissatisfied	9	4

Perform the chi-square test of independence on the two categorical variables. Use a .05 p-value. What does the test tell you?

9. We study 1,000 customers to determine whether level of product satisfaction is related to income level categories. Of the 1,000 people interviewed, 815 people are satisfied with the product; 390 people earn less than $20,000 and are satisfied with the product.

	Less than $20,000	$20,000–$50,000	More than $50,000	Total
Satisfied	390	325	100	815
Dissatisfied	10	75	100	185
	400	400	200	1,000

Perform the chi-square test of independence on the two categorical variables. Use a .001 p-value. What does the test tell you?

10.12 Integrating Framework

Managers solve problems, forecast and plan for the future, and control and allocate resources. To be effective in these roles, they must build mental models of how their departments or firms operate. Good mental models require an understanding of relationships between crucial business and economic variables. Over the last three chapters we have presented statistical methods for

1. *establishing* relationships (confidence intervals, hypothesis testing, chi-square test of independence) and
2. *measuring the degree of relationship* among variables (regression analysis).

Table 10.36 on page 592 outlines how the statistical tools from the last three chapters can help establish and measure relationships among business and economic variables.

Table 10.36
Integrating Framework for Detection of Relationships Among Variables

Tool	Dependent Variable	Predictor Variables	Sample Managerial Questions	Statistical Tools for Answering Questions
ANOVA studies	Quantitative	Categorical Quantitative	Do men watch TV more than women?	Dependent variable (hours of TV) is quantitative and the independent variable (gender) is categorical. Use a t-based confidence interval on the difference in means, or construct a confidence interval on the difference in medians.
			Do workers' compensation payments vary across three job classifications?	Dependent variable (payments) is quantitative and the independent variable (job classification) is categorical. Use the one-way ANOVA to test for differences in population means. Follow up with Tukey confidence intervals. Or, use the Kruskal–Wallis test on population medians, followed by Dunn's confidence intervals.
			Do the color and type of display affect volume of in-store traffic?	Dependent variable (number of customers) is quantitative and the independent variables (color and type of display) are categorical. Use the factorial ANOVA to test for interaction effect between color and type of display and main effects for each independent variable.
Regression analysis	Quantitative	Quantitative Categorical	Is manufacturing cost related to production run size and equipment age?	Dependent variable (cost) and independent variables (size of production run and age of equipment) are quantitative. Use multiple linear regression if the residual plots suggest that the model is adequate and the p-value of variance ratio is less than your acceptable level of significance. If residual plots suggest serious violations of assumptions, ask a statistician for help.
			Is number of units sold related to salespeoples' years of experience and participation in the profit sharing plan?	Dependent variable (units sold) is quantitative. One independent variable is quantitative (experience) and one is qualitative (1 = yes, 0 = no). Use multiple linear regression if the residual plots suggest that the model is adequate and the p-value of variance ratio is less than your acceptable level of significance. If residual plots suggest serious violations of assumptions, ask a statistician for help.
Test for independence	Categorical Quantitative	Categorical Quantitative	labor force mobility related to the level of the economy?	Both variables are categorical—high or low mobility and expansion or recession. Observations are data counts. Develop a cross-tabs table. Use the test for independence.
			Is distance from black neighborhoods related to whites' attitudes toward integration?	Attitude is a categorical variable—pro or con. The distance variable, which is quantitative, has been transformed into a categorical variable—less than 3 miles, 3–7 miles, more than 7 miles. Observations are data counts. Develop a cross-tabs table. Use the test of independence.

COMCEL

Date: October 10, 1992
To: Ann Tabor, CEO
From: Cherian Jain, V.P., Marketing Research
Re: Analysis of Market Research Study to Improve Sales of Model 76 Phones

SUMMARY
We should reduce the price of the Model 76 phone to $80 and run five ads per day on the most highly rated AM station in those cities where our retail stores are located. These actions will increase sales to about 35 units per store per week and will reduce our inventory.

SUPPORTING ANALYSIS
We selected 24 outlets with comparable sales from different cities across the country. We then tested the impact of four different prices and three different frequencies of ads on sales. We assigned each combination of price and advertising to two different outlets for one week. The ads were aired on the most highly rated AM station in each test city during the morning drive time. We then recorded the number of Model 76 phones sold during the test week.

Using regression analysis, we found the following relationship between sales vs. price and the number of radio ads aired per day:

$$\text{UNITS SOLD–PRED} = 60.89 - .529\,\text{PRICE} + 3.312\,\text{ADS}$$

The .529 numerical weight of the PRICE variable measures the effect of price on sales. Each dollar increase in price (between $80 and $100) reduces the mean number of units sold by about one-half phone.

The 3.312 numerical weight of the ADS variable measures the effect of number of ads per day on sales. Each additional ad results in a mean increase of over 3 phones sold per week.

To increase sales, the regression model suggests that we drop the price and increase the number of ads. The model predicts that our stores will sell 35.13 units per week at an $80 price and with five ads per day. Dropping the price below $80 or running more than five ads might further increase sales. However, we would be extrapolating the model, and extrapolation is risky. Before seriously considering prices under $80, we should run additional studies to see if we continue to obtain increasing sales with dropping prices.

Finally, we can use the above model to control sales. If an outlet charges $80 and runs five ads per day, it should sell about 35 units per week. If actual sales fall significantly below 35 units, we have a possible disturbance problem that must be diagnosed. If actual sales are significantly above 35 units, we may have an opportunity to improve sales by determining why sales were better than predicted.

CHAPTER 10 QUESTIONS

1. Why is it important for managers to predict, explain, and control?
2. Develop a *words-only* mental model based on the regression equation (10.1).
3. Distinguish between experimental and correlation regression studies.
4. Distinguish between cross-sectional and time-ordered studies.
5. Does lack of a linear relationship mean that two variables are completely unrelated?
6. During the *introduction phase* of a product, sales are initially very slow and then increase at an increasing rate. If we have time-ordered data, sales vs. time, would we expect a straight line to represent the data accurately?
7. In simple terms, what is a sample conditional mean?
8. Why isn't the sample conditional mean the same as the population conditional mean?
9. What does "minimizing the sum of squared deviations" mean?
10. What must be true in order for the SSE(rror) term to be zero?
11. Why are marginal t-tests necessary? What information do they provide that the analysis of variance table does not?
12. Suppose the sample regression coefficients are not zero. Why can't we conclude that the variables are related? Why must we do an ANOVA?
13. How do we calculate residuals?
14. If all the assumptions of the linear regression model are met, what should the residual plots look like?
15. If the original data are nonlinear, what should the plot of the residuals vs. the predictor variable look like?
16. If the plot of residuals vs. time follows a recurring up–down pattern, what does that pattern suggest?
17. If we compute the best fitting line by hand and all the residuals are negative, what does this mean?
18. *Logically*, why must prediction intervals be wider than confidence intervals?
19. When should we use prediction intervals and when should we use confidence intervals?
20. Why should we reduce the width of either confidence or prediction intervals?
21. Distinguish indicator variables from quantitative variables.
22. We have included a method of assigning a value to the inventory variable in a regression study—LIFO and FIFO. Show two different ways we could code this variable using a (0, 1) scheme.
23. Will the two different coding schemes produce different regression equations?
24. Will the two different coding schemes produce different predictions for y using their respective regression equations?
25. In the hospital study, how were we able to use only two indicator variables to represent three types of hospitals? Explain.
26. In simple terms, what is multicollinearity?
27. Why is multicollinearity more likely in a correlational regression study than in an experimental regression study?

28. Multicollinearity affects the stability of the sample regression coefficients. Why is this a problem?
29. Explain how a strategy to break the pattern reduces multicollinearity.
30. One explanation for a sign reversal is multicollinearity. What is another explanation?
31. Explain how a regression model can help managers detect potential problems.
32. Distinguish when regression analysis and the chi-square test of independence should be used.
33. Why can't we merely look at the cross-tabs data and determine whether the two categorical variables are related? Why must we test for independence statistically?
34. What role does the chi-square table (Appendix 6) play in the statistical test of independence?
35. Are the null hypotheses in the test of independence and regression analysis saying the same thing?

CHAPTER 10 APPLICATION PROBLEMS

Problems 1–7 use the following data set.

Shown is a data set for 16 skilled workers. DAYS (the number of days a worker exceeded quota during last quarter) is the dependent variable. There are five predictor variables. AGE is a *proxy* variable for experience in the labor force. A proxy variable is a substitute for a variable that we cannot directly measure. CLOSENESS of supervision is the degree to which workers are constantly watched and supervised. A score of 10 indicates very close supervision. SALARY is a worker's annual salary in thousands of dollars. TRAINING is the number of hours of skill training in the past quarter. EQUIP is the age in years of the equipment that a worker uses.

Worker	DAYS	AGE	CLOSENESS	SALARY	TRAINING	EQUIP
1	6	25	5	22	15	6
2	3	28	9	28	25	8
3	3	24	10	25	30	2
4	7	26	4	24	10	3
5	13	30	1	29	5	1
6	7	32	6	32	15	1
7	11	35	2	38	15	2
8	3	35	7	32	3	2
9	8	38	3	36	10	3
10	4	40	9	35	20	4
11	4	41	10	39	15	1
12	7	42	2	43	0	8
13	3	43	8	30	5	6
14	10	44	3	30	23	3
15	3	50	7	32	8	5
16	9	52	2	41	5	1

1. What is the unit of association? What type of study is it: cross-sectional vs. time-ordered; experimental vs. correlational?

2. Draw a scatter diagram between DAYS and each predictor variable. Do the predictor variables appear to be related to DAYS?

3. Use our software to compute the multiple regression model with all five predictor variables. Use the .05 *p*-value rule to test the null hypothesis.

4. Use our software to perform the follow-up *t*-tests. Are all the predictor variables needed in the model?

5. Remove all predictor variables (one at a time) that have *p*-values greater than .05. Use our software to compute the new regression model with the remaining predictor variables.

6. Use our software to compute the residuals from the regression model. Draw residual plots against each remaining predictor variable in the model. Have the linearity, equal variances, normality, and independence assumptions been met?

7. Explain how you could now use the new model to explain, predict, and control.

Problems 8–13 use the data set in the Appendix of this chapter.

The data set consists of 50 observations. JOBSATisfaction is the dependent variable. There are seven predictor variables—AGE, SALARY, GENDER, YEARS, EDUC, EXPER, and MANAG. GENDER and MANAG are indicator variables.

8. What is the unit of association? What type of study is it: cross-sectional vs. time-ordered; experimental vs. correlational?

9. Draw a scatter diagram between JOBSAT and each predictor variable. Remember, GENDER and MANAG are indicator variables that can take only two values—0 or 1. Do the predictor variables appear to be related to JOBSAT?

10. Use our software to compute the multiple regression model with all seven predictor variables. Use the .05 *p*-value rule to test the null hypothesis.

11. The correlation matrix indicates a multicollinearity problem. Use the backward elimination method to reduce the number of predictor variables in the model. Use the .05 *p*-value rule to eliminate variables.

12. Use our software to compute the residuals from the new regression model. Draw residual plots for each remaining predictor variable in the model. Have the linearity, equal variances, normality, and independence assumptions been met?

13. Explain how you could now use the new model to explain, predict, and control.

Problems 14–20 use the following data set.

A staff manager runs a planned change study to determine whether the size of the problem solving group and the amount of group problem solving training are related to performance on a group task. He selects four groups of two, four, and six workers for a total of 12 groups. For each set of four groups, he provides two groups with four hours of training and two groups with no training. Shown are the data.

GROUP	PERF	GROUPSIZE	TRAIN
1	50	2	0
2	52	2	0
3	68	2	4
4	72	2	4

(continued)

GROUP	PERF	GROUPSIZE	TRAIN
5	57	4	0
6	63	4	0
7	79	4	4
8	83	4	4
9	70	6	0
10	69	6	0
11	88	6	4
12	92	6	4

14. What is the unit of association? What type of study is it: cross-sectional vs. time-ordered; experimental vs. correlational?

15. Draw a scatter diagram between PERF and each predictor variable. Do the predictor variables appear to be related to PERF?

16. Use our software to compute the multiple regression model with both predictor variables. Use the .05 *p*-value rule to test the null hypothesis.

17. Use our software to perform the follow-up *t*-tests. Are all the predictor variables needed in the model?

18. Plot a scatter diagram of GROUPSIZE vs. TRAIN. Do the predictor variables appear to be related? Also check the correlation matrix from the computer output. Is multicollinearity a problem? Interpret the sample regression coefficients.

19. Use our software to compute the residuals from the regression model. Draw residual plots for each predictor variable in the model. Have the linearity, equal variances, normality, and independence assumptions been met?

20. Use our software to obtain a confidence interval on the mean task performance for a group of size three and with two hours of training. Use our software to obtain a prediction interval on the task performance for a single group of size three with two hours of training.

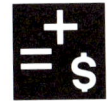

Problems 21–25 use the following data set.

All publicly traded firms are required to have their financial statements audited by an independent C.P.A. firm. When planning for the year's end, the comptroller is concerned about two things: the cost of the audit (in dollars) and the length of time the audit will take. The audit contract is negotiated by the Board of Directors. The comptroller, however, might be able to take steps to reduce audit time, and therefore the disruption to normal activities.

An organization of 30 comptrollers has pooled data to measure the effects of three variables on the amount of time needed (hours) to complete an audit. The first variable is sales—the larger the company, the more time an audit is likely to require. The second is the number of hours spent on internal audit—a function carried out within the firm by the company's own employees. The feeling is that the more work done by the company's employees, the less time an outside auditor will need to spend. The third is the strength of internal controls—how tightly the accounting process is controlled on a day-to-day basis. For this study, controls were categorized as either strong ($=1$) or weak ($=0$).

The following data were collected (sales are in $millions).

FIRM	HOURS	SALES	IN-AUDIT	CONTROL	FIRM	HOURS	SALES	IN-AUDIT	CONTROL
1	78.5	5.8	3,695.9	0	16	459.8	7.9	2,898.6	1
2	574.2	12.3	3,221.4	1	17	999.2	18.7	3,945.6	1
3	972.7	16.3	2,686.6	0	18	473.2	9.4	2,264.5	0
4	1,220.7	21.7	3,062.6	1	19	786.4	15.1	2,024.0	1
5	1,061.7	19.9	3,296.1	1	20	896.1	15.5	2,947.3	1
6	866.3	15.9	2,770.0	1	21	1,157.9	18.3	3,380.9	0
7	782.2	16.6	2,584.2	1	22	1,021.3	19.3	3,363.4	1
8	687.6	13.1	2,712.0	0	23	1,423.4	22.9	3,027.0	1
9	665.0	14.2	3,167.3	1	24	357.8	11.5	2,974.1	1
10	704.8	13.8	3,482.1	1	25	1,123.4	20.4	3,541.1	1
11	545.9	11.9	3,109.8	1	26	531.1	11.1	3,757.7	1
12	709.1	14.9	3,594.0	1	27	533.0	12.7	2,789.2	1
13	1,030.4	17.3	2,247.6	1	28	903.4	16.8	2,458.8	1
14	598.9	10.0	2,429.8	0	29	731.1	14.4	3,200.6	1
15	701.9	13.4	2,846.6	1	30	909.7	17.6	2,563.0	1

21. Draw a scatter diagram between HOURS and each predictor variable. Do the predictor variables appear to be linearly or nonlinearly related to HOURS?

22. Use our software to compute the multiple regression model with all three predictor variables. Were the auditors' assumptions correct about each of the predictor variables? Use the .05 p-value rule to draw your conclusions.

23. The auditors believed that SALES, IN-AUDIT, and CONTROL should be related to HOURS. If some of these independent variables are not significant in a multiple regression model, the reason could be that the independent variables are correlated. When two of the three variables are known, the third variable is redundant. Plot SALES and CONTROL against IN-AUDIT to check for multicollinearity. Do the graphs help to explain the results in Problem 22?

24. Use our software to compute the residuals from the final regression model. Draw residual plots for each predictor variable in the model. Have the linearity, equal variances, normality, and independence assumptions been met?

25. What policy implications could the comptrollers draw from this analysis?

26. Suppose that a particular cancer is indicated by a test using a count of chromosome effects, COUNT. There are two predictor variables: CIG is the number of cigarettes an individual smokes each day; ALCOH is the number of ounces of alcohol the individual drinks each day. The project manager has proposed the following regression model:

$$\text{COUNT-PRED} = b_0 + b_1 \text{CIG} + b_2 \text{ALCOH}$$

From previous studies, we know that the combined effect of heavy smoking and drinking produces a higher count of chromosome effects than would be predicted by each predictor variable singly.

   a. Is the above model appropriate given the known information?
   b. Propose a more realistic model that incorporates the idea that the combined effect of heavy smoking and drinking produces a higher count of chromosome effects than would be predicted by each predictor variable singly.

27. We wish to study whether female union members are earning the same amount of money, SALARY, as comparably situated male union members. Thus we include a GENDER variable in the model. According to Title VII and empirical studies of lifetime earnings, the only economically and legally justifiable factor explaining earnings differential is seniority. The plaintiffs use two measures of seniority: (1) years on job, YRS, and (2) age in years, AGE. The plaintiffs propose the following regression model:

$$\text{SALARY-PRED} = b_0 + b_1 \text{AGE} + b_2 \text{YRS} + b_3 \text{GENDER}$$

a. If females are represented as GENDER = 0 and males as GENDER = 1, and if females receive significantly lower salaries than comparably situated males, should the sign of the *sample* regression coefficient, b_3, be positive or negative? Discuss.

b. If females are represented as GENDER = 0 and males as GENDER = 1, and if females receive the same salaries as comparably situated males, what will the *population* regression coefficient for the GENDER variable equal? Discuss.

c. Suppose we wish to estimate the effect of YEARS on SALARY, after controlling for the impact of AGE and GENDER. Given the three predictor variables, is multicollinearity likely to be a problem? (*Hint:* Are AGE and YEARS likely to be related?)

d. If AGE and YEARS exhibit multicollinearity, will we be able to interpret the sample regression coefficient for the GENDER variable?

28. In *Segar v. Smith*, the plaintiffs introduced four regression models of annual salary using the following predictor variables: education, years of prior federal experience, years of prior nonfederal experience, and race. The RACE variable was coded as follows.

$$\text{RACE} = \begin{cases} 1 & \text{if agent is a minority} \\ 0 & \text{otherwise} \end{cases}$$

The study included several hundred agents of the Drug Enforcement Agency. Shown are the parameter estimates for the race coefficients and their *t*-values in the four models.

Year	Race Coefficient	*t*-Value	Two Tail *p*-Value
1976	−$1,864	−2.54	<.015
1977	−$1,119	−3.18	<.005
1978	−$ 866	−2.07	<.040
1979	−$1,026	−2.30	<.030

a. Have the plaintiffs shown that minority drug enforcement agents receive lower annual salaries than comparably situated white officers? Discuss.

b. The defendants argued that since the four multiple coefficients of determination, R^2, ranged between .42 and .52 (computations not shown above), the plaintiffs' case should be dismissed. The judge rejected this argument. Explain the judge's logic in arguing that the value of R^2 was not a critical factor in accepting the plaintiffs' four studies.

29. A substantial portion of a large shipment of oil was damaged due to sedimentation in some of the tanks or holds of an oil tanker. Oil chemists thought that sedimentation could have been due to the *shipper* neglecting to make sure that a particular type of oil (type A) was *not* present in all the tanks. Type A oil is suspected of causing sedimentation. Alternatively, the temperature at which the oil is loaded into the tanker and discharged at the port also may cause sedimentation. Loading and discharge temperatures are the responsibility of the *oil carrier*. Thus two different parties may have been responsible for the sedimentation and the damage. An arbitration panel had to decide which party should pay the major share of the damages. A third party provided regression analysis data to the arbitration panel. This study had the following variables:

Dependent variable: Percentage of sediment in the tanks, SEDIMENT
Predictor variables: Discharge temperature in Fahrenheit, DISCH
Loading temperature in Fahrenheit, LOAD
Presence of type A oil, TYPEA = 1 if type A oil is absent from tanks, 0 if otherwise.

Shown is the regression model based on 13 tanks of an oil tanker:

$$\text{SEDIMENT-PRED} = -4.97 - 3.19\text{TYPEA} + .014\text{DISCH} + .038\text{LOAD}$$

Parameter Estimates

Variable	Parameter Estimate	t-Value	Two Tail p-Value
INTERCEPT	−4.97	—	
TYPEA	−3.19	−7.22	<.001
DISCH	+.014	+1.02	>.300
LOAD	+.038	+1.36	>.100

a. Explain in simple terms the meaning of the sample regression coefficients for the three predictor variables.
b. Given the above data, which predictor variable appears to have the most significant impact on percentage of sedimentation? Discuss.
c. Given the above data, what do you think the arbitration panel concluded? That is, who was more responsible for the sedimentation damage—the shipper whose job is to ensure that type A oil is not present or the oil carrier who is responsible for the loading and discharge? Discuss.

30. Lenders who offer mortgages on single-family homes can usually get protection against borrower default by requiring mortgage guarantee insurance. One source of insurance is the Federal Housing Administration (FHA). The premium on such insurance becomes part of the purchaser's monthly payment.

    In forecasting demand for loans, the FHA believes the number of loans insured (the dependent variable) varies directly with the loan-to-value ratio (the amount borrowed/the market value of the house), the length of the loan (TERM), and the interest rate of the loan. In addition, FHA expects to insure fewer loans as the price of the insurance rises. The price of insurance is a fixed percentage of the loan.

    Data are collected over a number of quarters, and the following model* is developed to predict the number of mortgages that will require insurance:

---

*David L. Kasserman, "Default Risk and the Home Mortgage Insurance Industry," *Quarterly Review of Economics and Business* 18, no. 4 (Winter 1978): 59–68.

Variable	Parameter Estimate	Standard Error	t-Value
INTERCEPT	−79.21	16.85	−4.70
LOAN-VALUE	.58	.24	2.45
TERM	1.72	.69	2.51
INTEREST-RATE	2.37	.53	4.51
INSURE-PRICE	−94.54	15.19	−6.22

Number of observations: 58 R^2: .82

a. Given the size of the four *t*-values, would you conclude that all four predictor variables should be retained?

b. Interpret each of the regression coefficients in terms a manager would understand.

31. A critical step in auditing the financial statements of a firm involves assessing the strength of internal controls. One measure is compliance with established policies and procedures, e.g., having credit limits checked and authorized before processing a sales invoice. First, the auditor must make a judgment as to what the error rate (no authorization) is for the population of sales invoices that will be checked. This information is then used to determine the sample size, and later to test the hypothesis that the observed error rate is within acceptable bounds.

To assist in making the preliminary estimate of the population error rate, an auditing firm decides to construct a regression model based on a sample of 100 firms audited during the previous year. The dependent variable is the error rate (in percent). The auditors believe that error rates are related to (1) the volume of transactions processed during the accounting period, (2) the mean size of a sales invoice—large transactions are more likely to be properly handled, (3) the number of transactions per clerical worker during the period—high volume is expected to lead to higher error rates, and (4) the number of transactions per temporary worker—error rates are expected to be higher for this group because temporaries are less experienced and less committed than permanent employees. The results of the regression analysis appear here.

Variable	Parameter Estimate	Standard Error	t-Value
INTERCEPT	.56763		
VOLUME	.00011	.00002	5.50
AVESIZE	−.00261	.00064	−4.08
TRANS/CLERICAL	.00075	.00146	.52
TRANS/TEMP	.00458	.00144	3.18

R^2: .352

a. Can we say from these results that error rate is not related to the number of transactions per clerical worker? Explain.

b. If the volume of transactions rose by 1,000 over a previous period, would the error rate increase by .11% or by 11%, assuming that the other variables in the model stayed the same?

c. "Temporary employees are causing most of our errors in compliance." Evaluate.

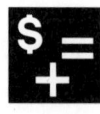

32. Banks, like other firms, can follow a strategy of growth through acquisition. An important consideration in any acquisition is, of course, the price. The purchase price of an acquired bank can be above, equal to, or below the acquired bank's net asset value—the market value of the acquired bank's assets less the market value of its liabilities. If the purchase price is above the net asset value, then the acquired bank is selling at a premium. If the price is below net asset value, then the bank is selling at a discount.

   Bankers believe that the growth rate of the bank to be acquired, as measured by the growth rate in deposits, has some influence on the purchase premium/discount. Another variable is profitability. In banking circles, one measure of profitability is the net interest spread (the difference between the rates paid depositors, and the rates charged to borrowers). Finally, the tax status of the transaction (taxable = 0, nontaxable = 1) should also have some influence, since shareholders of the acquired bank should demand a higher price to compensate for the additional taxes they will have to pay.

   Data have been collected for a number of bank acquisitions,* and the following model developed to predict the dependent variable—premium or discount—measured in percent:

Variable	Parameter Estimate	Standard Error	t-Value
Intercept	−42.95	20.26	2.12
Deposit growth	4.03	.85	4.72
Net interest spread	11.21	3.96	2.83
Tax status	−16.37	7.78	−2.10

   $F(4, 45) = 12.57 \quad R^2 = .53$

   a. Using a p-value of .05, would you conclude that all of the predictor variables should be retained?
   b. Interpret each of the regression coefficients in terms a manager would understand.

33. The IRS is always concerned about taxpayers' compliance with the tax laws. The tax code requires that when services are bartered (exchanged for other services), the fair value of those services should be reported as income. A staff member proposed that a predictive model could be developed from the data collected on past taxpayer audits. The proposed model would be used to predict which taxpayers were underreporting taxable income and should be audited.

   The dependent variable is the dollar amount of taxable barter income not reported by the taxpayer. The independent variables were (1) the amount of income from wages reported on form W-2, (2) the amount of self-employment income reported on Schedule C, and (3) the type of business engaged in by the taxpayer: professional = 1 and nonprofessional = 0.

---

*Adapted from: Randolph P. Beatty, John F. Reim, and Robert F. Schapperle, "The Effect of Barriers to Entry on Bank Shareholder Wealth: Implications for Interstate Banking," *Journal of Bank Research* 16, no. 1 (Spring 1985): 8–13.

Variable	Parameter Estimate	Standard Error
Intercept	−12,231.2	
W-2	.237	.063
Schedule C	.122	.015
Business type	1.572	709.797

Degrees of freedom: 96

a. Interpret the regression coefficients in managerial terms.
b. Which, if any, of the independent variables are linearly related to unreported barter income? Use a 1% level of significance (p-value < .01).
c. Does the intercept value of −12,231.2 mean that taxpayers, who report no W-2 income and no Schedule C income and are not professionals, *overpay* their income taxes by $12,231.20? Explain.
d. Suppose the IRS removed any insignificant independent variables from the model. What limitations do you see in using the final model to predict underreported (barter) income of future taxpayers?

34. Best Dairy Inc. knows that the Macho consumers have lower incomes than do the Status Seeker consumers. They wonder if Machos and Status Seekers also have different preferences for skim and whole milk. The marketing manager conducts a survey to determine if Machos and Status Seekers equally prefer skim and whole milk. He wants to verify that Best Dairy has meaningfully segmented its market. Best Dairy Inc. interviews 200 customers and cross-classifies them by the following two categorical variables. Use the .05 p-value rule to determine whether the two categorical variables are related.

	Machos	Status Seekers	Total
Skim	30	80	110
Whole	70	20	90
	100	100	200

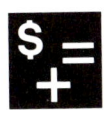

35. A stock analyst specializing in the retail industry wants to know if chain stores such as JC Penney stress the same focus—service or price—as do independents. She surveys 30 independents and 20 chains and determines whether they are price or service oriented. Here are the data. Use the .05 p-value rule to determine whether the two categorical variables are related.

	Service	Price	Total
Independents	25	5	30
Chains	4	16	20
	29	21	50

36. A human resource development manager for a large firm wishes to know if the percentage of extraverts and introverts (as measured by the Myers–Briggs Type Indicator) varies by management level. She randomly selects 100 upper-level managers, 400 mid-level managers, and 500 lower-level managers. Here are the data.

Use the .05 p-value rule to determine whether the two categorical variables are related.

	Extravert	Introvert	Total
Upper	65	35	100
Mid	250	150	400
Lower	330	170	500
	645	355	1,000

37. A personnel manager of a large company wants to assess employees' desires for flex-time among four different divisions of a large factory. The personnel manager selects a random sample of 200 employees from each division and asks each for his or her opinion of flex-time. The results are shown.

	Division 1	2	3	4
Favor	146	150	142	84
Oppose	54	50	58	116
	200	200	200	200

a. Convert the numbers in each column to percentages of the column total.
b. Based solely on the differences among the percentages in the first row, does it appear that there is a difference among divisions regarding the percentage that favor the proposed package? What tentative policy conclusions could the personnel manager draw?
c. Perform a chi-square analysis to determine whether the two categorical variables are related. Use the .05 p-value rule to draw your conclusions.
d. Explain how the results of the chi-square test help the manager to draw policy conclusions. In simple terms, what does the manager know after performing the test that he or she did not know before?

38. Elizabeth Dole, former U.S. Secretary of Labor, referred to a "glass ceiling" that allegedly keeps women and minorities out of the top echelons of corporate management. The personnel manager of a large corporation wants to be sure that women and minorities are not discriminated against in promotion decisions in his corporation. He examines all of the promotion decisions made over the past two years. The results are shown.

	White Males	Minorities	Total
Promoted	55	15	70
Not promoted	45	45	90
	100	60	160

a. Based on this sample of promotion decisions, does it appear that white males are favored in the promotion decision? Explain your conclusion in terms of the p-value of the test.

The personnel director repeated the study above, but this time he divided the sample into those that had an MBA degree and those that did not. The sample results are shown.

	MBA Group		No MBA Group	
	White Males	Minorities	White Males	Minorities
Promoted	30	10	25	5
Not promoted	15	5	30	40

    b. Does it appear that any difference in promotion rates is due to the education of the candidate and not minority status? Explain.

39.

Date: June 12, 1992
To: Bill O'Hara, Vice-President of Marketing
From: Cherian Jain, Manager of Marketing Research
Subject: Regression Analysis on Share of Market Data

I just reviewed the latest share of market report for our 30 sales territories. Our overall share of market nationally is 39%. While very good, there is much variation over our 30 sales territories. For example, we have only 10-11% SOM in Albany, NY, and Chicago but over 70% in Dallas and New York. I have been wondering why there is so much variation. I will be reviewing our share-of-market data base to see if I can draw some conclusions. I will forward my results to you when I have completed my regression analysis.

Use Data Base III and develop a memo along with the attached analysis.

40.

Date: February 3, 1992
To: Bill O'Hara, Vice-President of Marketing
From: Pam Ascher, National Sales Manager
Subject: Regression Analysis of Forces Affecting Atlanta Sales

In your January 24th memo, you asked me to review what factors affect sales in the Atlanta market. I have already sent you a preliminary analysis that indicated those factors that I believe affect sales.

I thought a more complete analysis is warranted. Accordingly, I will be sending you a more formal report that uses proven and sound statistical methods for drawing conclusions from the data. It will support my quick analysis and allow us to determine more exactly the impact of the various factors on sales. It will also allow us to make accurate predictions of future sales in the territory. What especially excites me is the possibility of taking what we learn in Atlanta and applying it throughout the Southern region and perhaps nationally. I look forward to your comments on my analysis.

Use Data Base II and develop a memo along with the attached analysis.

REFERENCES

MOSTELLER, F., and J. TUKEY. *Data Analysis and Regression Analysis*. Reading, Mass.: Addison-Wesley Publishing Co., 1977.

NETER, J., W. WASSERMAN, and M. KUTNER. *Applied Linear Statistical Models*, 2nd edition. Homewood, Illinois: Richard D. Irwin, 1985.

ROBERTS, H. *Data Analysis for Managers with Minitab*. Redwood City, Calif.: The Scientific Press, 1988.

APPENDIX

Job Satisfaction Data

OBS	Age	Gender	Salary	Years	Experience	Education	Management	Job Satisfaction
1	23	1	35.98	5	0	17	0	9.9
2	31	0	28.42	11	0	14	0	7.8
3	64	1	59.09	30	5	16	1	11.8
4	46	1	34.48	12	7	16	0	10.4
5	34	1	23.98	12	1	15	0	9.3
6	39	0	41.56	7	2	17	0	8.8
7	31	1	18.10	4	6	15	0	6.1
8	19	0	18.51	1	0	15	0	7.0
9	33	0	13.16	2	1	14	0	4.3
10	26	0	15.41	2	1	14	0	5.1
11	62	1	57.26	27	6	16	0	12.9
12	18	0	10.31	1	0	13	0	5.2
13	21	1	13.36	4	0	13	0	9.6
14	60	1	37.77	16	7	16	0	8.6
15	26	1	21.19	7	0	16	0	5.5
16	25	0	30.74	1	0	16	0	6.2
17	18	0	10.45	1	0	12	0	3.8
18	40	1	59.86	6	2	19	1	11.7
19	30	1	10.94	4	2	13	0	4.9
20	20	1	19.77	2	0	15	1	11.2
21	61	0	33.21	22	0	15	0	8.5
22	22	0	19.93	2	2	16	0	5.4
23	35	1	46.62	5	0	17	1	10.1
24	18	0	19.69	1	0	13	0	9.9
25	22	0	11.37	2	1	12	0	5.7
26	36	1	41.75	5	2	18	0	6.4
27	69	0	21.30	21	2	13	0	8.7
28	24	0	12.54	2	0	13	1	5.1
29	37	1	40.96	14	0	16	1	11.9
30	26	0	10.70	5	2	12	0	5.6
31	43	1	18.90	18	2	13	0	9.3

Gender: 1 if male, 0 if female.
Management: 1 if management responsibility, 0 if not.

(continued)

OBS	Age	Gender	Salary	Years	Experience	Education	Management	Job Satisfaction
32	40	1	38.60	9	1	16	0	5.6
33	43	0	41.48	7	1	16	1	10.6
34	27	0	27.58	2	0	16	0	9.3
35	70	0	50.55	6	9	16	1	10.2
36	37	1	55.52	16	0	19	1	6.8
37	32	0	12.00	5	3	12	0	6.2
38	30	0	19.91	9	0	13	1	10.2
39	29	0	17.22	4	0	13	0	8.4
40	36	0	17.48	9	0	12	0	6.8
41	31	0	19.40	5	2	14	0	10.1
42	20	1	18.48	2	0	15	0	8.3
43	46	1	35.99	11	8	14	0	11.2
44	20	1	17.71	3	0	14	0	9.0
45	46	1	49.56	7	5	18	0	8.6
46	62	0	30.66	7	12	16	0	9.7
47	34	0	15.21	4	3	15	0	4.3
48	48	1	43.93	22	0	16	0	10.5
49	34	1	39.64	12	0	16	0	8.9
50	29	1	25.70	13	0	13	1	13.1

11

Forecasting and Time Series Analysis

11.1 Data patterns and forecasting
11.2 Alternative forecasting approaches
    Quantitative forecasting approaches
    Qualitative approaches
11.3 Forecasting using regression analysis
    Autoregressive modeling
    Leading and coincident indicators
    Developing the model
    Analyzing residuals
    Mean absolute percentage error
    Limitations of regression models as forecasting tools
    Summary
11.4 Forecasting using the classical decomposition method
    Additive and multiplicative models
    Ratio to moving average method
    Deseasonalized data
    The trend pattern
    The cycle pattern
    Short-term forecasting
    Summary of the decomposition method
11.5 Qualitative forecasting methods
    Expert panels
    Delphi method
11.6 Key ideas and overview
Chapter 11 Questions
Chapter 11 Application Problems

CHAPTER OUTLINE

COMCEL Interoffice Communication

Date: August 13, 1993
To: Howard Bright, Manager, Norcross Plant
From: Ann Tabor, CEO
Re: Demand Forecasts for Car Phones in the Southern Region

I have seen your forecasts for the demand for our telephones in the Southern Region. If the forecasts materialize, we will be the industry leader. But frankly, I have my doubts about your numbers. They seem too optimistic to me. Since our production schedule depends so heavily on these forecasts, we need to be sure of our numbers.

How did you generate these forecasts? Please provide me with a detailed description of the forecasting methodology. I will feel better when I can concur with your forecasts.

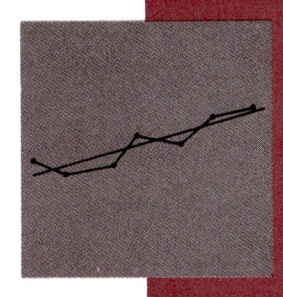

11.1 Data Patterns and Forecasting

Managers develop historical and forecasting models to predict the future and to detect significant deviations from expected behavior. Historical models look to the past. Under the assumption that the best estimate of the future is the recent past, managers expect continuity of performance. Whatever happened in the recent past should continue into the near future. If it does not, there may be a disturbance problem. Forecasting or planning models are forward looking. They serve two purposes. First, planning models set targets and goals for future performance. When actual future performance does not meet planned levels, managers may face a disturbance problem. Second, they provide basic input for developing production schedules and determining manpower, raw material, and capital equipment needs. In summary, accurate forecasts are essential in establishing, achieving, and monitoring progress toward business goals. Learning how to develop accurate forecasts is the goal of this chapter.

We will develop forecasts using time-ordered data. Time-ordered, or time series, data are data collected over time—data in chronological sequence. Forecasting begins by drawing a line graph of the historical data. The horizontal axis is time and the vertical axis is the level of the business or economic variable. Line graphs help managers see the systematic patterns underlying the data.

There are three common systematic patterns for time-ordered data: trend, seasonal, and cyclical. Time series data can include one or more of these patterns.

A *trend* pattern occurs when there is a long-term increase or decrease in the data. Figure 11.1 shows the product life cycle. Ignoring the roughness in the data, we see that, in Phase I, sales increase at an increasing rate—a nonlinear trend pattern. In Phase II, sales increase at a constant rate—a linear trend pattern. In Phase III, sales increase but at a decreasing rate. Sales begin to level off—a nonlinear pattern. In Phase IV, sales decrease at a nonlinear rate.

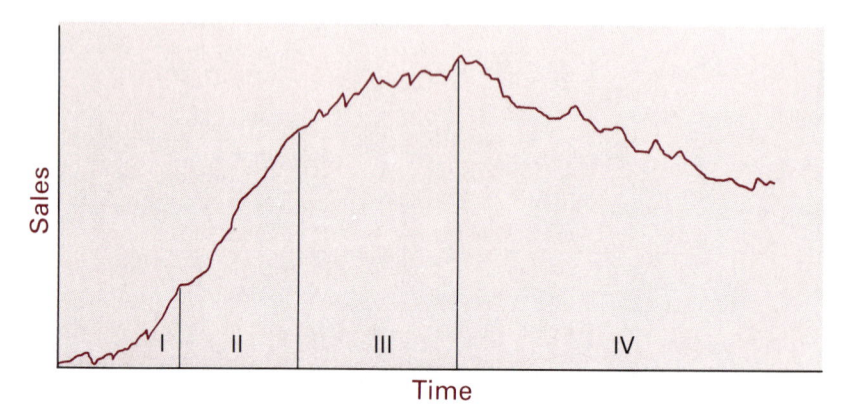

FIGURE 11.1 Product Life Cycle—Trend Patterns

FIGURE 11.2 Seasonal Pattern

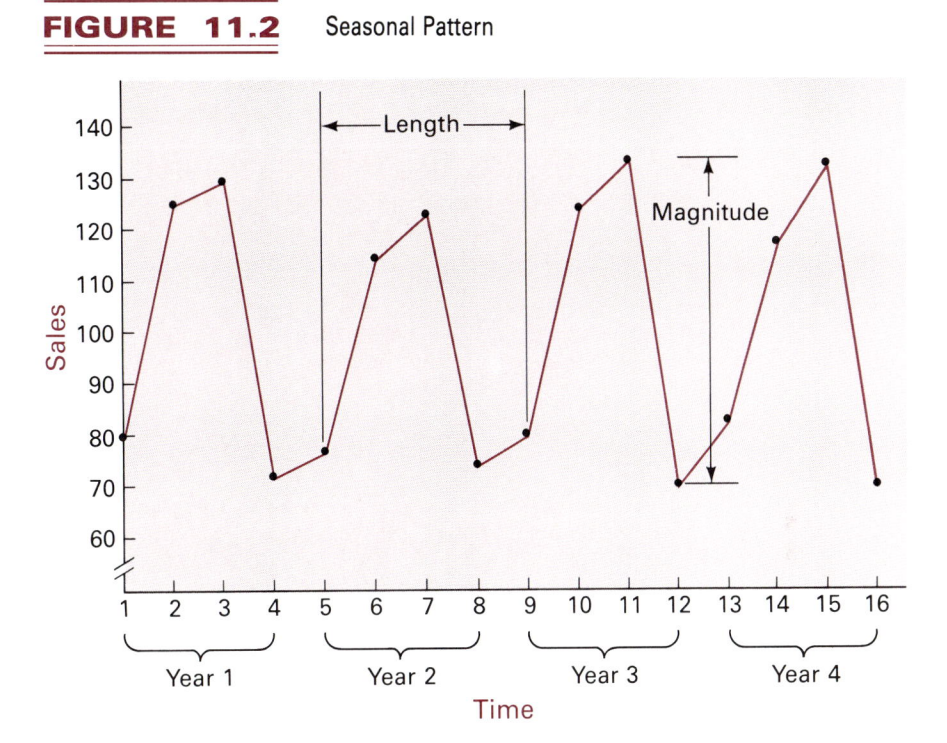

A *seasonal* pattern occurs when factors that are associated with a day of the week, a month, or quarter of the year influence the time-series data. The desire for long weekends may cause absenteeism to peak on Monday and Friday every week. High outdoor temperatures may cause sales of ice cream to peak during the summer months and drop during the winter months every year. To qualify as seasonal, the data pattern must be repetitive—occurring the same day of every week, the same month or same quarter of every year.

Figure 11.2 shows quarterly data with a seasonal pattern. The first and fourth quarters of every year are relatively weak sales periods. The second and third quarters are relatively strong sales periods. The pattern persists year after year. The magnitude of a seasonal pattern is measured as the peak (highest sales for the year) minus the trough (the lowest sales for the year). The length of a seasonal pattern is 1 year.

A *cyclical* pattern occurs when the data are influenced by business cycles that are longer than 1 year. Capital spending is an important determinant of the length of business cycles. Thus, when managers anticipate a slowdown in the economy, they cut back their capital outlays. As they cut back, unemployment increases and the economy slows. Consumers are less willing to buy big-ticket items such as cars or major appliances when they fear layoffs. Soon we find ourselves in a recession. Business cycles affect sales of a firm. Figure 11.3 shows sales data with a cyclical pattern.

FIGURE 11.3 Cyclical Pattern

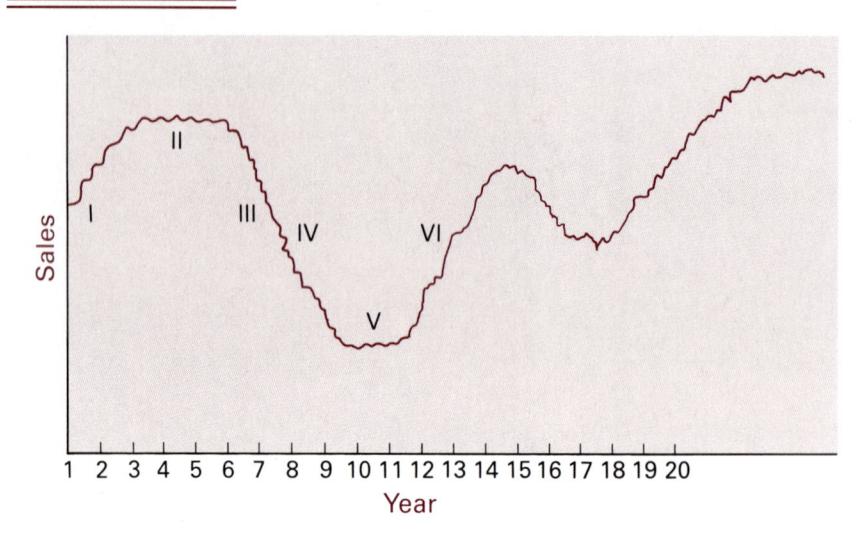

A business cycle can have up to six phases. These are growth (I), prosperity (II), warning (III), recession (IV), depression (V), and recovery (VI). The length and magnitude of cycles can vary from one cycle to the next.

The major distinction between seasonal and cyclical patterns is that the seasonal pattern is of constant length and recurs on a regular basis. Cycles vary in length and magnitude. Since World War II, business cycles have varied in length from 28 to 117 months.

11.2 Alternative Forecasting Approaches

Once we have graphed and reviewed the historical data, we develop forecasts. There are three forecasting approaches: time series, causal, and judgmental. The three approaches have different underlying assumptions, data requirements, and strengths and weaknesses. By the end of this section you should be able to:

1. explain the basic assumption underlying quantitative forecasting approaches;
2. distinguish between time series and causal forecasting approaches;
3. distinguish between quantitative and qualitative forecasting approaches; and
4. explain the major problem with qualitative approaches.

Table 11.1 summarizes the major forecasting approaches and lists some techniques that are used within each category.

Table 11.1

Forecasting Methods

	Quantitative Data Available		**Qualitative Data Available**
	Time Series Methods	**Causal Methods**	**Judgmental or Intuitive Methods**
How Forecast Is Made	Forecasts the continuation of *patterns* into the future	Forecasts the continuation of *relationships* into the future	Management or expert groups *subjectively* assess the future
Examples	Predicting the growth of phone sales for the upcoming year	Predicting how our price vs. competitors' prices and our advertising level affect car phone sales for the upcoming year	Predicting how car phones will look in the year 2000; predicting the percentage of car phones in the U.S. in the year 2010
Forecasting Methods	Decomposition method Exponential smoothing	Regression analysis Econometric models	Nominal group method Delphi method

Quantitative Forecasting Approaches

Quantitative approaches can provide accurate numerical short-term forecasts. Consider quantitative forecasting approaches when

1. you have past numerical data, and
2. you can assume that either the past data patterns or relationships among variables will continue into the near future.

This second condition, the *assumption of continuity*, is essential to all quantitative forecasting approaches. Continuity means that the recent past is a good guide to the near future. When sudden and major changes occur, quantitative forecasting approaches do not work well. For example, in 1973 forecasters severely overestimated gas consumption because they could not predict the Arab–Israeli war in June and the subsequent skyrocketing gas prices. Quantitative forecasting approaches seek to detect either (1) relationships among a set of business and economic variables—causal methods or (2) any of the three common data patterns discussed above—time series methods.

Relationship detection In Chapter 10 we used regression analysis to detect relationships between a dependent variable and a set of predictor variables using cross-sectional data. In Section 11.3 we use regression analysis to develop forecasts using time-ordered data. For a valid forecast, the relationship based on historical data must continue into the future.

Pattern detection These quantitative forecasting methods help us identify the trend, seasonal, and cyclical patterns. We develop forecasts by projecting these patterns into the near future. Pattern detection methods include moving averages (see Chapter 2), exponential smoothing, and the classical decomposition method. We present the decomposition method in Section 11.4. For a valid forecast, the detected patterns based on historical data must continue into the future.

Which quantitative approach should we use? Both approaches can produce accurate predictions. If we wish only to make predictions, then time series models based on data patterns are easier to build and maintain. If we also want to identify the predictor variables that affect the forecasted dependent variable for explanation and control purposes, we use regression models. But regression models are often more costly (Makridakis, Wheelwright, and McGee, 1983).

Qualitative Approaches

Qualitative approaches draw upon intuitive thinking, judgment, and accumulated knowledge. We will consider only group-based methods which require more than a single person to generate forecasts. We will present the Nominal Group and Delphi methods in Section 11.5.

Table 11.2

Some Forecasting Rules of Thumb Used by Experts

Type	Description	Example
Availability	The ease with which specific instances are recalled affects judgment.	Frequencies of well-publicized events (e.g., earthquakes) are overestimated.
Anchor and adjust	Predictions are made by anchoring on a value and then making adjustments.	Make sales forecast by taking last year's sales and adding 5%.
Wishful thinking	Managers' liking for outcomes affects their assessments.	Overestimate the likelihood of a cure for cancer by the year 2000.
Hindsight	Managers are not surprised about what happened in the past. They find plausible explanations.	Anyone could have foreseen the *Challenger* spacecraft disaster. After the crash some NASA officials said, "It was just a matter of time!" Why didn't they speak up before?
Selective perception	Managers look for information that is consistent with their own views.	If you think the stock market will drop, you seek out pessimistic forecasts and ignore optimistic ones.

The Nominal Group and Delphi methods minimize many of the following group interaction problems. When groups meet, they can make poor judgments. Ineffective group members rarely challenge one another and treat opinions as facts. Members often do not challenge questionable assumptions underlying their forecasts. Influential members stifle dissent and inhibit others from speaking. Ineffective group leaders interrupt colleagues, promote their own ideas early in the group discussion, and do not encourage and protect minority opinion.

The Nominal Group and Delphi methods still have problems because they both rely on judgments. In Chapter 4 we learned that judgments are often plagued by inconsistency and error. Business professionals have particular trouble in making judgments about the future. They may use rules of thumb that could result in poor forecasts. Table 11.2 provides examples of some poor forecasting rules of thumb.

Robin Hogarth (1987) has catalogued over 20 rules that can produce poor intuitive forecasts. Knowing these rules of thumb is an important step to minimizing their impact.

SECTION 11.2 EXERCISES

1. What is the basic assumption behind all quantitative forecasting methods? How can you be sure this assumption will hold?
2. Distinguish between time series (pattern detection) and causal (relationship detection) forecasting methods.
3. Distinguish between quantitative and qualitative forecasting methods. Provide examples of when each type of forecasting method might be used by a business organization.
4. With which component of a time series—T, S, C, or RF—would you associate each of the following:
    a. The steady increase of foreign car sales
    b. The drop in snow ski sales from April to October
    c. A flood closing our store and cutting sales by two-thirds
    d. A decrease in sales due to a recession
    e. The drop in sales of consumer products in January
    f. The explosive growth of PCs in the late 1980s
5. Suppose the date is December 1989. We wish to forecast the number of tourists to Eastern Europe for 1990. We have a data base for the period 1978–1988. If we used the data base to forecast, why might our forecast severely underestimate the number of tourists to Eastern Europe?

11.3 Forecasting Using Regression Analysis

In regression analysis we seek predictor variables to forecast the dependent variable. Detected relationships are assumed to continue into the near future. This section extends regression analysis to time-ordered data. By the end of this section you should be able to:

1. explain the terms: lagging, autocorrelation, autoregressive model, coincident indicator, and leading indicator;
2. develop, interpret, and use multiple regression models to make short-term forecasts;
3. explain the problem of using predictor variables that are coincident indicators in regression models based on time-ordered data; and
4. explain why the mean absolute percentage error (MAPE) is a useful measure of forecast accuracy.

EXAMPLE: FORECASTING UNITS SOLD AT COMCEL   Table 11.3 lists the units sold (in tens of thousands) of the deluxe mobile car phone for the past 16 quarters. It is now January 1, 1994. COMCEL wishes to forecast units sold for the first quarter of 1994.

Table 11.3

Units Sold Quarterly

Year	Quarter	SALES (tens of thousands)	SALES-1 (tens of thousands)
1990	1	3.40	—
	2	2.00	3.40 ← Sales from Quarter 1
	3	1.90	2.00 ← Sales from Quarter 2
	4	3.20	1.90
1991	1	4.80	3.20
	2	3.75	4.80
	3	4.13	3.75
	4	4.51	4.13
1992	1	5.61	4.51
	2	4.05	5.61
	3	4.63	4.05
	4	5.01	4.63
1993	1	6.03	5.01
	2	4.61	6.03
	3	5.08	4.61
	4	5.29	5.08 ← Sales from Quarter 3

Figure 11.4 graphs units sold over time. Units sold exhibit both a positive linear trend pattern and a seasonal pattern. Sales are relatively high in the first and fourth quarters and relatively low in the second and third quarters.

Regression analysis requires that we seek one or more predictor variables that explain the variation in units sold. An obvious first choice is sales from the previous quarter. Note that successive observations in Figure 11.4 are close to one another. Should our forecast of next quarter's sales be based, at least in part, on what we sold this quarter? We are asking: Is there a statistically significant relationship between sales in successive periods?

FIGURE 11.4 Line Graph of Sales

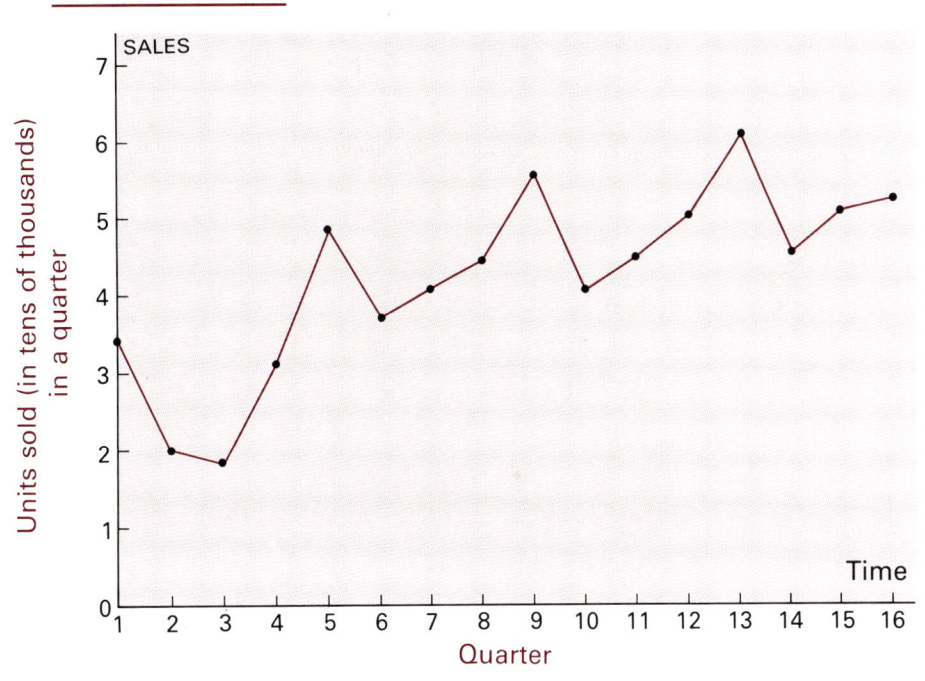

Autoregressive Modeling

We answer this question by creating a new predictor variable, SALES-1, where SALES-1 is the preceding value of SALES. We call this *one-quarter lagging.* (See the last column in Table 11.3.) To determine whether there is a relationship between SALES and SALES-1, we draw a scatter plot. SALES, the dependent variable, is measured on the vertical axis and SALES-1, a predictor variable, is measured on the horizontal axis.

We have labelled the data points in Figure 11.5 on page 620. The data point for quarter 3 in 1990 represents SALES = 1.90 (quarter 3) and SALES-1 = 2.00 (quarter 2). Figure 11.5 shows that the data points are upward sloping to the right, which suggests a positive linear relationship. That is, if sales in one quarter are low (high), sales in the following quarter will also be low (high). While the correlation is positive, it is not, however, perfect. All the data values do not lie on a straight line.

The term *autocorrelation* denotes the correlation between values of a variable and preceding values of the *same* variable. *Auto* means self or same. The data in Figure 11.5 are positively autocorrelated. Again, all that means is that successive observations are close to one another.

Can we use the predictor variable, SALES-1, to forecast SALES? Is SALES related to SALES-1? To find out, we fit a simple linear regression model to the data in Table 11.3. SALES is the dependent variable and SALES-1 is the predictor variable.

FIGURE 11.5 Scatter Plot of Sales and Sales Lagged by One Quarter

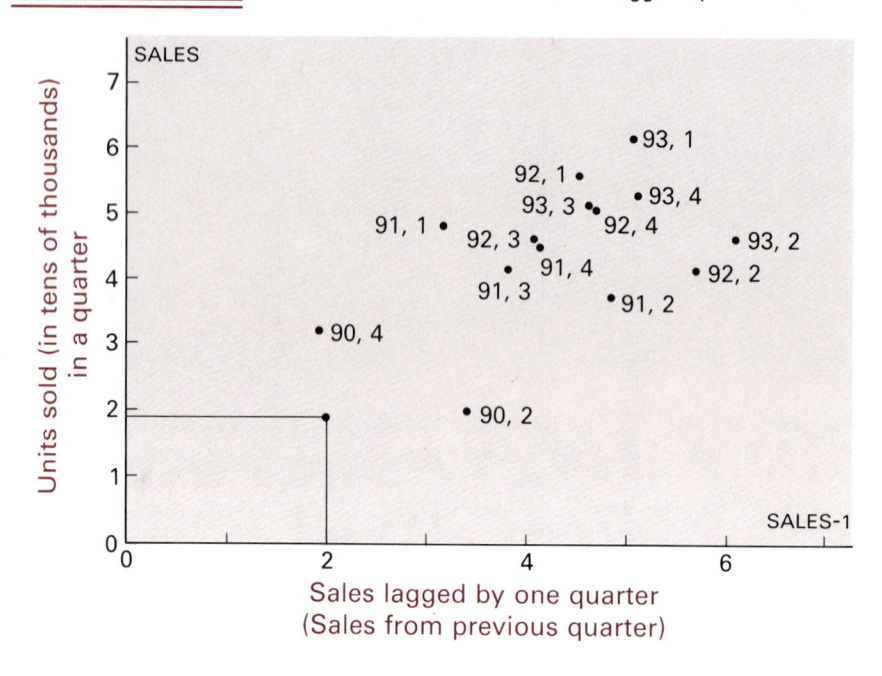

We have 15 observations from quarter 2, 1990, to quarter 4, 1993. We used a computer to develop the following simple linear regression model. Expression (11.1) is an **autoregressive model**.

We interpret the sample slope and intercept as we would in a typical regression model. Sales in any quarter are equal to a constant plus 63% of the sales the quarter before:

$$\text{SALES-PRED} = 1.67 + .63 \text{SALES-1} \tag{11.1}$$

An autoregressive model is one in which lagged values of the dependent variable are used to forecast the dependent variable.

The variance ratio of 8.34 has an interpolated *p*-value of less than .05 $[F(1, 13, .95) = 4.67]$. Thus we can use expression (11.1) to forecast units sold for the first quarter of 1994. We use 5.29, the actual sales for the fourth quarter of 1993, to forecast the sales for the first quarter of 1994:

$$\text{SALES-PRED} = 1.67 + .63(5.29) = 5.00, \quad \text{or } 50,000 \text{ phones}$$

Could we generate a more accurate forecast by bringing additional predictor variables into the model? The simple coefficient of determination provides an answer. The value of r^2 for this model is 39%. That is, 39% of the variation in units sold is explained by units sold in the preceding quarter. The relatively low r^2 value means that we should seek additional predictor variables.

In summary, when forecasting any dependent variable *Y*, consider using lagged values of *Y* as predictor variables. This is autoregressive modeling. Plot

Y vs. one-period-lagged values of Y. If the scatter plot indicates either a positive or negative autocorrelation, treat the lagged values of Y as a predictor variable. Also, consider variables with lags greater than one. Lagged values of two periods (Y-2) make sense if we believe that sales from two quarters ago also affect present-quarter sales. However, if the coefficient of determination is still relatively low for the final autoregressive model, seek predictor variables, X, other than lagged values of Y, to forecast Y. Examples include price, competitors' sales, and consumer income.

Leading and Coincident Indicators

We try to improve the forecasting power of the autoregressive model by adding another predictor variable—amount of advertising. We have also included lagged values of advertising, ADV-1, in Table 11.4. If lagged values of Y affect Y, doesn't it make sense that lagged values of X might also affect Y?

ADV, the level of advertising, in hundreds of thousands of dollars, is a *coincident indicator*. We believe that advertising in a quarter affects sales in the *same* quarter. ADV-1 is a potential *leading indicator*.* ADV-1 represents the possibility that advertising in one quarter affects sales in the *next* quarter.

Table 11.4

Quarterly Unit Sales and Predictor Variables

Year	Quarter	SALES (tens of thousands)	SALES-1	ADV (hundreds of thousands of dollars)	ADV-1
1990	1	3.40	—	1.10	—
	2	2.00	3.40	1.40	1.10
	3	1.90	2.00	3.30	1.40
	4	3.20	1.90	5.40	3.30
1991	1	4.80	3.20	1.50	5.40
	2	3.75	4.80	3.60	1.50
	3	4.13	3.75	3.70	3.60
	4	4.51	4.13	5.80	3.70
1992	1	5.61	4.51	1.90	5.80
	2	4.05	5.61	4.00	1.90
	3	4.63	4.05	4.10	4.00
	4	5.01	4.63	6.20	4.10
1993	1	6.03	5.01	2.50	6.20
	2	4.61	6.03	4.40	2.50
	3	5.08	4.61	4.50	4.40
	4	5.29	5.08	1.25	4.50

*Do not confuse the terms coincident and leading *indicators* with *indicator variables* from Chapter 10. Indicator variables represent categorical variables with two or more classes.

FIGURE 11.6 Scatter Plot of Units Sold vs. Amount of Advertising

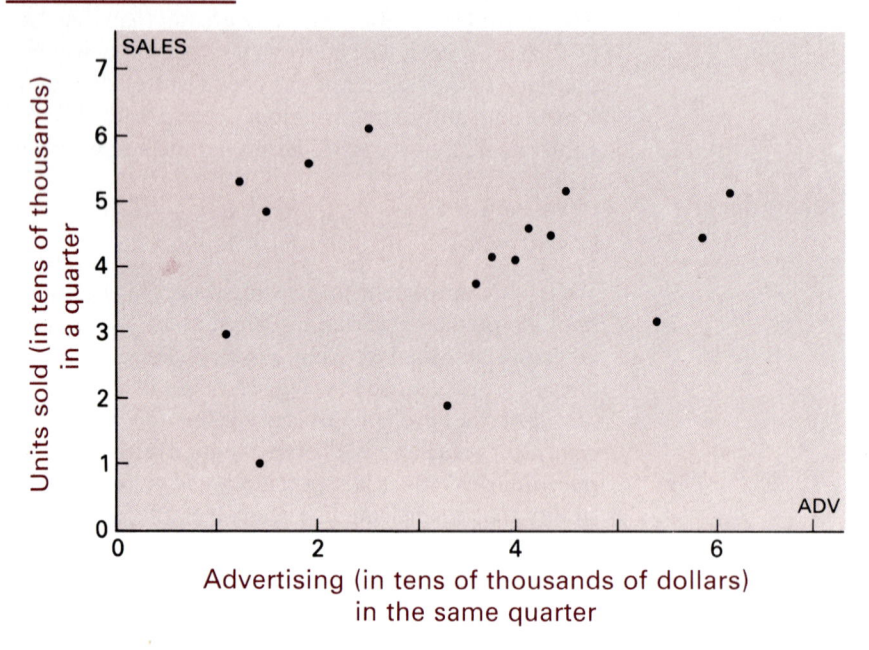

FIGURE 11.7 Scatter Plot of Units Sold vs. Amount of Advertising Lagged One Quarter

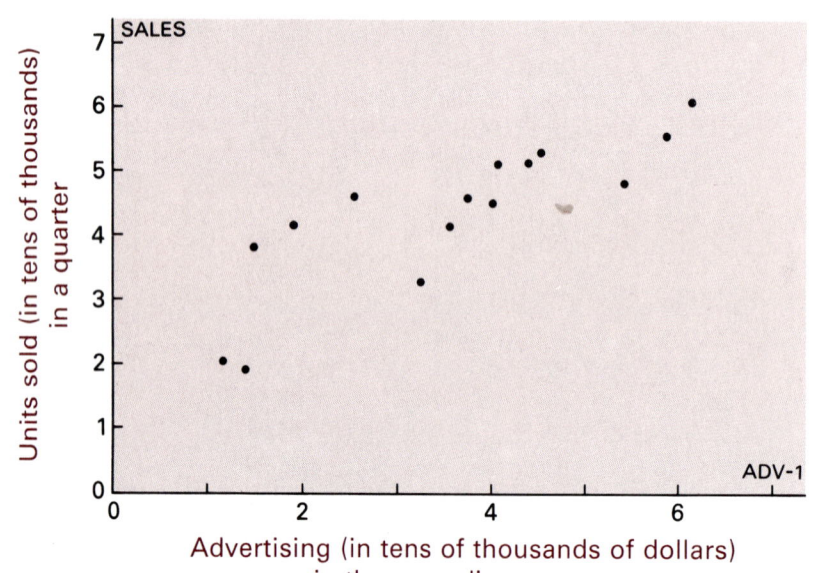

Developing the Model

Does it appear that either ADV or ADV-1 is related to SALES?

Figure 11.6 suggests that SALES and the coincident indicator, ADV, may not be related. It takes a circle or an ellipse parallel to the horizontal axis to encompass the data points. Figure 11.7 reveals that SALES and the leading indicator, ADV-1, probably are positively linearly related. Note that the swarm of points is upward sloping to the right. However, a graph is only suggestive and not a substitute for formal analysis. The ANOVA (not shown) indicates that ADV, ADV-1, and SALES-1 are significantly related to SALES.

Expression (11.2) is a multiple regression model of SALES with three predictor variables: SALES-1, ADV, and ADV-1. This computer-generated equation is based on 15 quarters of data—quarter 2, 1990, to quarter 4, 1993.

$$\text{SALES-PRED} = -.211 + .508\text{SALES-1} + .086\text{ADV} + .587\text{ADV-1} \qquad (11.2)$$

The *t*-tests in Table 11.5 indicate that we need *all* the predictor variables in the model, since the *p*-values are all less than .05.

The inclusion of ADV and ADV-1 increases the multiple coefficient of determination (not shown) to 98.6%. Thus, expression (11.2) accounts for almost all of the variation in SALES.

Analyzing Residuals

Next, we examine the residual plots to look for violations of the linear regression model assumptions (see Section 10.6). Because the data are time-ordered, plotting the residuals against time should be the first diagnostic check. Nonindependence occurs when the time sequence of residuals shows long strings of positive and negative values or when the residuals exhibit a sawtooth pattern. However, Figure 11.8 on page 624 suggests that the model satisfies the independence assumption. If the model violates the independence assumption, we should seek professional statistical help.

Next, we check for violations of the normality assumption and look for possible outliers. Standardize the residuals by dividing each one by the square root of the variance error term, MSE. If the normality assumption is met, then by the Empirical rule, about 68% of the standardized residuals should lie between

Table 11.5

t-Tests for Predictor Variables

Variable	Parameter Estimate	*t*-Value	*p*-Value
INTERCEPT	−.211	—	—
SALES-1	.508	13.89	.0001
ADV	.086	3.17	.0089
ADV-1	.587	21.58	.0001

FIGURE 11.8   Residual Plot vs. Time

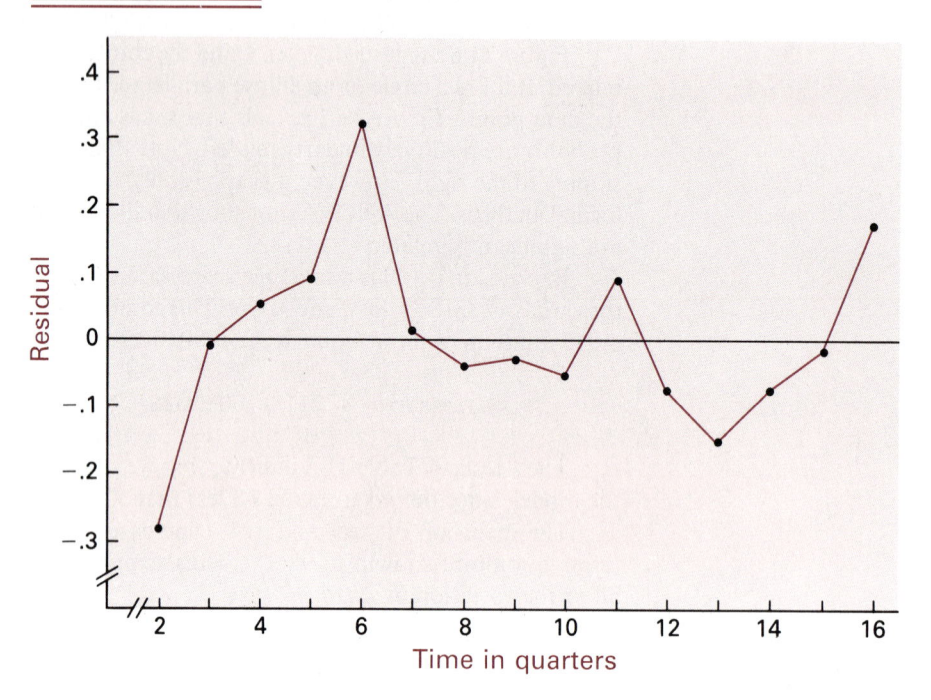

−1.00 and +1.00. About 95% should lie between −2.00 and +2.00. Almost all standardized residuals should fall between −3.00 and +3.00. If a standardized residual is beyond ±3, this data point should be considered a possible outlier.

The computer output shown in Table 11.6 indicates that there are no outliers. The normality assumption is difficult to check using the Empirical rule because percentages are very unstable when there are only 15 observations. However, 12 of 15 or 80.0% of the residuals are between −1 and +1, while 93.3% of the residuals are between −2.00 and +2.00. Although the percentage of residuals lying between −1 and +1 is a bit high to meet the normality assumption, the departure from the expected percentage is not serious enough to require corrective action, such as a data transformation on the dependent variable.

We should also plot the residuals against SALES-PRED and the predictor variables. The residual plots (not shown) do not suggest serious violations. If serious violations occur (see Section 10.6), seek professional statistical help.

Finally, Table 11.7, a correlation matrix for the three predictor variables, shows that multicollinearity is not a serious problem.

In summary, we have met to a large degree the assumptions underlying the linear regression model. Most importantly, we have met the independence assumption, which is commonly violated in time-ordered data. Multicollinearity is also not a serious problem. Therefore, we may use the model for explanation, prediction, and control.

Table 11.6

Residuals and Standardized Residuals

Year	Quarter	SALES	SALES-PRED from (11.2)	Residual	Standardized Residual
1990	2	2.00	2.28	−.28	−1.76
	3	1.90	1.91	−.01	−.06
	4	3.20	3.15	.05	.29
1991	1	4.80	4.71	.09	.56
	2	3.75	3.42	.33	2.10
	3	4.13	4.12	.01	.05
	4	4.51	4.55	−.04	−.28
1992	1	5.61	5.64	−.03	−.22
	2	4.05	4.10	−.05	−.28
	3	4.63	4.54	.09	.54
	4	5.01	5.08	−.07	−.42
1993	1	6.03	6.18	−.15	−.97
	2	4.61	4.69	−.08	−.53
	3	5.08	5.10	−.02	−.11
	4	5.29	5.12	.17	1.10

Table 11.7

Correlation Matrix for Three Predictor Variables

	SALES-1	ADV	ADV-1
SALES-1	1.000	.005	.154
ADV		1.000	−.167
ADV-1			1.000

Mean Absolute Percentage Error

We have repeated expression (11.2) below. The regression coefficients indicate the impact on units sold of each predictor variable, holding the other predictor variables constant.

$$\text{SALES-PRED} = -.211 + .508\text{SALES-1} + .086\text{ADV} + .587\text{ADV-1}$$

We can predict SALES for the first quarter of 1994 by inserting into (11.2) the known sales level for the fourth quarter of 1993, the known amount of advertising spent in the fourth quarter of 1993 (see Table 11.4), and the amount COMCEL will spend for advertising in the first quarter of 1994, $310,000. We obtain

$$\text{SALES-PRED} = -.211 + .508(5.29) + .086(3.10) + .587(1.25)$$

$$= 3.48, \quad \text{or 34,800 phones}$$

How good is the forecast? Since the multiple coefficient of determination is 98.6%, the forecast should be accurate provided the assumption of continuity holds. But how accurate is accurate? The *mean absolute percentage error*, or MAPE, is an excellent measure of forecasting accuracy. We compute the MAPE for expression (11.2). If the MAPE is small enough for our needs, we can then use the model for forecasting.

$$\text{Percentage error} = PE = \left(\frac{\text{Actual} - \text{Predicted}}{\text{Actual}}\right)100 \quad (11.3)$$

$$= \left(\frac{\text{Residual}}{\text{Actual}}\right)100$$

$$\text{MAPE} = \frac{\sum|PE|}{n} \quad (11.4)$$

where n is the number of periods of historical data.

Table 11.8 shows the MAPE calculations for the COMCEL sales data for the past 15 quarters. Over that time, the model's predictions of sales differed from the actual sales by 2.7%, on the average.

Table 11.8

Calculations of MAPE

Year	Quarter	ACTUAL SALES	SALES-PRED from (11.2)	Residual	PE (%)	|PE| (%)
1990	2	2.00	2.28	−.28	−14.0	14.0
	3	1.90	1.91	−.01	−.5	.5
	4	3.20	3.15	.05	1.4	1.4
1991	1	4.80	4.71	.09	1.9	1.9
	2	3.75	3.42	.33	8.9	8.9
	3	4.13	4.12	.01	.2	.2
	4	4.51	4.55	−.04	−1.0	1.0
1992	1	5.61	5.64	−.03	−.6	.6
	2	4.05	4.10	−.05	−1.1	1.1
	3	4.63	4.54	.09	1.9	1.9
	4	5.01	5.08	−.07	−1.4	1.4
1993	1	6.03	6.18	−.15	−2.6	2.6
	2	4.61	4.69	−.08	−1.8	1.8
	3	5.08	5.10	−.02	−.3	.3
	4	5.29	5.12	.17	3.3	3.3
						40.9

$$\text{Mean absolute percentage error} = \frac{40.9}{15} = 2.7\%$$

There are two reasons why the MAPE is useful. First, it is more informative than the actual forecasting error. From Table 11.8, the actual forecasting error (residual) for the first quarter of 1993 was −.15 unit, or 1,500 phones. That is, the model overestimated actual sales by 1,500 phones. How far off is that? Well, it depends on the actual sales for the period. An error of 1,500 units on actual sales of 2,000,000 car phones is trivial. An error of 1,500 units on actual sales of 1,500 units is critical. Second, many business professionals think in terms of percentages. They can tolerate small percentage errors, but must avoid large ones. The MAPE provides the type of information that professionals need and will use.

If the MAPE is sufficiently small, we can then use expression (11.2) for forecasting. In the COMCEL sales forecasting context: Is a mean forecasting error of 2.7% acceptable? Assume that the actual and predicted sales differed by as much as 2.7% for the first quarter of 1994. Could we then develop production schedules, determine manpower and raw material needs, and the like given a MAPE of 2.7%? An answer of yes means using the forecasted sales values in planning. An answer of no means developing additional regression models or using other forecasting methods to obtain a forecast with a lower MAPE.

Limitations of Regression Models As Forecasting Tools

A hypothetical regression model relating a company's quarterly sales to quarterly gross national product (GNP) is shown below. Assume the model is statistically significant and meets all the assumptions of the linear regression model. Why would it be difficult to forecast sales for the upcoming quarter? Please think about it before reading on.

$$\text{SALES-PRED} = 15.5 + .111 \text{GNP} \qquad (11.5)$$

GNP is a coincident indicator. To predict SALES for the first quarter of 1994, we must first predict the level of GNP. Experts often disagree on the forecasted GNP. Thus, forecasting by using a regression model with a coincident indicator is difficult. We must first forecast the value of the coincident indicator and then use it to forecast the value of the dependent variable. Using only lagged predictor variables reduces this problem. We use previous and already known values of the predictor variables to forecast future values of the dependent variable.

The coincident indicator, ADV, did not present a problem in model (11.2). Firms generally determine the amount of quarterly or monthly advertising for the upcoming year in their yearly budgets. Thus, the firm would know what it planned to spend over the next four quarters for advertising.

However, model (11.2) does have one limitation. We can forecast only one quarter ahead. We cannot predict sales for the second quarter of 1994 until we know the actual level of sales for the first quarter of 1994, which we will not know until the end of the quarter. Thus, the model (11.2) is somewhat limited.

Table 11.9

Forecasting Using a Four-Quarter-Lag Model

	1	2	3	4	1	2	3	4
1993	40	35	50	45				
1994					44[a]	40	52	48

[a] SALES-PRED = 12 + .80(40) = 44

We could make forecasts for more than one quarter if our model had variables with lags longer than one period. Consider the following autoregressive model:

$$\text{SALES-PRED} = 12 + .80 \text{SALES-4} \tag{11.6}$$

With expression (11.6) we can develop forecasts for the four quarters of 1994. We use the sales of each quarter in 1993 to forecast sales in the corresponding quarter of 1994. See Table 11.9.

In summary, a forecasting model with coincident indicators may be very good at explaining what affects any dependent variable, but it may not be very useful in forecasting. Including predictor variables with long lags increases the forecast horizon, the period of time over which we can use a model to make forecasts.

Summary

Managers often use time-ordered data to develop regression-based forecasting models. In this section, we have introduced three important extensions to the presentation of regression analysis in Chapter 10, namely,

1. Lagged values of Y to predict Y—autoregressive models
2. Lagged values of X to predict Y
3. MAPE as a measure of forecasting accuracy

How many lags should be included in a model? Roberts (1988) recommends that we include more, rather than fewer, lags. Then we can use the backward elimination method of Chapter 10 (or the more complex stepwise regression method) to remove those lagged variables that are not statistically related to Y.

Once we have developed our model, check for multicollinearity and do a residual analysis. First plot the residuals against time to see if the independence assumption is violated. Then plot the residuals against Y-PRED and the predictor variables. Take corrective action or get professional statistical help if needed. We use the validated model to make short-run forecasts on Y provided the MAPE is sufficiently low for our planning needs.

Chapter 11 Forecasting and Time Series Analysis

SECTION 11.3 EXERCISES

Use our software to solve the following exercises.

1. Shown are 20 quarters of sales data for ABC, Inc.

QTR	1	2	3	4	5	6	7	8	9	10
SALES	41	57	63	72	89	98	101	112	129	137

QTR	11	12	13	14	15	16	17	18	19	20
SALES	150	155	164	172	188	193	204	218	230	233

    a. Plot SALES vs. TIME (in quarters) on a line graph. We always start the analysis by plotting a line graph.
    b. We believe that SALES are affected by SALES-1, sales from the previous quarter. Draw a scatter diagram of SALES vs. SALES-1.
    c. Does the scatter diagram suggest positive autocorrelation, negative autocorrelation, or no autocorrelation?
    d. Develop a regression model of SALES vs. SALES-1. The data for the autoregressive model are SALES from periods 2–20 and SALES-1 from periods 1–19. There are 19 observations for fitting the regression model.
    e. Compute the MAPE for the 19 quarters of historical data. Should we use the regression model given the size of the MAPE? Discuss.
    f. Develop a sales forecast for quarter 21.

2. Shown are 20 quarters of data on the number of grievances filed in an industry.

QTR	1	2	3	4	5	6	7	8	9	10
GRIEV	0	47	71	81	70	61	48	27	49	47

QTR	11	12	13	14	15	16	17	18	19	20
GRIEV	50	82	91	65	96	26	70	63	3	43

    a. Plot GRIEV vs. TIME (in quarters) on a line graph.
    b. We do not believe that GRIEV is affected by GRIEV-1, the number of grievances in the previous quarter. Draw a scatter diagram of GRIEV vs. GRIEV-1 and verify.
    c. Does the scatter diagram indicate positive autocorrelation, negative autocorrelation, or no autocorrelation?

3. Shown are 20 quarters of data on the ending inventory levels of mobile phones in the Southern Region. The actual inventory levels were divided by 10 to obtain the data.

QTR	1	2	3	4	5	6	7	8	9	10
INVEN	10	40	15	50	10	60	20	50	30	40

QTR	11	12	13	14	15	16	17	18	19	20
INVEN	25	35	20	45	30	60	10	50	15	55

    a. Plot INVEN vs. TIME (in quarters) on a line graph.
    b. We believe that INVEN is affected by INVEN-1, inventory from the previous quarter. Draw a scatter diagram of INVEN vs. INVEN-1.
    c. Does the scatter diagram indicate positive autocorrelation, negative autocorrelation, or no autocorrelation?

    d. Develop a regression model of INVEN VS. INVEN-1. The data for the autoregressive model are INVEN from periods 2–20 and INVEN-1 from periods 1–19.
    e. Compute the MAPE for the 19 quarters of historical data. Should we use the regression model given the size of the MAPE?
    f. Develop a forecast of INVEN for quarter 21.

4. Shown are 20 quarters of data on sales and R&D expenditures (research and development). We believe that R&D expenditures in a quarter affect sales two quarters later.

QTR	SALES	R&D	QTR	SALES	R&D
1	40	10	11	81	40
2	37	20	12	97	30
3	50	20	13	110	35
4	70	15	14	89	45
5	60	20	15	103	50
6	60	30	16	117	35
7	72	35	17	131	40
8	88	25	18	98	50
9	101	25	19	112	55
10	80	35	20	134	25

    a. Plot SALES VS. TIME (in quarters) on a line graph.
    b. Draw a scatter diagram of SALES VS. R&D-2 (sales in quarter t and R&D expenditures two quarters earlier).
    c. Develop a regression model of SALES VS. R&D-2. The data for developing the regression model are R&D-2 from periods 1–18 and SALES from periods 3–20.
    d. Compute the MAPE for the 18 quarters of historical data. Should we use the regression model given the size of the MAPE?
    e. Develop a sales forecast for quarter 21.

5. Shown are 16 quarters of data. The dependent variable is SALES and a predictor variable is HS (housing starts). We believe that housing starts is a two-quarter leading indicator. We also believe that sales are affected by the previous quarter's sales.

QTR	SALES	HS	QTR	SALES	HS
1	100	700	9	427	710
2	120	400	10	452	520
3	190	550	11	485	600
4	218	600	12	505	610
5	271	725	13	526	770
6	315	500	14	553	580
7	378	550	15	582	650
8	397	610	16	604	680

    a. Plot SALES VS. TIME (in quarters) on a line graph.
    b. Since we believe that SALES is affected by SALES-1, draw a scatter diagram of SALES VS. SALES-1.

c. Does the scatter diagram indicate positive autocorrelation, negative autocorrelation, or no autocorrelation?
d. Draw a scatter diagram of SALES (periods 3–16) vs. HS-2 (periods 1–14). Do the two variables appear to be related?
e. Develop a regression model of SALES vs. SALES-1 and HS-2. The data for the regression model are SALES from periods 3–16, SALES-1 from periods 2–15, and HS-2 from periods 1–14.
f. Do the *t*-tests indicate that both predictor variables are needed?
g. Graph the two predictor variables. Does the graph indicate multicollinearity?
h. Compute the MAPE for the 14 quarters of historical data.
i. Develop a sales forecast for quarter 17.

6. In Exercise 4, note that the sales data contain a seasonal component (see the figure plotted in Exercise 4a). How many indicator variables would it take to represent the categorical variable, the quarter of the year? Explain.

7. In Exercise 1 there was a positive autocorrelation between SALES and SALES-1. Compare successive values of the series. Put a plus sign (+) between two data values if the second value of each pair is greater than or equal to the first, and a minus sign if the second value is less than the first.
   a. How would you explain how to recognize positive autocorrelation by looking at these pairs of successive changes? Discuss.
   b. Could a graph have a downward trend and exhibit positive autocorrelation? If so, create a small series to support your answer.

8. In Exercise 2 there was no autocorrelation between GRIEV and GRIEV-1. As in Exercise 7, identify the direction of pairwise changes (+ or −) from one period to the next. Can you predict the direction of pairwise changes based on the pattern of pluses and minuses? Explain.

9. In Exercise 3 there was a negative autocorrelation between INVEN and INVEN-1. Identify the direction of pairwise changes (+ or −) from one period to the next. How would you characterize a series that has negative autocorrelation in terms of these pairs of successive changes?

10. Interpret the following autoregressive model. EPS-PRED is the forecasted earnings per share for the firm for the upcoming quarter. Assuming the *t*-tests suggest keeping all the predictor variables in the model, explain in simple terms what the following model says about future earnings per share:

$$\text{EPS-PRED} = 1.75 + .5\text{EPS-1} + .4\text{EPS-2} + .1\text{EPS-3}$$

11.4 Forecasting Using the Classical Decomposition Method

In Section 11.3 we developed regression models to identify relationships between a dependent variable and a set of coincident and leading indicators. Regression models *explain* and *forecast* a dependent variable. In this section we use the decomposition method to identify the trend, seasonal, and cyclical patterns. Decomposition models do *not* contain predictor variables. Thus, they do not explain why the dependent variable varies. Decomposition models only provide forecasts. The forecasts are accurate provided that the assumption of continuity holds. The patterns found in the historical data must continue into the near future. By the end of this section you should be able to:

1. distinguish in pictures and words between an additive and a multiplicative decomposition model;
2. compute and explain raw seasonal indices;
3. compute and explain typical seasonal indices;
4. explain the differences among a seasonal pattern, no detectable seasonal pattern, and no seasonal pattern;
5. derive and explain deseasonalized data;
6. decide which trend expression should be used for forecasting;
7. compute and explain cyclical indices; and
8. make forecasts.

Additive and Multiplicative Models

Decomposition methods assume that values of the dependent variable, Y, are composed of up to four components: (1) trend, (2) seasonal, (3) cycle, and (4) random fluctuation:

$$\text{Actual data} = \text{Systematic pattern} + \text{Random fluctuation} \qquad (11.7)$$

$$= f[\text{trend }(T),\text{ seasonal }(S),\text{ cycle }(C)] + \text{randomness }(RF) \qquad (11.8)$$

The function (f) in equation (11.8) could be additive or multiplicative. Before formally defining the terms, we illustrate a major difference between the two functions. Table 11.10 contains two data sets. One is an *additive* function of a trend and seasonal pattern. The other is a *multiplicative* function of a trend and seasonal pattern. For simplicity, we have omitted cycle and random fluctuation.

Table 11.10

Time Series Data Sets with Additive and Multiplicative Functions of Trend and Seasonal Patterns

Period	Additive Model ($T + S$)	Multiplicative Model ($T \times S$)
1	70	70
2	110	108
3	110	112
4	150	102
5	230	294
6	270	300
7	270	232
8	310	198
9	390	518
10	430	492
11	430	360
12	470	294

Chapter 11 Forecasting and Time Series Analysis

FIGURE 11.9 Additive and Multiplicative Time Series

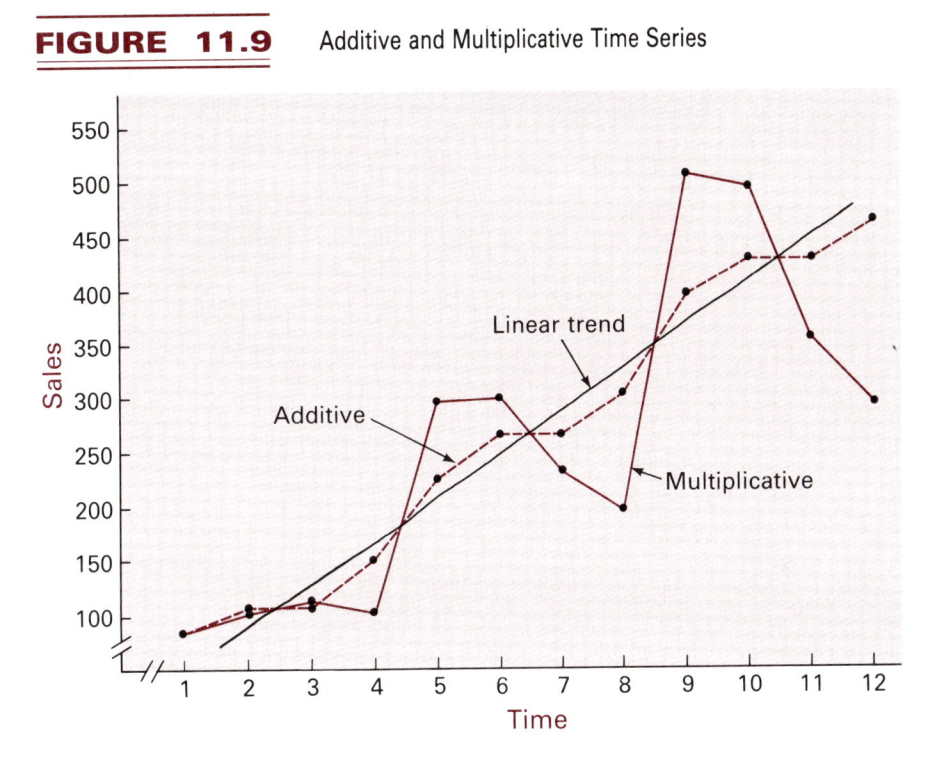

In Figure 11.9 we have superimposed a freehand linear trend line on the two data sets. The additive series has an upward linear trend and a seasonal pattern. Every year, quarters 1 and 2 are above the trend line and quarters 3 and 4 are below the trend line. The multiplicative series has the same upward linear trend and a seasonal pattern. Every year, quarters 1 and 2 are above the trend line and quarters 3 and 4 are below the trend line.

In the additive series, the magnitude (peak to trough) of the seasonal pattern does *not* change over the 12 quarters of data. As the trend values increase, the magnitude of the seasonal pattern does *not* change. In an additive series, the time series components are not related. In a multiplicative series, the magnitude of the seasonal pattern does change over the 12 quarters. As the trend values increase, so does the magnitude of the seasonal pattern. There is a positive multiplicative relationship between the trend and seasonal patterns.

The multiplicative function represents most time series data in business and economics. Firms with $100,000,000 sales generally have greater seasonal sales variation (peak to trough) than firms with only $100,000 sales. As sales increase, so does the magnitude of the seasonal variation around the trend line. Therefore, we will use the following multiplicative model in analyzing time series data:

Actual time series data: $Y = T \times S \times C \times RF$ (11.9)

Table 11.11

Car Phones Sold in Southern Region

Year	Quarter	TIME	Units Sold (hundreds)
1989	1	1	85
	2	2	133
	3	3	136
	4	4	94
1990	1	5	104
	2	6	154
	3	7	166
	4	8	115
1991	1	9	112
	2	10	184
	3	11	175
	4	12	140
1992	1	13	136
	2	14	205
	3	15	210
	4	16	144
1993	1	17	148
	2	18	229
	3	19	237
	4	20	170

Equation (11.9) says that we multiply the values of the trend, seasonal, cyclical, and random fluctuation components to obtain the Y-values.

The decomposition method identifies the trend, seasonal, and cyclical patterns underlying a time series, if these patterns exist. Random fluctuation does not exhibit a systematic pattern. Random fluctuation means that the data values are unpredictable.

We will apply the multiplicative decomposition model to the five years of data in Table 11.11. The data are the numbers of car phones (in hundreds) sold in COMCEL's Southern Region. Note that in Table 11.11 we have inserted a variable called TIME, which represents the 20 quarters of data. It is not a predictor variable in the sense of Chapter 10 or Section 11.3. It is a *proxy* variable that serves as a substitute for the predictor variable in regression-based forecasting models.

In Figure 11.10, the data show a distinct upward trend and seasonal pattern with a 1-year length. There may also be a cyclical component. We begin the analysis by identifying the seasonal pattern, if any.

Ratio to Moving Average Method

We use the ratio to moving average method to determine the seasonal component. First, using the historical sales data, we compute a moving average

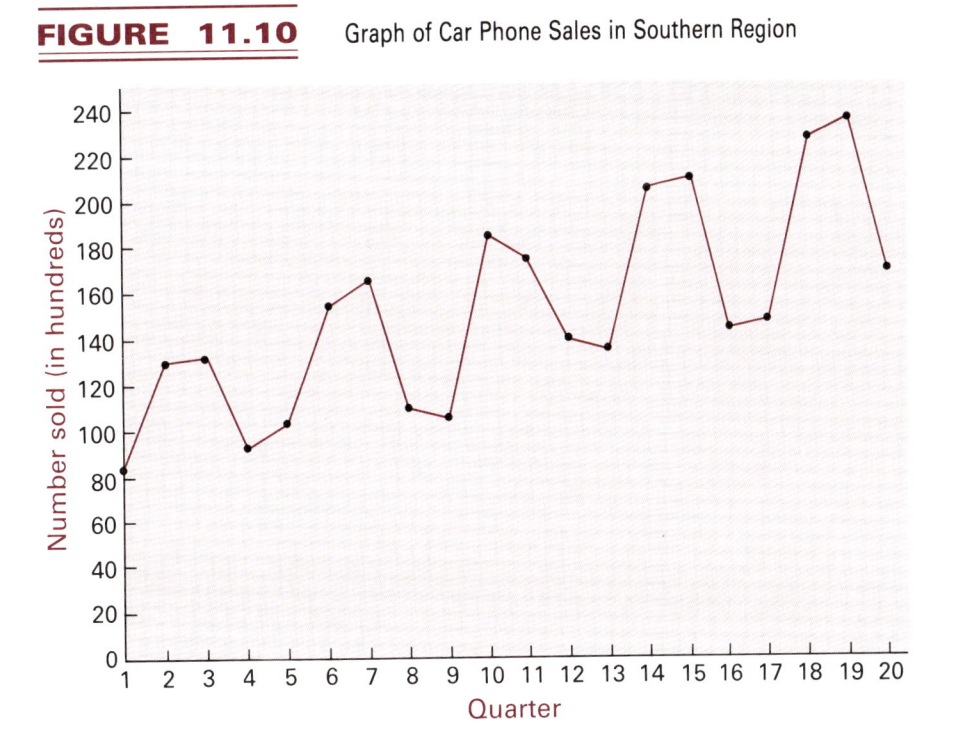

Chapter 11 Forecasting and Time Series Analysis

FIGURE 11.10 Graph of Car Phone Sales in Southern Region

that has the same length as the seasonal component in the data. For 1-year seasonal patterns, the length of the moving average should be 4 quarters (for quarterly data) or 12 months (for monthly data).

In Chapter 2 we first constructed moving averages. To compute a moving average of length four quarters (MA 4), take the first four values of the data set, add them, and compute the mean. Shown is the computation for the first value of the moving average for the COMCEL sales data in Table 11.11:

$$\text{First moving average value} = \frac{85 + 133 + 136 + 94}{4} = 112.00$$

COMCEL sold 85 units in quarter 1, as of March 31st; 133 units in quarter 2, as of June 30th; 136 units in quarter 3, as of September 30th; and 94 units in quarter 4, as of December 31st. March 31st is approximately the 90th day of the year, June 30th is the 180th day, September 30th is the 270th day, and December 31st is the 360th day. The mean of these four calendar dates is the 225th day of the year [(90 + 180 + 270 + 360)/4]. Thus the moving average value of 112 units sold is the mean sales as of the 225th day, August 15th. See the first entry under MA 4 in Table 11.12 on page 636.

To compute the second moving average value, delete the first data value and add the fifth data value. Add the four terms and compute the mean.

Table 11.12
Calculating a MA 4 and a Centered Moving Average

TIME	Calendar Date	Time Series	MA 4	Centered MA 4
1	3/31/89	85		Cannot determine
2	6/30/89	133		Cannot determine
	8/15/89		112.00	
3	9/30/89	136		114.38
	11/15/89		116.75	
4	12/31/89	94		119.38
	2/15/90		122.00	
5	3/31/90	104		125.75
	5/15/90		129.50	
6	6/30/90	154		132.13
	8/15/90		134.75	
7	9/30/90	166		135.75
	11/15/90		136.75	
8	12/31/90	115		140.50
	2/15/91		144.25	
9	3/31/91	112		145.38
	5/15/91		146.50	
10	6/30/91	184		149.63
	8/15/91		152.75	
11	9/30/91	175		155.75
	11/15/91		158.75	
12	12/31/91	140		161.38
	2/15/92		164.00	
13	3/31/92	136		168.38
	5/15/92		172.75	
14	6/30/92	205		173.25
	8/15/92		173.75	
15	9/30/92	210		175.25
	11/15/92		176.75	
16	12/31/92	144		179.75
	2/15/93		182.75	
17	3/31/93	148		186.13
	5/15/93		189.50	
18	6/30/93	229		192.75
	8/15/93		196.00	
19	9/30/93	237		Cannot determine
20	12/31/93	170		Cannot determine

$$\text{Second moving average value} = \frac{133 + 136 + 94 + 104}{4}$$

$$= 116.75$$

The moving average value of 116.75 is the mean sales as of the 315th day, November 15th. This is one quarter later (3 months or 90 days) than the calendar date for the first moving average value. See the second entry under MA 4 in Table 11.12. We computed the other 15 moving averages of length four quarters in the same way.

Figure 11.11 clearly shows that as a result of smoothing, the moving average of length four quarters contains no seasonal component. This is because the original data contain a seasonal pattern of length 1 year. Figure 11.11 also shows that as a result of averaging, the moving average has less random variation than the original data.

Of the original four components in model (11.9), the moving average contains only the T(rend) $\cdot$ C(ycle) components; the seasonal and random components have been eliminated. To isolate the S(easonal) $\cdot$ RF components, we must divide the actual data by the moving average data. The resulting values are called

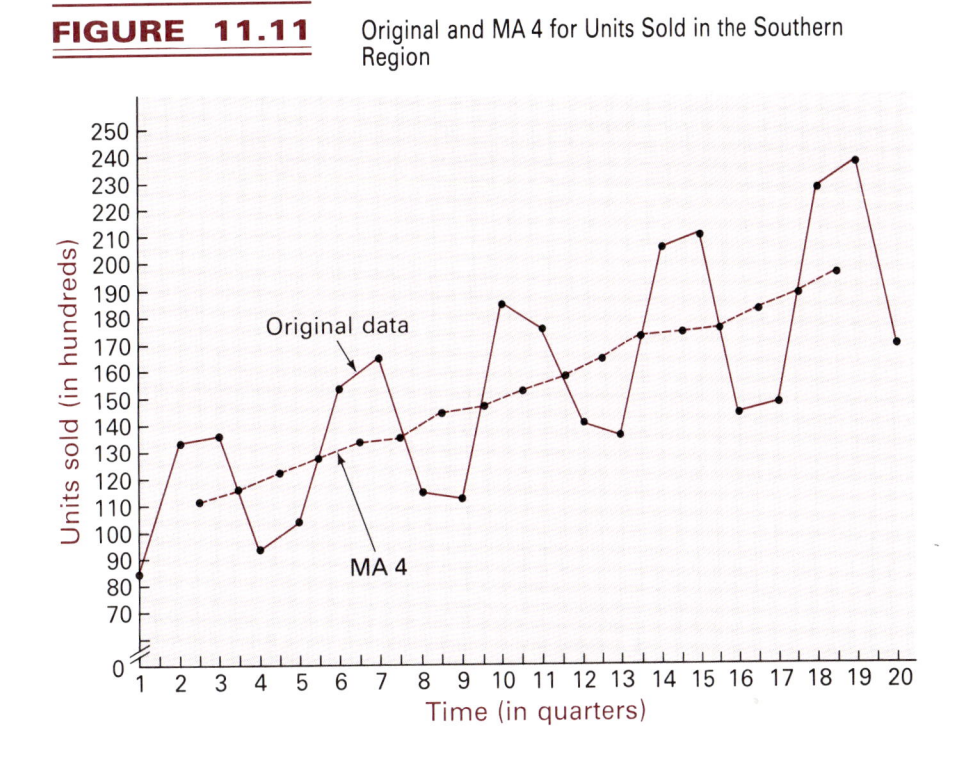

FIGURE 11.11 Original and MA 4 for Units Sold in the Southern Region

raw seasonal indices. The raw seasonal indices contain only two components, *S* and *RF*:

$$\text{Raw seasonal indices} = \frac{\text{Actual data values}}{\text{Moving average values}}$$

$$= \frac{T \times S \times C \times RF}{T \times C} = S \times RF \quad (11.10)$$

Centered moving average Expression (11.10) says to divide the original time series values by the moving average values. Now a problem arises. The original data are quarterly sales as of March 31st, June 30th, September 30th, and December 31st over five years. The moving average is the mean sales as of August 15th, November 15th, February 15th, and May 15th over the five years. We cannot divide the two time series because of the different calendar dates. However, by centering the moving average we can *line up* the moving average and original time series values. Only then is division meaningful.

We compute the mean of the first two moving average values of Table 11.12. The first value of the centered moving average is (112 + 116.75)/2, or 114.38. We place this value halfway between the August 15th and November 15th calendar dates—that is, September 30th. Now the first value lines up with the September 30th calendar date of the original time series. Notice how all the values of the centered moving average line up with the data in the original data set. Now we can divide the two time data sets as per expression (11.10).

Raw seasonal indices Raw seasonal indices measure the level of activity of a specific period (day, quarter, or month) compared to the mean activity for that year. The raw seasonal indices include the seasonal and random fluctuation components, *S* and *RF*.

For the COMCEL data, the raw seasonal index for quarter 3 in 1989 is the actual data value for quarter 3 divided by the centered moving average data value for quarter 3:

$$\text{Raw seasonal index for 1989 quarter 3} = \frac{136}{114.38} = 1.189 \text{ or } 118.9\%$$

Thus, the actual sales were 18.9% higher than the centered moving average for the same quarter. The seasonal and random fluctuation components account for the 18.9% increase. If the random component is small, the seasonal impact explains most of the 18.9% sales increase over the trend and cycle. Simply put, sales were strong in the third quarter—almost 19% above the centered moving average.

The raw seasonal index for quarter 4 in 1989 is 94/119.38 = .7874 or 78.74%. Actual sales were only 78.74% of the centered moving average, or trend and cycle, value. Thus, sales were weak in the fourth quarter. Table 11.13 contains the raw seasonal index calculations. The format of Table 11.13 makes it difficult to see if there is a seasonal pattern. We transferred the raw seasonal indices of Table 11.13 into a year-by-quarter table. See Table 11.14.

Table 11.13

Calculating Raw Seasonal Indices—*S* and *RF* Components

TIME	Calendar Date	Time Series	Centered MA	Raw Seasonal Indices
1	3/31/89	85	Cannot determine	
2	6/30/89	133	Cannot determine	
3	9/30/89	136	114.38	1.1890
4	12/31/89	94	119.38	.7874
5	3/31/90	104	125.75	.8270
6	6/30/90	154	132.13	1.1655
7	9/30/90	166	135.75	1.2228
8	12/31/90	115	140.50	.8185
9	3/31/91	112	145.38	.7704
10	6/30/91	184	149.63	1.2297
11	9/30/91	175	155.75	1.1236
12	12/31/91	140	161.38	.8675
13	3/31/92	136	168.38	.8077
14	6/30/92	205	173.25	1.1833
15	9/30/92	210	175.25	1.1983
16	12/31/92	144	179.75	.8011
17	3/31/93	148	186.13	.7951
18	6/30/93	229	192.75	1.1881
19	9/30/93	237	Cannot determine	
20	12/31/93	170	Cannot determine	

Table 11.14

Year-by-Quarter Table of Raw Seasonal Indices

Year	1	2	3	4
1989	Cannot determine		1.1890	.7874
1990	.8270	1.1655	1.2228	.8185
1991	.7704	1.2297	1.1236	.8675
1992	.8077	1.1833	1.1983	.8011
1993	.7951	1.1881	Cannot determine	

Quarters

Before continuing with the seasonal analysis, please compare the two sets of raw seasonal indices in Table 11.15 on page 640 with the indices in Table 11.14. Which set exhibits a seasonal pattern, which set exhibits wide variation but no seasonal pattern, and which set exhibits no seasonal pattern at all? Please think about it before reading on.

The raw seasonal indices in Table 11.14 exhibit a seasonal pattern. In each year, sales are low in the first and fourth quarters and high in the second and third

Table 11.15

Two Additional Year-by-Quarter Tables of Raw Seasonal Indices

Set A
Quarters

Year	1	2	3	4
1989	Cannot determine	1.4100	.4096	
1990	1.1500	.8691	.9774	.3089
1991	1.3567	.7900	.8311	1.2100
1992	.1056	1.5023	1.5109	1.3451
1993	.4530	1.6789	Cannot determine	

Set B
Quarters

Year	1	2	3	4
1989	Cannot determine	1.0003	.9989	
1990	1.0067	.9899	1.0001	1.0023
1991	.9999	1.0023	.9991	.9995
1992	1.0005	.9999	1.0100	1.0003
1993	.9995	1.0029	Cannot determine	

quarters. The pattern is stable and repeatable. Note that there is much variation between quarters in each year, but little variation within each quarter between years. That variation pattern suggests a *seasonal* component.

In contrast, Set A has much variability but no repeatable pattern—no detectable seasonal component. There is much variation within each quarter between years. For example, the first quarter raw seasonal indices varied from a low of .1056 to a high of 1.3567. There is no stable pattern from year to year. In short, there is much variation, but it is not a seasonal pattern. It is probably *random* fluctuation.

Set B also indicates a lack of any seasonal pattern. All indices are close to 1.0 in each quarter. The level of activity for each quarter is neither higher nor lower than the mean sales for the year. The indices in Set B represent sales of bread. As compared to ice cream or jewelry, bread sales are not affected by time of year— June weddings or Christmas—or temperature. Lack of variation within and between quarters over the five years indicates *no seasonality*.

Return to the COMCEL car phone study data. From Table 11.14 we have concluded that there is a seasonal pattern. Now we want to quantify it. Remember, each number in Table 11.14 consists of two components—seasonal and random fluctuation. Now we isolate the seasonal component by computing *typical seasonal indices*.

Typical seasonal indices Raw seasonal indices measure the level of activity of a *specific period* compared to the mean activity for that year. We speak of the raw seasonal index for the third quarter of 1991 or 1992. Typical seasonal indices measure the level of activity of a *typical period* compared to the mean activity for a *typical year*. We speak of a typical seasonal index for the third quarter or the first quarter. The raw seasonal indices contain the seasonal and random fluctuation components, whereas the typical seasonal indices contain only the seasonal component.

To obtain the typical seasonal indices, we must eliminate random fluctuation from the raw seasonal indices. We do this by computing *trimmed means*. Referring to Table 11.14, we eliminate the high and low raw seasonal indices for a quarter and then compute the mean of the remaining values. For example, to compute the trimmed mean for quarter 1, we eliminate the 1990 (the highest) and the 1991 (the lowest) quarter 1 raw seasonal indices. The trimmed mean is the mean of the remaining two indices, $(.8077 + .7951)/2 = .8014$. We would compute trimmed means in the same way for monthly data.

Here is the logic behind averaging. The differences among the raw seasonal indices for a given quarter over the five years are due to random fluctuation. By computing the trimmed means, we eliminate random fluctuation.

We must adjust the trimmed means to obtain the typical seasonal indices. The sum of the four trimmed means in Table 11.16 should be 4, for the following reason. Sales will be relatively strong in some quarters (or months) and the trimmed means will be greater than 1. Sales will be relatively weak in other quarters and the trimmed means will be less than 1. Strong quarters cancel out weak quarters and the mean of the four typical seasonal indices must be 1, or the sum must be 4. From Table 11.16, the sum of four trimmed means is 3.9906. The reason the sum is not 4 (or 12 for monthly data) is that we eliminated the lowest and highest raw seasonal indices within each quarter before computing the trimmed means. To make the adjustment, multiply each trimmed mean by 1.0024 (i.e., 4.00/3.9906) to obtain the four typical seasonal indices.

WARNING: Do not use the decomposition method unless you have five or more years of quarterly or monthly data. In computing the typical seasonal indices, we lose one year of data. (See Table 11.16.) First, we cannot determine the raw seasonal indices of the first two quarters of 1989 and the last two quarters of 1993. Then, we throw out two years of raw seasonal indices in computing the

Table 11.16

Typical Seasonal Indices Calculations

Year	Quarter 1	Quarter 2	Quarter 3	Quarter 4	
1989	Cannot determine		1.1890	.7874	
1990	.8270	1.1655	1.2228	.8185	
1991	.7704	1.2297	1.1236	.8675	
1992	.8077	1.1833	1.1983	.8011	
1993	.7951	1.1881	Cannot determine		
Trimmed means	.8014	1.1857	1.1937	.8098	3.9906
Typical seasonal indices	.8033	1.1885	1.1966	.8117	4.0000

trimmed means. That leaves only two raw seasonal indices for each period, which is barely enough to compute a meaningful typical seasonal index.

Deseasonalized Data

Before determining the trend pattern, we *deseasonalize* the data by removing the seasonal pattern from the original time series values. Deseasonalized data are also known as seasonally adjusted data:

$$\text{Deseasonalized data} = \frac{T \times S \times C \times RF}{S} = T \times C \times RF \quad (11.11)$$

Equation (11.11) says to divide the original data values by the typical seasonal indices to obtain deseasonalized data. In the COMCEL data set (see Table 11.17), for example, the deseasonalized data value for period 1 is 85/.8033 = 105.81, or 10,581 phones.

In Figure 11.12 the graph of the deseasonalized data is *smoother* than that of the original data, because the deseasonalized data do not contain the seasonal pattern. In fact, the trend pattern literally jumps out at us from the

Table 11.17
Deseasonalized, or Seasonally Adjusted, Data

Original Data (hundreds)	Typical Seasonal Indices	Deseasonalized Data (hundreds)
85	.8033	105.81
133	1.1885	111.91
136	1.1966	113.66
94	.8117	115.81
104	.8033	129.47
154	1.1885	129.58
166	1.1966	138.73
115	.8117	141.68
112	.8033	139.42
184	1.1885	154.82
175	1.1966	146.25
140	.8117	172.48
136	.8033	169.30
205	1.1885	172.49
210	1.1966	175.50
144	.8117	177.41
148	.8033	184.24
229	1.1885	192.68
237	1.1966	198.06
170	.8117	209.44

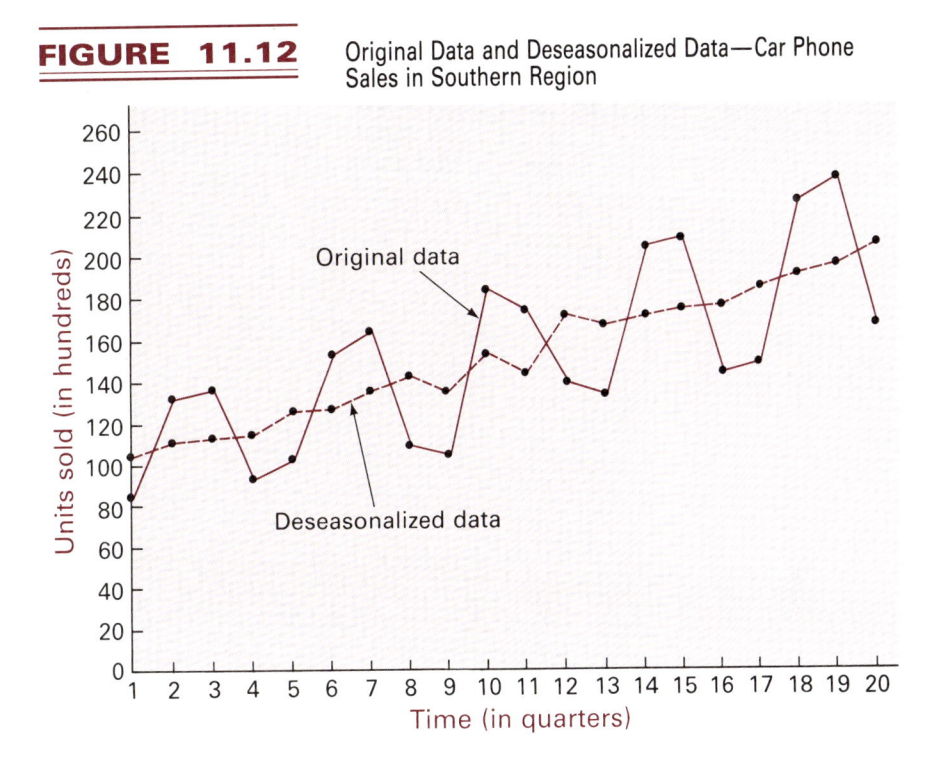

FIGURE 11.12 Original Data and Deseasonalized Data—Car Phone Sales in Southern Region

deseasonalized data. We will carry out the trend analysis next and it will quantify this observed trend pattern, just as the ratio to moving average method quantified the seasonal pattern.

WARNING: Do *not* deseasonalize the data if there is no stable seasonal pattern (see Table 11.15, Set A) or if there is no seasonal pattern at all (see Table 11.15, Set B). Deseasonalizing does not make sense when there is no seasonal pattern. Instead of using deseasonalized data for the trend analysis, we would use the *original* data.

The Trend Pattern

Table 11.18 on page 644 contains the data for determining the best-fitting trend line for the COMCEL data. The dependent variable is deseasonalized sales and the independent variable is TIME, 1, 2, 3, ..., 20. The deseasonalized data are always the dependent variable for the trend analysis, except when there is no stable seasonal component or no seasonal component at all. Then we use the original data.

In the regression models of Section 11.3, the independent variables were legitimate predictor variables. "Legitimate" means that we believed the predictor variables affected Y. In trend analysis, TIME, the independent variable, is a *proxy* variable. We know that TIME does not affect Y. It serves as a substitute for the predictor variables in regression-based forecasting models.

Table 11.18

COMCEL Sales Data for Trend Analysis

Period TIME	Deseasonalized Data Y	Period TIME	Deseasonalized Data Y
1	105.81	11	146.25
2	111.91	12	172.48
3	113.66	13	169.30
4	115.81	14	172.49
5	129.47	15	175.50
6	129.58	16	177.41
7	138.73	17	184.24
8	141.68	18	192.68
9	139.42	19	198.06
10	154.82	20	209.44

Our software package fits four best-fitting trend equations to the deseasonalized data—linear, exponential, power, and quadratic. Following are the equations of the four functions, as well as their graphs in Figures 11.13a–11.13d.

Trend	Equation	
Linear	Y-PRED $= a + b$TIME	(11.12)
Exponential	Y-PRED $= ae^{b\text{TIME}}$	(11.13)
Power	Y-PRED $= a\text{TIME}^b$	(11.14)
Quadratic	Y-PRED $= a + b\text{TIME} + c\text{TIME}^2$	(11.15)

For a linear trend equation, Y increases or decreases by a constant amount, b, each period. For an exponential trend, Y increases (or decreases) by an increasing (or decreasing) amount each period. A power trend equation is a very versatile curve. Its shape depends on its value of b. See Figure 11.13c on page 646 for some power curves. A quadratic trend equation is U-shaped—Y peaks or bottoms out.*

Returning to the COMCEL sales data, we used our software to compute the four trend lines for the 20 quarters of deseasonalized data (see Table 11.18). The software provides the MAPE for Y vs. Y-PRED for the 20 quarters of data for each curve. The results are given in Table 11.19 on page 647.

---

*Using the terminology of Chapter 10, equations (11.12) and (11.15) are linear in the parameters. That is, no regression coefficient appears as an exponent or is multiplied or divided by another regression coefficient. Equations (11.13) and (11.14) are not linear in the parameters. We will not present the four sets of least squares equations to determine the regression coefficients because there is no need. Use our software to determine the four best-fitting trend equations.

FIGURE 11.13a Linear Trend Patterns

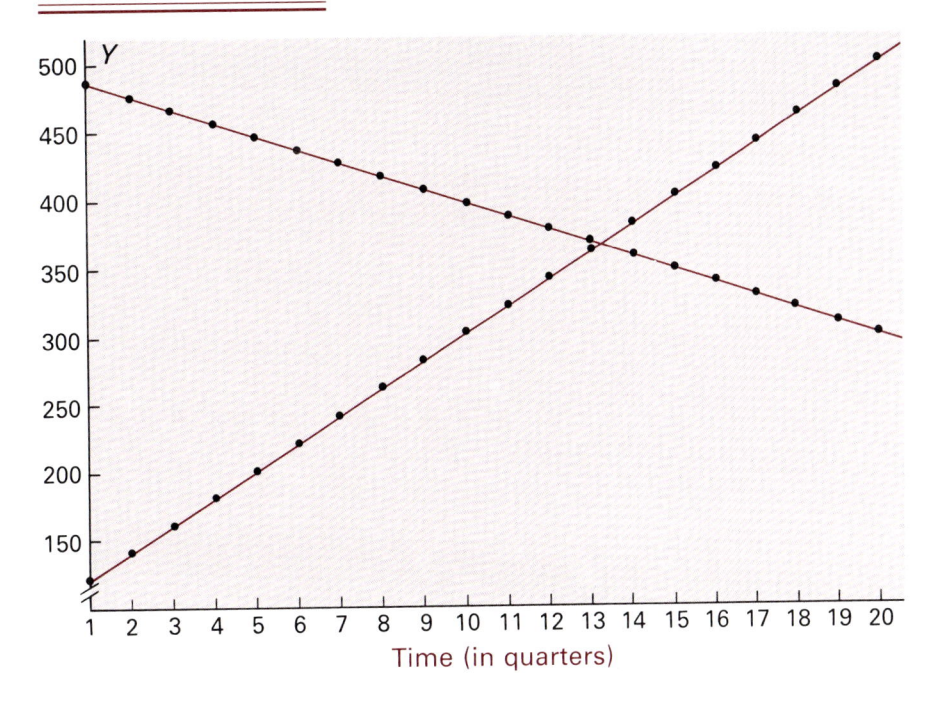

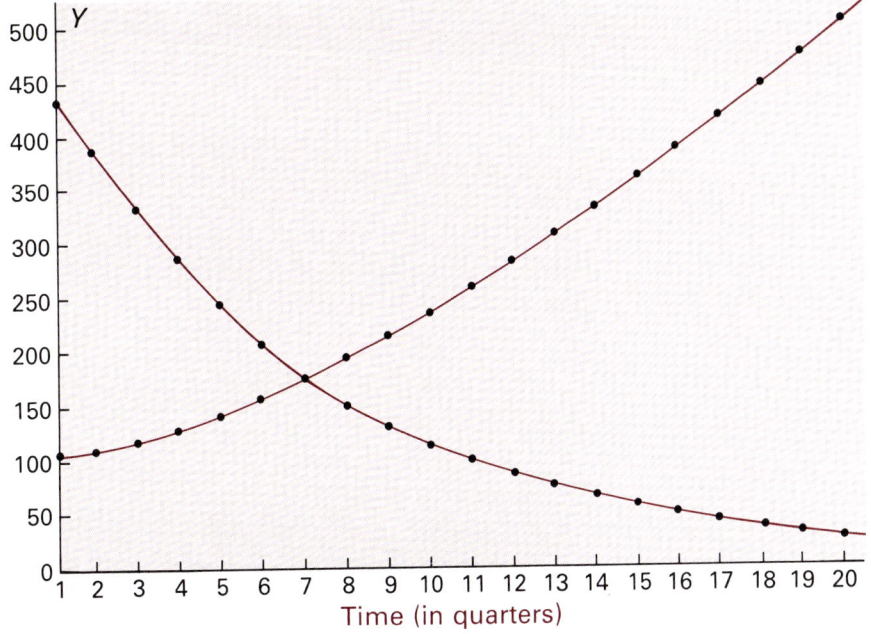

Time (in quarters)

FIGURE 11.13b Exponential Trend Patterns

Time (in quarters)

FIGURE 11.13c Power Trend Patterns

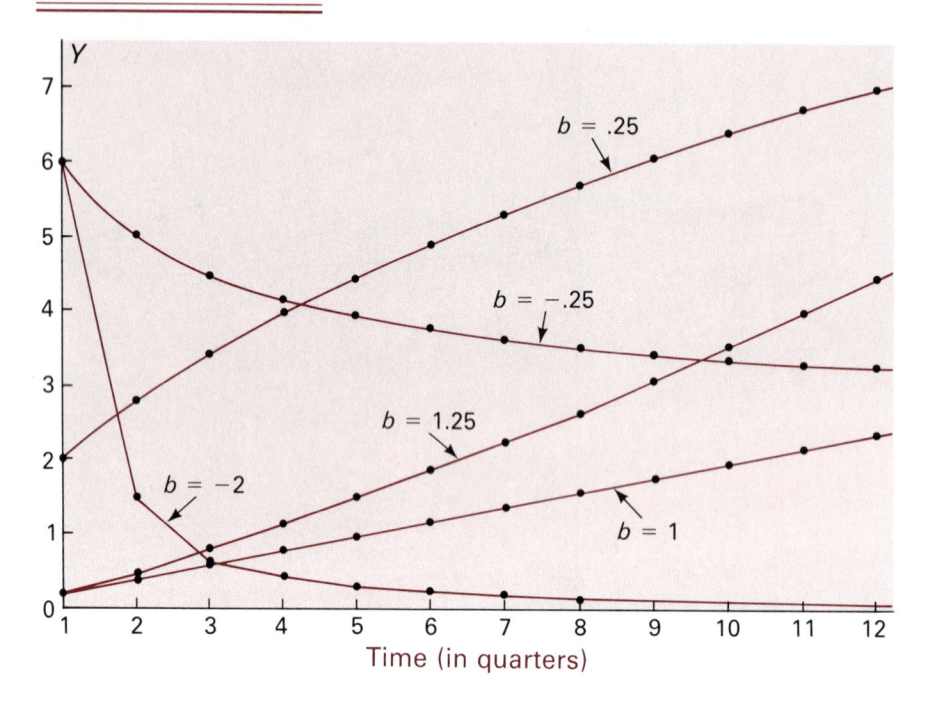

FIGURE 11.13d Quadratic Trend Patterns

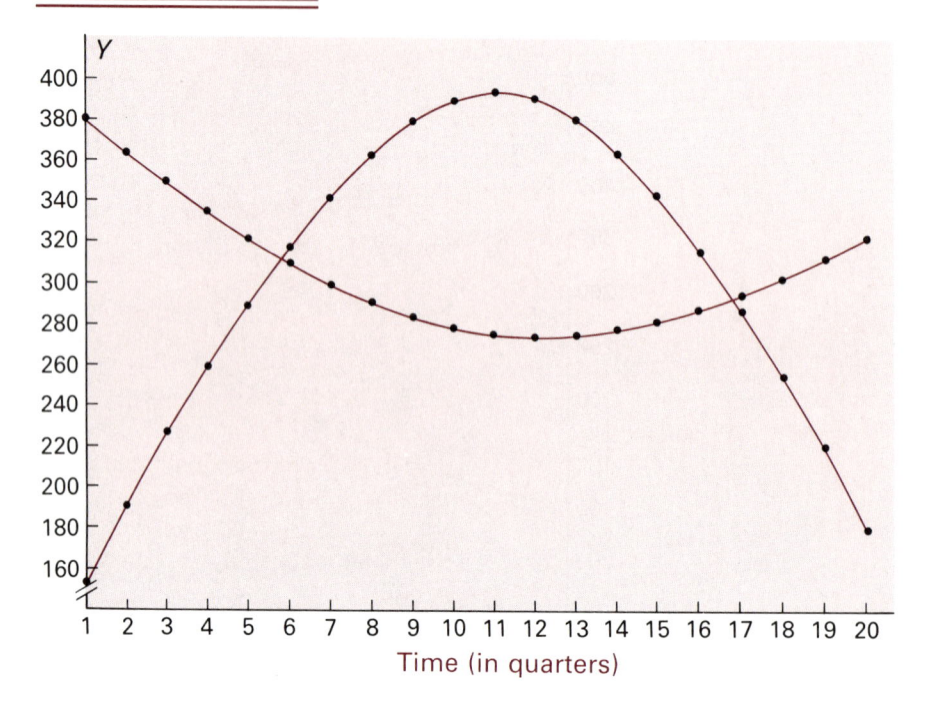

Table 11.19

Summary of Best-Fitting Equations for COMCEL Deseasonalized Data

Curve Type	Equation	MAPE	
Linear	Y-PRED $= 99.350 + 5.198$TIME	2.27%	(11.16)
Exponential	Y-PRED $= 105.091 e^{.0344 \text{TIME}}$	2.65%	(11.17)
Power	Y-PRED $= 90.915 \text{TIME}^{.239}$	5.49%	(11.18)
Quadratic	Y-PRED $= 101.023 + 4.742$TIME $+ .0217$TIME^2	2.96%	(11.19)

The best-fitting linear trend equation has an intercept of 99.350 and a slope of 5.198. It is the best-fitting linear line in the sense that it minimizes the sum of the squared deviations between Y and Y-PRED. The other three equations are likewise the best for their respective curves. Which trend equation should we select for forecasting? That is, which one is best *overall*? We recommend two strategies for making the selection.

Lowest MAPE Select the equation that has the lowest MAPE. In the COMCEL study, it is the linear trend equation. Over the past 20 quarters it has proven to be the best with a mean forecasting error of only 2.27%. If the assumption of continuity holds, it should produce the smallest forecasting errors over the next several quarters.

We could also select the curve that produces the lowest MAPE for the most recent one or two years. As the recent past may be more relevant for forecasting than the distant past, we could select that curve with the best most recent, not overall, performance.

When we forecast sales of consumer products, consider using a second strategy for selecting the overall best equation.

Product life cycle The product life cycle in Figure 11.1 on page 612 reflects a consumer product's sales growth and decline. During phase I, Introduction, sales increase slowly at first and then increase rapidly. During phase II, Growth, sales increase at a steady rate. During phase III, Maturity, sales, while still increasing, slow down as consumers lose interest in the product. During phase IV, Decline, sales peak and begin to drop. Sales will continue to drop unless the firm revitalizes the product or its marketing campaign.

The best overall trend equation depends on where a consumer product is in its life cycle. Here are some recommendations:

Phase	Consider using
Introduction	Exponential trend equation
Growth	Linear trend equation
Maturity	Power or quadratic trend equation
Decline	Quadratic or power trend equation

Since COMCEL has sold car phones for five years, sales are probably in the growth phase. Thus a linear trend equation is appropriate. In conclusion, use the linear trend equation as it is best according to both the MAPE and product life cycle strategies.

What should we do when the MAPE and product life cycle strategies recommend different trend equations? Select that trend equation that is easiest to explain to others. Usually, that will be the most straightforward. After all, if we cannot explain our forecast clearly, no one will listen. In explaining forecasts, use graphs. For example, do not try to explain a power curve in words. Graphs speak louder than words.

The Cycle Pattern

Before using the linear trend equation and the typical seasonal indices for forecasting, we must check for a cyclical pattern. If there is a cyclical pattern, our forecasts, which include only the trend and seasonal components, may be incorrect.

In the ratio to moving average method we constructed a centered moving average to determine the typical seasonal indices. This average contains the trend and cycle components. We can obtain the cycle component (if any) by

Table 11.20

Isolating a Possible Cyclical Pattern

Period TIME	Centered Moving Average $(T \times C)$	99.350 + 5.198TIME (T)	Cycle (C)
1	Cannot determine	104.55	Cannot determine
2	Cannot determine	109.75	Cannot determine
3	114.38	114.94	.995
4	119.38	120.14	.994
5	125.75	125.34	1.003
6	132.13	130.54	1.012
7	135.75	135.74	1.000
8	140.50	140.93	.997
9	145.38	146.13	.995
10	149.63	151.33	.989
11	155.75	156.53	.995
12	161.38	161.73	.998
13	168.38	166.92	1.009
14	173.25	172.12	1.007
15	175.25	177.32	.988
16	179.75	182.52	.985
17	186.13	187.72	.992
18	192.75	192.91	.999
19	Cannot determine	198.11	Cannot determine
20	Cannot determine	203.31	Cannot determine

dividing each centered moving average data value by the predicted trend value:

$$\frac{T \times C}{T} = C \tag{11.20}$$

Table 11.20 shows the computations for identifying a possible cycle component for the COMCEL data. The second column contains the values of the centered moving average taken from Table 11.12 and the third column contains the predicted trend values calculated from the best trend equation, linear equation (11.16). The values of the second column divided by the corresponding values in the third column give the cyclical indices in the fourth column.

In general economic terms, cyclical indices greater than 1 signify a booming economy. The economy is either in the growth (I), prosperity (II), or warning (III) phase (see Figure 11.3 on page 614). Cyclical indices less than 1 indicate a stagnant economy. The economy is either in the recession (IV), depression (V), or recovery (VI) phase.

Figure 11.14 is a plot of the cyclical indices for the COMCEL data. There does appear to be a cyclical pattern. The first cycle might have started in period 2 and concluded in period 11. A second cycle might have started in period 11 and concluded in period 18.

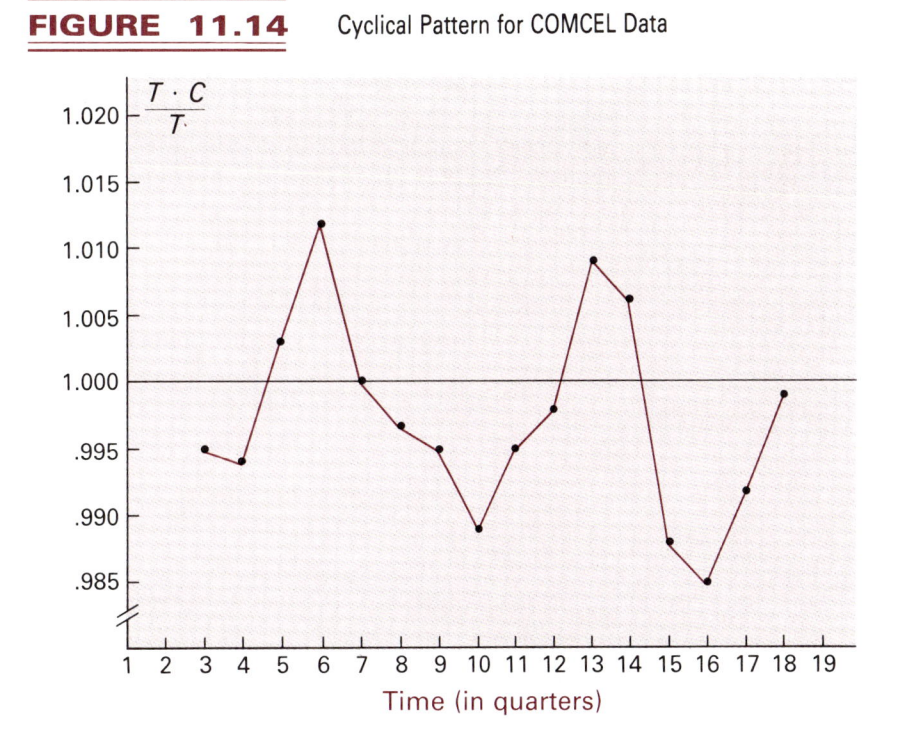

FIGURE 11.14 Cyclical Pattern for COMCEL Data

WARNING: Since cycles do not have constant lengths or magnitudes, it is difficult to estimate future cyclical indices. *If* history is any guide, it appears from Figure 11.14 that the economy is about to enter a growth phase in quarter 19 or 20. However, around periods 21–23 the economy may go stagnant. We may wish to include booming and stagnant economies in our forecasts.

Estimating cyclical indices involves more than looking at historic patterns such as Figure 11.14. It requires knowledge of the level of economic or industry activity during the periods to be forecasted. Such knowledge is often judgmental and perhaps the qualitative forecasting methods presented in Section 11.5 will be helpful.

Short-Term Forecasting

We have isolated the trend and seasonal patterns and a possible cyclical pattern. We can now prepare a forecast for the upcoming four quarters of 1994, periods 21–24. We develop the initial forecasts by multiplying the trend value for each forecast period by the appropriate typical seasonal index. Remember, we are using a multiplicative—*not* additive—decomposition model. Table 11.21 illustrates the forecasts for the next four quarters. The first quarter of 1994 is quarter 21. Remember, the historical data in Table 11.10 cover periods 1–20.

To forecast quarter 1 of 1994 (period 21), we multiply the trend value for the quarter from the second column by the typical seasonal index for the quarter in the third column. The forecast based on trend and seasonal index is 167.50, or 16,750 car phones. We generated the other three forecasts in the same way.

We can then incorporate cycle into the forecast by *estimating* the cyclical indices for periods 21–24. Suppose we estimate 1.02, 1.01, .99, and .98. Given the multiplicative model, we multiply the forecast values in Table 11.21 by these numbers. Our final forecast for the first quarter of 1994 is

Forecast for quarter 1, 1994 = (167.50)(1.02) = 170.85, or 17,085 phones

Including the estimated cyclical indices allows managers to do "what-ifying." They can prepare forecasts assuming that the economy will grow or that it

Table 11.21

Forecast Using Linear Trend Equation and Typical Seasonal Indices

TIME	Linear Trend Value 99.350 + 5.198TIME	Typical Seasonal Index	Forecast
21	208.51	.8033	167.50
22	213.71	1.1885	253.99
23	218.90	1.1966	261.94
24	224.10	.8117	181.90

Chapter 11 Forecasting and Time Series Analysis

FIGURE 11.15 Flowchart for the Decomposition Method

Flowchart (left column):

- Time, $t = 1, 2, \ldots$
  Orig. data: $T \times S \times C \times RF$
- Compute centered moving average.
- Compute raw seasonal indices.
- Compute typical seasonal indices.
- Deseasonalize original data.
- X: Time, $t = 1, 2, \ldots$
  Y: Deseasonalized data
- Select a best-fitting trend equation.
- Identify possible cyclical component.
- Generate forecast for two to six quarters.

Description (right column):

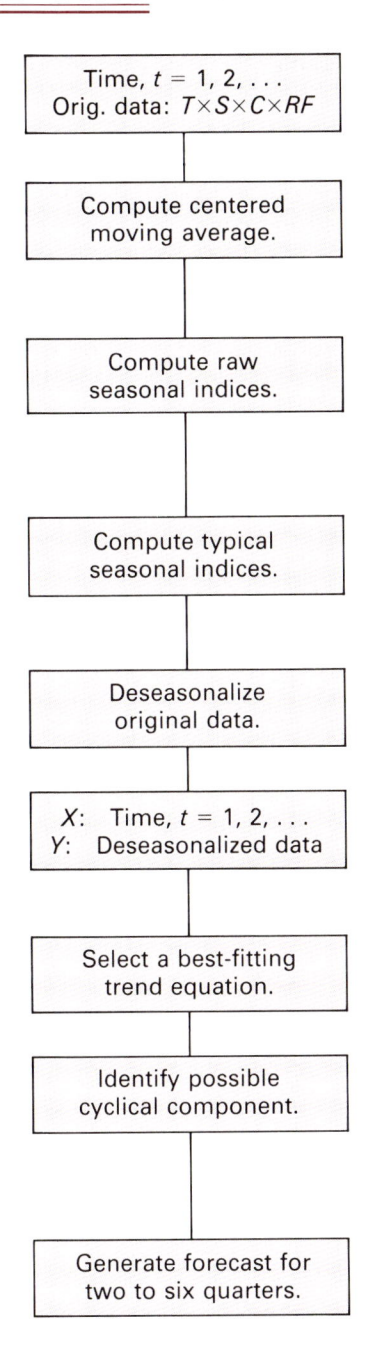

Begin with either monthly or quarterly data. Assume that the data are a multiplicative function of trend, seasonal, cycle, and random fluctuation.

First compute a MA 4 (quarterly data) or a MA 12 (monthly data). Center the moving average. The moving average contains only a trend and a cycle component.

Divide the original time series by the *centered* moving average. The resulting raw seasonal indices measure the level of activity in a specific period (quarter or month) compared to the mean activity for that year.

For each period eliminate the highest and lowest raw seasonal indices. Check the stability of indices for each period. If stable, compute the typical seasonal indices. These are used for forecasting.

Divide the original data by the typical seasonal indices. The resulting seasonally adjusted data contain only a trend, cycle, and random fluctuation component.

These are input data for the trend analysis. Use the original data if there is no stable seasonal or if there is no seasonal pattern at all.

The software package provides the best linear, exponential, power, and quadratic trend equations. Base the selection on the lowest-MAPE trend equation or use the product life cycle strategy.

Divide the centered moving average by the trend values from the selected trend curve. Plot the cyclical indices.

Assuming no cyclical pattern, forecast using the trend and seasonal patterns. For N periods of historical data, the first four forecast periods are $N + 1$, $N + 2$, $N + 3$, and $N + 4$. We can "what-if" the forecast by assuming either a booming or stagnant economy. Multiply the product of the trend and seasonal forecasts by the estimated cyclical indices.

will stagnate. They would select cyclical indices greater than 1 if they believe the economy will grow over the forecast period. They would select indices less than 1 if they believe the economy will stagnate. Making different assumptions about the economy or industry and incorporating them into the forecasts is called *"what-if"* analysis.

Table 11.21 provides a four-quarter forecast based on the trend and seasonal components. We could forecast more periods into the future, but that is risky. The decomposition method provides reasonably good forecasts for four to six quarters. Beyond that, the assumption of continuity may not hold. That is, whatever happened in the past is less likely to continue for the long term.

We suggest updating a forecast every quarter or as additional data become available, but forecasting only four to six quarters into the future.

One final reminder: If the data do not contain a stable seasonal pattern or a seasonal pattern at all, our forecast will consist of a trend component only—and possibly a cyclical component.

Summary of the Decomposition Method

Figure 11.15 summarizes the major steps in the decomposition method. We use the decomposition method to make short-term forecasts if there are at least five years of historical data. Our goal is to detect and quantify the trend, seasonal, and cyclical patterns if they exist. The decomposition method assumes that the recent past is a guide to the near future. That is, whatever happened recently will continue to happen. The decomposition method can produce accurate forecasts up to six quarters.

SECTION 11.4 EXERCISES

1. Complete the following table. Put a dash if the value cannot be calculated.

Year	Quarter	Value	MA 4	Centered Moving Average
1	1	4		
	2	6		
	3	10	___	___
	4	12	___	___
2	1	17	___	___
	2	20	___	___
	3	22	___	___
	4	26	___	___

Chapter 11 Forecasting and Time Series Analysis 653

2. Find the typical seasonal indices from the following raw seasonal indices:

	Quarter			
Year	1	2	3	4
1989	—	—	1.10	1.20
1990	.85	.90	1.15	1.30
1991	.80	.88	1.13	1.18
1992	.84	.75	1.20	1.15
1993	.86	.85	—	—

3. Does the following year-by-quarter table indicate a stable seasonal pattern? If not, why not?

	Quarter			
Year	1	2	3	4
1989	—	—	.8	1.2
1990	.6	1.4	1.2	.8
1991	1.3	.5	.3	1.9
1992	.2	1.0	1.1	.6
1993	1.1	.7	—	—

4. Shown are six months of inventory data (INVEN and INVEN-PRED). Compute the MAPE.

Period	Jan.	Feb.	March	April	May	June
INVEN	10	7	8	9	13	15
INVEN-PRED	8	6	9	11	13	14

5. Complete the following table:

Quarter	Original Value	Typical Seasonal Index	Deseasonalized Values
1	100	1.1	_____
2	120	.9	_____
3	140	1.2	_____
4	150	.8	_____

6. We fitted a linear equation to five years of deseasonalized quarterly sales data using the method of least squares. The resulting equation was

$$\text{SALES-PRED} = 15 + 3\text{TIME}$$

The typical seasonal indices for this series are

$$S_1 = .95; \quad S_2 = .90; \quad S_3 = 1.05; \quad S_4 = 1.10$$

Forecast the sales for quarters 21–24, which are quarters 1–4 of the sixth year.

7. Shown are the centered moving averages and the trend values for a time series. Compute and plot the cyclical indices.

Period	Trend	Centered Moving Average
1	50	60
2	61	68
3	52	59
4	65	66
5	54	53
6	65	60
7	58	56
8	70	70
9	63	66
10	72	77
11	66	70
12	77	80

8. Shown are eight periods of data.

Period	1	2	3	4	5	6	7	8
Y	3	4	5	6	8	12	13	23

Use our software to generate the best-fitting linear and exponential trend curves.
   a. Forecast the next three periods with both curves.
   b. Describe the differences between the forecasts for the linear and exponential trend equations.
   c. Which curve would you use for forecasting periods 9–11?

9. Shown are five years of quarterly data. Use our software to develop a forecast for periods 21–24.

1990	1	4	1993	1	23
	2	9		2	36
	3	10		3	37
	4	10		4	35
1991	1	10	1994	1	30
	2	19		2	47
	3	18		3	45
	4	18		4	39
1992	1	19			
	2	28			
	3	29			
	4	26			

a. Plot SALES vs. TIME. Do there appear to be trend and seasonal patterns?
b. Use our software to determine the typical seasonal indices (if any) and the four best-fitting trend curves. Using the MAPE strategy, select a trend curve for forecasting.
c. Forecast SALES for the next four quarters based on the trend and seasonal patterns.

10. Shown are time-ordered data for eight periods.

Period	1	2	3	4	5	6	7	8
Y	2	5	9	14	21	30	38	49

a. Plot a line graph of Y vs. TIME.
b. Draw a freehand best-fitting line.
c. Does it appear that a linear or power curve best represents the data? Describe in your own words the growth in sales.

11.5 Qualitative Forecasting Methods

Time series and regression methods provide accurate short-term forecasts. Both are useful when we have past numerical data and we can assume that either the past data patterns or relationships among variables will continue into the near future. Qualitative approaches do not require numerical data and are often used for making rough long-term forecasts. They are useful for making short-term forecasts when quantitative data do not exist. Qualitative approaches are also useful when we do *not* expect the future to be like the recent past. By the end of this section you should be able to:

1. explain and run a nominal group expert panel; and
2. explain and run a Delphi study.

Expert Panels

In its most basic form, an expert panel is simply a group of executives or professionals sitting around a table making forecasts about the future. Generally, a company brings together panel members from various departments, thereby providing a broad base of experience and judgment. Whenever possible, the panel members are provided with background reports on the economy and specific information about the products of the firm. The expert panel is one of the simplest and most widely used forecasting methods in industry.

An expert panel develops quick forecasts while pooling the best talent available from within or outside the firm. The major drawbacks of such panels are that they rely on judgment (see Table 11.2 for faulty rules of thumb), require costly executive time, and disperse forecasting responsibility. Moreover, groups can be ineffective.

We recommend the *nominal group method* for running expert panels. It will minimize some of the problems of face-to-face expert panel meetings. Van de Ven and Delbecq's (1974) nominal group method (NGM) produces more accurate decisions or judgments, and stronger feelings of accomplishment than free-flowing, or interacting, expert panels. Interacting groups have no formal rules or structures to organize or control members' participation. People speak when they have something to say; otherwise, they remain quiet.

The assumption underlying the nominal group method is that difference of opinion is important at arriving at a good forecast. Disagreements force group members to explain their underlying beliefs. Group members can "reality test" their assumptions and beliefs and thereby produce more accurate forecasts.

Here are the four steps in the nominal group method:

STEP 1. *Initial thoughts:* Group members *silently* and *independently* generate their forecasts. This can be done even before the meeting starts. Do not allow panel members to communicate during step 1.

STEP 2. *Round robin:* Each member now presents his or her forecast. Do not discuss or criticize the presentations. Permit only questions of clarification. The panel leader can make a presentation, but should go last to avoid putting pressure on others to conform. Also ask panel members to write down and hand in their forecasts.

STEP 3. *Discussion:* The panel explores and compares all the forecasts. Differences are examined, not ignored. The panel leader summarizes frequently and ensures that all forecasts are discussed, especially those suggested by junior team members. Panel members must make the assumptions behind their forecasts explicit. Assumptions are claims (not facts) about the future which support panel members' forecasts. Making assumptions explicit helps "reality test" the forecasts. The panel should strive for a synthesis that incorporates the best of each forecast.

STEP 4. *Closure:* Seek a consensus forecast. If that is not possible, have each member write down a final forecast and submit it to the expert panel leader. Ensure anonymity. The panel leader can then either select the forecast he or she believes is most accurate or compute the mean of the final forecasts.

The nominal group method is superior to the typical expert panel. Brightman (1988) presents suggestions for improving the effectiveness of the nominal group method.

Delphi Method

The name Delphi comes from the site of an ancient Greek temple where the gods of Greek mythology gathered to make forecasts of the future. In its modern form, the Delphi method is a forum for reaching a group consensus about either values or "futures" forecasting (Helmer, 1977).

Unlike most group meetings, the Delphi group members do not meet face to face and may not even know who the others are. All communication is done through writing or electronic mail using computers. This minimizes the problems associated with interacting groups.

We illustrate the Delphi method in the following example. COMCEL wants to estimate the percentage of automobiles that will have telephones as standard equipment by the year 2010. Since they are forecasting many years into the future, quantitative forecasting methods will not work. Therefore, COMCEL tries the Delphi method, as follows.

PHASE 1: *Selection of experts.* COMCEL selected 10 experts from a wide range of functional areas including research and development, marketing, and operations. This ensured a wide range of knowledge and perspective. It also selected 10 outside experts from the telecommunications industry, academe (marketing and sociology professors), and futurists (members of the World Future Society).

PHASE 2: *First-round forecasts.* The Delphi study team leader asked each member to estimate independently the percentage of automobiles with telephones as standard equipment by the year 2010. The group members returned their estimates to the team leader.

PHASE 3: *Summarize results and provide feedback.* The leader summarized and displayed the initial forecasts using descriptive statistics—quartiles and the median—and a box plot, as shown in Figure 11.16.

FIGURE 11.16   Results of Round 1 of the Delphi Study on the Percentage of Cars with Phones by the Year 2010

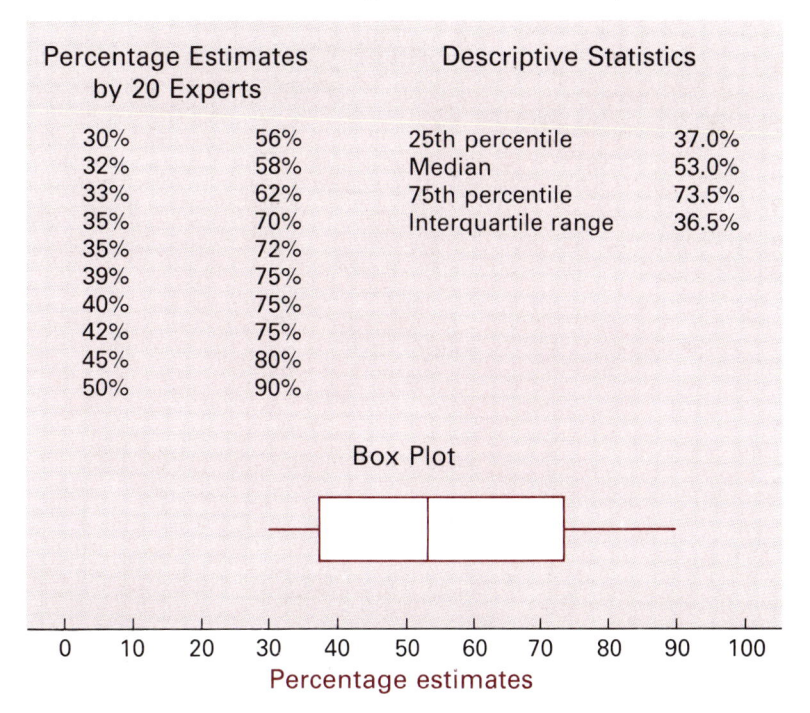

Percentage Estimates by 20 Experts

30%	56%
32%	58%
33%	62%
35%	70%
35%	72%
39%	75%
40%	75%
42%	75%
45%	80%
50%	90%

Descriptive Statistics

25th percentile	37.0%
Median	53.0%
75th percentile	73.5%
Interquartile range	36.5%

Box Plot

The leader sent this information to the group members who could revise their estimates based on the summarized data. Experts who wished to maintain their initially widely divergent estimates—below the 25th or above the 75th percentile—were asked to provide reasons for doing so. The study leader returned the summarized data together with the reasons for any widely divergent forecasts.

PHASE 4: Subsequent feedback. To further narrow the range of percentages, the leader repeated phase 3. The results are given in Figure 11.17. Note that the width of the interquartile range dropped from 36.5% in phase 1 to 9.0%. Had the group not reached a consensus (as evidenced by the small interquartile range), the team leader would have tried additional feedback sessions. Groups often can reach a consensus in three feedback sessions.

The Delphi method permits a spread of opinion to reflect group members' uncertainty. The goal is to narrow the interquartile range without pressuring the group members. Widely divergent views are still possible. However, members with widely divergent views must explain their positions in writing. In doing so, either they convince other members to change their positions or they move toward the median position.

The Delphi method has its strengths and weaknesses. It obtains estimates free of group power or political game playing. With the advent of electronic mail,

FIGURE 11.17 Final Results of the Delphi Study on the Percentage of Cars with Phones by the Year 2010

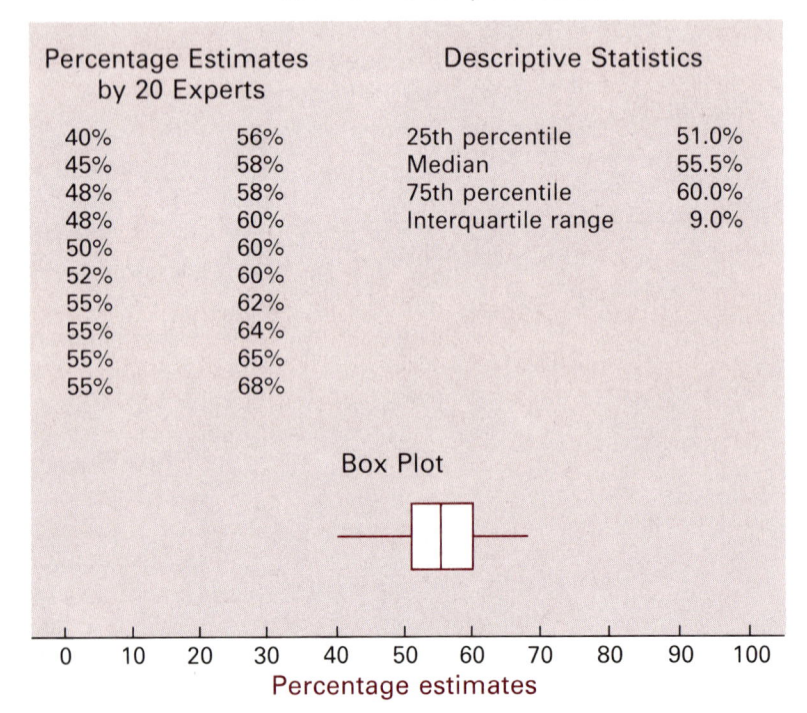

Percentage Estimates by 20 Experts		Descriptive Statistics	
40%	56%	25th percentile	51.0%
45%	58%	Median	55.5%
48%	58%	75th percentile	60.0%
48%	60%	Interquartile range	9.0%
50%	60%		
52%	60%		
55%	62%		
55%	64%		
55%	65%		
55%	68%		

Box Plot

Percentage estimates

it is quick and inexpensive. However, it can produce estimates with low reliability. Also, the study leader can influence the estimates by how he or she frames the questions and reports the findings from each round. Sachman (1975) evaluated the Delphi method and has suggested procedures to overcome its greatest shortcomings. In summary, the Delphi method is useful for reaching consensus on "futures" forecasting.

SECTION 11.5 EXERCISES

1. List the four steps of the nominal group method. Why is this method superior to an unstructured group approach for generating forecasts?
2. What is the Delphi technique? How does it differ from the nominal group technique?
3. A power generating firm is using a nominal group expert panel to estimate the percentage of Columbus, Ohio, metro area homes with insulation at the R30 or higher level by the year 2005. Should we expect that the percentages developed during phase I, the initial thoughts phase, will be similar? Discuss.
4. How might the group leader in a nominal group expert panel use descriptive statistics during the phase III discussion? Discuss.
5. What is the purpose of selecting participants from different functional fields to participate in a Delphi study? Could the strategy backfire? Discuss.

11.6 Key Ideas and Overview

We conclude this chapter on forecasting with the following key ideas:

1. Forecasting is an essential tool in planning. Managers cannot plan if they cannot forecast, nor can they detect deviations from plans if they have no plans. Predicting the future is akin to estimating a population parameter. Unfortunately, we cannot sample the future. In short, obtaining accurate forecasts can be difficult.
2. All quantitative forecasting approaches depend on the critical assumption that the past data patterns or relationships among variables will continue into the near future. If a major change takes place, quantitative models could become useless. For example, the equation used by the U.S. Army to forecast enlistments became useless after the abolition of the draft.
3. Quantitative forecasting approaches include time series methods and causal methods. We use the decomposition method when we are interested only in predicting Y and have at least five years of historical data. Time is the only independent (not a true predictor) variable. We use the regression method when we want to explain and predict future values of Y. Consider lagged variables of Y and X as true predictor variables. Check for multicollinearity and also check residuals against time to determine if the independence assumption has been met. Causal models are generally more costly to build and maintain.

4. The accuracy of quantitative forecasting methods depends on the existence and quality of historical data. If there are insufficient historical data or if the historical data are not representative of the future, use qualitative forecasting methods—the nominal group expert panel or the Delphi group method.

COMCEL

Date: August 17, 1993
To: Ann Tabor, CEO
From: Howard Bright, Manager, Norcross Plant
Re: Southern Region Forecasts

SUMMARY
We have reviewed our forecast and are still projecting that we will sell 86,533 units over the next year. The forecasts are based on the assumption that the forecasted pattern will continue over the next four quarters. The forecast is in line with the sales growth of our product and in line with the product life cycle for the car phone market in general.

SUPPORTING ANALYSIS
We developed the forecast using the method of time series decomposition. The data for the first five years showed a stable seasonal pattern and an underlying linear trend.

Since there is no way to know what the correct trend model is, we fitted several models to the deseasonalized data. We evaluated each model in terms of how well it would have predicted past sales values. The linear model showed the lowest mean absolute percentage prediction error—a mean of 2.27% per quarter. Moreover, we believe that the car phone market is now in the growth phase of the product life cycle. The linear model has proven to be an appropriate description of growth during this phase.

The data provided strong evidence of a seasonal pattern. Over the past five years, we have sold approximately 80% of trend in the first and fourth quarters and approximately 120% of trend in the second and third quarters. I assume that these seasonal indices also will remain the same for the coming year.

We will, of course, monitor these forecasts and make adjustments as needed.

CHAPTER 11 QUESTIONS

1. How does forecasting help managers detect future disturbance problems?
2. Describe a product or service that had an upward trend in the late 1980s. Describe one that had a downward trend in the 1980s.
3. Describe a product or service that has a seasonal pattern. Describe one that has no seasonal pattern.
4. Distinguish between seasonal and cyclical components.
5. Why is the assumption of continuity important in quantitative forecasting methods?
6. A travel agent is preparing a qualitative forecast for next year's number of air fatalities. That day the worst airline disaster in history occurs. How might this affect her forecast and what rule of thumb may she have fallen prey to?
7. Distinguish between regression and autoregression.
8. Explain the problem of using coincident predictor variables in regression models based on time-ordered data.
9. Explain why the mean absolute percentage error (MAPE) is a useful measure of the forecast accuracy.
10. Which of the four linear regression model assumptions is most often violated in time-ordered data? How can we assess the validity of the assumption?
11. What is a major limitation in using regression models for forecasting?
12. What is a leading indicator?
13. Distinguish between additive and multiplicative models.
14. Why must we center the moving average?
15. Why do we lose two data points at the beginning and end of the centered moving average time series for quarterly data? How many points would we lose for monthly data? What is the general rule?
16. Why can't all the typical seasonal indices be greater than 1?
17. What problems will we have if we try the decomposition method on a data set that contains only three years of data?
18. When might the product life cycle method be better than the lowest-MAPE approach in selecting a curve type for the trend component? (*Hint:* In the product life cycle context, when might the recent past not be effective in predicting the short-term future?)
19. Why are quantitative forecasting methods not effective beyond 12 to 18 months into the future?
20. Distinguish between the decomposition method and the regression method as forecasting approaches.
21. How do the nominal group expert panel and the Delphi method overcome many of the problems that face-to-face groups encounter?
22. How do box plots or stem-and-leaf displays help Delphi participants reach a consensus?

CHAPTER 11 APPLICATION PROBLEMS

1. Shown are 20 quarters of earnings per share (EPS) data for a *Fortune* 100 firm.

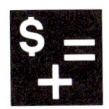

1	$1.50	6	$1.90	11	$2.15	16	$2.40
2	$1.75	7	$1.85	12	$2.10	17	$2.65
3	$1.70	8	$1.95	13	$2.25	18	$2.75
4	$1.75	9	$2.10	14	$2.40	19	$2.85
5	$1.80	10	$2.25	15	$2.45	20	$3.15

a. Plot a line graph of the EPS data. Do there appear to be trend and seasonal components?
b. Use regression analysis to develop a best-fitting straight line with EPS as the dependent variable and the proxy variable, TIME, as the independent variable. Plot the best-fitting line on the graph from part **a**.
c. Compute the MAPE for the linear equation in part **b**.
d. Develop a forecast for quarters 21–22 using the equation from part **b**.
e. TIME appears to be a reasonable proxy variable. For what is it a proxy? Could TIME be a proxy variable for the impact of previous quarters' earnings per shares? That is, could one quarter's EPS depend on the EPS from the previous quarter? Plot EPS vs. EPS-1 (one quarter lag).
f. Use regression analysis to develop a best-fitting line with EPS as the dependent variable and EPS-1 as the independent variable for the following data:

　　　　EPS　　from periods 2–20
　　　　EPS-1　from periods 1–19

g. Compute the MAPE for the autoregressive model.
h. Can you develop a forecast for periods 21–22? If not, develop a forecast for period 21.
i. Develop a line graph for the equations in parts **b** and **f**. Compare and contrast the two forecast equations. How are they similar and how are they different?

2. Shown are the number of grievances filed in a large firm for the past 20 quarters. The firm also records the ratio of the mean salary of skilled employees within the firm to the mean salary for the industry. A number less than 1 means that the firm pays its skilled workers less than the industry mean.

QTR	GRIEV	SALINDEX	QTR	GRIEV	SALINDEX
1	230	.90	11	190	1.18
2	290	.95	12	70	1.16
3	290	1.10	13	100	1.10
4	110	1.07	14	140	1.08
5	160	1.07	15	180	1.18
6	170	1.00	16	100	1.19
7	210	1.15	17	90	1.10
8	100	1.12	18	110	1.12
9	110	1.06	19	150	1.25
10	160	1.05	20	30	1.15

a. Plot a line graph with time on the horizontal axis for the GRIEVance data. Do there appear to be trend and seasonal components?
b. Use the decomposition package to determine the typical seasonal indices and the best-fitting line using the lowest-MAPE strategy. Plot the forecasted number of grievances for periods 1–20 on the line graph from part **a**.
c. Compute the MAPE for the forecasted number of grievances for periods 1–20.
d. Develop a forecast for quarter 21 using the trend and seasonal components.
e. Suppose we believe that the number of grievances is affected by the salary index (SALINDEX). Moreover, we believe that SALINDEX is a one-period leading indicator. Use regression analysis to develop a best-fitting linear line with GRIEV as the dependent variable and SALINDEX-1 as the independent variable

for the following data:

GRIEV from periods 2–20
SALINDEX-1 from periods 1–19

Graph the regression model and original data.
f. Compute the MAPE for the regression model.
g. Develop a forecast for period 21.

3. Shown are 60 months of hypothetical data on the number of mobile car phones bought, in tens of thousands.

	Jan	Feb	Mar	Apr	May	June	July	Aug	Sept	Oct	Nov	Dec
1989	.9	1.1	1.1	1.2	1.3	1.3	1.4	1.6	1.8	1.8	1.9	1.9
1990	1.7	1.9	2.0	2.2	2.1	2.3	2.6	2.9	3.4	3.2	3.5	3.5
1991	3.1	3.7	3.7	3.9	3.8	4.1	4.7	5.2	6.0	5.7	6.5	6.4
1992	5.7	6.1	6.7	7.0	7.0	7.8	8.6	9.8	10.9	10.5	11.5	11.6
1993	10.4	11.4	12.2	12.8	12.7	14.7	15.6	17.3	19.9	19.1	19.0	21.1

a. Plot a line graph of the SALES data. Do there appear to be trend and seasonal components?
b. Use the decomposition package to determine the typical seasonal indices and the best-fitting line using the lowest-MAPE strategy.
c. Compute the MAPE for the sales data for periods 1–60.
d. Develop a forecast for January to March of 1994 using the trend and seasonal components.

4. Shown are 24 quarters of sales data (in thousands of dollars) of a medium-size specialty women's clothing store. Sales are influenced by the timing of the sales promotions, including special one-day sales and other promotions.

TIME	SALES	TIME	SALES
1	80	13	110
2	91	14	81
3	121	15	90
4	110	16	120
5	81	17	111
6	89	18	81
7	119	19	89
8	111	20	119
9	80	21	112
10	90	22	79
11	122	23	90
12	109	24	122

a. Plot the data. Also use our software to compute the *raw* seasonal indices. Obtain a year-by-quarter table of raw seasonal indices. Does there appear to be a stable seasonal component?

b. Look at the raw seasonal indices closely. Can you detect a change in the pattern during the six years of data? Review your graph and the year-by-quarter table. When did a shift in the seasonal pattern happen?

c. What could account for the shift in the seasonal pattern?

5. Given are the total numbers of U.S. nuclear reactors built, being built, or planned (for power generation) between 1973 and 1982. *Source: U.S. Nuclear Regulatory Commission Reports.*

1973	214
1974	233
1975	236
1976	235
1977	221
1978	207
1979	188
1980	163
1981	162
1982	146

a. Plot a line graph.

b. Use the decomposition package to determine the best-fitting line for the data. (*Note:* Since the data are yearly, there are no seasonal indices.)

c. Forecast the numbers of nuclear reactors built, being built, or planned for 1983 to 1991.

d. What are the risks in using the trend analysis from the decomposition method to forecast nine years into the future?

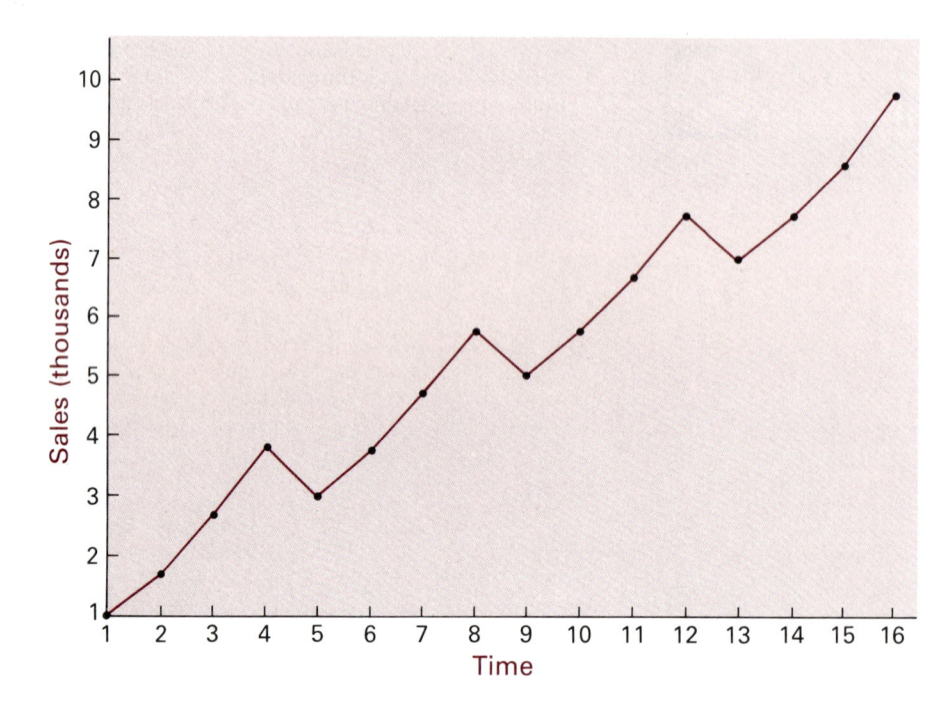

6. A line graph of sales for 16 quarters of data is shown in the figure. Without doing any calculations, would we obtain a lower MAPE on the historical data using an autoregressive model with a one-quarter lag (SALES-1) or a multiplicative time series decomposition model? Explain.

7. We have fitted the following autoregressive model to the monthly closing Dow–Jones Industrial Index for the years 1976 to 1981. The market peaked in December 1976 at about 980 and bottomed out about two years later at under 800. By March 1981 the market again had climbed into the 960 range.

$$\text{DJ-PRED} = 101 + .886\text{DJ-1}$$

The analysis of variance indicated that the predictor and dependent variables are significantly related.

If we had plotted the monthly closing Dow–Jones Index (DJ) vs. the Dow–Jones Index for the previous month (DJ-1), how would the graph look? Explain.

8. A firm's quality control department takes measurements of the diameter of a part. For proper functioning, the diameter should be close to the target value of 40 (in hundredths of an inch). Below are data taken from 16 successive time periods over several days.

TIME	DIAM	TIME	DIAM
1	39	9	41
2	40	10	46
3	39	11	31
4	41	12	32
5	35	13	44
6	30	14	32
7	31	15	46
8	48	16	37

a. Plot a line graph. Also draw a line representing the mean diameter over the 16 measurements.
b. Does there appear to be a trend? Does there appear to be any systematic pattern?
c. Given your answer in part b, if the production process continues to behave as it has for the past 16 observations, what would be your best prediction of future values of DIAM?
d. From the graph in part a, the mean level of the process is constant, the variability of the process about the mean level is relatively constant, and there is no pattern in the timing of the observations around the mean level. What do we call such patternless behavior?
e. Suppose we consider an autoregressive model between DIAM and DIAM-1 (the diameter lagged by one period) for the given data. Without actually determining the model, would we expect a significant relationship between DIAM and DIAM-1? Explain.
f. Suppose that observations 17, 18, and 19 are 70, 71, and 65. What might that suggest in terms of the production process's ability to produce properly functioning parts? As manager of the production process, what should you do? Discuss.

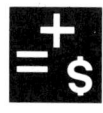

9. Shown are quarterly data on the discount rate charged by the Federal Reserve Bank of New York. The discount rate is the interest rate that the Fed charges its commercial bank customers to borrow money and is one of several tools it uses in managing the overall economy. *Source: Federal Reserve Bulletin* (Monthly).

Quarter	DISCOUNT	Quarter	DISCOUNT
March 1980	13.00%	September 1983	8.75%
June 1980	11.00%	December 1983	8.75%
September 1980	11.00%	March 1984	9.00%
December 1980	13.00%	June 1984	9.00%
March 1981	13.75%	September 1984	8.50%
June 1981	14.00%	December 1984	8.00%
September 1981	13.00%	March 1985	7.75%
December 1981	12.00%	June 1985	7.50%
March 1982	12.00%	September 1985	7.50%
June 1982	11.50%	December 1985	7.00%
September 1982	10.00%	March 1986	7.00%
December 1982	9.00%	June 1986	6.00%
March 1983	8.50%	September 1986	5.50%
June 1983	8.50%	December 1986	5.50%

    a. Plot a line graph of the DISCOUNT data.
    b. Develop an autoregressive model of DISCOUNT vs. DISCOUNT-1. Are the two variables significantly related?
    c. Determine the MAPE for the autoregressive model.
    d. Prepare a forecast for the March 1987 Federal Reserve Bank of New York discount rate.
    e. Using the 1987 *Federal Reserve Bulletin*, compare your forecast with the actual discount rate.

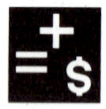

10. Shown are the mean sales (in thousands of dollars) per employee of corporations, SALES, in the United States from 1980 to 1988. *Source: The Fortune Directory*, Time, Inc.

1980	1981	1982	1983	1984	1985	1986	1987	1988
71.1	75.9	91.0	92.2	100.6	106.0	110.7	124.4	137.9

    a. Plot a line graph of mean sales per employee for 1980 to 1988.
    b. Use regression analysis to develop a best-fitting line with SALES as the dependent variable and SALES-1 as the independent variable.
    c. Are the two variables significantly related?
    d. Compute the MAPE for the historical data.
    e. Develop a forecast for the mean sales per employee for 1989.

11. We wish to forecast the number of mergers or acquisitions (for more than $1 million) that will take place in 1989. We believe that GNP may be a coincident indicator. *Source: Statistical Abstracts of the United States, 1990.*

Year	NUMBER	GNP (in billions of 1982 dollars)
1980	1,560	3,187
1981	2,329	3,150
1982	2,298	3,166

(continued)

Year	NUMBER	GNP (in billions of 1982 dollars)
1983	2,391	3,279
1984	3,164	3,501
1985	3,437	3,614
1986	4,381	3,717
1987	3,920	3,853
1988	3,487	4,024

    a. Develop a scatter plot of the two variables.
    b. Consider the following predictor variables, GNP and NUMBER-1. Determine whether one or both predictor variables are significantly related to the dependent variable.
    c. Do a residual analysis vs. time for the final regression model. Does it appear that the independence assumption has been met? Discuss.

12. We wish to forecast the percentage of eligible voters who will vote in the 1992 presidential election. Our data base includes data on two potential coincident indicators and the dependent variable for the last 15 presidential elections. The coincident indicators are (1) the indicator variable, presidential polls predicting a victory margin of 7.5% or more—yes or no, and (2) percentage of the civilian labor force unemployed. Code the indicator variable as: MARGIN = 1, if predicted victory margin is greater than 7.5% and 0, if otherwise. *Sources: Statistics of the Presidential and Congressional Elections*, U.S. Congress; *Employment and Earnings*, U.S. Bureau of Labor Statistics.

Election	PERCENT	MARGIN	UNEMPLOY
1932	52.4	Yes	23.6
1936	56.0	Yes	16.9
1940	58.9	Yes	14.6
1944	56.0	No	1.2
1948	51.1	No	3.8
1952	61.6	Yes	3.0
1956	59.3	Yes	4.1
1960	62.8	No	5.5
1964	61.9	Yes	5.2
1968	60.9	No	3.6
1972	55.2	Yes	3.3
1976	53.5	No	5.9
1980	52.6	Yes	5.1
1984	53.1	Yes	5.8
1988	50.2	Yes	4.3

    a. Consider the following three predictor variables: PERCENT-1 (the percentage of voters in the previous election), MARGIN, and UNEMPLOY. Determine whether all the predictor variables are significantly related to the dependent variable.
    b. Given the above data, can we make a prediction on the percentage of eligible voters who will vote in the 1992 presidential election? Discuss.

13. Given here are the daily attendance figures for five weeks for a movie theater in a mall.

Day	Week 1	Week 2	Week 3	Week 4	Week 5
Monday	150	135	155	175	125
Tuesday	175	165	165	135	145
Wednesday	135	150	150	165	145
Thursday	165	145	125	175	175
Friday	300	275	325	310	290
Saturday	600	650	700	600	610
Sunday	225	235	210	220	230

a. Plot a line graph of daily attendance.
b. Is there a 7-day seasonal pattern? Explain why such a 7-day seasonal pattern might exist.
c. Plot a moving average of length 3 days. Does the MA 3 still contain a seasonal pattern? Why or why not?
d. Plot a moving average of length 7 days. Does the MA 7 still contain a seasonal pattern? Why or why not?
e. Plot a moving average of length 21 days. Does the MA 21 still contain a seasonal pattern? Why or why not?

14. We believe that the number of people below the poverty level and the number of prisoners executed impact the number of violent crimes (murder, rape, aggravated assault, and robbery) committed each year. Our data include 1979–1988. *Sources: Crime in the United States*, U.S. Federal Bureau of Investigation; *Correctional Projections in the United States*, U.S. Bureau of Justice Statistics.

Year	VIOLENT (in millions)	POVERTY (in millions)	EXECUTE
1979	1.208	26.1	1
1980	1.345	29.3	1
1981	1.362	31.8	1
1982	1.322	34.4	2
1983	1.258	35.3	5
1984	1.273	33.7	21
1985	1.329	33.1	18
1986	1.489	32.4	18
1987	1.484	32.3	25
1988	1.566	31.9	11

a. Consider the following three predictor variables, VIOLENT-1 (the number of violent crimes in the prior year), POVERTY, and EXECUTE. Determine whether all the predictor variables are significantly related to the dependent variable, VIOLENT.
b. Does it appear that the independence assumption has been met for the final model? Discuss.

15.

Date: February 5, 1992
To: Pam Ascher, National Sales Manager
From: Bill O'Hara, Vice-President of Marketing
Subject: Forecast of Atlanta's Sales for Next Six Quarters

Your January 24 report generated more questions than it answered. You noted that sales have been steadily increasing and that the second and third quarters tend to be strong sales periods. Exactly how fast have sales been increasing? Exactly how strong are the second and third quarters? How weak are the first and fourth quarters?

I will also need for the upcoming planning meeting with Ann Tabor and the Senior Team a forecast for the Atlanta sales territory for the next six quarters. Keep the jargon and statistical "mumbo jumbo" to a minimum. You know how Ann likes straight talk. Please have the report on my desk by February 12.

Use Data Base III for your analysis. Your response to Bill O'Hara should include a brief memo and your analysis.

REFERENCES

BRIGHTMAN, H. *Group Problem Solving: An Improved Managerial Approach.* Atlanta: Georgia State University Business Press, 1988.

FARNUM, N., and L. STANTON. *Quantitative Forecasting Methods.* Boston: PWS/Kent, 1989.

HELMER, O. "Problems in Futures Research—Delphi and Causal Cross Impact Analysis." *Futures* 9 (1977).

HOGARTH, R. *Judgment and Choice.* New York: Wiley, 1987.

MAKRIDAKIS, S., S. WHEELWRIGHT, and V. MCGEE. *Forecasting: Methods and Applications.* New York: Wiley, 1983.

NEWBOLD, P., and T. BOS. *Introductory Business Forecasting.* Cincinnati: South-Western, 1990.

ROBERTS, H. *Data Analysis for Managers.* Redwood City, Calif.: The Scientific Press, 1988.

SACHMAN, H. *Delphi Critique.* Lexington, Mass.: Lexington Books, 1975.

VAN DE VEN, A., and A. DELBECQ. "The Effectiveness of Nominal, Delphi, and Interacting Group Decision Making Processes." *Academy of Management Journal* (December 1974): 605–621.

12

QUALITY CONTROL

12.1 The strategic importance of quality control
12.2 Types of quality
12.3 Control charting for variables
    Process control
    Process capability
    Basic control charts and problem solving
    Steps in building and using mean and standard deviation control charts
12.4 Control charts for attributes
    Control limits for a proportion nonconforming chart
12.5 Tools for controlling and improving quality
    Control charts
    Pareto charts
    Kepner–Tregoe problem analysis
    Frequency histograms
    Fishbone diagrams
    Scatter diagrams
    Experimental design
12.6 Vendor certification and acceptance sampling
    Acceptance sampling basics
    The inability of acceptance sampling to completely stop defectives
    Vendor certification
12.7 General principles
    General principles of quality
    General principles of statistical process control
    A final thought
Chapter 12 Questions
Chapter 12 Application Problems

CHAPTER OUTLINE

COMCEL Interoffice Communication

Date: September 10, 1993
To: Sang Kim, Quality Assurance Manager
From: Ann Tabor, CEO
Re: Costs of reworking defective parts

I have been looking at the cost figures for reworking our defective car phones. They have increased about 20% over last month's figures. The major problem is a defective touchtone circuit subassembly purchased from Widener Electronics. What is happening here? Haven't we negotiated an AQL of 1% with our supplier? If so, how are so many defective parts getting past inspectors? More importantly, why can't our supplier supply a steady stream of good touchtone circuits? Even if inspection stops poor subassemblies from entering our plant (and that is questionable), it does not ensure a steady stream of good parts.

Please follow up on this. We cannot afford to manufacture everything twice!

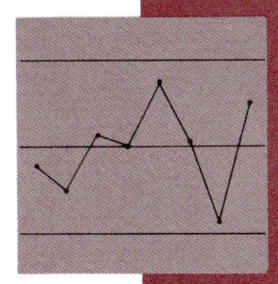

12.1 The Strategic Importance of Quality Control

In 1980 NBC ran a program entitled "If Japan Can... Why Can't We?" The program compared Japanese and American business practices and concluded that one major reason for Japanese success was their attention to quality. That was a remarkable turnabout, for before World War II, Japanese products were poorly constructed and could not compete in world markets. The program told how Dr. W. Edwards Deming, a leading American quality consultant, had introduced statistical quality control to the Japanese in the early 1950s. The Japanese enthusiastically adopted Deming's recommendations and Japanese product quality became the envy of the world. The program asked why American manufacturers had ignored Deming. While quality has become more important, it was not until 1989 that the aerospace industry held its First National Total Quality Management Symposium.

While quality rarely makes the headlines, its absence does. Consider the following problems:

1. In 1985, General Motors recalls 100,000 cars with *blushing paint*.
2. In 1986, faulty O-rings cause the *Challenger* space shuttle disaster.
3. In 1986, the Chernobyl nuclear plant in the USSR spews clouds of radiation that spread over several European countries.
4. In 1989, the Federal Aviation Administration cites recurring failures in maintenance at Eastern Airlines.
5. In 1990, a spacing error of 1.3 millimeters causes the $1.5 billion Hubble space telescope to send back blurry images. Its use will be limited until space-walking astronauts can install a new camera in 1993.

Poor quality caused all these problems.

The quality of the products or services of a firm is important to its financial success. Research by the Strategic Planning Institute (SPI) of Cambridge, Massachusetts, shows that firms that stress product quality have higher returns on investment (Gale, 1985). SPI asked 2,700 businesses to identify key product and service attributes (except price) and weight them in terms of customer importance. Each firm rated itself and its leading competitors on a scale from 1 to 10 on each attribute. SPI then compared the businesses' relative attribute scores against their return on investment (ROI). Relative quality was the only variable that *always* positively correlated with ROI. Figure 12.1 shows that the firms with the poorest relative quality product scores had a mean return on investment of about 12%. Firms with the highest relative quality product scores had a mean return on investment above 30%. Superior quality is a key to business success. As SPI noted, "Quality comes close to being a panacea (for business success)."

Dr. Deming (1986) uses the *Deming chain reaction* to explain the quality–ROI connection. Quality improvements reduce costs because there are fewer mistakes, less reworking, fewer delays, and better use of machines, people, and methods. The improved productivity helps capture a greater share of the market with better quality and lower prices.

FIGURE 12.1 Relationship Between Relative Quality and ROI

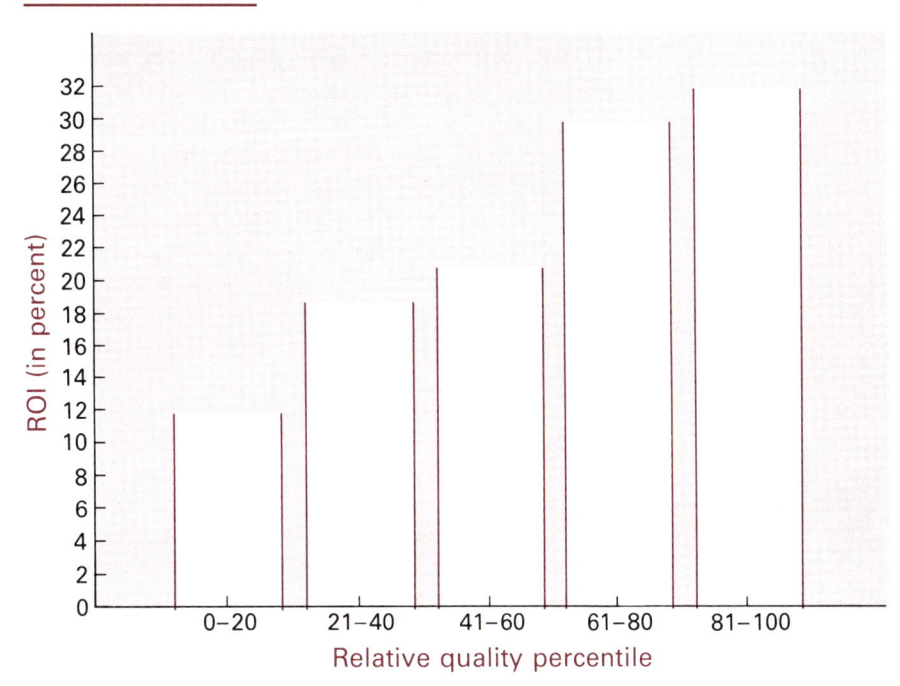

12.2 Types of Quality

What is quality? Are there different types of quality? Whose responsibility is it to monitor quality? By the end of this section you should be able to distinguish between design and manufactured quality.

A dictionary definition of quality is the degree of excellence. In that sense, a BMW is a better-quality car than a Yugo. Professionals who deal with quality use two other definitions.

Dr. J. M. Juran, a pioneer in the field, defines quality as "fitness for use" (1974). Fitness for use is the *design quality* definition. Under this definition, producing 1-foot rulers with a tolerance of plus or minus 2 inches is unacceptable quality. Such rulers are not fit for use because of their inaccuracy. Design quality must be considered carefully in planning the design, manufacture, and marketing of a product or service. Marketing research and product design departments ensure (or improve) design quality during product conception. They determine what customers want (and are willing to pay) and translate customer wants into engineering specifications. After selling the product, the marketing and sales departments ensure product quality by tracking and correcting after-sales problems. Synonyms for design quality are performance, reliability, serviceability, durability, and safety. Higher design quality often means higher cost.

P. B. Crosby, a well-known consultant, defines quality as "conformance to requirements" (1979). If a Mercedes Benz conforms to its engineering specification requirements, it is a quality car. If a Yugo conforms to its engineering specifications, it too is a quality car. Crosby warns not to talk of poor or good quality, but rather conformance or nonconformance. Conformance to requirements is *manufactured quality*. Under that definition, if a customer will accept a ruler with a tolerance of $\frac{1}{32}$ inch for a cost of $.39, then manufactured quality is the ability to produce rulers to that design specification. Manufacturing and statistical quality control departments ensure (or improve) manufactured quality by purchasing and inspecting raw materials, renovating or purchasing equipment, and improving or monitoring the manufacturing process. Synonyms for manufactured quality are conformance with manufacturing standards, performance of all required manufacturing steps, and subjection to required inspection tests.

Firms can improve manufactured quality in two ways. Through *inspection*, they can detect and scrap nonconforming products (rejects). As Deming has noted, an excessive number of rejects increases manufacturing costs and sales price, which can reduce market share. Alternatively, firms can *improve* their manufacturing processes so that a greater percentage of products conform to the engineering specifications and thus will not be rejected during inspection. Remember, inspection only finds rejects, but process improvements reduce the number of rejects. Deming urges continuous process improvement as the key to higher manufactured quality and lower product cost.

Figure 12.2 illustrates the connections between design quality and manufactured quality in designing, manufacturing, and marketing the COMCEL car phone unit. COMCEL's original market research showed that customers wanted a lightweight, attractive, durable, and indestructible phone unit that had reception as clear as present home phones. Product design specialists translated these features into engineering specifications. The designers wanted longer durability (i.e., longer mean time between failures—MTBF), but settled for 2,000 hours to keep costs down. Once the engineering specifications (specs) were approved, the manufacturing department sought reputable raw materials suppliers and developed manufacturing processes to meet the specs. The statistical quality control group instituted work-in-progress inspections and a company-wide quality improvement program to reduce costs and improve the manufactured quality. Finally, COMCEL developed after-sales support centers to ensure customer satisfaction.

Maintaining and improving quality must be a company-wide effort involving all levels of management, quality professionals, and employees. Top management must develop quality targets and policies; middle management must implement them and monitor their progress. The quality control organization typically includes the following departments: procurement quality control, product inspection, and product testing and performance. Procurement handles inspection of incoming raw materials and subassemblies and approves suppliers. Product inspection directs work-in-progress inspection and process control and capabilities studies. Product testing directs functional testing (does

FIGURE 12.2 Design and Manufactured Quality

The Design, Manufacturing, and Marketing Process

- Identify customer needs and wants.
- Translate into engineering specs.
- Purchase raw material from a certified vendor.
- Manufacture product, establish process control, and inspect final product.
- After-sales and service support.

Applied to COMCEL Car Phones

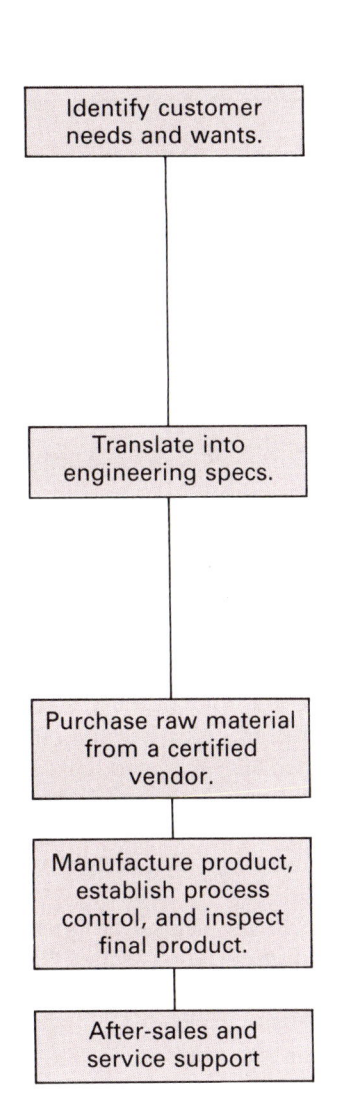

Customer Preferences
Lightweight
Attractive
Indestructible
Clear reception
Durable

Engineering Specifications
Weight: Phone handset unit weighs 10 ounces ± 5%.
Attractiveness: Phone handset is free of surface blemishes to the naked eye.
Shatterproof: Phone handsets can withstand between 4,600 and 4,900 pounds of pressure per square inch. The target value is 4,750 pounds per square inch.
Reception: The same standard as house phones
Durable: Mean time between failures (MBTF) is 2,000 hours or more.

Manufacturing Process
Add fillers and dyes to raw material.
Mold the phone headpiece.
Test the installed electrical assemblies.
Install the electrical assembly into the phone headpiece.
Test the product at outgoing inspection for conformance to engineering specifications.

Implement a customer "800 hot-line" to handle after-sales and service support.
Open 1-day repair centers in all major markets.

the product do what the customer wants?), reliability testing (does it do it without failures or breakdowns?), and customer support. However, quality assurance is too important to be left to a few professionals. Besides, there are not enough quality department personnel to do the job. The final responsibility for quality rests with those who produce the product or provide the service. Without their active participation, a company-wide quality control effort will fail.

SECTION 12.2 EXERCISES

1. How would a firm improve the design quality of its products?
2. How would a firm improve its manufactured quality?
3. According to retailer Sidney Marcus, of Neiman–Marcus, a BIC pen and a Rolex watch are both high-quality items. Explain how Marcus could put an item costing one dollar in the same class with an item costing thousands of dollars.
4. *Discuss the statement:* "Quality is not my job! That is what we pay inspectors for."

12.3 Control Charting for Variables

Quality professionals have developed tools to help monitor, control, and improve manufactured quality levels. We turn to these next. By the end of this section you should be able to:

1. plot mean and standard deviation process control charts and explain how to use them to determine whether a process is under control;
2. distinguish between natural tolerance limits and design specification limits;
3. compute and explain the process capability index;
4. explain why there will be many rejected units when natural tolerance limits exceed design specification limits;
5. explain when changing the process or the engineering specification is appropriate in order to overcome natural tolerance limits that exceed design specification limits;
6. explain why there may be problems even when the natural tolerance limits are less than the design specification limits;
7. compute upper and lower control limits for process control;
8. explain the differences between chance and assignable cause variation; and
9. determine when the manufacturing (or service) process is temporarily out of control and corrective action is needed.

Process Control

Before initiating a manufacturing or service process, we should do a *process control* study. Process control studies determine whether a process is stable, predictable, or under statistical control. A process that is under statistical control exhibits only random variation.

Table 12.1

Process Control Study Data

	Observation						
Shift	1	2	3	4	5	Mean	STD. DEV.
1	4,800	4,790	4,800	4,800	4,820	4,802	10.95
2	4,800	4,800	4,775	4,800	4,750	4,785	22.36
3	4,750	4,800	4,775	4,770	4,780	4,775	18.03
4	4,710	4,775	4,780	4,750	4,790	4,761	32.09
5	4,790	4,750	4,700	4,750	4,725	4,743	33.47
6	4,710	4,650	4,720	4,720	4,770	4,714	42.78
7	4,750	4,600	4,700	4,725	4,700	4,695	57.01
8	4,740	4,650	4,690	4,650	4,780	4,702	57.18
9	4,600	4,625	4,780	4,755	4,790	4,710	90.35
10	4,600	4,750	4,780	4,600	4,725	4,691	85.32

We illustrate the process control study idea. Before COMCEL started producing phones, it determined whether the molding process was under statistical control. For each of the first 10 shifts, COMCEL workers used a systematic 1-in-100 sampling procedure (see Section 6.6) to select five phone handsets. They then tested the phones for shatter resistance. Table 12.1 contains the shift mean and shift standard deviation shatter resistance based on the following equations:

$$\bar{x} = \frac{\sum x_i}{n} \qquad s = \sqrt{\frac{\sum (x_i - \bar{x})^2}{n - 1}} \qquad (12.1)$$

The sample size per subgroup, n, is 5 in the COMCEL study for the 10 subgroups. Generally, practitioners prefer 20 or more subgroups to run a process control study.

Figures 12.3 and 12.4 on page 678 show line graphs for the means and standard deviations for the 10 shifts. Both line graphs indicate that the molding process is *not* under statistical control because the shift means and shift standard deviations are not stable, or stationary (using terminology of Chapter 2). Rather, we see that

1. the shift mean shatter strength is dropping steadily; and
2. the shift standard deviation of shatter strength is increasing steadily.

COMCEL must look for *assignable causes* for the declining mean and the increasing standard deviation. Assignable causes explain the nonrandom patterns in Figures 12.3 and 12.4. Perhaps the molding equipment needs additional controls to maintain the proper shatter strength, or the molding supervisors need additional training. Since the standard deviation is also increasing, eventually some parts will not meet the engineering specifications. Such parts either will be

FIGURE 12.3 Example of a Process Not Under Control: Line Graph of Mean Shatter Strengths for Different Shifts

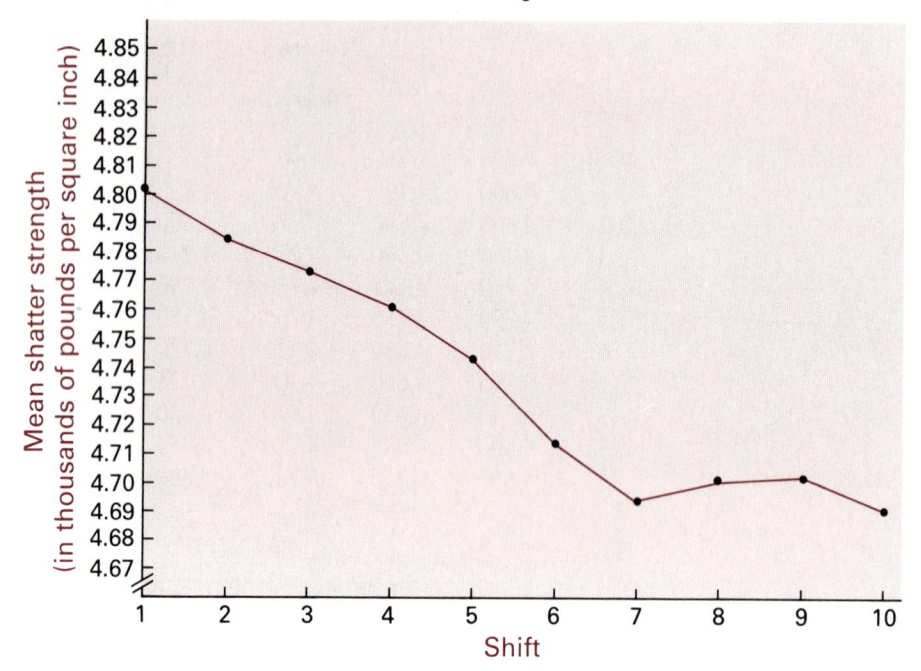

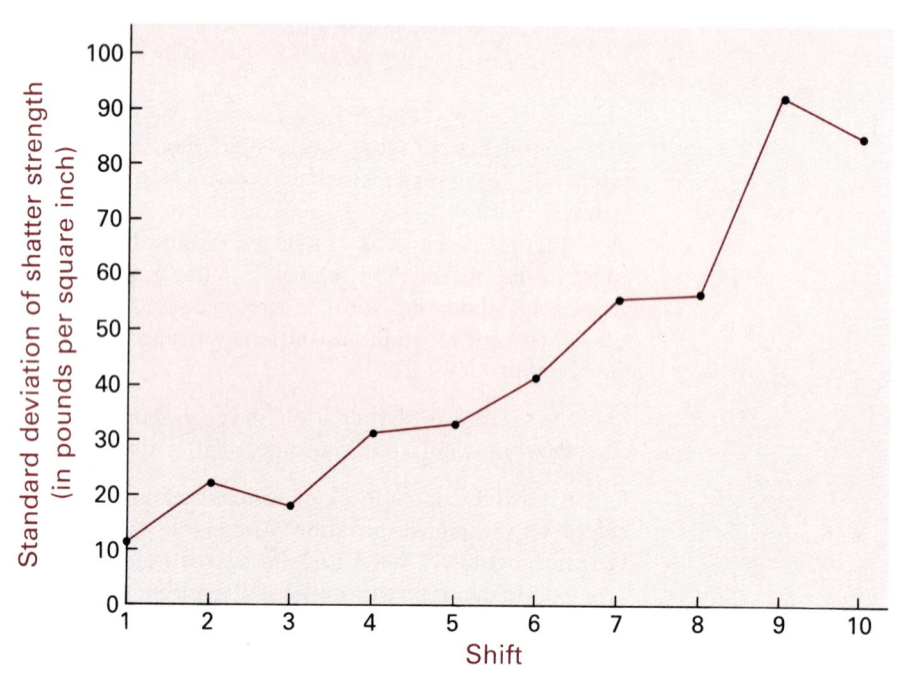

FIGURE 12.4 Example of a Process Not Under Control: Line Graph of Standard Deviation in Shatter Strengths for Different Shifts

found in final inspection and scrapped (then the parts must be remanufactured) or will slip through final inspection and cause customer complaints.

Before full-scale production begins, the firm must determine whether its manufacturing process is under *statistical control*. If the process is improving, we allow it to improve until it levels off. If the process is worsening, we try to correct the problem and wait until the process stabilizes. A process under statistical control exhibits merely random variation which results from machines, production methods, or workers that are incapable of producing *exactly* uniform parts. Random variation is also known as unexplainable variation or chance variation.

A process under statistical control exhibits only random variation. Random variation means:

1. The means and the standard deviations stay nearly constant from the start to the end of a process control study.
2. There are no *systematic* data patterns. The means and standard deviations do not exhibit an upward or downward trend, a cyclical pattern, a shift in performance level pattern, a widening or narrowing pattern, a meandering pattern (positive autocorrelation), or an oscillating pattern (negative autocorrelation) from the start to the end of a process control study.
3. Often, practitioners must go beyond visual checks to determine whether a process is under statistical control. They use control charts which we will discuss shortly.

Process Capability

Assume that COMCEL has achieved process control of its molding operation. The graphs of the mean and the standard deviation are stationary and exhibit only random variation. Now it must determine the molding operation's *process capability*. Process capability studies reveal to what extent a process can produce products within design specification limits set by engineering design. If the process cannot meet the limits, then the firm must either change its design specifications or, better yet, improve the manufacturing process. We will cover more on that later.

Process control and process capability are two different ideas. Process control determines whether a process is stable. Process capability determines whether the stable process can produce a sufficiently large number of parts within design specification limits.

We will illustrate the process capability study idea. The engineering design group of COMCEL determines that the handset shatter strength should be between 4,600 and 4,900 pounds per square inch (psi). The *lower specification limit* (LSL) is the lowest acceptable shatter strength—4,600 psi. The *upper specification limit* (USL) is the highest desired shatter strength—4,900 psi. The target value is 4,750 psi—halfway between the LSL and USL.

Using systematic sampling, the quality control group selects five handsets from each of 15 consecutive shifts and determines the shift means and shift standard deviations (see Table 12.2 on page 680). It also determines the overall

Table 12.2
Process Capability Study Data

			Observation				
Shift	1	2	3	4	5	Mean	STD. DEV.
1	4,705	4,780	4,715	4,750	4,780	4,746	35.25
2	4,750	4,800	4,775	4,740	4,750	4,763	24.39
3	4,740	4,740	4,775	4,770	4,780	4,761	19.49
4	4,710	4,775	4,780	4,780	4,810	4,771	36.81
5	4,770	4,750	4,780	4,750	4,725	4,755	21.21
6	4,735	4,700	4,755	4,770	4,755	4,743	27.06
7	4,750	4,800	4,775	4,725	4,790	4,768	30.54
8	4,740	4,750	4,775	4,770	4,780	4,763	17.18
9	4,840	4,780	4,780	4,755	4,790	4,789	31.30
10	4,770	4,750	4,780	4,800	4,725	4,765	28.72
11	4,690	4,750	4,750	4,720	4,720	4,726	25.10
12	4,800	4,775	4,780	4,750	4,800	4,781	20.74
13	4,790	4,790	4,740	4,810	4,810	4,788	28.64
14	4,750	4,720	4,780	4,750	4,770	4,754	23.02
15	4,750	4,760	4,775	4,720	4,790	4,759	26.55

$$\bar{\bar{x}} = \frac{4{,}746 + 4{,}763 + \cdots + 4{,}754 + 4{,}759}{15} = 4{,}762.13 \text{ psi}$$

$$\bar{s} = \sqrt{\frac{35.25^2 + 24.39^2 + \cdots + 26.55^2}{15}} = 26.96 \text{ psi}$$

mean ($\bar{\bar{x}}$) and the mean standard deviation ($\bar{s}$) using the following expressions:

$$\bar{\bar{x}} = \frac{\sum \bar{x}_i}{k} \qquad \bar{s}^2 = \frac{\sum s_i^2}{k} \qquad (12.2)$$

$$\bar{s} = \sqrt{\bar{s}^2}$$

The term k is the number of subgroups selected in the process capability study. In the COMCEL study, $k = 15$. The expressions of (12.2) assume that each of the k subgroups has the same sample size. In the COMCEL study, the sample size of each subgroup is 5. A process capability study should have at least 15 subgroups and a sample size of 5 or more per subgroup.

From the results in Table 12.2, we see that the mean of the 15 subgroup means, $\bar{\bar{x}}$, is 4,762 psi, which is close to the target value of 4,750 psi, and $\bar{s}$ is 26.96 psi.

Can the molding process produce handsets within the design specification limits of 4,600 psi to 4,900 psi? Figure 12.5 is a frequency histogram of the 75 individual observations in Table 12.2. The histogram of shatter strengths is

FIGURE 12.5 Frequency Histogram of 75 Handset Shatter Strengths

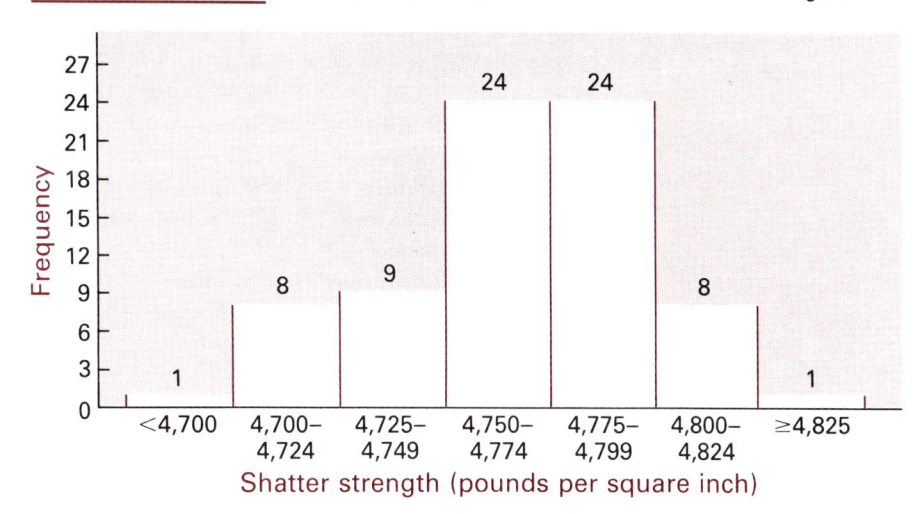

reasonably normal-shaped. Thus over 99% of the handsets will have a shatter strength within ±3 standard deviations of the mean of 4,762 psi. These two values are called the *lower and upper natural tolerance limits* (LNTL and UNTL).

Depending on the size of each subgroup, quality control professionals know that $\bar{s}$ is about 1%–7% less than the standard deviation, s. For simplicity, we use $\bar{s}$ rather than s in the following calculations:

$$\text{LNTL} = \bar{\bar{x}} - 3\bar{s} = 4{,}762 - 3(26.96) = 4{,}681 \text{ psi}$$

$$\text{UNTL} = \bar{\bar{x}} + 3\bar{s} = 4{,}762 + 3(26.96) = 4{,}843 \text{ psi}$$

Over 99% of the individual handsets will have a shatter strength between 4,681 psi and 4,843 psi. Since the design specification limits are 4,600 psi (LSL) and 4,900 psi (USL), there will be few, if any, rejects produced. In short, the molding process capability easily meets the design specification limits.

The process capability index (PCI) is the ratio of the width of the design specification limits (what the designers want) to the width of the natural tolerance limits (what the process can produce 99% of the time). This ratio, as given in expression (12.3), is meaningful only for a *centered* process. The process mean, $\bar{\bar{x}}$, must be centered (or close to) between the lower and upper specification limits. The molding operation is a (nearly) centered process since the $\bar{\bar{x}}$ of 4,762 psi is very close to 4,750 psi. Thus the PCI for the molding operation is a valid measure of process capability. Again for simplicity, we use $\bar{s}$ rather than s in the PCI calculation.

$$\text{PCI} = \frac{\text{USL} - \text{LSL}}{6\bar{s}} \tag{12.3}$$

The PCI for the molding process is (4,900 − 4,600)/(6 · 26.96), or 1.85. The width of the design specification limits is 1.85 times as large as the width of the natural tolerance limits. If the design specification limits satisfy customer needs in terms of shatter resistance, the molding operation will produce phone handsets that meet engineering specs *and* also satisfy customers' wants. However, if the present design specification limits are unacceptable to customers, the firm should tighten the design specification limits. It must then compare the width of the natural tolerance limits to the new width of the design limits. As long as the new PCI is greater than about 1.2–1.3, the firm can make parts that meet specs and satisfy its customers.

A process that has a PCI of less than 1 is in serious trouble. Such a process will produce many parts that will be rejected during final inspection. And as Deming has noted, rework leads to increased costs, lower market share, and lower profitability.

What options are available if the PCI is less than 1? One is to improve the process by reducing its natural variability. That is, make the standard deviation, or $\bar{s}$, smaller. That can be expensive because it may involve buying new equipment or installing new production methods. A second option is to have the marketing group review the lower and upper specification limits. Perhaps the range can be widened without displeasing the customer. If so, this will also increase the PCI. Japanese firms use the former approach. They strive to reduce the standard deviation, or $\bar{s}$, by continually improving the process.

In summary, the PCI provides useful information, as outlined in Table 12.3.

In situation 1 the process is not under statistical control. Look for assignable causes, such as (1) gross blunders, (2) lack of training, (3) need for better equipment or processes, or (4) poor supervision. Do not run process capability studies! Situation 2 typifies a process that is under statistical control. Also, the natural tolerance limits are well within the design specification limits. That is good provided the design specs meet consumer needs. Situation 3 represents a statistically controlled process in which design specification limits are too wide to meet customer wants. The product does not work well even though it is within specs. The solution is to tighten up the specs and ensure that the process can satisfy the new specs. In situation 4 we have a statistically controlled process in which the natural tolerance limits exceed the design specs. A large percentage of the parts will fail inspection even though the process is under control. That is unacceptable, and the firm must improve the process to remain competitive.

Basic Control Charts and Problem Solving

Process control and capability studies ensure that a manufacturing or service process is under statistical control and capable of meeting the design specification limits. Then the firm can begin full-scale production or service. Occasionally, problems will crop up and the process may temporarily go out of control. Control charts warn a firm when this is about to happen so that it can take corrective action.

In 1926 Walter Shewhart introduced the control chart (Shewhart, 1926). It is a visual aid that provides information about the level of manufactured quality. The

Table 12.3
Implications of Different PCI Values

Process Under Statistical Control?	PCI Value	Satisfied Customer?	Implications
1. No	—	—	Process is unstable in either the mean or the standard deviation. Correct the problem before starting the process capability study.
2. Yes	>1.3	Yes	Few if any rejects will be produced. Process will meet specs and satisfy customers. Begin manufacturing but should try to improve the process. Continuous improvement is essential to remain competitive.
3. Yes	>1.3	No	Customers are unhappy. Must tighten the design specification limits.
4. Yes	<1.0	No	The process produces many defective parts and must be improved. May require capital expenditures. Ask workers for their ideas.

control chart consists of three horizontal lines. The top line is the *upper control limit* (UCL), the bottom line is the *lower control limit* (LCL), and the centerline is the mean based on the process capability study data or the quality standard set by Engineering Design. The upper control limit is three standard deviations above the centerline and the lower control limit is three standard deviations below the centerline.

Quality control departments set up control charts, and workers on the production line or service operation maintain them. For that reason, control charts need to be simple to calculate and interpret. Two common control charts are charts for the mean and standard deviation.

CONTROL LIMITS FOR THE STANDARD DEVIATION CHART We begin by constructing a chart of the standard deviations—an *s*-chart. The centerline is the mean standard deviation for the 15 samples of size 5 from Table 12.2. Recall that the mean standard deviation is $\bar{s}$.

$$\text{Centerline of } s\text{-chart:} \quad \bar{s} = \sqrt{\frac{\sum s_i^2}{k}} = 26.96 \text{ psi}$$

Table 12.4

Factors for Constructing Mean and Standard Deviation Control Charts

Sample Size Per Subgroup	Upper/Lower A_3	Lower B_3	Upper B_4
2	2.659	0	3.267
3	1.954	0	2.568
4	1.628	0	2.266
5	1.427	0	2.089
6	1.287	.030	1.970
7	1.182	.118	1.882
8	1.099	.185	1.815
9	1.032	.239	1.761
10	.975	.284	1.716
15	.789	.428	1.572
20	.680	.510	1.490
25	.606	.565	1.435

Once we have calculated the centerline, we can use tables developed by quality control professionals (see Table 12.4) to determine the lower and upper control limits. Here are the calculations for the lower and upper control limits for $\bar{s}$ for the COMCEL study:

Upper control limit (UCL): $B_4 \bar{s} = 2.089(26.96) = 56.32$ psi (12.4)

Lower control limit (LCL): $B_3 \bar{s} = 0(26.96) = 0.00$ psi (12.5)

The values of B_3 and B_4, found in Table 12.4, help us construct 99% confidence intervals on $\bar{s}$. About 99% of the standard deviations for samples of size 5 should fall between the LCL and UCL if the process is operating properly. How the B_3 and B_4 values were determined need not concern us. The completed s-chart is shown in the lower panel of Figure 12.6.

CONTROL LIMITS FOR THE MEAN CHART   Next, we construct a control chart for the mean—the $\bar{x}$-chart. The centerline is the overall mean of the process capability data in Table 12.2:

Centerline of $\bar{x}$-chart: $\bar{\bar{x}} = \dfrac{\sum \bar{x}_i}{k} = 4{,}762$ psi

Here are the calculations for the lower and upper control limits for $\bar{x}$:

UCL: $\bar{\bar{x}} + A_3 \bar{s} = 4{,}762 + 1.427(26.96) = 4{,}800$ psi   (12.6)

LCL: $\bar{\bar{x}} - A_3 \bar{s} = 4{,}762 - 1.427(26.96) = 4{,}724$ psi   (12.7)

FIGURE 12.6 Control Chart for the Mean and Standard Deviation

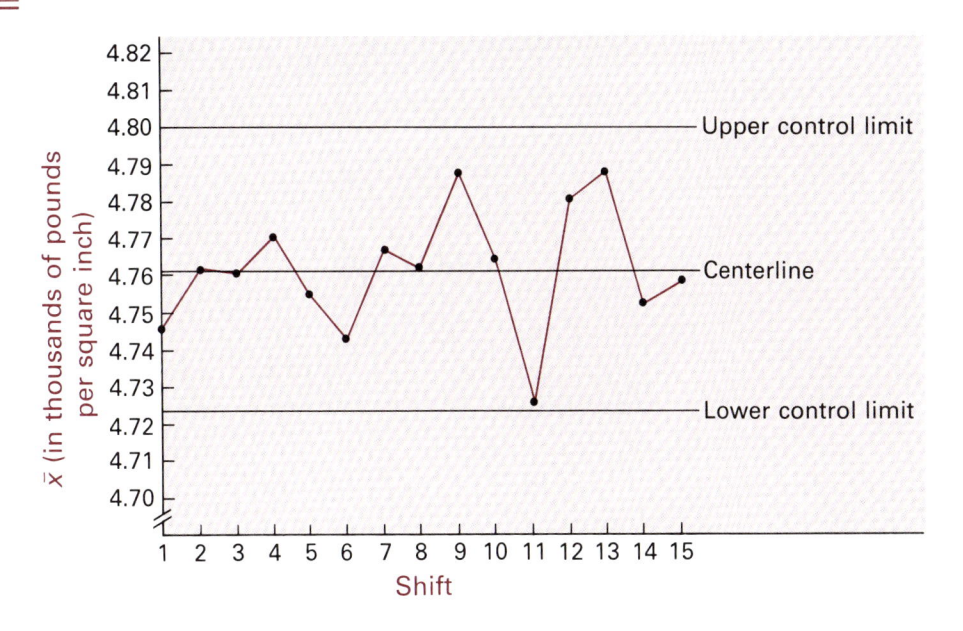

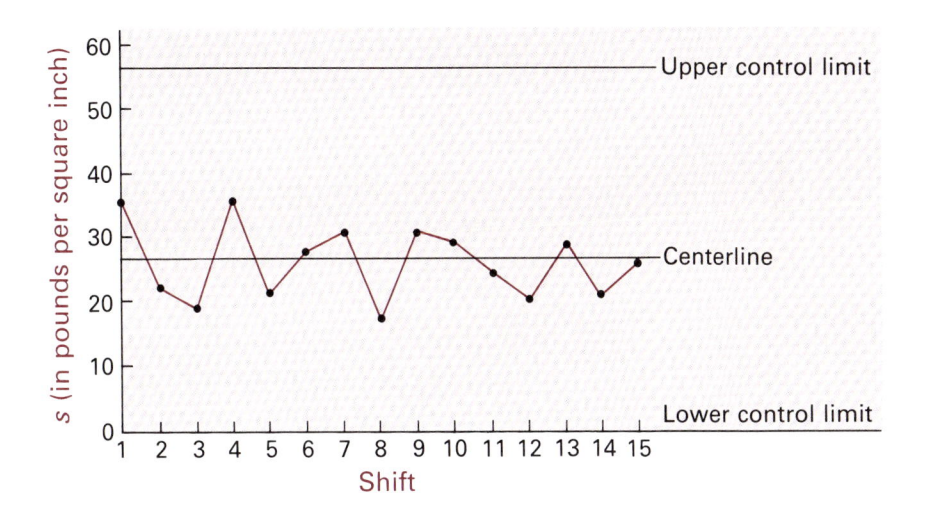

About 99% of the $\bar{x}$ values for samples of size 5 should fall between the LCL and UCL if the process is operating properly. The completed $\bar{x}$-chart is shown in the upper panel of Figure 12.6.

We can approximate the upper and lower control limits by using the general confidence interval expression from Chapter 7. The first expression in (12.8) is the general expression for a 99% confidence interval on the population mean. The second shows that $s/\sqrt{n}$ is the estimated standard error of the mean. However, since we do not know the value of the estimated standard deviation of the population, s, we use $\bar{s}$ rather than s. For this reason, the confidence interval approach only approximates the UCL and LCL.

$$\bar{\bar{x}} \pm 3 \text{ (Estimated standard error of the mean)}$$

$$\bar{\bar{x}} \pm 3\left(\frac{s}{\sqrt{n}}\right) \tag{12.8}$$

$$\bar{\bar{x}} \pm 3\left(\frac{\bar{s}}{\sqrt{n}}\right)$$

Apply expression (12.8) to COMCEL's molding operation data. The approximate UCL is 4,798 psi and the approximate LCL is 4,726 psi.

$$\text{UCL:} \quad \bar{\bar{x}} + 3\left(\frac{\bar{s}}{\sqrt{n}}\right) = 4{,}762 + 3\left(\frac{26.96}{\sqrt{5}}\right) = 4{,}798 \text{ psi}$$
$$\text{LCL:} \quad \bar{\bar{x}} - 3\left(\frac{\bar{s}}{\sqrt{n}}\right) = 4{,}762 - 3\left(\frac{26.96}{\sqrt{5}}\right) = 4{,}726 \text{ psi} \tag{12.9}$$

Figure 12.6 shows both control charts for the molding operation. It is common practice to place the $\bar{x}$-chart above the s-chart. Line workers will now take samples from each shift, compute the mean and standard deviation, and plot these values on the appropriate control charts.

THE 3-SIGMA RULE FOR DETECTING PROBLEMS   Shewhart (1926) said that a process is *temporarily* out of control when one point (an $\bar{x}$ or s value for a subgroup) falls outside of the control limits. Under this rule, neither the mean nor the standard deviation was temporarily out of control during the first 15 shifts in the COMCEL study (see Figure 12.6). That is, no point lies outside the 3-sigma control limits.

A process under control will occasionally produce subgroup means or standard deviations outside of their 3-sigma limits. How often will this occur? If a process under control produces parts with measurements that are normally distributed (see Figure 12.5), the probability of a data point lying outside the 3-sigma limits is only 26 in 10,000. Thus, if a point lies outside the limits, it is very likely a signal that the process is going out of control and someone needs to determine why.

We use control charts to identify the two following types of variation:

Chance variation is due to many factors that are uncontrollable on the production floor. Their impact makes it impossible to produce parts that are exactly uniform. However, the mean and standard deviation are under control, and there is no need for problem solving.

1. Subgroup means or standard deviations within the 3-sigma limits merely signal random variation, or **chance variation**. When chance variation is operating: (1) the process exhibits natural variability, and (2) the product cannot be readily improved except by redesigning the product or the manufacturing process.

Assignable cause variation is due to a special cause that must be corrected. In short, something is wrong, and management must take corrective action.

2. Subgroup means or standard deviations outside the 3-sigma limits signal that the process is temporarily out of control. Later we will discuss several tools to troubleshoot assignable cause variation.

Next, we illustrate how workers use control charts to monitor a process and initiate corrective problem solving action. Figure 12.7 on page 688 shows the means and standard deviations for the next 25 shifts—16–40. The means and standard deviations are based on systematic samples of size 5 taken during each shift.

On shift 28 the mean shatter strength dropped below the LCL. Using problem solving tools that we will discuss in Section 12.5, the quality control department and production workers determined the root causes. By the next shift, the mean was again within the 3-sigma control limits. On shift 33 the standard deviation was above the UCL. Again a joint problem solving effort reduced the standard deviation to within the 3-sigma limits by the next shift.

Firms also use median and range charts. Control charts are useful in *sensing* changes in the process mean or standard deviation. As we know, problem sensing is essential to timely problem solving. Delayed action can mean rework, extra cost, lost profitability, and lost market share. Quick detection and solution of quality problems are essential to the success of a firm.

ADDITIONAL RULES FOR DETECTING PROBLEMS   In the 1950s the Western Electric Company developed other rules to detect a process that is *temporarily* out of control. These rules are especially useful for $\bar{x}$-charts. In its system, a process is defined to be out of control when any of the following occur:

1. Two out of three successive data points lie outside the 2-sigma limits.
2. Four out of five successive data points lie outside the 1-sigma limits.
3. Eight successive points lie on one side of the centerline.

Each of these three data patterns has a chance of about 26 in 10,000 of happening if the process is under control. That is the same probability as with the 3-sigma rule. If these data patterns do occur, we take problem solving action. Always look for *unlikely* or *nonrandom* data patterns. As Deming (1951) has noted, "The control chart is no substitute for the brain."

An in-control process has the following characteristics:

1. Most of the means and standard deviations (data points) will occur near their respective centerlines.
2. A few points will occur near their respective control limits.
3. The points occur in a random fashion with no clustering, trending, or other departures from random variation.

Steps in Building and Using Mean and Standard Deviation Control Charts

Here are the steps for building and using control charts:

1. Decide on a subgroup sample size. A sample size between 5 and 10 is common. Use systematic sampling each shift (or day) to select your observations.

FIGURE 12.7 Control Chart for the Mean and Standard Deviation: Shifts 16–40

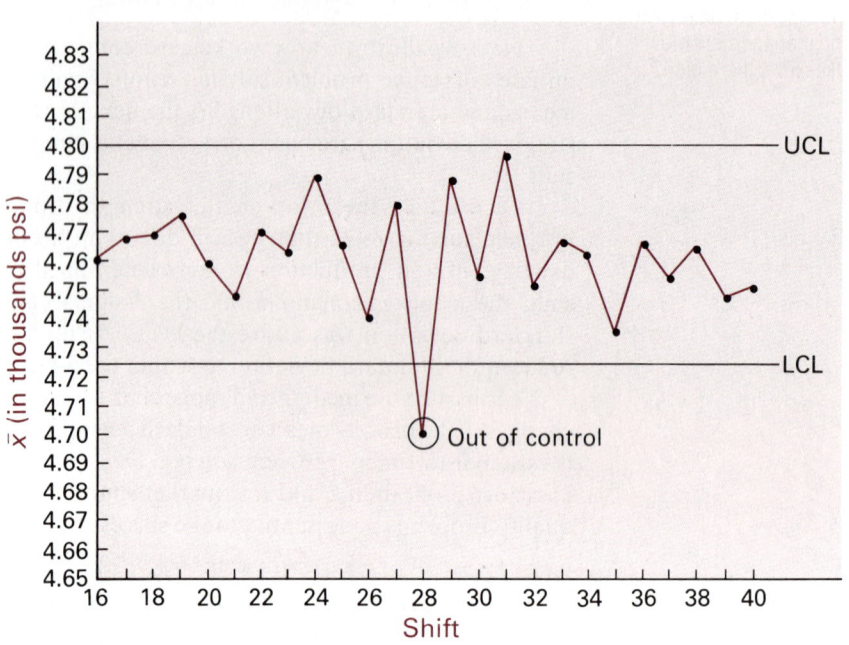

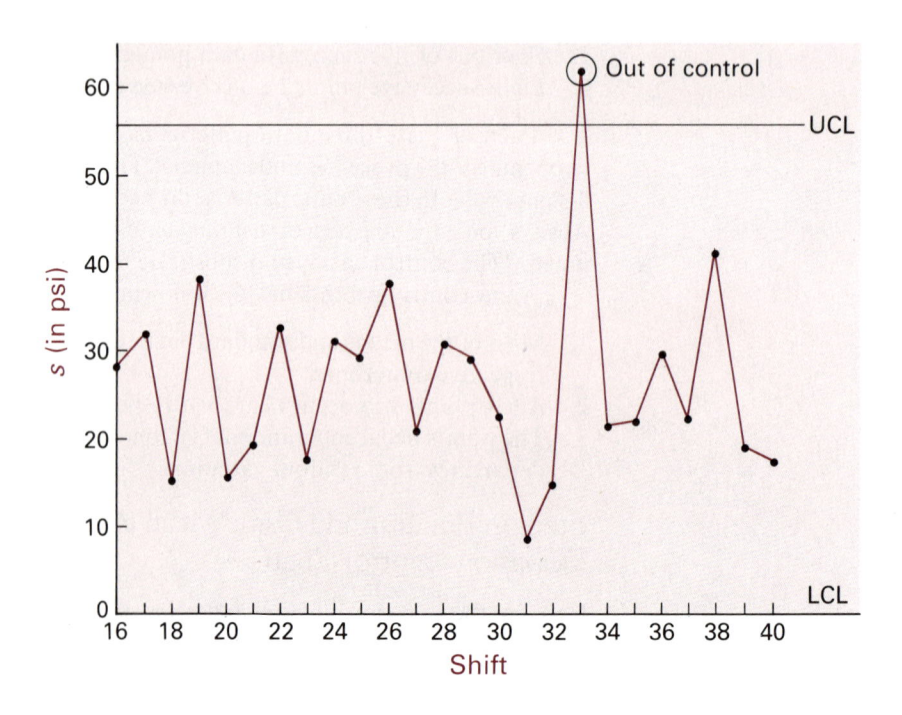

2. Select 15 or more subgroups.
3. For each subgroup, compute the sample mean and standard deviation.
4. Compute the overall mean ($\bar{\bar{x}}$) and the mean standard deviation.
5. $\bar{\bar{x}}$ is the centerline on the $\bar{x}$-chart and $\bar{s}$ is usually the centerline on the s-chart.
6. Calculate the control limits for the $\bar{x}$-chart using equations (12.6) and (12.7). Calculate the control limits for the s-chart using equations (12.4) and (12.5).
7. Draw the control chart. Place the s-chart just below the $\bar{x}$-chart.
8. Use the control limits to monitor future sample subgroup means and standard deviations. If a mean or standard deviation data point lies within the 3-sigma limits, take no action. When a single point falls outside either 3-sigma limit, determine the root causes and take corrective action. Alternatively, use the Western Electric Company rules to determine an out-of-control process.

In summary, we first establish process control. We do more than visually check for random variation. Beyond checking for systematic patterns, we can use control charts and apply the 3-sigma or Western Electric rules. Once the process is under statistical control, we then determine whether the process can meet the design specs. Then we use control charts to monitor the process and to initiate problem solving to correct assignable cause variation. This is the joint responsibility of all employees.

SECTION 12.3 EXERCISES

1. Draw a line graph of a process under statistical control and a line graph of a process not under statistical control. Explain your graphs.

2. We select eight subgroups of five items each and weigh them. The subgroup means (in ounces) and standard deviations are shown here.

Shift	1	2	3	4	5	6	7	8
$\bar{x}$	5.1	5.3	4.8	5.1	5.2	5.0	4.9	5.3
s	.4	.5	.7	.8	.8	.9	1.2	1.5

   a. Construct a process control chart for the mean and the standard deviation.
   b. Is the process under statistical control? Explain.

3. Suppose the Mobile Phone Engineering Design group sets a target value for mean-time-to-failure at 2,000 hours with a USL of 2,100 hours and an LSL of 1,900 hours. The firm runs a process capability study by taking 20 subgroups of five phones and running time-to-failure tests. Here are the sample mean data for the 20 subgroups.

1	2,105	6	2,117	11	2,038	16	2,124
2	2,145	7	2,049	12	2,061	17	2,040
3	2,071	8	2,001	13	2,131	18	2,036
4	2,039	9	2,018	14	2,051	19	2,116
5	2,106	10	2,017	15	2,081	20	2,102

a. Plot the data. Do the data appear to exhibit only random variation?
b. How close is $\bar{\bar{x}}$ to the target value?
c. If we started full-scale production, would most of the phones be within specs on mean-time-to-failure? Discuss.
d. *Discuss the following statement:* A process can be in a state of statistical control and yet still be performing badly. Under what conditions is this true?

4. Which of the following four processes appear to be under statistical control? Discuss.

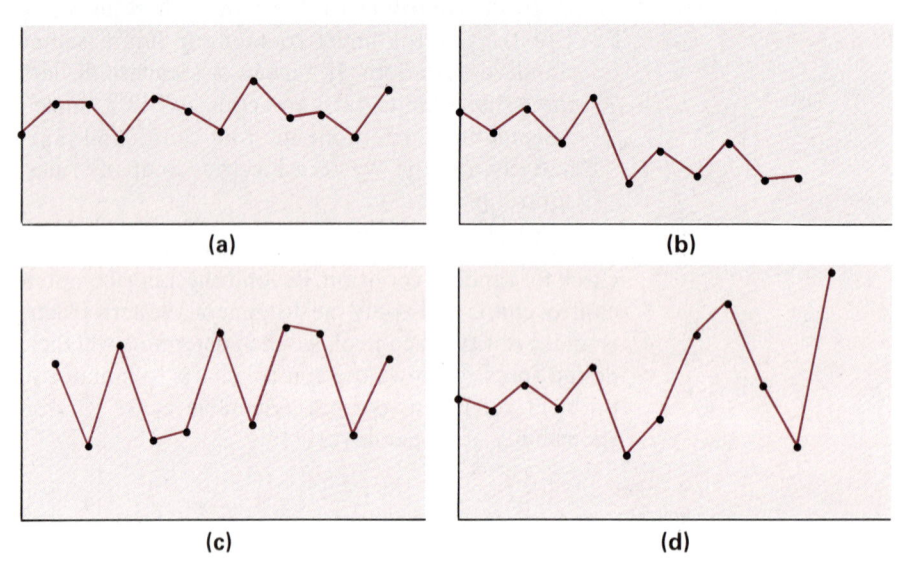

(a)

(b)

(c)

(d)

5. A sample of 10 items was selected each hour over an 8-hour period. Inspectors measure the shatter strength of the parts. The mean of the eight standard deviations was 100 pounds per square inch (psi). The mean of the eight sample means was 2,800 psi.
   a. Calculate the upper and lower natural tolerance limits for the process.
   b. The lower and upper design specification limits are 2,400 psi and 3,200 psi. The target value was 2,800 psi. Calculate the process capability index (PCI).
   c. Is it necessary to know the target value to compute the PCI?
   d. Calculate the lower and upper control limits for the mean.
   e. Calculate the lower and upper control limits for the standard deviation.

6. A sample of four items was selected each hour over a 5-hour period and the lengths were measured. The mean of the five sample standard deviations was 1.0 cm. The mean of the five sample means was 17.5 cm.
   a. Calculate the upper and lower natural tolerance limits for the process.
   b. The lower and upper design specification limits are 15 and 20 cm. Calculate the process capability index (PCI).
   c. Given the value of the PCI, should a firm start producing the product?

7. This problem demonstrates that a PCI is valid only if the process is centered. Suppose the target value for a process is 50 seconds with an LSL of 40 seconds and a USL of 60 seconds. Suppose that $\bar{\bar{x}}$ is 50 seconds and $\bar{s}$ is 1 second.
   a. Compute the PCI for the centered process.
   b. Would most of the parts be acceptable? Discuss.

Suppose that $\bar{\bar{x}}$ is 60 seconds and $\bar{s}$ is 1 second.
   c. Compute the PCI for the noncentered process.

d. Would most of the parts be acceptable? Discuss.
e. Explain why PCIs are valid only for centered processes.

8. A firm that makes batteries samples 5 items per shift over 10 shifts. Inspectors measure the battery weight. The mean of the 10 standard deviations was .25 ounce. The mean of the 10 sample means was 20.5 ounces.
   a. Calculate the upper and lower natural tolerance limits for the process.
   b. The lower and upper design specification limits are 19 ounces and 22 ounces. Calculate the process capability index (PCI).
   c. Calculate the lower and upper control limits for the mean.
   d. Calculate the lower and upper control limits for the standard deviation.

9. This problem illustrates how we can use control charts to determine whether the process is under statistical control. Shown are sample means and standard deviations based on subgroups of size 5 each. The variable being measured is time in seconds.

	$\bar{x}$	s		$\bar{x}$	s
1	64.32	16.15	11	59.01	11.74
2	65.90	12.32	12	67.79	13.00
3	61.36	12.19	13	61.80	8.08
4	58.92	11.81	14	66.92	16.58
5	51.44	10.68	15	64.29	13.97
6	62.17	11.63	16	21.50	10.59
7	55.10	16.55	17	51.69	7.53
8	60.96	8.90	18	57.83	15.80
9	53.19	9.64	19	53.13	13.24
10	59.51	12.32	20	59.19	13.84

   a. Compute the overall mean and the mean standard deviation.
   b. Set up *initial* control limits for the mean. Are any of the first 20 subgroup means outside the limits?
   c. What should you do about those sample means that are outside of the limits?
   d. Suppose you can determine the assignable cause for the out-of-control data point and you correct the problem. Now you eliminate that data point and recompute the *final* control limits. Do this for the above data set.
   e. Based on part **d**, is the process under statistical control? Discuss.

10. Refer to Exercise 8. Given here are the mean and standard deviation for the next 7 shifts based on taking 5 items per shift. Is the process ever temporarily out of control? Use the 3-sigma rule. Explain.

Shift	11	12	13	14	15	16	17
$\bar{x}$	20.55	20.20	20.45	20.78	20.35	20.99	20.55
s	.10	.45	.25	.75	.15	.35	.15

11. Explain the difference between chance and assignable cause variation.

12. Explain how a manufacturing process with a PCI of 1.8 could still have serious problems.

13. The lower and upper design specification limits for a product's weight are 19 ounces and 21 ounces. What must $\bar{s}$ be so that the PCI will equal 1.5? What could a firm do to reduce $\bar{s}$?

14. Suppose a sample mean falls outside of the 3-sigma control limits. We must seek an assignable cause. What is the probability that such a point could occur without there being an assignable cause? Explain.

15. *Thought question:* Why not adopt a 1-sigma rule? That is, if one sample mean falls outside the 1-sigma limits, we look for an assignable cause. What problems do you foresee with such a rule? Is there any advantage to such a rule? *Hint:* Use the normal tables to compute the probability that one sample mean will fall outside the 1-sigma limits.

16. Suppose that the PCI for a process is 1.4, and the customer is satisfied with the product. Does that mean that the firm need not attempt to improve the process? Discuss.

12.4 Control Charts for Attributes

We cannot always determine product quality by measuring length, weight, or shatter strength. For example, the engineering design specification for phone handset attractiveness is that it should be free of surface blemishes to the naked eye (see Figure 12.2). An inspection will conclude that either the surface is free of blemishes, or it is not. If the product is without a blemish, it *conforms*. If the product has blemishes, it is *nonconforming*. The attribute—free of surface blemishes—determines the quality. In the previous section we set up control charts on variables such as shatter strength. We now turn to control charts for attributes.

By the end of this section you should be able to:

1. plot *p* (proportion nonconforming) charts; and
2. determine the upper and lower control limits.

We will discuss how to conduct initial process control studies and track process performance using control charts. We will consider only the proportion nonconforming, or *p*, chart.

COMCEL inspectors check each phone handset for surface blemishes before shipping to distributors. If they find one or more blemishes, the product is nonconforming. Finishers must then buff out the blemishes in a final polishing operation. COMCEL believes that blemished phones will alienate customers.

Table 12.5 shows the proportion of nonconforming handsets (one or more blemishes) for the first 10 production days. COMCEL inspects a sample of 500 handsets each day. Table 12.5 represents data for 10 subgroups, whereas practitioners would prefer about 20 subgroups.

The line graph of proportion nonconforming in Figure 12.8 exhibits only random variation. That is, the data stay nearly constant from the start to the end of the process control study. The data also do not exhibit a trend, a cyclical pattern, a widening or narrowing pattern, a performance level shift pattern, a meandering pattern, or an oscillating pattern. The process is under statistical control. As we begin full-scale production, we must develop control charts for the proportion nonconforming.

Table 12.5
Initial Process Control Study Data

DAY	Sample Size	Number Nonconforming	Proportion Nonconforming (p)
1	500	11	.022
2	500	14	.028
3	500	6	.012
4	500	8	.016
5	500	11	.022
6	500	7	.014
7	500	11	.022
8	500	6	.012
9	500	13	.026
10	500	11	.022

FIGURE 12.8 Proportion Defective for Process Control Study

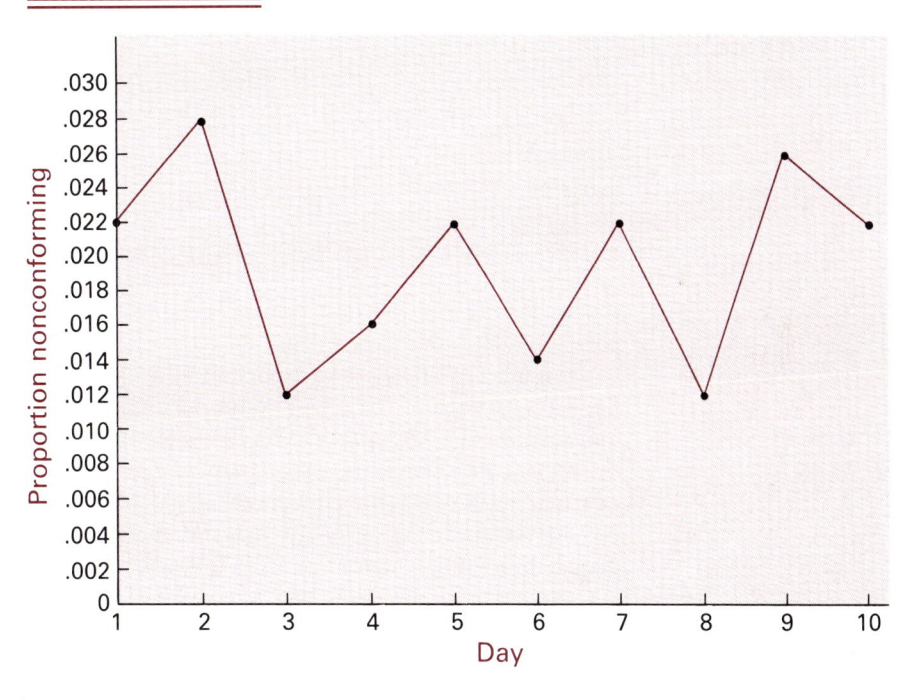

Control Limits for a Proportion Nonconforming Chart

When the sample size of each subgroup is the same, the centerline for the control chart is the mean proportion nonconforming from the process control study:

$$\bar{p} = \frac{\sum p_i}{k} \quad \text{where} \quad p_i = \frac{\text{Number of defectives in subgroup } i}{\text{Sample size}} \quad (12.10)$$

In expression (12.10), k is the number of subgroups taken for the study. From Table 12.5, the centerline of the p-chart is:

$$\frac{.022 + .028 + \cdots + .022}{10} = .0196$$

Below are the equations for the upper and lower control limits. In these expressions, n is the size of each sample that is inspected for defects.

$$\begin{aligned}
\text{UCL:} \quad & \bar{p} + 3(\text{Estimated standard error of the proportion}) \\
&= \bar{p} + 3\sqrt{\frac{\bar{p}(1-\bar{p})}{n}} \\
&= .0196 + 3\sqrt{\frac{.0196(1-.0196)}{500}} \\
&= .0196 + .0186 = .0382
\end{aligned} \qquad (12.11)$$

$$\begin{aligned}
\text{LCL:} \quad & \bar{p} - 3(\text{Estimated standard error of the proportion}) \\
&= \bar{p} - 3\sqrt{\frac{\bar{p}(1-\bar{p})}{n}} \\
&= .0196 - 3\sqrt{\frac{.0196(1-.0196)}{500}} \\
&= .0196 - .0186 = .001
\end{aligned} \qquad (12.12)$$

As long as the proportion nonconforming falls between .001 and .0382, no corrective action need be taken.

Figure 12.9 shows the proportion nonconforming based on samples of 500 handsets for each of the next 15 days—11–25. On day 22 the process produced an exceptionally high proportion of nonconforming handsets—a point above the upper control limit. Look for an *assignable cause*. An analysis revealed that a new and improperly trained worker had run the molding operation. By the next day he had been properly trained and the proportion nonconforming again dropped to within chance-variation bounds.

Here is a thought question. Why are we concerned if p falls below the lower control limit? After all, isn't that good? Why must we determine why the proportion nonconforming has dropped so low? Think about it before reading on!

A data point falling below the lower control limit means there may be an assignable cause for the very low proportion nonconforming. If we can determine the causes, we may be able to *permanently* reduce the proportion nonconforming. For example, suppose the operator had incorrectly set the molding temperature that day. He has accidentally discovered a way to reduce surface blemishes (assuming it does not reduce shatter strength). Now unless we had sought an assignable cause, we might have lost an opportunity to make a permanent process improvement.

FIGURE 12.9 *p*-Chart for 15 Days of Operations

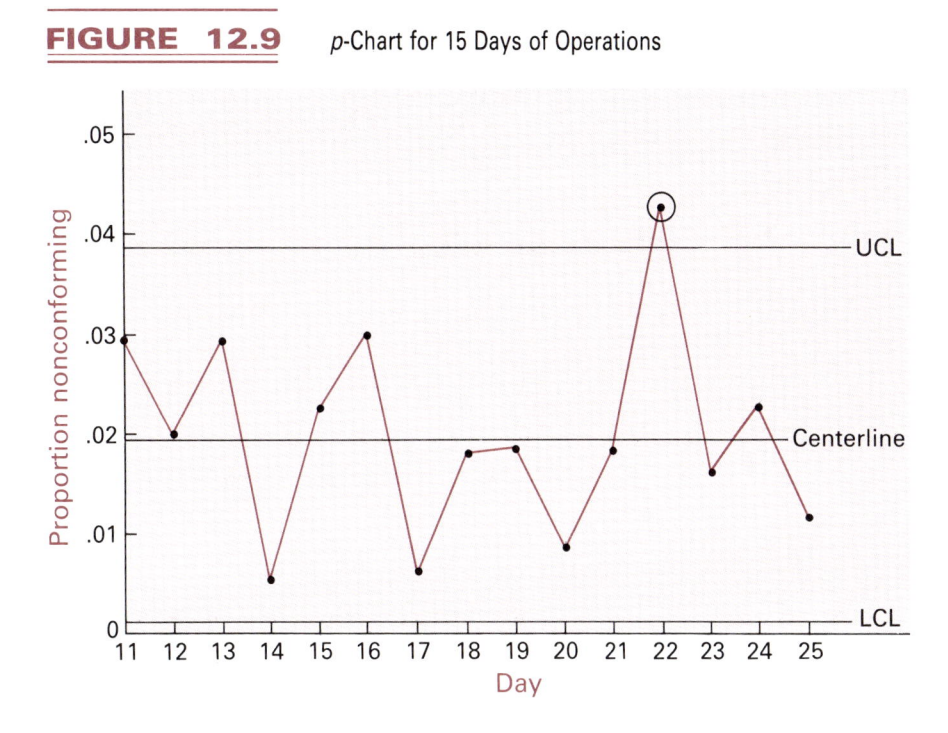

In summary, control charts for variables and attributes help us determine when problem solving action is needed. Quality professionals use a variety of tools to correct and improve processes. We have already presented some of them; others are new and are used mainly in the quality field.

SECTION 12.4 EXERCISES

1. Inspector A selects an item from an assembly line and measures its width. Inspector B examines the item's finish and declares it to be either conforming or nonconforming. Suggest an appropriate control chart for each inspector.

2. A company selects a sample of 200 items per day for a 10-day period.

Day	Sample	Number Nonconforming	Proportion
1	200	7	.035
2	200	12	.060
3	200	8	.040
4	200	10	.050
5	200	13	.065
6	200	9	.045
7	200	11	.055
8	200	10	.050
9	200	14	.070
10	200	6	.030

a. Compute $\bar{p}$ for the 10 days of data.
b. Compute the lower and upper control limits for the process.
c. Construct a control chart for this attribute for days 11–15. Is the process ever out of control? What should you do?

Day	11	12	13	14	15
Proportion Nonconforming	.055	.070	.040	.075	.105

3. The following are the results of the inspection of 10 samples of 100 units each.

Sample	Number Nonconforming
1	3
2	6
3	1
4	4
5	8
6	2
7	3
8	1
9	6
10	5

Set up the centerline and the upper and lower control limits for the proportion nonconforming for this process.

4. Is the following process under statistical control? Does the proportion nonconforming plot suggest only random variation?

Day	Sample	Proportion of Nonconforming Parts
1	100	.04
2	100	.06
3	100	.03
4	100	.07
5	100	.02
6	100	.08
7	100	.01
8	100	.09
9	100	.00
10	100	.10

5. What must the sample size be for each subgroup so that a process with a $\bar{p}$ of .02 will have a UCL of .05?

6. Do the two p-charts at the top of page 697 suggest processes that are under statistical control? Discuss.

Chapter 12 Quality Control

(a)

(b)

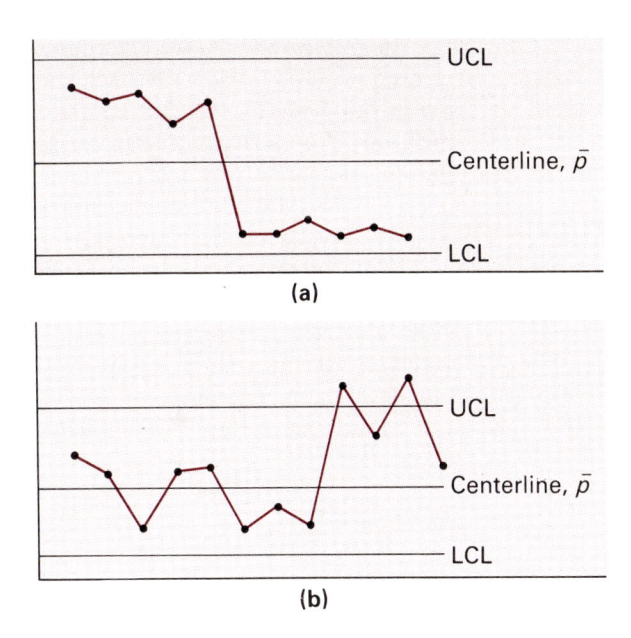

7. Suppose that the workers take a different size sample for each subgroup for inspection. Will this have any effect on the LCL and UCL?

8. The control limits for a *p*-chart are based on the assumption that *p* is approximately normally distributed. If this is so, then the probability of a *p* falling outside the control limits is roughly .0026. Based on Table 7.10, if we expect the proportion nonconforming to be about .10 for a process, what size sample per subgroup must we take to ensure normality?

12.5 Tools for Controlling and Improving Quality

Company-wide quality programs have two goals: (1) to control present manufactured quality and (2) to improve manufactured and design quality. Control charts for attributes and variables help with the first mission. They warn when a process is temporarily out of control and we must take corrective action. Improving manufactured quality is mandatory when an operation's PCI is under 1.0. Such a processs cannot consistently produce units within the design specification limits. Unless we can reduce the process variation ($6\bar{s}$), the operation will produce many rejects. Improving manufactured quality also means improving processes with PCIs above 1.3. That is the spirit behind the maxim: Process improvement must be continuous. Finally, improving design quality entails bettering product performance, durability, or serviceability.

In this section we use our problem solving model from Chapter 1 to illustrate how seven important problem solving tools can help to control and improve quality. (Refer again to Figure 1.1 on page 2.)

In *problem sensing* we determine whether a process is out of control or is in need of improvement. We will show how control charts and Pareto charts aid in problem sensing. During *diagnosis/alternative generation* we clarify the problem or opportunity. Then we seek and evaluate possible root causes of the out-of-control process, or we determine the major obstacles to improving a process. Finally, we develop alternative solutions. We will show how Kepner–Tregoe problem analysis, frequency histograms, fishbone diagrams, and scatter diagrams aid in problem diagnosis and alternative generation. In *decision making/implementation* we select and implement an alternative action. Then we determine whether the action has reestablished process control or accomplished the desired improvement. We will show how experimental design can aid in the decision making phase. By the end of this section you should be able to use and explain the following seven tools for controlling and improving quality:

Problem Sensing

1. Control charts
2. Pareto charts

Diagnosis/Alternative Generation

3. Kepner–Tregoe problem analysis
4. Frequency histograms (or stem-and-leaf displays)
5. Fishbone diagrams
6. Scatter diagrams

Decision Making

7. Experimental design

Among these, only the Pareto chart and fishbone diagram are new problem solving tools.

Control Charts

Control charts are essential for monitoring and controlling the quality level. As long as $\bar{x}$, s, or p falls within its respective control limits, the process is under control. When a process goes out of control, workers and management should immediately determine the root causes and take corrective action.

Pareto Charts

Where should a firm concentrate its quality improvement efforts? There may be hundreds of quality areas that need improvement. The Pareto chart helps sort out the "vital few" from the "trivial many." Named after an Italian economist, Pareto charts are among the most commonly used graphic techniques in quality improvement programs. They organize problem sensing data.

Chapter 12　Quality Control

Table 12.6

Types of Defects in Manufacturing Heaters

Defect Category	Percentage Defects
Cratered paint	45%
Bent fan	36%
Bad motor	10%
Frayed wires	5%
Loose hose	4%
	100%

A basic Pareto chart shows the breakdown of problems by type and percentage. The horizontal axis displays problem type and the vertical axis measures the percentage occurrence of each problem.

Pareto charts determine which quality problems occur most frequently, are most costly, or have the greatest impact on market share. We build a Pareto chart by (1) listing problem categories and (2) gathering data on the frequency of the different problems. The problem solving team then selects the several most common or most expensive problems to correct or to improve first. Often, several defects account for over 80% of the problems. These are the vital few we must correct.

As an illustration for building a Pareto chart, consider the data for defects found during the manufacturing of heaters in Table 12.6. Figure 12.10 presents a **Pareto chart** of these results.

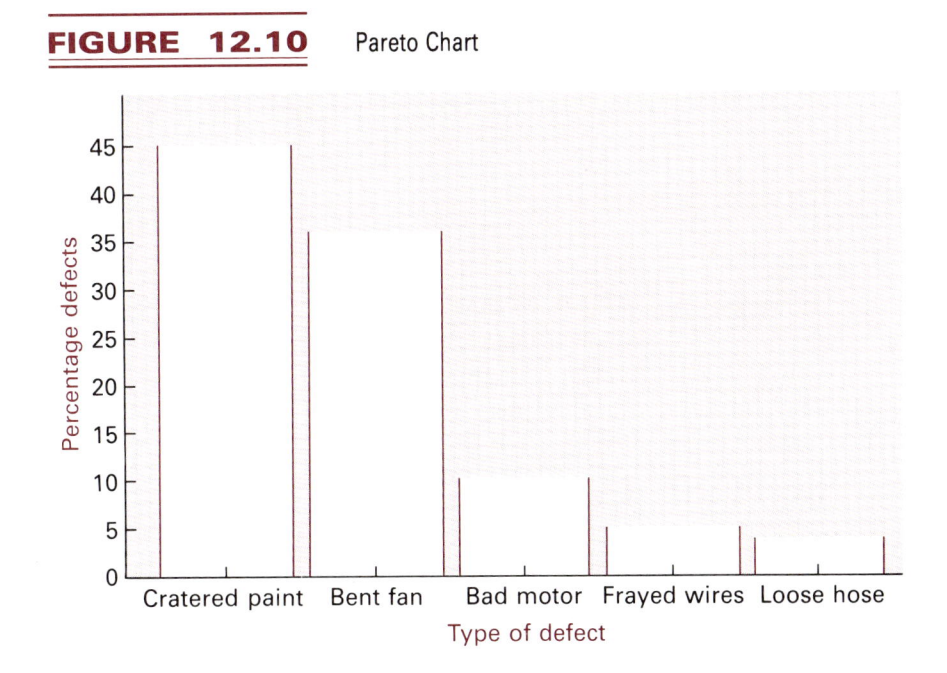

FIGURE 12.10　Pareto Chart

Cratered paint and bent fans are the major causes of defective heaters. Together, they account for 81% of the rejects. The next most common problem occurs only 10% of the time. Clearly, cratered paint and bent fans are the two vital areas that must be improved. It is not worthwhile at this point to spend time correcting loose hoses or frayed wires. They are not major defects.

The Pareto chart resembles the relative frequency histogram from Chapter 2. While they are similar, there is one major difference. In a relative frequency histogram, the horizontal axis displays values of a quantitative variable such as income, claims processed, days to complete a project, or group productivity. The horizontal axis for a Pareto chart displays problem type, a qualitative variable. The vertical axis for both graphical tools is percentage occurrence.

Table 12.7 contains after-sales warranty problems for COMCEL phones. The first two columns of Table 12.7 contain the data for a basic Pareto chart. Excessive static, volume fluctuation, and signal interference are the three most common warranty problems. The next most common problem happens only 3% of the time.

Should COMCEL focus its product redesign effort to eliminate these three problems? The answer is yes, but only if the firm's goal is to reduce the *number* of complaints.

Reducing excessive static, volume fluctuation, and signal interference may not help COMCEL reduce *quality dollar losses*. The third column of the table shows the costs of repairing the various warranty problems. Note that signal interference, limited channel usage, and total failures are the three most costly problems. While the latter two problems are rare (2% and 1% of the total), they are costly to correct.

Should COMCEL focus its product redesign efforts to eliminate these three problems? The answer is yes, but only if it wants to reduce the total warranty *costs*.

Table 12.7

Types of Warranty Problems

Problem	Percentage Problem	Annual Warranty Cost	Reason for Switch to Competitors
Excessive static	40%	$ 6,700	30%
Volume fluctuation	30%	7,500	1%
Signal interference	20%	46,000	2%
Broken handset	3%	1,000	20%
Limited channel usage	2%	27,000	6%
Surface blemishes	2%	500	5%
Total failures	1%	15,500	35%
Auto number recall failure	1%	8,750	1%
Sticky buttons	1%	1,750	0%

Reduced signal interference, limited channel usage, and total failures may not help COMCEL reduce *market share losses*. Excessive warranty work can cause customers to switch to competitors' phones. The fourth column shows the percentage of customers who switched because of the nine problems. Note that excessive static, total failures, and broken handsets are the three major causes. Perhaps COMCEL should focus its product redesign effort in these three areas.

Basic (column 2) and dollar-based Pareto charts (columns 3 and 4) indicate which defects must be corrected. However, charts alone are useless unless we have clear goals (reduce complaints, minimize warranty cost, or minimize lost market share) and collect the requisite data.

Through control and Pareto charts we have identified areas to improve. Now we enter the diagnosis/alternative generation phase. We begin by specifying the problem clearly. The Kepner–Tregoe (1988) problem analysis method is particularly useful. Frequency histograms (or stem-and-leaf displays), fishbone diagrams, and scatter diagrams are also very useful in seeking and evaluating possible root causes.

Kepner-Tregoe Problem Analysis

We first discussed the Kepner–Tregoe (K–T) problem analysis method in Chapter 9. It transforms ambiguous symptoms, facts, and assumptions into a clear problem statement. We start by asking (and answering) a series of questions. We have illustrated these questions in the context of the cratered paint problem identified by the Pareto chart in Figure 12.10.

What is the deviation (vs. what it isn't)?
  What exactly is *cratering*? Use more precise language to describe cratering. The term "cratering" is vague.

When did the deviation occur (vs. when didn't it occur)?
  When (shift and day) did the cratering begin?

Where did the deviation occur (vs. where didn't it occur)?
  Where is the cratering occurring on the heaters? On the top, bottom, or sides?
  Where in the manufacturing process is the cratering occurring or where is the cratering first noticed?
  Is the cratering occurring on heaters from all shifts? From all plants?

How much, how many, to what extent did the deviation occur (vs. to what extent didn't it occur)?
  Is the cratering problem increasing, decreasing, or remaining constant? Is cratering worse on the Monday and Friday shifts vs. the other weekdays?
  How many paint craters are there on each heater?

Answering these questions will require additional data. In fact, a major value of the K–T method is that it identifies the data necessary to generate a clear problem statement. Having a clear problem statement increases the chance of identifying the causes of the paint cratering—the why.

The K–T method aids the identification of possible root causes. The problem solver looks for changes in equipment, processes, personnel, or suppliers that might explain the onset of a problem. The problem solver also reviews the problem statement for possible root causes. For example, suppose the paint cratering happens on only one shift. What root cause might that suggest? Suppose the paint cratering happens only on the bottom of the heater. What root cause might that suggest?

Frequency Histograms

Frequency histograms (and stem-and-leaf displays) can help evaluate possible root causes. Suppose that COMCEL's molding operation produces about 9% rejects. This is clearly unacceptable. The quality team undertakes a project to reduce process variation and thereby reduce the number of rejects. COMCEL is considering the following root causes areas.

People:	Improper supervision
Raw materials:	Too many plastics vendors of varying quality
Equipment:	Old or poorly maintained equipment or too few controls on the present equipment
Methods:	Outdated manufacturing methods or too complex methods
Product design:	Too stringent design specification limits

Deming (1982) and Juran and Gryna (1980) suggest that about 85% of all quality problems can be corrected only by management. Note that all the above possible root causes are under management's control.

COMCEL suspects that raw material differences among its three plastics suppliers cause the excessive process variation. The firm uses frequency histograms to compare plastic shatter strength for the last 260 lots of material from each of its three vendors.

Figure 12.11 shows that all three vendors' raw materials have roughly the same mean shatter strength, about 4,750 pounds per square inch. However, vendor B's raw material is the most consistent. Note the tightness of its frequency histogram. COMCEL should now consider making vendor B the firm's sole source. Alternatively, it can work with the two other vendors to help them reduce their shatter strength variation.

Fishbone Diagrams

Fishbone, or Ishikawa, diagrams are visual aids that help generate and evaluate the diagnosis of potential problem root causes or help find ways to make process or product improvements. We will illustrate how a fishbone diagram helped determine why the mean shatter strength at the COMCEL molding operation dropped below the LCL during shift 28 (see Figure 12.7).

FIGURE 12.11 Shatter Strength of Plastic from Three Vendors

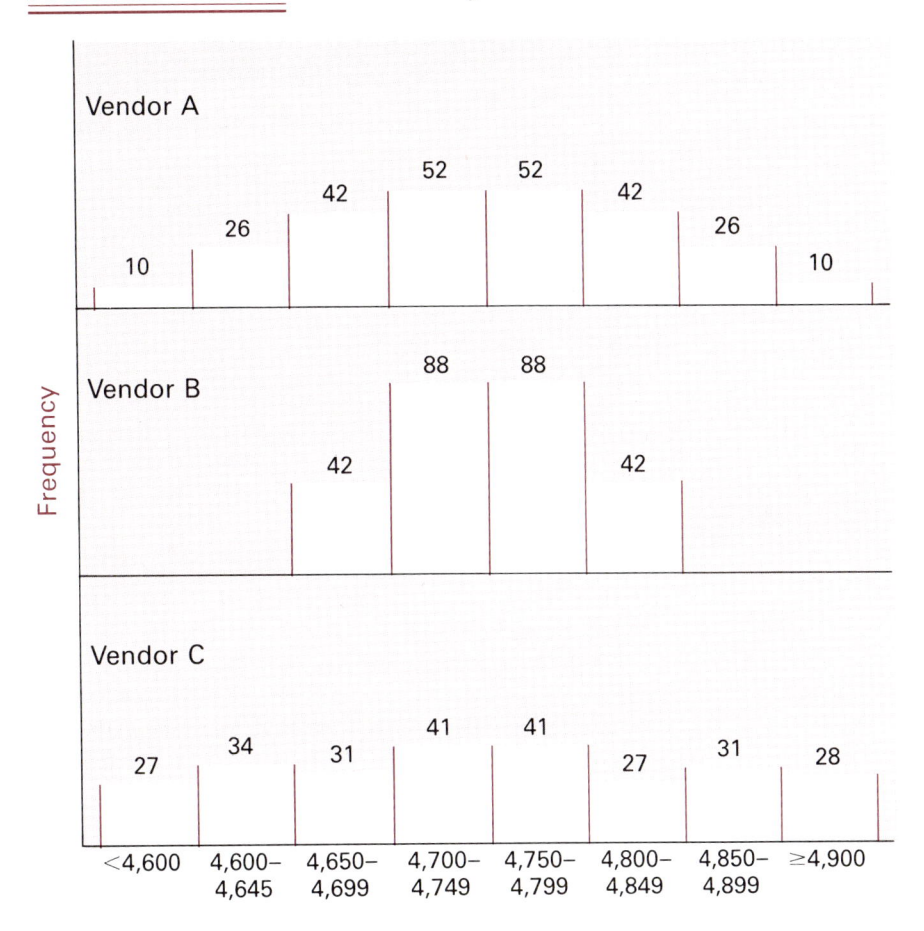

Vendor A: 10, 26, 42, 52, 52, 42, 26, 10

Vendor B: 88, 88, 42, 42

Vendor C: 27, 34, 31, 41, 41, 27, 31, 28

Bins: <4,600 | 4,600–4,645 | 4,650–4,699 | 4,700–4,749 | 4,750–4,799 | 4,800–4,849 | 4,850–4,899 | ≥4,900

Frequency (y-axis)

A fishbone diagram contains a goal box into which we place the goal of our investigation—in this case, determine the reason why $\bar{x}$ was below the LCL on shift 28. The quality team then generated three or four potential major cause areas. These are shown as the "large bones" in the diagram in Figure 12.12 on page 704. Good sources for major cause areas are the four M's: *methods*, *manpower*, *materials*, and *machines*. Alternatively, the group may generate its own list. Starting with each major bone, the group brainstormed two to six possible specific causes, or "small bones." Then it ranked the specific causes and investigated the most promising ones.

A brainstorming session produced the fishbone diagram in Figure 12.12. The quality team thought that either a new molding supervisor or a new plastics vendor was the most likely cause. Together with the purchasing and engineering departments, they determined that the cause was the new vendor. When

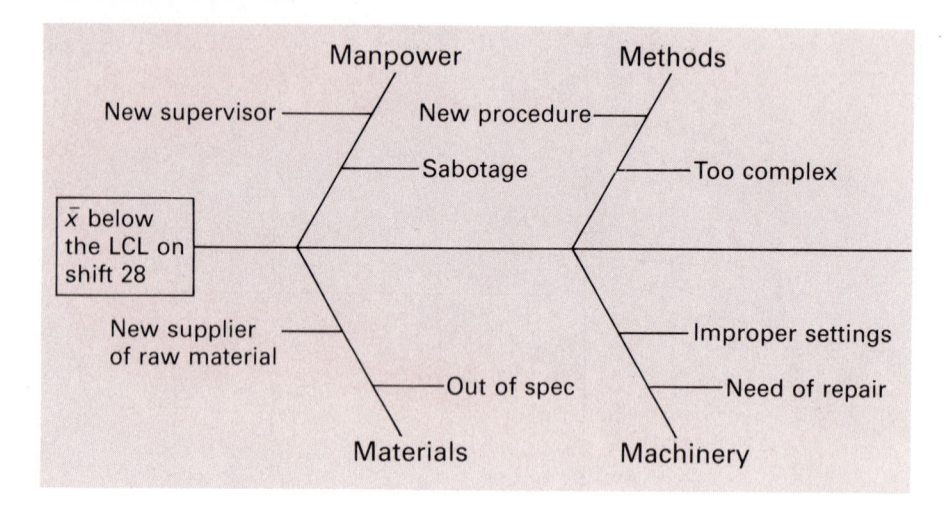

FIGURE 12.12   Fishbone Diagram

```
                    Manpower              Methods
       New supervisor ─┐    New procedure ─┐
                       │                   │
                       ├─ Sabotage         ├─ Too complex
  ┌─────────┐          │                   │
  │ x̄ below │──────────┴───────────────────┴──────────────
  │ the LCL │          │                   │
  │ on      │          │                   │
  │ shift 28│          │                   │
  └─────────┘          │                   ├─ Improper settings
    New supplier ──────┤                   │
    of raw material    │                   ├─ Need of repair
                       └─ Out of spec      │
                    Materials              Machinery
```

COMCEL returned to its previous supplier, the mean shatter strength rose to within the control limits (see shift 29 in Figure 12.7).

Returning to the paint cratering problem, the quality improvement team used the Kepner–Tregoe problem analysis method to develop a clear problem statement (see goal box of Figure 12.13). The team generated five major cause areas—the four M's and a specification category. Then it brainstormed possible specific causes within each of the five categories. The team believed that cratering was due to either (1) the heaters touching one another during painting or (2) wide daily temperature fluctuations in the painting booths. The team evaluated and rejected the touching hypothesis. **Fishbone diagrams** help quality teams focus on the problem, actively search for causes, suggest critical data, and maintain and improve quality. Best of all, they are easily learned. However, do not develop fishbone diagrams until you have a clear understanding of the problem. Determining the root causes of a poorly defined problem is difficult.

> A fishbone diagram is a visual aid that helps identify major problem cause areas or product improvement areas. Using brainstorming, specific causes or ways to improve the process/product are generated and then evaluated.

Scatter Diagrams

We first encountered scatter diagrams in Chapter 3 and more recently in Chapters 10–11. Recall that they are useful in showing possible relationships between two quantitative variables. Place one variable on the vertical axis and the other variable on the horizontal axis. A data point is an (X, Y) value.

Returning to the paint cratering problem, the quality team next evaluated the temperature hypothesis. They recorded the daily mean temperature in the painting booth and the percentage of cratered heaters over a 10-day period. They then developed the accompanying scatter diagram.

Figure 12.14 clearly indicates that as the temperature drops below 68°F, the

Chapter 12 Quality Control

FIGURE 12.13 Fishbone Diagram for Cratered Paint Problem

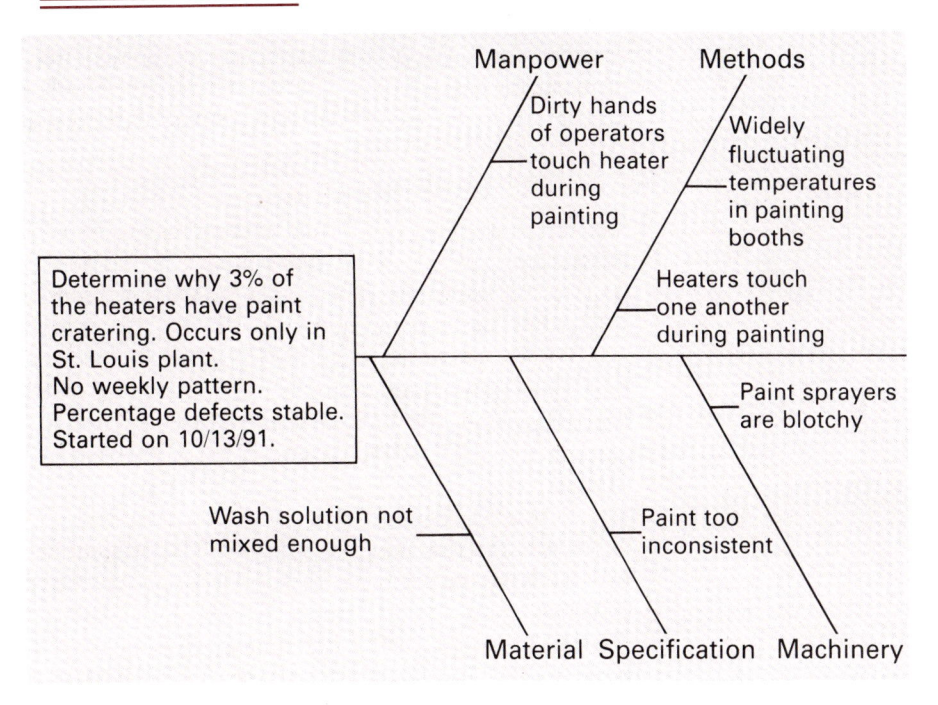

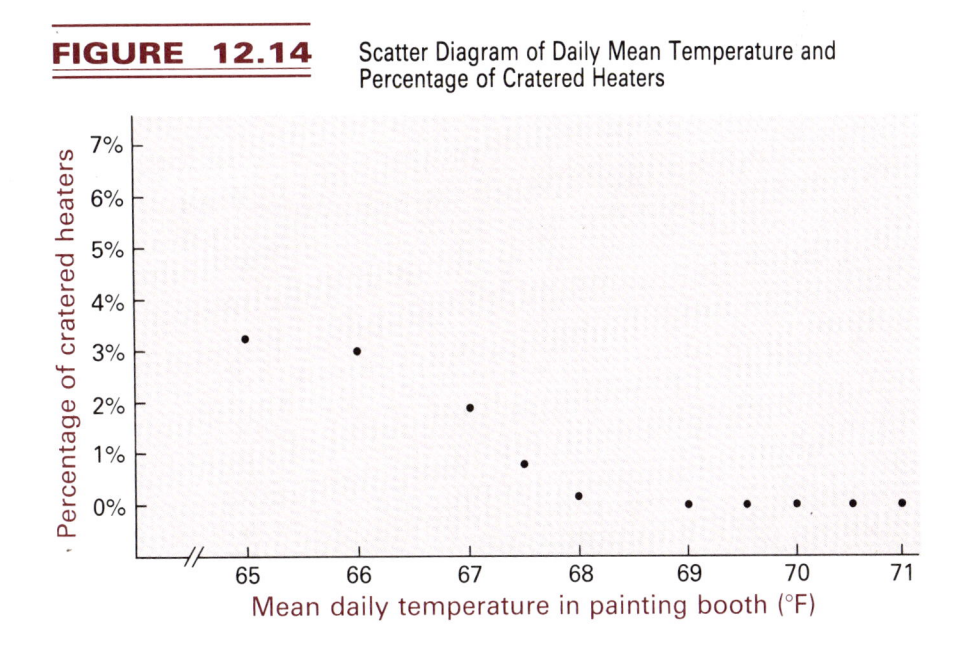

Determine why 3% of the heaters have paint cratering. Occurs only in St. Louis plant. No weekly pattern. Percentage defects stable. Started on 10/13/91.

Manpower:
- Dirty hands of operators touch heater during painting

Methods:
- Widely fluctuating temperatures in painting booths
- Heaters touch one another during painting

Machinery:
- Paint sprayers are blotchy

Specification:
- Paint too inconsistent

Material:
- Wash solution not mixed enough

FIGURE 12.14 Scatter Diagram of Daily Mean Temperature and Percentage of Cratered Heaters

percentage of cratering increases. To eliminate cratering, the firm needs to keep temperature above 68°F in the painting booths.

Having determined the root causes of a problem, we then must select a corrective action and monitor its impact. Sometimes, as in the paint cratering problem, the best action is obvious. Increase the booth temperature. Other times, firms must use formal experiments to choose the best action to implement.

Experimental Design

Sometimes we must run formal experiments to improve processes or products. After testing a change, study the results. What did we learn? If the planned change is successful, implement it permanently. We first discussed how to conduct formal studies in Chapter 6 and more recently in Chapter 9.

We will illustrate how COMCEL used experimental design to determine that a new raw material supplier was the cause of the mean shatter strength dropping below the LCL on shift 28 (see Figure 12.7). The experiment also confirmed that COMCEL could solve the problem by returning to the original supplier.

COMCEL conducted a one-factor, two-level, random experiment. The factor was the raw material supplier. The original and new vendors were the two levels in the study. Both suppliers' manufacturing processes were under statistical control and the material used in the study was representative of current production. COMCEL produced 10 phones with raw material from both suppliers. The firm then tested the shatter strength of the 20 phones. Table 12.8 contains the data for the formal study.

The variance ratio of 29.50 in Table 12.9 indicates that there is a significant difference between the two suppliers' raw materials (p-value $< .01$). The mean shatter strength for the new material, 4,685 psi, is below the LCL of 4,724 psi. The

Table 12.8

Data for a One-Factor, Two-Level Experiment

	Original Vendor	New Vendor
	4,760	4,690
	4,800	4,650
	4,725	4,710
	4,775	4,730
	4,770	4,690
	4,700	4,630
	4,790	4,700
	4,750	4,660
	4,750	4,710
	4,760	4,680
$\bar{x}$	4,758 psi	4,685 psi
s	29.46 psi	30.64 psi

Table 12.9
ANOVA Table for Raw Material Study

Sources of Variation	Sum of Squares	Degrees of Freedom	Variance	Variance Ratio
Between	26,645	1	26,645	29.50
Within	16,260	18	903.33	
Total	42,905	19		

mean shatter strength for the original material, 4,758 psi, is in the middle of the control chart limits. COMCEL should return to its original supplier or ask the new supplier to increase the shatter strength of its plastics.

Finally, we monitor the corrective action to determine whether it has had the desired impacts. For example, the control chart in Figure 12.7 indicates that by returning to its original supplier, COMCEL reestablished control over the molding process.

In summary, firms that use a systematic problem solving model and the seven tools we've presented can control and improve both process and product. Managers can and do use many of the seven tools in more than one problem solving phase. These tools reduce the chance that poor quality products will "make it out the door." However, no amount of process control and improvement can assure zero defects because many manufacturing companies purchase as much value (raw material or subassemblies) as they add in their own manufacturing. Thus, ensuring the quality of purchased items is crucial. In the next section we discuss several strategies for ensuring high quality of purchased items.

SECTION 12.5 EXERCISES

1. The Department of Decision Sciences gives a common final examination in basic statistics. Over the last 10 quarters the mean grade has been 75. This past quarter the mean grade was below 60, over three standard deviations below the historical mean. Draw a fishbone diagram to help identify possible root causes. Use the following major bones—Final exam, Students, Teachers—to brainstorm two possible sub-causes for each major bone.

2. Refer to Table 12.7. Draw a Pareto chart for annual warranty cost and a Pareto chart for reasons for switching to competitors. Include only the top six causes for each chart.

3. Suppose you notice that sometimes your portable CD player does not work properly. Develop a list of questions that you should ask to develop a clear problem understanding. Use the Kepner–Tregoe problem analysis method to frame your questions.

4. A department store wishes to develop a Pareto chart on reasons for returning clothing. Develop five possible reasons that might account for returning clothing.

5. Refer to Exercise 3. Would asking *why* the portable CD player does not work be appropriate to developing a clear problem statement?

6. Why is a fishbone diagram ineffective until we have a clear statement of the problem?

12.6 Vendor Certification and Acceptance Sampling

Given that purchased materials can run as high as 90% of manufactured cost, firms must establish effective supplier quality control systems. For many years, firms relied solely on incoming inspection. Inspectors tested samples from incoming lots and either accepted or rejected the lots. Firms are now relying less on incoming inspection for two reasons. First, incoming inspection cannot completely stop defective raw materials or subassemblies from entering a plant. Second, the goal of effective supplier quality control is to obtain good parts, not merely to stop defective parts. Finding and working with high-quality vendors are replacing or at least complementing incoming inspection. Perhaps in the near future, incoming inspection will become obsolete. By the end of this section you should be able to:

1. distinguish acceptance sampling from other inspection methods;
2. explain and demonstrate why an acceptance sampling plan cannot stop all raw material or subassembly defects from entering a firm; and
3. understand strategies to implement and maintain a vendor certification program.

Acceptance Sampling Basics

The degree to which a firm uses incoming inspection depends on the past quality performance history of the vendor, the importance of the part, and its intended use. There are several levels of incoming inspection.

No inspection Firms accept all incoming lots without inspecting them. A "no-inspection" policy is becoming the norm, but only with high-quality vendors. In lieu of testing, firms develop programs to certify high-quality vendors and work with them to improve their processes. We will cover more on this later.

100% inspection Firms inspect every piece of every lot they receive. However, this is costly, time-consuming, and impractical for destructive testing (testing that destroys the product). A firm may have hundreds of vendors supplying thousands of parts. Furthermore, 100% inspection is not 100% effective at finding defective parts. Fatigue and stress can cause inspectors to make mistakes. However, the National Aeronautics and Space Administration (NASA) still relies on 100% inspection of incoming parts, since a defective part can cause a shuttle disaster.

Acceptance sampling Acceptance sampling is a process that evaluates a portion of each incoming lot and, based on the test results, accepts or rejects it. Acceptance sampling is still used because of its low cost, although Deming and others argue that quality comes not from inspection but from process improvement.

There are several types of acceptance sampling plans. *Single-sampling plans* require inspectors to take one sample of size *n* from each incoming lot. Based on the test results, the firm accepts or rejects the lot. Vendors must then replace rejected lots. American firms use what is called MIL-STD-105D single-sampling

Table 12.10

Some MIL-STD-105D Single-Sampling Plans for Normal Inspection[a]

		Acceptable Quality Levels					
		1.0%		2.5%		6.5%	
Lot Size	Sample Size	Accept	Reject	Accept	Reject	Accept	Reject
51 to 90	13	0	1	1	2	2	3
91 to 150	20	0	1	1	2	3	4
151 to 280	32	1	2	2	3	5	6
281 to 500	50	1	2	3	4	7	8
501 to 1,200	80	2	3	5	6	10	11
1,201 to 3,200	125	3	4	7	8	14	15
3,201 to 10,000	200	5	6	10	11	21	22

[a] Taken from the master table, Table II-A of MIL-STD-105D.

plans. *Double-sampling plans* require that inspectors draw two samples, if needed, before making a yes/no decision. *Multiple-sampling plans* allow inspectors to select more than two samples if needed to make a decision.

Table 12.10 illustrates some MIL-STD-105D single-sampling plans.

The acceptable quality level (AQL) is the maximum percentage of incoming defective pieces that a receiving firm can tolerate. Of course, receiving firms prefer lots with 0% defective, but vendors argue that it is not possible to ship lots with 0% defective. They say that the receiving firm should be satisfied if the maximum percentage of defectives is 1% or 2.5%. Vendors and receiving firms *negotiate* the AQLs.

Suppose that a receiving firm and its vendor have agreed to a 1% AQL. Further suppose that the vendor ships lots of 2,000 parts each. Using Table 12.10, the receiving firm will select a random sample of 125 pieces from each lot to inspect. If the receiving firm finds three or fewer defectives in the sample of 125, it accepts the lot. If it finds four or more defectives, it rejects the lot. This set of acceptance and rejection rules constitutes one MIL-STD-105D sampling plan. Each of the other 20 sets of acceptance and rejection rules in Table 12.10 constitutes a different MIL-STD-105D sampling plan.

Even low-AQL sampling plans will not stop defectives from entering a plant. Every defective item that the receiving firm receives from a vendor may cause serious problems. It makes no difference if a defective piece comes from a lot that is .1% defective or 1% defective. Defects are defects! Acceptance sampling plans cannot keep all defective pieces from entering a firm. We will illustrate this idea next.

The Inability of Acceptance Sampling to Completely Stop Defectives

Suppose that a firm using a 1% AQL sampling plan receives 100 lots of 2,000 parts each. The receiving firm takes a random sample of 125 pieces from each lot. The firm accepts the lot if it finds three or fewer defective parts. How effective will acceptance sampling be in stopping defective pieces from entering the firm? Assume that all lots contain exactly 1.0% defectives, the negotiated AQL.

Incoming inspectors will randomly select and test 125 pieces from each lot, or 12,500 pieces in total [(125)(100 lots)]. Of the 12,500 pieces we expect to find 125 defectives, or 1.0%. Moreover, we expect to accept about 96% of the incoming lots. Why? Because the Poisson distribution (see Chapter 5) tells us that for lots with a 1% defective rate, inspectors will find three or fewer defectives in the random sample of 125 pieces about 96% of the time:

$$P[\text{three or fewer defectives when } \lambda = (125)(.01) = 1.25] = .96$$

$$P[\text{four or more defectives when } \lambda = (125)(.01) = 1.25] = .04$$

Based on the Poisson distribution, about 96% of the lots will be accepted and 4% of the lots will be rejected. That is, samples from 96 lots will have three or fewer defectives. Samples from 4 lots will have four or more defectives. Consider the 100 lots in Table 12.11.

Given these data, how many defective parts will enter the receiving firm? We

Table 12.11

100 Hypothetical Lots of 2,000 Parts Each Containing 1% Defectives

Lot	Sample Size	Number of Defectives	Action
1	125	3	Accept
2	125	2	Accept
3	125	1	Accept
4	125	1	Accept
⋮	⋮	⋮	⋮
90	125	0	Accept
91	125	2	Accept
92	125	3	Accept
93	125	2	Accept
94	125	3	Accept
95	125	1	Accept
96	125	0	Accept
97	125	6	Reject
98	125	4	Reject
99	125	4	Reject
100	125	5	Reject

125 defectives

106 defective parts found in lots 1–96
19 defective parts found in lots 97–100

have shown the calculations below:

Number of accepted lots	96
Number of defectives in accepted lots	(96)(2,000 parts)(.01) = 1,920
Number of defectives found in accepted lots	106
Total number of defectives entering plant	1,920 − 106 = 1,814

The 96 accepted lots contain 1% defectives. That accounts for 1,920 defective parts. Inspectors found 106 defectives in the 96 lots they ultimately accepted. Therefore, 1,814 defectives got past incoming inspection. Had the firm accepted all 100 lots without testing, then (100)(2,000)(.01) = 2,000 defective parts would have entered the firm. Thus, acceptance sampling kept *only* 186 defective parts from entering the plant.

Acceptance sampling is not very effective at stopping defective pieces from entering a plant when incoming lots consistently have a percentage of defectives at or near the AQL. Then why use acceptance sampling at all? Acceptance sampling plans are quite effective in rejecting lots with very high percentage defectives. For example, suppose a lot actually contains 10% defects. According to the Poisson distribution, the chance or finding three or fewer defectives in a random sample of 125 is only about .2%:

$$P[\text{three or fewer defectives when } \lambda = (125)(.1) = 12.5] = .002$$

Even if incoming inspection were successful in stopping defects, it does not ensure a continuous supply of good parts. Vendor certification programs can.

Vendor Certification

Most manufacturing companies buy as much value (raw material or subassemblies) as they add in manufacturing. The only way to ensure good quality of purchased items is to have good suppliers. *A company that wants to receive good parts and materials must buy from reputable suppliers.* Firms should not select vendors solely on the basis of cost. They must choose vendors on their ability to be competitive and to provide evidence that they are using statistical process control principles in manufacturing their parts. If suppliers use statistical process control, there is generally less need to do incoming inspection.

Vendor certification programs identify and rank reputable vendors and seek long-term cooperative, not adversarial, relationships. In his book, *The Chain of Quality*, J. M. Groocock, a practicing quality professional at the TRW organization, discusses how to make vendor certification programs work (1986). His suggestions include developing quality-of-purchased-items policy statements and joint vendor–firm quality improvement activities.

Here are a few statements taken from TRW's quality-of-purchased-items policy:

1. The primary objective is progressively to reduce the proportion of purchased items that are defective.

2. The division will purchase only from approved suppliers.
3. The division will establish a relationship of cooperation with its approved suppliers, with the purpose of helping them supply products conforming to the defined requirements.

Firms rank vendors through vendor surveys. Those vendors that score high are certified. Surveys generally include the following items:

1. Does the vendor have written statistical process control procedures?
2. How does the vendor handle its suppliers?
3. Is the vendor's information system for quality data adequate and used?
4. Are quality control personnel competent and aggressive?
5. Is top management committed to the quality effort?
6. How do the vendor's engineering and quality control personnel keep abreast of the customer's quality requirements?

The customer and vendor must have a successful "marriage." Suppliers must be viewed as team members, not adversaries. Quality will result when the receiving firm and vendor establish a sound and mutually profitable long-term relationship. Here are some ideas offered by Kenneth Kivenko, a quality professional (1984):

1. Explain the needed quality standards clearly to the vendor.
2. Get to know key vendor personnel. Build relationships.
3. Provide engineering support to vendors when they are having problems meeting your quality standards for incoming parts.
4. Hold "vendor days" at your plant. Show vendors how their products are used in your manufacturing process.

Acceptance sampling and vendor certification programs are useful. Acceptance sampling stops lots with a high percentage of defectives from entering the plant, but it will not improve the overall quality of incoming lots. Only a reputable vendor who will work with your company can do that. Vendor certification programs have greater success in ensuring a continuous stream of good parts and raw materials than do acceptance sampling plans.

SECTION 12.6 EXERCISES

1. A firm receives shipments of electronic components in lots of size 1,000 units. The negotiated AQL is 1%.
   a. What size sample should the firm take at incoming inspection?
   b. Describe the acceptance and rejection rules using the sampling plan.
   c. The firm finds eight defective components in a random sample of 80. What action should it take?

2. A firm receives shipments of subassemblies in lots of size 7,500 units. The negotiated AQL is 6.5%.
   a. What size sample should the firm take at incoming inspection?
   b. Describe the acceptance and rejection rules using the sampling plan.
   c. The firm finds 18 defective parts in a random sample of 200. What action should it take?

3. Dr. Deming noted in his 1986 book, *Out of Chaos*, that "incredibly, courses and books in statistical methods still devote time and pages to acceptance sampling." What does he mean by that statement?

4. We made the statement that acceptance sampling is useful in stopping shipments with a very high percentage of defective parts from entering a plant. Assume that 100 lots of size 1,000 are shipped to a plant. Assume that each lot contains 10% defective parts. The negotiated AQL is 1%. Why would a very large percentage of these lots be rejected at incoming inspection?

5. Describe the major difference between vendor certification programs and acceptance sampling plans to control incoming quality of parts and subassemblies.

6. *Comment on the following statement:* Select the low-cost vendor for subassemblies even if it does not use statistical process control principles in its manufacturing.

12.7 General Principles

Our basic premise is that a high-quality product is a customer's right. For this to be more than a slogan, firms should adopt the philosophy that quality is more than just $\bar{x}$-, s-, p-charts or vendor certification programs. It is more than techniques—Pareto charts, fishbone diagrams, and the like. It is an attitude. Quality occurs when workers and management commit themselves to controlling and improving quality. A commitment to quality should not be this month's pet project, but an ongoing and constant commitment.

We conclude the book with a set of principles to improve quality based on Deming's writings.

General Principles of Quality

PRINCIPLE 1: Management should make workers feel secure in controlling and improving quality. It should encourage workers to ask questions when they do not understand some aspect of operations and to report out-of-control processes, even if it means delaying schedules. Management should encourage workers to actively seek process improvements, rather than being passive operators.

PRINCIPLE 2: Avoid purchasing from lowest-bid vendors, unless they are high-quality suppliers. Low cost may mean low-quality inputs, which will cause quality problems.

PRINCIPLE 3: Institute quality circles or teams at all levels of the firm and train them. Quality circles are groups of 5 to 10 workers who periodically meet to control and improve quality. The leader may be a middle manager, foreman, or an hourly employee. Using the seven problem solving techniques discussed in this chapter, quality circles can achieve significant results in quality improvement, cost reduction, productivity, and safety.

PRINCIPLE 4:   Instill pride of workmanship. Years ago, workers were craftsmen. Since automation, workers have taken less responsibility for their work. That must change. Managers and workers must regain pride of workmanship and service.

General Principles of Statistical Process Control

PRINCIPLE 5:   Variability is a fact of life. No two purchased items entering a plant are the same. No two finished products leaving a plant are the same. There are item-to-item, day-to-day, and week-to-week variations. It is impossible to eliminate variation, but it is possible to reduce and control it.

PRINCIPLE 6:   Use control charts to identify out-of-control processes.

PRINCIPLE 7:   Take quick and effective problem solving action for an out-of-control process. Use the seven problem solving tools to help identify root causes.

PRINCIPLE 8:   Strive to improve the product and the process. Use the seven problem solving tools to help determine how.

PRINCIPLE 9:   Use vendor certification and acceptance sampling programs to improve the quality of purchased items or raw material.

A Final Thought

The Information Age is here. Each day, business professionals are swamped by data. Moreover, their day is highly fragmented. They have only a few minutes to review and digest the data before their next meeting or interruption. They can learn to do quick and simple analyses and to develop *mental models* on the state of their department or firm. Mental models suggest opportunities or emerging problems. These models need not be complex or mathematical. Rather they can be simple, verbal or visual.

Throughout this book we have intertwined quantitative statistical tools with qualitative problem solving concepts. We believe that this unique combination can improve developing mental models. And better mental models make for better problem solvers, decision makers, and business professionals.

COMCEL
COMCEL

Date: September 15, 1993
To: Ann Tabor, CEO
From: Sang Kim, Quality Assurance Manager
Re: Rework costs

SUMMARY
The jump in rework costs was due to two factors. First, we changed to a new supplier who offered us a unit price well below that of our former supplier. Our mistake was in selecting a vendor on the basis of price alone. Poor subassembly quality leads to higher costs for us. I suggest we switch back to our previous supplier and initiate a joint effort to improve the quality of their subassemblies. As you know, our philosophy had always been to buy from the low-cost vendor. That must change. I recommend that quality, not cost, should be our prime concern in selecting a vendor.

Second, we did negotiate our contract on the basis of an AQL of 1%. But even at that level, we cannot stop all defective assemblies from entering our plant.

SUPPORTING ANALYSIS
Dr. W. Edwards Deming, a leading authority in the quality area, points out that firms must cease relying on inspection. In his 1986 book, *Out of Chaos*, he argued that a company's aim should be to do away with using inspection to ensure quality. It does not work.

As for now, we should continue our acceptance sampling procedure. However, it will *not* stop defective subassemblies from entering our plant. In fact, it will not stop lots with relatively high levels of defective subassemblies from entering our plant.

For example, if a lot of 2,000 subassemblies has 66 bad units (3.3% defectives) there is a 41% probability of its being accepted by our inspectors. Here is why. Our sampling plan tells us to take a random sample of 125 assemblies from the lot of 2,000. If we find three or fewer defective assemblies, we accept the lot. Based on the Poisson distribution:

$P[$ three or fewer defectives when $\lambda = (125)(.033) = 4.125] = .41$

For a lot that is 10% defective (very poor), there is only a .2% probability of its being accepted by our inspectors:

P[three or fewer defectives when λ = (125)(.10) = 12.5] = .002

Our plan keeps out really bad lots, but it does not keep out moderately bad lots (such as 3.3% defective). Even with incoming sampling, many defective subassemblies enter the plant and cause us problems during manufacturing. The only way to ensure good-quality subassemblies is to work with a reputable and willing vendor to improve its statistical quality control. Through such efforts, the quality of purchased subassemblies will improve.

CHAPTER 12 QUESTIONS

1. Distinguish between design and manufactured quality.
2. Should (or can) ensuring manufactured quality be the sole responsibility of a quality control department?
3. A Ford Company ad says that "Quality is job #1!" What do you think that means?
4. What is the purpose of *process control* studies?
5. What is the problem with an increasing standard deviation in a process control study?
6. How does a *process capability* study differ from a *process control* study?
7. What information does the process capability index (PCI) provide?
8. If the PCI is 2.0, there can still be serious problems. Explain.
9. What remedies would you suggest for a process with a PCI of .5?
10. Distinguish the purpose of control charting vs. process control studies and process capability studies.
11. If a data point ($\bar{x}$ or s) falls above or below the 3-sigma limits, is it possible that there is no problem? How often will this happen? What assumption must be true?
12. What problem might you have if you use a fishbone diagram without first clearly defining the problem?
13. How do basic Pareto charts differ from relative frequency histograms?
14. What advantage do dollar-based Pareto charts have over basic Pareto charts?
15. Why doesn't 100% incoming inspection of raw material and subassemblies stop all defects from entering a plant?
16. What is the negotiated AQL and what does it mean?
17. What role does the Poisson distribution play in understanding sampling plans?
18. Can MIL-STD-105D sampling plans stop all defects from entering a plant?
19. Acceptance sampling cannot stop defects from entering your plant. What use, if any, is it?
20. Why are vendor certification programs and joint supplier–customer efforts needed to improve incoming quality?

CHAPTER 12 APPLICATION PROBLEMS

1. A firm produces car batteries. Each shift, inspectors use systematic sampling to select five batteries. They determine how long an engine will crank (in seconds) at 30° before needing to be recharged. The firm has set a lower specification limit of 85 seconds and an upper specification limit of 115 seconds. Shown are the process control and capability data based on the first 10 production shifts.

	Observation				
Shift	1	2	3	4	5
1	101	104	100	103	101
2	102	102	105	101	100
3	100	100	103	104	100
4	100	103	102	101	104
5	103	101	102	104	103
6	104	102	100	103	105
7	104	103	103	102	100
8	102	102	101	104	100
9	105	104	103	102	102
10	105	103	101	103	102

   a. Are the process mean and standard deviation under control?
   b. Compute $\bar{s}$. Is the process capability index greater than 1.3?
   c. Compute $\bar{\bar{x}}$ and set up the LCL and UCL for the mean cranking time.
   d. Set up the LCL and UCL for the standard deviation in cranking time.

2. Given are the cranking time data for the next 15 shifts for the battery manufacturer in the previous problem.

	Observation				
Shift	1	2	3	4	5
11	105	105	104	100	102
12	105	104	105	101	101
13	104	104	100	103	103
14	104	101	104	103	101
15	102	101	103	103	105
16	102	103	102	104	102
17	102	101	105	104	102
18	115	113	112	113	111
19	103	104	103	103	101
20	102	104	105	103	103
21	103	100	101	103	104
22	102	103	101	103	101
23	102	100	104	108	101
24	102	104	103	101	101
25	100	102	102	101	101

a. Is the process ever out of control according to the $\bar{x}$- and s-charts for the next 15 shifts?
b. If either statistic was out of control, was the firm able to correct the problem(s)? Explain.
c. Had you been the line manager, how would you have sought the root causes of the out-of-control production process?

3. Journal adjustments are made at the monthly closing only when there have been incorrect entries posted in the journal accounts. Shown are the number of adjusting entries made for the first 10 monthly closings for four major accounts. Each account has over 20,000 postings each month.

	Account			
Month	1	2	3	4
Jan.	100	98	102	94
Feb.	96	95	104	100
Mar.	102	104	103	98
April	90	100	100	98
May	103	100	100	93
June	100	95	100	101
July	104	103	100	97
Aug.	101	99	104	102
Sept.	104	100	103	99
Oct.	93	97	103	102

a. Is the journal adjustment process stable in the mean and standard deviation? Defend.
b. If so, set up control limits for the mean and standard deviation.

4. Given are the number of adjusting entries for the four journal accounts for the next 10 months.

	Account			
Month	1	2	3	4
Nov.	96	95	103	96
Dec.	100	96	105	99
Jan.	102	101	100	105
Feb.	101	95	102	104
Mar.	110	85	103	91
April	104	97	101	102
May	99	99	98	99
June	102	104	102	99
July	95	102	96	104
Aug.	98	96	98	96

a. Is the process ever out of control according to the $\bar{x}$- or s-charts?
b. Even though the process is under control, should a firm be satisfied with the number of adjusting entries needed each month?

5. A library at a major university employs 10 research librarians to help researchers locate articles and books. The 10 librarians have kept records on the number of search requests per day. The mean for the past three months has been 18 requests per librarian per day. The mean standard deviation in the number of daily searches has been 4. The library quality team developed the following control limits for the mean number of search requests:

$$\text{LCL}(\bar{x}): \quad 18 - .975 \cdot 4 = 18 - 3.9 = 14.1 \text{ requests}$$

$$\text{UCL}(\bar{x}): \quad 18 + .975 \cdot 4 = 18 + 3.9 = 21.9 \text{ requests}$$

Using the Western Electric Company rules:
a. Was the process ever out of control in the mean number of requests per day over the next 10 days?
b. Did the library regain control of the daily mean number of search requests after the process went out of control?

Day	Mean Requests per Librarian
1	18.2
2	20.0
3	17.3
4	15.9
5	18.0
6	19.4
7	15.0
8	15.1
9	19.1
10	17.9

6. A firm produces wooden handles for umbrellas. The standard reads: *The handles shall be free of blemishes or rough spots.* Each shift, the inspector randomly selects 500 handles and inspects them for blemishes and rough spots. Shown are the data for the first 10 shifts.

Shift	Sample Size	Number of Nonconforming Handles
1	500	3
2	500	4
3	500	2
4	500	5
5	500	3
6	500	4
7	500	2
8	500	5
9	500	3
10	500	5

a. Determine the sample proportion nonconforming for the first 10 shifts. Is the manufacturing process in control?
b. Compute $\bar{p}$ for the first 10 shifts. Determine the LCL and UCL.

7. Shown are the numbers of nonconforming umbrella handles (see Problem 6) for the next 15 shifts—11–25.

Shift	Sample Size	Number of Nonconforming Handles
11	500	3
12	500	4
13	500	3
14	500	2
15	500	3
16	500	4
17	500	10
18	500	11
19	500	10
20	500	4
21	500	3
22	500	5
23	500	2
24	500	3
25	500	2

    a. Is the process ever out of control for the next 15 shifts?
    b. If it was, was the firm able to correct the problem immediately? Explain.

8. Shown are data on the amount of time (in minutes) for a pill to enter or diffuse into the bloodstream. Each hour, an inspector randomly selects four pills and runs diffusion tests.

Hour	Observation 1	2	3	4
1	2.00	1.98	2.02	1.98
2	2.02	1.98	2.02	2.00
3	2.00	1.97	2.02	1.97
4	2.00	1.98	2.03	2.00
5	2.00	1.98	2.02	1.96
6	2.00	1.98	2.02	2.00
7	2.03	1.98	2.02	2.00
8	2.00	1.98	2.02	2.00
9	2.35	2.33	2.35	2.31
10	2.37	2.33	2.36	2.33
11	2.33	2.30	2.34	2.33
12	2.35	2.30	2.35	2.31
13	2.32	2.32	2.35	2.31
14	2.38	2.34	2.33	2.35
15	2.33	2.30	2.35	2.31

Are the mean and standard deviation of the process under control? Explain.

9. For the following problem, use the Kepner–Tregoe method to develop *what*, *where*, *when*, and *extent* questions:

   Electrodoor manufactures a line of garage door openers. All three products are electronically triggered by a tiny transmitter in the car. The openers lower the garage door if it is raised and raise it if it is lowered. All three openers have a very short range so that one opener cannot open other garage doors on the same block. With the exception of the weight of the door that it will open, the three products in the line are identical.

   Electrodoor introduced its line in the San Francisco area in April 1991. Until that time, it had sold its products exclusively in Arizona and New Mexico. At first, sales in the San Francisco area exceeded expectations. However, in September, complaints began to roll in. One customer complained that without touching the transmitter, his garage door opened. Another complained that the door came down in the middle of the car as she was backing out of her garage and almost took off her head. These were not isolated complaints. In the last quarter of 1991, over 40% of the door openers in the San Francisco area had exhibited the same problem. Only customers who lived in a wedge between the ocean and the bay were complaining. It appeared that the area of complaints was wider at the ocean end and narrower at the bay end. (Based on a case in *The Rational Manager*, by Kepner and Tregoe, McGraw-Hill, 1965.)

10. Assume that each lot of size 75 entering a plant contains exactly 1% defectives. The firm uses a MIL-STD-105D plan with an AQL of 1%. Thus it takes a simple random sample of 13 and accepts the lot if it finds no defective parts in the sample. Use the Poisson probability distribution from Chapter 5 to determine the probability of accepting lots that actually have 1% defectives. Interpret your results. *Hint:* Compute the following probability:

    $$P[D = 0 \text{ defectives when } \lambda = (13)(.01) = .13]$$

11. For the following problem, use the Kepner–Tregoe method to develop *what*, *where*, *when*, and *extent* questions.

    A plant makes two types of quarter panels for cars. Metal sheets are first cut into identical-size blanks and are stacked 40 to a pallet. The pallets are then delivered to the stamping operation. Here stamping presses shape the blanks into hood panels. There is always a supply of blanks at 8 A.M., the beginning of the day shift, for the operators of the four stamping presses. The stamping operators use the starter supply while they wait for the morning shift to produce more blanks. The SD and DD panels differ in only one respect–the depth of draw, or curvature of the quarter panels, after the stamping operation.

    Lines 1 and 2 stamp 80 DD (deep draw) panels per hour. Line 4 stamps 50 DD panels per hour, and line 3 stamps 80 SD (shallow draw) panels per hour. All except line 2 have four pallets of blanks at the beginning of the morning shift. Line 2 workers have complained that with only two stacks, they sometimes have to stop and wait for the morning shift to produce more blanks for stamping. They have demanded equal treatment with the other lines.

    On Wednesday at 11:00 A.M., the plant manager calls an emergency meeting. This morning at about 9:30 A.M., the stamping press on line 2 started producing nearly 12% rejects. After the morning break at 10 A.M., the stamping press on line 1 also started producing about 12% rejects. The problem is excessive burrs and other rough spots. The normal rate is under 2%. The manager reports that engineering has not found anything wrong with the four presses.

    Several supervisors argue that sabotage may be the problem. Everyone agrees that the workers could cause excessive burrs by mispositioning a blank in the press.

Moreover, the supervisor on line 2 had sent a worker home for allegedly drinking on the job the day before. When he returned this morning the supervisor again confronted him and demanded an apology. For 30 minutes they argued while the workers on line 2 watched from the sidelines. Finally the supervisor sent the worker home again. The union has threatened to file a grievance. During the meeting the group learns that at 11:20 A.M. the stamping press on line 4 also started producing about 12% rejects. Only line 3, which is run by the most respected supervisor, is not yet experiencing any excessive rejects. (Based on the case entitled "Can You Analyze This Problem?" by P. Stryker in the *Harvard Business Review*, May–June 1965, pp. 73–78.)

12. Refer to Problem 10. Given an AQL of 1%, what must the percentage of defectives be in each incoming lot such that the receiving firm would accept 100% of the lots based on the sample of 13? In other words, what must λ be to obtain a Poisson probability of zero? (*Hint:* Try proportion defects of .005 and .0025.)

13. The accompanying information (from which two Pareto charts could be constructed) illustrates the types of errors in typed documents in a major law firm. The Before column reflects the breakdown of errors before the firm began a quality improvement effort. The After column reflects the breakdown of errors after the quality improvement effort.

	Before	After
Spelling errors	50%	—
Missing words	35%	—
Improper punctuation	10%	70%
Improper formatting	3%	20%
Additional words	1%	5%
Incorrect upper- and lowercase lettering	1%	5%

   a. What did the quality improvement program stress? Did it focus on the most important problems? Was it successful?
   b. Has there been a drop in the overall number of typing errors?
   c. Now what action should the firm take to further reduce typing errors?

14. The following data represent the number of types of nonconformities for a production process that produces electronic circuits. Develop two Pareto charts, one for each week. What problem should the firm attempt to solve first? How should it go about solving the problem?

	Missing Component	Wrong Component	Failed Component
Week 1	10	20	70
Week 2	11	17	72

15. The traffic at a major shopping mall has dropped about 20% in March 1992 vs. March 1991. Use a fishbone diagram to generate possible root causes. Identify four major branches and several subbranches, or subbones for each major branch.

16. The College of Business does exit interviews with a random sample of undergraduates each year. The college wants to determine how to improve the education that students receive. Shown is a hypothetical data set based on 18 students. The

symbol "×" represents a student's suggestions on how to improve undergraduate education.

Student	Eliminate Multiple Choice Exams	Less Lecturing, More Cases	Less Theory, More Practice	More Internships
Joe K.			×	
Andrea T.		×		
Bob G.				×
Nat T.			×	
Jeanette T.			×	
Arlene B.			×	
Rebecca G.		×		
Lutfus S.	×			
Trisnadi I.			×	
Sang L.			×	
Carlos K.		×		
Pam B.				×
Ellen A.				×
Beth T.			×	
David A.		×		
Dwight T.			×	
Yezdi B.			×	
Juan S.	×			

Construct and interpret a Pareto chart on ways to improve undergraduate training of business students at the college.

17. Assume that lots of size 75 entering a plant contain 10% defectives. The firm uses a MIL-STD-105D plan with an AQL of 1%. Thus it takes a simple random sample of 13 and rejects the lot if it finds one or more defective parts in the sample. Use the Poisson tables in Appendix II to determine the probability of rejecting lots that actually have 10% defectives.

18. An overnight parcel delivery service wishes to develop a control chart for the proportion of overnight parcels that are *not* delivered within the specified time limit. Shown are data for a small shipping center.

Day	Number of Overnight Parcels	Number Not Delivered on Time
1	10,000	10
2	9,000	7
3	9,000	10
4	11,000	10
5	13,000	12
6	12,000	14
7	9,000	9
8	10,000	8
9	15,000	16
10	12,000	9

a. Is the delivery process stable? Discuss.
b. In terms of late deliveries, the firm has set a desired target value proportion of .002 or less. Has it met its target over the past 10 days? Calculate

$$\bar{p} = \frac{\text{Total number not delivered on time}}{\text{Total number of parcels delivered}}$$

c. Set up an LCL and UCL for the proportion of overnight parcels that fail to arrive within the specified time. Use 10,000 for the normal or typical sample size.
d. Suppose the firm wants to reduce late deliveries. What quality improvement tool should it use first? Discuss what analysis the firm should carry out.

19. The marketing director for a college continuing education program is tracking the proportion of people who sign up for one or more self-improvement courses each quarter. Using a mailing list of 10,000 names, the director has obtained the following results for the last 15 quarters.

Quarter	Number Signing Up for 1 or More Courses in a Quarter
1	405
2	505
3	599
4	705
5	610
6	500
7	415
8	521
9	605
10	735
11	620
12	570
13	455
14	535
15	635

a. Is the proportion signing up for one or more courses stable? Discuss.
b. Suppose the process were stable. Is a stable process desirable in this problem? From the director's viewpoint, what should the line graph look like? Discuss.

20.

Date: October 21, 1992
To: Sang Kim, Quality Assurance Manager
From: Howard Bright, Plant Manager
Subject: Possible Ramifications of Ed Margate Dismissal

I was recently talking to Sarah Teman about the dismissal of Ed Margate for allegedly drinking on the job. You'll recall that Sarah dismissed him on Wednesday, September 30th. I'm wondering if the work groups retaliated for his dismissal. If so, how did they do it? I keep hearing rumors of a slowdown, but that's all they are right now—rumors. I need some hard data. Your statistical process control charts may be helpful. If the work groups did take a *job action*, I may consider talking to the union as this is illegal under our present contract.

I need your report by the end of month.

> Use Data Base IV for your analysis. Your response to Howard Bright should include a brief memo and your analysis.

REFERENCES

BRIGHTMAN, H. *Group Problem Solving: An Improved Managerial Problem Solving Approach*. Atlanta: Georgia State University Business Press, 1988.

CROSBY, P. B. *Quality Is Free*. New York: McGraw-Hill, 1979.

DEMING, W. E. *Out of Chaos*. Cambridge: Massachusetts Institute of Technology, Center for Advanced Engineering Studies, 1986.

DEMING, W. E. *Quality, Productivity, and Competitive Position*. Cambridge: Massachusetts Institute of Technology, Center for Advanced Engineering Studies, 1982.

DEMING, W. E. *Elementary Principles of the Statistical Control of Quality*. Tokyo: Nippon Kagaku Gijutsu Remmei, 1951.

GALE, BRADLEY. *Quality As a Strategic Weapon*. Cambridge: The Strategic Planning Institute, 1985.

GROOCOCK, J. M. *The Chain of Quality*. New York: Wiley, 1986.

JURAN, J. M., and F. M. GRYNA. *Quality Planning and Analysis*. New York: McGraw-Hill, 1980.

JURAN, J. M., ed. *Quality Control Handbook*, 3d ed. New York: McGraw-Hill, 1974.

Quality Problem Solving Summary. Princeton, New Jersey: Kepner-Tregoe, Inc., 1988.

KIVENKO, K. *Quality Control for Management*. Englewood Cliffs, New Jersey: Prentice-Hall, 1984.

SHEWHART, W. "Quality Control Charts." *Bell Systems Technical Journal* (1926): 593–603.

WALTON, MARY. *The Deming Management Method*. New York: Dodd, Mead, and Company, 1986.

APPENDICES

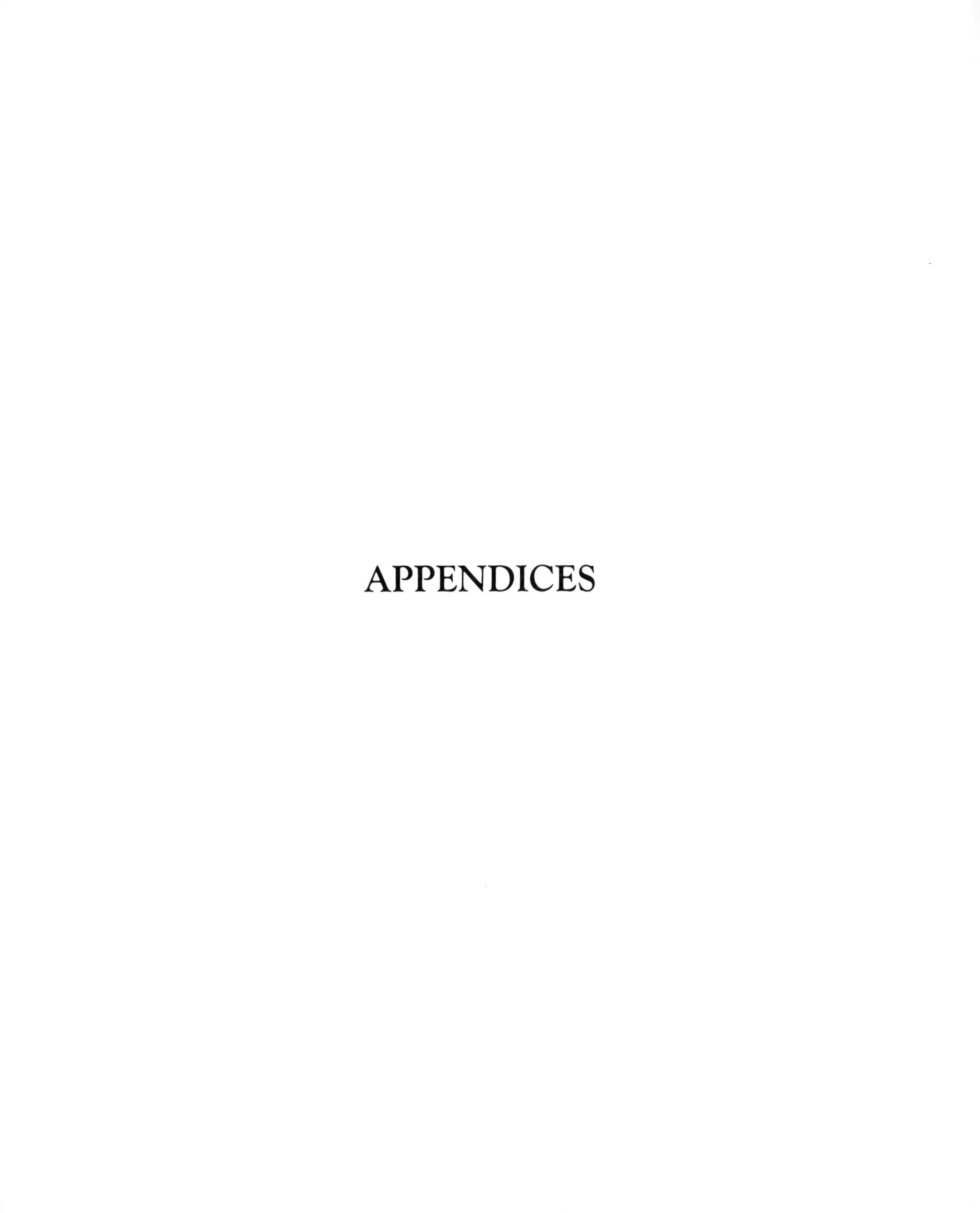

APPENDIX 1 The Binomial Table

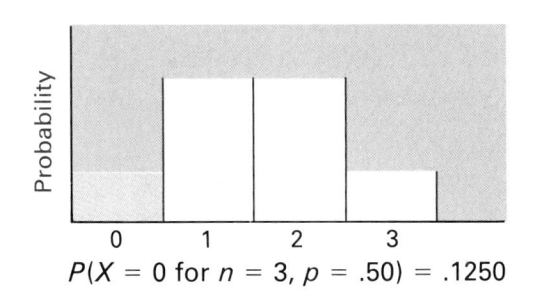

$P(X = 0$ for $n = 3, p = .50) = .1250$

$n = 1$

p / x	.01	.02	.03	.04	.05	.06	.07	.08	.09	.10
0	.9900	.9800	.9700	.9600	.9500	.9400	.9300	.9200	.9100	.9000
1	.0100	.0200	.0300	.0400	.0500	.0600	.0700	.0800	.0900	.1000

	.11	.12	.13	.14	.15	.16	.17	.18	.19	.20
0	.8900	.8800	.8700	.8600	.8500	.8400	.8300	.8200	.8100	.8000
1	.1100	.1200	.1300	.1400	.1500	.1600	.1700	.1800	.1900	.2000

	.21	.22	.23	.24	.25	.26	.27	.28	.29	.30
0	.7900	.7800	.7700	.7600	.7500	.7400	.7300	.7200	.7100	.7000
1	.2100	.2200	.2300	.2400	.2500	.2600	.2700	.2800	.2900	.3000

	.31	.32	.33	.34	.35	.36	.37	.38	.39	.40
0	.6900	.6800	.6700	.6600	.6500	.6400	.6300	.6200	.6100	.6000
1	.3100	.3200	.3300	.3400	.3500	.3600	.3700	.3800	.3900	.4000

	.41	.42	.43	.44	.45	.46	.47	.48	.49	.50
0	.5900	.5800	.5700	.5600	.5500	.5400	.5300	.5200	.5100	.5000
1	.4100	.4200	.4300	.4400	.4500	.4600	.4700	.4800	.4900	.5000

$n = 2$

p / x	.01	.02	.03	.04	.05	.06	.07	.08	.09	.10
0	.9801	.9604	.9409	.9216	.9025	.8836	.8649	.8464	.8281	.8100
1	.0198	.0392	.0582	.0768	.0950	.1128	.1302	.1472	.1638	.1800
2	.0001	.0004	.0009	.0016	.0025	.0036	.0049	.0064	.0081	.0100

	.11	.12	.13	.14	.15	.16	.17	.18	.19	.20
0	.7921	.7744	.7569	.7396	.7225	.7056	.6889	.6724	.6561	.6400
1	.1958	.2112	.2262	.2408	.2550	.2688	.2822	.2952	.3078	.3200
2	.0121	.0144	.0169	.0196	.0225	.0256	.0289	.0324	.0361	.0400

Appendix 1 The Binomial Table

n = 2 (Continued)

x \ p	.21	.22	.23	.24	.25	.26	.27	.28	.29	.30
0	.6241	.6084	.5929	.5776	.5625	.5476	.5329	.5184	.5041	.4900
1	.3318	.3432	.3542	.3648	.3750	.3848	.3942	.4032	.4118	.4200
2	.0441	.0484	.0529	.0576	.0625	.0676	.0729	.0784	.0841	.0900

x \ p	.31	.32	.33	.34	.35	.36	.37	.38	.39	.40
0	.4761	.4624	.4489	.4356	.4225	.4096	.3969	.3844	.3721	.3600
1	.4278	.4352	.4422	.4488	.4550	.4608	.4662	.4712	.4758	.4800
2	.0961	.1024	.1089	.1156	.1225	.1296	.1369	.1444	.1521	.1600

x \ p	.41	.42	.43	.44	.45	.46	.47	.48	.49	.50
0	.3481	.3364	.3249	.3136	.3025	.2916	.2809	.2704	.2601	.2500
1	.4838	.4872	.4902	.4928	.4950	.4968	.4982	.4992	.4998	.5000
2	.1681	.1764	.1849	.1936	.2025	.2116	.2209	.2304	.2401	.2500

n = 3

x \ p	.01	.02	.03	.04	.05	.06	.07	.08	.09	.10
0	.9704	.9412	.9127	.8847	.8574	.8306	.8044	.7787	.7536	.7290
1	.0294	.0576	.0847	.1106	.1354	.1590	.1816	.2031	.2236	.2430
2	.0003	.0012	.0026	.0046	.0071	.0102	.0137	.0177	.0221	.0270
3	.0000	.0000	.0000	.0001	.0001	.0002	.0003	.0005	.0007	.0010

x \ p	.11	.12	.13	.14	.15	.16	.17	.18	.19	.20
0	.7050	.6815	.6585	.6361	.6141	.5927	.5718	.5514	.5314	.5120
1	.2614	.2788	.2952	.3106	.3251	.3387	.3513	.3631	.3740	.3840
2	.0323	.0380	.0441	.0506	.0574	.0645	.0720	.0797	.0877	.0960
3	.0013	.0017	.0022	.0027	.0034	.0041	.0049	.0058	.0069	.0080

x \ p	.21	.22	.23	.24	.25	.26	.27	.28	.29	.30
0	.4930	.4746	.4565	.4390	.4219	.4052	.3890	.3732	.3579	.3430
1	.3932	.4015	.4091	.4159	.4219	.4271	.4316	.4355	.4386	.4410
2	.1045	.1133	.1222	.1313	.1406	.1501	.1597	.1693	.1791	.1890
3	.0093	.0106	.0122	.0138	.0156	.0176	.0197	.0220	.0244	.0270

x \ p	.31	.32	.33	.34	.35	.36	.37	.38	.39	.40
0	.3285	.3144	.3008	.2875	.2746	.2621	.2500	.2383	.2270	.2160
1	.4428	.4439	.4444	.4443	.4436	.4424	.4406	.4382	.4354	.4320
2	.1989	.2089	.2189	.2289	.2389	.2488	.2587	.2686	.2783	.2880
3	.0298	.0328	.0359	.0393	.0429	.0467	.0507	.0549	.0593	.0640

x \ p	.41	.42	.43	.44	.45	.46	.47	.48	.49	.50
0	.2054	.1951	.1852	.1756	.1664	.1575	.1489	.1406	.1327	.1250
1	.4282	.4239	.4191	.4140	.4084	.4024	.3961	.3894	.3823	.3750
2	.2975	.3069	.3162	.3252	.3341	.3428	.3512	.3594	.3674	.3750
3	.0689	.0741	.0795	.0852	.0911	.0973	.1038	.1106	.1176	.1250

Appendix 1 The Binomial Table A-3

n = 4

x \ p	.01	.02	.03	.04	.05	.06	.07	.08	.09	.10
0	.9606	.9224	.8853	.8493	.8145	.7807	.7481	.7164	.6857	.6561
1	.0388	.0753	.1095	.1416	.1715	.1993	.2252	.2492	.2713	.2916
2	.0006	.0023	.0051	.0088	.0135	.0191	.0254	.0325	.0402	.0486
3	.0000	.0000	.0001	.0002	.0005	.0008	.0013	.0019	.0027	.0036
4	.0000	.0000	.0000	.0000	.0000	.0000	.0000	.0000	.0001	.0001

x \ p	.11	.12	.13	.14	.15	.16	.17	.18	.19	.20
0	.6274	.5997	.5729	.5470	.5220	.4979	.4746	.4521	.4305	.4096
1	.3102	.3271	.3424	.3562	.3685	.3793	.3888	.3970	.4039	.4096
2	.0575	.0669	.0767	.0870	.0975	.1084	.1195	.1307	.1421	.1536
3	.0047	.0061	.0076	.0094	.0115	.0138	.0163	.0191	.0222	.0256
4	.0001	.0002	.0003	.0004	.0005	.0007	.0008	.0010	.0013	.0016

x \ p	.21	.22	.23	.24	.25	.26	.27	.28	.29	.30
0	.3895	.3702	.3515	.3336	.3164	.2999	.2840	.2687	.2541	.2401
1	.4142	.4176	.4200	.4214	.4219	.4214	.4201	.4180	.4152	.4116
2	.1651	.1767	.1882	.1996	.2109	.2221	.2331	.2439	.2544	.2646
3	.0293	.0332	.0375	.0420	.0469	.0520	.0575	.0632	.0693	.0756
4	.0019	.0023	.0028	.0033	.0039	.0046	.0053	.0061	.0071	.0081

x \ p	.31	.32	.33	.34	.35	.36	.37	.38	.39	.40
0	.2267	.2138	.2015	.1897	.1785	.1678	.1575	.1478	.1385	.1296
1	.4074	.4025	.3970	.3910	.3845	.3775	.3701	.3623	.3541	.3456
2	.2745	.2841	.2933	.3021	.3105	.3185	.3260	.3330	.3396	.3456
3	.0822	.0891	.0963	.1038	.1115	.1194	.1276	.1361	.1447	.1536
4	.0092	.0105	.0119	.0134	.0150	.0168	.0187	.0209	.0231	.0256

x \ p	.41	.42	.43	.44	.45	.46	.47	.48	.49	.50
0	.1212	.1132	.1056	.0983	.0915	.0850	.0789	.0731	.0677	.0625
1	.3368	.3278	.3185	.3091	.2995	.2897	.2799	.2700	.2600	.2500
2	.3511	.3560	.3604	.3643	.3675	.3702	.3723	.3738	.3747	.3750
3	.1627	.1719	.1813	.1908	.2005	.2102	.2201	.2300	.2400	.2500
4	.0283	.0311	.0342	.0375	.0410	.0448	.0488	.0531	.0576	.0625

n = 5

x \ p	.01	.02	.03	.04	.05	.06	.07	.08	.09	.10
0	.9510	.9039	.8587	.8154	.7738	.7339	.6957	.6591	.6240	.5905
1	.0480	.0922	.1328	.1699	.2036	.2342	.2618	.2866	.3086	.3280
2	.0010	.0038	.0082	.0142	.0214	.0299	.0394	.0498	.0610	.0729
3	.0000	.0001	.0003	.0006	.0011	.0019	.0030	.0043	.0060	.0081
4	.0000	.0000	.0000	.0000	.0000	.0001	.0001	.0002	.0003	.0004

$n = 5$ (Continued)

x \ p	.11	.12	.13	.14	.15	.16	.17	.18	.19	.20
0	.5584	.5277	.4984	.4704	.4437	.4182	.3939	.3707	.3487	.3277
1	.3451	.3598	.3724	.3829	.3915	.3983	.4034	.4069	.4089	.4096
2	.0853	.0981	.1113	.1247	.1382	.1517	.1652	.1786	.1919	.2048
3	.0105	.0134	.0166	.0203	.0244	.0289	.0338	.0392	.0450	.0512
4	.0007	.0009	.0012	.0017	.0022	.0028	.0035	.0043	.0053	.0064
5	.0000	.0000	.0000	.0001	.0001	.0001	.0001	.0002	.0002	.0003

x \ p	.21	.22	.23	.24	.25	.26	.27	.28	.29	.30
0	.3077	.2887	.2707	.2536	.2373	.2219	.2073	.1935	.1804	.1681
1	.4090	.4072	.4043	.4003	.3955	.3898	.3834	.3762	.3685	.3602
2	.2174	.2297	.2415	.2529	.2637	.2739	.2836	.2926	.3010	.3087
3	.0578	.0648	.0721	.0798	.0879	.0962	.1049	.1138	.1229	.1323
4	.0077	.0091	.0108	.0126	.0146	.0169	.0194	.0221	.0251	.0284
5	.0004	.0005	.0006	.0008	.0010	.0012	.0014	.0017	.0021	.0024

x \ p	.31	.32	.33	.34	.35	.36	.37	.38	.39	.40
0	.1564	.1454	.1350	.1252	.1160	.1074	.0992	.0916	.0845	.0778
1	.3513	.3421	.3325	.3226	.3124	.3020	.2914	.2808	.2700	.2592
2	.3157	.3220	.3275	.3323	.3364	.3397	.3423	.3441	.3452	.3456
3	.1418	.1515	.1613	.1712	.1811	.1911	.2010	.2109	.2207	.2304
4	.0319	.0357	.0397	.0441	.0488	.0537	.0590	.0646	.0706	.0768
5	.0029	.0034	.0039	.0045	.0053	.0060	.0069	.0079	.0090	.0102

x \ p	.41	.42	.43	.44	.45	.46	.47	.48	.49	.50
0	.0715	.0656	.0602	.0551	.0503	.0459	.0418	.0380	.0345	.0312
1	.2484	.2376	.2270	.2164	.2059	.1956	.1854	.1755	.1657	.1562
2	.3452	.3442	.3424	.3400	.3369	.3332	.3289	.3240	.3185	.3125
3	.2399	.2492	.2583	.2671	.2757	.2838	.2916	.2990	.3060	.3125
4	.0834	.0902	.0974	.1049	.1128	.1209	.1293	.1380	.1470	.1562
5	.0116	.0131	.0147	.0165	.0185	.0206	.0229	.0255	.0282	.0312

$n = 6$

x \ p	.01	.02	.03	.04	.05	.06	.07	.08	.09	.10
0	.9415	.8858	.8330	.7828	.7351	.6899	.6470	.6064	.5679	.5314
1	.0571	.1085	.1546	.1957	.2321	.2642	.2922	.3164	.3370	.3543
2	.0014	.0055	.0120	.0204	.0305	.0422	.0550	.0688	.0833	.0984
3	.0000	.0002	.0005	.0011	.0021	.0036	.0055	.0080	.0110	.0146
4	.0000	.0000	.0000	.0000	.0001	.0002	.0003	.0005	.0008	.0012
5	.0000	.0000	.0000	.0000	.0000	.0000	.0000	.0000	.0000	.0001

$n = 6$ (Continued)

p\x	.11	.12	.13	.14	.15	.16	.17	.18	.19	.20
0	.4970	.4644	.4336	.4046	.3771	.3513	.3269	.3040	.2824	.2621
1	.3685	.3800	.3888	.3952	.3993	.4015	.4018	.4004	.3975	.3932
2	.1139	.1295	.1452	.1608	.1762	.1912	.2057	.2197	.2331	.2458
3	.0188	.0236	.0289	.0349	.0415	.0486	.0562	.0643	.0729	.0819
4	.0017	.0024	.0032	.0043	.0055	.0069	.0086	.0106	.0128	.0154
5	.0001	.0001	.0002	.0003	.0004	.0005	.0007	.0009	.0012	.0015
6	.0000	.0000	.0000	.0000	.0000	.0000	.0000	.0000	.0000	.0001

p\x	.21	.22	.23	.24	.25	.26	.27	.28	.29	.30
0	.2431	.2252	.2084	.1927	.1780	.1642	.1513	.1393	.1281	.1176
1	.3877	.3811	.3735	.3651	.3560	.3462	.3358	.3251	.3139	.3025
2	.2577	.2687	.2789	.2882	.2966	.3041	.3105	.3160	.3206	.3241
3	.0913	.1011	.1111	.1214	.1318	.1424	.1531	.1639	.1746	.1852
4	.0182	.0214	.0249	.0287	.0330	.0375	.0425	.0478	.0535	.0595
5	.0019	.0024	.0030	.0036	.0044	.0053	.0063	.0074	.0087	.0102
6	.0001	.0001	.0001	.0002	.0002	.0003	.0004	.0005	.0006	.0007

p\x	.31	.32	.33	.34	.35	.36	.37	.38	.39	.40
0	.1079	.0989	.0905	.0827	.0754	.0687	.0625	.0568	.0515	.0467
1	.2909	.2792	.2673	.2555	.2437	.2319	.2203	.2089	.1976	.1866
2	.3267	.3284	.3292	.3290	.3280	.3261	.3235	.3201	.3159	.3110
3	.1957	.2061	.2162	.2260	.2355	.2446	.2533	.2616	.2693	.2765
4	.0660	.0727	.0799	.0873	.0951	.1032	.1116	.1202	.1291	.1382
5	.0119	.0137	.0157	.0180	.0205	.0232	.0262	.0295	.0330	.0369
6	.0009	.0011	.0013	.0015	.0018	.0022	.0026	.0030	.0035	.0041

p\x	.41	.42	.43	.44	.45	.46	.47	.48	.49	.50
0	.0422	.0381	.0343	.0308	.0277	.0248	.0222	.0198	.0176	.0156
1	.1759	.1654	.1552	.1454	.1359	.1267	.1179	.1095	.1014	.0938
2	.3055	.2994	.2928	.2856	.2780	.2699	.2615	.2527	.2436	.2344
3	.2831	.2891	.2945	.2992	.3032	.3065	.3091	.3110	.3121	.3125
4	.1475	.1570	.1666	.1763	.1861	.1958	.2056	.2153	.2249	.2344
5	.0410	.0455	.0503	.0554	.0609	.0667	.0729	.0795	.0864	.0938
6	.0048	.0055	.0063	.0073	.0083	.0095	.0108	.0122	.0138	.0156

$n = 7$

p\x	.01	.02	.03	.04	.05	.06	.07	.08	.09	.10
0	.9321	.8681	.8080	.7514	.6983	.6485	.6017	.5578	.5168	.4783
1	.0659	.1240	.1749	.2192	.2573	.2897	.3170	.3396	.3578	.3720
2	.0020	.0076	.0162	.0274	.0406	.0555	.0716	.0886	.1061	.1240
3	.0000	.0003	.0008	.0019	.0036	.0059	.0090	.0128	.0175	.0230
4	.0000	.0000	.0000	.0001	.0002	.0004	.0007	.0011	.0017	.0026
5	.0000	.0000	.0000	.0000	.0000	.0000	.0000	.0001	.0001	.0002

$n = 7$ (Continued)

x \ p	.11	.12	.13	.14	.15	.16	.17	.18	.19	.20
0	.4423	.4087	.3773	.3479	.3206	.2951	.2714	.2493	.2288	.2097
1	.3827	.3901	.3946	.3965	.3960	.3935	.3891	.3830	.3756	.3670
2	.1419	.1596	.1769	.1936	.2097	.2248	.2391	.2523	.2643	.2753
3	.0292	.0363	.0441	.0525	.0617	.0714	.0816	.0923	.1033	.1147
4	.0036	.0049	.0066	.0086	.0109	.0136	.0167	.0203	.0242	.0287
5	.0003	.0004	.0006	.0008	.0012	.0016	.0021	.0027	.0034	.0043
6	.0000	.0000	.0000	.0000	.0001	.0001	.0001	.0002	.0003	.0004

x \ p	.21	.22	.23	.24	.25	.26	.27	.28	.29	.30
0	.1920	.1757	.1605	.1465	.1335	.1215	.1105	.1003	.0910	.0824
1	.3573	.3468	.3356	.3237	.3115	.2989	.2860	.2731	.2600	.2471
2	.2850	.2935	.3007	.3067	.3115	.3150	.3174	.3186	.3186	.3177
3	.1263	.1379	.1497	.1614	.1730	.1845	.1956	.2065	.2169	.2269
4	.0336	.0389	.0447	.0510	.0577	.0648	.0724	.0803	.0886	.0972
5	.0054	.0066	.0080	.0097	.0115	.0137	.0161	.0187	.0217	.0250
6	.0005	.0006	.0008	.0010	.0013	.0016	.0020	.0024	.0030	.0036
7	.0000	.0000	.0000	.0000	.0001	.0001	.0001	.0001	.0002	.0002

x \ p	.31	.32	.33	.34	.35	.36	.37	.38	.39	.40
0	.0745	.0672	.0606	.0546	.0490	.0440	.0394	.0352	.0314	.0280
1	.2342	.2215	.2090	.1967	.1848	.1732	.1619	.1511	.1407	.1306
2	.3156	.3127	.3088	.3040	.2985	.2922	.2853	.2778	.2698	.2613
3	.2363	.2452	.2535	.2610	.2679	.2740	.2793	.2838	.2875	.2903
4	.1062	.1154	.1248	.1345	.1442	.1541	.1640	.1739	.1838	.1935
5	.0286	.0326	.0369	.0416	.0466	.0520	.0578	.0640	.0705	.0774
6	.0043	.0051	.0061	.0071	.0084	.0098	.0113	.0131	.0150	.0172
7	.0003	.0003	.0004	.0005	.0006	.0008	.0009	.0011	.0014	.0016

x \ p	.41	.42	.43	.44	.45	.46	.47	.48	.49	.50
0	.0249	.0221	.0195	.0173	.0152	.0134	.0117	.0103	.0090	.0078
1	.1211	.1119	.1032	.0950	.0872	.0798	.0729	.0664	.0604	.0547
2	.2524	.2431	.2336	.2239	.2140	.2040	.1940	.1840	.1740	.1641
3	.2923	.2934	.2937	.2932	.2918	.2897	.2867	.2830	.2786	.2734
4	.2031	.2125	.2216	.2304	.2388	.2468	.2543	.2612	.2676	.2734
5	.0847	.0923	.1003	.1086	.1172	.1261	.1353	.1447	.1543	.1641
6	.0196	.0223	.0252	.0284	.0320	.0358	.0400	.0445	.0494	.0547
7	.0019	.0023	.0027	.0032	.0037	.0044	.0051	.0059	.0068	.0078

Appendix 1 The Binomial Table

$n = 8$

x \ p	.01	.02	.03	.04	.05	.06	.07	.08	.09	.10
0	.9227	.8508	.7837	.7214	.6634	.6096	.5596	.5132	.4703	.4305
1	.0746	.1389	.1939	.2405	.2793	.3113	.3370	.3570	.3721	.3826
2	.0026	.0099	.0210	.0351	.0515	.0695	.0888	.1087	.1288	.1488
3	.0001	.0004	.0013	.0029	.0054	.0089	.0134	.0189	.0255	.0331
4	.0000	.0000	.0001	.0002	.0004	.0007	.0013	.0021	.0031	.0046
5	.0000	.0000	.0000	.0000	.0000	.0000	.0001	.0001	.0002	.0004

x \ p	.11	.12	.13	.14	.15	.16	.17	.18	.19	.20
0	.3937	.3596	.3282	.2992	.2725	.2479	.2252	.2044	.1853	.1678
1	.3892	.3923	.3923	.3897	.3847	.3777	.3691	.3590	.3477	.3355
2	.1684	.1872	.2052	.2220	.2376	.2518	.2646	.2758	.2855	.2936
3	.0416	.0511	.0613	.0723	.0839	.0959	.1084	.1211	.1339	.1468
4	.0064	.0087	.0115	.0147	.0185	.0228	.0277	.0332	.0393	.0459
5	.0006	.0009	.0014	.0019	.0026	.0035	.0045	.0058	.0074	.0092
6	.0000	.0001	.0001	.0002	.0002	.0003	.0005	.0006	.0009	.0011
7	.0000	.0000	.0000	.0000	.0000	.0000	.0000	.0000	.0001	.0001

x \ p	.21	.22	.23	.24	.25	.26	.27	.28	.29	.30
0	.1517	.1370	.1236	.1113	.1001	.0899	.0806	.0722	.0646	.0576
1	.3226	.3092	.2953	.2812	.2670	.2527	.2386	.2247	.2110	.1977
2	.3002	.3052	.3087	.3108	.3115	.3108	.3089	.3058	.3017	.2965
3	.1596	.1722	.1844	.1963	.2076	.2184	.2285	.2379	.2464	.2541
4	.0530	.0607	.0689	.0775	.0865	.0959	.1056	.1156	.1258	.1361
5	.0113	.0137	.0165	.0196	.0231	.0270	.0313	.0360	.0411	.0467
6	.0015	.0019	.0025	.0031	.0038	.0047	.0058	.0070	.0084	.0100
7	.0001	.0002	.0002	.0003	.0004	.0005	.0006	.0008	.0010	.0012
8	.0000	.0000	.0000	.0000	.0000	.0000	.0000	.0000	.0001	.0001

x \ p	.31	.32	.33	.34	.35	.36	.37	.38	.39	.40
0	.0514	.0457	.0406	.0360	.0319	.0281	.0248	.0218	.0192	.0168
1	.1847	.1721	.1600	.1484	.1373	.1267	.1166	.1071	.0981	.0896
2	.2904	.2835	.2758	.2675	.2587	.2494	.2397	.2297	.2194	.2090
3	.2609	.2668	.2717	.2756	.2786	.2805	.2815	.2815	.2806	.2787
4	.1465	.1569	.1673	.1775	.1875	.1973	.2067	.2157	.2242	.2322
5	.0527	.0591	.0659	.0732	.0808	.0888	.0971	.1058	.1147	.1239
6	.0118	.0139	.0162	.0188	.0217	.0250	.0285	.0324	.0367	.0413
7	.0015	.0019	.0023	.0028	.0033	.0040	.0048	.0057	.0067	.0079
8	.0001	.0001	.0001	.0002	.0002	.0003	.0004	.0004	.0005	.0007

n = 8 (Continued)

x \ p	.41	.42	.43	.44	.45	.46	.47	.48	.49	.50
0	.0147	.0128	.0111	.0097	.0084	.0072	.0062	.0053	.0046	.0039
1	.0816	.0742	.0672	.0608	.0548	.0493	.0442	.0395	.0352	.0312
2	.1985	.1880	.1776	.1672	.1569	.1469	.1371	.1275	.1183	.1094
3	.2759	.2723	.2679	.2627	.2568	.2503	.2431	.2355	.2273	.2188
4	.2397	.2465	.2526	.2580	.2627	.2665	.2695	.2717	.2730	.2734
5	.1332	.1428	.1525	.1622	.1719	.1816	.1912	.2006	.2098	.2188
6	.0463	.0517	.0575	.0637	.0703	.0774	.0848	.0926	.1008	.1094
7	.0092	.0107	.0124	.0143	.0164	.0188	.0215	.0244	.0277	.0312
8	.0008	.0010	.0012	.0014	.0017	.0020	.0024	.0028	.0033	.0039

n = 9

x \ p	.01	.02	.03	.04	.05	.06	.07	.08	.09	.10
0	.9135	.8337	.7602	.6925	.6302	.5730	.5204	.4722	.4279	.3874
1	.0830	.1531	.2116	.2597	.2985	.3292	.3525	.3695	.3809	.3874
2	.0034	.0125	.0262	.0433	.0629	.0840	.1061	.1285	.1507	.1722
3	.0001	.0006	.0019	.0042	.0077	.0125	.0186	.0261	.0348	.0446
4	.0000	.0000	.0001	.0003	.0006	.0012	.0021	.0034	.0052	.0074
5	.0000	.0000	.0000	.0000	.0000	.0001	.0002	.0003	.0005	.0008
6	.0000	.0000	.0000	.0000	.0000	.0000	.0000	.0000	.0000	.0001

x \ p	.11	.12	.13	.14	.15	.16	.17	.18	.19	.20
0	.3504	.3165	.2855	.2573	.2316	.2082	.1869	.1676	.1501	.1342
1	.3897	.3884	.3840	.3770	.3679	.3569	.3446	.3312	.3169	.3020
2	.1927	.2119	.2295	.2455	.2597	.2720	.2823	.2908	.2973	.3020
3	.0556	.0674	.0800	.0933	.1069	.1209	.1349	.1489	.1627	.1762
4	.0103	.0138	.0179	.0228	.0283	.0345	.0415	.0490	.0573	.0661
5	.0013	.0019	.0027	.0037	.0050	.0066	.0085	.0108	.0134	.0165
6	.0001	.0002	.0003	.0004	.0006	.0008	.0012	.0016	.0021	.0028
7	.0000	.0000	.0000	.0000	.0000	.0001	.0001	.0001	.0002	.0003

x \ p	.21	.22	.23	.24	.25	.26	.27	.28	.29	.30
0	.1199	.1069	.0952	.0846	.0751	.0665	.0589	.0520	.0458	.0404
1	.2867	.2713	.2558	.2404	.2253	.2104	.1960	.1820	.1685	.1556
2	.3049	.3061	.3056	.3037	.3003	.2957	.2899	.2831	.2754	.2668
3	.1891	.2014	.2130	.2238	.2336	.2424	.2502	.2569	.2624	.2668
4	.0754	.0852	.0954	.1060	.1168	.1278	.1388	.1499	.1608	.1715
5	.0200	.0240	.0285	.0335	.0389	.0449	.0513	.0583	.0657	.0735
6	.0036	.0045	.0057	.0070	.0087	.0105	.0127	.0151	.0179	.0210
7	.0004	.0005	.0007	.0010	.0012	.0016	.0020	.0025	.0031	.0039
8	.0000	.0000	.0001	.0001	.0001	.0001	.0002	.0002	.0003	.0004

$n = 9$ (Continued)

p\x	.31	.32	.33	.34	.35	.36	.37	.38	.39	.40
0	.0355	.0311	.0272	.0238	.0207	.0180	.0156	.0135	.0117	.0101
1	.1433	.1317	.1206	.1102	.1004	.0912	.0826	.0747	.0673	.0605
2	.2576	.2478	.2376	.2270	.2162	.2052	.1941	.1831	.1721	.1612
3	.2701	.2721	.2731	.2729	.2716	.2693	.2660	.2618	.2567	.2508
4	.1820	.1921	.2017	.2109	.2194	.2272	.2344	.2407	.2462	.2508
5	.0818	.0904	.0994	.1086	.1181	.1278	.1376	.1475	.1574	.1672
6	.0245	.0284	.0326	.0373	.0424	.0479	.0539	.0603	.0671	.0743
7	.0047	.0057	.0069	.0082	.0098	.0116	.0136	.0158	.0184	.0212
8	.0005	.0007	.0008	.0011	.0013	.0016	.0020	.0024	.0029	.0035
9	.0000	.0000	.0000	.0001	.0001	.0001	.0001	.0002	.0002	.0003

p\x	.41	.42	.43	.44	.45	.46	.47	.48	.49	.50
0	.0087	.0074	.0064	.0054	.0046	.0039	.0033	.0028	.0023	.0020
1	.0542	.0484	.0431	.0383	.0339	.0299	.0263	.0231	.0202	.0176
2	.1506	.1402	.1301	.1204	.1110	.1020	.0934	.0853	.0776	.0703
3	.2442	.2369	.2291	.2207	.2119	.2027	.1933	.1837	.1739	.1641
4	.2545	.2573	.2592	.2601	.2600	.2590	.2571	.2543	.2506	.2461
5	.1769	.1863	.1955	.2044	.2128	.2207	.2280	.2347	.2408	.2461
6	.0819	.0900	.0983	.1070	.1160	.1253	.1348	.1445	.1542	.1641
7	.0244	.0279	.0318	.0360	.0407	.0458	.0512	.0571	.0635	.0703
8	.0042	.0051	.0060	.0071	.0083	.0097	.0114	.0132	.0153	.0176
9	.0003	.0004	.0005	.0006	.0008	.0009	.0011	.0014	.0016	.0020

$n = 10$

p\x	.01	.02	.03	.04	.05	.06	.07	.08	.09	.10
0	.9044	.8171	.7374	.6648	.5987	.5386	.4840	.4344	.3894	.3487
1	.0914	.1667	.2281	.2770	.3151	.3438	.3643	.3777	.3851	.3874
2	.0042	.0153	.0317	.0519	.0746	.0988	.1234	.1478	.1714	.1937
3	.0001	.0008	.0026	.0058	.0105	.0168	.0248	.0343	.0452	.0574
4	.0000	.0000	.0001	.0004	.0010	.0019	.0033	.0052	.0078	.0112
5	.0000	.0000	.0000	.0000	.0001	.0001	.0003	.0005	.0009	.0015
6	.0000	.0000	.0000	.0000	.0000	.0000	.0000	.0000	.0001	.0001

p\x	.11	.12	.13	.14	.15	.16	.17	.18	.19	.20
0	.3118	.2785	.2484	.2213	.1969	.1749	.1552	.1374	.1216	.1074
1	.3854	.3798	.3712	.3603	.3474	.3331	.3178	.3017	.2852	.2684
2	.2143	.2330	.2496	.2639	.2759	.2856	.2929	.2980	.3010	.3020
3	.0706	.0847	.0995	.1146	.1298	.1450	.1600	.1745	.1883	.2013
4	.0153	.0202	.0260	.0326	.0401	.0483	.0573	.0670	.0773	.0881
5	.0023	.0033	.0047	.0064	.0085	.0111	.0141	.0177	.0218	.0264
6	.0002	.0004	.0006	.0009	.0012	.0018	.0024	.0032	.0043	.0055
7	.0000	.0000	.0000	.0001	.0001	.0002	.0003	.0004	.0006	.0008
8	.0000	.0000	.0000	.0000	.0000	.0000	.0000	.0000	.0001	.0001

Appendix 1 The Binomial Table

$n = 10$ (Continued)

p \ x	.21	.22	.23	.24	.25	.26	.27	.28	.29	.30
0	.0947	.0834	.0733	.0643	.0563	.0492	.0430	.0374	.0326	.0282
1	.2517	.2351	.2188	.2030	.1877	.1730	.1590	.1456	.1330	.1211
2	.3011	.2984	.2942	.2885	.2816	.2735	.2646	.2548	.2444	.2335
3	.2134	.2244	.2343	.2429	.2503	.2563	.2609	.2642	.2662	.2668
4	.0993	.1108	.1225	.1343	.1460	.1576	.1689	.1798	.1903	.2001
5	.0317	.0375	.0439	.0509	.0584	.0664	.0750	.0839	.0933	.1029
6	.0070	.0088	.0109	.0134	.0162	.0195	.0231	.0272	.0317	.0368
7	.0011	.0014	.0019	.0024	.0031	.0039	.0049	.0060	.0074	.0090
8	.0001	.0002	.0002	.0003	.0004	.0005	.0007	.0009	.0011	.0014
9	.0000	.0000	.0000	.0000	.0000	.0000	.0001	.0001	.0001	.0001

p \ x	.31	.32	.33	.34	.35	.36	.37	.38	.39	.40
0	.0245	.0211	.0182	.0157	.0135	.0115	.0098	.0084	.0071	.0060
1	.1099	.0995	.0898	.0808	.0725	.0649	.0578	.0514	.0456	.0403
2	.2222	.2107	.1990	.0873	.1757	.1642	.1529	.1419	.1312	.1209
3	.2662	.2644	.2614	.2573	.2522	.2462	.2394	.2319	.2237	.2150
4	.2093	.2177	.2253	.2320	.2377	.2424	.2461	.2487	.2503	.2508
5	.1128	.1229	.1332	.1434	.1536	.1636	.1734	.1829	.1920	.2007
6	.0422	.0482	.0547	.0616	.0689	.0767	.0849	.0934	.1023	.1115
7	.0108	.0130	.0154	.0181	.0212	.0247	.0285	.0327	.0374	.0425
8	.0018	.0023	.0028	.0035	.0043	.0052	.0063	.0075	.0090	.0106
9	.0002	.0002	.0003	.0004	.0005	.0006	.0008	.0010	.0013	.0016
10	.0000	.0000	.0000	.0000	.0000	.0000	.0000	.0001	.0001	.0001

p \ x	.41	.42	.43	.44	.45	.46	.47	.48	.49	.50
0	.0051	.0043	.0036	.0030	.0025	.0021	.0017	.0014	.0012	.0010
1	.0355	.0312	.0273	.0238	.0207	.0180	.0155	.0133	.0114	.0098
2	.1111	.1017	.0927	.0843	.0763	.0688	.0619	.0554	.0494	.0439
3	.2058	.1963	.1865	.1765	.1665	.1564	.1464	.1364	.1267	.1172
4	.2503	.2488	.2462	.2427	.2384	.2331	.2271	.2204	.2130	.2051
5	.2087	.2162	.2229	.2289	.2340	.2383	.2417	.2441	.2456	.2461
6	.1209	.1304	.1401	.1499	.1596	.1692	.1786	.1878	.1966	.2051
7	.0480	.0540	.0604	.0673	.0746	.0824	.0905	.0991	.1080	.1172
8	.0125	.0147	.0171	.0198	.0229	.0263	.0301	.0343	.0389	.0439
9	.0019	.0024	.0029	.0035	.0042	.0050	.0059	.0070	.0083	.0098
10	.0001	.0002	.0002	.0003	.0003	.0004	.0005	.0006	.0008	.0010

Appendix 1 The Binomial Table

$n = 15$

p\x	.01	.02	.03	.04	.05	.06	.07	.08	.09	.10
0	.8601	.7386	.6333	.5421	.4633	.3953	.3367	.2863	.2430	.2059
1	.1303	.2261	.2938	.3388	.3658	.3785	.3801	.3734	.3605	.3432
2	.0092	.0323	.0636	.0988	.1348	.1691	.2003	.2273	.2496	.2669
3	.0004	.0029	.0085	.0178	.0307	.0468	.0653	.0857	.1070	.1285
4	.0000	.0002	.0008	.0022	.0049	.0090	.0148	.0223	.0317	.0428
5	.0000	.0000	.0001	.0002	.0006	.0013	.0024	.0043	.0069	.0105
6	.0000	.0000	.0000	.0000	.0000	.0001	.0003	.0006	.0011	.0019
7	.0000	.0000	.0000	.0000	.0000	.0000	.0000	.0001	.0001	.0003

p\x	.11	.12	.13	.14	.15	.16	.17	.18	.19	.20
0	.1741	.1470	.1238	.1041	.0874	.0731	.0611	.0510	.0424	.0352
1	.3228	.3006	.2775	.2542	.2312	.2090	.1878	.1678	.1492	.1319
2	.2793	.2870	.2903	.2897	.2856	.2787	.2692	.2578	.2449	.2309
3	.1496	.1696	.1880	.2044	.2184	.2300	.2389	.2452	.2489	.2501
4	.0555	.0694	.0843	.0998	.1156	.1314	.1468	.1615	.1752	.1876
5	.0151	.0208	.0277	.0357	.0449	.0551	.0662	.0780	.0904	.1032
6	.0031	.0047	.0069	.0097	.0132	.0175	.0226	.0285	.0353	.0430
7	.0005	.0008	.0013	.0020	.0030	.0043	.0059	.0081	.0107	.0138
8	.0001	.0001	.0002	.0003	.0005	.0008	.0012	.0018	.0025	.0035
9	.0000	.0000	.0000	.0000	.0001	.0001	.0002	.0003	.0005	.0007
10	.0000	.0000	.0000	.0000	.0000	.0000	.0000	.0000	.0001	.0001

$n = 15$ (Continued)

x \ p	.21	.22	.23	.24	.25	.26	.27	.28	.29	.30
0	.0291	.0241	.0198	.0163	.0134	.0109	.0089	.0072	.0059	.0047
1	.1162	.1018	.0889	.0772	.0668	.0576	.0494	.0423	.0360	.0305
2	.2162	.2010	.1858	.1707	.1559	.1416	.1280	.1150	.1029	.0916
3	.2490	.2457	.2405	.2336	.2252	.2156	.2051	.1939	.1821	.1700
4	.1986	.2079	.2155	.2213	.2252	.2273	.2276	.2262	.2231	.2186
5	.1161	.1290	.1416	.1537	.1651	.1757	.1852	.1935	.2005	.2061
6	.0514	.0606	.0705	.0809	.0917	.1029	.1142	.1254	.1365	.1472
7	.0176	.0220	.0271	.0329	.0393	.0465	.0543	.0627	.0717	.0811
8	.0047	.0062	.0081	.0104	.0131	.0163	.0201	.0244	.0293	.0348
9	.0010	.0014	.0019	.0025	.0034	.0045	.0058	.0074	.0093	.0116
10	.0002	.0002	.0003	.0005	.0007	.0009	.0013	.0017	.0023	.0030
11	.0000	.0000	.0000	.0001	.0001	.0002	.0002	.0003	.0004	.0006
12	.0000	.0000	.0000	.0000	.0000	.0000	.0000	.0000	.0001	.0001

x \ p	.31	.32	.33	.34	.35	.36	.37	.38	.39	.40
0	.0038	.0031	.0025	.0020	.0016	.0012	.0010	.0008	.0006	.0005
1	.0258	.0217	.0182	.0152	.0126	.0104	.0086	.0071	.0058	.0047
2	.0811	.0715	.0627	.0547	.0476	.0411	.0354	.0303	.0259	.0219
3	.1579	.1457	.1338	.1222	.1110	.1002	.0901	.0805	.0716	.0634
4	.2128	.2057	.1977	.1888	.1792	.1692	.1587	.1481	.1374	.1268
5	.2103	.2130	.2142	.2140	.2123	.2093	.2051	.1997	.1933	.1859
6	.1575	.1671	.1759	.1837	.1906	.1963	.2008	.2040	.2059	.2066
7	.0910	.1011	.1114	.1217	.1319	.1419	.1516	.1608	.1693	.1771
8	.0409	.0476	.0549	.0627	.0710	.0798	.0890	.0985	.1082	.1181
9	.0143	.0174	.0210	.0251	.0298	.0349	.0407	.0470	.0538	.0612
10	.0038	.0049	.0062	.0078	.0096	.0118	.0143	.0173	.0206	.0245
11	.0008	.0011	.0014	.0018	.0024	.0030	.0038	.0048	.0060	.0074
12	.0001	.0002	.0002	.0003	.0004	.0006	.0007	.0010	.0013	.0016
13	.0000	.0000	.0000	.0000	.0001	.0001	.0001	.0001	.0002	.0003

Appendix 1 The Binomial Table A-13

$n = 15$ (Continued)

p\\x	.41	.42	.43	.44	.45	.46	.47	.48	.49	.50
0	.0004	.0003	.0002	.0002	.0001	.0001	.0001	.0001	.0000	.0000
1	.0038	.0031	.0025	.0020	.0016	.0012	.0010	.0008	.0006	.0005
2	.0185	.0156	.0130	.0108	.0090	.0074	.0060	.0049	.0040	.0032
3	.0558	.0489	.0426	.0369	.0318	.0272	.0232	.0197	.0166	.0139
4	.1163	.1061	.0963	.0869	.0780	.0696	.0617	.0545	.0478	.0417
5	.1778	.1691	.1598	.1502	.1404	.1304	.1204	.1106	.1010	.0916
6	.2060	.2041	.2010	.1967	.1914	.1851	.1780	.1702	.1617	.1527
7	.1840	.1900	.1949	.1987	.2013	.2028	.2030	.2020	.1997	.1964
8	.1279	.1376	.1470	.1561	.1647	.1727	.1800	.1864	.1919	.1964
9	.0691	.0775	.0863	.0954	.1048	.1144	.1241	.1338	.1434	.1527
10	.0288	.0337	.0390	.0450	.0515	.0585	.0661	.0741	.0827	.0916
11	.0091	.0111	.0134	.0161	.0191	.0226	.0266	.0311	.0361	.0417
12	.0021	.0027	.0034	.0042	.0052	.0064	.0079	.0096	.0116	.0139
13	.0003	.0004	.0006	.0008	.0010	.0013	.0016	.0020	.0026	.0032
14	.0000	.0000	.0001	.0001	.0001	.0002	.0002	.0003	.0004	.0005

$n = 20$

p\\x	.01	.02	.03	.04	.05	.06	.07	.08	.09	.10
0	.8179	.6676	.5438	.4420	.3585	.2901	.2342	.1887	.1516	.1216
1	.1652	.2725	.3364	.3683	.3774	.3703	.3526	.3282	.3000	.2702
2	.0159	.0528	.0988	.1458	.1887	.2246	.2521	.2711	.2818	.2852
3	.0010	.0065	.0183	.0364	.0596	.0860	.1139	.1414	.1672	.1901
4	.0000	.0006	.0024	.0065	.0133	.0233	.0364	.0523	.0703	.0898
5	.0000	.0000	.0002	.0009	.0022	.0048	.0088	.0145	.0222	.0319
6	.0000	.0000	.0000	.0001	.0003	.0008	.0017	.0032	.0055	.0089
7	.0000	.0000	.0000	.0000	.0000	.0001	.0002	.0005	.0011	.0020
8	.0000	.0000	.0000	.0000	.0000	.0000	.0000	.0001	.0002	.0004
9	.0000	.0000	.0000	.0000	.0000	.0000	.0000	.0000	.0000	.0001

$n = 20$ (Continued)

p \ x	.11	.12	.13	.14	.15	.16	.17	.18	.19	.20
0	.0972	.0776	.0617	.0490	.0388	.0306	.0241	.0189	.0148	.0115
1	.2403	.2115	.1844	.1595	.1368	.1165	.0986	.0829	.0693	.0576
2	.2822	.2740	.2618	.2466	.2293	.2109	.1919	.1730	.1545	.1369
3	.2093	.2242	.2347	.2409	.2428	.2410	.2358	.2278	.2175	.2054
4	.1099	.1299	.1491	.1666	.1821	.1951	.2053	.2125	.2168	.2182
5	.0435	.0567	.0713	.1868	.1028	.1189	.1345	.1493	.1627	.1746
6	.0134	.0193	.0266	.0353	.0454	.0566	.0689	.0819	.0954	.1091
7	.0033	.0053	.0080	.0115	.0160	.0216	.0282	.0360	.0448	.0545
8	.0007	.0012	.0019	.0030	.0046	.0067	.0094	.0128	.0171	.0222
9	.0001	.0002	.0004	.0007	.0011	.0017	.0026	.0038	.0053	.0074
10	.0000	.0000	.0001	.0001	.0002	.0004	.0006	.0009	.0014	.0020
11	.0000	.0000	.0000	.0000	.0000	.0001	.0001	.0002	.0003	.0005
12	.0000	.0000	.0000	.0000	.0000	.0000	.0000	.0000	.0001	.0001

p \ x	.21	.22	.23	.24	.25	.26	.27	.28	.29	.30
0	.0090	.0069	.0054	.0041	.0032	.0024	.0018	.0014	.0011	.0008
1	.0477	.0392	.0321	.0261	.0211	.0170	.0137	.0109	.0087	.0068
2	.1204	.1050	.0910	.0783	.0669	.0569	.0480	.0403	.0336	.0278
3	.1920	.1777	.1631	.1484	.1339	.1199	.1065	.0940	.0823	.0716
4	.2169	.2131	.2070	.1991	.1897	.1790	.1675	.1553	.1429	.1304
5	.1845	.1923	.1979	.2012	.2023	.2013	.1982	.1933	.1868	.1789
6	.1225	.1356	.1478	.1589	.1686	.1768	.1833	.1879	.1907	.1916
7	.0652	.0765	.0883	.1003	.1124	.1242	.1356	.1462	.1558	.1643
8	.0282	.0351	.0429	.0515	.0609	.0709	.0815	.0924	.1034	.1144
9	.0100	.0132	.0171	.0217	.0271	.0332	.0402	.0479	.0563	.0654
10	.0029	.0041	.0056	.0075	.0099	.0128	.0163	.0205	.0253	.0308
11	.0007	.0010	.0015	.0022	.0030	.0041	.0055	.0072	.0094	.0120
12	.0001	.0002	.0003	.0005	.0008	.0011	.0015	.0021	.0029	.0039
13	.0000	.0000	.0001	.0001	.0002	.0002	.0003	.0005	.0007	.0010
14	.0000	.0000	.0000	.0000	.0000	.0000	.0001	.0001	.0001	.0002

Appendix 1 The Binomial Table

$n = 20$ (Continued)

x \ p	.31	.32	.33	.34	.35	.36	.37	.38	.39	.40
0	.0006	.0004	.0003	.0002	.0002	.0001	.0001	.0001	.0001	.0000
1	.0054	.0042	.0033	.0025	.0020	.0015	.0011	.0009	.0007	.0005
2	.0229	.0188	.0153	.0124	.0100	.0080	.0064	.0050	.0040	.0031
3	.0619	.0531	.0453	.0383	.0323	.0270	.0224	.0185	.0152	.0123
4	.1181	.1062	.0947	.0839	.0738	.0645	.0559	.0482	.0412	.0350
5	1698	.1599	.1493	.1384	.1272	.1161	.1051	.0945	.0843	.0746
6	.1907	.1881	.1839	.1782	.1712	.1632	.1543	.1447	.1347	.1244
7	.1714	.1770	.1811	.1836	.1844	.1836	.1812	.1774	.1722	.1659
8	.1251	.1354	.1450	.1537	.1614	.1678	.1730	.1767	.1790	.1797
9	.0750	.0849	.0952	.1056	.1158	.1259	.1354	.1444	.1526	.1597
10	.0370	.0440	.0516	.0598	.0686	.0779	.0875	.0974	.1073	.1171
11	.0151	.0188	.0231	.0280	.0336	.0398	.0467	.0542	.0624	.0710
12	.0051	.0066	.0085	.0108	.0136	.0168	.0206	.0249	.0299	.0355
13	.0014	.0019	.0026	.0034	.0045	.0058	.0074	.0094	.0118	.0146
14	.0003	.0005	.0006	.0009	.0012	.0016	.0022	.0029	.0038	.0049
15	.0001	.0001	.0001	.0002	.0003	.0004	.0005	.0007	.0010	.0013
16	.0000	.0000	.0000	.0000	.0000	.0001	.0001	.0001	.0002	.0003

x \ p	.41	.42	.43	.44	.45	.46	.47	.48	.49	.50
0	.0000	.0000	.0000	.0000	.0000	.0000	.0000	.0000	.0000	.0000
1	.0004	.0003	.0002	.0001	.0001	.0001	.0001	.0000	.0000	.0000
2	.0024	.0018	.0014	.0011	.0008	.0006	.0005	.0003	.0002	.0002
3	.0100	.0080	.0064	.0051	.0040	.0031	.0024	.0019	.0014	.0011
4	.0295	.0247	.0206	.0170	.0139	.0113	.0092	.0074	.0059	.0046
5	.0656	.0573	.0496	.0427	.0365	.0309	.0260	.0217	.0180	.0148
6	.1140	.1037	.0936	.0839	.0746	.0658	.0577	.0501	.0432	.0370
7	.1585	.1502	.1413	.1318	.1221	.1122	.1023	.0925	.0830	.0739
8	.1790	.1768	.1732	.1683	.1623	.1553	.1474	.1388	.1296	.1201
9	.1658	.1707	.1742	.1763	.1771	.1763	.1742	.1708	.1661	.1602
10	.1268	.1359	.1446	.1524	.1593	.1652	.1700	.1734	.1755	.1762
11	.0801	.0895	.0991	.1089	.1185	.1280	.1370	.1455	.1533	.1602
12	.0417	.0486	.0561	.0642	.0727	.0818	.0911	.1007	.1105	.1201
13	.0178	.0217	.0260	.0310	.0366	.0429	.0497	.0572	.0653	.0739
14	.0062	.0078	.0098	.0122	.0150	.0183	.0221	.0264	.0314	.0370
15	.0017	.0023	.0030	.0038	.0049	.0062	.0078	.0098	.0121	.0148
16	.0004	.0005	.0007	.0009	.0013	.0017	.0022	.0028	.0036	.0046
17	.0001	.0001	.0001	.0002	.0002	.0003	.0005	.0006	.0008	.0011
18	.0000	.0000	.0000	.0000	.0000	.0000	.0001	.0001	.0001	.0002

2 APPENDIX Cumulative Poisson Distribution

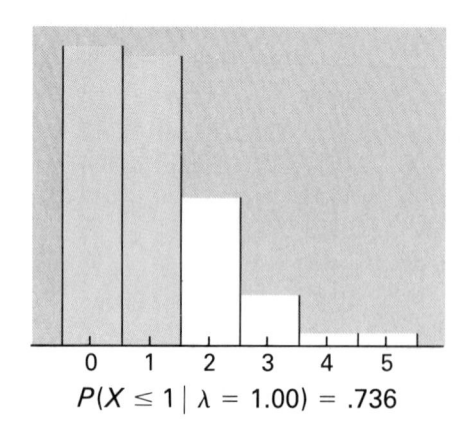

$P(X \leq 1 \mid \lambda = 1.00) = .736$

x \ λ	.02	.04	.06	.08	.10	.15	.20	.25
0	.980	.961	.942	.923	.905	.861	.819	.779
1	1.000	.999	.998	.997	.995	.990	.982	.974
2		1.000	1.000	1.000	1.000	.999	.999	.998
3						1.000	1.000	1.000

x \ λ	.30	.35	.40	.45	.50	.55	.60	.65
0	.741	.705	.670	.638	.607	.577	.549	.522
1	.963	.951	.938	.925	.910	.894	.878	.861
2	996	.994	.992	.989	.986	.982	.977	.972
3	1.000	1.000	.999	.999	.998	.998	.997	.996
4			1.000	1.000	1.000	1.000	1.000	.999
5								1.000

x \ λ	.70	.75	.80	.85	.90	.95	1.0	1.1
0	.497	.472	.449	.427	.407	.387	.368	.333
1	.844	.827	.809	.791	.772	.754	.736	.699
2	.966	.959	.953	.945	.937	.929	.920	.900
3	.994	.993	.991	.989	.987	.984	.981	.974
4	.999	.999	.999	.998	.998	.997	.996	.995
5	1.000	1.000	1.000	1.000	1.000	1.000	.999	.999
6							1.000	1.000

Source: Daniel, Wayne and James Terrell, *Business Statistics for Management and Economics*, Fifth Edition. Copyright © 1989 by Houghton Mifflin Company. Used with permission.

Appendix 2 Cumulative Poisson Distribution

x \ λ	1.2	1.3	1.4	1.5	1.6	1.7	1.8	1.9
0	.301	.273	.247	.223	.202	.183	.165	.150
1	.663	.627	.592	.558	.525	.493	.463	.434
2	.879	.857	.833	.809	.783	.757	.731	.704
3	.966	.957	.946	.934	.921	.907	.891	.875
4	.992	.989	.986	.981	.976	.970	.964	.956
5	.998	.998	.997	.996	.994	.992	.990	.987
6	1.000	1.000	.999	.999	.999	.998	.997	.997
7			1.000	1.000	1.000	1.000	.999	.999
8							1.000	1.000

x \ λ	2.0	2.2	2.4	2.6	2.8	3.0	3.2	3.4
0	.135	.111	.091	.074	.061	.050	.041	.033
1	.406	.355	.308	.267	.231	.199	.171	.147
2	.677	.623	.570	.518	.469	.423	.380	.340
3	.857	.819	.779	.736	.692	.647	.603	.558
4	.947	.928	.904	.877	.848	.815	.781	.744
5	.983	.975	.964	.951	.935	.916	.895	.871
6	.995	.993	.988	.983	.976	.966	.955	.942
7	.999	.998	.997	.995	.992	.988	.983	.977
8	1.000	1.000	.999	.999	.998	.996	.994	.992
9			1.000	1.000	.999	.999	.998	.997
10					1.000	1.000	1.000	.999
11								1.000

x \ λ	3.6	3.8	4.0	4.2	4.4	4.6	4.8	5.0
0	.027	.022	.018	.015	.012	.010	.008	.007
1	.126	.107	.092	.078	.066	.056	.048	.040
2	.303	.269	.238	.210	.185	.163	.143	.125
3	.515	.473	.433	.395	.359	.326	.294	.265
4	.706	.668	.629	.590	.551	.513	.476	.440
5	.844	.816	.785	.753	.720	.686	.651	.616
6	.927	.909	.889	.867	.844	.818	.791	.762
7	.969	.960	.949	.936	.921	.905	.887	.867
8	.988	.984	.979	.972	.964	.955	.944	.932
9	.996	.994	.992	.989	.985	.980	.975	.968
10	.999	.998	.997	.996	.994	.992	.990	.986
11	1.000	.999	.999	.999	.998	.997	.996	.995
12		1.000	1.000	1.000	.999	.999	.999	.998
13					1.000	1.000	1.000	.999
14								1.000

Appendix 2 Cumulative Poisson Distribution

λ \ x	5.2	5.4	5.6	5.8	6.0	6.2	6.4	6.6
0	.006	.005	.004	.003	.002	.002	.002	.001
1	.034	.029	.024	.021	.017	.015	.012	.010
2	.109	.095	.082	.072	.062	.054	.046	.040
3	.238	.213	.191	.170	.151	.134	.119	.105
4	.406	.373	.342	.313	.285	.259	.235	.213
5	.581	.546	.512	.478	.446	.414	.384	.355
6	.732	.702	.670	.638	.606	.574	.542	.511
7	.845	.822	.797	.771	.744	.716	.687	.658
8	.918	.903	.886	.867	.847	.826	.803	.780
9	.960	.951	.941	.929	.916	.902	.886	.869
10	.982	.977	.972	.965	.957	.949	.939	.927
11	.993	.990	.988	.984	.980	.975	.969	.963
12	.997	.996	.995	.993	.991	.989	.986	.982
13	.999	.999	.998	.997	.996	.995	.994	.992
14	1.000	.999	.999	.999	.999	.998	.997	.997
15		1.000	1.000	1.000	.999	.999	.999	.999
16					1.000	1.000	1.000	.999
17								1.000

λ \ x	6.8	7.0	7.2	7.4	7.6	7.8	8.0	8.5
0	.001	.001	.001	.001	.001	.000	.000	.000
1	.009	.007	.006	.005	.004	.004	.003	.002
2	.034	.030	.025	.022	.019	.016	.014	.009
3	.093	.082	.072	.063	.055	.048	.042	.030
4	.192	.173	.156	.140	.125	.112	.100	.074
5	.327	.301	.276	.253	.231	.210	.191	.150
6	.480	.450	.420	.392	.365	.338	.313	.256
7	.628	.599	.569	.539	.510	.481	.453	.386
8	.755	.729	.703	.676	.648	.620	.593	.523
9	.850	.830	.810	.788	.765	.741	.717	.653
10	.915	.901	.887	.871	.854	.835	.816	.763
11	.955	.947	.937	.926	.915	.902	.888	.849
12	.978	.973	.967	.961	.954	.945	.936	.909
13	.990	.987	.984	.980	.976	.971	.966	.949
14	.996	.994	.993	.991	.989	.986	.983	.973
15	.998	.998	.997	.996	.995	.993	.992	.986
16	.999	.999	.999	.998	.998	.997	.996	.993
17	1.000	1.000	.999	.999	.999	.999	.998	.997
18			1.000	1.000	1.000	1.000	.999	.999
19							1.000	.999
20								1.000

Appendix 2 Cumulative Poisson Distribution

λ \ x	9.0	9.5	10.0	10.5	11.0	11.5	12.0	12.5
1	.001	.001	.000	.000	.000	.000	.000	.000
2	.006	.004	.003	.002	.001	.001	.001	.000
3	.021	.015	.010	.007	.005	.003	.002	.002
4	.055	.040	.029	.021	.015	.011	.008	.005
5	.116	.089	.067	.050	.038	.028	.020	.015
6	.207	.165	.130	.102	.079	.060	.046	.035
7	.324	.269	.220	.179	.143	.114	.090	.070
8	.456	.392	.333	.279	.232	.191	.155	.125
9	.587	.522	.458	.397	.341	.289	.242	.201
10	.706	.645	.583	.521	.460	.402	.347	.297
11	.803	.752	.697	.639	.579	.520	.462	.406
12	.876	.836	.792	.742	.689	.633	.576	.519
13	.926	.898	.864	.825	.781	.733	.682	.628
14	.959	.940	.917	.888	.854	.815	.772	.725
15	.978	.967	.951	.932	.907	.878	.844	.806
16	.989	.982	.973	.960	.944	.924	.899	.869
17	.995	.991	.986	.978	.968	.954	.937	.916
18	.998	.996	.993	.988	.982	.974	.963	.948
19	.999	.998	.997	.994	.991	.986	.979	.969
20	1.000	.999	.998	.997	.995	.992	.988	.983
21		1.000	.999	.999	.998	.996	.994	.991
22			1.000	.999	.999	.998	.997	.995
23				1.000	1.000	.999	.999	.998
24						1.000	.999	.999
25							1.000	.999
26								1.000

λ \ x	13.0	13.5	14.0	14.5	15	16	17	18
3	.001	.001	.000	.000	.000	.000	.000	.000
4	.004	.003	.002	.001	.001	.000	.000	.000
5	.011	.008	.006	.004	.003	.001	.001	.000
6	.026	.019	.014	.010	.008	.004	.002	.001
7	.054	.041	.032	.024	.018	.010	.005	.003
8	.100	.079	.062	.048	.037	.022	.013	.007
9	.166	.135	.109	.088	.070	.043	.026	.015
10	.252	.211	.176	.145	.118	.077	.049	.030
11	.353	.304	.260	.220	.185	.127	.085	.055
12	.463	.409	.358	.311	.268	.193	.135	.092
13	.573	.518	.464	.413	.363	.275	.201	.143
14	.675	.623	.570	.518	.466	.368	.281	.208
15	.764	.718	.669	.619	.568	.467	.371	.287
16	.835	.798	.756	.711	.664	.566	.468	.375
17	.890	.861	.827	.790	.749	.659	.564	.469

(Continued)

λ \ x	13.0	13.5	14.0	14.5	15	16	17	18
18	.930	.908	.883	.853	.819	.742	.655	.562
19	.957	.942	.923	.901	.875	.812	.736	.651
20	.975	.965	.952	.936	.917	.868	.805	.731
21	.986	.980	.971	.960	.947	.911	.861	.799
22	.992	.989	.983	.976	.967	.942	.905	.855
23	.996	.994	.991	.986	.981	.963	.937	.899
24	.998	.997	.995	.992	.989	.978	.959	.932
25	.999	.998	.997	.996	.994	.987	.975	.955
26	1.000	.999	.999	.998	.997	.993	.985	.972
27		1.000	.999	.999	.998	.996	.991	.983
28			.1000	.999	.999	.998	.995	.990
29				1.000	1.000	.999	.997	.994
30						.999	.999	.997
31						1.000	.999	.998
32							1.000	.999
33								1.000

λ \ x	19	20	21	22	23	24	25
6	.001	.000	.000	.000	.000	.000	.000
7	.002	.001	.000	.000	.000	.000	.000
8	.004	.002	.001	.001	.000	.000	.000
9	.009	.005	.003	.002	.001	.000	.000
10	.018	.011	.006	.004	.002	.001	.001
11	.035	.021	.013	.008	.004	.003	.001
12	.061	.039	.025	.015	.009	.005	.003
13	.098	.066	.043	.028	.017	.011	.006
14	.150	.105	.072	.048	.031	.020	.012
15	.215	.157	.111	.077	.052	.034	.022
16	.292	.221	.163	.117	.082	.056	.038
17	.378	.297	.227	.169	.123	.087	.060
18	.469	.381	.302	.232	.175	.128	.092
19	.561	.470	.384	.306	.238	.180	.134
20	.647	.559	.471	.387	.310	.243	.185
21	.725	.644	.558	.472	.389	.314	.247
22	.793	.721	.640	.556	.472	.392	.318
23	.849	.787	.716	.637	.555	.473	.394
24	.893	.843	.782	.712	.635	.554	.473
25	.927	.888	.838	.777	.708	.632	.553
26	.951	.922	.883	.832	.772	.704	.629
27	.969	.948	.917	.877	.827	.768	.700
28	.980	.966	.944	.913	.873	.823	.763
29	.988	.978	.963	.940	.908	.868	.818

Appendix 2 Cumulative Poisson Distribution

(Continued)

x \ λ	19	20	21	22	23	24	25
30	.993	.987	.976	.959	.936	.904	.863
31	.996	.992	.985	.973	.956	.932	.900
32	.998	.995	.991	.983	.971	.953	.929
33	.999	.997	.994	.989	.981	.969	.950
34	.999	.999	.997	.994	.988	.979	.966
35	.1000	.999	.998	.996	.993	.987	.978
36		1.000	.999	.998	.996	.992	.985
37			.999	.999	.997	.995	.991
38			1.000	.999	.999	.997	.994
39				1.000	.999	.998	.997
40					1.000	.999	.998
41						.999	.999
42						1.000	.999
43							1.000

3 APPENDIX The Normal Table

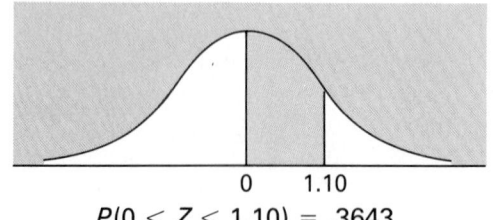

$P(0 < Z < 1.10) = .3643$

z	.00	.01	.02	.03	.04	.05	.06	.07	.08	.09
0.0	.0000	.0040	.0080	.0120	.0160	.0199	.0239	.0279	.0319	.0359
0.1	.0398	.0438	.0478	.0517	.0557	.0596	.0636	.0675	.0714	.0753
0.2	.0793	.0832	.0871	.0910	.0948	.0987	.1026	.1064	.1103	.1141
0.3	.1179	.1217	.1255	.1293	.1331	.1368	.1406	.1443	.1480	.1517
0.4	.1554	.1591	.1628	.1664	.1700	.1736	.1772	.1808	.1844	.1879
0.5	.1915	.1950	.1985	.2019	.2054	.2088	.2123	.2157	.2190	.2224
0.6	.2257	.2291	.2324	.2357	.2389	.2422	.2454	.2486	.2517	.2549
0.7	.2580	.2611	.2642	.2673	.2704	.2734	.2764	.2794	.2823	.2852
0.8	.2881	.2910	.2939	.2967	.2995	.3023	.3051	.3078	.3106	.3133
0.9	.3159	.3186	.3212	.3238	.3264	.3289	.3315	.3340	.3365	.3389
1.0	.3413	.3438	.3461	.3485	.3508	.3531	.3554	.3577	.3599	.3621
1.1	.3643	.3665	.3686	.3708	.3729	.3749	.3770	.3790	.3810	.3830
1.2	.3849	.3869	.3888	.3907	.3925	.3944	.3962	.3980	.3997	.4015
1.3	.4032	.4049	.4066	.4082	.4099	.4115	.4131	.4147	.4162	.4177
1.4	.4192	.4207	.4222	.4236	.4251	.4265	.4279	.4292	.4306	.4319
1.5	.4332	.4345	.4357	.4370	.4382	.4394	.4406	.4418	.4429	.4441
1.6	.4452	.4463	.4474	.4484	.4495	.4505	.4515	.4525	.4535	.4545
1.7	.4554	.4564	.4573	.4582	.4591	.4599	.4608	.4616	.4625	.4633
1.8	.4641	.4649	.4656	.4664	.4671	.4678	.4686	.4693	.4699	.4706
1.9	.4713	.4719	.4726	.4732	.4738	.4744	.4750	.4756	.4761	.4767
2.0	.4772	.4778	.4783	.4788	.4793	.4798	.4803	.4808	.4812	.4817
2.1	.4821	.4826	.4830	.4834	.4838	.4842	.4846	.4850	.4854	.4857
2.2	.4861	.4864	.4868	.4871	.4875	.4878	.4881	.4884	.4887	.4890
2.3	.4893	.4896	.4898	.4901	.4904	.4906	.4909	.4911	.4913	.4916
2.4	.4918	.4920	.4922	.4925	.4927	.4929	.4931	.4932	.4934	.4936
2.5	.4938	.4940	.4941	.4943	.4945	.4946	.4948	.4949	.4951	.4952
2.6	.4953	.4955	.4956	.4957	.4959	.4960	.4961	.4962	.4963	.4964
2.7	.4965	.4966	.4967	.4968	.4969	.4970	.4971	.4972	.4973	.4974
2.8	.4974	.4975	.4976	.4977	.4977	.4978	.4979	.4979	.4980	.4981
2.9	.4981	.4982	.4982	.4982	.4984	.4984	.4985	.4985	.4986	.4986
3.0	.4987	.4987	.4987	.4988	.4988	.4989	.4989	.4989	.4990	.4990

4 APPENDIX Table of Random Numbers

Line	(1)	(2)	(3)	(4)	(5)	(6)	(7)	(8)	(9)	(10)	(11)	(12)	(13)	(14)
1	10480	15011	01536	02011	81647	91646	69179	14194	62590	36207	20969	99570	91291	90700
2	22368	46573	25595	85393	30995	89198	27982	53402	93965	34095	52666	19174	39615	99505
3	24130	48360	22527	97265	76393	64809	15179	24830	49340	32081	30680	19655	63348	58629
4	42167	93093	06243	61680	07856	16376	39440	53537	71341	57004	00849	74917	97758	16379
5	37570	39975	81837	16656	06121	91782	60468	81305	49684	60672	14110	06927	01263	54613
6	77921	06907	11008	42751	27756	53498	18602	70659	90655	15053	21916	81825	44394	42880
7	99562	72905	56420	69994	98872	31016	71194	18738	44013	48840	63213	21069	10634	12952
8	96301	91977	05463	07972	18876	20922	94595	56869	69014	60045	18425	84903	42508	32307
9	89579	14342	63661	10281	17453	18103	57740	84378	25331	12566	58678	44947	05585	56941
10	85475	36857	53342	53988	53060	59533	38867	62300	08158	17983	16439	11458	18593	64952
11	28918	69578	88231	33276	70997	79936	56865	05859	90106	31595	01547	85590	91610	78188
12	63553	40961	48235	03427	49626	69445	18663	72695	52180	20847	12234	90511	33703	90322
13	09429	93969	52636	92737	88974	33488	36320	17617	30015	08272	84115	27156	30613	74952
14	10365	61129	87529	85689	48237	52267	67689	93394	01511	26358	85104	20285	29975	89868
15	07119	97336	71048	08178	77233	13916	47564	81056	97735	85977	29372	74461	28551	90707
16	51085	12765	51821	51259	77452	16308	60756	92144	49442	53900	70960	63990	75601	40719
17	02368	21382	52404	60268	89368	19885	55322	44819	01188	65255	64835	44919	05944	55157
18	01011	54092	33362	94904	31273	04146	18594	29852	71585	85030	51132	01915	92747	64951
19	52162	53916	46369	58586	23216	14513	83149	98736	23495	64350	94738	17752	35156	35749
20	07056	97628	33787	09998	42698	06691	76988	13602	51851	46104	88916	19509	25625	58104
21	48663	91245	85828	14346	09172	30168	90229	04734	59193	22178	30421	61666	99904	32812
22	54164	58492	22421	74103	47070	25306	76468	26384	58151	06646	21524	15227	96909	44592
23	32639	32363	05597	24200	13363	38005	94342	28728	35806	06912	17012	64161	18296	22851
24	29334	27001	87637	87308	58731	00256	45834	15398	46557	41135	10367	07684	36188	18510
25	02488	33062	28834	07351	19731	92420	60952	61280	50001	67658	32586	86679	50720	94953
26	81525	72295	04839	96423	24878	82651	66566	14778	76797	14780	13300	87074	79666	95725
27	29676	20591	68086	26432	46901	20849	89768	81536	86645	12659	92259	57102	80428	25280
28	00742	57392	39064	66432	84673	40027	32832	61362	98947	96067	64760	64584	96096	98253
29	05366	04213	25669	26422	44407	44048	37937	63904	45766	66134	75470	66520	34693	90449
30	91921	26418	64117	94305	26766	25940	39972	22209	71500	64568	91402	42416	07844	69618
31	00582	04711	87917	77341	42206	35126	74087	99547	81817	42607	43808	76655	62028	76630
32	00725	69884	62797	56170	86324	88072	76222	36086	84637	93161	76038	65855	77919	88006
33	69011	65795	95876	55293	18988	27354	26575	08625	40801	59920	29841	80150	12777	48501
34	25976	57948	29888	88604	67917	48708	18912	82271	65424	69774	33611	54262	85963	03547
35	09763	83473	73577	12908	30883	18317	28290	35797	05998	41688	34952	37888	38917	88050
36	91567	42595	27958	30134	04024	86385	29880	99730	55536	84855	29080	09250	79656	73211
37	17955	56349	90999	49127	20044	59931	06115	20542	18059	02008	73708	83517	36103	42791
38	46503	18584	18845	49618	02304	51038	20655	58727	28168	15475	56942	53389	20562	87338
39	92157	89634	94824	78171	84610	82834	09922	25417	44137	48413	25555	21246	35509	20468
40	14577	62765	35605	81263	39667	47358	56873	56307	61607	49518	89656	20103	77490	18062
41	98427	07523	33362	64270	01638	92477	66969	98420	04880	45585	46565	04102	46880	45709
42	34914	63976	88720	82765	34476	17032	87589	40836	32427	70002	70663	88863	77775	69348
43	70060	28277	39475	46473	23219	53416	94970	25832	69975	94884	19661	72828	00102	66794
44	53976	54914	06990	67245	68350	82948	11398	42878	80287	88267	47363	46634	06541	97809
45	76072	29515	40980	07391	58745	25774	22987	80059	39911	96189	41151	14222	60697	59583

APPENDIX 4 (*Continued*)

Line	(1)	(2)	(3)	(4)	(5)	(6)	(7)	(8)	(9)	(10)	(11)	(12)	(13)	(14)
46	90725	52210	83974	29992	65831	38857	50490	83765	55657	14361	31720	57375	56228	41546
47	64364	67412	33339	31926	14883	24413	59744	92351	97473	89286	35931	04110	23726	51900
48	08962	00358	31662	25388	61642	34072	81249	35648	56891	69352	48373	45578	78547	81788
49	95012	68379	93526	70765	10592	04542	76463	54328	02349	17247	28865	14777	62730	92277
50	15664	10493	20492	38391	91132	21999	59516	81652	27195	48223	46751	22923	32261	85653
51	16408	81899	04153	53381	79401	21438	83035	92350	36693	31238	59649	91754	72772	02338
52	18629	81953	05520	91962	04739	13092	97662	24822	94730	06496	35090	04822	86774	98289
53	73115	35101	47498	87637	99016	71060	88824	71013	18735	20286	23153	72924	35165	43040
54	57491	16703	23167	49323	45021	33132	12544	41035	80780	45393	44812	12515	98931	91202
55	30405	83946	23792	14422	15059	45799	22716	19792	09983	74353	68668	30429	70735	25499
56	16631	35006	85900	98275	32388	52390	16815	69298	82732	38480	73817	32523	41961	44437
57	96773	20206	42559	78985	05300	22164	24369	54224	35083	19687	11052	91491	60383	19746
58	38935	64202	14349	82674	66523	44133	00697	35552	35970	19124	63318	29686	03387	59846
59	31624	76384	17403	53363	44167	64486	64758	75366	76554	31601	12614	33072	60332	92325
60	78919	19474	23632	27889	47914	02584	37680	20801	72152	39339	34806	08930	85001	87820
61	03931	33309	57047	74211	63445	17361	62825	39908	05607	91284	68833	25570	38818	46920
62	74426	33278	43972	10119	89917	15665	52872	73823	73144	88662	88970	74492	51805	99378
63	09066	00903	20795	95452	92648	45454	09552	88815	16553	51125	79375	97596	16296	66092
64	42238	12426	87025	14267	20979	04508	64535	31355	86064	29472	47689	05974	52468	16834
65	16153	08002	26504	41744	81959	65642	74240	56302	00033	67107	77510	70625	28725	34191

Source: R. Schaeffer, W. Mendenhall, and L. Ott. *Elementary Survey Sampling* (Boston, Mass.: Duxbury Press, 1986), pp. 308–311. Used with permission.

5 APPENDIX Student *t* Tables

df	2-sided 20% CI or 1-sided 60% CI	2-sided 40% CI or 1-sided 70% CI	2-sided 60% CI or 1-sided 80% CI	2-sided 80% CI or 1-sided 90% CI	2-sided 90% CI or 1-sided 95% CI	2-sided 95% CI or 1-sided 97.5% CI	2-sided 98% CI or 1-sided 99% CI	2-sided 99% CI or 1-sided 99.5% CI
1	.325	.727	1.376	3.078	6.314	12.706	31.821	63.657
2	.289	.617	1.061	1.886	2.920	4.303	6.965	9.925
3	.277	.584	.978	1.638	2.353	3.182	4.541	5.841
4	.271	.569	.941	1.533	2.132	2.776	3.747	4.604
5	.267	.559	.920	1.476	2.015	2.571	3.365	4.032
6	.265	.553	.906	1.440	1.943	2.447	3.143	3.707
7	.263	.549	.896	1.415	1.895	2.365	2.998	3.499
8	.262	.546	.889	1.397	1.860	2.306	2.896	3.355
9	.261	.543	.883	1.383	1.833	2.262	2.821	3.250
10	.260	.542	.879	1.372	1.812	2.228	2.764	3.169
11	.260	.540	.876	1.363	1.796	2.201	2.718	3.106
12	.259	.539	.873	1.356	1.782	2.179	2.681	3.055
13	.259	.538	.870	1.350	1.771	2.160	2.650	3.012
14	.258	.537	.868	1.345	1.761	2.145	2.624	2.977
15	.258	.536	.866	1.341	1.753	2.131	2.602	2.947
16	.258	.535	.865	1.337	1.746	2.120	2.583	2.921
17	.257	.534	.863	1.333	1.740	2.110	2.567	2.898
18	.257	.534	.862	1.330	1.734	2.101	2.552	2.878
19	.257	.533	.861	1.328	1.729	2.093	2.539	2.861
20	.257	.533	.860	1.325	1.725	2.086	2.528	2.845
21	.257	.532	.859	1.323	1.721	2.080	2.518	2.831
22	.256	.532	.858	1.321	1.717	2.074	2.508	2.819
23	.256	.532	.858	1.319	1.714	2.069	2.500	2.807
24	.256	.531	.857	1.318	1.711	2.064	2.492	2.797
25	.256	.531	.856	1.316	1.708	2.060	2.485	2.787
26	.256	.531	.856	1.315	1.706	2.056	2.479	2.779
27	.256	.531	.855	1.314	1.703	2.052	2.473	2.771
28	.256	.530	.855	1.313	1.701	2.048	2.467	2.763
29	.256	.530	.854	1.311	1.699	2.045	2.462	2.756
30	.256	.530	.854	1.310	1.697	2.042	2.457	2.750
40	.255	.529	.851	1.303	1.684	2.021	2.423	2.704
60	.254	.527	.848	1.296	1.671	2.000	2.390	2.660
120	.254	.526	.845	1.289	1.658	1.980	2.358	2.617
∞	.253	.524	.842	1.282	1.645	1.960	2.326	2.576

6 APPENDIX Percentiles of the χ^2 Distribution

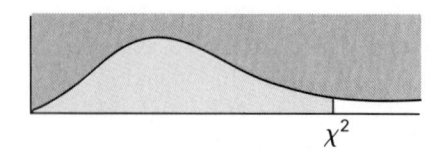

df	$\chi^2_{.5}$	χ^2_1	$\chi^2_{2.5}$	χ^2_5	χ^2_{10}	χ^2_{90}	χ^2_{95}	$\chi^2_{97.5}$	χ^2_{99}	$\chi^2_{99.5}$
1	.000039	.00016	.00098	.0039	.0158	2.71	3.84	5.02	6.63	7.88
2	.0100	.0201	.0506	.1026	.2107	4.61	5.99	7.38	9.21	10.60
3	.0717	.115	.216	.352	.584	6.25	7.81	9.35	11.34	12.84
4	.207	.297	.484	.711	1.064	7.78	9.49	11.14	13.28	14.86
5	.412	.554	.831	1.15	1.61	9.24	11.07	12.83	15.09	16.75
6	.676	.872	1.24	1.64	2.20	10.64	12.59	14.45	16.81	18.55
7	.989	1.24	1.69	2.17	2.83	12.02	14.07	16.01	18.48	20.28
8	1.34	1.65	2.18	2.73	3.49	13.36	15.51	17.53	20.09	21.96
9	1.73	2.09	2.70	3.33	4.17	14.68	16.92	19.02	21.67	23.59
10	2.16	2.56	3.25	3.94	4.87	15.99	18.31	20.48	23.21	25.19
11	2.60	3.05	3.82	4.57	5.58	17.28	19.68	21.92	24.73	26.76
12	3.07	3.57	4.40	5.23	6.30	18.55	21.03	23.34	26.22	28.30
13	3.57	4.11	5.01	5.89	7.04	19.81	22.36	24.74	27.69	29.82
14	4.07	4.66	5.63	6.57	7.79	21.06	23.68	26.12	29.14	31.32
15	4.60	5.23	6.26	7.26	8.55	22.31	25.00	27.49	30.58	32.80
16	5.14	5.81	6.91	7.96	9.31	23.54	26.30	28.85	32.00	34.27
18	6.26	7.01	8.23	9.39	10.86	25.99	28.87	31.53	34.81	37.16
20	7.43	8.26	9.59	10.85	12.44	28.41	31.41	34.17	37.57	40.00
24	9.89	10.86	12.40	13.85	15.66	33.20	36.42	39.36	42.98	45.56
30	13.79	14.95	16.79	18.49	20.60	40.26	43.77	46.98	50.89	53.67
40	20.71	22.16	24.43	26.51	29.05	51.81	55.76	59.34	63.69	66.77
60	35.53	37.48	40.48	43.19	46.46	74.40	79.08	83.30	88.38	91.95
120	83.85	86.92	91.58	95.70	100.62	140.23	146.57	152.21	158.95	163.64

Source: W. J. Dixon and F. Massey, Jr. *Introduction to Statistical Analysis*, 2nd edition (McGraw Hill Book Co. Inc.). Used with permission.

7 APPENDIX The *F* Distribution

APPENDIX 7 The F Distribution (*Continued*)

df for denominator	Percentile	1	2	3	4	5	6	7	8	9
1	.025	0	.03	.06	.08	.10	.11	.12	.13	.14
	.05	0	.05	.10	.13	.15	.17	.17	.18	.19
	.90	39.9	49.5	53.6	55.8	57.2	58.2	58.9	59.4	59.9
	.95	161	200	216	225	230	234	237	239	241
	.975	648	800	864	900	922	937	948	957	963
	.99	4,052	5,000	5,403	5,625	5,764	5,859	5,928	5,981	6,022
	.995	16,211	20,000	21,615	22,500	23,056	23,437	23,715	23,925	24,091
	.999	405,280	500,000	540,380	562,500	576,400	585,940	592,870	598,140	602,280
2	.025	0	.03	.06	.07	.12	.13	.15	.17	.18
	.05	0	.05	.10	.14	.17	.19	.21	.22	.23
	.90	8.53	9.00	9.16	9.24	9.29	9.33	9.35	9.37	9.38
	.95	18.5	19.0	19.2	19.2	19.3	19.3	19.4	19.4	19.4
	.975	38.5	39.0	39.2	39.2	39.3	39.3	39.4	39.4	39.4
	.99	98.5	99.0	99.2	99.2	99.3	99.3	99.4	99.4	99.4
	.995	199	199	199	199	199	199	199	199	199
	.999	998.5	999.0	999.2	999.2	999.3	999.3	999.4	999.4	999.4
3	.025	0	.03	.06	.10	.12	.15	.17	.18	.20
	.05	0	.05	.11	.15	.18	.21	.22	.25	.26
	.90	5.54	5.46	5.39	5.34	5.31	5.28	5.27	5.25	5.24
	.95	10.1	9.55	9.28	9.12	9.01	8.94	8.89	8.85	8.81
	.975	17.4	16.0	15.4	15.1	14.9	14.7	14.6	14.5	14.5
	.99	34.1	30.8	29.5	28.7	28.2	27.9	27.7	27.5	27.3
	.995	55.6	49.8	47.5	46.2	45.4	44.8	44.4	44.1	43.9
	.999	167.0	148.5	141.1	137.1	134.6	132.8	131.6	130.6	129.9
4	.025	0	.03	.07	.10	.14	.16	.18	.20	.21
	.05	0	.05	.11	.16	.19	.22	.24	.26	.28
	.90	4.54	4.32	4.19	4.11	4.05	4.01	3.98	3.95	3.94
	.95	7.71	6.94	6.59	6.39	6.26	6.16	6.09	6.04	6.00
	.975	12.2	10.6	9.98	9.60	9.36	9.20	9.07	8.98	8.90
	.99	21.2	18.0	16.7	16.0	15.5	15.2	15.0	14.8	14.7
	.995	31.3	26.3	24.3	23.2	22.5	22.0	21.6	21.4	21.1
	.999	74.1	61.2	56.2	53.4	51.7	50.5	49.7	49.0	48.5
5	.025	0	.03	.07	.11	.14	.17	.19	.21	.22
	.05	0	.05	.11	.16	.20	.23	.25	.27	.29
	.90	4.06	3.78	3.62	3.52	3.45	3.40	3.37	3.34	3.32
	.95	6.61	5.79	5.41	5.19	5.05	4.95	4.88	4.82	4.77
	.975	10.0	8.43	7.76	7.39	7.15	6.98	6.85	6.76	6.68
	.99	16.3	13.3	12.1	11.4	11.0	10.7	10.5	10.3	10.2
	.995	22.8	18.3	16.5	15.6	14.9	14.5	14.2	14.0	13.8
	.999	47.2	37.1	33.2	31.1	29.8	28.8	28.2	27.6	27.2
6	.025	0	.03	.07	.11	.14	.17	.20	.22	.23
	.05	0	.05	.11	.16	.20	.23	.25	.28	.30
	.90	3.78	3.46	3.26	3.18	3.11	3.05	3.01	2.98	2.96
	.95	5.99	5.14	4.76	4.53	4.39	4.28	4.21	4.15	4.10
	.975	8.81	7.26	6.60	6.23	5.99	5.82	5.70	5.60	5.52
	.99	13.7	10.9	9.78	9.15	8.75	8.47	8.26	8.10	7.98
	.995	18.6	14.5	12.9	12.0	11.5	11.1	10.8	10.6	10.4
	.999	35.5	27.0	23.7	21.9	20.8	20.0	19.5	19.0	18.7

df for denominator	Percentile	\multicolumn{9}{c}{df for numerator}
		10	12	15	20	24	30	60	120	∞
1	.025	.14	.15	.16	.17	.17	.18	.19	.19	.20
	.05	.20	.21	.22	.23	.23	.24	.25	.26	.26
	.90	60.2	60.7	61.2	61.7	62.0	62.3	62.8	63.1	63.3
	.95	242	244	246	248	249	250	252	253	254
	.975	969	977	985	993	997	1,001	1,010	1,014	1,018
	.99	6,056	6,106	6,157	6,209	6,235	6,261	6,313	6,339	6,366
	.995	24,224	24,426	24,630	24,836	24,940	25,044	25,253	25,359	25,464
	.999	605,620	610,670	615,760	620,910	623,500	626,100	631,340	633,970	636,620
2	.025	.18	.20	.21	.22	.23	.24	.25	.26	.27
	.05	.24	.26	.27	.29	.29	.30	.32	.33	.33
	.90	9.39	9.41	9.42	9.44	9.45	9.46	9.47	9.48	9.49
	.95	19.4	19.4	19.4	19.4	19.5	19.5	19.5	19.5	19.5
	.975	39.4	39.4	39.4	39.4	39.5	39.5	39.5	39.5	39.5
	.99	99.4	99.4	99.4	99.4	99.5	99.5	99.5	99.5	99.5
	.995	199	199	199	199	199	199	199	199	200
	.999	999.4	999.4	999.4	999.4	999.5	999.5	999.5	999.5	999.5
3	.025	.21	.22	.24	.26	.27	.28	.30	.31	.32
	.05	.27	.29	.30	.32	.33	.34	.36	.37	.38
	.90	5.23	5.22	5.20	5.18	5.18	5.17	5.15	5.14	5.13
	.95	8.79	8.74	8.70	8.66	8.64	8.62	8.57	8.55	8.53
	.975	14.4	14.3	14.3	14.2	14.1	14.1	14.0	13.9	13.9
	.99	27.2	27.1	26.9	26.7	26.6	26.5	26.3	26.2	26.1
	.995	43.7	43.4	43.1	42.8	42.6	42.5	42.1	42.0	41.8
	.999	129.2	128.3	127.4	126.4	125.9	125.4	124.5	124.0	123.5
4	.025	.22	.24	.26	.28	.30	.31	.33	.34	.36
	.05	.29	.31	.33	.35	.36	.37	.40	.41	.42
	.90	3.92	3.90	3.87	3.84	3.83	3.82	3.79	3.78	3.76
	.95	5.96	5.91	5.86	5.80	5.77	5.75	5.69	5.66	5.63
	.975	8.84	8.75	8.66	8.56	8.51	8.46	8.36	8.31	8.26
	.99	14.5	14.4	14.2	14.0	13.9	13.8	13.7	13.6	13.5
	.995	21.0	20.7	20.4	20.2	20.0	19.9	19.6	19.5	19.3
	.999	48.1	47.4	46.8	46.1	45.8	45.4	44.7	44.4	44.1
5	.025	.24	.26	.28	.30	.32	.33	.36	.37	.39
	.05	.30	.32	.34	.37	.38	.40	.42	.44	.45
	.90	3.30	3.27	3.24	3.21	3.19	3.17	3.14	3.12	3.11
	.95	4.74	4.68	4.62	4.56	4.53	4.50	4.43	4.40	4.37
	.975	6.62	6.52	6.43	6.33	6.28	6.23	6.12	6.07	6.02
	.99	10.1	9.89	9.72	9.55	9.47	9.38	9.20	9.11	9.02
	.995	13.6	13.4	13.1	12.9	12.8	12.7	12.4	12.3	12.1
	.999	26.9	26.4	25.9	25.4	25.1	24.9	24.3	24.1	23.8
6	.025	.25	.27	.29	.32	.33	.35	.38	.40	.41
	.05	.31	.33	.36	.38	.40	.41	.44	.46	.48
	.90	2.94	2.90	2.87	2.84	2.82	2.80	2.76	2.74	2.72
	.95	4.06	4.00	3.94	3.87	3.84	3.81	3.74	3.70	3.67
	.975	5.46	5.37	5.27	5.17	5.12	5.07	4.96	4.90	4.85
	.99	7.87	7.72	7.56	7.40	7.31	7.23	7.06	6.97	6.88
	.995	10.2	10.0	9.81	9.59	9.47	9.36	9.12	9.00	8.88
	.999	18.4	18.0	17.6	17.1	16.9	16.7	16.2	16.0	15.7

APPENDIX 7 The F Distribution (*Continued*)

df for denominator	Percentile	1	2	3	4	5	6	7	8	9
7	.025	0	.03	.07	.11	.14	.18	.20	.22	.24
	.05	0	.05	.11	.16	.20	.24	.26	.29	.30
	.90	3.59	3.26	3.07	2.96	2.88	2.83	2.78	2.75	2.72
	.95	5.59	4.74	4.35	4.12	3.97	3.87	3.79	3.73	3.68
	.975	8.07	6.54	5.89	5.52	5.29	5.12	4.99	4.90	4.82
	.99	12.2	9.55	8.45	7.85	7.46	7.19	6.99	6.84	6.72
	.995	16.2	12.4	10.9	10.1	9.52	9.16	8.89	8.68	8.51
	.999	29.2	21.7	18.8	17.2	16.2	15.5	15.0	14.6	14.3
8	.025	0	.03	.07	.11	.15	.18	.20	.23	.24
	.05	0	.05	.11	.17	.21	.24	.27	.29	.31
	.90	3.46	3.11	2.92	2.81	2.73	2.67	2.62	2.59	2.56
	.95	5.32	4.46	4.07	3.84	3.69	3.58	3.50	3.44	3.39
	.975	7.57	6.06	5.42	5.05	4.82	4.65	4.53	4.43	4.36
	.99	11.3	8.65	7.59	7.01	6.63	6.37	6.18	6.03	5.91
	.995	14.7	11.0	9.60	8.81	8.30	7.95	7.69	7.50	7.34
	.999	25.4	18.5	15.8	14.4	13.5	12.9	12.4	12.0	11.8
9	.025	0	.03	.07	.11	.15	.18	.21	.23	.23
	.05	0	.05	.11	.17	.21	.24	.27	.29	.31
	.90	3.36	3.01	2.81	2.69	2.61	2.55	2.51	2.47	2.44
	.95	5.12	4.26	3.86	3.63	3.48	3.37	3.29	3.23	3.18
	.975	7.21	5.71	5.08	4.72	4.48	4.32	4.20	4.10	4.03
	.99	10.6	8.02	6.99	6.42	6.06	5.80	5.61	5.47	5.35
	.995	13.6	10.1	8.72	7.96	7.47	7.13	6.88	6.69	6.54
	.999	22.9	16.4	13.9	12.6	11.7	11.1	10.7	10.4	10.1
10	.025	0	.03	.07	.11	.15	.18	.21	.23	.25
	.05	0	.05	.11	.17	.21	.25	.27	.30	.32
	.90	3.29	2.92	2.73	2.61	2.52	2.46	2.41	2.38	2.35
	.95	4.96	4.10	3.71	3.48	3.33	3.22	3.14	3.07	3.02
	.975	6.94	5.46	4.83	4.47	4.24	4.07	3.95	3.85	3.78
	.99	10.0	7.56	6.55	5.99	5.64	5.39	5.20	5.06	4.94
	.995	12.8	9.43	8.08	7.34	6.87	6.54	6.30	6.12	5.97
	.999	21.0	14.9	12.6	11.3	10.5	9.93	9.52	9.20	8.96
12	.025	0	.03	.07	.11	.15	.19	.21	.23	.26
	.05	0	.05	.11	.17	.21	.25	.28	.30	.33
	.90	3.18	2.81	2.61	2.48	2.39	2.33	2.28	2.24	2.21
	.95	4.75	3.89	3.49	3.26	3.11	3.00	2.91	2.85	2.80
	.975	6.55	5.10	4.47	4.12	3.89	3.73	3.61	3.51	3.44
	.99	9.33	6.93	5.95	5.41	5.06	4.82	4.64	4.50	4.39
	.995	11.8	8.51	7.23	6.52	6.07	5.76	5.52	5.35	5.20
	.999	18.6	13.0	10.8	9.63	8.89	8.38	8.00	7.71	7.48
15	.025	0	.03	.07	.12	.16	.19	.22	.24	.27
	.05	0	.05	.11	.17	.22	.25	.28	.31	.33
	.90	3.07	2.70	2.49	2.36	2.27	2.21	2.16	2.12	2.09
	.95	4.54	3.68	3.29	3.06	2.90	2.79	2.71	2.64	2.59
	.975	6.20	4.77	4.15	3.80	3.58	3.41	3.29	3.20	3.12
	.99	8.68	6.36	5.42	4.89	4.56	4.32	4.14	4.00	3.89
	.995	10.8	7.70	6.48	5.80	5.37	5.07	4.85	4.67	4.54
	.999	16.6	11.3	9.34	8.25	7.57	7.09	6.74	6.47	6.26

df for denominator	Percentile	\multicolumn{9}{c}{df for numerator}
		10	12	15	20	24	30	60	120	∞
7	.025	.25	.28	.30	.33	.35	.36	.40	.42	.44
	.05	.32	.34	.37	.40	.41	.43	.46	.48	.50
	.90	2.70	2.67	2.63	2.59	2.58	2.56	2.51	2.49	2.47
	.95	3.64	3.57	3.51	3.44	3.41	3.38	3.30	3.27	3.23
	.975	4.76	4.67	4.57	4.47	4.42	4.36	4.25	4.20	4.14
	.99	6.62	6.47	6.31	6.16	6.07	5.99	5.82	5.74	5.65
	.995	8.38	8.18	7.97	7.75	7.65	7.53	7.31	7.19	7.08
	.999	14.1	13.7	13.3	12.9	12.7	12.5	12.1	11.9	11.7
8	.025	.26	.28	.31	.34	.36	.38	.41	.43	.46
	.05	.33	.35	.38	.41	.42	.44	.48	.50	.52
	.90	2.54	2.50	2.46	2.42	2.40	2.38	2.34	2.32	2.29
	.95	3.35	3.28	3.22	3.15	3.12	3.08	3.01	2.97	2.93
	.975	4.30	4.20	4.10	4.00	3.95	3.89	3.78	3.73	3.67
	.99	5.81	5.67	5.52	5.36	5.28	5.20	5.03	4.95	4.86
	.995	7.21	7.01	6.81	6.61	6.50	6.40	6.18	6.06	5.95
	.999	11.5	11.2	10.8	10.5	10.3	10.1	9.73	9.53	9.33
9	.025	.26	.29	.32	.35	.37	.39	.43	.45	.47
	.05	.33	.36	.39	.41	.43	.45	.49	.51	.53
	.90	2.42	2.38	2.34	2.30	2.28	2.25	2.21	2.18	2.16
	.95	3.14	3.07	3.01	2.94	2.90	2.86	2.79	2.75	2.71
	.975	3.96	3.87	3.77	3.67	3.61	3.56	3.45	3.39	3.33
	.99	5.26	5.11	4.96	4.81	4.73	4.65	4.48	4.40	4.31
	.995	6.42	6.23	6.03	5.83	5.73	5.62	5.41	5.30	5.19
	.999	9.89	9.57	9.24	8.90	8.72	8.55	8.19	8.00	7.81
10	.025	.27	.30	.33	.36	.38	.40	.44	.46	.49
	.05	.34	.36	.39	.43	.44	.46	.50	.52	.55
	.90	2.32	2.28	2.24	2.20	2.18	2.16	2.11	2.08	2.06
	.95	2.98	2.91	2.84	2.77	2.74	2.70	2.62	2.58	2.54
	.975	3.72	3.62	3.52	3.42	3.37	3.31	3.20	3.14	3.08
	.99	4.85	4.71	4.56	4.41	4.33	4.25	4.08	4.00	3.91
	.995	5.85	5.66	5.47	5.27	5.17	5.07	4.86	4.75	4.64
	.999	8.75	8.45	8.13	7.80	7.64	7.47	7.12	6.94	6.76
12	.025	.28	.30	.34	.37	.39	.41	.46	.49	.52
	.05	.34	.37	.40	.44	.46	.48	.52	.55	.57
	.90	2.19	2.15	2.10	2.06	2.04	2.01	1.96	1.93	1.90
	.95	2.75	2.69	2.62	2.54	2.51	2.47	2.38	2.34	2.30
	.975	3.37	3.28	3.18	3.07	3.02	2.96	2.85	2.79	2.72
	.99	4.30	4.16	4.01	3.86	3.78	3.70	3.54	3.45	3.36
	.995	5.09	4.91	4.72	4.53	4.43	4.33	4.12	4.01	3.90
	.999	7.29	7.00	6.71	6.40	6.25	6.09	5.76	5.59	5.42
15	.025	.28	.31	.35	.39	.41	.43	.49	.51	.55
	.05	.35	.38	.42	.45	.47	.50	.54	.57	.59
	.90	2.06	2.02	1.97	1.92	1.90	1.87	1.82	1.79	1.76
	.95	2.54	2.48	2.40	2.33	2.29	2.25	2.16	2.11	2.07
	.975	3.06	2.96	2.86	2.76	2.70	2.64	2.52	2.46	2.40
	.99	3.80	3.67	3.52	3.37	3.29	3.21	3.05	2.96	2.87
	.995	4.42	4.25	4.07	3.88	3.79	3.69	3.48	3.37	3.26
	.999	6.08	5.81	5.54	5.25	5.10	4.95	4.64	4.48	4.31

APPENDIX 7 The *F* Distribution (*Continued*)

df for denominator	Percentile	\multicolumn{9}{c}{df for numerator}
		1	2	3	4	5	6	7	8	9
20	.025	0	.03	.07	.11	.16	.19	.22	.25	.27
	.05	0	.05	.12	.17	.22	.26	.29	.31	.34
	.90	2.97	2.59	2.38	2.25	2.16	2.09	2.04	2.00	1.96
	.95	4.35	3.49	3.10	2.87	2.71	2.60	2.51	2.45	2.39
	.975	5.87	4.46	3.86	3.51	3.29	3.13	3.01	2.91	2.84
	.99	8.10	5.85	4.94	4.43	4.10	3.87	3.70	3.56	3.46
	.995	9.94	6.99	5.82	5.17	4.76	4.47	4.26	4.09	3.96
	.999	14.8	9.95	8.10	7.10	6.46	6.02	5.69	5.44	5.24
24	.025	0	.03	.07	.12	.16	.20	.23	.25	.28
	.05	0	.05	.12	.17	.22	.26	.29	.32	.34
	.90	2.93	2.54	2.33	2.19	2.10	2.04	1.98	1.94	1.91
	.95	4.26	3.40	3.01	2.78	2.62	2.51	2.42	2.36	2.30
	.975	5.72	4.32	3.72	3.38	3.15	2.99	2.87	2.78	2.70
	.99	7.82	5.61	4.72	4.22	3.90	3.67	3.50	3.36	3.26
	.995	9.55	6.66	5.52	4.89	4.49	4.20	3.99	3.83	3.69
	.999	14.0	9.34	7.55	6.59	5.98	5.55	5.23	4.99	4.80
30	.025	0	.03	.07	.12	.16	.20	.23	.26	.28
	.05	0	.05	.12	.17	.22	.26	.30	.32	.35
	.90	2.88	2.49	2.28	2.14	2.05	1.98	1.93	1.88	1.85
	.95	4.17	3.32	2.92	2.69	2.53	2.42	2.33	2.27	2.21
	.975	5.57	4.18	3.59	3.25	3.03	2.87	2.75	2.65	2.57
	.99	7.56	5.39	4.51	4.02	3.70	3.47	3.30	3.17	3.07
	.995	9.18	6.35	5.24	4.62	4.23	3.95	3.74	3.58	3.45
	.999	13.3	8.77	7.05	6.12	5.53	5.12	4.82	4.58	4.39
60	.025	0	.03	.07	.12	.16	.20	.24	.26	.29
	.05	0	.05	.12	.18	.23	.27	.30	.33	.36
	.90	2.79	2.39	2.18	2.04	1.95	1.87	1.82	1.77	1.74
	.95	4.00	3.15	2.76	2.53	2.37	2.25	2.17	2.10	2.04
	.975	5.29	3.93	3.34	3.01	2.79	2.63	2.51	2.41	2.33
	.99	7.08	4.98	4.13	3.65	3.34	3.12	2.95	2.82	2.72
	.995	8.49	5.80	4.73	4.14	3.76	3.49	3.29	3.13	3.01
	.999	12.0	7.77	6.17	5.31	4.76	4.37	4.09	3.86	3.69
120	.025	0	.03	.07	.12	.16	.20	.24	.27	.29
	.05	0	.05	.12	.18	.23	.27	.31	.34	.36
	.90	2.75	2.35	2.13	1.99	1.90	1.82	1.77	1.72	1.68
	.95	3.92	3.07	2.68	2.45	2.29	2.18	2.09	2.02	1.96
	.975	5.15	3.80	3.23	2.89	2.67	2.52	2.39	2.30	2.22
	.99	6.85	4.79	3.95	3.48	3.17	2.96	2.79	2.66	2.56
	.995	8.18	5.54	4.50	3.92	3.55	3.28	3.09	2.93	2.81
	.999	11.4	7.32	5.78	4.95	4.42	4.04	3.77	3.55	3.38
∞	.025	0	.03	.07	.12	.17	.21	.24	.27	.30
	.05	0	.05	.12	.18	.23	.27	.31	.34	.40
	.90	2.71	2.30	2.08	1.94	1.85	1.77	1.72	1.67	1.63
	.95	3.84	3.00	2.60	2.37	2.21	2.10	2.01	1.94	1.88
	.975	5.02	3.69	3.12	2.79	2.57	2.41	2.29	2.19	2.11
	.99	6.63	4.61	3.78	3.32	3.02	2.80	2.64	2.51	2.41
	.995	7.88	5.30	4.28	3.72	3.35	3.09	2.90	2.74	2.62
	.999	10.8	6.91	5.42	4.62	4.10	3.74	3.47	3.27	3.10

df for denominator	Percentile	df for numerator 10	12	15	20	24	30	60	120	∞
20	.025	.29	.33	.36	.41	.43	.45	.52	.55	.58
	.05	.36	.39	.43	.47	.49	.52	.57	.60	.64
	.90	1.94	1.89	1.84	1.79	1.77	1.74	1.68	1.64	1.61
	.95	2.35	2.28	2.20	2.12	2.08	2.04	1.95	1.90	1.84
	.975	2.77	2.68	2.57	2.46	2.41	2.35	2.22	2.16	2.09
	.99	3.37	3.23	3.09	2.94	2.86	2.78	2.61	2.52	2.42
	.995	3.85	3.68	3.50	3.32	3.22	3.12	2.92	2.81	2.69
	.999	5.08	4.82	4.56	4.29	4.15	4.00	3.70	3.54	3.38
24	.025	.30	.33	.37	.41	.44	.47	.53	.57	.61
	.05	.36	.40	.44	.48	.50	.53	.59	.62	.66
	.90	1.88	1.83	1.78	1.73	1.70	1.67	1.61	1.57	1.53
	.95	2.25	2.18	2.11	2.03	1.98	1.94	1.84	1.79	1.73
	.975	2.64	2.54	2.44	2.33	2.27	2.21	2.08	2.01	1.94
	.99	3.17	3.03	2.89	2.74	2.66	2.58	2.40	2.31	2.21
	.995	3.59	3.42	3.25	3.06	2.97	2.87	2.66	2.55	2.43
	.999	4.64	4.39	4.14	3.87	3.74	3.59	3.29	3.14	2.97
30	.025	.30	.34	.38	.43	.45	.48	.55	.59	.64
	.05	.37	.40	.44	.49	.52	.54	.61	.65	.68
	.90	1.82	1.77	1.72	1.67	1.64	1.61	1.54	1.50	1.46
	.95	2.16	2.09	2.01	1.93	1.89	1.84	1.74	1.68	1.62
	.975	2.51	2.41	2.31	2.20	2.14	2.07	1.94	1.87	1.79
	.99	2.98	2.84	2.70	2.55	2.47	2.39	2.21	2.11	2.01
	.995	3.34	3.18	3.01	2.82	2.73	2.63	2.42	2.30	2.18
	.999	4.24	4.00	3.75	3.49	3.36	3.22	2.92	2.76	2.59
60	.025	.31	.35	.40	.45	.48	.52	.60	.65	.72
	.05	.38	.42	.46	.51	.54	.57	.65	.70	.76
	.90	1.71	1.66	1.60	1.54	1.51	1.48	1.40	1.35	1.29
	.95	1.99	1.92	1.84	1.75	1.70	1.65	1.53	1.47	1.39
	.975	2.27	2.17	2.06	1.94	1.88	1.82	1.67	1.58	1.48
	.99	2.63	2.50	2.35	2.20	2.12	2.03	1.84	1.73	1.60
	.995	2.90	2.74	2.57	2.39	2.29	2.19	1.96	1.83	1.69
	.999	3.54	3.32	3.08	2.83	2.69	2.55	2.25	2.08	1.89
120	.025	.32	.36	.41	.46	.50	.53	.63	.70	.79
	.05	.39	.43	.47	.53	.56	.60	.68	.74	.82
	.90	1.65	1.60	1.55	1.48	1.45	1.41	1.32	1.26	1.19
	.95	1.91	1.83	1.75	1.66	1.61	1.55	1.43	1.35	1.25
	.975	2.16	2.05	1.95	1.82	1.76	1.69	1.53	1.43	1.31
	.99	2.47	2.34	2.19	2.03	1.95	1.86	1.66	1.53	1.38
	.995	2.71	2.54	2.37	2.19	2.09	1.98	1.75	1.61	1.43
	.999	3.24	3.02	2.78	2.53	2.40	2.26	1.95	1.77	1.54
∞	.025	.32	.37	.42	.48	.52	.56	.68	.76	1.00
	.05	.39	.43	.48	.54	.58	.62	.72	.80	1.00
	.90	1.60	1.55	1.49	1.42	1.38	1.34	1.24	1.17	1.00
	.95	1.83	1.75	1.67	1.57	1.52	1.46	1.32	1.22	1.00
	.975	2.05	1.94	1.83	1.71	1.64	1.57	1.39	1.27	1.00
	.99	2.32	2.18	2.04	1.88	1.79	1.70	1.47	1.32	1.00
	.995	2.52	2.36	2.19	2.00	1.90	1.79	1.53	1.36	1.00
	.999	2.96	2.74	2.51	2.27	2.13	1.99	1.66	1.45	1.00

Source: Reprinted from Table 5 of Pearson and Hartley, *Biometrika Tables for Statisticians*, Volume 2, 1972, published by the Cambridge University Press, on behalf of The Biometrika Society, by permission of the authors and publishers.

8 APPENDIX Table of Studentized Range Values

Within df	Experiment-wise confidence level	2	3	4	5	6	7	8	9	10	11	12	13	14	15
1	.95	18.0	27.0	32.8	37.1	40.4	43.1	45.4	47.4	49.1	50.6	52.0	53.2	54.3	55.4
	.99	90.0	135	164	186	202	216	227	237	246	253	260	266	272	277
2	.95	6.09	8.3	9.8	10.9	11.7	12.4	13.0	13.5	14.0	14.4	14.7	15.1	15.4	15.7
	.99	14.0	19.0	22.3	24.7	26.6	28.2	29.5	30.7	31.7	32.6	33.4	34.1	34.8	35.4
3	.95	4.50	5.91	6.82	7.50	8.04	8.48	8.85	9.18	9.46	9.72	9.95	10.2	10.4	10.5
	.99	8.26	10.6	12.2	13.3	14.2	15.0	15.6	16.2	16.7	17.1	17.5	17.9	18.2	18.5
4	.95	3.93	5.04	5.76	6.29	6.71	7.05	7.35	7.60	7.83	8.03	8.21	8.37	8.52	8.66
	.99	6.51	8.12	9.17	9.96	10.6	11.1	11.5	11.9	12.3	12.6	12.8	13.1	13.3	13.5
5	.95	3.64	4.60	5.22	5.67	6.03	6.33	6.58	6.80	6.99	7.17	7.32	7.47	7.60	7.72
	.99	5.70	6.97	7.80	8.42	8.91	9.32	9.67	9.97	10.2	10.5	10.7	10.9	11.1	11.2
6	.95	3.46	4.34	4.90	5.31	5.63	5.89	6.12	6.32	6.49	6.65	6.79	6.92	7.03	7.14
	.99	5.24	6.33	7.03	7.56	7.97	8.32	8.61	8.87	9.10	9.30	9.49	9.65	9.81	9.95
7	.95	3.34	4.16	4.69	5.06	5.36	5.61	5.82	6.00	6.16	6.30	6.43	6.55	6.66	6.76
	.99	4.95	5.92	6.54	7.01	7.37	7.68	7.94	8.17	8.37	8.55	8.71	8.86	9.00	9.12
8	.95	3.26	4.04	4.53	4.89	5.17	5.40	5.60	5.77	5.92	6.05	6.18	6.29	6.39	6.48
	.99	4.74	5.63	6.20	6.63	6.96	7.24	7.47	7.68	7.87	8.03	8.18	8.31	8.44	8.55
9	.95	3.20	3.95	4.42	4.76	5.02	5.24	5.43	5.60	5.74	5.87	5.98	6.09	6.19	6.28
	.99	4.60	5.43	5.96	6.35	6.66	6.91	7.13	7.32	7.49	7.65	7.78	7.91	8.03	8.13
10	.95	3.15	3.88	4.33	4.65	4.91	5.12	5.30	5.46	5.60	5.72	5.83	5.93	6.03	6.11
	.99	4.48	5.27	5.77	6.14	6.43	6.67	6.87	7.05	7.21	7.36	7.48	7.60	7.71	7.81
11	.95	3.11	3.82	4.26	4.57	4.82	5.03	5.20	5.35	5.49	5.61	5.71	5.81	5.90	5.99
	.99	4.39	5.14	5.62	5.97	6.25	6.48	6.67	6.84	6.99	7.13	7.26	7.36	7.46	7.56
12	.95	3.08	3.77	4.20	4.51	4.75	4.95	5.12	5.27	5.40	5.51	5.62	5.71	5.80	5.88
	.99	4.32	5.04	5.50	5.84	6.10	6.32	6.51	6.67	6.81	6.94	7.06	7.17	7.26	7.36
13	.95	3.06	3.73	4.15	4.45	4.69	4.88	5.05	5.19	5.32	5.43	5.53	5.63	5.71	5.79
	.99	4.26	4.96	5.40	5.73	5.98	6.19	6.37	6.53	6.67	6.79	6.90	7.01	7.10	7.19
14	.95	3.03	3.70	4.11	4.41	4.64	4.83	4.99	5.13	5.25	5.36	5.46	5.55	6.64	5.72
	.99	4.21	4.89	5.32	5.63	5.88	6.08	6.26	6.41	6.54	6.66	6.77	6.87	6.96	7.05
16	.95	3.00	3.65	4.05	4.33	4.56	4.74	4.90	5.03	5.15	5.26	5.35	5.44	5.52	5.59
	.99	4.13	4.78	5.19	5.49	5.72	5.92	6.08	6.22	6.35	6.46	6.56	6.66	6.74	6.82
18	.95	2.97	3.61	4.00	4.28	4.49	4.67	4.82	4.96	5.07	5.17	5.27	5.35	5.43	5.50
	.99	4.07	4.70	5.09	5.38	5.60	5.79	5.94	6.08	6.20	6.31	6.41	6.50	6.58	6.65
20	.95	2.95	3.58	3.96	4.23	4.45	4.62	4.77	4.90	5.01	5.11	5.20	5.28	5.36	5.43
	.99	4.02	4.64	5.02	5.29	5.51	5.69	5.84	5.97	6.09	6.19	6.29	6.37	6.45	6.52
24	.95	2.92	3.53	3.90	4.17	4.37	4.54	4.68	4.81	4.92	5.01	5.10	5.18	5.25	5.32
	.99	3.96	4.54	4.91	5.17	5.37	5.54	5.69	5.81	5.92	6.02	6.11	6.19	6.26	6.33

Number of treatment levels

APPENDIX 8 Table of Studentized Range Values (*Continued*)

Within df	Experiment-wise confidence level	2	3	4	5	6	7	8	9	10	11	12	13	14	15
30	.95	2.89	3.49	3.84	4.10	4.30	4.46	4.60	4.72	4.83	4.92	5.00	5.08	5.15	5.21
	.99	3.89	4.45	4.80	5.05	5.24	5.40	5.54	5.56	5.76	5.85	5.93	6.01	6.08	6.14
40	.95	2.86	3.44	3.79	4.04	4.23	4.39	4.52	4.63	4.74	4.82	4.91	4.98	5.05	5.11
	.99	3.82	4.37	4.70	4.93	5.11	5.27	5.39	5.50	5.60	5.69	5.77	5.84	5.90	5.96
60	.95	2.83	3.40	3.74	3.98	4.16	4.31	4.44	4.55	4.65	4.73	4.81	4.88	4.94	5.00
	.99	3.76	4.28	4.60	4.82	4.99	5.13	5.25	5.36	5.45	5.53	5.60	5.67	5.73	5.79
120	.95	2.80	3.36	3.69	3.92	4.10	4.24	4.36	4.48	4.56	4.64	4.72	4.78	4.84	4.90
	.99	3.70	4.20	4.50	4.71	4.87	5.01	5.12	5.21	5.30	5.38	5.44	5.51	5.56	5.61
∞	.95	2.77	3.31	3.63	3.86	4.03	4.17	4.29	4.39	4.47	4.55	4.62	4.68	4.74	4.80
	.99	3.64	4.12	4.40	4.60	4.76	4.88	4.99	5.08	5.16	5.23	5.29	5.35	5.40	5.45

Number of treatment levels

Source: H. Harter, D. Clemm, and E. Guthrie. *The Probability Integrals of the Range and the Studentized Range* (Wright Air Development Center, 1959). Used with permission.

ANSWERS TO ODD-NUMBERED EXERCISES AND PROBLEMS

ANSWERS to Section Exercises

SECTION 1.1

1. a. H
   b. E
   c. O
   d. B
   e. E
   f. O
   g. O and E
   h. O

3. The fourth quarter always has the highest rate of return, averaging about 6.6%. The third quarter always has the smallest return rate, about 2.5%. The returns have ranged from 2.5% to 7%. Average return rate is approximately 4%.

SECTION 2.1

1. a. TO
   b. CS
   c. CS
   d. TO

3. One variable can signal that a problem exists. We must look for a cause (second variable).

SECTION 2.2

1. a. Overlapping classes, not exhaustive, unequal class widths
   b. Not exhaustive, unequal class widths
   c. Unequal class widths

3. a.
   5 | .23 .26 .30 .45 .49 .55 .65 .95 .95
   6 | .13 .20 .30 .30 .50 .65 .69 .70 .70 .72 .72 .74 .90
   7 | .00 .00 .00 .00 .15 .15 .20 .20

   b. 5.00–5.49   5
      5.50–5.99   4
      6.00–6.49   4
      6.50–6.99   9
      7.00–7.49   8

5. a.
Cum. Freq.	Cum. %
0	0
6	25
16	66.7
21	87.5
23	95.8
24	100

   b. Most of the time expect fewer than 9 accidents per month
   c. Might signal disturbance problem

SECTION 2.3

1. What was different this time?
3. Yes; no

5. Skewed toward higher values

B-1

SECTION 2.4

1. Has a constant mean over time
3. Upward trend
5. Nonstationary
7. a. Nonstationary
   b. S-shaped
   c. About 10 years
   d. 1981; conservation, high energy costs

SECTION 2.5

1. 2 minutes, 1 (minute)^2, 1 minute
3. a. Increase mean, no change in standard deviation
   b. Doubles mean and doubles standard deviation
5. Same mean; bank B has greater standard deviation because 40 of 50 loans in classes far from the mean.
7. .3; .46

SECTION 2.6

1. a. 2.9
   b. 3.2, 1.79
   c. Six
   d. Ten
3. Skewed: At least 75% of data between 80 and 120; at least 89% of data between 70 and 130.
   Bell-shaped: 68% of data between 90 and 110; 95% of data between 80 and 120; all data between 70 and 130.
5. a. 16%
   b. 97.5%
   c. 2.5%
7. Use Chebyshev's rule since data may not be normal.

SECTION 2.7

1. a. 35, 29, 40.5, 11.5
   b. 36.47, 34.91
   c. Trimmed mean closer to median; mean is larger.

3.
Freq.	%	Cum. Freq.	Cum. %
2	16.7	2	16.7
5	41.7	7	58.3
3	25.0	10	83.3
2	16.7	12	100

   Close to 3;
   3

5. a. 50th
   b. 25th
   c. 75th

SECTION 2.8

1. a. Skewed to right
   b. No outliers
3. a: Visualize important features of data
   b. 4, 2.5, 5.5, 3
   c. Salesman 6; determine root causes
5. Yes; no spread in 50% of middle values of ranked data

SECTION 2.9

1. 5, 6, 7, 8.67, 11.67, 15, 13.67, 13.33, 12.67, 16.67
3. 0, 1, −1, −.67, .33, 0, 4.33, −5.33, 1.33, −.67
5. Steady increase.
   Residuals for period 5–6 may be outliers.

SECTION 3.1

1. Diagnosis looks for causes—requires a second variable
3. Look for changes or differences.

SECTION 3.2

1. a. Q
   b. Q
   c. C
   d. C
   e. C
   f. Q
   g. C
   h. C
3. None

SECTION 3.3

1. a. Men: Sample size 11, mean = 3.18, SD = 2.60;
      Women: Sample size 9, mean = 3.67, SD = 3.57
   b. Men: Median = 3, IQR = 2.5;
      Women: Median = 2, IQR = 2.0
3. b. Property agents older than life agents
5. Previous performance rating, salary, four levels

SECTION 3.4

1.
	Managers	Nonmanagers
Yes	15	15
No	15	35

3. a. 30%
   b. 50%
   c. 70%
   d. 48%
   e. Yes

5. a.
	Debt	No Debt
Above median	6	6
Median or below	8	4

b. Yes
c. Sample is small. Another sample might yield different conclusion.

7.
	Pro	Con	No Opinion
D	12	12	6
R	12	12	6
I	16	16	8

9.
	Pro	Con	No Opinion
D	10	10	10
R	20	5	5
I	10	25	5

SECTION 3.5

1. a. Salaries nonlinearly related to sales
   b. No relationship
   c. Two different nonlinear relationships
3. Positively linearly related
5. Yes. Note that data points vary from line. Other variables affect GPA.
7. Percentage returns rapidly increase up to $4, then level off.

SECTION 3.6

1. a. No relationship
   b. C this month related to Y next month
   c. Reordered data show relationship
3. Scatter diagram—a period's X and Y values. Lagged diagram—a period's Y value and an X value from one or more earlier periods.
5. Changes in R&D will positively affect sales 9 months later.

SECTION 3.7

1. Variance measures variability in one data set. Covariance measures the relationship between two variables (diagnosis).
3. a. x: mean = 4, SD = 2.58; y: mean = 11, SD = 5.16
   b. 13.33
   c. 1
   d. All data points lie on straight upward sloping line.
5. .205   .854   .005
7. a. Points swarm upward to right
   b. Points swarm downward to right
   c. Totally scattered

SECTION 4.2

1. a. No, no uncertainty
   b. Yes
   c. No, nothing measured
   d. No, not a repeatable action
   e. Yes
   f. Yes
3. a. No, nothing counted
   b. Yes, action repeatable
   c. {1, 2, 3}
5. a. .10
   b. .12
   c. Relative frequency only approximates the true probability.
7. Probabilities can't sum to more than 1.
9. a. Simple
   b. {0, 2, 3, 4, 5}

SECTION 4.3

1. a.

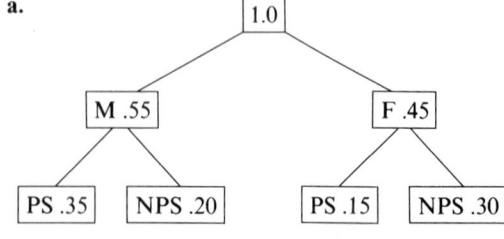

```
           [1.0]
           /    \
       [M .55]  [F .45]
        /  \     /  \
  [PS .35][NPS .20][PS .15][NPS .30]
```

   b. .55, .45

3.
	Male	Female
PS	.35	.15
Not PS	.20	.30

5. a.
	Promoted	Not Promoted
B or better	.10	.70
Less than B	.15	.05

b. .25

7. **a.**

	<2	2–5	>5
Club member	.04	.06	.10
Not member	.20	.40	.20

   b. .20, .20, .04

9. Tree diagram:
   - 1.0
     - LM .361
       - P .083
       - A .278
     - HM .639
       - P .417
       - A .222

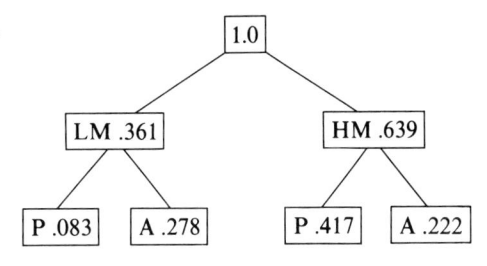

SECTION 4.4

1. **a.** .85
   b. .30

3. Tree diagram:
   - 1.0
     - C .50
       - D .20
       - ND .30
     - NC .50
       - D .50
       - ND 0

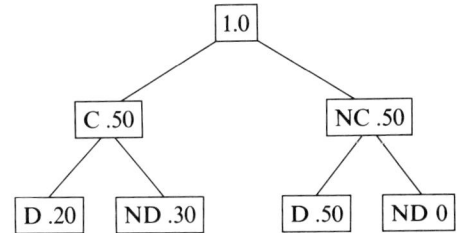

   b. .50
   c. 0
   d. 1.0

SECTION 4.5

1. Knowledge that one event has occurred has no effect on the probability that the other will occur.
3. **a.** Conditional
   b. Joint
   c. Simple
5. Equal to, events are independent

SECTION 4.6

1. **a.** Joint
   b. Conditional
   c. Conditional
   d. Joint

3. **a.** .20
   b. .60
   c. Independent

   d.

	≤5%	>5%
≤75	.32	.08
>75	.48	.12

5. **a.** .40
   b. .40
   c. Yes

SECTION 4.7

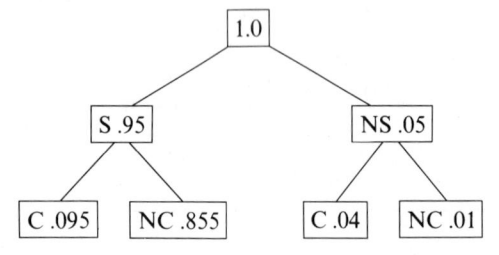

1. a. .04
    b. .855
    c.
    ```
                      1.0
                  /         \
              S .95         NS .05
             /    \         /    \
         C .095  NC .855  C .04  NC .01
    ```
    d. .296

    b. Manager 2
    c. Manager 1—statistically independent

5. a.

	Win	Lose
≥ 60	.63	.07
< 60	.02	.28

    Coherent probabilities
    b. .93

3. a.

	Manager 1 A	Manager 1 Not A	Manager 2 A	Manager 2 Not A	Manager 3 A	Manager 3 Not A
B	.24	.16	.7	−.4	0	.5
Not B	.36	.24	.1	.6	.3	.2

SECTION 4.8

1. Availability error
3. Availability error

SECTION 4.9

1. a. Relative frequency
    b. Personal
    c. Personal

SECTION 5.2

1. a. Discrete random variable, $\{0, 1, 2, \ldots, 100\}$
    b. Not a random variable; for x tickets, $Y = 6x$
3. Probability distribution consists of a random variable (outcomes) and a rule for assigning probabilities to values of the random variable.
5. $\mu = 1.5$, SD $= 1.02$. μ is the long-run average.

7. a.

x	$P(X \leq x)$
1	.45
2	.70
3	.85
4	.95
5	1.00

    b. .85
    c. .05
9. a. $\mu = .87$, SD $= 1.13$
    b. The distribution is skewed to the right.

SECTION 5.3

1.
	Success	Failure
a.	Worker present	Worker not present
b.	American-made	Foreign-made
c.	Loan default	Loan paid
d.	Parcel valued above $100,000	Parcel valued at or below $100,000

3. a. X = number of times wildcatter strikes oil in 10 wells
   b. .3487
   c. .2511
   d. Number of wells drilled divided by the number of times oil was found

5. a. .2508
   b. .0001
   c. .0123
   d. .8337
   e. $\mu = 4$ loans, SD = 1.55 loans. Ten loans is more than 3 standard deviations from μ—a rare happening.

7. $\mu = 3.5$ claims, SD = 1.02 claims

9. $P(3$ or more defectives if $p = .10) = .0702$
   $P(3$ or more defectives if $p = .30) = .6172$
   More likely that proportion defective is .30.

SECTION 5.4

1. .0001; demand for deluxe phone has decreased.
3. Joel will reject 22.62% of the lots.
5. a. .2641, producer's risk
   b. .3918, consumer's risk
   c. As sample size increases, producer's risk increases and consumer's risk decreases.
7. Do not use binomial model. The probability does not remain constant over trials.

SECTION 5.5

1. A fixed length of time or area of space over which something will be counted in integers
3. a. .130
   b. .603
   c. $\mu = 3.2$, SD = 1.79
   d. Count number of people in 50 cars. Divide the total by 50 to get the mean number of persons per car.
5. a. .567, .908
   b. Low probability (.092) of one or fewer accidents. But only one accident happened. Workshop has worked.
7. $\mu = 9$ employees; .015

SECTION 5.6

1. When measurement of variable is affected by many chance factors
3. a. .6826
   b. .9802
   c. .9902
   d. .95
   e. .9974
   f. .0013
   g. .9987
   h. .1044
   i. .3239
   j. 0
5. a. .9772
   b. .0228
   c. .9974
   d. .0013
   e. .0215
7. a. 61.65
   b. 57
   c. 2.28%
9. a. .1587
   b. .0228
   c. $\mu = 5.51$ ounces
   d. $P(\text{overflow}) = .0000$
      Yes, very small probability of cup overflowing. Either mean greater than 5 ounces or standard deviation larger than .25 ounce or both.

SECTION 5.7

1. Ten possible samples. Sample means are 3.5, 4.0, 4.5, 5.5, 4.5, 5.0, 6.0, 5.5, 6.5, 7.0
3. The sampling distribution of the sample mean peaks as the sample size increases. The spread of the distribution of the sample means also shrinks as the sample size increases.

SECTION 6.2

1. The percentage of the population that favors brand X is somewhere between 35% and 45%.
3. The margin of error must increase.

5. a.
Samples	Means
2, 4	3
2, 6	4
2, 8	5
2, 10	6
4, 6	5
4, 8	6
4, 10	7
6, 8	7
6, 10	8
8, 10	9

   b. Since the population mean is 6, the maximum margin of error is 3.

   c.
Sample	Means
2, 4, 6, 8	5
2, 4, 6, 10	5.5
2, 4, 8, 10	6
2, 6, 8, 10	6.5
4, 6, 8, 10	7

   d. The maximum margin of error is 1.
   e. When the sample size increases the maximum margin of error decreases.

7. a. 38.3%
   b. 68.26%
   c. The confidence levels have declined because the standard deviation has doubled from 2 cm. to 4 cm.

SECTION 6.3

1. The target population is the set of elements of interest. The sampling frame is the physical list of elements or sampling units that will actually be sampled.
3. Street address
5. The frame could be the list of 100 branch offices. Once a sampling unit is selected, then the survey elements, the employees, can be sampled.

SECTION 6.4

1. See text.
3. No. Stratified sampling is a survey *design*. Survey *methods* include personal interview, telephone interview, and mailed questionnaires.
5. Response error arises because the respondent did not understand the question, did not have the information, or did not answer truthfully. Nonresponse error occurs when the element cannot be located or refuses to answer.
7. People who live on the first floor are likely to be older because older people have trouble climbing the stairs. Therefore, the study results could overrepresent the characteristics of older people.
9. Selection errors: (1) The target population is not represented by the frame. Spanish-speaking people in Miami are mostly Cuban-Americans, whereas those in western states are mostly Mexican-Americans. (2) Some people do not have phones, may have unlisted numbers, or may simply not be listed in the latest version of the telephone directory.

   Must use same diction and voice inflection. Also problem of common understanding of survey wording.

   New immigrants may be suspicious of telephone survey.

SECTION 6.5

1. 480 429 368 475 365
   11 130 119 162 167

3. Ineligible units cause a problem because the resulting sample will be smaller than desired since ineligibles are discarded.

Duplicate sampling units cause a problem because the duplicates have a higher chance of selection. This situation could cause the service organization to look worse than if all customers were weighted equally.

SECTION 6.6

1. (1) The variation of the measurement of interest within each stratum is smaller than the variance among the strata. (2) An estimate is needed for each stratum (factory, regional office) as well as an estimate for the target population.

3. Proportional allocation considers only the size of each stratum in allocating the total sample. Use when stratum variances similar and sampling cost per stratum similar.

5. Stratified sampling would result in no reduction in the margin of error over simple random sampling unless it is cheaper to survey an item under the stratified plan than the simple random sampling plan.

7. You don't have to know the population size and you don't have to carry around a table of random numbers. "Interview every 10th person walking through the door" is a simple direction for field personnel to follow.

9. Unless the measurement of interest is related to the name of the employee, the population (frame) is random.

11. Small businesses and professional corporations frequently have their home residences listed after the office numbers. This income group would have a greater chance of selection if the next number is selected. The correct procedure is to skip businesses and professional numbers and select the next kth number.

13. If the opinions of white- and blue-collar workers are expected to be similar within any factory, but expected to vary by factory, a stratified sampling plan would be considered and each factory would be sampled. If the opinions are expected to differ by type of worker but not by factory, then one or two factories can be sampled with a large number of workers sampled from each factory.

SECTION 6.7

1. a. Personal interview
   b. Personal interview
3. Combination of personal interview and telephone
5. The interviewer's facial expressions, etc., affect the answers given. You can determine if survey has the interviewer-bias problem by reinterviewing the same respondents using different interviewers and comparing the results.

SECTION 6.8

1. a. Since respondents have a tendency to compress time (think of the past six weeks as the past month), they may overstate the number of times they visited a shopping mall in the past month.
   b. Personal and potentially embarrassing question
   c. The words "caloric" and "polyunsaturates" may not be familiar to all respondents.
   d. The words "you" and "service" could be ambiguous.
   e. Double question
   f. Ambiguous question. What does "frequent user" mean?
   g. Biased question. People will say they shop at all "upscale" stores, even listing stores that don't exist!

3. For aided-recall form: Pro—Consumer may have considered many other brands but just can't think of the names. Con—Consumer may have considered only the one he or she bought, but doesn't want to be considered a poor shopper and might say he or she looked at all brands.

SECTION 6.9

1. Nothing is changed or manipulated, and there is no random assignment of experimental units to treatments in an observational study. Data are simply collected.
3. A properly conducted experiment seeks to show that a factor caused the observed changes in the dependent variable by (1) equalizing experimental units through randomization and (2) controlling for other variables that might affect the dependent variable.
5. Randomization *tends* to equalize groups of experimental units on *all* possible factors.
7. a. Despite the random selection, this is not an experiment. The employees were not assigned, they were merely classified.
   b. Other explanations are possible. People who are employed longer usually make more money and have managerial positions. A managerial position may have better working conditions than a nonmanagerial position.

SECTION 6.10

1. A small variation in a factor is unlikely to produce noticeable effects on the dependent variable. Vary the factor enough so the dependent variable has a chance to reflect the change.
3. Random error is the variation within a treatment caused by all the other variables not considered in the study. Randomization does *not* reduce random error, but tends to equalize it within each treatment.
5. Inconclusive. If accidents go down during selective enforcement, the difference could simply be due to differences in the weather or road construction during the two periods. Consider a control group. Randomly assign high-accident locations to two groups. Put selective enforcement in one and not in the other. Compare the changes before and after for the two groups.

SECTION 7.1

1. A statistic is calculated from a sample. Statistics vary from sample to sample. A population parameter is a fixed, but unknown, value of a population.
3. a. All members of general public who might use product
   b. Proportion of target population who prefer brand A
   c. .40
5. Desired level of confidence, population variability, the sample size, and the sample design
7. a. Two target populations—number of claims processed per day under old method and under small groups
   b. Long-run mean numbers of claims under each method
   c. The mean numbers of claims processed per day during sample period under each method

SECTION 7.2

1. a. 4
   b. 1.63
   c. 4
   d. 1.15
   e. $\mu = \mu_{\bar{x}}$
   f. $1.63/\sqrt{2} = 1.15$
3. $\mu \quad\quad \sigma$
   $\mu_{\bar{x}} \quad\quad \sigma_{\bar{x}}$
   $\bar{x} \quad\quad s$
5. normal shape, $\mu_{\bar{x}} = 50.0$ cm., $\sigma_{\bar{x}} = .083$ cm.
7. a. .1587
   b. .4013
   c. .1336

Answers to Section Exercises

SECTION 7.3

1. Probability sample, population distribution is normal or sample size large enough so that sampling distribution of the sample mean is normal, and parameter of interest is fixed (nonstationary time series data not appropriate).
3. Sample size large enough so that t value equals z value.
   a. (41.51, 48.49)
   b. (40.84, 49.16)
   c. (39.54, 50.46)
5. a. 4, 2.12
   b. Use 2.12 to estimate σ
   c. (2.69, 5.31)
   d. Simple random sample, population is normal
7. a. 2,000 hours, 7.5 hours
   b. 95% of all intervals will contain the mean of the population.
   c. No, the CI does not contain 2,000 hours.
9. a. All cigarettes that have been or will be produced by the manufacturer.
   b. The mean nicotine level per cigarette
   c. Simple random sample and normal population of nicotine measurements
   d. (.494, .506)

SECTION 7.4

1. a. (11.42, 18.58)
   b. At most 17.90
   c. At least 12.81
3. a. No, bank loans cannot take on negative values.
   b. Use the Central Limit Theorem.
   c. $28.46, $24.66 (with fpc)
   d. ($601.67, $698.33)
   e. $609.43
   f. $707.36
5. $682.30

SECTION 7.5

1. a. Null and alternative hypotheses should be expressed in terms of population means, not sample means.
   b. Not exclusive and exhaustive
   c. Valid
3. $H_0: \mu = \$3,500$ per month
   $H_1: \mu \neq \$3,500$ per month
5. Since $\bar{x} = 2.8 <$ critical value $= 2.822$, fail to reject null; new advertising no better than old advertising approach.
7. Since $\bar{x} = 173 >$ critical value $= 168.02$ feet, fail to reject null; stay with present brake system.
9. a. Type I error
   b. Type II error
   c. Small level of significance
   d. No, failing to reject null does not prove that null is true.
11. Reject null
13. No; must sample the entire population.

SECTION 7.6

1. Variance between strata is greater than variance within a stratum, or want CI for each stratum.
3. (45.27 hours, 45.71 hours)

SECTION 7.7

1. No, according to Cochran's table—sample size too small.
3. a. .112
   b. yes
5. a. (.21, .36)
   b. No, only those in sampling frame

SECTION 7.8

1. Variance of population, sampling design, level of confidence, and acceptable margin of error
3. 2,402

SECTION 7.9

1. Population highly skewed and sample size less than 30
3. a. 6
   b. $n = 10$
   c. (4, 8)
   d. Interval too wide to be of practical value
5. (5.1%, 7.7%)

SECTION 7.10

1. a. z, t, chi-square
   b. t and chi-square
   c. z and t
   d. Chi-square
   e. z and t
   f. z
   g. Chi-square
3. (3.38, 9.58)
5. a. (.057, .113)
   b. (.047, .175)
   c. Not safe to use

SECTION 8.2

1. Shape: Normal, nonnormal, skewed;
   Center: Mean, median;
   Spread: Standard deviation, interquartile range
3. Neither transformation can be used because of negative numbers or the value of zero.
5. a. Sample suggests skewed population.
   b. Log transform slightly better at eliminating outliers and normalizing the data than square root transform.

SECTION 8.3

1. Check for highly asymmetric population.
3. Population variances are equal.
5. a. 29.3
   b. 18 df
   c. SE = 2.5
   d. (−1.3, 9.3)
   e. Zero in CI; cannot conclude there is a difference.
   f. Population is normal, simple random sample, population variances are equal
7. a. (1.4 hours, 10.6 hours)
   b. 95% confident that Company 2's transistors last from 1.4 to 10.6 hours longer.
9. (−.9, 1.3); since zero in CI, Anderson is treating its toxic waste.

SECTION 8.4

1. (−.069, .269); cannot detect any difference.
3. a. Long-term cure rates of those given the drug
   b. (−.05, .21); cannot detect any difference since 0 in interval.
5. (.068, .086); 90% confident that proportion of whites employed exceeds blacks by 6.8% to 8.6%.

SECTION 8.5

1. Populations skewed and sample sizes are small.
3. a. Median-new: 64.5; Median-current: 72.5; 80.6% are positive, suggesting a difference between population medians
   b. Lower bound $= -2$, upper bound $= 15$; cannot conclude there is a difference between population medians.
5. a. Each sample should be normal and have the same variance.
   b. Samples should be highly skewed.

SECTION 8.6

1. a. 2.98
   b. .21
   c. 2.74
3. a. (.82, 11.96)
   b. Since 1 is in the interval, cannot detect a difference.
5. (.60, 15.19); CI includes 1, so cannot detect a difference.
7. No, both populations are not normally distributed.

SECTION 8.7

1. Populations are not normally distributed, samples independent, and the population medians are (nearly) equal.
3. a. Median-Clouds: 20.95; Median-Springs: 20.70
   b. M-calculated $= 462.5$; cannot detect a difference.
   c. (.59, 10.38); cannot detect a difference since 1 in interval.
5. M-calculated $= 59.25$; cannot detect a difference between dispersions of two stocks.

SECTION 9.1

1. A control group does not receive a treatment and serves as a basis for comparison with those groups that did receive a treatment.
3. Diagnosis means knowing what is distinctive about a problem or what has changed. Knowing the "IS" and "IS NOTS" is essential for determining distinctiveness or changes.
5. Experimentation tests potential problem causes.
7. Some changes must have occurred that triggered the problem.

SECTION 9.2

1. b. No. Spread between group means is large, spread within groups is small.
   c. Point-of-purchase promotion
3. b. No. Spread between group means is small, spread within groups is large.
5.
T1	T2	T3	T4
1	1	3	1
2	2	2	2
3	2	1	3
2	3	2	1

7.
T1	T2	T3	T4
0	6	7	9
2	2	3	2
4	4	3	8
3	7	7	4

SECTION 9.3

1. Variance equals sum of squares divided by degrees of freedom.
3. a. (19, 16, 3)
   b. (29, 27, 2)
   c. (1, 0, 1)
   d. At least 2 observations per treatment
5. a. 5.67; 3, 4, 10
   b. 110
   c. 86, 24
   d. 8, 2, 6

   e.
Source of Variation	Sum of Squares	df	Variance	Variance Ratio
Between	86	2	43	10.75
Within	24	6	4	
Total	110	8		

   f. $VR = 10.75 > F(2, 6, .95) = 5.14$, reject null.
7. $VR = 18.20 > F(2, 12, .90) = 2.81$, reject null.

9. a. No, no random assignment
   b. Null: Both charge same mean price; Alternative: Mean prices are different.
   c. Prices at each type of store normally distributed and have the same variance.
   d. $VR = 8.04 < F(1, 6, .99) = 13.7$, fail to reject null.
11. a. No, nothing changed
    b. Null: Population mean scores the same; Alternative: Not all population mean scores the same.
    c. Ranks will probably be normally distributed for midrange candidates.

    d.
Source of Variation	Sum of Squares	df	Variance	Variance Ratio
Between	41.46	3	13.82	7.76
Within	35.50	20	1.78	
Total	76.96	23		

    $VR = 7.76 > F(3, 20, .95) = 3.10$, reject null.

SECTION 9.4

1. Alternative hypothesis is that not all population means are the same. Don't know which means are different.
3. Increases the CI width, which maintains the probability of a Type I error over all pairwise comparisons.
5. Detailed write-up and call-back better than control. Cannot detect difference between detailed write-up and call-back.
7. Role better than case and lecture. Cannot detect difference between case and lecture.
9. Wider intervals make it more difficult to find a difference between population means.

SECTION 9.5

1. To compare three or more locations of distributions, and populations not normally distributed or variances unequal.
3. a. All samples have outliers.
   b. Null: All population medians the same; Alternative: Not all population medians the same.

   $H = 9.18 >$ chi-square $(2, .90) = 4.61$, reject null.
   c. Medians for populations 2 and 3 are different; no other differences
5. $H = .04 <$ chi-square $(2, .95)$, fail to reject null.

SECTION 9.6

1. 2 independent variables, 2 levels each; yes, but not discussed in this chapter
3. Row means and column means
5. a. 253, 105, 1.5
   b. $VR = 1.5 < F(1, 16, .95)$, no interaction
   c. $VR = 253 > F(1, 16, .95)$, difference in population means of promotions

d. VR = 105 > $F(1, 16, .95)$, difference in population means of incomes
7. **a.** Crossed profiles suggest an interaction.
   b. No, discovery learning better for higher-SAT students; lecture better for lower-SAT students.
9.

Source of Variation	Sum of Squares	Degrees of Freedom	Variance	Variance Ratio
Factor A	170	2	85	6.44
Factor B	450	1	450	34.09
AB interaction	14	2	7	.53
Within	316	24	13.2	
Total	950	29		

a. 3 levels
b. 5 observations per cell
c. No VR < 1
d. VR = 6.44 > $F(2, 24, .95)$, some difference in population means for A
e. VR = 34.09 > $F(1, 24, .95)$, difference in population means for B

SECTION 10.2

1. **a.** Job performance
   b. Age, salary, years on job
   c. Worker
   d. Data on each worker
   e. Correlational
   f. Cross-sectional
3. **a.** Percent rejected
   b. Amount of filler
   c. Cabinet
   d. Data on each cabinet
   e. Experimental
5. **a.** GPA
   b. Math SAT, study hours
   c. Accounting requires basic math skills. The amount of study hours generally affects performance.
7. What is the maximum range of production runs that we can actually run? How old are the newest and oldest machines in production? We have "pulled apart" if answers are 333 units to 1,000 units, and 1 to 5 years.

SECTION 10.3

1. **b.** Yes
   c. Have not done formal statistical analysis
3. **b.** Both variables linearly related to SALES
5. **a.** Positive relationship
   b. Two distinct clusters
   Married doctors have more insurance than single doctors with the same income.

SECTION 10.4

1. SALARY-PRED = 8.43 + 1.015PROD
   As PROD increases by 1, SALARY-PRED increases by 1.015 (or $1,015)
3. For men:
   SALARY-PRED = 1,974.63 + 45.95MONTHS
   For women:
   SALARY-PRED = 1,902.47 + 13.16MONTHS
   Slopes different; men's salaries appear to increase faster.
5. STOCK-PRED = 1.13 + .56NYSE
   Half as volatile as the market
7. **a.** Motivation means: 3.75, 7.50
   Skill means: 4.00, 7.25
   Multivariate means 2.0, 5.5, 6.0, 9.00
   b. PERF-PRED = −1.208 + .05417SKILL + .075MOTIV
   c. Predicted = 9.126 vs. 9.0 actual; difference due to all other variables that affect performance.

SECTION 10.5

1. a. 4
   b. 40
   c. 2.61
3. .311
   Yes; predictor variables account for only 31% of Y's variation.
5. Null: None of variables linearly related to creditworthiness;
   Alternative: At least one predictor variable linearly related.
7. a. Females; VR = 22.6, $p < .01$;
      Males; VR = 46.5, $p < .01$

   b. .764: Almost 77% of variation in salaries accounted for by months on job;
      .869: Almost 87% of variation in salaries accounted for by months on job
9. a. SALES-PRED = $-2.16 + .28$DISPOS
   b. VR = 758.71; yes
   c. Only one predictor variable. ANOVA and t-test should reach same conclusion.
   d. 98.7% of variation in sales is associated with variation in disposable income.

SECTION 10.6

1. No, unless variables in equation are correlated with "true" causal variables.
3. Is histogram of standardized residuals normal-shaped?
5. a. Yes; no curvilinear pattern or expanding pattern of residuals
   b. Histogram of standardized residuals not normal
   c. No, usually a problem for time-ordered data

SECTION 10.7

1. a. (3.41, 6.39)
   b. (4.50, 5.30)
   c. Prediction intervals set ranges for individuals. Confidence intervals set ranges on mean performance for all employees.
3. a. ($2,045.58, $2,443.90)
   b. ($2,181.70, $2,307.78)
   c. Beyond range of sample
5. a. ($1,988.32, $2,185.22);
      width of interval: $196.90
   b. ($2,181.70, $2,307.78); width of interval: $126.08
   c. ($2,315.40, $2,542.68); width of interval: $227.28
   d. Narrowest and therefore most meaningful interval at center of range of MONTHS data. Making predictions far from the center of the data produces wide prediction or confidence intervals.

SECTION 10.8

1. (i) TYPE = 1 if mutual, TYPE = 0 if stock;
   (ii) TYPE = 1 if stock, TYPE = 0 if mutual
3. $t = -.094$, $p > .05$. The relationship between number of innovations and asset size is the same for mutual and stock companies.
5. Answers vary.
7. (i) APPR = 1 if concentration approach, APPR = 0 if multisegment;
   (ii) APPR = 1 if multisegment approach, APPR = 0 if concentration
9. SALES-PRED = $b_0 + b_1$FEET $+ b_2$COMM $+ b_3$FEET $\times$ COMM
   Sales grow faster as square feet increases in departments that are on commission vs. those that are not on commission.

SECTION 10.9

1. a. All data values on straight line upward sloping to the right.
   b. Data values scattered about a line upward sloping to the right.
   c. Data values totally scattered.
   d. Data values scattered about a line downward sloping to the right.
   e. All data values on a straight line downward sloping to the right.
3. a. No multicollinearity
   c. Y-PRED = 1.97 + .526x1 + .792x2
      Y-PRED = 4.32 + .769x1
      Y-PRED = 3.50   + .929x2
   d. Lack of multicollinearity
   e. corr(x1, x2) = .28 vs. corr(Y, x1) = .66 and corr(Y, x2) = .87
5. No, multicollinearity is present when predictor variables are related.
7. No. We cannot control the values of the predictor variable—out of our control. We only record the data.

SECTION 10.10

1. a. 4
   b. $p \gg .10$
   c. Would not reject null
3. a. Income ($\leq 50{,}000$ and $> 50{,}000$); ownership of 1 or more partnerships (yes and no)
   b.
	No	Yes
$\leq 50{,}000$	200	200
$> 50{,}000$	200	400

   c. 50%
   d. 66.7%
5. Chi-square calculated = 125.00, reject null
7. Chi-square calculated = 17.43, reject null
9. Chi-square calculated = 199.55, reject null

SECTION 11.2

1. Continuity. Must verify that patterns and relationships that held in the past will continue in the future.
3. Quantitative forecasting methods require the existence of reliable and relevant historical data. Qualitative methods are used when reliable historical data are not available.
5. With the destruction of the Berlin Wall and the democratization of Eastern Europe, tourism should dramatically increase over the next several years.

SECTION 11.3

1. c. Positively autocorrelated
   d. 12.26 + .984SALES-1
   e. 3%. Since the MAPE is quite low, managers would probably use the autoregressive model.
   f. 241.69
3. c. Negatively autocorrelated
   d. 61.49 − .827INVEN-1
   e. 29.0%. Since the MAPE is quite high, managers might be reluctant to use the autoregressive model.
   f. 16.03 units (160 car phones)
5. c. Positively autocorrelated
   d. Slight positive relationship, one outlier
   e. 10.701 + .904SALES-1 + .101HS-2
   f. Yes
   g. No
   h. 1%
   i. 622.61
7. a. Tend to be either always positive or always negative
   b. Yes; successive differences tend to be negative.
9. Tend to alternate between positive and negative changes.

SECTION 11.4

1. 8, 11.25, 14.75, 17.75, 21.25;
   9.625, 13, 16.25, 19.5
3. No stable seasonal pattern
5. 90.9, 133.3, 116.7, 187.5
7. 1.2, 1.11, 1.13, 1.02, .98, .92, .97, 1.00, 1.05, 1.07, 1.06, 1.04

9. a. Yes—trend and seasonal pattern
   b. Quadratic curve slightly better than linear curve
   c. 35.48, 54.62, 52.46, 46.64

SECTION 11.5

1. The nominal group technique is superior because all ideas are given a chance to be heard. Ideas are evaluated based on merit, not on status of group members.
3. No. Many factors affect percentage and experts will disagree.
5. Avoids selective perception of an issue; makes it more difficult to reach consensus.

SECTION 12.2

1. Seek new methods, better worker and supervisor training, and technology to improve performance and reliability.
3. Both products conform to engineering and marketing requirements.

SECTION 12.3

1. Under control: no systematic pattern;
   Not under control: trend or cycle pattern
3. a. Only random variation
   b. 2,072.4 hours is far away from target of 2,000 hours
   c. No
   d. Process that is not centered
5. a. LNTL = 2,500 psi, UNTL = 3,100 psi
   b. 1.33
   c. No
   d. LCL = 2,702.5 psi, UCL = 2,897.5 psi
   e. LCL = 28.4 psi, UCL = 171.6 psi
7. a. 3.33
   b. Yes; LNTL = 47 seconds, UNTL = 53 seconds
   c. 3.33
   d. No; LNTL = 57 seconds, UNTL = 63 seconds
   e. Noncentered processes will produce many nonconforming parts.
9. a. 57.80 seconds, 12.60 seconds
   b. LCL = 39.82 seconds, UCL = 75.78 seconds; subgroup 16 below LCL
   c. Look for assignable causes.
   d. LCL = 41.59 seconds, UCL = 77.83 seconds
   e. Yes
11. Chance variation: when sample statistics vary within 3-sigma limits;
    Assignable variation: when sample statistics vary outside 3-sigma limits (or vary as per Western Electric rules)
13. $\frac{2}{9}$; better machines, materials, methods, supervision, training may reduce "natural variability."
15. About 32% of time an $\bar{x}$ would fall outside of limits even if process were under control. Bad: Will look for assignable cause variation when only random variation present—wild goose chase. Good: May detect an out-of-control process sooner than with 3-sigma rule.

SECTION 12.4

1. A: Use $\bar{x}$ and s control chart;
   B: Use p control chart
3. Centerline = .039, LCL = 0, UCL = .097
5. 196 per subgroup
7. As n varies, so do the LCL and UCL limits.

SECTION 12.5

1. Teachers: Poor preparation, poor teaching;
   Students: Low math ability, not prepared;
   Exam: At 8:00 A.M., very difficult
3. What is problem? When did it start? How often does it happen? Where does the problem happen? On all CDs?
5. Gets at root causes—premature until problem understood.

SECTION 12.6

1. a. 80
   b. Accept lot if 2 or fewer defects; otherwise reject
   c. Reject
3. Acceptance sampling cannot ensure a steady stream of good raw material.
5. Acceptance sampling stops lots with high percent defectives from entering plant. Vendor certification increases chances that vendors ship lots with little or no defectives.

ANSWERS to Application Problems

CHAPTER 2

1. **a.** Machos (000)
   ```
   20 | 0
   21 | 0  .5
   22 | 0  0  .5  .5
   23 | 0  .5  .75
   ```
   Status Seekers (000)
   ```
   27 | .5  .5
   28 | 0  0  0  0  .5  .5
   29 | 0  0
   ```
   b. No outliers, use mean and standard deviation.
   Machos: $22,175, $1,142.91
   Status Seekers: $28,200, $ 537.48
   c. Status Seekers have higher mean incomes but less variability.

3. **a.** 2.5%
   b. 2.5%
   c. Staffing okay
   d.
   ```
   <10              80
   10.00–14.99      10
   15.00–19.99      10
   20.00–24.99      20
   25.00–29.99      10
   >30              70
   ```

5. **a.** Box plot
   b. Outliers; use first quartile, median, third quartile, and interquartile range.
   Atlanta: 2.25, 2.90, 3.65, 1.40
   Houston: 5.35, 6.20, 7.15, 1.80
   c. Houston gives bigger discounts.
   d. Housing available, economic conditions, number of people looking

7. **a.** Both line graphs stationary
   b. Hourly means: 9.97 ounces, .043 ounce
   Hourly ranges: .37 ounce, .149 ounce
   c. Disturbance problem
   d. Disturbance problem
   e. Take corrective action. Determine why process mean and range so far from normal conditions.

9. **a.** Managers: .8, .40
   Staff: .3, .46
   Hourly: .25, .43

   b. Managers differ
   c. Offer flexible benefits to all. Only managers would select.

11. **a.** Upward sloping line graph
    b. 839.6, 799.5, 587
    c. Data not stationary, descriptive measures meaningless
    d. Early dip, sales increase sharply, level off
    e. 1,219 units

13. **a.** 71, 11
    b. Outliers: firm 4 and firm 7
    c. Determine the root causes.

15. **a.** 4.1, 2, 2
    b. Skewed data
    c. 7.46, 1
    d. Standard deviation affected greatly by outlier

17. **b.** Stationary
    c. 62.3 hours, 5 hours
    d. 52.3 hours to 72.3 hours
    e. Something is out of ordinary. Determine causes.

19. **b.**

	Cum. Freq.	Cum. %
Less than 1.0	1	3.1%
1.00–1.49	3	9.4%
1.50–1.99	10	31.3%
2.00–2.49	24	75.0%
2.50–2.99	31	96.9%
Above 3.00	32	100%

    d. Only 3.1% of firms have current ratios as low as XYZ. Why?

21. **b.** Sales follow product life cycle.
    c. Declining sales period; improve product, remove product, etc.

23. **a.** 36 students
    b. Cannot predict
    c. Forecast horizon limited to one quarter

B-21

CHAPTER 3

1. **a.** Row: 27.3%, 72.7%; 77.8%, 22.2%; 50%, 50%
       Column: 30%, 70%; 80%, 20%; 55%, 45%
    b. No
    c. Based on sample data only
3. **a.** With inducement: Sample size 6,
       mean = 19.0 days, SD = 3.2 days;
       No inducement: Sample size 6,
       mean = 29.8 days, SD = 3.3 days
    b. Yes
    c. Cross-tabs tables describe categorical data
5. **a.** Years in residence
    b. Yes, nonlinearly
    c. One-way tables describe mixed data
7. **a.** Row: 83.3%, 16.7%; 20%, 80%
    b. Independents more service-oriented, chains more price-oriented.
    c. Not mixed data
9. **a.** **Participative Management**

	Yes	No
Sample size	5	5
Mean	59.4	79.4
SD	9.3	11.3

    b. Appears to reduce the mean number of grievances

11. **a.** Row: 40%, 60%; 10%, 90%
    b. Yes, big differences in row percentages
13. **a.** Underweight column:
       12.5%, 87.5%; 17.5%, 82.5%
       Overweight column: 83.3%, 16.7%; 80%, 20%
    b. No, similar column percentages within each cross-tabs table
15. **b.** lag 0: −.024; lag 1: −.169; lag 2: .402
    c. No, even highest correlation (lag 2) not related to number of fraud cases
17. **b.** Paper industry: Product quality not related to ROI
       Stereo industry: Product quality linearly positively related
19. **a.** Acres per farm steadily increasing, number of farms steadily decreasing
    b. Less than 1 million farms with a mean size over 550 acres
21. **b.** 1960–1981: Both increased steadily
       1982–1985: Medical care increased more rapidly than the energy index
       1986–1987: Again medical care increased more rapidly, energy cost declined
23. **a.** No
    b. Expected profits, amount of financial assistance, amount of training

CHAPTER 4

1. **a.**

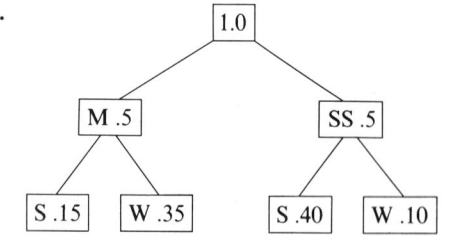

    ```
                  1.0
                /     \
              M .5    SS .5
             /   \    /   \
          S .15 W .35 S .40 W .10
    ```

    b. .65
    c. .5
    d. .778
    e. Relative frequencies
    f. Dependent
    g. Segment market and use different advertising for different segments.

3. **a.**

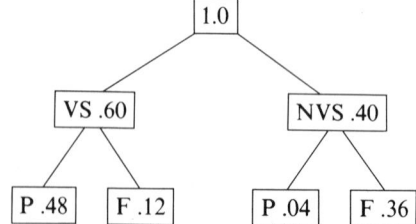

    ```
                  1.0
                /     \
             VS .60   NVS .40
             /   \    /   \
          P .48 F .12 P .04 F .36
    ```

    b. .92, .75
    c. Yes. Passing test increases chance of correctly predicting success from .60 to .92. Failing test increases chance of correctly predicting not success from .40 to .75.
5. **a.** 1
    b. .20, .30, .50

Answers to Application Problems

c. .95, .05, .00
7. a. Incoherent probabilities, P(negative finding AND meet goal) cannot equal −.1
   b. Answers vary.
   c. Positive market research finding a perfect indicator of meeting goal
9. a. Probabilities do not sum to 1.
   b. Multiply each probability by 1/.9.
11. a. Yes, probability of GPA above 3.5 changes with knowledge of SAT score.
    b. Cross-classify 1,500 students and convert to relative frequencies.
    c. Relative frequencies
13. a.

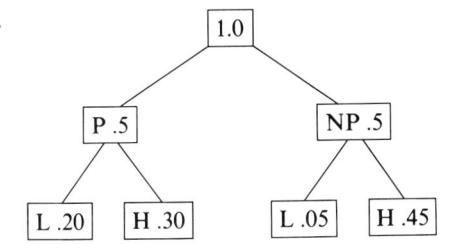

```
                1.0
          /            \
      P .5              NP .5
     /    \            /     \
  L .20  H .30      L .05   H .45
```

   b. .8
   c. .25

d. .4
e. No, having programs reduces chance of absenteeism.
15. a. Probabilities are consistent.
    b. .133
17. a. .15
    b. .95
    c. .75
    d. Strong need for capital investment
19. a. All the probabilities must be equal.
    b. No, different antecedents
21. a. .639
    b. .361
    c. .099
    d. .105
    e. No, two conditional probabilities very similar
23. a. Somewhat, rare event (probability .02) but could happen
    b. Yes, .0004 represents an exceptionally rare event
25. a. .875
    b. .724
    c. Yes, using group increases probability of B or better from .70 to .875.

CHAPTER 5

1. a. .3955
   b. .1562
   c. .3280
   d. Probability of a sale does not change within a neighborhood.

3. a.
x	P(X = x)
0	.050
1	.149
2	.224
3	.224
4	.168
5	.101
6	.050
7	.022
8	.008
9	.003
10	.001

   b. .034
   c. Each sale is independent of the others. Large number of potential buyers and the probability that anyone will purchase a disk player is very small. No one buys 2 or more players on a single purchase.

5. a. Zenith. Zenith's standard deviation is 1.6% of its mean; Apex's standard deviation is 6.1% of its mean.
   b. .6915, .0228; Apex has greater probability
   c. .9332, .9772; Zenith has greater probability
   d. The distributions have different means and standard deviations.

7. a. X = number of consumers in the awareness stage who adopt product, $\{0, 1, 2, 3, 4, 5\}$; Y = number of consumers through the trial stage who adopt product, $\{0, 1, 2, 3, 4, 5\}$
   b. .0004, .7373
   c. Try various strategies to bring all consumers to trial stage.

9. a. .368
   b. .019

11. Project A: μ = \$16,250, SD = \$38,304
    Project B: μ = \$14,000, SD = \$16,248
    Project A is riskier—similar mean but much larger SD

13. a. .9772
    b. .5000

15. a. .6826

      b. .9332
      c. SD = 2%
17. **a.** .007
    b. Something is wrong—very small probability of no calls.
19. **a.** .0192
    b. The mean could be closer to 1,600 hours. Battery quality as measured in hours has deteriorated. Need for problem solving action.
21. **a.** .0047
    b. The mean number of shares increased as investors forgot the crash of 1987.
23. **a.**

x	P(x)
0	.449
1	.360
2	.144
3	.038
4	.008
5	.001

    b.

Expected	Actual
45	45
36	37
14	13
4	4
0	1

Good fit

    c. .449 + .360 + .144 = .953. 95.3% of the bags should have 2 or fewer rotten potatoes. Sample entire bag. If more than 2 potatoes are rotten, reject the bag.

25. **a.** The highest mean profit ($4 million) is from Strategy 3.
    b. Strategy 3 is least risky by this measure.

CHAPTER 6

1. No. The confidence interval (.48, .54) contains .50.
3. **a.** Population — All major airports in the United States
    Sample — Ten randomly selected airports.
    b. Population — All taxpayers who filed for the year
    Sample — A random sample of taxpayers
    c. Population — All hourly, support, and professional workers
    Sample — Randomly selected workers from the three groups
5. 24 = MS, Mississippi
   14 = IN, Indiana
   13 = IL, Illinois
   29 = NH, New Hampshire
   20 = MD, Maryland
   26 = MT, Montana
   46 = VA, Virginia
   12 = ID, Idaho
7. Use stratified sampling with the countries as strata. Use a mailed questionnaire or FAX.
9. **a.** All people who live in New York City who have phones
    b. No. This was a convenience sample. The 100 people were not selected at random from the entire city. Respondents had to be in the shopping mall and select themselves by entering the research booth.
    c. Margin of error has no meaning for a convenience sample. The sample may not be representative of the target population.
11. **a.** Town A already has a fire station; town B does not. Town A has more crime than town B.
    b. Use proportional sampling. Since 70% of the people live in town A, randomly select 700 families from town A for your sample. Randomly select 300 families from town B for your sample.
13. The sample of size 10 contains only 2 men, while the target population contains about 50% men. The makeup of the sample does not mirror the target population. Stratified random sampling should have been used since women have similar weights and men have similar weights, but the average weight of each group is very different.
15. **a.** A large number of the observations could come from his early data entries and overestimate the average over all 5,000 data entries. A large number of observations could come from his later data entries and underestimate the average over all 5,000 data entries.
    b. The target population is *ordered*. Errors tend to fall systematically as the clerk gains more experience. Use a systematic sampling design.
17. The primary customers of Domino's pizzas are young, single, high school and college students. Amstar's sample excluded these people. The sample was not representative of the target population.

Answers to Application Problems B-25

19.	Experimental Factor	Level of Feedback		scale: Poor, mediocre, average, good, outstanding
	Levels	Two levels: No feedback, Feedback		
	Dependent variable	Level of service measured along a 5-point	Experimental units	Customers who have their cars serviced in our shop

CHAPTER 7

1. **a.** (.779, .821)
   b. Simple random sample, sample size large enough so that sampling distribution of sample proportions is normal.
3. **a.** $H_0: \mu \geq 22$ days
   $H_1: \mu < 22$ days
   b. Type I: Believe that approaches have reduced accounts payable, but they have not.
   Type II: Believe that approaches have not worked, but they have.
   c. Implementation cost of an ineffective method; develop new and unneeded ways to reduce accounts payable
   d. Critical value = 21.18 days, reject the null
   e. No, only correct decision or Type I error
5. **a.** $H_0: \mu \leq 1,750$ cartons
   $H_1: \mu > 1,750$ cartons
   b. Type I: Switch to individual branding, but no better than family branding.
   Type II: Stay with family branding but individual branding better.
   c. All costs associated with switching to IB
   Opportunity cost associated with lost sales
   d. Critical value = 1,878.2 cartons per week, do not reject null
   f. Yes, either correct decision or Type II error
7. **a.** Population proportion could be above or below .50; can't say.
   b. Reducing ME by increasing sample size will eventually cause both the lower and upper bounds to be either below .50 (a minority) or above .50 (a majority).
9. **a.** (2.22 minutes, 2.78 minutes); 90% confident that the mean time for all 50 operators to resolve complaint is between 2.22 and 2.78 minutes.
   b. Workers have improved. Upper limit below 3.20 minutes.
11. 247
13. **a.** (92%, 104%); 95% confident that median productivity is between 92% and 104%.
    b. Frequency of population is highly skewed or contains outlier(s).
    c. Sample data contain an outlier—138%.
15. (70.12 cartons, 74.88 cartons); 90% confident that mean sales over 2,000 stores is between 70.12 and 74.88 cartons per week.
17. **a.** Yes
    b. (4,626 ppsi, 4,674 ppsi); 95% confident that mean impact resistance between 4,626 and 4,674 ppsi.
    c. (22.93 ppsi, 60.86 ppsi); 95% confident that standard deviation in impact resistance between 22.93 and 60.86 ppsi.
    d. Meeting mean performance level, but not meeting variability target.
    e. Diagnose causes of increased variability.
19. **a.** At least 51,179 miles
    b. Switch to new brake pads
    c. Not interested in drawing inferences about sample mean, only the population mean.
21. **a.** At most 13.2%
    b. Blacks underrepresented—potential racial discrimination. The "at most" figure should have been equal to or greater than 26% for no discrimination.
23. (.335, .399)

CHAPTER 8

1. **a.** Shapes near normal and similar variabilities
   b. ($5,470, $6,410); 80% confident that Status Seekers have higher mean incomes than Machos by $5,470 to $6,410.
3. **a.** Data skewed; use test for difference between two population medians.
   b. (−75, 100); cannot detect any difference since zero in interval.
5. M-calculated = 59.25; cannot detect a difference
7. **a.** (.01, .05); 95% confident that control groups produce between 1% and 5% more defects than cross-trained groups.

b. Yes; zero not in interval.

9. (1.63, 16.77); the variance before is between 1.63 and 16.77 times larger than the variance after the campaign. There has been a reduction since 1 is not in the interval.

11. (.14, .26); there is a difference since 0 not in the interval. Cochran's table assures us the sample size is sufficient.

13. (.59, 3.51); cannot detect a difference between the two population variances since 1 is in interval.

15. a. (6.21%, 7.79%); 90% confident that workers led by participative leadership have between 6.21% and 7.79% higher productivity than workers led by an autocratic leadership.
b. Data are not proportions. Can take on values larger than 1.

17. (188.4 hours, 211.6 hours); 80% confident that Vendor A's fixed disks last between 188.4 and 211.6 hours longer than Vendor B's disks.

19. a. $\hat{p}$ female = .78; $\hat{p}$ male = .90; (−.02, .26); cannot detect a difference since 0 is in the interval.

21. a. $\hat{p}$ black = .069; $\hat{p}$ white = .203; (.095, .173); between 9.5% and 17.3% more whites assigned nonutility jobs than blacks.

23. a. Lower bound = −9,000; Upper bound = 30,000. Since interval contains 0, cannot detect a difference.
b. No, the difference could be due to factors other than gender—for example, length of service or field of study.

25. M-calculated = 310.5; cannot detect a difference between income dispersions in two cities.

CHAPTER 9

1. a. Randomly select, divide into groups, and assign participants.
b. Role and case are similar and both better than the lecture.

3. a. Factorial design
b.

	Lecture	Case
Sensing	85	50
Intuitive	40	85

c. Crossed profiles

5. a. One factor—need for independence
b. Two levels—low and high
c. 2 × 2 factorial design
d.

	Low Need	High Need
Participative	20	100
Autocratic	100	30

7. a. Displays A and C have outliers on high side. Display B's values show little dispersion and all less than the other two displays.
b. $H = 9.50 >$ chi-square $(2, .95) = 5.99$, reject null.
c. Displays A and C are better than B; no difference between A and C.

9. a. Yes
b. No, but need analysis of variance to draw inferences about *population* means.
c. VR = 18.24 > $F(2, 12, .95)$, reject null
d. Plastic and lubricant are better than standard blade; cannot detect other differences.

11. a. Crossed profiles
b. VR = 60 > $F(1, 8, .95)$; there is an interaction.
c. Use lecture to teach sensing managers; use case method to teach intuitive managers.

13. a. Much spread in means, little spread within groups
b. VR = 17.33 > $F(2, 12, .99)$, reject null
c. Brainstorming and Analogy are better than control group; cannot detect other differences.

15. a. Much spread in means, little spread within groups
b. VR = 63.1 > $F(2, 15, .95)$, reject null; letter has highest "goodwill."
c. Becomes harassment

17. a. Two factors
b. 200 subjects
c. Identify middle- and high-income customers. Randomly select 100 from each target population. Randomly split both groups into two subgroups. Assign each subgroup at random to different promotion. Record change in usage before and after the study.

19. a. Differences between individuals, within sweeteners, etc.
b. Sugar appears to be most preferred.

21. Spread of rates is small within each country. Spread between countries is large. Conclusion: France < West Germany < United States

23. a. Factorial design
b.

	Low Need	High Need
<20K	$400	$520
30K–50K	$580	$700
>75K	$900	$1,800

Nonparallel profiles

CHAPTER 10

1. Worker, cross-sectional, correlational study
3. DAYS-PRED = 11.38 − .02AGE − 1.01CLOSENESS + .04SALARY + .10TRAINING − .32EQUIP; VR = 23.86, $p < .05$
5. DAYS-PRED = 11.75 − 1.02CLOSENESS + .10TRAINING − .33EQUIP
7. Coefficients indicate direction and size of impact on DAYS-PRED. Can use equation for prediction of DAYS. If actual days falls far below DAYS-PRED, should find out why.
9. AGE, SALARY, YEARS, EXPER, and EDUC appear to be positively linearly related to SATIS. Males have higher SATIS than females. So too for managers vs. nonmanagers.
11. Only GENDER, SALARY, and EDUC remain in the model.
13. Coefficients indicate direction and size of impact on SATIS. Can use equation for prediction of SATIS. If actual job satisfaction falls far below the predicted job satisfaction, should find out why.
15. Yes
17. Yes
19. Yes
21. SALES and CONTROL linearly related; IN-AUDIT does not appear to be related.
23. Multicollinearity may be present.
25. External auditors ignore the results of internal auditors. Spend less time on internal audits and strengthen controls.
27. a. Positive
    b. Zero
    c. Yes
    d. Yes, because the purpose of the study is to test the significance of GENDER after controlling for AGE and YEARS.
29. a. If TYPEA oil is absent, sediment goes down by 3.19%. As the discharge temperature increases by 1 degree, sediment increases by .014%. As loading temperature increases by 1 degree, sediment increases by .038%.
    b. Only TYPEA variable is significant.
    c. Shipper at fault
31. a. No; variable is not significant only *after* controlling for other predictor variables.
    b. .11%
    c. Incorrect; cannot compare regression coefficients directly.
33. a. W-2: For every dollar reported on W-2, taxpayers do not report 23.7 cents.
       Sch-C: For every dollar reported on Schedule C, taxpayers do not report 12.2 cents.
       Bus. type: Professionals fail to report a mean of $1.57 more than nonprofessionals after controlling for other two variables.
    b. Only W-2 and Sch-C are statistically significant.
    c. No, intercept has no physical meaning.
    d. Not a random sample of all taxpayers—only those audited for suspected failure to report barter income. Cannot be used to predict underreported taxes for all taxpayers.
35. Chi-square calculated = 19.76, reject the null. Independents stress service; chains stress price.
37. a. 73%, 27%; 75%, 25%; 71%, 29%; 42%, 58%
    b. Division 4 seems to oppose flex-hours. Try it in other three divisions.
    c. Chi-square calculated = 64.28, reject null.
    d. Not all divisions favor flex-hours; have 95% confidence in that assertion.

CHAPTER 11

1. a. Upward trend but no seasonal component.
   b. 1.44 + .0709TIME
   c. 4%
   d. $2.93, $3.00
   e. Impact of previous quarters' earnings per share
   f. −.02 + 1.05EPS-1
   g. 4%
   h. $3.29; cannot predict quarter 22.
   i. Similar: Both have similar MAPEs for the historical data; both equations predict EPS; both are quantitative forecasts.
      Different: The equations generate quite different forecasts; the autoregressive model explains as well as predicts; the autoregressive model's predictions do not increase every quarter as do the linear TIME trend equation predictions.
3. a. Yes, nonlinear trend and a seasonal pattern.
   c. S-JAN = .8972, S-FEB = .9535, S-MAR = .9506, S-APR = .9557, S-MAY = .8893, S-JUNE = .9384, S-JULY = .9831, S-AUG = 1.0578, S-SEPT = 1.1515, S-OCT = 1.0580, S-NOV = 1.1082, S-DEC = 1.0568
      $1.018 \exp^{.0496 \text{TIME}}$
   c. 1.67%
   d. 18.8 or 18,800; 21.0 or 21,000; 22.0 or 22,000
5. b. 218.97 + 8.04TIME − 1.63TIME^2, 3.85%

    c.   110, 81, 48, 12, −27, −69, −115, −164, −216
    d.   Negative values impossible
7.   Upward linear pattern
9.   b.   .0545 + .966DISCOUNT-1; yes
    c.   5.30%
    d.   5.37%
11. b.   Neither variable related, but each variable is significant when considered alone, due to multicollinearity.

    c.   No, shows upward pattern. Do not use model for forecasting.
13. b.   Heavy attendance typically occurs every weekend.
    c.   Still a seasonal pattern
    d.   No seasonal pattern
    e.   No seasonal pattern

CHAPTER 12

1. a.   No systematic patterns; process under control.
    b.   1.61 seconds; yes
    c.   102.28 seconds; LCL = 99.98 seconds, UCL = 104.58 seconds
    d.   1.55 seconds; LCL = 0 seconds, UCL = 3.36 seconds
3. a.   Yes
    b. $\bar{s}$ = 3.54 errors;
       LCL = 0 errors,
       UCL = 8.01 errors;
       $\bar{\bar{x}}$ = 99.68 errors;
       LCL = 93.92 errors,
       UCL = 105.43 errors
5. a.   On days 7–8—not random variation.
    b.   Yes, in days 9–10—returned within the 2-sigma limits.
7. a.   Yes, on shifts 17–19
    b.   No. Control not restored until shift 20.
9.   Exactly *what* is wrong with opener?
    Where (what streets) in San Francisco are complaints occurring?
    Is anyone outside of San Francisco complaining?
    When did complaints begin?
    Is there a pattern to the complaints? More on the weekend or weekdays?
    What time of day does the problem happen?
    When the problem occurs, does every garage door opener malfunction or only one or two garage door openers?
    Of the people in the wedge, are all customers complaining?
    Are all three types of openers having the same problem?
    Are garage door openers manufactured by other firms also having the problem?
11.   Exactly *what* are nicks and burrs?
    Where are nicks and burrs occurring on the panels?
    Are nicks and burrs occurring in the blanking operation?
    When did nicks and burrs start on each line?
    How many nicks and burrs are on each panel?
    Are the nicks and burrs at the same place on all the defective panels?
    What percentage of the panels on the four lines are experiencing nicks and burrs?
    How many lines are experiencing nicks and burrs?
13. a.   Sought ways to reduce spelling errors and missing words in the documents. These two problems accounted for 85% of the typing errors. The program was successful because the after column shows that typists no longer misspell or omit words from the documents.
    b.   Can't tell. Pareto chart indicates only the percentage of defects by category, not the actual number.
    c.   Reduce improper punctuation

15.

Major bones	Subbones
Stores in mall	Major store became vacant, new mix of stores
State of economy	Recession, major local firm closing
Other malls	New mall opened nearby, competitor mall added a food court
Weather	Too cold, mall closed because of weather, icy roads

17.   .727
19. a.   "Cyclical" pattern—a sine wave
    b.   No; director wants increasing enrollment.

INDEX

Acceptable quality level, 709–711
Acceptance sampling, 708–711
Addition rule, 178
Additive model, 632–633
Alternative generation, 6–7
Analysis of variance
    Kruskal–Wallis, 472–475
    one-factor design, 456–464
    two-factor design, 479–487
Assignable cause variation, 5, 677
Assumption of continuity, 615, 659
Autocorrelation, 544–546, 619
Autoregressive model
    analyzing assumptions, 623–625
    definition, 620
    limitations in forecasting, 627
    model development, 623

Binomial distribution
    assessing assumptions, 234–236
    binomial expression, 225–226
    binomial table, 228
    business problem solving, 231–236
    definition of success, 224
    mean and standard deviation, 228–229
Bivariate data, 96
Box plot, 65–67
    multiple, 102–103

Causal models, 569, 614–615
Centered process, 681
Central Limit Theorem, 257–260
Chebyshev's rule, 53–55
Chi-square distribution, 370–371
Cluster sampling, 290–291
Cochran's rules, 358
Coefficient of multiple determination, 534
Coincident indicators, 621–622
Compensatory rivalry, 311
Confidence intervals
    assumptions, 335, 340, 358, 367, 371, 402, 410, 413, 422, 426

Confidence intervals (*continued*)
    definition, 331–332
    Dunn's multiple comparisons, 476–478
    one mean, one-sided, 338–341
    one mean, two-sided, 332–336
    one median, 364–368
    one proportion, 357–359
    one standard deviation, 369–372
    reducing width, 553–554
    regression model predictions, 551–554
    setting level of confidence, 336
    stratified sampling, 353–355
    two means, 402–406
    two proportions, 409–411
    two standard deviations, 419–424
    Turkey HSD, 467–472
Confidence level
    impact on margin of error, 277
Consumer's risk, 233
Control charts
    attributes, 692–695, 698
    variables, 682–689, 698
Control groups, 311
Convenience sampling, 285
Correlation, 136
Crosby, Philip, 674
Cross-correlation
    interpretation, 136, 140–142
    lagged relationship, 137–140
Cross-tabs table, 104–105
Cumulative frequency, 30–31
Cyclical pattern, 613, 648–650

Data
    bivariate, 96
    cross-sectional, 22, 100–124, 262
    nonstationary series, 42–43, 677
    rescaling, 36–37
    sources, 274–275
    time-ordered, 23, 127–142, 262, 612–614
    transformation, 393–396
    univariate, 96
    yes/no, proportion, 48–50

Decision making, 12–13, 584–585
Decision making errors
    costs, 343–344
Decomposition method
    cycle pattern detection, 648–650
    seasonal pattern detection, 634–642
    short-term forecasting, 650–652
    trend pattern detection, 643–648
    types of models, 632–634
    when to use, 631
Degrees of freedom, 332, 460–461, 485, 532
Delphi method, 656–659
Deming, W. Edwards, 672, 674
Deseasonalized data, 642–643
Design quality, 673–674
Diffusion of treatment, 311
Discrete probability distribution, 217–221
    mean and variance, 219–221
Dunn's multiple comparisons, 476–478

Element, 280
Ellipse test, 117–118
Empirical rule, 52–53
Event
    complementary, 164
    compound, 163–164
    probability, 165–166
    relative frequency, 164–165
    simple, 163
Experimental factor, 304, 480
Experimental level, 304, 480–481
Experimental unit, 305
Experimentwise error, 468
Exploratory data analysis, 15, 390–398, 450–455, 481–483
Extraneous factors, 306
Extrapolation, 551

F distribution, 421–422, 462–463
Finite correction factor, 341
First-order model, 515
Fishbone diagrams, 702–704

Frequency histogram
  class width, 27
  definition, 26
  open-ended classes, 28–29
  problem solving, 702–703

Histogram
  bell-shaped, 35–36
  skewed, 37–38
  symmetric, 34–35
History effect, 310–311
Hogarth, Robin, 617
Homoscedasticity, 539
Hypotheses, 342–343, 448–449
Hypothesis testing
  decision making, 345–347, 349–350
  determining costs of errors, 343–344, 349
  developing hypotheses, 342–343, 348
  setting significance level, 344–345, 349
  versus confidence intervals, 351

Inductive inference, 109–110
Interaction effect, 481–483, 560–563
Interquartile range, 60–62

Joint probability table, 171–172
Judgment errors, 188–189
  anchor and adjust, 616
  availability, 197–198, 616
  concreteness, 198–199
  hindsight, 616
  noncoherency, 193–196
  overlooking the base rate, 189–193
  selective perception, 616
  wishful thinking, 616
Judgmental models, 614–616
Juran, J., 673

Kahneman, David, 168
Kepner–Tregoe method, 447–449, 701–702
Kruskal–Wallis analysis of variance, 472–475

Law of large numbers, 165, 167
Leading indicators, 612–622

Line graph
  multiple, 128–130
  single, 40–43, 283

Mann–Whitney interval, 414–417
Manufactured quality, 674
Margin of error
  calculation, 332, 338, 354, 358, 402, 410, 468
  definition, 12, 29, 275
  influences on, 275–278, 406
Mean
  confidence intervals, 332–341, 402–406
  control chart, 684–686
  histogram data, 46–47
  nonstationary data, 68–70
  raw data, 45
  weakness, 55
  when to use, 62
  yes/no data, 49
Mean absolute percentage error, 625–627, 647
Median
  confidence interval, 364–368
  histogram data, 57–58
  raw data, 56–57
  when to use, 62
Mental model, 2, 29–30, 66
MIL-STD-105D, 709–711
Mood test, 425–429
Moving averages, 70–74
Multicollinearity
  definition, 569–571
  detection, 576–578
  impact on regression model, 571–576
  minimizing, 576–580
Multiplication rule, 191
Multiplicative model, 632–652

Natural tolerance limits, 681
Nominal group expert panel, 655–656
Nonparametric methods
  Dunn's multiple comparisons, 474–478
  one median, 364–368
  three or more medians, 472–475
  two medians, 412–417
  two variabilities, 425–429

Nonresponse error, 282
Normal distribution
  assessing assumptions, 255–256
  business problem solving, 249–255
  importance, 244–246
  properties, 246–247
  z-scores, 247–248

Observational study, 306
Ogive, 31
One-way table, 101–102, 451, 463
Outlier
  Chebyshev's rule, 54
  Empirical rule, 53
  explanations of, 39
  impact on moving average, 77–78
  impact on regression model, 544
  impact on width of confidence interval, 367
  Tukey's rule, 64

Pareto charts, 698–701
Percentage table
  column, 107, 186
  joint, 106–107
  row, 107–108, 186
Planned change study
  definition, 305–308
  potential problems, 309–313
  terminology, 303–313
  when to run, 446–449, 489, 504, 706–707
Poisson distribution
  acceptance sampling, 710–711
  assessing assumptions, 242
  business problem solving, 240–242
  definition of trial, 238
  mean and standard deviation, 242–243
  Poisson expression, 238
  Poisson table, 238–239
Population, 12, 45
Population parameter, 322, 373
Pounds's strategy, 3
Prediction interval, 551

Probability
  basic rules, 166
  conditional, 180–181, 183–184, 189–196
  joint, 171, 177–178, 185–186, 224, 587
  personal, 167–169, 214, 262
  relative frequency, 165, 214, 262
  union, 177–178
Probability tree, 172–175, 190–191, 195
Problem classification
  disturbance, 2, 390–391
  managerial, 2, 390
Problem diagnosis, 6–7, 97–98, 144, 215, 446–449
Problem sensing, 3, 30, 96–97, 144, 214, 233, 584, 686–688, 698–701
Prob-value, 347–348
Process capability index, 681–682
Process capability study, 253–255, 679–682
Process control study, 676–679
Producer's risk, 232
Product life cycle, 647–648
Proportion
  computation, 48–50
  confidence interval, 357–359, 409–411
Pull apart strategy, 510–511, 553–554

Qualitative forecasting, 616–617, 655–659
Quality
  importance of, 672–673
  types of, 673–676
Quality circle, 713
Quality control
  acceptance sampling, 708–711
  control charts, 682–695
  process capability study, 253–255, 679–682
  process control study, 676–679
  tools for improving quality, 697–707
  vendor certification, 711–712
Quantitative forecasting, 615–616, 659–660
Questionnaire construction, 297–303

Random error, 312
Random experiment, 162–163
Random variables
  continuous, 216–217, 244–256
  discrete, 216–217, 223–243
Random variation, 5, 676, 679, 686
Randomization, 308, 312
Range, 47–48
Raw seasonal index, 637–640
Regression analysis
  assessing assumptions, 538–549
  backward elimination method, 579–580
  business problem solving, 582–585
  goals, 507–509
  indicator variables, 555–567
  model estimation, 520–527
  multicollinearity, 569–580
  regression coefficients, 507–508
  significance testing, 529–536, 567–568
  types of studies, 510–512
  when to use, 504–505
Relationships
  clusters, 120–124, 517
  detection, 504–505
  lagged, 130–134
  linear, 117–118, 515
  nonlinear, 118–120, 516
Relative frequency histogram, 29
Residual analysis, 538–549
Residual plot, 74–77, 540–548
Response error, 282

Sample, 12, 45, 322, 325
Sample proportion, 48–50, 357
Sample size
  impact on margin of error, 275–276, 373
  determination, 360–363
Sample statistic, 323, 373
Sampling distribution
  one sample mean, 257–259, 276–278, 324–328
  two sample means, 399–401
  variance ratio, 420–421
Sampling frame, 280–281
Sampling units, 280
Scatter diagram, 115–117, 513–517, 704–706

Seasonal pattern, 613, 634–642
Second-order model, 516
Selection error, 281–282
Shewhart, Walter, 682, 686
Simple random sampling, 284–286, 290
Spread charts, 452–454
Standard deviation
  confidence intervals, 369–372, 419–424
  control chart, 683–684
  impact on margin of error, 277–278, 323
  interpretation, 48
  weakness, 55
  yes/no data, 50
Standard error, 326–327
Statistical control, 679
Statistical independence, 181–182
Stem-and-leaf display
  comparing two data sets, 391–398
  one data set, 24–26
Stratified random sampling, 287–290
Studentized range values, 468–469
Sum of squares, 459–460, 483–485, 531–532
Survey methods, 293–296
Survey sampling design, 280 ,
Systematic sampling, 289–290

t-Table, 332
Target population, 280–281, 322
Test of independence
  computation, 585–589
  purpose, 110, 506
Three-sigma rule, 686–687
Time series models, 614–615, 659
Tree diagram, 110
Trend pattern, 612, 643–648
Trend pattern equations, 644–647
Trimmed mean, 59–60
Tukey, John, 64, 468
Tukey HSD intervals, 467–472
Tversky, Amos, 168
Type I error, 343
Type II error, 343
Typical seasonal index, 640–642

Univariate data, 96

Variables
- categorical, 99–100, 504–505, 510, 555–567
- dependent, 101, 305, 504–505, 510
- explanatory (predictor), 101, 510

Variables (*continued*)
- intervening, 110–112
- quantitative, 99–100, 504–505
- random, 216–221

Variance ratio, 420–421, 532–533, 706–707

Vendor certification, 711–712

Western Electric rules, 687

z-Scores, 247–248

HINTS FOR WRITING MEMOS FOR END-OF-CHAPTER APPLICATION PROBLEMS

1. Your memo must quickly establish the following:
   - **What** is the problem?
   - **Why** should the reader care?
   - **What** do you want the reader to do?
2. Create informative headings **before** writing your memos. Use "white space" to create a readable and attractive page. For example,

---

Problem

Over the past quarter the reject rate increased from 1% to 4% in the Abilene plant. This increased our rework cost by $70,000. Failure to understand the new quality control procedures caused the jump in the reject rate.

Recommendation

We request $5,250 for Qualtrain Inc. to conduct three one-day workshops for all supervisory and hourly workers.

Supporting Data

On March 12, we interviewed 100 randomly selected workers and supervisors in the Abilene plant and found ...

---

3. Focus paragraphs clearly—one idea and supporting points. Each paragraph that has more than three sentences should contain a cover sentence that provides an overview. Keep paragraphs to 10 lines or less.
4. Use the active voice. It is more forceful than the passive voice, it reduces the risk of being misunderstood, and it requires fewer words.
5. Use personal pronouns such as **you** and **we**. Personally addressing your audience will produce better responses.
6. Simplify sentences by using lists whenever possible (see hint #1).
7. Avoid long sentences and words, use only one adjective before a noun, and state sentences in positive form. Minimize phrases that begin with **of, with,** or **for.**

From Jerry A. Dibble and Beverly Y. Langford's *Communication Skills and Strategies: Guidelines for Managers at Work*. Atlanta, GA: By the Authors, 1990. Used with permission of the authors.